THE KING'S CARDINAL

The Rise and Fall of Thomas Wolsey

———

PETER GWYN

PIMLICO

Published by Pimlico 2002

2 4 6 8 10 9 7 5 3 1

First published in Great Britain by Barrie & Jenkins Ltd 1990
First Pimlico edition 1992
Reissue 2002

Pimlico
Random House, 20 Vauxhall Bridge Road,
London SW1V 2SA

Random House Australia (Pty) Limited
20 Alfred Street, Milsons Point, Sydney,
New South Wales 2061, Australia

Random House New Zealand Limited
18 Poland Road, Glenfield,
Auckland 10, New Zealand

Random House (Pty) Limited
Endulini, 5A Jubilee Road, Parktown 2193, South Africa

The Random House Group Limited Reg. No. 954009
www.randomhouse.co.uk

A CIP catalogue record for this book
is available from the British Library

ISBN 0-7126-6833-0

Papers used by Random House are natural,
recyclable products made from wood grown in sustainable forests.
The manufacturing processes conform to the environmental
regulations of the country of origin

Printed and bound in Great Britain by
Mackays of Chatham plc

To Nikolai Tolstoy
whose efforts to explain the tragic
events in Austria in the early Summer
of 1945 I so much admire

CONTENTS

THE KING'S CARDINAL

PREFACE

I am very conscious that this book could not have been written without the support and encouragement of a large number of friends. In the first place I could not have survived financially for the twelve years that it has taken me to write it without the generosity of Romy and Richard Briant and my sister and brother-in-law Alison and David Kingsley. Much of it was written and researched in the Upper Reading Room of the Bodleian, and to the spirit of that beautiful room and those who worked in it during my time I owe a special debt: in particular I would like to thank Ian Archer, Mark Curthoys, Trevor Dean, Jeremy Gregory, Trevor Griffith, David Katz, Sarah Kochan, Simon Payling and Blair Worden; as also the staff of the Bodleian – especially Helen Rogers – whose willingness to help more than compensated for the vagaries of the library's administration. To other friends, and relatives, in Oxford and elsewhere who were kind enough to put up with Wolsey for so long, a further debt is owed: in particular Catherine Bennett, Roland Dannreuther, Kathleen Davies, Eileen Gwyn, Catherine La Farge, Christl and Michael Lethbridge, Frances and Roger Little, Iain and Nigel McGilchrist, Paul Nabavi, Audrey Nevin, John Nightingale, Emma Rees Mogg, Robert Sackville-West, Lotte and Nicky Spice, Mark Stephenson, Kate and Bryan Ward-Perkins and Lucas Wilson.

As for libraries and archival repositories other than the Bodleian, I would like to thank the staff of the Guildhall Library, the Kent Record Office, the Lincoln Record Office, the Northumberland Record Office, the Westminster Abbey Muniments, the West Sussex County Record Office, the Wiltshire Record Office for kindly answering enquiries or allowing me to consult their records. I have found working in the Reading Room of the British Library positively harmful to research; not so its Manuscript Room, or the Public Record Office, whose staff have shown great patience in deciphering documents that have defeated me.

Susan Brigden, M.L. Bush, C. Dyer and Richard Hoyle very kindly read and commented on particular chapters, while M. Bowker, Christopher Brooke, Pierre Chaplais, C.R. Cheney, J.A. Guy, Peter Partner and J.A.F. Thomson have all been kind enough to answer enquiries, while Simon Thurley took a lot of trouble over possible illustrations. My inadequate linguistic skills have been buttressed by a number of people including Trevor Dean and Bryan Ward-Perkins already mentioned, Mrs A. Rainton, and above all Richard Roberts.

Throughout the enterprise Alistair Ricketts has acted as my unofficial editor and adviser on all literary matters. More recently my 'official' editor – though she would not approve of the inverted commas – Sue Phillpott has removed a large number of words to the great advantage of the reader and with the minimum of pain to myself.

It will quickly become apparent that on many aspects of the Tudor period Sir Geoffrey Elton and I do not agree. This has not prevented him from taking an interest in my work and on a number of occasions offering excellent advice. Steve Gunn, Steve Thompson and Greg Walker, all of whom began their research while this book was in progress and with some justification could have taken a protectionist stance, have gone out of their way to share their knowledge and ideas to my great benefit. The contribution of three other Tudor historians has been immeasurable. It was Jack Scarisbrick's treatment of Wolsey's foreign policy in his *Henry VIII* that provided its starting point, and though I have come to take a different view to his on many matters of detail, his approach to the writing of history remains a source of inspiration. Cliff Davies commented on my first piece of writing on Wolsey, has read much of this book in its various stages, and has throughout these twelve years been a most supportive critic. George Bernard may not have read every word of every draft, but everything in this book has been discussed with him – and occasionally fought over – so that in many ways it is as much his book as mine. Furthermore his practical help in all the minutiae of scholarly activity has helped to overcome the disadvantages of attempting to write this kind book while situated on the outer fringes of academe.

Finally I must acknowledge two longer-term debts. Paddy McGrath was my tutor at Bristol, and he and his extended family have remained close friends ever since. Those who have had the advantage of having been taught by him will readily understand how much I owe to that combination of scepticism and commitment that are to me his hallmark. My father was a teacher of history, and it was his bedtime stories that, for better or for worse, made the past for me such an exciting world to inhabit. Sadly he died before he could know that the teaching and writing of history would occupy so much of my time. He might have been surprised that I could write so many words. I hope he would have been pleased.

Notes to the Notes

I have deliberately geared the notes to the Calendars of the State Papers rather than to the documents themselves. This is not because the documents have not been consulted – and where a quote is only to be found in the original, or in the rare cases where the calendars are defective, or there is no calendar, the document reference is given – but because they provide the most readily available means for anyone to check my sources, and are in themselves the best finding list to the documents. Where no page reference is given a document number is to be assumed.

The secondary sources relate very precisely to the bibliography at the back. A single name indicates that only one work by that author is to be found there; initials distinguish one author with the same name from another; where there is no author, or for those authors with more than one work, short titles to the work, or to the periodical in which it appears, have been used.

Abbreviations

AC	Archaelogia Cantiana
AHR	Agricultural History Review
AJLH	American Journal of Legal History
BBCS	Bulletin of the Board of Celtic Studies
BIHR	Bulletin of the Institute of Historical Research
BL	British Library
BP	Borthwick Papers
CS	Camden Society
CWE	The Complete Works of Erasmus (Toronto, 1974-)
CWM	Complete Works of St Thomas More (Yale, 1963-)
EcHR	Economic History Review
EDR	Ely Diocesan Records
EETS	Early English Text Society
EHR	English Historical Review
HJ	Historical Journal
HLQ	Huntingdon Library Quarterly
JEH	Journal of Ecclesiastical History
JWCI	Journal of the Warburg and Coutauld Institutes
KCA DR	Kent County Archives, Diocesan Records
LP	Letters and Papers, Foreign and Domestic, of the reign of Henry VIII, 1509-47, ed. J.S. Brewer, J. Gairdner, R.H. Brodie (1862-1920)
LP Add	Letters and Papers, . . . , Addenda, ed. R.H. Brodie (1929-32)
LRO	Lincoln Record Office
Mil. Cal.	Calendar of State Papers, Milan (1385-1618), ed. A.B. Hinds (1912)

NH	*Northern History*
OHS	Oxford Historical Society
PP	*Past and Present*
PRO	Public Record Office
Rymer	*Foedera, Conventiones, Litterae, etc.* (edn. 1704-35)
SH	*Southern History*
Sp. Cal.	*Calendar of State Papers, Spanish* ed. G.A. Bergenroth, P. de Gayangos (1862-86)
Sp. Cal. F.S.	*Further Supplement to the calendar of State papers, Spanish*, ed. G. Mattingly (1954)
SR	*Statutes of the Realm* (11 vols, 1810-28)
SS	Selden Society
St. P	*State Papers of the reign of King Henry the Eighth* (1830-52)
TRHS	*Transactions of the Royal Historical Society*
TRP	*Tudor Royal Proclamations 1: The Early Tudors (1485-1553)*, ed. P.L. Hughes and J.F. Larkin (1964)
Ven. Cal.	*Calendar of State Papers, Venetian*, ed. R. Brown, C. Bentinck, H. Brown (9 vols, 1864-98)
VCH	*Victoria County History*
WAM	Westminster Abbey Muniments
WSRO	West Sussex Record Office

Introduction

THIS BOOK IS AN ATTEMPT TO UNDERSTAND AND EXPLAIN THE POLITICAL career of Thomas Wolsey. There will be very little about his private life, not because it is thought to be of little interest, but because there is virtually no evidence for it. He had a mistress, or concubine, as clerical mistresses were called. Her name was 'Mistress Lark'. She bore him two children, a girl, Dorothy, who was sent to Shaftesbury Abbey, a much favoured convent for the daughters of the wealthy, and a boy, Thomas Winter, whom Wolsey publicly acknowledged as his 'nephew'.[1] Having said that, one has said almost everything that is known about an aspect of his life that one would really like to know much more about, for it is not necessary to be too Freudian to acknowledge that emotional and sexual matters contribute to an understanding of a person's character. There is hardly more information about what nowadays might be called Wolsey's 'leisure activities'! There is one reference to hunting, and that very late in his life.[2] He was to be a great builder, as parts of Hampton Court and Christ Church College, Oxford, still bear witness to. He possessed quantities of tapestries, jewels and plate, and may have had a particular liking for 'Damascene carpets', by which was presumably meant oriental carpets.[3] He kept a chapel choir, which in 1518 Henry considered to be so much better than his own that he insisted that some of Wolsey's choirboys should be transferred to the royal choir [4] – and Henry did have rather a habit of insisting that anything he fancied should be his! Still, almost none of these things sheds much light on Wolsey's personality because it is almost impossible to decide what represents a genuine personal taste, and what the style and preferences of any wealthy man of his time. As for what he read, or even the books that were on his shelves, here information of almost any kind is lacking: only four surviving books have been closely associated with him, two of which are merely liturgical, and there is no surviving catalogue of his libraries.[5] Given that one is anxious to penetrate the

---

[1] Pollard, *Wolsey*, p.306. Since A.F. Pollard wrote, no further information about Mistress Lark or her children by Wolsey seems to have come to light.

[2] *LP*, iv, 4773.

[3] Much excellent work is currently being done on all aspects of Wolsey's artistic patronage; the following papers were presented to a Wolsey conference at Cambridge in September 1988: T. Campbell, 'Wolsey's patronage of tapestries'; P. Glanville, 'Goldsmith's work in the age of Wolsey'; P. Lindley, 'Wolsey's patronage of renaissance sculpture'; S. Thurley, 'The domestic buildings of Cardinal Wolsey'; and H. Wayment 'Wolsey and stained glass'. These will appear in *'Cardinal Wolsey: Church, State and Art'*, ed. S.J. Gunn and P. Lindley, and add enormously to our knowledge and understanding of these very important matters. Whether in the end they bring us any closer to Wolsey, the man, is in my view doubtful.

[4] *LP*, ii, 4023, 4024, 4025, 4043, 4053, 4055.

[5] The two literary works are: Aelfric, 'First Book of Homilies in Anglo-Saxon' (BL, Royal MS. 7.C.xii) and *Nova legenda Anglie* (1516) (Merton Coll. Lib. 87.B.13); the others are a gospel-book (Magdalen Coll MS. latin 223) and epistle-book (Christ Church MS. 101).

workings of Wolsey's mind, this is a grievous handicap.

Another is the suspicion, not to say hostility, with which Wolsey has been viewed. His first biographer and household servant, George Cavendish, declared that he had only decided to write a life of his master because 'since his death I have heard divers sundry surmises and imagined tales made of his proceedings and doings which I myself have perfectly known to be untrue' – and he made it clear that the 'surmises' had not been complimentary.[1] Some hundred and seventy years later, in 1724, an Oxford don and cleric, Richard Fiddes, explained that there were two reasons for his wanting to write a life of Wolsey. The first was by way of paying a debt that his university owed to Wolsey's generous patronage. The second was out of a desire to do 'justice to his injured memory', for 'it may be questioned whether in all the histories that are extant, a like instance can be found in any nation of so general a prejudice, as that under which his name has suffered'.[2] Not a lot has changed since then. It is true that in the late nineteenth century there was briefly something of a sea change. England was at the zenith of her Imperial power and 'great statesmen' were fashionable. Macmillan's commissioned biographies of 'Twelve English Statesmen', and Wolsey was one of the twelve. The result was the appearance in 1891 of *Cardinal Wolsey* , an on the whole favourable biography by a leading historian of the time, Mandell Creighton. Since then, however, things have only got worse. Two doyens of Tudor history, A.F. Pollard and Sir Geoffrey Elton, have not taken a favourable view.[3]

Moreover Pollard's *Wolsey* is the last major assessment to have been attempted, and that as long ago as 1929. For want of much attention, the field has been left to the American actor, Orson Welles, whose portrayal of Wolsey in *A Man for All Seasons* – a most successful film biography of Sir Thomas More, which appeared in 1966 but has been much shown since on television[4] – has probably done more to fashion current perceptions of Wolsey than anything else – and it is not a flattering portrayal.

What Orson Welles portrayed was everybody's idea of a Renaissance cardinal, an overweight and overdressed spider occupying the centre of a web of intrigue, and bearing a much closer resemblance to the emperor Nero than to anyone remotely religious. The question of Wolsey's size is an intriguing one. The most famous image of him to have survived, the portrait by an unknown artist in the National Portrait Gallery in London, suggests that he was of ample proportions.[5] But it was never intended to be an accurate representation, and the only other near contemporary portrait, though admittedly French and dating from 1567, suggests a much thinner man.[6] What there is not is any remotely detailed description of his physical appearance, so that not even the colour of his hair is known. The Venetian

---

[1] Cavendish, p.4.

[2] Fiddes, p.ii.

[3] Pollard's *Wolsey* has dominated our perception of Wolsey since it first appeared in 1929 – and in many ways this book is a refutation of it. Elton's unhappiness with the cardinal is apparent in all that he has written about him, but can be most readily and, in this context, most usefully gauged in his introduction to the Fontana edition of Pollard's *Wolsey*, reprinted in his *Studies*, i, pp.109-28.

[4] Originally a play by Robert Bolt.

[5] See plate 1; also Strong, pp.335-6.

[6] See plate 2; also Campbell, *Journal of the Warburg and Courtauld Institutes*, xl.

ambassador, Sebastian Giustinian, thought him 'very handsome',[1] and another Venetian ambassador found him 'hale and of good presence'.[2] Neither description suggests that he was thin, but there has to be a suspicion that since his death the poor cardinal's girth has increased, even as his fame has diminished! The poet John Skelton referred to

> ... a flap afore his eye,
> Men wene that he is pocky.[3]

Skelton's explanation is unlikely, even though one of the articles brought against him at his fall accused him of having endangered the king's person by blowing upon him when knowing himself to have 'the foul and contagious disease of the great pox broken out upon him'.[4] There was Mistress Lark, but insofar as there is any evidence at all, it points to his having been faithful to her; and surely if he had been promiscuous, international gossip would have soon got hold of it. As it is, there was nothing, and what seems more likely is that Wolsey had some kind of disfigurement to his eye which gave Skelton the opportunity to make an easy gibe.[5]

Whether Wolsey deserves his bad press will be a major theme of the book. What may be helpful at the start is to explain some of the more obvious reasons for it – and in doing so Mr Welles's portrayal may be of some help. At its simplest, the English are not very fond of cardinals. They associate them with an excess of wealth and power, at least unseemly in a man of the cloth – and perhaps nothing has done more harm to Wolsey's reputation than his apparent penchant for dressing up in scarlet. The English also associate cardinals with decadent and superstitious religious practices, with incense and all the mumbo-jumbo that popery is allegedly prey to. Above all they are foreign and, thus, not to be trusted. And in Wolsey's case, all these prejudices have been aggravated by the simple fact of chronology. Living on the eve of the English Reformation, and in some people's eyes being one of its principal causes, he has had to bear a weight of criticism, which if he had been born earlier he would have escaped. The myth of a 'waning Middle Ages' and of a late medieval church suffocating under the burden of its own excesses has inevitably been a dominant theme of England's Protestant historiography – and one of the earliest and most savage attacks on Wolsey was made by one of England's first Protestants, William Tyndale, in his *Practice of Prelates* of 1530.

Thus Wolsey has not fared well at the hands of one of the strongest strands of English cultural and intellectual life, the Protestant tradition. Neither has the closely allied Whig tradition treated him any better.[6] At its heart lies a pride in this country's achievements, but especially its nurture of parliamentary democracy, the common law – and common sense! What it is opposed to is kings and queens before they became 'constitutional', their favourites, meddlesome clerics – and anything in

---

[1] Rawdon Brown, ii, p.314 (*LP*, iii, 402).

[2] *Ven. Cal.*, iii, 232.

[3] Skelton, p.308, ll.1169-70. This edition of Skelton's poems appears to be the best available.

[4] Art.6; see *LP*, iv, 6075, taken from Herbert, pp.294-302.

[5] *Sp. Cal.*, F.S., p.164 for a specific reference to Wolsey being in danger of losing an eye.

[6] Both Pollard and Elton seem to me to be very much part of these two traditions, if the latter in a rather secular guise. For Pollard see Galbraith; also Neale – though the quickest way to understand Pollard's view of Wolsey is to consult his index.

the least bit intellectual! While it has never been suggested that there was much of the intellectual about Wolsey, in other respects he has scored badly. He was both a royal favourite and a meddlesome priest, and as such despised both parliament and the common law. Moreover, he suffers from another handicap. The Whig tradition is nothing if not teleological. Everything that has happened in English history has had as its purpose the creation of this miraculous construct, parliamentary democracy. Some things, and especially people, have contributed more than others. Wolsey has contributed not at all, and in this sense he has been seen as unimportant. Or, to put it another way, he has been thought of as a medieval figure, representative of a way of doing things which, thankfully, we have grown out of. By contrast, his successor as the king's leading councillor, Thomas Cromwell – who at least in one account believed in parliament and the civil service[1] – is a modern figure and, therefore, of great interest.

I am neither very Protestant nor very Whiggish, and it is probably true, though this may be to underestimate the underlying strength of these two strands of English intellectual and cultural life, that fewer and fewer English men and women are. But, whatever one's attitudes, it is easy enough to appreciate that the Protestant and Whig traditions have tremendously distorted our view of Wolsey. What we have for the most part is a caricature out of Gerald Scarfe, or at the least an Old Master so covered with grime and coats of varnish that it is no longer possible to appreciate the portrait underneath. The process of cleaning has been begun by others, but in some ways this has only made things worse: bits of a different Wolsey have been revealed, but the result is a confusing mosaic of dark and light that makes no sense at all. It is time to attempt a complete restoration – despite the risks that this entails. In the end too much may be removed, or the retouching may be obtrusive, but there is this safeguard that the historian is usually not in a position to destroy the evidence, even if he distorts it.

Before embarking upon this task, a general word about the evidence may be helpful. First there are the 'State Papers'. The great majority of what has survived relate to the conduct of foreign policy, essentially letters to and from English representatives abroad, those to them usually only in draft form. There are also the letters of foreign representatives in England to their respective heads of state, which, because they have been easy of access and are presented in a straightforward chronological order, have been overused, or at any rate, much misinterpreted. Records of the royal Council, especially in its non-judicial capacity, are extremely patchy, and anything approaching a 'Home Office' archive is lacking. As for legal records, they survive in great quantity, but they are not especially relevant to a political biography, and both because of their quantity and their technical nature are difficult to use effectively. On the other hand, the problem as regards Wolsey's involvement with the English Church is the severe shortage of evidence.

What all this adds up to is distinct bias towards Wolsey's conduct of foreign policy, a bias which goes a long way to explain one of the most common misconceptions about him, which is that he was only interested in foreign affairs –

---

[1] The reference is to Elton's many treatments of Thomas Cromwell, but see especially *Reform and Renewal*, and 'Political creed of Thomas Cromwell' in *Studies*, ii.

and especially their more showy manifestations, such as the Field of the Cloth of Gold. He was interested in such things, if only because as the king's chief councillor he had to be, but, as will become all too apparent, he was interested in much else besides. What is also lacking is any significant private archive, and not just for Wolsey, but for all the leading figures of the time. There are very few private letters, let alone diaries, and thus precisely the kind of material that might shed light on the most intriguing questions of all, those to do with the motivation of the leading figures, are missing. This is obviously a great disadvantage to the historian. It has also been of some disadvantage to Wolsey's reputation because it has increased the reliance on the contemporary literary sources, and three out of the four major ones present a distinctly unflattering portrait.

Wolsey's first biographer, and household servant, George Cavendish, undoubtedly meant to present his master in a favourable light, or at least, as was indicated earlier, to put the record straight. However, his *Life and Death of Cardinal Wolsey* was not written until some thirty years after Wolsey's death, in the late 1550s, and the passage of time did not make for accurate recollection. Moreover, it is important to bear in mind that it is not until after Wolsey's political disgrace in 1529 that his work becomes anything like a primary source – and for this reason a fuller discussion of the work will be postponed until the final chapter. The simple point to make here is that he did not join Wolsey's household until probably 1522. His job as gentleman usher only required him to act as a cross between a social secretary and travel agent much involved in planning the frequent movement from place to place of Wolsey's large household. As such, until the special circumstances of Wolsey's last year, he was not close to Wolsey, and certainly not informed about matters of state. This comes out very clearly in his book. Only two-fifths of the way through it the matter of Henry's divorce takes centre stage, and about half of it is devoted to Wolsey's last year when he was no longer a councillor. Thus, as a source for Wolsey's political life it has severe limitations.[1]

The two contemporary historians, Polydore Vergil and Edward Hall, were much less close to Wolsey than Cavendish. Arguably, however, they were both intellectually and politically more literate, though neither was anywhere near the centre of English political life. Something else they shared was a strong dislike of Wolsey. An Italian by birth and upbringing, Vergil came to England in 1502 to be deputy collector of Peter's Pence – an infrequent and not very onerous papal tax – to a fellow countryman, Adriano Castellessi,[2] who happened to be well in with Henry VII; in 1504 Henry had made him bishop of Bath and Wells, perhaps encouraged to do so by his elevation to the office of cardinal the previous year. Vergil quickly established himself in the cultural and intellectual life of London and in 1506 Henry VII asked him to write a history of England. Not surprisingly, the resulting *Anglica Historia* is an especially important source for that king's reign and when it first appeared in 1535 ended with Henry VII's death. However, in a subsequent edition published in 1555, the year of Vergil's death, he continued the history down to

---

[1] Sadly, there is nothing very helpful on Cavendish, but see R.S. Sylvester's introduction to the EETS edition, referred to henceforth as Cavendish; for a modernized text see *Two Early Tudor Lives*, the second life being William Roper's *The Life of Sir Thomas More*.

[2] In earlier work he often appears as Cardinal Hadrian.

1537, so that it included the whole of Wolsey's career – and Wolsey's first appearance in the book sets the tone for what follows. Commenting on the marriage of Louis XII to Henry VIII's sister, Mary, in 1514, Vergil wrote:

> English affairs thus daily prospered, and in this prosperity Thomas Wolsey gloried exceedingly, as though he alone were responsible for the great good fortune, in that his authority was now supreme with the king. But he was also more hated, not only on account of his arrogance and his low reputation for integrity, but also on account of his recent origins. [1]

Why Vergil came to hate Wolsey is a complicated story. It has to do in part with rivalries at Rome between Vergil's original patron, Castellessi, and Silvestro Gigli, another Italian favoured by Henry VII, who appointed him bishop of Worcester; and for a time, at any rate, Gigli was very much in favour with the new king and with Wolsey, and much more so than Castellessi was. It also had to do with rivalries at court between intellectuals, or 'humanists' favoured by the old king, such as Vergil, and those favoured by the new king, such as yet another Italian, Andrea Ammonio. Appointed Latin secretary to Henry VIII, Ammonio, in cahoots with Gigli, had designs on Vergil's post as deputy collector. Vergil thought, perhaps correctly, that Wolsey favoured Ammonio's designs. It is worth mentioning, however, that in 1514, only a year before the crisis in their relationship occurred, Wolsey had been quite prepared to use Vergil, on a trip to Rome, to push his own claims for a cardinal's hat, something which was very much a priority of his and the king's at this time. In February 1515 Vergil returned, but without having achieved anything, not that this was in the first instance held against him. However, very soon Ammonio brought to Wolsey's attention the fact that Vergil had begun to write letters back to Castellessi in which he was extremely rude about Wolsey. The result was that for a few months Vergil found himself in the Tower, and the following year lost his post as deputy collector. It is not clear from all this that Vergil deserves much sympathy, for in fuelling the opposition to Wolsey in Rome he had been acting in direct contradiction to the king's wishes. Moreover, the episode cannot have been so unpleasant for him, for he was to stay in England until 1553. Still, it certainly did not predispose him towards Wolsey – and the way he got his own back was to launch a sustained attack on him in his history. [2]

Edward Hall, the author of *The Union of the Two Noble and Illustre Famelies of York and Lancaster*, probably never came into contact with Wolsey. It is, therefore, unlikely that his antagonism derived from any personal animus, which has to be an argument for taking it more seriously. What does need to be borne in mind is that Hall had a very definite point of view. How typical it was of his London mercantile background is difficult to determine; he himself became a lawyer, but as under-sheriff of the City, he remained closely associated with its affairs. It is not at all clear that such circles were hostile to Wolsey, at least not in any consistent way. What Hall did share with many Englishmen was an intense francophobia. He was also very anti-clerical, supportive of the break with Rome, and indeed everything that

---

[1] Vergil, p.225.

[2] D. Hays's introduction to Vergil and *JWCI*, XII; also Chambers, 'English representation'. For Vergil's offending letter to Castellessi see *LP*, ii, 215.

Henry VIII did. He may even have been a Protestant, though there are difficulties in calling anybody that in the 1530s and 1540s when the religious divisions were still so confused.[1] Still, none of these things was likely to have made Hall sympathetic to someone who was not only a cardinal, but who was rather inclined to favour an alliance with the French. Not surprisingly, given his Protestant bias, Hall was not very sympathetic to Sir Thomas More, wondering, when commenting upon his execution, whether he should be called 'a foolish wiseman or a wise foolish man'.[2] It is a comment that has not influenced subsequent judgments on the future saint nearly as much as his many adverse comments on Wolsey – but then More was a common lawyer, a Speaker of the House of Commons, and, though obviously very Catholic, had never dressed up in red!

The present point is not that either Vergil or Hall was necessarily wrong about Wolsey – though this will become the argument – but that they were expressing not facts but their interpretation of them. In other words, their works are not primary sources, however tempting as readily available and contemporary accounts of Wolsey's political career it may be to use them as such. And just because their works have been of such easy access, their influence has been very pervasive, and always will be, even when historians are aware of the pitfalls. Most of the adverse judgments about Wolsey can be traced directly back to them, for it did not need the advent of the computer for it to become virtually impossible to remove or amend something once it has got into print. And if by any chance the source for these judgments is not Vergil or Hall, it is probably John Skelton.

In a recent study, it has been persuasively argued that Skelton was not just the crude 'Wolsey-basher' that he has usually been taken to be, nor was he even the paid hack of the Howards, that leading noble family supposedly dedicated to bringing Wolsey down.[3] Nevertheless, in two poems especially, *Speke Parott* and *Why come ye nat to Courte?*, Henry VII's poet laureate and tutor to his son and eventual heir, savaged Wolsey in one Skeltonic couplet after another. In some ways this has made it easier, for, unlike the two historians, it has been obvious to all that the poet was making no pretence at objectivity. Yet a few lines of poetry can be more destructive than any amount of prose; witness Dryden's portrayal of the first earl of Shaftesbury as Achitophel, or Shelley's two-line assassination of Castlereagh: 'I met murder on the way . . . /He had a face like Castlereagh'.[4] The force of Skelton's attack is cumulative, and thus does not lend itself to brief quotation; but, even when not at his rudest, his verse has had an enormous influence on the way people have looked at Wolsey. Take, for instance, his answer to his own question, 'Why come ye nat to Courte?'

> *To whyche court?*
> *To the kynges courte?*
> *Or to Hampton Court?*

---

[1] Surprisingly little work has been done on Hall, but see full entry in Bindoff; also McKisack, *Medieval History*.
[2] Hall, p.817.
[3] In G. Walker's *John Skelton*, which appeared too late for me to make as much use of it as I would have liked to; but my debt to the author predates its publication.
[4] Shelley, *The Mask of Anarchy*, l.5.

Nay, to the kynges court!
The kynges courte
Shulde have the excellence;
But Hampton Court
Hath the preemynence![1]

Here is the classic expression of the view of Wolsey as *alter rex*, or, indeed, as not just another king but as almost the sole source of power. It is a view that will be strenuously resisted in this study – but one has a suspicion that in the end Skelton will win out!

The reason for discussing these sources has not been to win sympathy for the poor historian, but, firstly, to alert the reader to some of the more obvious dangers that anyone trying to understand Wolsey must face, and, secondly, to draw attention to my approach, which to some extent has been dictated by the difficulties that the sources present. What follows is something akin to a detective story, in which all the evidence will be treated as clues to be shared with the reader. Of course, all history has an element of the detective story about it – or, to put it another way, involves interpretation. But often it is only the answers that are given, not the workings out; or these are relegated to the footnotes. There are good reasons for this: workings out are often rather confusing, and anyway it is answers that many readers want. Answers will be given here. Indeed, it is hoped that they may be the more persuasive for having the reasons behind them so fully discussed. The result is a more combative and argumentative work than some people will like, but at least they have been warned. And there is this advantage, that by allowing the reader to follow my reasoning so closely, by presenting alternatives, and even occasionally following false trails, he or she will be in a much better position to spot the mistakes, or just to make up his, or her own mind. Such an approach is perhaps especially appropriate where such a major work of restoration is being attempted.

[1] Skelton, p.289, ll.402-9.

CHAPTER ONE

FROM BUTCHER'S CUR TO LORDLY PRELATE

THE FIRST QUESTION THAT ANYONE INTERESTED IN WOLSEY IS BOUND TO ask is how it was that a not particularly well-connected fellow of Magdalen College, Oxford, became a cardinal and lord chancellor of England, and for fifteen years was Henry VIII's leading councillor – and it is an answer to such a question that this chapter seeks to provide. In doing so, it focuses on a subject which is anyway at the very heart of this book, the nature of the relationship between Wolsey and his king. Inevitably, the concentration will be on what attracted the two men to each other in the first place and the chronology of the early stages of the relationship. In particular, it will seek to determine at what moment Wolsey became Henry's leading councillor, or, as most accounts would have it, took over the reins of government. By and large it has been an early date that has been favoured; as early as the autumn of 1511, when England joined the Holy League against France, but certainly by the early summer of 1513 when Henry VIII, accompanied by Wolsey, led an expedition into France.[1] Such datings will be resisted, as, indeed, will be the view that Wolsey ever held the reins of power, if this is taken to mean that Henry VIII did not. Instead, the argument will be that at least until the signing of peace with France in 1514, the lord privy seal, Richard Fox, with years of experience behind him as one of Henry VII's leading advisers, played as important a role in major decision making as Wolsey did, even though he was increasingly anxious to retire. One consequence of this argument is that the decisions themselves, mainly to do with the conduct of foreign policy, will only be discussed insofar as they relate to Wolsey's rise to prominence. Another is that this chapter concerns itself not only with his relationship with Henry, but with such people as Fox, and Fox's alleged arch-rival, Thomas Howard earl of Surrey. This in turn will inevitably lead to a first look at the nature of early Tudor politics, and in particular at what has become something of an obsession with Tudor historians, the workings of 'faction'. But before any of this is done, some simple biographical information is required.[2]

The precise date of Wolsey's birth is not known, but it was probably in late 1472 or early the following year. His father, Robert, appears to have been a successful innkeeper and butcher in the Ipswich area.[3] Thomas was sent to Magdalen College, Oxford, having probably first attended the college's school;[4] at any rate it would have been quite normal for a person of his social and financial standing to have done so.[5] Though many details are missing, he clearly had a successful, if not

---

[1] See p.12 ff. for a full discussion of this issue.

[2] Wolsey's entry in Emden, *Oxford* remains the best source for this.

[3] I have discovered nothing that adds much to Redstone and Cameron; also useful are A.F. Pollard, pp.11-25 and Ridley, *The Statesman and the Fanatic*, pp.1-9, 18-28.

[4] There is no precise answer to the question of why Magdalen, but the college owned extensive property in East Anglia and the bishops of Norwich were entitled to fill four places from those in the diocese; for which see *Statutes of the Colleges of Oxford*, ii, p.17.

outstanding, academic career. He would have read first of all for a Bachelor of Arts degree, in his day normally taking four years to complete, followed by three years reading for a Master of Arts. There would then usually have been two years as 'regent in practice', essentially a junior teaching post, and only after this would he have started on his theology degree course. To obtain a B.Th. required at the very least a further seven years' study, but by the time Wolsey left the university in 1501 he had not taken his degree – not altogether surprising when one starts to do the arithmetic. Even if, as Cavendish had it from Wolsey himself,[1] he became a B.A. when only fifteen, probably in 1488 – and this would have been unusually young[2] – he could not have become a B.Th. until at the earliest 1498, and more reasonably 1500. If such distractions as his year as master of Magdalen School and his two years as bursar are then added, there was hardly time for him to have obtained the degree by 1501[3] – as anyone studying for a further degree today would surely confirm! In fact, nothing would be known about his academic attainments if in 1510 he had not obtained a grace to proceed to degrees of B.Th. and D.Th.,[4] something that would not have been granted if he had not gone a long way to meet the statutory requirements as to length of study and academic attainment.[5] There is documentary evidence for his having been bursar of Magdalen College and master of Magdalen School. There is nothing, however, in the records to support the college tradition that he was dismissed from the former office for financial impropriety in connection with the building of the college's most beautiful tower.[6] He certainly was not dismissed from his fellowship, which one might have thought would have been an inevitable consequence. In 1500-1, just prior to his resignation from the college, he held the mastership of the school and the quite senior post of dean of divinity, which does not suggest that he was in any way in disgrace. And there is nothing surprising about his resignation. Through the patronage of the marquess of Dorset, whose sons he had taught at Magdalen School, in October 1500 he became rector of Limington in Somerset. With the benefice came an income of £21, and thus some measure of financial security; and, more to the point, it was a statutory requirement that on obtaining a benefice worth more than £8 a year, a fellow should resign.[7]

Limington is the scene for another story not entirely to the credit of the young Wolsey. According to Cavendish, Wolsey managed to offend the local squire, Sir Amyas Paulet, and as a consequence was put in the stocks.[8] Unfortunately Cavendish gave no explanation for this but later two were given – one that Wolsey was a drunkard, the other that he was a fornicator![9] Be that as it may, as lord chancellor Wolsey supposedly got his revenge by insisting that Paulet be confined to

[5] Stainer, pp.23, 55.

[1] Cavendish, pp.4-5.
[2] He is more likely to have entered at fifteen and have graduated at eighteen or nineteen.
[3] McConica, *Collegiate University*, pp.165, 181-5, 295-6; Stainer, pp.31 ff.
[4] *Register of the University of Oxford*, pp.67, 296-7.
[5] J.M. Fletcher, pp.194-5.
[6] Macray, iii, p.19. See also A.F. Pollard, p.12 for a full discussion, though predictably he is unwilling to clear Wolsey completely of financial indiscretion.
[7] *Statutes of the Colleges of Oxford*, p.46. It was a requirement that was almost universal, though the value of the benefice varied; at New College it was 10 marks (£6 10s.).
[8] Cavendish, pp.5-6.

the Middle Temple, where he was made to supervise the building of a new gatehouse adorned with decoration in praise of the miscreant he had punished so many years previously. For Cavendish, the story served as a warning to all in authority to have a certain humility, because the wheel of fortune never stops going round – and who knows where it will deposit one next? In other words it was a moral fable, but based on how much truth? For Cavendish morality was always more important than accuracy, but it is doubtful that, even to point the moral, he would have gone to the trouble of a complete fabrication. What seems more likely is that he picked up gossip, itself derived merely from the fact that Paulet was for a time treasurer of the Middle Temple[1] – but to become such is not quite the same as being a prisoner there! Moreover, it is unlikely that Wolsey was resident at Limington long enough for any conflict between him and Paulet to have arisen. Clerical careerists were not inclined to linger in their first benefices, and it is much more likely that Wolsey was never resident at Limington. Very soon after resigning his fellowship he became chaplain to the archbishop of Canterbury, Henry Deane; and it must have been soon after because Deane died in 1503, having only been appointed in 1501. Thus, one way and another, the story as Cavendish presented it looks to have been so garbled as to bear little relation to the truth.

The patronage of a marquess and an archbishop of Canterbury made a promising beginning, but by 1503 both were dead. For a time Wolsey had to make do with service in the household of Sir Richard Nanfan, governor of Calais, where he seems to have resided until Nanfan's death in 1507. Only then did he make the vital transference to the royal household, becoming chaplain to Henry VII. As such, his duties were not in any sense confined to the saying of the office, or preaching, or indeed to any more general spiritual duties. There was very little specialization amongst household servants, whether royal or otherwise, clerical or secular. Someone with Wolsey's university training would have been expected to perform every kind of administrative duty, and in the royal household this would have included serving on missions abroad. Wolsey's experience at Calais especially equipped him for such work, and in 1508 he was sent both to Scotland and the Low Countries. Surviving correspondence between him and his royal master suggests that even within such a short time his views were being taken seriously,[2] and his appointment as dean of Lincoln in February 1509 is further evidence of the good impression that he was making. However, in April Henry VII died. As chaplain, Wolsey not surprisingly took part in the funeral service, but he may not have been immediately appointed chaplain to the new king.[3] Whether it is right to deduce from this that Margaret Beaufort, Henry VIII's grandmother, had taken against him is another matter.[4] There is no evidence that she had; and by November he was not

[9] The informants were the Elizabethans, Sir Roger Wilbraham (fornication) and Sir John Harrington (drunkenness); see Ridley, *The Statesman and the Fanatic*, p.20.

---

[1] A.F. Pollard, p.13.

[2] *Letters and Papers Illustrative*, i, pp.425-52.

[3] LP,i,20 for Henry VII's funeral. It is Wolsey's absence from any lists drawn up for Henry VIII's coronation (LP,i,82) which has led to the speculation that he must have temporarily lost his position as chaplain.

[4] A.F. Pollard, p.13.

only once again royal chaplain, but also almoner – but by then Margaret was dead.

It is on such slender evidence – the coincidence of her death on 30 July and Wolsey's reappointment to the royal household on, as has been assumed wrongly, 8 November, that the stuff, or should one say the fantasy, of faction has been built.[1] In fact, all that is known for certain is that by that date he already held both offices; and my guess would be that he was appointed almoner on Thomas Hobbs's death in September, and that probably he had never ceased to be a royal chaplain. But whatever the truth of this, from November 1509 Wolsey's career was to proceed in leaps and bounds. In April 1510 he was appointed registrar of the Order of the Garter. There followed a burst of ecclesiastical preferments, culminating in February 1513 in the deanery of York. The successful campaign in France during the summer of that year, in the organization of which he played a leading part, brought him the rather doubtful benefit of the bishopric of Tournai, his claim to which in the face of a French rival he never made effective. However, by March 1514 Wolsey was bishop of Lincoln, and by September he had been translated to York. On 10 September 1515 he became a cardinal, and on 24 December lord chancellor. In May 1518 he obtained his first commission as legate *a latere*, thereby securing at least a legal supremacy over the English Church, and by maintaining pressure on the papacy he was to have it periodically renewed, and enlarged, until in January 1524 he became legate *a latere* for life.[2] Meanwhile in July 1518 he had obtained the bishopric of Bath and Wells *in commendam*, which is to say he held it in conjunction with York. In 1523 he exchanged it for Durham, and in 1529 he exchanged Durham for Winchester, while all the time remaining archbishop of York. In addition, in November 1521 he had been granted the abbacy of St Albans, which he thus held *in commendam* with his bishoprics.[3] Pluralism, or the holding of a number of ecclesiastical offices at the same time, was a commonplace of the period, and had been for much of the Church's history. Nevertheless, though common on the continent, in an English context the practice of holding *in commendam* was unprecedented. Thus John Morton, whose political authority under Henry VII was similar to Wolsey's under Henry VIII, became archbishop of Canterbury and a cardinal, but never held more than one episcopal office, nor did he combine such an office with an abbacy. It will be argued subsequently that the difference is to be explained not by Wolsey's greater greed, but by Henry VIII's greater standing in European affairs. That, however, raises the question as to why Henry was so anxious to promote Wolsey in this very generous way.

Broadly, there have been two responses to such a question. One has it that Henry was weak and lazy, a natural victim to every scheming courtier or ambitious cleric. Like most weak people, according to this argument, he was also a poor judge of men, and, though he could put his faith in somebody as statesmanlike as Thomas Cromwell, he was just as likely to be seduced by Tom, Dick or Harry – but even

---

[1] LP,i,257 (31); it is a royal grant to Wolsey as almoner rather than his appointment to the office. The fact that Wolsey had not obtained the office on the death of John Edenham in July may lend credence to some version of the conspiracy theory, but it does not have to. Hobbs had been a royal chaplain for much longer than Wolsey and was a very strong candidate for the office; see his entry under 'Hobbys' in Emden, *Oxford*.

[2] See p.265.

[3] See Wolsey's entry in Emden, *Oxford* for all the above details.

more by a Catherine, Anne or Jane! Admittedly in such a scenario Wolsey is a slight anomaly. He did, after all, hold a position of considerable power for fifteen years, which suggests a modicum of constancy on Henry's part. However, the way round this has been to concentrate on Wolsey's particularly effective – some have even thought magical – powers of seduction on a young and therefore more than usually impressionable Henry. Not until he grew up would he try to take the reins of power into his own hands, only to fall even more swiftly into the clutches of somebody else. Or to put it another way, the more Henry tried to be king, the more obviously his weaknesses were exposed. However, in the context of Wolsey's rise to prominence the key has been seen to be an essentially passive Henry being manipulated by a very active Wolsey – a view which can easily complement that of an excessively greedy Wolsey.[1]

The counter-argument, if not exactly the reverse of the first because it has never been suggested that Wolsey was weak, has placed the emphasis on a powerful Henry dominating all that he surveyed, and insofar as there was factional fighting very much the puppeteer rather than the puppet. It is the Henry of the Holbein portraits, bull-like in his bulk and arrogance. It is the Henry who got through six wives and in the process executed two of them; the Henry of the Field of Cloth of Gold, the Henry who no sooner had he been proclaimed Defender of the Faith by one pope than he repudiated the authority of another and took the English Church into schism – and, as it turned out, into the Protestant camp. And if this was what Henry was like, then the explanation for Wolsey's rise is simply that Henry saw him as a suitable instrument for his own ambitions – and when he ceased to be such, he was dismissed.[2]

Contrasts of this kind are helpful in finding one's way about, but they also distort and exaggerate. In the course of this book, it is hoped, some shading will emerge. Henry, after all, was not a bull, and to get through six wives is not necessarily a sign of strength. Nevertheless, of these two ways of looking at Henry it is the latter that will be adopted here.[3] There are many reasons for this, but, not I hope too perversely, the best way of explaining the decision is to show how the alternative view has developed. In so doing, it will be possible to examine in some detail the influence that the major literary sources have exerted on subsequent

---

[1] The *locus classicus* is Elton's *Henry VIII* of 1962, but see *inter alia* his 'King of hearts' in *Studies*, i, pp.100-8, a review of J.J. Scarisbrick's *Henry VIII*, a biography which began the counter-attack to Elton's view, and remains in my view the most stimulating history of the reign. Meanwhile, Elton's view has been developed to present a picture of Henry as the victim of faction; in particular by his former pupil, D.R. Starkey – perhaps most characteristically in *History Today*, 32 (1982) – and by E.W. Ives in *Anne Boleyn* and *Faction in Tudor England*. For an important review of all these historians' work, in which their view of Henry VIII is seriously questioned, see Bernard, *HJ*, 31.

[2] Arguably this Henry is more my own construct, and it is important to point out that the dominant Henry can be either a 'goody', as in Pollard's *Henry VIII*, or a 'baddy', as in W.G. Hoskins's *The Age of Plunder* and J. Hurstfield's 'Was there a Tudor despotism?', both of which quote Sir Walter Raleigh: 'Now for King Henry the eight: if all the pictures and patterns of a merciless prince were lost in the world, they might all again be painted to the life, out of the story of this king.' L. Baldwin Smith's *Henry VIII* is also relevant, see p.23, n.2 below.

[3] My views on Henry VIII are very close to those of G.W. Bernard, no doubt because we have so often discussed the king's personality together, but see especially his *War, Taxation and Rebellion*, pp.40-5, 60-6.

interpretations. What will also emerge is a more informative chronology of Wolsey's rise than the mere recital of the principal offices he held in Church and state.

The notion that it was a passive Henry – in the words of Sir Geoffrey Elton, the most influential modern exponent of the view, a 'bit of a booby and a bit of a baby'[1] – manipulated by the wily Wolsey goes back, like so much else that is unfavourable to him, to Polydore Vergil. Indeed, Vergil is virtually the only contemporary source for Wolsey's political career before 1515. Hall is surprisingly laconic; his first mention of Wolsey is not until his appointment as bishop of Lincoln in February 1514, by which time, in most accounts, Wolsey had already masterminded the 1513 campaign in France.[2] He does, however, suggest that Wolsey was behind the diplomatic revolution of the summer of 1514, whereby Henry, having spent a year or two fighting the French, suddenly deserted the Habsburgs and Ferdinand of Aragon, and married his sister to the king of France.[3] As Hall hated the French, it provides him with the occasion of awarding the first black mark; but as regards Wolsey's rise to influence, all he ventures is that, when in the November of that year Wolsey was translated to York, he 'bare all the rule about the king, and what he said was obeyed in all places'.[4] Obviously, Cavendish has something to say about Wolsey's rise, but, as was made clear earlier, his account of his career prior to 1523 was derivative, if, in part, derived from Wolsey himself. Nevertheless, in some respects Cavendish's account is of a man willing and able to take advantage of a 'young and lusty' king only too happy to place all 'troublesome business' in someone else's hands.[5] To that extent he is an exponent, and source, of the passive view of Henry. However, he makes some rather important qualifications – of which more later – and anyway does not attempt anything like such a detailed account as Vergil. As for Skelton, that most influential jibe, already quoted, about the pre-eminence of Hampton Court over the king's court puts him firmly in the same camp. It is he who, along with William Tyndale,[6] ascribed Wolsey's ascendancy to

> . . . sorsery
> Or such other loselry
> As wychecraft or charmyng;[7]

As for one of the most important non-literary sources for Wolsey's early years as leading royal councillor, the reports of Sebastian Giustinian, the Venetian ambassador – and incidentally one of the shrewdest of all Wolsey-watchers – they are disappointing on this subject; but then, arriving in England in April 1515, when Wolsey's influence with the king was obvious to everybody, Giustinian can be excused for seeing it as already a fact of English political life.[8]

It is Polydore Vergil who produced the first full account of the Machiavellian young cleric twisting the tail not only of an even younger monarch but of all that

[1] Elton, 'King of hearts', p.104.
[2] Hall, p.567.
[3] Ibid, p.569.
[4] Ibid, p.581.
[5] Cavendish, pp.11-14.
[6] Tyndale, *Exposition and Notes*, p.308.
[7] Skelton, p.295, ll.663-5.
[8] Calendared in *LP* and *Ven. Cal.*, but for full transcripts see Rawdon Brown. For his first comments on Wolsey see ibid., p.110 (*LP*,ii,666).

monarch's councillors, and in the process knifing in the back the person who had, in his account, done most to promote his career, the bishop of Winchester, Richard Fox.[1] And in developing his account, Vergil presents a political scenario for the first years of Henry VIII's reign which has very much centre stage the rivalry between Fox and Thomas Howard earl of Surrey for the heart and mind of the new king. Both these men had been of great importance in the previous reign. Fox had come over with Henry Tudor in 1485, was immediately appointed royal secretary, and then in 1487 keeper of the privy seal, at the same time obtaining his first bishopric, that of Exeter.[2] Others followed quickly: Bath and Wells in 1492, Durham in 1494, and Winchester, the wealthiest see in England, in 1501. Though none was held *in commendam*, as in Wolsey's case, these promotions are evidence of Henry VII's confidence in him. He never seems, however, to have quite succeeded to the pre-eminent position that Cardinal Morton maintained in that king's affairs until his death in September 1500; nor, for instance, did he succeed Morton as archbishop of Canterbury. Nevertheless, an area in which Fox always seems to have played a particularly important role was in the conduct of foreign affairs.[3] He was chief English negotiator for the Treaty of Etaples with France in 1492, and for the Magnus Intercursus, an important commercial treaty with the Low Countries, in 1496. He was also much involved in the protracted negotiations with Scotland which had culminated in the marriage of Henry's eldest daughter, Margaret, to James IV in 1503, and in the equally protracted negotiations which had led to Catherine of Aragon's marriage, first to Prince Arthur in 1501, and second to Prince Henry in June 1509, by which time the prince had become Henry VIII.

Along with his father, the first Howard duke of Norfolk, the earl of Surrey had had the misfortune to choose the losing side in 1485.[4] The father had paid for the mistake with his life on the field of Bosworth. The son was attainted, but four years later was restored to his earldom, and sent north as lieutenant-general of the Scottish marches under Prince Arthur. This in effect made him the king's leading representative in the area. As such he had put down the Yorkshire rising of 1489, and in the autumn of 1496 had successfully resisted a Scottish invasion. In 1501 he had been appointed lord treasurer, and by this time had also recovered much of the Howard property lost at the attainder; and for the rest it was mostly a question of waiting for the relevant people to die.[5] Thus, long before Henry VII's death, though still without his dukedom, Surrey had re-established himself as a leading magnate and royal councillor. This meant he had had to work alongside Richard Fox, and there is no evidence from Henry VII's reign that they had not worked well together.[6] Nevertheless, according to Vergil, the new reign saw them fighting for supremacy, and in that fight, again according to Vergil, Wolsey saw his opportunity.

[1] See Vergil, pp.194-200 for his account of Wolsey's rise. It appeared first in the 1555 edition; those of 1534 and 1546 ended with Henry VII's death.

[2] There has been no recent detailed study of Fox, so that E.C. Batten's introduction to *Registers of Richard Fox* of 1889 still provides the best biographical information. But for a recent pen portrait see Oakley, pp.285-300.

[3] Called by S.B. Chrimes, in his *Henry VII*, p.109, 'Henry VII's ace negotiator'.

[4] Tucker's is the only recent life – though I am not happy with the interpretation.

[5] Virgoe.

[6] Tucker, pp.68-9.

Vergil states that Fox, realizing that he could not counter the Howard influence alone, picked on Wolsey as an effective ally, took every opportunity to promote him in the eyes of the new king, and, to cut a long story short, succeeded only too well. More even than Cavendish, Vergil describes the complete seduction of the young Henry by a Wolsey prepared to turn his own house into 'a temple of all pleasures', the better to distract the king from affairs of state. And in that temple Wolsey set about convincing the king 'that the governing of the kingdom was safer in the hands of one than of several, and that it was right for it to be committed to someone other than Henry himself until such time as he had reached maturity – and thus he put Wolsey in charge of affairs'. However, Fox was then to find, along with all Wolsey's old friends, that his friendship was no longer valued. Vergil does not in fact state that Wolsey engineered Fox's resignation in May 1516, or indeed Archbishop Warham's as lord chancellor in the previous December – though this has not prevented subsequent historians from suggesting it[1] – but he comes fairly close to doing so. According to him, Wolsey had by this time already become 'so proud that he considered himself the peer of kings', so that by his arrogance and ambition he had 'raised against himself the hatred of the whole people and, in his hostility towards nobles and common folk, procured their great irritation at his vainglory'. At the beginning, admittedly, Wolsey's rule may have had 'a shadowy appearance of justice' but 'because it was only a shadow' this quickly disappeared, 'Wolsey conducting all business at his own pleasure . . . It was certainly as a result of this that several leading councillors . . . withdrew gradually from court. Canterbury and Winchester were among the first to leave.'[2]

Vergil's message is clear. Fox had been hoist by his own petard, the petard in question being his own protégé, Thomas Wolsey. Is it right? A lot depends on the answer, much more than merely an account of the early years of Henry VIII's reign – though Vergil's happens to be the only coherent interpretation of those years. What it has done is provide subsequent historians with a framework which has an upstart Wolsey dominating if not a weak, at least a youthful and inexperienced king to the exclusion of the rest of the political nation, until by the end of the 1520s king and political nation had had enough, and Wolsey was thrown out. Obviously, if Vergil got the early scenario wrong, then the rest of the framework is seriously undermined. If he got it right, then most of what follows here is wrong! It is, therefore, important to look at the matter in some detail. Did the rivalry between Fox and Surrey dominate the first years of Henry's reign? What was Wolsey's relationship to Fox? How did it affect his relationship with Henry? And, perhaps most important of all, is it possible to decide which view of Henry is correct, because, as has already been indicated, on that depends an interpretation of Wolsey's career? It is with these sorts of questions, arising out of Polydore Vergil's 'conspiracy theory', that the rest of this chapter will concern itself.

One of the problems in trying to arrive at some answers is the severe shortage of evidence for the early years of Henry's reign. To take first the question of Fox's

---

[1] Most notably G.W. Bernard in *Early Tudor Nobility*, pp.21-3, but see also A.F. Pollard, p.109. For a more sceptical view see Scarisbrick, *Henry VIII*, p.42.

[2] For all the quotations above see Vergil, pp.194-200, though I have translated from the original Latin given there.

rivalry with Surrey, there are only a handful of documents that throw any light on the matter, and over half of these are rather generalized references to Fox being in a position of great influence.[1] This leaves only two documents of any significance – and it has to be admitted that on first reading they may appear to confirm Vergil's account. The first in chronological order is a letter of Lord Darcy to Fox in about August 1509.[2] In it he reported back London gossip brought north by merchants to the effect that

> the Lord Privy Seal [Fox] seeing of his own craft and policy he cannot bring himself to rule the king's grace and put out of favour the earl of Surrey, the earl of Shrewsbury, the bishop of Durham, Mr Marney, Mr Brandon and Lord Darcy, now he will prove another way, which is to bring in and bolster himself to rule all with the duke of Buckingham and the earl of Northumberland. And doubtless, fast they curse and speak evil of my Lord Privy Seal.

What this letter does not confirm are some of the later elaborations of the Vergil thesis, for there is no hint that Fox was at the head of a clerical 'peace' party, and Surrey an aristocratic 'war' party[3] – and of course there is no mention of Wolsey, but then it is very early. Still, as regards the central issue, the rivalry between Fox and Surrey, it could hardly be more convincing – until one reads on. 'My Lord,' Darcy continued, 'good it is to have a good eye, though much be but sayings. As I hear, I will warn you, my lord of Durham and Mr Marney whilst I live. And further show this as you think seems good to the king's grace, or otherwise'.[4] The picture immediately alters. If, as alleged, Darcy had been part of the Surrey faction, he would hardly have written to Fox about it, nor would he have wanted to inform him of the names of other members of it. Moreover, he would not have suggested that Fox inform the king of such gossip if he seriously believed that Fox was involved in a battle for the heart and mind of the young Henry with his rival Surrey. Indeed, it was precisely because he did not believe it to be true that he thought Fox, and perhaps the king, should know about it, for all such idle gossip was dangerous.

Darcy's comment that 'much be but sayings' provides a suitable warning as regards any discussion of faction in the early Tudor period, and his letter serves as a reminder, if one is ever needed, that gossip is not always true! What is required is to submit such evidence to various tests: where has it come from and why? And is it probable? Why, for instance, should two men who seem to have got on perfectly well under Henry VII have suddenly fallen out? The answer is that supposedly they each saw themselves as a 'king-maker', but in fact nothing that is known about either of them suggests that this is at all likely. Fox appears to have been the very model of a loyal and most conscientious servant of the Tudor state. Admittedly, Surrey had made the mistake of fighting for Richard III at Bosworth, but given how much his family owed the Yorkists, this may not have been held so much against him for it suggested a capacity for loyalty that could be harnessed to the new regime, which seems to have been what happened. His initial mistake certainly inclined the

---

[1] For ambassadorial comments to that effect in 1510 see *Ven. Cal.*, ii, 64; *Sp. Cal.*, ii, pp. 40-2.

[2] *LP*, i, 157 (PRO SP1/229/fo. 8).

[3] For these see R.H. Brodie in *LP*, i, intro., xiii f; A.F. Pollard, pp. 10-11, 17; Scarisbrick, *Henry VIII*, pp. 25-6; Tucker, pp. 94 ff.

[4] *LP*, i, 157.

earl to extreme caution and a determination not to repeat it – and attempting to be a 'king-maker' had to be a risky business. Nor does Surrey really look to have been a man anxious to head a 'war faction'. His experience was almost entirely bound up with the defence of England's boundary with Scotland,[1] which is why, when war with France came in 1513, he was left behind, thereby being given the opportunity of becoming the great victor of Flodden. But, if defence of the northern boundary was your major concern, the last thing you would have wanted is a war with Scotland's traditional ally, France, and thus one suspects that as regards foreign policy as well Surrey would have been all caution.

Much more likely candidates for a 'war faction' are the young companions with whom Henry surrounded himself on becoming king. Inevitably it was something of a magic circle, the brightest and the best of England's youth, or at least of those who were closely connected with the Tudor regime. On the hunting ground, in the tiltyard, at the elaborate court entertainments and other royal diversions such as gambling, the likes of Edward and Henry Guildford, Charles Brandon the future duke of Suffolk, Thomas Knyvet, but above all Edward Howard, a younger son of the earl of Surrey, were constantly at Henry's side. These men probably did see war as an opportunity to win fame and fortune, and certainly when the fighting broke out they were immediately in the thick of it; so much so that by April 1513 Knyvet and Howard were both dead, killed in glorious, if rather futile, naval engagements with the French.[2]

But if this group constituted a 'war faction', it almost certainly lacked Surrey as its head, despite the fact that he was the father of its most prominent member. Unfitted by temperament and policy for such a role, he also seems not to have got on with his son. The evidence for this is provided by Charles Brandon, himself a leading member of this magic circle, and Edward Howard's closest friend and executor.[3] In October 1514 Brandon made it clear to Wolsey that he viewed the Howard family with the gravest suspicion.[4] To have been such a friend of one member of a family and so suspicious of all the others would have been difficult if that friend had been especially close to his family, and the fact that Edward made none of his relatives an executor also points to an uneasy relationship.[5] He was also temperamentally different from his father, and indeed from his eldest brother Thomas, the future 3rd duke of Norfolk.[6] What, however, Brandon's comments do suggest is a certain confidence that Wolsey would be sympathetic to critical comments about the Howards. And there is a much earlier letter of Wolsey's in which he himself was critical, and to none other than Richard Fox – and this letter provides the second piece of evidence directly relating to rivalry between Fox and Surrey, and the only one to give any real indication as to where Wolsey stood.

Writing from 'Windsor the last day of September [1511], with the rude hand of

---

[1] Tucker, pp.51-74.

[2] Gunn, *Charles Brandon*, pp.6-8; Starkey, 'The king's privy chamber', pp.80 ff.

[3] Gunn, *Charles Brandon*, p.8.

[4] *LP*,i,3376 – Suffolk to Wolsey, 20 Oct.

[5] Gunn, *Charles Brandon*, p.8.

[6] Very much my own judgement, based on the readily available sources, without the benefit of S. Vokes's research into the early career of Thomas, the future 3rd duke, which appeared too late to be consulted. But I am thankful to her for a number of conversations on the subject.

your true and humble priest', Wolsey ventured to remark that Surrey

> at his last coming to the king . . . had such manner and countenance showed on him
> that on the morrow he departed home again, and yet is not returned to court. With a
> little help now he might be utterly, as touching lodging in the same, excluded: whereof
> in my poor judgement no little good should ensue . . . Mr Howard [Edward]
> marvelously incenseth the king against the Scots; by whose wanton means his grace
> spendeth much money, and is more disposed to war than peace. Your presence shall be
> very necessary to repress this appetite.[1]

Here surely is incontrovertible evidence that Fox and Surrey were in conflict, that
Wolsey sided with the former, and indeed saw him as his patron – proof, in other
words, that Vergil has got it right? Moreover, it would appear that Fox was rather in
favour of peace and the Howards in favour of war.

In fact the letter supports none of these points – or, at least, not to the extent
that a first reading might suggest. Perhaps the first thing to emphasize is not just that
it is the sole piece of documentary evidence that bears directly on the matter, but its
chronological isolation. It happens to be the earliest letter to have survived between
Wolsey and Fox; the next is not until almost a year later. And it is not until May of
the following year that there is anything like a sequence. Moreover, it is not as if
there are letters between other people that might throw additional light on the
political groupings at court. It must, therefore, be wrong to attach too much
significance to remarks about the Howards that may represent very temporary
feelings. And that they were temporary is suggested by a letter from Sir Edward
Howard to Wolsey in November 1512, thanking him for his kindness towards him in
his absence, which he had only just learnt about from Brandon, and also for the
'great reward' which the king had sent him, as he put it, at Wolsey's instance.[2] In
1513 letters from Edward's elder brother, Thomas, to Wolsey are friendly enough in
tone.[3] It will, in fact, be a theme of this study that one of Wolsey's gifts was an
ability to get on with people, and that, for instance, far from antagonizing the
nobility of England, he always strove to be conciliatory. What this does not have to
mean, however, is that he was a close friend of all of them, or that he was in all
circumstances unwilling to criticize them – and, indeed, the notion of getting on
may imply some measure of insincerity. Moreover, there is always a problem in
interpreting letters between 'establishment' figures, for they are written in a coded
insincerity always difficult to decipher, but especially if it comes from a different era.
So I am not claiming that these letters are proof of a genuine friendship, only that
they indicate that Wolsey and the Howards were perfectly capable of getting on
with one another. In other words, they had just the sort of good working
relationship one would expect to find amongst leading courtiers and royal
councillors when there was firm direction from the top.[4]

What else can one learn from Wolsey's letter to Fox? He did indeed talk of
peace, but very much in the context of Anglo-Scottish relations. It is an important
qualification, for even as Wolsey wrote Henry was moving towards war on a number

---

[1] Richard Fox, p.54 (LP,i,880). It provides a full transcript.
[2] LP,i,1480.
[3] LP,i,1852, 1883, 1965.
[4] For a full discussion of this topic see pp.178-9, 565-70.

of fronts. In May 1511 Lord Darcy had been allowed to take a small force to Spain in order to aid Ferdinand of Aragon in a 'crusade' against the Moors, while a small English force was aiding Margaret of Austria against the incursions of the duke of Gelders. Six weeks later England, together with Ferdinand, the Swiss and the Venetians, had joined a Holy League in defence of Pope Julius II against the 'schismatic' Louis XII. Thus, English foreign policy was moving strongly and fairly swiftly in the direction of conflict with France, so that if Fox was at the head of a 'peace faction' he had definitely lost the argument – and there is not much hint of this in the letter. It is possible that Wolsey was merely stringing Fox along, and had already secretly joined the winning 'war faction' – or, as some people would have it, that Wolsey and Henry alone constituted the 'war faction' against all the former king's councillors who were frightened by the aggressive stance adopted by the new king.[1] But there is no hint of that either, and there is another, simpler, explanation. What Wolsey, and it is implied Fox, disliked about conflict with Scotland – and indeed about something else Wolsey mentioned, Darcy's 'crusade', on which the king had spent £1,000 – was that 'the king's money goeth away in every corner'. And why was this so worrying? Because they were all too aware that in any major conflict with France very large sums of money would be needed. This is, of course, to go beyond the actual wording of the letter, but it makes more sense of it, especially given the fact that for the next two years both Wolsey and Fox were going to be up to their necks in organizing England's war effort. If this interpretation is correct, then Wolsey's criticisms of the Howards should be taken not as evidence of a deep-seated hatred of his political patron's greatest rivals, nor of a fundamental disagreement over foreign policy, but rather as a reflection of his annoyance that Howard incompetence was not helping the conduct of the king's affairs. In other words, what one is witnessing is not factional intrigue, but the normal ups and downs of men working under considerable pressure.

It may seem that we have moved a long way from Vergil's 'conspiracy theory', but if the conclusion reached so far is correct, Vergil's explanation for Wolsey's rise is seriously undermined. If there was no major conflict between Fox and Surrey, then there was no need for Fox to push his protégé in the king's direction in order to further the struggle. Moreover, it is beginning to look as if Henry's role in affairs was rather greater than the 'conspiracy theory' or, indeed, any factional view of his reign allows. And, of course, the greater Henry's role and the stronger his personality, the less likely is it that he would fall victim to anybody's seductive powers, even Wolsey's. But before Henry's personality is looked at in more detail, it may be helpful to take a little further the relationship between Wolsey and Fox. For one thing, some evidence of it has survived, and there is hardly enough evidence of any kind for this early period for it to be ignored. For another, it will help further to establish the way in which politics worked and to stake out the chronology of Wolsey's increasing influence.

Probably the only point that should be retained from Vergil's account of Wolsey's rise is that he and Fox did have a close relationship, and that, naturally enough in its early stages, the vastly experienced and by all accounts highly astute Fox was the dominant partner. Cavendish confirms this, while adding another

[1] Tucker, p.98.

patron, Sir Thomas Lovell, 'a very sage counsellor and witty, being master of the king's wards and constable of the Tower'.[1] In fact, Wolsey's letter to Fox of September 1511 provides the only piece of documentary evidence of any special relationship with Lovell, for in it Wolsey mentioned that Lovell, referred to as 'Mr Treasurer' (that is treasurer of the household), was the one person to whom he might disclose the chief concern of Fox's letters, and his reply – for the comments about the Howards and foreign policy had merely provided a coda. This was which candidate Henry should support in what was thought to be, as it turned out wrongly, an imminent papal election. Fox's and Wolsey's preferred candidate, ironically, was Polydore Vergil's patron, Cardinal Castellesi, who by 1515 was to be completely out of favour with Wolsey. What is more relevant here is the tone Wolsey adopted towards Fox. He told the bishop of Winchester that he had spoken to the king about Castellesi and had found him

> very conformable and agreeable to my saying. Howbeit I durst not further wade with his grace as touching your letters of recommendation, as well for the 'renouelyng' of your letters and the dates of the same, as also we have no sure knowledge of the pope's death otherwise than is before said. Your lordship, I trust, is no thing miscontent with that I presumed to break your instructions; for assuredly . . . I am half afraid that you be displeased for as much as I have received no writing from you this long season. I trust you will take my doing (which proceded of good will, thinking that it was for the best) in good part.[2]

It is the letter of one who saw himself as the junior partner but who was prepared to take the initiative, not because he was desperately anxious to supplant his senior, but because his senior was not around to make the decisions for himself. If he had been, it was Wolsey's view that

> this matter would be soon brought to your purposes. And my lord, for divers urgent causes it is thought very expedient that you should repair to the king; for all his great matters be deferred on to your coming: which is daily looked for and desired of all those that would the king's causes should proceed in good train.[3]

For those who would see Fox as the ambitious leader of a faction, his absence from court at what was apparently a critical time needs some explanation, and for those who see Wolsey as entirely consumed with ambition it may come as a surprise to see him begging Fox to come to court in order to take up what was assumed by Wolsey to be his natural role, not as the head of a faction but as a leading royal councillor. A year later Wolsey was still writing with 'a rude hand' and was still deferring to a senior, who was not as in touch with the day-to-day events at court as he was.[4] By 1513 a change had taken place but one foreshadowed in the earlier letters. War with France had by then become a reality, and preparations for various expeditions, including one led by the king himself, were very much under way. In May Fox was instructed to take charge of the victualling of the various fleets and

---

[1] Cavendish, p.7.
[2] Richard Fox, pp. 52-3 (*LP*, i, 880).
[3] Richard Fox, p.53 (*LP*, i, 880).
[4] Richard Fox, pp. 56-8 (*LP*, i, 1356).

armies assembling at Southampton and Portsmouth, and in this connection seven letters from him to Wolsey have survived,[1] all written 'with the shaking hand of your loving brother', presumably shaking because of Fox's health and age, of which more shortly. There is no doubt that Fox now saw himself in a subordinate role to Wolsey, as an executor rather than as a maker of policy. On the other hand, the letters convey no sense that Fox felt that he had been deliberately demoted or pushed aside by his former protégé. The feeling is rather of a man reluctantly being dragged back into the political arena because in the special circumstances he could hardly avoid it. As bishop of Winchester and lord privy seal, he was by far and away the most important royal councillor in the area of the assembling forces, and his experience in the conduct of war, including Henry vii's expedition to France in 1492, had to be invaluable. Thus his letters were peppered with advice. Much of it had to do with the details of victualling: Wolsey must instruct the lord admiral, Thomas Howard, to see that the victuallers return immediately; he must see that escorts were provided to protect the victualling ships; he must send down Edward Radcliffe, the second clerk of the kitchen, to inspect some casked beef before it went bad. Other advice touched on major policy matters such as Maximilian's probable reaction to the recently made truce between Ferdinand and Louis xii, and James iv of Scotland's likely reaction to England's invasion of France. And with each letter Fox became increasingly anxious to be kept informed, though well aware that Wolsey might not himself have time to write. Then, when no replies came, he got upset, especially since, as he did not hesitate to point out, 'some part of them were matter of charge'.[2] Nevertheless, the tone throughout remained warm, the overall impression very much that of a man anxious to be as helpful as possible, partly because he knew only too well the enormous strain that Wolsey was under; indeed at one point he commented that if Wolsey was not soon delivered of his 'outrageous charge and labour', he 'shall have a cold stomach, little sleep, pale image and a thin belly *cum rara egestione*: all which and as deaf as a stock, I had when in your case'.[3]

What emerges from this spate of correspondence is that, despite the fact that Fox no longer saw himself as Wolsey's senior in royal government, he bore no resentment. It is also clear that he saw Wolsey as occupying a central position in that government. Does that mean that by May 1513 Wolsey had reached the top, and that, for instance, one can definitely begin to talk about Wolsey's foreign policy? Many distinguished historians have thought so, and some indeed would put it even earlier, associating the English decision to join the Holy League in the autumn of 1511 with Wolsey's increasing ascendancy, despite the fact that such a view rather conflicts with the idea of Wolsey as a subordinate in Fox's 'peace faction'.[4] In this account a note of caution will be sounded. It is not that Wolsey's

---

[1] Richard Fox, pp.60 ff. (*LP*,i,1858, 1881, 1885, 1899, 1912, 1960, 1976).

[2] Richard Fox, p.73 (*LP*,i,1976).

[3] Richard Fox, p.70 (*LP*,i,1912).

[4] Commenting on England's adherence to the Holy League against France in Nov. 1511, Pollard wrote: 'The peace party . . . had received a shot between wind and water. Its mainstays had been Foxe and Warham; but how could they resist when the silver trumpet called them not to convocation, but to war? Henry and Wolsey were at one, but Warham at least held out.' (A.F. Pollard, p.17). Later he has Wolsey in 'full control' during 1513 and 1514 (ibid, p.108). For Scarisbrick, 'if Wolsey mattered, as he

importance by this time is denied, because everything points to it; but what it also points to is that, with the increased activity in foreign affairs brought about by war with France, Fox too resumed a more active role. Despite his age and infirmity, he accompanied Henry and Wolsey on the expedition to France, even suffering, if not quite a war wound, at least a nasty kick from a horse, so that 'for some days he could neither sit nor stand'.[1] This did not, however, prevent him from playing a major part in decision-making, so that when, at a vital stage in the siege of Tournai, a delegation from the city met Henry and Maximilian, it was Fox, not Wolsey, who summarized the earlier negotiations.[2] When a little later Maximilian's behaviour caused offence to the English, it was with Fox as well as Wolsey that Margaret of Austria met to try and put things to rights.[3] And in the following year Fox's involvement was to continue.

The year 1514 saw one of those diplomatic volte-faces that were to characterize what is usually referred to as 'Wolsey's foreign policy'. Having appeared at the beginning of the year to be determined to carry on the war with France, if anything on an even larger scale, the English unceremoniously ditched their allies and unilaterally made peace with the French. And to celebrate the new alliance, a marriage was arranged between the recently widowed, and physically much the worse for wear, Louis XII, and Henry's youngest and by all accounts rather attractive sister, Mary. It was a bold manoeuvre intended to consolidate the position of European importance that the successful campaign of the previous year had helped to secure. England was now able to influence French policy and, in alliance with France, to dominate the rest of Europe – or at least that was the intention. When Wolsey's handling of foreign affairs comes to be looked at in detail it will be seen that this simple idea, of using the French as a lever to exert maximum influence on the other powers of Europe, lay at its heart. Thus, it is not surprising that historians, from Edward Hall onwards, have credited the peace with France to Wolsey, and seen it as further confirmation that the control of England's foreign policy was now completely in his hands.[4] Moreover, in August 1515 Henry wrote to the pope that no one had 'laboured and sweated' for this peace as much as Wolsey had,[5] while in July of the following year Wolsey himself claimed that he had been its author.[6] Almost certainly, both were exaggerating Wolsey's role in the interests of diplomacy, something that Wolsey was very prone to do; and the reason for thinking this is a letter that Fox wrote to Wolsey on 17 April 1514.

The letter is unfortunately much mutilated, but what emerges is that both men were still working very closely together on some important negotiations, so much so that Fox advised that, other than the king, no one should know of them in case

---

did, by 1512, he mattered still more by the end of 1513. It was his firm hands which had largely shaped the campaign in France of that year . . .' (*Henry VIII*, p.41). There was gossip to the effect that Wolsey and Ruthal were responsible for the French and Scottish campaigns of 1513; see Ruthal to Wolsey, 24 Oct. 1513 (*LP*,i,2394).

[1] Recorded in John Taylor's diary of the expedition (*LP*,i,2391, p.1059).
[2] Cruickshank, p.148.
[3] *LP*,i,2367, 2372.
[4] Hall, p.569.
[5] *LP*,i,5140.
[6] In conversation with the Venetian ambassador; see Rawdon Brown, i, p.111 (*LP*,ii,666).

'some folks . . . would say that we were over much busier than is needed, and if none effect come thereof, they might give cause of mockery'.[1] To the proponents of 'faction', by 'some folks' Fox will have meant the Howards; but he need not have done. All he was really saying was that the negotiations were at a critical stage, and therefore the fewer people who knew about them the better. It is just the kind of remark that anybody involved in tricky negotiations is inclined to make, but it does not have to follow that he sees the whole world as his enemy – or even just the Howards. Fox was being cautious, and very sensibly so.

But can the negotiations referred to in the letter be associated with a possible French alliance? It is difficult to see what else Fox could have had in mind, and there are anyway some details that point to such a conclusion. The 'Mr Poynings' he referred to was almost certainly Sir Edward Poynings, lieutenant of the recently captured Tournai, who is known to have been used as a go-between with the French.[2] The second half of the letter had to do with excuses being proffered by the Habsburgs, Maximilian and Margaret of Austria, for delaying the long contracted marriage between the Archduke Charles and Mary, and it is this that provided England with some justification, however spurious, for marrying Mary to Louis. And that both Fox and Wolsey were already involved in negotiations with the French is indicated by a letter they wrote, probably in February, to their agent with the pope, Silvestro Gigli, declaring their intention to act as the pope's instrument in bringing about universal peace.[3] In his reply, Gigli reported back the pope's praises for their dexterity in persuading Henry to make peace with France.[4] It is not obvious that Henry needed much persuading, but these letters do seem to suggest that insofar as Wolsey was the author of the French alliance, he has at least to share the authorship with Fox. Furthermore, in their letter to Gigli the two men had declared they were of one mind not only on this particular issue, but on everything.[5] All the evidence so far points to the truth of this. Is there any reason to suppose that by the time of Fox's resignation two years later, some serious disagreement or dislike had emerged?

When, in early 1519, Wolsey summoned a legatine council to discuss reform of the Church, he received a letter in which Fox compared his joy on receiving the news to Simeon's joy on seeing, after so many years of waiting, the infant Messiah.[6] It was heady stuff indeed, and there was more to come, including a good deal of praise for Wolsey's 'great skill in business'. Of course, when Fox wrote the letter he had been out of office for three years, and perhaps he had got over the hurt of being forced out – or was this, perhaps, his bid to get back into office? In fact, there is not the slightest hint of either of these things, and his praise of Wolsey is quite consistent with everything that is known about Fox's attitude to him before his resignation. Furthermore, it confirms the central point of what amounted to his

---

[1] Richard Fox, p.75 (*LP*,i,2811).

[2] *LP*,i,2888 – the draft of a letter from the Council to Poynings, interestingly in Fox's handwriting.

[3] *LP*,i,2611.

[4] *LP*,i,2928. It is his reference to the pope receiving their letter of 7 Feb. which suggests the probable date for *LP*,i,2611.

[5] 'We twain, *qui non solum in hac sanctissima causa verum in omnibus aliis sumus semper unius animi . . .*' (*LP*,i,2611).

[6] Richard Fox, pp.114-17 (*LP*,iii,1122, where it is placed, wrongly, in 1521).

resignation letter in 1516: that, after so many years of deep involvement in high politics, he was anxious to devote his old age to the service of God;[1] and like Simeon, he was by this time an old man, probably in his late sixties.[2] He had been deaf for a number of years, and was to become blind.[3] Finally, there is no doubt at all that despite his very busy career in royal service, he had a very genuine interest in religious matters, both pastoral and intellectual. He was an increasingly active diocesan bishop, and at the time of his resignation was engaged in the founding of a college at Oxford, to be called Corpus Christi, a chief purpose of which was to promote that new interest in biblical studies awakened by such as Colet and Erasmus.

And what of Fox's resignation letter? Written on 23 April 1516, it was in fact a response to an urgent appeal from Wolsey to come to court, where his services were in great demand.[4] This alone makes the notion that Wolsey was trying to get rid of him a trifle odd, as does the fact that in explaining why he had not answered the appeal, he made the point that he had already obtained the king's licence to be occupied in his diocese. He then made a personal appeal to Wolsey to show some sympathy for his point of view:

> But, my lord, to serve worldly with the damnation of my soul and many other souls whereof I have the cure, I am sure you will not desire . . . I assure you, my lord, my absence from you is neither to hunt nor hawk, nor to take none other worldly pleasure, nor for ease of my body, nor yet for quietness of mind: which is troubled night and day with other men's enormities and vices more than I dare write. Whereof I remember you showed me you had some knowledge, when you were bishop of Lincoln: and of them I assure you there is plenty here with much more. But I have provided the medicine which I trust shall do good service.[5]

If Fox was really pushed out, then this whole paragraph has to be some kind of deception, if only a self-deception to hide the cruel reality that he was no longer needed. But it does not read like that, nor does such a view make much sense in the context of what else is known of his relationship with Wolsey. Moreover, almost exactly one year later history repeated itself. Henry and Wolsey were once again anxious for Fox's advice, and this despite the fact that he was no longer in office. And once again Fox had to remind Wolsey that he had 'left the keeping of his privy seal' by licence of the king,[6] which can only mean that far from his resignation being sought by anyone, he had actually had to seek it out. Wolsey's reply has not survived, but on 10 May Fox was able to write that it was to his

---

[1] Richard Fox, pp.82-4 (*LP*,ii,1814).

[2] In April 1527, when giving evidence about Henry's marriage to Catherine, he stated that he was seventy-nine.

[3] He called himself 'deaf as a stock' in a letter to Wolsey, 12 May 1513, implying that he had been for some time (Richard Fox, p.70). The first report of his blindness was by the Venetian ambassador in June 1523 (Ven. Cal., iii, 687), and Batten's opinion was that it happened in 1521 (*Registers of Richard Fox*, p.112).

[4] '. . . understand by my fellow, William Purdie, that of late your said lordship [Wolsey] divers times asked of him when I intended to be there, and that finally you commanded him to send to me for my coming thither' (Richard Fox, p.82).

[5] Richard Fox, p.83 (*LP*,ii,1814).

[6] Richard Fox, p.93 (*LP*,iii, 2207, where misdated to 1522).

greatest comfort that you have benignly accepted the excuses that I made to your good lordship for my not coming to you at that time, and that it will please your good lordship to declare and show my said excuses to the king's grace as his highness shall be contented. My lord, your good lordship hath done more for me in this behalf than I can write or think . . . [1]

Even if one is not prepared to accept the tone of the letter as genuine, the fact that Fox had had to seek the king's permission to withdraw from court hardly fits a conspiratorial view of his resignation. It does, however, leave open the possibility that the reason why Fox had chosen to withdraw was because of increasing disillusion with the way Wolsey was running things, but especially foreign policy. In accepting such a view, one would have also to accept that Fox was a consummate liar, but then it is possible that thirty years in politics would have been a good training for this!

The notion that Fox, and indeed others, especially the earl of Shrewsbury, were unhappy with Wolsey's 'takeover' of royal government takes us both chronologically and thematically too far from the chief concerns of this chapter for it to be discussed in detail here. As regards Fox's attitude to England's foreign policy, the conclusion will be that what has been taken as evidence for his dissatisfaction with Wolsey's handling of it, in fact reflects only the misinterpretation and wishful thinking of the Venetian ambassador, Giustinian.[2] What Fox really thought will, of course, never be known, but Giustinian's reports describe a man using all his diplomatic experience, and incidentally still very much in the know, despite his earlier resignation, to ward off a very importunate ambassador eager for any crumbs of comfort. At the very least, the case for an unhappy Fox is not proven – and to see him as such goes very much against the grain of everything else that is known about his relationship with Wolsey, and more generally about the politics of the early years of Henry's reign.

What has emerged is something much less dramatic than the usual picture of a fight to the death between Fox and Surrey, in which both eventually lost out to the thrusting and ruthless younger man. As regards Fox, the probability is that, a comparatively old man when Henry VIII succeeded to the throne, he was already looking towards retirement. First, however, he saw it as his duty to see the young king in – and perhaps to save him from time to time from the injudicious advice of a Howard. Increasingly, however, he left the weight of day-to-day business to his younger colleague, Thomas Wolsey, whom he saw as his natural successor. However, the outbreak of a major war with France in 1513 temporarily changed all this. Reluctantly but loyally, Fox came out of retirement, accompanied the king and Wolsey to France, and played a very active role in the difficult diplomacy of 1514. But as soon as he felt that things had returned to something like normal, he sought the king's permission to retire. One consequence of his withdrawal was, indeed, to leave Wolsey in a more dominant position, but the evidence all points to Wolsey neither seeking nor even welcoming his retirement. This is not to make Wolsey into a saint, and indeed the cynic may say that the reason why he got on with Fox was precisely because the ageing bishop represented no threat – though to

[1] Richard Fox, p.96 (*LP*, add.,185 (10 May 1517).
[2] See pp.70-1.

accept such a view would be to ignore the warmth that permeates much of their correspondence.[1] And if this view of the relationship between Fox and Wolsey is correct, then the story – heavily dependent upon Vergil's account – of Wolsey's rise to power is rescued from the caricature and exaggeration that it has been too often embellished with. The time has now come to create a new version, and one that must have at its heart the relationship between Wolsey and his King.

The magic that makes a relationship is by definition hard to pin down, and that which bound Henry to Wolsey is no exception. What, however, every contemporary commentator, whether friend or foe, agreed about was what Giustinian referred to as Wolsey's 'vast ability', also describing him as being 'learned, extremely eloquent . . . and indefatigable'.[2] For Cavendish, it was Wolsey's 'very wit and what wisdom was packed into his head' that had first brought him to the notice of Richard Fox,[3] while it was his miraculous embassy to Maximilian probably in 1508 – Richmond to Dordrecht and back in three and half days, and thought 'to be almost beyond the capacity of man' – that won him the admiration of Henry VII,[4] and his 'wisdom and other witty qualities' that caught the second Tudor's eye.[5] Even if, as seems likely, Wolsey did not perform his embassy to Maximilian quite as speedily as stated,[6] for Cavendish the story represented a symbolic truth: if Wolsey wanted to achieve something, nothing could stop him. And Cavendish relates what was for him a rather similar episode, though this time he was himself an eye-witness, at least to some of it. This took place at Compiègne in 1527 following some rather stormy negotiations with the French, at which, however, Wolsey had eventually got his way. Cavendish describes what then happened as follows:

> the next morning after this conflict, he [Wolsey] rose early in the morning about four of the clock, sitting down to write letters into England unto the king, commanding one of his chaplains to prepare him to mass, in so much that his said chaplain stood revested [in his vestments], until four of the clock at afternoon. All which season my lord never rose once to piss, nor yet to eat any meat, but continually wrote his letters with his own hands, having all that time his nightcap and keverchief on his head.[7]

As with the previous episode, there is something almost miraculous for Cavendish about Wolsey's behaviour, though on this occasion it was his master's capacity to concentrate for so long that caused him to marvel.

This view of Wolsey, as a man who combined both enormous ability and unstoppable determination, is not the invention of a doting household servant. Even Vergil admitted that Wolsey was intelligent and daring, and when he portrays

[1] In this matter of tone piecemeal quotation is no substitute for reading the letters in full, and I would like to stress how easily this can be done by consulting Richard Fox.
[2] Rawdon Brown, ii, p.314 (LP, iii, 402).
[3] Cavendish, p.7.
[4] Ibid, pp.7-10.
[5] Ibid, p.13.
[6] Ibid, p.195; Ridley, *The Statesman and the Fanatic*, pp.26-7.
[7] Cavendish, pp.58-9.

Fox trying to convince the king of Wolsey's ability it is his 'sound judgement, vigilance and hard work' that Vergil has Fox specifically mention.[1] This is not to say that he agreed with Fox's assessment, but even his criticisms of Wolsey testify to the man's ability. And if one turns from the literary evidence to the documents that went out under Wolsey's name, what immediately impresses is not only their quantity and length – each one frequently over five thousand words – but the range of business they cover. It might be the formation of an alliance with a foreign power, or a 'universal peace treaty'; an enclosure commission or a new constitution for the Augustinian canons; the founding of a college at Oxford or the settling of a dispute in Chancery – and often all these things at much the same time! The multiplicity is endless and the workload staggering; but Wolsey was evidently able, both physically and mentally, to take it in his stride.

Of course, what one has described is no more than anyone in a similar position, from the first pharaoh to Margaret Thatcher, has to cope with; and given that for fifteen years Wolsey was closely involved with every aspect of royal government, that he had these qualities should come as no surprise. Why it might is because, as was pointed out in the Introduction, there has been a tendency to hide Giustinian's man 'of vast ability' under the glitz and razzmatazz of Renaissance politics, in the process turning Wolsey into some kind of strutting peacock devoted only to self-glorification and self-indulgence.[2] The truth is much more sober, which is not to deny a glamorous side to politics. It is also true that ability and hard work can combine very happily with intense ambition – and even worse! Whether this was so in Wolsey's case is best dealt with as the story unfolds, but it is right to start with the fact that Wolsey was a man of enormous ability, for it provides the simple answer to the question why he became the king's leading minister.

There are many more descriptions of the young Henry VIII than there are of the early Wolsey. All are extremely complimentary. William Lord Mountjoy, writing to Erasmus in May 1509, referred to his 'exceptional and almost more than human talents',[3] while in 1511 Andrea Ammonio wrote to the same correspondent about the king 'who every day shows himself in a more godlike guise'.[4] As for Erasmus himself, his praise of Henry and his court – the only court in the world, he wrote to a friend in 1518, that he would consider being a part of[5] – is almost too well known to be quoted,[6] and like all his praise of potential or actual patrons has to be viewed with some suspicion. On the other hand, it is hard to see why Erasmus should have bothered to conceal his true feelings when writing to Cochlaeus in 1529. His purpose was to explain to the Catholic polemicist why he was convinced that Henry was the true author of the royal attacks on Luther, and one reason he gave was his

---

[1] Vergil, pp.194 ff.

[2] Thus Elton in *Studies*, p.110 writes of 'the childish flamboyancy, the spirited deviousness of mind, the overpitched ambitions and overcharged emotions which made up so large a part of Wolsey's personality'. Elton's 'Wolsey' in my view tells us much more about his own personality than Wolsey's, just as he believes Pollard's 'Wolsey' tells us more about Pollard – and no doubt the same will be said about my 'Wolsey'!

[3] CWE, 2, p.147.

[4] CWE, 2, p.160.

[5] CWE, 6, pp.62-3.

[6] For praise of Henry VIII's court see *inter alia* CWE, 3, pp.86-7, 94-5; 5, pp.392-3, 411; 6, pp.62-3, 356-8, 364-5, 377-80, 387, 405.

first-hand knowledge of Henry's great ability as a young man, for when he was 'no more than a child, he was set to study. He had a vivid and active mind, above measure able to execute whatever tasks he undertook. He never attempted anything in which he did not succeed . . . You would say he was a universal genius.' And amongst the many pursuits at which Erasmus claimed Henry excelled were riding, music, mathematics, reading and disputations, 'of which he is very fond' and in which he conducted himself 'with remarkable courtesy and unruffled temper'.[1] What the humanist did not dwell on were Henry's more martial accomplishments, those jousts and tourneys with which he was so obsessed, or even hunting, in which, Giustinian reported, he never took part 'without tiring eight or ten horses, which he causes to be stationed beforehand along the line of the country he may mean to take, and when one is tired, he mounts another, and before he gets home they are all exhausted'.[2] What also caught Giustinian's imagination, as it did many other observers, was Henry's physical appearance, for he found him

> *extremely handsome; nature could not have done more for him; he is much handsomer than the king of France; very fair, and his whole frame admirably proportioned . . . He is extremely fond of tennis, at which game it is the prettiest thing in the world to see him play, his fair skin glowing through the shirt of the finest texture.*[3]

The eulogy is the more convincing in that it faithfully echoed his first impression of the king, which four years at court had done nothing to dim.[4]

The young Henry's ability to charm, almost to mesmerize all those he came into contact with, is vitally important in capturing the mood of the early years of his reign, when his relationship with Wolsey was formed. There is no doubt that he was determined to cut a great figure on the European stage, and that he was fortunate enough to be endowed with many of the necessary attributes. This does not mean that he was foolishly over-confident and impetuous, determined to charge into battle at the earliest opportunity; in fact, he was to wait five years, until he got to France, and then with rather more support than his father had in 1492. Neither should the war with France be seen as mere bravado or just a chivalric gesture. There was something of that in it, but then chivalry was an essential part of the panoply of kingship. Any king with ideas of dominating Europe would have to present himself as an embodiment of chivalric virtues;[5] and however much Christianity had tried to soften or disguise them, it remained true that in the end there had to be a man in armour on a horse performing daring deeds before such virtues could be displayed. The point would have been perfectly clear to Henry, as it was to his rivals Francis I and Charles V, that great kings had to be warriors as well as

[1] LP,iv,5412.
[2] Rawdon Brown, ii, p.312 (LP,iii,402).
[3] Ibid.
[4] Rawdon Brown, i, p.76 (LP,ii,409); see also ibid, i, pp.79, 86 for the equally enthusiastic reactions of his fellow Venetians, Nicolo Sagudino and Piero Pasqualigo; also LP,i,2351 for that of a correspondent of the duke of Milan, Paulo da Laude.
[5] See, for instance, Sir Robert Wingfield's assessment of Francis I in Nov. 1516: 'He is young, mighty, insatiable; always reading or talking of such enterprises as whet and inflame himself and his hearers . . . his trust is that by his valour and industry the things which have been lost lettyn and spoiled by his ignoble predecessors shall be recovered, and that the monarchy of Christendom shall rest under the banner of France, as it was wont to do.' (LP,ii,2536).

judges and patrons. For a French king this meant making good his claim to Milan and Naples, for an English king it meant an invasion of France. When Henry VIII looked around for a model of kingship, it is not surprising that he alighted upon his namesake, Henry V[1] – and what had he done on becoming king but lead an army into France, thereby winning everlasting renown on the field of Agincourt? During the course of this book it will become apparent that in practice English foreign policy was never solely directed to winning battles in France; indeed a French alliance was often the desired aim, but the contradiction between the field of Agincourt and the Field of Cloth of Gold, on which the kings of England and France embraced each other as loving brothers, is not as great as may first appear. Or, to put it another way, Henry was to find other means of maintaining his honour than waging war.

For the modern reader, the trappings of chivalry may confuse and trivialize. Such notions as nationalism, or great power rivalry – or whatever the current jargon is – are more readily understood. But while the language changes, the competitive nature of the relationship between states does not, and somewhere not far below the surface has to lurk power, not exclusively of a military kind but with the capability of being translated into that – as, for instance, quite commonly in the early sixteenth century by the hiring of mercenary troops. In February 1513 Ferdinand of Aragon, who after over forty years of political life knew something about these matters, made the significant comment that, while English soldiers might be strong and courageous, their inexperience of continental warfare was such that they could not compete with the best in Europe.[2] His explicit conclusion was that in the forthcoming campaign they would need to be supplemented with German troops. Implicit was the belief that Henry was not a major force to be reckoned with, and could be easily manipulated. This Ferdinand had done the previous year, when he had made use of English help to capture Navarre for himself while ignoring the English aim of capturing Guienne; and he was, as he thought, about to do it again, this time by unilaterally signing a truce with England's declared enemy, France, while pretending to be England's ally. This time it did not work out as he intended, because England chose to ignore his defection and conducted a successful enough campaign without him. Moreover, when the following year Ferdinand tried to perform the same trick, he found the English had got there before him. And one of the chief reasons they were able to outmanoeuvre him was that in 1513 they had shown they were indeed a military force to be reckoned with, while, if the truth be told, Ferdinand was militarily and financially very stretched, and thus for Louis XII a potential victim rather than an ally.[3]

It has to be said that English historians have tended to take a rather dim view of the 1513 campaign.[4] But in desperately trying to calculate some material advantage,

[1] Gunn, 'French wars', pp.36-7; Scarisbrick, *Henry VIII*, pp.22-3.

[2] *LP*,i,1656.

[3] I have not thought it helpful to provide detailed references to my very general treatment of foreign policy in this chapter, but it is based upon a detailed study of the calendared documents.

[4] For a typical view see Elton, *Reform and Reformation*, p.39: 'The 1513 expedition, spectacularly mounted and much dreaded by the French, turned into a futile sideshow with almost no effect upon the

and, not surprisingly, given the enormous expense of waging war, coming up with a large deficit, they have missed the whole point. By showing that he could deliver, not just money – and the general perception was that he was extremely wealthy[1] – but also military and naval might, Henry secured for himself a leading role in Europe, at least until the 'divorce' seriously weakened his hand. And it was Henry himself, and only he, who took the decision to play that role. Seen in this light, the notion of a 'peace' or 'war' faction becomes an irrelevance. Instead, there were only royal councillors giving advice to a king who knew the direction that he wished to take, and, moreover, was much more active in getting what he wanted than is frequently allowed. The myth of a lazy king devoting himself entirely to pleasure, while the likes of Wolsey and Thomas Cromwell got on with the hard work, does not stand up to scrutiny.[2] Admittedly Henry sometimes gave this impression; and harassed councillors, trying to get him to read or sign something which they thought important and he did not, may occasionally have despaired. But where it is possible to follow the king at work over a period of time, for instance in the spring of 1518 or in August and September 1523, what is striking is his close attention to business, a quickness of mind that enabled him immediately to grasp the essentials, and the strong feeling that he was very much in control of all that was being done on his behalf.[3] In confirmation of this there is the judgement of that astute French ambassador, Jean du Bellay, that there was nothing that went on, whether inside or outside the court, that Henry was not aware of.[4]

There are, of course, many different styles of governing a country, or indeed, of running any large organization. Some have found delegation impossible, and like Philip II of Spain have immersed themselves in paperwork; but while such people get good marks for effort, they are not necessarily good at making decisions. Indeed too much immersion may make decision making all the more difficult, and certainly there was more to being an effective king than shutting oneself up in the Escorial, or its equivalent. Henry's style should not deceive, and though there were many who were deceived by him, there was almost no one who doubted that he was in charge – and certainly not those, such as Wolsey and Cromwell, who worked most closely with him.[5] In this respect it is interesting that both More and Wolsey are alleged to have made almost precisely the same comment: that Henry, in order to get his own way, would have been willing to go to any lengths, whether this meant cutting off a

war. . . . The knight of Christendom came as near to being a figure of fun as ever he was to do in his long reign.'

---

[1] Rawdon Brown, ii, p.313 (*LP*,iii,402) for Giustinian's assessment that Henry VIII was 'very rich indeed'.

[2] One of the few historians in recent years to reject the myth has been L.B. Smith, whose extended essay on the king's character in his *Henry VIII* deserves more recognition; in this context see ibid, pp.39-49; also Bernard, *War, Taxation and Rebellion*, pp.40-5.

[3] See pp.205 ff.

[4] *LP*,iv,4206.

[5] Cromwell's 'Remembrances at my next going to the court' are especially instructive in this respect; and they, for instance, make it clear that it was Henry who decided the fate of More and Fisher; for which see *LP*,viii,892.

subject's head or losing half a kingdom.[1] They also agreed that it was vital to think before one spoke to him because, as Wolsey said on his deathbed, once an idea was put into his head, 'you shall never pull it out again'.[2] It could be that these judgements reflect merely the views of their contemporary biographers, only too conscious that their subjects had been treated badly; but they receive support from almost everything that Henry is known to have said and done.

None of this is supposed to make Henry into a Superman, and certainly not into the bluff King Harry of popular mythology, though this was a role he could play well. The choices that he made were often not, at least to the present writer, very attractive ones, nor, in spite of the warmth and charm he could exhibit, at least when young, was he at bottom an attractive character. Much more than his first great minister, he wore his egotism close to the surface, and as he aged and life became more difficult – probably at a personal level but certainly in the 1530s and 40s at a political level – the suspicion and animal cunning came to the fore. Flawed he obviously was, and to argue that he was a powerful personality is not to imply that there was not weakness or insecurity as well. It has been suggested, for instance, that he had difficulties with sex: the fact of his six wives, his very few mistresses – by the standards at any rate of his great rival Francis I – and only four children who survived for any length of time (and even then the two males, his illegitimate son by Elizabeth Blount, Henry Fitzroy, and Edward VI, were both dead before they were out of their teens) may suggest that something was amiss.[3] And despite his cunning he was very capable of great errors of judgement – but then what leading political figure has not been? The key to political success lies in a capacity to recover from one's mistakes, and in this art Henry was extremely skilled, as indeed was Wolsey. But the one thing Henry was not was someone who could be easily manipulated, whether by an individual or a faction, and even those he fell head over heels in love with, such as Anne Boleyn and, to a lesser extent, Catherine Howard, though they obviously affected what he did, were never able to manage him to any significant extent. All of this leads to only one conclusion: that Wolsey rose to a commanding position in royal government because Henry chose that he should, and all that remains to be stressed in this chapter is that there was nothing very surprising in Henry's choice.

Even the rags to riches element in Wolsey's story, or as this chapter title has it, the rise from 'butcher's cur to lordly prelate', has been much exaggerated. In this respect John Skelton who, especially in *Why come ye nat to Courte*, could not put the theme down, has done his work only too well. Wolsey's

> . . . *gresy genalogy,*
> He came of the sank royall
> That was cast out of a bochers stall![4]

---

[1] Roper, pp. 20-1 and Cavendish, p.179.

[2] Cavendish, p.179 – Wolsey's advice to Sir William Kingston if he ever became a royal councillor. More's advice to Cromwell on becoming a councillor was the more ambiguous: 'ever tell him what he ought to do, but never what he is able to do . . . For if a lion knew his own strength, hard were it for any man to rule him.' (Roper, pp.56-7).

[3] The difficulties in any kind of 'psycho-history' hardly need spelling out – but they will not prevent speculation, and as long as the limitations are borne in mind, it is good that they do not. Here, I am following L.B. Smith, pp.63-6.

is the one thing that almost everybody knows about him. In part, this is because Skelton was mining an already well-worked vein of English satirical writing, of which John Lydgate's *Fall of Princes* is but the best of many.[1] It thrived then presumably for the same reason that it remains alive and well today, that anyone who betters himself is open both to the envy of those whom he has left behind and the contempt and jealousy of those whose social position he now shares, and threatens. The upstart courtier or despised royal favourite is a stock figure because he represents but the most extreme example of the parvenu who, almost by definition, has more wealth, more ambition, and above all more pride than is good for him.

> *What thyng to God is mor abhomynable*
> *Than pride upreised out of poverte?*[2]

asked Lydgate in the fifteenth century, and for John Skelton in the sixteenth, Wolsey with his

> *Presumcyon and vayne glory,*
> *Envy, wrath and lechery,*
> *Covetys and glotiny;*
> *Slouthfull to do good,*
> *Now frantick, now starke wode!*[3]

was living proof that to 'set up a wretche on hye' was asking for the worst possible trouble.[4] But it must always be remembered that the satirical view is a very partial one. In the 1980s we laugh with *Spitting Image* at Ronald Reagan and Margaret Thatcher, the former having risen from the Hollywood 'B' movie to the White House, the latter from the corner shop to 10 Downing Street. No doubt there is much that is comic and unlikeable about both people. But they happen to be the two most successful politicians in the Western world with a proven capacity to capture the imagination, or at least the vote, of millions of people. Moreover, it is almost certainly the case that if the one had been a WASP and the other a member of the English aristocracy, they would still not have escaped the eagle eye of the satirist, though the topos would be different. In other words, *Spitting Image* is no more right about these two figures than Skelton was about Wolsey, and in many respects both are demonstrably wrong.

That someone from Wolsey's urban and retailing background had got to university in the early sixteenth century should come as no surprise, for, along with the sons of yeomen and lesser gentry, it was for such people, rather than those from the ruling classes, that the universities largely catered.[5] Once there, the great

---

[4] Skelton, p.291, ll.492-4.

[1] See Walker, pp.139-43.
[2] Lydgate, bk 2, ll.239-40.
[3] Skelton, p.293, ll.574-8.
[4] Ibid, p. 293, ll.585.
[5] A large, and not uncontroversial, subject but see *inter alia* Aston, Duncan and Evans, p.50; McConica, *Collegiate University*, pp.666-89; McConica, 'Scholars and commoners'.

likelihood was that such a person would go into the Church, and, as a graduate, have a successful ecclesiastical career. If he did well, he was very likely to end up in royal service, which had always been staffed with a high proportion of clerics.[1] Admittedly some changes in the career structure of the educated were taking place. It is probable that the fifteenth century saw an increasing number of laymen in royal service,[2] and the universities themselves were a comparatively new phenomenon, the full exploitation of which it had taken some time to develop. About two hundred years earlier William of Wykeham, like Wolsey a lord chancellor and founder of an Oxford college, and like him from a comparatively humble background (in his case that of the tenant farmer), had not gone to university, but in his day it was not the most normal route to the top. By Wolsey's time the successful cleric did as a rule go to university, and to that extent he is a typical figure.[3] However, the really fast route lay through a study of law, increasingly both civil and canon law, then into the household of the archbishop of Canterbury in some legal capacity, and then into royal service.[4] Typical of those who took that route were two clerical lawyers, Archbishop Warham, whose career lay through Winchester, New College and the Canterbury Court of Arches, and Tunstall, who transferred early from Oxford to King's Hall, Cambridge, and then to Padua, whence he returned to become Warham's chancellor before transferring to royal service as master of the rolls in 1516. Wolsey's career with its more university and schoolmasterly flavour, and his study not of law but of theology, is just that little bit different, and when he entered the service of the archbishop of Canterbury it was as a chaplain rather than a legal administrator. This slight difference serves to draw attention to that element of personality as opposed to qualifications that played a vital part in Wolsey's rise. However, as against the Skeltonic view, what needs to be emphasized is that for someone entering royal service Wolsey's early career was not all that unusual, nor were his social origins. The English episcopacy had always been largely recruited from below the top ranks of society. Of the nineteen men appointed to bishoprics by the Yorkist kings only four had come from the nobility,[5] and, of the twenty-four prior to Wolsey appointed to the plum see of Winchester from the time of the Norman Conquest only six appear to have come from noble families.[6] As for Wolsey's contemporaries, while Tunstall, though illegitimate, came from a Northern gentry family, Warham was of yeoman stock, as was Richard Fox. John Fisher's father was a mercer of Beverley; the father of Nicholas West, bishop of Ely, was a baker from Putney; and of all Wolsey's episcopal colleagues only Audley of Salisbury came out of the top drawer.

Moreover, it needs to be stressed, especially given the English dislike of 'meddlesome priests', that high-flying clerics had always played a leading role in

[1] See R. G. Davies.
[2] Storey, 'Gentleman-bureaucrats'.
[3] See R. G. Davies, p.55.
[4] Aston, T.H., p.30; Aston, Duncan and Evans, pp. 80-1, where it is suggested that, contrary to what has been normally held, in all but the really top jobs 'theologians' were doing increasingly well during the fifteenth century; R. G. Davies, p. 55; Storey, BP, 16 (2nd edn., 1972), pp. 13-17.
[5] J.R Lander, p.120.
[6] By my calculation the six were Walkelin, William Giffard, Henry of Blois, Aymer de Valence, Henry Beaufort and Peter Courtenay – this out of twenty-two.

English politics. Starting with William the Conqueror's first archbishop of Canterbury, Lanfranc, the list of powerful ecclesiastical personalities is very long, through Becket and Langton in the twelfth and thirteenth centuries, Winchelsey and Stratford in the fourteenth, Arundel, Beaufort and Chichele in the fifteenth, and in the present context most relevantly, and just getting on into the sixteenth century, Cardinal John Morton. Morton, indeed, prefigures Wolsey in all manner of ways, some of which will be looked at in more detail later, but most obviously in his general management of all the king's affairs, both secular and ecclesiastical.[1] And if, nevertheless, one feels that there was something about the scale of Wolsey's dominance that separates him from these predecessors, the explanation is almost certainly not to be found in his greater ambition and greed, but in the increasing power and centralized control of the Crown. Without anticipating too much, it needs to be borne in mind that for much of the Middle Ages Church and state were in some degree of conflict, resulting most famously in the murder of Thomas Becket in his own cathedral on 29 December 1170. But if the king was in conflict with the Church, he was unlikely to give to a churchman the necessary trust and confidence to make him his chief minister; and for much of the Middle Ages even royal control of episcopal appointments was not completely secure. Moreover, for an ecclesiastical statesman to dominate the political scene he needed, paradoxically, the support of a strong king because unlike a nobleman's, the wealth and military might of a bishop derived most usually from office alone. Of course, along with their expertise in law and administration, it was precisely this lack of family affinity or influence that made such an ecclesiastical statesman attractive to kings, and that Henry vii looked to Morton and sought with success to make him a cardinal with unusually extensive powers over the English Church, should come as no surprise. But in the present context the essential point is that, whatever Morton's role in Henry's campaign for the throne of England, it was the king who chose to give him a dominating position in government, just as it was his son who chose to give Wolsey a similar position. And if a cleric was chosen to be the king's leading councillor, and as a consequence become a prince of the Church, it was inevitable that he would live in some style.

From Skelton onwards, Wolsey's ostentatious life-style has attracted unfavourable comment. Interestingly, lay figures, such as the Cecils, who made immense private fortunes as leading councillors to Elizabeth and James i, have to a great extent escaped criticism;[2] and perhaps the expectation is that as a churchman, Wolsey should have behaved better. In a later chapter it will be argued that the expectation is unwarranted, or at the very least that it involves a judgement about how the Church should present itself, a judgement that has by no means always come down on the side of apostolic poverty – and justifiably so. Wolsey did pour money into

[1] It was C.S.L. Davies who first impressed upon me the relevance of Morton's career to a study of Wolsey, for which I am extremely grateful. Unfortunately there is no adequate study of Morton's political career, though see C.S.L. Davies, EHR, cii (1987) for his vital contribution to the accession of Henry vii; and for his churchmanship, see Harper-Bill, JEH, 29.

[2] I do not mean to imply that there has been none – and, for instance, Robert Cecil has received more criticism than his father, William – but I do believe that the general perception is that Wolsey's ostentation was *sui generis*, and that is a mistake.

building, purchased tapestries and carpets, and commissioned all kinds of beautiful objects, from illuminated manuscripts through to jewellery and silver.[1] His chief London residence from 1514, York Place, was the traditional home of archbishops of York, but it seems to have been largely rebuilt by Wolsey. Very little detail about this has survived, but the new work was considered impressive enough by Henry VIII for him to appropriate it on Wolsey's fall in 1529, and in the process it acquired the new name of Whitehall.[2] Wolsey's chief out-of-town residence was the building most associated with him, Hampton Court.[3] This in 1515 he leased from the Knights Hospitallers, though it had been used by Henry VII. Again, the details of Wolsey's quite clearly extensive rebuilding are not known, but when Bishop Sherburne visited it in 1525 he found it a 'most splendid and magnificent house',[4] a view shared by a French envoy in 1527.[5] However, in 1525 Wolsey had surrendered Hampton Court to the king, or rather he seems to have exchanged it for Richmond. For some, this has been seen as confirmation that, as Skelton would have it, Henry was becoming fed up with being constantly outshone by his minister, most visibly in the matter of palaces, but given that an exchange was involved – and apparently, unlike his father, Henry had never taken to Richmond – this seems very unlikely. Wolsey certainly continued to use Hampton Court a lot, but was anyway by 1525 making increasing use of two manor houses belonging to St Albans, whose abbot he had become in 1522, the More and Tittenhanger, and the more likely conclusion is that the exchange was agreeable to both men.[6]

What is not in doubt is that wherever Wolsey was in residence, or when, for instance, in 1527 he travelled to France, he lived in great style – and to his first biographer's obvious admiration. In his conclusion, Cavendish referred to him as 'my late lord and master, the rich and triumphant legate and Cardinal of England',[7] while earlier he went to great lengths to describe the magnificence of Wolsey's household, which according to him numbered some five hundred people.[8] It may be that present-day Western man is not quite as impressed by magnificence as his sixteenth-century counterpart, though much fascination – and repulsion – with glamour, and royalty, still abounds. But it is important to appreciate that in Wolsey's time magnificence of all kinds was expected from princes, whether of Church or state, and that for Wolsey to have dressed down would have won him very few marks indeed.[9] All his colleagues, including his episcopal ones, lived in some style.[10] Warham's household consisted of well over two hundred people,[11] and he is alleged to have spent £33,000 on the building of a new 'palace' – as

---

[1] See p.xv.

[2] *King's Works*, pp.300-6.

[3] *King's Works*, pp.126-35.

[4] *LP*,iv,1708.

[5] *LP*,iv,3105, p.1407.

[6] The Hampton/Richmond exchange remains something of a mystery, but see *King's Works*, p.127.

[7] Cavendish, p.187.

[8] Cavendish, p.21. I have found it impossible to reconstruct in any detail the workings of Wolsey's household, but see *LP*,iv,2972, 3216, 4623, 6185 for various lists, mainly to do with tax assessments. They indicate that it certainly numbered over four hundred, so Cavendish's figure is not so far out.

[9] A fifteenth-century churchman's comment that 'though he was poor, *the which made a man to be reputed no great wisdom*, yet he would do such service as he could', may be of some relevance. The italics are mine.

significantly bishops' major residences were called – at Otford.[1] And he had a reputation for a certain personal abstemiousness and frugality![2] Although the figure has to be an exaggeration, he did virtually rebuild Otford, and on such a magnificent scale that its courtyard was larger than Hampton Court's – and this despite the fact that his two predecessors, Bourchier and Morton, had spent a lot of money on rebuilding Knole, only a stone's throw away.[3] If only to suggest that there was nothing very personal in Henry's acquisition of Hampton Court, it is worth pointing out that in the 1530s he was to acquire, by exchange, both Knole and Otford from the then archbishop of Canterbury, Thomas Cranmer, whom nobody has ever accused of wanting to upstage Henry![4]

What is difficult about Wolsey's outward show is not that it occurred, because any cardinal and lord chancellor would have had to exhibit a good deal, but deciding how far it reflected a genuine personal preference. Given how little can ever be known about Wolsey's inner feelings, there is probably no way of arriving at a confident answer, but in resisting what has been the received and, admittedly not unnatural view, that he positively revelled in it, it would be wrong to go too far in the other direction. On such a matter Cavendish, who must have been present at many of Wolsey's entertainments, may provide a valuable insight, as regards both Wolsey's attitude in this matter and, even more importantly, his relationship with Henry. 'It pleased the king's majesty', he writes,

> for his recreation to repair unto the cardinal's house (as he did divers times in the year), at which time there wanted no preparations or goodly furniture with viands of the finest sort that might be provided for money or friendship. Such pleasures were then devised for the king's comfort and consolation as might be invented or by man's wit imagined. The banquets were set forth with masques and mummeries in so gorgeous a sort and costly manner that it was an heaven to behold. There wanted no dames or damsels meet or apt to dance with the maskers or to garnish the place for the time, with other goodly disports.[5]

He then goes on to describe a particular occasion when the king arrived, apparently unexpectedly, disguised as a shepherd, as indeed were those who accompanied him. The first that Wolsey and his guests knew about it was a volley of cannon, not perhaps the usual way to announce a band of shepherds, but then these were dressed in fine cloth of gold and crimson satin! Anyway, Wolsey sent the lord chamberlain, Lord Sandys, and the master of the revels, Sir Henry Guildford, to see who they were, and the story was that they had travelled many miles across the sea, drawn to Wolsey's household by the fame of his splendid banquets and the beautiful damsels

---

[10] Heal, *Of Prelates and Princes*, pp.39-40; Hembry, 'Episcopal palaces' – the archbishop of Canterbury had a choice of twenty-one residences, and Winchester fifteen.
[11] M.J. Kelly, 'Canterbury jurisdiction', pp.9-12.

---

[1] Stoyel, *Archaeologia Cantiana*, c (1984), p.261, but the figure derives from William Lambarde's *A Perambulation of Kent* (1576).
[2] M.J. Kelly, 'Canterbury jurisdiction', pp.39-40.
[3] Stoyel, p.261.
[4] Ridley, *Thomas Cranmer*, pp.137-40. For Henry's exchanges with noblemen see Miller, *English Nobility*, pp.217-19.
[5] Cavendish, p.25.

that graced them. They requested Wolsey's permission to dance and play at dice and this he duly granted. All their winnings, amounting to over two hundred crowns, were then placed before him, he was asked to throw for them, and to everyone's delight, so Cavendish alleges, he won. He then asked whether there was not amongst them some particular nobleman worthy enough for him to give up his seat to at the head of the banquet. Yes, there was, but Wolsey would have to pick him out himself from amongst their company. This he did, but to everyone's amusement he chose not Henry, but Sir Edward Neville, who apparently much resembled the king. This diversion over, Henry and his courtiers went away to change, to be greeted on their return by an entirely new banquet at which were 'served two hundred dishes or above of wonderous costly meats and devises subtly devised. Thus passed they forth the whole night with banqueting, dancing and other triumphant devices, to the great comfort of the king and pleasant regard of the nobility there assembled.'[1]

Cavendish explains that he had given this lengthy description so that the reader might 'understand what joy and delight the Cardinal had to see his prince and sovereign lord in his house so nobly entertained and pleased; which was always his only study';[2] and it is precisely for the same reason that it is repeated here. The evening's entertainment could not have taken place in the first flush of Henry's and Wolsey's relationship; if Lord Sandys was truly present as lord chamberlain, it must have occurred after 1526. But it may nevertheless serve to capture a vital aspect of their mutual attraction: a shared delight in the good things of life, an enormous vitality and almost animal energy, and a feeling that together they could set the world alight. This hyperbole may worry, and much of the time the discussion between them would have been of a much more mundane nature, whether to do with the small change of royal patronage or how to react to trouble in East Anglia. But the suggestion is that the reason why Henry chose Wolsey to be his leading minister was that in him he had discovered someone who could share in his dreams and who at the same time, and most vitally, had the ability to turn them into a reality. In the end, such a conclusion can only be guesswork, a feeling one gets after long absorption in the lives of the two men, but it may be given some further weight if one glances briefly at the other councillors surrounding Henry at the start of his reign.

Enough has already been said about Richard Fox, obviously clever enough, but ageing and anxious to turn his thoughts to less temporal matters. Also discussed earlier was Thomas Howard duke of Norfolk, who, although he had made himself into a more than loyal and not incompetent royal servant, was, in his late sixties, even older than Fox, and by temperament and circumstances seemingly cautious and a little on the dour side. His son, the future third duke, will be considered more fully later, but he had one characteristic that alone would have excluded him from the kind of role that Wolsey was to play, and that was his dislike of responsibility.[3] As for the two other dukes, Charles Brandon, duke of Suffolk, and Edward Stafford 3rd duke of Buckingham, the former was to remain an extremely close friend to

[1] Cavendish, p.28.
[2] Ibid.
[3] See pp.569-70.

Henry, and had enjoyed a rise almost as spectacular as Wolsey's – in his case from mere esquire to duke in under five years – and though very good in the tiltyard and a not incompetent soldier, he never showed any significant political ambition, one reason, perhaps, why he retained the king's favour for so long.[1] Buckingham appears as almost the ageing Hamlet of Henry's court, very uncertain about what he wanted from life, or from Henry, and as a result unwilling to put in the amount of work necessary to become an active member of his Council.[2]

As for the others, Charles Somerset, in 1514 created earl of Worcester, was obviously a highly skilled diplomat and administrator, but he was well into his fifties, and never seems to have exhibited the necessary oomph to land a star role. Ruthal was a very competent pen-pusher, but no more than that. Lord Darcy was on the slide for reasons that are not entirely clear, but he shows no sign of ever having possessed the qualities needed to perform the kind of role that Wolsey was to play. He was also part of the old king's regime, and this probably did not help anyone who aspired to play a leading role in the new king's court. The spectacular evidence for this is, of course, the dismissal and execution of two of Henry VII's leading councillors, Empson and Dudley, a very deliberate, not to say ruthless, political act. They suffered for allegedly arbitrary and illegal actions taken against the king's subjects and, whether true or not, their removal contributed to that enormous feeling of elation and liberation that the new reign ushered in. 'Heaven smiles, earth rejoices; all is milk and honey and nectar,' wrote Lord Mountjoy in his famous letter to Erasmus,[3] while Thomas More in a coronation poem wrote more sharply that 'this day is the limit of our slavery, the beginning of our freedom, the end of sadness, the source of joy'.[4] But despite the downfall of Empson and Dudley, there was in fact a good deal of continuity as regards royal councillors, with Fox and Norfolk very much in evidence at the start of the reign, and no mad rush dramatically to alter England's stance in European affairs. Rather there was a change in tempo, and with it an inevitable change of personnel, with Wolsey's rise to prominence being the most obvious example. If this scenario is correct, it confirms a central argument of this chapter, that Wolsey did not have 'to wade through blood' to get to the top. As the choice of a king who had quickly established his authority, there was never likely to have been any serious opposition to his rise. Moreover, as will emerge, Wolsey was never in the business of stirring up opposition to himself, and indeed seems to have been exceptionally good at what might be called 'man-management' – even if the men were noblemen. But, in fact, none of his potential rivals constituted much of a threat, even if they had wanted to; not even Richard Fox, nor the man whom Wolsey succeeded as lord chancellor in December 1515, William Warham.

Warham had been appointed archbishop of Canterbury in 1503 and lord chancellor in the following year. By 1515 he was in his mid-sixties. As has been mentioned already, his progress to the top was typical of the successful ecclesiastical careerist, and he seems to have possessed something of the necessary caution –

[1] See pp.571-2.
[2] See 165 ff.
[3] CWE, 2, pp.147-8.
[4] More, Latin Epigrams, p.138.

which is not to deny him many good qualities. What he could never have been was someone to excite Henry, and indeed, as a result of a serious quarrel between him and other bishops, led by Richard Fox, Henry had become distinctly tetchy with Warham as he obstinately refused to settle the dispute. Moreover, as will be shown in the following chapter, during 1515 he became involved in a major dispute with Henry over the important matter of the relationship between Church and state. All this means that Henry was probably keen to replace him as lord chancellor with someone, such as Wolsey, with whom he had a much better, not to say very close, relationship; and no doubt Wolsey was keen to get the job. What does not seem to be the case, however, is that in December 1515 Warham was either dismissed by Henry or manoeuvred out by the thrusting Wolsey. Admittedly, the combined weight of Cavendish, Hall and Vergil is for a Warham unhappy with Wolsey's increasing prominence,[1] but a letter written only about six weeks after Warham's resignation, and by someone who had many dealings with him, must surely count for more, especially as the writer was Thomas More. And what More told Erasmus was that Warham was only too delighted to have obtained greater privacy and the leisure to enjoy his books, adding significantly that the archbishop had only secured his liberty 'after some years of strenuous effort'.[2] And when in June Colet wrote to Erasmus he confirmed that Warham was now 'living happily at leisure'.[3]

What More also mentioned in his letter to Erasmus was that Wolsey had been appointed in Warham's place and was winning 'golden opinions'.[4] Why this may have been so will be the subject of a separate chapter, but before he ever became lord chancellor Wolsey had, on 10 September 1515, been created a cardinal. The reason why, and what it meant for him and for his master, must be tackled next.

---

[1] Cavendish, pp.15-17; Hall, p.583; Vergil, p.231.
[2] CWE, 3, p.233 (LP,ii,1552).
[3] CWE, 3, p.312 (LP, ii, 2941 – but wrongly dated).
[4] CWE, 3, p.233 (LP, ii, 1552).

CHAPTER TWO

CHURCH AND STATE IN EARLY SIXTEENTH-CENTURY ENGLAND

O N 10 SEPTEMBER 1515 POPE LEO X CREATED WOLSEY CARDINAL.[1] THIS decision had nothing to do with religion and all to do with Francis I's invasion of Northern Italy, which had started the previous month and which, not unnaturally, Leo viewed with great alarm. English support was now of great importance to him and thus he was willing, at last, to give way to the systematic pressure for Wolsey's elevation that had been applied by the English court for well over a year.[2] As recently as April, when the new French king's intentions were not entirely clear, Leo had declared that it would be quite impossible to create Wolsey cardinal without at the same time satisfying Francis's and Maximilian's desire for the creation of their own cardinals, and that this would require some time to sort out.[3] Four months later, and only three days before Francis's great victory at Marignano, this argument was forgotten and Wolsey was created cardinal on his own.

The pope's motives need to be fully understood. For instance, far from wanting to further his own interests in England at the expense of the Crown, the opposite is true. Many of the concessions he granted, including the bestowal of legatine powers on Wolsey, actually involved him in financial loss and some diminution of papal involvement in the affairs of the English Church – but this was the price he was prepared to pay for English diplomatic and, if possible, military support.[4] More importantly, he was not primarily interested in pleasing Wolsey, but Henry. To please Wolsey some more private and particular favour would have been the obvious course, something that the king might not have been aware of, and that therefore would not make him suspicious of his councillor's advice. To make Wolsey cardinal was the most public act possible, involving, amongst other things, a day of high ceremonial in London. And it certainly did please the king. As he explained to Leo, he esteemed the distinction bestowed upon a subject for whom he had the greatest affection as if it had been bestowed upon himself.[5] But in stressing that the creation of an English cardinal brought honour to the English, Henry was not telling the whole story. There were more practical reasons – not to do with the ambitions of his leading councillor but with his own relations with the English Church. These were more complicated than has sometimes been presented. Two *causes célèbres*, both concerned with the position of the Church in England and both of them occurring even while pressure was being put on the pope to create Wolsey cardinal, will provide some insight not only into Henry's attitudes, but also Wolsey's. One

---

[1] *LP*,ii,892.
[2] For these first efforts back in May 1514 see *LP*,i,2932 – a letter from Vergil in Rome to Wolsey; for Leo x's early resistance to the idea see *LP*,i,3300. See also *LP*,i,3140, 3304, 3495-7.
[3] *LP*,ii,374.
[4] On the general subject of papal relations with the secular powers in the late Middles Ages see Thomson, *Popes and Princes*.
[5] *LP*,ii,960; more generally for Henry's involvement see *LP*,i,3140, 3300, 3497; ii,763.

involved a certain Richard Hunne, the other Henry Standish.[1]

Before discussing these incidents a word of warning is necessary. Although at the time the Standish affair was felt to be much more important, by and large it is Richard Hunne who has captured the historical headlines. This is not surprising. The Standish affair, though it had its exciting moments, failed to produce any dead bodies and had no obvious hero or villain. The Hunne affair, in contrast, has all the classic ingredients: a dead body, a number of villains, including a stagey gaoler, and a popular hero in Richard Hunne, the upright citizen of London doing battle with the church establishment. And not only was Hunne upright, but he also took a critical view of the Roman Catholic Church, thereby becoming one of John Foxe's martyrs.[2] All this has led to the significance of the Hunne affair being exaggerated: on close inspection it appears to be merely one more example of tension between the laity and clergy in the early sixteenth century, albeit a tension which was not as great as it had been. It is also a misleading example, because it suggests that the danger to the Church came primarily from below – in this instance from the citizens of London – whereas the real danger came from above and in particular from Henry VIII himself.

Richard Hunne was a London tailor of some wealth and standing who,[3] in 1511, refused to pay a mortuary fee for the burial of his infant son. A year later the aggrieved rector, Thomas Dryffeld, took him before the archbishop's court of audience where it was decided that Hunne should pay. This decision was almost certainly correct, though Hunne's defence, that as the bearing sheet was his, it could not be demanded as the child's mortuary fee, did raise issues which were recognized both by the canon lawyers and by such critics of ecclesiastical jurisdiction as Christopher St German.[4]

Having been defeated in the archbishop's court, Hunne took about six months to decide on his next step. According to Thomas More, Hunne had been set on a famous victory over the Church from the start,[5] but if so, this six-month delay seems unaccountable. It seems more probable that something happened during the second half of 1512 to persuade him to resume battle. One can only guess at what that might have been. It was not, apparently, because he was excommunicated for non-payment, as he was later to deny this before King's Bench.[6] It may have been the opening of proceedings against him for heresy, or at least a hint that this was about to happen, that prompted him to act. Perhaps this was what Thomas Dryffeld's chaplain had in mind when, on 27 December 1512, he refused to begin evensong unless the 'accursed' Hunne left the church. Such a scenario would mean that Hunne's main motive in bringing two cases before King's Bench in the Hilary term

---

[1] *Inter alia* see E. J. Davis, *EHR*, xxx (1915); Derrett; Fines, *EHR*, lxxviii (1963);Milsom; M. J. Kelly, 'Canterbury jurisdiction, pp.127-47; Ogle; Schoeck, 'Common law and canon law'; Smart; Wunderli.

[2] Foxe, *Acts and Monuments*, pp.183-205.

[3] More stated that Hunne was 'well worth a thousand marks' (More, *CWM*, 6, p.318), that is £666 13s. 4d. Whether this figure referred to income or capital, it is a considerable amount of money, putting him just below London's ruling élite of successful overseas merchants.

[4] Ogle, pp.55-6; St German, *CWM*, 9, pp.194-5.

[5] *CWM*, 6, pp.326-7.

[6] For the evidence for this, and indeed for all the details of the various cases brought by or against Hunne, see Milsom, pp.80-2.

1513 was to defend himself.[1] First he sued the chaplain for defamation of character.[2] Then he issued a writ of praemunire against the rector and everyone connected with the mortuary case, including the summoner Charles Joseph (later to become his gaoler and perhaps even his murderer), on the grounds that the Church had no jurisdiction in this matter. With these two cases in progress, the church authorities may have been reluctant to accuse a leading citizen of heresy. It would look as if they were deliberately trying to influence the outcome, and if the judgments went against them, this would not help to convict Hunne of heresy. The contrary view, prevalent at the time in some London circles, alleged that the heresy prosecution was a defensive measure by the church authorities.[3] The problem with this is that it does not explain the delay of nearly two years between the start of Hunne's proceedings in King's Bench, early in 1513, and his first interrogation for heresy the next year. If the authorities really thought that they could quash the praemunire charges by convicting Hunne of heresy, the sooner they acted the better. Nor is the suggestion that the Church was motivated by desire for revenge on Hunne convincing. Many people brought charges of praemunire against the clergy,[4] but despite allegations to the contrary by such arch-critics as Simon Fish, there is little evidence that they were accused of heresy as a result.[5] What seems to have happened is that, possessing evidence that Hunne was a heretic, the church authorities waited until December 1514 to proceed against him because by then it looked as if King's Bench was about to decide against him.[6]

Was Hunne a heretic? Probably he was, which is not the same as saying that he was a paid-up member of a Lollard cell. But according to the evidence of his heresy trials, he did possess Lollard literature, he was prepared to defend a convicted Lollard, Joan Baker, and he did deny any obligation of the laity to pay tithes. He did also make highly critical remarks about the church establishment, including a statement that the bishops and priests were just like the scribes and pharisees who had crucified Christ.[7] It looks suspicious, at any rate, and if More's evidence that Hunne haunted the midnight lectures patronized by Lollards is not an invention, the case against him hardens.[8]

What perhaps more than anything else has led people to be suspicious of the

---

[1] This is argued by J. D. M. Derrett in 'Hunne and Standish', pp.222-4, following More's statement in his *Supplication of Souls*, pp.59-60 that this is precisely what the church authorities did.

[2] Baker, ii, *pp.240-1* for the interesting legal aspects of his case.

[3] Hall, p.573; Wriothesley, p.9.

[4] Baker, ii, *pp.66-8.*

[5] 'If any man . . . dare be so hardy to indict a priest of any such crime, he hath, ere the year go out, such a yoke of heresy laid on his neck, that it maketh him wish that he had not done it . . . Had not Richard Hunne commenced an action of praemunire against a priest, he had been yet alive, and no heretic at all but an honest man' – from Fish's *Supplication for the Beggars*, p.28. See Bowker, 'Some archdeacons' court book', pp.310-12 for the suggestion that there was a widespread dislike of heresy trials, but, leaving the Hunne affair aside, the only evidence that they were rigged or that accusations of heresy were lightly or unfairly made comes in Bishop Nix's letter to Warham in 1504; see p.45 below.

[6] Derrett, p.217.

[7] Foxe, *Acts and Monuments*, iv, pp.183-4, 186-90 for the charges. Foxe transcribed them from Fitzjames's registers, but they are no longer to be found there. Evidence about Hunne has a tendency to disappear, but for new material for the heresy trial see Fines, *EHR*, xxviii (1963). All these accusations were common Lollard beliefs; see Thomson, *The Later Lollards*, pp.162-70.

[8] CWM, 8, p.126.

Church's motives in the Hunne affair is that the heresy trial took place only after his death and that the final sentence was that his already dead body should be burnt – an act of revenge seemingly the more vindictive for being so gratuitous. But it was never the intention of the church authorities to burn heretics. Instead what they sought was the return of erring sheep to the fold – or, to put it more technically, the abjuration of those accused. The problem in Hunne's case was simply that since he was already dead, he was in no position to abjure, and therefore under canon law had to be burnt – and it was only the fact of his unexpected death that had resulted in the posthumous trial. It is usually alleged that such a trial was to the Church's advantage, on the grounds that its case against Hunne was so weak that had he been alive, he would have been able to demolish it.[1] Indeed, such an argument has been necessary, for it is the only explanation that anyone has been able to give as to why Dr William Horsey, the bishop's vicar-general, might have had Hunne murdered, which is what the coroner's court found that he had done. In fact, Hunne's death was almost certainly a grave blow to the church authorities. Two days before, in the course of a preliminary examination before the bishop of London, he had made a partial confession. While denying that he had spoken the precise words alleged against him, he did admit to having 'spoken words somewhat sounding to the same'. More to the point, he asked God's mercy for what he had done and submitted himself to the bishop's 'charitable and favourable correction'.[2] After this, the church authorities must have been extremely confident of Hunne's successful conviction and subsequent abjuration, and there was thus no need to murder him. As it was, after his death, they had to do the best they could without their star witness.

The trial itself appears to have been conducted with the utmost formality. It was presided over by three bishops and one suffragan bishop. It was conducted in public. It lasted for at least a week, and though no detailed account of what took place has survived, it is known that considerable evidence was presented to show that Hunne had both possessed and made use of Lollard literature.[3] And it seems most unlikely that the Church needed the posthumous trial in order to save Dr Horsey. Whether or not Hunne was a heretic could not have affected Horsey's fate one way or another, for the Church had no licence to murder heretics. What the Church may have been guilty of was political ineptitude, for undoubtedly the trial added fuel to an already overheated situation. Amongst other things, Hunne's conviction meant that his children would be disinherited, and this in turn was likely to provoke moves in their defence – as indeed, it did.[4] Tactically the church authorities would have been well advised to keep a low profile. That they chose not to suggests that they were genuinely convinced that Hunne was a heretic and, that being the case, they considered it impossible for tactical considerations to be taken into account.

It must also be remembered that heresy was a serious and persistent problem for bishops of London and, like his predecessors, Bishop Fitzjames was determined to grapple with it.[5] All the evidence suggests that he was an extremely conscientious

[1] Ogle, pp.66-8.
[2] Foxe, *Acts and Monuments*, iv, p.184.
[3] Fines, *EHR*, lxxviii.
[4] See p.40 below.

churchman.[1] Certainly his determination to stamp out heresy was such that, probably in 1513, at the time when the Hunne affair was brewing, he contemplated heresy proceedings against the dean of St Paul's, John Colet, and may have suspended him briefly from preaching. Usually this is taken to be yet another black mark against the bishop but this is unfair.[2] The 'conservative' Fitzjames did not accept Colet's criticism of the Church: too wealthy, too worldly, too much emphasis upon rites and ceremonies, too great a veneration of images, too great a concentration on the 'good works' themselves, rather than the spirit with which they were performed. The Bishop of London's objection was that these criticisms coincided with those voiced by the Lollards. No wonder they went to hear the dean's sermons! Colet, of course, was no Lollard. Whether his views were heretical or not is another matter. It is not known why Fitzjames did not in the end proceed against Colet. Perhaps he felt that the dean had too many friends in high places, including, possibly, the archbishop of Canterbury, or perhaps, like modern historians, he could not quite decide whether his views were heretical.[3] There was no such difficulty with the Lollards. For well over a century the Church had been 'persecuting' them and the guidelines were well drawn. During 1510 and 1511 twenty-two people had abjured this heresy in the diocese of London, among them Joan Baker whose views Hunne had defended.[4] If a wealthy citizen such as Hunne was even thought to sympathize with Lollard views, it made a great deal of sense to investigate and, if sufficient evidence was forthcoming, to proceed against him. It made no sense at all to have him murdered in the bishop's prison.

Was Richard Hunne murdered and if so, by whom? On the morning of 4 December 1514, only two days after his interrogation by the bishop, his body was discovered hanging from a beam in his cell in the bishop's prison. A coroner's jury decided that he had been murdered, and named William Horsey, along with the gaoler and summoner, Charles Joseph, and his assistant, John Spalding. The Church maintained that Hunne had committed suicide, and the Crown appears to have agreed; certainly Horsey's plea of 'not guilty' was accepted by King's Bench, and there is no evidence that any proceedings were taken against the other two.[5] Most historians have inclined towards the coroner's view. This is surprising. To begin with, our only record of the inquest derives entirely from an anticlerical booklet published in the late 1530s.[6] What is more, the evidence itself is totally

---

[5] On heresy in London see Brigden, 'The early Reformation in London', pp.87 ff; Thomson, *The Later Lollards*, pp.139-71 and *EHR* lxxvii (1963); for Fitzjames and heresy see S. Thompson, p.124.

[1] S. Thompson, 'English and Welsh bishops', pp.166-8. My generally favourable view of Fitzjames owes a good deal to Thompson's work. (He points out that Fitzjames personally examined candidates for ordination, probably the only bishop at this time to do so. S. Thompson, 'Bishop in his Diocese', p.76.)

[2] Dickens, pp.66, 91. For Elton, Fitzjames was an 'old bigot'! (*Reform and Reformation*, p.57).

[3] Lack of evidence will probably always prevent this episode from being dealt with satisfactorily but see *inter alia* Allen and Kaufman; for contemporary comment see *CWE*, 2, p.248; 3, pp.48, 296.

[4] Thomson, *The Later Lollards*, p.238; S. Thompson, 'English and Welsh bishops', p.124 refers to 60 heresy cases in the London diocese for 1510-12.

[5] The matter has been complicated by Fish's statement that Horsey paid £600 for a pardon, but there is no other evidence that he did, and, as More pointed out, since Horsey never received a pardon it would have been difficult for him to pay for one! (*CWM*, 6, 326). Despite this, many historians have accepted that a 'fine' was imposed; see Ogle, p.109; Schoeck, p.29.

unbelievable. Is it likely, as is stated in the booklet, that Horsey, if he was planning to murder Hunne, would have asked his forgiveness beforehand? Would he have chosen the two obvious suspects, Hunne's gaolers, to carry out the crime? Would he have accompanied them? Would he, when they got to the cell, have shouted 'Lay hands on the thief'? Why shout anything? Why 'thief'? And there are plenty of other oddities. There is the suggestion that physical pressure was used on Hunne by the church authorities, which if true would be almost the only occasion that there is evidence for this.[1] Moreover, it would surely have been considered counter-productive in the case of an important London citizen in a position to make public what had happened to him. One way and another, the more the evidence is looked at, the less likely does it seem that Richard Hunne was murdered either by Horsey or at his instigation – even, that is, if one accepts that Horsey was the sort of person likely to contemplate committing murder.

But to maintain that Horsey was not responsible in no way discounts the possibility that Hunne was murdered by somebody else, and in Charles Joseph, the summoner *cum* gaoler, there is at least a plausible candidate. On admittedly rather limited and partial evidence, he does appear to have been an unsavoury character who, along with his other professions, may also have been a professional pimp. Not only did Joseph have access to Hunne's cell, but he also had a number of motives. Unlike Horsey, he had been cited by Hunne in the praemunire case, but as Hunne was apparently on the point of losing his case, this alone does not appear to be a sufficient reason to commit murder. What may have supplied a motive was Joseph's dismissal from the post of summoner by Horsey only a few weeks before Hunne's death. If this had taken place, it would have put Horsey in a position to make an offer that Joseph would have found difficult to refuse: his reinstatement as summoner in return for murdering Hunne – the only difficulty being that such a surmise brings one straight back to why Horsey would have wished Hunne dead, and for that no explanation has ever been discovered.[2]

A theory that avoids this problem is that Joseph murdered Hunne at his own instigation in an effort to win back Horsey's favour – and it is just conceivable that Horsey may have given the false impression that he would like to see Hunne dead.[3] But if Joseph was the murderer, why did the church authorities not press the case against him themselves? Such a move would have had its obvious dangers, but, to take the most cynical view, Joseph's reputation would surely have made it a possible ploy, and one that would have been tactically sounder than faking a suicide, for at least it offered to the citizens of London a sacrificial lamb, or rather wolf. As it was, the authorities stuck by Joseph throughout, despite his damaging confession that he had committed the murder at Horsey's instigation and indeed in Horsey's presence.[4]

---

[6] 'The enquirie and verdite of the quest panneld of the death of Richard Hune wich was found hanged in Lolars Tower.' Probably the only copy now resides in the Parker Library, Corpus Christi College, Cambridge, the BL copy having been destroyed in the war. I am very grateful to the college authorities for allowing me to consult it. It is transcribed in Hall, pp.573-80 and Foxe, iv, pp.190-7. For its dating see E. J. Davis, *EHR*, xxx (1915).

---

[1] Thomson, *The Later Lollards*, p.230.

[2] For this view and much new information about Joseph, see Wunderli.

[3] The parallel might be with Henry II's famous outburst against Thomas Becket, leading, unintentionally perhaps, to the latter's martyrdom.

Moreover, it would appear that the Crown accepted Joseph's plea of 'not guilty' at the same time that it accepted Horsey's.[1] There is a lot that needs to be explained about Joseph's involvement in the Hunne affair, but the evidence does not appear to be sufficient to convict him of murder, whether at his own or someone else's instigation. However, if he really had been dismissed by Horsey, at the very least this means that he was a biased witness, and it has always to be remembered that the only evidence produced at the coroner's inquest that implicated Horsey was Joseph's confession. Hunne might, of course, have died as a result of an accident, or from natural causes, and in either case the church authorities might have felt that some cover-up was required. But this explanation was never put forward by anyone with any inside knowledge.[2] This leaves suicide, the explanation favoured at the time by the authorities, and later by Thomas More.[3] This would discount the evidence at the inquest, but as we have seen, much of that was unbelievable. Moreover, it is certainly quite feasible that Hunne took his own life. For over three years he had been waging war against the Church, and by December 1514 he was losing on every front. About to be defeated in King's Bench and to be convicted of heresy, with all the public humiliation that entailed, he may well have felt suicidal.

If this is so, then an important consequence follows. Hunne was one of Foxe's 'martyrs', and it is as a martyr that he has been portrayed ever since. Even today, when the Protestant tradition of historiography is no longer so strong, we are still expected to feel a great deal of sympathy for Hunne and none at all for the church authorities. Whether actually stated or not, the implication is that murder and cover-ups are to be expected from the late medieval Church.[4] But if Hunne was not murdered, and if there was therefore no cover-up, then the affair ceases to provide evidence of a wicked Church. It also, and rather importantly for Wolsey's reputation, ceases to provide evidence that Wolsey was the sort of person who would have connived at this kind of action.

But it is not only 'Protestant' historians who have thought that Hunne was murdered. Whatever the status and reliability of the surviving account of the inquest, a coroner's jury did return a verdict of murder. It is also clear that other people at the time agreed, or at least felt that Hunne had been treated badly. Polydore Vergil, in a letter of March 1515, referred to people crying out indiscriminately against the clergy because 'a heretic' had been put to death by the bishop of London.[5] When he came to write the *Anglia Historia* he was not so certain that the bishop was responsible, but he had no doubt that 'an uproar' had resulted.[6] The London chroniclers, Richard Arnold and Charles Wriothesley, both indicate

---

[4] Cf. Fitzjames's contention that Joseph's accusation against Horsey was only made 'by pain and durance' – in his supposed letter to Wolsey printed in ' The enquirie and verdite' and quoted in Ogle, pp.81-2.

---

[1] This was More's contention; see CWM, 6, p.326. Certainly there is no evidence for any action being taken against Joseph or his alleged accomplice, John Spalding.

[2] A view tentatively put forward by Elton in *Reform and Reformation*, p.53.

[3] CWM, 6, pp.316-30. More's writing is just as polemical as Fish's or Foxe's – but I confess to finding his case more convincing.

[4] Ozment, p.213, for a recent general account, in which there is reference to 'episcopal arrogance' and 'damage to lay respect . . . for many irreversible'.

[5] LP, ii, 215.

[6] Vergil, p.229.

that strong feelings were aroused,[1] and so does Hall.[2] It is known that a City delegation went to Fitzjames to object to 'certain perilous and heinous words as been surmised by him to be spoken of the whole body of the city touching heresy'[3] – not evidence, of course, that the City Fathers thought that Hunne had been murdered or that he was not a heretic, but only that they were critical of the bishop's handling of the affair. It is also known that, at Henry's request, a full inquiry into the matter, in which he himself participated, was conducted by members of his Council at Baynard's Castle.[4] Concern was also shown in parliament. A bill was introduced to secure the restitution to Hunne's children of his property forfeited to the Crown as a result of his posthumous conviction for heresy. Another bill endeavoured to bring a charge of murder irrespective of what action the Crown took. Both bills failed to get through the Lords, but they are yet another indication that many people felt Hunne had been treated badly.[5] It is therefore clear that if the Hunne affair is not evidence for a 'wicked' Church, it does show that there was a willingness to think that the Church was wicked. It is, in other words, evidence of that difficult and complex notion, anticlericalism.

The death of a wealthy London citizen in a bishop's prison was bound to arouse comment and suspicion. Such a man was likely to have influential friends in City circles who would have been active on his and his children's behalf – it was presumably the City members of parliament who had introduced the two bills concerning Hunne in the House of Commons. Furthermore, whether Hunne was a heretic or not, it was unusual for a man of his standing to be accused of heresy, and it was also unusual, though not irregular, for anyone to be convicted of heresy after their death.[6] These things may have secured sympathy for Hunne from people who would not normally have been critical of the Church. And, of course, there were people in London who did hate the Church – the Lollards. No doubt, given an opportunity to express their anticlerical feeling with some impunity, they also contributed to the 'uproar'. But it must not be assumed that sympathy for Hunne necessarily implied strong antagonism towards the Church in general for there is just not sufficient evidence for such an equation to be made.

The religious life of London continued after 1515 very much as it had done before.[7] There continued to be Lollards, and they continued to be persecuted. There was opposition to tithes, with a major dispute orchestrated by the City Fathers beginning in 1519 and ending ten years later with a compromise in the Church's favour. But such disputes were endemic in London – there had been a particularly prolonged one in the 1450s – and what is more they were not about tithes *per se*, which would have been heretical, but about how the assessment was arrived at and the actual amount demanded.[8] In the 1520s the occasional clergyman did have disputes with his parishioners. There is some evidence that Londoners

---

[1] Wriothesley, p.9.
[2] Hall, p.573.
[3] Quoted in E. J. Davis, EHR xxx, p.478.
[4] CWM, 6, p.318.
[5] LJ, i, p.41; A. F. Pollard, pp.39-41.
[6] Thomson, *The Later Lollards*, p.167.
[7] What follows relies very heavily on Brigden, 'Early Reformation', and VCH, *London*, i, pp.207-87.
[8] Brigden, JEH, 32 (1981); Thomson, EHR, lxviii (1963).

were increasingly conducting their litigation before secular rather than ecclesiastical courts, a trend that, as regards cases to do with 'breach of faith' and the payment of debts, was nation-wide, as secular courts showed themselves more willing to take cognizance of such cases and provide better remedies for the aggrieved parties.[1] As for that matter with which the Hunne affair had begun, his opposition to the payment of a mortuary fee, contrary to what has often been implied – in part by a rather too uncritical use of the Hunne affair – there is surprisingly little evidence in the surviving records of ecclesiastical courts of widespread opposition to its payment, whether in London or elsewhere: for instance, between 1519 and 1529 only six cases were brought before the bishop of Norwich's consistory court, while in the archdeaconry of Chester there were only eight between 1504 and 1529.[2] Such figures lend little support to St German's contention that 'mortuaries increased daily',[3] which is not to say that on occasions people did not object to their payment, or that some clergy did not abuse their right to exact this, and other, payments. In 1515 there was discussion of mortuaries in parliament, while in 1529 an Act was passed to regulate their payment.[4] What needs to be stressed, however, is that, both in 1515 and 1529, feelings were inflamed – and were being manipulated. It is, therefore, terribly important to get, as it were, behind the headlines and the rhetoric, and if this is done the picture of a Church in its death throes, wracked by abuse, and quite unable to answer to the spiritual needs of its flock seems very far from the truth.

It is only in recent years that the vitality of late medieval religious life has come to be fully appreciated.[5] In the first three decades of the sixteenth century, the laity appear to have been pouring money into the Church: for enlarging and beautifying their parish churches, for setting up chantries, for having obits said for the repose of their souls, contributing to lay fraternities, and much else besides. It is a rich and varied picture, and one from which London should not be excluded. Indeed, such was the Londoners' liking for religious processions and festivals that they threatened to get out of hand so that in 1523 the bishop and the City's Common Council were forced to agree that in future all festivals for the dedication of particular churches should be held on one day each year, 3 October.[6] This agreement may serve to make the point that the religious life of the city was not all conflict and dissatisfaction with the church authorities. If it had been, one would have expected a more headlong rush towards Lutheranism. In fact there was no rush at all, but rather government pressure in the 1530s to accept even the limited changes which were then being introduced.[7] London was a great commercial centre, and as such it was

[1] Woodcock, *Medieval Ecclesiastical Courts*, pp.89-92.

[2] St German CWM, 9, p.195; see also Houlbrooke, *Church Courts*, pp.124-6; Haigh, *History*, p.395. But for larger numbers in the archdeaconry of Leicester see Bowker, *The Henrician Reformation*, p.53, though she admits the evidence is 'scrappy and difficult'. And in 'Some archdeacons' court books' she takes a generally optimistic view of the late medieval Church.

[3] St German, p.195.

[4] Lehmberg, pp.91-2.

[5] A vast and controversial subject with a literature to match – but for revisionist views see *inter alia* Haigh, *History*, 68 (1963); Harper-Bill, *JEH*, 29 (1987); O'Day and Heal; Scarisbrick, *Reformation*; and for a measured restatement of the previous orthodoxy see Dickens, 'The shape of anti-clericalism'.

[6] *VCH, London*, i, p.256.

composed, both socially and ethnically, of a great variety of people – not an easy place for the Church to control or satisfy. It is not, therefore, surprising that heterodox views were to be found there. But the suggestion often made that London's reaction to the Hunne affair is evidence of a strong tide of anticlericalism which, growing through the 1520s, led inevitably to the 'break with Rome' and protestantism, is the result either of wishful or lazy thinking.[1]

The problem of anticlericalism can be approached in another way. It is inconceivable that an organization such as the Church, so pervasive, so closely involved with almost every aspect of life, with power not only to summon anyone before its courts, to extract money in fees and tithes, to supervise all testamentary matters, but also to grant or withhold eternal salvation, should not attract criticism, just as all governments will attract criticism.[2] And one of the features of the Church was that, for better or worse, it was inextricably bound up with royal government, its popularity depending to some extent on the popularity of a particular monarch. Anticlericalism was inevitable, but insofar as it can be measured, it was less strong in the first two decades of Henry VIII's reign than in the past. There was nothing then to compare with the attacks on papal power in the second half of the fourteenth century that had resulted in the famous statutes of provisors and praemunire. And it was not only papal power that had earlier come under attack. In the 1370s and 1380s there had been moves in parliament to remove clerics from high office as well as attempts to ensure that the clergy contributed a much greater share to national taxation. During the Peasants' Revolt of 1381 the archbishop of Canterbury had been summarily executed, while in 1385 there had been an attempt in parliament to deprive the Church of all its temporal possessions. Out of all this agitation had emerged John Wyclif and the Lollard heresy, with their message that the existing church institutions and those who ran them had nothing to do with the true Church of God. The anticlericalism of the late fourteenth and early fifteenth century involved not only the new heresy which, as it turned out, was fairly rapidly brought under control (though never eliminated), but also a systematic attack on the extent of ecclesiastical jurisdiction. In 1450 violence erupted with the murder of two bishops, while in 1456 rebels in Kent demanded that all pluralist clerics should be put to death and the remainder castrated.[3] The 'uproar' resulting from the death of Richard Hunne bears no comparison with the strength of anticlericalism in this earlier period.

There is little to suggest that in the period in which anticlericalism was so overt the state of the Church was any worse than at any other time. The difference lay in the prevalence of plague, economic difficulties, major continental wars, heavy taxation, minority governments, and much political instability. All this suggests that in order to understand anticlericalism, economic and political factors need to be considered just as much as, if not more than, the condition of the Church itself. Given that anticlericalism was always present, it was there to be exploited by

[7] Brigden, 'Early Reformation', pp.118-48.

---

[1] Dickens, *English Reformation*, pp.90ff. as a *locus classicus* – and despite my strong disagreement with him, I remain an admirer of his work.

[2] My approach to anticlericalism has been much influenced by R.W. Southern.

[3] Storey, *The End of the House of Lancaster*, p.9.

anyone in a position to do so – by rebels, by noble factions, and by the Crown itself. In the early sixteenth century, it was the Crown that was doing the exploiting, as it sought to recover control over areas of the Church in which it had lost ground during the previous fifty years.

The second half of the fifteenth century was a period of recovery for the Church.[1] No bishops were murdered and there was no anticlerical legislation. Instead, in 1462 Edward iv, anxious for church support, granted to it a charter of liberties.[2] The main intention of this charter was to alter the existing practice as regards 'benefit of clergy' by which clerics were protected from punishment in a secular court as long as they could prove that they were clerics. Previously, they could only claim the benefit after sentence had been passed in the secular court. Now they could claim it immediately. Furthermore, if the claim was challenged, its validity was to be decided in an ecclesiastical court, though a secular judge would be present. The charter also stated that all cases concerning tithes should be determined in the ecclesiastical courts, and prohibited any attempt to have them transferred to a secular one by means of the writ of 'praemunire facias'. The practice of using this writ to remove many kinds of cases from ecclesiastical courts had been developed by the common lawyers after the statute of praemunire of 1393. It was intensely disliked by the Church, so this concession was greatly welcomed, and as it turned out, it was to be the only real gain resulting from the charter. The clauses relating to benefit were never put into effect, unlike the one prohibiting the use of the writ of praemunire facias, which appears to have been interpreted in the widest sense so as to include not just tithes but matters traditionally within the jurisdiction of the Church.[3] Partly as a result of this, the thirty years following the grant of Edward iv's charter witnessed a great increase in the activities of the ecclesiastical courts, especially in one of its most important, the consistory court of Canterbury. Not only was there more business before it, but that business included cases relating to breach of faith and other matters which for almost two hundred years had been considered outside the Church's jurisdiction by the secular courts.[4]

Richard iii confirmed the Church's charter of liberties.[5] Henry vii did not. Instead, his reign witnessed a sustained attack on those liberties, an attack which included two statutes actually curtailing benefit of clergy.[6] The first, in 1489, prohibited clerics not in holy orders – that is below the order of sub-deacon – from claiming benefit more than once, and to ensure that they did not, they were to be branded on their thumb after their first claim.[7] The second Act, in 1497, deprived those not in holy orders of any benefit in cases involving the murder of their masters.[8] Neither Act was very drastic, and together they could hardly have solved

---

[1] This may be considered an over-bold statement – and the subject is under-researched. The best introduction, with a good bibliography, is probably J.R. Lander, *Government and Community*, pp.105-51.

[2] Wilkins, iii, pp.583-5; Scofield, i, pp.390-2.

[3] See Firth, for a detailed discussion of the charter; also *Registrum Thome Bourgchier*, pp.xxxii ff. and 102-7.

[4] Houlbrooke, 'The decline of ecclesiastical jurisdiction', p.240; Woodcock, pp.79-92.

[5] Wilkins, iii, p.616.

[6] *Inter alia* Condon, pp.110-32; M.J. Kelly, 'Canterbury jurisdiction', pp.97-110.

[7] 4 Hen. vii, c.13 (*SR*, ii, p.538).

[8] 12 Hen. vii, c.7 (*SR*, ii, p.639).

the problem of abuse of benefit, which was considered at the time, probably mistakenly, to be great.[1] Even so, they were a public declaration that church liberties were not immune from secular interference.

However, the main thrust of the attack was in the law courts themselves. During the last two law terms of Henry VII's reign ten cases of praemunire were brought before King's Bench, eight of which were by the new attorney-general, John Ernley. The bishop of Norwich's registrar and summoner were amongst those cited, but the cases were not confined to the diocese of Norwich. None of the cases was successful, but given that in the previous sixteen years only six praemunire cases were brought, it does look as if Ernley was deliberately testing the law in order to establish the extent of the Crown's jurisdiction with regard to the Church, and perhaps to extend it. The record specifically states that Ernley had brought his prosecutions 'for the king himself', and even if this was merely a legal formula, Henry VII's known close attention to all matters of government suggests that he would have been fully aware of what his attorney-general was up to.[2] Moreover, a list of eighty-four people 'ill-used' by Henry VII cited seventeen churchmen, of whom two, the abbots of Gloucester and Cirencester, 'were hardly dealt withal for praemunire'. Also named were none other than Bishop Fitzjames and Dr Horsey, the latter, it was stated, being imprisoned 'contrary to conscience'. Unfortunately no details are given.[3] There is other evidence of Henry VII's direct intervention in church affairs, though much of it is difficult to interpret – it would be interesting to know, for instance, why the bishop of Salisbury had to pay '1000 marks for a very light cause'[4] – but it looks as if Henry was unhappy with the concessions made to the Church by his Yorkist predecessors, and was anxious to win back lost ground.

Henry VII does not come across as someone especially interested in political theory, but he was probably well aware of the theoretical justification for his moves against the Church – and, if he was not, one of his closest ministers during the later part of his reign certainly was. Edmund Dudley wrote *The Tree of Commonwealth* in 1510 while awaiting execution for alleged treason, though he had been guilty merely of being a too willing executant of his master's wishes. In the circumstances, he must have considered his words carefully. He was aware that some of Henry VII's actions against individual churchmen had been unfair, for it was he who drew up that list already referred to of those 'ill-used' by the king. However, his book makes it clear that he fully supported Henry's policy: it was the prince's role not to assist the Church, but rather to assist 'his maker and redeemer of whom he hath all his power and authority'; moreover, not only was his ability to correct the wicked much greater than the Church's could ever be, but 'the root of the love of God . . . within this realm must chiefly grow by our sovereign lord the king'.[5] This last statement almost suggests that he envisaged a spiritual function for the prince, such as Henry VIII was to claim from time to time in the 1530s. Certainly he envisaged an ecclesiastical one – that is to say, he thought it the prince's duty to control the

---

[1] Gabel; but also Baker, ii, pp.327-34; Bellamy, *Crime and Public Order*, pp.154-5; Blatcher, pp.56-7.

[2] Houlbrooke, 'The decline of ecclesiastical jurisdiction', pp.239-41; M. J. Kelly, 'Canterbury jurisdiction', pp.104-8.

[3] See Harrison for a full transcript.

[4] Included in Dudley's list.

[5] Dudley, pp.32-3 for all these quotations.

external activities of the Church, its organization and jurisdiction. Such a view was no novelty. Deriving from Roman law, it had become an integral part of civil law, and as such was very much alive throughout the Middle Ages, despite the challenge of Gregorian views that asserted the primacy of the Church and papacy in all temporal matters. Amost a commonplace of the English legal profession, the notion seems to have been fully grasped by Henry VII, and certainly by his son.[1] There is some doubt whether the alterations to the latter's coronation oath made with his own hand date from the beginning of his reign or from the 1530s, but they indicate very clearly Henry's view that the royal obligation to maintain the liberties of the Church should be in no way 'prejudicial to his jurisdiction and dignity royal'.[2] And that this view was not merely the by-product of the 'break with Rome' of the 1530s is made abundantly clear by the position he took up in 1515 in the Standish Affair – an affair that would not, however, have occurred unless the Church had not already begun to resist the threat to its liberties posed by the Crown.

Shortly after the 1504 parliament, the much-harassed bishop of Norwich, Richard Nix, wrote a letter to the archbishop of Canterbury stating that 'lay men be much bolder against the Church than ever they were. If your Lordship help not, having the great seal in your hand, I and other of your subjects can no thing do.' He added that if the archbishop would support him, he would bring charges of heresy against all those who threatened the church courts with praemunire[3] – precisely what some people alleged Fitzjames had done in the Hunne affair. In fact, as was mentioned earlier, it is very hard to find any evidence that the Church did proceed in this way,[4] but that Nix could think of doing so is an indication of the strong feelings aroused in church circles by the new wave of anticlericalism fomented by the Crown lawyers. It also suggests that the Church was not going to take it lying down. The convocation of 1504 – that is, the Church's assembly or parliament – made it clear to Henry VII that during his reign the liberties of the English Church had been undermined, and it hoped that he would do something to put this right[5] – presumably a hint that even at this late stage he would renew its charter of liberties. In 1510, during the first parliament of the new reign, a bill had been introduced to confirm the Church's liberties, but without success.[6] At the same time convocation determined to resist the activity of certain 'wicked men' who were threatening to trample the Church under foot.[7] In his opening sermon the dean of St Paul's, John Colet, strongly criticized the faults of the clergy, but also very much emphasized 'the dignity of priesthood . . . the which is greater than either the king's or emperor's: it is equal with the dignity of angels'.[8] This meant, amongst other things, that the clergy should not be brought before the secular courts.

Colet's sermon to the 1510 convocation is famous, though more for its call for

---

[1] Ullmann.

[2] BL, Tib. E. VIII, fo. 89. Ullmann suggested that they were, but the 1530s does seem more likely.

[3] PRO, SCI/44/fo. 83; quoted in Houlbroke, 'The decline of ecclesiastical jurisdiction', p.241.

[4] See pp.42-3, above.

[5] *Registrum Ricardi Mayew*, p.55.

[6] LJ, i, pp.4-6.

[7] Wilkins, iii, p.651 – the summons to the 1510 convocation; see also M. J. Kelly, 'Canterbury jurisdiction', pp.95-147 – an outstanding piece of work that should have been published.

[8] Lupton, p.297; for the whole sermon ibid, pp.293-310.

reform than for extolling the clerical orders. A speech to the 1514 convocation by John Taylor, who, as prolocuter, presided over the debates in the lower house, has been too often ignored.[1] Like Colet, he attacked the deficiencies of the Church, that only encouraged the laity to trample on its liberties. Churchmen did nothing but quarrel amongst themselves. Monks were arrogant and idle. Secular priests – that is, those not in religious orders – led 'foul and dissolute' lives, and committed crimes which led to them being 'sold publically in fetters by the secular power, like condemned criminals'. Taylor's message was that the Church must reform or there would be no Church left, but throughout his speech he stressed that the 'following of righteousness' and the Church's liberties went hand in hand, and, calling the leaders of the Church to arms, he reminded them that 'neither the threat of harm nor exile, privation, mockeries, calumnies, hatred, not even the parade of death before their eyes', had prevented their predecessors from fighting for these two things. Taylor's speech is all the more remarkable in that, unlike Colet, he was not an obvious 'reformer', rather a successful career churchman, who under Wolsey was to become master of the rolls, and often employed on diplomatic missions. The fact that such a man could make so forceful a speech is the clearest indication possible of the strength of the clergy's feelings on the eve of their battle with the Crown. The issues in this battle may appear trivial: whether the minor clerical orders should receive 'benefit of clergy', or whether cases of 'breach of faith' should be tried in the secular or ecclesiastical courts. But each one of them raised the question that had dominated so much of medieval polemic: who on this earth should have the final word, pope or emperor, Church or state? In 1515 both sides drew back from the brink. Fifteen years later it was to be a different story.

As has already been indicated, the battle in 1515 was not over Richard Hunne, though the feelings aroused by his mysterious death undoubtedly contributed to the heightening of tension. The specific issue was an Act of 1512 which had prohibited all clerics not in holy orders from claiming 'benefit' for certain serious offences, such as any murder committed in a holy place, in any occupied house, or on the king's highway.[2] The Act was for a trial period, to be reconsidered in the next parliament. The Church had, therefore, very good warning that the bill would again be before parliament in 1515, and it is almost certain that they had determined to fight it long before there was any question of defending Dr Horsey – and since he was in holy orders the Act did not affect his position one way or the other. The Church would have been encouraged to fight by certain resolutions taken at the Fifth Lateran Council, which was dominated by concerns similar to those being expressed in England by the likes of Colet and Taylor – the need for reform, but also to resist lay interference.[3] In two bulls of 1514 the whole panoply of the Church's defence against such interference was specifically restated.[4] The call from Rome was clear, and the English clergy were in the mood to answer it.

---

[1] BL, Vit. B. ii, fos. 80-1. In the quotations that follow I have made use of R.E. Brock's translation in his 'Career of John Taylor', pp. 309-15.
[2] 4 Hen. VIII, c.2 (SR, iii, p.49).
[3] Jedin, i, pp.128 ff.
[4] The two bulls were *Supernae dispositionis arbitrio* (5 May 1514) and *Regimini universalis ecclesiae* (4 May 1515); see Schroeder, pp.488-98, 500-3.

Early in 1515, probably to coincide with the opening of parliament on 5 February, the distinguished abbot of Winchcombe, Richard Kidderminster, delivered a sermon at St Paul's Cross in which he attacked the Act of 1512.[1] In it he argued that since minor orders were just as 'holy' as major ones, those belonging to them could not be sentenced in the secular courts. More controversially, he went on to argue that nobody in holy orders could even be tried there and that the existing practice, quite irrespective of the fate of the disputed Act, was wrong. Immediate exception was taken to the sermon, and pressure from parliament led to Henry calling a conference at Blackfriars to debate the issues it raised. The spokesman for the 'secular' side was Henry Standish, the warden of the Grey Friars in London and provincial of the Franciscan order. The fact that he was a Franciscan is not without significance. The convocation of 1512 had forwarded to Rome a whole series of complaints against the orders of friars[2] – part of a wider running battle between 'secular' clergy and friars that had, for instance, occupied much time at the Lateran Council.[3] And amongst the mendicant orders none was so critical of the wealth and pretensions of the 'secular' clergy as the Franciscans. Thus in the battle between Crown and Church it is no surprise to find Standish on the side of the Crown.

The main thrust of his argument, both at the first Blackfriars conference and subsequently, was that the Act of 1512 was for the 'public good'. It was therefore very much the concern of the Crown, who had a duty to ensure that the 'public good' was upheld, irrespective of whether the matter in question was ecclesiastical or secular; indeed, as regards the 'public good' there was no such distinction. And in arguing thus, Standish was drawing on that tradition of the civil law already referred to, that gave to the Crown control of the 'ecclesiastical' or external affairs of the Church as distinct from 'spiritual' or inward matters. He also argued that many papal decrees had not been observed in England, and that anyway their observance depended both on their formal acceptance by the Crown and on local custom. Since in England it had been the practice for all clergy, whether in major orders or not, to be 'convented' before the secular courts and only to be handed over to the ecclesiastical ones for sentencing, papal decrees to the contrary should have no effect. Standish also argued for a distinction between major and minor orders. If his earlier reasoning concerning the sovereignty of the 'public good' was correct, to do so was surely unnecessary – but as the Act of 1512 affected only those in minor orders, to emphasize the distinction was no doubt tempting.

The Church's argument was that clerical exemption from secular jurisdiction derived from 'divine law', and to prove it they cited two texts: 'Touch not the Lord's anointed' and 'Honour thy Father'. The point of the first text is clear: as the Lord's anointed, the clergy could not be arrested or tried. As regards the second, it was

---

[1] Found in Keilwey, a major, and sometimes questioned source for the Standish affair, used extensively in his own translation by A. Ogle in his *Lollards' Tower*, pp.140 ff. For important discussions on the *Reports* see A. F. Pollard, pp.44, n.2 and Simpson. Many of the doubts about its authenticity as a source for this episode have been removed by J.A. Guy's discovery of an early sixteenth-century version; see Guy, *EHR*, xvii, p.497, n.2 – though this does not prevent it from being biased against the clerical position. I am grateful to J.A. Guy for providing me with a photocopy of his discovery.

[2] *Registrum Ricardi Mayew*, pp.50-2.

[3] Jedin, i, pp.135-6.

well understood that by 'Father' was implied the layman's spiritual as well as natural father, and since it would be against all reason to suppose that a child could have jurisdiction over its father, so it was for a layman to have jurisdiction over a priest. Moreover, as 'divine law' was superior to all other kinds of law, its formal acceptance by a ruler was obviously not required, neither could local practice override it. But it was also argued that the 'positive law' of the Church did not require formal 'acceptance' by a ruler. Thus papal decrees forbidding secular interference in church affairs were to be obeyed, whether formally 'received' or not. In making their case the church spokesmen had gone well beyond the particular issues raised by the Act of 1512, for the whole thrust of their argument was to show that 'divine law' prohibited the subjection of the clergy to any form of secular jurisdiction, and that therefore existing English practice was quite wrong. If it persisted, ecclesiastical censures would follow. It was aggressive stuff, but then the Church was in aggressive mood.[1]

It is not entirely clear what the outcome of the first Blackfriars conference was. Neither is it possible to date precisely the events which followed it, although their sequence seems clear enough. Shortly after it had ended, the Commons requested that the abbot of Winchcombe should publicly renounce the views he had expressed in his St Paul's Cross sermon. The request was, however, refused, and when Standish continued to publicize his views in a series of lectures, he was summoned before convocation to answer a number of questions in what turned out to be the first steps in proceedings against him for heresy. On the central issues Standish stuck to his guns but, fearing the consequences, he appealed to the king, as indeed did the Church. A second Blackfriars conference was called, probably some time in November. Both sides repeated and developed their arguments, Standish getting full support from John Veysey, a doctor of civil law and dean of the Chapel Royal who, even before the second conference began, had informed the king 'that the conventing of clerks before the temporal judges, as had always been the custom in the realm of England, might well stand with the law of God, and with the liberties of the Holy Church'.[2] But, of course, the new development which had to be thrashed out was the validity of convocation's moves against Standish. On this issue the Church suffered a real setback, for the judges declared that here convocation was guilty of praemunire, presumably for their partial reliance, in putting forward their case, on papal decrees which had not received the royal assent. Furthermore, they went on to argue that the Church had no role to play in parliament: the bishops were present in the House of Lords only by reason of their temporal possessions, and therefore the king was perfectly at liberty not to summon them.[3] In other words, they were there on sufferance and had no say in the government of the country except that graciously allowed them by the Crown. It is not known what the bishops' reaction to this broadside was, but a detailed defence against the praemunire charge has survived.[4] Amongst other things, the point was made that it

---

[1] By drawing together the various arguments put by both sides it has proved difficult to provide satisfactory references, but see Ogle, pp.140 ff. For a sermon putting forward the clerical view see PRO, SP6/3/5/ fos. 45-85 (LP, v, 1021, where wrongly dated; see M. J. Kelly, 'Canterbury jurisdiction', p.139, n.2).

[2] Ogle, p.150.

[3] Ibid, p.151.

was the duty of the Church to investigate possible cases of heresy, and it was thought quite unreasonable for parliament to be able to criticize the Church with impunity, while convocation could make no criticism of the laity without the threat of a praemunire charge.

What was now at issue was the very role of the Church in English society. It was high time that the king intervened directly. A further conference was called, this time at Baynard's Castle, with Henry himself presiding and with everybody who was anybody being present – including Wolsey. Indeed, it was Wolsey who opened the proceedings by kneeling before Henry and declaring that

> to his knowledge none of the clergy had ever meant to do anything in derogation of the king's prerogative, and for his own part he owed his whole advancement solely to our lord the king; wherefore he said he would assent to nothing that would tend to annul or derogate from his royal authority for all the world. Nevertheless, to all the clergy this matter of conventing of clerks before the temporal judges seems contrary to the laws of God and the liberties of the Holy Church, the which he himself and all the prelates of Holy Church are bound by their oath to maintain according to their power.[1]

Wolsey then requested that Henry should allow the matter to be decided at Rome, to which Henry replied that he thought the Church's case had been fully answered by Dr Standish and others. This was too much for Richard Fox, who angrily retorted, 'Sir, I warrant you Dr Standish will not abide by his opinion [but] at his peril', whereupon Standish asked his famous question, 'What should one poor friar do alone against the bishops and clergy of England?'[2] After a pause for tempers to cool, Warham formally presented the Church's case, reminding Henry that many holy fathers had resisted attempts by the Crown to limit 'benefit of clergy' and some had even suffered martyrdom in this cause – a reference, as everyone there would have known, to his predecessor, Thomas Becket.[3] His case was answered by Chief Justice Fineux, who pointed out that since the practice of 'conventing' clergy had long been accepted by the English Church, this presupposed that for all this time it had never been considered contrary to the laws of God. Turning to the problem that had led to the Act of 1512 – the widespread feeling that handing clerics over to the ecclesiastical courts for sentencing was tantamount to letting them off – he argued that ecclesiastical law made no provision for cases of felony – which Warham denied – and that therefore there was no point in handing over clerics who had committed felonies to a court which was in no position to sentence them. To this Warham made no reply.[4]

At this point Henry gave his judgment:

> By the ordinance and sufferance of God, we are king of England, and kings of England in time past have never had any superior but God only. Wherefore know you well that

---

[4] PRO, SP1/12/ fos. 18-21 (LP, ii, 1314).

[1] Ogle, pp.151-2.
[2] Ibid, p.152 for this exchange.
[3] Ibid, p.152. J.M.D. Derrett in his important, but to my mind confusing, article wrongly attributes Warham's remarks to Wolsey; see Derrett, pp.234-5.
[4] Ogle, p.152.

we will maintain the right of our Crown and of our temporal jurisdiction as well in this point as in all others, in as ample a wise as any of our progenitors have done before us. And as to our decrees, we are well informed that you yourselves of the Spirituality do expressly contrary to the words of many of them, as has been well shown to you by some of our spiritual Counsel: nevertheless, you interpret your decrees at your pleasure. Wherefore, consent to your desire more than our progenitors have done in time past we will not.[1]

All that remained was for Warham to make a last despairing plea for the whole matter to be decided at Rome, but all he received for his pains was a royal silence.

The crisis of 1515 was largely a political one, the culmination of a conflict between Crown and Church which had originated in the second half of Henry VII's reign when he and his leading lay councillors had determined to assert greater control over the Church, and in particular to win back concessions granted to it by the Yorkist kings. These moves the Church determined to resist, though there may also have been at this time within the Church a more aggressive spirit abroad, associated with a greater interest in reform. The conflict was about spheres of activity within society, rather than about theology and religious observance, but this does not mean that the conflict was not serious; three conferences within the course of one year is evidence that it was. What has puzzled historians and has led them to underestimate the seriousness of the situation, is that apparently very little resulted from these conferences. Actually more came of them than has usually been realized, even if on the face of it their result was a stalemate: the Act of 1512 limiting benefit of clergy was not renewed but, on the other hand, the clerical demand for the end of the practice of 'conventing' was not met. But in reality the Church had suffered a defeat, even if the extent of that defeat was to be partially obscured by Wolsey's political skill.

To understand the nature of the defeat, a return must be made to Henry VIII's attitude towards the Church. It has been said of him that 'if there is any single thread to his theological evolution it is his anticlericalism'.[2] The only quarrel with this statement must be with the word 'evolution'. The claims that Henry made for supremacy over the English Church in the 1530s, even his view that 'all spiritual things, by reason whereof may arise bodily trouble and inquietation, be necessarily included in a prince's power', and that as a result God had assigned to the prince power over the Church's 'person, acts and deeds'[3] – all this was implicit in the stance that he took in 1515. His declaration that 'kings of England . . . have never had any superior but God only' could hardly have been clearer. The English Church was subordinate to the Crown and had only a delegated authority; if what the Church was doing was not conducive to the 'public good', the Crown had a duty to intervene. This is what Standish and Veysey had argued, and to their argument Henry had given his full assent. Henry VIII was determined to be master of his Church. The instrument of his mastery was to be Thomas Wolsey.

Evidence of Wolsey's direct participation in the two *causes célèbres* is extremely meagre. There is the letter which Fitzjames may have written to him asking for his

[1] Ogle, pp.152-3 – but, like the above, a translation from Keilwey, *Reports*; see p.47, n.1 above.
[2] Scarisbrick, *Henry VIII*, p.417.
[3] Ibid, p.279.

aid in protecting Horsey from the bias of a London jury.[1] There is also the summary of the speech which he made while kneeling before Henry at Baynard's Castle.[2] That is about it, and one is thus forced back on conjecture. It does seem inconceivable that a man as close to Henry as Wolsey was in 1515, a man whom Henry was pushing for cardinal and was just about to make lord chancellor, could have been ignorant of Henry's views on the Church. Indeed, the assumption must be that Henry and his chief minister had discussed the two affairs in some detail, and that each knew beforehand what the other was going to say at Baynard's Castle. Both, of course, would also have been well aware of the strength of clerical feeling. The fact that the only copy of the Church's defence to a possible charge of praemunire for questioning Standish on a suspicion of heresy is in the hand of Brian Tuke, at the time Wolsey's secretary, is not evidence of Wolsey's whole-hearted support for the clerical party, but only that he had detailed knowledge of their position, for whatever his personal views he would have needed to have such information.[3] And at this point it is important to stress, especially in view of the emphasis which has been placed on Henry's determination to exert his 'superiority' over the Church, that the main purpose of the conference at Baynard's Castle was to put an end to a dangerous dispute. Although Henry had no intention of conceding anything to the Church on the principles at stake, equally there was no intention of widening the divisions – and in practice the offending bill was dropped. Wolsey's role in all this was to act as mediator – his favourite role, and one that he was supremely good at. Hence his kneeling and his recognition of the king's prerogative, but hence also his statement that 'conventing of clerks' was 'contrary to the laws of God'. His was a conciliatory speech, quite unlike Warham's with its talk of martyrdom, and quite unlike his former patron Fox's interjection concerning Standish, which must have raised the temperature a good deal. Wolsey's immediate tactics seem clear enough: he wanted to 'cool' the situation.

But what of Wolsey's long-term aims? Or, to put it another way, was he entirely neutral in the conflict, or, if, as seems likely, he was not, which side did he favour? Wolsey was, of course, a cleric, indeed a bishop, and by the end of the affair a cardinal. In his speech at Baynard's Castle he pointed out that as bishop he had sworn to maintain the 'laws of God and the liberties of the Holy Church'. He also requested, as Warham did, that the matter might be determined at Rome. But by far and away the major ingredient in Wolsey's rise was his personal relationship with Henry VIII. This being so, it seems unlikely – though bearing in mind the precedent of Henry II and Thomas Becket, not impossible – that in a conflict between Church and state he would side wholeheartedly with the Church.

Furthermore, not all churchmen opposed the Crown's case for 'superiority' – Standish and Veysey to name but two. Standish, being a Franciscan, was a rather special case, but Veysey's career seems to have been very typical of the careerist cleric. About ten years Wolsey's senior, he too had gone to Magdalen College, Oxford, but unlike Wolsey, he had studied civil law, becoming a doctor in 1495. He had then embarked upon a successful ecclesiastical career, including spells as vicar-

[1] Foxe, *Acts and Monuments*, iv, p.196.
[2] Ogle, pp.151-2.
[3] *LP*, ii, 1314; see M. J. Kelly, 'Canterbury jurisdiction', pp.135-6.

general in two different dioceses. He accumulated innumerable benefices and canonries, and by 1515 was dean of Exeter as well as of the Chapel Royal and of St George's, Windsor. Perhaps royal favour did influence his judgment at the second Blackfriars conference, but then most successful ecclesiastical careers depended to some extent on royal favour. If Veysey could side with the Crown, no doubt a number of other leading clerics could do so as well, but how many is not known. One of the many surprising incidents in 1515 had been Fox's outburst against Standish. As has been shown, there was no more devoted servant of the Crown than Richard Fox – almost the quintessential clerical politician.[1] Furthermore, he was no friend to Warham, having spent most of the previous ten years in dispute with him. In particular, he and a number of other suffragan bishops had strongly resisted Warham's attempt to extend the jurisdictional privileges of the see of Canterbury, in the process hindering both the Church's efforts at reform and its resistance to secular interference.[2] Yet at Baynard's Castle Fox had, most unusually, lost his temper, and made it very clear that he stood with Warham and against the king. Notwithstanding that Fox was on the point of retiring from politics and had been increasingly preoccupied with his diocese, his opposition is nevertheless an indication of how high feeling was running in some church circles at least. It is also a reminder of the problems facing the historian in trying to define the relationship between Crown and Church at any given time.

Most historians have emphasized the conformity of the early Tudor episcopacy with the royal will.[3] This has been misleading and has, for instance, obscured the importance of the Standish affair. Of course, almost by definition leading clerics were also leading servants of the Crown, which needed the Church's support just as the Church needed the Crown's. Despite the papacy and its claims to temporal supremacy, much of the time there was no conflict. Insofar as there was the potential for it, it was one that people had learnt to live with. Henry could claim that he had no superior but God and yet consider himself a very loyal son of the pope. Wolsey could be both a prince of the Church and yet the king's chief minister. Neither appears to have suffered overmuch from schizophrenia. That said, there was always likely to be conflict between a confident monarchy determined to exert its authority to the full and the entrenched vested interest that was the Church.

So, whose side was Wolsey on? The answer must be – the Crown's. Time and again one comes back to the point that Henry made Wolsey what he was, that their relationship was a personal one, that Wolsey's own ambitions were subsumed in Henry's, and – what will appear more clearly in the following chapters – that it was the desire to make royal government fairer and more effective that was the main driving force behind Wolsey's life's work. At the same time he was a cleric who took his religious duties seriously. He was also a consummate politician – hence the stand he took in 1515. As archbishop of York, even as cardinal, Wolsey was not master of

---

[1] See p.7 above.

[2] M. J. Kelly, 'Canterbury jurisdiction', pp.42-94.

[3] Thus Dickens could write: 'Amongst the higher clergy the impressive feature is the virtual unanimity with which they followed the lead of the king.' (*English Reformation*, p.124). Admittedly in recent years the consensus has been challenged, especially by Scarisbrick, both in his *Henry VIII*, pp.273-81, 329-31 and *Reformation*, pp.61 ff; see also Bernard, *JEH*, 37 (1986).

the English Church. To be in a position to override Canterbury, he required to be legate *a latere*. Already in 1515 he and Henry were working on that,[1] but until he could obtain such a commission there was no point in unnecessarily antagonizing Warham and his supporters, and indeed it was never Wolsey's policy to antagonize anybody unnecessarily. Much of his performance at Baynard's Castle had been directed towards the bishops rather than towards Henry, who needed no reassurance that Wolsey was not his enemy. The bishops, and Warham in particular, did, and thus his appearance of supporting Warham's efforts to get the issues raised by the Standish 'affair' settled at Rome. Wolsey did approach the pope, not, however, to get his views on the principles at stake, but to ask for a bull prohibiting anyone being admitted to minor orders unless he at the same time became subdeacon, that is, took holy orders. This Leo granted, though not without pointing out that the proposal was not in accordance with the laws of the Church.[2] It was a skilful move by Wolsey. It saved the Church's face by obviating the need for it to endure any secular limitation of 'benefit'. At the same time it removed the Crown's main objection to benefit, that it applied as much to people who had not the slightest intention of pursuing a career in the Church as to genuine clerics. That it seems not to have been very effective might suggest that it was a purely tactical move by Wolsey to dampen things down, but against this is the fact that towards the end of the 1520s Wolsey returned to the problem. In 1528 he secured a bull giving him authority greatly to simplify the machinery whereby a 'criminous clerk' could be degraded from both major and minor orders, and thus handed over to the secular courts for sentencing.[3] The bull is indicative of Wolsey's not always acknowledged determination to solve a problem once identified. More relevantly it suggests that he did not share Warham's and the clerical party's resistance to all innovations, however beneficial, that might infringe in any way upon the Church's liberties.

At this point it may be helpful to mention another problem that was causing friction between Crown and Church and one which, as in the case of benefit of clergy, led in 1519 to a conference presided over by Henry himself. It concerned the innumerable sanctuaries, which, as a consequence of the peace associated with any sanctified place, provided a refuge from arrest.[4] The most common sanctuary was the parish church, and for it there were elaborate rules, governing such matters as the area of the church that constituted the sanctuary, the length of time any person might remain there, and what was to happen when that time elapsed. Forty days were allowed before the fugitive, if he was still determined not to face trial, had to confess his crime and then abjure the realm – that is to say, go into permanent exile. Such a fate might appear harsh, and certainly the taking of sanctuary was not intended as an easy option, but it should be remembered that it was only permitted for offences for which the penalty was death. Given this choice, permanent exile might well seem more attractive. Furthermore, there were many opportunities for taking advantage of the privilege. One might escape from one sanctuary to another,

---

[1] *LP*, ii, 780, 966.

[2] Rymer, xiii, p.495; *LP*, ii, 1105, 1281.

[3] Wilkins, iii, p.713; Bellamy, *Criminal Law*, pp.138-40.

[4] The standard account is Thornley, but see also Baker, ii, pp.334-46. I am very grateful to A. G. Rosser for his comments on what I originally wrote on this subject – and for the Westminster sanctuary see his *Medieval Westminster*.

thus prolonging the period of protection, or one might escape altogether – and the often very long journey from the sanctuary to the nearest port, from where a fugitive was supposed to begin his exile, offered ample opportunity for this. More open to abuse were the private sanctuaries, those created by a grant either from the pope or from the Crown. Many imposed no time limit, and the area involved was often quite extensive. They could, therefore, provide the professional criminal with a permanent refuge, not to say convenient base from which to conduct his operations.

It is hard to assess just how serious a hindrance to law enforcement sanctuaries were, or, indeed, whether they were becoming more so. Both contemporary comment and particular cases at least suggest that the privilege was frequently abused;[1] and what is certain is that Henry VII's reign had witnessed a new determination to tackle the problem.[2] One of the ways chosen was for judges to insist that any holder of the privilege must produce a royal, not a papal, charter granting it to them, on the grounds that the prerogative of mercy, of which the right of sanctuary formed a part, pertained in England only to its king. Or, in other words, the judges were asserting the king's 'imperial' jurisdiction.

The discussion in Star Chamber on 10 November 1519 centred on the claims of the order of St John of Jerusalem and Westminster Abbey to possess the privilege of sanctuary.[3] The former's claim was quickly dismissed on the grounds that it did not possess a royal charter. Wolsey appears to have accepted this decision, for later in the conference he opened a debate on the principles involved by pointing out that in the Old Testament it had been princes who had created sanctuaries. Other examples of royal initiative were produced, and reference made both to the first English king and to Romulus; the conclusion reached was that not only was the creation of sanctuary a royal prerogative but that anyone who relied on a papal grant was guilty of praemunire. It is not quite certain from Keilwey's *Reports* whether this conclusion was delivered by Wolsey himself, but his opening remarks suggest that he was in full agreement with it. It also seems clear that he shared the judges' desire to reform the abuse of the privilege. But since Westminster Abbey's sanctuary, unlike most others, was based upon a royal grant, it was in a strong position to resist any attempt at reform. Chief Justice Fineux tried to get round the problem by arguing that the abuse of a privilege must result in its removal.[4] Wolsey's solution was not so radical. Long before the conference took place he had set up a commission to establish the precise boundaries of the Westminster sanctuary, the lack of which was one of the reasons for the abuse. He had also insisted on all its sanctuary men taking an oath not to commit treason, murder or felony outside the sanctuary, while still resident there, in an effort to stop them using it as a base for their criminal activities. However, on the second day of the conference he had had to admit that the oath had been ineffective; furthermore, Abbot Islip made it clear that he considered it to be invalid as contrary to the existing and perfectly legal

---

[1] Baker, ii, p.340.

[2] Thornley, p.197, though for a different view see Kaufman, 'Henry VII and sanctuary'.

[3] Keilway, pp.190-2 is the source, but extensively summarized in Gasquet, *The Eve of the Reformation*, pp.51 ff. Ives, 'Crimes, sanctuary and royal authority' is very important, especially for the events leading up to the discussion, which I have not been able to tackle.

[4] Keilway, p.191.

privileges.[1]

The abbot of Westminster's rejection of the oath, and thus of Wolsey's solution, ended the conference – and there is no evidence that during the 1520s the Abbey's sanctuary was in any way modified. Must the conclusion be that this episode illustrates Wolsey's ineffectiveness as a reformer – an ineffectiveness deriving in great measure from the fact that his heart was not really in reform? To the extent that Westminster's sanctuary remained, and no doubt continued to harbour all manner of rogues, the answer must be yes.[2] But Westminster was a special case. Given its royal charter, its sanctuary was virtually unassailable unless one was prepared to abolish all private sanctuaries. There is no evidence that Wolsey ever contemplated such a step, and thus there was little he could do. On the other hand, during the 1520s the judges continued to attack the problem of sanctuary, with the result that it became virtually impossible to plead sanctuary with success.[3] Considering how closely Wolsey worked with the judges in Chancery and Star Chamber, it seems most unlikely that he was opposed to what they were doing – indeed, there is evidence to the contrary. In 1526 a William Gilbank, having at first taken sanctuary in Colchester Abbey, removed himself to that of the Crutched Friars in the same town. A certain John Veer was deputed by Wolsey to arrest him. This meant tackling the prior about the rights of his house to provide sanctuary and, in particular, whether he possessed a royal grant. The prior's rather lame reply – that he possessed no grant himself but he assumed the head of the order had one – led Gilbank to the conclusion that his protection might suddenly be removed, and he decided that the sooner he confessed to a coroner and abjured the realm the better.[4] Here was a minor victory for Wolsey's insistence on a more effective supervision of the privilege of sanctuary. His failure with Westminster is merely evidence of the intractable nature of so many of the matters in need of reform.

The question of whether Wolsey was an effective reformer is one that will recur constantly. Here it has been raised merely as a coda to the Standish affair. Sanctuary was never such a divisive issue as benefit of clergy because, though it raised similar theoretical issues, it was only of real concern to the few custodians of private sanctuaries. This made it much easier for the Church as a whole to accept that the privilege was open to abuse and hence more willing to accept royal interference – and as his presence at the discussions in 1519 indicate, interfere was what Henry intended to do.[5] Wolsey was of the same mind, even to the extent of accepting that the granting of the privilege was entirely in the gift of the Crown – this incidentally having the important practical consequence that very few private sanctuary holders could substantiate their claims. On the other hand, Wolsey's aim was reform, not revolution. He did not take on the Church directly by seeking to abolish all private sanctuaries at one stroke, as was done in 1540. As he saw it, the best way of reforming the Church was to secure its co-operation, and this would include the co-operation of such a man as John Islip, abbot of Westminster.

[1] Keilway, pp.191-2.
[2] LP, iv, 2935-6, 3334 for evidence of continuing trouble – including the possibility of an attack on Wolsey's London residence, York Place.
[3] Baker, ii, 345.
[4] LP, iv, 2385.
[5] For Henry's stated intentions at the discussion see Baker, ii, p.343.

A policy emerges. In 1515 Wolsey's immediate task was to end the serious conflict between Crown and Church which, brewing for some time, had come to a head with the Standish affair. To do this he had tried to solve the problem of criminous clerks in a way that would meet the criticisms of the laity without unnecessarily antagonizing the Church. And that he did not wish to antagonize the latter is not evidence of *parti pris*, but that he realized that without greater powers he was in no position to make the Church do what he, or his master, wanted. Henry's involvement has been little understood. Historians have been so obsessed with their vision of the power-hungry and extravagantly ambitious Wolsey, that they have seen his wish to be made legate *a latere* as merely evidence of this vision. But would a Henry, who had made his views on the subject of clerical pretensions so abundantly clear in 1515, have supported efforts to secure such an appointment, if it would only have served to further Wolsey's own pretensions? The answer must be no. What, then, was the reason for Henry's support? It must have been because he had every confidence that Wolsey's domination of the English Church meant, in fact, domination by the Crown – a domination, indeed, such as had never previously been achieved. In 1515 Henry did not change his views; merely his tactics. He still intended to control the Church, but he would achieve this through a papal legate who happened also to be his leading councillor.

The change of tactics was not without its difficulties, the chief one being that the legatine commission had yet to be obtained, and in 1515 Leo x would go no further than to make Wolsey a cardinal. And not everyone would be fooled by the fiction that it was a papal legate who was reforming the Church rather than a king's leading councillor – and not everyone would want to be reformed! But undoubtedly the legatine powers would help to disguise the fact, or at least soften the blow that it was the Crown that was taking the initiative in the Church's affairs. Moreover, they would make it very difficult for any opponent in the future to do what the Church had tried to do in 1515, that is to appeal over the head of the king to the pope, for in effect Wolsey, as far as the English Church was concerned, had become the pope.

The news that Wolsey had been created a cardinal reached the English court at the end of September 1515, and on 15 November the cardinal's hat, brought from Rome by the protonotary of the papal court, was carried through the city of London in great splendour. It was then placed on the high altar of Westminster Abbey to await the ceremony of installation, on Sunday the 18th. As was only fitting on this great occasion, the mass was sung by the archbishop of Canterbury assisted by the bishops of Lincoln and Exeter. Also present were the archbishops of Armagh and Dublin and six other bishops, including Fisher of Rochester and Wolsey's old patron, Fox of Winchester. The papal bull was read out by none other than the dean of the Chapel Royal, John Veysey, and the sermon was delivered by the dean of St Paul's, John Colet. The laity were equally well represented. For some unknown reason Henry himself seems to have graced only the sumptuous banquet which followed the service, but present at the Abbey had been the dukes of Norfolk and Suffolk, the marquess of Dorset, the earls of Essex, Shrewsbury, Surrey and Wiltshire, along with nine barons, a goodly number of knights, the judges, City Fathers, and really anybody who was anybody.[1]

In his sermon Colet dwelt not only upon those virtues of Wolsey that had led to

56

his 'high and joyous promotion', but on Henry's as well, because that promotion had been secured by 'the great zeal and favour that our holy father, the pope, hath to his grace' – thereby indicating that he, at least, appreciated that aspect of Wolsey's elevation which so many historians have missed. He then stressed the need for humility. This has always been taken as a timely warning to a man who was singularly lacking in that quality. He may have intended something of the sort, but it is highly unlikely, and not just because it was hardly the occasion for personal criticism. The point that Colet stressed about humility was service: 'Remember that our Saviour in his own person said to his disciples: "I came not to be ministered unto but to minister . . ." My lord cardinal, be glad, and enforce yourself always to do and execute righteousness to rich and poor.' Justice to rich and poor alike was something that Wolsey always believed in, and as lord chancellor he strove to make it a reality. Colet also stressed 'the high and great power of a cardinal' who 'representeth the order of seraphim, which continually burneth in the love of the glorious Trinity' and is therefore 'metely apparelled with red'.[1] Wolsey's obsession with dressing up in red, along with his love of ceremonial, has come in for a good deal of criticism.[2] It did not worry Colet, and neither is it likely to have worried another great reformer of the time, Giles of Viterbo, who placed a great deal of emphasis upon magnificent church ceremonial.[3]

More will be said on the subject of ceremonial later, as also on Wolsey's relationship with Colet. Meanwhile, the service at Westminster Abbey and the subsequent banquet provide a fitting end to this discussion of the Hunne and Standish affairs and the way in which they helped to mould Henry's and Wolsey's policy towards the Church. Most of the leading participants were present, many of whom had taken diametrically opposed views on the issues that had emerged during the course of the year. One would give anything to know what they were all thinking, as Wolsey lay 'grovelling' on the floor of the Abbey while they were asked to pray for him.[4] No doubt there was much apprehension, but also hope – hope amongst some that as a prince of the Church he would defend its liberties, and amongst others that as the Crown's leading councillor he would ensure that the Church did not exceed its proper role. And amongst all shades of opinion there may have been an awareness that things might never be quite the same in the Church. But to discover whether their hopes and fears would be realized they would all have to wait a while. The ceremony was merely symbolic of a new policy. It could only become a reality when Wolsey became legate *a latere*, and that was not to happen until 1518.

---

[1] Lupton, pp.193-8 (*LP*, ii, 1153), a transcript of a document in the College of Arms giving a detailed description of Wolsey's installation, including Colet's sermon.

---

[1] Lupton, p.197.
[2] Elton's description of him 'flaunting his scarlet, his maces, his tapers, his canopies, the trappings of his mule' (*Reform and Reformation*, p.64) is a good example.
[3] O'Malley, pp.135-8.
[4] Lupton, p.198 – for the 'grovelling'.

CHAPTER THREE

THE MAKING OF THE TREATY OF LONDON

THE YEAR 1518 HAS SOME CLAIM TO BEING CALLED WOLSEY'S *ANNUS MIRABILIS*. On 17 May he was created legate *a latere*, a position he had been working hard to obtain for well over two years. It was true that for the time being he would have to put up with a fellow legate in Cardinal Campeggio and that his legatine powers would only last for as long as Campeggio remained in England. It was also true that the initial grant of these powers by Leo X was for the sole purpose of enabling the two cardinals to promote the papal plans for a five-year truce in Europe and a crusade against the Turk. Still, as legate *a latere* Wolsey would have authority over the whole English Church, not excluding those religious orders previously exempt from episcopal jurisdiction, while even the archbishop of Canterbury would have to recognize his superiority. Thus, if Leo X could be persuaded to prolong Wolsey's new powers after Campeggio's departure, and perhaps even to enlarge their scope, then at last he would be truly in a position to govern the English Church, and maybe even to reform it.

That was for the future. What of the price demanded by Leo X, his plans for European peace and a crusade? This Wolsey refused to pay, or rather he made very certain that it was his own plans for peace that dominated the attention of the European powers in the summer and autumn of 1518, and these did not include a crusade. On 3 October a treaty of universal peace was proclaimed in London at St Paul's Cathedral. In fact, it was but one of a number of treaties drawn up at this time collectively referred to as the Treaty of London, the central purpose of which had been the renewal, on even more favourable terms to England, of the Anglo-French alliance of 1514. Still, in all the elaborate ceremonials that accompanied its signing, it was the universal peace that was given the greatest prominence, and that brought the greatest honour to its architects, the king of England, and his leading councillor, Cardinal Wolsey. Undoubtedly, the Treaty of London was a great diplomatic coup, as to a lesser extent was the obtaining of Wolsey's legatine powers. The purpose of this chapter will be to show how both these events were brought about.

The year 1518 had not begun well. This was partly for a reason quite outside Wolsey's control. Ever since the midsummer of the previous year a 'new malady' had made its presence felt. It derived its name, the 'sweating sickness' from the heavy sweating that accompanied it, resulting in complete dehydration. It lasted usually for no more than four or five hours and never more than twenty-four, by which time the sufferer was either dead or on the way to a full recovery.[1] While Wolsey survived four attacks in one month,[2] Henry rushed from one improvised residence to another, often accompanied by as few as half a dozen people, in a desperate effort to

---

[1] Rawdon Brown, ii p.113 (*LP*, ii, 3558); see also p.440-2 below.
[2] Rawdon Brown, pp.126-9 (*LP*, ii, 3634, 3655) – this in Aug. 1517.

escape the contagion. He succeeded, but some about him, including Lord Clinton and Lord Grey, succumbed.[1] Hall suggests that in some towns over half the inhabitants died – probably an exaggeration, for there is no other evidence for any dramatic fall in population, but indicative perhaps of the panic that the 'sweating sickness' caused. The Michaelmas law term of 1517 was adjourned and the court's Christmas celebrations were kept to a minimum, though it was Hall's view that by then the outbreak was over.[2] This was not a view that Henry shared. Having spent February and March 1518 lurking at Windsor, he was off on his travels again, spending the next two months in Reading, Abingdon and finally Woodstock, all the time desperately anxious for news of the latest victims of the 'sweat'.[3] For the historian, the epidemic has this advantage: by separating Henry from his leading minister it necessitated a constant interchange of letters, many of which have survived. For Henry and Wolsey it can only have contributed to their anxieties. Although the previous summer Wolsey had been able to write that 'your realm, our Lord, be thanked, was never in such peace nor tranquility',[4] external affairs were in no such good order, and had not been so for some time.

That Wolsey's foreign policy appeared to be so unsuccessful is, given his reputation in this field, surprising, especially as the failure looks predictable, and not only with the benefit of hindsight. Many of those involved in the execution of England's foreign policy warned that it was running into difficulty, and on occasions even suggested changes. Its ostensible aims were simple enough. Francis I was to be deprived of the fruits of his great victory in September 1515 over the Swiss at Marignano, the chief outcome of which had been the assertion of his claim to the duchy of Milan and with it the French domination of Northern Italy. With Milan safely in his hands, it was possible for Francis both to dominate the papacy and to achieve what, since at least 1494 and the first invasion of Italy, had been the ultimate goal of French policy in the peninsula – the conquest of Naples. The ostensible aim of England's foreign policy was to ensure that none of this happened. Instead, the French were to be kicked out of Northern Italy and then pursued back into their own country, though not, in the first instance at any rate, by direct military intervention by the English. The fighting was to be done by the Swiss and the Emperor Maximilian. England's role was confined to providing them with money, and, indeed, she never even got round formally to breaking off diplomatic relations with the supposed enemy.[5]

This rather curious stance may be the first clue that Wolsey's real intentions were not quite as stated, but for the moment it is the defects of the stated policy that must be considered. The chief of these was that England appeared to have linked herself not with genuine allies who shared her aims but with those whose ambitions were essentially mercenary. Prompt and regular payment was what the Swiss and

---

[1] *LP*, ii, 3748, 3788.
[2] Hall, p.592.
[3] *LP*, ii, 3985 ff.
[4] *LP*, ii, app.38.
[5] Wolsey's detailed instructions to Pace give the best indication of English policy at this time; for which see *LP*, ii, 1065, 1095, but also *LP*, ii, 1943 (BL, Vit. B. xix, fos. 98-102v.), which has been placed in May 1516, but must be before Maximilian's retreat from Milan, and is probably an answer to Pace's letter of 4 Feb. (*LP*, ii, 1480).

Maximilian wanted, and the more money the better. If this was not forthcoming, then there was always the possibility that the French might be more generous, which was precisely what happened. At Fribourg in November 1516 the Swiss succumbed to French money, and in the following March at Cambrai Maximilian did the same.[1] England was left looking exposed, not to say foolish, and apparently with nowhere very obvious to go. Still, this is perhaps unfair, and certainly anticipates events.

Back in the late autumn of 1515, when the English plans for an alliance were drawn up, it was of course known that the Swiss were mercenaries by tradition, which is no doubt why 'divers in England saith that they be villains, and disdaineth to hear speak of them'.[2] But some of the Swiss were also motivated by a strong desire to avenge Marignano, a defeat that had lost them not only their pride but also territory obtained just three years previously, when they had helped to throw the French out of Northern Italy. Thus, there were grounds for believing that they might be an effective instrument against the French; and in addition there remained their most obvious qualification – despite Marignano, where they had been heavily outnumbered, they were still the best infantrymen in Europe. Against this, the division of the Swiss confederation into thirteen cantons meant that they were never an especially united force, and in 1515 only five – those most affected by the French occupation of Milan – consistently supported the English.

But if the Swiss were not entirely dependable, they were as the Bank of England in comparison with Maximilian. His unreliability was notorious, and England's willingness to place so much faith in him would have seemed remarkable in any circumstances.[3] At this time there were additional reasons for mistrusting him. It would be a brave man who would ascribe to Maximilian any consistent aims, but certainly in 1515 neither the fate of Milan, nor indeed any attack on the French, was his primary concern. Instead, it was the need to defend the gains of his long-drawn-out, if intermittent, war with Venice, begun as long ago as 1508. It is true that France, by being Venice's ally, became his enemy; but Milan was not Verona, and it was the defence of the latter from Venetian attack, not the recapture of the former from the French, that was Maximilian's chief preoccupation in Northern Italy – and it was a preoccupation which helped England not at all.[4]

What of other possible allies? Given the continuing French obsession with his kingdom of Naples, Ferdinand of Aragon had good cause to dislike their presence in Italy. Unfortunately his track record made it difficult for the English to place much trust in him; neither, in 1515, did he have much to offer. He was old and ailing, and by the end of January 1516 he would be dead, leaving his grandson, Charles, free to take possession of his Iberian inheritance. This was not Charles's only inheritance. The Spanish kingdoms of Aragon and Castile came to him via his mother, Joanna – nicknamed the Mad – who was the heir both to her mother, Isabella's, kingdom of

[1] Knecht, pp.67-8.
[2] LP, ii, 1003.
[3] See Brandi, pp.96-9 for an excellent pen portrait: 'unstable, easily tempted by wild plans, usually without patience, and always without money' – which follows closely Julius ii's judgement reported by Pace to Wolsey, 12 May 1516 (LP, ii, p.lxxviii). Also Pace's own assessment that Maximilian 'doth as oftentimes change his mind as the weathercock doth change his turn' (LP, ii, 2034).
[4] Mallet and Hale, pp.221-3.

Castile, and her father's, Ferdinand's, kingdoms of Aragon and Naples. The title of duke of Burgundy, and with it the Burgundian inheritance – in 1515 approximating to what is now Belgium and Holland, then commonly referred to as the Low Countries – had already come to Charles from his father, Philip the Handsome, who had died in 1506. Philip's father – Charles's paternal grandfather – was none other than Maximilian, head of the house of Habsburg, whose territorial centre was Austria. On Maximilian's death in 1519, Charles was not only to succeed to the Habsburg inheritance, but was also to be elected Holy Roman Emperor in his place. It was a mighty inheritance that would force this shy and introverted man into the very centre of European politics, where amongst other things he was to be, along with Francis I, Henry's, and thus Wolsey's, leading rival.[1] But in 1515 this was in the future. Charles was then only fifteen, and therefore what mattered, as far as Henry and Wolsey were concerned, was not his views but those of his advisers – and these mattered a great deal. As the whole history of Anglo-French conflict during the previous hundred and fifty years demonstrated, no policy directed against the French was likely to succeed without, at the very least, the benevolent neutrality of the house of Burgundy. In 1515 not even this could be guaranteed. At the beginning of that year Charles was officially declared to have come of age. The regency of his aunt, the pro-English Margaret of Savoy, thereby came to an end, and Charles's government was now dominated by the so-called 'regents', his former tutor, William of Croy, lord of Chièvres, and the chancellor of Burgundy, John Sauvage. While not in any committed way pro-French, they were not prepared to allow the young duke to be dragged into war with France at Henry's bequest, as had happened in 1513. Instead, they immediately set about restoring good relations with the new French king, Francis I – which is precisely what Wolsey did not want.[2]

Lastly, the Pope – and it is extremely difficult to make any simple statement about Leo X's intentions.[3] This is due in part to the complexities of his personality, but even more to the complexities of his situation: ruler of the Catholic Church and of the papal states and, as head of the Medici family, effectively ruler of Florence, it required a considerable juggling act on his part to keep in play the conflicts of interest that resulted. No wonder he, and even more his cousin, the future Clement VII, at this time his close adviser, have been accused of being over-cautious. Probably Leo would have preferred the French not to have been in Northern Italy. But once they were there he was prepared to make the best of it.[4] At the famous meeting between him and Francis at Bologna in December 1515, despite the French king's recent military victories, Leo had not emerged altogether the loser. Just who in reality secured the greater benefits from the Concordat of Bologna, by which the relationship between the papacy and the French Church was from henceforth to be governed, is difficult to evaluate – the usual answer has been the French Crown, whose right of nomination to major benefices in France, was formally conceded. But from Leo's point of view the mere fact that the concordat replaced the long-hated

[1] Brandi, pp. 21 ff. This remains in my view the best biography, and has been much relied upon in all that follows.

[2] See Brandi, pp. 45-61 for a useful introduction to the rivalry between Margaret on the one hand and Chièvres and Sauvage on the other.

[3] Pastor, vii, pp. 3, 88.

[4] Pastor, vii, pp. 108 ff.

pragmatic sanction of Borges of 1438, whereby all papal rights in France had been severely curtailed, was an enormous feather in his cap. Territorially, he had had to endure the loss of Parma and Piacenza to Francis, and Modena and Reggio to his supposed ally, the duke of Ferrara all of which was very painful and, incidentally, soured relations between the papacy and France. On the other hand, Leo was given a free hand to remove the duke of Urbino and replace him with his own nephew, Lorenzo de' Medici, even though the duke's neutrality during the war had been of great help to Francis. The result of all this was that, while during the next three years Leo x did find continuing French influence in Italy irksome, there was no great incentive for him to ally with England to throw the French out.[1]

One way and another, the anti-French alliance that Wolsey concocted in the aftermath of Marignano was a pretty ramshackle affair: a few Swiss cantons and an emperor who bore all too close a resemblance to that famous knight of la Mancha, Don Quixote. The surprising thing is that in March 1516 it came very close to success. Urged on by the English envoys, Richard Pace and Sir Robert Wingfield, the Swiss and Maximilian were converging on a very inadequately defended Milan. By 25 March their two armies were poised for attack only nine miles from the city, at which point Maximilian decided to sit 'still in pensiveness, and was angry with every man that did move him to set forward'.[2] That evening he announced his decision not to besiege Milan and the next day he was off, taking with him the gunpowder, thereby effectively preventing the Swiss from pressing on with the siege alone.[3]

Why Maximilian retreated at this juncture need not concern us. All sorts of reasons were given at the time, by those like Pace who were very critical, and by those like Wingfield, whose many years at the Imperial court had made him so great a devotee of Maximilian's that even as regards this episode he would have nothing said against him. Two brief comments may be helpful. Maximilian's complaint that the promised English money had not arrived was true as far as it went – and poor Pace suddenly found himself having to serve as a human surety that it would eventually be paid. On the other hand, on the day that Maximilian decided to retreat the money was less than a fortnight away, and if he could have got within nine miles of Milan without it, he could surely have continued for just a little longer.[4] The truth seems to have been that he had very little wish to attack the city, and the lack of money was merely an excuse. As has been made clear, it was Venice, not France, that was his main enemy, so to have provoked the wrath of France would not have been at all to his advantage. During the spring and summer of 1516 Maximilian was to occupy himself chiefly with the defence of Brescia and Verona, though without much success. As early as May he had managed to lose Brescia, and though he hung on to Verona for longer, by the end of the year he had decided to cut his losses and sell it back to Venice. By then he had also come to terms with the French.

[1] Knecht, pp. 47-65; Pastor, pp. 134 ff.

[2] LP, ii, 1721.

[3] It is very hard to provide adequate footnotes when detailed events are so briefly summarized, but the evidence on which this account is based can easily be consulted in the various calendars of state papers (LP, Sp. Cal., Ven. Cal.).

[4] LP, ii, 1721, 1729, 1754, 1877.

But if there was something a little strange about Maximilian's performance before Milan, it was as nothing compared with Henry's and Wolsey's reaction to it. Far from drawing the obvious conclusion that Maximilian should never be trusted again, after just a brief period of disillusionment, they were to offer him an equally prominent part in an even more grandiose scheme to bring the French down.[1] This entailed the construction of a new league consisting of Henry, Maximilian, Charles and, if possible, the pope, the principal purpose of which was to raise an annual pension for the Swiss, who in return would spearhead a military effort against the French. In essence it was the same policy as before, but instead of the rather ad hoc arrangements which had come to grief at the siege of Milan something rather more formal and, with luck, more effective was to be put in their place.

Not altogether surprisingly, it did not turn out that way. The débâcle before Milan had done nothing to improve relations between the emperor and the Swiss,[2] and the fact that the English envoys, Pace and Wingfield, were locked in their own private battle, the result largely of the latter's resentment that Pace should have been preferred to him as royal secretary, did not help either.[3] Nor did another rivalry, this in the Swiss camp between Matthew Schinner, cardinal of Sion, an influential figure in Swiss politics, whose violently anti-French sentiments made him anxious to restore good relations with the emperor as quickly as possible, and Galeazzo Visconti, the recently appointed captain-general of the Swiss army, who, since his major concern was to remove the French from Milan, was far less ready to forgive and forget the emperor's recent behaviour.[4] None of this assisted Wolsey's plans, but a more serious hindrance was the continuing refusal of Charles's leading ministers, Chièvres and Sauvage, to help.[5] Wolsey's answer to this was, to say the least, high-handed: to engineer their removal from office! This was to be achieved by paying the emperor to make a 'descent' on the Low Countries so as to be able to persuade his young grandson, Duke Charles, to appoint councillors more amenable to Wolsey's direction.[6] Meanwhile he proceeded to negotiate with the duke's ambassadors in England as if the regents had already been dismissed. On 29 October 1516 a treaty was concluded with them and with Schinner, representing Maximilian, that apparently gave Wolsey everything he wanted.[7] Its main purpose was to supply that pension for the Swiss that was ostensibly at the centre of Wolsey's strategy. He also sought to retain control of the timing of any attack on the French by the insertion of a clause whereby any refusal by the French to meet an English claim to *redditus et emolumentia* – a deliberately catch-all phrase designed to cover anything from the return of Henry's sister Mary's dowry as dowager queen of France to any revenue resulting from Henry's claim to the throne of France (which all

[1] LP, ii, 1753, 1784, 1863, 1890, 1942.
[2] LP, ii, 1746, 1816-7, 1877-8, 1890-2, 1896.
[3] See especially LP, ii, 1582, 2095, 2177, but it is present in all their correspondence; see also LP, ii, pp.lx-lxvii, xcv.
[4] LP, ii, 1817, 1965, 1982-3, 2040, 2076-7, 2090, 2151-2, 2157.
[5] LP, ii, 2099, 2132, 2165, 2217, 2219, 2317, 2322, 2331.
[6] LP, ii, 2387 (BL, Vit. B. xix, fos.267-71) – what Wolsey called 'certain weighty matters of secrecy' in a letter to Pace of 27 Sept. 1516. Also LP, ii, 2501.
[7] Rymer, xiii, pp.556-72; LP, ii, 2486, 2497. For the negotiations, chiefly with Schinner, see 2445, 2449, 2462-4, 2472. For the agreement of Charles's ambassadors see LP, ii, 2499, 2630.

English kings since Edward III had claimed) – could be taken as a *casus belli*.[1]

Potentially this treaty was a great coup, deliberately designed to cause the regents maximum embarrassment, but especially because only three months previously, at Noyon, they had signed a treaty with France which should have prevented Duke Charles from making any alliance with the English.[2] The question now was whether Wolsey would be able to force the regents to honour what had been signed on their behalf, or, alternatively, whether his plan to get them dismissed would work. Throughout the winter of 1516-17 English diplomacy did its utmost to achieve one or the other solution, but to no avail. The regents felt confident enough to repudiate what their ambassadors had agreed[3] – a confidence which was apparently in no way shaken when in January Maximilian eventually made his long-expected 'descent'.[4] Indeed, the English ambassadors reported back that the regents seemed as strongly entrenched as ever.[5] What was worse, these same ambassadors were soon confirming the suspicion that before his arrival Maximilian had followed the regents' example by coming to terms with the French, even though this had meant selling his beloved Verona back to the Venetians.[6]

Thus, by the spring of 1517 it had come to this. England had spent the previous twelve months financing Maximilian's defence of a city which he had then proceeded to sell. She had financed his 'descent' to the Low Countries in an effort to bring about an effective league against the French, only to learn that he had gone and joined up with them. Meanwhile, Richard Pace had spent this time endeavouring to keep at least some of the Swiss cantons faithful to the English, only to find that in November 1516 at Fribourg the French had outbid him.[7] It is difficult to estimate what all this had cost, but it was probably somewhere in the region of £35,000.[8] What, on the face of it at least, seems much clearer is that it had been money down the drain.

It might be thought that the time was thus long overdue for England to cut her losses, perhaps even for her to do what everybody else was doing and make her own terms with the French – but not a bit of it. Wolsey's efforts to create some kind of anti-French alliance persisted, and with them inevitably the expenditure of yet more money. What is even more bizarre is that now the money was to be given to none other than the regents, the very people whom he had been spending most of the winter trying to get rid of. A year had passed since Ferdinand's death, and it was

---

[1] *LP*, ii, 2640, 2663, 2902, 2958, 2991-2 – when the phrase is mentioned for the first time. I am assuming that earlier references to objected 'invasion clause' are to it, but I may have jumped to the wrong conclusion.

[2] 13 August 1516.

[3] Knecht, p. 67.

[4] Maximilian and Charles met up on 29 Jan. 1517 (*LP*, ii, 2861).

[5] *LP*, ii, 2863, 2891.

[6] Agreement made by representatives of Maximilian and Francis at Brussels on 3 Dec. 1516. For their suspicions and confirmation see *LP*, ii, 2862, 2891, 2910, 2921, 2930, 2940.

[7] *LP*, ii, 2562, 2565, 2659.

[8] The 'somewhere' needs to be stressed, as should the fact that my figure is for what I believe to have been paid out as distinct from what was promised. Wolsey's estimate in Sept. 1516 – and much continued to paid out after this date – was considerably higher: over £80,000 on Maximilian's behalf (*LP*, ii, 2404-5), though for a much lower estimate in April 1517 see *LP*, ii, 3106.

high time that Charles claimed his inheritance in Spain. And once he had done this, so the English thinking went, he would be in a position seriously to turn his attention to some great exploit against the French. There was also the hope that once he had got to Spain the influence of the Burgundian regents might be lessened. At any rate, the decision was made for England to help finance Charles's voyage to his new kingdoms of Aragon and Castile – and this took place in September.[1] Two months earlier an extremely showy embassy had been sent over from the Low Countries for the purpose, no less, of confirming that long-resisted treaty of the previous October.[2] Is this evidence that at last Wolsey's policy was beginning to work? Well, not obviously so. For one thing that rather essential clause, as far as the English were concerned, to do with *redditus et emolumentia*, was omitted.[3] More puzzling was the attitude taken towards the provision of the Swiss with money, which, it will be remembered, had been at the heart of Wolsey's strategy. In September Pace was reporting from Switzerland that since the new league 'hath been concluded to the king's great cost, and your grace's singular wisdom and intolerable labours, no man has had any mind to this thing that should be concluded with the Swiss'.[4] And by the following month he was back in England, with no treaty with the Swiss concluded. Indeed, nobody seemed at all interested in it – which is odd, because without it there was really no hope of any serious moves against the French. The only conclusion to be drawn is that insofar as it had been Wolsey's intention ever since the autumn of 1515 to organize a major offensive against the French, it had met with no success whatsoever.

What has been briefly described is, however, not only a policy that appears to have failed, but one that was doomed almost from the start; and, furthermore, many informed people had thought it likely to fail and had not been afraid to say so. This last point needs to be considered in more detail, and this will provide an opportunity to look more generally at the nuts and bolts of foreign policy during Wolsey's time: how was the information on which it was based obtained, by whom, and other related matters.

During April and May 1517, a busy but not unrepresentative period, Henry and Wolsey received at least seventy letters from their diplomatic representatives in Europe. The English effort was being concentrated in the Low Countries, what with Maximilian's 'descent', and attempts to get the regents to agree to an alliance against France. The main burden of the negotiations there was borne by two extremely competent diplomats, Charles Somerset earl of Worcester, and Cuthbert Tunstall. They were very different. Worcester, an illegitimate son of Henry Beaufort 3rd duke of Somerset, had been involved in most of the major diplomatic events under Henry VII, who had first made him chamberlain of the royal household and then in 1505 raised him to the peerage as Lord Herbert. Henry VIII had

---

[1] The amount was 100,000 Flemish florins, with a florin being anything between 2s 2d and 3s 3d. For the loan see *inter alia* LP, ii, 3143- 4, 3402, 3439-42.

[2] This on 5 July (LP, ii, 3437); see also Rawdon Brown, ii, 95-103 (LP, i, 3455, 3462) for detailed descriptions. But the embassy was largely ceremonial, the effective confirmation having been signed in Brussels on 11 May (LP, ii, 3225).

[3] LP, ii, 3191, 3221-2.

[4] LP, ii, 3693.

confirmed him in his household post and had continued to make great use of him in the conduct of diplomacy. He had played an important role during the 1513 campaign in France, while in 1514 he had accompanied Henry's sister, Mary, to her marriage with Louis XII, and had then become involved in the refortification of the recently captured town of Tournai. In the same year he was created earl of Worcester. His mission to the Low Countries in early 1517 had been his next big job, and many others followed. Worcester was, thus, an extremely experienced diplomat. Aristocratic, and, indeed, related through the Beauforts to the Tudors, he was perfectly at home in the courts of Europe. But he was much more than a mere ceremonial figure, as his despatches during the early months of 1517 make clear. And perhaps it should be added that, though he was in no sense a dependant of Wolsey's, the two men appear to have worked well together.

Tunstall's background was quite different, though he too was illegitimate. Educated at Oxford, Cambridge and Padua, and graduate in both canon and civil law, he was quickly picked up by Archbishop Warham, becoming his chancellor and commissary of the prerogative court of Canterbury. Such positions were traditional starting points for a successful career in both Church and state, and so it turned out for Tunstall. Having been in 1516 appointed master of the rolls, in 1522 he became bishop of London, and in the 1523 keeper of the privy seal. In his humanist interests, or rather the combination of these with an active career in the royal service, Tunstall is in many ways a representative figure of the early sixteenth century. Knowing both Greek and Hebrew, he was in touch with leading continental humanists such as Erasmus, and also, of course, with humanist circles in England. In 1517 he was a comparative newcomer to diplomacy, his experience beginning with that embassy to the Low Countries, two years before, made famous by More's involvement and his writing of at least part of *Utopia* during it.[1] Despite his manifold duties at home, during the next twelve years Tunstall was constantly used for important embassies abroad, no doubt because he was good at diplomacy.[2] In the early sixteenth century the diplomatic careerist had not yet arrived – at least not in England – but it would be a mistake therefore to underestimate the diplomatic skills of men like Tunstall and Worcester. Indeed, they were clearly 'pros' to their finger tips, and all the more effective for having a wide experience of government.

The diplomat with the most difficult task during these years was Richard Pace, who had to try to keep the peace between Maximilian and the Swiss at the same time as trying to prevent the Swiss from going over *en bloc* to the French.[3] His career was not dissimilar from Tunstall's, at least until madness and perhaps Wolsey's displeasure intervened. Like Tunstall, Pace studied at Padua, but also probably at Bologna and Ferrara. Then in 1509 he became secretary to Cardinal Bainbridge who was just starting his embassy at Rome, and on his master's death in 1514 he was taken up first by Wolsey and then, almost immediately, by the king. Indeed, while on his embassy to the Swiss in 1516, he was appointed royal secretary, and it was

[1] Surtz, *Catholic Historical Review*, xxxix (1953-4), pp. 272-97

[2] But cf. Brewer's 'cold cautious character . . . His habitual caution and timidity foiled his first and better judgment-' (*LP*, ii, p. cxiii).

[3] Wegg is still very useful, but on Pace's early career in Bainbridge's household at Rome see Chambers, 'English representation', pp. 390-3.

during this time that he wrote – in the public baths at Constance, he alleged – his *De Fructu*. This suggests a further similarity with Tunstall, his humanist interests, and, if his ecclesiastical career was not to be as distinguished, he did hold many important benefices, which included succeeding Colet as dean of St Paul's. Pace's career will have to be looked at again.[1] All that needs to be said here is that his linguistic skills and scholarly reputation well equipped him for his many diplomatic missions, especially to Italy where his previous experience in the service of Cardinal Bainbridge in Rome would serve him in good stead.

Someone who gave Pace a good deal of trouble in these years was Sir Robert Wingfield, the English ambassador to Maximilian; Wingfield even devoted part of a report he wrote in June 1516 to explaining why he thought Pace was a bad choice as royal secretary.[2] Wingfield comes quite close to being that figure it was denied then existed, the career diplomat, and, ironically, he also appears to have been the weak link in the diplomatic chain. First sent on a mission to the Emperor Maximilian by Henry VII in 1508, he remained with him on and off until the summer of 1517, all the time, as he himself remarked, gathering white hairs in the cold snowy mountains of Germany.[3] One has some sympathy with Wingfield, chasing around Europe after that most peripatetic of emperors. But as a colleague his sense of his own importance must have been tiresome, and he showed no capacity to analyse or evaluate the man he was paid to report on. Violently anti-French,[4] he considered that all Maximilian's deeds and thoughts proceeded *ex Spiritu Sancto*[5] – despite all the evidence to the contrary.

Someone with as great an experience of diplomacy as Wingfield but from a very different background, was Thomas Spinelly. He belongs to that rather special category of foreigners, often Italian, who made a career for themselves acting for states other than their own.[6] Originally a Florentine merchant based in Flanders, he came to act as Henry VII's agent at the court of Margaret of Austria – then regent in the Low Countries – and continued in that post under Henry VIII.[7] In 1513 he was knighted. Spinelly's contacts at Margaret's court appear to be very close, so much so that at one stage Wolsey feared that he might be passing on English secrets to the new regents. In fact, his mistrust probably arose just because Spinelly's reports were so accurate and well informed, and anyway it soon passed.[8]

The last diplomat to deserve special mention is William Knight. In 1512 he had taken part in the ill-starred expedition to Guienne, from whence he had reported to Wolsey the inadequacies of the English commanders. In May 1515 he had been accredited to the court of the Duke Charles. He returned in February 1516, only to be sent back in the January of the following year, along with Worcester, this time

---

[1] See pp.550-5 below.

[2] *LP*, ii, 2095; see also *LP*, ii, 1582.

[3] *LP*, ii, 463.

[4] *LP*, ii, pp.lx-lxi, 982, 1265.

[5] *LP*, ii, 1817 – Pace to William Burbank, 23 April 1517.

[6] cf. Andrea Ammonio from Lucca, the king's Latin secretary, friend of More and Erasmus and enemy of Vergil; also the Casali family from Bologna, from the mid-1520s active on royal service in Rome and Venice; and the Genoese Jean-Joachim de Passano in the service of Louise of Savoy.

[7] Behrens.

[8] *LP*, ii, 2700. Spinelly was subsequently deputed to accompany Charles to Spain which suggests that the suspicion of him did not last long.

with the specific task of negotiating with Maximilian. This was never easy, but Knight very quickly got the measure of the emperor, and it was he who in February reported the well-known words of Maximilian to Charles: '*Mon fils vous allez tromper les Français; et moi, je vais tromper les Anglais.*' At the same time Knight strongly recommended to Wolsey that the policy of trying to build up an anti-French alliance should cease, as being a waste of money.[1] Knight was always very ready with advice, but then in early 1517 so were most of England's diplomats.

A major source of information for all governments was the Roman Curia, if only because it was necessary for all the powers of Europe to have some kind of representation there. There was all the routine ecclesiastical business to be dealt with: provisions, annates, appeals, dispensations. But much of it was not routine. The monarchs of Europe were always wanting particular favours from the papacy, whether it was the granting of the cardinal's hat to a royal favourite, or permission to raise a clerical tenth. Then again, quite apart from any more general European significance the spiritual headship of Europe gave it, Italy had for some time been the most contentious area in Europe, and there the papacy was a leading temporal power. Thus, for one reason or another, everybody wanted papal support, and Rome had become the diplomatic centre of Europe. It is, therefore, surprising, especially given the usual picture of a Wolsey only too anxious to please the papacy, that during the years 1515-18 there was no English diplomat resident in Rome. Instead, Wolsey relied on foreign churchmen with close connections at the Curia, in particular Cardinal Adriano Castellessi, bishop of Bath and Wells, and Silvestro Gigli, bishop of Worcester. As these two men spent most of their time fighting each other, at least until the summer of 1517 when Cardinal Adriano became involved in a plot to overthrow the pope and had to flee from Rome, English representation was particularly unsatisfactory. However, this does not appear to have prevented reasonably accurate accounts of Leo x's intentions from reaching Wolsey.[2]

English diplomats and agents were not the only sources of information. Robert Wingfield's brother, Richard, as lord deputy of Calais,[3] and successive governors of Tournai were also well placed to gather news and, of course, in their exposed positions it was important that they did so, especially any news of French troop movements. It was they who were most involved in the organization of the English spy network.[4] This was concentrated not only on Francis i's movements and intentions, but also on those of the White Rose, Richard de la Pole, the last survivor of a family whose claim to the English throne had caused Henry vii, and indeed to some extent his son, so much anxiety. De la Pole was at this time resident in the Imperial city of Metz, where he had been banished in 1514 by Louis xii as part of the peace treaty with England. There English spies were constantly sent to infiltrate his household, not only in order to collect information but also to attempt, though without success, his assassination.[5]

Yet another source of information was the foreign ambassadors in England, whether they were resident or sent on particular missions. The reports that they sent

---

[1] LP, ii, 2930.
[2] Chambers, 'English representation', pp.439 ff.
[3] Lord deputy of Calais from c.1515 to 1519.
[4] *Inter alia* LP, ii, 2369, 2872, 2967, 3120; LP, ii, app. 32.
[5] Cruickshank, *Tournai*, pp.208 ff.

back home are also a major source for the historian, especially at this time those of the Venetian ambassador, Sebastian Giustinian. Arriving in April 1515, he sent back a vivid account of the running battle that he conducted with Wolsey during the next four years, from which both emerge with some credit. Giustinian was in a difficult position. Venice had no real quarrel with England but, as an ally of France and the chief enemy of England's ally Maximilian, her relationship with England could not be easy. Giustinian tried to avoid an open breach, while at the same time putting in a good word for France. Wolsey's chief aim was to separate Venice from France, and to this end he used every means at his disposal. Affable, charming, conciliatory, conspiratorial – or on the other hand aggressive, insolent, rabid, almost violent – he could be all these things in turn, but the historian must be careful, just as Giustinian was, to take into account the element of calculation in these changing moods.[1]

Moreover Wolsey had a second purpose, almost as important as the first. He wanted to use Giustinian to pass messages and warnings, via the Venetian ambassador in France, to the French king.[2] This obviously makes the interpretation of Giustinian's reports all the more difficult. For instance, when in the summer of 1515 Henry and Wolsey boasted – and the assumption throughout this study is that in their dealings, as with everything else, king and minister worked very closely together[3] – that Francis I would do whatever England told him to, this was not mere arrogance or presumption.[4] Rather their intention was first to warn Venice that it was England who was the real power on the European scene. Secondly, with the string of complaints that inevitably followed, they were hoping that England's worries about Francis's activity would be passed on to the French king, and that he would take the hint. All this comes out quite clearly in a report of an after-dinner conversation with Wolsey that Giustinian sent back to Venice in July 1515. First came the boast. Francis would not cross the Alps into Italy this year, unless Henry allowed him to. Then came the complaints, and they were many: 'He never writes hither; he does not communicate any of his secrets; he treats all Englishmen as enemies . . . ; he has sent the Duke of Albany into Scotland.' Wolsey then mentioned that Henry had offered his services in reconciling the French and the Swiss after the Swiss defeat at Marignano, but instead of thanks he had got no reply at all.

> Think, sir ambassadors [the out-going ambassador was with Giustinian during the conversation], whether this to be borne, and say if these are the fashions of confederates. Per Deum, Rex noster decrevit servare honorem at existimationem suam. This, indeed, I tell you, that should he alter his style, this King will change his mind; let King Francis evince regard and esteem and trust in him, communicating his affairs, treating his Majesty's subjects well, and not attacking our ships; in this case the

---

[1] There is no substitute for reading his reports – and very good reading they are too.

[2] For evidence that Giustinian was in contact with his French colleague and that Henry and Wolsey were aware of this, see especially Rawdon Brown, ii, p.172 (*LP*, ii, 4009); also ibid, ii, p.311 (*LP*, iii, 402).

[3] See Giustinian's comment about Wolsey's 'very warm language, similar to that uttered by the king when we had audience of him' (Rawdon Brown, i, p.111); but for a fuller discussion of the way Henry and Wolsey conducted their business relations see pp.207 ff. below.

[4] Rawdon Brown, i, pp.104, 110-1, 115-7 (*LP*, ii, 652, 666, 716).

King will keep the covenant agreed on, and not swerve thence unless goaded by legitimate causes.

Wolsey followed this up with one of his favourite ploys, which was to stress that friendship with France was opposed by everyone in England except himself, and thus that he could maintain it only if the French did what he told them to. His final throw was another boast – that the pope would do what he and Henry wanted him to do – which was, of course, quite untrue. But merely to suggest that this was the case would put pressure on the ambassador because there was just the outside possibility that Wolsey was right, or knew something that the ambassador did not. And in this kind of way the ambassador was put at a disadvantage.[1]

'Pressure diplomacy' was the name of the game, and throughout his four years in London Giustinian was being either cajoled, or threatened, or, most dangerous of all, given helpful advice by a master in the art of negotiation. But if sometimes Wolsey's purpose was to use him to put pressure on Venice's ally, France, his principal objective was that already referred to, the breaking of their alliance – and he was unscrupulous about the methods he employed. His favourite gambit was to suggest that he had reason to believe that France was playing a double game, even to the extent of secretly negotiating with Venice's arch-enemy, Maximilian.[2] This warning would be uttered as if Wolsey was conferring a special favour: I am only giving you this information out of my great regard for you, and what is more you should believe it because a cardinal would not lie.[3] It should be said at once that Giustinian was never really fooled – as he once informed the Doge, 'his right reverend lordship never says what he means'[4] – but, nonetheless, everything Wolsey said was reported back. Wolsey did not succeed in destroying Venice's faith in France but it must have given her much cause for thought. And as regards this particular piece of 'advice',[5] there was good reason for taking it seriously. At Cambrai in March 1517 an elaborate plan was worked out for dividing up Northern Italy between Maximilian, Charles and Francis, under which Venice would have been divided between the first two.[6] Wolsey got wind of this,[7] but he had used the possibility of something similar happening long before Cambrai. Thus, on most occasions when he suggested to Giustinian that France was conspiring against Venice, he was indulging in what might be called a diplomatic lie, but one that could not easily be ignored. This made life difficult for Giustinian, and it continues to make life difficult for the historian who is always having to decide what was or was not a diplomatic lie.

There are other problems. An ambassador would not be human if, in his reports home, he did not try and present his own conduct in the most favourable light, often by stressing the difficulties he faced. There was also a strong temptation to

---

[1] Rawdon Brown, i, pp.110-1 (*LP*, ii, 666).

[2] Rawdon Brown, *Court of Henry VIII*, i, pp.182, 209, 256, 267, 274, (*LP*, ii, 1585, 1730, 2205, 2259, 2264).

[3] Rawdon Brown, i, pp.156-7, 267 (*LP*, ii, 1380, 2259).

[4] Rawdon Brown, ii, pp.50-1 (*LP*, ii, 3081).

[5] Rawdon Brown, i, pp.110-111. The whole document is a very good example of the effect that Wolsey's constant pressure had on Giustinian.

[6] *LP*, ii, p.1019)

[7] *LP*, ii, 3033.

flatter his superiors. These two things combined in Giustinian to produce this recurrent scenario: everybody in England loves Venice, and indeed myself, with the one great exception, Wolsey. He, unfortunately, has managed to gain control of the government. But do not despair. There is plenty of opposition to him, and very soon all will be well.[1] In this kind of way, Giustinian exaggerated the extent of opposition to policies or people that his government was opposed to, and it was a tendency that all ambassadors shared.[2] Furthermore, they were not as well informed as a superficial reading of their reports might indicate. It must never be forgotten that they were not privy to the inner workings of the government's mind, and, as has been shown in Giustinian's dealings with Wolsey, for the most part they had to rely on what was being deliberately fed to them, which was not always the truth. For all these reasons their reports are the most difficult evidence to evaluate, which, nevertheless, does not prevent Giustinian's from providing the most complete picture of Wolsey at work that has survived.

One more episode described by Giustinian will serve to bring out some of these points. On 10 February 1517 he reported interviews with both Henry and Wolsey at which he had informed them of Venice's recovery of Verona from Maximilian.[3] This news, he wrote, had been received by both men with astonishment. If Giustinian was right, then their conduct of foreign policy must be considered very incompetent indeed: the English diplomatic machinery should have got wind of such an important matter before Henry and Wolsey were told about it by the Venetian ambassador. Even if they did not know about it, they should have been sufficiently aware of the possibility to contain their astonishment. In fact, the truth is rather different. For at least the previous six weeks news had been reaching England of Maximilian's negotiations with the French, despite the fact that on 8 December he had confirmed his earlier treaty with England.[4] It is true that to begin with Wolsey did not believe the news; or rather, because he was aware that the emperor might be tempted to 'play on both hands, using the nature of a participle which taketh *partem a nomine et partem a verbo*', he wanted it closely checked. This he asked to be done in a letter written on Christmas day, well over a month before the interview with Giustinian.[5] In the meantime, though there was little hard information to be had – not surprisingly as Maximilian was doing every thing possible to confuse the issue – the drift of the reports coming in to Wolsey was that Maximilian had indeed done a deal with the French. Confirmation was provided by a letter from Cardinal Schinner of 4 February – essentially an apologia for Maximilian's surrender of Verona.[6] This may or may not have reached England

---

[1] See especially: 'Neither the right reverend Canterbury nor Winchester, nor the illustrious duke of Suffolk, nor many other lords who are accustomed to discuss state affairs here, were present at this conclusion, a fact which has caused incredible surprise and universal dissatisfaction, the general inference being that the right reverend Cardinal of York is the beginning, middle and end of this result.' (Rawdon Brown, i, p.326); also ibid, p.264 (LP, ii, 2222).

[2] This will discussed more fully in connection with Wolsey's downfall; see pp.572-6 below.

[3] Rawdon Brown, ii, pp.29-32 (LP, ii, 2896).

[4] On 28 Nov. Robert Wingfield reported pressure on Maximilian to come to terms with the French; on 5 Dec. Tunstall reported that this had happened, only two days after it had; for which see LP, ii, 2605, 2633.

[5] LP, ii, 2700.

[6] LP, ii, 2869.

before the 10th – four to five days was about the average time letters took from the Low Countries, where Schinner was – but the point is that neither Henry nor Wolsey would have needed that letter to alert them that Maximilian's 'sale' of Verona was on the cards.

Why, then, did they show 'astonishment'? Of course, Giustinian may have exaggerated. The recovery of Verona was a great coup for Venice, and one, what is more, which Wolsey had always maintained would not take place. Not surprisingly, therefore, Giustinian was in the mood to enjoy his moment of glory, and to share that enjoyment with his superiors. But it is unlikely that he would have wholly invented Henry's and Wolsey's reaction, so the question remains. The answer is probably that by playing dumb they gave nothing away and hoped to gain more information. In particular, even after Schinner's letter they were anxious to ascertain whether the report was true. They had heard so many rumours, but nothing definite, and it was definite information that they wanted and obtained from Giustinian. That they were play-acting is suggested by Henry's remark that if the surrender of Verona had taken place with the consent of the emperor, then he was content; and furthermore he rejoiced at whatever proved to be for the welfare and prosperity of Venice. In fact, of course, Maximilian's agreement with France was a body blow to English plans. Henry's assertions that it did not matter can only be evidence that, throughout the interview, he was well in control of his feelings because he had been well prepared for the news.

This has been a long story to make a small point, but it is, unfortunately, on such points that an interpretation of Wolsey's foreign policy has to rest. If Giustinian's reports of his interviews with Wolsey and Henry are taken at their face value, then a very misleading view of the conduct of foreign policy at this time results. If treated with care, much can be revealed. Meanwhile they have distracted from the general point being made, that in the conduct of foreign policy Wolsey did not fly blind. From the reports of his own ambassadors and other royal officials resident abroad, from his spy network, and from his conversations with foreign ambassadors, he kept himself fully informed about what was going on in Europe, so that ignorance cannot be the excuse for the apparent failure of his policy. But it has been suggested that his policy ran counter to the information and expert advice that he was receiving – and this suggestion needs to be looked at more closely.

On the central issue of Maximilian's trustworthiness Wolsey hardly required much new information, for he had had plenty of experience in dealing with him in 1513. But Pace's letters during 1516 and early 1517 were a never-ending stream of abuse about the emperor. He blamed him for the débâcle in front of Milan; he blamed him for taking money intended for the Swiss; and he blamed him for a general unwillingness to co-operate with the Swiss.[1] In January 1517 he reported that in Switzerland it was common knowledge that Francis i and Maximilian were about to meet, and he warned Wolsey to be on his guard because 'Judas [Maximilian] does not sleep'.[2] And as 'Judas' moved to the Low Countries and news of him became the responsibility of other English ambassadors, they took up the same refrain. We have

[1] LP, ii, 1746, 1877-8, 1923, 2151, 2366, 2473.
[2] LP, ii, 2798.

already seen that they were predicting the 'sale' of Verona long before it happened. They were also quick to point out that though Maximilian had promised to remove the regents, he showed no sign of doing so.[1] Their removal was vital to the success of Wolsey's policy. Yet the English diplomats clearly thought that there was no hope of Maximilian ever doing it, and by March 1517 they were suggesting that they should no longer be asked to push the issue, since such efforts were bound to be counter-productive.[2] In fact, William Knight had already made this point when he wrote from Brussels on 16 February, saying that he would have liked to prevent the earl of Worcester from making any overture to Maximilian about removing the regents, because, since the emperor was getting on so well with them, they were bound to hear from him of Wolsey's plan![3] Worcester, of course, was acting under Wolsey's instructions, so that Knight's comments ran completely counter to what Wolsey was trying to achieve.

Knight's despatch of 16 February was in effect a critique of Wolsey's handling of affairs, but, as he explained to him, if he was not 'so plain', he would be deceiving 'the king and your grace, which I will never do during my life'.[4] And apparently his fellow ambassadors were just as anxious not to deceive! Only four days earlier Worcester and Tunstall were advising Henry to shut his purse,[5] while on 18 February Tunstall pointed out that it was foolish to think that Charles would ever confirm the league with Maximilian and Henry so long as the clause containing English financial claims on France remained; far better not to go pushing for its inclusion because to do so would only result in 'strangers' taking the bridle of English affairs. Henry should draw his foot out of the affair gently as if he perceived it not, giving good words for good words, 'which yet they give us, thinking our heads to be so gross that we perceive not their abuses.'[6] Shortly afterwards Tunstall was instructed to continue to push for the confirmation of the league, though a complicated compromise over the controversial clause, involving Maximilian's arbitration, was grudgingly suggested.[7] Tunstall remained unconvinced, as his joint letter with Worcester of 6 March addressed to Henry made clear:

> And whereas your Grace in your said letter showeth unto us many great reasons moving the same to put the exclusion of the words 'proventus et emolumenta' in the Emperor's arbitrement, which thing was seen to your most honourable council expedient, albeit our advice in our letters of the xiith. of the last month was to the contrary, after we saw your Grace's pleasure we endeavoured ourselves to our best to the accomplishment of the same.[8]

However, all too soon Tunstall was reporting that their best endeavours were getting nowhere,[9] and in the end Charles confirmed the treaty only with the

---

[1] LP, ii, 2891, 2910.
[2] LP, ii, 2992.
[3] LP, ii, 2930.
[4] LP, ii, 2930.
[5] LP, ii, 2910.
[6] LP, ii, 2940 – in fact a joint letter but it was expressly stated that Tunstall was making this point.
[7] LP, ii, 2958.
[8] LP, ii, 2992 (BL, Galba B. v, fo.129v.).
[9] LP, ii, 3047, 3049, 3054.

disputed clause left out[1] – just as the ambassadors had always predicted. It is very hard to escape the conclusion the the men on the spot always got it right and Wolsey always got it wrong – unless, that is, Wolsey's real intentions were not understood by them.

At this stage it may be helpful to recall that the ostensible aim of English foreign policy from 1515 to 1518 was to remove the French from Northern Italy. This was not achieved, for under the Treaty of London of October 1518 the duchy of Milan was left in French hands. The argument so far has been that the aim was never likely to have been achieved because no other European power shared it sufficiently to make a reliable ally. Furthermore, most of the people involved in the conduct of English policy quickly became aware of the improbability of its success – but not, apparently, Wolsey or Henry. It is very puzzling. Enough has been written to indicate that Wolsey was not a fool, and yet during these years he appears to have acted like one. This paradox has suggested to some a possible explanation for English failure at this time: her policy did not succeed because Wolsey was not fully committed to it, having been forced into an anti-French posture because of Henry's intense rivalry with the new French king, whose nearness in age and similar accomplishments could only have fuelled the competitive spirit of someone who saw himself as the natural successor of the victor of Agincourt, Henry V. And as against the warrior king can be contrasted a Wolsey dedicated to peace. The resulting tension, so it has been argued, was not helpful to the smooth conduct of English foreign policy, and in particular it was responsible for much that went wrong in the period 1515-18.[2]

To see whether such a view can be sustained, it is necessary to return to the late autumn of 1515 when it appeared that the English intention was not only to drive the French out of Northern Italy, but also to recover Henry's rights in France by means of an English invasion, led perhaps by Henry himself.[3] During the following February both Pace and Wingfield were still referring to such a possibility,[4] but early in March Pace had received instructions from Wolsey, asking for a delay to all invasion plans, mainly because there was no way in which England could be ready to invade from the north until August at the earliest. He, therefore, suggested that once Milan was taken, Maximilian and the Swiss should spend the early summer consolidating their position in Northern Italy rather than, as was originally intended, pressing on into south-east France.[5] When by the end of March it became clear that Milan was not going to fall, at least for the foreseeable future, then it was Pace's turn to ask for delay. And by 23 April he was having to explain that not only was any immediate Imperial-Swiss invasion of France no longer possible, but that even Wolsey's revised date for an English invasion 'must be set apart (after my

---

[1] *LP*, ii, 3094, 3223-5, 3232.

[2] The interpretation is Scarisbrick's in his *Henry VIII*, pp.56-96. In resisting it, I wish to stress my admiration for the way in which the interpretation was put forward.

[3] *LP*, ii, 1065, 1095.

[4] *LP*, ii, 1470, 1564, 1565, 1593.

[5] *LP*, ii, 1943 (BL, Vit. B. xix, 98-102v.) In *LP* it is dated to late May 1516, and this dating is accepted by Scarisbrick (*Henry VIII*, pp.61-2) and this materially affects his interpretation. But in fact it has to be a letter written *before* Wolsey knew of Maximilian's retreat from Milan on 24 March; I suspect an answer to Pace's letter of 4 Feb. (*LP*, ii, 1480).

judgment) unto such time as your grace shall have knowledge of the end of this business here'.[1]

What emerges from this, therefore, is not that in the spring of 1516 Wolsey was being 'soft' on war, but that circumstances had dictated some modification and delay to the very ambitious schemes for a joint invasion of France that, ostensibly at any rate, had been at the forefront of English plans. But what of the two pieces of evidence that appear to suggest that there was at any rate a difference of emphasis between Wolsey and Henry in this matter? In the same letter to Pace in which he had asked for a delay, Wolsey had made another, rather curious, request. Could Pace and Wingfield, with all the skill at their command, try and make it appear that the request for delay had not originated with the English, and could they instead persuade the emperor and the Swiss to 'make an instance to you to be a mean unto the king that they proceed no further but only into the duchy of Milan'?[2] This has been taken to mean that when Wolsey made this request to the English ambassadors Henry either did not know about it, or more probably did know, but was not convinced that it was necessary.[3] If, however, Wolsey could persuade the emperor and the Swiss to ask for delay themselves, then Henry would have little option but to agree. And sure enough, Henry did agree, for in a draft letter to Pace dated sometime in April 1516 he wrote that he was 'right well contented' with the proposal that the Swiss should spend the summer establishing themselves in the Duchy of Milan, and that in the meantime better provision could be made for an invasion of France the following year.[4] The second piece of evidence comes in a letter from Wolsey to Silvestro Gigli, bishop of Worcester, at this time the most trusted English representative at Rome, written on 22 May. In it he remarked that though Henry himself was committed to an invasion of France, all his councillors had dissuaded him from crossing the sea until his allies were equally ready, lest, as on other occasions, he should be left in the lurch.[5]

In the spring of 1516 Henry was bursting to go to war and was only with difficulty restrained by his more cautious and peace-loving councillors, of whom the most important was Thomas Wolsey: is that really the truth? The answer must be no. Something has already been said about the difficulties of interpreting the correspondence of foreign diplomats, and most of those difficulties apply to English diplomatic correspondence. What were Wolsey's intentions when he wrote those letters to Pace and to the bishop of Worcester? The answer seems clear enough; he genuinely wanted delay. Why did he want delay? Because England had made no military preparations, and therefore could not take part in an invasion even if she wanted to. Other reasons, as Wolsey's letter to Pace also made clear, were an inability to finance three armies – those of England, the emperor, and the Swiss – and a basic mistrust of Imperial and Swiss intentions.[6] No English army, not enough money, and no trust, are any of these things reasons that could be made known to England's allies? Would such information inspire confidence in English leadership?

[1] LP, ii, 1816 (PRO, SP1/13/fos.123-5).
[2] LP, ii, 1943 (BL, Vit. B. xix, fo.100).
[3] Scarisbrick, p.62.
[4] LP, ii, 1753 (PRO, SP1/13/fo.91v.).
[5] LP, ii, 1928 (Martene and Durand, iii, p.1274).
[6] LP, ii, 1943.

Wolsey was in an extremely difficult position. He had to delay, but he did not want the reasons for this to be known. The only solution was for Pace and Wingfield to try and manipulate a request for delay out of the allies, and for their own good reasons. Just how far Wolsey himself was manipulating the truth emerges if his letter to the bishop of Worcester is looked at in more detail.[1]

He began it by declaring that relations between Henry VIII and Charles had never been better, despite a little difficulty from some of Charles's ministers who remained apprehensive about the French. The truth was that relations were not at all good, and that 'some ministers' were none other than the regents, Chièvres and Sauvage, whose pro-French policy was not at all to Wolsey's liking. Wolsey then went on to stress England's good relations with Maximilian, who treated the king of England like a son, and with the Swiss who would certainly not desert to the French. In fact, whether he treated Henry like a son or not, Maximilian had just destroyed the English plans by his flight from Milan. Realizing that praise of Maximilian at this juncture might seem a little strange, Wolsey even provided an excuse for his behaviour: it was all due to the knavery of the banker, Frescobaldi, who had failed to get the English money to Maximilian on time. Of course, the truth was that, whatever the inadequacies of the banker, the real 'knave' was Maximilian, as Wolsey knew perfectly well. And it was following his defence of Maximilian that Wolsey introduced the picture of the warlike Henry restrained by his cautious councillors; and by now his reasons for doing so should be clear. He was trying to persuade Leo X, via the bishop of Worcester, that England was still a power to be reckoned with, and that, whatever the temporary setbacks, the anti-French alliance, with England at its centre, still had credibility. True, England had not yet invaded France, but Henry had every intention of doing so whenever his councillors judged that the moment was right. Furthermore, when she did invade, Henry himself would lead so large an army across the Channel that the French would be defeated, whatever England's allies chose to do. The implicit corollary of all this was that it would be very much in Leo X's interests to side with the English.

In both these letters, to Pace and the bishop of Worcester, Wolsey was trying to get his ambassadors to put the best possible case for the apparent inadequacies of England's anti-French manoeuvring. They are not evidence of any difference of opinion between Wolsey and Henry, and no such difference could provide the explanation for the failure of English policy. This is not to say that either man had really intended to invade France in 1516. Indeed, it seems most unlikely that either seriously entertained such a plan during the three and a half years under review, the main reason for saying this being that there is virtually no evidence for any large-scale military preparations. So what has to be explained is why there was so much talk of invasion, not only in early 1516, but during the next eighteen months.

To do this we must return to the autumn of 1515 to assess the precise circumstances that had to led to England getting involved in any kind of anti-French alliance. The fact was that Francis I had moved too quickly for everyone, had got into Italy by an unexpected route, on 14 September had won the great battle of Marignano before his enemies could co-ordinate their plans, and with the support of Venice had secured the effective mastery of Northern Italy. No wonder Leo X was

---

[1] *LP*, ii, 1928 (Martene and Durand, pp.1269-75).

anxious to come to terms with him. It is, of course, true that success creates its own problems; it not only concentrates the minds of existing enemies, but also creates new ones. Thus in September, when Wolsey first put out feelers for some plan to curb the French, he got a favourable response: Maximilian, Ferdinand, the duke of Milan, and the Swiss were all found to be eager for English support.[1] Pace's mission to the Swiss was the English answer to the response, and was in that sense well-timed. But if the English intention had seriously been to prevent French expansion in Northern Italy, the mission had been incredibly badly timed. Francis I had made no secret of his desire to recover Milan, and England had had all summer to try to prevent it. Why had she not joined the anti-French league from its inception? Why, indeed, not invade at an earlier date? The time for a successful invasion was when Francis and his army had been struggling to cross the Alps, not after he had won a great battle, and was in a position to turn his attention back to the North. But rather than doing anything very practical, Henry and Wolsey had spent much of their time loudly proclaiming that Francis would never cross the Alps because England would not allow him to. When they were not doing that they were busy negotiating with him – and, as it happens, it is those negotiations that provide the key to England's foreign policy.

The message that England had spent the spring and summer trying to get across to Francis was that though she was anxious for his friendship, this would be impossible to achieve if Francis insisted on acting in an unfriendly manner. If he would not return all the jewels and plate owing to the dowager queen of France, Mary Tudor, if he insisted on sending the duke of Albany to Scotland in order to deprive Henry's other sister, Margaret, of her rightful position as regent for her own son, James V, if he refused to provide English merchants with adequate compensation for acts of piracy committed by Frenchmen, if, above all, he refused to take Henry into his confidence – then no friendship was possible. On the other hand, if Francis would only show some sign of valuing her friendship, then England would remain his most faithful ally. One way of getting this message across was to make use of the Venetian ambassadors; hence all that boasting to Giustinian about not letting Francis invade Italy, and even threats that if it did take place Henry would invade France.[2] And if the stick, as it were, could be most effectively wielded by the Venetians, the carrots could be delivered by English envoys to France. One such carrot was the prospect of returning Tournai to Francis.

The capture of Tournai had been the high point of Henry's campaign in France in 1513, and in the following year its future had been very much at the centre of the peace negotiations.[3] Obviously, the French were anxious to recover what would otherwise always be a symbol of defeat, and moreover, as a French enclave in the Low Countries, it had some strategic importance. On the English side, there was some reluctance to relinquish what had just been so splendidly won, but there were disadvantages in retaining Tournai, especially the cost of garrisoning it and rebuilding its fortifications. Thus its return to France was never non-negotiable. Instead it was seen as a useful bargaining counter, but one to be played only if great

---

[1] LP, ii, 981-2.
[2] Rawdon Brown, i, pp.102 ff (LP, ii, 652, 666, 847).
[3] Cruickshank, Tournai, passim.

advantages accrued. In 1514 England had got more or less what she wanted from Louis XII without having to use it, and thus Tournai had been retained. On 1 January 1515 Francis had succeeded to the throne and he quickly brought up the subject of its return, offering to pay the costs England had incurred in winning it.[1] The English response was not discouraging, but it was made clear that rather more than the costs would be required. Moreover, the English envoys in France strongly recommended that if Tournai was to be returned, it should not be made part of any renewal of the peace treaty between the two countries, because then people would think that England had had to relinquish it in order to secure the renewal. Instead the envoys suggested that a separate agreement should be made, to be kept secret until the two kings had met, when it would be announced as a gracious and entirely voluntary gesture of goodwill on Henry's part.[2] In other words, not only was it important to secure real gains from the surrender of Tournai, but it was equally important not to lose any face over it. The difficulty, however, was that Francis was unwilling to pay a sufficiently high price. Furthermore, if the carrot did not work, neither did the stick.

Wolsey's problem was how to bring effective pressure to bear on Francis, a problem made much more difficult by Francis's marriage alliance with Charles of Burgundy made in March 1515,[3] and the generally pro-French policy of Charles's regents which this alliance reflected. It meant not only that Wolsey could not expect any practical help from them, but, much more important – because he was not really thinking of going to war with France – it prevented him from using the threat of an English alliance with Charles to put pressure on Francis. Indeed, all the pressure that Wolsey was able to muster in the summer of 1515 was verbal, just those boasts made to the Venetian ambassador of what England would do if Francis ignored her. Unfortunately for Wolsey, Francis called his bluff. He was willing to continue the payment of the French pension that his predecessor, Louis XII, had agreed to. He was willing to entertain the possibility of a summit meeting with Henry, but only after he had returned from Italy.[4] He was willing to make the occasional friendly noise. That, however, was all, and as Wolsey frequently pointed out to Giustinian, it was not enough.[5]

At this stage it is important to stress that Wolsey, and indeed Henry, had very much wanted to make favourable terms with Francis, and expended a great deal of effort towards that goal. As soon as the news of Louis XII's death reached England, a high-powered delegation consisting of the duke of Suffolk, Nicholas West (shortly to become bishop of Ely), and Sir Richard Wingfield had been sent over to open negotiations. Suffolk and Wingfield remained until the middle of April. West stayed until the middle of May in order to witness Francis's confirmation of a treaty signed in London on 5 April, by which the French, while agreeing to continue the pension, had refused to meet any other English demands.[6] Thus, almost as soon as

[1] *LP*, ii, 175 – Francis I in conversation with the English ambassadors as reported 18 Feb.
[2] *LP*, ii, 175.
[3] 24 March; see Knecht, p.37.
[4] *LP*, ii, 437.
[5] See especially Rawdon Brown, i, pp.110-11 (*LP*, ii, 666).
[6] *LP*, ii, 175, 184, 189, 192, 231, 296, 304 for continuing negotiations with Francis; *LP*, ii, 301 for the treaty; *LP*, ii, 428 for Francis I's confirmation.

West had returned, Sir William Sidney was sent over to reopen negotiations with Francis, who was by now on his way to join his army for the invasion of Italy. Sidney crossed early in July, caught up with Francis at Lyons, but their meeting achieved nothing.[1] Neither did the arrival in London in August of an envoy from Francis, who brought with him a formal announcement of Francis's intentions to recover the duchy of Milan.[2] This was hardly news to the English court, but coupled with the refusal of the envoy to discuss any of the disputed issues it represented a slap in the face for Henry who, it will be remembered, had been saying that this would never happen without his permission. At this point Wolsey may have planned to send yet another envoy. Instructions have survived for Richard Wingfield, outlining in great detail the arguments he should put to Francis. Their dating is very uncertain, and it seems that they were never in the end presented to the French king. Nevertheless, they are indicative of the English determination to come to terms with him, and also of the great difficulties involved. Mention is made of all the contentious issues – the English merchants' complaints, Mary's dowry, Albany – but perhaps the most interesting section relates to Tournai. It was hoped that Francis would raise the matter himself, because he would undoubtedly have heard of the English plans to refortify the town and should have been worried by them. However, if he did not raise it, Wingfield, though only in a private capacity, was to do so himself. He was then to hint at the many inconveniences to France of the English plans, and to imply that this was the right moment, before the fortifications were up, for Francis to strike a bargain.[3] In other words, Wingfield was to cast a fly in the hope that Francis would bite. In the event it looks as if Wingfield never made his cast, but it would have been only one amongst the many that Wolsey had made during the spring and summer of 1515, all to no avail.

It looks as if Wolsey made one more bid to tempt Francis. On 26 October 1515 the French ambassador officially informed Henry of his master's great victory at Marignano over the Swiss. Henry was not especially delighted, and even managed to get into a quarrel about how many Swiss had been slain on the battlefield, suggesting that the ambassador had greatly exaggerated the numbers and declaring anyway that the Swiss troops were as nothing compared with the German. It was a typical combative performance, and Wolsey, when presented with the news, behaved in an equally typical way. He was delighted to hear of Francis's victory – hardly a truthful statement, but then neither was his denial of any warlike preparations by England. Partly, it depended on one's interpretation of the phrase. There was indeed very little physical preparation by England, but by late October Pace was already on his way to Switzerland with offers of money and military help to whoever might oppose the French. Nevertheless, in a private interview shortly afterwards Wolsey tried to revive the French interest in negotiations. There was no prince whom Henry loved more than the king of France, and indeed these two princes were so alike in their great abilities and virtues that they really ought to love one another. And after the soft soap, the hard talk: the ambassador should remind his master 'that the time is no longer such as it used to be', which vague as it was,

[1] LP, ii, 468, 613, 740-1.
[2] Rawdon Brown, i, p.124 (LP, ii, 847).
[3] LP, ii, 827 (BL, Calig. D. vi, fo.245).

may have been a hint that following his great successes opposition to Francis was mounting and therefore he would increasingly need English support. Less vague was Wolsey's statement on Scotland. If Francis would recall Albany, the English would not insist on Margaret, Henry VIII's sister, being the effective guardian of her children, though they would want her to retain the courtesy title and be allowed unrestricted access to them. If Albany was not recalled, then Henry was determined to aid his sister, and to that end had recently made a treaty with Ferdinand who had agreed to support England in any war with Scotland, in return for England's support in Guienne. Wolsey ended the interview by once more turning on the charm. Henry's affection for Francis was again stressed, and if only the French king would treat him a little better, then of course Henry would not make any treaty with the king of Aragon, or any other person hostile to Francis.[1] Unfortunately for Wolsey, by early November the dying Ferdinand was not much of a threat, but then this had been Wolsey's great difficulty throughout 1515: he had very little to threaten Francis with. He was to spend the next two years trying to rectify this.

If this point is understood, a lot that has so far been inexplicable makes sense. Why did Wolsey allow himself to become entangled with the completely untrustworthy Maximilian and the not so trustworthy Swiss? Why, when the untrustworthiness and incompetence of these allies had been made patently clear in the débâcle before Milan, were Henry's hopes of success apparently so quickly revived? Why, though he and Wolsey had shown a little displeasure at what had taken place there, were they willing to go on encouraging Maximilian to greater efforts? And it must be stressed that neither was taken in by Maximilian's customary consummate performance. The constant wearing of the garter and the flattery, as when he praised the style of Henry's Latin and French secretaries, made not the slightest difference to their extremely cold-eyed view.[2] In June 1516 Wolsey informed Pace that Henry quite agreed with his unfavourable assessment of the emperor, but this only meant that Pace must use him accordingly.[3] Shortly afterwards Wolsey was advising him to play Maximilian along, and then in July he wrote to say that though the Council thought the emperor's conduct strange, 'it was necessary to use policy therein and dissemble for a time.'[4] Maximilian's offer of the Imperial title made no impression on Henry: 'We think they mean nothing . . . touching the vicary general of the Empire, which we set little by.'[5] Neither Henry nor Wolsey ever set much store by Maximilian, but the point was that if pressure was to be brought to bear on Francis, they had to make use of what was available, and Maximilian just happened to be one of the few people who was.

This same need to make the best of what was available explains Wolsey's desperate efforts to build up some kind of anti-French league in the summer of 1516, despite the overwhelming difficulties which the creation of such a league presented: in essence Maximilian's untrustworthiness and the regents' opposition. The regents' treaty with Francis at Noyon in August 1516 was a severe blow to Wolsey, but was not sufficient to put him off completely. He argued, quite correctly, that it was in

[1] *LP*, ii, 1113 – an account by the French ambassador of these various interviews.
[2] *LP*, ii, 2648, 2679, 2866.
[3] *LP*, ii, 2082.
[4] *LP*, ii, 2178.
[5] *LP*, ii, 2218 – this a letter of Henry's to Wolsey and thus no diplomatic reason for it.

many ways unfavourable to Charles. The loss of Navarre; the surrender of his claim to Artois; the recognition of Francis's claim to Naples, which was to be admitted as the young French princess's dowry despite the fact that the prospective husband was already the *de facto* ruler of that kingdom; the disparity of ages between Charles who was seventeen and the Princess Louise who was less than a year old – all these things, Wolsey believed, made it most unlikely that Noyon would hold.[1] But in order to make sure that it did not, he was prepared, as we have seen, to risk paying for Maximilian's 'descent' into the Low Countries to remove the pro-French regents. When he hit on this plan Wolsey knew there was a possibility that Maximilian might deceive him, but he had been prepared to take a risk because any alliance, however fudged or improbable, was better than none. Without one he had no bargaining counters, and it was these that he was desperately seeking.

Here we have the explanation for Wolsey's rejection of the sound advice of the ambassadors that the chasing after such an alliance should be given up because it was unobtainable on any reasonable terms. Instead, the ambassadors were instructed to go on working for it, even if this meant giving up the crucial clause concerning the English financial demands on France. Moreover, continuing to work for an alliance meant in the end coming to terms with the very people England had spent so much time and money trying to remove – Charles's regents, Chièvres and Sauvage. As it happened, by the early summer of 1517 this was not such a bitter pill to swallow because by then Wolsey found himself with some kind of hold over them. Now their main concern was to get Charles to Spain in order to establish his rule there; they needed money and naval assistance, and England could provide both. The result was that in the July they sent over to England a most splendid embassy, headed by the young James de Luxemburg, son of the governor-general of Flanders, son-in-law of Chièvres and a close friend of Charles himself. Giustinian reported back to Venice that never did ambassadors receive such honours, and he and his secretary have left behind detailed descriptions of all the ceremonials and amusements, which included the 'supernatural feats' of Henry VIII in 'changing his horses and making them fly rather than leap, to the delight and ecstasy of everybody'.[2] Present at these ceremonials was the recently arrived French ambassador, and there seems little doubt that they were put on as much to impress him as to please the young James de Luxemburg. It was two months later, on 19 September, that Pace, still out in Switzerland, commented that since the league had been formed, one of the main purposes of which was supposedly to provide money for a Swiss army, 'no man has had any mind to this thing that should be concluded with the Swiss'.[3] One has some sympathy with Pace. For almost two years he had had the thankless task of keeping the Swiss in play, despite the machinations of Maximilian, the French and the rival Swiss factions. His efforts were not entirely in vain, for he had, at least, helped to provide England's aggressive posture with some credibility – and in the process had secured for himself the office of royal secretary. What, however, he seems never to have realized – and the same goes for most of his fellow diplomats – is what Wolsey's policy was all about, that was

[1] *LP*, ii, 2387.
[2] Rawdon Brown, ii, pp. 95 ff. (*LP*, ii, 3455, 3462).
[3] *LP*, ii, 3693.

somehow to get the French to sit round a table and agree to favourable terms. And no sooner had Charles's ambassadors left than this process began.

In presenting this explanation of Wolsey's foreign policy from 1515 to the autumn of 1517 the intention is not to reverse completely the earlier picture of failure. There were failures during this period. Wolsey had not wanted the attack on Milan to fail. The Treaty of Noyon had been a blow and Maximilian's acceptance of it an even greater one. It had also been a setback that Maximilian had been unable or unwilling to remove the regents and that he had to wait over five months for Charles's confirmation of the treaty originally signed in London in October 1516. There had in one sense been one damned failure after another. However, when Wolsey's intentions are understood, the failures do not appear quite so stupid or pointless. The policy had always been risky, but the risks had from the first been calculated, and the disasters on the way allowed for. And in the end the prize was won – the Treaty of London of October 1518.

Just a few more comments and qualifications are required. One of the points that emerges from this analysis is not that Henry and Wolsey differed in their warlike intentions, but that during this period neither was warlike. In support of this view there is the curious fact, already mentioned, that despite all Wolsey's moves against France there was never any official break between the two countries and, as a consequence, the French pension continued to be paid.[1] Perhaps of even more significance was the enormous restraint shown by England in her relations with Scotland, and, since the banning of the duke of Albany from Scotland was to be one of the important English gains in the Treaty of London, it is now necessary to look in some detail at the part Scottish affairs played in the lead up to it.[2] When, after James IV's death at Flodden, Margaret, Henry VIII's sister, had become regent to her not yet two year old son, James V, the English had assumed that they would have a dominant say in the affairs of Scotland. It did not turn out that way. Factional struggles amongst the Scottish nobility led to the demand that Margaret be replaced by John Stuart duke of Albany. As James's cousin and heir-presumptive, Albany had some claim to the post, but from the English point of view he was unacceptable. He had been born and brought up in France, and furthermore he had so distinguished himself in the service of the French Crown that he had been created lord high admiral. It is not therefore surprising that the English, in their negotiations with Louis XII in 1514, had insisted that Albany be prevented from going to Scotland, and Louis had felt compelled to agree. Francis I had no such inhibitions. Indeed, it would obviously be to his immediate advantage to be able to threaten England with a Scottish attack led by his 'client' Albany, if by any chance Henry took it into his head to invade France while he was away in Northern Italy. Thus in the spring of 1515 Albany was allowed to leave France. He arrived in Scotland on 18 May, and by September, Margaret was in exile in England. If ever there was an excuse for England to invade Scotland this was it, but all that happened were some inconclusive and intermittent negotiations. In April 1516 a Scottish delegation accompanied by the French ambassador to Scotland arrived in

---

[1] Its payment was secured by the Anglo-French treaty of 5 April 1515.
[2] In what follows I have relied heavily on Eaves, *Scottish Diplomacy* and it should be consulted for detailed references.

London, to be followed about ten days later by Margaret, who until then had lingered in the North. She was given a royal welcome by her brother, but this did not prevent a six month truce, to last until the end of November, being arranged with the Scottish delegation.

Despite frequent border raids on both sides, this truce was extended until the end of January 1517, by which time a major agreement had been reached which involved, amongst other things, Margaret's return to Scotland. She was to be given all the honour due to her rank, her jewels and personal belongings were to be returned and her lawful revenues guaranteed, but she was to have no effective power. It appears, therefore, to have been a face-saving operation as far as the English were concerned, with Albany the real winner. The arrangement had also extended the truce until the end of November 1517, by which time Albany had felt secure enough to return to France, having left behind him a regency council. At Rouen in August he negotiated a treaty whereby, if England invaded Scotland, France would not only provide aid but would invade England. The treaty also contained an unsatisfactory marriage alliance: Francis's promise of his younger daughter for James v, but only if she was not required by one of the two Habsburg princes, Charles or Ferdinand; if she was, James would have to make do with the hope that Francis would father another daughter. The Scots had hoped for rather more favourable treatment, and it looks as if the French were dragging their feet, anxious not to allow Scottish affairs to stand in the way of their negotiations with England, which were just beginning. Furthermore, Albany managed to negotiate yet another extension of the truce with England – this time for two years, until the end of November 1519. Meanwhile, Scotland itself in the autumn of 1517 was in more turmoil than ever. In September the rivalries on the regency council came to a head after the murder of Seigneur de la Bastie, the man Albany had left behind in charge of the Scottish Marches. The murder had been carried out by a faction led by the Hume family which was favourable to Margaret. Lord David and John Hume, together with William Cockburn, were declared traitors by the Scottish parliament, but escaped over the border. The Scottish parliament asked for their return, but with no success. All the same, Henry showed no real inclination to further Margaret's complaints about her treatment at the hands of Albany's supporters, which since her return to Scotland in June had been frequent and shrill. The Scottish parliament had no more success with Albany when they requested his immediate return to Scotland. When he heard of this, Henry made a lot of noise, even threatening war with France if Albany should be allowed to return, but it is significant that Stephen Poncher, the bishop of Paris, who was leading the negotiations with Henry at this time, was of the view that England would not break them off over this issue. It is perhaps equally significant that Albany did not return.

This summary of Anglo-Scottish relations, brief as it is, may suffice to make the point that despite a lot of diplomatic noise and many border raids, neither England nor France was prepared to allow Scottish affairs to get in the way of their real intentions. England in particular had showed a good deal of restraint. The natural expectation that Flodden would lead to a greater say in Scottish affairs had had to be suppressed, while Henry had had to endure the public humiliation of his sister's plight. Yet none of this had been allowed to prevent constant negotiations with Scotland, which always led to yet another extension of the truce. Why was England so patient? It was because an invasion of Scotland would almost certainly have led to war with France, and war with France was what she did not want.

But what of all the English talk of war with France? It has been shown already that such talk was not confined to Henry. Indeed, it has been argued that late in 1515 and early 1516 an invasion of France was official English policy. After the spring of 1516 the talk was less open, but the alliance worked for by Wolsey throughout the remainder of that year and during the first half of the next did contain elaborate details concerning the number of men and ships that each of the confederates would provide, and Giustinian even reported the names of the generals who would command the invading forces. It is true that these armies would only be raised if France was to invade territory belonging to a confederate, or inflict 'grave damage', but such conditions were sufficiently vague to allow the possibility of an attack on France if one was desired. Moreover, it was Wolsey who had been anxious to add to the reasons for going to war any failure by the French to pay any money that they rightfully owed to England.

The contradiction between all the talk of war and invasion and the view that the English had no intention of going to war is more apparent than real. Talk is one thing; doing is quite another. In the late autumn of 1515 England had to talk of war, and indeed she had to continue to talk of war, for otherwise her policy possessed no credibility. It has not been sufficiently grasped that England was asking her allies to take on the all-conquering French. It is true that both Maximilian and the Swiss had reasons of their own for wanting to do this, and that they were going to receive English money for doing it. But in one sense they were merely doing England's dirty work. What was to happen if they were badly beaten? What guarantee was there that England would pay? What guarantee was there that England would not desert them just whenever it suited – which was, indeed, what she intended to do? It was no good talking of a great alliance against the French, indeed posing as the leader of such an alliance, if no convincing reasons were produced for pursuing such a line. For England to say that she was worried about Milan was just not good enough. The obvious reason, the most convincing, was the one that she gave: she was prepared to lead a French alliance because her king wished to recover his rights in France.[1] To that end she was prepared to put an army in the field, admittedly not today, perhaps not tomorrow or even the day after; but offer to do it some day she had to. In other words, talk of an English invasion of France was a diplomatic smoke screen intended to deceive her allies. It should not deceive historians.

One consequence of this analysis is that it suggests that Wolsey was not very interested in the 'balance of power'. The occupation of the duchy of Milan gave France great territorial gains as well as great strategic and, though less easy to compute, great economic advantages. Of course it was not a new phenomenon in 1515. Ever since France's first invasion of Italy in 1494 the duchy had frequently been in French occupation. That occupation had not been welcomed by the other European powers and, indeed, a great deal of money and effort had been expended, in particular by the papacy and by Ferdinand, to get the French out. England had not participated in this, and for an obvious reason. Milan affected no vital English

[1] *LP*, ii, 982 (BL, Vit. B. xviii, fo.187v.), 1095, 1244.

interest, and a French occupation was arguably of some benefit as it kept French armies well away from areas such as Calais and the Low Countries that did concern England. Wolsey's view of the matter was no different from his predecessors'. Of course, he could and did make diplomatic noises. He could also point out to Maximilian, or to the pope, or to the Venetians, the great dangers to them of the French occupation. However, concerning the more theoretical threat that might result from any change in the balance of power, not even diplomatic noises were heard. And during all the negotiations that took place with the French during 1515 the issue of the French invasion of Northern Italy was never raised by the English, and when they did come to terms with France in 1518 the French were left in occupation of Milan. The evidence seems clear. England did not mind France having the duchy. What she wanted was for her to have obtained England's permission first.[1]

Another consequence of this analysis is that papal concerns were not the priority for Wolsey that has often been alleged.[2] On 10 September 1515 Leo x had hurriedly created Wolsey a cardinal in an effort to buy English help against the rapidly advancing French. By late October Wolsey was planning to oppose the French in Northern Italy. There thus appears to be a possible causal connection between these two events, which historians have found all too seductive. In fact, by the time Pace had arrived in Switzerland in November 1515 Leo was already deep in negotiations with the victorious Francis, and during September at their famous meeting at Bologna the two men had come to terms. Admittedly the terms of their agreement were kept secret, but Wolsey soon discovered that no effective help was to be expected from the pope in any of his moves against France.[3] It was not until November 1517 that Leo was persuaded to join, and then only secretly, an anti-French league,[4] by which time Wolsey himself was negotiating hard with the French.

Nor had the pope been especially helpful over Wolsey's more private concern, his appointment to the bishopric of Tournai. This whole episode, in its detail extremely complicated, is in essence quite simple.[5] Wolsey had wanted to become bishop of Tournai. No doubt personal ambition was involved, and when the possibility had first arisen, in the autumn of 1513, he was not yet an English bishop. The point that is usually overlooked is that after the recent English occupation of the city it made political sense to appoint an English bishop, and Wolsey was the obvious candidate. Two major difficulties stood in his way. In June 1513 Leo x had appointed Louis Guillard, son of the vice-president of the Paris parlement, to the bishopric. Guillard was only twenty-one, under the canonical age. This did not prevent him from receiving the necessary papal bulls for taking possession of the see,

---

[1] It has not perhaps been sufficiently appreciated that in coming to terms with France in 1514 England was prepared to accept French ambitions in Northern Italy; see LP, i, 2956-7, 3129, 3477.

[2] The notion that Wolsey's conduct of foreign policy was governed by such concerns was central to A.F. Pollard's interpretation in Wolsey, pp. 111-64, 336, recently reformulated in Wilke, pp.114 ff. and accepted by Elton in Reform and Reformation, pp.69-72, 85-7. However, it has been most effectively challenged by D.S. Chambers in 'Cardinal Wolsey', and Scarisbrick in Henry VIII, pp.46 ff. and 107 ff.

[3] LP, ii, 2243, 2259, 2387, 2420, 2473, 2486, 2544, 2798, 2889, 2930; also Pastor, pp.160 ff.

[4] LP, ii, 3801.

[5] For this episode see Cruickshank, Tournai, pp.143-87.

but it did mean that technically he would remain only bishop-elect until his twenty-seventh year. This gave Wolsey a glimmer of hope; even more so did Guillard's refusal to take the oath of loyalty to Henry after the English occupation of Tournai in September, for Wolsey now had grounds for approaching the pope, who in the early summer of 1514 appointed him administrator of the see until Guillard would take the oath.

At this point the second difficulty came into play. The town of Tournai comprised only a small proportion of the see, which meant that most of it was outside English jurisdiction. It soon became apparent that, despite the papal blessing, it was impossible for Wolsey to establish effective control of the diocese, especially as Guillard proved to be a very astute adversary who had, of course, French backing. The details of the ensuing battle are not significant, but Leo's reluctance to help Wolsey is. Late in 1516 Leo not only confirmed Guillard's clear title to the bishopric, but empowered him to call on the secular arm to help him obtain his rights, thereby giving Francis the ideal excuse for reconquering Tournai. This hardly suggests that a grateful pope was eager to reward his loyal servant Wolsey, and that, after exerting a great deal of pressure, Wolsey and Henry persuaded Leo to revoke the bull and to have Wolsey's appointment reconfirmed does not seriously affect the conclusion to be drawn. In order to safeguard its temporal interests in Italy, the papacy was prepared to sell its vast reservoir of spiritual and ecclesiastical favours to the highest bidder. Sometimes this was Wolsey, but it was just as often others, and over the bishopric of Tournai it was Francis and Guillard who usually won. There was never any question of one person or state monopolizing the bidding: possessing something that no other power had, the papacy was in a very strong position to sell to whom it wanted, and at an advantageous price. In these circumstances the only sensible course was the one that Wolsey adopted – to seize opportunities as and when they occurred. This he had done in 1515 in order to become a cardinal, and would do again in 1518 in order to obtain his legatine powers. What he did not do was to allow the course of English foreign policy to be dictated to by a papal auction that he was never in a position to control. As for the bishopric, in the end Wolsey was happy enough to surrender all claim to it in return for a suitable pension.

But to return to the arrival in London of the French ambassadors towards the end of June 1517, in time to witness those elaborate ceremonials in honour of a rival embassy, from Charles and the regents, which had, it will be remembered, so impressed the Venetian ambassador. The suggestion was made earlier that they were also intended to impress the French,[1] at a time when they had every reason to be increasingly apprehensive of the Burgundian court. Despite Noyon and Cambrai and despite the proposed marriage between Charles and Francis's daughter, Louise, they must, by the summer of 1517, have realized that once Charles was established in Spain it was most unlikely that he would abide by these agreements – indeed, the likelihood was that he would wish to destroy them. No king of Spain would willingly return the recently conquered Navarre or recognize the French title to the kingdom of Naples. Even more worryingly, he might not accept any French

[1] See p.81 above.

presence in Italy. And who was it helping to bring about Charles's establishment in Spain, but the English? Clearly it was time for the French to take the English more seriously. This, of course, is what Wolsey had been trying to get them to do for the previous three years, and thus by the autumn of 1517 the right climate for successful negotiations had been created.[1]

But success did not immediately follow, and the reason is simple. The negotiations failed because, in Wolsey's view, the French were still not prepared to concede enough. In particular, they were not prepared to pay enough for Tournai, or sufficiently to compensate the English merchants who had suffered at the hands of French pirates.[2] At the end of November the two French envoys sent over earlier in the month to conclude, it was hoped, an agreement left empty-handed.[3] In December English commissioners were sent to Calais in an effort to settle the merchants' complaints, but returned to England with their business unfinished only to find Wolsey in a very bad mood.[4] For the time being all negotiations with France were broken off, and there was even talk of war. In February 1518 Richard Fox wrote to Wolsey to inform him that Portsmouth and the Isle of Wight were in no condition to withstand a French attack, and at about the same time the garrisons of Calais and Tournai were put on the alert.[5] On 15 March Henry spent an hour and a half providing the Venetian ambassador with 'manifest proof of the deceit of the King of France'.[6] However, three days later Pace, back in England in his new post as royal secretary, reported that Henry had received two letters from the French king as well as a favourable report from the envoy sent over to France some weeks before to congratulate Francis on the birth of a son – which offered a new negotiating point, for it opened up the possibility of a marriage between the dauphin and Henry's daughter, Mary.[7] It was a possibility that the French were quick to exploit. Stephen Poncher, bishop of Paris and in charge of negotiations on the French side, wrote to Wolsey on 8 April urging him to reopen them, and to show that he meant business he sent over his secretary with a number of proposals, including a marriage alliance.[8] At about the same time news reached Wolsey of the appointment of Cardinal Campeggio as legatus a latere so that in this capacity he could come to England to explain the pope's plan for a five-year truce in Europe and a crusade against the Turk.[9] It was these two initiatives, from the French and the papacy, which Wolsey seized upon and turned into his greatest triumph, the Treaty of London.

But before that treaty is examined, attention must turn to somewhat shadowy and

<hr />

[1] Knecht, pp.68-71, 77-8 is disappointing on this; but in this context it is worth making the important, but not always appreciated, point that because one side thinks they have gained an advantage does not mean that the other side does not think the same – and both may be right.

[2] LP, ii, 3714; LP, ii, app. 38.

[3] Rawdon Brown, ii, pp.135 ff. (LP, ii, 3788, 3804).

[4] Rawdon Brown, ii, p.140 (LP, ii, 3844); LP, ii, 3858; for the commercial negotiations themselves see LP, ii, 3520-1, 3773, 3803, 3861; LP, ii. app.38. More was one of the commissioners.

[5] LP, ii, 3874, 3907, 3918, 3952; LPAdd, i, 209.

[6] Brown, ii, p.168 (LP, ii, 4009).

[7] LP, ii, 4014.

[8] LP, ii, 4063-4.

[9] LP, ii, 4034.

sinister events which were taking place at Abingdon and Woodstock in the spring of 1518 – events which suggest that there was some opposition in high places to Wolsey's conduct of foreign policy. One of the consequences of the epidemic of 'sweating sickness' that England had been suffering from since the previous summer was, as was noted at the beginning of this chapter, the disruption of Henry's normal routine. Staying out of London as much as possible, and keeping his household down to a bare minimum, he decided to spend the early spring in the Thames valley. He was at Abingdon by 27 March, and there he stayed for the next three weeks – which happen to be some of the best documented weeks of Henry's life. Given the physical separation of king and leading minister, and the crucial state of the negotiations with France, there was need for a constant stream of letters between the two men. Indeed, at one stage Henry insisted that a train of horses be set up so that messages could be sent every seven hours.[1]

Not all the communications were about foreign policy. On 3 April Pace wrote that Henry thanked Wolsey for the final clause in his letter 'touching great personages', and praised Wolsey's special regard for his safety. At the same time he was anxious for Wolsey to know that he had taken effective measures on his own account, for

> at such time as his Grace had perfect knowledge of the coming of the said great personages unto him, his Grace did secretly provide that they should be advertised by their own servants resident in the court, as well of the strait lodging here as the penury of horse meat, and for these respects to bring with them a very small company. And Sir Henry Marney is executor of the king's pleasure, and doth look thereunto wisely and faithfully, as well within this town as nigh thereunto.[2]

Three days later Pace reassured Wolsey that Henry had not forgotten what Wolsey had written concerning some of the nobles at that time with the king.[3] This is all the specific information that has survived about the episode, or at least all that can be precisely dated, but there are one or two hints of continuing concern.

First, when John Clerk, the future bishop of Bath and Wells, arrived at Woodstock on 27 April carrying letters from Wolsey he was ordered by Henry 'that in no wise he should make mention of London matters before his Lords'. Henry also asked Clerk to put it about that Wolsey would arrive at Woodstock within five or six days, when in fact there were no plans for Wolsey to come there. Then, at the Council meeting that evening Henry went out of his way to praise Wolsey, saying that there was no man living 'that pondereth more the surety of his person and the common wealth of this his realm'. Meanwhile, Wolsey was informed that Sir Thomas Lovell would be coming up to see him 'for reasons be known', arriving in London on 1 May.[4]

Unfortunately, those reasons are not known to us. However, there is a possibility that Lovell took with him the famous letter written in Henry's own hand in which he warned Wolsey to 'make good watch on the duke of Suffolk, on the duke of Buckingham, on my lord of Northumberland, on my lord of Derby, on my

---

[1] LP, ii, 4060.
[2] LP, ii, 4057 (PRO, SP1/16/fo.210).
[3] LP, ii, 4060.
[4] LP, ii, 4124.

lord of Wiltshire, and on others which you think suspect, to see what they do with this news'.[1] The letter is undated, but the reasons for connecting it with this episode are these. Henry began by stating that 'the most of this business I have committed to our trusty councillor this bearer to be declared to you by mouth' – and Lovell was certainly a trusty councillor, having been close to Henry's father even before Bosworth. There was undoubtedly a marked concern about 'great personages', and the two who head Henry's list, the dukes of Suffolk and Buckingham, were with him at Abingdon and Woodstock and were both present at the Council meeting on 27 April at which Henry had so deliberately praised Wolsey's concern for his surety. Of course, the letter can be interpreted as indicating that Henry was informing Wolsey of disquiet for the first time, which if so would appear to rule out any connection between the letter and this particular episode, because Wolsey did know of the disquiet prior to any communication with him via a 'trusty councillor'. But the reference to 'others which you think suspect' surely suggests that Wolsey did have prior knowledge, because without more information than was contained in Henry's letter there would be no good reason for Wolsey suspecting anyone else. And in late April 1518 there was indeed important 'news' – the successful revival of negotiations with France. A close alliance with the French would have been a dramatic reversal of the apparent aims of English foreign policy during the previous three years, and that it was considered controversial is suggested by two pieces of evidence. First there was Henry's warning to Clerk not to mention 'London matters' to anyone with him at Woodstock. Now 'London matters' could have referred to anything: perhaps to the controversial and much disliked measures to cope with the 'sweating sickness'.[2] But it could have referred to the French negotiations. Certainly these were kept secret for as long as possible, a fact confirmed by the second piece of evidence. When, towards the end of June, a French envoy arrived in London with more proposals, Henry considered the matter of such importance that he made a secret dash to Greenwich to consult with Wolsey[3] – despite his intense fear of the sweating sickness.[4] And it was only on his return to Woodstock on 5 July that he announced to the members of his Council the advanced state of the negotiations.[5]

Whether or not Henry's famous letter should be ascribed to the end of April 1518, the fact remains that at this time the attitude of some of the nobility was cause for some concern. However, it was probably never much more than that, deriving more from general warnings from abroad than from any specific information nearer home. Of the general warnings there were a number. As early as October 1515 the bishop of Worcester was reporting from Rome that Francis I had alleged that there was about to be an insurrection in England headed by the nobles.[6] In May 1516 Pace reported from Trent in Northern Italy rumours of opposition to Wolsey's handling of affairs.[7] In February 1517 Henry instructed his ambassadors in the Low Countries

[1] *LP*, iii, 1 (BL, Add. 1938, fo.44). There it is placed at the beginning of 1519. Scarisbrick places it in 1520 or early 1521 and associates it with the downfall of Buckingham (*Henry VIII*, p.120).
[2] See pp.440-2 below.
[3] *LP*, ii, 4276.
[4] *LP*, ii, 4279.
[5] *LP*, ii, 4293.
[6] *LP*, ii, 1042.
[7] *LP*, ii, 1931.

to deny Maximilian's suggestion that he, Henry, was unpopular with his noblemen.[1] But the most relevant warning, which almost certainly led directly to Henry's and Wolsey's worries in the spring of 1518, came in February of that year, via the bishop of Worcester, from the pope. And on the 27th Wolsey replied that it was quite impossible to express Henry's gratitude for the information that there was a party in England plotting in conjunction with the French. The bishop was to reassure the pope that there was nothing to fear. No one was more loved and respected than Henry, and as for Wolsey himself, if he offered to resign he was quite sure neither the king nor the nobility would allow him to. On the other hand he could well believe that the French would stick at nothing to disturb the peace of the realm.[2]

It is, of course, most unlikely that Wolsey would have wished to admit to the pope that he was on the point of being overthrown, but there are other reasons for suggesting that Wolsey's apparent lack of concern was exaggerated. If one thing has emerged from this account of his handling of foreign policy it is that it was often unsuccessful, and certainly misunderstood, even by those whose task it was to implement it. For those who were not so close to Wolsey it must have appeared especially disastrous. Large sums of money were leaving the country, some of it provided by the taxpayers, and the results both in terms of prestige and real benefits were nil. It would therefore have been very surprising if there had not been a lot of criticism, both of his policies and of Wolsey himself. It was during this period, following his appointment as cardinal in September and lord chancellor in December 1515, that the full extent of his power became apparent. It was argued earlier that there had been no 'coup' by Wolsey then, and that, for instance, neither Warham nor Fox had been forced out of office by him.[3] But this does not mean that people would not have been suspicious of what had taken place and extremely jealous. As lord chancellor Wolsey had made it very clear that he thought royal justice should not allow for any distinction between 'high' and 'low', and to show that he meant business cases had been brought against the earl of Northumberland, the marquess of Dorset, and Lords Burgavenny and Hastings. Wolsey's policy at home had much to recommend it, but coupled with his unsuccessful foreign policy and his rapid rise to power, it almost certainly meant that in the spring of 1518 there was some opposition to him. Its extent, however, should not be exaggerated.

One source for evidence of such opposition, discussed earlier in this chapter, is Giustinian's reports,[4] and the fact that he wrote about it should alert us to the possibility of some exaggeration. It was reassuring both to himself and his employers to believe that, but for Wolsey, the hated English policy would have been different, and the situation that Giustinian was in led him to clutch at straws. The other evidence for opposition should be treated with equal caution. It suited Maximilian in the spring of 1517 to embarrass Henry with news of internal opposition, while it was in the French interest in 1518 to put it around that Wolsey was about to be deposed. The point is not that all talk of opposition from foreign sources should be

---

[1] *LP*, ii, 2958.
[2] *LP*, ii, 3973. See also *LP*, ii, 4161.
[3] See pp. 6 ff. above.
[4] See pp. 70-1 above.

discounted, only that it must be treated with the greatest care. It was one thing for someone at the English court to let slip a few critical remarks to a foreign ambassador; but quite another for him to want, or be able, to translate that criticism into action. And in the spring of 1518 there is no real evidence of any significant opposition.

It is known why Suffolk was viewed with some suspicion at this time. During the negotiations with the French in the previous November he had apparently put the French ambassadors 'in comfort of the restitution of Tournai'.[1] This is in itself a rather interesting misdemeanour, for one of the arguments here has been that both Henry and Wolsey were themselves keen to return Tournai – but for the best possible price. So they must have been annoyed, and perhaps a little suspicious, to find Suffolk undermining their bargaining position by suggesting to the French that Tournai was theirs for the asking. Moreover, given his previous close relationship with Francis, Suffolk must anyway have seemed the most likely leader of any plot, if, as the pope alleged, it was being master-minded by the French. Far less is known about Buckingham, also mentioned in Henry's letter, and what little there is makes him a most unlikely collaborator with the French.[2] Neither is there any evidence that any of the other noblemen were pro-French, and it is most unlikely that either Henry or Wolsey thought that they were. But if that is the case, why the fuss at Abingdon and Woodstock? A possible scenario might be as follows.

Late in February 1518, Wolsey received warning of a 'plot'. He did not take it too seriously. The secret negotiations with the French continued. Henry decided to celebrate Easter at Abingdon with very little ceremony and a much diminished court on account of the sweating sickness. He did, however, want his sister, Mary, Suffolk's wife, to be present, and it may be that Suffolk saw this as an opportunity to get back into favour. At any rate, he wrote to consult Wolsey on the subject,[3] and both Suffolk and his wife certainly did come. But on 29 March Pace wrote to tell Wolsey that Buckingham also intended to be present.[4] Immediately warning signals began to flash. On 3 April Pace thanked Wolsey on Henry's behalf for his advice about 'great personages', and also reported the precautions that had already been taken.[5] It is perhaps important to stress that in 1518 neither Henry nor Wolsey had any knowledge of Buckingham's interest in prophecies concerning his own succession to the throne; that was only to come to light in the autumn of 1520, and was to result in his trial and execution for high treason – and there is no evidence that prior to this they had had any desire to destroy him. Indeed, only two years before, Wolsey had been helping to plan the marriage of Buckingham's son and heir. What is true is that Buckingham had never been very close to Henry and had been given no place of trust or responsibility, nor was he often at court. Thus, when he announced his intention of coming, and with Suffolk already present, the possibility that the papal warning of a plot might be justified had to be taken seriously. But there appears to have been no panic, certainly no arrests or

[1] LP, ii, 4061; for this episode and, more generally, Suffolk's francophilia see Gunn, Charles Brandon, pp. 56-62.
[2] See pp.159-60 below.
[3] LP, ii, 4035.
[4] LP, ii, 4043.
[5] LP, ii, 4057.

interrogations, not even any hint that they were under suspicion. Instead a few discreet measures were taken to ensure that the number of retainers that the two noblemen brought with them to court, or stationed in the neighbourhood, was severely restricted. In other words, presumably because it did not altogether believe in its existence, the government's response to the possibility of a plot was very restrained. All the same, there had been just enough in it for Henry to feel the need to suggest that an eye should be kept not only on Buckingham and Suffolk but also on any other noblemen whose loyalty to the regime was in any way suspect. Hence his famous letter.

Meanwhile, serious negotiations with the French were being revived. On 8 April the bishop of Paris had written to Wolsey urging him to work for peace between the two countries, as he had done in Louis XII's time.[1] On the 14th he wrote again to thank Wolsey for his favourable response, at the same time informing him that an envoy was on the way with further proposals.[2] It was to discuss these and the results of the negotiations between the envoy and Wolsey that Henry had made his dash to Greenwich during the first weekend in July, and it was these results that he presented to his councillors at Woodstock. They apparently judged them 'to be not only for the great tranquility and wealth of the realm alone, but also for the common quietness and wealth of all Christendom'.[3] Nevertheless it took three more months, and some very hard bargaining, to complete the negotiations. Most of that bargaining was between Wolsey and the bishop of Paris, who arrived in London at the very beginning of August. Information about it is scanty, partly because it was conducted with unusual secrecy.[4] However, enough is known to identify the areas of conflict, and to suggest that by and large it was the French who gave way.

As we noted earlier, the occasion, or excuse, for the reopening of negotiations in the spring of 1518 was the birth of the dauphin on 28 February, and the possibility of a marriage between him and Henry's daughter, Mary. It was to be laid down in the Treaty of London that the marriage would not take place until the dauphin was fifteen, so that with the high sixteenth-century mortality rate and the changeability of diplomatic relations the likelihood of it taking place was never very great. Meanwhile the betrothal would serve as an earnest of good intentions, and a symbol of what it was hoped would be a long and loving relationship between England and France.[5]

Under the terms of the marriage settlement Mary's dowry was fixed at 330,000 gold crowns – a figure only reluctantly agreed to by the French, after a good deal of haggling.[6] With any marriage settlement haggling was to be expected, but in this case matters were complicated by the most difficult item on the agenda, the return

---

[1] LP, ii, 4063.

[2] LP, ii, 4166.

[3] LP, ii, 4293.

[4] Giustinian reported More 'declaring that the Cardinal of York "most solely", to use his own expression, transacted this matter with the French . . . so that the king himself scarcely knows in what state matters are' (LP, ii, 4438). In fact, as has been shown, Henry was intimately involved in what was going on, but Giustinian did find it particularly hard to obtain information at this time, which may suggest that he normally found out only what Wolsey wanted him to.

[5] Rymer, xiii, pp.632-42 (LP, ii, 4475).

[6] LP, ii, 4479, LP, ii, app.52.

to France of Tournai.[1] As was indicated earlier, the problem here was to get the right balance: neither monarch could afford to lose too much face: Henry by appearing to give it up for too little, Francis by having to pay too much. And less defensively Wolsey was anxious to exploit this expensive bargaining-counter for something that could not be measured in financial terms – real diplomatic advantage. What precisely Wolsey had hoped for in 1515 is not known but there had been talk of territorial compensation.[2] In the autumn of 1517 the French were offering 900,000 francs, which Wolsey estimated as equivalent to £100,000.[3] A year later the French agreed to pay 600,000 crowns, or about £120,000. Of this, 50,000 francs was to be paid on the day that they re-occupied the city, the rest in twice yearly instalments of 25,000 francs. In fact these payments would cease long before the sum of 600,000 crowns was reached, because by a complicated arrangement the sum the French owed for Tournai would be written off against the 330,000 gold crowns to be paid them as Mary's dowry. The amount that the English would receive was, therefore, 270,000 gold crowns, or £54,000.[4]

At first glance this appears to have been a poor price, for it nowhere near covered the cost of the five and a half year occupation of Tournai. A conservative estimate puts this at £250,000, though some of this, perhaps as much as £15,000, had been recovered from the citizens of Tournai by way of an annual levy.[5] This puts the English financial loss at £180,000, rather more than the Crown's annual income. Admittedly, for this figure Mary, in theory, obtained a husband. On the other hand Francis obtained a newly built citadel which had cost the English over £50,000. Of the two, the citadel may have looked the better asset, though as it turned out it was not to be so. Mary never got the dauphin as her husband, but in 1521 Francis lost Tournai to Charles v and, what was even worse, from 1525 Francis found himself having to pay the English for a city that he no longer possessed. However, none of this was calculable in 1518. The problem here is to know how much to make of the English loss. Of course, it would have been better to have recovered much more for Tournai, but there were limits to what the French were willing to pay. As it is, both over the price for Tournai and the figure fixed for the dowry the French did in the end agree to pay rather more than they had initially intended, which suggests that Wolsey got the best bargain available.[6]

It is anyway undoubtedly a mistake to concentrate on the book-keeping aspects of the treaty, for the occupation of Tournai had never been a financial venture. What its capture and occupation had given Wolsey was an important diplomatic weapon without which there might well not have been any treaty at all. Moreover, the treaty of London not only committed France to paying England £5,000 per annum for Tournai, but also guaranteed the previous commitment, under the treaties of 1514 and 1515, to pay her an annual sum of £10,000. Fifteen thousand

[1] Rawdon Brown, ii, pp.210, 222 (*LP*, ii, 4413, 4457) – but the Tournai aspects of the negotiations are the least well documented.
[2] *LP*, ii, 192, 231.
[3] *LP*, ii, app.38.
[4] Rymer, xiii, pp.646-7 (*LP*, ii, 4476); Cruickshank, *Tournai*, pp.240 ff. I confess that I would not go to the stake for this figure – but it the best that I can do!
[5] Cruickshank, *Tournai*, pp.275-9.
[6] *LP*, ii, 4479; *LP*, ii, app.52.

pounds a year was a considerable sum for one sovereign state to pay to another, equivalent to about a tenth of the revenues of the English Crown. But again, it is not just a question of money. That France was prepared to pay so much is evidence for the success of Henry and Wolsey's aggressive policy. The payment symbolized England's dominant role in the relationship, one that her actual financial and military strength did not merit.

The restoration of Tournai was probably the most important single item on the agenda in September 1518, but one that appears to have caused almost as much difficulty was the vexed question of whether or not the duke of Albany should be allowed to return to Scotland.[1] The English were determined to prevent this. The French position was more ambiguous. It has already been argued that they had no intention of allowing Scottish affairs to get in the way of successful negotiations with England, and this, even before the Treaty of London, had led to Scottish mistrust of their actions. On the other hand, they did not want completely to sever their traditional links with Scotland which, if the English alliance did not survive, would once again be of the utmost importance. The compromise they arrived at was probably a secret agreement that Albany would not be allowed to return during James v's minority. There is no definite proof for this, but at the time various people suggested that this was indeed what had happened, and various draft clauses have survived.[2] Even more convincing is the circumstantial evidence. When the time came for Scotland to join the treaty of universal peace, made at the same time as the treaty between England and France, she refused. Moreover, she showed every sign of being highly suspicious of what had been agreed between those two countries. She also proved very reluctant to renew the truce with England, which was to expire in November 1519, and it needed a combined Anglo-French embassy and a French threat to leave her completely in the lurch before she would agree to do so. Meanwhile Albany was to remain in France until November 1521.[3] By that time the Anglo-French alliance formed in London in 1518 was on the point of breaking up. It does, therefore, look as if the exclusion of Albany from Scotland was one of the English gains from the bargaining in September 1518, even though there was no reference to it in any of the public treaties. If this is so, it marked the successful conclusion of English efforts to oust him that had started the moment that Albany had set foot in Scotland three years previously.[4]

The French response to the English attempts to prevent French piracy and to obtain compensation for English merchants was, inevitably and with justification, to make counter-claims. The legal battles had been joined at various meetings to settle the rival claims in the late autumn and early winter of 1517, but with no success – and there is a suspicion that these meetings were anyway a cover to allow more serious political negotiations to continue informally. And once the right political climate had been established, it did not prove too difficult, as part of the London negotiations, to draw up procedures by which merchants from both

---

[1] Rawdon Brown, ii, pp.215, 231 (LP, ii, 4424, 4491); LP, ii, 4357, 4479; LP, ii, app.52.

[2] LP, ii, 4577; Ven. Cal.,ii, 1120, 1140; see also LP, ii, 4471.

[3] For the whole of this paragraph see Eaves, pp.66-101. It is worth pointing out that in November 1517 the French were maintaining that if Albany wanted to be in Scotland there was nothing they could do to stop him (LP, ii, 3804).

[4] Rymer, xiii, pp.649-53 (LP, ii, 4477).

countries could have their grievances looked into – not that the procedures seem to have been all that successful, but then establishing the rights and wrongs in such cases is always difficult. Nor did the Treaty of London do anything very much to eliminate piracy in the English Channel, even if the restoration of normal relations between England and France would have made life more difficult for the pirates.[1]

Two more personal matters had also been harming Anglo-French relations. First, there was the refusal of the French to return jewels and plate which the English claimed rightly belonged to the 'French queen', Henry's sister, Mary. This issue had been strongly pushed by the English in 1515.[2] In 1518 there was much less concern, though it was on Wolsey's agenda, and before the final negotiations he raised the matter with Mary's new husband, the duke of Suffolk.[3] But none of the various treaties signed in October provided for the return of the dowry, and there is no evidence that the matter was debated. This is curious. If Wolsey had tried and failed one would have expected some mention to have survived; possibly Suffolk's indiscretions with the French envoys during the previous year disinclined Wolsey to raise the matter.

The second personal matter concerned Wolsey's own tenure of the bishopric of Tournai. With the surrender of the town there was no chance of winning the battle against his French rival, Louis Guillard, and very little point as by 1518 Wolsey was archbishop of York and had just been made bishop commendatory of Bath and Wells. But Francis was quite prepared to accommodate Henry's leading minister and the chief architect of the French alliance. In return for giving up all claims to the bishopric Wolsey gained a pension of about £1,200 a year which, considering that he had never secured anything like the full revenues from the diocese of Tournai was an extremely good bargain.[4]

The pension does not, though, explain Wolsey's pursuit of a French alliance. For one thing he was not dependent on the French for pensions of this kind. In 1517 Chièvres granted him one of between £300 and £400 a year and was soon making offers of Spanish bishoprics.[5] Admittedly the pension was not as much as he received in lieu of Tournai, but was a little more than he had been receiving regularly from France since the Anglo-French alliance of 1514. As has been shown, the latter had in no way inhibited Wolsey from being a constant thorn in the French side, nor did the acceptance of one pension mean the rejection of another, unless, that is, a formal declaration of war against the donor's country was involved, which was not the case at this time.

Moreover, it must be stressed that Wolsey was not the only person in Europe in receipt of a foreign pension. The French were always free with such payments and, for instance, after 1525 they were going to spend annually about £4,000 on pensions to important Englishmen. Admittedly over half this amount went to Wolsey, but the dukes of Norfolk and Suffolk and the earl of Shrewsbury received about £100 a

[1] *LP*, ii, 4613, 4652, 4663-4.
[2] *Inter alia LP*, ii, 468, 826, 828.
[3] *LP*, ii, 4357, 4388, 4448. For this and Mary's dower income; see Gunn, *Charles Brandon*, pp.59-60.
[4] Rymer, xiii, p.610, *LP*, ii, 4352-4 – the figure given is 12,000 *livres tournois*.
[5] *LP*, ii, 3345, 3347, 3872, 3935, 4245-6, 4384-5. For very useful notes on both the French and Spanish pensions see A.F. Pollard, pp.116-7, 321, 324.

year each, and even Sir Thomas More received £30.[1] The English did not provide pensions on anything like the same scale. This is probably not because they possessed greater moral rectitude, but because they could not so readily afford them. All the same, when it suited them they were willing to pay out. When Cardinal Schinner left England in November 1516 he was granted a pension of £666 13s 4d, in addition to presents worth about £900.[2] Chièvres, on the other hand, when offered a pension in the autumn of 1518, turned it down, though graciously declaring that he would not mind a gratuity.[3] He gave no reason for his refusal, which is a pity because it might have helped to define contemporary attitudes. If Chièvres thought that it was unbecoming for a leading minister to accept a foreign pension, he was probably exceptional. Presumably there was some expectation that the recipient would at least look favourably on the country that bestowed it. Like the business man's lunch, the pension created a favourable climate; it might even incur some minor obligations, but not much more than that. After all, the pensions were not usually kept secret, and all Wolsey's gains would have been known about by Henry, who never made any objection. Moreover, the practice was just too common to have been an effective way to control another country's foreign policy; it would have meant that the highest bidder would always take the prize, and this does not seem to have happened. Wolsey did well from foreign gifts and pensions, and not just from French ones; that he did rather better than most people merely indicates his greater standing.

To see England's or any other country's foreign policy as consisting of a private auction sale whereby leading royal ministers sought to feather their own nests is too naïve. We have seen how for three years Wolsey struggled to force the French to come to terms. The policy was expensive and difficult, involving the whole English diplomatic service, the royal Council, and above all the king himself. Henry's involvement cannot be overestimated, as Pace's correspondence with Wolsey during the spring and early summer of 1518 makes clear. Not only did Henry want to be informed of every detail, but he had to be persuaded of the correctness of every move.[4]

Pace's correspondence also reveals a disagreement between Henry and Wolsey, one that sheds some light on Wolsey's methods and may help to confirm the interpretation of his intentions offered here. In April 1518 Wolsey was most anxious for Pace to return to the Swiss. Henry to begin with opposed the idea, then agreed, only for Pace to fall ill. And in the end he never went.[5] Henry had argued, quite reasonably, that when England was striving to get on good terms with the French, to send Pace on a mission to try to break the French alliance with the Swiss could only be considered provocative, and therefore counter-productive. Wolsey's reasons for wanting to send him have not survived, but they can be guesssed at. Such a move was entirely consistent with his policy over the previous three years, which

[1] Inter alia LP, iv, 3619.
[2] LP, ii, 4023, 4074.
[3] LP, ii, 3647.
[4] See especially Pace's comment to Wolsey 'that no letter be sent unto his highness under your grace's pacquet, but his highness doth read them every word'. (LP, ii, 4089).
[5] LP, ii, 4014, 4057-8, 4071, 4082, 4085, 4228, 4277, 4360.

had been to apply the greatest possible pressure on the French. It was to that end that he had secured the alliance with Maximilian, Charles, and Leo x, one of the principal aims of which was to subsidize a Swiss army. As we have seen, once that alliance was confirmed, in the early summer of 1517, little was done about the Swiss, and indeed Pace had soon been recalled. The reason seems clear enough. No sooner had Wolsey completed his alliance than he began serious negotiations with the French, and for the time being did not need the threat of the Swiss army. When, by the end of 1517, the negotiations broke down, Wolsey once again needed to exert pressure. If the anti-French alliance was to break up too soon, then Wolsey's hold on the French would be greatly weakened. Thus, in order to remind France of the existence of the alliance at a crucial time in his negotiations with them, Wolsey wanted Pace to return to Switzerland. The difference between Henry and Wolsey was not serious because both were fully agreed about the main aim of English policy, as indeed they were always to be. When from time to time disagreements occurred they were only ever over means, and that these did occur is not all that surprising.[1] Both were, after all, intelligent and powerful personalities. More interestingly, the disagreements provide evidence for Henry's close involvement in the conduct of foreign policy – something that has not always been appreciated.

In October 1518 Wolsey secured the alliance with the French that he had been looking for during the previous three years; or perhaps it would be more correct to say that he recovered the alliance that he had made with Francis's predecessor in August 1514. Francis had formally renewed that alliance but he had completely ignored its spirit. He had been less than generous to Henry's sister Mary, the dowager queen of France; he had allowed Albany to go to Scotland and supplant Henry's other sister, Margaret; he had shown scant interest in the complaints of English merchants. Above all, he had made it perfectly clear that the English were to have no say in the conduct of his foreign policy. By 1518, Francis's attitude to an English alliance had changed. Wolsey's diplomacy was not the only reason for this. Francis's occupation of the duchy of Milan meant that he was now much more interested in the preservation of the status quo than he had been three years earlier. He also knew that Charles's accession to the Spanish throne constituted a serious threat to his Italian gains, and perhaps to much else. It was time for him to look around for friends, or at least to try and do something about the English, who for three long years had been behind every move to thwart him. If England's aggressive policy towards him was to continue in the changed circumstances of 1518, then Francis would be faced with a very serious situation, because the anti-French coalition would no longer be merely a paper one. Thus, though circumstances had undoubtedly helped, Wolsey's aggression had also played a part in forcing Francis to make the vital move towards him in 1518. And that aggression continued during the negotiations in September, as he used the threat of his alliance with Charles and Maximilian, and in particular their reluctance to see Tournai returned to the French, to extract better terms from Francis.[2] In the end, Francis was prepared both to pay more for Tournai than he would have liked and to risk jeopardizing the ancient alliance with the Scots. He was also ready to be much more deferential to

---

[1] See pp.153, 381-2 below.
[2] LP, ii, 4479.

Henry and Wolsey than he had been in the past.[1] This is not to say that the English had everything their own way, or that the French were humbled; given their successes in 1515 and their vastly superior financial and military resources, it would have required more than the ad hoc alliance that Wolsey had cooked up with Maximilian and his motley crew to achieve that. But in the end the French had come to London, and if only in the symbolic sense, this constituted a victory for Henry and Wolsey.

But to what end? To answer this, the reasons which had originally led Wolsey to seek a French alliance back in 1514 must be touched upon. Very simply, he had calculated that, given the lack of any reliable allies, a serious campaign in France might well end in disaster. He had also grasped that despite her great financial and military resources, France was the country most amenable to English pressure, precisely because it did make some sense to threaten an invasion. It was close, the possession of Calais provided a secure harbour for both men and provisions, while the possession of a rightful claim to the throne of France provided a justification. To invade Spain or the Low Countries had none of these advantages: no rightful claim, difficult logistics and the worst possible disruption of trade, which was increasingly concentrated on Antwerp. These considerations were not lost on the rulers of these countries, with the result that first Ferdinand and later Charles could afford to be unreliable allies: England might huff and puff, but it was most unlikely that she would do more. What had completely thrown Wolsey's calculations was Francis's initial unwillingness to accept his logic. Instead of deferring to the English, he had virtually ignored them. Wolsey had therefore set out to show Francis the error of his ways by forcing him to acknowledge how dependent on the English he really was. The Treaty of London is evidence that Wolsey had succeeded. But if France could be brought to heel, why not the rest of Europe?

To answer this question, we must consider that aspect of the London negotiations which resulted in a treaty of universal peace on 2 October. That it was initially signed only by England and France may throw some doubts on its universality, but the terms themselves were impressive enough. The signatories were to live in peace with one another, which meant that not only invasion of one another's territory, but also any unfriendly or harmful action, was prohibited. No aid or asylum was to be given to rebels, and any outside request for their return had to be complied with within twenty days. Another clause prohibited the hiring of foreign troops. As all armies were heavily dependent upon such troops, especially those from the Swiss cantons, this was an eminently sensible attempt at least to limit the scale of warfare. The most important provisions concerned the action to be taken in the event of any breach of the peace. Any aggressor was to be requested to curb his actions forthwith, and to make reparations for any injury or loss he had inflicted. If he refused, everyone else was to declare war on him within one month, and within two was to be at war. It was expected that the pope, Maximilian and Charles would sign the treaty within four months, thereby, along with Henry and Francis, becoming 'principal contraherents', with the right to nominate other adherents who would have eight months to make up their minds. In this way it was hoped that almost

[1] *LP*, ii, 4664.

every state in Europe would become signatories.[1]

Nothing Wolsey had done until this moment quite prepares one for this treaty, and it has been a puzzle to everyone who has given it any thought.[2] Even Wolsey's authorship is not absolutely certain. A rough draft in his own hand is suggestive, perhaps more significant is the general assumption by contemporaries that he was responsible.[3] But when it comes down to it very little is known about its origins, what precedents were used, what sources of inspiration tapped. One obvious source would be the great Erasmian polemics against war; the most famous of these, 'Dulce Bellum Inexpertis', first appeared in the much revised edition of his Adages of 1515, while The Complaint of Peace, dedicated to one of the regents, John le Sauvage, was published in December 1517. Thus, the dates fit well, while Wolsey certainly knew who Erasmus was if only because the great author had frequently badgered him for gifts and favours – not, incidently, with much success. Furthermore, it is probably safe to assume that he would have been aware of Erasmus's views on war, for he was surrounded by people who were. By 1518 such a close friend of Erasmus as Sir Thomas More had become a royal councillor – and he was, as it happened, with the king at Woodstock during the spring of 1518. There was Andrew Ammonio, the king's Latin secretary, responsible for much of Wolsey's correspondence with the papacy. There was Richard Pace who had just become the king's secretary and had been for a short time Wolsey's. Cuthbert Tunstall, appointed master of the rolls in May 1516, had during the three years under discussion become one of Wolsey's most trusted diplomats. All these men were close to Erasmus and close to Wolsey, and no doubt the rights and wrongs of warfare were discussed by them, perhaps in Wolsey's hearing. Nevertheless, to have a secondhand acquaintance with someone's views is very different from being deeply imbued, and there is no evidence for Wolsey having first-hand acquaintance with any work of Erasmus.

Mention of Erasmus does, however, suggest a point that must be made in any discussion of Wolsey's universal peace treaty. By far the most influential writer of his day had for some years before 1518 been clamouring for peace, and he was influential just because he had important friends in high places, not only in England but throughout Europe. Europe was, thus, prepared, even eager for peace, so that Erasmus could write in a letter to the German humanist, Wolfgang Faber, on 26 February 1517: 'At this moment, nonetheless, I should be almost willing to grow young again for a space, for this sole reason that I perceive we may shortly behold the rise of a new kind of golden age.'[4] Inspiration is difficult to assess, but for that reason should not be ignored.

But if 'affairs everywhere were tending towards peace',[5] it was not only inspiration or Erasmus that had brought it about. Europe had been in an almost continuous state of war ever since the first French invasion of Italy in 1494. A war weariness was setting in that disposed rulers to accept unpalatable facts which they would have challenged when feeling more buoyant or more financially solvent. By

---

[1] Rymer, xiii, pp. 624-ff (LP, ii, 4469).
[2] See especially Mattingly, Journal of Modern History, x; Scarisbrick, Henry VIII, pp. 70-4.
[3] LP, ii, 4357; also LP, ii, 4137 for important minutes in Ruthal's hand. Contemporary comment includes that by Erasmus, Fox, and Giustinian.
[4] CWE, 4, p.261.
[5] Guicciardini, p.303.

his adherence to the Treaty of Noyon in 1516 Maximilian had accepted that for the time being he was not going to obtain any territorial gains from Venice, and by that same treaty Charles accepted the French occupation of Milan, while Francis in effect accepted the Spanish occupation of Naples. What may also have greatly contributed to these moves towards peace was the death of Ferdinand early that same year, the youthfulness of his successor, Charles, and his urgent need to establish his rule in Spain. Only when this had been achieved could he don his grandfather's mantle as the chief opponent of the crown of France; and in 1521 Europe would be at war again, war weary or not.

In 1518 there was another consideration which inclined some people towards peace, and that was the Turk. In a series of successful campaigns during 1516 and 1517 Selim I had defeated the Syrian and Egyptian sultans with the result that he found himself in control of much of the Middle East. As he already held much of the Balkans and the Greek peninsula, he appeared to be ominously poised for an attack on Christian Europe, whether along the Mediterranean to Italy and Spain or by land through Hungary. In 1517 and again in 1518 Leo X had made serious efforts to concentrate the minds of the European leaders on this threat. On 6 March 1518 a five-year truce amongst the European powers was solemnly declared in Rome, the purpose of which was to facilitate a crusade. To show that he meant business Leo nominated four papal legates *a latere* to attend upon the four principal rulers of Europe to obtain their adherence to his proposals.[1]

A Wolsey devoted to peace might have been expected to respond enthusiastically to his spiritual prince's call, but in fact his response was lukewarm.[2] He never rejected the truce, but he made certain that the papal proposals were completely subordinated to his own. Rightly or wrongly, he never took the Turkish threat very seriously, and thus might justifiably have felt that the plans for a crusade were an irrelevance as far as European peace was concerned.[3] He could have had no such excuse when rejecting Francis I's proposal in September 1516 that England should become a signatory to the Treaty of Noyon. As we have seen, it was this treaty that had removed, for a time at any rate, the real obstacles to European peace, essentially by the acceptance by its signatories of the status quo in Italy, and its contribution to European peace was in reality much greater than anything that would be achieved by the Treaty of London. But what was Wolsey's reaction? Not only did he reject Francis's offer to join, but he did everything in his power to destroy it. The only conclusion that can be drawn, as also from his reaction to Leo X's proposal for a European truce, is that if Wolsey was devoted to peace, it was to peace on no one else's terms but his own.[4]

Such a conclusion is not intended to engender cynicism. If it does, it seriously misleads. For one thing, Wolsey himself was not a cynic, but believed passionately that it was his duty to work for the greater glory of Henry. For another, it could easily obscure what is, after all, the logical consequence of this conclusion, which is

---

[1] Pastor, vii, pp.213 ff.
[2] *Inter alia LP*, ii, 4003, 4028, 4034, 4040, 4047, 4135, 4243.
[3] Cf. his comment to Giustinian: 'Guard yourselves more against the Christian Turk than the real Turk.' (*LP*, ii, 4047). It should be said that Erasmus took a not dissimilar view in letters to More and Warham, March 1518.
[4] *LP*, ii, 2340, 2377, 2387.

that having obtained a favourable peace Wolsey would work hard to maintain it. It was not only that the peace treaty guaranteed the favourable terms obtained from France, though that was its most important function. It also obviated the danger that Francis might use his new alliance with England to advance yet further his Italian ambitions,[1] and these ambitions were much more troublesome to England in 1518 than they had been three years previously. This had nothing to do with Wolsey's alleged love of the papacy, but was a consequence of Ferdinand's death. With his successor Charles as both king of Naples and duke of Burgundy it was harder than ever before to isolate the affairs of Italy, and the particular danger for England was that in the furtherance of his Italian ambitions Francis might get dragged into a war in the Low Countries, thereby threatening vital English trading interests.

Peace was also a much cheaper way of securing England's dominant role in European affairs than subsidizing expensive anti-French alliances. Ever since Henry had joined the Holy League in November 1511 royal expenditure had been outrunning royal income by a considerable amount, despite the £290,000 received from parliamentary and £115,000 from clerical taxation. Between April 1512 and June 1513, admittedly the period of greatest military involvement, over £600,000 was paid out by the treasurer of the Chamber for the purposes of war, and when it is borne in mind that Henry viii's ordinary revenues were running at just over £100,000 a year, the financial strain that war produced can be easily understood.[2] More will have to be said about England's ability to finance the ambitious foreign policy that both Henry and Wolsey were determined to pursue,[3] but there seems little reason to doubt – though it is nowhere mentioned – that the high cost of war combined with England's comparative lack of financial resources provided a strong incentive to work for the peace of Europe, especially when that peace did so much to uphold the honour and prestige of the English monarch. Where others had failed to bring about peace England had succeeded. The treaty had been signed in London with the greatest possible publicity, while England's pivotal position was built into it by the fact that adherents only signed an agreement with England, not with each other. Henry and Wolsey as the peacemakers of Europe! It was an exciting and honourable role, and for the next three years they played it with the utmost panache. The caveat must be that circumstances change, and it would not always be in England's interests for the maintenance of peace to be the principal aim of English foreign policy. When that happened, it will be shown that Wolsey had no great difficulty in adapting.

Richard Fox informed Wolsey that the Treaty of London was 'the best deed that was ever done for the realm of England, and, after the King's Highness, the laud and praise thereof shall be to you a perpetual memory'.[4] Something for which Wolsey has not received so much praise is that first acquisition, on 17 May 1518, of legatine

---

[1] The fact that the French were opposed to Maximilian and Charles becoming principal signatories of the universal peace treaty – and perhaps to the treaty itself – is instructive; see *LP*, ii, app. 52.

[2] For these figures I have relied on Wolfe, *Crown Lands*, pp. 76 ff; Schofield, 'Direct Lay Taxation', table 40, pp. 415-6; M.J. Kelly, 'Canterbury jurisdiction', app. ii, pp. 292 ff. Some of the adding up, however, is mine!

[3] See pp. 355 ff. below.

[4] Fox, *Letters*, p. 112 (*LP*, ii, 4540).

powers with which this chapter began.[1] What this meant for Wolsey and the English Church will be considered in another chapter. This will conclude with some attempt to disperse some of the myths and misconceptions that have grown up concerning the way in which these powers were obtained.

When in late March 1518 Henry had been informed of Leo x's decision to send Cardinal Campeggio to England as legate *a latere* in order to further the papal plans for a crusade, his initial reaction was to suppose that, though it was not really the English practice to admit such officials, it would be all right as long as Campeggio confined his activity to doing just that.[2] Wolsey had other ideas. If Leo wanted his legate to enter England, why not insist that he make Wolsey legate with him? Henry had immediately taken the point.[3] On 11 April a request was sent to Rome, and, whatever Leo's personal feelings may have been, he had little option but to agree if he wanted his own plans to proceed.[4]

Three things should be said about this episode. Henry's comment that it was not the English practice to admit legates *a latere* was substantially correct. The rules and precedents were against doing so, though exceptions had been made.[5] Second, other countries took a very similar attitude to papal legates, while that same year Maximilian and Cardinal Gurk used precisely the same tactics as Henry and Wolsey to ensure that Gurk was made a co-legate with Cardinal Cajetan, who was the Pope's choice as papal legate for Germany.[6] The last point is that Leo's grant to Wolsey in 17 May predated Campeggio's arrival in Calais by about a month,[7] so that the commonly stated view that he was delayed there until the grant was made is incorrect.[8] The real reason for his enforced delay was that Wolsey was anxious for Leo to grant him a further request. It concerned the unfortunate Adriano Castellessi. Wolsey's relationship with this cardinal had never been very good, and had worsened considerably during the winter of 1514-15 when he had discovered that Polydore Vergil was writing rude comments about him to Castellessi. Subsequently, their relationship appeared to improve, but probably only because it was difficult for Wolsey to do much about a man who had been a loyal friend of the English Crown for well over twenty years and, perhaps more importantly had great influence in the Curia. However, in the summer of 1517 Castellessi gave Wolsey his opportunity by becoming implicated in a plot to murder Leo. The trouble was that it soon became clear that his involvement had only been slight, and Leo, who always found decisive action difficult, proved reluctant to move against him. One reason for this was that he knew that Wolsey was less concerned for his, the pope's, safety

[1] *LP*, ii, 4170.

[2] *LP*, ii, 4034.

[3] *LP*, ii, 4055.

[4] *LP*, ii, 4070, 4073, 4179.

[5] Macfarlane, pp.319-22. For Henry's refusal in 1513 to allow Bainbridge to enter the country as legate see *LP*, i, 2512, 2517, 2611.

[6] Pastor, vii, p.244.

[7] Campeggio wrote from Lapalisse, en route from Lyons to Paris, on 28 May (*LP*, ii, 4194) and was in Calais by at least 21 June (*LP*, ii, 4243).

[8] A.F. Pollard, pp.115-16 is muddled; he realized that Castellessi's deprivation was also involved but gives Wolsey's legatine appointment as the first reason for Campeggio's delay; Scarisbrick in *Henry VIII*, pp.69-70 has it as the only reason. He also places Campeggio's stay in Boulogne.

than with getting his hands on the bishopric of Bath and Wells, held by Castellessi for the last fourteen years, and which Wolsey intended to hold *in commendam* with York. Leo saw no point in making unnecessary concessions to Wolsey, and thus resisted the demand for Cardinal Castellessi's deprivation, a demand which was also being pushed by Castellessi's main rival for English favour at the Roman Curia and fellow English bishop, Silvestro Gigli.[1] It appears to have been Gigli's idea to keep Campeggio waiting in Calais until Leo gave in on this point,[2] and whosoever idea it was it worked. On 5 July Castellessi was deprived both of his cardinal's hat and of his English bishopric.[3] As soon as Wolsey heard the news he sent over a knight of the garter to escort Campeggio from Calais to London where he was received with the greatest honour possible.[4]

This, briefly, is the story of Campeggio's first journey to England, and Wolsey's acquisition of his first legatine commission. Leo had intended that it should last only for as long as Campeggio remained in England. Moreover, he must have hoped that as a result of granting it Wolsey would help Campeggio to further the papal project for a crusade. As it turned out, Wolsey was to remain a legate *a latere* until his downfall, while his interest in the crusade, as has been shown, was minimal. His real reasons for wanting to become legate will provide the subject of another chapter.

---

[1] *LP*, ii, 4271, 4284; also Chambers, 'English representation', pp. 439-45; Pastor, vii, pp. 170 ff.
[2] *LP*, ii, 4179 – Gigli to Wolsey 20 May, and thus after Wolsey's appointment as legate *a latere*.
[3] *LP*, ii, 4289, 4350.
[4] *LP*, ii, 4333, 4348.

CHAPTER FOUR

'WHERE CONSCIENCE HATH THE MOST FORCE':
WOLSEY AND THE LAW

IN SOME RESPECTS IT IS POSSIBLE TO ATTACH TOO MUCH SIGNIFICANCE TO Wolsey's appointment as lord chancellor in December 1515.[1] In describing his rise to power, considerable emphasis has been placed on his growing relationship with the king, rather than on his holding of any particular office. Before 1515 he had held no important political office, and yet this had not prevented him from playing a significant role in royal government. Moreover, the office of lord chancellor, for all its prestige, did not automatically ensure that the incumbent became the king's most influential minister. Neither Wolsey's immediate predecessor, William Warham, nor his two successors, Thomas More and Thomas Audley, achieved that eminence, whereas Thomas Cromwell, who did, never became lord chancellor. It is not quite so obvious, therefore, as is usually assumed that it was an office that a power-hungry Wolsey was bound to seek. Power did accrue, including some patronage and a considerable income,[2] but these came to anyone in royal favour. And there was one considerable drawback to the office: it involved a lot of work.

By the early sixteenth century this work was largely judicial, and in particular required the holder of the office to preside over both his own court of Chancery and the judicial activity of the king's Council sitting in Star Chamber.[3] It has been estimated that during the fourteen years that Wolsey was lord chancellor over nine thousand cases were brought before these two bodies.[4] They came in different shapes and sizes, many of them getting no further than an initial bill of complaint and therefore not requiring much attention from Wolsey. In any case he often delegated the essential work. Nevertheless the numbers are impressive, particularly since during his tenure of office the number of cases dealt with annually by the lord chancellor significantly increased. During the four legal terms, that is, for about six months of each year, Wolsey would spend the best part of every morning at Westminster Hall

> and there commune sometimes with the judges and sometimes with other persons. And that done he would repair into the Chancery, and sitting there until eleven of the clock, hearing suitors and determining of divers matters. And from thence he would divers

---

[1] Rymer, xiii, pp.529-30. The great seal was given to him on 22 Dec. and he took the oath on the 24th.

[2] Just how much of either is not clear. Many chancery appointments were in the gift of the master of the rolls, but the chancellor did appoint the eleven masters of chancery. He received £419 15s. 0d. for diet, £40 for clothes and £200 for sitting in Star Chamber, but his real income was considerably more; see Maxwell-Lyte, pp.1-19; W.J. Jones, pp.86ff.

[3] Referred to frequently as Star Chamber, despite all the problems surrounding the dating of its emergence as a separate body from the king's Council.

[4] For Chancery see Metzger, 'Das Englische Kanzleigericht', and his own English summary in 'Medieval Chancery'. For Star Chamber see Guy, Cardinal's Court and More, pp.37-93. Despite some disagreements, I would like to acknowledge J.A. Guy's help in the legal aspects of Wolsey's career. The extent to which I am indebted to his labours will emerge from the footnotes that follow.

times go into the Star Chamber, as occasion did serve, where he spared neither high nor low, but judged every estate according to their merits and deserts.[1]

Perhaps what is most surprising about the time and effort that Wolsey put in, is that although the 'high' did appear before him, most of his cases concerned the purely private interests of individuals of no particular political significance. Why, then, did he bother? It was not as if he was short of things to occupy himself with, including many more glamorous or more important than determining whether or not George Blundell of Little Crosby in Lancashire had a life interest in the manor of Crosby,[2] or what to do about an organ-builder's bad debts.[3] One obvious answer – so obvious, perhaps, that it can easily be overlooked – is that he had no choice. Henry VIII wanted him to be lord chancellor, and that being so, it was not for Wolsey to refuse. In any event, it seems likely that Wolsey was happy to take up the burdens of the chancellorship, not so as to satisfy his vanity, or to achieve his own private ends – both have been alleged[4] – but because he genuinely believed that there was an important job for him to do.

However, before looking more closely at Wolsey's intentions, more detail about his work as lord chancellor is called for. Of the nine thousand and more cases already referred to, 7,526 came before Chancery[5] and about 1,685 before the Council in Star Chamber.[6] Chancery was, thus, though not the one on which Wolsey left most mark, by far the busier of the two judicial bodies. It had been in existence for well over a hundred years, and so its procedures and jurisidictional scope were well-established, as was its popularity. The number of cases coming before it under Wolsey increased, though not by very much, to about 540 a year; Morton and Warham had presided over an average of about five hundred.[7] In Star Chamber the increase appears to have been much more dramatic: in Henry VII's reign the number of cases averaged 12.5 per annum, while under Wolsey it averaged 120.[8]

Such an increase might suggest that Wolsey took positive steps to popularize the Council's judicial activity,[9] but if so this did not involve the introduction of any new category of cases. By far the largest category, comprising 41 per cent, was concerned with disputed title to land, however much this had to be disguised in order to justify bringing such cases before the Council rather than the common law courts.[10] A second category had to do with disputes over rival claims to jurisdiction

---

[1] Cavendish, p.24.

[2] Guy, *Cardinal's Court*, pp.127-8.

[3] Ibid, p.71.

[4] Cf. 'The chancellor gloried in his presidency of the council, drew suits unto himself especially those involving his conciliar colleagues and pompously demonstrated his political power and personal intelligence in star chamber.' (Guy, *Cardinal's Court*, p.34). See also A.F. Pollard, pp.74, 80.

[5] Metzger. 'Medieval Chancery', p.80, n.5.

[6] Guy, *Cardinal's Court*, p.51. The records for Star Chamber are far less complete than those for Chancery. They are also mainly undated, so there are great difficulties in assigning a case to a particular chancellor.

[7] Averages given by Ives in *TRHS*, 5 ser, xviii, p.166, but other figures are to be found. Pronay's are considerably higher: 605 a year for 1500-15, and 770 a year for 1515-29; see Pronay, pp.88-9. See also Guy, *More*, p.50.

[8] Ibid, p.38; Guy, *Cardinal's Court*, p.15.

[9] This is the main burden of Guy's work.

within towns: sometimes, as in Norwich, between the town government and the Church, and sometimes, as in Newcastle, between the town government and certain of its guild merchants. Another category concerned trade and commerce and included cases brought against people who had offended against proclamations regulating economic activity as well as against those who had failed to pay their debts. Yet another category had to do with disputes between landlord and tenant, over such matters as enclosure, poaching, rights of way and tithes. The Council also dealt with testamentary and defamation cases. In fact, as it was in theory open to anyone to bring any kind of complaint, there was nothing that might not provide the subject of a case, even if the Council might merely refer it to one of the regular law courts. In other words, the only limits to its jurisdiction were those it chose to make, and the choices it was making were no different in Wolsey's time than they had been previously. A category that has been traditionally associated with the Council in Star Chamber included all cases to do with the perversion of justice and good government, whether by royal officials, juries, or anyone else. It is not, of course, surprising that the Council should have wanted to concern itself with such cases, but their number was comparatively small, comprising only about 15 per cent.

A brief survey of the cases coming before Chancery during Wolsey's period of office reveals a very similar picture. There were, it is true, some categories which, if not peculiar to Chancery, were particularly associated with it. For instance, unlike the common law courts, Chancery was prepared to recognize that a man holding his land by copyhold tenure had legal rights. It was also prepared to recognize the increasingly popular, though still controversial, form of conveyance, the enfeoffment to uses. Like Star Chamber, however, it was happy to deal with commercial matters, especially those concerned with that most difficult of areas, contractual obligation and debt. But its involvement here was much greater: it has been estimated that whereas 28 per cent of cases in Chancery during this period involved commerce, in Star Chamber it was only 3 per cent.[1] On the other hand, as in Star Chamber, by far the largest category of cases in Chancery involved disputed title to land, and the proportion of such cases in both courts was very similar: 46 per cent in Chancery compared with 41 in Star Chamber.[2] Moreover, it would appear that, as in Star Chamber, it was here that the increase in Chancery business, such as it was, occurred. In fact, it has been suggested that by the 1520s there had been a significant reversal in the proportion of property to commercial cases compared with the 1470s, when commercial cases had predominated.[3] Whether this was so or not – and the statistics are fraught with problems – what does seem reasonably clear is that Wolsey made no alteration to the scope of Chancery's jurisisdiction. As with Star Chamber, he allowed no new kinds of cases to be brought before him. This being so,

[10] Guy, *Cardinal's Court*, pp. 51-71 for this and all the categories that follow. They are based on the study of the 473 cases for which there is sufficient evidence to make some categorization possible, though the fact that the second largest category is a miscellaneous one indicates how difficult the exercise is and suggests that one should not set too much store by it.

[1] Metzger, 'Medieval Chancery', p.84. Life for the 'layman' is made more difficult by the fact that while Guy made use of Metzger's work, he reworked the categories, thereby producing different figures; see Guy, *More*, p.39.

[2] This is Guy's estimate; see *More*, p.39.

[3] Guy, 'Equitable jurisdiction', pp.84.

one obvious explanation for the increasing popularity of these two courts during his period of office is ruled out.

In trying to arrive at other explanations, it is necessary to establish how the kind of jurisdiction that has just been outlined had first come to be associated with the office of lord chancellor. Originally the chancellor – he seems only to have assumed the style of lord chancellor in the sixteenth century – had performed the function of royal secretary, a role that he quickly grew out of but without acquiring any very specific new functions. What special function he had remained, however, essentially administrative rather than judicial, and by the end of the thirteenth century he can perhaps best be described as the chief executive officer of the Crown, especially associated with that increasingly important – though almost impossible to define – institution, the king's Council. One function of this body was to respond to the many petitions and complaints that the king's subjects addressed to him, and as the number of these increased it became no longer convenient to deal with them on an ad hoc basis. Some more regular machinery was required, and the chancellor was the obvious person to set this up. Not only did he already possess the necessary prestige, but as a consequence of his original secretarial function he was still responsible for preparing, and authenticating with the great seal of England, the written commands of the king. He was, thus, in a good position to implement the royal response to petitioners' requests for help. When precisely the chancellor began to act in a judicial capacity is not known, and there was probably no precise date, but by the early fourteenth century a court of Chancery was in existence, and by the end of that century it was well established.[1]

However, the emergence of this court did not prevent the king's subjects from still wishing to appeal directly to him, nor was it intended to, for the notion that they should be able to was so intimately bound up with the belief in kingship itself that to prevent them would have been unthinkable, as well as politically unwise. As one plaintiff put it in 1499: 'All and every of the king's true subjects ought of right to be contented to sue and be sued before the king's highness, which is the head of justice, and in his absence before the lords of his most honourable council.'[2] Moreover, Chancery, like any other institution, quickly developed a life of its own – its own procedures, its own criteria for handling problems, and its own vested interests. In the process it lost a great deal of its initial flexibility. Thus as Chancery developed there took place what was essentially a re-run of what had occurred nearly two hundred years earlier at its emergence. The Council found that it was having to spend a considerable amount of time on legal business, and in order to cope it was having to develop its own procedures. One of these was that the lord chancellor now presided over the judicial business of the Council, and, not surprisingly therefore, many of its procedures were borrowed from Chancery.[3]

The Council, thus, ceased to be a body to which the subject appealed in exceptional circumstances, but instead became, though admittedly as only part of its function, a court to which in the normal course of events the legal profession

---

[1] An archivally significant date is 1387 when petitions to the chancellor first began to be calendared separately; see Pronay, p.88. See also Baldwin, pp.236-61, and, for an excellent survey for a non-scholarly audience, Underhill, pp.1-96.

[2] *Select Cases in the Council of Henry VII*, p.xxxiii.

[3] The most obvious being the English bill of complaint with which a plaintiff began his suit.

could recommend its clients to make recourse. This much had already taken place before Wolsey became lord chancellor.[1] And although no essential changes were made during his period in office – that is, no decisive break was made between the Council's judicial and other activities – the increase in judicial business eventually made such a formal separation virtually inevitable, if it was to continue to perform its other even more vital function of advising the king about every conceivable aspect of royal government. It is not, therefore, surprising that the break did occur under Cromwell's supervision, during the 1530s.

One obvious reason why administrative and judicial machinery ceases to function effectively is that the problems it was designed to deal with change. In theory it is possible for the machinery to adapt, but in practice it is often easier for new machinery to be set up. And new problems do appear to have contributed to the emergence of Chancery. Enfeoffment to uses, copyhold tenure and unwritten contractual arrangements were all matters that, during the formative years of the common law, had either not existed or else had not been considered sufficiently important for the Crown to take an interest in them. By the fifteenth century this was no longer the case, but the difficulty was that the common law courts proved to be unwilling to take account of them. The only remedy was a petition to the king and his Council, but more especially to that new extension of the king's Council, the court of Chancery.

It is not, however, nearly so obvious that any new concerns of litigants and their lawyers contributed to the emergence of Star Chamber. What seems to have happened is that the notion that any subject could petition the king was exploited by the common lawyers to enable their clients to approach what they took to be just another court – that is, Star Chamber. The fact that its procedures were more effective than the common law courts was by way of being a bonus. That this was so has been obscured until recently by the failure to recognize the great extent to which both Star Chamber and Chancery were dominated by disputes to do with property. In theory such cases should have been brought before the common law courts, but in order to get round this the lawyers, with at least the tacit consent of successive chancellors, had developed legal fictions.[2] In Star Chamber the fiction would be that the plaintiff's case had been prejudiced by the use of violence, usually in the form of riot. Since riot was defined as the assembly of three or more persons for an unlawful purpose, it was not difficult to allege that one had taken place. Moreover, to bring a property dispute even before the common law courts it had been usual to allege some degree of violence, if only forcible entry or trespass.[3] In Chancery, the fiction was that the plaintiff's case had been prejudiced in the common law courts by the defendant's unfair retention of vital documents. In both cases a fiction was used because people preferred to have their cases tried before the conciliar courts rather than the common law courts.

The question of whether litigants and their legal advisers were really making choices is important, because if they were, then various judgments commonly made

---

[1] *Select Cases in the Council of Henry VII*, passim, is essential reading.
[2] Apart from the works by Guy and Metzger already cited, Ives, *TRHS*, 5 ser, xviii, pp.165ff. and Blatcher should be consulted.
[3] Guy, *Cardinal's Court*, p.54.

about Wolsey's attitude to the law – even the fairly neutral one that he deliberately set out to popularize the conciliar courts – have to be rethought. Of course, insofar as there were some matters that the common law courts refused to consider, one cannot talk about choice, but the number of such cases was small. For instance, only 6 per cent of all cases coming before Chancery during Wolsey's time turned on the issue of enfoeffment to uses – and this was precisely the same percentage as from 1474-83.[1] As for cases to do with copyhold tenure, their number has been estimated as low as forty for the whole of Wolsey's period in office.[2] But more than any statistics, the legal fictions themselves suggest that a choice was being exercised, for if people had not been anxious to bring cases before the conciliar courts rather than the common law courts, there would have been no need to invent them.

Another approach to this question of choice is to look at what was happening in the common law courts. Here the picture that emerges seems to be one of falling popularity, and this over a considerable period. Using the profits of sealing fees as a measure of the amount of business coming before its two most important courts, King's Bench and Common Pleas, it has been shown that business began to decline in the 1430s, reaching a low point in the 1520s. In the 1530s there was a recovery of a sort, to be sustained in the next decade, but it was not until the 1550s that a really substantial increase took place, bringing the figures to above those for the first two decades of the previous century.[3] The fact that the common law courts had for so long been losing business does not in itself prove that a choice was being made, even when coupled with the increase of business in the conciliar courts. Neither do the figures correlate quite as well as at first glance they appear to. Even at their lowest ebb the common law courts dealt with many more cases than the conciliar courts, and the fall in numbers in the former in no way corresponded to the increase in the latter. Moreover, when business in the common law courts did pick up, there was no falling off in business in the conciliar courts. The relationship between the varying fortunes of the two systems of law is thus not very clear-cut, but that there was some connection seems sufficiently likely to merit a closer examination of the state of the common law itself.

The defects of the common law at this time have been much, arguably too much, emphasized. There has never been a period when its workings have not been heavily criticized, and the criticism has always followed a similar pattern: over-complexity leading to absurd anomalies, long delays, and perhaps above all expense – so great that only the wealthy can afford to make use of it. A problem that is less prevalent now was the enormous difficulty experienced in getting people to appear in court. During the Easter term 1470 eighty defendants to actions of trespass brought by private individuals, that is in civil cases before King's Bench, put in an appearance. Three hundred and fifty did not. In the Michaelmas term 1488 before that same court, 838 civil cases had to be delayed, 685 of them because of the non-appearance of the defendant.[4] And not only was non-appearance just as prevalent in civil suits brought before other common law courts, but also in criminal cases.[5]

---

[1] Guy, 'Equitable jurisdiction', p.84.

[2] Metzger, *Das Englische Kanzleigericht*, p.152.

[3] Blatcher, pp.10-63. During the 1530s business in Common Pleas picked up quite dramatically, while that in King's Bench continued to fall.

[4] Blatcher, pp.64-5.

That it existed on such a scale suggests some serious defects in the machinery of law enforcement, but for the moment it is the point of view of the plaintiff in a civil case that will be our concern. A study of the enrolment of civil suits in King's Bench reveals that many plaintiffs were so disheartened that they abandoned their cases at an early stage, precisely because of this failure of the defendant to turn up.[1]

Non-appearance was not such a problem in the conciliar courts even though the theoretical penalties under the common law, resulting in the distraint of goods or outlawry, were if anything more severe.[2] One reason for this may have been that in the conciliar courts the initiative in serving the processes by which a defendant was compelled to appear, begun either by a summons under the privy seal or a subpoena, lay not with the disinterested sheriff but with the plaintiff who would be much more determined to ensure the appearance of the defendant.[3] A more important factor may have been the defendant's realization that behind the plaintiff loomed the figure of the lord chancellor, and in the case of Star Chamber the lords of the king's Council as well. By the early sixteenth century the common law processes had become all too familiar, and the ways and means of escaping them, or of at least minimizing their consequences, had been brought to a fine art. To borrow a metaphor used by the historian of King's Bench, the result was that the penalties for non-appearance were viewed in rather the same way as many people today view library fines – irksome but not sufficiently so to make one return the book.[4] This was not the view taken, as yet, of the conciliar processes. Defendants were still too reluctant to risk the wrath of the lord chancellor.

The greater effectiveness of the conciliar processes must have encouraged plaintiffs and their legal advisers to make use of these courts. They would also have had to take into account which courts provided them with the best chance of winning their case, and, having won it, of having the decision enforced. Again, it looks as if on both counts the balance of advantages lay with the conciliar courts. The common law's insistence upon correct pleading meant that many cases were lost on a technicality. The wrong date, the wrong name, the wrong place – any of these could lead to the defendant suing out a writ of error before King's Bench, thereby effectively putting an end to the case against him; and as the errors could be either in the indictment itself or in any of the writs of process required to secure his appearance, there were plenty of opportunities for them to creep in. Of course, there is much to be said for the law being on the side of the defendant,[5] though perhaps rather less so in civil than in criminal cases. And whether or not the bias served the interests of justice, it did not serve the interests of the plaintiff. The conciliar courts, on the other hand, did not offer such opportunities for the defendant to escape. The great virtue of the English bill used in these courts was its

---

[5] Ibid, p.65; Bellamy, *Crime and Public Order*, p.158; Hastings, pp.175-83.

[1] Blatcher, p.73.

[2] Ibid, pp.65-81.

[3] Ibid, pp.71ff.; Bellamy, *Crime and Public Order*, pp.91-3; Guy, *Cardinal's Court*, pp.82-5.

[4] Blatcher, p.68. Baker compares them to gas and electricity bills; see Baker, ii, p.90.

[5] And was thought to be so at the time; see Sir John Fortescue's comment that it was better that twenty guilty men escaped than a single innocent man escaped, quoted in Bellamy, *Crime and Public Order*, p.156.

flexibility and greater concern with matter than with form. The plaintiff was allowed to state his complaint with a good deal of freedom, and the defendant was forced to answer it in a reasonably direct way. Some formulae were involved, and there were those legal fictions already mentioned, but dealing with these was simplicity itself compared with the technicalities of pleading before the common law courts.[1]

As regards the effectiveness of any decisions, the balance was not so obviously in favour of the conciliar courts, and at least in one respect not at all. For in theory, only the common law courts could pronounce a final judgment in matters of land ownership. All that the conciliar court could do was to pronounce on the merits of the particular case brought before it: on the evidence presented, X had a better case than Y and therefore 'in conscience' should enjoy possession of the land in dispute. What it could not say was that X owned the land.[2] Many conciliar decrees explicitly reflected their provisional nature: X should enjoy the land until such time as Y could produce further evidence, or even until Y had proved his case in the common law courts.[3] But even if the decree took a more positive line, sometimes going so far as to forbid further litigation, in theory its provisional nature remained. And one suspects that practice was of rather greater concern to the plaintiff than theory: he wanted protection or repossession now rather than for the future, and against the particular person who was threatening his enjoyment of the land. The difficulty for the historian is to decide which of the two kinds of courts did best provide this kind of protection, if only because neither seems to have been very good at it.

In the common law courts the incidence of non-appearance was obviously a major stumbling block, so much so that the suspicion must be that many disputes were settled out of court; otherwise why should a plaintiff, knowing as well as the modern historian the improbability of any conclusion to the case, spend a considerable amount of time and money in even beginning to sue? And if this is so, the initial writ was merely a way of bringing sufficient pressure to persuade the defendant to begin negotiations – a tactic not unknown today! Nevertheless, it would appear that the conciliar courts were better designed to settle disputes, even if in the event they frequently did not. Flexibility, and not just of the bills of complaint, was the keynote of most conciliar procedures at this time. And this reflected an essential difference in approach between the two jurisdictions. The common law's main concern was not to find remedies to disputes, but rather to tackle the much more specific task of deciding, by jury, whether or not the defendant had indeed done what the plaintiff had accused him of doing. The fact, for instance, that the defendant had clearly wronged the plaintiff but not precisely in the manner alleged, was not the common law courts' concern. It was not their task to bring the parties together, or to act as arbitrators; and, moreover, their reliance on the jury not only to pass judgment on the facts but to some extent still actually to obtain them, by their answers to questions concerning the case, meant that the common law court lacked the machinery to get to the bottom of a complicated case.

---

[1] *Inter alia*, Baker, ii, pp.70*ff*; Guy, *Cardinal's Court*, pp.79ff.; W.J. Jones, pp.177ff.
[2] Metzger, 'Medieval Chancery', pp.86-7.
[3] Guy, *Cardinal's Court*, p.108.

It was very different with conciliar courts. There the plaintiff's complaint and the defendant's answers were written down at great length and then given in open court, with any additional points being made by counsel. Lengthy depositions were taken from witnesses, who themselves were submitted to detailed questioning. And when all the evidence had been presented, the chancellor was still left with a number of options before proceeding to a determination. He could refer the matter to judges, who had power to hear and consider all the evidence, for their expert opinion. On the basis of their report he could then proceed to a decision. On the other hand, if he felt that a less technical approach was required, he could bind the parties to accept arbitration. Judges or other legal experts would always be included as arbitrators, but important 'non-experts' would also be chosen. Often the latter would come from the locality in which the disputes had arisen, and since the commission for arbitration would often sit in that locality, it was much easier to arrive at all the facts. Another option was to attempt a compromise. This was the most flexible approach of all, but it had this disadvantage that unlike an arbitration award it was not enforceable at common law. It was, however, better than nothing, and was presumably only attempted where other approaches were deemed unlikely to succeed. It should be said that these options were more likely to be used in Star Chamber than in Chancery, but the essential point applies to both courts. Both were actively looking for remedies, and to that end were making use of men of the greatest expertise and authority, while the common law court's task was the much more passive and circumscribed one of passing judgment on the facts presented. It may be that the mere fact of going to law would encourage people to settle out of court, and that therefore in practice the differences between the two approaches were not as great as they now seem to the historian. It should also be stressed that the conciliar courts do not appear to have been much more successful at arriving at a formal determination to a case than their so-called rivals. The danger is to exaggerate the advantages of the conciliar courts, but in view of their growing popularity we have to conclude that they offered some real benefits.

This popularity did not originate with Wolsey. However unreliable the statistics, they all point to the trends already noticed: a decline in the number of cases before the common law courts, and an increase in the number before the conciliar courts. Both trends had begun by 1450 and were maintained in the sixty-five years before Wolsey's appointment. This being so, the personal contribution of any particular chancellor can only have been small. Since it was the litigants themselves who chose to bring their suits before the conciliar courts, the most dramatic thing that any chancellor could have done would have been deliberately to limit access to them. This he could have done in a number of ways: for instance, by accepting the common law view that enfeoffment to uses was an invalid transaction, or that non-written contracts and obligations should have no force at law. Or he might have refused to accept the fictitious reasons alleged by many litigants for bringing their cases before the conciliar courts. And that Wolsey recognized them to be fictitious is suggested by his decision in 1527 to allow defendants who denied any riot in their answers to be represented by attorneys and allowed to go home;[1] if they had behaved even halfway as badly as was usually

---

[1] Guy, *Cardinal's Court*, p.89.

alleged, it is unlikely that they would have been allowed this freedom. Wolsey, in fact, did nothing to make life harder for litigants to apply to his court. Indeed, he has been accused of going out of his way to encourage people to bring their suits before him from a mixture of discreditable motives including an overwhelming confidence in his own ability to settle any dispute and his personal antipathy to the common law deriving from his own ignorance of it. More generally, it is thought that he was too lenient and too flexible in his approach to the law, with the result that too many cases appeared before him that were frivolous or vexatious, or did not properly belong to the conciliar court. This, allegedly, had two consequences: it clogged up the conciliar machinery so that it ceased to be effective, and it posed a serious threat to the common law courts, whether this was Wolsey's intention or not.[1] All these matters must now be looked at.

The charge that Wolsey knew no law cannot be true, and is anyway largely beside the point. What is true is that he was not trained as a common lawyer, but this was equally true of his predecessors who, churchmen like Wolsey, had not been eligible for such training. On the other hand, unlike Wolsey, many chancellors, such as his two immediate predecessors, Warham and Morton, had been trained in canon and civil law. But not so Thomas Rotherham, chancellor from 1474 to 1483, who apparently reformed the office with some distinction.[2] And though a training in canon and civil law may have been of some help, the fact was that the conciliar courts based their decisions on common law. But the point is that the one thing that no chancellor lacked was expert legal advice. In Chancery he was supported by a trained staff, including the master of the rolls, eleven masters in chancery and the so-called six clerks.[3] In Star Chamber his support was even more impressive, though not so formally organized. Most of the judges and many other leading common lawyers were fellow royal councillors, and it was to such people that much of the essential legal work of the Council was delegated.[4] Moreover, the fact that all the major courts were situated either in Westminster Hall itself or in adjoining rooms such as Star Chamber, made it very easy for the lord chancellor to consult with the judges at work there – which, according to Cavendish, Wolsey was accustomed to do.[5] Just occasionally he would ask the advice of the judicial bench as a whole, as he did in 1526 when he asked whether a peacock should be considered a game bird and therefore wild, or a domesticated fowl – an apparently trivial matter but one of some legal consequence, because only a domesticated animal could be taken feloniously. And domesticated the judges decided a peacock was.[6]

If one looks at Wolsey's personal qualifications for the chancellorship, they turn out to be more promising than is usually implied. As bursar of Magdalen College, and in the posts that followed, he would have been much involved in legal matters. The formal designation of chaplain to Henry VII conceals the fact that much of his work at court would have been administrative and legal. And once he became

---

[1] This a central criticism of Guy's work; see ibid, 119ff. But see also Baker, ii, pp.77-80; Blatcher, pp.27-9.

[2] Pronay, p.92.

[3] W.J.Jones, pp.100ff.

[4] Guy, *Cardinal's Court* pp.28-9 for a list of attenders.

[5] Cavendish, p.24.

[6] Baker, ii, p.318.

almoner to Henry VIII, which he had by at least November 1509, he would have been directly involved in handling those bills of complaint that were still being presented to the king in person. The following year he was a royal councillor sitting in Star Chamber and directly concerned with its legal proceedings. Thus, when five years later he was appointed lord chancellor, he may not have equalled some of his predecessors in knowledge and experience but he surely possessed enough of each to perform the office adequately, and, given his natural abilities and capacity for hard work, to perform it with distinction. Be that as it may, any responsibility that Wolsey, or indeed any other lord chancellor, may bear for the popularity of the conciliar courts can only have been marginal, for, insofar as it can be explained at all, this was due to intrinsic differences in approach between them and the common law courts.

Nevertheless, it is precisely Wolsey's personal contribution that inspired the author of the most important book on his activity in Star Chamber to call it *The Cardinal's Court*. It could only be on the basis of a study of Star Chamber that such a claim could have been made, because as we have seen the figures for Chancery do not suggest any great increase in business under Wolsey. For Star Chamber just such an increase has been discovered for, as we noted earlier, the average number of cases handled there rose from 12.5 cases a year under Henry VII to 120 under Wolsey. The difficulty is to decide how far we can trust these figures – not from the point of view of any particular historian's counting, but of what he has had to count with. Not only have the Council registers for this period disappeared, leaving us only edited extracts prepared for the Elizabethan lord chancellor, Sir Thomas Egerton, but what has survived – a mass of papers associated with particular cases – is extremely difficult to use because so much of it is undated.[1] And without dates the statistics can offer only a crude impression. It has been possible to arrive at a yearly average for the whole of Henry VII's reign, but there are no figures for any particular year. This means that we will never be able to tell precisely what impact Wolsey made, for rather than any dramatic jump when he took over, the rate of increase might have been steadily building up under his predecessor. Furthermore, the figure of 12.5 a year must wildly underestimate the amount of business for the earlier period, for not only does the identification, during the last twenty-five years, of about a hundred more cases for Henry VII's reign suggest it, but even more so does the comment made in 1494, that the then chancellor had been so busy that he had 'kept not the Star Chamber this eight days'.[2] If there had been only 12.5 cases a year, this could hardly have deserved a mention.

But if the figures must be treated with the utmost caution, there is other evidence to suggest that the number of cases before the Council in Star Chamber during Wolsey's period as lord chancellor was growing. Most convincing are the indications that legal business was occupying too much of the Council's time, and the various attempts by Wolsey to ease the workload.[3] The decision taken in June 1517 to sit in Star Chamber on Mondays, Tuesdays, Thursdays and Saturdays may provide the first evidence of increasing business, especially when taken in

---

[1] See especially Guy, *Journal of the Society of Archivists*, v (1975).
[2] Quoted in Guy, *Cardinal's Court*, p.14.
[3] Ibid, pp.23-50 for what follows.

conjunction with a further decision in October of that year that the Council should also sit on Wednesdays and Fridays, which under the previous arrangement had been reserved for Chancery sittings. Also in 1517, Wolsey set up a temporary tribunal or 'under-court' to sit at Westminster in order to hear poor men's causes. In the following year this temporary arrangement was renewed, and soon became permanent.

In late 1525 and early 1526 Wolsey was busy with various schemes for reforming the royal household, central amongst which was one to separate off the legal work of the Council. The task was to be undertaken by twenty-eight named royal councillors, not of the first rank, together with 'the residue of the judges', 'the remnant of the barons of the exchequer', the attorney-general, and serjeants-at-law. Some such move was inevitable once the number of cases before the Council rose beyond a certain point: a body whose principal duty was to advise the king on all matters of policy and administration could not allow its time to be dominated by essentially legal matters. Sometime during the 1530s Cromwell was to take the inevitable step of implementing Wolsey's scheme of ten years earlier. A privy council was set up to provide advice on policy and to involve itself in administrative decisions, while the legal work was to continue to be carried out in Star Chamber in what was from this date a formal court separate from the Council, though sharing its personnel.[1]

In 1526 Wolsey drew back from implementing his own scheme, perhaps because, unlike Cromwell, he was himself lord chancellor and it would not so obviously relieve him from the pressure of work. That some relief was needed is suggested by his decision in June 1529 to delegate his work in Chancery to a commission,[2] though no doubt the divorce proceedings had a good deal to do with it. Instead of a separation of functions Wolsey hit upon a policy of delegating suits to the localities in which they originated. In May 1526 it was decided to set up commissioners in every shire to deal with these suits. In fact this does not seem to have happened, but cases were sent to the Council in the Marches of Wales, which in the previous year had been reorganized under the titular leadership of the Princess Mary, and to the duke of Richmond's Council in the North established in that same year. There were other reasons for such a policy. Since one of the problems for litigants was the expense not only of their own journeys to London but also of their witnesses', the hearing of their case in their own locality should have resulted in cheaper and quicker justice. Nevertheless, the projected reforms of 1525 and 1526, plus the decision in February 1527 to have all 'minute cases' (presumably those of relatively little importance) remitted to the assize judges, suggest that this policy of delegating was largely motivated by the desire to limit the amount of time that the Council needed to set aside for legal business. It has been argued that the policy was not a success.[3] This may be true, although the lack of any systematic records for Mary's and Richmond's Councils makes any assessment almost impossible. Some

[1] A controversial subject because of Elton's belief that Cromwell instituted a privy council, and that this had great constitutional and political significance; for which see inter alia Elton, Tudor Revolution, pp.316 ff., and Guy, 'The privy council'. For my own part, I am yet to be convinced that anything significant happened to the king's Council in the 1530s; for which see pp.202 ff. below.

[2] LP,iv,5666; the legatine court opened on 18 June.

[3] Guy, Cardinal's Court, p.48.

115

cases were returned to Star Chamber, the litigants apparently being unwilling to be fobbed off with what they took to be second best. But if this was the case, it only strengthens the view that it was they who wanted the Council in Star Chamber, not the Council, and more specifically Wolsey, who wanted them.

What is the evidence for Wolsey wishing people to bring their complaints before him? There were two principal ways in which he could have encouraged them. He could have set out to publicize the work of his courts, and especially that of Star Chamber; or, by deliberately going out of his way to favour the plaintiff, who was undoubtedly at most disadvantage in the common law courts, he could have encouraged the legal profession to advise its clients to make use of his courts. It has been suggested that he did both these things. To take the question of publicity first: not long after he became lord chancellor, on 2 May 1516, Wolsey made an important speech before a great assembly of the Council at which the king himself was present.[1] There he spoke of the 'enormities' which were prevalent in the kingdom, 'to the derogation of indifferent justice, as well as the causes of the continuance of the same enormities. For the redress and reformation whereof the same most reverend father advertised his highness in the name of the whole councillors of certain provisions by their diligent study excogitate.' As if to emphasize that he meant business, Wolsey chose the same day for the appearance of the 5th earl of Northumberland before the Council for an offence which probably had to do with the 'ravishment' of a royal ward. And whatever the offence, it involved the public humiliation of a leading nobleman, one which ended with the earl being committed to the Fleet prison. Then in May 1517 there was a second great assembly, convened so that the king could pardon four hundred or so Londoners who had taken part in 'the Evil May Day riots', but Wolsey took the opportunity to refer again to 'the enormities and things misbehaved and misordered within this Realm'.[2] Two years later, on 27 October 1519, he delivered a 'notable oration' concerning the 'due administration of justice', following it up the next day by hearing the submission of Sir William Bulmer for wearing the duke of Buckingham's livery in the king's presence, and at the same time passing sentence upon two Surrey Justices of the Peace accused of 'great maintenance, embracery, and bearing' – all different ways of corrupting a jury.[3] There seems little doubt that all these occasions were stage-managed for maximum effect. What effect was intended is not so clear, but they were almost certainly not attempts to popularize the conciliar courts.

'Enormities' is a rather general term, used not of defects in the common law but rather of abuses of it, especially by the powerful, such as the earl of Northumberland, and those such as the Surrey JPs whose task it was to administer the law. In other words, the propaganda was towards better law enforcement rather than the provision of better remedies for private problems. In practice, of course, the two things could not be separated. If a genuine riot accompanied a dispute over property, or if the claim quite often made in a bill of complaint that the plaintiff could not obtain justice in the local courts because of the undue influence of his

[1] Ibid, pp.30-1. The information for all these Star Chamber set pieces is derived from Huntingdon Library California, Ellesmere MS, 2654, fos.22-5; 2655, fos.10, 15.

[2] Ibid, pp.31-2.

[3] Ibid, p.32.

opponents was true, then indeed 'enormities' were being committed. Even if they were not, it could be that litigants might be more willing to pretend that these things were occurring in order to get their private suits before Star Chamber, if it was known that a chancellor was anxious to put an end to them. Whether or not this happened under Wolsey, and whether he publicized the conciliar court in other ways – through, for instance, the justices of assize – is not known. Given that the conciliar courts were already popular, to have wasted time on such efforts would appear to have been uncharacteristically foolish, but, if he did, he had by 1527 clearly repented, because we know that in that year he was sending at least some categories of cases back to them. What is more likely is that his prestige and known abilities provided an additional attraction to litigants and their legal advisers; if they were looking for genuine remedies he may well have seemed an ideal man to provide them, as a brief glance at one or two particular cases will demonstrate.

The first two decades of the sixteenth century saw a number of disputes over property and claims to wardship in the counties of Lancashire and Cheshire between the earl of Derby and Sir Thomas Butler of Warrington. Butler on more than one occasion claimed that he could obtain no justice either at the local assizes or at the duchy of Lancaster's courts, because the earl 'was and is of such strength and power in the said county'.[1] He therefore wished his complaints to be considered before the Council in Star Chamber. There was probably something in Butler's claim, though given the importance of his own family he probably exaggerated the Derby influence in order to justify his appeal to Star Chamber. The advantage of doing this was not necessarily just to receive a fair trial, but a trial which would be better able to take into account that along with the strictly legal issues involved there was also a conflict between two leading families. To resolve such a conflict compromises would have to be made, to secure which both the procedures and the prestige provided by the Council in Star Chamber would be useful. One would like to add to these advantages Wolsey's chairmanship of the proceedings, but if this ever did come into Butler's calculations it cannot have been the chief attraction, because he first brought his troubles to the Council long before Wolsey became lord chancellor.[2] What has survived, though, is a letter from Derby to Wolsey, probably written in January 1521, in which he refers to another dispute that came before Star Chamber, this time with tenants from his lordship of Holland.[3] Here the tenants seem to have won, despite the fact that it was admitted by the Crown 'that the said earl by the rigour of the common law might put the said tenants from the said leases and liberties without any offence doing to the said law'.[4]

Would Derby have given way to his tenants without the intervention of Wolsey and the Council in Star Chamber, and, by extension, would there have been any hope of a settlement with Butler without such intervention? It may not be beside the point that Derby was heavily in debt to the Crown, and by an agreement renewed in 1517 had been forced to set aside the revenues of certain of his manors for the repayment of his debt.[5] Consequently, Derby may well have been anxious to

[1] PRO STAC 2/19/372.
[2] Ibid; LP,iii,1923. For a comprehensive treatment of these disputes see Coward, p.116.
[3] LP,iii,1923 (i).
[4] PRO E 315/313 A, quoted in Wolfe, pp.192-3.
[5] Coward, pp.147-8.

please the Crown in the hope that some of the debt might be cancelled. And in his letter to Wolsey he did express the hope that 'by your good mediation and my reasonable petition and consideration seen afore your grace I doubt not that I shall have some favour at the King's hand and yours'.[1]

Disputes between leading families were not infrequently brought before Star Chamber. In Wolsey's time the peace of Leicestershire was disturbed by rivalry between Thomas marquess of Dorset on the one hand and Lord Hastings and his relative by marriage, Sir Richard Sacheverell, on the other. In 1516 all three appeared in Star Chamber to be examined about their illegal retaining and this was followed by charges being brought against them in King's Bench. Despite this, in 1525 Sacheverell turned up at the Leicestershire assizes 'with such a company that he ruleth the whole court', and that this was not merely a partial view is suggested by the fact that the two judges presiding over the assize, Sir Robert Brudenell and Sir Anthony Fitzherbert, felt compelled to order him and his followers to leave. Sacheverell's behaviour on this occasion led Dorset to file an 'information' against him, thereby suggesting that Sacheverell was guilty of a wrong done to the Crown rather than to himself, for such a procedure was more usually used by the Crown. However, one suspects that Sacheverell's effort during the preceding years to 'use himself in manner of comparison with the lord marquess' may have had a good deal to do with Dorset's action. In 1527 it was the turn of Lord Hastings, for in that year his dispute with Dorset over the exercising of certain offices in the county was brought before Star Chamber and then submitted to arbitration.[2]

Kent was another county whose whose leading families' rivalries came to the attention of Wolsey and the Council. Most prominent was that between the Nevilles, led by Lord Bergavenny, and the Guildfords, and in 1516 Bergavenny was accused, not for the first time, of illegal retaining, and suffered the same fate as Dorset, Hastings and Sacheverell.[3] There is no evidence to suggest any great rivalry between two other predominantly Kentish families, the Boleyns and the Wyatts, but given their close relationship with the king, it is perhaps not surprising to find that in February 1528 Thomas Boleyn, recently created Viscount Rochford, and Sir Henry Wyatt treasurer of the chamber, promised Wolsey in Star Chamber that they would abide by the decision of the two chief justices and chief baron of the Exchequer in a dispute over property.[4]

At about the same time a much more serious dispute over property mainly in Lincolnshire, but also in Norfolk and Suffolk, was brewing. It concerned the inheritance of Lord Willoughby, who died in 1526, and the leading protagonists were Lord Willoughby's brother and male heir, Sir Christopher Willoughby, on the one hand, and Lord Willoughby's second wife and their daughter Katherine on the other. What made the conflict especially difficult to resolve was the support that the two women received from the duke of Suffolk. In 1527 he had secured the wardship of the daugter, with the obvious intention of getting his hands on the Willoughby inheritance, thereby establishing himself as a dominant figure in Lincolnshire. The

[1] LP,iii,1923 (i).
[2] Guy, Cardinal's Court, pp.60-1,99.
[3] Ibid, p.31; PRO STAC 2/19/372 for Sir Edward Guildford's report on Bergavenny's retaining; for more on Bergavenny see pp.185-7 below.
[4] LP,iv,3926.

matter was complicated in law because Lord Willoughby had contrived in 1512 to settle half his estate on Sir Christopher, but then, following his second marriage, he had bequeathed the whole of it, including the lands already promised to his brother, to Katherine. What, however, complicated it even more were the personalities and positions of those involved. At one point Sir Christopher decided to take the law into his own hands by making a forcible entry, despite a previous order from Wolsey and the Council not to, into one of the disputed manors – Eresby in Lincolnshire. As a consequence, Suffolk and Lady Willoughby brought a bill of complaint against him before Star Chamber.[1] Wolsey was only involved with the beginnings of this dispute, which seems to have led to genuine disturbances of the peace and was to continue through most of the 1530s.[2] Sir Thomas More, after succeeding Wolsey as lord chancellor, was to make an attempt to settle the matter, but with no real success.[3] This may serve as a reminder that the lord chancellor and his fellow councillors were often unsuccessful in putting an end to major disputes between leading families. At the same time, it is easy to see why they offered the best hope for a solution: they had great authority, they could command the best legal expertise available, and in Wolsey they had a man who, if his conduct of foreign policy is anything to go by, was a past master at just the kind of negotiations that any successful solution would entail. The great sadness is that the documents do not really allow for any proper evaluation of Wolsey's personal contribution to any particular case, with perhaps the exception of that which involved the prior of Norwich and the City Fathers.

This was the kind of dispute that was all too common in the later Middle Ages, arising as it did out of competing claims to jurisdiction over a particular area between secular and religious bodies, but the problems of Norwich do appear to have been especially intractable.[4] They had defeated the effort of Wolsey's predecessor, Warham, to solve them, and in fact conflict between the church and the city had been intermittent since at least the 1420s. What was in dispute was the prior's jurisdiction both over an area of the city called Tombland, including the fairs that were held there, and over land outside the city owned by the priory but to which the citizens of Norwich had rights of commons. Wolsey's settlement involved the Priory surrendering all claims over Tombland, while in return the citizens gave up their rights of commons. In achieving this various other compromises were arrived at. The priory was to be exempt from all tolls within the city, and the citizens were to be given priory land just outside, which, in order to make it viable, had to be drained. Indicative of his personal interest is the fact that this was apparently carried out at Wolsey's expense. The episode involved him in at least one trip to Norwich;[5] in the drawing up of a 'book' in which the conflicting claims

---

[1] See James, *Past and Present*, 48, for an extended treatment, though some of the detail is wrong; for instance Suffolk obtained the wardship in 1527 rather than, as he states, 1529. See also Gunn, *Charles Brandon*, pp.95-6.

[2] PRO STAC 2/2/279; STAC 2/20/400; *LP*,iv,3997, vii,223.

[3] Guy, *More*, pp.59-60, though Guy is surely a little too optimistic about More's achievement.

[4] Guy, *Cardinal's Court*, pp.68-9; *Select Cases in the Council of Henry VII*, p.clxi.

[5] In autumn 1517, on his pilgrimage to St Mary of Walsingham. An eighteenth-century history of Norwich mentions a visit in the company of Catherine of Aragon on 2 March 1520, Blomefield, iii, p.194, but I have not been able to confirm this.

were set out; in an an ultimatum in 1522 to settle the matter within the week or else to submit to a decision imposed by outside commissioners, in drawing up a composition, or agreement, late in 1523, and in a threat of *quo warranto* proceedings in 1524. In August of that year a final agreement was reached, and in 1525 it was incorporated into a new city charter.[1]

Wolsey was instrumental in at least two other similar, though relatively minor, disputes: one between the Charterhouse and the city of Hull concerning an area of the town called the Trippett and a rather more complicated franchise case concerning Bishop's Lynn.[2] In both cases solutions appear to have been found, and although the second did not, it seems, involve the conciliar courts, it illustrates Wolsey's skill at bringing constructive pressure to bear. Here the key seems to have been provided by the use of the *quo warranto* proceedings to challenge the franchisal rights of everyone in Bishop's Lynn, and then to discontinue the proceedings when the parties agreed to settle their differences – a ploy he had also used at one point in his negotiations with the the prior and city of Norwich.

The Norwich episode shows Wolsey at his best,[3] using that same mixture of carrot and stick that was such a feature of his conduct of foreign policy, and without which no agreement would probably ever have been reached. Even so, it took him about seven years from his first visit to the city in the autumn of 1517 to the signing of the final agreement. The case, therefore, illustrates not only his skill, but also the difficulties that he, and indeed any lord chancellor, faced. As in the disputes between leading families, what was involved was not simply a matter for the law – for in law both sides could usually produce a reasonable case – but a conflict of interest, which did not disappear just because a legal decision had been made. What was required was a genuine compromise, one sufficiently satisfactory to both sides as to create a vested interest in maintaining it. This was difficult to achieve, requiring a real mutual desire to settle – which almost by definition was lacking, at least initially – for otherwise there would have been no need to appeal to the lord chancellor. Fortunately, this desire did not have to depend upon goodwill, which was invariably in short supply. Self-interest informed by good legal advice, could bring it about, if only through fear of the consequences of not attempting to settle. It was this that gave Wolsey and his colleagues their chance.

It was, of course, the plaintiff who took the initiative in bringing a dispute to the lord chancellor's attention, and, as we have noted earlier, it has been suggested that Wolsey as lord chancellor was a plaintiff's judge. One reason behind this suggestion is that it would provide an explanation for the increase in business. Believing him to be 'a soft touch', people would have been encouraged to bring to him cases that a stricter lord chancellor would not have entertained. And the result of Wolsey's softness may have been a too high proportion of essentially frivolous or vexatious suits. The suggestion also fits well with a certain view of his character: the self-

---

[1] *Norwich, the Records*, i, pp.cx, 43-4; ii, pp.cxxxvii-ix, 369-71.

[2] I owe the information about Hull to Dr P. Heath. For Bishop's Lynn see Garrett-Goodyear, pp.251-3.

[3] Though not according to John Palsgrave, who in his polemic against Wolsey wrote: 'As for one thing I must needs mislike, that his grace, being chancellor, should take up in manner all the great matters depending in suit in England, . . . and would suffer no way to take effect that had been driven by other men. And hereof to show thee one example, call to mind the matter between the prior of Norwich and the city.' (*LP*,iv, p.2562).

important Wolsey who would find enormous pleasure in the ever-growing number of people appealing to him for help, and the over-confident Wolsey who believed that only he could solve other people's problems. The trouble with both these approaches is that they do not relate very closely to what Wolsey actually did as lord chancellor; and the trouble with what he actually did is that, as has already been suggested, the evidence rarely permits one to evaluate Wolsey's personal contribution to the legal proceedings. Moreover, to attempt to do so requires a considerable degree of expertise in the handling of legal records, and, to complicate the issue further, two people with just such expertise have come up with contradictory answers.

F. Metzger in his study of Wolsey's work in chancery, has emphasized his formal correctness and indeed his genuine effort to deter frivolous or vexatious suits. Wolsey appears to have insisted that the mainpernors who in theory guaranteed that a plaintiff's complaint was genuine, should be real people rather than the fictional Does, Roes and Smith that had been increasingly allowed by his predecessors. He was the first lord chancellor to insist that bills of complaint should be signed by the plaintiff's counsel and countersigned by a master in chancery. He also insisted on the strict rule of proof and was quite willing to refer a case back to the common law court if a plaintiff failed to show sufficient reason why he should not.[1] On the other hand, J.A. Guy has argued that in Star Chamber Wolsey deliberately relaxed the rules to the great advantage of the plaintiff. He appears not to have insisted that the plaintiff produce sureties for the payment of damages to a wronged defendant.[2] He made no effort to scrutinize bills of complaint, as his successor More was to do.[3] He allowed the plaintiff to start the procedure by which the defendant was forced to appear in court before he had filed his bill of complaint, and to alter it right up until the moment the defendant had put in his first appearance, which must have made it that much more difficult for him to prepare his defence.[4]

It would almost seem as if these two historians were writing about different people and, when Guy makes a point of saying that Wolsey in Star Chamber did not insist on bills of complaint being signed by counsel, a procedure which Metzger maintains that Wolsey introduced into Chancery,[5] the non-expert comes near to despair. Of course, one way of explaining the contradictions would be to emphasize the different attitudes of the two courts rather than the personality of a particular lord chancellor – and this approach does seem to offer the best remedy to despair! Chancery, being the older and better established court, took a stricter view of procedural matters than the Council in Star Chamber. As time went by, and inevitably once it became a formal court, stricter procedures were to be introduced into Star Chamber. Meanwhile the flexibility which may have favoured the plaintiff had very little to do with Wolsey, but quite a lot to do with the stage in its evolution that the court had reached. However, more important than any difference between the two institutions is what they shared in common: that concern to listen to the

[1] Metzger, 'Medieval Chancery', pp.80-6.
[2] Guy, *Cardinal's Court*, p.81.
[3] Guy, *More*, pp.89-90.
[4] Guy, *Cardinal's Court*, pp,81-2.
[5] Ibid; Metzger, 'Medieval Chancery', p.81.

complaints of the king's subjects. In this sense they were both plaintiffs' courts, and would have failed in their duty if they had put difficulties in the plaintiff's way, even if this meant that they were sometimes taken for a ride. Put in this context, Wolsey's alleged leniency becomes almost meaningless. The chancellor was there to favour the plaintiff in the initial stages of a case. But, once the case was under way the plaintiff could expect no special treatment. Even the unfriendly Edward Hall considered that Wolsey was severe on perjury 'so that in his time it was less used',[1] and a number of people ended up in Westminster Hall with papers on their heads declaring them to be perjurers.[2] Of course, not all perjurers were plaintiffs, but if Wolsey was known to be severe on perjurers it must have at least deterred plaintiffs from making false complaints.

Someone who was both a plaintiff and, insofar as she deliberately based her case in Star Chamber on a forger's evidence, a perjurer was Joan Staunton. Her suit, over land in Kidlington Oxon, can be seen as just of that frivolous and vexatious kind that Wolsey's leniency attracted,[3] because it would appear that she had no case to make – and certainly it led the acting clerk of the council, Sir Thomas Elyot, to wonder how Wolsey and his colleague might be spared the barking of such a bitch.[4] However, Wolsey's contemptuous dismissal of her case and the fact that the perjurer was condemned to spend a whole day in a pillory suspended by her ears, hardly supports the view of the over-lenient lord chancellor. Moreover, it must always have been the case that until the evidence had been presented in court and, for instance, in Joan Staunton's case, it was shown that vital documents had been forged, it was very difficult to be certain whether a suit was merely frivolous and vexatious. This being so, such suits are an inevitable part of any legal system. It is not known whether the defendant to Joan Staunton's suit received any costs or damages, but probably he did. A defendant in another case was awarded 6s for being forced to appear in court without sufficient cause being laid against him,[5] and this was not a unique occurrence. Indeed, whatever the nature of his complaint, a plaintiff always risked the possibility of having to pay costs, and this must have acted as some deterrent to the wilful misuse of the conciliar courts.[6]

According to Hall, there was a class of litigant that Wolsey did go out of his way to encourage: 'The poor men perceived that he punished the rich, then they complained without number, and brought many an honest man to trouble and vexation.'[7] It is not necessary, of course, to take Hall's rather jaundiced view of a chancellor who went out of his way to encourage the poor to bring their cases before him. The real difficulty is to decide whether the proposition is true. It does receive some support, though, from the fact that by three orders of 1517, 1518 and 1520 Wolsey felt compelled to set up 'under-courts' sitting in Westminster specifically to

---

[1] Hall, p.585.

[2] BL Lansdowne 639, fos.46v, 47v, 48v, 54v. Thomas Palys, Thomas Leke, John Caunton and William Gibbs respectively.

[3] For Guy the moment (April 1529) when 'disillusionment probably hit its peak'. (Guy, Cardinal's Court, pp.125-6).

[4] For Elyot's comments on the dorse of Joan Staunton's bill of complaint see PRO STAC 10/4 pt.2/355.

[5] BL Lansdowne 639, fo.16v.

[6] Guy, Cardinal's Court, pp.63-4.

[7] Hall, p.585.

hear poor men's causes, for this does suggest that there were too many cases to be dealt with by the existing machinery.[1] In 1520 these under-courts emerged in the more formal shape of the 'king's most honourable Council in his Court of Requests', and though the personnel changed, this embryo court of requests remained in being for the rest of Wolsey's period as chancellor. At the same time litigants could still bring their complaints before two councillors specially appointed to attend upon the king, and these two may have provided the poor with additional access to conciliar jurisdiction. There is, thus, no doubt that concern was shown for the special needs of the poor. What is more difficult to decide is just how poor the 'poor' were, and how far Wolsey was responsible for any increasing concern for their affairs during his period of office. There must have been some kind of yardstick by which to judge the poverty of a litigant, for in a case in 1519 the Council decided that the plaintiff was a gentleman with sufficient income to make use of the common law courts.[2] However, what that yardstick was is not known, and by and large historians have been reluctant to allow that the poor really benefited. For Wolsey's period Guy has come across only three litigants, out of a total of 1,268 whose social origins he has been able to discover, who were allowed to sue as paupers;[3] but as the bulk of the records for poor men's causes have either not survived, or have not been fully sorted, too much cannot be made of these figures.[4] What is of some interest is Guy's finding that of the 753 plaintiffs whose social origins are known, 245 were either yeomen, craftsmen or labourers.[5] Admittedly the great majority of these belonged to the first category,[6] which would undoubtedly have included some quite wealthy people, but that over 30 per cent came from such categories is some evidence for a special concern for the less powerful.

Direct evidence for Wolsey's concern for poor men's causes can be found in the detailed instructions drawn up for the reconstructed Council in the Marches of Wales in 1525, in which it was stated that the Council was to publicize the fact that the complaints of the poor and disadvantaged would be very much its concern. Their cases would always be considered first so as to save them as much inconvenience as possible, and, moreover, they were to be given free legal advice.[7] The more general provision of free legal advice for the poor was something that the Venetian ambassador, Giustinian, specifically mentioned in his final report to the Venetian Senate in 1519, and in other ways, too, he praised Wolsey's treatment of their cases: he had 'the reputation of being extremely just: he favours the people exceedingly, and especially the poor; hearing their suits, and seeking to despatch them instantly; he also makes the lawyers plead gratis for all paupers.'[8] Enough has already been said about the dangers of taking ambassadorial comments at their face value to deter us from relying too heavily on Giustinian's favourable assessment, but there seems no reason for him to have written in this way unless he was at least

[1] Guy, *Cardinal's Court*, pp.40-5.
[2] Ibid, p.154,n.110.
[3] Ibid, p.109.
[4] Ibid, p.154,n.103.
[5] Ibid, p.109.
[6] 191 out of 245.
[7] BL. Vitellius C i, fos.13v, 16, summarized in Skeel, pp.49-51.
[8] Rawdon Brown, ii, p.314 (*LP*,iii,402).

reflecting a commonly held view. But, as so often, a word of caution must be introduced. Conciliar concern for poor men's causes was no innovation of Wolsey's. It was inherent in the notion that all the king's subjects, irrespective of rank or condition, could appeal to him for justice; and from at least the early fifteenth century, when statutory provision had been made for free legal assistance, it had been realized that to make this notion a reality some practical help would have to be provided.[1] As recently as 1495 an Act had been passed that entitled poor people, at the direction of the chancellor, not only to free legal advice but also to free legal writs.[2] Wolsey may have used his discretionary powers more widely than some of his predecessors, but in showing a concern for the poor he was merely continuing and building upon their work.

On 17 July 1517 Wolsey and the Council considered two cases concerning a certain John Cole.[3] In the first they decided that Cole's cattle had been wrongfully detained, and that not only should they be returned but he should be awarded 20 marks in costs. The second case was more difficult. One Roger Langford maintained that Cole had stolen two of his oxen. This Cole denied, arguing that confusion had arisen from the fact that two out of twenty oxen he had purchased happened to be the same colour as Langford's. Wolsey and his colleagues felt that there was no way of proving that the two oxen were Langford's, but that Cole was partly responsible for the dispute because of his refusal to allow Langford to inspect them at the time that Cole had made the purchase. The Council, therefore, came to a decision worthy of Solomon, awarding one ox to Langford and allowing Cole to keep the other, while both were to pay their own costs. There is no suggestion that the Council thought that either case was frivolous or vexatious: these were genuine disputes which one has to presume the local courts had failed to resolve. One cannot fail to be impressed at the time and trouble taken over them, and that this happened in such cases can only have increased the king's subjects' confidence in royal justice and thus contributed to good government. But was it cost-effective? Should the Crown's leading councillors have concerned themselves with such trivial matters? If they were dragged in every time an ox was stolen, then conciliar jurisdiction would grind to a halt. In fact this did not happen. It has been estimated that during Wolsey's time the average length of litigation in Chancery was twenty months, a considerably shorter time than in Elizabeth's reign, and for Star Chamber about a year.[4] Neither figure suggests that the system was not coping, even if the pressure of business, in Star Chamber at least, was creating problems which Wolsey's delegation of suits either to the localities or to under-courts at Westminster was not entirely solving. If business continued to increase, a greater formality would have to be introduced. This was to happen in the 1530s, but insofar as flexibility had been one of the chief attractions of conciliar jurisdiction, the changes were not all to the good.

[1] Baldwin, pp.276-7.
[2] 11 Henry VII c.12.
[3] BL Lansdowne 639, fos.52v-3.
[4] Metzger, 'Medieval Chancery', p.81; Guy, *Cardinal's Court*, p.113; and for scepticism about the claim that More was able to clear the enormous backlog of cases that had built up under Wolsey, see Guy, *More*, p.92.

Something that might have helped to relieve the pressure on the conciliar courts would have been a greater confidence amongst litigants in the workings of the common law courts, and arguably this was a matter Wolsey should have shown more concern for. Indeed a frequent criticism has been that he deliberately set out to sabotage the common law.[1] Recent research has gone a long way to answer this criticism.[2] It has been shown that leading common lawyers were closely involved in the workings of the conciliar court. This was especially true of Star Chamber, much of whose judicial work was carried out by the judges prominent amongst whom was the chief justice of King's Bench from 1495 to 1525, Sir John Fineux, whose great contribution to the reform of the common law is only now beginning to be appreciated.[3] And it was the common lawyers who were advising their clients to take their cases to Chancery and Star Chamber, and appearing there on their behalf. At the same time it is clear that Wolsey was quite prepared to return cases to the common law courts, especially in what one might call criminal matters. The people involved, such as the noblemen had up for illegal retaining in 1516, or Sir John Savage who in the same year was implicated in the murder of a Gloucestershire justice of the peace, might initially appear in Star Chamber, but their cases were actually tried in King's Bench. One of the things that Wolsey was to be accused of in 1529 was the increase in injunctions,[4] whereby common law courts were prevented from taking any action while the chancellor was considering the case, but it has proved impossible to find evidence for this. Ironically, it was the common lawyer, More, who as chancellor came into conflict with the judges over his use of injunctions – though in his view it was the judges who were at fault by failing to use their own discretion to mitigate the rigours of the common law.[5]

At a more personal level, there is no evidence at all of a concerted hostility to Wolsey amongst leading common lawyers. True, he did show some 'dexterity' in persuading Lewis Pollard, a justice of Common Pleas, of the legality of the 1522 loan,[6] and he did clash with Sir Anthony Fitzherbert, another justice of Common Pleas, over the question of probate jurisdiction in York, though whether he or Fitzherbert was in the right it is impossible to say.[7] But there is certainly no evidence that Wolsey ever conducted any vendetta against Fitzherbert, whom he had personally installed as a justice of Common Pleas, calling upon him 'to minister justice indifferently to rich and poor and not to have a peakish heart but fortitude in all his judgments'.[8] Fitzherbert seems to have been one of the more active justices of Wolsey's time, being especially involved in Northern affairs, and in 1524 was a

---

[1] Such a view underlies Pollard's treatment of Wolsey's legal work (A.F. Pollard, pp.59-98), but see *inter alia*, Baker, ii, pp.77-80. It really derives from Maitland's argument that the existence of the common law was at this time under serious threat from Roman law and equity; for a discussion of which, see ibid, ii, pp.24ff.

[2] For what follows see Guy, *Cardinal's Court*, pp.29, 65, 131; *More*, pp.40-9; Metzger, 'Medieval Chancery', pp.83-9.

[3] Baker, ii, pp.53ff.

[4] Art. 21 (*LP*,iv,6075).

[5] Guy, *More*, pp.86-9.

[6] *LP*,iii,2393 Sir Richard Wingfield to Wolsey, 17 July 1522.

[7] Wolsey's treatment of Fitzherbert comprised art.31 of the accusations brought against him in 1529 (*LP*,iv,6075).

[8] Quoted in Boersma, p.6.

member of an important commission to Ireland. It is true that he never became a chief justice, but any opportunities for doing so occurred after Wolsey's fall anyway.[1] All in all, Wolsey's alleged 'rebuke' to Fitzherbert appears to have been an isolated incident, and should not be used to support any general theory of strong antagonism between Wolsey and the common lawyers. Furthermore, if the argument presented here, that the main feature of Wolsey's chancellorship was continuity rather than innovation, is correct, then any sustained attack by him on the working of the common law is ruled out. For, as St German pointed out in his many works on conciliar jurisdiction written at this time, the two systems of law – the chancellor's and the common lawyer's – had co-existed for many years and necessarily complemented one another.[2]

Nevertheless it would be misleading to suggest that there was no worry expressed in Wolsey's time at the increasing role of the chancellor's 'conscience' in judicial matters and the possible threat that this posed to the common law. The mere fact that St German felt it necessary to defend the chancellor is evidence to the contrary, even if legal historians have recently tended to argue that any anxieties on this score were ill-founded.[3] It now seems clear that there was never any separate corpus of conciliar law deriving from Roman and civil law, but that conciliar judgments were based upon the common law, if approaching it from a rather different perspective from that of the common law courts. The chancellor's task was to complement the common law by providing particular remedies in cases where the common law's intentions were defeated, either by the particularities of the case in question or by the refusal of the common law courts to take cognizance of new areas of litigation.[4] A lot would depend on how many new areas there were and how frequently particular remedies, or, looking at it from another standpoint, worrying exceptions to the existing law were made. Too many new areas or too many exceptions would undermine the common law even if there was no positive determination by any chancellor to do so – and one person at least, the anonymous author of A Replication of a Sergeant at the Laws of England, writing in answer to St German's first dialogue of his Doctor and Student, thought that this was what was happening in the 1520s. The consequence, according to the 'sergeant', was legal chaos, for 'if the subject of any realm shall be compelled to leave the law of the realm, and to be ordered by the discretion of one man, what thing may be more unknown or more uncertain?'[5] But one 'replication' does not make a summer, and there is no reason to suppose that this attack on the chancellor's 'conscience' was typical of the views of the legal profession;[6] indeed, the fact that so many of its members were deeply involved in the workings of the conciliar courts suggests quite the opposite. However, even St German was worried that the notion of 'conscience', if too widely interpreted, might be used to subvert the common law. A

---

[1] Boersma, p.8.

[2] See especially his 'A Little Treatise concerning Writs of Subpoena' in Hargrave, pp.332 ff.

[3] See Guy, Christopher St German, pp.81, 94; also Guy, More, pp.42-9; Baker, ii, pp.24ff., St German, Doctor and Student.

[4] Metzger, 'Medieval Chancery', pp.83ff.

[5] Hargrave, p.325.

[6] If the 'sergeant' was an unsuccessful lawyer, his attack could be attributed to sour grapes, but recently the future lord chancellor Thomas Audley has been suggested; see Baker, ii, 198-200.

writ of subpoena, used by the conciliar courts to summon people before them, should not, he argued, lie against statute, or against the maxims of the common law. He was also strongly against Chancery attempting to review decisions already taken in the common law courts, something that Wolsey would be accused of doing in the articles laid against him in 1529.[1] There is no real evidence to suggest that he did, but when in that dispute between the earl of Derby and his tenants already referred to he defended the latter's position while admitting that the earl 'by the rigour of the common law' was technically in the right, he was coming very near to doing so.[2] Moreover, along with the theoretical worries expressed by both the 'sergeant' and St German, real disputes were taking place between the two jurisdictions – such as More's with the judges over his use of injunctions and the even more serious one of 1482 in which Chief Justice Huse in consultation with his fellow justices took the view that an injunction against a plaintiff in a common law suit was not enforceable.[3] Furthermore, the very development of the notion of 'conscience' in the second half of the fifteenth century is evidence of an awareness of the potential for conflict and of the need to develop a defence against attack by the common lawyers.

All in all, there seems little point in denying that there was a problem, but it was one that probably had little to do with the intentions of any particular lord chancellor and a good deal to do with the preferences of litigants and their legal advisers. No one was forcing them to make use of Chancery and Star Chamber, except perhaps the common law courts. If these refused to deal with matters that litigants thought important, or to alter their procedures, then they had only themselves to blame if people were increasingly ignoring them.

In fact, rather more was being done to reform the common law during the early sixteenth century than has sometimes been allowed for, especially in King's Bench. Important procedural changes involving the use of the fictitious bill of Middlesex and the writ of *latitat* were being developed, and by the action of assumpsit the common law was moving into areas such as defamation and the enforcement of promises of all kinds, including failure to pay debts, which previously it had been reluctant to consider. Probably the real breakthrough did not occur until the early 1540s, by which time the cost of these new procedures had fallen considerably, permitting business in King's Bench to begin to recover.[4] And it was not until the second half of the century that the common law courts were willing to concern themselves with another growth area, copyhold tenure.[5] Of course, given the conservatism of the legal profession at any period, it takes time for new procedures to be recognized. Going to law is risky enough without attempting to introduce innovations, which may be successfully challenged by one's opponents. People require some degree of certainty concerning the workings of the law before they can be expected to make use of it, and it is probable that more injustice would result from too much change than actually results from too little. Historians have, perhaps, a tendency to overlook this, and are consequently overcritical of the time

---

[1] Art.10 (*LP*,iv,6075).
[2] PRO E 315/313 A, fo.43v, transcribed in Wolfe, p.192.
[3] Blatcher, pp.4-5.
[4] Ibid, pp.111-37; Baker,ii, pp.*51-61, 220-98*.
[5] Baker,ii, pp.*184-7*.

it takes for changes in the law to take place. Chief Justice Fineux, for example, was clearly a great reforming and interventionist judge, but if the profession would not follow him – and many innovations, such as the bill of Middlesex, had been available for many years before they were widely used – there was little he, or the lord chancellor, could do. Precisely because this is a question of usage, reform is unlikely to be achieved by any fiat from on high. And when governments have tried to hurry lawyers along, the lawyers have usually been quite successful in resisting.[1]

Given Wolsey's responsibility for the administration of justice and his enthusiasm for tackling any problem that came his way it is a little surprising that only one reference to his concern for law reform has survived; and since it appears in a letter to Wolsey from one of the least endearing of Tudor personalities, the future lord chancellor and betrayer of Thomas More, Richard Rich, it is difficult to attach much weight to it.[2] What can be said is that Wolsey made no effort to resist any of the changes that were taking place; indeed, he may even have been sympathetic, which is more than can be said for many of the common lawyers. But whatever his personal views, he had no intention of battling with the common lawyers in order to bring them about. Late in 1522, or early 1523, considerable worries were expressed about judgments being made by John Stokesley, deputed to be sole judge in certain conciliar cases. The precise nature of these worries is not clear, but they appear to have had to do with his giving judgments in property cases. It may be that some common lawyers saw this as a raid on their own preserve – though, as we have seen, many property cases were appearing in the conciliar courts, and with their connivance. They may also have been worried that he was departing too far from common law precedents. But whatever the nature of the anxiety, Wolsey responded by setting up a high powered commission of inquiry, consisting entirely of trained common lawyers and including the chief baron of the Exchequer and two justices of Common Pleas.[3] Their task was to 'examine such cases as Mr Stokesley hath given judgement in the White Hall, and to make report whether they be allowable or not'. Their decision appears to have been that they were not, for shortly afterwards Stokesley was removed from the Council.[4] It was a minor victory for the common law, and one that was made possible by Wolsey's intervention – further proof that he was never its inveterate enemy.

There can be no doubt that Wolsey was an extremely active lord chancellor, who used that office's existing machinery to the full. In the process he may have further increased the popularity of Chancery and Star Chamber, and in doing so may also have focused attention on the differences in procedure and attitude between the conciliar and common law courts, raising some worries that the former's might swamp the latter's. But far from this being deliberate, he took the view – and it was almost certainly the majority view – that the two systems were necessary and

[1] A rather topical subject, but see Cromwell's unsuccessful attempt to introduce land registration in the 1530s (Elton, *Reform and Renewal*, pp.144-9).

[2] *LP*,iv,4937 a letter of Nov. 1528 in which Rich expressed a wish to present his own ideas on legal reform.

[3] One of the chief justices being Fitzherbert. More was one of the common lawyers on the commission, for a complete list of which, see Guy, *Cardinal's Court*, p.45.

[4] BL Lansdowne 639, fo.56v.

complementary. After his fall in October 1529 the king was to ask him, apparently on the advice of his judges and learned counsel, to surrender York Place, the London residence of the archbishops of York. Wolsey argued that no individual archbishop had the right to surrender something that belonged to the office rather than to the man. In doing so, he took the opportunity to warn Henry's councillors

> to put no more [into Henry's head] than the law may stand with good conscience, for when you tell him 'this is the law' it were well done you should tell him also that 'although this be the law, yet this is conscience'. For law without conscience is not good to be given unto a king in counsel for a lawful right, but always to have a respect to conscience before the rigour of the common law . . . Therefore, in his royal place of equal justice [the king] hath constituted a chancellor, an officer to execute justice with clemency where conscience is oppressed by the rigour of the law. And therefore the court of Chancery hath been heretofore commonly called the Court of Conscience because it had jurisdiction to command the high ministers of the common law to spare execution and judgement where conscience hath most effect.[1]

The circumstances may suggest special pleading on Wolsey's part, but his words carry conviction. They also provide a succinct account of the history and role of the lord chancellor that could hardly be bettered. It was a role that Wolsey performed with distinction.

One aspect of the lord chancellor's role not mentioned here by Wolsey was his special responsibilities for law enforcement. Many of these responsibilities – and they were perhaps especially associated with supervising the work of the justices of the peace – he had acquired in the fifteenth century. By an Act of 1429 JPs were instructed to inform the chancellor of anyone suspected of taking part in a riot, unlawful assembly, insurrection or any similar offence who, in order to escape arrest, had fled into another county. An Act of 1439, which laid down certain property qualifications for JPs, also gave discretionary powers to the chancellor to appoint anyone whom he considered suitable for the office, irrespective of the property qualifications if there were not sufficient people who possessed them. An Act of 1487 laid down that the chancellor should act as a final court of appeal for any complaints against JPs.[2] This association between chancellor and JPs probably only reflects the growing importance of the latter office during the fifteenth century, but it does illustrate the kind of supervisory role that the chancellor was expected to play over the whole range of judicial machinery. Also included here would have been the sheriffs, assize judges and the great number of extraordinary commissioners set up to deal with particular problems. Of course, the king's involvement in all aspects was also substantial. It would appear, for instance, that he personally chose the sheriff for each county from a list of three drawn up by the chancellor, and he would no doubt have had views about all other appointments,[3] even if the donkey work was done by the chancellor and his officials. It must also be true that, insofar as

---

[1] Cavendish, p.117.

[2] Pronay, pp.97-99.

[3] See *inter alia* Henry's concern to to appoint a successor to Compton as sheriff of Worcestershire in 1528 (*LP*, iv, 4476); for his close interest in the commissioners for the general proscription see Goring, *EHR*, lxxxvi, p.685.

the maintenance of law and order depended to a great extent upon the political stability of the regime, the personality and effectiveness of the king had to be of the utmost importance, however little he involved himself in the day to day detail of law enforcement. Political stability was not a problem under Henry VIII, or at least not until the 1530s when the divorce and ensuing 'break with Rome' imposed considerable strains. However, unlike Edward IV who personally sat on a number of local commissions, Henry VIII saved himself for the exceptional cases, such as that against Buckingham in early 1521 where he personally examined the chief witnesses, and he did make those few rather stage-managed appearances in Star Chamber which have already been mentioned.

At the heart of Wolsey's law enforcement policy was what he called 'the indifferent ministrations of justice to all persons as well high as low', and it was in Star Chamber that it was most publicly put into effect. The high and mighty were indeed made to appear there. The earl of Northumberland did so in May 1516, and in the same year the marquess of Dorset, Lord Bergavenny, Lord Hastings and Sir Richard Sacheverell, as we have seen; in 1517 it was the turn of Thomas Pygot, serjeant-at-law, and Sir Andrew Windsor, keeper of the great wardrobe, summoned because of an affray between their servants; the next year Sir Robert Sheffield, a royal councillor who had been Speaker of the House of Commons in Henry VIII's second parliament; in 1519 Lord Edward Howard and two other Surrey JPs and Sir William Bulmer, a prominent royal official in the North of England, who, as we noted earlier, was forced to appear for wearing the livery of the duke of Buckingham. In 1524 and 1525 two other important Northern figures, Sir Robert Constable and Thomas Dacre, appeared.[1] A list of other prominent men who at some time or other found themselves before Wolsey would include Sir William Brereton, Sir William Compton, Sir Henry Grey, Sir John Hussey and Sir Christopher Willoughby. Most of these men were royal councillors, and at least two, the marquess of Dorset and Sir William Compton, were personally close to the king. All, in one way or another, were taught 'the law of Star Chamber, that they shall beware how from thenceforth they shall redress their matter with their hands' – Wolsey's words when, in a letter of August 1517, he informed Henry of the affray between Pygot's and Sir Andrew's servants. Later in the same letter, he made his famous reference to 'the new law of Star Chamber'.[2] There was in fact no such thing, but what it presumably reflected was a new determination on his part to ensure that the laws were enforced, irrespective of who broke them.

It has recently been shown that there were only nine official prosecutions in Star Chamber during Wolsey's chancellorship,[3] which, given his public pronouncements on the many 'enormities usually exercised in this his Realm',[4] might seem a disappointingly low figure, suggesting, perhaps, that he was all talk and no action. In fact, the figures mislead. Tudor government relied very heavily, even in what might be considered criminal matters, on private initiatives, which it could and did encourage, for instance by making public its willingness to act. This

---

[1] For all these appearances see Guy, *Cardinal's Court*, pp.30-5, 72-8, 121-3.
[2] LP,ii, app.38.
[3] Guy, *Cardinal's Court*, pp.72-8.
[4] Guy, *Cardinal's Court*, p.30.

could be done by using the JPs or assize judges as its mouthpieces, by issuing proclamations, or by setting up special commissions to hear complaints. But in the end it was up to the private individual to respond. Though not an official prosecution, any resulting case was very much to do with law enforcement. A good example would be a suit brought by one Alice Swettenham, initially against John and George Cotton and others for the murder of her husband, and subsequently, in conjunction with her father-in-law, against Sir William Brereton and others for the 'maintaining and comforting' of the murderers. Her husband had been hit while playing bowls 'so that his brain came forth before and behind his head'. Not surprisingly, he never regained consciousness and was dead within a quarter of an hour.[1] Wolsey and the Council may have had some sympathy for the widow, but it was the involvement of John Fitton and Thomas Bulkely, and above all Brereton, that concerned them most. These people, so the Swettenhams maintained, were 'so kindred and allied, and so many belong unto them' within the county of Chester, that they had successfully prevented the Swettenhams from obtaining justice there – hence their appeal to Wolsey and the Council.[2] In allegedly helping the murderers to escape arrest, the three had allowed the man who had delivered the fatal blow, a servant of Brereton's, to escape to a sanctuary at Knowle church in Warwickshire, while a relation of Brereton's had released from prison, 'without any authority of the law',[3] another who had taken part in the fatal assault. Wolsey and the Council went to considerable lengths to discover all the facts: a special commission was sent to Knowle to examine the murderers,[4] while Wolsey himself on two occasions in 1518 examined Brereton, who was put to the considerable expense and inconvenience of appearing each day in Star Chamber during the lengthy investigations.[5] The Council's conclusion was that Brereton had been guilty of 'comforting' felons, and as a result in November 1518 he was fined 500 marks, to be paid in twice yearly instalments of 50 marks; if he defaulted part of his estates would become the property of the Crown.[6]

The fact that the comparatively humble Swettenhams could not only take on the Breretons, a leading Cheshire family and moreover one with court connections,[7] but actually win, reflects well on early Tudor justice, and in particular on Wolsey's administration of it. It may be that the Swettenhams had been encouraged to bring their complaint to the Council by Wolsey's various orations on the subject of law enforcement, and certainly his handling of their complaints would have provided clear evidence that he had meant what he said. However, Wolsey did not confine his activity to speeches, or indeed to merely responding to private initiatives. In October 1518 the assize judges were required to report to the Council all those who had seriously offended against justice, 'that is to say, who be retainers or oppressors, or maintainers of wrongful causes, or otherwise misbehaved

---

[1] *Lancashire and Cheshire Cases in Star Chamber*, p.20.

[2] Ibid, p.23.

[3] Ibid, p.121.

[4] Ibid, p.21.

[5] Ibid, p.22.

[6] Guy, *Cardinal's Court*, p.116.

[7] For Brereton's career see Ives, *Trans of the Historical Society of Lancashire and Cheshire*, cxxiii, and Ives (ed.), *Letters and Accounts of William Brereton*.

persons'.[1] Early in the following year local inquiries were instituted into the activities of all royal officials concerned with the administration of justice,[2] and any suspected of negligence were to be summoned before the Council and not to be allowed to depart 'until such time as they have made their purgation why they have not done their duties.'[3] In November 1519 detailed instructions were drawn up concerning the duties of the sheriff and his officials.[4] These, along with a revised oath to be sworn by the sheriff on taking office, were to be published. Wolsey appears to have been very anxious personally to acquaint not only the sheriffs but also the JPs with what their duties entailed. In what may have been a new departure, he encouraged the latter to attend each year the swearing-in of the sheriffs, when they could themselves be 'new sworn', and a homily would be read exhorting them to provide 'equal right to the poor and to the rich'.[5] In July 1526 Wolsey summoned an extraordinary meeting of the JPs to which one hundred and ten turned up, and all were required to give written answers to twenty-one articles concerning the prevalence of offences against justice in their localities.[6]

The extent of Wolsey's concern for law and order may have been obscured by the lack of any significant new legislation on the subject during his chancellorship. Instead, he concentrated on personally supervising the local officials, and tactically this was sound. A crooked or merely biased sheriff could still cause considerable harm, albeit a harm limited by his brief tenure of office, which was usually just one year.[7] It was still the sheriff who was responsible for the execution of common law writs, and by delaying them or by making a false return – stating, for instance, that a defendant could not be found in his county – he could make life very difficult for a plaintiff. He was also still responsible for the empanelling of juries, and thus in the best possible position to produce one that was favourable either to his own or someone else's interests.[8] All this made it very important that a close check should be kept on his activities. Similarly, the increasing use made of JPs who were not merely royal officials, but, like Sir William Brereton, leading lights in their locality, and thus in the best possible position to abuse the system made it all the more necessary to supervise their work.

How effective were Wolsey's efforts to encourage a sense of responsibility and service in royal officials? Certainly his activities did sometimes result in their punishment. Perhaps the best example concerns Sir John Savage – like Brereton, a member of a leading Cheshire family, but one which through royal favour had extended its influence throughout the counties adjoining the Welsh border. Amongst the many offices that Savage held was that of sheriff of Worcestershire – most unusually, for life. In June 1516 he was summoned before the Council accused not only of 'negligence' but also of 'cherishing' the murderers of a Gloucestershire JP, John Pauncefote, who earlier in that year had been killed while travelling to

[1] Guy, *Cardinal's Court*, p.33.
[2] BL. Lansdowne 639, fo.54v.
[3] Guy, *Cardinal's Court*, p.33.
[4] Ibid, pp.32-3; *LP*,ii,2579.
[5] Guy, *Cardinal's Court*, p.120.
[6] Ibid.
[7] For instance, Sir John Savage's appointment as sheriff of Worcestershire for life.
[8] *Inter alia* Bellamy, *Crime and Public Order*, pp.13-4, 91-2; Blatcher, pp.63-89.

attend the quarter sessions at Cirencester.[1] Sir John Savage's son, another John Savage, was also fully implicated in the murder, and it was he who, by taking refuge in the Clerkenwell sanctuary of the priory of St John of Jerusalem, turned what was really a rather sordid case of murder into an interesting legal and constitutional matter. This last aspect is not the present concern, though it certainly complicated Wolsey's efforts to teach the Savage family 'the new law of Star Chamber'. In November 1520 Sir John Savage did receive a royal pardon, but only after he had lost all his offices in Gloucestershire and Worcestershire and had agreed to pay a fine of 4,000 marks to the Crown and 1,000 marks to the widow and children of John Pauncefote. The 'pardon' may appear suspiciously lenient – and the whole question of the use made of pardons will be considered later – but what had happened was that a family which had, it emerged, systematically abused their position to further their own interests, even to the extent of involving themselves in the murder of another royal official, had been very severely punished.

Sir John Savage's abuse of his office does seem to have been rather exceptional, and few other royal officials were treated even as harshly as he was. However, he was by no means the only one to be taken to task. Another who was summoned before the Council, in his case for failing to execute a royal writ, was the sheriff of Cumberland, Sir John Ratcliffe.[2] Then in 1519 the activities of three Surrey JPs, Sir Matthew Browne, Sir John A Legh and Lord Edmund Howard, were closely investigated, and in July information against all three was brought by the attorney-general – in itself an unusual procedure – to the effect that 'the good rule and execution of justice in the county of Surrey hath been of long time letted and misused by the great maintenance, embracery and bearing' of the three defendants.[3] Lord Edmund Howard quickly confessed and may have escaped the £100 fine the two others eventually received. Knowledge of their activities may have resulted directly from those local inquiries into the administration of justice that Wolsey had instituted early in 1519. Also probably associated with them is an 'abbreviate of the deposition of certain Justices of the Peace of the county of Lincoln concerning sundry misorders of divers particular persons within the said shire'.[4] Most of these depositions concerned the activities of Sir John Hussey, not only a leading Lincolnshire JP, but also a royal councillor much involved in judicial work at Westminster.[5] It is a little worrying that in the previous year Hussey had been requested not to sit on the Council while the complaint of one Alice Hardiman, that he had protected the murderers of her husband, was investigated.[6] In fact the Council decided that he had not, but

> moved with pity and compassion to the intent the same Alice should cease her exclamations against the same Sir John, have willed the same Sir John to pay to the said Alice six pounds thirteen shillings and four pence for her costs . . . not intending that by the same payment that the said Sir John should be deemed and taken a convict of the said maintenance and bearing, but only of pity and compassion.[7]

[1] Ives, 'Crime, sanctuary, and royal authority', pp. 296 ff.
[2] BL Lansdowne 639, fo. 57v undated, but c. 1523-4.
[3] Guy, Cardinal's Court, p. 73.
[4] PRO STAC 2/26/395.
[5] In 1537 to be executed for his ambiguous role in the Lincolnshire rebellion of the previous year.
[6] BL Lansdowne 639, fo. 47v.

One hopes that this is not another way of saying that Alice was bought off, just as one hopes that the fact that no action appears to have been taken against Hussey following the complaints of 1519 was not because he had too many friends in high places. There is no means of telling,[1] but the mere possibility that there may have been some kind of cover up for someone in the royal favour – and it should be said that there is no evidence that Hussey was especially close to Wolsey – does raise the question of Wolsey's integrity as lord chancellor, especially as regards his work in Star Chamber. Did some people escape punishment there because they were politically important to him, and – which is more usually alleged – were some people punished because they were his enemies?[2]

The great difficulty – one that will also be encountered when the subject of political factions is discussed – is that the evidence almost never gives any hint as to the motivation behind a particular action. This being the case, almost everything depends on one's preconceptions about the way either Wolsey or the political system operated.

As regards Wolsey and Star Chamber, one illuminating test case concerns Sir Robert Sheffield, whose father had been a successful lawyer in Lincolnshire.[3] The father had managed to obtain as Sir Robert's wife a sister of the 2nd earl of Derby, but this marriage into the nobility had not discouraged him from following his father into the law, and from 1495 to 1508 he was recorder of London, usually representing the City in parliament. He was also a royal councillor, and at the beginning of Henry VIII's second parliament in February 1512 he was elected Speaker of the House of Commons, evidence of some royal favour. The following parliament of 1515 was dominated by church matters. As a City MP Sheffield may have been particularly concerned about the mysterious death of his fellow citizen Richard Hunne in the bishop of London's prison, but he was also involved in the much more serious conflict between Church and state arising from the public debate between the abbot of Winchcombe and Friar Standish over benefit of clergy. On this second issue Sheffield appears to have taken an anticlerical stance, and that, according to his own as well as some others' interpretation, was the reason for his subsequent downfall.[4] In any event, after 1515 things began to go so wrong for him that on his death in August 1518, after spending a good part of the previous two and a half years in prison, he owed to the court as the result of a fine the very large sum of 8000 marks (£5,333 6s. 4d.).[5]

How had this happened? Sheffield's explanation, which he had apparently given to the king in person,[6] was that he had been maliciously accused by Wolsey of complicity in a murder merely because of his anticlerical stance in the 1515 parliament. If the explanation were to be accepted, one would have to find Wolsey

---

[7] Ibid.

[1] I think that it is not too naïve to suppose that many complaints against officials, both then and now, are unjustified and, of course, the evidence that there was some investigation may not have survived.

[2] Implicit in much of what Guy has argued; see his *Cardinal's Court*, pp.34, 76-8.

[3] Ibid, pp.76-8; A.F.Pollard, pp.45,52; Roskell, pp.311 ff.

[4] PRO SP 1/16/fo.130 (*LP*,ii,3951) for the contemporary accusation.

[5] *LP*,ii,4616.

[6] *LP*,ii, 3487, 3951.

guilty of a deliberate perversion of justice which, even if justified politically on the grounds that he intended Sheffield's fate to be seen as a warning against laymen attacking the Church, would reflect no credit on him at all. However, there are many reasons for not accepting Sheffield's explanation. First, there is the fact that in the end he admitted that he had consistently lied to the Council and withdrew his allegations against Wolsey.[1] Of course, he may have done this in a last desperate effort to rescue something from a most difficult situation; and it should be said in Sheffield's favour that the chief evidence for his complicity in the murder was provided by the two people who were accused of doing it and who would have had a good motive for placing the blame on someone whom they had reason to believe was not in Wolsey's favour. Thus, though Sheffield's confession should be taken into account, it is not by itself a convincing reason for exonerating Wolsey. The main reason, which relates to a point that has already been made in a different context, is that Wolsey never acted alone in Star Chamber. For instance, when in July 1517 Sheffield was committed to the Tower for 'the complaint he made to the King of my lord cardinal',[2] there were nineteen other councillors present, including the duke of Norfolk and three judges.[3] It is therefore most unlikely that a trumped-up charge could have been brought against Sheffield. For even if one takes the view that his colleagues were all so frightened of Wolsey that they would do whatever he told them, this would not explain why his treatment of Sheffield was not made the basis of one of the many charges brought against him at his downfall. Moreover, it has to be remembered that Sheffield was a sufficiently important man to make his allegations against Wolsey to the king in person. Furthermore, in the conflict between Church and state in 1515 he had taken the king's side. The fact, therefore, that Henry made no effort to intervene on his behalf suggests quite strongly that Henry himself had no doubt about the justification for the action taken by Wolsey against him. Indeed, it looks as if it was immediately after his interview with Henry that Sheffield was brought before the Council for contempt.[4] Finally, much of the motivation for either a personal or a political attack on Sheffield by Wolsey disappears, if the view put forward in chapter 2, that Wolsey was not the leader of the clerical party, is accepted.

Of course, once Sheffield made his allegations against him, Wolsey would have had to take them seriously. It could not have been in the public interest, let alone his own, for an accusation that the lord chancellor of England had perverted the course of justice to have gone unanswered. Once Sheffield began to talk, Wolsey was forced to intervene, but not, as is so often implied, out of a personal desire for revenge. And it is worth pointing out that any attack on Wolsey – whether made by Sheffield or by Thomas Lucas, a solicitor-general under Henry VII, who in 1518 was committed to the Tower for scandalous words against Wolsey,[5] or even by John

---

[1] PRO SP 1/16/fo.143 (LP,ii,3951); PRO STAC 10/4 pt.2/127-32; these two accounts of Sheffield's examinations are virtually identical.

[2] LP,ii,3487 Thomas Allen to Shrewsbury 27 July 1517.

[3] BL Lansdowne 639, fo.49.

[4] LP,ii,3487.

[5] BL. Lansdowne, 637, fo.47. Lucas's quarrel with Wolsey may have had something to do with his running battle with Buckingham in which for the most part he seems to have been the loser and he was not a man to mince his words; for which see Baker, pp.77, 108-9, 244-5.

Roo, a serjeant-at-law committed to the Fleet in 1527 for a masque he had produced at Gray's Inn which Wolsey thought contained a veiled attack on him[1] – was immediately a matter of public concern just because Wolsey was not a private person but the leading royal servant.

If there is, then, good reason for not accepting Sheffield's explanations for his trials and tribulations, another is required, and it might go something like this: the original charge in 1516 of some involvement by Sheffield in a murder – of the kind, for instance, that Sir William Brereton or Sir John Savage was accused of – was genuine, and he was thus rightly fined or at least bound by recognizances.[2] He seems to have been worried that additional charges might be made, for he took the precaution of suing out a pardon in Chancery that covered all possible offences that he might have committed.[3] He also went on to the attack by challenging Wolsey's motives. But the attack boomeranged when the king refused to accept the allegations, and in July 1517 he found himself hauled before the Council and then put in the Tower for having made them. At about the same time further evidence came to light concerning his complicity in the murder. Thus, when in February 1518 he had to face three separate interrogations by Wolsey he found himself in an impossible situation, conceded all the charges, both for the complicity in the murder and for the many personal attacks on Wolsey, and threw himself on the mercy of the king and Council. He was again committed to the Tower, but sometime before his death in August he was fined and then released. The view that he died while still in the Tower,[4] which has previously lent colour to the portrayal of a Wolsey driven by personal animosity, is not sustained by the evidence of his will.[5] That Sheffield was buried in the Austin Friars – which is the only reason so far produced for suggesting that he did die in the Tower, on the grounds that it was commonly used for the burial of those who had died there[6] – turns out to have been his own choice, because his wife was buried there.

In the end, of course, everyone must make their own judgement, and as we have seen, given the difficulties that the evidence presents, people's preconceptions will play a large part in that judgment. But the argument presented here is that Sheffield was no innocent victim of Wolsey's spite, but rather that he was treated with commendable fairness, and that even the fine, though large, was justified.[7]

If this view of Wolsey's treatment of Sheffield is accepted, it becomes very

---

[1] Hall, p.719; A.F.Pollard, p.220,n.3 for Warham believing that Wolsey had over-reacted; see also LP,iv,2854.

[2] PRO E/38/216/fo.176,though the document gives no reason for the fine. But it is most unlikely that it could have had anything to to with a verbal attack on Wolsey, and from the evidence of his examination the verbal attack was merely an aggravating factor (PRO STAC 10/4 pt.2/127-32).

[3] PRO C/66/627, m.17 (LP,ii,2537). The question of whether or not the pardon prevented further action did become an issue in Feb. 1518; Wolsey gave Sheffield considerable time to consider with his counsel whether to stand by it, though indicating that he did not himself think such a course of action was in Sheffield's best interests (PRO STAC 10/4 pt.2/129). On the subject of pardons generally see Blatcher, pp.53 ff, 81-7.

[4] It seems to have derive from A.F. Pollard, p.52 and was followed by Guy in Cardinal's Court, p.78.

[5] PRO PROB 11/19/fo.15.

[6] A.F. Pollard, p.52, n.2.

[7] Cf. Sir John Savage's fine of 5,600 marks to the Crown and an additional 1,000 marks to the widow and children of the murdered man.

difficult to accept the more general charge that Wolsey deliberately used his position as lord chancellor to further his own personal and political interests. It is not the only case that could be used to support the charge: two others that might, one concerning Henry Standish, and the other Thomas lord Dacre, are examined elsewhere.[1] But the Sheffield case is the best, partly because a possible motive is discernible and partly because the allegation of Wolsey's bias was actually made at the time. Although there was no mention of it in any of the accusations made against Wolsey at his fall, there were amongst the articles drawn up at that time three references to personal bias in legal matters, one of which was very personal indeed. Article 38 accused him of committing to the Fleet prison Sir John Stanley until he released a farm which he held of the abbot of Chester, to one Legh of Adlington. And the reason why Wolsey wanted Legh to have the farm, at least according to the article, was that Legh had married one Lark's daughter, 'which woman the said Lord Cardinal kept, and had with her two children'. Poor Stanley was allegedly so upset by Wolsey's treatment of him that 'upon displeasure in his heart, [he] made himself a monk in Westminster, and there died'.[2] No record of the case has been traced, so it is not possible to make any convincing judgment on the validity of the charge. It does, however, seem a little unlikely that Wolsey would have stooped to a deliberate perversion of justice merely to help his mistress's husband, when he was in a position to do so much for him in quite legitimate ways. And to become a monk at Westminster was, to say the least, an idiosyncratic response to the loss of a case in Star Chamber.[3] Nothing is known of the other two cases singled out, the one concerning a disputed lease of parsonage with which Wolsey's newly founded Cardinal College was involved, the other the use of an injunction in favour of Sir George Throckmorton. Three comparatively trivial cases seem a meagre catch for people looking to discredit a fallen minister, and that so little was found is perhaps the best evidence that Wolsey was in no sense a corrupt lord chancellor.[4]

Nevertheless, one apparently worrying aspect of the cases that had to do with law enforcement is that most of the culprits do seem to have escaped comparatively lightly. If Sir William Brereton and Sir John Savage were really guilty of aiding and abetting murderers, was a fine, even if quite a large one, a sufficient punishment? It becomes even more worrying when twenty years after he had been punished in Star Chamber, Brereton was discovered still troubling the peace of Cheshire.[5] Sir John Savage's heavy fine in 1520 did not prevent him and his family from feuding with other local gentry, and on more than one occasion they were back before Wolsey in Star Chamber.[6] The three Surrey JPs in trouble in 1519 were not as a consequence

---

[1] See pp.218-20, 291.

[2] *LP*,iv,6075.

[3] Entry into a religious order in later life by devout laymen who were previously married is a much under-researched subject, but was not uncommon and the evidence of Stanley's will suggests that his reasons for entering Westminster had nothing to do with Wolsey's alleged treatment of him. In drawing up art. 38 it may have helped that Stanley had died the previous year; see B. Harvey, p.387, n.7.

[4] Cf. the greater number of charges against Empson and Dudley (Public Records, app.ii, p.228; also Harrison, *EHR*, lxxxvii).

[5] *LP*,xiii,519.

[6] Ives, 'Crime, sanctuary and royal authority', pp.318-9.

removed from the commission of the peace, and although Sir John Hussey was never found guilty of any of the various offences alleged against him, it is nonetheless a little surprising that he continued to play such an active part in government, both in Lincolnshire and at the Council table.[1] And if all these people were inadequately punished, is it not also true that far too few were made even to answer for their abuse of justice? It has been calculated that 28 cases of some kind of maladministration by an official were brought before Star Chamber in Wolsey's period, to which can be added 44 others which bore directly on the problem of law and order – a grand total of 66 cases out of the 473 brought before Wolsey, for which there is enough evidence to make any classification possible.[2] Even with the admittedly important qualification that it was never Wolsey's intention that Star Chamber should play a major role in criminal jurisdiction, and that when cases were brought there it was his usual practice to transfer them to King's Bench, the number might still appear too few. What had become of all those 'enormities and things misbehaved and murdered within this realm'?

It is easy enough to raise the question, but almost impossible to answer it – though not for lack of evidence. Enough of the records of Wolsey's judicial activities has survived to lead one to suspect that the discovery of more would not alter the general picture. As for the common law courts, all too many records survive, though perhaps because of this they have not been studied in quite the same detail. In any event, one is still left with the insoluable problem of trying to decide what proportion of serious crime was detected; or, to relate this problem to the present context, does the fact that comparatively few cases came to Wolsey's attention merely reflect that very few serious crimes involving the maladministration of justice were committed? One will never know. Even Wolsey's frequent references to 'enormities' are not very helpful. It was the practice of royal government in the late medieval and early modern period to use emotive terms in describing society's ills. Any new law or administrative move was justified as providing a remedy to almost unspeakable evils, but just because the evils are so unspeakable it is difficult to take the government's view as a realistic assessment, especially when the same few evils are so frequently referred to. If things were as bad as royal governments maintained, life would have been intolerable for most people most of the time, and the evidence does not suggest that this was so. Why, then, did royal governments and indeed parliament, use such extreme language? The question has not been much studied.[3] It may in part be a question of style: the English language in the fifteenth and early sixteenth centuries was more colourful and more emotional. It may be that there was a greater need to justify government action of any kind. But perhaps, most obviously, there were advantages in exaggerating the extent of a problem. If, for instance, instead of talking about 'enormities', Wolsey had merely said that it had come to his notice that one or two local officials were a little lax in their enforcement of the law, it would hardly have encouraged anyone to take the problem of law enforcement seriously. Moreover, he did not always speak in such

[1] Especially in the various under courts set up by Wolsey; see Guy, *Cardinal's Court*, pp.38-9, 42.
[2] Ibid, p.53.
[3] See Ives, 'Agaynst taking awaye of Women', p.25 for the suggestion that the Abduction Act of 1487 was not the result of an increase in the number of women being abducted. See also pp.447 below for further comments on early sixteenth-century language.

extreme terms, as a well-known letter of his written to Henry in the autumn of 1517 attests: 'And for your realm, our Lord be thanked, it was never in such tranquility. For all this summer I have had neither of riot, felony, nor forcible entry, but that your laws be in every place indifferently ministered without leaning of any manner.'[1] There is no reason to suppose that Wolsey was deliberately lying, and indeed, since Henry could so easily have checked his assessment, it would have been extremely foolish of him to do so. Rather, what it shows is that both the view taken and the language used depended to a great extent upon one's audience.

My suggestion would be that many historians have failed to take this into account, and have taken the rhetoric of early Tudor pronouncements on law and order at its face value.[2] What may give some support to this are the very facts that are produced to show that law enforcement was an exceptionally difficult problem. It now seems reasonably well established that only between 10 and 30 per cent of all those brought to trial were convicted and, what is more, that the number of defendants who escaped trial by not putting in an appearance was sometimes as high as 80 per cent, and only rarely fell under 50 per cent.[3] The elaborate process by which defendants should have been forced to appear, leading eventually to distraint of goods or outlawing if they failed to respond, had, by the end of the fifteenth century, become very ineffective.[4] However, the vast majority of those defendants who did put in an appearance escaped trial by the payment of money, either as a fine, if they admitted their guilt, or for a pardon. As a result, very few people actually had their cases submitted to a jury and even fewer were found guilty. If, for instance, one combines the figures for the Michaelmas terms of 1488 and 1490, it emerges that of the 112 defendants who appeared only six were actually tried, only three were found guilty, and only one failed in the end to receive a pardon – and as a consequence was executed.[5]

These are remarkable figures, but the conclusion need not be that the system was in total chaos. Indeed, for the figures to have been in one sense so bad – and there is no reason to suppose that those of 1488 and 1499 were untypical – suggests that at the very least the early Tudors had a different perception of what was acceptable, or, perhaps even more importantly, realistic. This is not to say that early Tudor society was more violent than others, or that crime was less easily detectable. Both have been suggested, and some play is frequently made of the fact that there was no police force.[6] Yet the presence of a police force today does not prevent a great many cases going undetected, nor indeed has it put an end to violence. Moreover, there is no good reason to believe that our society is any better than early Tudor society at preventing the rich and the powerful from abusing the

---

[1] LP,ii, app.38, this same letter in which he told Henry of his intention of teaching Thomas Pygot and Sir Andrew Windsor the 'law of Star Chamber'.

[2] The new breed of historians of crime are more cautious and by and large take a far less gloomy view of the prevalence of serious crime; see Sharpe, *Social History*, 7.

[3] Bellamy, *Crime and Public Order*, pp.156-8; Blatcher, pp.50-1, 63-5.

[4] Blatcher, pp.65-8.

[5] Ibid, pp.50-3.

[6] See Stone, pp.199-270 for a classic 'whig' view of a gradual diminishing of aristocratic violence; also C.S.L.Davies, *Peace, Print and Protestantism*, p.51. I would agree with Sharp that 'the system provided well enough for the needs of a rural and small town society'. (*Social History*, 7, p.192).

legal system. What is different is that the nobility and landed gentry have been forced, over a very long period of time, to share their power with other sections of the community, and there has also occurred a greater specialization of functions, of which the emergence of a police force is but one example. The near monopoly of power exercised by the nobility and landed gentry has thus been broken. Whether that monopoly resulted in an early Tudor version of the Hobbesian nightmare portrayed by some historians is another matter, but all that its breakdown means is that nowadays it is more likely to be the wealthy business man, the large industrial company or a powerful trade union that abuses the system rather than the nobleman or the country squire. Things have changed, but not all that much and not necessarily for the better.

The intention of this detour has been to provide some criteria by which to judge Wolsey's achievements in this field. If early Tudor society is thought of as violent and disorderly, then what he did will not appear to add up to very much. But if the more optimistic view offered here is taken, then his achievement will appear much more considerable. Only a comparatively few people appeared before him in Star Chamber on what may loosely be called criminal charges, because only comparatively few people deserved to; and those who were guilty 'got away' with only a fine or a pardon not because Wolsey lost his nerve or was weak, but because he held the accepted view that these were appropriate punishments. As regards the powerful, an appropriate punishment meant ensuring that they were made fully aware that they were not above the law, but this did not usually mean that they were deprived of their natural role as leaders in their localities, partly because that was difficult to do. An occasion on which it might have been attempted was when the action involved was treasonable, though even in such cases the Crown was well aware that to cut somebody's head off solved very little because the victim's family and friends remained to seek their revenge. Thus attainders were often reversed, and kings were usually anxious – but some more anxious than others[1] – to restore to favour families that had been in opposition to them. In other words, the realities of the power structure in late medieval and early modern England imposed a certain degree of leniency and compromise upon the Crown's and Wolsey's treatment of the powerful, but only in the way that a different power structure demands different compromises today.

But it was not just a question of effective political manipulation. There were also genuine ambiguities that were difficult to reconcile. On the one hand, early Tudor society was one in which the arts of war were very much extolled and the joust and tourney were still the major recreations of the great, and on the other hand it condemned the riot and the brawl. It was a society in which the great man's retinue was still an essential part of any royal army, yet one which declared that 'illegal' retaining was undesirable. It was a society which still considered 'good lordship' a cardinal virtue, but saw 'maintenance', the use of undue influence to protect one's servants' or clients' legal interests, as an evil. No judgement upon the effectiveness of law enforcement can be made without these ambiguities being kept in mind.

[1] For Henry VII being more grudging or more controlled about restoration than Edward IV see Lander, *Crown and Community*, pp.353- 4.

What needs to be done is to concentrate on the Crown's ability to define and then impose acceptable limits to the exercise and influence of the great, while not expecting these limits to be narrow ones. Thus in Wolsey's period Sir William Brereton was forced to appear in Star Chamber for aiding and abetting murderers, but he was not as a result deprived of office and influence in Cheshire. In 1516 George Neville Lord Bergavenny was charged, not for the first time, with illegal retaining, but he continued to act as royal councillor and in any war his 'legal' retinue was always welcome to the Crown. That at about the same time Thomas Grey marquess of Dorset was charged with the same offence is of particular interest because, unlike Bergavenny, he was personally close to the king – and, it should be said, remained so after his case had been tried. It is perhaps too often assumed that a person's appearance in Star Chamber in such a case involved his disgrace and downfall, and it is an assumption based upon a misconception about the Crown's and Wolsey's intentions. These were well explained by Wolsey in that letter to Henry in the autumn of 1517, already quoted, in which he commented on the affray between the servants of Thomas Pygot and Sir Andrew Windsor:

> I trust at the next term to learn them the law of Star Chamber that they shall beware how from thenceforth they shall redress their matter with their hands. They be both learned in the temporal law, and I doubt not good example shall ensue to see them learn the new law of the Star Chamber which, God willing, they shall have indifferently ministered to them according to their deserts.[1]

What Wolsey wanted to do was to teach them, and, by their example, others that no one, especially those with responsibility for the administration of justice, should see themselves as being above the law. But learning their lesson was never intended to entail their dismissal from office, for if that were the case there would have been no point in teaching them. And in fact Thomas Pygot retained his important office of king's serjeant until his death in 1520, while so successful did Andrew Windsor's career continue to be that in December 1529 he was created a lord. Admittedly, this elevation came after Wolsey's downfall, but there is nothing to suggest that relations between him and Wolsey were seriously impaired by the events of 1517. Windsor continued to play a most active part in the administration of conciliar justice, and he could only have done this if Wolsey had been confident that he had indeed learnt his lesson.

We noted earlier that there had never been any such thing as that 'new law of Star Chamber', and that what Wolsey had in mind was simply to put into effect the laws of the realm as they then existed. In attempting to sum up his efforts at law enforcement, we should perhaps emphasize this new determination. There is little doubt that, following the departure of the elderly, and politically not very influential, Warham, the arrival of someone with Wolsey's enormous vitality and persuasion marked a new departure, and the fact that he was so close to his monarch must have added further to his authority. Just as this helped to make the conciliar courts even more popular and effective than they had been earlier, so it also helped to ensure that the machinery of justice was well maintained and the law better enforced. Of course, Wolsey did not solve the problems of law and order, because

[1] *LP*, ii, app. 38.

there are never any solutions to them. This being so, one should not be surprised that during the fifteenth and sixteenth centuries the same difficulties – such as illegal retaining and maintenance – and the same solutions, for instance in the form of barely effective statutes, keep recurring. But this is no more evidence of royal ineffectiveness than the similar failure to cope with human fraility today. These problems do not go away; they can only be kept within limits. One way of doing this is for authority constantly to reiterate that such practices are undesirable, and another is to make examples of those offenders who are caught. Wolsey did both.

That the powerful were brought within the law is evidence of Wolsey's success in this area of government, and is much to his credit – but not to his alone. At this level, law and order is much more a political than a 'police' problem, and there is no way that the high and mighty would have submitted to correction if behind the figure of the lord chancellor had not loomed that of Henry VIII. Moreover, always necessary to any successful policy of law enforcement is a high degree of political stability, and for that Henry's father and his ministers must take some of the credit, though just how much and in what ways is still a matter of considerable controversy.[1] It has been argued that in this vital area of law enforcement Henry VII made very little sustained effort.[2] My own inclination is rather to the opposite view that he did too much, and if that is right one last suggestion about Wolsey's attitude in this area may be made.

One of the chief agencies of Henry VII's administration, at least by 1500, was the 'king's Council learned in the law'. Its most famous members were Richard Empson and Edmund Dudley, those two of his father's ministers that Henry VIII felt it expedient to sacrifice at the beginning of his reign because of their unpopularity. Both had legal training and experience, as had all those known to have been members. Like any Tudor council, its duties were multifarious: for instance, it heard suits between parties in just the same way as the Council in Star Chamber did. However, the main thrust of its activity was in that area that particularly concerned the king's own rights and the collection of revenue resulting from them. Moreover, unlike the Council in Star Chamber, it did itself initiate the majority of the cases that came before it. It was thus an especially hard-nosed body with a tendency to forget about the rights of the subjects in pursuing, however legitimately, the king's.[3]

Wolsey made no attempt to revive the Council Learned, which had ceased to function as a conciliar court at Henry VII's death. Instead, he worked essentially through the normal channels; that is, Chancery and the king's Council sitting in Star Chamber. And though his chancellorship may have witnessed a significant increase in the latter's legal business, the body itself was not only well established but, unlike the Council Learned, consisted of anybody of real importance, including nobles, who had been notably absent from the Council Learned. There may not have been anything overtly sinister about their exclusion; it could be that they were not put on it for the good reason that they were not learned in the law. But whatever the explanation, the result was a specialized and unrepresentative

---

[1] For the original controversy see Cooper, *HJ*, 2, pp.103-29; Elton, *Studies*, pp.45-99. But see also Condon, *passim*; Lander, *Crown and Nobility*, pp.267 ff. for this and what follows.
[2] Chrimes, p.185 ff.
[3] See n.1 above, also Somerville, *passim*.

body, that did arouse antagonism.

If, along with his use of bonds and recognizances to attach leading subjects to the Crown under financial penalty, it is permissible to see the Council Learned as in some way characteristic of Henry VII's approach to government, and if one then compares this approach with what Henry VIII and Wolsey were doing, the picture that emerges might also be described as a gradual 'return to normalcy'. This is not to say that Henry VIII and Wolsey were more complacent, but they were more relaxed and confident; and what was absent was that sense of strain, almost paranoia, that had been discernible during the previous reign. There were going to be difficulties for them. There was a serious riot in London in May 1517. There was the suspicion of an aristocratic plot, probably in 1518. There was considerable opposition to the 'Amicable Grant' in 1525. There was widespread discontent following the bad harvest of 1527. Arguably, indeed, by the end of the 1520s the rather heady confidence of the earlier period of Wolsey's ascendancy was dwindling. Nevertheless, the overall impression is of stability and of a government which felt itself to be very much in control of its own affairs. As a result, there was less of an obsession with furthering the Crown's own interests, and less of a need 'to keep all Englishmen obedient through fear'. Instead, the emphasis could now be placed on 'the indifferent ministration of Justice to all persons high as well as low'. Moreover, it was a justice that was ministered at the highest level by a chancellor who did not doubt that 'the king ought of his royal dignity and prerogative to mitigate the rigour of the law, where conscience hath the most force.'[1]

[1] Cavendish, p.117.

CHAPTER FIVE

PEACE OR WAR: THE CALAIS CONFERENCE OF 1521

ON 2 AUGUST 1521 WOLSEY ARRIVED AT CALAIS TO PRESIDE OVER A conference the ostensible purpose of which was to put an end to fighting that had broken out earlier in the year between French and Imperial forces. When, nearly four months later, the conference broke up, the fighting still continued. Clearly Wolsey had been unsuccessful in bringing about peace, but he did not return to England empty-handed. On 24 November a treaty had been signed with the emperor committing England to a Great Enterprise against France. What had happened to turn the erstwhile architect of that universal peace treaty, signed with so much pomp and ceremony in October 1518, into the iron cardinal determined to turn Europe into a battlefield in order to win back for his master the throne of France? It is the purpose of this chapter to find out, and in the process a central question about Wolsey's approach to foreign policy – his attitude to peace – will have to be answered.[1]

In some ways, of course, the matter has been prejudged. In chapter 3 it was shown how fortuitous, in many ways, that universal peace treaty had been. For differing reasons, both Henry's great rivals, Francis and Charles, had been anxious for peace in 1518, as had the pope. Indeed, it was Leo x's plans for peace that Wolsey had upstaged by his more effective performance in London. Furthermore despite appearances, peace had not been Wolsey's central aim in 1518. Instead, what he had sought and finally achieved was a sufficient hold on the French to make them accept an alliance in which England would be the dominant partner. Or at the very least, his hope had been that he could use this alliance to dominate the affairs of Europe – and hence a map of Europe drawn up by him and the French to suit their particular interests, the maintenance of which was to be guaranteed by those elaborate provisions to maintain peace that were outlined earlier.[2] If this view is correct, it would not be possible to accept Wolsey's commitment to peace as being genuinely motivated by Christian beliefs, or as in anyway disinterested – but this interpretation of Wolsey has been strongly defended by some historians, and, moreover, it is his conduct at the Calais conference that supposedly provides the vital evidence.[3]

As it happens, the maintenance of the French alliance, so central to the Treaty of London for reasons of state, would have to become even more so to any policy that had peace as its central objective. There are two reasons for this. The first is the paradoxical one that France was England's natural enemy, and had been from time

[1] This chapter follows very closely my article 'Wolsey's foreign policy', HJ, 23.
[2] See pp. 97 ff.
[3] Scarisbrick, Henry VIII, p.49 and more generally, pp.41-240. Scarisbrick's treatment of Wolsey's foreign policy is entirely responsible for my interest in Wolsey and thus the fons et origo of this book! Despite my many disagreements with his interpretation, I would like to express my great admiration for the skill with which it is presented. For other accounts of Wolsey's concern for peace, see Mattingly, Journal of Modern History, x, and Russell, BIHR, xliv.

immemorial. If Englishmen wanted to win honour and glory they fought the French, and to this general rule Henry VIII was no exception. Furthermore, as was shown earlier, the English Crown considered it had a rightful claim to the French throne, while at a more mundane level an invasion of France was the most practical campaign that the English could embark on. Thus in order to maintain peace, a French alliance had to be made attractive enough to resist the ever-present temptation of an Imperial alliance and a war against France.

The second reason arises from the general European situation. In the early 1520s Charles V was much more likely than Francis I to disturb the peace of Europe, despite the fact that in 1521 it was Francis who started the war. At the Treaty of Noyon in 1516, Charles, in order to facilitate his journey to Spain to establish his claim to the kingdoms of Aragon and Castile, had been compelled to make concessions to the French, the most important of which was his acceptance of the French occupation of the duchy of Milan.[1] This occupation gave the French a stranglehold on communications between the Mediterranean and the rest of Europe and, thus, a position of great power. This the Treaty of London confirmed. In January 1519 Maximilian died. Charles succeeded to his grandfather's possessions in Germany and Eastern Europe, and by the end of June had defeated Francis in the election for the Imperial title. Charles was now, potentially at least, very strong, and at the same time the question of who was in control of Milan was now a vital concern to him. Sooner or later Charles would have to challenge the French position in Northern Italy.[2]

Looking at what Wolsey was doing in the time between the Treaty of London and his arrival in Calais in August 1521, it soon becomes apparent that the French alliance was of some importance to him. If it was not, the expenditure and effort that he lavished on the famous meeting between Henry and Francis in 1520 at the Field of Cloth of Gold are totally inexplicable. To remove the prejudices built up over at least two hundred years of enmity, something out of the ordinary was necessary; something that could, as it were, outshine even Agincourt. Despite the scepticism of some historians, the Field of Cloth of Gold remains the most convincing evidence that Wolsey genuinely desired peace.[3] And there is other evidence. Certainly, both he and Henry were constantly talking about it.[4] Certainly, they were constantly informing both the French and the Imperialists that they would consider any invasion of each other's territory as an infringement of the Treaty of London; and if that occurred, they both declared their intention to come to the aid of the injured party.[5] Furthermore, though the Field of Cloth of Gold was the centrepiece of English diplomatic activity, it was immediately preceded and followed by meetings between Henry and the emperor. Every effort appears to have been made to keep both sides happy and to prevent the inevitable suspicion that these summit meetings caused.[6] All in all, England's behaviour appears scrupulously correct, never more so than in March 1521: the emperor's offer of a marriage

[1] Dumont, iv, pp. 224-5; see also pp. 80-81, 86-7 above.
[2] For Imperial policy at this time, see inter alia LP, iii, 1106, 1446.
[3] Elton, Reform and Reformation, p. 84 for such scepticism; otherwise Russell, Field of Cloth of Gold.
[4] LP, iii, 689; Ven. Cal., ii, 1259. 1298; iii, 60, 184.
[5] LP, iii, 1212, 1257, 1283.
[6] LP, iii, 936.

between himself and the Princess Mary, together with an offensive alliance against France, was turned down, and Cuthbert Tunstall, Henry's special envoy to the emperor, was recalled. As Wolsey explained to Henry, 'in this controversy betwixt these two princes it shall be a marvellous great praise and honour to your grace so by your high wisdom and authority to pass between and stay them both, that you be not by their contention and variance brought in to the war'.[1]

The evidence that, at least until March 1521, England was determined to maintain the peace of Europe does seem convincing – that is, until the negotiations prior to Tunstall's recall are looked at more closely. To begin with, it is a little surprising that there were any negotiations for a marriage at all, for was not Mary, by the Treaty of London, betrothed to the dauphin? It becomes even more surprising when it is discovered that the negotiations were begun at Henry's meeting with Charles at Canterbury in May 1520, just before the Field of Cloth of Gold, and were continued at Gravelines and Calais in July immediately after. It is true that this marriage proposal, along with the plan to mount a joint invasion of France, was at once disclosed by Henry to Francis. Henry also made comforting noises about having persuaded Charles and his advisers to give up their evil designs.[2] These might be convincing if the negotiations had ended there and then, but they did not. Instead, Tunstall was sent to the emperor in an effort to bring them to a conclusion. This did not happen, but it is important to decide just how serious the negotiations were.

It looks as if both sides were quite serious, but in the end not serious enough.[3] That the Imperialists were anxious for them to succeed is not surprising. As has been argued already, it was they who had most to gain from the disruption of the status quo established by the Treaty of London. This could best be done by removing the linchpin of that treaty, the Anglo-French alliance – and they were in some hurry. In Rome a race had been taking place between the emperor and the French to see who could first secure a papal alliance, and early in 1521 it looked as if the French might win. If the emperor could secure immediate English support, this might convince the pope that Charles was strong enough to provide effective protection against the French, and thus remove one of the chief obstacles to a papal alliance with him.[4] Charles was also anxious to obtain help in putting down a serious revolt that had broken out during his absence in Germany – the so-called revolt of the comuneros. Thus he was insisting on a package deal with the English: a defensive alliance with the pope, an offensive alliance with the Swiss, aid against the rebels, and a new meeting between himself and Henry.

If the Imperial attitude is easy to appreciate, the English one is not because, as Henry and Wolsey made clear to the emperor, they felt no immediate pressures.[5] They therefore had no need, and very little intention, of being rushed into any

---

[1] LP,iii,1213; the recall is LP,iii,1214.

[2] LP,iii,936.

[3] LP,iii,1044, 1098, 1149, 1162, 1213.

[4] Pastor, viii, pp.1-36.

[5] 'For remembering the good amity that is betwixt us and France and our daughter honourably bestowed there, considering also that we be in peace with all Christian princes, what need have we to care for further amities, alliances or intelligence with the pope or the emperor than we have already.' (LP,iii,1150).

grandiose schemes; hence their insistence on a marriage alliance first, discussion about other matters later. But did they want even a marriage alliance, and, if so, why? The essential point about the proposed marriage terms is that Charles was to be free to marry whom he liked until Mary came of age, which would not be until February 1528. Such a generous time allowance hardly suggests great eagerness on England's part, but it might be that the marriage was merely a means of keeping in with the Imperialists so as to influence their actions in the direction of peace. On the other hand, would this require Tunstall to spend two months with the emperor involved, on the face of it, in hard bargaining? At one stage he was instructed by Henry, if things were going badly, to bypass Charles's leading councillors, Chièvres and Sauvage's successor as chancellor, Mercurino Gattinara, considered to be ill-disposed towards the English, and to seek a private interview with the emperor. He was, then, to press on Charles the great disadvantage of Mary's marriage to the dauphin, especially if as a result the dauphin succeeded to the throne of England. With the sealing off of the Channel and the French possession of Milan, Charles's lands would be effectively cut in two. This was a threat, albeit a distant one, and there seems no reason for it unless some sort of alliance with the emperor was really wanted.[1]

When Wolsey suggested to Henry the recall of Tunstall, he gave two main reasons. Firstly, the negotiations were being used by the Imperialists to blacken Henry's good name with the French, thereby improving their own standing with them.[2] Secondly, the Imperialist position was sufficiently weak for them sooner or later to have to come begging 'on their hands and feet', for, 'if they attempt any thing by hostility, your grace not consenting thereto, they shall be utterly undone.' Nowhere in the letter is there any reference to the need to maintain the peace of Europe as something to be worked for because good in itself. Instead, only the negative point is made, that it would be wrong for England to be dragged into a war of the emperor's and Francis's making.[3]

A policy is beginning to emerge. Throughout 1520, and indeed 1521, Wolsey posed as the honest broker trying to resolve the ever-growing conflict between the emperor and the French king. Of course, he more or less had to do this; the Treaty of London had been such a success that, whatever his motives in bringing it about, he could only lose face by abandoning it too quickly. And the role did have positive attractions. It gave England a dominating and extremely honourable position in Europe without the expense of providing an army – and if one thing is certain about Wolsey's policy at this time it is that he did not want to fight a major campaign.[4] Thus, he was quite prepared to stand by the Treaty of London, but only so long as a better alternative did not turn up. Keeping his options open was always a central article of faith, and as early as the Canterbury meeting in May 1520 he began to consider how best to do this. One option was the Imperial alliance, but only if the terms were right. In March 1521 they were not, and so for the time being Wolsey continued to act as the peacemaker of Europe. The only difficulty was that late in

---

[1] Ibid.
[2] LP,iii,1257, 1258, 1283 for English efforts to thwart these moves.
[3] LP,iii,1213.
[4] LP,iii,1270, 1362, 1367, 1371, 1383, 1395, 1488.

February Robert de La Marck, duke of Bouillon, had defied the emperor and marched into Luxemburg. If he had been an Italian, one would call La Marck a *condottiere* – given some additional status by the possession of an hereditary title, and in La Marck's case the lordship of Sedan, situated on France's border with the Holy Roman Empire. Not surprisingly, La Marck took full advantage of the Habsburg-Valois rivalry, changing sides whenever it suited him, but when he marched into Luxemburg he was undoubtedly acting on Francis's behalf, despite the inevitable statements to the contrary. An Imperial army had little trouble in driving him out, but by May showed every indication of wishing to follow up this success by marching into French territory. Meanwhile the French had captured Navarre. The expected conflict between Habsburg and Valois had begun.

It led immediately to great diplomatic activity on Wolsey's part. Special envoys were sent to both Francis and Charles carrying with them the same message: the disadvantages of war would far outweigh the temporary gains that either might win; they should therefore submit their disputes to England's mediation; if they refused, she would have to intervene against the aggressor.[1] Charles's initial response was favourable,[2] unlike Francis's.[3] Indeed, it was in order to persuade the latter to accept English mediation that it was first suggested that Wolsey should come to Calais so as to conduct the negotiations more easily. On about 9 June Francis accepted this, and on the 13th Charles was informed of this. So far so good: that is to say, Henry and Wolsey had behaved with the utmost correctness and in the new situation had showed every indication of standing by the Treaty of London.

It was on 16 June 1521 that John Lord Berghes, an important councillor of Charles v, and an especially close adviser of his aunt, Margaret, who was known for her pro-English sympathies, put forward an idea whose attraction was so powerful that it would eventually lead to an English invasion of France in 1523. In an after-dinner conversation with the English ambassadors at the Imperial court, Berghes stressed the need to strengthen the good relations between their two countries, 'considering the subtle and colourable demeanour used by the French king'. He went on to suggest that Wolsey should immediately come to Calais, 'at the which journey may be well treated and concluded such perfect intelligence and straight conjunction as the wealth of the parties requireth, without suspicion of the Frenchmen, having themselves consented and desired the same.'[4] Here is the genesis of the famous plot to deceive the French. It was formally presented to Henry in a memorandum brought back from the Imperial court by Sir Richard Wingfield. On 1 July, before Wingfield had had time to return with the English reply, Philip Haneton, a special envoy from the emperor, arrived with the task of persuading Henry and Wolsey.[5] As in January and February, so now a lot of pressure was being applied by the Imperialists for an English alliance. This time round it was to succeed.

It was to succeed for the reason that most negotiations succeed: both parties were now sufficiently determined to be willing to make the necessary compromises.

[1] *LP*,iii,1271, 1283.
[2] *LP*,iii,1304, 1315.
[3] *LP*,iii,1303, 1304, 1310, 1315, 1331.
[4] *St.P*,vi,p.72 (*LP*,iii,1352).
[5] *LP*,iii,1362, 1371.

On both occasions the Imperialists had wanted an immediate English declaration against the French. On both occasions they failed, but the second time they did not let it end the negotiations. The explanation is that, now that they were at war, they wanted the alliance more then ever – just, of course, as Wolsey had predicted. When Haneton was sent they were under the impression that a French army, having occupied Navarre, was marching into Castile, a Castile hardly yet recovered from a major rebellion. By 16 July the situation had changed for the better, with the news that Navarre had been reoccupied. This gave the Imperialists a breathing space, and also lessened the need for an immediate English declaration. Even so, faced with a war on a number of fronts – in the Pyrenees, on the north-western border of France, and also in Italy – the English alliance remained a priority.

This also explains why the Imperialists were prepared to give way on another issue. Before accepting their plan to deceive the French, Wolsey insisted on receiving from Charles a written promise that he would not negotiate with the French while talks with the English continued. At the same time, he refused to make a similar promise on Henry's behalf.[1] This insistence is a little surprising; with the outbreak of war, there hardly seems any need for it. But Wolsey had been around long enough to know that alliances changed all too quickly.[2] It was apparent that in 1521 neither Charles nor Francis was in a position to deliver a major blow, least of all Charles, who was desperately short of money and needed to return to Spain before embarking upon anything too ambitious.[3] It would have been a disaster for Wolsey if the peacemaker of Europe had been shown up as nothing but a wolf in sheep's clothing, and for the emperor then to have earned good marks with the French for making the discovery. England would have been left without an ally and without a role, and it was this that Wolsey was determined to prevent.[4]

Wolsey secured these concessions because the Imperialists needed him, but it was just as true that he needed them. Once war had broken out between the emperor and Francis, it was virtually impossible for England to escape being drawn into it. This was not only because, under the provisions of the Treaty of London, England was bound to come to the aid of the injured party if diplomacy failed. There were also the separate treaties between Henry and the emperor which had emerged from their two meetings, at Canterbury and Gravelines, in 1520, stipulating that if either was attacked the other must come to his aid. It was to these treaties that the emperor usually appealed; they involved none of the delays allowed for by the Treaty of London, and delay was not what the emperor wanted.[5] Wolsey, as we have seen, did, and that is one of the reasons why, in the spring and early summer of 1521, the Treaty of London had its uses, even if it left him with a number of problems.

[1] St.P,i,p.17 (LP,iii,1383) also LP,iii,1415, 1419.
[2] He was quite good at changing them himself!
[3] LP,iii,1446 for Gattinara's assessment of the Imperial position
[4] Gattinara's comments at the Imperial Council meeting in August show that he was aware of Wolsey's worries on this score, while in November they were used by Charles to bring pressure on England; see LP,iii,1507, 1770.
[5] Neither of these meetings is well documented. During 1521 reference was usually made to the 'Treaty of Canterbury'. What has survived is a treaty made at Calais, so presumably the terms were discussed at Canterbury and confirmed at Calais; see LP,iii,908.

How was Wolsey to turn any delay to his advantage? He could, of course, put all his efforts into attempting to end the conflict. If successful, he would avoid being drawn into a war and he would achieve another diplomatic triumph. Extremely attractive, but not very practical. It is true, as has been seen, that both Francis and Charles had to begin with tentatively accepted the English mediation, but, once the news of the French capture of Navarre had reached him, Charles on 1 June turned it down.[1] This was a body blow to Wolsey. If he could not even get the contending parties to the conference table, what would become of 'the immortal fame and renown' that the Treaty of London had brought him?[2] The Imperial offer that Haneton brought with him a month later, allowing Wolsey still to pose as peacemaker, solved the immediate, but not the long term, crisis. It was just possible that, having got to Calais, he could still have persuaded both sides to end the war, but it was not at all likely. Much more so was the possibility that the two sides would come to terms without bothering with Wolsey's good offices – and then where would he be?

Furthermore, there had always been a major flaw lurking behind the successful facade of the Treaty of London. At some point, in order to maintain it, England might be forced to go to war, and – here was the real rub – the war would not be of England's choosing. It was all very well coming to the aid of the aggrieved party, but almost by definition this meant coming to the aid of the losing side, for only the losing side was likely to accept English intervention. Even before Haneton's arrival, it looks as if the English had decided that Charles would win,[3] and the information Haneton brought about the Imperial military and financial position must have confirmed this view.[4] Thus, even if there was a good case for saying that the French had started the war, once they began to lose and their territory was invaded, they had only to accept Wolsey's offer to mediate for them to become the aggrieved party. England would then be dragged into the worst possible war, propping up her natural enemy against her successful friend. On the other hand, if this was too ghastly to contemplate, what sort of terms was a successful emperor likely to offer someone who had refused to help when the going was rough, and had only been a hindrance when things started to go well? What all this adds up to is: in July 1521 England was in a strong bargaining position because the Imperialists needed English support. The longer she delayed giving it, the weaker that position would become. It was this that made the role of the genuinely impartial mediator too risky to contemplate.[5]

It is not, in any case, at all certain how much Wolsey wanted her to play that role. Here the earlier negotiations should be recalled. It may, then, appear that in a certain sense he had merely been waiting for Haneton to arrive.[6] He had very quickly seen the disadvantages of the Treaty of London and had taken steps to

---

[1] *LP*,iii,1326, 1357.

[2] Giustinian's praise of Wolsey in September 1518; see *LP*,ii,4453.

[3] *LP* 1370.

[4] *LP*,iii,1371.

[5] See the assessment to this effect of England's ambassador in the Low Countries, Sir Thomas Spinelly, writing to Wolsey on 21 July. (*LP*,iii,1428).

[6] He was certainly very eager to see him, insisting on a meeting as soon as he arrived, despite the resident Imperial ambassador's view that this was inconvenient; see *LP*,iii,1381.

minimize them: the meetings with the emperor in the summer of 1520, the defensive alliance that was then signed, negotiations for a marriage between Charles and Mary, despite her prior betrothal to the dauphin, and Tunstall's mission during the winter of 1520-1. The Imperial alliance had been kept warm, ready for use when required. In the summer of 1521 that moment had come, and the real bargaining could begin.[1]

One word of warning is necessary. The conclusion to be drawn is not that there was a 'master plan' by which in 1520 Wolsey knew that he would be allied to the emperor in 1521, and invading France in 1523. Indeed, the whole emphasis is otherwise. No one was more aware than Wolsey that plans go awry, that situations change, and that changed situations need different policies: it is really because of this that it is difficult to accept a very serious commitment on his part to universal peace. Wolsey's skill was to be ready for any eventuality, and this held good as much after Haneton's mission as before. Wolsey crossed the Channel with the intention of achieving an Imperial alliance, but he was not yet certain what terms he could secure. If they were not good enough, there would be no alliance.[2] The great advantage of the Imperialists' plan to use a peace conference as a cover to deceive the French was that it helped to keep Wolsey's options open for a little longer. If the Imperialists proved intransigent, he would play the peacemaker more seriously, if only to give himself time to think what to do next.

In support of this account of Wolsey's intentions, there has survived an interesting document listing six alternative terms for an Imperial alliance.[3] Despite the fact that it appears to be a formal document, written in Latin and signed both at the beginning and end by Henry himself, it unfortunately lacks a date. In *Letters and Papers* it was associated with the Treaty of Windsor of 1522, but for a number of reasons it must be placed earlier, sometime between March and August 1521. It cannot be earlier than March because the terms assumed that the war between the emperor and the French king had already started. It cannot be later than the Bruges treaty of 25 August because most of the points mentioned in the alternatives were decided at that time.[4] These vary in the degree to which they commit the allies to an all-out attack on France. The fifth is the least aggressive: universal peace and the restoration of the status ante bellum,[5] with only a marriage treaty and defensive alliance to provide for any future French attack. The second is the most aggressive, with the recovery of Milan as a specific aim of a war with France. All the

---

[1] See *Sp.Cal.*, ii, 337 for the assessment of the Imperial ambassador at Rome to this effect.

[2] It is the uncertainty about the terms, and the sense in which all was still to play for, that provides the answer to the question posed by Scarisbrick: why, if all he wanted was an Imperial alliance, did not Wolsey just send over ambassadors? See his *Henry VIII*, p.84.

[3] BL, Galba B,vii, fos.288-90 (*LP*,iii,2333).

[4] In particular, pt.4 suggests that, after a marriage alliance, there should be a two-year truce to allow England time to prepare for war, and for Charles to return to Spain. But Charles's return was decided at Bruges, and when the Treaty of Windsor was signed he was already on his way. What first suggested to me that the document was misplaced was the assumption made throughout that France was still in possession of the duchy of Milan, which after November 1521 was not the case.

[5] This may suggest a date close to Haneton's mission in very early July. At that date Navarre had not been recovered by the Spanish, so that this provision would have restored it to them. After November 1521 it would require the restoration of Milan to France, not a very likely way of gaining an Imperial alliance.

alternatives suggest a major concern of Wolsey's throughout the negotiations: namely, the need to secure time for England to make serious military preparations; he was not going to be rushed, because England was not in a position to conduct a major campaign. He was also concerned to ensure that the annual French pension would be paid by the emperor if, as a result of any Imperial alliance, the French ceased to do so.[1] Only if none of the terms was acceptable to the emperor would the English consider a radical and undoubtedly unsatisfactory alternative: an alliance with the French involving a defence of the duchy of Milan, French help in settling the affairs of Scotland, the continuance of trade between the two countries, and an increase in the pension from £16,000 to £20,000 a year. I have been able to discover no moves in the direction of such an alliance at any time during the Calais and Bruges negotiations. The assumption can only be that Wolsey got what he wanted from the Imperialists.

Wolsey arrived at Calais on 2 August, and almost immediately he was involved in some hard bargaining with the Imperial delegation;[2] indeed, at one point he threatened to call off any meeting with Charles, and thus in effect all plans for an Anglo-Imperial alliance, because the Imperialists were proving too intractable.[3] As it was, on 14 August he set off for Bruges – for the benefit of the French his excuse for this visit being the need to persuade the emperor not to withdraw his delegation from the Calais conference[4] – and there the bargaining continued. The two matters most in dispute concerned the Imperial acceptance of the responsibility for the annual French pension – what in the negotiations was referred to as the indemnity – and the details of the marriage terms. On both of these Wolsey seems to have got his way. He certainly secured the indemnity and appears to have obtained slightly more than the going rate for Mary's dowry.[5] This left the most important matter, and one that Wolsey had stipulated could be discussed only with the emperor himself: when would England actually have to declare war?[6] As has already been mentioned, Wolsey won this argument as well. Under the terms of the Treaty of Bruges, signed on 25 August, England was not expected to do this until March 1523, unless, that is, the present war between the French and the Imperialists had not ended by the beginning of November, when England was supposed to come in on the Imperial side immediately. It was therefore embarrassing that, when the deadline arrived, the war was still in progress. However, Wolsey was able to secure an extension until the end of the the month,[7] and in the end was able to delay England's declaration of war against France until 29 May 1522.[8] But the price for all these concessions by the Imperialists – including the various extensions that Wolsey had won – was that

---

[1] Three of the six points specifically mention this.

[2] St.P,i, p.27 (LP,iii,1462).

[3] LP,iii,1479-81.

[4] LP,iii,1480.

[5] LP,iii, 1480; Sp.Cal.,ii, 355, pts 7,8. The Imperial ambassadors argued that the amount of money settled on Mary should be one-tenth of the marriage portion she brought with her. They therefore objected to Wolsey's demand for 20,000 marks a year, since the portion was only 100,000 marks. The figure reached at Bruges was less favourable to Mary but still above the Imperialists' assessment of the going rate; by my calculation the figure had dropped from £13,000 a year to £10,000.

[6] LP,iii,1479.

[7] LP,1802.

[8] LP,iii,2292.

England had to provide money, ships and men for Charles's return to Spain.[1]

The postponement of the declaration of war was a major victory for Wolsey,[2] but its purpose must not be misunderstood. It did give him more room for manoeuvre, and one such manoeuvre might just possibly have been a break with the emperor. But its main purpose was quite different. Wolsey genuinely wanted time for English military preparations to be made, for only then could the 'Great Enterprise' against France become a reality. This was also why he was willing to help Charles return to Spain. Only then, once the rebellions were settled, could Charles raise sufficient money and troops to make a joint invasion of France effective. After Bruges, the 'Great Enterprise' was the major aim of English foreign policy, and this represents a change of emphasis. As has been shown, initially the Imperial alliance was partly a means of getting England out of a difficult situation, almost a defensive measure. On the other hand, if the emperor really could be tied down, and detailed plans for a joint invasion of France in strength be worked out, then there was a golden opportunity to win honour and glory. At Bruges, this began to happen.

No wonder Henry got excited. So did Wolsey – but with this very important proviso: he was all too aware of the difficulties yet to come, and therefore determined to move cautiously. This explains the differences between him and Henry that occurred while Wolsey was at Calais. The first concerned who should command a force of six thousand archers to be sent to the immediate aid of the emperor,[3] the second whether the English merchants should make their usual autumn trip to Bordeaux to buy wine.[4] The point about both is that Henry was anxious to get things moving, while Wolsey wanted business as usual. In Wolsey's view there was no point in antagonizing the French until England was ready to declare war, and in the summer and autumn of 1521 she was not.[5]

Both Wolsey and Henry were delighted with the new Imperial alliance.[6] That being the case, why did Wolsey spend over three months at Calais pretending that he was interested in peace? In fact the explanations have already been given. To have suddenly blown his cover, and to have changed overnight his role of peacemaker to that of warmonger, as well as losing him room for manoeuvre, would have resulted in a damaging loss of credibility. As it was, when England did declare war, she did so as the defender of the Treaty of London, having apparently attempted every diplomatic means at her disposal to reconcile the warring parties. England had right on her side, and that always has its uses.[7]

There was also the question of how to secure time to make the necessary

---

[1] LP,iii,1508; Sp.Cal,ii,355 for the provisions of the Treaty of Bruges.

[2] Sp.Cal.,ii,358 for Gattinara's comment on Juan Manuel's worries about the English efforts to secure a truce: 'I should much like the king of England to be persuaded to declare against France.' Manuel's letter was dated 6 September 1521.

[3] LP,iii,1393, 1448, 1453, 1454, 1459,1462,1473, for the disagreement about who should command the force. Henry wanted an aristocrat, Wolsey preferred Sir William Sandys; in other words, Wolsey was anxious to play the whole thing down, though at one stage he did rashly promise to lead the force into battle himself. St.P,i, p.31 (LP,iii,1462).

[4] LP,iii, 1533, 1544, 1558, 1577, 1594, 1611, 1629.

[5] Scarisbrick, Henry VIII, pp. 86,89-96 for both disputes, and the argument that they indicate a major divergence over policy between the two men.

[6] LP,iii,1515, 1539, 1543 (St.P,i, pp.49, 50; vi, p.85).

[7] LP,iii,2292.

preparations for war. It all boils down to a simple point that has never been sufficiently emphasized: the difference between a truce and a peace. It was the former that Wolsey was working for when he returned to Calais at the end of August, and he wanted it the better to prepare for war. So did Charles.[1] It is true that Charles would have preferred an immediate English declaration, but that was because he was involved in the war already and was naturally anxious to come out of it with as much credit as possible. But he knew that he was short of money, he knew that he ought to return to Spain, and he knew that he was not ready for a major showdown with Francis. Thus, at Bruges, he came to see some advantages from a peace conference orchestrated by Wolsey and his own delegation, the purpose of which was to secure a truce at the moment of maximum advantage to himself.

This was the plan, and throughout most of September it worked very well.[2] By the beginning of October this was no longer the case, and by the beginning of November relations between Wolsey and the emperor were definitely bad. The rift was caused by the difficulties in deciding when the moment of maximum advantage had arrived. For Wolsey, the present war was so much men and money down the drain, thus hindering the 'Great Enterprise'. Unless there were immediate and decisive successes to be gained, the sooner a truce was made the better.[3] Charles's desire for a truce fluctuated, depending entirely on how the war on France's north-eastern border was going. By early October the Imperialists were on the retreat, having already abandoned the siege of Mézières. Francis was now crossing the River Scheldt, poised either to raise the siege of Tournai or to do battle with the emperor outside Valenciennes. Charles was quite anxious for a truce, despite disliking many of its conditions. However, with things moving in their direction, the French were dragging their feet.[4] To overcome this, Wolsey decided to impose the greatest possible pressure by sending delegations from Calais to negotiate directly with the two princes. But it was now the turn of the Imperialists to prove obstructive. By early November, the situation had changed. It was clear that Francis's attempt to relieve Tournai had failed and that it was only a matter of time before the city would fall to the Imperialists. In Italy, also, the war was going well, with the French on the verge of losing Milan. On the other hand, the news of the French capture of Fuenterrabia, on Spain's north-west border with France, close to the disputed kingdom of Navarre, on 19 October was very unwelcome, and for the emperor any truce that involved the acceptance of this unpleasant fact was out of the question, unless there was absolutely no alternative.[5]

There is no doubt that Wolsey was angry with the emperor's refusal to respond favourably to his diplomatic initiatives – and with reason.[6] They had been made, as he thought, in order to rescue Charles from a difficult situation.[7] No wonder he

---

[1] *LP*,iii, 1446, 1507.

[2] *LP*,iii, 1560, 1568, 1573.

[3] *LP*,iii,1694 for Wolsey's argument that the present war was hindering the eventual Anglo-Imperial success; *LP*,iii,1518, 1538, 1762 for his view that if the war was going well, a truce should be delayed.

[4] *LP*,iii,1670, 1683 for their impossible demands.

[5] *LP*,iii,1695-6, 1707, 1727-8, 1742, 1749, 1763, 1776 for negotiations with Francis I. *LP*,iii,1694, 1705-6, 1714-5, 1733, 1735-6, 1752-3, 1768-9, 1777-8, for negotiations with the emperor.

[6] *LP*,iii, 1766 – for Margaret's description of Charles's anger.

[7] *LP*,iii, 1736.

wrote to the delegation sent to Francis I that he was for his part

> *sore tempested in mind by the untowardness of the chancellors and orators on every side putting so many difficulties and obstacles to condescend to any reasonable condiction of truce and abstinence of war, that night nor day I could have no quietness nor rest, so that almost my appetite and sleep . . . are sequesterate from me.*

Here, so it has been suggested, speaks a man worn out in the service of universal peace.[1] That this is not so is shown by a letter Wolsey wrote to Henry a little later, on about 14 November. He had just received an explanation from the emperor of why this was the wrong moment to make a truce. In effect, the reasons have already been given: the war was going too well, except in and around Navarre where it was going too badly. Wolsey, as the apostle of peace, should have been distressed to hear this news. In fact, he wrote as follows:

> *And, Sir, if the enterprise of Tournai succeed, and the expedition against Milan take effect, and the Spaniards determine themselves to revenge these outrages of the French king done against Naverre, Biscay, Fuenterrabia and other countries under the obeisance of the crown of Spain, his [the French king's] dominions, power and substance shall be so well shaken, diminished, and extenuated, before you set forth your enterprises against him, that, God willing, he shall be easy enough to meddle with. And thus, Sir, the affairs standing in such train, as it is before expressed, better it is to suffer these princes to ruffle with the said French king, and invest him on all parts, for the consumption of his treasure, which is almost clearly extenuated, than suddenly to take this truce now, when he can do no more harm than he hath done. And to the intent your grace may understand in what state the matters of Italy stand, I send unto the same, at this time, certain copies of such news as lately came from thence; whereby there is some good hope and appearance that the affairs of the French king be like to decay there, and proceed from evil to worse.[2]*

The quarrel with the emperor was very quickly over because it had only ever been a quarrel over immediate tactics, not long-term aims. The truce could well be delayed until after Wolsey's return to England. Meanwhile at Calais, there was a meeting with the Imperial delegation and the papal nuncio Ghinucci in order to discuss the terms of the alliance in the light of developments since the meeting at Bruges, and the inclusion of the papacy. On 24 November a new treaty was signed, and on the 27th Wolsey sailed for Dover.[3]

Thus ended the conferences of Calais and Bruges. For Wolsey they had been a *tour de force*.[4] It was true that all was not yet settled. The search for a truce, with Charles's connivance, continued. So also did the bargaining; that was not settled until Charles's visit to England the following summer, if indeed then. There was also a lot of work to be done if England was going to be ready for war, and to that end a commission was set up in March to look into the whole question of England's

[1] Scarisbrick, *Henry VIII*, p.92.

[2] *St.P*,i, p.90 (*LP,iii, 1762*).

[3] *LP*,iii,1802, 1810.

[4] Arguably an even greater one if peace had been his aim - though in the end unsuccessful. One of the difficulties of the 'peace' theory is that it requires Wolsey to be deceiving not only the French, but also the pope, the emperor, and even Henry VIII. Perhaps this was beyond even Wolsey?

military potential.[1] Still, if his return to England was to bring him no rest, Wolsey must have derived some satisfaction from what had so far been achieved. For four months he had hoodwinked the French into believing that he was concerned with peace, while all the time he had been negotiating with the emperor on how best to bring them to their destruction. In doing this, he had engineered a situation in which even greater honour and fame might accrue to his master than that which had resulted from the Treaty of London.

Mention of Henry's honour may serve to introduce some final thoughts about Wolsey's intentions at Calais and Bruges. The picture of him that has emerged from this account is that of the skilful political operator: opportunist, pragmatist, tough negotiator – these are the words that seem best to describe him. What they leave out is the whole question of motivation. Many motives have been ascribed to him, most of them unfavourable. Self-glorification – already touched on in another context – comes obviously to mind, and this could include an excessive desire for material things. It was an aspect of his character that contemporaries were well aware of:[2] the Imperialists were always bribing him with a bishopric, the French with a pension.[3] However, as an explanation for what he did it does not help very much: as everybody was offering him rewards, it was easy for him to retain his freedom of action. However, one thing that not everybody could offer him was the papacy. The one person who might be able to do so was Charles v, and at Bruges he did offer to support Wolsey's candidature at the next election. This has led some historians to see this as the key to Wolsey's action in 1521: Wolsey wanted an Imperial alliance because he wanted to be pope. It now seems clear that this is not the case because he never genuinely wanted to become pope. Even so, the view still persists that the papal connection, very much nurtured by the cardinal protector of England and the pope's cousin and chief confidant, Giulio de' Medici (later Clement vii, provides the best explanation for Wolsey's foreign policy. Without becoming too involved in the intricacies of papal politics, we must offer some comment on this view.[4]

It may have been noticed that up until now there has been no reference to any papal connection. This has not been deliberate, but merely reflects the fact that it was during this time very little discussed.[5] What evidence there is suggests that in responding to the Imperial proposals for an alliance Wolsey had no knowledge of the papal alliance with the emperor of 28 May.[6] It is true that from mid-July onwards the new English ambassador at Rome, John Clerk, was reporting back the pope's very strong anti-French feelings; but it is clear from these same reports that Clerk's instructions were to defend Wolsey's ostensible policy of trying to maintain

[1] See p.355 below.

[2] 'The statesmen in Rome, however, are persuaded that the cardinal will do what is most lucrative for himself . . .' – Juan Manuel to Charles v, 13 June 1520, *Sp.Cal*,ii, 281.

[3] A.F. Pollard, p.116, n.3.

[4] See p.85, n.2 above.

[5] I refer to questions of foreign policy affecting the Imperial alliance, not to such matters as the presentation to Leo x of Henry's *Assertio Septem Sacramentum*: those were discussed.

[6] Haneton and the resident Imperial ambassador were not to inform the English of it, unless they were proving obstinate (*LP*,iii, 1371) Apparently they were not, for it was not until 25 July that Wolsey wrote to Henry that from something in the Imperial ambassador's letter he suspected that there was some agreement between them and the pope, 'which as yet be kept to themselves secret'. (*LP*,iii,1439).

the peace of Europe. Certainly there is no hint that he was to begin negotiations for an anti-French league.[1] Just before he left for Calais, Wolsey did hint to the papal nuncio that he might be able to help Leo x against the French,[2] but it was not until 25 August, the day the Treaty of Bruges was signed, that he wrote to Clerk informing him of the plot to deceive the French,[3] and not until 13 September that Clerk told the pope.[4] In other words, Wolsey told the pope of what he was doing only after the moves had been decided. At no time was there any consultation or negotiating with the pope because the pope was not in Wolsey's confidence.

Furthermore, it is clear that the pope was extremely suspicious of Wolsey's activities at Calais, even after he knew of the Anglo-Imperial alliance. The fact is that because of the pope's desire for immediate military success against the French in Italy and Wolsey's plans for future military success in France, papal and English policies were not close. Leo x dreaded Wolsey's desire for a truce and late in September suggested to the Imperial ambassador in Rome that someone ought to speak to the king of England and show him what sort of person Wolsey was.[5] Wolsey, for his part, must have been pleased that the pope had sided with the emperor just because it increased the new alliance's chances against the French, but he was in no sense led by him. In late October, he warned the emperor 'not to regard matters of Italy and the pope so greatly as to damage the rest of his dominions'.[6] On 20 November he made his views even clearer. After discussing the forthcoming inclusion of the papacy in the Anglo-Imperial alliance with the Imperial delegation, he went on to say that neither Henry nor Charles should be led by the pope, but rather they should lead him.

In 1521 Wolsey did rather well out of the pope: greatly extended legatine powers both in scope and length of tenure, and the title of *Defensor Fidei* for Henry, though it might be said that the king had earned this himself with his famous book against Luther – the *Assertio Septem Sacramentorum*. In return, he gave very little. The explanation is that on the whole Leo x was more anxious for his help than Wolsey was for Leo's. But the real point that is being made here is that as regards foreign affairs Wolsey considered the papacy just as he did any other foreign power – something to be manipulated for his master's benefit. There was no 'special relationship', and therefore it cannot provide the key to what went on at Calais and Bruges.

Another explanation of what went on there concentrates on Henry's dynastic problems: a marriage between Mary and Charles was the best solution to the increasingly worrying fact that Catherine of Aragon had failed to provide Henry with a male heir.[7] It does not seem very convincing. The marriage would not come

---

[1] *LP*,iii,1402-3, 1430, 1477. For a contrary view, see Wilkie, p. 121: 'The progression of events during the following months was the direct result of the new understanding between de' Medici and Wolsey which Clerk's arrival in Rome was intended to implement.'

[2] *LP*,iii,1486.

[3] *LP*,iii,1510.

[4] *LP*,iii,1574.

[5] *Sp.Cal.*,ii, 359. His reports provide a running commentary on papal suspicions of Wolsey from the time of Clerk's arrival.

[6] *LP*,iii,1694 point 8. The emperor's concern for Italy was going to be much more damaging for Wolsey, and, indeed, the policy begun at Calais and Bruges would eventually flounder on this issue.

[7] Wernham, pp.98-101.

into effect for at least seven years, and a costly war against France appears to be a high price for something that was so uncertain. Be that as it may, the chief defect of this thesis is that it is impossible to find any evidence for it. There was some discussion of the marriage terms, but nothing to suggest that this was anything more than the usual haggling. Certainly, if it was the central purpose of English foreign policy in 1521, Wolsey and Henry kept surprisingly quiet about it.

Perhaps the best explanation is provided by Wolsey himself. On his return from the successful negotiations at Bruges, he sent Henry an assessment of the young emperor. It was a favourable one, particularly so because Charles had made it clear that, just as Henry had done, so he intended to place the burden of affairs on Wolsey's shoulders.

> Wherefore, Sir, you have cause to give thanks to Almighty God, which have given your grace so to order and convene your affairs, that you be not only the ruler of this your realm, which is an angle of the world; but also by your wisdom and counsel, Spain, Italy, Almaine [Germany] and these Low Countries, which is the greatest part of Christendom, shall be ruled and governed. And as for France, this knot now being assuredly knit, shall not fail to do as your grace shall command. What honour this is to your highness, I doubt not but that your grace, of your high wisdom can right well consider.[1]

This letter should not, of course, be taken at its face value – if there is one thing that all Wolsey's subsequent actions make clear it is that he did not trust Charles an inch – but it does contain an essential truth. Henry's honour is the explanation for Wolsey's foreign policy.[2] As has been shown, Wolsey was far too astute not to appreciate that particular policies had particular drawbacks, and this applied as much to the conduct of war as to the search for peace. The important thing was to dominate affairs, and by this means bring honour and glory to his master – and, of course, to himself. Not that I would want to end this chapter on a cynical note. At the end of his life, Wolsey realized that a choice had always had to be made between serving the king and serving God. He had chosen to serve the king, but in doing this he made the same choice as almost every other politically conscious man did in the sixteenth century.[3] He devoted his considerable talents and energies to his chosen task, and, as far as the negotiations at Calais and Bruges were concerned, his monarch was extremely grateful.[4]

---

[1] St.P, vi, p.86 (LP,iii,1515).
[2] Recent historians have had difficulty taking it seriously, a notable exception being L.Baldwin Smith; see L.B. Smith, pp.161- 7.
[3] See pp.637-8 below for Wolsey's apparent regrets.
[4] Wolsey received not only praise, but also St Albans Abbey; see LP,iii,1759.

Chapter Six

Patronage and the Politics of the Court

O N 8 APRIL 1521 A ROYAL MESSENGER ARRIVED AT THORNBURY CASTLE IN Gloucestershire, the principal residence of Edward Stafford 3rd duke of Buckingham. He brought with him a request for the duke to attend upon the king. To someone in Buckingham's position this was not unusual and there is no evidence that it aroused any suspicion in his mind. He set off almost immediately. Within a week he had been committed to the Tower of London, and within just over a month he had been found guilty of high treason before the court of the lord high steward of England. On 17 May he was taken under a guard of five hundred men to Tower Hill. Here he admitted that he had offended against the king, but only through negligence and lack of grace, a rather less fulsome confession of guilt than was usual in such circumstances.[1] Nevertheless, he expressed the hope that his disgrace and execution would provide an example and warning to all other noblemen. He then recited the penitential psalms, gave the customary forgiveness to his executioner, 'after which he took off his gown, and having had his eyes blindfolded, he laid his neck on the block, and the executioner with a woodman's axe severed his head from his body with three strokes'.[2]

The sudden and dramatic destruction of England's leading nobleman, a son, moreover, of the man who had first raised the Tudor standard against the house of York, was bound to cause a stir both at home and abroad. At home it was ordinary Londoners who were most affected; or at least it was only they who were prepared publicly to show their grief for a man who, for reasons which are not altogether clear, had always been popular with them.[3] Abroad, there was only some embarrassing comment. Francis I mischievously offered to come to the aid of his 'brother-in-distress', thereby implying that the English nobility was in full revolt, with perhaps the further implication that this could have been brought about only by Henry's incompetence. His offer was politely but firmly turned down.[4] What Buckingham's fellow peers thought about his destruction is not known. Publicly, however, they, or at least the forty per cent of them who had taken part in his trial, were quite clear that he was guilty of high treason. Historians have tended to disagree.[5] The execution has usually been seen as a put-up job, either by Henry or by Wolsey. The king, like all good Tudors, is supposed to have had a strong aversion

---

[1] L.B. Smith, *Journal of the History of Ideas*, xv.

[2] *Ven. Cal.*, iii, 213; see also Hall, pp. 622-4. Since I wrote this Barbara Harris has published her *Edward Stafford*. My debt to her important article (*AJLH*, xx) will emerge in the subsequent footnotes.

[3] Rawcliffe, p. 43; Kennedy, pp. 210-11.

[4] *LP*, iii, 1245, 1268, 1293. For Charles's less mischievous regrets see *LP*, 1328.

[5] For the classic case against Wolsey see Mattingly, *Catherine of Aragon*, pp. 160-1, but see *inter alia* Davies, *Peace, Print and Protestantism*, pp. 165-6, Elton, *Reform and Renewal*, pp. 81-2. Against the tide, neither Scarisbrick (*Henry VIII*, pp. 120-2) nor Bernard (*Power of the Early Nobility*, pp. 199-20) has seen Wolsey as the 'culprit'. See also Fiddes, p. 275.

to anyone who looked like an 'over-mighty subject', but especially one, such as Buckingham, who could boast a claim to the throne through both John of Gaunt and Thomas of Woodstock, sons of Edward III. Wolsey, as the upstart son of an Ipswich butcher, is supposed to have disliked all noblemen, but especially those who might successfully compete with him for royal favour. In other words, Buckingham's fall has been much used to support various theories concerning both the character and policies of Henry and Wolsey. Rather less attention has been paid to the event itself, and in particular the question, why April 1521?

It was Polydore Vergil who first outlined a conspiratorial view of Buckingham's downfall, and predictably it was one in which Wolsey played the leading role. He had Wolsey first of all working to secure the removal of any potential ally of Buckingham's. Thus, one of his brothers-in-law, the 5th earl of Northumberland, had been hauled before Star Chamber in 1516, and another, the earl of Surrey, had been packed off to Ireland in May 1520, not to return until Buckingham had been executed.[1] That Wolsey was planning Buckingham's destruction five years before it took place may seem a little too far-sighted, even for someone of his intelligence, while not to have bothered to remove Surrey's father, the duke of Norfolk, who might have been expected to show some concern at the fate of his son's father-in-law, seems an unlikely oversight. And why wait until nearly a year after Surrey had gone to Ireland before moving against Buckingham? Where do Buckingham's alleged grumblings about the waste of money and general futility of the Field of Cloth of Gold fit into such a scenario? They could hardly have been predicted by Wolsey in 1516! However, it is arguable that it was Wolsey's fear of Buckingham exploiting the endemic francophobia of the English ruling classes in order to mount a successful attack on Wolsey's handling of foreign policy, that triggered his own counter-attack. Surrey's removal to Ireland just before the Field of Cloth of Gold, when Buckingham's complaints may have already become audible, at first glance supports such an interpretation.

We have only Vergil's word for it that Buckingham was unhappy about the Field of Cloth of Gold, and his presence there with the most splendid entourage does not support this notion. Moreover, by April 1521 the French alliance was very much under review, and by the end of the year England was to be associated with the emperor in the Great Enterprise against the French. This makes it difficult to make too much of a connection between foreign policy and Buckingham's fall, even if after his execution Wolsey was to make some play of the duke's dislike of the French in his complicated manoeuvring with the French king.[2] Moreover, it was Henry, not Wolsey, who had sent Surrey to Ireland,[3] so either the king also was planning Buckingham's destruction, or Wolsey had had a stroke of luck! As with all conspiracy theories, the possible permutations are endless, and in the end not all that convincing – especially if there is a much more simple explanation.

Buckingham was executed for the very good reason that on the evidence presented to them a panel of twenty peers found him guilty of high treason. That they did so in May 1521 is because it was not until the previous autumn, at the

---

[1] Vergil, pp. 263, 265, 279.
[2] LP, iii, 1293, 1556.
[3] Quinn, pp. 334-5.

earliest, that the government had any notion that the duke had been indulging in treasonable thoughts – and it perhaps needs to be stressed that he was never accused of more than that. Thus the fact that no evidence for any major conspiracy against the Crown has ever been found in no way points to the duke's innocence. As a precautionary measure, two of his sons-in-law, Lords Bergavenny and Montagu, were arrested, but they were soon released.[1] That Buckingham had 'imagined' the deposition and death of the king was due to his having taken heed of the prophecies of one Nicholas Hopkins, a Carthusian monk of the priory of Henton in Somerset, to the effect that Henry would have no male heir and that Buckingham would succeed him. When, back in 1511 or 1512, Buckingham had first listened to Hopkins, Henry had no heir; but on the last occasion, in March 1519, the Princess Mary was three years old. If Buckingham was to become king, therefore, not only Henry but also his daughter would have to die first, whether from natural or unnatural causes neither Hopkins nor Buckingham chose to make explicit. However, a good deal of evidence was produced at the trial to show that the latter was not averse to giving fate, or God, a helping hand.[2] In September 1519 he apparently told Bergavenny that if Henry should die, he intended to be king 'whoever would say to the contrary'. Later in the same year he informed one of his relatives and estate officials, Charles Knivet, that if Henry had dared to arrest him for the unlawful retaining of Sir William Bulmer, his intention had been to put into effect a plan devised by his father to murder Richard III: the stabbing of the monarch while in private audience with him. In February 1520 Buckingham informed his chancellor, Robert Gilbert, that he considered that everything that Henry VII had done 'had been done wrongfully', while Henry VIII had not behaved much better. Despite this, he had decided to put off his 'treason' for a more convenient time because it could only be successful 'if the lords of the kingdom would show their minds to each other, but some of them were afraid to do so'. He had also on various occasions been very critical of Wolsey, calling him an 'idolator' for using magic to retain the king's favour, and king's 'bawd' for using less transcendental means to achieve the same end. He had also made it clear that on his becoming king Wolsey would lose his head.[3]

Following Vergil, historians have tended to be so obsessed with conspiracy theories that they have refused to take the lengthy indictment against Buckingham very seriously. This has been a mistake, for it is utterly damning. For anyone to condone prophecies predicting his succession to the throne, to couple this with highly critical comments about the reigning monarch and his leading councillor, and, furthermore, to hint that he was willing to depose the king just as soon as he could find the necessary backing, was political suicide. This was especially so if, like Buckingham, you had not only a claim, however remote, to the throne, but were probably the most powerful nobleman in England and related by blood or by marriage to most rivals for that position.[4] Furthermore, even in the technical sense

[1] Hall, p.623; Ven.Cal.,iii,209. Wolsey was to deny to Francis that their arrests had anything to do with Buckingham's (LP,iii,1293), but this seems unlikely.

[2] For the charges and evidence brought against Buckingham see LP,iii, 1284, much expanded upon, with transcripts of related documents, in J.S. Brewer's introduction; see LP,iii, pp.cxxix-xxxi. See also Public Records, app.ii, pp.230-4.

[3] LP,iii,1284 (ii).

Buckingham probably had committed high treason. Concern has been shown by recent historians over the question of whether in the fifteenth or early sixteenth centuries 'overt action' was required for a conviction of high treason, or whether mere words or 'imaginings' were sufficient.[1] There was not a great deal that was 'overt' about what Buckingham had done, and thus if the law required 'overt action', he ought to have been acquitted. But his fellow peers were as concerned as recent historians with the question of what constituted high treason. They specifically asked John Fineux, the chief justice of King's Bench, who was present throughout the trial to provide legal advice as to whether words alone were sufficient, and his answer was yes.[2] Whether he was right can only ever be a matter of interpretation, but there is no reason to suppose that he merely gave the answer that the Crown wished to hear. There were precedents for his judgment in both Edward iv's and Henry vii's reign, most of them involving the court of the lord high steward, the very court in which Buckingham was tried.[3]

This court, and specifically the way in which Buckingham's trial was conducted, has received unfavourable comment. Most of it has been misplaced, or at least anachronistic. Given that Buckingham had a right to be tried by his fellow peers and that parliament was not sitting, it was the only court that could have dealt with his case. There was, in fact, some discussion about whether parliament should be called,[4] and the reason it was not was probably due to the inconvenience of such a step rather than to any Machiavellian plot to pervert the course of justice.[5] Buckingham was tried by a jury consisting of twenty of the fifty noblemen alive at the time.[6] Was it packed? The numbers alone suggest that it was not: to find twenty people guaranteed to be willing to pervert the course of justice is quite a tall order. Moreover, the government had only a limited choice. Five of the fifty were not eligible for selection because they were either minors or lunatics,[7] and one, the earl of Surrey, was busy in Ireland. Three peers – the duke's brother the earl of Wiltshire, and his sons-in-law, the Lords Bergavenny and Montagu – were excluded as being too close to the duke; indeed, as has been mentioned, the last two were briefly imprisoned. On the other hand, it may be that two others, Lords Berkeley and Berners, were excluded for the opposite reason, that they were too antagonistic.[8] The largest number of absentees, about twelve, was from the North; and though this meant the exclusion of Buckingham's brother-in-law, the earl of

---

[4] He had married a Percy, while his three daughters had married respectively George Neville Lord Bergavenny, Ralph Neville earl of Westmorland and Thomas Howard earl of Surrey; see Rawcliffe, pp. 22-3.

[1] See especially Bellamy, *Law of Treason*, though, unlike most other commentators, he takes the view that the important 1352 Act of treason did not insist on 'overt acts'; see ibid, p.122, n.7. For an excellent summary of the legal position on the eve of the trial see Harris, *AJLH*, 20, pp.21-3. My interpretation of the trial relies very heavily on her account.

[2] Harcourt, p.470.

[3] B. Harris, *AJLH*, 20, pp.16-22.

[4] *LP*, iii, 1204.

[5] In addition to B. Harris, *AJLH*, 20 see Levine, 'Fall of Edward duke of Buckingham'.

[6] B. Harris, *AJLH*, p.17 calculates 49 noblemen. Both calculations include Thomas Docwra, prior of the order of St John.

[7] The minors were the earl of Derby and the Lords Clinton, Grey of Powis and Grey of Wilton, and the lunatic was Lord Burgh.

Northumberland, and another son-in-law, the earl of Westmorland, it does suggest that the reason for this mass exclusion, rather than anything sinister, was the practical difficulties of getting down south at short notice and an unwillingness to empty the North of its noblemen.[1] And if most of Buckingham's relatives were excluded, the court was presided over by the father of his son-in-law, the duke of Norfolk.

Thus, if there was some selection, it was not entirely determined by the desire to secure a conviction. Neither does it appear that the trial itself was conducted unfairly, given that the strong presumption at the time was that anyone accused of high treason was likely to be guilty. This may offend modern sensibility, but should not prejudice one's treatment of a particular case. And it should be said that in 1534 a jury of noblemen sitting in the same court under which Buckingham had been tried was to find William Lord Dacre not guilty of treason. Though Fineux's advice was available to Buckingham as to others in the court, he had no defence lawyer. Neither was he given any prior information about the charge. This was standard practice. He does, however, appear to have been allowed to cross-examine some of the witnesses testifying against him. If so, this was a departure from the norm, and one much in his favour.[2] The likelihood is that Buckingham's fellow peers were convinced by the evidence presented that he was guilty. Of course, it is just possible that that evidence was a complete fabrication, but if Henry and Wolsey were prepared to go to such lengths, they could have done so at any time – which brings us back again to the question of why they waited until April 1521 to make a move. If we can accept that it was only in the few months before this date that the Crown had any idea that Buckingham had been 'imagining' treason, then the question is solved.

Unfortunately it is impossible to be certain about this. The bulk of the evidence against the duke was provided by three members of his household: Robert Gilbert, his chancellor, John Dellacourt, his chaplain and confessor, and Charles Knivet, the relative and estate official already referred to. Edward Hall believed that it was Gilbert who talked first.[3] He certainly had plenty of opportunity to do so, for he was often sent by Buckingham to discuss his master's business with Wolsey, as he was at the end of November 1520.[4] However, there appears to have been no obvious reason for Gilbert to turn against his employer. He had been with Buckingham for about twenty years, and enjoyed a position of great responsibility and remuneration. On the other hand, Buckingham was extremely difficult to work for. Many of his officials were dismissed, challenged in the law courts, arbitrarily put in prison, or had their lands seized. Some no doubt deserved their fate, but it is doubtful whether

---

[8] This is alleged in B. Harris, *AJLH*, 20, p.17, but she provides no evidence. Berners was involved in complicated legal transactions with Buckingham (Rawcliffe, pp.140-1), which may have caused conflict, but it seems more likely that it was his residency in Calais as lord deputy that was the reason for his absence. I have found no information about any quarrel between Berkeley and Buckingham.

---

[1] For worries about emptying the North of noblemen in 1526 see *LP*,iv,1910. Other northern noblemen were the Lords Clifford, Conyers, Dacre, Darcy, Latimer, Lumley, Monteagle, Ogle, Scrope and Stourton.

[2] Hall, p.623; Harris, *AJLH*, 20, p.20.

[3] Hall, p.623.

[4] *LP*,iii,1070.

this would have been true of John Russell whom Buckingham turned on in 1508. He had been Buckingham's secretary for seven years, and his subsequent successful career in royal service – he became in 1525 secretary to the Princess Mary and a member of her Council of the Welsh Marches – hardly suggests disloyalty or corruption. Yet Buckingham accused him of embezzling over £3,000, and when he had the temerity to defend himself against the charge the duke seized his estates. Given this precedent, it is not inconceivable that, though Gilbert had no particular grievance, by 1520 he was so fed up with such a difficult master that he was prepared to tell all. The same may have been true of Dellacourt.[1] Knivet, on the other hand, had an obvious motive. Some time in 1520 – Vergil says just before Buckingham's departure for the Field of Cloth of Gold in very early July, though it may have been a little earlier[2] – he was dismissed from his post as surveyor of the duke's lands in Kent. As a result, he may have begun hinting to royal officials that he had information that would be of interest.

There is one other candidate for the role of first informer, one Margaret Gedding, former nurse to Buckingham's children and lady-in-waiting to his wife, Eleanor. The evidence is frustratingly slight, but it is known that by 26 November 1520 Buckingham was worried about what Gedding may have told Wolsey, and that whatever it was, Knivet was involved.[3] Some information about the government's handling of Knivet survives in the form of a letter to Wolsey from an unknown correspondent, and, perhaps even more irritatingly, undated, has survived. The letter is of great interest. It suggests very strongly something that has been so far only implied: that the information about the duke's treasonable activities came to Wolsey, rather than Wolsey going in search of it. The letter begins: 'Please it your grace to be remembered as touching the matter that I showed unto your grace at the More of Charles Knivet, wherein you advertised and commanded me that I should handle it further the best I could to bring it to light and better knowledge.' There is no suggestion in this, or in the rest of the letter, that Wolsey thought the matter of the utmost urgency or importance, but merely that it should be followed up – and after all someone in Wolsey's position would have learnt to be sceptical of the many rumours and innuendoes that came his way, especially when, as in his case, the source was so biased. The letter makes it clear that the correspondent had not yet obtained any very concrete information, but only that he suspected the likelihood of 'some great matter . . . or else is Charles a marvellous, simple, insolent body'. What also emerges is that Buckingham's other dismissed servants had already made Wolsey aware of the general dissatisfaction with the government, and his reaction to this earlier information is instructive. Far from wishing to arrest Buckingham, Wolsey had gone out of his way to warn him not to indulge in foolish talk: he did

---

[1] For Buckingham's relations with Gilbert, Russell and Dellacourt, and more generally with his household officials see Rawcliffe, pp.90-1, 139-40, 151, 164-70, 195-6, 229-30, 247-9.

[2] Vergil, p.27. After Buckingham's execution, Knivet was to state that he left Buckingham's service of his own accord in September 1520, but since this was in furtherance of his claim for compensation for loss of office following disclosure of Buckingham's plottings, the statement must be questioned; see LP,iii,1289 (ii). The September date does, however, better fit the scenario being presented here, for if Knivet began to talk in May 1520, it is harder to explain why Buckingham was not picked up until almost a year later.

[3] LP,iii,1070.

not mind so much what the duke said about himself, but 'he should take heed how that he did use himself towards the King's highness'. Meanwhile, Wolsey's correspondent chose to give him a brief lesson in the art of extracting information from those unwilling to give it by telling him how Henry VII would have dealt with such a task – 'circumspectly, and with convenient diligence, for inveighing, and yet not disclose it to the party nor otherwise by a great space after, but keep it to himself, and always grope further, having ever good wait and espial to the party'. There is in all this the slight feeling of someone trying to teach his grandmother how to suck eggs, but perhaps only if the usual picture of the Machiavellian Wolsey is strongly adhered to.[1]

Whoever came forward first, one thing is clear: by the end of 1520 Buckingham's household was a very leaky vessel indeed, and it could only have been a matter of time before the Crown would have to take the leaks seriously. No wonder, then, that when Buckingham requested permission in November to go to Wales with three or four hundred men he was turned down. There was probably nothing untoward about the request: the duke was extremely unpopular with his Welsh tenants and he was probably wise to fear for his safety if he visited them. But, of course, by this time the Crown had good grounds for being highly suspicious, even if all the details of the case against the duke had not yet been assembled. The refusal is, thus, not evidence of a general distrust of him, but of a particular distrust arising out of information only recently received.[2] Nevertheless, the question remains: how eager was the Crown to make use of that information to destroy Buckingham? The fact that the information was not looked for suggests that it was not especially welcomed. Such a view is supported not only by Wolsey's warning to Buckingham not to make critical remarks about Henry: there is evidence of similar warnings, some from Henry himself.[3] The prosecution of Sir William Bulmer in 1519 for wearing Buckingham's livery in the royal presence, referred to earlier, may have been just such an occasion.[4] No direct moves were made against Buckingham in this instance, just as none had been made against any of the noblemen, including Buckingham, involved in the rumoured 'conspiracy' of 1518. On the face of it, therefore, it does not look as if either Henry or Wolsey was anxious to destroy him, which is not to say that they trusted him. Indeed, it has to be remembered that the duke's relations with the Crown had never been good, and this inevitably affected his relations with Wolsey.

Despite the advantage of his father's attempt to topple Richard III and despite being for some time a royal ward, Buckingham had obviously been viewed with some suspicion by Henry VII. Given the pretext of two not very serious offences, Buckingham's mother's marriage and his own entry into his estates when not yet of age, both without royal licence, Henry imposed heavy enough fines to affect the duke's financial position for some years.[5] No wonder, then, that the duke was given to making rude remarks about him. He was not, however, alone in this – indeed, on

---

[1] LP,iii,1283a, transcribed fully in LP,iii, pp.cxiii-cxiv.
[2] LP,iii,1070 for the request. For Buckingham and Wales see pp.170-1 below.
[3] LP,iii,1283a for Wolsey's warning; LP,iii,1245 for Henry's.
[4] Guy, *Cardinal's Court*, p.74; Hall, p.599 for Henry's alleged comments to Buckingham on this occasion, and LP,iii,1284 (ii) for Buckingham's alleged anger.
[5] Rawcliffe, p.36.

the accession of Henry VIII it was rather the thing to do. But as it turned out Buckingham's relationship with the new king was not much better. Although he was immediately admitted to the Council, he was never a frequent attender. In 1509 his first attempt to secure the confirmation of his, as he saw it, hereditary office of great constable of England came to nothing, Henry only allowing him to exercise it for the day of his coronation.[1] In May 1510 he had become involved in a quarrel with Henry concerning the honour of his youngest sister who, although married, was being courted by one of the king's favourites, Sir William Compton, probably on the king's behalf.[2] During the following year the duke's brother, the earl of Wiltshire, initially a close companion of the king much involved in the heavy round of jousting and revelling with which the new reign began, appears to have fallen from favour, though the reason for this is not clear.[3] In 1514 Buckingham failed to obtain any serious reduction of his debt to the Crown. Earlier he had been relieved of the need to meet a bond for £400, but nearly £4,000 of the £7,000 debt remained, and this he had to continue to pay off in annual instalments of 500 marks.[4] Too much should not be made of this. The payment was not chickenfeed, but for someone who was spending about £1,000 a year on rebuilding his chief residence at Thornbury, and could in 1519 spend £1,500 on entertaining the king at Penshurst it was hardly crippling.[5] Rather it must have been, like so much else in Buckingham's relationship with the Crown, extremely irritating, all the more so if he considered that there had been little justification for the debt in the first place.

Irritating also must have been his failure once again, during 1514, to have his right to the office of great constable confirmed. This second attempt, involving lengthy legal proceedings before the royal Council, was much more serious than the first. Buckingham claimed that the office was hereditary, being vested in three estates that had been in the Staffords' possession for almost a hundred years; or rather two estates, for the third was now held by the Crown. This, of course, weakened his case in law. Of more political consequence was the fact that all three estates formed part of the Bohun inheritance. Ever since Henry IV's marriage to one of the Bohun heiresses, this inheritance had caused difficulties between the Stafford family and successive kings of England. The other heiress had married Thomas Woodstock duke of Gloucester, and their daughter and heir had married first the 3rd and second the 5th earl of Stafford, Buckingham's great-great-grandfather. Thus, the emphasis placed on the Bohun inheritance recalled one strand of the Stafford family's claim to the throne; and if one strand, why not the other, which in a Tudor context was probably the more serious? Buckingham's grandfather had married a Margaret Beaufort, not the mother of Henry VII, but her cousin. Given the two strands, Buckingham's claim to the throne was no worse than Henry VIII's, and though it is possible to exaggerate the Tudor neurosis about potential rivals, the fact that Buckingham's claim to the great constableship also emphasized his royal connection probably did not greatly please the king. However, of greater concern

[1] *LP* ,i,94; Rawcliffe, pp.37-8.

[2] *LP*,i,474.

[3] Hall, pp.505, 512.

[4] *LP*,i,3483. More generally for Buckingham's financial relationship with the Crown see Rawcliffe, pp.138 ff.

[5] B. Harris, *Edward Stafford*, p.89; Rawcliffe, pp.137-8 for expenditure at Thornbury and Penshurst.

was Henry's determination not to allow any one family to establish an hereditary claim to such a prestigious office. It is interesting, given the suspicion that Tudor judges never went against the interests of the Crown, that in this case they did not entirely take Henry's view. They found that Buckingham did have a legitimate claim to the office, though at the same time declaring that the Crown had an equal right not to make use of his services. It was a compromise almost designed to cause the maximum irritation to Buckingham. In effect he had won the case, but was to be denied the fruits of victory. This can only have confirmed his probably mistaken view that the Tudors were determined to treat him unfairly.[1]

The most surprising thing about Buckingham's attempt to become hereditary great constable is that he made it at all. It is true that Tudor noblemen and gentry were second to none in prosecuting any legal claim, but to do so in a matter which so closely concerned the Crown indicated a great lack of tact and political sensitivity. So too, admittedly in a matter of less importance, did his refusal to take part in a joust, this probably in 1517.[2] It may be that the excuses he gave were valid. He was out of practice, and anyway he had vowed that he would never again run against the king, which in the circumstances was rather convenient because he had been asked to do just that. However, if Henry would allow him to take part on his side, he was willing to overlook his own lack of preparation – which suggests that it had only ever been an excuse. And despite the compliment implied in this concession, his answer did amount to a refusal, and one that strengthens the impression that his strenuous efforts to obtain the office of great constable also suggest: that he wanted, even expected, his relationship with Henry to be conducted on his own terms. If this impression is correct, it explains why the relationship was never good. Henry was not a man to stand on ceremony. He had great charm and an easy manner with those about him; the famous episode in More's garden at Chelsea in which the bluff King Hal was to be seen walking up and down with his arm around his royal servant and friend is evidence of this.[3] No ceremony, but as More, and indeed Wolsey, knew all to well, he never forgot that he was king, and had no intention of putting up with other people's conditions if he could possibly help it.

For a nobleman of his high rank and wealth, Buckingham was not often at court. His visit to Henry's makeshift court at Abingdon in the spring of 1518 has already been discussed: there were obviously some worries about him at that time, but nevertheless he went away with royal gifts of a 'goodly courser, a rich gown, a like jacket, doublet, and hose'.[4] Two years previously he had also been present at court, and apparently in good favour with the king. In fact he turned up on most occasions when he ought to have done or when he had particular reason for doing so, but no more than that. He was present in October 1518 for the signing of the Treaty of London,[5] which, if he did suffer from francophobia, he cannot have

---

[1] Rawcliffe, pp.37-9.
[2] Ellis, 3 ser,i, pp.216-7 (*LP*,ii,2987, though he suggests 1519. I have followed the editors of *LP* in dating it to 1517, thereby associating it with the great joust of 7 July 1517 in which Buckingham did not take part; see Rawdon Brown,ii,pp.101-3; Hall, p.591).
[3] Roper, pp.20-21.
[4] *LP*,ii,4075.
[5] *LP*,ii,4469.

enjoyed any more than his attendance at the Field of Cloth of Gold. More to his taste may have been the expedition to France in 1513, though by all accounts he did not play a very distinguished part.[1] It is important to get the balance right. Apart from the episode concerning Buckingham's sister in 1510, there appears to have been no open quarrel between the king and premier senior duke, no obvious animosity, no deliberate slights; only a certain wariness, a certain unease, a refusal by Henry to take Buckingham into his confidence, and an unwillingness on Buckingham's part to try very hard to obtain that confidence. That part of Buckingham at any rate did wish to play a role commensurate with his wealth and standing seems clear. Why otherwise would he have wished to become great constable? Why otherwise would he have complained that his services to the Crown were not well rewarded, while all the royal favours went to mere 'boys'?[2] But the point is that the other half of Buckingham was not prepared to perform the services without which there would be no rewards.

The suggestion being made here is that Buckingham was not excluded from power and influence by a king with an ingrained hostility towards all noblemen, particularly those with a claim to the throne. All the indications are that Henry VIII got on very well with his nobility, and was prepared to make extensive use of those who were willing and able to do him service. Two who did possess these qualifications were the 2nd and 3rd dukes of Norfolk. Both held major offices of state, both were given crucial military commands, and were in every respect indispensable servants of the Crown. Yet, as is well known, their family had been the most loyal supporters of the Yorkist regime, the 2nd duke's father dying on the field of Bosworth, fighting for Richard III. If an excuse was needed not to make use of the family, there was none better. Nor did it matter if a nobleman possessed a claim to the throne. One of Henry's great favourites throughout the 1520s was Henry Courtenay earl of Devon, who in 1525 he created marquess of Exeter. Yet Courtenay was a grandson of Edward IV. It was not who you were by birth that mattered to Henry, though he preferred it if you were well bred, but what your attitude to him was.[3] This was something that Buckingham never made up his mind about. He was obviously a proud man with something of a temper. When asked in April 1521 by Francis I what the duke was like, the English ambassador to France replied that he was 'a high-minded man that were in a rage', which Francis, with no doubt some eye to the situation, said squared with his own assessment of him as a man 'so full of choler that there was nothing could content him'.[4] In addition, Buckingham was determined to play an imposing role on whatever stage he appeared; hence that lavish expenditure on his entertainment of the court at Penshurst in 1519, and his even more lavish expenditure on himself and his retinue at the Field of Cloth of Gold. But of real service – of, for instance, regular attendance at Council meetings[5] – there was very little, and it does not appear to have been Henry who deliberately prevented him from performing it. The

---

[1] The evidence for this is mainly negative; that is none of the accounts of the expedition make much mention of him; see Rawcliffe, pp.100-1.

[2] LP,iii,1284 (iii), from Gilbert's deposition.

[3] Bush, History, iv for the argument that the Tudors' suspicion of those with a claim to the throne has been exaggerated.

[4] LP,iii,1245.

impression is rather of a man too proud to involve himself in the real business of government because to do so would mean working with, and even under, people – amongst whom he included Wolsey, and came perhaps to include Henry himself – when what he wanted was to be on top. At the very least he seems to have thought that the Tudors owed him something, and when they failed to meet his expectations he turned in upon himself, concentrating his energies on overhauling his estates and rebuilding Thornbury Castle in the finest manner possible.[1] There were no rivals, only monks who could foretell the future and fuel his dreams of what might be if Henry VIII was no longer king of England.

But what of Buckingham's relationship with Wolsey? If the evidence presented at Buckingham's trial is to be accepted, then it must also be accepted that Buckingham did resent Wolsey's power and influence with the king. There is, however, no evidence that Wolsey returned this resentment, and, as will be shown shortly, there is no good reason why he should have done. Furthermore, as regards their dealings with one another there is no evidence of great ill-will – if anything, rather the opposite. For instance, when Buckingham was anxious not to take part in the royal joust it was to Wolsey he wrote in his ultimately successful efforts to get his way, at the same time making it clear that he was extremely grateful to Wolsey for all he had done to further his cause on previous occasions. Of course, too much should not be made of this; Wolsey's help was worth a few compliments. But at least, on the evidence of this letter alone, relations were not so bad that there was no communication between the two men.[2] Indeed, on one matter it is known that they worked quite closely together. On his visit to court in May 1516 Buckingham had had a long conversation with Sir Richard Sacheverell, during the course of which Sacheverell had floated an idea, put to him by Wolsey only the night before – with the intention no doubt that it would be passed on [3] – that it was high time that Buckingham brought his son to court. In itself the idea is of some interest because it rather confirms the impression that Buckingham was reluctant to become too closely involved with the Crown. His son was by this time fifteen, and it would have been very usual for the son of a leading nobleman to serve some apprenticeship in the royal household. And that he raised the matter is further evidence of Wolsey's inclination to give good advice to Buckingham: if the son's appearance was delayed too long, Henry would begin to wonder why.

Buckingham's explanation was that he considered the court too risky a place for the health of an only son, especially because of the great danger of contracting the plague there. Only when his son was married and had an heir would it be all right for him to appear. The rather lame explanation elicited the inevitable inquiry – which may have been Buckingham's intention – about what marriage plans had been made for the boy. When the duke said none, Wolsey had suggested a daughter of the countess of Salisbury. It is quite an interesting choice. The countess was a daughter of the duke of Clarence and thus a niece of Edward IV. Such a marriage could only

---

[5] Guy credits him with attendance at only one meeting though there are many gaps in the evidence; see Guy, 'Court of Star Chamber', app. ii.

---

[1] For a good contemporary description of Thornbury see LP, iii, 1286.

[2] LP, ii, 2987.

[3] LP, ii, 1893.

strengthen the Stafford claim to the throne, which, if there was any worry about it, makes Wolsey's suggestion extremely foolish. In fact, it does not look as if there was, for two years later the marriage took place.[1] What did matter was that Buckingham's son married someone of whom Henry approved, and although in the late 1530s the countess of Salisbury's family was to fall foul of him, in 1516 it was very much in favour. No less so was the earl of Shrewsbury, lord high steward and a most conscientious servant of the Crown.[2] It was for this reason that when Buckingham foresaw difficulties concerning Wolsey's first proposal, Wolsey had suggested a Talbot match as an alternative. In making these proposals, Wolsey was doing nothing unusual. The Crown had always taken an interest in the marriages of its leading subjects, and Wolsey, as Henry's chief minister, was performing a very traditional role – and, it should be said, doing it with his customary tact. There was no suggestion of dictating to Buckingham; here, simply, was an offer to make the Crown's good offices available if they were required, with admittedly the implication that they would only be made available if the marriage met with royal approval. And that Wolsey did not offend Buckingham is suggested by the fact that he was very shortly to take up Wolsey's first proposal and bring it to a successful conclusion.

There was, however, an area that provided possibilities for conflict between Buckingham and Wolsey, and indeed between Buckingham and the Crown, and this was the law. No one was more obsessed with his legal rights than the duke, and whether upholding his claims to property, chasing up unpaid debts or suing his own officials for failure to carry out their duties, he was constantly asserting them. Between 1498 and 1521 he brought 128 separate actions before the courts of King's Bench and Common Pleas, while 43 additional cases were brought on his behalf by his senior officials.[3] With these cases Wolsey was not involved; neither does the frequency with which Buckingham went to law suggest that he felt that the common law courts were biased against him. But when Buckingham's legal affairs came before the king's Council sitting in Star Chamber, then Wolsey was involved – and the cases did not always go Buckingham's way. For instance, it seems likely that Star Chamber upheld John Russell's claim that his former master had wrongfully seized his estates; at any rate the Crown never accepted that Russell had gone in for large-scale embezzlement – the alleged justification for the duke's action – for otherwise it would hardly have appointed him to the Council in the Marches of Wales.[4] On another occasion Wolsey intervened directly to ensure that one of Buckingham's Welsh marcher tenants was 'indifferently handled and truly according to his desire, setting apart all rancour, malice or partiality, and without delays unreasonable'.[5] This meant that he should not be tried before Buckingham's own officials, and demonstrates Wolsey's well-known concern for 'indifferent justice' – a concern which might not endear him to noblemen determined, and perhaps even accustomed, to get their own way in legal matters.

Here is also a reminder that legal matters and government policy could

[1] The date favoured by Rawcliffe (Rawcliffe, p.136), though it is sometimes placed in the following year.
[2] For this episode see Bernard, *Early Tudor Nobility*, pp.11-26, though his interpretation differs.
[3] Rawcliffe, pp.164-81.
[4] Ibid, pp.166-7, 230.
[5] Ibid, pp.170-1.

interrelate, especially where certain sensitive areas such as the Welsh Marches were concerned. The government was bound to be interested in Buckingham's activities as a marcher lord, even if Buckingham might interpret that interest as unnecessary interference. In 1518 the king's Council arbitrated in a dispute between Buckingham and his tenants in the lordship of Brecon and Hay. The tenants had refused to 'redeem the great session', that is to say they had objected to the common practice by which all defaulters before a lordship's court were automatically pardoned at the end of the session on the payment of a fixed sum levied on the marcher tenants as a whole, not just on those found guilty. 'Redeeming the great session' had become a device by which marcher lords taxed their tenants. It did not further the maintenance of law and order, and was thus viewed with increasing suspicion by the Crown. In a complicated settlement the king's Council, headed by Wolsey but including, it should be stressed, Buckingham's fellow peers and relations by marriage, the duke of Norfolk, the earl of Surrey and Lord Bergavenny – the latter especially close to Buckingham – decided that while in this instance redemption should be paid, in future tenants should have the right to refuse. Past debts to Buckingham, other than arrears of rent, were to be cancelled. Efforts were made to prevent arbitrary action by the duke's officials; for instance, any tenant arrested merely on the suspicion of felony was to be allowed bail.[1]

On the other hand, the penalties for breaking the settlement were severe, and of much greater financial consequence to a tenant than to the duke, so that its effect was in some ways to strengthen the duke's position. The settlement has been called 'a powerful exercise of royal sovereignty in the Marches',[2] which is fair enough so long as it is also seen as a careful balancing act to ensure that both Buckingham's legal and financial rights and the good government of the lordship were effectively provided for. Though the Crown had delegated much of the administration of law and order to the marcher lords in return for certain military obligations, it had not thereby surrendered its overall responsibility for these lordships. This the 1518 settlement made clear, as did Henry's letter to Buckingham in that same year accusing him of failing to impose on his tenants bonds for good behaviour. The result of this failure was that 'many and diverse murders, rapes, robberies, riots, and other misdemeanours have been of late and daily committed, and left clearly unpunished'.[3] The duke was given just under three months to put the matter right. What he thought of Henry's letter, or indeed of the Council's settlement, is not known. Almost certainly he did not like them, and no doubt they added to his discontent and frustration. However, what they are not evidence of is any partial or sustained policy by the Crown or Wolsey to do him down.

And why should Wolsey want to do Buckingham down? The usual explanation, deriving almost entirely from Vergil's account, is that he saw the duke as a dangerous political rival. But given the poor relationship between Henry and Buckingham, this explanation will not do. There was never any possibility that Buckingham would usurp Wolsey's position. There is no evidence that Henry's visit to Penshurst in the summer of 1519 led to closer relations between the two men; and

---

[1] Pugh, *Marcher Lordships*, pp.32-5, 44-6, 135-8.
[2] Ibid, p.45.
[3] Quoted by Skeel, pp.35-6.

though, for instance, the duke may have disliked the junketings on the Field of Cloth of Gold, there is no evidence that Henry did, nor that he was losing confidence in Wolsey's general conduct of foreign policy. Some very few noblemen, perhaps only the dukes of Norfolk and Suffolk, had the necessary standing and influence at court to pose a real threat to Wolsey's position. Buckingham did not. Of course, if he were somehow to have succeeded to the throne, then Wolsey's position, even life, would have been in jeopardy. In this most obvious sense Wolsey had a vested interest in preventing this, but as long as Henry VIII was alive, or had a legitimate heir, Wolsey's duty as a royal servant and loyal subject dictated this as well. Once information reached him of Buckingham's dreams of becoming king, he had to take decisive action, whatever his personal feelings. This would have included bringing the information to the king's attention. When precisely he did this is not known, but once informed Henry took an active interest in all aspects of the case, personally supervising the interrogation of the witnesses,[1] and probably himself masterminding the duke's arrest; certainly Sir William Compton, groom of the stool, and other household servants were involved in it.[2] Henry's involvement is not very surprising; the matter did after all concern him intimately, but it needs mentioning just to make the point that if the downfall of Buckingham had been a 'frame-up', both Henry and Wolsey would have been responsible. The argument here, however, is quite otherwise. Until information reached them that Buckingham was listening to prophecies about his succession to the throne, both Henry's and Wolsey's attitude towards him had been perfectly correct if, especially in Henry's case, no more than that. Once it had done so, however, it is difficult to see how they could have reacted other than they did, even if Buckingham's relations with the Crown had been much better – but then if they had been the duke would probably not have spent his time indulging in such speculations.

If this explanation of Buckingham's downfall is correct, a number of consequences follow, the most important being that the whole notion of an inherent antagonism between 'butcher's cur' and pure-bred nobleman is seriously undermined. Far from planning the duke's destruction, it would appear that Wolsey did his best to save him from himself. Moreover, there is plenty of evidence of Wolsey getting on with the nobility. His first benefice had been a gift of the Grey family, presumably as a reward for teaching the three sons of the 1st marquess of Dorset at Magdalen School. When, twenty years later, their mother was anxious to settle with the eldest, the 2nd marquess, her highly complicated affairs – not only had she been an heiress and in her own right a baroness, but on being widowed she had married none other than Buckingham's brother, the earl of Wiltshire, all the while producing a great many children – it was to Wolsey that she and the 2nd marquess looked to in order to draw up 'Articles of Agreement'.[3]

Two years later it was the Howards who were seeking Wolsey's help in settling their family affairs. The resulting 'Order . . . to limit John earl of Oxenford in the ordering of the expenses of household and other his affairs in his younger years, as also for his demeanour towards the countess his wife' was an attempt to provide a

---

[1] *LP*,iii, 1233.
[2] Hall, p.622.
[3] *LP*,iii,2703.

solution to a family tragedy brought about by the disturbing behaviour of the 14th earl of Oxford.[1] Not only was he incapable of managing the De Vere estates, but he drank too much, ate too much, kept wild and riotous company, wore 'excessive and superfluous apparel' and, worst of all, treated his wife, who was a daughter of the 2nd duke of Norfolk, with none of the 'gentleness and kindness' expected of a husband and a nobleman. It is not known whether Wolsey's 'Order' did solve all the problems – and two years later the earl was dead – but it sheds light on many aspects of early Tudor life, such as attitudes to marriage and, more relevantly, to the nobility. It is permeated with a real concern for the preservation of a nobleman's patrimony and a belief in aristocratic values as a vital ingredient in the better maintenance of the common weal, and yet its author was supposedly antipathetic to such values. If he was, on this occasion he managed to conceal it with remarkable skill! Moreover, in drawing up the 'Order' he would have had to work very closely with the principal parties involved, and in the process he appears to have won the genuine gratitude of the countess of Oxford, who at one stage acknowledged that he was 'the setting forward of me; for I have nothing, nor was never like to have had, if it had not been for your gracious goodness.'[2]

Wolsey's 'Articles of Agreement' for the Grey family and 'Order' for the De Veres and Howards are of particular interest, because here were private matters – insofar as anything to do with aristocratic families can be thought of as private – being dealt with by Wolsey, insofar as his position permitted, in a private capacity. That his help was sought in this way may therefore be taken as evidence of a real trust in his ability to produce solutions. Moreover, it confirms something that Cavendish pointed out, but that has been overlooked, that Wolsey's career was successful not only because he secured the confidence of the king, but also because 'his sentences and witty persuasions in the Council chamber was always so pithy' that people, 'as occasion moved them, assigned him for his filed tongue and ornate eloquence to be their expositor unto the king's majesty in all their proceedings'.[3] Admittedly, Cavendish does not single out noblemen as a class who sought his help, but they more than anyone had dealings with the king, and, though the surviving evidence is meagre, what there is suggests that Wolsey's good offices were constantly made use of by them.

The distinction between the private and the public is not one, however, that should be overstressed. The evidence hardly permits any real assessment of Wolsey's private feelings towards individual noblemen, or theirs towards him – and in any age it is difficult for public men to have private feelings. Insofar as the politics of the time very much centred on the relationship between the Crown and nobility, anyone at the hub of royal government such as Wolsey, as lord chancellor and leading royal councillor, was bound to be intimately involved in the affairs of the nobility.

Wolsey was also a cardinal and papal legate. In December 1515 there took place at Bologna a famous meeting between Francis i and Pope Leo x. Although Francis came as the conqueror of Northern Italy, his demeanour throughout was modest,

---

[1] BL Hargrave, 249, fo.226 printed in *Archaeologia*, xix, pp.62-5.
[2] LP,iii,2932 (4).
[3] Cavendish, p.64.

not to say subservient. Indeed, he seems to have spent much of his time grovelling at the pope's feet which, as the Imperial ambassador rather archly remarked, were almost kissed away by his attentions and those of the French nobility who accompanied him.[1] Leo, it is true, was a Medici, and thus a member of the great banking family which for most of the fifteenth century had controlled the government of Florence. Nevertheless, in comparison with a king of France or a member of the French aristocracy, the crème de la crème of European society, a Medici was nothing. The Vicar of Christ, on the other hand, was everything, and the fact that the French had spent the last five or six years in bitter conflict with the papacy in no way affected this. Wolsey was not pope, but the English nobility would not have found it in the least demeaning to pay him, as a cardinal and prince of the Church as well as the king's leading councillor, the greatest respect. Moreover, it needs to be stressed that they were used to clerical lord chancellors, some of whom, such as John Morton only fifteen or so years earlier, had also been cardinals. Although in England leading churchmen had very rarely been drawn from the nobility, or even leading gentry, this had in no way prevented them from playing a leading role, not only in royal government but in society as a whole. Most English historians, perhaps because not familiar with either cardinals or aristocrats, have found it curiously difficult to accept this – at least when they have turned their attention to Wolsey. Instead, they have latched on to Cavendish's loving descriptions of the great pomp and ceremony with which Wolsey surrounded his daily life, in which the nobility played a great part, and have seen it as evidence not only of moral failure but of political insensitivity in thereby so obviously antagonizing the ruling classes. Nobody would have been more surprised at this use of his work than Cavendish himself. The lesson to be drawn from Wolsey's life was indeed that in any final judgment all is vanity, but it was precisely because Wolsey's life had been so great and glorious that it drew the lesson so well. And when Cavendish wrote, 'thus in great honour, triumph, and glory he [Wolsey] reigned a long season, ruling all things within this realm appertaining to the King by his wisdom', he meant every word of it.[2]

Cavendish also informs us that the English nobility were quite happy for their children to serve an apprenticeship in Wolsey's household, for Wolsey had in his household 'of lords nine or ten, who had each of them allowed two servants; and the earl of Derby had allowed five men'. Sadly, the remaining evidence provides only a few names. The most famous noble member of his household was the 6th earl of Northumberland, Henry Percy, for it was while he was serving there that he allegedly fell in love with Anne Boleyn, and may even have entered into a precontract of marriage with her. The earl of Derby, mentioned by Cavendish, also appears in a list of young noblemen who in 1527 accompanied Wolsey on his mission to Amiens to negotiate with Francis.[3] Others were Lords Monteagle and Vaux; Sir John Dudley, the future duke of Northumberland; 'master Ratclyfe' (probably the future 2nd earl of Sussex); 'master Willowby' (perhaps the future 1st Lord Willoughby of Parham); 'master Parker' (probably the son and heir of Lord

---

[1] Ibid, pp.24-5.
[2] Ibid, p.20.
[3] LP,iv,3216; Calais, p.38 for identification of the names.

Morley); and 'master Stourton' (the future 7th Lord Stourton) and Edward Seymour, the future Lord Protector. Other noblemen who may have been brought up in Wolsey's houshold were the Irish peer, James Lord Butler,[1] and Christopher Lord Conyers.[2]

On the death of his father in 1521, the earl of Derby had been made a royal ward, and though it is not entirely clear why he ended up in Wolsey's household, it is hardly likely that he had much say in the matter.[3] As regards the others, there is no reason to doubt that their parents, at least, had been free to choose Wolsey's household as a training ground for their children; and clearly it made an enormous amount of sense. It was very common for children of aristocratic and leading gentry families to send their children away to other households, including those of leading churchmen: the future 4th duke of Norfolk was to be a page with successive bishops of Winchester, Stephen Gardiner and John White – a fact to which his grandson the earl of Arundel referred when instructing his own younger son William in all things to 'reverence, honour and obey my lord bishop of Norwich as you would any of your parents . . . and in all things esteem yourself my lord's page; a breeding which youths of my house far superior to you were accustomed to'.[4] Arundel's instructions may serve to make the point that there had always been a familiar, if respectful, relationship between the nobility and leading churchmen, the latter being, just as much as the nobility, pillars of their local communities, living in palaces and enjoying the income from vast estates. The more important the bishop, the more likely it was that the nobility should seek to enter their sons in his household; and what better training, other than service in the king's household, for a young Tudor nobleman than service in Wolsey's?

Of course the willingness of the nobility to entrust their children to Wolsey's care may not by itself be evidence of a great liking for him; they may just have been making a cynical calculation that while the king chose to favour this man it could only be advantageous for their children to be associated with him. The evidence does not exist that would allow a judgement on this. But there is enough evidence to challenge the usual assumption that Wolsey's 'rule' was somehow inimical to the nobility as a class. Merely to point out that there was nothing unusual about a leading churchman of Wolsey's background playing a major role in royal government goes some way to undermine it, but it could be that his especially egocentric personality and his apparent dominance over the king caused the nobility unusual concern. Or, to put it another way, perhaps by becoming a royal favourite Wolsey destroyed the subtle balance between king and political nation, of which the nobility composed the most important part, thereby imposing great strain on the body politic until the nobility rose up against him and engineered his downfall. Were the nobility excluded from high office, banished from the royal Council, deprived of the fruits of royal patronage? Or looking at it more from Wolsey's point of view, did he spend his fifteen years in high office feeling so insecure about his relationship with the king that he was constantly having to

---

[1] St.P, ii, p.50 (*LP*,iii,1011).
[2] *LP*,ii,2481.
[3] Coward, pp.21-88.
[4] Quoted in Paul V.B. Jones, pp.32-3.

exclude possible rivals from the court, whether nobles such as the earl of Surrey, or other clerics, such as Richard Pace, who as the king's secretary became far too close to Henry for Wolsey's comfort – or so it has been alleged? Then there was that newly formed body composed of gentlemen of the privy chamber, who as personal servants and constant companions of the king played, it has been claimed, a significant political role, and were seen by Wolsey as such a threat that from time to time he felt the need to 'purge' them. It is issues such as these that must now be addressed.

Even at a first glance it becomes obvious that the nobility were just as active in royal government as they had ever been, and in some ways perhaps a little more so than during Henry VII's reign. Traditionally kings had made use of noblemen to dominate those regions of their kingdom where they themselves lacked a local affinity. It was always a balancing act between allowing them so much power that they themselves posed a threat to royal authority, or so little that the area became ungovernable. In early Tudor times it was in the North that this balancing act can best be studied (and will be in the next chapter). What is perfectly clear is that neither Henry VIII nor Wolsey was anxious to weaken the position of the nobility there, and indeed their problem was to find a nobleman who could provide a leadership effective enough not only to deal with the wild men of those northern upland valleys, but also to defend the border from the constant threat from Scotland. In the more settled Midlands and South the problems of good government were not so acute, but no attempt was ever made to weaken the position of particular noblemen, while the Crown was perfectly happy to build up the power and influence of a new magnate, such as Charles Brandon duke of Suffolk in first Suffolk and then Lincolnshire.[1] And as regards the government of the localities the nobility was made use of in every conceivable way.

First and foremost they served on the important commissions of the peace, which, appointed for each county and sitting in quarter sessions, were increasingly used for every kind of government intervention in local affairs as well as acting in their main capacity as a judicial body with very wide responsibilities for law enforcement. During Wolsey's lord chancellorship probably every eligible nobleman sat as a justice of the peace on at least one commission, and most on more than one. This remains as true for the last years of Wolsey's chancellorship as for the first; the slight drop in figures from thirty-six nobles for 1514-15 to thirty-one in 1528-9 being accounted for by the absence of some of the later lists of commissions. There was during this time a slight increase in the number of clerical JPs, but it is extremely doubtful that this was some deliberate ploy by Wolsey to undermine the influence of the local nobility and gentry. In 1528-9 there are known to have been only thirty-eight clerical JPs, which averages less than one per commission – hardly an invasion. In fact the clerical representation was concentrated in the counties close to the Welsh and Scottish borders. The reason for this was that from 1525 members of the newly constituted Councils of the North and of the Marches of Wales, which included a significant, but not overwhelming, clerical presence, were automatically

---

[1] For Suffolk see Gunn, Charles Brandon, pp.32 ff., and more generally Bernard, Early Tudor Nobility, pp.173-208.

placed on these commissions. But, as will be argued in the following chapter, that was for no other reason than that they were particularly well qualified for the heavy legal burdens that these Councils had to bear.[1]

The commissions of the peace were but one of a number of different commissions that were at work in Tudor England and on which noblemen sat. Many were of an ad hoc kind. Thus in 1522 Wolsey instituted a major survey of England's wealth and military potential, and to carry it out the nobility were very much called into service. Indeed, when writing to the English ambassadors with Charles v, Wolsey gave the impression that the various commissions entrusted with the survey were entirely made up of noblemen; at the same time he explained to Henry that it would be inconvenient to go to war with France immediately, given 'the employment of the nobles in viewing the people'.[2] Three years later Wolsey decided to supplement the already large subsidy granted by parliament in 1523 with a request for a voluntary aid, otherwise known as the Amicable Grant, to pay for an immediate invasion of France. Given the many recent demands for money, which included not only the first payment of the subsidy but an anticipation of the next, not to mention the heavy loans of of 1522-3, it was clear that a good deal of persuasion would be needed to secure this new demand. Consequently 'the greatest men of every shire' were appointed commissioners for the Amicable Grant.[3] Unfortunately no lists of the commissioners have survived, but we know that these included in East Anglia the dukes of Norfolk and Suffolk, the earls of Essex and Oxford and Lord Fitzwater; in Kent Lord Cobham; in Berkshire Viscount Lisle, and in the North and West Ridings of Yorkshire Lords Conyers and Latimer.[4] When in 1527 the harvest failed, noblemen were put on the commissions to search for grain, set up to cope with the shortages.[5]

In 1525, and again in 1528, there were disturbances, especially in parts of East Anglia. In the end they may not have amounted to much, though large assemblies of angry people had always to be taken seriously – and were. The Crown looked to the nobility and the leading gentry to put them down, for only they could quickly get together the necessary armed forces. Thus when, in May 1517, the London apprentices had gone on the rampage it was the duke of Norfolk and his son, the earl of Surrey, along with the earl of Shrewsbury and Lord Bergavenny, who had restored order in the City.[6] When in August 1525 there was trouble at Coventry it was the leading nobleman in the area, the marquess of Dorset, who headed the commission set up to deal with it. In fact by the time he had been appointed, the trouble was probably over. Nevertheless, Dorset informed his fellow commissioner and relative, Sir Henry Willoughby, that he intended to take with him to Coventry between thirty and fifty armed men, and trusted that Willoughby would bring some as well.[7]

---

[1] My own calculations from the printed lists of JPs; see *LP*,i, app.1; iii,1379, 2993, 3495; iv,1525, 2002, 5083, 5243, 5510.

[2] *LP*,iii,2126.

[3] Hall, p.694.

[4] Ibid, p.696, *LP*,iv,1235, 1260, 1305, 1321, 1325; iv, app.6.

[5] *Inter alia LP*,iv,3822.

[6] *Inter alia* Rawdon Brown, ii, p.71 (*LP*,ii,3204).

[7] Pythian-Adams,pp.253-7.

The main feature of the government's response to the disturbances in East Anglia, both in 1525 and in 1528, was the co-operation between the likes of Norfolk and Suffolk with Wolsey, prompting him, on the first occasion, to thank the two dukes for their 'wise, discreet and politic' handling of the situation, 'wherein you have deserved high and great praise'.[1] Arguably they deserved even more praise for the handling of the situation in 1528, when bad harvests, food shortages, trade embargoes, and illness were making life very difficult for the inhabitants of East Anglia – and for those who governed them. By this date, in most accounts, an aristocratic faction led by the two dukes was already plotting Wolsey's downfall. Of such plotting there is not the slightest hint in any of the many letters they wrote to the cardinal from East Anglia at this time. Indeed, on 9 March Norfolk wrote him a long letter, the tone of which could hardly have been more friendly.[2] He begged Wolsey to inform the lord admiral, Lord Lisle, that the pirates who had captured a small trading ship had in their turn been captured by the men of Dunwich. At Norfolk's command they had been put in prison until instructions were received from the lord admiral as to what he wanted done with them; meanwhile the cost of keeping them in prison would be charged to him. Norfolk then turned to a more important matter, his meeting with forty of the most substantial clothiers in the locality. After great difficulty he had persuaded them to start up work again and take back their laid-off men, but he urged Wolsey to persuade the London clothiers 'not to suffer so many cloths to remain in Blackwell Hall unbought', for if the East Anglian clothiers could not sell their cloth, they would have to lay the men off again. Finally, he turned to a matter of great personal concern to Wolsey, his new college at Ipswich. He 'had been to Ipswich and saw a platt [plan] made of the whole house of St Peter's, which your grace shall see at my coming, and I trust my poor advice in your building there shall save your grace large money'. As it happened, Norfolk's coming up to see Wolsey was delayed, for no sooner had he finished the letter than he received a royal command to remain at home. This threw his plans into confusion, for amongst other things he was short of ready cash which he had intended to obtain while in London. In the circumstances, the tone of his postscript was very reasonable. He would, of course, obey the royal command, but nevertheless hoped that he would be allowed to come up to London, 'though I do not tary VI days in going, coming, or abiding there'.[3] And one reason that he gave for wishing to come up was that he might still be able to consult with Wolsey. At the same time, he made it clear that if he had thought that there was 'any danger in time of my absence' he would not have made even this request. In fact, both Henry and Wolsey took the view that at this critical time Norfolk's place was in East Anglia, and, apart from a brief visit to London in June, this is where he remained for much of the rest of the year.[4] But as this letter, and his more than busy career, make very plain, a nobleman such as Norfolk was a linchpin of Henrician government, whether dealing with the side effects of piracy, the problems of large-scale unemployment or the threat of insurrection; and this was as true in Wolsey's time as

---

[1] LP,iv,1324.
[2] PRO SP1/47/fo.89v (LP,iv,4044).
[3] PRO SP1/47/fo.91 (LP,iv,4045).
[4] LP,iv, 4192, 4320.

later.

All the same, however useful the nobility might be in the maintenance of good government at home, it was on horseback and doing daring deeds on the battlefield that they really came into their own. Chivalric ideas still permeated the top levels of English society, and to win renown in the tiltyard or on the battlefield was still the ideal of every self-respecting nobleman and knight. More mundanely, it was only the wealthy landowner who could afford to provide men and weapons for the king's armies. During the time that Wolsey was a leading royal councillor no attempt was made to undermine the noblemen's military role. Armies continued to be recruited in the traditional way, largely from the retinues provided by them and by the leading gentry. All the important military expeditions were led by noblemen: the marquess of Dorset to Guienne in 1512; the earl of Surrey – soon to be restored to the dukedom of Norfolk – against the Scots in 1513; his son, by then himself earl of Surrey, in Ireland from 1520 to 1522, and against the French and Scots in 1522, 1523 and 1524; and the duke of Suffolk against the French in 1523. Moreover, when expeditions against the French in 1525 and against the Imperialists in 1528 were planned, appointed to command them were, respectively, Norfolk and Suffolk. It is true that in 1521 Wolsey opposed Henry's wish to appoint a nobleman to command an English force to be sent to provide immediate help for the emperor. But only a very small force of archers was involved, and anyway Wolsey's objection had nothing to do with any inherent hostility towards the nobility, and everything to do with the very tricky diplomacy he was currently engaged in, the success of which depended upon maintaining some appearance of neutrality as between Habsburg and Valois. To appoint a nobleman to command the force could only draw attention to it and thus to the breach of neutrality that sending the force involved – as, in the end, Henry accepted. Once war against the French had been openly declared, no more was heard from Wolsey about not having a nobleman to command a royal army.[1]

The only point in commenting on the vital military role that the nobility continued to play during this period is that, like so much else, it must undermine the notion of a Wolsey inimical to their interests and way of life. Indeed, insofar as Henry and he pursued a forward foreign policy, it could be argued that quite the opposite was true. When in 1513 Henry led over to France what was probably the largest expeditionary force that had hitherto left English shores, he took with him twenty-seven noblemen out of a total of forty-seven alive at the time. This sixty-two per cent turn-out becomes even more impressive if the eleven noblemen involved in the campaign against the Scots of that same year, the four who were too young to take part, and the one, Edward Lord Burgh, who was a lunatic, are removed from the reckoning. And of the three noblemen so far unaccounted for, all sent their sons to France, so presumably they considered themselves too old for active campaigning.[2] What this adds up to is that, whether in France or in Scotland, all the nobles who could possibly do so fought on Henry's behalf in 1513. It was an excellent turn-out, and no doubt both Henry and Wolsey worked hard to attain it. It may also indicate that the young King Henry had succeeded in capturing the

---

[1] *LP*,iii,1393, 1448, 1453-4, 1459, 1462, 1473.

[2] Very much my own calculations; but for those who took part in the 1513 campaign see *LP*,i,2052-3.

imagination of a nobility whose pride and morale, if not their real power, had suffered a good deal during the previous reign. I suggested earlier that the main purpose of this expedition was to make a point about English power, and to establish a bargaining position as a result of which England could play a dominant role in European affairs.[1] Such a view does not exclude the possibility that the expedition was also seen as a means by which the winning of honour and glory abroad might secure the loyalty of an at least mildly discontented nobility. In other words, not only may Henry VIII have captured the nobility's imagination, but he may have deliberately set out to do so.

Alas, there is very little evidence for all this; nothing to compare, for instance, with the speech made to the 1472 parliament, perhaps by the chancellor, Robert Stillington, in which one of the chief justifications for a campaign against the French was that since the Norman conquest internal peace had never long prevailed 'in any King's day, but in such as have made war outward'.[2] The appearance in 1513 of a new and slightly expanded translation of Titus Livius's biography of Henry V may be a straw in the wind. It does not appear to have been commissioned by the king (though this has been alleged),[3] but its message – that the virtuous king with justice, and therefore God, on his side would be successful in battle and thereby win great honour and lasting fame – was calculated to rally the nobility of England behind a king who shared both the name and some of the qualities of the great victor of Agincourt. And Lord Berners's translation of Froissart's *Chronicles*, the first volume of which appeared in 1523 when England was again at war with France, was made 'at the high commandment of my most redoubted sovereign, Lord King Henry the Eighth'.[4] Berners's purpose was to spur on 'the noble gentlemen of England' by enabling them 'to see, behold, and read the high enterprises, famous acts, and glorious deeds done and achieved by their valiant ancestors'. And if two translations hardly make a very convincing case, Henry's and Wolsey's determination to conduct a forward foreign policy was bound to enhance the role of the nobility.

As I have argued elsewhere in this book, a forward foreign policy did not necessarily mean war; peace could bring just as much honour as long as it was achieved in the right way. The signing of the Treaty of London in October 1518 had been a great coup for Wolsey, and had brought great honour to his master. Not surprisingly it had been accompanied with the greatest ceremonial possible: the marriage settlement by which the Princess Mary was betrothed to the dauphin was signed by no less than three dukes, a marquess and three earls.[5] Two years later even more noblemen graced the Field of Cloth of Gold than had taken part in the expedition of 1513, and with retinues almost as large.[6] And whatever its diplomatic significance, the event itself was a glorious celebration of chivalry. When, by 1522,

---

[1] See pp.22 ff. above.
[2] Quoted and fully discussed in Lander, *Crown and Nobility*, pp.228-30.
[3] Scarisbrick, *Henry VIII*, p.23, n.3, but the unknown author's prologue strongly suggests otherwise; see Kingsford, pp.3-4.
[4] Froissart, p.xvii; more generally Ferguson, pp.23 ff; Gunn, 'French wars', pp.34-7; Scarisbrick, *Henry VIII*, pp.22-4.
[5] *LP*,ii,4475; more generally Angelo, pp.131-6.
[6] 32 as compared with 27, but the first figure does include four sons of the marquess of Dorset; see Russell, *Field of Cloth of Gold*, pp.191-5. But the real point is that a lot went.

the alliance with France had broken down, the Emperor Charles paid a visit to England to inaugurate the Great Enterprise against England's former ally. On arriving at Canterbury he was greeted by no less than eighteen noblemen, nine of whom were to put their signature to the ensuing Treaty of Windsor.[1] By 1527 England's ally was once again France, in a year that saw much diplomatic ceremonial, the highlight had been an exchange between the two monarchs of the premier chivalric orders – that of St Michael and the garter.[2]

All in all, the evidence is overwhelming that Henry and Wolsey set out to create an impression, not only at home but throughout Europe. Whether it was as warrior or peacemaker did not matter very much. Both involved a deliberate use of ceremonial and courtly entertainments for propaganda purposes. In all these the nobility's presence was vital, even if it meant that they had to take part in the dancing and 'disguising' along with the more traditional jousting and tourneying. And it should be said that by and large Henry and Wolsey were indeed impressive. Many foreign observers reported favourably. One such, Francesco Chieregato, writing to Isabella d'Este in July 1517, described in great detail the entertainment offered to the Archduke Charles's ambassadors. At their first meeting with Henry were present

> the Queens [Catherine or Aragon and Mary dowager queen of France and subsequently duchess of Suffolk] the dukes, the marquess, and all other barons all arranged in cloth of gold with chains around their necks; everything glistened with gold. They were banqueted daily until Tuesday week, first by the cardinal, then by the lord mayor of London, and by various noblemen in succession.

One day there was a solemn mass, on another 'a most stately joust . . . at which all the princes and barons of the kingdom were present', followed by a supper which appears to have lasted for seven hours. In conclusion Chieregato declared that 'the wealth and civilization of the world are here; and those who call the English barbarians appear to me to render themselves such'.[3] There is just the suspicion that the whole thing had gone to his head, perhaps literally as well as metaphorically; but then, of course, it was meant to.

Whether or not there was an element of calculation in all this, it is certainly true that Henry VIII seems to have been at ease in the company of his nobility – and why not? Something has already been said about the young Henry; his outstanding gifts, his great charm and imposing physical presence.[4] Although it was his elder brother who had been christened Arthur, it was Henry who really deserved the name, for he it was who determined to make his court into a second Camelot where knightly pursuits and, in keeping with the new fashions, Renaissance pastimes such as masquing and music-making, flourished. Or to put it more prosaically, Henry VIII, unlike his father, had been brought up at court, and, since the death of his elder brother in 1502, had expected to succeed to the throne without having to fight for it. The precise nature of Henry VII's rule has been much debated. The notion of the 'New Monarchy' has rather gone out of fashion, and with it the belief that

[1] LP,iii,2288, 2333 (vi).
[2] Ven.Cal.,iv,188, 201, 205; Angelo, pp.211-34.
[3] Ven.Cal.,ii,918; see also Rawdon Brown,ii, 224-8 (LP,ii,4481).
[4] See pp.20-2.

Henry VII set out deliberately to remove the stranglehold which the nobility had supposedly secured during the travails of the fifteenth century. Nevertheless, the fact that, having spent most of his formative years in precarious exile in Brittany, he had not had the typical upbringing and training for someone of his high social status; that he had had to to obtain the throne on a battlefield in which many of the nobility were on the other side, including such as the Howards; that for most of his reign he had faced the possibility of foreign intervention on behalf of rivals, however spurious, to his throne – none of this can have helped to foster good relations with the ruling classes. One must not exaggerate. There were lots of noblemen at Henry VII's court, many of whom played an active part in his government; but he was reluctant to create new peers (only nine new creations in almost twenty-four years), he was not generous with rewards, and his determination to extract every financial advantage from the royal prerogative was not to their advantage. Above all, there was his extensive use of bonds and recognizances, so that by the end of his reign about four-fifths of the nobility were under some kind of financial obligation to the Crown, in many cases for no very good reason.

Undoubtedly, the son's style, reflecting both the different circumstances of his accession and his different personality, was not like the father's. His earliest companions had been taken from such noble families as the Bourchiers, Howards, Nevilles and Staffords, and, as has been stressed already, he loved to participate in the pursuits that such families enjoyed.[1] Amongst his closest personal friends during the 1520s were Henry Courtenay, created marquess of Exeter in 1525, and Thomas Grey marquess of Dorset, and they, as gentlemen of the privy chamber, were in constant attendance on him.[2] And Henry was quite happy to create new noblemen. Someone whom he raised from a mere esquire in 1509 to a dukedom in 1514 was another close friend, Charles Brandon. Thomas Howard earl of Surrey was a hardly a close friend, if only because he was nearly fifty years older than the king, but he too in 1514 became a duke, though restored to a title that his father had previously held. Along with the three dukes Henry created during Wolsey's time – the third being his illegitimate son, who became duke of Richmond in 1525 – he also created five new earls, one marquess, four viscounts and four barons. His father only managed three earls, two of whom were restorations, and the other was a foreigner who appears to have died, with his title, in less than a year. As for the elevation of those not previously connected with the nobility, the number seems on close inspection to dwindle to two or three, of whom the best example is Giles Daubeney, created Lord Daubeney in 1486, leaving only two 'new creations' for the remaining twenty-two years of his reign.[3]

One way and another, there is good reason to believe that during the 1510s and 1520s the nobility would have been well satisfied with their king, and with his leading councillor. And even if they did not especially like Wolsey – though there is precious little evidence that they did not – so far no reason has been discovered to suppose that they found his presence in any way inimical to their interests, or that it prevented them from playing that leading role both at court and in the localities to

[1] Gunn, *Charles Brandon*, 6-8; D.R. Starkey, 'King's privy chamber', pp.80 ff.
[2] D.R. Starkey, 'King's privy chamber', pp.129-31.
[3] *Inter alia* Chrimes, pp.137-9.

which their high rank entitled them. However, for such a conclusion to carry conviction there are two aspects of Henry VIII's government that need further consideration: his relationship with his Council and courtiers, and the way in which royal patronage was bestowed. Both matters were of some concern to the nobility. It was all very well to adorn the court, to take part in the king's pastimes, even to perform a key military role, but if real power was denied the nobility and if, for instance, Wolsey had managed to gain complete control both over the advice that reached the king and the favours that he bestowed, then indeed they may have had a genuine grievance against 'the butcher's cur'.

But before these important matters are looked at, it is necessary to make the point that however anxious Wolsey may have been to get on with the nobility, and more generally with the ruling classes – and the distinction between the nobility and leading gentry was fairly artificial – both as lord chancellor and a leading royal councillor, he was bound to have to do things that would not be popular with them. Most obviously, the duke of Buckingham would not have welcomed having his head chopped off, and may well have blamed Wolsey for this unfortunate occurrence! And it was after Sir William Bulmer had been hauled up before the Council in Star Chamber in 1519 that the duke was alleged to have contemplated Henry's assassination. As we saw in chapter 4, a number of noblemen, among them the earl of Northumberland and Lord Bergavenny, were brought before Star Chamber. Others, such as the earl of Derby, had to appear there at the instigation of those who felt maltreated by them.[1] None of them would have been especially delighted at having to put in an appearance, particularly when the verdicts went against them. 'Indifferent justice' did mean what the words suggest, that both high and low would be treated impartially. The high-born of any period have a tendency to believe that decisions should go in their favour; and the fact that, contrary to normal practice, noblemen were made to answer on oath in Star Chamber, may also not have endeared its presiding royal councillor to them.[2] And outside Star Chamber Wolsey may have ruffled the *amour propre* of a section of society unaccustomed to being thwarted in other ways. It has been suggested that they would have strongly resented the prosecutions for illegal enclosure that some, including the dukes of Norfolk and Suffolk, found themselves caught up in.[3] It is a suggestion that should be treated with some caution. Most of the ruling classes were not directly involved in enclosure, and insofar as they were royal councillors they almost certainly supported any moves to do something about a practice that was considered by many to be harmful to the common weal.[4] Still, at the very least, to have to appear or to be represented in court would have caused inconvenience and expense. What also may have depleted the nobility's resources was Wolsey's decision to transfer from local commissioners to a committee of leading royal councillors, headed by himself, the responsibility for assessing them for tax purposes.[5]

What none of this shows, though, is any undifferentiated animosity or personal spite by Wolsey against the ruling class. If they offended against the law or did

---

[1] See p.117 above.
[2] Guy, 'Court of Star Chamber', p.224.
[3] Scarisbrick, 'Cardinal Wolsey', pp.63-6.
[4] For further detail see pp.411 ff. below.
[5] Schofield, p.201.

things detrimental to the common weal, then it was his job to bring them to book, just as it was his task to criticize them if, as sometimes happened, they failed to carry out the king's instructions. And that they appreciated this is indicated, for instance, by the fact that, despite his appearance in Star Chamber in 1516 the 5th earl of Northumberland was prepared to entrust his eldest son to Wolsey's care. Historians have been too quick to assume an arrogance or lack of tact, when all Wolsey was doing was trying to ensure that the king's policy was being carried out in the best possible way. Thus, in August 1524 he was prepared to tell the duke of Norfolk off, but only because his failure to carry out instructions was endangering the king's policy towards Scotland.[1] Moreover, it is quite wrong to see Wolsey as somehow pitted against the rest. When in May 1525 the request for an Amicable Grant led to serious unrest, Henry was warned to keep an eye on the Lords Bergavenny and Henry Stafford, respectively the duke of Buckingham's son-in-law and son, on the grounds, presumably, that they might be tempted to avenge the duke's fall; but the warning came not from Wolsey but from none other than the dukes of Norfolk and Suffolk.[2] Similarly, the suggestion that a 'good watch' should be kept, probably in 1518, on at least six leading noblemen, including the dukes of Buckingham and Suffolk, came from the king himself.[3] It was always true that the greatest threat to any king was likely to come from the ranks of the nobility, and as Henry's leading councillor it was one of Wolsey's tasks to protect him; but it was a task that he shared with his fellow councillors, not excluding those of noble rank.

And it is worth stressing the participation of his fellow councillors, not only in matters of treason but in anything concerning the interests of the nobility. Admittedly, when he was asked to intervene in the private affairs of, in the one instance, the Grey family, and the other, the De Vere and Howard families, Wolsey seems to have acted alone, but the point about both these matters was that they were private. When matters came before him as lord chancellor, whether in Chancery itself or in Star Chamber, he never acted alone. Thus, as we have seen, when in 1518 Wolsey had arbitrated in the case between the duke of Buckingham and his tenants in the lordship of Brecon and Hay, his fellow arbitrators had been the duke of Norfolk, the earl of Surrey and Lord Bergavenny.[4] Those deputed to arbitrate in 1527 in a dispute between the marquess of Dorset and Lord Hastings were Wolsey himself, the 3rd duke of Norfolk, Thomas Boleyn, by that time Viscount Rochford, the two chief justices, the chief baron of the exchequer, the bishop of Bath, John Clerk, Sir Humphrey Coningsby and Sir Thomas More.[5] A year later Boleyn himself was in dispute with a leading member of Henry's household, Sir Henry Wyatt, and both men promised Wolsey to abide by the decision of the two chief justices and chief baron of the Exchequer.[6] Thus, unless one assumes that everyone else in and around Henry's court were mere yes-men, the simple truth is that Wolsey was never in a position to have done the nobility down, even if he had wanted to. And on the really big occasions, as when in 1516

---

[1] LP,iv,571; see also pp.568-9 below.
[2] LP,iii,1.
[3] LP,iv,1319.
[4] Pugh, *Marcher Lordships*, p.135.
[5] LP,iv,3719.
[6] LP,iv,3926.

Northumberland had submitted, or in 1519 when Sir William Bulmer had admitted his fault in wearing the duke of Buckingham's livery in the royal presence, then not only were Wolsey's fellow councillors present, but so also was the king himself.

In Wolsey's time, it is possible to identify a handful of what might be labelled, if a little anachronistically, opposition peers, or at least peers whose faces somehow did not fit. Obviously Buckingham was one. So also was the earl of Northumberland, who never obtained the high office and position in the North of England that his rank and family name entitled him to.[1] Another Northern nobleman who obviously felt that he had been wrongly overlooked was Lord Darcy. His does seem to have been a rather difficult personality, made worse by his disappointment, but the reason why he was overlooked may have been that he lacked the local power and influence to perform the role that the Crown was looking for in that area. What is interesting about Darcy is that at an early stage he claimed Wolsey as a friend, and still failed to obtain what he wanted.[2] Probably he exaggerated – or is this an example of the Machiavellian Wolsey discarding friends when they ceased to be of use? There is no way of knowing, though a similar claim for his relationship with Richard Fox was rejected earlier in this book. When in 1529 Henry was looking for information to use against Wolsey, Darcy saw his opportunity to draw up an indictment of Wolsey's administration of the North. We shall return to this in chapter 7, but if he thought that on Wolsey's downfall his time had come, he was to be disappointed yet again, and in 1537 he was beheaded for his part in the Pilgrimage of Grace. At the very least, therefore, one can say that Wolsey was not the only reason for his failure to get on with the Tudor regime.

Someone who was constantly in trouble, whether with his tenants, with rival familiies such as the Butlers of Warrington or with officials of the duchy of Lancaster, was the 2nd earl of Derby; and he was also, it will be remembered, on Henry's list of noblemen to be watched in 1518. In many ways he does exhibit those characteristics that made the enforcement of 'indifferent justice' with regard to the nobility and leading gentry so difficult: in particular, a willingness to use his enormous influence in Lancashire and Cheshire purely for his own advantage.[3] That he found himself in trouble with the Crown, and with Wolsey, is not surprising – and not at all to Wolsey's discredit. How they got on at a personal level is not known, but on his death in 1521 the earl bequeathed 'to my lord cardinal's grace a gold ring with a point of a diamond set in the same, and £20 in gold, beseeching his grace to be good to mine executors and favourable for the confirmation of my Chantry, beadhouse and free school'[4] – obviously something of an insurance policy, but all the same, would Derby have bothered to remember someone he hated or despised?

Unfortunately, even less is known of Wolsey's relationship with George Neville Lord Bergavenny, though Wolsey would have often sat in council with him, as well as having to mete out various punishments, even in 1521 having him imprisoned; and it is precisely these contacts, and the ambiguities inherent in them, that are so

---

[1] See pp. 220 ff. below.

[2] LP,i,2576: 'You and I were bedfellows and each of us broke our minds to [the] other in all our affrays. . .
' Darcy to Wolsey 15 Jan. 1514.

[3] See pp. 117-18 above.

[4] LP,iii,1923 (3).

intriguing. No nobleman was more in trouble with the first two Tudors than Bergavenny, usually for illegal retaining. In 1516 he was again charged with this offence, though what seems to have been behind the charge was a long-standing quarrel with the Guildford family, Bergavenny's chief rivals for power in the county of Kent.[1] The two half-brothers, Sir Henry and Sir Edward Guildford, pursued very successful careers in and around the royal household, and had the great advantage, unlike Bergavenny, of a father who had risen with the 2nd duke of Buckingham for Henry Tudor in 1485 and thereafter dedicated his life to him. However, if Bergavenny's troubles in 1516 are ascribed to a conspiracy by a Tudor monarch and the Guildfords to do him down, it would have to be pointed out that his two brothers, Sir Edward and Sir Thomas Neville, were as much in favour with Henry VIII as the Guildfords were. Neither is it at all clear that Bergavenny suffered any serious consequences from his brushes with Star Chamber and King's Bench in 1516. In 1521 he was in trouble again, on this occasion 'from a small concealment proceeding from negligence':[2] or in other words for failing to report to the Crown the treasonable words spoken to him by his father-in-law, the duke of Buckingham.

This time, for a brief period at any rate, the consequences were substantial. They included a recognizance of 10,000 marks, the payment of which appears to have entailed the possibility of losing his chief residence, the manor of Birling in Kent. He also had to surrender the office of lord warden of the Cinque Ports to none other than Sir Edward Guildford.[3] However, from these dire punishments Bergavenny did recover. In March 1522 he received a general pardon, and by the end of that year, though he had to find a large number of people to stand as surety for him, he was released from his recognizance. At the same time the threat of losing Birling was partially lifted, though as late as 1530 he was still having to pay out for its full recovery.[4] In 1523 he contributed a retinue to Suffolk's abortive expedition to France.[5] There continued, however, to be some suspicion of him – sufficient, as we have seen, to prompt two of his fellow noblemen to warn Henry to keep an eye on him. Nevertheless, in June of that year he was sufficiently in favour to join in the ceremonies centring on the elevation to the peerage of the king's illegitimate son, Henry Fitzroy.[6] And in all these ups and downs at no point was Bergavenny dropped from the commissions of the peace for the three counties he was most associated with, Kent, Surrey and Sussex. Even more surprising, he was one of the peers who most frequently attended royal Council meetings, continuing to do so even after 1521.[7]

It is very hard to know what to make of a man who, suspected of Yorkist leanings in Henry VII's reign and found guilty of misprision of treason in Henry VIII's, was yet extremely active in all military matters on behalf of the Crown, and whose advice was most sought after by Henry VIII. Bergavenny was wealthy, and could raise a

---

[1] PRO STAC 2/16/365-70; Clark, pp.14 ff; Guy, *Cardinal's Court*, p.31.

[2] *LP*,iii,1293.

[3] *LP*,iii,1290; Clark,p.17.

[4] *LP*,iii,2140, 2712; iv,6363 (1) though much remains uncertain; and to date he lacks a detailed study.

[5] *LP*,iii,3288.

[6] *LP*,iv,1431 (2).

[7] Guy, 'Court of Star Chamber', app.ii cites 18 attendances, with only the dukes of Norfolk and Dorset attending more often.

large retinue. Moreover, the fact that his chief power and influence lay in Kent meant that his retinue was conveniently placed for an expedition to France; but it was also, from another point of view, dangerously close to London. Perhaps the nearest we can get is to suggest that he was too powerful and too useful to the Crown for his support not to be strongly desired, and yet, given some of his activities and connections, he could never be completely trusted – a point confirmed by the fact that he, and indeed his younger brother, Sir Edward, gave less than wholehearted support to the 'break with Rome'. In other words, Bergavenny was a rather difficult customer, but the Crown's handling of him, far from indicating any desire to destroy an overmighty subject, is evidence of skilful management of a potentially very important member of the political nation. This is also true of those other noblemen whose relationship with Henry VIII was not always of the best during the period of Wolsey's ascendancy. All were treated with the respect due to their rank and position, all were made use of to varying degrees in the conduct of government and in court ceremonial – unless, that is, they were actively disloyal or showed an unwillingness to abide by the rule of law. When that happened, the Crown intervened. Only in the case of the duke of Buckingham did it feel compelled to take extreme measures.

Curiously, the only nobleman for whom it is possible to make a case that he personally mistrusted Wolsey is that most trustworthy and in most respects uncontroversial figure, George Talbot earl of Shrewsbury; the mere fact that Shrewsbury was that kind of man may suggest that the case is not all that convincing.[1] As lord high steward he was heavily involved in court ceremonial. He was a frequent attender at Council meetings, and, though not a lot of evidence has survived for this, he was no doubt active on the Crown's behalf in those areas of the Midlands where he possessed considerable land and influence; it is no surprise to find him on the commissions of the peace for the counties of Derbyshire, Leicestershire, Nottinghamshire, Shropshire, Staffordshire, Worcestershire and the three Yorkshire Ridings. He was also an important military figure. He led a large contingent to France in 1513, and in 1522 was appointed lieutenant general in the North. He may not have been the first choice for the post: the obvious candidate, given his previous experience in the North, was the future 3rd duke of Norfolk, but at that time he was needed for the war with France. Shrewsbury was also a rather reluctant candidate, Wolsey reporting to Henry that he had had some difficulty in persuading him to accept.[2] But then campaigning in the North was never very popular, and Shrewsbury was not a man to seek the limelight. Nevertheless, we know that someone, probably Wolsey, judged him 'to be as active a captain as can be chosen within your realm, meet, convenable, and necessary to be appointed for the leading of the army against Scotland',[3] and so off to the North he dutifully went.

However, back in May 1516 he had not been quite so dutiful in turning up at court, where Henry was most anxious for his presence.[4] There is nothing sinister

[1] Bernard, *Early Tudor Nobility*, pp.11-29. One of our few disagreements, but I am most grateful for much discussion on the subject.

[2] St.P,i,p.18 (*LP*,iii,1383).; see Bernard, 'Fourth and fifth earls of Shrewsbury', pp.164 ff. for the 1522 Scottish campaign.

[3] St.P,i,p.30 (*LP*,iii,1462(2).)

[4] *LP*,ii,1832, 2018

about Henry wanting him there. As lord steward, Shrewsbury was an important
figure in the royal household, who might, for instance, be expected to grace the
Whitsuntide celebrations. But he was reluctant to come, and moreover was strongly
advised not to by his servant Thomas Allen, whose letters are a principal source for
this episode and who was at this time very active in London on his master's behalf,
and in contact with Wolsey.[1] Shrewsbury maintained that serious illness prevented
him from coming, for even if he himself was on the mend, the chaos caused by the
illness of other members of his household made a journey to London
administratively very difficult.[2] The suggestion has been made that the talk of
illness should be interpreted as a mild protest or coded message by which a trusty
servant was informing the king that he did not like the way that his recently
appointed lord chancellor was running his affairs – something rather similar to the
present one-day strike.[3] Henry certainly did not act upon the message, nor is there
any evidence that he understood it in the way that has been suggested – but that
does not mean that Shrewsbury did not intend it. There were a number of reasons
why Shrewsbury might have wanted to stay away. It was a little embarrassing for
him that the earl of Northumberland, the father of the man he was hoping to have
as his son-in-law, had recently been made to acknowledge his guilt before the king
and Council in Star Chamber.[4] And Wolsey's suggestion, however well
intentioned, that rather than a Percy, he should take a Stafford as a brother-in-law
would not have been very welcome either; and he quickly turned it down.[5] The
drive taking place against illegal retaining had led to a number of noblemen being
temporarily in trouble before the Council, and Allen reported that a servant of
Shrewsbury's had been rather carelessly wearing his master's livery.[6] England's
foreign policy was going badly and because its purpose was being very much kept
under wraps, it lent itself to rumour and misunderstanding. Moreover, it was only
recently that two very senior councillors, Warham and Fox, had resigned from high
office, with Wolsey replacing the former as lord chancellor, and this had also led to
rumour and unease. More pertinently, Shrewsbury was himself involved in a case
before Star Chamber. The details are obscure.[7] It seems to have involved the duchy
of Lancaster, whose chancellor, Sir Henry Marney, was not his favourite fellow
councillor, so he must have been delighted when he heard that Wolsey had put him
in his place, by informing the chancellor that he 'had done more displeasure unto
the king's grace, by reason of his cruelty against the great estates of this realm, than
any man alive'.[8] And indeed, a feature of the whole episode is that both Allen, and
another correspondent of Shrewsbury's, and one of those in trouble over retaining,
Sir Richard Sacheverell, made it clear on more than one occasion that the earl was

---

[1] *LP*, ii, 2018 for Sir Richard Sacheverell's similar advice see *LP*, ii, 1893.

[2] *LP*, ii, 1815, 1887.

[3] This is the essence of Bernard's argument; see his *Early Tudor Nobility*, pp. 16-18.

[4] *LP*, ii, 1836, 1861.

[5] *LP*, ii, 1969-70.

[6] *LP*, ii, 2018.

[7] *LP*, ii, 1959. Marney was chancellor of the duchy 1509-23.

[8] *LP*, ii, 1959; also *LP*, ii, 2018. But by 1521 Wolsey and Marney were happily co-operating (*LP*, iii, 4057, 4088, 4124), and Marney's appointment as keeper of the privy seal in 1523 suggests at least a working relationship.

very much in Wolsey's good books.[1] Indeed there is not a hint in any of the correspondence that Shrewsbury saw Wolsey as some bogey figure.

In the spring of 1516 rumour and speculation were rife, but if the argument of the first chapter is accepted, that Wolsey had not knifed his former patron, Richard Fox, in the back, and that Warham's retirement was not enforced, rumour and speculation was probably all that it was – and if Shrewsbury had come to court he would have been in better position to appreciate this. Moreover, the earl does not seem the sort of person who would have wanted to make coded signals to anybody, let alone to his king. So, if in the spring of 1516 he was deliberately keeping away, it is likely that it had more to do with the state of his private affairs, such as his marriage negotiations with the Percys, than with any dislike of the new cardinal, who certainly showed no dislike of him. Indeed, one of Wolsey's tasks as the king's leading councillor was to keep the likes of Shrewsbury happy.

It will by now be clear that any evidence which would afford an assessment of a particular nobleman's happiness is extremely scanty, and in all cases difficult to interpret. What must be true is that access to royal patronage and favour would have been a vital ingredient in how a nobleman viewed his king. If he felt that he was being denied his just rewards, or that other people were getting more than they deserved, he was unlikely to take a favourable view; he might even in certain circumstances be tempted to oppose him. Moreover, if he thought that this situation arose out of the stranglehold that the king's leading councillor had obtained over the exercise of royal patronage, his opposition and resentment would naturally focus on him – and the same would go for any others who might have expected to enjoy some of the fruits, however small and however indirectly, of royal favour. In fact, Wolsey never commanded such a monopoly of patronage, or anything approaching it. This, at least, was his own assessment of the matter, if Cavendish is to be believed. The circumstances in which he made it were, admittedly, unusual. In disgrace at Esher in 1529, Wolsey summoned his household officers and servants. His chief purpose for doing this was to dismiss them until such time as it became clearer what was to become of him, but he was also anxious to justify his past behaviour towards them in the light of criticism recently put to him by one who was at this time probably the most important member of his household, Thomas Cromwell. According to Cromwell, while Wolsey had been in royal favour he had only rewarded those members of his household who were clerics: just those people, Cromwell had added with some bitterness, who had deserted him at his downfall. Hurt by this accusation, Wolsey had launched into a defence; in 'floods of tears', he explained to the assembled household:

> There was never thing that repenteth me more that ever I did than doth the remembrance of my oblivious negligence and ungentleness, that I have not promoted or preferred you to condign rooms and preferments according to your demerits. Howbeit it is not unknown unto you all that I was not so well furnished of temporal advancements as I was of spiritual preferments. And if I should have promoted you to any of the king's offices and rooms, then I should have incurred the indignation of the king's servants, who would not much let to report in every place behind my back that there could no office or room of the king's gift escape the cardinal and his servants.[2]

[1] LP,ii,1959, 2018.

In arguing thus, Wolsey may have conveniently overlooked the amount of secular patronage that the holder of two episcopal sees, an abbacy and the office of lord chancellor held directly in his own hands; and for local families in particular, such as the Boweses, Eures and Tempests in the diocese of Durham, such patronage would be important.[1] Still, as he implied, in comparison with the Crown he had little to offer, so it is what he had to say about royal patronage that is of most interest. His claim was that he had never interfered in what might be called the small change of royal patronage, and the surviving evidence very much supports this. The people who day in, day out, were in receipt of it were either members of the royal household, or else in some other way connected with royal service. Members of Wolsey's household did not normally benefit; that is the fact. Of course, it could have been that only royal servants whom Wolsey considered to be favourably disposed towards him were rewarded and that in this circumscribed way he was manipulating royal patronage. The problem of arriving at the truth is common to all discussions of the exercise of royal patronage: that the circumstances surrounding any particular grant are rarely known. It needs to be stressed, though, that such evidence as has survived suggests quite strongly that Wolsey had little say in who got what.

The gamut of what the king had to offer was extremely various, ranging from important offices of state to minor posts in the royal kitchens, and from grants of large estates to stewardships of decaying castles. Add to these a whole range of licences and exemptions from existing statutes, all of which offered some pecuniary advantage to the receiver.[2] The most prestigious and financially rewarding office to become vacant during Wolsey's time was that of lord treasurer – after the lord chancellor, the most important office of state. When Wolsey first began to acquire political influence it was held by Thomas Howard 2nd duke of Norfolk, and had been since 1501. In December 1522, aged nearly eighty, he resigned, to be succeeded by his son and heir, the earl of Surrey. In a letter written two days before his appointment was confirmed, Surrey informed Wolsey that he had spoken to the king on the subject, that Henry had been very gracious, but had told him to get in touch with Wolsey, so he was now writing to make an appointment with him for 9.00 or 10.00 a.m. the following day.[3] It would be possible to interpret all this as vital evidence that Henry had left the appointment completely in Wolsey's hands, but further thought suggests otherwise. The impending resignation of so important a person from so important a post must have been known to the king for some time before it took place, and, given Norfolk's age, would anyway have been foreseen. The likelihood, therefore, is that the decision to appoint the son was taken long before he saw the king. No doubt it had involved discussion between Henry and Wolsey, but there is no good reason for believing that the king's would not have been the decisive voice. After all, it was he who had appointed Wolsey and, perhaps even more relevantly, had raised his close friend Charles Brandon from

[2] Cavendish, pp.107-8.

---

[1] For Durham see James, *Family Lineage*, pp.29 ff.

[2] A lot more work on the royal patronage and the household in the early Tudor period needs to be done, but for a good impressionistic account see L.B. Smith, *Henry VIII*, pp.78-84.

[3] *LP Add*,356.

esquire to duke in the space of five years, so he was quite capable of making choices. In such a scenario Surrey's interview with Henry becomes something of a formality or courtesy call, and that with Wolsey only a matter of sorting out the details. Even if this reconstruction is faulty, the bits of evidence do not point in any convincing way to Wolsey as the man who made the appointment; and for Surrey to have given Wolsey less than twenty-four hours' notice of what, in this scenario, would have been a crucial interview, would have been a curious way to go about securing such an important post. And what the episode certainly cannot be taken as is evidence of a desire by Wolsey to do the house of Howard down, although those who are predisposed to think along these lines would want to draw attention to the following coda.

Surrey succeeded his father as lord treasurer in 1522. In 1524, on his father's death, he did not succeed him as earl marshal. How is one to interpret this? Was it a deliberate blow to Howard *amour propre*, or was it instead, or as well, a political balancing act? In other words, if Surrey was to have the treasurership, perhaps it was only fair that Suffolk became earl marshal, with the possible advantage to Wolsey that the division of spoils would help to maintain a rivalry between his two most powerful opponents? Clearly, some notion of fairness, if not balance, was involved. Surrey had been given a succession of important military and administrative posts in Ireland, in the North and against the French. Suffolk, on the other hand, ever since his marriage without initial royal consent to Henry's youngest sister Mary in early 1515, had been given very little responsibility, until, that is, the summer of 1523 when he was given command of the important expeditionary force to France; and it should be mentioned that it was in that summer that he secured the reversion of the office of earl marshal which, on the old duke's death in the following year, was to give him the office itself. Surrey in 1523 was heavily involved in the North, so that the attention paid to Suffolk should not be seen as any demotion of himself. Still, it does look as if there was in that year a deliberate decision to make more use of Suffolk, and his receipt of the high and particularly honorific office of earl marshal was part of this. However, it is surely of much greater relevance that it was an office that was almost tailor-made for Suffolk. Most of its duties had to do with the ceremonial and chivalrous side of court life, with which Suffolk had been intimately involved all his life, and he had already held the related though less important office, of master of the horse.[1] In other words, Suffolk's appointment was sensible, if, and only for that reason, rather obvious. And in the context of the present argument probably the most important aspect of the appointment is that it was in an area so closely connected with the whole panoply of kingship, as well as with Henry's particular interests, that it is hardly conceivable that he would not have made the decision himself.

Given all this, it seems unlikely that Surrey would have greatly resented his failure to obtain the earl marshalship, and indeed there is no evidence that he did. On the other hand, in October 1527 the Spanish ambassador reported that one of the reasons why the king's new favourite, Anne Boleyn, was antagonistic towards Wolsey was because he had some years previously deprived her father of an

---

[1] Gunn, *Charles Brandon*, pp.11-4, 66-74, 97-100, 121-3. In 1533 Suffolk was forced to resign in favour of Surrey, by then 3rd duke of Norfolk and uncle to the new queen.

important office.[1] Here is a specific accusation that Wolsey did manipulate the higher reaches of royal patronage, and to the detriment of one of the triumvirate of Norfolk, Suffolk and Thomas Boleyn that allegedly brought him down in 1529. What the Spanish ambassador seems to have been referring to is an episode which had taken place eight years before, and for which some evidence, mainly in the form of letters from Boleyn to Wolsey, has survived.

In May 1519 on an embassy to the court of Francis I, Boleyn was informed in a letter from Wolsey that the office of treasurer of the household, to become vacant as a result of Sir Thomas Lovell's wish to resign, was going to Sir Edward Poynings rather than to himself.[2] Poynings' elevation would make available the lesser office of comptroller of the household, but Boleyn was not going to be given that either. This double blow must have been very distressing for someone who, ever since his involvement in putting down the Cornish rebellion of 1497, had played an active part in Tudor government, especially, since 1512, in the conduct of diplomacy, and who might justifiably have felt that this service deserved some reward. It was even more distressing because when, four years previously, he had asked Henry whether on Lovell's resignation as treasurer, expected at any moment, he might succeed him, he had been promised that while that office was likely to go to Poynings, the comptrollership would definitely be his. What is more, Henry had repeated his promise in January 1519 just before Boleyn's departure for France. In wondering why the promise had not been fulfilled, Boleyn wrote that he supposed it was because Wolsey had perceived some fault in him[3] – and in so wondering he may appear to prove the case for the Machiavellian Wolsey. A closer reading of the letter, however, dispels such an impression.

There are two points to be addressed here. The first concerns the degree of Wolsey's involvement in the proposed appointments. The second, and perhaps more relevant to the question of subsequent Boleyn resentment, is to try to decide whether what was happening was a deliberate attempt to do Sir Thomas down. The suggestion will be that Wolsey did have a hand in the appointments, but that this in itself does not prove that there was dirty work afoot. Indeed, the argument will be that part of Wolsey's intention was to benefit Boleyn. It is important to bear in mind that the basic proposal, that on Lovell's retirement as treasurer, Poynings would succeed him, was at least four years old. Both Lovell and Poynings were outstanding Tudor servants, and that one should succeed the other was very right and proper; and it may be said in passing that there is nothing to associate Poynings and Wolsey in any factional sense. It is also noticeable, though given his long association with the royal household not at all surprising, that Boleyn carried out his own negotiations with Henry. On neither of the occasions when the matter was discussed was Wolsey present, nor is there any suggestion that the proposals were Wolsey's. What makes it likely that he did have something to do with them as they emerged in May 1519 is the reason that Boleyn was given for Henry's promise to him not being fulfilled: that it was Henry's intention in the fairly near future to create Poynings a baron. When that happened, Boleyn would succeed him, and

[1] Sp.Cal.,iii (ii), p.432.
[2] LP,iii,223 Boleyn to Wolsey. Wolsey's letter has not survived.
[3] LP,iii,223.

meanwhile it was thought not very sensible to put Boleyn in as comptroller for such a short period. Instead – and this had been Wolsey's reason for writing to Boleyn – it was thought important that whoever was appointed to that office should be someone approved of by Boleyn, so that when he did succeed Poynings, treasurer and comptroller would get on well together. What Wolsey was doing, in other words, was trying to devise the best possible solution to the problems raised by Sir Thomas Lovell's retirement, to ensure both that the administrative requirements of government were well served, and that the rewards of patronage were best distributed amongst the many claimants.

In stating this, one is making an important point about Wolsey's role in government. There is no evidence at all that it was he who made the really important decision that both Poynings and Boleyn should be rewarded. Wolsey's job was to implement Henry's decisions in the best way possible, whether they had to with the making of war and peace, obtaining a 'divorce', or, as in this case, with the exercise of royal patronage. Although it follows from this that there was no deliberate attempt to do Boleyn down, this is not to say that Boleyn did not have some grounds for feeling aggrieved. He had, after all, failed to obtain a post that he had been promised only a month before and, as he himself pointed out to Wolsey, it was a poor reward for his services as ambassador; and if he had realized that his absence from the court might be used as an argument for his non-appointment, he would not have agreed to go to France.[1] But if Boleyn was not unreasonably a little put out, how far did he blame Wolsey for what had happened? Since the main evidence for what he was thinking comes from letters he wrote to Wolsey, only a very cautious answer can be given, but he does appear to have appreciated that the real decision-maker had been Henry. At any rate, he was not averse to applying a little gentle pressure on Wolsey to persuade the king to honour his original promise. And when he wrote that he supposed Wolsey had perceived some fault in him, he seems to have been looking for a denial in the hope that this would force Wolsey to prove it by strongly furthering his cause. It is a common enough gambit and it is not one that works with anyone you genuinely believe to be hostile. And if this is to read too much or too little into Boleyn's response, what is not in doubt is that in the September he was writing to Wolsey that he surrendered any claim that he might have had to the comptrollership resulting from Henry's previous promise, and this because he perceived 'the favourable mind that your grace beareth to me, intending my advancement to the treasurership, wherein I think myself more bounden to your grace than ever I can deserve.'[2] Boleyn may not have been entirely sincere here – who can tell? – but probably by October 1521, on Poynings's death, and certainly by April of the following year, he had become treasurer.[3] It may also be the case that for a short time after his return from France, he did hold the office that he had originally been promised.[4]

With the death of the chancellor of the duchy of Lancaster, Sir Richard Wingfield,

---

[1] LP,iii,223.

[2] LP,iii,447.

[3] LP,iii,1712, 2481.

[4] Called comptroller by Henry in Sept. 1520 (St.P,ii,p.57). Cf. Ives, *Anne Boleyn*, pp.15-17 for a different account of this episode.

while on an embassy to Spain in the summer of 1525, an opportunity occurred for a reshuffle amongst certain quite important office-holders. The appointment of a new chancellor would in itself, of course, probably create a vacancy, but it was not the only office that Wingfield had held. Making the numerous new appointments was bound to be a complicated business, at the end of which not everyone might feel well done by. For those of a conspiratorial mind it is worth stressing at the outset that there has never been any suggestion that Wolsey had Wingfield murdered, so that the opportunity to fill these vacancies, even assuming that Wolsey would have considered them his to fill, was not of his own creation, nor is there any evidence that he welcomed it.[1] What follows, therefore, does not require a conspiracy theory to explain it.

The office of chancellor of the duchy was a major one, the holder exercising judicial and administrative responsibilities over a large area. He was paid a salary of £66 13s. 4d., a large enough sum, but probably, like so many Tudor salaries, merely the tip of the iceberg. It was bound to be much sought after, but it required a man of some proven judicial and administrative ability. From this distance in time it is obvious that the man to replace Wingfield was Sir Thomas More, and he was in fact to be appointed, though not without at least one other person being seriously considered. On 18 September Wolsey wrote to Henry that:

> it might like your highness to understand that yesterday I received a letter from Sir Richard Weston wherein he desireth me to be a mediator unto your grace for him, that he may have the office of steward of your duchy of Lancaster which Sir Richard Wingfield had, offering for the same to leave the office of master of your wards, or his annuity of one hundred pounds by year, of the which his desire and offer I thought convenient to advertise your grace, not doubting that by good means Sir William Compton shall be satisfied with the said stewardship or office of master of your wards, being offices more meet for him than the chancellorship of your said duchy.[2]

Sir William Compton was, as groom of the stool, head of the privy chamber, a newly formed department of the royal household, membership of which brought one into daily and intimate contact with the king. As such, Compton was bound to have been favoured by Henry. Someone who had occupied a very similar position, but at a time when the privy chamber as a formal subdepartment of the royal household did not exist, was Charles Brandon, and his meteoric rise has already been mentioned. Although never ennobled, Compton was most generously rewarded, so that at his death in 1528 he was one of the wealthiest men in the kingdom, with an annual landed income somewhere in the region of £2,000 and moveables worth nearly £4,500. And, as with Brandon, it should be stressed that it was his master, not Wolsey, who was showering these rewards upon him. Obviously in 1525 he was being considered for the office of chancellor of the duchy, but equally obviously he was not Wolsey's choice, a fact which has been taken as evidence of Wolsey's hatred of him – for which, it should be stressed, there is precious little support elsewhere. And surely Wolsey's letter to Henry is evidence of no such thing? Compton's career had been wholly in the royal household, and though, as groom of

---

[1] On the other hand William Roper suggested Wolsey plotted to send More to Spain in order to get him out of the way; see Roper, pp 19-20. There is no reason to suppose that Roper was right; see p.374.

[2] St.P,i,pp.162-3 (LP,iv,1646).

the stool, he did perform some administrative and financial tasks, Wolsey was only expressing an obvious truth when he said that he was not the person best qualified for the office under consideration. On the other hand, it is understandable that after fifteen years of close personal service to the king Compton would have been looking for further promotion and that the king would be anxious to provide it. There was thus a problem. Compton did deserve something quite important. The lesser offices of steward of the duchy or master of the wards might do, but not the chancellorship; this at least was Wolsey's view, and a perfectly sensible one. In fact, the solution arrived at was to give Compton More's former office of under-treasurer of the Exchequer. Compton, as keeper of the privy purse, an office which went with being groom of the stool, did have some experience of finance. Moreover, the under-treasurer received the large annual salary of £173. It does not seem, therefore, that in the end Compton had very much to complain about, nor is there any evidence that he did.

Neither is there any evidence that More complained, though, as with Compton, it has been suggested that he had some grounds.[1] Wingfield had combined the chancellorship with a lesser duchy office – though one worth £100 a year – that of steward of the south parts. But More was not given this: instead it went to Sir William Kingston, a man, who it has been alleged was close to Wolsey.[2] Here, surely, is evidence of a deliberate slight by Wolsey of a man of whom he was jealous and, because of the king's great liking for him, a little afraid? It was a slight, moreover, which may have had financial consequences for More. His salary as under-treasurer had been £173, but that of chancellor of the duchy was only £66 13s 4d, with additional annual sums of just under £100; thus without the stewardship his promotion appears not to have brought additional remuneration, though we must be cautious about this. If the remuneration of other offices is anything to go by, the £160 odd for the chancellorship is probably only a very minimum figure. Furthermore, only three months before becoming chancellor, More had been given the admittedly lesser stewardship of Hertfordshire and Middlesex.[3] At about the same time he also acquired a French pension of about £35,[4] while in June 1526 he received a licence to export cloth.[5]

In any event, remuneration does not seem to have been More's problem at this time, nor, as with all the other men so far looked at, is there convincing evidence that he was disliked or feared by Wolsey. If anything, the opposite was true. In 1523 Wolsey had gone out of his way to obtain from Henry a further £100 for More as a reward for his good services as Speaker of the House of Commons.[6] And in that same year More was frequently acting as the king's unofficial secretary, and, as a consequence, was at times in almost daily correspondence with Wolsey.[7] The surviving letters indicate a very good working relationship between the two men. This goes beyond and behind the mutual flattery which is certainly present and is

---

[1] Guy, More, pp.26-7 and for the details that follow.
[2] Somerville, Duchy of Lancaster, p.430.
[3] Ibid, p.606.
[4] LP,iv,3619.
[5] LP,iv,2248; see also Guy, More, pp.24-5.
[6] LP,iii,3267.
[7] More, Correspondence, pp.275 ff.

always hard to interpret. At one point More referred to a letter of Wolsey's as 'one of the best made letters for words, matter, sentence, and couching that ever I read in my life',[1] which may seem a little excessive, were it not that Wolsey's letters are to this day very impressive. But the point is that Wolsey need not have reminded Henry about the additional £100 owing to More, nor need he have continually praised him in his letters to Henry.[2] In August 1524 the University of Oxford thanked Wolsey for prevailing on More to accept the office of high steward of the university.[3] It seems a little improbable that More would have needed much prevailing upon, but it is just as improbable that, given Wolsey's very close involvement with Oxford, the university would have offered More the post without the cardinal's full consent. Nothing that occurred between August 1524 and September 1525, when More became chancellor of the duchy, offers any reason for believing that Wolsey would have wished to alter his favourable view of More, while a letter that he wrote to More shortly after the appointment seems warm enough to suggest that all was well between them.[4] And just suppose, finally, that despite the weight of evidence to the contrary, Wolsey was suspicious of More; would the supposed slight have been a very intelligent way of giving vent to such suspicion? In such a scenario it would simply have annoyed someone very close to the king without doing that person any serious harm. Machiavelli would surely have done it better!

Wolsey's role in the appointment of a new chancellor of the duchy of Lancaster in 1525 was the same as his role in the appointment of the household officers between 1519 and 1521. What he had tried to do was to redistribute royal patronage in the most effective way. And that this was always his purpose is confirmed by his actions in the summer of 1528. To examine them in detail might seem to be unnecessarily repetitious if the issue of royal patronage were not so relevant to possible reasons for Wolsey's downfall. If Wolsey did monopolize it, then the motivation for an aristocratic faction is obvious. If, as is argued here, he did not, it becomes very difficult to explain why men who were doing very well during his tenure of high office should have been desperate to see him go. Moreover, it is often alleged that by 1528 the opposition to Wolsey was gaining ground – which the events surrounding the appointments about to be discussed would appear at first glance to corroborate. And there happens to be a rather unusual amount of evidence relating to these appointments.

On 30 June 1528 Wolsey wrote to Henry, then at Tittenhanger, a St Albans manor where he had taken refuge from the sweating sickness:

> This present hour it has come to my knowledge that it hath pleased Almighty God to call unto his mercy, Sir William Compton. And forasmuch as the said Sir William had divers great rooms and offices, as well of your grace's gift as of divers other men, both spiritual and temporal, it shall be well done, if it may stand with your high pleasure, to stay the gift and disposition of the same offices for a while, and that your letters may be sent forth to such other persons as he had offices of to do the semblable till your pleasure

---

[1] Ibid, p.280 (*LP*,iii,3291).

[2] Ibid, pp.284, 288, 299 (*LP*,iii,3302, 3326, 3363).

[3] Mitchell, p.127.

[4] More, *Correspondence*, p.321 (*LP*,iv,1696) Wolsey to More c. Oct.1525.

may be further notified unto them in that behalf. In thus doing, your grace shall provide
for such your servants as your pleasure shall be to advance and do good unto, and in
respecting of the gift no hurt, but good, can ensue.[1]

Here, in Wolsey's own words, is a statement of precisely that attitude to royal
patronage that I have argued here is the one he took. It was the king's servants, not
his, who were to be rewarded, and the clear implication is that it was the king who
would make the choices. Wolsey's only concern was that they should be
implemented as smoothly as possible. The question then arises whether Wolsey's
words can be taken at their face value, or whether they merely mask self-interest.
What this letter could demonstrate is his realization that after Compton's death
Henry would immediately be bombarded with all kinds of requests, and that those
physically nearest to the king, such as his own alleged enemies in the privy
chamber, were more likely to have their requests accepted. Hence his call for a
moratorium so that he could the more effectively bring his own influence to bear. In
support of such a view is the fact that five days later he wrote another letter
specifically asking that Compton's most important post, that of under-treasurer,
should not be filled until he and Henry had had a chance to talk about it. He added
that he had a plan by which the office would be given to an 'able person, to your
pleasure', and which would also 'provide for divers other your good servants'.[2]
Again one must note Wolsey's concern that royal patronage should be shared out,
resulting in these rather complicated reshuffles. But, again, was his concern merely
to share it amongst his friends? That his proposal for a moratorium was not very
sinister is suggested by the fact that at almost precisely the same time as he made it,
Thomas Heneage, recently transferred from Wolsey's household to the king's, was
writing to inform him that Henry did not intend to grant any of Compton's offices
'unto such time as he hath knowledge from your grace how many offices he had of
his gift, and what they be'.[3] In other words, Henry, quite independently of Wolsey,
had come to the conclusion that a pause would be a good idea. In practice,
however, the pressure of suitors made it difficult to put the idea into effect.

On the very morning that the news of Compton's death reached the court,
Heneage informed Wolsey that 'divers there is that maketh suit to the king for his
offices',[4] and by the following day he was able to report that already a front-runner
for the post of under-treasurer had emerged in the person of Sir John Gage.[5] That
same day Wolsey received the first request, from Lord Sandys, for support in
obtaining some of Compton's offices.[6] The speed of all this is remarkable, and the
pressure to grant quickly must have been great. Moreover, it proved quite
impossible to prevent the patrons of the non-royal offices which Compton had held
from filling the vacancies immediately. Henry himself was anxious that the office of
steward of Furness Abbey should be bestowed upon Sir Thomas More and Sir
William Fitzwilliam jointly.[7] Meanwhile, sometime before he knew of this, Wolsey

[1] St.P,i, p.304 (LP,iv,4438).
[2] St.P,i,p.309 (LP,iv,4468).
[3] St.P,i,p.304 (LP,iv,4438).
[4] St.P,i,p.304 (LP,iv,4438).
[5] LP,iv,4449.
[6] LP,iv,4450.
[7] LP,iv,4476.

had written to the abbot requiring him to write what was the equivalent of a blank cheque: a grant of the stewardship duly signed and sealed, leaving Wolsey and/or the king to make the appointment.[1] In fact, even Wolsey's letter was too late, because the abbot replied that, alas, he had already filled the post, the lucky recipient being the earl of Derby.[2] But why had Wolsey written to the abbot? Was he using the very moratorium that he had suggested in order to go behind Henry's back to secure his own nominees? Or was he merely trying to get hold of as many non-royal offices as possible so as to be in a better position to make an intelligent distribution of all the Compton offices ? If Derby was to get Furness it would not make much sense for him to get a royal stewardship as well. In support of the former view might be the fact that Henry was a little put out to discover that Wolsey had already granted Compton's stewardship of Sarum.[3] Wolsey's explanation for his action has not survived. The office was theoretically in the gift of the bishop of Salisbury, but owing to the then bishop, Campeggio's, absence, Wolsey was the effective grantor. Maybe he felt that offices in his own gift should be excluded from the moratorium, a perhaps understandable but not very creditable view of the matter? On the other hand, it may be that Henry had simply been misinformed of Wolsey's actions.

There is some reason for giving Wolsey the benefit of the doubt, for in another case, unconnected with Compton's death but in which Henry's will was thwarted, there is no doubt at all about Wolsey's innocence. The king had wanted to give various offices in the gift of the duke of Richmond to Sir Edward Seymour and Sir Giles Strangeways, but before he could do so they had been filled by Richmond's Council, who, as the nine-year-old duke was made to explain to his natural father, had been given by Wolsey, allegedly speaking for the king, *carte blanche* to make all appointments theoretically in his gift.[4] And that this was not merely a cover-up for another snatch and grab by Wolsey is suggested by the fact that Thomas Magnus, a member of the duke's Council, had to explain to Wolsey precisely what had happened – which would not have been necessary if Wolsey himself had been pulling the strings.[5]

Private patrons moved fast in these matters, no doubt partly in an attempt to prevent royal interference. And normally the Crown, also, was no sluggard when it came to dispensing its own patronage. Why both Henry and Wolsey wanted a pause on this occasion was because of the exceptional number of offices that Compton's death made available; but the rush for offices permitted no breathing space. Be that as it may, the point here is Henry's active interest. He it was who requested Wolsey to draw up for him a complete list of Compton's offices because it was he, Henry, who would be doing the giving.[6] People he favoured would do well. Those he did not would be unlucky. In saying this it is important not to give the impression that the bestowing of his patronage was either too conscious or too whimsical. The notion of the ever bountiful king always ready to listen to the requests of his loyal

[1] LP,iv,4522.
[2] LP,iv,4522.
[3] LP,iv,4488.
[4] LP,iv,4522.
[5] LP,iv,4547.
[6] LP,iv,4438, 4456.

subjects was a powerful one, and one that it was important to maintain. Everybody was to be allowed to ask, and lots did. In the scramble much would depend not only on who asked, but when, and with whose backing.

One man whose backing would undoubtedly have been very useful was Wolsey's, and, as Henry made quite explicit during this episode, he much appreciated Wolsey's counsel.[1] Consequently, many people on this occasion, and indeed throughout Wolsey's period in high office, did ask him to intervene with the king on their behalf. What is not very clear is whether his interventions were decisive. One difficulty in trying to evaluate the evidence is that just because a person wrote to Wolsey did not mean that Wolsey would favour him. All that can be said for certain is that the people known to have written to him in 1528 did not do very well. Sir Thomas Denys, for instance, was very anxious to become under-treasurer. He had been for a time chamberlain of Wolsey's household, and he had the support of Heneage, Wolsey's former servant, who wrote to him on Denys's behalf.[2] Denys then wrote to Wolsey himself, amongst other things claiming that his legal training made him better qualified for the office than the previous three incumbents.[3] He did not get the job. Another person who wrote was John Mordaunt. He had apparently approached Wolsey on the last occasion that the office had fallen vacant back in 1525. Earlier in 1528 he had asked Wolsey for the office of treasurer of the chamber, vacated by Sir Henry Wyatt, but it had gone to Brian Tuke.[4] For the under-treasurership he was prepared to give 500 marks to Wolsey's college at Oxford and £100 to the king, but even so it was not to be.[5] One who wrote more than once for virtually any of Compton's offices was Sir George Throckmorton.[6] He had connections with Wolsey, including an uncle who was a master of Chancery, and he did receive something. But it was not very much, nor was it in the king's gift, for what he received was the stewardship of the bishop of Worcester's lands, an office, like that of Sarum, effectively in Wolsey's gift because of an absentee foreign bishop.[7] Giving this office to Throckmorton meant denying Sir William Kingston.[8] It was Kingston who, it may be remembered, in 1525 had obtained the duchy office of steward of the south parts instead of More, and who, it has been said, largely on the evidence of a comment from the Venetian ambassador in 1519, was a 'creature' of Wolsey's.[9] It is therefore surprising to find him being denied patronage by the man who supposedly controlled his every move. In 1528 he did receive some of Compton's offices, but probably the person who favoured him was the man in the best position to do so, the king himself.[10]

Another of Wolsey's so-called 'creatures', and someone whom he had favoured for the stewardship that Kingston had obtained in 1525, was Sir Richard Weston,

[1] St.P.,i,p.310 (LP,iv,4476).

[2] LP,iv,4449.

[3] LP,iv,4544.

[4] LP,iv,4452.

[5] LP,iv,4452. In a P.S. Mordaunt asked Wolsey to burn his letter, but interestingly Wolsey did not comply.

[6] LP,iv,4483, 4734 and in the second letter he refers to having written at various times.

[7] Bindoff, iii, p.451.

[8] LP,iv,4456 for Kingston wanting it.

[9] See pp.558-9.

[10] LP,iv,4687 for various stewardships.

and he it was who secured the main prize in 1528, the office of under-treasurer. Whether he was the person whom Wolsey had hoped to talk about with Henry and whose appointment was in his view the best, is not known.[1] If so, it was probably not because he was one of Wolsey's 'creatures', but because he happened to be an extremely experienced royal servant whose career had begun in Henry VII's reign, at a time when Wolsey had no influence at all. In 1518 he had become master of the wards, in 1525 treasurer of Calais. There is nothing odd about his appointment, and certainly nothing to suggest that it was due to Wolsey's special favour.

The same can be said of all the people who shared in the distribution of Compton's old offices.[2] Almost all were closely connected with Henry and his household, whether they were aristocrats such as the marquess of Exeter,[3] who happened also to be a leading member of the privy chamber, or merely a page of the wardrobe of the king's beds, as Thomas Garton was.[4] These, as was made clear earlier, were just the kind of people who were always in receipt of royal patronage, for the obvious reason that they were favoured by the king. Indeed, it was the obligation of the head of any household, as Cromwell's complaints to Wolsey quoted earlier make clear, to favour the interests of its members. In this respect the only difference between the king's household and anyone else's was that it was considerably larger, while its head had considerably more to give.

When in 1528 Sir John Russell informed Wolsey, his former master, that Henry had appointed him constable of Kenilworth Castle, this came as news to Wolsey.[5] It had been Henry himself, or at least someone present with him at Tittenhanger, who had written to Richmond's Council to secure offices for Strangeways and Seymour.[6] It was Henry who had wished to appoint Sir Edward Baynton steward of Sarum and Sir Edward Ferrers sheriff of Warwickshire – unless, that is, Wolsey had 'any further and more perfect knowledge of any other person or persons for the said room more convenient and expedient'.[7] That Henry did not always get his way is not to be ascribed to the machinations of Wolsey, or indeed of anyone else. The exercise of royal patronage was extremely complex. There was an enormous demand for it, as the speed at which decisions were normally taken indicates. Compromises were inevitable, not least because other patrons would not always do what the king wanted. Chance also played a part, if only because one had to get one's request in so quickly; absences from court could prove fatal. But the main argument here has been that on the whole Henry got his way.

As against all this, it could be suggested that the distribution of patronage in the summer of 1528 and Henry's apparently dominant role was unusual, and reflects only the particular circumstances of those months. It was a time when the king's relationship with Wolsey was being subjected to various strains, largely as a result of the difficulties in obtaining Henry's divorce. One symptom of these strains may have been the disagreement, which flared up at about the time of Compton's death,

[1] LP,iv,4468.
[2] LP,iv,4687, 4896, 5083, 5243, 5406, 5510, 5624, 5906.
[3] LP,iv,5083, constable of Warwick Castle.
[4] LP,iv,4896.
[5] LP,iv,4556.
[6] LP,iv,4536.
[7] St.P,i,p.310 (LP,iv,4476).

between king and cardinal about the appointment of a new abbess of Wilton. 'The matter of Wilton' will be discussed in some detail in chapter 8,[1] but, as will be shown, Wolsey's handling of the election resulted in his receiving the most severe dressing down from his master, in the course of which he was accused of greatly abusing his legatine powers and corruptly furthering the interests of his newly founded colleges. Henry did not usually criticize Wolsey in this way, so that in this respect the times were out of joint, but, if the analysis of earlier episodes has been correct, not in the matter of the exercise of royal patronage. The evidence of what took place in the summer of 1528 merely confirms in rather more detail that it was Henry who played the leading role. Wolsey's was to act as his patronage secretary, with the task not only of recommending, but of sorting out, smoothing over and generally introducing a little order into the rather messy way that the system operated – a system, it should be said, which worked on the assumption that the king had a never failing supply of favours to distribute when in fact the number was limited and their availability unpredictable. It was therefore extremely difficult to find rewards for everyone; hence the juggling acts that we have seen Wolsey having to perform.

What has emerged so far is a Wolsey rather different from the one usually portrayed. He did not destroy the duke of Buckingham. He was not antagonistic to the interests of the nobility as a group, or, insofar as the evidence permits any judgement, to any particular nobleman. It was Wolsey's job to ensure that the king's government was carried out in the best possible way. This could sometimes lead him to be critical of what individual noblemen or leading gentry were doing, and even, on rare occasions, to initiate legal action. On the other hand, he was on many more occasions brought in by them to help sort out their affairs. Finally, he did not prevent them from having access to the king, at least as regards royal bounty and favour. But what of real political power and influence? The usual answer has been that this was denied the ruling classes. Indeed, ever since Polydore Vergil first presented it, the most accepted scenario has been one in which Wolsey conspired to prevent potential rivals from establishing any kind of relationship with the king, the most notable victim being Thomas Howard 3rd duke of Norfolk. Whether Norfolk was treated in this way is better left until his role in Wolsey's downfall is discussed.[2] Here we must consider the more general question of whether Wolsey did establish a monopoly over the advice that was offered to the king.

Already the thrust of the evidence is that he did not. The nobility's involvement in all aspects of government has been stressed, and the same went for leading gentry. From now on the distinction between the nobility and other leading groups within the political nation will become increasingly irrelevant. Those such as Compton, Boleyn before he was ennobled, the Guildfords, the Nevilles and the Wyatts were just as important, and in some cases just as wealthy, as many noblemen. In late medieval government it was the king's councillors and his Council that provided the formal channel for advice, and the role of the councillor and the kind of response the king or prince should give to the advice offered him was

[1] See pp. 321-3 below.
[2] See pp. 565 ff. below.

201

at the heart of a large corpus of political writing. More's *Utopia*, especially Book 1, is such a work. In the same year that it was published, 1516, Erasmus's *Education of a Christian Prince* also appeared. Two years previously in Florence Machiavelli had finished perhaps the most famous, though by no means the most typical, of such works, *The Prince*, while in 1515 Claude Seyssel proffered to the new king of France, Francis I, the experience that he had garnered over many years as royal councillor in the form of his *La Monarchie de France*. All these books saw the problem of counsel as one of the keys to good government.

By and large English historians have taken the view that in Wolsey's time the king's Council ceased to perform the advisory or more generally political role of earlier years, and this despite the fact that its judicial role had been greatly increased by him.[1] This view cannot be sustained. Evidence that royal councillors, whether in Council or in a more informal way, were discussing all sorts of policy matters, and in particular helping in the formation and execution of foreign policy, can be discovered throughout the period of Wolsey's chancellorship. In January 1516 the Venetian ambassador reported having a long audience with both Wolsey and Norfolk, during the course of which the latter was very forthcoming on the issues of the day.[2] When in February of that year the French ambassador presented a letter from his master, Henry consulted with Norfolk and Suffolk,[3] while in the October the Venetian ambassador reported a Council meeting at which Wolsey, the royal secretary and bishop of Durham Thomas Ruthal, the bishop of Norwich Richard Nix, Norfolk, Lovell and Marney were present.[4] In January 1522 the Imperial ambassadors reported to Charles V that Wolsey had summoned them to a Council meeting at which four or five of the king's most intimate councillors had been present. A few days later they were present at another Council meeting at which Wolsey had been able to make them some answers to the questions they had raised, but only on those points on which he knew the king's mind; for the rest, he and his fellow councillors needed time to consult further with the king. On the following Friday, sitting with what the ambassadors described as the larger part of the Council, Wolsey reported the conclusions of their consultations – which unfortunately for the ambassadors were that there were certain difficulties![5] The following January the Imperial ambassadors had to wait until Henry had conferred with his Council before he could see them. And having seen them, he ordered that some of the Council, headed by Wolsey, should discuss the issues further.[6] In June 1523 Wolsey wrote to Lord Dacre, at the time actively involved on the Northern border, that when Scottish affairs had been discussed in Council it would have been very useful to have had his advice. As Dacre could not be spared, would he please

---

[1] *Inter alia* Davies, *Peace, Print and Protestantism*, p.165; Elton, *Tudor Revolution*, pp.61-75; Guy, *Cardinal's Court*, p.29. ('Although the minister [Wolsey] could not refuse the advice of the Howards and Brandons, Marneys and Lovells, who attended both the council and the royal court, he could render consultation to the barest minimum, and the council was abrupt even with leading councillors. Discussion of affairs of state was almost entirely confined to domestic issues.') Recently Guy has performed something of a volte-face. See also A.F. Pollard, pp.99 ff.

[2] *Ven.Cal.*, ii, 673.

[3] *Ven.Cal.*, ii, 682.

[4] *Ven.Cal.*, ii, 791.

[5] *Sp.Cal., F.S*, pp.31, 38, 42 for these three episodes.

[6] *Sp.Cal., F.S*, p.176.

give his opinion on three matters which Wolsey then proceeded to outline.[1]

It would be tedious to list the sixty or more similar references to the Council's active involvement in policy matters,[2] but it should be stressed that they are to be discovered just as frequently at the end of Wolsey's period as at the beginning. Indeed, the emergence of 'the king's great matter', that is, his search for a divorce, if anything increased the need for Henry to consult with not only his councillors but also a wider sample of the political nation, and ultimately with parliament itself, though this only after Wolsey's fall. In October 1528 the French ambassador was reporting that 'in truth he [Wolsey] has been for ten days wonderfully burdened. The king came to him from Hampton Court to Richmond every morning and did not leave the Council till the evening.'[3] The imminent arrival of Cardinal Campeggio was the occasion for this perhaps slightly unusual run of Council meetings attended by the king – though, as will be suggested shortly, attend Council meetings he certainly did. Moreover, one thing that all the ambassadorial coverage suggests is that Council meetings at which policy matters were discussed were the norm. So the sixty references are almost certainly the tip of an iceberg. The conclusion must, therefore, be that Wolsey did not preside over a one-man band, nor indeed did he even preside. Henry did that. Moreover, there is very little trace in any of the many letters that Wolsey wrote of that 'thoughtlessness and self-aggrandizement' that he has so often been accused of.[4] As we have seen, he could be critical when people were failing to carry out instructions, but he could also show considerable patience, even when fellow councillors were advocating different and, in his view, damaging policies. Thus, when Richard Pace was bombarding him with excessive praise of the duke of Bourbon's abilities and willingness to do Henry's bidding, Wolsey bent over backwards not to offend the prickly royal secretary.[5] In his inevitably difficult relationship with Warham, whose position he had in a number of ways usurped, Wolsey worked very hard to keep the older man happy. When in January 1523 Warham was ill, he seems to have been genuinely touched by Wolsey's offer to allow him to convalesce at Hampton Court.[6] In April 1525, at a most difficult time for both Wolsey and the government as opposition to the Amicable Grant increased, he was very supportive, pointing out to his 'dearest friend' that someone in Wolsey's position would always take the brunt of any criticism of royal government, 'but whatever be spoken, the fruits which a tree brings forth will prove its goodness.'[7] Wolsey was good at the art of man-management, as More himself admitted when he acknowledged the way in which by praising him in a letter addressed to himself but which Wolsey knew would be read to Henry, the cardinal had managed both to 'give me your thanks and get me his [the king's]. I were, my good lord, very blind if I perceived not, very unkind if I ever forgot, of what gracious favour it proceedeth.' And even under the enormous

[1] LP,iii,3114.
[2] And I am quite sure that I will have missed a good many.
[3] LP,iv, app.206.
[4] Guy, *Cardinal's Court*, p.131. But see also Elton, *Reform and Reformation*, pp.49 and pp.63-72.
[5] See pp.385-6, 552 below.
[6] LP,iii,2767. For an excellent treatment of their relationship see Bernard, *War, Taxation and Rebellion*, pp.96-109.
[7] LP,iv, app.39.

stress of the final months before his downfall, Wolsey could show a sensitivity to the pressures that the English envoys at Rome were also under.[1]

It may have already become apparent – though it is a matter that will be considered in more detail in chapter 13 – that, far from being riven by faction, Henry's councillors worked well together, often in difficult circumstances, to ensure the effectiveness of the king's government. The composition of the Council was very much the same mix as it had always been: noblemen, such as the two Norfolks and Suffolk; leading churchmen, such as Clerk and Tunstall, household officials such as Sir Henry Wyatt; and men such as Thomas More, or his predecessor as chancellor of the duchy of Lancaster, Richard Wingfield, often with a legal background and a tradition of service to the Crown.[2] Undoubtedly there was a pecking order, and one that reflected the fact that the Council was expected to turn its attention to every conceivable matter, whether it was dilapidated dovecotes in Sussex or complaints to be presented to the emperor for his refusal to play his full part in the Great Enterprise. As regards policy, it was upon a small group of councillors that the king relied: again the two Norfolks, father and son, and Suffolk, Ruthal and Tunstall, Fitzwilliam, Lovell, More and Wingfield, and perhaps also Richard Pace, Henry Marney, Thomas Boleyn and Henry Wyatt. It is not a precise list. Important people were often away on the king's business, leading armies, or on diplomatic missions. If we bear in mind that Marney and Ruthal died in 1523, the 2nd duke of Norfolk and Lovell in 1524 and Wingfield in 1525, it becomes clear that the inner ring, sometimes referred to as a privy or secret council, was indeed small.[3] This is not altogether surprising: the number of close advisers that anyone has tends to be limited. Henry VII relied at any one time on about seven,[4] Elizabeth perhaps on even fewer.[5] It is a feature of every study of the royal Council from the late fourteenth century to at least the end of the sixteenth that it was the principal officeholders – lord chancellor, lord treasurer and lord privy seal – together with one or two household officials or special friends of the monarch, who made up the inner ring.[6] In the metaphysical search for a privy council whose formation in the 1530s supposedly signified a new and 'modern' way of conducting the king's business, the more vital fact that important matters had always been dealt with by a small group has been obscured.[7] So also has the fact that a formal body with its own staff, assigned membership, and recognized procedures for implementing its decisions and recording of them, had been in existence for at least a hundred years before Wolsey, and, more relevantly, before the supposed architect of the new form of Council, Thomas Cromwell.[8] In fact, as we saw in chapter 4, all that happened in the 1530s was that the legal work of the Council was formally hived off to the court of Star

[1] See St.P,vii, p.193 (LP,iv,5797).

[2] Inter alia Guy, Cardinal's Court, pp.23-9; Lander, Crown and Nobility, pp.204-16.

[3] Guy, Cardinal's Court, p.28. For references to a 'privy' or secret council see LP,iii,1252 (St.P,ii,p.66); iv,5016; Sp.Cal.,iii (ii),p.105; Sp.Cal.,F.S,, p.38, 78, 124.

[4] Chrimes, p.113.

[5] S.L. Adams, p.63.

[6] Inter alia, A.L. Brown, pp.95-109; Chrimes, Administrative History, pp.133, 161-2, 223-5; Catto, 'King's servants', p.81; Ross, p.308; Select Cases, pp.xxix-li.

[7] The metaphysics largely provided by Elton; see especially Tudor Revolution, 316-69; Studies,iii, pp.21-38; but followed by his pupils, Guy and Starkey, though they have sought to modify their master's chronology; see Guy, 'Privy Council', pp. 59 ff; D.R. Starkey, History Today, 37,pp.27-31.

Chamber, so as to prevent its agenda from becoming clogged up.[1] A similar process had taken place in the twelfth and and early thirteenth centuries to bring about the court of King's Bench, and in the late thirteenth and fourteenth centuries to establish the court of Chancery.

However, the essential point being made here is that the king's Council, as the most important consultative and administrative body in the realm, did not go into abeyance in Wolsey's time. Then, as now, it can be difficult to express opinions contrary to one's boss – something that Tunstall had in mind when in December 1525 he wrote to Henry from Toledo begging him not to think that he was dissatisfied with the 'determination' of the king and Council. However, as Henry had admitted him, 'being of your own making, to be of your most honourable Council', he thought it right to give his opinion, and had been encouraged to do so by declarations often made by Henry in Council 'that, whatsoever our opinions be, we may have liberty to show them without displeasure'.[2] And in a letter to Wolsey he asked him to mitigate the king's displeasure, expressed in royal letters of 30 October, at certain words in a letter he had written to Brian Tuke, which he believed Henry had misunderstood.[3] If the ambassadors with the emperor could not write freely to the king and Council, it might hinder affairs.

Tunstall's two letters contain many insights into the workings of the upper reaches of Henry's government. They confirm that to offer advice on important policy matters was considered, at least by one of its members, to be an integral part of the Council's role. They also help to confirm an underlying theme of this study, that in a real sense Henry did rule. For one thing, it is strongly implied that he frequently sat in Council. Usually it is held that he appeared only on a few very important occasions or set pieces: for instance, when on 14 May 1517 those who had been arrested for their part in the Evil May Day riots were pardoned.[4] In contrast, his father is often said to have sat regularly, thereby confirming once more that a hardworking father had been succeeded by a lazy son.[5] One of the problems in arriving at any conclusions on this subject is that information about Council meetings for both reigns is extremely scanty; for Henry VII's reign only 135, or about a six a year, are known of, when, during the legal term at least, the Council may have sat every day. Of these 135, the king is known not to have sat in less than half.[6] For Wolsey's period, 580 meetings of the Council in Star Chamber have been identified, but with Henry VIII appearing in only a handful.[7] The conclusion should not, though, be that the usual view is correct. What in essence has survived are selections made by late sixteenth- and early seventeenth-century officials of the ›court of Star Chamber, together with often undated documents relating to

[8] Inter alia, A.L. Brown, 96-8; Chrimes, Administrative History, pp.216 ff; Harriss, pp.32 ff. Catto, 'King's servant', pp.82-84.

---

[1] See p.115 above.
[2] LP,iv,1800.
[3] LP,iv,1801.
[4] Guy, Cardinal's Court, pp.29-35 for this and other appearances.
[5] Inter alia, Davies, Peace, Print and Protestantism, p.156; Elton, Reform and Reformation, pp.33-4; Guy, Cardinal's Court, p.9-21, 29.
[6] Chrimes, Henry VII, pp.102-3Select Cases of Henry VII, pp.xix, xxxiii-xxxiv, 7 ff.
[7] Guy, Cardinal's Court, p.27.

particular cases.[1] One result of this is that the evidence is very much weighted towards judicial matters, and even on the known figures it seems that neither king was an active participant in the everyday judicial work of the Council. At the beginning of his reign at least, Henry VII may have sat a little more frequently than his son did, but it looks as if he soon realized that this was a waste of his time; at any rate from 1497 it was thought necessary to appoint a president of the Council. Moreover, it had not been customary for previous kings regularly to preside over the judicial and administrative work of their Councils, much of it of a fairly routine nature. Like Henry VIII, they only did so in exceptional circumstances.[2] What they wanted was advice and support, but it is precisely in this area that the sources are so deficient, as indeed they have continued to be. Policy matters tend not to get into minutes of any kind, or, if they do, only in the most laconic form: a heated discussion lasting an hour may result in only one line, if that. If one combines the nature of the sources with the usual bias against Wolsey, one can quite see why he has been thought, erroneously, not to have allowed the Council a political role. What has contributed to the error is precisely the notion that Henry VIII was weak and lazy, at least when young, and therefore happy to allow Wolsey to take the reins of government into his capable hands.

Tunstall's letter is not the only piece of evidence that Henry sat in Council. Already mentioned are the half-dozen set pieces and du Bellay's references to the the ten days he was present in October 1528. It is known that ten years earlier Henry was presiding over Council meetings at Abingdon and Woodstock.[3] And in January 1523 the Imperial ambassadors reported that after dinner the king was some time in Council.[4] An interesting variation on this was noted in June 1525, when Margaret of Austria's envoys reported a meeting with the Council during which Henry, in an adjoining room, occasionally put in an appearance.[5] This could be taken as evidence of the lazy Henry who did not bother to attend the whole meeting; but the head of any organization may wish to reserve his interventions to particular moments in a discussion; and as far as international relations are concerned, the whole point of having foreign secretaries, or their equivalents, is to keep the head of state in reserve. Still, it is a reminder that evidence does need interpretation, and the evidence of Henry's direct involvement in government is not only sparse, but difficult to interpret. Hence the wildly differing assessments of the part he played – at least by historians. Contemporaries never seem to have doubted that he was a powerful personality, whose presence could never be forgotten – a perception not to be dismissed lightly.

Part of the reason for the difficulty in assessing the evidence is the one already touched upon: that it is the consequences of decisions – in the early sixteenth century letters patent, writs and so on, along with the more familiar correspondence – rather than the making of them which produce evidence that survives. And since it was the king's task to make decisions rather than implement them, he does not figure in surviving evidence in the way that much less important figures do; and if

[1] Guy, *Cardinal's Court*, pp.1 ff.
[2] A.L. Brown, pp.96-7; Chrimes, *Administrative History*, p.236.
[3] LP, iv, 4061, 4124, 4125, 4288, 4293.
[4] *Sp. Cal., F.S*, p.176.
[5] *Sp. Cal.*, iii (i), p.194.

importance depended upon extant handwriting, it would be people such as Ruthal and Pace, and even humbler figures such as the clerks of the Council, who would come out on top – which would be plainly absurd. It is not that Henry did not like writing letters, or even that he was incapable of writing them; he was a highly educated man, perfectly literate, and not just in his own language. As now, important people had secretaries, and might barely glance at the bulk of the letters that went out under their name. Most of Wolsey's letters were written by others, and in 1517 Richard Fox could marvel that he had found the leisure to write to him in his own hand, clearly taking it it as a special compliment.[1]

The major problem for a biographer of Wolsey is that much of the business between king and cardinal was conducted in private, without any record of what was said surviving, and this makes it very difficult to assess the dynamics of the relationship. And at this point it is important to stress that they did meet frequently, because it has been argued that one of the problems Wolsey faced in retaining the confidence of and, in some accounts, domination over the king is that he was with him so little.[2] What is true is that once he became lord chancellor he was forced to be in London much of the year, presiding over Chancery and Star Chamber. London was also the most convenient place to conduct the day to day running of foreign policy. It was there that the foreign ambassadors resided, and it was well placed to be a centre of communications with the continent. And if he was not at his London residence, York Place, he was usually at Hampton Court, even after he had exchanged it with Henry for the palace of Richmond, probably in 1525, or, if not there, at either Tittenhanger or the More, two manor houses belonging to the the the abbey of St Albans. Henry also spent a good deal of time in and around London, but mainly at his palace at Greenwich, or, if he wished to be right in the City, at Bridewell. He was also often at Windsor, the usual venue for the court's Christmas festivities, and those connected with St George and the knights of the garter in April and May. In July and August Henry went on progress, visiting his leading subjects' country houses, and also staying at the many royal manor houses, such as Ampthill and Woodstock. Mentioned already has been his visit to the duke of Buckingham at Penshurst in 1519. In 1526 he was in Sussex and Hampshire and in the following year spent most of August at his new palace of Beaulieu in Essex, while Wolsey was in France. In fact, even in a more normal year, it was not Wolsey's practice to go on progress with Henry, so that during the summer months their usual means of communication was by letter.

Just how often they met during the remainder of the year is hard to establish. Writing in probably June 1528, Heneage reported Henry's remark that Wolsey was 'always accustomed to be with him as upon Monday night';[3] and that there were regular weekly meetings is confirmed by Cavendish, though he has it that they took place on Sunday.[4] Evidence for these meetings is, however, difficult to pick up, presumably because, since they were regular there was no need for any special

---

[1] Richard Fox, p.97 (LP Add,185): 'And much I marvel when you could find the leisure to write it yourself. I know perfectly that it came of your special good heart and affection towards me.'

[2] The notion underlies all Starkey's work on the privy chamber and faction first presented in 'King's privy chamber'; see also Scarisbrick, *Thought*, 52, pp.251-6.

[3] St.P,i,p.289 (LP,iv,4335).

[4] Cavendish, p.24.

arrangements to be made. One has to rely on the reports of foreign ambassadors. They could not have been aware of every meeting of king and cardinal, but nevertheless they do report their meetings sufficiently to confirm that they were very frequent. Thus, in May 1519 Giustinian recorded that Wolsey had visited Henry at Greenwich twice within three days,[1] while another Venetian ambassador in letters of 13 and 17 January, 19 February and 28 March 1526 reported that Henry and Wolsey were together at Greenwich.[2] In December 1522 the Imperial ambassadors found Wolsey at court,[3] and on January 1523 the king and cardinal kept them in conversation for two consecutive days.[4] None of these meetings appears to have required any special arrangements, but on occasions these had to be made. Thus, in 1518 Henry had dashed up to London from Woodstock to have a secret meeting with Wolsey to consult about the negotiations with the French.[5] In October 1523 Henry agreed to move to Windsor to be near enough to Wolsey to consult about the many military and foreign policy issues which were then preoccupying them both, and in fact shortly after this Henry stayed at Wolsey's 'poor house' in London.[6] April 1525 was also a difficult time, what with the Amicable Grant and the consequences of the Imperial victory at Pavia to be decided upon, and again the reaction of both Henry and Wolsey was to consult in person. On this occasion it appears to have been Henry who took the initiative, but Wolsey's response was that nothing could be more advantageous, offering to put Henry up at the same 'poor house', if that would facilitate the meeting.[7]

Henry and Wolsey did meet and, when they were geographically close, probably very often. When they did not, letters passed between them almost daily, and it is such of these which have survived – not many, alas – that provide one with the best opportunity of making some assessment of how king and cardinal worked together. Twenty-four letters have survived for August and September 1523, and they are additionally interesting because many of them were written by Thomas More, acting as royal secretary, something he seems to have done quite a lot while the actual secretary, Richard Pace, was on his long mission abroad.[8]

One thing that emerges from this correspondence is that the normal practice was for letters addressed to the king to go directly to him rather than, as is often implied, for them to be opened first by Wolsey.[9] More importantly, Henry either read or had read to him virtually all letters addressed to Wolsey that in any way related to his own affairs.[10] Sometimes those about him complained of his

[1] Rawdon Brown, ii p.268 (Ven.Cal., ii, 1215).

[2] Ven.Cal.,iii,1201, 1203, 1220, 1235.

[3] Sp.Cal.,F.S, pp.177 ff.

[4] Sp.Cal.,F.S, p.181.

[5] LP,ii,4276.

[6] LP,iii,3485, 3568.

[7] LP,iv,1234.

[8] Thomas More, Correspondence, pp.275 f; St.P,i,pp.135 ff; the latter includes Wolsey's letters direct to Henry.

[9] See especially Thomas More Correspondence, p.275 (LP,iii,3270).

[10] See especially ibid, p.295 (LP,iii,3355) for More reporting to Wolsey that he had 'distinctly read' to Henry a letter from Wolsey to himself, four letters from Margaret of Scotland, two to Henry and two to Surrey, and two letters devised by Wolsey to be sent to her. In 1521 Pace informed Wolsey that Henry 'readeth all your letters with great diligence'; see St.P,i, p.79 (LP,iii,717).

dilatoriness in grappling with his correspondence,[1] but in fact a portion of each day was devoted to this task; on 1 September More mentioned that he had spent over two hours going through it.[2] Much went through on the nod, but this is what one would expect. However, if Wolsey was anxious to draw Henry's attention to a particular matter, he was in the habit of adding his own comments in the margins,[3] or he would ask whoever was in attendance on the king specifically to bring it up.[4] Many of the policy initiatives to be found in these letters came from Wolsey, but again one would expect this. Indeed, this was what he was paid to provide. On 1 September Henry agreed to Wolsey's redrafting of instructions to Sir Richard Wingfield, while a letter Wolsey had written to Margaret of Scotland he 'so well liked that I never saw him like thing better'.[5] On the other hand, Henry himself was all the time putting forward his own views. More's letter to Wolsey on 26 August was full of the king's advice on Scottish affairs.[6] On 12 September Wolsey was instructed to convey Henry's views on strategy to English and Imperial commanders in France,[7] and on 20 September he was presented with two thousand words on why the siege of Boulogne should not be raised.[8] It was a brilliant presentation of the arguments, many of which were to prove all too prescient; but in fact the siege was to be abandoned and the alternative strategy of a march into the bowels of France adopted. This is not evidence of a weak and easily led Henry. Wolsey himself had only just changed his mind, and received praise from Henry for doing so, for 'his highness esteemeth no thing in counsel so perilous than one to persevere in the maintenance of his advice because he has once given it'. And the reason why Wolsey had changed his mind, and why Henry did as well, despite his serious reservations, is that the commanders in the field were so strongly in favour of abandoning the siege.[9] Moreover, Henry was quite consciously raising his reservations with Wolsey so that 'such final determination may be taken by his grace and yours, as shall, with God's grace, bring his affairs to good and honourable effect'.

What we have here is evidence of that genuine partnership that was referred to at the beginning of this book. Wolsey was Henry's leading councillor because the king trusted him to carry out his wishes, but it was Henry who was king, and Wolsey was never allowed to forget it. Thus, Wolsey was told to arrange a marriage for a member of the royal household.[10] The king noticed that copies of letters from Surrey to Margaret of Scotland, which had been sent to Wolsey, had not been sent on to him, and he wanted the omission remedied. In the same letter he also 'much desireth . . . thinketh it very necessary, . . . also requireth'. He concluded by having sent back to Wolsey all the Scottish documents 'to be by your good grace again sent unto his highness, with your most politique counsel thereupon'.[11] How Wolsey must

---

[1] Elton, Tudor Revolution, pp.68-9 for some examples.
[2] More, Correspondence, p.283 (LP,iii,3291).
[3] LP,iii,3477, 3515; iv,2392.
[4] More, Correspondence (LP,iii,iv,2535) Wolsey to More in Sept-Oct 1526.
[5] Ibid, pp.279-82 (LP,iii,3291).
[6] Ibid, pp.275-8 (LP,iii,3270).
[7] Ibid, p.285 (LP,iii,3320).
[8] Ibid, pp.289-95 (LP,iii,3346).
[9] Gunn, EHR,ci, pp.607-11.
[10] More, Correspondence, pp.288-9 (LP,iii,3340).
[11] Ibid, pp.295-7 (LP,iii,3355).

have cursed when it was all deposited back on his desk, but if these were the king's wishes, so be it, and sure enough the missing material with Wolsey's additional comments were soon back with Henry.[1] Even the evidence of Wolsey taking the initiative turns out to support the view of a king genuinely in charge.

On 7 December 1523 Wolsey reported to Henry that he had 'incontinently devised new instructions' for the duke of Suffolk, the English commander in France, and what he meant by this was that he had sent them without Henry seeing them.[2] This could be taken as evidence that it was really Wolsey who was running affairs, but to do so would be to ignore the explanation Wolsey gave to Henry. Firstly, there was the necessity for speed. There was, after all, a war being fought, and though I am reluctant to make too much of the difficulties of communication in the early sixteenth century, clearly Wolsey was right to want to get instructions off as quickly as possible, especially as Sir William Fitzwilliam, who was already deputed to go out to Suffolk, was with Wolsey and waiting to leave. His second reason was that he 'had well incorporated in my mind your full deliberation and intent in that matter, as well by such consultation as I lately had with your grace therein, as also by the knowledge of your pleasure signified unto me by the said Sir Thomas More'. And two further comments. First, it was Wolsey who had sought the meeting with Henry 'for the better furtherance and advancement' of the king's affairs, which 'may be more perfectly communicated and more speedily set forth by groundly consultation in presence than by letters in absence'.[3] Secondly, if Wolsey had not 'incorporated' Henry's mind in drawing up the new instructions, he would not have got away with it because he immediately sent the king a copy of them.

All these letters do need to be interpreted, and in the end everyone must make up his or her mind – since these letters have been printed, they can quite easily be consulted. The conclusion here is that they firmly support the view of a Henry, while confident of Wolsey's great abilities, very much on top of his own affairs. It is a view that is confirmed by much else, including the earlier suggestion in this chapter that it was the king who exercised his own patronage and was perfectly happy to consult with people other than Wolsey. It is also confirmed by the considerable amount of evidence of foreign ambassadors' dealings with him. None of them gave any indication that Henry was ever out of his depth or incompetent. Indeed, they all present a picture of a man fully informed of all that was going on in foreign affairs, and, like Wolsey, possessed of all the skills of a good negotiator, including an ability to turn on and off the charm as the occasion required.[4] If one were to take a modern analogy, Henry's role was that of chairman of the board, responsible ultimately for everything, including the hiring and firing of all who worked in the firm. His councillors are the directors, some of them part-time, others more actively involved. Wolsey is the managing director, responsible for the day-to-day running of affairs, and in a strong position to influence what happened, just as long as he retained the confidence of his chairman. Like all analogies, it only goes so far, and in particular it leaves out that essential element which is so hard to capture,

[1] Ibid, p.287 (LP,iii,3359).
[2] St.P,i,p.149 (LP,iii,3613).
[3] More, *Correspondence*, p.301 (LP,iii,3485).
[4] See Bernard, *War, Taxation and Rebellion*, pp.40-5 for an excellent treatment of Henry's role in the conduct of foreign policy.

but which must have had its effect on those who served Henry: the magic of kingship. But it may help to explain how it is that one can ascribe to Wolsey such an active role in the king's government, while still maintaining that Henry was the dominant force. And if he was, then much else falls into place. With the king in command and perfectly accessible to the upper reaches of the political nation, it was always likely that the nobility would be happy to co-operate with a man such as Wolsey, so obviously a master of all the political skills. What also follows is that it is unlikely that Wolsey ever felt seriously threatened by other members of the political élite. This was not an environment in which faction flourished. Many people have thought otherwise, and in particular it has been commonly supposed that Wolsey was brought low by a group of noblemen seizing upon the opportunity to do him damage presented by the king's wish for a new wife. But more of that when the question of why Wolsey was dismissed from office in October 1529 is discussed.

CHAPTER SEVEN

THE NORTH, IRELAND AND WALES

WOLSEY SPENT LESS THAN SIX MONTHS IN THE NORTH OF ENGLAND, AND then only after his fall from favour. However, an enormous amount of his time and energy was spent on its affairs. Partly this was because as archbishop of York from 1514 until his death in 1530, and as bishop of Durham from 1523 until 1529, he had specific responsibilities in the area. But the major reason was that the North posed serious problems for royal government which demanded constant attention from any important servant of the Crown. And perhaps it would be helpful to state at the outset that these problems were insoluble: there were too many of them, and any attempt to solve one would only aggravate another. This point needs stressing if only because historians, like journalists, are apt to believe in solutions, and have sometimes suggested that the Tudors did have a solution to the problems of the North. Put at its simplest, their answer was to remove the 'feudal barons' from power and influence in the North and to replace them with 'modern', 'bureaucratic' Councils, staffed by royal nominees and closely controlled from the centre.[1]

In such a scheme, Wolsey puts in a rather muted appearance as the architect in 1525 of a Council of the North – otherwise referred to as the duke of Richmond's Council – but even this had been foreshadowed by those set up by the Yorkist kings, and was but a pale shadow of what was to come. Wolsey thus earns few marks from such historians, being always considered more medieval than modern, whatever that is supposed to mean. In reality, the problems facing Wolsey in the 1520s were much the same as those facing Elizabethan statesmen in the 1580s and 1590s. The differences were those of detail, and it is the detail that historians have tended to ignore. For the people having to deal with the day-to-day problems of the North, they were of the utmost importance. All that was really open to Tudor statesmen was to 'make and mend', and this was something that Wolsey was very good at.

The underlying problem was that the North had a border with a traditionally unfriendly country only too willing to make trouble, especially when England was involved in continental matters. In 1496 and 1497 James IV had invaded England on Perkin Warbeck's behalf, and when in 1513 Henry VIII had taken an army to France, James could not resist the opportunity to invade yet again. There followed his defeat and death at Flodden, but for England the Scottish threat remained. The intervention of the duke of Albany in Scottish affairs, with his close connections with France, had foiled English efforts to set up a government in Scotland with which they could co-operate. In the summer of 1517 Albany had returned to France, but by the end of 1521 he was back and during the following three years, a period

---

[1] The most interesting work on the North in recent years has been done by M.E. James; see *Family Lineage*; *BP*, 27, 30; *NH* 1. In taking issue with him I have been much influenced by Bush, *NH*, 6. And I am most grateful to M.L. Bush and R.W. Hoyle for commenting on an earlier draft.

when England was actively engaged in a war with France, a Scottish invasion was a constant threat. At the end of May 1524, Albany left Scotland for good, and by the end of that year a truce between the two countries was signed. During the next three years this was constantly renewed until in December 1528 a five-year truce was arranged at Berwick, along with a major redress of grievances.[1]

Two things had greatly contributed to the improved relations between the two countries following Albany's departure. First and foremost, there was the new English alliance with France, signalled by the Treaty of the More in August 1525. Only in conjunction with France could Scotland be a real threat to England, and both countries knew this. Secondly, in February 1525, a new faction headed by the earl of Angus had taken over the government in Scotland – a faction which owed much of its success to English support, for the return of Angus and his brother to Scotland had been engineered by Wolsey.[2] But the underlying reason for the good relations – something that was stressed in a previous chapter – was English restraint.[3] Evidence of what might otherwise appear to be too Sassenach a view can be found in the English reaction to the overthrow of Angus in 1528 by a faction led by the young king, James v. Neither James nor the new faction were by inclination friends of England, and there is no doubt that the overthrow of Angus was a major defeat for Wolsey, who was for some time, and according to some of his advisers on the spot, for too long, reluctant to accept it.[4] Yet despite Scotland's continuing isolation and the insecurity of James's position, the English reaction was not to wage war but to negotiate the Treaty of Berwick. All this is not to suggest that Wolsey was a saint. There was constant English intervention in Scottish affairs, and Wolsey was, as usual in his conduct of foreign policy, quite prepared to heighten tension and to use force – in this case border raids – in order to exert pressure to achieve his ends. But in the North the direction of this pressure was always towards peace. The conquest of Scotland was never one of Wolsey's aims, which is also to say that it was never one of Henry's. Scottish affairs were peripheral to their European design, to be coped with only insofar as they affected it, and with as little expenditure as possible. But that did not prevent both men having to spend a great deal of time on Scottish affairs, nor did their pacific intentions enable them to escape from the reality that the North was a border which had to be kept in some kind of military preparedness.

This reality had dictated the way in which the North was governed for the last two hundred years. It had led to the creation of the office of warden of the Marches to rule over those areas adjoining the boundary, an arrangement duplicated on the Scottish side – and by the early sixteenth century there were on both sides three in number, West, Middle and East. In the Marches the wardens possessed wide-ranging powers chiefly designed to enable them to raise an army whenever one was needed but also to perform any judicial and administrative functions relating to border warfare. Much older than the Marches was the great ecclesiastical Palatinate of Durham, but its *raison d'être* was much the same as that of the many other

---

[1] For Anglo-Scottish relations at this time Eaves and Rae are indispensable.
[2] Rae, pp.157 ff.
[3] See pp.82-4.
[4] *LP*,iv,4924, 4986, 5070.

franchises and honours still in existence in the early sixteenth century. By delegation of special powers to men likely to be resident in the area the Crown hoped to create an effective defence against the Scots – all of which enables the simple point to be made that the Crown had been interfering in the affairs of the North long before the Tudors came to power.[1]

The purpose of this interference had not been to weaken the power of the Northern nobility, which was after all partly of its own creation, in practice providing a more effective defence against the Scots than any administrative unit that the Crown might construct. It was, in the Tudor period, too administratively complicated, and perhaps above all too expensive, to keep anything approaching a professional army in being. The Crown had still to rely very heavily on the nobleman's retinue, and, thus, also to live with the possibility that it might be used against itself – but the obsession with this possibility has been the historians' rather than the Crown's. Kings had to behave peculiarly badly for noblemen to revolt – and almost all kings who did face major rebellions had either succeeded to the throne as minors, like Richard II and Henry VI, or had wrested the throne from somebody else, as both Henry IV and Henry VII had done. It is therefore misleading to see the Northern nobility as in some abstract way a constant threat to the Crown. Indeed, by and large it was quite the opposite, and it was for this reason that the Crown appointed the great noblemen to such important offices as the wardenship of a March. Here was the ideal solution, because the nobles brought to the office their own authority and influence in the area. Unfortunately, it was not always possible.

It is sometimes implied that there was an unlimited supply of important Northern noblemen available for royal service. In fact, at any one time there were at the most only three or four: a Neville or a Percy, and perhaps, though not as powerful, a Clifford or Dacre. If any of these, for whatever reason, were unavailable, there were obvious difficulties – and the reason need not have been suspicion of their loyalty: sheer incompetence, or the minority of one of them, would have just the same consequence. Another difficulty was that the nobility's estates did not fit neatly into the administrative divisions. Percy lands were everywhere.[2] Although most often associated with the county of their title and their great residence at Alnwick Castle, the Percys owned even more land in Yorkshire, the county of their origin; and also with their ownership of the great honour of Cockermouth, a great deal in Cumberland. North of Cockermouth was the barony of Gilsland owned by the Dacre family, and it was this, with their chief residence at Naworth Castle, that made the Dacres possible candidates for the wardenship of the West March; but they also owned the barony of Morpeth, away towards the west coast of Northumberland. The chief centre of the Clifford family was Skipton in the West Riding, but they also possessed important estates in Westmorland and some in Cumberland.[3] A detailed political map of the North showing the distribution of the leading family estates would comprise concentrations of holdings with a wide and uneven spread. Furthermore, though this mosaic of holdings would be repeated throughout England, the suspicion is that in the North they were more tightly

---

[1] Reid, pp.1-40; Storey, *EHR*, (1957), lxxii.
[2] Bean.
[3] James, *NH*, p.44

packed and the possibility for friction greater than elsewhere. Certainly there was friction and rivalry in the North, exacerbated by the royal administrative divisions, in particular the wide powers granted to the wardens. This office gave the occupant power over other people's tenants, possibly over the tenants of his chief rival, and this both rival lord and tenant could and did resent. The evidence, at least for the first twenty years of Henry VIII's reign, is that these rivalries were not welcomed by the Crown – indeed, nothing made the good administration of the North more difficult.

In the 1520s the most open rivalry was to be found in the West March between the Dacre and Clifford families.[1] It had begun at least as early as 1513 when Thomas Lord Dacre felt compelled to request royal intervention in order to ensure that the Clifford tenants carried out his instructions as warden.[2] It then grumbled on for the rest of Dacre's life, but only really surfaced after his death in 1525. In that year Henry Lord Clifford was created earl of Cumberland, and succeeded Dacre as warden of the West March just before the latter's death. Dacre had held the post for almost forty years, so his replacement by Clifford was bound to cause problems as the new warden strove to establish himself in what had become a Dacre stronghold. He immediately had difficulty in gaining possession of various subsidiary royal offices, such as the captaincy of Carlisle and stewardship of Penrith that customarily went with the office of warden. In an effort to secure himself in these offices, he abruptly terminated all leases attached to them, previously granted by Dacre, and put in tenants of his own. Dacre resistance was so great that in order to put an end to the 'inquietation', Wolsey wrote to Clifford ordering him to restore immediately the former leaseholders until such time as he and the king's Council could discuss the matter with him. Though addressed to 'my entirely beloved friend', Wolsey's letter was a rebuke,[3] and it is not certain how great a friend to Clifford Wolsey was. The matter is of some importance. Clifford was to remain warden for only two years, to be replaced at the end of 1527 by his rival, William, the new Lord Dacre, and it could be argued that he only lasted so short a time because he had received insufficient support from the Crown, and in particular from Wolsey. Back in the autumn of 1517 Clifford had spent a fortnight in the Fleet prison, put there by Wolsey. His offence is unknown – probably it had to do with his bad relations with his father and his riotous life-style – but if there was almost certainly good reason for his imprisonment, it cannot have helped his future relations with Wolsey.[4] On the other hand, what evidence there is suggests that his relations with Henry, with whom he had been brought up, were good and all his life he was to be a loyal servant of the Crown.[5] Could it be, therefore, that Wolsey was never reconciled to him being chosen as warden by Henry, and thus failed to give him the backing he should have done? In favour of such a view is the fact that though Thomas Lord Dacre had lost office in 1525 the family had not been disgraced, and Wolsey's relations with Thomas's brother, Sir Christopher, and with his son and heir, William, were good. There is also the evidence of the extremely interesting letter that Lord Percy wrote

[1] *Clifford Letters*, pp.23-4; Hoyle, pp.92-3; James, *NH 1*, p.46,n.24.
[2] *LP*,i,2443.
[3] *Clifford Letters*, pp.89-90 for Wolsey's letter. See also *LP*,iv,2003-4, 2052, 2110.
[4] *Clifford Letters*, pp.21-2; HMC, app.iv, p.447.
[5] James, *NH, i*, pp.67-8.

to Clifford in October 1526, in which Percy reported a conversation he had overheard during which his father had warned Wolsey 'that there was no trust in you [Clifford], and desired his Grace to put no confidence in you, for you were all with my Lord of Norfolk'.[1] Thus, it could be that Clifford's removal from office was connected with the more important struggle for power at court between Norfolk and Wolsey.

In chapter 13 it will be argued that no such struggle occurred, whatever gossip there may have been to the contrary in Northern circles – and it is almost certainly such gossip that Percy's father was drawing upon in his conversation with Wolsey. But whether the argument is correct, the notion of such a struggle, in which Clifford, as a supporter of Norfolk, was to suffer, is not necessary to explain Clifford's removal from office in 1527, nor, indeed, is it likely that personal feeling came into it. This removal occurred at the end of a year which had seen great disturbances in the North as a result of the activities of Sir William Lisle. The failure of the royal administration in the North to cope with Lisle led to major alterations both in organization and personnel. These will be discussed later, but one of the victims of the reshuffle was Clifford. The Crown appears to have taken the view that he had not been an effective warden, one reason being that he was not influential enough in the West March to dominate it in the way that the Dacre family had done – and, of course, one of the reasons why Clifford had failed to dominate there was that he was being constantly undermined by the Dacres. The one worry about this explanation is that almost all evidence for Clifford's removal from office is lacking. It must therefore remain a suggestion, but one that is strengthened by subsequent events.

Clifford was not disgraced. He remained as captain of Carlisle – this perhaps an attempt partly to soften the blow and partly to balance the rival forces in the West March and thus to lessen the conflict. But if it was a deliberate balancing act, it was one that did not work. Within months, his successor, William Lord Dacre, was being ordered not to interfere in tenancies granted by Clifford, in the same way as Clifford in 1526 had been ordered not to interfere in tenancies granted by the then Lord Dacre.[2] More importantly, both the new Warden General of the East and Middle Marches, the former Lord Percy, now Earl of Northumberland, and the Council of the North,[3] were finding it impossible to put an end to the quarrelling between the two families.[4] By October 1528 Thomas Magnus, one of Wolsey's closest advisers on Northern matters and a member of Richmond's Council, was advising that the captaincy of Carlisle should be returned to the new warden, but he clearly felt that rather more than this was required to provide a solution:

> There is no little trouble nor business between the earl of Cumberland [Clifford] and the said Lord Dacre, not only to the inquieting of their servants, friends, and lovers in Cumberland and Westmorland, but also the countries there, by the occasion of the same, be the more further from good rule. Wherefore, your said Grace should do a good and blessed deed to set some good order between them.[5]

[1] Clifford Letters, p.105.
[2] LP,iv, 4419.
[3] Otherwise Richmond's Council.
[4] LP,iv, 3971, 4790, 4855.

The evidence is that Wolsey was no more successful than Northumberland or Richmond's Council had been in resolving the conflict, though perhaps it would be fairer to say that if he was successful, conflict soon broke out again after his fall, even though in August 1529 Magnus's advice was taken and the captaincy of Carlisle was granted to Dacre.[1] In 1534 Dacre was accused of high treason for collusion with the Scots. Though acquitted, he was fined £10,000 and removed from the wardenship.[2] There is little doubt that the Clifford influence was behind these charges and it was Clifford who succeeded him. But Clifford's second term as warden of the West March was hardly more successful than his first. It is true that he retained the post until his death in 1542, but in 1537 the Crown decided that his rule was so inadequate that they appointed a deputy, Sir Thomas Wharton, giving him such extensive powers that in effect it was he who performed the warden's duties.[3] As a postscript it is worth quoting the duke of Norfolk's comment in 1537, a time when Clifford's tenure was under review – 'no man can serve his highness better than Lord Dacre there' [4] – though he recognized that he was debarred from office by virtue of the charge of treason made against him in 1534. By 1549 this was deemed to be no longer a bar. Dacre once again became warden of the West March and remained so until his death in 1562.

It looks very much from all this as if the natural leaders in the West March were members of the Dacre family, and it was to these natural leaders, other things being equal, that the Crown looked to exercise its authority there. The problem was that though this was the case, the Dacres were not without rivals – and not just the Cliffords. Or to put it another way, it was not that the Dacre family was too strong but that it was too weak – too weak always to impose its will, even with royal support.

What has been described so far is merely the tip of an iceberg. In August 1523 the earl of Surrey found 'the greatest dissensions' amongst the gentlemen of Yorkshire, who would have fought each other, given half a chance, if they had met, and he singled out six factions who were particularly at loggerheads. Though he had taken immediate steps to end the conflicts, he still required, so he informed Wolsey, the sending out of royal letters to ensure that they would stop quarrelling and be ready to serve him at a day's notice.[5] In October of the same year he wrote that he was forced to lead in person the Lancashire contingent for 'there is some little displeasure amongst them, and no man among them by whom they will be ruled.'[6] These letters underline the point that not only were local rivalries inimical to 'good government' in the North, but they seriously hampered its defence. Families were unwilling to put aside their mutual dislike, even in the face of the common enemy from over the border. The result was that time and again the senior military man in the area, whether it was Surrey in 1523 or Dacre or Shrewsbury on earlier occasions,

[5] St.P,iv,p.516 (LP,iv,4828).

---

[1] LP,iv, 5906 (6).
[2] Clifford Letters, pp.23-4.
[3] Bush, NH, 6, pp.40 ff; James, BP, 27, pp.26 ff.
[4] LP,xii,919.
[5] LP,iii,3240.
[6] LP,iii,3482.

had great difficulty in persuading the leading Northern families to turn up on time and with the right number of men; hence the great number of requests for royal intervention in order to get them to do so.[1] The conclusion to be drawn is that in no sense was the Crown looking to 'divide and rule', if only because the divisions were already all too apparent. The rifts between noble and gentry families – and those of the latter were usually the consequence of the former – benefited the Crown not one iota. Recognizing this, the Crown expended a considerable amount of time and effort to minimize their harmful effects. It was precisely in an attempt to solve these problems that great noblemen were used to govern the North, for only they had the necessary power and prestige to impose order on 'a cumbrous country'.[2]

There was, however, one considerable difficulty. For reasons which will shortly be discussed, the obvious candidate for great office in the North, the 5th earl of Northumberland, was considered unsuitable. The result was a power vacuum into which the rather less powerful noblemen such as Dacre and Clifford only uneasily fitted, and then only in 'normal' circumstances. When times were abnormal, as for instance from 1522 to 1524 when Albany threatened invasion, the need for a great nobleman was so strong that one had to be found even if he lacked his own power base in the North: thus in 1522 the earl of Shrewsbury, and in 1523 and 1524 the earl of Surrey. When, by the end of 1527, circumstances were again unusual – this time as a result of Lisle's activities – the 5th earl of Northumberland had died, enabling his heir to be given high office.

There is no reason to suppose that Wolsey had any doubts about the wisdom of appointing such men. He almost certainly recommended Shrewsbury in 1522, because Surrey, the obvious choice, given his previous experience of the North, was already involved in directing the war with France, and when he was no longer needed for that purpose, he was immediately given the Northern command.[3] As for the 6th earl of Northumberland, he had very close connections with Wolsey, who almost certainly favoured his appointment. However, it can of course be argued that just because the circumstances resulting in these appointments were unusual, and for the period from 1522 to 1524 very much involved with military matters, they can tell us little about Wolsey's more general attitude to the day-to-day administration of the North and to the question of who should be in charge. And, after all, neither Shrewsbury nor Surrey was resident in the North for any length of time, and having so little local influence neither could be the threat to royal government in the area that a Northern nobleman might be.

What of the 'disgrace' of Thomas Lord Dacre in 1524-5? Is there not here some evidence of Wolsey's suspicion of Northern noblemen? Certainly Dacre was not afraid to act independently. In September 1522, he had made a truce with Albany without either his immediate superior, the earl of Shrewsbury's, or Wolsey's permission.[4] In the following September he was arousing both Henry's and Wolsey's suspicion by his unwillingness to carry out their instructions to use the 'great rod' against the Scots.[5] Also, beginning in 1522, there was mounting criticism of Dacre's

[1] LP,i,2443; iii,2536, 2598, 2621, 3241, 3306, 3310, 3412; iv, 278 and no doubt many others.

[2] Called this by Magnus in a letter to Dacre, 3 Dec.1523 (LP,iii,3599).

[3] See Bernard, 'Fourth and fifth earls of Shrewsbury', pp.164 ff. The letter concerning Shrewsbury's suitability for a command in the North is LP,iii,1462.

[4] LP,iii,2536 for Dacre's own account of the event.

rule in the North, leading two years later to specific charges being made against him, charges that were to result in his removal from office.[1] Before looking at Dacre's 'disgrace' in more detail, it is worth making the point that whatever Wolsey's general attitude towards the Northern nobility was, it took him at least seven years to do anything about Dacre's rule. Furthermore, it is not at all clear that even by 1524 he was anxious to remove him. On the other hand, there is plenty of evidence that Dacre himself wished to retire, at any rate from the wardenship of the East and Middle Marches.[2] He had never had any illusions about his effectiveness in these two areas; his family lacked real power in both of them, but especially in the Middle March, and he had always found it difficult to assert his authority as warden.[3] For over a decade he had done his best to perform a rather thankless task, and now that he was well into his fifties he seems to have genuinely desired a respite. He may also have guessed which way the wind was blowing and have been anxious to get out before the storm broke over his head. When in November 1523, following Surrey's resignation, Dacre was reappointed to the wardenship of the East and Middle Marches, he made his feelings known, agreeing to serve only until the following Easter in the expectation that he would then be succeeded by Lord Percy.[4] Thus, in one sense, Dacre's 'fall' in 1524 was one that he sought himself. Moreover, it was not as great as has often been assumed. As well as suspicion of his handling of Scottish affairs, there had also been some praise. Wolsey had, for instance, taken the view that even his unauthorized truce with Albany was greatly to England's advantage, though this was partly because, being unauthorized, it could easily be repudiated.[5] Moreover, Wolsey never failed to recognize that Dacre's knowledge of Scottish affairs was of great value to the Crown[6] and in 1524-5, at a time when important negotiations with Scotland were taking place, he had no intention of dispensing with it. In 1525 Dacre returned from London without any of his wardenships and bound by heavy recognizances, but also as one of the chief commissioners to treat with the Scots.[7] His treatment in London had been severe. Wolsey and the Council appear to have accepted much of the criticism of his wardenship, and no doubt they were right to do so,[8] but they also seem to have

---

[5] *LP*, iii, 3291.

---

[1] *LP*, iii, 2271, 3304, 3306, 3286; iv, 133, 218, 220, 279, 682, 701, 726, 822, 893, 1223, 1239, 1429, 1460, 1517. For the charges and Darcy's replies see Hodgson, v, pp.31-40.

[2] *LP*,iii,3544; iv,218, 220. For the bishop of Carlisle's comment that the Dacres were not loved in the East and Middle Marches see *LP*,iii,2271.

[3] *LP*,iii,3544. This was one of the chief points that he made in his defence: he had endeavoured to keep the East and Middle Marches in as good order as the West, 'albeit his power was not so good of the one as the other'; see Hodgson, v,p.33.

[4] *LP*,iv,220.

[5] *LP*,iii,2537.

[6] *Inter alia*, Wolsey's marginal note to Surrey's recommendation that Dacre succeed him: 'True it is that there is no man so meet as the Lord Dacre is, as well for his great wisdom and experience, as for his power ready at hand to withstand excursion to be made by the Scots from time to time.' (*LP*,iii,3515). For Wolsey remitting all to Dacre's wisdom see *LP*,iii,1950; for Fox's favourable assessment see Richard Fox, pp.137-8; for Surrey being unable to spare Dacre see *LP*,iv,726.

[7] *LP*,iv,1665, 1725.

[8] Hodgson, v,pp.31-40. The chief burden of the case against Dacre was that he had been unable to maintain law and order because he was too closely involved with those who were causing the disorder.

realized that the rule of the North was virtually impossible without the co-operation of the Dacres. Further evidence for such a view is provided by the appointment in August 1525 of Dacre's brother, Sir Christopher, to the Council of the North, and in the following August to the post of deputy-warden of the East March.[1]

Dacre's 'disgrace' touches upon an issue which is central to any assessment of Wolsey's handling of Northern affairs. There is little doubt that behind much of the criticism of Dacre rule in the East and Middle Marches lay Percy resentment at exclusion from office there, just as behind the criticism of his rule in the West March lay Clifford resentment. As long ago as 1513 Dacre had had to ask for royal letters to be sent to the 5th earl of Northumberland in order to get him to provide a Percy retinue for the defence of the border.[2] During the 1522 campaign against Scotland the rivalry between the two families was such that even the Percy retainers thought that the Dacres had missed an opportunity to betray Lord Percy and Lord Ogle to the Scots during the burning of Kelso.[3] In December of the following year, Dacre refused a request from the 5th earl for a loan of £100.[4] In fact, bearing in mind that at the same time the earl had made complaints against Dacre's brother, the refusal had been couched in a conciliatory tone, but this may only have been because during 1523 the open criticism of Dacre's rule pointed to the undesirability of unnecessarily offending the man who was probably its greatest exponent. Amongst the criticism was a paper concerning 'the reformation of things necessary upon his Grace's East and Middle Marches . . . and also for the ministering of justice within his Grace's county of Northumberland, for the commonwealth and quietness of the King's true subjects'. Its main recommendation was for 'some great and discrete nobleman to be made warden of the East and Middle Marches to live in the county and keep all men in their duty.' The paper was signed by Sir William Eure, John Widdrington, John Horsley and Lionel Gray. All these men appear to have had strong Percy connections, and there can have been little doubt which 'great and discreet nobleman' they had in mind.[5]

Thus, Percy pressure was involved in bringing about Dacre's removal from office – and in one sense why not? Wealthier and more influential than any other family, including the Dacres, the Percys were the natural rulers of the East and Middle Marches – indeed, of the entire North. Even in the West March where, it has been suggested, the Dacres were the natural rulers, the Percys' ownership of the great

---

BL Lansdowne, 1, fo.105 states that on 1 Feb.1525 Dacre confessed to the 'bearing of thieves . . . Whereupon he is committed to the keeping of the warden of the Fleet and his recognizance, taken and knowledged the 31 January last part as well for himself and his sureties, is decreed by the said most reverend father [Wolsey] to be utterly void, prostrate, and cancelled.' See also BL Vespasian C xiv (pt.2), fo.267; LP,iv,302. For a different account see Guy, Cardinals' Court, pp.122-3.

[1] LP,iv,2401, 2402; Reid, p.104.
[2] LP,i,2443.
[3] LP,iii,2402.
[4] LP,iii,3603.
[5] LP,iii,3286 though it should be said that Dacre was not mentioned by name. For a fuller treatment of the Dacre/Percy conflict see James, BP, 30, pp.28 ff. James makes the point that those who signed were closely connected with the Crown, but since all the leading gentry were likely to have had connections both with the Crown as well as Northern noblemen it hardly carries the weight he wishes it to. The conflict between local clientage and Crown service was never as great as he suggests and there is little evidence that it was growing.

honour of Cockermouth gave them considerable influence. With their great estates in Sussex as well, they were in a different league from any of their Northern competitors. For the 1523 subsidy, the 5th earl was assessed for an income of £2,920,[1] while a modern historian has estimated that his real income in that year was much nearer £4,000.[2] Dacre's may have been in the region of £1,500.[3] Thus, if Henry and Wolsey were indeed anxious to make use of the natural leaders of the North, then one would expect members of the Percy family to be fully employed there. In fact, until very late in 1527, this was not the case; and the man who was never appointed to high office was the man one would most expect to have been – Henry Percy 5th earl of Northumberland.

How did this come about? The first difficulty about the 5th earl, as far as the Crown was concerned, was that when, after his father's murder at Cocklodge in 1489, he succeeded to the title, he was only eleven. This may have resulted in some financial advantage for the Crown, but it also meant that for the next decade the earl would not be available for employment in royal service. However, his long minority does not explain why after 1498 he was still denied important office. What makes this even more surprising is that he appears to have made a successful start to his career. In 1492 he was present at the signing of the Treaty of Étaples. Two years later he played a prominent part in the ceremonies surrounding the installation of the infant Prince Henry as Knight of the Bath and duke of York. In the following year he became a knight of the garter and in 1497 he helped to put down the Cornish rebels at Blackheath – all this before he received livery of his lands in May 1498. In 1501 he was appointed constable of Knaresborough, and from this time on he served on various local commissions as well as continuing to play a full part in ceremonies at court. He also took part, though probably only in an honorific capacity, in the negotiations for the proposed marriage between Duke Charles and Princess Mary, Henry VIII's daughter.[4] If none of this is particularly surprising for a young nobleman brought up as a royal ward, there is also nothing in it to suggest royal disfavour. Yet despite its favourable beginnings, the 5th earl's career in royal service never really took off. One explanation for this may have been his 'ravishment' of Elizabeth Hastings, which is to say that the Crown had claimed successfully that she was a royal ward and that therefore the 5th earl, by arranging her marriage, had trespassed on the royal prerogative. On the face of it, the offence does not seem very serious, but towards the end of Henry VII's reign it was dangerous for anyone to be found encroaching upon royal rights, and what may have inclined the king to take a serious view was the fact that the 5th earl had already been involved in a series of disputes and incidents with Thomas Savage, archbishop of York and Henry's leading representative in the North.[5] But for whatever reason, Northumberland's punishment was severe – in 1505 a fine of £10,000, later reduced to £5,000 to be paid in annual instalments of 1,000 marks. To ensure that the

[1] LP,iv,331.

[2] Bean, p.140, who puts his income in 1523 at c. £3,900. The nobility's average income was £1,000; see Miller, 'Early Tudor peerage', p.127.

[3] I owe this information to R.W. Hoyle.

[4] For biographical information see inter alia Fonblanque, pp.310-360, a splendid though not entirely reliable source.

[5] James, BP, 30, pp.18-9; Select Cases, pp.41-4. For the dispute with Savage see PRO STAC/2/24/79.

money was paid, certain Percy estates were to be administered by royal feoffees, and their revenues to come to the Crown.[1] All this cannot have made for continuing good relations between the Percys and Tudors, but too much can be read into it. There is little doubt that Henry VII was determined to ensure that no one, not even a Percy, should trespass on his rights, but this does not mean that he was conducting a vendetta against any particular family, or that he saw Northumberland as a 'feudal magnate' or 'over-mighty subject'.

At this stage, it is worth asking what reason had the early Tudors for fearing the Percys? They were wealthy and could, in theory at any rate, put into the field a very considerable force. One estimate puts it as high as eleven thousand men, comprising about seven thousand foot soldiers and four thousand horse.[2] And if this seems a little exaggerated, the 5th earl did take a retinue of over five hundred men to France in 1513,[3] and for the Scottish campaign of 1523 raised a force of about eight hundred and fifty.[4] Even these numbers are large, but not such as seriously to challenge the Tudor regime – except in peculiar circumstances, and then in combination with other noblemen. In 1536, the 'break with Rome' and subsequent dissolution of the monasteries and other religious changes, real or imagined, did produce the peculiar circumstances, and the result was the Pilgrimage of Grace. This, for a time, did pose an extremely serious threat, but in the end it was quite easily overcome, just because in the crisis the leading noblemen remained loyal to the Crown.[5] Without the peculiar circumstances, and given the rivalries amongst the Northern families, it is hard to see what steps a disgruntled Percy could take to challenge the Tudor state.

One possibility was to combine with that other disgruntled nobleman, the duke of Buckingham. In 1509, there was a rumour emanating from Northumberland's servants that Buckingham should become 'protector of England' and that the 5th earl should 'rule all from the Trent North'. If this did not come about and 'their Lord had not rooms in the North as his father had' – that is to say, the wardenship of the East and Middle Marches – 'it should not long be well'.[6] The 5th earl never did become warden of any March, but neither did things go especially badly, and perhaps too much should not be made of an isolated report of servants' gossip. It has already been shown that there was no conspiracy to destroy Buckingham – only that the duke's unwillingness to play the role of a royal servant meant that his relationship with Henry could not be close.[7] The same may well be true of the 5th earl, though the evidence is so slight that any assessment must be tentative. Although he failed to obtain high office, he was never completely disgraced, and certainly not at the time of Buckingham's downfall in 1521, even though Wolsey was forced to deny rumours that he had been.[8] Thus, if he was ever very close to the

[1] Bean, p.143; James, BP, 30, pp.21-2.
[2] James, BP, 30, p.27, n.101.
[3] Ibid, 27, n.102; LP,i,2053.
[4] Fonblanque,i, p.552, but James gives the figure as 762; see BP, 30, p.27, n.102.
[5] Inter alia, Bernard, Early Tudor Nobility, pp.38-58; C.S.L. Davies, Past and Present, 41, pp.54-76. Fonblanque, i, p.458 gives a figure of nearly 35,000 for the rebel army.
[6] LP,i,157.
[7] See pp.159-72.
[8] LP,iii,1293.

duke – if, for instance, he was one of the noblemen whom the duke had found to be too frightened to plan concerted action against Henry's government[1] – he clearly was not considered to be so in 1521. He had, however, come under suspicion in 1518, being one of the noblemen, along with Buckingham, Suffolk, Derby and Wiltshire, on whom Henry had asked Wolsey to keep a close watch. Although in March 1510 he had been released from all recognizances entered into in Henry VII's reign for his 'ravishment' of Elizabeth Hastings, six years later he was once more in trouble with the Crown, for an offence that may have again concerned the royal rights to wardship. At any rate, at about this time he was defendant in a Star Chamber case during the course of which he appeared not only before an unusually large number of royal councillors, but also the king himself.[2] He was then placed in the Fleet prison, and was only released after a telling-off from the king.[3] The Crown's treatment of the 5th earl in 1516 was very public, very conscious, and must have been, for the earl, very humiliating, but again some caution must be exercised in drawing any conclusion. The Crown was not saying 'down with all noblemen', or even 'down with all Northern noblemen', but was publicly making the point that nobody, not even a Percy, was above the law. The worst that can be said, therefore, is that the 5th earl was a victim of Wolsey's drive to assert the principle of 'indifferent justice',though it was careless of the earl, if not downright foolish, to have infringed upon the royal prerogative a second time – if that was his offence.

Be that as it may, in the following year he was asked to escort Margaret of Scotland for part of her journey back over the border.[4] In 1520 he took an active part at the Field of Cloth of Gold.[5] In 1522 he was a member of the council set up to advise the new lieutenant of the North,[6] and incidentally a personal friend, the earl of Shrewsbury, and in the following year he took part under Shrewsbury's successor, the earl of Surrey, in further campaigning against the Scots. In June 1525 he was present at the ceremonies at which Henry's illegitimate son, Henry Fitzroy, was created duke of Richmond,[7] but when in the next month the lapsed Council of the North was resuscitated with Richmond as its nominal head, Northumberland was not put on it.[8] In fact, this is not quite so surprising as is sometimes made out. Since the council's function was primarily legal, it was composed largely of lawyers, not of noblemen for whom such work on any regular basis would have been inappropriate and uncongenial. When, on the other hand, a military council had been needed, as in 1522, Northumberland was made a member. It is, therefore, a little surprising that in 1525 he was not given what was essentially a military post, that of deputy-warden of a March – Richmond having been made warden-general – particularly as his fellow noblemen, the earls of Cumberland and Westmorland, were.

[1] *LP*,iii,1284 [3].

[2] James states that the case involved another abducted heiress, but none of his references appear to support this view; see *BP*, 30, p.26.

[3] BL Lansdowne 639, fos.45v-6; Vespasian C xiv (pt.2), fo.266v; Guy, *Cardinals' Court*, pp.27, 31 though he sheds no light on what the charges were.

[4] *LP*,ii,3209, 3278. Fonblanque, i, p.350 quotes the relevant letters in full. It should be said that Northumberland showed himself very reluctant to perform this duty.

[5] Russell, *Field of Cloth of Gold*, pp.51-4.

[6] *LP*,iii,2412.

[7] *LP*,iv,1431.

[8] Reid, pp.103 ff.

Before we attempt to make sense of this very patchy evidence, Northumberland's relations with Wolsey himself must be considered. It may be assumed that Wolsey had been much involved in the 5th earl's appearance before the king and Council in 1516. Nevertheless, relations between the two men were not irredeemably harmed by this episode, for otherwise it would have been very strange for the earl to have entrusted to Wolsey at least the later stages of his eldest son's upbringing.[1] Just as with Buckingham, some pressure may have been put upon him to bring his son to court. Moreover, there were some advantages, even for a disgruntled nobleman, in establishing a connection with the cardinal. However, the fact is that he need not have placed his son in Wolsey's household, and he chose to do so. Furthermore, during the crisis brought about by his son's 'affair' with Anne Boleyn, both the father and Wolsey combined to force the son to break it off, this probably in 1522.[2] In 1523 Wolsey defended Northumberland against the king's charge that the Percy retinue had worn the cross keys of the See of York during the Scottish campaign.[3] Of course, Wolsey's defence was not disinterested; the charge was aimed almost as much against himself as against the 5th earl. But Wolsey could have made use of the incident to do the earl down, and did not. In 1526 Northumberland was involved in a case before the Council of the North in which it appears – though, as is so often the case, the evidence is ambiguous – that Wolsey put in a kind word for him.[4] Then in October of the same year, when the earl was in London, he took the trouble to warn Wolsey not to trust the earl of Cumberland because he was in league with the duke of Norfolk.[5]

What to make of all this? Certainly it is not evidence of abiding enmity between the two men, or of any vendetta on Wolsey's part to discredit the earl. What does emerge from some of the evidence is strong antagonism between the earl and his son, antagonism which Wolsey was attempting to put an end to early in 1527.[6] As has been shown, he was quite often drawn into the nobility's family quarrels, a role that required great tact and sensitivity and not one that can easily be associated with his alleged opposition to its concerns.[7] It is not known in this case how successful he was and, in any event, the death of the 5th earl in May of 1527 removed the problem. What, however, the antagonism between father and son probably does explain is Wolsey's otherwise bizarre and heartless request that the son should not attend his father's funeral.[8] It may also explain why the plan to create the son warden of the East and Middle Marches, in the early 1520s, never came to anything:

[1] Cavendish, pp.29-34 is the main source for the 6th earl's presence in Wolsey's household, but though it is confirmed by other references such as LP,iv,4082, 4093 nothing gives us a precise date.

[2] Again this date is conjectural, but Anne really only appeared at court in 1522 and by September 1523 Percy was engaged to be married to Mary Talbot.

[3] LP,iii,3563. Fonblanque, i, pp.357-8 quotes the relevant passage in full.

[4] LP,iv,2729.

[5] Clifford Letters, pp.105-7. It predates Wolsey's good word, which was in December, and was perhaps a consequence of it.

[6] Ibid for crucial evidence of the quarrel; also Cavendish, pp.29-34.

[7] See pp.172-3 above.

[8] Fonblanque, i, p.379: 'Before Ambrose came unto me I was coming unto my house at Topcliffe towards the funeral of my late lord and father, whose soul J'hu pardon; . . . but seeing I know my lord grace's [Wolsey's] pleasure contrary, I will not come to the funeral to Beverly, the which to have been at I would have been very glad.' The fact that he would have liked to have been at the funeral may suggest

his father's dislike would have made his position untenable.[1]

The more one looks at the evidence usually put forward for a deliberate policy, whether Henry VIII's or Wolsey's, to destroy the power of the Percys, the less convincing it appears. What emerges is a more complicated picture, at the heart of which must be the personality of the 5th earl, however shadowy that now appears. Undoubtedly, he was never trusted sufficiently, nor considered competent enough, to be given high office. What may be significant is the fact that, though brought up at Henry VII's court, he failed to become an intimate of the young Prince Henry. Of course he was thirteen years older, but then the first boon companions of the future Henry VIII were almost all of them considerably older. Those who did manage to become close at an early stage – Brandon, Compton, the Howards and the Guildfords – all became important figures in the new reign, and remained close until either they or Henry died.[2] Why the 5th earl did not will probably never be known, but his failure to do so may well explain much that followed. In many ways his career parallels the duke of Buckingham's, not only in that he was never brought into the inner circle of government, but that his reaction to this exclusion was similar. He retired to his estates and concentrated his energies on administering them effectively – and successfully, for if wealth is a measure of a nobleman's power, the 5th earl was undoubtedly more powerful by the end of his life than when he succeeded to the title.[3] And if, as in the case of the duke, the Crown always viewed him with some suspicion, so, like the duke he was usually treated with the respect due to a great peer of the realm. The great difference between him and Buckingham was, of course, that he steered clear of treasonable speculation. But, just as Buckingham's execution cannot be taken as evidence of any theoretical or general hatred of the nobility, neither can the 5th earl's exclusion from high office be taken as evidence for any such hatred of the Northern nobility, or of the Percy family.

If one reason for being so sure about this is that Percy wealth was greater by the end of the 1520s than it had been at the beginning of Henry VII's reign, another is the evident willingness of both Henry VIII and Wolsey, insofar as it was practical, to make use of the nobility in their rule of the North. The re-establishment in 1525 of a Council of the North under Richmond – often referred to as Richmond's Council – in no way contradicts this. The increased government activity in the North, brought about by Albany's return to Scotland in 1521 and the ensuing threat of an invasion by the Scots, had, almost incidentally, brought to Wolsey's attention the more general problem of law and order – or rather the lack of it. When the new bishop of Carlisle, John Kite, had arrived in the North in 1522 his special task was to act as councillor and treasurer to Lord Dacre in the fight against Albany. He soon

rather better relations between the two than I have suggested, but it could equally well indicate remorse or perhaps even pleasure at his father's death!

---

[1] Hall states that in 1523 the 5th earl turned down an offer of a wardenship, as a result of which he 'was not regarded of his tenants, which disdained him and his blood, and much lamented his folly'; see Hall, pp.651-2. If Hall was correct, our puzzle would be solved: the 5th earl never received high office because he did not want it. But it seems unlikely, while no hint of such an offer has survived, and the documentation for Northern concerns in 1522 and 1523 is quite extensive.

[2] D.R. Starkey, 'King's privy chamber', pp.80 ff. but the detail needs checking in Gunn, *Charles Brandon*, pp.6-11, 66-71.

[3] Bean, pp.135-43.

found, however, that the more serious problem was caused by the English:

> There is more theft, more extortion by English thieves, than there is by all the Scots of
> Scotland. There is no man which is not in a hold strong that hath or may have any
> cattle or moveable in surety through the bishopric and from the bishopric till we come
> within eight miles of Carlisle, all Northumberland likewise. Exhamshire, which longeth
> to your Grace, worst of all, for in Exham self every market day there is fourscore or
> 100 strong thieves, and the poor men and gentlemen seeth them which did rob them and
> their goods and neither complain of them by name, nor say one word to them. They
> take all their cattle and horse, their corn as they carry it to sow or to the mill to grind,
> and at their houses bid them deliver what they will have, or they shall be fired and
> burnt. By this ungracious mean not looked to all the country goeth, and shall more, to
> waste.[1]

It may be that Kite overreacted to his first immersion in the realities of the North,
but he was no innocent, having served for some time in both Ireland and Spain.
Moreover, his gloomy view of the matter was to be echoed on many occasions
during 1523 and 1524 by the earl of Surrey. But while Kite concentrated on what
were endemic problems of any border country, especially one with difficult terrain,
Surrey tended to emphasize the rivalry between the leading families, which was
characteristic of the whole of England, but compounded here by being placed in a
border context.

In his analysis of the causes of disorder, Surrey made two important points.[2]
First, that most of the Northumberland gentry had close connections with thieves.
Dacre was charged with this in 1524,[3] and the charge was true. He was closely
connected with such families, or clans, as the Armstrongs and Carletons, who,
based in the border valleys of Liddesdale, Redesdale, and Tynedale – valleys difficult
of access and providing little settled employment – were in effect professional cattle
thieves and robbers.[4] This was their way of life and, furthermore, in any conflict
with Scotland it was they who provided the best soldiers. Thus, any successful
warden would have to rely on their military help while hoping to keep their
peacetime activities sufficiently under control so that the more settled parts of the
North – and there were many – were not too inconvenienced. A careful balancing
act was required, and it looks as if by 1524 Dacre, even on his own admission, was
failing to achieve it.[5] Thus, though in the mounting criticism of Dacre's rule, the
not impartial role of both the Cliffords and the Percys has been emphasized, much
of that criticism was probably deserved. At the same time, Wolsey, though most
anxious that Dacre should have a fair hearing,[6] and well aware, as indeed was
Surrey, that Dacre's knowledge of Scottish affairs was indispensable,[7] also saw,
especially when the prospects for a long-term peace with Scotland were good, that
some new initiative must be made to establish law and order in the North.

[1] LP,iii,2328.
[2] LP,iii,3240 for this analysis, but all Surrey's letters in 1523 and 1524 should be consulted.
[3] Hodgson, pp.31 ff.
[4] Hodgson, pp.31 ff.
[5] LP,iii,3544; iv,22. Though Dacre defends himself in these letters, he also admits difficulties and not
just on account of his gout!
[6] St.P,iv,pp.153-6 (LP,iv,701).
[7] See p.219, n.7 above.

Surrey's second explanation for the disorder in the North was that people were highly sceptical of the seriousness of the government's intentions to launch a new initiative, and would remain so until someone was appointed to 'continue among them to see justice administered'.[1] As always, it was easier to provide the explanation than the solution. Wolsey's immediate answer, early in 1524, was to press Dacre to be more active,[2] and by June he was able to write that he and Henry were pleased that Dacre now took such pains for the correction of malefactors, at the same time pointing out that to persist in so doing would be the best way to put an end to the mounting criticism against him.[3] In the following month special commissions were set up for Yorkshire and Northumberland to put an end to the 'enormities' there.[4] Both commissions were headed by Surrey, now duke of Norfolk, and included the king's attorney-general, Ralph Swillington. Interestingly, the commission for Northumberland included Dacre – further evidence of Wolsey's reluctance to move against him. But, if any persistent effort to enforce law and order was to be made, by 1524 Dacre could not be considered the right man to implement it, and anyway, he did not want to. Neither did Norfolk: almost from the moment he set foot in the North, early in 1523, he had been pleading for his recall with a persistence that suggests that his pleading was genuine[5] – and twenty years later he was remembering with horror the time that he had spent in the North on this occasion.[6] And if Norfolk would not serve, it seems unlikely that many other noblemen would have been eager to do so. To spend long periods up there, involved for the most part in judicial matters, was not an exciting prospect for a nobleman whose estates and interests were elsewhere – and if Dacre and Northumberland were considered ineligible, it would have to be someone from further south. But in order to compensate for his lack of local influence any southern candidate would have to be a man of more than ordinary prestige,[7] and this further narrowed the choice. Indeed with Norfolk so unwilling and Shrewsbury having been in 1522 a reluctant and not especially successful lord lieutenant in the North,[8] it gave Wolsey virtually no choice at all. The duke of Suffolk might just have been considered, but he had no experience of Northern affairs, and anyway there is no reason to suppose that he would have welcomed a posting to the North any more than Norfolk had. Thus when it comes down to it, the choice of the duke of Richmond, far from being part of a long-term plan to increase royal authority in the area at the expense of the nobility's, appears to have been merely an expedient forced upon Henry and Wolsey

---

[1] *LP*,iii,3240.

[2] *LP*,iv,133, 220, 279, 332, 404.

[3] *LP*,iv,405.

[4] *LP*,iv,497.

[5] *LP*,iii,3365, 3384, 3509, 3515.

[6] *LP*,xvii,940.

[7] For even a Clifford doubting his influence in the West March see Cumberland's letter to Wolsey in November 1525 (*LP*,iv,1762). One of the points that an unknown writer made about holding office in the North, was that he must be 'enabled to support a plenteous and liberal home of meat and drink; otherwise I shall not be regarded amongst them, but shall be held in [approby] and derision', this because he lacked land in the area; see *LP*,iv,1764. The unknown man may have been Ralph Neville earl of Westmorland, appointed vice-warden of the East and Middle Marches in 1525. For the general problem of ever more 'foreign noblemen' see Bush, *NH*, 6, pp.59 ff.

[8] Bernard, 'Fourth and fifth earls of Shrewsbury', pp.164 ff.

for want of an alternative.

Henry Fitzroy was an illegitimate son of Henry VIII by Elizabeth Blount. Until created earl of Nottingham and duke of Richmond and Somerset in July 1525, he had lived in relative obscurity – not all that surprising since he was at the time only six years old. Given his age, his appointment as lieutenant-general north of the Trent and warden-general of the Marches four days after his elevation to the peerage, can only have been to provide a figurehead, albeit one intended to be as prestigious as possible.[1] The real work, as in the earlier appointments of this kind involving legitimate royal children, was to be carried out by a Council of the North attached to the duke's household made up entirely of people with considerable experience of Northern affairs.[2] One such was Thomas Magnus, archdeacon of the East Riding, very much in Wolsey's confidence and used by him for all manner of tasks, but perhaps especially for Scottish diplomacy. Wolsey's close relationship with Magnus and many of Richmond's councillors, and the fact that ten out of the seventeen members of the Council were lawyers, of whom only half were trained in the common law, has been seen as evidence of an intention to obtrude a personal, and clerical rule on the North, though mistakenly so.[3] Given Wolsey's involvement in Northern affairs during the previous decade, their closeness to him could hardly have been avoided. And how close is close? If they were merely 'Wolsey's yes-men', one would expect them to have been removed from office at his fall and this was not the case.[4] Someone who was appointed to the Council was the same Sir William Bulmer who in 1519 had got all too close to Wolsey when he was forced to appear before the king's Council in Star Chamber for wearing the duke of Buckingham's livery in the royal presence. Whether this episode made him a particular friend is surely another matter.

Since the main public function of the Council was to provide justice, the presence of a large number of lawyers is not very surprising. That half of the lawyers were churchmen and therefore not trained in the common law is only significant if some major clash between common and civil law is assumed. It has, however, been shown that there was no such clash.[5] Neither was it Wolsey's intention that Richmond's Council should replace the existing common law machinery, that provided by the commissions of oyer and terminer, the assizes, and quarter sessions.[6] In the running of this machinery its members would play an important part, but the Council itself would have the same kind of supervisory role as the king's Council in Star Chamber, the only difference being that as it was on the spot it could perform the role all the more effectively. It also had administrative functions, but the temptation may be to read too much into this. For instance, much is often made of the fact that Richmond himself was made warden-general; the suggestion being that the warden's functions were assumed by Richmond's Council. In fact it was the

---

[1] *LP*,iv,1431, 1510 his appointments in the North were dated 22 July 1525.
[2] Reid, pp.103-5.
[3] R.B. Smith, pp.154-6.
[4] Virtually no one was deliberately dropped. Reid's list of councillors suggests that Frankleyn may have been, but the evidence for this is not altogether convincing and he was certainly restored to it; see Reid, pp.113 ff.
[5] See pp.125 ff.
[6] Guy, *Cardinal's Court*, pp.123-4; Reid, pp.102 ff.

deputy-wardens – initially the earls of Cumberland and Westmorland – who did most of the work, and were able to deal directly with Wolsey.[1]

With a Clifford or a Neville appointed to high positions in the North, it is not possible to argue that the setting up of Richmond's Council marks a major step in the Crown's usurpation of the noblemen's position there. Rather, it was the best available solution to a number of different problems, not least the financial one. To set up as resident overlord of the North someone from elsewhere would have cost the Crown a lot of money.[2] Of course, even a Northern nobleman cost something, wardens of Marches received fees, were given other offices with fees attached, and so on. But the Northern nobleman did at least have his own residences and household to provide a basis. Anyone else would have to start de novo, and, moreover, would have to outshine his Northern compeers in display and hospitality. By giving to Richmond the estates that belonged to Henry's grandmother, Margaret Beaufort countess of Richmond, many of which were in the North as they derived from attainted Neville land, the Crown provided him with an income of over £4,000, and it was out of this income that his Council's activity was funded.[3] There were precedents for what might be called the royal solution, Edward IV's gift of lands to his brother Richard, which provided the basis for Richard's rule in the North, being the most obvious.[4] The alternative, tried on the Welsh Marches,[5] of using a bishop, whose position could financed out of his episcopal revenues, was not available here, because the obvious candidate as archbishop of York and from 1523 bishop of Durham was Wolsey, and he was rather occupied elsewhere!

The argument presented here that the choice of Richmond and his Council was almost one of force majeure rather than one eagerly sought by Henry and Wolsey cannot be proved, for no statement of their reasons for making the choice has survived. However, that it may be the right argument is suggested by subsequent events, and in particular by the rapid ending of the Council's jurisdiction in the Marches and the appointment in December 1527 of Henry Percy 6th earl of Northumberland as warden of the East and Middle Marches. It is only fair to state that these events have been used to support a quite different argument, one which sees them as a defeat for the alleged new policy of direct intervention in Northern affairs inaugurated in 1525, and a defeat that was brought about by pressure from the Percy family to be restored to their rightful place at the head of Northern society.[6] What is common to both views is the fact that the experiment of giving a Council of the North some jurisdiction over the Marches had not been a success. In a letter to Wolsey, written in August 1526, Magnus had pointed out some of the dangers and

---

[1] LP,iv,1727, 1762, 1764, 2003, 2176, 2401-2, 2729, 3230, 3370, 3404, 3421, 3477, 3501.

[2] That it was perceived to be cheaper at the time, see especially Surrey's letter to Wolsey in Nov.1523: 'Also if my Lord Dacre be well written to by the king's highness, and your grace . . . I doubt not he will occupy as warden for 40s. a day; and I having of the king's highness £5 a day, £3 may be saved.' (St.P,iv, p.55 LP,iii,3515). In a marginal note Wolsey accepted this. See also LP,iv,2004.

[3] For all matters relating to Richmond, including transcripts of most of the relevant documents, see Nichols, Henry Fitzroy Duke of Richmond.

[4] Ross, pp.198-203.

[5] See Chrimes, Henry VII, pp.249-51 for the Welsh precedents; the bishops acted as presidents of the council in the Marches of Wales under the titular leadership of the prince of Wales.

[6] James, BP, 30, pp.10 ff.

inconveniences that resulted from Tynedale men – these some of the most unruly men in the North – having to come into Yorkshire to act as pledges for the good behaviour of those left behind.[1] Just over a year later, most of Richmond's Council were crying out for a great nobleman to be resident in Northumberland.[2] The reason for their distress was the activity of Sir William Lisle and his eldest son, Humphrey, who in July 1527 had broken out of Newcastle prison, releasing at the same time a number of fellow prisoners.[3] Ever since, and in league with many of the most troublesome Northern clans such as the Armstrongs, Carletons and Dodds, these two had been terrorizing the Marches while using Scotland as a bolthole.[4] Neither Richmond's Council nor the deputy-wardens, especially Sir William Eure in the Middle March who had borne the brunt of Lisle's rampaging, were able to bring Lisle to justice, and by the beginning of November the situation appeared to be out of control.[5]

The Lisles had close connections with the Percys. Sir William's father had fought at Flodden in the Percy retinue, while in 1522 Sir William himself had fought under Sir William Percy, the 5th earl's brother. On 25 March 1525 the earl had appointed him constable of Alnwick.[6] But the Lisles, as lords of Felton, were quite an important family in their own right, having rather more status and wealth than a typical border clan such as the Armstrongs. Moreover, in 1523 Sir William, as captain of Wark (a royal appointment), had been the hero of the hour when he had successfully defended the castle against the invading Scots. This had led Henry to ask the earl of Surrey to pass on to Lisle his monarch's congratulations.[7] However, though a cut above the border 'clans', the Lisles had close contacts with them, especially in Redesdale where the Lisles held property. Like the clans, they were of the utmost help to the Crown in times of war, but found peacetime irksome, and were always willing to take the law into their own hands, as, for instance, Sir William's contretemps with Roger Heron, with whose family he was often at loggerheads, demonstrates. When Sir William subsequently appeared before Richmond's Council with his son Humphrey, he was alleged to have said that he had already 'ruffled' with Wolsey, and now had every intention of plucking him by the nose.[8] Furthermore, the son had apparently put an apparitor, acting on behalf of one of Wolsey's legatine commissarys, in the stocks.[9] Following their examination, father and son were indicted at Newcastle assizes for riot and forcible entry and were placed in Newcastle prison from which, as we have seen, they subsequently escaped.[10]

Even before he embarked on his embassy to Amiens and Compiègne in July 1527, Wolsey had become directly involved in the Lisles' activities, but on his

[1] LP,iv,2402.
[2] LP,iv,3552.
[3] LP,iv,3230, 3244.
[4] LP,iv,3383, 3404, 3421.
[5] LP,iv,3421, 3501, 3521, 3552.
[6] James BP, pp.10 ff; Hodgson, pp.244 ff.
[7] LP,iii,3506, 3531.
[8] LP,iv,2402.
[9] LP,iv,2450.
[10] LP,iv,2450, 3231.

return in late September he was faced with an increasingly serious crisis. The Lisles were by now plundering the Marches and the adjoining country more or less at will, and they were able to do so mainly because they were able to use Scotland as a comparatively safe base from which to mount their raids.[1] Wolsey's response was first to put pressure on the Scots to move against the Lisles.[2] Secondly, in December 1527 he appointed the 6th earl of Northumberland warden of the East and Middle Marches with a special brief to put an end to the Lisles' activities.[3]

On Sunday 25 January 1528 the earl was returning from church to his castle at Alnwick when he was met by fifteen penitents in white shirts and with halters around their necks. On his approach, they knelt and 'submitted themselves without any manner of condition unto the king's gracious mercy'.[4] The leader of the group was Sir William Lisle. The appointment of the 6th earl had brought almost immediate success, but does this mean that to him should go the credit? And if so, should the episode be seen as evidence that the North was ungovernable without the active co-operation of the Percy family, a fact of life that, in making the earl's appointment, Henry and Wolsey had had reluctantly to come to terms with?[5] The Lisles certainly claimed the 6th earl as their 'good lord', and thus someone from whom they could expect mercy, and in return he did go to some lengths to save not Sir William's life, as is sometimes stated, but his two sons.[6] And the reason he gave to Wolsey for doing so was because 'William Lisle is kyned and allied of the borders amongst them that I must need put my life in trust with many times', if he was to serve successfully as Henry's warden.[7]

The earl's point is a fair one. Families such as the Lisles were just as much a fact of Northern life as the Percys. They would not disappear or quickly change their ways, however strong and frequent were the exhortations from the South for them to do so, and besides, in times of conflict with Scotland, their warlike propensities were of great advantage to the English Crown. All this may not have been fully appreciated by the Crown, or even by Wolsey, though it might be more accurate to say that it wished to play it both ways just because there were two different problems: defending the border against the Scots, and maintaining law and order when there was no immediate Scottish threat. The Crown was happy enough to congratulate a Lisle for his defence of Wark, but equally happy to put him in prison

---

[1] Wolsey was informed of their break-out in a letter from Magnus dated 4 July 1527 while on his way to Amiens, but he knew of their activity well before that; see *LP*, iv, 2450, 3230, 3244. It would appear that Wolsey was on the point of releasing Lisle, in return for good sureties, when he broke out of prison.

[2] On 8 July Wolsey suggested to Henry an approach to Scotland (*LP*, iv, 3244), and from at least 12 Aug. Henry wrote either to James or to Angus at regular intervals until the Lisles surrendered.

[3] *LP*, iv, 3628, 3629; Fonblanque, i, pp. 556-8.

[4] *LP*, iv, 3849, 3850.

[5] This the essence of James's argument in *BP*, 30, pp. 13-14.

[6] Ibid, p. 14 for the view that the 6th earl sought Sir William's pardon. That it was only the two sons' pardon is clear from (1) Tuke's letter to Wolsey (*LP*, iv, 4204) in which he refers only to the younger son aged about 13; (2) Wolsey's letter to the 6th earl (*LP*, iv, 4082) in which he refers only to the request for the pardon of the eldest son and 'for the sparing of putting to execution of Sir William Lisle's elder son'; (3) the 6th earl's letter to Wolsey (*LP*, iv, 4093) in which he wrote: 'I sent unto my Lord of London and wrote to Mr. Tuke to move your Grace and move others to save some of their lives.' There is nowhere any reference to a pardon for Sir William, which, given his record, is surely not at all surprising.

[7] *LP*, iv, 4093; quoted in James, *BP*, 30, p. 14.

for ruffling with the sheriff of Northumberland. This ambiguity was all very well when one was sitting in London, but it undoubtedly made life difficult for those in the North who had to deal with the likes of the Lisles.

It is not clear whether the Lisles presented a particular difficulty to the 6th earl because of his family's close connection with them. It was his father whom Sir William Lisle had known well and who had made him constable of Alnwick and, given that father and son got on so badly, the suggestion that Sir William would have assumed that he would receive special treatment from the son is probably wrong. Indeed, that he could even have hoped for it is more likely to be an indication of his desperate plight, something that the emphasis often placed on the 'feudal' relationship between the Percys and the Lisles rather obscures.

The fact is that in January 1528 the Lisles had little option but to submit. Admittedly, it is hard to assess how effective the English appeal to the earl of Angus – at this time still in control of Scottish affairs – to do something about the Lisles was. The 6th earl was to deny that he had received any help from that quarter,[1] and both Henry and Wolsey had complained that not enough was being done.[2] This Angus had denied and, given the prospect of Albany's return and his own overthrow that the improving relations between England and France opened up, it seems likely that he would have been anxious to do everything he could to keep in with Henry and Wolsey.[3] His problem was that his control over the Scottish Marches, where the Lisles were harbouring, was not all that secure. Still, he was probably able to do enough to persuade the Lisles that Scotland could not for long remain a safe haven.[4] More important in exerting pressure on the Lisles was Wolsey's decision to order the new warden of the East and Middle Marches to go into the trouble spots such as Redesdale and Tynedale, where the Lisles were getting a lot of support, and to extract pledges whereby certain individuals from each family were made responsible for the good behaviour of the rest.[5] Such a ploy was by no means new, but Northumberland was able to get across that in this instance the government meant business – helped no doubt by the proclamations, issued on Wolsey's orders, calling upon the rebels to submit to the king's mercy and threatening excommunication and terrible punishment on their families if they did not do so.[6] By the end of January Lisle was thus a desperate man, unsure of his base in Scotland but all too sure that the new warden was determined to bring him to justice. The offer of a pardon, which it must be stressed came not from the warden but from the Crown, may well have seemed to him the only possible way of saving anything from an impossible situation. Whether Lisle was helped to this conclusion by the fact that the person he would have to submit to was a Percy is impossible to tell, but if he hoped for some special treatment, he was soon to be disappointed, at least insofar as his own person was concerned. By the beginning of April, various parts of his anatomy were decorating conspicuous public places in Newcastle.[7]

[1] LP,iv, 3914.
[2] LP,iv,3924, 4105, 4116.
[3] LP,iv,3704, 3705, 3773-6, 3778, 3791, 3794.
[4] For Anglo-Scottish relations at this time and Angus's attitude towards Sir William Lisle, see Rae, pp.157 ff.
[5] LP,iv,3689, 3816.
[6] LP,iv,3629 [2], 3816.

Nevertheless, it remains true that where the deputy wardens and Richmond's Council had failed, the 6th earl had succeeded, and it may be that the prestige of a Percy was an important factor in the Crown's ability to tighten the noose around the rebels' necks. This is not, however, the same thing as saying that the rebels' activities forced the Crown to return to a Percy rule of the North, nor does it give any support to the suggestion that the Percys encouraged the rampages of the Lisles in 1527 in order to force the Crown to turn to them.[1] The difficulty with this latter point is that, as an explanation, it is not required. The Lisles' quarrel with the Herons, with which the whole episode had begun, has every appearance of being genuine, and was certainly all too typical, while their rampage following their break-out from prison appears to have been one long act of revenge against the sheriff of Northumberland who had tried to intervene in the original quarrel.[2] Furthermore, it seems too altruistic of Sir William to have risked his own life and those of his family merely to further the interests of the Percys! And, of course, if the argument presented here can be accepted, there was no need for the Crown to be forced into accepting Percy rule. Its objection had been to a particular Percy, the 5th earl of Northumberland. There was, at least initially, no objection to his son. Indeed, it looks very much as if, brought up in Wolsey's household, he had been groomed for high office in the North. What had almost certainly prevented an earlier appointment were those major disagreements with his father already referred to. Once the father died, in May 1527, the way was left clear for the son's appointment, which took place only six months later. The activities of the Lisles may well explain the precise timing, but there is no reason to suppose that it would not have come about at some stage, and sooner rather than later.

Henry and Wolsey had always understood that only by co-operating with the leading noblemen in the North could its good government and safety be insured. The problem had been to find a suitable nobleman. In January 1528 with the success in bringing the Lisles to book, it must have seemed as if the search was over. But as it turned out, the 6th earl was to be something of a disappointment – not because he was 'overmighty', but because he was unstable, subject to depression and what looks like hypochondria – or, as he called it, 'my old disease'.[3] It is perhaps a little harsh to suggest that his affair with Anne Boleyn, while still in Wolsey's household, provides the first indication of this instability, but it certainly did not help his relationship with his father, who had been planning for some time to marry him to Mary Talbot, a daughter of the earl of Shrewsbury. When, late in 1523 or early 1524, the marriage took place it turned into something of a disaster, perhaps partly the result of a dependence upon male favourites strong enough to suggest some quite strong homosexual element in his make-up. At any rate, his affection for them led him to give away such large amounts of money and land that in 1537 one of the royal commissioners who surveyed his estates on his death could write: 'Never have I seen

---

[1] As suggested by James; see his *BP*, 30, pp.12-4, 30-2.

[2] The animus against the sheriff, Sir William Ellerker, emerges very clearly in Humphrey Lisle's confession; see *LP*,iv,4336.

[3] The easiest source for the 6th earl's character is Fonblanque, i, pp.378 ff., where many of his letters are quoted at some length.

a finer inheritance more blemished by the follies of the owner and untruth of his servants.'[1]

It is against this background that Wolsey's efforts in 1528 to supervise the management of the 6th earl's household must be seen. Often taken as yet more evidence of Henry VIII's and Wolsey's implacable pursuit of the Percys, it is in fact evidence of their desire to save them from themselves. The case is paralleled by a similar desire to save the De Vere and Grey families from the efforts of a particular head of each family to dissipate its inheritance.[2] The real question to ask is not whether the 6th earl was badly treated but why, given his instability, he was chosen to rule over the East and Middle Marches. It could be argued that it was his weakness and malleability that attracted the Crown, but that would be to ignore the circumstances surrounding his appointment. What was looked for was someone tough enough to deal with the Lisles, and Wolsey must have hoped that the 6th earl would prove to be such – and however much he was aided and abetted by others such as Angus, and indeed Wolsey, the earl did rise to the occasion. But it may be that Wolsey underestimated the difficulty of keeping him up to the mark; and indeed, almost immediately he was forced to give him a severe telling-off for going behind his back in his efforts to save the lives of Lisle's two sons.[3] Is there evidence here of the autocratic Wolsey, suspicious of any potential rivals and all too anxious to browbeat his own protégé? It seems unlikely, and neither of the two people the earl consulted, Tunstall and Tuke, was in any serious sense a rival of Wolsey. The straightforward explanation for Wolsey's reaction is that the earl had done the wrong thing: if it was his considered view that Lisle's sons should be pardoned, his correct course of action was to have raised the matter with Wolsey. And what is sometimes overlooked is that Wolsey did take the earl's advice and the sons were spared.[4] Still, by late 1528 Wolsey was having to reassure Henry that the earl would, given time, prove 'conformable to his Highness's pleasure in giving better attendance, leaving off his prodigality, sullennness, mistrust, disdain and making of parties'.[5] It could hardly have been a more damning indictment, and it brings one back to the central problem that, whatever the theoretical solution, the real difficulty in governing the North was to find the right person. That Henry and his two leading councillors, Wolsey and Cromwell, persevered for so long with one who appears to have been so unsuitable only confirms the central argument of this chapter, that they were prepared to put up with a great deal from a Percy.

In stressing Henry's and Wolsey's desire to make use of the nobility in the running of Northern affairs, the danger has been perhaps to play down the role that both men saw the Crown playing. The emphasis was on co-operation, not surrender. When in 1524 criticisms of Dacre's rule were mounting, Wolsey wrote to Norfolk that he considered that some of the complainants 'exceed the limits of humble and conformable subjects, when they absolutely affirm in their supplication that they cannot nor ever will be contented to be ordered by Lord Dacre, not to

---

[1] *LP*, xii, 548; for a modern assessment of his character and its effect on the Percys' financial affairs see Bean, pp. 145ff.

[2] Bernard, *HJ*, 25, pp. 671-85 is good on this.

[3] *LP*, iv, 4082; for a transcript see Fonblanque, i, pp. 390-2.

[4] *LP*, iv, 4082.

[5] Fonblanque, i, p. 404.

favour or love him in their hearts, but rather to depart the country. For such saying implieth in it great presumption, and is not to be pretermitted under silence, for as much as it becometh not them to refuse any officer which the king shall constitute, though he were of much inferior degree than the Lord Dacre is'.[1] Thirteen years later Henry was expressing a similar idea when he wrote to that same duke that 'we will not be bound of a necessity to be served there with Lords, but we will be served with such men, what degree so ever they be of, as we shall appoint to the same'.[2] Neither man was saying that they disliked or were suspicious of the nobility – and it should be added that noblemen continued to be used as much in the 1530s and 1540s as in the 1520s. The point they were making was that a servant of the Crown in carrying out the king's commands should be obeyed as if he was king, and therefore the servant's own status was of no consequence. In practice they were perfectly well aware that it was, but as the choppings and changings of the 1520s indicate, whomever they chose to govern the North, they had absolutely no intention of leaving him to his own devices.

Wolsey was immersed in all the details of Northern government: the conduct of war, the raising of money, the settling of quarrels, the maintenance of law and order – all was grist to his mill. And in obtaining the necessary information and implementing his decisions he did not – nor indeed could he – rely only on noblemen; people such as Thomas Magnus and his colleagues on Richmond's Council were also indispensable. Moreover, all royal servants, including the likes of Dacre and Surrey, were expected to do Wolsey's bidding. Indeed, one's overriding impression is of the immense pressure that Wolsey exerted to ensure that his instructions were carried out – the kind of pressure that, for instance, had led to Lisle's surrender. The pressure may not have been there all the time; and it appears that the Scottish threat, for instance, concentrated his mind on the problems of the North in the early 1520s. But any leading minister must have his priorities, and obviously the North was not always going to be Wolsey's.

How successful was Wolsey in tackling the problems of the North? At the start of this chapter a warning was given against thinking that anybody could have solved them: they were too intractable, and the solution to one problem was probably going to be detrimental to the solving of another. It must also be admitted that the detailed work needed to come up with an answer has yet to be done; and because of the inadequacies of the sources it will never be possible to do it very satisfactorily. But as always the real difficulty is elsewhere. There is at all times considerable 'disorder', and how one measures its containment depends upon so many assumptions. The easy way out would be to say that good order was present when those responsible for it declared that it was. But the men on the spot had a penchant for announcing that all had never been better, only to have to admit in their next despatch that all had never been worse – not that we should be critical. Like us, they found any assessment difficult; and until the next incident happened no doubt all did look well, and in one sense was. The obsession with trends – are things getting better or worse? – obscures the fact that events are often random and unpredictable, and certainly the men of Redesdale and Tynedale were not thinking

[1] St.P,iv, p.155 (LP,iv,701).
[2] St.P,i,p.548 (LP,xii [1],1118); quoted in Bush, NH, 6, p.40.

of the historian's tidy graph when they planned their next crime! And if one draws comparisons between the state of the North in Wolsey's time and at others it is the similarities that are striking. By the 1580s, for instance, a permanent Council of the North had been at work for forty years, but this had prevented neither the rebellion of the Northern earls in 1569, nor the ambushing of the sheriff of Northumberland and the murder of his brother in 1586. Furthermore when the ambushers were brought to trial the jury was very much on their side and found the murderer not guilty. And in 1596 two members of the Council of the North could write to Lord Burghley: 'We find that the gentlemen, to the great overthrow of justice, do too much favour their blood.'[1] Such difficulties would have been well understood by Wolsey and those who served under him in the North.

The accepted view of Wolsey's success in the North is that all was bad until in 1525 he re-established a Council of the North under the duke of Richmond's nominal headship. There may be something in this, though it may owe rather too much to Dacre's critics. Dacre's own view was that there had been no increase in crime during his long period of office[2] – but then he was hardly likely to think otherwise. What needs to be stressed is that from 1515 when Albany first set foot in Scotland until 1524 when he left for the last time, the threat he posed was the Crown's, and therefore Dacre's, chief priority: more general considerations regarding the good government of the North came second. But as the Scottish threat subsided so a concern for law and order gradually crept up Wolsey's list of priorities. At about the same time the number of cases appearing before Star Chamber was increasing so rapidly that he began to look for ways of lightening the load: the result was Richmond's Council for, as well as exercising a more general supervisory role, it also acted as a court to which private suits could be brought. Whether the Council really solved the problems that it was designed to solve has been hotly debated. Lord Darcy took the rather jaundiced view that those in the North desired 'to live under the king without commissioners, for at present if we do well, the commissioners get all the thanks, and if either we or any of the commissioners do badly the whole blame is laid to us'.[3] His assessment was more than a little biased, but it is a warning against a too easy acceptance that the Council of the North was indeed the answer to the endemic problems.

In April 1528 Thomas Magnus reported to Wolsey the successful conclusion of assizes held at York and Newcastle. Twenty-four offenders had been executed, amongst them 'two great thieves' from Tynedale and two from Redesdale. The result was that, in his view, the county of Northumberland was now 'in reasonable good order'.[4] This assessment will serve as a final judgment on Wolsey's involvement with the North, just as long as it is borne in mind that to secure even partial good order was quite an achievement. The credit for this was due not only to Wolsey, for nobody had worked harder to achieve it than Magnus himself. Towards the end of 1528 he was back in Newcastle, having spent ten weeks in difficult negotiations with the Scots, resulting on 14 December in the Treaty of Berwick.

[1] Reid, p.286.
[2] LP,iv,220, 279; Hodgson,iv, pp.35-40.
[3] LP,xii(2),186 the essential point being that he had not been put on the Council.
[4] LP,iv,4186.

However, even before he had returned to Newcastle he received letters from Henry and Wolsey instructing him to return to Berwick for yet more talks. Back he went, despite his sixty-five years and his 'wanting powers, [feblished] and made weak with many winter journeys' – and this, he added, was 'the sorest winter' he had yet suffered.[1] It may not have been of much consolation to him that the one person who was almost certainly working harder was Wolsey himself; more so might have been the realization that the negotiations were of the greatest importance for the good rule of the North. As long as the disturbers of the peace had been able to take refuge on the other side of the border, there could be no real progress towards the taming of the border clans. A permanent peace with Scotland rather than administrative innovations in the North offered the way forward, and Wolsey's continual efforts to bring this about can only be to his credit. And in support of such a view is the fact that one of the matters that Magnus raised with James v on his return to Berwick was the possibility of concerted action against one of the most troublesome border clans, the Armstrongs of Liddesdale.[2]

The lordship of Ireland and the North presented Henry VIII and Wolsey with many similar problems. Both were wooded regions a long way from the centre of government. Both were inhabited by 'wild men' who showed much more interest in raiding other people's cattle and burning other people's corn than in their own agricultural pursuits. And if the northern clans such as the Armstrongs and the Dodds bear many obvious similarities to such Gaelic tribes as the MacMurroughs and the O'Byrnes, so also do the great Northern families such as the Nevilles and Percys to Anglo-Irish families such as the Butlers and Geraldines. That said, it is on the differences between the regions that we will concentrate here, for it is these which will provide a key to an understanding of the Crown's handling of Irish affairs during the period of Wolsey's ascendancy.[3]

The first essential difference is that the Crown's control of the lordship of Ireland was significantly weaker than its control of the North. Indeed, by the early sixteenth century it was virtually non-existent. This had not always been the case. The hundred years following the first Anglo-Norman invasion of Ireland in 1169 had been a period of such great expansion and consolidation that by 1300 much of Ireland was governed in the same way as England.[4] There was a chancery, an exchequer and a developed legal administration. There were twelve counties, including Connacht, Cork and Kerry in the west, in which the king's writ ran just as it did in the English counties. There were also, it is true – as in the North of England and Wales – many 'liberties', such as Kilkenny, Ulster and Wexford, where royal administration and justice were delegated to a particular noble family. Some indication of the English success in Ireland is provided by the fact that between 1278 and 1306 more than £40,000 was provided by the lordship for Edward i, while for much of that period the Irish exchequer was receiving on average £6,300 a year.[5] By

---

[1] *LP*,iv,5070.
[2] *LP*,iv,5289.
[3] This account relies heavily on two important articles: S.G. Ellis, *IHS*, xx, pp. 235-71; Quinn, pp.318-44. Since I wrote this both have produced important reworkings of their original research; see Quinn's chapters in Cosgrove, pp.638-87 and S.G. Ellis, *Tudor Ireland* and *Reform and Revival*.
[4] Lydon, passim; Otway-Ruthven, p.174.

the early sixteenth century that amount was down to under £1,000, barely enough to pay for the lordship's royal officials.[1] And by the same time the number of counties had been decimated: in 1515, according to a contemporary estimate, there were only five half-counties – Louth, Meath, Dublin, Kildare and Wexford – and the inclusion of Wexford appears anyway to have been wishful thinking.[2] Anything resembling effective English control was confined to those first four, the so-called 'obedient shires' or 'English Pale' surrounding the city of Dublin.[3] In theory the royal 'liberties' remained, but English control, even where the holder of the liberty was entirely loyal to the Crown – as were in this period the Butlers of Ormond and Tipperary – was really only nominal. And when the holder was one such as James Fitzgerald earl of Desmond, who during this period was in effect an independent prince with his own client lords, control was hardly even nominal. In 1529 an Imperial envoy to Desmond was told that the earl could put into the field of his own account a force of 16,000 foot soldiers and 1,500 horsemen,[4] while his allies and clients could produce a further 6,620 foot soldiers and 1,130 horsemen. But when the earl of Surrey was sent over in 1520 to restore order in the lordship, he brought with him just 400 of the king's guard and 24 gunners, and money to raise a further 100 Irish horsemen[5] – figures that give some indication of the military problem facing the English Crown in Ireland in the early sixteenth century.

In an anonymous reform programme of 1515 Desmond appears at the top of a list of '30 great captains of the English noble folk that followeth the same Irish order and keepeth the same rule, and every of them maketh war and peace for himself without any licence of the king, or any other temporal person, save to him that is strongest, and of such that may subdue them by the sword'.[6] The 'Irish order' was more graphically described by the Imperial envoy when he remarked of Desmond's men that they were much given to theft and murder and showed no skill in anything except in daring death like animals.[7] Amongst Desmond's following were some of the sixty 'chief captains' of 'the king's Irish enemies' mentioned elsewhere in the reform programme, and even some of these called themselves kings.[8] The most important were the heads of the O'Neill family of Tyrone and the O'Donnell of Tyrconnell, families which dominated the northern province of Ulster. Not perhaps in the same league, but situated in the heart of Leinster – a province which had seen more continuous English occupation than any other – were such 'Irish enemies' as the MacMurroughs and the O'Byrnes. But as the anonymous writer was at pains to point out, as well as 'the chief captains' there were 'diverse petty captains, and every of them maketh war and peace for himself without licence of the chief captains'.[9] Ireland in the early sixteenth century was, thus, a patchwork of

---

[5] Lydon, p.132.

[1] Ellis, *IHS*, xx, 239, n.12.
[2] *St.P*, ii, p.9. The dating is tentative.
[3] Lydon, pp.260ff.
[4] *LP*,iv,5501 [2] a paper prepared by Desmond for Charles and carried to him by the Imperial envoy.
[5] *LP*,iii,670.
[6] *St.P*,ii, p.6.
[7] *LP*,iv,5501 [1].
[8] *St.P*,ii, pp.1-7.
[9] *St.P*,ii, p.5. For an agreement between a 'chief-captain' and 'petty captain' see O'Faolain, pp.23-4.

usually competing but nonetheless interlocking entities, whose precise mix and strength was entirely dependent upon the personalities of those who governed the individual pieces. Moreover, the racial origins of these leaders, whether Gaelic or Anglo-Irish, and their nominal relationship to the English Crown, had little bearing on the question of effective English control. The English Pale was but one piece of an ever revolving kaleidoscope of power groupings, and by no means the biggest and brightest.

Moreover, even within the English Pale all does not seem to have been well. To begin with, the Irish way of life, including such things as dress, language, hairstyle, and even their liking for the moustache, was as dominant inside the Pale as outside – which, considering that most of 'the common people' there were of Gaelic origin, is not all that surprising. The presence of this large fifth column was thought to threaten the security of the Pale, constantly under attack from the Irish without, but for some commentators at least the problem went deeper. It was not only that the 'Irish' within were potential allies of the enemy but that they were temperamentally ungovernable. So although some commentators put their faith in education, especially of the Irish chiefs, the easier solution of importing ready-made Englishmen was increasingly favoured.[1]

Another point that commentators frequently made was that though the Irish exchequer received very little, the lords of the Pale did very well for themselves from all manner of exactions from their tenants. The most controversial of these was 'coyne and livery', which was a lord's right to billet his men and horses upon his tenants free of charge, and it was a right which was much used – and abused.[2] Another was a tribute called 'black rent', exacted by one lord or family from another family or area. For instance, the county of Meath paid £300 a year to the O'Connors,[3] and when in early 1528 the vice-deputy, Delvin, in the absence of the lord deputy, Kildare, the Crown's chief representative in Ireland, attempted to put an end to this payment he was promptly kidnapped by them.[4] As this episode shows, these exactions as well as being burdensome in themselves were also evidence of royal weakness. Coyne and livery was, or could become, merely a way of subsidizing the lord's private army, 'black rent' merely a protection racket imposed upon the Palesmen by the Irish chiefs.[5] But then, however one approaches the lordship of Ireland in the early sixteenth century, the predominant impression is of English weakness and a resulting lack of good government, so much so that the writer of the 1515 reform programme could lament that 'there is no land in the world of so long continual war within himself nor of so great shedding of Christian blood, nor of so great rubbing, spoiling, praying, and burning, nor of so great wrongful extortion continually as Ireland'.[6]

Perhaps what has been presented is rather an English view. After all, the Crown

---

[1] Taken from the four Irish Reform programmes of about the period; see Carew MSS, 1-2; LP,iv,2405; St.P,ii, pp.1-31. For a detailed discussion see Bradshaw, pp.32 ff. My own view is that Bradshaw exaggerates their importance while minimizing the difficulties in governing Ireland.

[2] For contemporary comment see *inter alia* St.P,ii, pp.9-10, 14.

[3] St.P,ii,p.9.

[4] St.P,ii,pp.127, 129.

[5] For black rents paid to Kildare see Lydon, pp.275-6.

[6] St.P,ii, p.11.

did have a nasty habit of winning any military encounter, and moreover, what looked like bad government from London or even Dublin might not seem so from Connacht or Leinster – no doubt cattle raids could be fun! Furthermore, most of the evidence comes from harassed royal servants, from noblemen and their retainers anxious to exaggerate the evil doings of their rivals, or from the 'reforming' gentry and merchants of the Pale and major Irish ports. All these people had a vested interest in painting as black a picture as possible; and there is some evidence that all was not entirely black, for, as in England, the fifteenth century saw considerable building activity in Ireland, which suggests increasing economic prosperity. From the English viewpoint, however, the problems of governing Ireland must have appeared great, and in many ways significantly greater than those of governing the North, where, after all, royal control had been reasonably effective for hundreds of years.

But in one crucial respect Ireland posed less of a problem than the North. Whereas the Northern border was dominated by a Scottish Crown sufficiently organized and powerful to mount a serious invasion of England, the sheer political chaos of Ireland meant that it posed no such threat. It is true that an earl of Desmond or an O'Neill could put into the field a sizeable army, but even more than most sixteenth-century armies they were liable to fragmentation. Thus when O'Neill was anxious to take on the new lord lieutenant of Ireland in 1520 he was effectively prevented from doing so by his great rivals, the O'Donnells. And if the earl of Desmond wished to attack the English Pale, he had first to march through the territory of his great rivals, the Butlers. The smaller Irish families, mainly of Gaelic origin, such as the O'Connors of Offaly or the MacMurroughs of Carlow, might well prove a nuisance to an English lord deputy in Ireland, but they hardly posed a threat to the English Crown.

All the same, there was the potential for danger. In the conflict between York and Lancaster, for example, Ireland had played a part, and that mainly on the Yorkist side. Thus, in Henry VII's reign both Lambert Simnel and Perkin Warbeck, though especially Simnel, had received support from Ireland, which was a convenient base for a rival claimant, or foreign power, from which to launch an attack on the English throne. Its value as such was something that the fifteenth-century English author of the *The Libelle of Englyshe Polycye* had been well aware. On no account, he argued, must England lose Ireland, because it acted as a buttress against foreign intervention and gave England vital control of the Irish Channel.[1] This belief may not have been restated in Wolsey's time, but there is little doubt that the possible use of Ireland by foreign powers or rival claimants – and often the two went together – did help to concentrate the minds of the first two Tudor kings on the problems of the lordship. It was because of his justified suspicions that his lord deputy, the 8th earl of Kildare, was giving support to Perkin Warbeck that Henry VII made his one serious effort to solve them, when in 1494 he had sent over Sir Edward Poynings with a force of about seven hundred men.[2] In the 1520s the earl of Desmond's alliances with first France and then the emperor caused some concern. The difficulty is to decide just how much, and whether that concern was

---

[1] *Libelle of Englyshe Polycye*, pp. 34-40; also Lydon, p. 242.
[2] *Inter alia* Lydon, pp. 272 ff.

the main reason for the Crown's involvement with Ireland. Or alternatively, was it thought that there was a 'final solution' for Ireland, not to prevail in Wolsey's time, or even in Henry VIII's, but one that was already clearly articulated and in which the twin props were reconquest and colonization? To arrive at some answers to these questions, Henry's and Wolsey's relationship with Gerald the younger, 9th earl of Kildare, must be looked at.

The Fitzgeralds of Kildare, the senior branch of the Geraldine family, made up, with their allies and clients, the most important political grouping in Ireland. This is not necessarily because it was the wealthiest or because it could put the most men into the field, but because its undoubted power and wealth were concentrated either in or just outside the English Pale, especially in the counties of Kildare and Meath. From land in these counties the family received just under £900 a year,[1] but it had many other sources of revenue and profit. These included not only booty from the 'hostings' – that is raids on competing families – and a large number of 'tributes' extracted from Irish chieftains, but also the English Crown's Irish revenues if, as was more often than not the case, the head of their family was lord deputy. What this all added up to is difficult to estimate. Sir William Darcy suggested in 1515 that the earl of Kildare spent £10,000 a year,[2] which seems too high an estimate – and much more than any English noble family was spending at this time – but then another contemporary thought that by using his position as lord deputy to levy coyne and livery on all inhabitants of the Pale, not just on his own tenants, the 9th earl obtained the equivalent of £36,000 a year.[3] Whatever the real figure, there is no disputing that the Kildare wealth and power had been increased by the fact that, but for a brief interregnum in the 1490s, the 8th earl had been lord deputy from 1478 until his death in 1513. The chief consequence of this was that the family increasingly controlled royal patronage in the Pale.[4] There had been some attempt to check this process: when the earl was restored to office in 1496 the appointment of the two most important posts in the Irish administration, those of lord chancellor and chief justice, had been taken out of his hands and reserved for the Crown; and in 1522 six more offices were placed in this category.[5] But even when a Kildare was not lord deputy it was a very brave man who would dare to criticize or oppose him. When in 1515 Sir William Darcy did so, he was dismissed from the Irish Council. In that year the 9th earl had been summoned to the English court, and it may have looked as if one could get away with criticism because his days in office were numbered. In fact he returned with even greater powers, so Darcy's gamble, if that is what it was, did not pay off.[6] But for most people the prospect of a Geraldine come-back – even if, as in the 1520s, the 9th earl was often out of office and, indeed, often in custody in England – must always have weighed heavily enough to prevent opposition to the family's wishes.

One way in which the earls of Kildare had strengthened their position was by

[1] S.G. Ellis, IHS, p.240, n.14.
[2] Bush, NH, 6, pp.40 ff; James, BP, 27, pp.26 ff.
[3] St. Pii, p.13. The average income of the nobility was £1,000; Buckingham's was in excess of £5,000 and Northumberland's £3,900.
[4] Ellis, IHS, xx, pp.246-8.
[5] Ibid.
[6] Ibid, p.248.

marrying into such powerful Gaelic families as the O'Neills of Tyronne. Perhaps of even greater concern to the English Crown was their kinship, if by the sixteenth century at some remove, with the Fitzgeralds earls of Desmond, whose power and independence of royal control has already been mentioned. It is not, therefore, surprising that the 8th earl of Kildare was called 'the Great Earl', and earned for himself the title of 'all-but-king of Ireland'. Something else that he might have been is that rather elusive being – at least in this work – 'the over mighty subject', though his receipt of a great deal of royal favour would suggest that, even in his case, much caution needs to be exercised before such a label be pinned on him. Still, it was not all royal favour, for despite being lord deputy of Ireland for most of Henry VII's reign and for the first four years of Henry VIII's, he had been, in 1494, attainted for treason. So eventually was the 9th earl, but it would seem that almost from the moment that he succeeded his father as lord deputy in 1513 he was viewed with some suspicion. Unfortunately, little is known of the circumstances surrounding his summons to the English court in 1515, but it would appear from Sir William Darcy's paper presented to the royal Council on 24 June of that year that one reason was that he had been making war without 'the assent of the Lords and King's Council'[1] – though who was meant by the 'Lords' and whether the Irish or English Council was intended is not made clear. But though Darcy's paper was an indictment of Kildare rule, by 1516 the 9th earl had returned to Ireland, not only still lord deputy, but having acquired many marks of royal favour, including permission to call a parliament and a licence to endow a perpetual college at Maynooth. In March of that year he was granted a new patent as lord deputy, which gave him authority to appoint his own nominees to the (since 1496) reserved posts of lord chancellor and chief justice.[2]

Royal favour did not last long. In the autumn of 1519 he was summoned back to England, though, again, exactly why is not altogether clear. Nearly twenty years later Robert Cowley, a client of Kildare's only significant rival, Piers Butler of Ormond, gave as the reason a list of 'enormities' committed by Kildare, which he presented in person before the king's Council.[3] Amongst these was his 'disinheriting the king of his hereditaments', a failure to make any account of the Crown's Irish revenues, and his wrongful retaining of Irishmen. But whatever the reason, when the earl of Surrey arrived to take up his post of lord lieutenant of Ireland in May 1520, he found much of the country in rebellion. What is more, he was convinced that Kildare, who was still retained in England, was largely responsible for this state of affairs. His reports led to Kildare's examination by Wolsey. He was for a time placed in custody, and when not in custody was bound not only to remain in London and to appear in Star Chamber at a certain date, but also not to have any communication with Ireland without Wolsey's express permission. Despite all this, by August 1524 he was once again lord deputy, only for the whole process to start up again two years later. In the late autumn of 1526 he was summoned back to London again to be examined by Wolsey, and put into custody. And after Wolsey's fall, the process was to be repeated. In 1532 he became lord deputy for the third time, but by

[1] *Carew MSS*, i, p.6.
[2] Quinn, p.322.
[3] *Carew MSS*, i, 126.

the end of 1533 he was back in the Tower of London, and on this occasion there was to be no return, for on 12 December 1534 he was to die while still in the Tower. Yet even without death intervening another come-back had virtually been ruled out. In the previous June his son and heir, 'Silken Thomas', had led the Geraldines in a full-scale revolt. It was not successful, and with its failure the Kildare ascendancy came to an end.[1]

However, long before these last dramatic events, the Crown was surely becoming increasingly impatient with the Kildare domination. A man is not constantly recalled, accused of all manner of offences and put in the Tower of London, if his performance is perfectly satisfactory. Moreover, the arguments presented at the time to support Kildare's various reappointments merely confirm the fact that the Crown was deeply suspicious of him. It was Surrey who argued for the first of Kildare's reappointments, in 1521, within only a year of having taken over the lordship from him. This was not because he was greatly in favour of Kildare; as just mentioned he considered him largely responsible for the difficulties he was facing.[2] But his difficulties in restoring royal control had convinced him that unless Henry was prepared to invest much more money and many more men in Ireland than previously, there was little alternative to Geraldine rule. Seven years later he took precisely the same view:

> So to look upon the poor land of Ireland that it take not more hurt this year than it hath done in any year since the first conquest, which was never so likely to ensue as now considering the great weakness as well of good captains of the Englishry, as lack of men of war, and also great dissention between the greatest bloods of the land, and the Irish never so strong as now. The premises considered on my truth I see no remedy, the king not sending the Earl of Kildare thither, but only to continue his brother in authority for this summer.[3]

To antagonize the Geraldines, and with no effective power to put in their place, would have been a recipe for disaster – or, in other words, if one could not beat the Geraldines, one should join them.

With all this, Wolsey agreed. At about the same time that he received Norfolk's letter, he presented a paper to the king in which he argued that the situation in Ireland was so bad that it was quite the wrong moment to antagonize the Geraldines unnecessarily. Kildare should be retained in office as lord deputy, but should remain in England while Lord James Butler, the earl of Ormond's heir, should be given the task of defending the Pale. With Kildare still deputy, the Geraldines would not wish to come out in open revolt, and at the same time Kildare himself could be held accountable for their good behaviour, which was really to say that he would serve as a hostage but with honourable status.[4] However, it is clear that in 1528 Wolsey saw

---

[1] For this sequence of events see Quinn, pp.333 ff.

[2] St.P,ii, pp.66-70 (LP,iii,1252).

[3] St.P,ii, pp.135-6. In the same letter he advised that money should be given to the Butlers to help them in their fight with Desmond, while two months earlier he had urged Wolsey not to abolish coyne and livery in the diocese of Cashel on the grounds that this would seriously weaken the Butler's military strength (LP,iv,4277. Quinn's suggestion (Quinn, pp.333-5) that Norfolk switched from support of Ormond to support of Kildare to further his factional struggles at the English court does not seem convincing. There is no evidence that he was ever anti-Butler. His reasons for preferring Kildare as deputy were entirely pragmatic.

the retaining of Kildare, even as an absentee deputy, as merely a temporary measure 'until a more mature consultation were taken and had therein'.[1] And thus, as with Norfolk, his support for a continuation of the Kildare ascendancy is not evidence that he liked it. In fact, it is usual to suggest quite the opposite, that he was profoundly antagonistic towards the 9th earl of Kildare, rather in the same way that he is alleged to have been antagonistic towards the 3rd duke of Buckingham, the 5th earl of Northumberland – and, indeed, towards all noblemen.

There are two main sources for Wolsey's dislike of Kildare. One is Polydore Vergil, who produces a most complicated scenario in which Wolsey's hatred for Kildare is a sub-plot in his great rivalry with the earl of Surrey: in order to get him to Ireland, he must first disgrace Kildare.[2] It is not very convincing, if only because it was almost certainly Henry rather than Wolsey who chose Surrey as lord lieutenant in 1520.[3] The other, and perhaps more important, source is Richard Stanyhurst's account of Ireland in the reign of Henry VIII, first published by Holinshed in 1577. It includes a vivid description of Kildare's interrogation by Wolsey before the Council after his third summons to England in 1526 – a description which leaves the reader in no doubt that it was Kildare who got the better of the argument. As regards the main charge against him, that while ostensibly going to arrest his 'cousin Desmond' he had deliberately ensured that Desmond escaped, Kildare pointed out that the only evidence for this had been provided by people who have 'gaped long for my wreck, and now at length for want of better stuff are fain to fill their mouths with smoke.' He then gave Wolsey a lesson in the conduct of Irish affairs.

> Little know you my lord, how necessary it is not only for the governors but also for every nobleman in Ireland, so to hamper their neighbours at discretion, wherein if they waited for process of law they might hap to lose their own lives and lands without the law. You, in England, hear of a case and feel not the smart that vexeth us.

Finally, he denied Wolsey's charge that he saw himself as 'King of Kildare', declaring that he would give anything to exchange for one month his 'kingdom' for Wolsey's.

> I sleep in a cabin, when you lie soft in your bed of down. I serve under the cope of heaven, when you are served under a canopy. I drink water out of a skull, when you drink wine out of golden cups. My courser is trained to the field, when your gennet is taught to amble. When you are begraced and belorded, and crouched and kneeled unto, then I find small grace with our Irish borderers, except I cut them off by the knees.[4]

It is wonderful stuff, but it is almost certainly fiction. Not only has no contemporary account of the interrogation survived, but there is no evidence that

---

[4] St. P., ii, pp.136-40 (LP,iv.4541).

[1] St. P,ii, p.138 (LP, iv, 454).
[2] Vergil, p.265.
[3] Quinn, pp.324-5.
[4] Holinshed, iv, pp.280ff. quoted extensively in Fitzgerald, pp.176-9 where Stonyhurst's account seems to be accepted. Both Ellis and Quinn are more sceptical.

any verbatim account was ever made at any Council meeting. Moreover, the little documentary evidence that has survived does not suggest that Wolsey had any particular animus against Kildare. Of course, he would conduct the investigations into Kildare's rule in Ireland and be responsible for his treatment while in England, but then he was paid to do that. It is also true that in 1521 Wolsey thought that Kildare's great rival, Piers Butler earl of Ormond, 'for his wisdom and puissance', would be the most suitable successor to Surrey.[1] By 1528 he was rather more doubtful about Piers, 'his age, unwellness, and other passions considered', but he wrote highly of his son, Lord James Butler, who had spent much of the 1520s in England, may even have been in Wolsey's household, and was generally well liked.[2] This last point is of some importance, for if Wolsey showed any preference for the Butlers over the Geraldines it was a preference shared by almost every Englishman who thought at all seriously about Ireland – except the Grey family. In 1520 Kildare had taken as his second wife Elizabeth Grey, sister of Thomas marquess of Dorset. Whether the marriage was arranged by the king is not known, but given that Kildare was in England in response to a royal summons, it cannot have happened without royal knowledge and consent, and it was probably seen as a way of binding Kildare to the English court.[3] But Wolsey was closely involved with the Grey family, who had been his first patrons, and in May 1523 the new countess of Kildare considered it worth her while to write to Wolsey on her husband's behalf.[4] Thus, this second marriage gave Kildare a personal link with Wolsey, making it a little less likely that there should be any strong animus between them.

If there was someone at court who seems to have disliked Kildare, it was the king. It was he who in 1521 had refused to send him back to Ireland when Surrey, his man on the spot, had suggested such a move. Henry took the view that for this to happen so soon after Kildare's imprisonment could only reflect dishonourably on himself, and would discourage all those who, unfavourably inclined towards Kildare, had loyally supported Surrey. Moreover, it might give Kildare an opportunity to take revenge for his treatment in England by joining up with the Irish rebels.[5] And it was Henry, against the advice of Wolsey and Norfolk, who in 1528 refused to allow him to remain as lord deputy. Indeed , he considered that Kildare 'goeth fraudulently about to colour that the King should think that his grace could not be served there, but only by him', and replaced him with Piers Butler.[6] In fact the suspicion with which the 9th earl was viewed throughout the 1520s, but especially by the king, only makes his treatment the more puzzling, for though between 1518 and 1529 he was twice dismissed from office, he was also twice reappointed.

Wolsey's assessment in 1528, strongly endorsed by Norfolk, that to do without Kildare would endanger the security of the English Pale is the simple solution to the

---

[1] St.P, i, p.73 (LP,iii,1675).

[2] St.P,ii, pp.136-40 (LP,iv,4541). For Butler being in Wolsey's household see St.P,ii, pp.49-51 (LP,iii,1011, 1628); also Ives, Anne Boleyn, p.44, who makes no qualification. For the Butlers being preferred see inter alia LP,iii,1011, 1628; iv,81, 4422, 4562.

[3] Quinn, pp.329-30.

[4] St.P,ii, p.101 (LP,111,3049.

[5] St.P,ii, pp.69-70 (LP,iii,1252).

[6] St.P,ii, p.140, n.1 (LP,iv, 4502).

puzzle. Kildare was too strongly entrenched there to be dismissed, unless the Crown was prepared to intervene in the affairs of Ireland with much more vigour and perseverance than hitherto. Did the Crown in Wolsey's period ever even contemplate such intervention? The nearest it got to it was early in 1520 when Surrey was sent to Ireland as lord lieutenant, but the episode is deceptive. Once he had re-established good order, his main task was to make an on-the-spot assessment of the situation and report back.[1] With him went Sir John Stile, with a special responsibility for assessing the financial situation in the Pale, which after almost twenty years of unbroken Geraldine administration was an unknown quantity. Surrey arrived in Ireland in May 1520 to find a state of chaos, with both O'Neill in the north-east and the earl of Desmond in the south-west up in arms, so it was not until June of the following year that he felt able to give his considered view on the long-term future of the lordship. By then he had no doubt that 'this land shall never be brought to good order and due subjection, but only by conquest.' One way of achieving this was to do it gradually, taking one county one year, another the next. Such a policy would require a force of at least 2,500 men. The other was to attempt a speedier conquest, in which case at least 6,000 men would be required. But even with that number the conquest would take a long time, for Ireland was five times as large as Wales, which had taken Edward I ten years. Moreover, for conquest to be successful, it would require not only the building of fortified towns and castles, but also the importation of English colonists, for unless Irish customs were rooted out no reconquest could ever be permanent.[2]

This was Surrey's assessment in 1521, and it may have been deliberately pessimistic in order to try to introduce a note of reality into the discussion of Irish affairs at court.[3] No direct reaction to his assessment has survived, but given the Crown's horrified reaction to an earlier modest request for reinforcements, which, it was estimated, would raise the cost of his army to between £16,000 and £17,000 a year,[4] it is not difficult to guess how a proposal to at least double the army's size would have been received, especially as it was quickly followed by Stile's gloomy views on the Crown's financial prospects in Ireland.[5] Within months of Surrey's assessment being submitted, his recall was under discussion, not least by Surrey himself, who as soon as he was aware of just how little help would be forthcoming, was most anxious to extract himself from a situation which offered him no chance to shine. In the end he did not get away until March 1522, and not before he had had to make a hurried trip to London and back in order to take part in discussions about his successor.[6] And in these one of the chief considerations, as Wolsey pointed out in a long letter from Calais in October 1521, was the desirability of spending as little money on his successor as possible.[7] In effect, this meant that he would have to be

[1] This was Surrey's own view of his task; see St. P, ii, p. 73 (LP, iii, 1377); also St. P, ii, p. 37 LP, iii, 924.

[2] St. P, ii, pp. 72-5 (LP, iii, 1377) Surrey to Henry, 30 June 1521.

[3] This is Bradshaw's view; see Bradshaw, p. 64. But since most people shared Surrey's pessimism, I am not convinced.

[4] St. P, ii, pp. 66-8 (LP, iii, 1252).

[5] St. P, ii pp. 77-82 (LPiii, 1447).

[6] Surrey first asked for his recall in June 1521; see St. P, ii, p. 74 (LP, iii, 1377). For the events leading up to his final recall see St. P, ii, pp. 84-93.

[7] St. P, i, pp. 72-3 (LP, iii, 1675).

an Irishman.

When in the spring of 1521 Henry had rejected Surrey's request for reinforcements, the period of European peace inaugurated by the Treaty of London in 1518 had come to an end. In March hostilities between Francis I and Charles V had begun, and Henry made it very clear to Surrey what in this situation his priorities were: first, and very much foremost, Europe; second, Scotland because it seemed likely that the government there would seek to take advantage of England's European involvement; lastly and a long way behind these two, Ireland. But it is almost certain that the particular circumstances of that year made very little difference.[1] Europe had always been Henry's and Wolsey's main concern. All that had happened was that peace in Europe had given them a breathing space to look at other less important matters, amongst them Ireland.[2]

However, even the maintenance of peace cost money. In the month following Surrey's arrival in Dublin, Henry crossed to France to meet with Francis at the Field of Cloth of Gold at a cost of about £15,000, considerably more than he was to spend on Surrey's expedition. On his return to England in the middle of July he was quickly writing to a lord lieutenant increasingly involved in fighting rebel Irishmen, to press upon him the need for caution and restraint: 'now at the beginning politique practices may do more good than exploit of war, till such a time as the strength of the Irish enemies shall be enfeebled and diminished, as well as getting their captains from them as by putting division amongst them, so that they join not together'.[3] In October he was even more certain of the need for 'sober ways, politique drifts, and amicable persuasions', rather than 'rigorous dealing, commination [denunciations], or any other enforcement by strength or violence', for to spend large sums of money merely 'to bring the Irishry in appearance only of obeisance . . . it were a thing of little policy, less advantage, and no effect'.[4] What Surrey had to do was to persuade the Irish of the great benefit that would accrue to them from the rule of law, nor need it be English law if the Irish felt that to be too extreme and vigorous; any reasonable laws would do as long as they were kept, and as long as the Crown's lands wrongfully retained by the Irish were returned.[5] It does not say very much for Henry's concern for his lordship of Ireland that the only thing that seemed to interest him in October 1520, when he had comparatively few distractions on the continent, was the recovery of his lands. Once these returned, all he was willing to do then was to spend the absolute minimum merely to maintain some kind of presence in Ireland. What this means is that Surrey's period as lord lieutenant from 1520 to 1522, far from being crucial evidence that the Crown had any serious intentions towards Ireland, on the contrary turns out to be good evidence that it had not.

It also shows that at the heart of the Crown's unwillingness to take Ireland very

---

[1] St.P,iii, pp.66-68 (LP,iii,1252).

[2] There is no direct evidence for this, but the circumstantial evidence seems convincing: Ireland was included amongst a number of other matters that the king intended to tackle in an undated memorandum placed at the end of 1519, that has the appearance of a programme for the new era of peace; see LP,iii,576.

[3] St.P,ii, p.34 (LP,iii,860).

[4] St.P,ii, p.52 (LP,iii,1004).

[5] St.P,ii, pp.52 ff. (LP,iii,1004).

seriously was its great reluctance to spend money on it. It is true that throughout the later Middle Ages there had been a vague hope that Ireland could once again become a source of revenue, just as it had been in the late thirteenth century; and that this hope was still alive at the time of Surrey's expedition is suggested by the expectation that it might be paid for partly out of Irish revenues.[1] The hope proved illusory, and though Irish 'reformers' might continue to hold out the promise of financial gain if Ireland was taken in hand,[2] Sir John Stile's gloomy assessment of the financial situation there probably weighed more heavily. What is clear, however, is that, unless large amounts of money were spent, little could be achieved – and certainly not the reconquest of Ireland. To take one example, most people commenting on Irish problems saw the Irish lords' right to coyne and livery – that is their right to billet troops and horses on their tenants free of charge – as an abuse that ought to be tackled. But, as was pointed out to the Crown at the time of Surrey's expedition, if the practice was abolished large additional sums would have to be found for any defence of the Pale.[3] It was not, therefore, the right time to do anything about it. In 1528 Surrey himself made virtually the same point when he advised Wolsey against agreeing to the archbishop of Cashel's request that no coyne and livery be levied in his diocese, for Ormond's military strength depended upon it.[4] Thus, until the Crown was willing to provide adequate funding from England for military expenditure in Ireland, nothing could be done to remedy a major abuse.

Probably the cheapest solution to the problem of finding a successor to Surrey would have been the return of Kildare, but this, as we have seen, Henry was not prepared to countenance. For a brief moment, he toyed with the possibility of an English successor, in particular William Devereux Lord Ferrers, who with his military and Welsh experience had some qualifications,[5] but when Wolsey explained that any Englishman would prove more expensive to maintain than an Irishman, he quickly plumped for the only possible Irish alternative to Kildare, Piers Butler earl of Ormond.[6] Not only did he have considerable resources in Ireland, but his recent loyal service to Surrey also recommended him.[7] The choice was not a success. Without additional Crown backing – and of course it was the belief that this would not be required which had inspired the choice – his resources proved inadequate. This was largely because his power base was in Kilkenny and Tipperary, which was excellent for containing the earl of Desmond, lying to the west of him, but not for governing the English Pale.[8] And in the English Pale it soon emerged that the Geraldines and their supporters were not prepared to accept this rule. A policy of sustained pressure designed to secure Kildare's return was adopted. Early in 1523 the Crown gave way and Kildare returned, but the quarrelling between the Butlers and the Geraldines continued. In December 1523 Robert Talbot, on his way

[1] St.P,ii, p.54 (LP,iii,1004).
[2] Bradshaw, pp.78-9; Quinn, p.329.
[3] LP,iii,670 [2].
[4] LP,iv, 4277.
[5] St.P,i, pp.69-70 (LP,iii,1646).
[6] St.P,i, pp.72-3, 76-7; ii, pp.88-91 (LP,iii,1675, 1709, 1718).
[7] Inter alia St.P,ii, p.58 (LP,iii,1037).
[8] This was well understood by all those involved; see inter alia St.P,ii, pp.129, 136 (LP,iv,4265, 4541); LP,iv,8193.

to keeping Christmas with Ormond, was murdered by some Geraldines. Feeling it must intervene, the Crown sent out a high-powered commission which in July 1524 not only brought about an elaborate settlement of all outstanding disputes between the two families, but laid down elaborate procedures to be followed in the event of further quarrelling.[1] In many ways the settlement seems to have favoured Ormond, and certainly Kildare agreed to forgo a number of financial claims on him. However, on its return to England, the commission left behind a new lord deputy – none other than Kildare.

How far Ormond resented his own early loss of office and Kildare's appointment in his stead is uncertain. He had earlier asked for the return of his rival to Ireland because he was finding it impossible to maintain order in Kildare, and in November 1523 he had even agreed to pay the earl an annuity of £100 to enable him the better to achieve that task.[2] All this was an admission of defeat, and it may be that Ormond was quite relieved to return to his own lands, while still retaining a place on the Irish Council as treasurer. In any event, despite the settlement, the quarrelling between the two families continued. Charges and counter-charges were put before the king, both sides making use of their contacts at court. The result, in the late summer of 1526, was a summons to both Kildare and Ormond to come to England. There followed a most unsatisfactory year in Ireland during which there were two vice-deputies in charge, first Kildare's brother, Sir Thomas Fitzgerald, and then the pro-Butler Lord Delvin. Then in 1528 Delvin was kidnapped by the O'Connors, almost certainly with Geraldine backing. Such a direct challenge to royal authority in Ireland demanded a response – but what? On 4 August Henry made his decision.[3] Despite Wolsey's and Norfolk's advice to the contrary,[4] he rejected a Geraldine solution and Piers Butler – since earlier in the year earl of Ossory rather than Ormond – became lord deputy for the second time.

When in June 1528 Norfolk had written to Wolsey on the subject of Ireland, he made the point that in his opinion 'the malice between the earls of Kildare and Ossory' was 'the only cause of the ruin of that poor land'.[5] In this, of course, he exaggerated, but there is little doubt that here was the key to the failure of the Crown's preferred policy between 1522 and 1528. The hope had been that Piers Butler would prove strong enough to keep the Pale in reasonably good order and at least to defend it from outside attack, but not so strong as to be the worry that Kildare had become by 1520. And that even Piers Butler was viewed with some suspicion is evidenced by Wolsey's suggestion to Henry in November 1521 that his son, Lord James Butler, should be retained in England so as to provide some kind of check on his father's activities.[6] In the event Piers Butler had not proved strong enough to keep even reasonably good order, and Kildare had to be resorted to again. But with Kildare came the old worries, well expressed by an anonymous writer in the 1520s when he made the point that although Kildare as lord deputy was undoubtedly strong enough to reform the Pale he had chosen not to do so, perhaps

[1] St.P,ii, pp.104-8 (LP,iv,537).
[2] LP,iv,81 [2].
[3] LP,,iv,4556, 4562, 4609.
[4] LP,iv,4459, 4540-1.
[5] St.P,ii, pp.135-6 (LP,iv,4459).
[6] St.P,i, pp.91-2 (LP,iii,1762).

because he did not wish the king's laws to press too heavily on his own kinsmen.[1] Or in other words, the price for having Kildare as lord deputy was to allow him to have his own way. After Piers Butler's failure and given their heavy commitment in Europe, it was a price that Henry and Wolsey were just about prepared to pay, but only if they could get Kildare and Butler to co-operate. Despite great efforts, they failed. The faults were probably not all with Kildare, but it would appear that the Crown took Butler's criticism of Kildare's rule seriously, and an increasingly important reason for doing so was the activity of Kildare's relation, James Fitzgerald, earl of Desmond. Desmond was dangerous. He had a large army, he was virtually independent of royal control, and, as was mentioned earlier, he was quite prepared to negotiate with the Crown's enemies, whether Francis I or Charles V.[2] In the second half of the 1520s the most important task of the lord deputy was at the very least to contain Desmond, but preferably to bring him under royal control. In 1526 the Crown took the view that Kildare had failed in this task – indeed it had evidence that he had deliberately failed, which, if correct, was tantamount to treason.[3] But treason or not, Kildare's failure to do anything about Desmond must have confirmed the view, probably held by Henry and Wolsey from at least 1515, that he was not to be trusted.

But what real alternative was there to Kildare? Wolsey in 1528 could only come up with the stop-gap solution of leaving Kildare in nominal charge while giving the actual task of reasserting royal authority to the Butlers. It had this much to be said for it – that it made some concessions to the reality of Kildare's continuing power and influence in the lordship. Henry's solution to go all out for the Butlers, despite their earlier failure, was thought to be unrealistic by both Wolsey and Norfolk, and so it proved. Sandwiched between the two branches of the Geraldine family, Ossory and his son found their task too much, with the result that the Crown was forced to consider intervening more directly in Irish affairs – exactly what, during the previous six years, it had desperately tried to avoid. The death of Hugo Inge, archbishop of Dublin and chancellor of Ireland, in August 1528 gave an opportunity for this process to begin. Inge's successor as both archbishop and chancellor was John Allen who had hitherto been involved at the highest level in the administration of Wolsey's legatine powers. His appointment is thus a strong indication that Wolsey at this late date intended to take Ireland more seriously. Shortly after Allen had been consecrated archbishop in Dublin in June 1529, Henry Fitzroy duke of Richmond was made lord lieutenant of Ireland, while the administration of the lordship was placed in the hands of a secret council which included Allen.[4] In the following month the master of ordinance, Sir William Skeffington, was chosen as special commissioner, essentially to act as the military arm of the secret council. Skeffington did not arrive in Ireland until 24 August, less than a month before Wolsey was dismissed as lord chancellor, but there seems no reason to suppose that his instructions had not been drawn up by Wolsey.[5] If so,

---

[1] LP,iv,2405 (3).
[2] LP,iv, 4878, 4911, 4919, 5002, 5322, 5501, 5620, 5756, 5938; Carew MSS,i,126. Most of the evidence derives from 1528-9, but the historian of seventeenth-century Ireland, Sir James Ware, says that Desmond began his plotting in 1524; see Ware, p.77.
[3] Carew MSS,126; Holinshed, vi, pp.281; Quinn, IHS, xii, pp.333-4.
[4] LP,v,398; Quinn, IHS, xxi, pp.336-7.

Wolsey was probably also responsible for an agreement made between Skeffington and Ossory (even though it was not actually signed until November 1529), whereby Kilkenny, Tipperary and Ormond were to be made into 'English' counties, committed indeed to Ossory's charge, but as a justice of the peace administering English laws. At the same time his power to retain men was limited: he could only do so when the security of the three counties was threatened, not for his own private purposes.[1]

What was to happen elsewhere is not known, but in itself this agreement suggests a determination to control the power of a noble family in its own area of influence – a radical departure. The same agreement bound Ossory to settle all future quarrels with the earl of Desmond by arbitration, but by November 1529 there was a new earl, Thomas the Bald, and he was anxious to co-operate with the English. It could, therefore, be that the curbs placed on Ossory's power are significant only as part of a wider settlement with the new earl of Desmond. At any rate, his succession dramatically altered the political scene in Ireland, removing as it did the pressure that a possible conjunction between the two branches of the Geraldine family had posed since at least 1526. By the end of June 1530 the secret council was no more. Shortly afterwards Kildare was allowed to return to Ireland, to be appointed in July 1532 lord deputy for the third and last time.

The experiment of a 'secret council' in 1529 is of some interest to a biographer of Wolsey. The fact that John Allen, who had worked so closely with him in England, was a member, and Wolsey's own suggestion in his memorandum to Henry in the previous year that the time had come for 'a substantial debatement and consultation' on the problems of Ireland,[2] both point to Wolsey's close involvement in the experiment despite it having been begun so shortly before his loss of office. But while this suggests that he had come to think that the only way forward was for much greater control of Irish affairs from England, there is no hint that he saw the corollary of this as being either reconquest or recolonization. What seems, rather, to have happened is that for differing reasons the two families through which the Crown had tried to govern what was left to it in Ireland had proved unsatisfactory, the Geraldines because they were too strong, and the Butlers because they were not strong enough. As a result, the Crown had had to look for an alternative, and that alternative was 'the secret council'. In other words, the experiment was a response to the pressure of events – something that was characteristic of the conduct of Irish affairs throughout the period of Wolsey's ascendancy. The only possible evidence of a major initiative, Surrey's period as lord lieutenant from 1520 to 1522, turns out in this account to be no evidence of such at all. It has been argued by one historian that after Surrey's return to England in 1522 a deliberate policy of limiting the period of tenure of any lord deputy was implemented, in order to prevent either Kildare or Ormond becoming too powerful.[3] It is not an interpretation which I find acceptable; instead, I argued that in 1522 both Henry and Wolsey made a genuine decision in favour of Ormond, a decision which Geraldine power in the English Pale

[5] St.P,ii, pp.147-50 (LP,iv,5903).

---

[1] Ormond Deeds,iv,149.
[2] St.P, ii, p.137 (LP,iv,4541).
[3] Quinn, pp.330-6.

was strong enough to reverse.

Any assessment of Wolsey's personal contribution to Irish affairs is seriously hampered by lack of evidence. Only two documents give any direct insight: his letter to Henry of October 1521 in which he pressed strongly for an Irish successor to the earl of Surrey on the grounds of cost-effectiveness,[1] and his memorandum in 1528 following the kidnapping of the vice-deputy, Lord Delvin.[2] Neither document suggests that if Wolsey had been given a free hand in Ireland he would have wished to pursue a more interventionist policy. If he had, one might have expected him to take a greater interest than he appears to have done in the affairs of the Irish Church. It is true that a memorandum drawn up just before Surrey's departure to Ireland early in 1520 made the point that Wolsey should send a legatine commissary to Ireland in order to get the Irish Church behind Surrey's efforts.[3] But Surrey made no reference to such a person, so it can only be assumed that if he was ever sent, he was not very active. At a later stage, perhaps in 1524, Wolsey does appear to have appointed someone to look after his legatine interests in Ireland. Who this person was is not known, but whoever it was, he was very gloomy about his ability to do anything effective. One reason he gave was that he was getting no co-operation from the Irish chancellor and archbishop of Dublin, Hugh Inge.[4] The other, and more significant reason, was that there was considerable doubt whether Wolsey's legatine powers had any authority in Ireland.[5] In 1528 Wolsey sought to remedy this uncertainty by securing a bull which specifically included Ireland within his legatine jurisdiction. At about the same time he sought another bull to enable him to redraw the ecclesiastical map of Ireland by severely reducing the number of dioceses, thereby greatly increasing the revenues of those remaining and making it much easier to attract Englishmen to them.[6] And if by appointing Englishmen to top positions he could have secured effective control of the Irish Church, he might have been able to use the Church to spearhead the anglicization of Ireland. Or, if this was too ambitious, the new diocese could at least have provided the means of financing competent English administrators.

These moves to assert greater English control over the Irish Church provide further evidence that by the late 1520s Wolsey was being forced to take Ireland more seriously, but perhaps more significant is the time that it took him to make them. Why did he wait until 1528? One possible reason was that, though it was easy enough to point out the need for action, it was most unlikely that any action would be effective. Control of the Irish Church was not possible without a greater degree of political control. It was no good appointing Englishmen to Irish dioceses if they could be prevented from exercising their authority by unfriendly Irish chiefs. The same would apply for Wolsey's legatine powers, whether or not they were boosted by additional papal bulls. They could and would be ignored just as long as political control was lacking. In other words, though in theory the Irish Church may have

---

[1] St. P, i, pp. 72-3 (LP, iii, 1675).

[2] St. P, ii, pp. 136-40 (LP, iv, 4541).

[3] LP, iii, 670.

[4] St. P, ii, pp. 102-4 a letter to Wolsey 1 June [1524] by an unknown John, sometimes thought to be John Allen, but more likely to be John Rawson, prior of Kilmain.

[5] St. P, ii, 102-4.

[6] LP, iv, 80; Taunton, pp. 123-4; LP, iv, p. 1077.

seemed a way into Ireland for the English, in practice it was not. Wolsey may well have realized this and thus have been in no hurry to attempt something that would almost certainly end in failure. Another reason, probably the most important, was that neither the Irish Church nor Ireland itself was high on his list of priorities.

When, earlier, Ireland was compared with the North of England, it was argued that though there were obvious similarities between the problems facing the Crown in both areas and in its responses to them, there were two important differences. The first was that the Crown's control of Ireland was significantly weaker than its control of the North. Consequently, though in both areas the Crown preferred to delegate much of its power to leading families, such a policy was much riskier in Ireland because the great Irish families, in particular the Fitzgeralds, were less amenable to royal control. This being so, one might have expected the Crown to intervene in Irish affairs much more than it did in the North. That it did not was due to the second major difference – the lack in Ireland of any strongly organized opposition to the Crown such as was provided in the North not indeed by any English noble family but by the Crown of Scotland. Especially because of its close relationship with France, Scotland was a threat that could never be ignored, and so the Crown had to spend a lot of time and energy on the defence of its northern border.

In Ireland none of the great families were sufficiently powerful by themselves to pose the same kind of threat; neither in this period were they capable of successfully combining. This meant that a very small English presence in the English Pale, coupled with the geographical fact of the Irish Channel was sufficient to protect the English Crown from the worst effects of its lack of political control. It could, therefore, choose to ignore the problems of Ireland, despite the fact that they were in many ways greater than those in the far North. The honour and reputation of the English monarch did not depend upon what happened in Ireland, an unimportant backwater, but on playing a leading role in European affairs; Ireland was seen merely as a drain on valuable English resources. The result was that Irish affairs were only to be taken even moderately seriously when there was little else going on, or when even the small English presence there was threatened. To lose Ireland altogether would have been a blow to Henry's honour and, perhaps, even a threat to his security. To reconquer it would have required a great deal of time, effort, and above all money. For better or for worse, neither Henry nor Wolsey considered that Ireland was worth all this. One consequence of this is that the lordship does not provide a glorious chapter in the cardinal's life – but then it has not done so for many English politicians and at least, unlike his immediate successors, he avoided a Kildare Rebellion![1]

With scenery every bit as mountainous and wooded as both Ireland and the North, to many observers Wales still appeared to be inhabited by wild men, speaking their own language, and preserving their own customs – all of which spelt trouble. 'Thieves I found them and thieves I shall leave them,' lamented that scourge of the Welsh and lord president of the Council, Rowland Lee,[2] which is perhaps why he

[1] The rebellion, led in the 9th earl's son, 'Silken Thomas', broke out in autumn 1534 on the death of his father in the Tower, and took almost a year to put down.

[2] LP, xii [2], 1237.

decided to leave so few: within six of his nine years' presidency he is alleged to have hanged over five thousand of them.[1] No doubt his office inclined him to take a gloomy view, but it cannot be denied that there was a problem of law and order. What is less certain is how serious it was.

Wales's problems can most conveniently be divided into two kinds. First, there were those that were endemic to all pastoral and mountainous regions in which tribal loyalties persisted, and second those that were a legacy of the English conquest and the resulting administrative chaos. By the early sixteenth century Wales had not yet been incorporated into the English administrative system, nor had it any centralized system of its own. To the west was the so-called principality of Wales, established in 1284 by the Statute of Rhuddlan, and consisting of the counties of Anglesey, Caernarvon and Merioneth presided over by the justice of North Wales, the counties of Cardigan and Carmarthen by the justice of South Wales, and the county of Flint by the justice of Chester. In these counties English law and legal proceedings were in use, though less in civil than in criminal matters. However, it can be argued that similarities with the English counties were fewer than the nomenclature suggests, the main reason being that in the Welsh counties there were no justices of the peace. One important consequence was that these counties were governed by a much smaller circle of leading gentry, the sheriffs, constables of castles and other royal officials, than their English equivalents. What remained of Wales – rather more than half – was made up of a mosaic of marcher lordships of varying sizes, each, to the despair of the historian, with its own distinctive customs and practices, and varying considerably in size. What they shared was a high degree of independence, for in them the royal writ did not run and 'life and death, lands and goods' were 'subject to the pleasure of peculiar lords'.[2]

In the early sixteenth century the marcher lords were no longer the political problem they had been for much of the Middle Ages. Moreover, especially after the attainder of the 3rd duke of Buckingham in 1521, the Crown was by far and away the greatest marcher lord. The only lordships of any size that it did not possess were Gower, which was in the hands of that most active of royal servants, Charles Somerset, created earl of Worcester in 1514, and Powys, the two halves of which were owned respectively by Lord Dudley and Lord Powis, neither of whom posed any threat to the Tudor monarchy. The new problem was that the marcher lords had become an anachronism. In the twelfth and thirteenth centuries they had had a *raison d'être*. Then the Crown had been willing to surrender many of its rights to those it hoped would prove loyal supporters, willing and able to provide a plentiful supply of men and weapons and with a vested interest in ensuring that its conquest of Wales was permanent.[3] By Henry VIII's accession the last serious rebellion – Glendower's – had occurred some hundred years previously, and then only in exceptional circumstances.[4] With no one to keep in submission, marcher lords had declined into being merely holders of hereditary sinecures which provided them, usually in their absence, with money and patronage. In this respect the greatest

---

[1] By the Welsh chronicler Ellis Griffith; see HMC, *Wales*, i, pp.ix-x. For Griffith see Thomas Jones.

[2] R.R. Davies, p.3.

[3] Ibid, pp. 67 ff.

[4] Owen Glendower's rebellion had broken out in 1400 and was to last for about ten years. The exceptional circumstances arose from Henry IV's usurpation.

beneficiary was the Crown which, as the greatest marcher lord, had a vested interest in their continuing existence; but it was a very moot point whether this vested interest was also shared by royal government.

The most difficult problem that the marcher lordships created was that the multiplicity of jurisdictions made it easy for criminals to move from one to another, thus avoiding capture or, if captured, pleading that they were not subject to the jurisdiction of the particular lord in whose lordship their arrest had occurred. Attempts had been made to overcome these difficulties, but while the separate jurisdictions remained they were unlikely to be very successful. Another problem arose from the predominantly financial concerns of the marcher lords, which in the mid-fourteenth century had led to the practice of 'redeeming the Great Session'.[1] The Great Session, or session in eyre, was the highest court of a lordship, competent to deal with all manner of cases, both civil and criminal, with the one exception of treason, which was reserved for the Crown. The advantage to a marcher lord was that in return for dissolving the session and issuing a general pardon he received an agreed sum of money, or 'fine', for which there was also an agreed machinery for assessment and collection. If he went ahead and held the session, he would probably in theory have obtained more from the ensuing judicial fees, but collecting them would have been much more problematic. There were also advantages for those paying the redemption 'fine' – which in a lordship meant all its inhabitants – the main one being that they were freed from the obligation of attending the Great Session and from paying any fine for non-attendance. In addition, in order to secure the redemption fine the marcher lord was prepared to make concessions. He might, for instance, agree not to interfere with any existing liberties and franchises within his lordship. During the fifteenth century these mutual advantages seem to have resulted in a willing acceptance of the practice by both sides. By the early sixteenth century the tenants were no longer so happy with it and were exerting considerable pressure to bring the practice to an end.

Why this should have been so is not entirely clear. The Great Session was only ever an occasional court, and the bulk of judicial business was performed in lesser courts, so that it is difficult to see how the practice seriously affected the administration of justice, as it was alleged it did. The practice of issuing pardons to people charged with criminal offences was extremely common at every level of Tudor judicial activity, but elsewhere the custom of people who were not charged with a crime being required to pay pardons for those who were did not occur. This custom was extremely difficult to enforce, and it looks as if it was not a greater concern for law and order that motivated the early sixteenth-century marcher tenants, but rather the dislike of a tax which they no longer considered brought them sufficient benefits. But whatever the motivation behind their new attitude, the tenants succeeded in making the question of the redemption of the Great Session a central issue of the government of Wales during the first decades of the sixteenth century. Moreover, increasingly, the Crown took their view of the matter. What may have helped its change of mind was that when, after the attainder of Buckingham, Henry VIII himself became marcher lord of Brecon, his own attempt to redeem the Great Session there met with the tenants' refusal to pay

[1] Griffiths, *Principality of Wales*, pp. 27 ff.

the redemption money. This may help to confirm that what was at issue here was not really any great concern for good government – although much talked about by both sides – but financial considerations. If the tenants refused to pay the redemption money, obviously the advantages of the practice to the marcher lords ceased, and as the Crown was marcher lord not only of Brecon but of many other lordships, the fact that the financial advantages of 'redeeming the Great Session' had been put in doubt made it at least easier for the Crown to accept the tenants' argument.

Another practice peculiar to Wales for which there were demands for abolition was the levying of commorths.[1] In theory these were voluntary gifts of money to anyone in financial distress, but in practice almost anything – a marriage of a daughter, the upkeep of a house, or even the paying of a judicial fine – could provide the excuse for levying one and their voluntary nature was disregarded. They had become a form of irregular taxation, one imposed not by the lord but by anyone powerful enough for his request for a commorth not to be denied. Amongst such were undoubtedly the lord's officials, whose abuse of their position did constitute a further problem. Of course, such abuse by officials was not confined to the Marches of Wales, but the almost unlimited power that a marcher lord enjoyed over his tenants, the fact that he was almost always an absentee (the most notable absentee being the king), and therefore in no position to supervise his officials very closely, the possibility that he might himself benefit from the abuse of his officials, the great number of lordships and thus the great number of officials – all this makes it likely that marcher officials constituted more of a threat to good government than those elsewhere.

However, as regards good government, the problems peculiar to Wales were probably less important than those endemic to all pastoral and mountainous areas, which we have come across already in discussing the problems of the North and Ireland. When in 1533 Thomas Holt, a member of the Council in the Welsh Marches, was listing 'the greatest things that be amiss at this time in Wales', the 'great stealing of cattle' by the poorer Welsh gentry figured prominently.[2] He also specifically mentioned the complicity in this activity of 'under-officers and gentlemen that be younger brethren and bastards', who because of the prevalence of partible inheritance were in possession of uneconomic holdings but whose aspirations were too grand to permit them seriously to look for regular employment. For such people the stealing of cattle had become a way of life, especially since they often had sufficient influence and family connections to prevent any effective action being taken against them – and even if it was, local juries were often unwilling to return a verdict of guilty. And if one adds to the cattle stealing of the poorer Welsh gentry the inevitable disputes and rivalries between all manner of gentry families of the kind to be found throughout Henry's kingdom, there can be little doubt that there was plenty to occupy Henry and Wolsey in Wales.

However, the 'wildness' of Wales can be exaggerated. Much of it, including most of Glamorgan, was very similar in economic and social structure to many English regions.[3] Increasingly the English system of inheritance and land tenure,

---

[1] *Glamorgan County History*, p.275; Owen, p.27-8.
[2] *Wales and Monmouthshire*, app.3 for Holt's memorandum.

resulting in the bulk of a family's land remaining with the eldest son, was adopted;[1] and this was but one aspect of an 'anglicization' of Wales that had been going on for two hundred years. This was in marked contrast to the situation in Ireland, where, as we have seen, Irish laws and customs showed no sign of dying out, even within the English Pale. Moreover, although as a consequence of Glendower's revolt various penal statutes against the Welsh had been passed, including a ban on their holding of office, these had been more honoured in the breach than in the observance.[2]

In 1496 Sir Rhys ap Thomas was appointed justiciar of South Wales, the most important office in that area. Admittedly, he had the advantage of special links with the Tudor monarchy, forged when he had provided crucial support for Henry VII in 1485. But over fifty years before, his grandfather, Griffith ap Nicholas, had had no such advantage, and, though officially only deputy-justiciar, he had in effect been the most powerful political figure in west Wales.[3] Arguably an even more successful Welsh family than the house of Dinefwr, to which ap Nicholas and ap Thomas belonged, though admittedly one that had chosen to adopt an English surname, were the Herberts, who, in the person of William Herbert 1st earl of Pembroke, had not only dominated much of Wales throughout the 1460s but had also played an important role at the court of Edward IV.[4] These two families were, however, only exceptional in the degree of success they had achieved. Most of the offices, both in the principality and in the marcher lordships, were held by Welshmen. Not surprisingly, therefore, there is little evidence for any strong Welsh resentment against an alien oppressor. The pattern of political control and patronage was in many respects similar to that which pertained in England: the Crown and leading families dominated. Whether these leading families were of English or Welsh origin was not an issue. Admittedly, Englishmen could be heard to make rude remarks about the Welsh, but they were most commonly made by Englishmen living in the border counties, who suffered from the activities of the Welsh cattle thieves – but it was the fact that they were cattle thieves, not that they were Welsh, that mattered.

The suggestion that is being made here is that unlike Ireland and the North, Wales in the early sixteenth century did not present the Crown with a political problem. The difficulty for the Crown in the North had been that it was still an active border which had to be defended against an organized enemy. In Ireland the problem was one of trying to maintain some kind of political control; the problem of lawlessness was a symptom of the much larger problem of endemic Irish resistance to English rule. Neither of these conditions pertained to Wales. The Welsh Marches were in no real sense an active border, and had not been so for almost two hundred years.

Not surprisingly, then, Wolsey attempted no fundamental alterations to the way in which Wales was governed. Instead, his efforts were directed to making the existing machinery work more effectively. The key to this was close supervision of

---

[3] *Glamorgan County History*, p. 308.

---

[1] Though not formally abolished; see J.B. Smith, pp. 157 ff.
[2] Griffiths, *Principality of Wales*, p. xix.
[3] Ibid, pp. 162ff.; LLoyd, passim.
[4] Ross, pp. 76-8.

the marcher lordships, not only to ensure that each was well governed, but to secure the greatest possible co-operation in criminal matters with each other and with the adjoining shires. To achieve this various means were used. Indentures were drawn up between the Crown and marcher lords by which the latter promised to carry out the Crown's instructions, any default resulting in payment of money to the Crown. Within the lordships every man between the ages of eighteen and seventy was made to enter into a bond as a guarantee of his good conduct, and to ensure his appearance at the lord's court when required.[1] The attempt to impose severe financial penalties on all those who misbehaved was central to the Crown's efforts in the marcher lordships. It was neither a new policy nor, indeed, was it confined to Wales.

Under its indentures with the marcher lords, the Crown insisted that the pursuit of criminals into another lordship was not to be prevented by the officers of that lordship, nor was the criminal to be given any hope of escaping punishment by pleading that he was not a resident of the lordship or county where his arrest had taken place. Efforts were also made to prevent a criminal 'abjuring', a process whereby someone who had committed a crime could, by promptly confessing, avoid being tried and sentenced. Instead, he was to be banished from the realm – though, since in the case of a tenant the realm was taken to refer merely to the area under the jurisdiction of his marcher lord, his exile was not especially onerous.[2] These provisions went some way, in theory, towards solving the problem of the many rival jurisdictions. In practice much depended on the efficiency and good intentions of the marcher officials, something that the Crown in its many interventions in Welsh affairs showed itself to be well aware of. As it was, one of the greatest impediments to good government in Wales came from the actions of those whose chief responsibility was to try to bring it about. Before any attempt is made to evaluate the Crown's success or failure in Wales, it is important to stress that considerable attention was paid to Wales during this period – for there is a tendency to dismiss what was done there as merely 'business as usual'. Certainly nothing very new was attempted, and what constituted the major thrust of the policy, the system of indentures and bonds, was only the stock response to the problems that areas such as Wales presented to royal government. Moreover, it has been suggested here that as regards the few positive reforms attempted, the Crown's financial self-interest may have played a part. Whether this means that any assessment of Wolsey's involvement with Wales must be critical is another matter.

In 1518 letters were sent by the Crown to the marcher lords accusing them of failing to bind their men to good behaviour, 'by means thereof many and diverse murders, rapes, robberies, riots, and other misdemeanours have been of late and daily committed'. They were given just under three months to remedy this omission.[3] In the same year Wolsey and other royal councillors gave judgment in Star Chamber that the tenants of the duke of Buckingham's lordship of Brecon and Hay had the right to some say in whether or not the Great Session should be

---

[1] B.L. Vitellius C i, fo.14; Theophilus Jones, p.363; Pugh, *EHR*, lxxi, pp.436 ff.

[2] Pugh, *EHR*, lxxi, pp.436 ff.; Pugh, *Marcher Lordships*, pp.245 ff.

[3] BL Add. MS.32091, fos.107-9, printed in Skeel, pp.35-6; this to Buckingham as lord of Brecon and Hay.

redeemed.[1] And the issue came up again in Star Chamber in 1524, when the tenants of the lordship of Gower and Kelvey challenged the right of the marcher lord, the earl of Worcester, even to hold a Great Session, let alone redeem it.[2] This time the decision went against the tenants. Wolsey, who as lord chancellor was involved in it, may have been influenced by being embroiled, yet again, with the tenants of Brecon and Hay, the important difference being that on this second occasion the lord was now the Crown. This time round the Crown put considerable pressure on the tenants to redeem – which they formally agreed to do, while insisting that this should not be seen as a precedent.[3] But in practice they showed an extreme reluctance to pay the redemption fee. By 1528 this counter-pressure was largely successful, for in a royal ordinance of that year the Crown agreed never to redeem the Great Session without the consent of the majority of the tenants of Brecon and Hay.[4]

The biographer of Wolsey does well to concentrate on the Star Chamber cases for they provide one of the few bits of evidence that Wolsey was fully aware of the problems of Wales. There is also the elaborate set of instructions prepared in 1525 for Princess Mary's Council and household, set up in that year to administer the affairs of Wales.[5] Given its intimate connection with the administration of justice, and the setting up in the same year of the duke of Richmond's Council to perform a similar role in the North, the assumption that Wolsey was deeply involved in the decision to send the princess to Wales is probably justified. It has often been suggested that a major reason for doing so was the realization that lawlessness was on the increase in Wales. The evidence for this comes solely from the preamble to the instructions.[6] It must always have been tempting to justify any such royal initiative by a dire assessment of the existing state of affairs and the obvious benefits of what was being proposed. It was apparently 'the long absence of any Prince' which explained why 'the good order, quiet, and tranquillity of the country' had been subverted, and so Henry, 'by mature deliberation and substantial advice of his Council', had decided to remedy the omission. It seems hardly likely that he, or indeed Wolsey, genuinely believed that Princess Mary's presence in Wales would solve the problems of law and order; although it might marginally help by providing the already well-established Council in the Marches with some additional status. In particular, her household could become a centre of hospitality, thereby reminding the Welsh gentry of both the power and the generosity of the Crown. In fact the whole point of the exercise seems to have been to show the Tudor flag, and probably the only reason for not having acted earlier was the hope that a 'Prince of Wales' might yet appear and Mary's youth – she was nine in 1525.

The notion that things were going from bad to worse in Wales receives little support, therefore, from the sending of Mary there in 1525. Moreover, a Council in

---

[1] Pugh, *Marcher Lordships*, pp.45-6; *Registrum Caroli Bothe*, pp.35-6, a letter to the bishop of Hereford of the same date as that to Buckingham.

[2] Pugh, *Marcher Lordships*, pp.271ff.

[3] Ibid, p.46.

[4] *LP*,iv,5098-9; Theophilus Jones, i, pp.353-64 (though he gives 1533 or 1584 as the date); Pugh, *Marcher Lordships*, p.46; Skeel, pp.54-5.

[5] BL Vitellius C i, fos.7v ff; quoted in Madden, pp.4 ff.; also Skeel, pp.49 ff.

[6] *Inter alia* Skeel, p.49. For the preamble itself see BL Vitellius C i, fo.7v (Madden, p.2).

the Marches had been in almost continuous existence since 1471, and despite its title its jurisdiction had always covered not only the marcher lordships but also the counties of the principality, the palatinate of Chester, and the English counties adjoining the Welsh border – Shropshire, Herefordshire, Worcestershire, and Gloucestershire. Its powers had certainly been extensive, with authority to try civil as well as all criminal cases, and they do not seem to have been added to in any way in 1525. Nevertheless, the new instructions remain impressive in their detail and their scope. One thing which catches the eye is the apparently genuine concern for poor suitors whose cases were to be dealt with before any others and who were to receive free legal advice.[1] The instructions also contained much about the need to supervise the marcher officials and to prevent abuse by the councillors. Commorths were not to be levied, nor were Great Sessions to be redeemed[2] – this last provision striking a slightly false note, given what the Crown was attempting to do in its lordship of Brecon.

What the 'Instructions' of 1525 also show is a real awareness of the problems of Wales and a determination to tackle them, albeit in ways that had been tried before. Whether a different approach should have been used will be considered later, but of some relevance here is the suggestion already made that Mary's Council was not a response to a dramatically worsening situation. What may have helped to bring Wales to Henry's and Wolsey's notice was the death in 1525 of Sir Rhys ap Thomas. For almost thirty years he had held the most important post of justiciar of South Wales, while his son, Sir Griffith ap Rhys, had been chamberlain of South Wales from 1509 until his death in 1521 and had also been active on the Council in the Marches.[3] There appears to have been no sustained criticism of their 'rule', as there had been in the North about Dacre's – a tribute, perhaps, to their skill, but also a consequence of the more normal conditions that prevailed in South Wales. The decision not to appoint Sir Rhys's grandson, Rhys ap Griffith, as his successor in the office of justiciar of South Wales has been seen as a deliberate move against an 'over-mighty' family,[4] but given that he was only in his late teens or early twenties, the less Machiavellian reason that he was considered too young is probably correct. Since he may have been brought up in Wolsey's household and was married in 1524 to Katherine Howard, sister of the 3rd duke of Norfolk, he evidently did not lack friends in high places.

Given the paucity of evidence, the reasons for sending Mary to Wales in 1525 must in the end remain speculative. The continuing failure of Henry and Catherine of Aragon to produce a prince of Wales, the decision to set up a Council of the North headed by the duke of Richmond, a desire to facilitate access to royal justice but also to relieve pressure on the central courts and particularly Star Chamber, and the continuing recognition that a Council was required to supervise the governing of an administratively very confused area in which law and order was not everywhere well maintained – all these things played their part. The most prominent lay figure on the new Council was a former member, Walter Devereux

[1] BL Vitellius C i, fo.16.
[2] Ibid, fo.14.
[3] Griffiths, *Principality of Wales*, pp.162 ff.; D. Jones, pp. 81 ff; LLoyd, pp.54 ff.
[4] LLoyd, pp.62-4.

Lord Ferrers. He was by way of being a professional soldier, serving in France both in 1513 and 1523. What he lacked was political skills, or so Wolsey argued in opposing Henry's desire to appoint him Surrey's successor in Ireland in 1521.[1] He must have seemed a more suitable choice for the less politically sensitive Wales, for what he lacked in nous was made up for by his unquestioned loyalty, his experience in Welsh affairs, and the fact that his estates lay on the Welsh borders. Unfortunately it was to turn out otherwise.

Almost all the lay members of Mary's Council had, like Ferrers, considerable experience of Welsh affairs, in some cases going back almost thirty years.[2] Four members out of fifteen were clerics, a proportion which hardly supports the general thesis – though not one accepted in this study – that Wolsey strove for a clerical dominance of government. Admittedly the Council's president, John Veysey, was bishop of Exeter, but then his predecessors had also been bishops. Moreover, Veysey almost certainly owed his successful career not, as has been alleged, to Wolsey but to his close association with the court as dean both of the Chapel Royal and St George's, Windsor. This is not to suggest that he and Wolsey did not get on, or that Wolsey did not approve of his appointment to the presidency, for which his proven administrative and legal ability, together with his intimate association with the court, made him the obvious choice. Nevertheless his presidency is often deemed to have been something of a fiasco,[3] and one for which Wolsey, even if not as close to Veysey as is sometimes alleged, must share some of the responsibility – always assuming that the verdict is correct.

One of the great difficulties in arriving at any verdict is the almost complete lack of evidence about the activities of the Council for this period. The view that all was bad derives entirely from memoranda and letters of the early 1530s, including a letter from a fellow councillor of Veysey, Sir Edward Croft, in which he stated that Wales was 'far out of order': he wanted a man to be sent down 'to use the sword of justice . . . otherwise the Welsh will wax so wild it will not be easy to bring them into order again'.[4] He was critical of the clerical element on the Council because, he alleged, as churchmen they had no power to inflict the death penalty – a remark which seems to have been a complete red herring. Both under Veysey and most spectacularly so under Veysey's successor and fellow bishop, Rowland Lee, the Council did impose the death penalty.[5] He also commented on the lord president's absence – and this has contributed to the view that Veysey was indolent. At about the same time Henry informed Veysey that he had received many complaints that not only was cattle-stealing on the increase in the Marches, but it was going unpunished. Much of the blame for this must rest with the Council which was to rectify the matter immediately.[6]

There is other evidence from this period that all was not well with Wales, and it would be foolish to argue that the criticisms were without foundation. All the same,

---

[1] St.P,i, p.72 (LP,iii,1675).
[2] For its membership see Madden, p.xxxiv.
[3] Elton, *Reform and Reformation*, p.203; *Glamorgan County History*, pp.562-3; P. Williams, *Council in the Marches*, pp.13-5.
[4] LP,vi,210.
[5] *Glamorgan County History*, p.565; P. Williams, pp.15ff.
[6] *Glamorgan County History*, p.563.

there may have been a tendency to take them too seriously. Royal complaints were often on the sharp side, and the fact that Veysey was a bishop who had been closely associated with Princess Mary may not have helped him much in the early 1530s, even though he had been careful to comply with the king's wishes over the divorce. He may also have lacked the enormous energy and drive of his successor, Rowland Lee – though it is partly the chance survival of Lee's letters to Cromwell that enables us to make a judgement on Lee's dynamism. At the time of his replacement by Lee in 1534 he was already in his early seventies, which alone may explain quite a lot. But, given his earlier record, it seems most unlikely that he was incompetent or that in Wolsey's time at least he was presiding over a rapidly deteriorating situation, a view supported by the bits of evidence that have survived. Sometime in 1525 or 1526, the prior of Llanthony was requested to make an indenture for the administration of justice in his lordship that was entirely in line with the instructions given to the Council to make new indentures with all the marcher lords.[1] On 1 September 1526 Veysey reported that he had received the king's commission and Wolsey's instructions, and had sent monitions to the shires for their execution.[2] He also excused his hasty writing on the grounds that he was so busy. In March 1528 he could write 'that these parts under the Princess's authority are in great quietness'.[3] Four months later he informed Wolsey that the matter between Lord Ferrers and 'young Mr Rhys' was pacified[4] – but this proved to be premature.

It was suggested earlier that there had been no great political intent behind the decision in 1525 not to appoint Rhys ap Griffith to his grandfather's office of justiciar of South Wales. Be that as it may, the intrusion of a stranger into his family's sphere of influence was resented by the young Rhys ap Griffith, leading to those matters which in July 1528 Veysey hoped had been pacified. However, in the following March ap Griffith was complaining to Wolsey that Lord Ferrers's deputies continued to vex his poor tenants, and in order to prevent this, he asked to become a deputy himself and also chamberlain of South Wales, the post his father had held, offering to pay Lord Ferrers whatever sum Wolsey thought appropriate.[5] Nothing seems to have come of this request, and by the middle of June he was a prisoner in Carmarthen castle for having, allegedly, attempted to kill Lord Ferrers. It was further alleged that a hundred and forty of his supporters, spurred on by his wife, the former Lady Katherine Howard, had marched on the town in an effort to rescue their leader.[6] The difficulty with the so-called 'Welsh insurrection' of Rhys ap Griffith is to decide whether it was indeed an insurrection, and, if so, how Welsh was it. Of course, if one hundred and forty men did march on Carmarthen the matter was of some seriousness, but there is reason to doubt this. For one thing, in Lord Ferrers' bill to Star Chamber, out of the hundred and forty he could only produce twenty-seven names.[7] Moreover, when the alleged hundred and forty got

---

[1] W.R.B. Robinson, p.350.

[2] LP,iv,2448.

[3] LP,iv,4079.

[4] LP,iv,4470.

[5] LP,iv,5345.

[6] For Ferrers' bill of indictment against ap Griffith see PRO STAC 18/234, printed in D. Jones, pp.192-5; see also LLoyd, pp.75ff.; Rees, pp.45 ff; W.L. Williams, pp.1 ff.

to Carmarthen they do not seem to have done anything – which, given that they were supposed to have been summoned from all the counties of Carmarthen, Cardigan, and Pembroke, would indicate a curious loss of nerve. And if it was obvious that an insurrection had been planned with the murder of Lord Ferrers as one of its aims, it is strange that the reaction of the Council in the Marches was to put both Ferrers and ap Griffith under bonds to appear before Star Chamber, meanwhile releasing ap Griffith. For what happened in Star Chamber we are dependent on the account of the soldier and chronicler Ellis Griffith, an anglicized Welshman who spent much of his life in the service of Sir Robert Wingfield. No lover of the House of Dinefwr, he appears to have concurred with the views of many who lived within twenty miles of Sir Rhys ap Thomas that 'there was not in possession of the poor yeoman any land which, if he fancied it, he did not obtain'.[1] Nevertheless, when reporting on the trial he wrote that he had heard there 'the ugliest accusations and charges that two gentlemen could bring against each other'[2] – which in the circumstances was surely a vote for ap Griffith. And according to him, Wolsey took a similar view, censuring both men but being more severe on Lord Ferrers, whom he accused of bad temper and a lack of sense in quarrelling with someone young enough to be his son. But at the same time, he took the precaution of not allowing Rhys ap Griffith to return to Wales.[3]

This account of the early stages of the so-called 'Welsh insurrection' does not support the view that it was Wolsey who saved ap Griffith from execution in 1529 – this for a number of rather speculative reasons, including the wish, at a critical juncture in his own career, to keep in with the 3rd duke of Norfolk whose brother-in-law ap Griffith was.[4] It suggests, rather, that the main reason why ap Griffith was not executed then was that there had been no insurrection. Ellis Griffith makes no mention of 'Welsh' backing for ap Griffith, and even if, unlikely as it is, as many as a hundred and forty did rise in his support, this does not add up to anything like Owen Glendower's revolt of some hundred years earlier. In fact, far from being a national uprising, the 'insurrection' of 1529 was just another skirmish between rival families of the kind that Wolsey spent much of his time trying to contain. In 1529 Wolsey may have thought that in the case of Ferrers and ap Griffith he had done just that. As it turned out, he was wrong. Further incidents occurred, not unlike those leading up to Kildare's rebellion in Ireland in 1534: in both cases the head of an important family was prevented from returning to his area of influence, and the response was disturbances designed to bring pressure on the Crown to allow his return. The difference was that the support for ap Griffith was never strong enough to threaten English control. Instead, a disgruntled ap Griffith was tempted into opening up negotiations with James v of Scotland – which constituted an act of treason and was thus of a quite different order from anything he had been involved in in 1529. And the result was a quite different treatment – his execution on 4 December 1531.

There were other rivalries in Wales, including one between two successful

---

[7] David Jones, p.194.

[1] HMC, *Wales*,i, p.x.
[2] Thomas Jones, p.11.
[3] HMC, *Wales*,i, pp.ix-x.
[4] Suggested by Williams (W.L. Williams, p.23), but rejected by Lloyd (Lloyd, p.98).

courtiers with interests in the area, Sir Ralph Egerton, a member of Mary's Council, and William Brereton,[1] but only that between Ferrers and ap Griffith appears to have caused any concern – and, it has been suggested here, not very much at that. Indeed, that Wales did not cause much concern to Wolsey, has been, in this account, the underlying theme. This explains why he did not set in motion the kind of changes that between 1536 and 1543 were to result in the abolition of the marcher lordships and the incorporation of Wales into the English political, legal and administrative systems: since there was nothing dramatically wrong with Wales, there was no need for any dramatic changes. By 1536, when the first 'act of union' was passed, the situation had altered somewhat.[2] There were, for instance, serious doubts about whether the vital legislation by which Henry effected his 'break with Rome' was legally enforceable in Wales, while as its revenues as marcher lord dwindled, especially with the ending of the practice of 'redeeming the Great Session', the financial advantages of extending the parliamentary subsidy to Wales grew ever more obvious. What is not so clear is that a belief that the 'good government' of Wales would be best served by union played any vital part in the Crown's thinking. At any rate, the man who knew most about Wales, Veysey's successor as president of the Council in the Marches, Rowland Lee, was strongly opposed to union on the grounds that the Welsh gentry were not up to running an English system of local government; indeed, it was they who, in his view, were largely responsible for Wales's many ills.[3] That he took this view is a warning not to see the union as self-evidently the only way forward. That his assessment turned out to be far too gloomy confirms the view put forward here that there was not much wrong with Wales that a little bit of attention could not cope with – and that at least Wolsey had provided.

[1] Ives, *Bulletin of the John Ryland Library*, 52, pp.364 ff.
[2] Roberts, pp.49-70, but see also Rees, pp.27-100.
[3] LP,x,453.

CHAPTER EIGHT

THE CARDINAL LEGATE AND THE ENGLISH CHURCH

O NE OF THE BYPRODUCTS OF WOLSEY'S SKILFUL DIPLOMACY IN 1518 HAD
been his appointment by Leo x to the office of legate *a latere*. Admittedly, the
appointment was to last only for as long as his fellow legate *a latere*, Cardinal
Campeggio, remained in England, and the only specific power it gave Wolsey was to
help Campeggio in furthering the papal plans for a crusade.[1] However, the mere fact
of being legate *a latere* did in theory give Wolsey the kind of supremacy over the
English Church that he and Henry had been looking for. Under canon law a legate
a latere had very extensive powers, including the right to make visitations, to
appoint to all benefices in ecclesiastical patronage, to summon church councils, and
to make new constitutions for the clergy and those in religious orders. In theory,
also, all other ecclesiastical jurisdiction had to give way. Consequently, Warham,
as archbishop of Canterbury only *legatus natus*, would have to concede precedence
to Wolsey, though otherwise the primacy lay with Canterbury rather than York.[2]
And as it turned out, the papacy's continuing desire for English support made it
comparatively easy for Wolsey not only continually to renew his legatine commission, until in January 1524 he was made legate *a latere* for life, but also greatly to
enlarge the specific powers granted to him.[3]

Many people have argued that the acquisition of these powers was for Wolsey an
end in itself. Cavendish describes a disagreement between Wolsey and Warham
before the former's appointment as legate.[4] It had to do with ecclesiastical etiquette
– roughly speaking, whose cross should be carried before whose in whose province –
and the point of the story has usually been taken to be that Wolsey found the
primacy of Canterbury irksome to his over-developed *amour propre*.[5] Moreover,
Canterbury was a wealthier see than York, and one source of this wealth derived

---

[1] See pp.102-3 above. This chapter could not have been written without the help of Stephen
Thompson. The references to his important thesis, 'English and Welsh bishops', are comparatively few
only because it was completed after this chapter was written.

[2] Pollard, pp.165-7 remains one of the best accounts of the distinction between legate *a latere* and *legatus
natus*.

[3] M.J. Kelly, 'Canterbury jurisdiction', pp.166 ff. for the best available survey of the various extensions
based in part on his search of the Vatican archives, which I have not been able to do. However, I have
given his references to them, as they are not available in print, and may be of some use: 10 June 1519
(Reg.Vat, 1200, fos 34-41v; KCA, DR c/R7 (Fisher's Register), fos.100v- 101v;*LP*,iii,475). Jan. 1520
(Reg.Vat, 1200, fo 344). Jan. 1521 (Reg.Vat, 1177, fo.50; Rymer, xiii, p.734). 1 April 1521 (Reg.Vat,
1202, fos.39 ff; Rymer, xiii, pp.739-42). July 1521 (Reg.Vat, 1202, fo 110). Jan. 1523 (*LP*,iii,2521,
2771, 2891). Jan. 1524 (*LP*,iv,14, 115, 126 not discovered by Kelly in Vatican register). 21 Aug. 1524
(Wilkins,iii, 703-4). See also M.J. Kelly, 'Canterbury jurisdiction', pp.168-71.

[4] From this point Wolsey will usually be referred to just as legate rather than more correctly legate *a
latere*.

[5] Cavendish, pp.15-16. Cavendish writes that this disagreement took place before Wolsey became
cardinal, but if it occurred at all, it could only have done after, when there were genuine reasons for
disputing who legally had precedence. In a parallel case, Eugenius iv had ruled that Cardinal Kemp had

from its archbishop's many jurisdictional rights throughout the southern province, including his right to prove the wills of the wealthy and to conduct *sede vacante* visitations.[1] York had similar rights, but the province was much smaller, the number of dioceses it contained far fewer, and its inhabitants by and large less wealthy. But as legate *a latere*, Wolsey was able to lay claim to all Canterbury's jurisdictional rights and revenues, and indeed to all such rights and revenues belonging to any churchman. The suggestion has been, therefore, that along with his obsession with self, it was his insatiable greed that motivated his ecclesiastical policies as legate, and that, if he occasionally talked of reform, this was mere window-dressing for what was in reality a systematic exploitation of the English Church for his own ends. An assessment along these lines raises many issues. For one thing, it makes it difficult to pass a favourable judgment on some of his other activities: someone who could so cynically milk an institution of which he was head is hardly likely to have performed his other duties responsibly.

Moreover, in discussing Wolsey's administration of the Church, much more than a judgement on his character is involved. The English Reformation, begun dramatically by Henry VIII's 'break with Rome' in the early 1530s, is one of the major events of English history, with consequences that are still working themselves out today. In this event, Wolsey is usually assigned an important role, although in line with the usual assessment of his performance, it is not one that brings him any credit. The cardinal, it is argued, personified all that was wrong with the late medieval Church: its concern with pomp and ceremony, its excessive wealth, its over-involvement with secular affairs – and in support of this argument is the way that Wolsey was portrayed by such Protestant polemicists as William Tyndale. If, therefore, there was in the early sixteenth century a steady stream of people disenchanted with the existing state of the Church, it only needed a Wolsey to turn that stream into a flood whose direction led straight to Martin Luther. But as well as being a representative figure, Wolsey was by virtue of his legatine powers, a unique one – and this, it has been suggested, had certain consequences. Instead of the papacy being remote and ineffectual, it suddenly became in the figure of the pope's chief representative in England, a very active presence that many people would rather have done without. For, as the duke of Suffolk remarked, 'it was never merry in England whilst we had Cardinals among us'.[2] In reminding people of the pope's existence, Wolsey succeeded in disturbing the *modus vivendi* between Church and state which had emerged during the later Middle ages, and in doing so had revived an age-old conflict. The people who felt the new papal pressure most were not the laity, but rather the clergy, who suddenly found their own well-established rights under threat. This, so the argument continues, hardly put them in the right frame of mind to rush to the support of the papacy when it found itself in direct conflict with Henry VIII over the divorce. And even if they had wanted to, Wolsey's legatine domination over them in the 1520s had not been the ideal preparation for doing

precedence over Archbishop Chichele, despite the fact that Kemp was then only archbishop of York. For the disagreement see M.J. Kelly, 'Canterbury jurisdiction', pp.150-1.

---

[1] Visitations made following the death or translation of a bishop and before the consecration of his successor. See Register of Henry Chichele for the best account of Canterbury's powers.

[2] Cavendish's version; see Cavendish, p.91; Hall, p.758.

serious battle with the Crown in the 1530s, for by then they had lost the will to stand up for themselves. The indictment could hardly be more damning, but it does not have to be accepted, nor should it be.[1]

Perhaps the first thing to try to establish is what use Wolsey made of his legatine powers, leaving the more difficult questions of intent and motivation until later. His first appointment as legate, on 17 May 1518, gave him authority to promote, along with Campeggio, the papal crusade.[2] By the end of August his powers had been widened to enable him, again along with Campeggio, to conduct visitations of the English religious houses, whether 'exempt' or not – that is, irrespective of whether they were normally free of episcopal jurisdiction.[3] In December, he summoned the bishops to a council at Westminster Abbey for the following March, in order to consider how best to go about reform of the Church. Sadly, little is known about what happened at it. Probably all the bishops were asked to attend: only two summonses have survived, those for the bishops of Hereford and London,[4] but their standard form suggests that they were sent out to more than just two. Moreover, there is evidence to believe that Fox of Winchester,[5] Oldham of Exeter,[6] and Penny of Carlisle received summonses, the latter asking to be excused attendance on the grounds of ill health.[7] Even less helpful is the fact that only two accounts of what was discussed at the meeting have survived, both in their differing ways unsatisfactory. The Venetian ambassador reported that what Wolsey was really after was 'certain pecuniary contributions'.[8] These could have been intended for the crusade, but it is unlikely that they were the main item on the agenda. There was no mention of the crusade in the summonses, and no evidence of any moves by Wolsey to obtain a contribution for one has survived. Moreover, Fox, in what appears to be his letter of acceptance, concerned himself only with the prospects for reform that Wolsey's acquisition of legatine powers had opened up.[9]

The second report derives from an account of a speech that John Fisher, bishop of Rochester, is alleged to have made at what his anonymous early biographer called a 'synod of bishops', summoned shortly after Wolsey had acquired his 'powers legatine'[10] – and this does look to be the March meeting. Far from having to do with a crusade, the speech was a powerful attack on the state of the Church, an attack Fisher said he felt all the freer to make because he was addressing only his fellow churchmen. He concentrated on two issues: the vanity of costly apparel and 'this vanity in temporal things', which involved the clergy too much in affairs of state. He himself was constantly being interrupted by messengers from 'higher authority',

---

[1] A rather composite picture of Wolsey's ecclesiastical reputation, but see Dickens, *English Reformation*, pp.38-41, and more recently Haigh's comment: 'But while no charge against Wolsey was too gross to be impossible, Wolsey was not the Church' (*History*, 68, p.394).

[2] Rymer, xiii, pp.621-2.

[3] *LP*, ii, 4170.

[4] GRO, MS 9531/9/fo.136; *Registrum Caroli Bothe*, p.65.

[5] Richard Fox, pp.114-17.

[6] *LP*, iii, 63.

[7] *LP*, iii, 77.

[8] *LP*, iii, 162.

[9] Richard Fox, pp.114-17.

[10] Ortory, pp.255-9.

so that 'by tossing and going this way and that way, time hath passed, and in the meanwhile nothing done but attending after triumphs, receiving of ambassadors, haunting of prince's courts, and such like, whereby great expenses rise that might be better spent many other ways'.[1]

Fisher's biographer took a jaundiced view of Wolsey's intentions, maintaining that he called the synod 'rather to notify to the world his great authority, and to be seen sitting in his pontifical seat, than for any great good that he meant to do'. He added that Fisher was quick to realize this, and implied that the main target of his attack was Wolsey himself.[2] This seems unlikely. Whatever reservations the future saint may have had about Wolsey as a man of God, he must have realized, as his episcopal colleague Fox had, that Wolsey's legatine powers, his closeness to the king, and his proven administrative and political ability offered a unique opportunity for reform.[3] To jeopardize this by launching a personal attack would have made no sense. Moreover, although the faults that he highlighted have commonly been associated with Wolsey, they were also part and parcel of almost every cry for reform during the late Middle Ages and were a common theme of sermons.[4] More specifically, in the convocation of 1487 Archbishop Morton had criticized some London clergy for being too ostentatious in their dress.[5] In the convocation of 1510 the main burden of Colet's famous speech had been to warn against what he called 'creeping secularity', something that he considered to be an even greater danger than heresy itself.[6] And in that same convocation, of the three new canons passed, one was a condemnation of improper dress.[7] What all this means is that Fisher's speech, far from being a personal attack on the new legate, concerned itself with issues that were very much at the centre of reform long before Wolsey ever came to prominence. It therefore needs no disapproval of Wolsey to explain why Fisher should have raised them. In fact, if the speech was ever delivered – and there has to be a question mark over this – it provides evidence that at the March meeting there was a genuine discussion of the present state of the Church. And if so, then it rather looks as if Wolsey's oft-declared concern for reform was not the mere window-dressing that it has commonly been taken to be.

At any rate, the meeting did result in something positive being done, for out of it emerged new legatine 'constitutions' for the Church – or at least for the southern province of Canterbury, because no evidence that they were ever published in Wolsey's own northern province has survived. However, one would expect legatine constitutions to apply to both, and the fact that the bishop of Carlisle – Carlisle

---

[1] Ibid, p.258.

[2] Ibid, p.255.

[3] In fact if conflict at the 1523 convocation is discounted, for which see pp.286 ff. below, there is no evidence that the two men did not get on, and when Wolsey had his important conversation with Fisher about the divorce in 1527, he began by saying: 'My Lord, you and I have been of an old acquaintance, and the one hath loved and trusted the other'; see St. P, i, p.198 (LP, iv, 3231). Of course, Wolsey was intending to please Fisher in beginning thus, but if his remarks were blatantly untrue, it would have hardly have been a very intelligent opening gambit.

[4] Owst, pp.210-86.

[5] Harper-Bill, JEH, 29, p.12.

[6] Printed in Lupton, pp.293-304; for Kelly's redating to 1510 from 1512 see Kelly, 'Canterbury jurisdiction', p.112. Harper-Bill in History, lxxiii, p.191 retains the traditional dating without comment

[7] Kelly, 'Canterbury jurisdiction', p.114.

being one of the three Northern dioceses – was summoned to the March meeting supports this assumption. The dioceses in which they are known to have been published are Hereford and Lincoln in 1519, and Ely in the following year. The silence concerning the others should not be taken as proof that they were not published there, for there is nothing about these three that would explain why they might have been singled out. In Hereford, as well as the constitutions being read out in English so that they would be better understood – they would have been published in Latin – printed copies were provided.[1] In Lincoln the lack of copies led to demands that unless they were produced they would not be agreed to and there was other opposition.[2]

Its extent should not be exaggerated. At four of the eight Lincoln meetings at which the constitutions were presented no objections were raised, and only in the archdeaconries of Bedford and Huntingdon were the protesters in a majority. And in Hereford and Ely there seems to have been no protest.[3] Still, that there was some in Lincoln is of interest. It arose in part from a suspicion of the legatine powers. A certain Dr Harrington argued that it was not in anyone's power, not even a papal legate's, to legislate for the English Church without the prior consent of the clergy.[4] He was probably incorrect. In granting Wolsey legatine powers Leo x had envisaged that Wolsey would consult with the bishops and heads of religious houses before taking any action,[5] and in calling the March meeting Wolsey had complied with both the letter and the spirit of the pope's commission. On the other hand, there is no indication in them that any formal consent was required. No such consent had been obtained in the thirteenth century for the most famous of the English legatine constitutions, those of Cardinals Otto and Ottobuono.[6] Moreover, the very notion of consent is contrary to the nature of legatine authority: depending so directly on the papal *plenitudo potestatis*, it could hardly require any further legitimization. In the fifteenth century the English canon lawyer, William Lyndwood, in his famous commentary on the constitutions of the English Church, the *Provinciale*, had pointed out very clearly that no English bishop or council had power to repeal or override legatine constitutions, precisely because they derived from a superior authority, that of the pope.[7] Thus, Wolsey's decision to issue his constitutions without the formal consent of convocation was almost certainly in order. And when convocations – there was both a northern and southern convocation – were summoned in 1523 to coincide, as was the normal practice, with the calling of parliament, there is no indication that Wolsey saw any need, or that there was any call by others, to have the constitutions ratified.

It looks, therefore, as if the opposition was confined to the diocese of Lincoln;

---

[1] *Registrum Caroli Bothe*, p.66.

[2] *Visitations in the Diocese of Lincoln*, xxxiii, pp.148-52; see also Bowker, *Secular Clergy*, pp.124-6, though the implication that the contents of the legatine constitutions are known is misleading.

[3] For Ely see EDR B/2/1/fos.18 ff.; discussed in Heal, 'Bishops of Ely', pp.51-3.

[4] *Visitations in the Diocese of Lincoln*, xxxiii, 148.

[5] Rymer, xiii, p.740, from the legatine commission of April 1521 which greatly increased the scope of Wolsey's powers.

[6] Williamson, p.164. I have found this article to be the most useful work on the general issue of the role and authority of papal legates.

[7] *Lyndwood*, pp.11, 154.

and this is in many ways surprising, for even if there was nothing illegal about the constitutions, they were something of a novelty – no new legatine constitutions had appeared since 1268 – and novelty is usually unwelcome, as is reform. Dr Sheffield, who led the opposition in the archdeaconry of Bedford, had long been in dispute with his bishop for holding a benefice without licence while under age. Another opponent had been cited to appear before the bishop for non-residence.[1] Such people would have had cause to fear any attempt, from whatever source, at a more strict enforcement of canon law, and their fear would have been even greater if they had had reason to believe that the attempt would be effective.

Stout-hearted resistance to arbitrary intervention, or self-interested and obscurantist opposition to genuine reform – such a question is at the heart of the interpretative problem rather more than the facts, and in the end it is one's own value judgements that will provide the answer. Still, it would help to know what the legatine constitutions consisted of, but, since no copy has survived, one can only guess. Probably they were a comprehensive restatement of the existing canons, similar to those that, as archbishop of York, Wolsey had issued for the northern province only the previous year.[2] It is known that some had to do with clerical dress, and others with the conduct of all those in clerical orders, but especially the bishops.[3] What there is no specific evidence for are articles affecting the financial interests of the clergy – the fees they could charge for conducting burial services and the like – and the conditions relating to the holding of benefices, including non-residence and pluralism. However, in any comprehensive restatement such matters would have been included and no doubt would have been of greater concern to the majority of the clergy than more overtly religious matters, such as doctrine and liturgical practice, that are more readily associated with reform. Or, to put it more simply, few clergy would have welcomed reform if it involved financial loss, and this perhaps rather obvious point is worth making in order to counter the tendency to ascribe only the best motives to opposition to Wolsey's legatine authority and only the worst to Wolsey for wishing to exercise it.

It had been Wolsey's intention to call a second meeting of bishops for 9 September 1519, but in the event he decided to postpone it. This was not because he had lost interest in reform, but because the presence of the plague in London made such a meeting dangerous; and anyway it may have seemed more sensible to wait until after a meeting with the heads of religious houses, called for 12 November,[4] for the relationship between the bishops and the religious orders would have to figure on any agenda for reform. Again, the problem is the very meagre evidence for the meeting. It did take place, and the intention was to include delegates from at least the three major religious orders – the Augustinians, Benedictines and Cistercians – and probably from all.[5] This mix of orders was unusual, and, given their autonomy, would hardly have come about but for Wolsey's legatine authority. It also touches

---

[1] Bowker, *Secular Clergy*, pp.125-6.

[2] Wilkins,iii, pp.662-82.

[3] *Registrum Caroli Bothe*, p.66: 'de habitu clericorum deque vita moribusque ordinandorum . . alia capitula et articulos prelotos tangentes'.

[4] Wilkins,iii, p.661; Richard Fox, p.122 (*LP*,iii,414) in which he accepts Wolsey's arguments for postponement.

on an issue that provided the most obvious justification for the meeting – the question of supervision. A large number of religious orders were exempt from any kind of episcopal supervision. Amongst the 'exempt' were all the orders of Friars, the most prominent of which were the Dominicans and Franciscans, and, amongst the earlier monastic orders, the Cistercians, which with their sixty-two houses comprised the third largest such order in England.[1] In theory the two largest, the Augustinians and Benedictines, were subject to episcopal supervision, but in the course of time many of their wealthier houses such as the Benedictine abbeys of Glastonbury and St Albans had secured exemption; and it was probably the aim of any self-respecting house of any size to aspire to the ranks of the 'exempt' – and not necessarily for the wrong reasons. Self-respect may be a better guarantee of the health of an institution than any amount of outside control; and, moreover, because a house was exempt did not mean that it was free of all supervision. Most orders had their own machinery for conducting visitations, and it is by no means certain that these were less effective than episcopal ones. For instance, the Cistercians appear to have been in good order at this time, in part because of the regular visitations by the distinguished head of their order, Marmaduke Huby.[2] Moreover, it must be borne in mind that when bishops complained about exempt houses, their own financial interests were at stake, for visitations resulted in the payment of procurations to the visitor. And in any conflict between bishop and monastic head, personal and not always very creditable considerations must sometimes have been involved. The insistence on his house's right to exemption by the rather pushy and aggressive abbot of St Werburg's, Chester, John Birchenshawe, must have annoyed his bishop, whatever the rights and wrongs of the abbot's claims. And it is not surprising that a major dispute, in which Wolsey became involved, arose between them.[3]

Nevertheless, the health of a monastic institution, especially a large one, undoubtedly affected more than just the well-being of its own members. If monks were regularly visiting the nearby taverns or consorting with local women, then the religious life of the diocese was being undermined; as it could be in ways that are less easily appreciated today. A central purpose of the religious orders was the continual offering up of prayers for the dead, and many local families would have contributed large sums of money in an effort to ensure the salvation of their ancestors' souls. Thus, if for whatever reason services were not being properly conducted, not only the present but past generations were threatened with eternal damnation. Less dangerous, for the soul at least, was the deep involvement of monks and nuns in the economic life of the community as farmers, landlords, employers, bankers, teachers and almsgivers, and any financial scandals or unfair practices could not be entirely separated from the institution's religious purposes and standing.[4] Finally, religious

---

[5] Pantin (ed.), *English Black Monks*, pp.118-19 for the Benedictines; *Butley Priory*, pp.36-9 for the Augustinians; *LP*,iii,475 for the Cistercians.

---

[1] Together the three orders comprised about 80 per cent of all monastic houses. For a useful summary of facts and figures see Hughes, pp.31 ff.

[2] Knowles, *Religious Orders*, iii, pp.33-8. For Richard Redman's visitations of the Premonstratensians see ibid, pp.39-51.

[3] Burne, pp.1-35.

[4] See especially Haigh, *Reformation and Resistance*, pp.118 ff.

houses were responsible for the appointment of many parish priests; in the diocese of Lincoln as many as 40 per cent of all benefices were in their gift, as compared with under 3 per cent in the gift of the bishop.[1]

All this is not merely supposition. The bishop of Winchester, Richard Fox, was for a time sufficiently worried about the well-being of the important Benedictine abbey of Hyde to visit it every fifteen days.[2] More generally, complaints were made that he was too harsh in his treatment of the religious, especially of those nuns who showed a reluctance to abide by their rule and remain within the walls of their nunneries. When Wolsey passed these complaints on, Fox was unrepentant. Indeed, he declared that if he had Wolsey's 'power and authority', he would endeavour 'to mure and enclose their monasteries acccording to the ordinance of the law'[3] – and as a translator of the rule of St Benedict he could speak with some authority.[4] And it was Fox who, as deputy to Silvestro Gigli, the absentee bishop of Worcester, drew Wolsey's attention in 1515 to the 'inordinate, heady, and unreligious dealing of the canons of Saint Augustine besides Bristol', as they attempted to elect a new abbot. 'This is a perilous matter', he wrote, 'for the evil example that may come thereof, and therefore according to your good beginning I beseech you hold your good hand to it.'[5]

Other bishops known to have taken a particular interest in the religious orders were Blythe of Coventry and Lichfield,[6] Fisher,[7] Nix of Norwich,[8] Sherburne of Chichester,[9] but above all Longland. In 1519 he was asked to preach before the monks of Westminster on the occasion of Wolsey's and Campeggio's joint legatine visitation.[10] On becoming bishop of Lincoln in 1521, he concentrated his attention on the 111 monastic institutions within his vast diocese, visiting in person any that showed signs of disarray.[11] One of the houses that he was not able to do much about, though by his own account much needed to be done, was Thame; and the point about Thame was that as a Cistercian house it was exempt from his jurisdiction. In an effort to get round this, in 1526 he sought Wolsey's help as legate. Wolsey in his turn instructed his Cistercian commissary, perhaps best thought of in this context as his deputy, the abbot of Waverley, to conduct a visitation of the wayward house.[12] As it happened, Longland was to be disappointed with the abbot's performance, finding his injunctions lacking in specific criticisms and constructive proposals for reform.[13] He did not despair, though, and in the following year, again with Wolsey's

---

[1] Bowker, *Henrician Reformation*, pp.44-f.,122-3. In Chichester the bishop presented to 23 out of 278 benefices, though during his long episcopate Sherborne was able to increase that number to 32; see Lander, 'Diocese of Chichester', pp.191 ff.

[2] Richard Fox, p.95 (*LP*,iii,2207).

[3] Ibid, pp.150-1.(*LP*,iv,3815).

[4] Ibid, pp.86 ff.

[5] Ibid, pp.79-80 (*LP*,ii,730).

[6] *Visitations c.1515-1525*.

[7] S. Thompson, 'The bishop in his diocese', p.75.

[8] *Visitations of the Diocese of Norwich*.

[9] Lander, 'Diocese of Chichester', pp.163 ff.

[10] Longland.

[11] Bowker, *Henrician Reformation*, pp.12, 17-28.

[12] Perry, p.712 for the abbot's authorization, and for transcripts of all the documents see ibid, pp.704-22; also *Visitations in the Diocese of Lincoln*,xxxv, p.209.

help, he secured the appointment of a new abbot who he was confident would put all to rights.[1]

The 'reform' of Thame is a good illustration of the problems that the 'exempt' monastic houses posed for the bishops, and the ways in which Wolsey's legatine powers could be called on, at least in theory, to overcome them. In practice they had not, in the case of Thame, worked all that well, and for an interesting and, given Wolsey's reputation for high-handedness, rather surprising reason. He had chosen to exercise his legatine powers indirectly, by appointing as his legatine commissary a leading abbot of the order who already possessed visitorial powers granted to him by the head of the order, the abbot of Cîteaux. This policy had the disadvantage that it could result, as in the case of Thame, in ineffectual action being taken. On the other hand, it had the great advantage that the Cistercians were not greatly antagonized by Wolsey's intervention and might therefore be more willing to accept a measure of reform. And, in fact, a feature of Wolsey's take-over of the English Church was the care that he took not to cause unnecessary offence. Did he go too far in this direction, for what may have been needed, after all, was a more vigorous intervention, and one that took less account of the susceptibilities of the various interest groups within the Church?

Such questions can never be far away in any discussion of Wolsey's legatine rule – and at some point an answer will have to be attempted. For the moment, what is being stressed is just how careful he was not to tread on any toes. Thame is one example; his consultations with leading churchmen in March and November 1519 are another. And from the November meeting emerged new statutes for the Augustinian and Benedictine orders, a feature of which was, again, Wolsey's desire to go through what might be called constitutional channels. As regards the Benedictines, this meant calling upon their two distinguished presidents, John Islip abbot of Westminster and Richard Kidderminster abbot of Winchcombe,[2] to summon a general chapter for 26 February 1520, where the legatine statutes were presented and accepted. How Wolsey arrived at these is not known. It was usual for the Benedictines to appoint a committee of 'definitors' to perform such a task, and it may be that at the meeting of monastery heads in November 1519 such a committee was set up. At any rate, it seems unlikely that new statutes could have been drawn up without close consultation with members of the order, the more so because Islip, as a royal councillor very active in Star Chamber, was well known to Wolsey.[3] Still, what efforts Wolsey made at conciliation were not entirely successful, for in an oft-quoted letter to him, members – though how many is not known – pointed out that:

> beyond all doubt, if everything should tend, in the reform of the said order, to over-great austerity and rigour, we should not have monks enough to staff all our many very great monasteries . . . For in these stormy times (as the world now decays towards its end) those who desire a life of austerity and of regular observance are few, and indeed most rare.[4]

[13] *Visitations in the Diocese of Lincoln*, xxxv, p.214.

---

[1] For Longland's request to Wolsey for help in appointing a new abbot see *LP*,iv,5189, though there dated 1529; see also Knowles, *Monastic Orders*,iii, pp.70-2.

[2] Knowles, *Religious Orders*,iii, pp.91-9 for portraits of both men.

[3] Pantin (ed.), *English Black Monks*, pp. 117-22.

It has to be said that a hundred years earlier very similar objections had been made to Henry v's attempts to reform the Benedictines, and there has to be a suspicion that this was an instinctive reaction to any outside interference, rather than a reasoned commentary on the nature of the intended reform.[1] Still, it serves to reinforce the point that not everybody in England welcomed change, and thus the need for Wolsey to move with caution.

No copy of Wolsey's legatine statutes for the Benedictines has survived, though in June 1520 the prior of Worcester, William More, is known to have paid twenty pence for one.[2] As with the legatine constitutions, it is unlikely that they contained anything very novel. And what is certain is that those for the Augustinian order, of which a copy has survived, did not.[3] These were initially published under Wolsey's own authority as legate – an action which at first glance might appear to gainsay the thrust of the present argument. But it so happened that a general chapter of the Benedictines was anyway due to be summoned in 1520, and therefore Wolsey's asking for one caused the minimum of inconvenience. An Augustinian chapter was not due until the following year, and thus a problem arose. Should Wolsey insist on a special meeting being summoned, with all the administrative complications this involved? Should he wait until 1521 to publish the new statutes, thereby allowing them to be formally accepted by the chapter, but also running the risk of seeing the impetus for reform brought about by his newly acquired legatine powers diminish? Or should he, having first consulted with at least some members of the order, go ahead and publish the statutes immediately but in doing so stress that not only was he anxious to hear what the general chapter of 1521 had to say about them, but was willing to make alterations in the light of its discussions? It was the last course of action that Wolsey adopted.[4] However one estimates his sincerity in asking for the order's views, again what emerges, despite appearances, is the degree of tact that Wolsey was prepared to show.

Probably he showed equal tact when he turned his attention to the remaining religious orders, but sadly the information is so meagre that it is not even always possible to state with certainty that he did anything. His use of the Cistercian abbot of Waverley as a legatine commissary may exemplify the way in which he made himself the effective head of this order in England. Unlike the Cistercians, the Premonstratensians, with thirty-one houses, had secured independence from their founding abbey – in their case, Prémontré – though only as recently as 1512.[5] The abbot of Welbeck became *ex officio* head of the order, but what that abbot's relationship with Wolsey was, or whether, indeed, there was any legatine interference in the affairs of the order, is not known. The same is true of the Carthusians and Gilbertines. The presence in England of both these orders was

---

[4] Hughes, p.67 for this translation; Latin text in Pantin (ed.), *English Black Monks*, pp.123-4.

[1] Knowles, *Religious Orders*, ii, pp.182-4.

[2] William More, p.108. More's journal contains further evidence of the 1520 general chapter.

[3] Wilkins, iii, pp.683-8; see also *Chapters of the Augustinian Canon*, pp.xxxv-viii.

[4] Wilkins, 688: 'Et si quid religiosis huiusmodi onerosum nimis et importabile, sive aliquid addendum vel minuendum in eisdem statutis compertum ficerit, id tune moderare et reformare, ac eisdem addere vel diminuere, secundum quod res expostulare videbitur curabimus'.

[5] For the history of this order during this period see Colvin, pp.227 ff; Knowles, *Religious Orders*, pp.39-52.

small – perhaps as few as nine Carthusian and ten Gilbertine houses[1] – and they may have escaped Wolsey's attention on this account. On the other hand, his usual thoroughness would suggest otherwise, and, as there is so little information about any aspect of these orders for the 1520s, it seems reasonable to assume that Wolsey did intervene, despite the lack of evidence.

What of the friars, or mendicant orders? Together the various orders of friars owned about 180 houses, and numbered between 1,500 and 3,000 members.[2] Most historians have taken a somewhat gloomy view of their performance during the fifteenth and early sixteenth centuries,[3] a view that was shared by none other than Thomas More whose fictional friar in the first book of Utopia was made the butt of hangers-on at Cardinal Morton's household – and of More's readers ever since.[4] Much of the contemporary criticism may have been exaggerated, a consequence of the long-standing battle between the friars and secular clergy which was touched upon in connection with the Hunne affair;[5] and if the evidence of wills can be taken as an indication of genuine attitudes, it would seem that many laymen thought highly enough of the friars to believe that their presence at a funeral improved the deceased's chances of salvation.[6] Be that as it may, the friars constituted such a large part of the religious landscape of England that it is hard to believe that Wolsey would have ignored them, though again there are difficulties in establishing what precisely he did.

Best documented is Wolsey's intervention in the affairs of the Franciscan Observants. Although a very small order with no more than six houses, they were, because of royal patronage and their reputation for holy living, much more important than their numbers suggest.[7] In particular, Greenwich, founded in 1481 by Edward IV, but with its foundation confirmed in 1485 by Henry VII, played an important role because of its very close proximity to the royal palace.[8] It was at Greenwich in June 1509 that Henry VIII and Catherine of Aragon were married, and that the Princess Mary was baptized in February 1516, with Wolsey as one of her godfathers. So it is not inappropriate that in the crisis brought about by Henry's desire for a divorce from Catherine the majority of the Observants sided with Catherine and Mary. Indeed, the irony is that an order which the first Tudor monarch had done so much to encourage was the first to be suppressed, and this as early 1534.[9] Wolsey, too, had his difficulties with it. In the summer of 1524 both Clement VII and Francisco Quinones, the general of the order, wrote in an effort to

---

[1] Knowles and Hadcock, pp.135-6, 194-9.

[2] For the lower figure see Hughes, p.70, for the higher Knowles, Religious Orders, iii, p.52.

[3] Knowles, Religious Orders, iii, p.52.

[4] CWM, 4, pp.83-4, 347.

[5] See p.47 above.

[6] Scarisbrick, in Reformation, p.6 says one in five gave money to friars, while Bowker, in Henrician Reformation, p.48, suggests 22 per cent for the archdeaconry of Lincoln but in the archdeaconry of Buckingham nothing was given. See also Whiting, SH, 5, p.70.

[7] For the Franciscan Observants in England K.D. Brown is now the major work. Sadly it was not available to me when I was writing this chapter, but I am grateful for the author's comments on my own treatment of the order. See also Knowles, Religious Orders, iii, pp.10-13, 206-11.

[8] King's Works. pp.96 ff.

[9] Knowles, Religious Orders, pp.206-11.

persuade him not to carry out his intended visitation of the Greenwich house.[1] The new pope went out of his way to stress the importance of the order in the battle against Luther. He asked Wolsey to think more about the good of Christendom than of England alone by treating the Greenwich Observants with the utmost gentleness and tact; with some vehemence, he asked the English envoy at Rome to pass on the message, 'For God's sake use mercy with these Friars.'[2] In reply, Wolsey assured the pope that he would use such tact that no complaints would arise, but he refused to give way.[3] 16th January 1525 was set aside for the visitation, which was to be conducted by John Allen, responsible for most of the legatine visitations, and by Henry Standish, the same man who in 1515 had done battle with the English clergy.[4]

That Standish was chosen is yet further evidence that Wolsey never held his actions in 1515 against him, but it may nonetheless have been a controversial choice.[5] The bishop of St Asaph, as he had become by 1525, was probably the most distinguished English Franciscan of his time, but he was not an Observant, and between the Observants and the Conventual Franciscans there was no love lost. His appointment, therefore, as joint visitor, though making some sense, may explain the vigour of Greenwich's opposition – of which the pleas of the pope and the general were but an early salvo – just as much as any dislike of legatine interference. When that salvo failed to head off the visitation, a number of the Greenwich friars decided to sabotage it by staging a mass walk-out. However, a new day was arranged, and it was made clear that those who did not attend would be expelled from the order. At the same time, one of the most eminent of the Greenwich friars, John Forest, confessor to Catherine of Aragon, and a future Catholic martyr, was called upon to preach against his offending brothers at Paul's Cross. Some were for a time 'put in the porter's ward in the cardinal's palace', while a lay-brother, William Renscroft, was sent to the Greyfriars' house in London until he 'submitted himself, and was assoiled of the said bishop [Standish] by the authority of the cardinal, and so delivered home again'.[6] For some this is yet another episode to be held against Wolsey. It may be that in carrying through the visitation, Wolsey was acting illegally, because it looks as if in the summer of 1524 the Observants had managed to secure a two-year restraint from legatine interference that was only lifted in November 1525 – after the visitation had taken place. If this is so, it would further help to explain the vigour of Greenwich's resistance, as does the mere fact that they had such powerful friends. But if Wolsey did act illegally, it was one of the very rare occasions that he did; and the powerful are not always in favour of reform.

Very little is known of Wolsey's legatine involvement with the remaining orders of friars. Apparently he had intended to carry out a visitation of the London Greyfriars himself, accompanied by the king. In what precise capacity Henry would

---

[1] *LP*,iv,477, 478.

[2] *LP*,iv,610.

[3] *LP*,iv,759.

[4] *Monumenta Franciscana*, p.190 for an account of the visitation.

[5] It was K.D. Brown who suggested I reconsider my rather over-optimistic remarks about the choice of Standish.

[6] *LP*,iv,587, 1777. I remain sceptical about the illegality, if only because in most cases Wolsey showed a great concern to act within the law and the gaps in the evidence make any certainty impossible.

have acted is a little unclear, but his intention to take part is at any rate evidence of his support for Wolsey's legatine activities. As it happened, the day chosen, 9 March 1525, was the moment when confirmation of the Imperial victory at Pavia reached London, and the visitation was postponed. When later in the year, it did take place it was carried out once again by John Allen.[1] There is no evidence of any resistance, but neither is there any further information about what took place, nor evidence of any other legatine connection with the Franciscans. The small order of Austin Friars had run into financial difficulties as a result of a plenary indulgence secured in 1516 to help finance their Oxford house.[2] It was thought that the provincial of the order, Edmund Bellond, may have pocketed some of the money, so the prior-general, the Venetian Gabriel della Volta, was brought in, and early in 1520 Bellond was removed from office. In April 1522, his financial affairs were examined by John Dowman and Richard Wolman, both distinguished clerical lawyers and administrators with close connections with Wolsey,[3] and it seems likely, although there is no direct evidence, that they were acting in some legatine capacity. In any event, their investigations failed to solve the problems of the order. By the end of 1522 Bellond's successor, William Wetherall, had in turn been replaced by John Stokes, only for Wetherall to be reinstated in 1526. This time he managed to secure his tenure of office for six years by virtue of Wolsey's legatine powers – something that was to backfire on him when, following Wolsey's downfall, he was accused by the prior-general of destroying the liberties of his province. Still, it provides some definite proof of Wolsey's involvement with the order, though whether Wetherall was worthy of the cardinal's support cannot be established.

For legatine involvement with the important Dominican order there is only one piece of evidence. A full discussion is best left until later, but what it shows is Bishop Longland once again calling upon Wolsey's legatine authority to interfere in the affairs of an 'exempt' house – in this case, King's Langley. As regards the Carmelites and the very small order of Crutched Friars, there is nothing. For involvement with any order of nuns, there is only one dramatic episode – the so-called 'Matter of Wilton' – but, as with King's Langley, it is better that consideration of it is postponed. Still, the final tally is not unimpressive: the two largest religious orders, the Augustinians and Dominicans, had had new statutes provided, while in one way or another the Cistercians, the Conventual and Observant Franciscans, the Dominicans and the Austin Friars had accepted Wolsey's legatine authority; and probably all the others had as well. Only in the rather special case of the Greenwich Observants had he faced any serious opposition, in part because of the sensitivity he showed to the pride and susceptibilities of the different orders. There remains the important question of what qualitative difference his interference made, but before this is looked at some outline of the legatine machinery itself is called upon.

Precisely when Wolsey began to organize his legatine administration is not known.

---

[1] *Monumenta Franciscana*, pp.190-1.

[2] Roth, pp.431 ff for the whole episode.

[3] *LP*,iii,2163. Dowman acted as auditor in Wolsey's court of audience; Wolman was Wolsey's vicar-general at Bath and Wells 1518-22, and also presented the case against the validity of Henry VIII's marriage to Catherine when the matter appeared before Wolsey's legatine court in 1527.

As early as 1519 he was asked by John Colet to arbitrate as legate in a dispute that, as dean of St Paul's, he was having with his residentiary canons. The result was an elaborate composition, or legal agreement, which would have had to be drawn up by some officials, though perhaps at that date not by those with formal responsibilities for legatine matters.[1] Still, the likelihood is that similar appeals would have been made, which would have forced a consideration of the setting-up of some permanent machinery. On the other hand, since Wolsey's legatine commissions were for a long time granted only for limited periods, this would not have encouraged more formal arrangements. As mentioned earlier, originally they had to do either with the proposed crusade or with the reform of the religious orders. When, in January 1521, Wolsey secured a renewal of his commission, it included a passing reference to reform of the secular clergy, however eminent[2] – an indication that he did mean business; and by then he had already issued his legatine constitutions. However, it was not until April of that year that he was granted a number of specific powers to intervene in the administration of the Church as a whole: to grant dispensations and exemptions, to absolve from excommunication, to license preachers, to grant university degrees and the like.[3] Then, in July, his commission was extended for five years, and amongst a number of additional powers granted was one allowing him to appoint by 'prevention' his 'familiars' – that is, members of his household to any benefice in ecclesiastical patronage.[4] Only then did it make sense to set up a legatine machinery, and the first indication that he was doing so may come from two letters to him from Archbishop Warham. Both are full of complaints of interference in his jurisdiction by Wolsey's officials, despite Wolsey's having promised him that this would not happen. If it continued, Warham lamented, he 'should be as a shadow and image of an archbishop and legate [legatus natus], void of authority and jurisdiction, which should be to my perpetual reproach, and to my Church [Canterbury] a perpetual prejudice'.[5] Maddeningly, on neither letter did Warham record the year, only the month – March and April respectively – but the suggestion here is that they should be assigned to 1522.[6] And at any rate, by October 1522 a legatine court was definitely in being, because the proceedings of a testamentary case before it on 2nd of that month have survived.[7] It was in this same month that a draft composition between Wolsey and Warham was drawn up, a final version being signed the following January.[8]

The composition concerned itself with one aspect of their respective jurisdictions, that to do with testamentary matters. The proving of those wills which had previously been part of the archbishop's prerogative, that is wills of those with bona notabilia in more than one diocese, was now to be administered jointly by

---

[1] Registrum Statutorum et Consuetudinem Ecclesiae Cathedralis Sancti Pauli Londiniensis, pp.249-63.

[2] Rymer,xiii, p.734.

[3] Ibid, pp.739-42.

[4] M.J. Kelly, 'Canterbury jurisdiction', p.171, where he gives as his source Reg.Vat. 1202, fo 110.

[5] LP,iii,127; for the other letter see LP,iii,98.

[6] M.J. Kelly, 'Canterbury jurisdiction', p.182. Certainly their appearance in LP in 1519 seems too early, because it was not until June 1519 that Wolsey knew that his legatine powers would continue after Campeggio's departure.

[7] LP,iii,2625.

[8] LP,iii,2633, 2752. See also M.J. Kelly, 'Canterbury jurisdiction', pp.182-7; Kitching, pp.191-213.

officials appointed by both Wolsey and Warham, and the resulting probate fees were to be divided equally between them. The value to be given to *bona notabilia* was not specified, which is strange, because it was precisely this that had been at issue in that major dispute between Warham and his suffragans only ten years before.[1] The figure then agreed was £10 or over – and probably the same was assumed in 1523, for that amount was specifically mentioned in the composition between Wolsey and Bishop Longland made the following year.[2] Where the testator left goods worth over £100, the proving of his will was reserved for Wolsey's commissaries alone,[3] as was the will of anyone who left goods in the exempt jurisdictions of Westminster, St Albans, Bury, and Bewley.

Little evidence of the workings of the joint-prerogative court that was set up as a result of this composition has survived. Its two leading officials were John Allen acting on Wolsey's behalf, and John Cocks acting on Warham's. Under them were two registrars, Robert Toneys and John Barrett, the former Wolsey's and the latter Warham's. Records of one or two of the cases have survived in a formulary prepared for Thomas Cromwell's vicegerential probate court, which was modelled on it.[4] A few more are known about as a consequence of Warham's complaints to Wolsey, to be considered in due course, about the workings of the court. These, however, are just the tip of the iceberg, for in the year before Wolsey's fall and the disbandment of the court, Warham received as his share of its revenues £315 1s 9d.[5] How many cases this represented is impossible to calculate because it is not known what fees were charged, but it has to be in three figures. And whatever the fees, they do not appear to have been excessive, for otherwise some reference to this would surely have been included in the many charges prepared against Wolsey in 1529. Instead, there is only a reference to probate fees in the diocese of York, and even then the accusation is that Wolsey had used his position as lord chancellor to protect his diocesan officials from legal action by those who were dissatisfied with the fees they had charged.[6]

What is true is that the whole question of ecclesiastical fees, including probate fees, did become an issue in the first sessions of the Reformation parliament, and in the course of a debate on the subject Sir Henry Guildford declared that 'he and others, being executors to Sir William Compton, knight, paid for probate of his will to the cardinal and the archbishop of Canterbury a thousand marks' – a statement which, according to Edward Hall, opened the floodgates to all manner of complaints about 'excess of fines' exacted by the bishops.[7] These complaints should be treated with some caution: modern research does not support them,[8] while the circumstances in which they were made were hardly conducive to an impartial

---

[1] M.J. Kelly, 'Canterbury jurisdiction', pp. 42-94.

[2] LRO Bishop's Possessions, Manional, unnumbered box. I am grateful to M. Bowker for a copy of this document and for much other help.

[3] Kitching, p. 195 states that the goods worth £100 had to be in one diocese, but this worries me.

[4] BL Add.MSS, 48012.

[5] *LP*, v, 450.

[6] *LP*, iv, 6075 art. 31. The article does not specify that only wills in the diocese of York were at issue, but since the archbishops of York appears not to have exercised any prerogative jurisdictions over wills until the Elizabethan period I am assuming this to be so; see Kitching, p. 193.

[7] Hall, p. 765.

[8] See Bowker 'Some archdeacons' court books', pp. 294-301.

view. Moreover, the writers of the preamble to the statute of 1529, which laid down a new tariff, were extremely vague about the old one,[1] perhaps because the detail would not have supported their case that it had been excessive.

Nobody likes paying fees, and in 1529 the Commons were given a unique opportunity to vent their dislike. So, also, was Sir Henry Guildford. With his close connections with the court he would have been well aware of the popularity in royal circles of any attack on the clergy, but, arguably, especially one directed against the far too independent-minded archbishop of Canterbury. Indeed, it may be that Guildford was put up to it by the king himself, if only because the accusation seems most improbable. Admittedly, Compton had been extremely wealthy. His movables alone were estimated to be worth nearly £4,500,[2] but even so it is hard to arrive at any credible rate which would produce a fee of £666.[3] It is known, however, that one reason for Compton's wealth was his expropriation of royal revenues, something which, prior to his death, was preying on his mind. On 31 August 1527 he wrote to Sir Henry Guildford asking that in addition to any bequests to the king, a sum of 1,000 marks should be paid to him 'as a recompense'.[4] Given that this was the very sum mentioned in Guildford's accusation, it could be that it was the payment of this debt that the joint prerogative court had been asking for. Certainly, it would be wrong to use the accusation as proof that the fees asked for by that court were excessive, for the only precise information that we have – the £300 a year for Warham's share – suggests otherwise.

One thing that Wolsey's composition with Warham made clear was that he considered himself entitled to prove all wills, and that in allowing Warham a share in some he was making a concession. In support of his claim he served notice of his intention to appoint commissaries to every diocese, who, apart from looking after his own interests, could be appealed to by anyone who felt that his case might be more fairly or efficiently treated by them.[5] In other words, Wolsey was challenging the testamentary jurisdiction of the English episcopate. In agreeing to the composition, Warham had conceded the validity of Wolsey's claim, thereby making it virtually impossible for anyone else to resist it. In fact, nothing is known of Wolsey's negotiations with the bishops on this matter. All that has survived is a reasonably complete copy of the composition he made with Longland of Lincoln,[6] plus fragmentary, if at least direct, evidence of similar compositions with the bishops of Chichester, Ely, Hereford, and Norwich.[7] However, what underlay the charges of praemunire brought in 1530 against a number of bishops, including those of Chichester, Ely and Norwich just mentioned, but also Bath and Wells, Coventry and Lichfield, Rochester, Bangor and St Asaph, was that these men had made

[1] SR, p.286.

[2] Bernard, EHR, xcvi, p.772.

[3] In 1524 the executors of Sir Thomas Lovell paid £66 13s 4d for his probate in the joint-prerogative court with some additional fees to various officials amounting to about £20. His wealth is not known, but given his many years in royal service it must have been considerable; see LP,iv,366.

[4] LP,iv,3395. For Sir William Compton's will see LP,iv,4442.

[5] LP,iii,2752.

[6] 135 LRO, Bishop's Possessions, Marional, unnumbered box.

[7] For Chichester BL Add MSS 34317, fo.33; for Ely LP,iii,599; for Hereford Registrum Caroli Bothe, pp.189-90; and for Norwich LP,iv,5589.

compositions with Wolsey in his capacity as legate.[1] True, these charges were in essence political, which is to say that they were a way of browbeating into submission leading representatives of a Church that was proving dangerously unsympathetic to Henry's wishes.[2] Nevertheless, it seems unlikely that Henry would have gone so far as to invent the compositions, and if so there is evidence for ten having been made – enough surely to suggest that no bishop escaped? As for their timing, that with Longland was dated 24 March 1524.[3] A letter from West of Ely to Wolsey concerning their composition is dated 20 January – the year is missing, but it is probably 1524.[4] And the composition with Booth of Hereford, on the evidence of a later receipt, was probably made in March 1524.[5] All in all, therefore, it looks as if early 1524 is the best date for Wolsey's composition with the bishops that can be arrived at.

By these compositions, the bishops bought back from Wolsey their episcopal rights, which in theory had been superseded by his legatine authority. These included the right to appoint to benefices, to make visitations, to hold ecclesiastical courts, and to prove the wills of testators whose goods and chattels were confined to their particular diocese. With these rights went the related fees. They, in fact, never made up a very large proportion of a bishop's revenue, the bulk of which came from episcopal land. Just how much derived from this source, referred to as 'spiritualities', is difficult to calculate, partly because it was a variable figure depending in part on whether a bishop had conducted a visitation of his diocese in a particular accounting year.[6] In 1535, the famous survey of ecclesiastical wealth, the Valor Ecclesiasticus, put the annual revenue of the English and Welsh bishops from their estates, or 'temporalities', at £26,100, and that from their spiritualities at only £3,450, a mere 12 per cent of their total revenue.[7] In the poorer dioceses such as Carlisle and Rochester, though, the proportion of the bishops' revenue from spiritualities was nearer to 25 per cent.[8]

The price that the bishops had to pay Wolsey for the recovery of their rights appears to have been a third of their spiritualities. Certainly this was true for Hereford, where Booth paid Wolsey the sum of £10 over a period of three years.[9] A third was also mentioned by Bishop West in his letter to Wolsey on the subject, though he rather rashly added that he would not mind if Wolsey took all the profits of his jurisdiction; his desire to recover his rights was 'not for any profit or advantage that I trust or intend to have by the same, but only for quietness and good order'.[10] For Chichester, there is a reference to the bishop paying £20 a year, which, it has been suggested, meant a rate of a half rather than a third. However, Chichester's

[1] Guy, EHR, xcvii, pp.482-3.
[2] In saying this, I am disagreeing with Guy's interpretation in EHR, xcvii and following Bernard in JEH, 37 and Scarisbrick in Cambridge Historical Journal, xii.
[3] LRO Bishop's Possessions, Manorial, unnumbered box.
[4] LP,iii,599, where it is placed in 1519. But Heal ('Bishops of Ely', pp.46-7) argues for 1523 or 1524, and of these two I prefer the latter, for that with Warham was only signed in January 1523.
[5] Registrum Caroli Bothe, pp.189-90.
[6] Heal, Of Prelates and Princes, pp.62-4.
[7] Ibid, p.328.
[8] Ibid, p.62.
[9] Registrum Caroli Bothe, pp.189-90.
[10] PRO SP 1/19/fo.168 (LP,iii,599).

spiritualities stood at £66 in 1522, which would fit the more likely proportion of a third – more likely because one would expect a standard rate.[1] Whatever the rate, the amount of money involved was not very great; but given that they were merely paying for the exercise of rights which had been theirs for hundreds of years, the bishops could not have been pleased at the prospect of paying anything at all.

The workings of another part of Wolsey's legatine machinery, the legatine court of audience, are, like so much of that machinery, rather shadowy. It is known to have been in existence by October 1522.[2] The names of a number of its officials, or auditors, have survived.[3] On seven occasions between 1525 and 1528 proceedings are known to have taken place against those who had failed to appear before it.[4] A priest, Sir Christopher Nelson, brought a case against a certain John Cooke, who had reported him to the bishop of Winchester for making indecent advances to a young married woman. As a result, Sir Christopher had found himself for a short time in the bishop's prison, and had subsequently been expelled from the diocese. Apparently William Burbank, one of the auditors of Wolsey's court, was a relative of Sir Christopher's, and this seems to have provided the expelled priest with an opportunity for gaining his revenge on Cooke. However, a letter from Bishop Fox convinced Burbank that Cooke had no case to answer, and he put an end to the proceedings.[5] Superficially, at any rate, the episode reflects some credit both on Fox's diocesan administration, and on Wolsey's legatine court.

The outcome in two other cases is not known. One involved an attempt by a widow to prove a fictitious will.[6] The other appears to have been a case of defamation, in the course of which the plaintiff's lawyer made an interesting plea on behalf of his client: that her case had been prejudiced by being cited both to appear within the month of August, which the law recognized as a time when no one be compelled to do so, and at places where it was not safe for her to attend.[7] This looks very much like a legal fiction or technicality of the kind used in the secular courts to bring cases before Chancery or Star Chamber, and it is tempting to suggest other similarities – for instance, that the legatine courts provided the same opportunity to escape from the excessive legalism and vested interests of the diocesan courts which the conciliar courts offered in the secular field. In fact, these faults do not appear to have been a major feature of the church courts, which have emerged reasonably unscathed from the scrutiny of recent research.[8] Moreover, there existed already, in the archbishop of Canterbury's courts of arches and audience, a body which would provide an alternative to , and perhaps a check on, the inferior ecclesiastical courts. So it is not at all clear that Wolsey's legatine court had any very obvious function. Instead, it may have merely made an already complicated picture even more so. In

---

[1] BL MS Add 34317, fo 33; for its interpretation see S.J. Lander, 'Church courts', p.227.

[2] LP,iii,2625.

[3] John Allen, John Bell, William Benet, William Burbank, William Clayburgh, William Clayton, John Dowman, Richard Duke, Roland Lee and Edward Steward; see M.J. Kelly, 'Canterbury jurisdiction', pp.178-80.

[4] PRO C/85/188/ fos.16 ff.

[5] LP,iv,5095.

[6] LP,iii,2625.

[7] *Associated Architectural Societies' Reports and Papers*, xxviiii, p.638.

[8] Houlbrooke; Bowker, 'Some archdeacons' court books'.

1521 Lewis More, the rector of All Hallows, London Wall, became involved in a dispute over the refusal of a parishioner, Robert Cockered, to pay his tithes. In one form or another, the case came before the bishop of London's consistory and commissary courts, the archbishop of Canterbury's courts of arches and audience, King's Bench who sent it back to the ecclesiastical courts, and to Wolsey's legatine court. The latter seems to have had no more success in resolving the case than any of the others, because Cockered refused to turn up, and the whole episode illustrates the comparative ease with which people could spin out a case indefinitely.[1] Wolsey's court could only have made this even easier.

However, to suggest that Wolsey's court was unnecessary is not to say that it was badly conducted or that its chief purpose was to add to his already considerable revenues, for the little bits of evidence that have survived do not suggest this. In November 1526 the archbishop of Canterbury advised the rector of St Mary Aldermary, London, Clement Browne, to resign, following a dispute with his parishioners about the repair of the chancel. The reason he gave was that if the parishioners found that their case against the rector was being delayed by the archbishop's favouring of him, they would bring the case before the cardinal's court where, by implication, the rector was unlikely to fare well.[2] On the face of it at least, the advice is not to the archbishop's credit, but, perhaps, a little to the legate's.

A better-known case had to do with the will of John Roper, an important official in King's Bench and father of William, the son-in-law and biographer of Sir Thomas More;[3] and it was the small amount of money that was left to William in his father's will that was at the heart of the dispute.[4] The case had initially gone before the joint-prerogative court,[5] but in February 1525 Warham wrote to Wolsey that Roper's widow had been summoned to appear before Wolsey's 'commissaries at your chapel at York Place' – which I take to be a reference to Wolsey's legatine court of audience. This pleased Warham not one bit; rumour had it, he told Wolsey, that no testament could take effect 'otherwise than your grace is content', and many people told him that it had been 'a great oversight in me that I would make such a composition with your grace which should turn so many men to trouble and vexation'.[6] However, it was not so much the composition itself that pained Warham but the fact that it was not being observed, insofar as a matter which should have gone before the joint-prerogative court had been removed from it. His grief is not surprising, for he had a half-share in the revenue of that court, no share in that of Wolsey's court of audience. At the same time, it is not altogether surprising that the case had been brought before Wolsey's court. The will, as is the habit with wills, had resulted in a family quarrel, and the suggestion had been made

---

[1] Brigden, *JEH*, 32, pp.289-90.

[2] *LP*,iv,2619.

[3] Baker, ii, pp.54-7 for biographical information.

[4] He was to have what was left after various large legacies to the widow and two younger sons had been paid; see Roper, pp.xxxv-vi. But his father had secured his succession to the post of protonotary, and so may have felt that he had sufficiently provided for him.

[5] *LP*,iv,1118 makes this clear, though not picked up by Kelly in his discussion of the case; see M.J. Kelly, 'Canterbury jurisdiction', pp.190-1.

[6] *LP*,iv,1118.

that Roper's widow had exercised undue influence over her husband just before his death in favour of the younger sons.[1] So it seems probable that it was William Roper who had approached Wolsey's court, rather than any initiative being taken by the court. Wolsey's response to Warham's complaint appears to have been a soothing letter, for on 6 March Warham felt able to write that he was glad to see how graciously Wolsey had taken his 'plain-writing . . . Unless I had had in your grace's undoubted favour and benignity towards me very singular trust and confidence to write without displeasure not only the plainness my mind, but also such reports as were brought unto me, I would in no wise have attempted to disclose my said mind and reports so openly.'[2] He agreed with Wolsey that nothing further should be done until they had had a chance to discuss the matter, and the result appears to have been that the case proceeded before the joint-prerogative court.[3]

This whole episode is evidence of Wolsey's tactful handling of Warham.[4] It also demonstrates that Wolsey's legatine court was not, as has been alleged, 'one of the most aggressive and powerful tribunals in the history of the English Church to his time'. The simple fact is that there is not sufficient evidence concerning the workings of the court for any such conclusive judgement to be made, and inherently it is unlikely to be correct. It would, of course, intervene in matters which touched upon Wolsey's legatine rights, but the great bulk of the business before it would depend upon the voluntary choice of its clients. The service it provided, at this distance in time, may not appear very necessary, but if it was much used, this could only have been because it was popular.

An aspect of Wolsey's legatine powers which does not appear to have resulted in any controversy was his right to grant dispensations and licences of the kind that would normally have been obtained from the papacy, despite the fact that the papal power to make such exemptions had, throughout the Middle Ages, come in for a fair share of criticism.[5] Undoubtedly too many exceptions were made and not enough care was taken to find out whether they were justified, and in 1514 the Fifth Lateran Council had tried to do something about this.[6] In themselves, however, they were not a bad thing. It made perfectly good sense to allow a beneficed clerk leave of absence in order to further his studies, and it was humane to allow people within the prohibited degree of affinity to get married in certain circumstances. But if it became merely a question of paying, the whole justification for canon law would be seriously undermined. The difficulty was that with the best will in the world, the papal Curia was not in the best position to check the genuineness and particular circumstances of requests that were reaching it from all parts of Christendom and, given the distances involved, the procedures were bound to be complicated and expensive. Moreover, a large proportion of the papal revenue came from the granting of these requests, so the potential for abuse was great.[7] Arguably, therefore, a resident papal legate was in a much better position to prevent such

---

[1] LP,iv,1518; for the will see LP,iv,72.

[2] Henry Ellis, 3 ser, ii, p.43 (LP,iv,1157).

[3] The reason for saying this is that the examination of the witnesses on 23 March 1526 took place before John Cocks, Warham's commissary in the joint-prerogative court; see LP,iv,1518.

[4] M.J. Kelly, 'Canterbury jurisdiction', p.181.

[5] For the criticisms of theologians asembled at Alcala in 1479 see Jedin, i, p.41.

[6] Ibid, p.131.

abuse than a distant Curia. Whether Wolsey did, in fact, do so is impossible to say. It is not even known what machinery he set up to administer the grants, but it must have been quite considerable because in the twelve months for which there is evidence, about a hundred were made. Moreover, the fees from these amounted to about £200, a considerable sum.[1]

There is one scrap of evidence that shows that some kind of check on Wolsey's granting of exemptions was made: when Bishop Fox discovered in 1527 that a fellow of Winchester College had secured a dispensation from Wolsey by falsely maintaining that his fellowship did not require continual residence, the fellow was ordered to explain why he should not incur the appropriate canonical penalties for misrepresentation.[2] Of course, the episode reflects more credit on Fox's episcopal administration which detected the misrepresentation than on Wolsey's legatine administration which failed to, but the fact that the fellow considered that a misrepresentation was required may suggest that the securing of a dispensation from Wolsey was not a complete formality. But if Wolsey ever did intend to use his powers to grant licences and exemptions in order to bring about the reform of the English Church, no evidence for it seems to have survived. Moreover, it could be that his possession of these powers may marginally have made matters worse, for easier access to them may well have encouraged an anyway endemic abuse of the pope's *plenitudo potestatis*.

Wolsey's legatine authority gave him the power to summon church councils, and in 1523 he attempted to do so, though the precise results of his efforts are not at all clear. In that year a parliament was called in order to secure financial help for the Great Enterprise against France. Following the usual practice, convocations of the northern and southern provinces were also called. But, as reported to the earl of Surrey, no sooner had southern convocation assembled on 22 April, and

> *a mass of the Holy Ghost at Paul's was done, my lord cardinal [adcited] all of them to appear before him in convocation at Westminster, which so did; and there was another mass of the Holy Ghost; and within six or seven days the priests proved that all my lord cardinal's convocations should do, it should be void because that their summons was to appear before my lord of Canterbury, which things so espied, my lord cardinal hath addressed out of new citations into every country commanding the priests to appear before him eight days after Ascension [22 May], and then I think they shall have the [3rd] mass of the Holy Ghost. I pray God the holy ghost be amongst them and us both.*[3]

Surrey's unknown correspondent got the date wrong, or perhaps it was changed after he wrote, for none of the surviving summonses for a legatine convocation gives 30 May as the date for its first meeting. He was also much puzzled by the number of invocations to the Holy Ghost, but he was clearly under the impression that a specially summoned legatine council, or convocation, was to meet, which is

---

[7] The best introduction to this subject is Southern, pp.100-69. See also Thomson, *Popes and Princes*, with a useful bibliography.

[1] PRO SP 1/39/fos,19-29 (*LP*,iv,2360); the period covered is July 1525 to July 1526.

[2] Houlbrooke, p.185.

[3] Henry Ellis, 1 ser, ii, pp.221-2.

important, because, apart from the seven surviving summonses, there is no direct evidence that it did. Moreover, the one outcome of all these proceedings that is well documented, the clerical subsidy, was issued in the traditional manner – that is, in the name of the two separate provinces of Canterbury and York.[1] In other words, there was no legatine subsidy. There is also the puzzling fact that while five out of the seven summonses give 8 June as the date of the legatine convocation, two give the 2nd.[2] But for this, one would be inclined to believe that a formal legatine convocation did meet, for it would have been strange to have gone to the considerable trouble of calling the meeting only for it then not to have taken place.

Whether or not it met must remain an open question. But this has not prevented historians alleging that at the convocation there was considerable opposition to Wolsey, led by none other than John Fisher and Richard Fox with strong initial support from an influential cleric, Rowland Phillips.[3] The only direct source for this is Polydore Vergil. Enough has already been said about his unreliability where Wolsey is concerned to inject at once a note of caution, but since, as dean of Wells, Vergil was entitled to, and probably did, attend the convocation, in this instance his account must be taken seriously. This does not prevent it from being confused. He fails to mention the formal summons for a legatine convocation already discussed. Instead, he begins with Wolsey, after the northern and southern convocations had met separately, asking Warham whether he would mind them meeting together at Westminster Abbey under his chairmanship – a request which Vergil believed Warham readily granted because he realized that it would only increase Wolsey's unpopularity.

> Thereafter the prelates and clergy met for some days in Wolsey's 'senate'. There sat Wolsey in person on a golden chair. At first he began to promise much concerning matters of religion, but then he began to deal with financial questions, on account of which the convocation had been summoned. But the man was 'headlong and erratic in all his judgments', and when a little later he learnt that there were legal impediments to prosecuting the business in the province of Canterbury except under Canterbury's authority, he dismissed the prelate to St. Paul's Cathedral and himself returned to his own provincial convocation.[4]

There follows a discussion of the opposition in parliament to the demand for a very large subsidy, and Vergil then raises for the first time the question of clerical opposition, which according to him surfaced only when the two convocations had re-formed into their traditional constituents.

[1] Wilkins, iii, p.699.

[2] The five summonses for 8 June are that for Wolsey's vicar-general at Bath and Wells (*Registers of Thomas Wolsey, John Clerke, etc*, pp.27-8; for the bishop of Chichester (WSRO Ep1/1/4/fos. 104-6); for the bishop of Hereford (*Registrum Caroli Bothe*, pp.142-4); for the bishop of London, (GRO Register Tunstall, 9531/10/fo.34); for the prior of Butley (*Butley Priory*, pp.44-6). The two for 2 June are for the bishop of Lincoln (Wilkins, iii, p.700 though not in the extant registers); for the bishop of Rochester (KCA, DR c/R7/fo.110). Rochester's summons for 2 June was issued on 7 May but so also was Wolsey's vicar-general's for 8 June.

[3] See Elton, *Reform and Reformation*, p.92; Guy, *EHR*, xcvii, pp.483-4; M.J. Kelly, 'Canterbury jurisdiction', pp.174-7; A.F. Pollard, pp.187-91.

[4] Vergil, p.305.

For many opposed him [Wolsey], and especially Richard bishop of Winchester, John bishop of Rochester, and above all Rowland Phillips vicar of Croydon and canon of St Paul's, who was a splendid preacher. This last speaker Wolsey summoned while the discussion was going on and so frightened him that he afterwards appeared no more in convocation, thereby very gravely impairing his integrity. Upon the leader thus withdrawing from a prolonged dispute, the rest gave way.[1]

It is slightly curious that in such a trio Phillips should have been the leader and, if true, may suggest that neither Fisher nor Fox was as opposed to the clerical subsidy as Vergil implies. Moreover, the additional information concerning their and other clerical opposition at this time is not very convincing. A recent suggestion that, in order to punish Fox for his opposition, Wolsey had him assessed for the clerical subsidy at twice the amount he should have been, is incorrect, because the figure of £2,000 used to support it relates not to the subsidy but to the loan of 1522.[2] It is true that Fox was one of those who was specifically excluded from the General Pardon with which, as was customary, the parliament ended, but exclusion in matters of current legal concern was perfectly normal, and, for instance, it was for just such a reason that a fellow bishop of Fox's, Richard Nix, was also excluded from the 1523 General Pardon.[3] And anyway, if Fox's exclusion was a punishment, why were Fisher and Phillips not punished in the same way? Whether Phillips was silenced in the manner that Vergil suggests, it is impossible to say. He was not afraid of controversy, and was to spend part of the 1530s in prison because he was of the 'papish sort'.[4] But, there is no other evidence of any opposition by him to Wolsey, and he was quite happy, probably in March 1524, to write to Wolsey on behalf of the prior of Binham, a dependent house of St Albans, whom he recommended as a good religious man and a former scholar of his at Gloucester College.[5]

Recently, it has been suggested that Wolsey deliberately engineered a charge of treason against Geoffrey Blythe, bishop of Coventry and Lichfield in order to forestall any possible opposition from him in the 1523 convocation,[6] but this receives little support from contemporary sources. Hall mentions the case, but fails to make any connection with clerical opposition.[7] Vergil fails even to mention it. Given both these writers' willingness to discredit Wolsey, this suggests that any connection between the case and the 1523 convocation is coincidental. Moreover, the precise timings do not fit all that well. Blythe was imprisoned on 28 March which, though after he would have received his summons to the southern convocation, was before he would have had any knowledge of Wolsey's intention to hold a legatine convocation – and thus it would have been difficult for the bishop to

---

[1] Ibid, p.307.

[2] M.J. Kelly, 'Canterbury jurisdiction', p.175 for the suggestion; for the correction *LP*,iii,2483 [1]; Goring, *EHR*, lxxxvi, p.701, n.2.

[3] Nix was excluded in connection with the *quo warranto* proceedings at King's Lynn. It may be this that prompted Elton to name him amongst Wolsey's opponents in 1523 (*Reform and Reformation*, p.92), but there is no other evidnce for it.

[4] *LP*,vi,1672.

[5] *LP*,iv,183. Gloucester College was the first Benedictine Hall in Oxford. It stood on the site now occupied by Worcester College.

[6] Heath, *BIHR*, xlii, pp.101-9.

[7] Hall, p.655.

have been contemplating opposition to one! It is also unlikely that he would have made plans to oppose a clerical subsidy before knowing how much was going to be asked for. Furthermore, there is nothing in Blythe's career to suggest that he would contemplate opposition of any kind. What probably happened is that an allegation was made against Blythe – perhaps by 'a certain Welshman' – that could not be ignored, even if it was not taken very seriously. He was tried by a commission comprising his secular peers headed by the duke of Suffolk, and was acquitted. It is true that Wolsey did not make any public statement about Blythe until he addressed the House of Lords on 10 June, the opening day of the second session, when he announced his acquittal. But rather than this being to his discredit, it may be that his chief concern was to play down the whole episode, for there is nothing in Wolsey's career to suggest that he would have seen any private or public advantage in the trial of a fellow bishop.

The case for strong opposition to Wolsey at the convocation of 1523 has really only ever rested on the not unbiased account of Polydore Vergil, and recent attempts to extract additional evidence do not stand up to close scrutiny. Nevertheless, the mere sequence of events does suggest a surprising uncertainty in Wolsey's handling of them. Why, for instance, did he not formally summon a joint legatine covocation in the first place? One answer might be that his initial attempt to summon such a convocation in an informal way resulted from a snap decision which, in the event, did not turn out well. Alternatively, he may have always envisaged calling one, but thought that it would be easier to allow the traditional processes for calling the separate convocations to take their course, only to be genuinely taken by surprise by the legal objections raised at the joint assembly. Or perhaps he had always realized that there would be opposition, and so did not wish to signal his intention until the last possible moment. But whatever was in his mind, the fact that he did in the end feel it necessary to summon a joint convocation formally, which he then may never have allowed to meet, does suggest some kind of defeat, or at least a tactical retreat. It needs to be borne in mind that his position was complicated by having to pursue at least two, if not three, differing aims. The ostensible reason, as given in his summonses and hinted at by Vergil, was reform of the Church, but it is not necessary to share Vergil's cynicism in order to accept his view that money was Wolsey's major concern.[1] He had, after all, already held meetings to discuss reform, and had taken a number of steps as a consequence. No doubt a joint convocation would provide an opportunity to monitor these steps and to exhort the clergy to greater efforts. But in 1523 it was the Great Enterprise against France, and the need to finance it, that was uppermost in his mind. It was because of this that a parliament had been summoned, and it was because a parliament was called that a convocation was also summoned. And the main reason why these assemblies were ever called was to provide the Crown with money. However, at the same time the need to call convocation did provide Wolsey with an opportunity to demonstrate his legatine authority just when he was beginning to put that authority on a regular footing: the composition with Warham had already been negotiated, and those with the other bishops were in the pipeline. In the end he may have had to compromise and concede to worries expressed about the legality of

---

[1] Vergil, p. 305.

a joint convocation, in order to obtain the money. Certainly he would have been very reluctant to do anything to jeopardize its collection. All this is not to say that there was large-scale opposition, but that there was sufficient for Wolsey to have to show some flexibility – and in doing so he secured the largest clerical subsidy that had hitherto ever been granted.[1]

The question of the extent of opposition within the Church to Wolsey's legatine powers is naturally of great importance. But the opposition so far noted, at the convocation of 1523 and at some of the meetings in the diocese of Lincoln summoned to hear the legatine constitutions of 1519, does not add up to much, and it might be expected that it would have been greater. Nothing was more characteristic of the Middle Ages than disputes over rival jurisdictions, as much within the Church as amongst the secular authorities. A glance at the history of the English Church in the thirty years before Wolsey's appointment as legate confirms this. In the 1480s and 1490s there had been the opposition to John Morton's attempts to extend his powers as archbishop of Canterbury over both the secular clergy and the monastic orders, which led to serious conflict between him and Abbot Wallingford of St Albans,[2] and with the bishop of London, Richard Hill. Both episodes involved appeals to Rome and, during the course of the second, Morton appears to have excommunicated the bishop and arrested one of his leading officials.[3] Warham continued Morton's aggressive attempts to extend Canterbury's jurisdiction, especially as regards testamentary matters, and soon found himself faced with widespread opposition, spearheaded by Bishop Fox. The ensuing battle, which split the episcopacy into two camps, was taken to Rome, but the pope thought it wiser to pass the buck, and authorized Henry VIII to settle the matter, which with some difficulty and increasing annoyance, he did during the course of 1513.[4] The details of this dispute can be ignored; the fact that it took place, and the fierceness with which it was waged, is the necessary background for assessing the amount of opposition to Wolsey.

It will be evident that the person who was most directly affected by Wolsey's legatine authority was Warham. There was, to begin with, the question of status and dignity already touched upon, resulting, if Cavendish can be trusted – and there has to be a doubt about this – in a dispute about whether the crosses of Canterbury or York should have precedence.[5] Technically, once he became legate, Wolsey was correct to insist on his superior rank, but this need not have helped to reconcile Warham to his demotion. Then, as has been shown, there was the threat to his prerogative and jurisdictional rights that Wolsey's legatine authority posed, and with it a possibility of serious financial loss. Furthermore, it had been Wolsey who, in 1515, had succeeded him as lord chancellor; and even if, as was argued earlier,[6] Warham had been quite willing to resign, in retrospect Wolsey's succession may have begun to rankle. At his age it was perfectly seemly to retire gracefully from

[1] M.J. Kelly, 'Canterbury jurisdiction', pp.307-8. Wolsey estimated that it would bring in £120,000; see LP,iii,2483 [3].
[2] Knowles, JEH, 3, pp.144-58.
[3] Harper-Bill, JEH, 29, pp.6 ff. for both episodes.
[4] M.J. Kelly, 'Canterbury jurisdiction', pp.42-94.
[5] Cavendish, p.16.
[6] See pp.31-2 above.

secular affairs, but then to be pushed around by the same man in spiritual matters, and in matters concerning the dignity of his see, about which Warham held strong views, may well have injected an element of paranoia into his attitude towards Wolsey.

Warham's initial reaction to Wolsey's acquisition of legatine powers was to resist them, and the occasion that he chose to make his stand was the calling of that legatine meeting of bishops for 14 March 1519 referred to earlier. According to Wolsey, the calling of that meeting had been discussed with, and agreed to, by Warham some time before the formal summonses were sent out and, what is more, it was the king who had ordered Warham to discuss the matter with the new legate *a latere*. But having appeared to go along with Wolsey, however reluctantly, Warham had then proceeded, on 2 December 1518, to issue his own summonses for a provincial council to meet to discuss reform before Wolsey's.[1] It seems most unlikely that Wolsey would have invented the king's involvement or Warham's preknowledge of his own intentions, so it must be concluded that Warham's decision to summon his own council was intended as a slap in the face for Wolsey and, less directly, for Henry. No wonder Wolsey was put out:

> Assured I am that his grace [Henry] will not I should be so little esteemed that you should enterprise the said reformation to the express derogation of the said dignity of the see apostolic, and otherwise than the law will suffer you, without mine advice, consent, and knowledge, nor you had no such commandment of his grace, but expressly to the contrary.

This being the case,

> necessary it shall be that forthwith you repair to me, as well to be learnt of the considerations which moved you thus besides my knowledge, and also to have communication with you for divers things concerning your person, and declaration of the same of the king's pleasure.[2]

The tone of Wolsey's letter was sharp, not to say threatening, and it may well be that one of the 'things concerning your person' was contained in a letter from one of Warham's chaplains, Thomas Gold, written on 14 February, in which he described to Warham the efforts of 'this great tyrant' and the archbishop's 'great adversary' to persuade the king's Council to bring a charge of praemunire against him. Happily Wolsey's efforts had been thwarted by the councillors' 'great love and favour' towards Warham, 'wherefore you may be glad that your great adversary is thus discomforted, and greater discomforted shall be shortly by God's grace'. Gold also reported a meeting he had had with the bishop of Norwich, Richard Nix, who had told him

> that he would assuredly stick by you . . . saying moreover that the cardinal laid no manner of thing to his charge as yet, but that he would that he should keep his day this

---

[1] On 7 Feb. 1519; Wolsey's having been summoned for 14 March. A copy of Warham's summons is to be found in BL MS Add 48012, fo.53v.

[2] Wilkins, iii, pp.660-1(*LP*,iii,77 (2)). It is not dated but presumably written fairly soon after Warham's summonses had been sent out on 2 Dec.

next Lent [the legatine convocation of March 1519], . . . also he said that if the king would not suffer him to have his lawful defence in the case of praemunire he would tell him that he would forsake him as his liege man . . . Therefore, I take of this bishop that he is stiffly set to this matter, which you know hath been always stiff in his causes.[1]

'Stiffly' almost seems a euphemism, for what Nix was proposing was treason; but in fact no formal charge of praemunire against either him or Warham has survived for this date. Furthermore, it is unlikely that Wolsey would have wanted to take a step which would undoubtedly have raised the ecclesiastical temperature, thus making the general acceptance of his legatine powers much more difficult. Neither is Gold's suggestion that Wolsey had been defeated in Council over the matter very likely: the royal support of his legatine powers tells against this, and moreover neither Gold nor his named source, 'Doctor Sexten' – perhaps John Sixtinus, a friend of Erasmus and Colet and resident in London at this time – was in a position to obtain accurate information of what went on in the Council, though no doubt there were leaks.

Nevertheless, Gold's letter leaves no doubt that Warham and Nix were fearful of praemunire charges, and that Warham may even have been threatened with such a charge if he would not toe the line. It is worth remembering here that in October 1518 a charge of praemunire had been brought against Henry Standish, who only a few months earlier had been appointed bishop of St Asaph. It is often alleged that these charges were brought by Wolsey in order to take revenge on a man who in 1515 had dared to take on the English clergy and had been Henry's rather than his own choice for St Asaph.[2] The allegation has never been very convincing. It would have been the height of political folly to move against a man who was so in favour with the king without having first secured the royal consent – which would hardly have been forthcoming if Wolsey's motivation had been merely to gratify a personal whim. What is not usually stressed is the precise charge, which was that Standish had allowed himself to be consecrated bishop before he had received the royal assent and done homage for his temporalities – and the person who had consecrated him was Warham. Given that Standish was Henry's personal choice, the charge was ludicrous, but if Standish was technically guilty so also was Warham; and, in fact, Warham's action in 1518 was to provide the basis for the charge of praemunire brought against him early in 1532.[3] It seems possible therefore that the charge against Standish in the autumn of 1518 was an oblique way of putting pressure on Warham to accept the consequences of Wolsey's new position. Whether anything more direct was tried is not known. People close to Warham believed it likely, and it may be that Warham was only saved from a praemunire charge because he gave way. His council never took place. Wolsey's did.[4]

But if the major battle between Wolsey and Warham ended in the spring of 1519, there continued to be the occasional skirmish. As has been shown, it was not until late in 1522 that the two men reached an agreement on jurisdictional matters,

---

[1] PRO SP 1/18/fo.37 (*LP*,iii,77 [6]).

[2] Guy, *Cardinal's Court*, pp.76, 164-5 for the suggestion and documentation; see also Elton, *Reform and Reformation*, pp.56-7.

[3] Scarisbrick, *Henry VIII*, p.330

[4] Kelly's suggestion that Warham failed to turn up for the legatine council depends in my view on a misdating of *LP*,iii,120. Though placed in 1519 in *LP*, the suggestion in AC, i, p.20 of 1523 seems to me more likely; but see M.J. Kelly, 'Canterbury jurisdiction', p.167.

and not without some huffing and puffing from Warham. Nevertheless, the final result was not altogether unfavourable to him: if he had to share the revenue from his prerogative probate, he had at least had his rights to these fees, previously challenged by Fox and his supporters, confirmed. Indeed it may well be that, given the new impetus to their collection that resulted from the setting up of the joint-prerogative court, he may not have suffered any financial loss.[1] And, at any rate, to share the revenue was a great deal better than no revenues at all, an outcome which he must have considered a real possibility when he first pondered on the consequences of Wolsey's legatine appointment. In 1525 there had been some excitement over John Roper's probate, but it had not taken a great deal of effort on Wolsey's part to calm Warham down. Another cause not so much of disagreement but of hurt was Wolsey's usurpation of Warham's role as the dominant influence at Oxford university, despite the fact that Warham retained the office of chancellor of the university. In their preoccupation with securing Wolsey's favour, the university often forgot to consult with Warham, who sometimes let his displeasure be known. In 1518 he reacted to their rather tardy notification of the appointment of a new bedel, a nominee of Wolsey and of Bishop Atwater of Lincoln, by remarking that he would prefer it if the university asked his opinion about appointments before they were made, rather than after.[2] And when in 1522 all the statutes and privileges of the university were surrendered to Wolsey, who had been asked to produce new ones without, apparently, any consultation with its chancellor, one senses Warham's annoyance beneath his dry observation that doubtless Wolsey was as devoted to the well-being of the university as he was.[3] But however irritated the former fellow of New College may have been by the former fellow of Magdalen's interference and munificence, he never allowed his irritation to develop into open conflict.

In reviewing every aspect of their relationship through the 1520s, the impression from their many surviving letters is not of great hostility, but rather of a willingness to put up with each other, and certainly to co-operate together in the king's service. In 1520 Wolsey took some trouble to further Warham's efforts at Rome to secure the papal privileges granted for previous jubilee celebrations to commemorate Becket's martyrdom, but which were not on this occasion forthcoming.[4] In 1521 there was a gracious exchange of presents, Wolsey's being a costly jewel for Becket's shrine.[5] In January 1523 Warham, who had been ordered to bed by his doctor, thanked Wolsey for his advice to live on 'high and dry ground as Knowle and such other', and also for his offer of 'a pleasant lodging at Hampton Court' until the archbishop had fully recovered his health.[6] Even when the two men were in disagreement, Wolsey was usually gracious and nearly always suggested a meeting to sort the matter out.[7] Admittedly, in the major dispute over their respective reforming councils, Wolsey

[1] Here I am following Kelly ('Canterbury jurisdiction', pp.186-7), though in general he takes a gloomier view of their relationship than I do.

[2] Mitchell, pp.86-7.

[3] Ibid, p.116.

[4] LP,iii,695, 756; the celebrations took place every fifty years, and were due in 1520.

[5] LP,iii,1218.

[6] LP,iii,2767; for another offer of lodgings by Wolsey, this time in Aug. 1525, see LP,iv,1591.

[7] LP,iii,98; iv,1157.

had been less forthcoming, but even so he had ended his letter by pointing out to Warham that the nearness of Mortlake, which belonged to the archbishop of Canterbury, to Richmond, where Wolsey was going to stay, would make it possible for both of them 'with little pain often to repair together as the case shall require'.[1] Wolsey's concern on this occasion to save Warham pain may have been somewhat lacking in sincerity, but it is difficult not to take Warham's comments to Wolsey in 1525 at something near their face value. They were made in a letter written at the height of the difficulties over the collection of the Amicable Grant, and Warham took it upon himself to offer Wolsey some consolation. Given the circumstances, Wolsey must expect to receive a good deal of abuse. He, Warham, was being called an old fool. Wolsey must expect worse, because that was always the fate of those most in favour with the king, 'do he never so well; but, whatever be spoken, the fruits which a tree brings forth will prove its goodness'.[2] The phrasing of this letter is surely too particular and too apposite to be passed off as merely the conventional pleasantries of the Tudor establishment.

All the same, the evidence of this one letter should not be allowed to weigh too heavily in any final assessment of the two men's relationship, for they were very different characters. As a somewhat buttoned-up but successful lawyer and civil servant with genuine scholarly interests, Warham was both the caricature of a Wykehamist and a representative figure of the late medieval English Church, and his ascent up the ladder of promotion, from New College, through the administration of the archbishop of Canterbury, to royal service, and then to the lord chancellorship and the see of Canterbury seems almost preordained. Wolsey's rise, with its curious schoolmasterly beginnings, had required much more energy and personality, but also much more luck. There was a twenty-year difference in age and little reason for Warham to think very warmly of Wolsey. For his part, Wolsey may well have thought Warham a bit of a bore, and certainly from time to time the archbishop caused him trouble. But the argument presented here is that neither man – but especially Wolsey, if only because he was in the dominant position – allowed their differences to get so out of hand as to prevent them working together in a perfectly civilized way.

The only other leading churchman with whom Wolsey had, from time to time, any serious difficulties was Richard Nix, bishop of Norwich since 1501. Unlike both Wolsey and Warham, his early career had been in ordinary diocesan administration, acting as vicar-general to Richard Fox at both Bath and Wells, and Durham. This did not prevent him from siding against his former patron and with Warham in the conflict over Canterbury's prerogative jurisdiction, perhaps because of the support he had received from Warham in his conflict with Henry VII's attorney-general, John Ernley.[3] And as has already been shown, early in 1519 he had sided with Warham against Wolsey over the latter's legatine powers, even expressing a readiness to forsake the king over the matter.[4] Despite, however, being

---

[1] Wilkins, iii, p.661.
[2] LP,iv, app.39. It is quoted by Bernard in his excellent assessment of the relationship between the two men; see Bernard, *War, Taxation and Rebellion*, pp.96-107.
[3] M J. Kelly, 'Canterbury jurisdiction', pp.104-8.
[4] See pp.290-1 above.

'always stiff in his causes',[1] Nix did at some point give way and make a composition with Wolsey; no doubt Warham's surrender had left him in such an exposed position that he felt he had very little alternative. However, trouble broke out again in connection with Wolsey's illegitimate son, Thomas Winter, who from 1526 to 1528 was archdeacon of Suffolk and subsequently until 1530 archdeacon of Norfolk. All seems to have been well while Winter held the former office, but when he moved a difficulty immediately arose because of Wolsey's wish to replace him at the archdeaconry of Suffolk with one of his chaplains, 'doctor Leigh' – perhaps Rowland Lee the future bishop of Coventry and Lichfield.[2] Nix had other ideas, and appointed one of his leading diocesan officials, Edmund Steward, which, as the office was in his gift, he had every right to do. Whether Wolsey had intended to 'prevent' 'doctor Leigh' by virtue of his legatine authority, or whether he had assumed Nix would go along with his choice and make the appointment on his behalf is not known. But at any rate Nix, having in August 1528 claimed Wolsey as his 'good lord, the which I esteem a great treasure to me', got his way and Steward remained as archdeacon.[3] However, in the following May, Nix informed Wolsey that he had become positively ill on hearing of the cardinal's 'heavy mind and displeasure' towards him.[4] What had caused this was Nix's challenge to Wolsey's right to testamentary jurisdiction in the archdeaconry of Norfolk. Nix argued that in claiming and enforcing this right Wolsey had broken their composition, the purpose of which had been to exclude Wolsey's legatine interference in the diocese in return for an agreed share of the bishop's revenue from spiritualities.[5] Wolsey's defence is nowhere stated, but presumably he would have argued that the issue had nothing to do with his legatine powers and thus nothing to do with their composition, but entirely concerned the rights of the archdeacon of Norfolk on whose behalf he was acting.

Wolsey's position, if this it was, might be more compelling had the archdeacon not been a teenager who happened to be his illegitimate son. It is also possible that in enforcing the archdeacon's jurisdictional rights Wolsey may have intended to get his own back on Nix for his swiftness in appointing Steward to the archdeaconry of Suffolk. On the other hand, he may merely have been anxious to protect his son's legally justified rights, which for better or worse he always viewed as his own. Nix was a crusty and combative man who was inclined to overreact, and it would be quite wrong to assume that his position was the correct one.[6] But, whatever the rights and wrongs of this particular episode, there is no doubt that in the late 1520s relationships between the two men were not good. Moreover, in none of the surviving letters between the two men are there those touches of any personal regard to be found in those between Wolsey and Warham. Nix, not being nearly so involved in national affairs, would not have known Wolsey as well as Warham did,

---

[1] PRO SP 1/18/fo.37 (LP,iii,77 [6]).

[2] LP,iv,4659.

[3] PRO SP 1/50/fo.20 (LP,iv,4659); Fasti, iv, p.34.

[4] LP,iv,5589.

[5] Ibid.

[6] See LP,iv,5491, 5492 for Nix's 'fury and fretting melancholy' in this matter. For the English envoys having fun with Clement VII at Nix's expense see LP,iv,4120; and called 'a devilish man' in a letter to Cromwell 5 Jan. 1530 (LP,iv,6159).

and he was anyway almost certainly a more difficult man to deal with. But if Wolsey's handling of Warham, and indeed other people, is anything to go by, he would have treated the bishop of Norwich as tactfully as the situation allowed – and Wolsey's tact is one of the explanations of the surprising fact that, when all is said and done, the amount of opposition to his legatine rule was surprisingly small.

What may also have helped Wolsey in avoiding opposition is the amount of patronage and therefore power that he had at his disposal. The more one can offer people, the more willing they are to do one's bidding – or, at least, that is one view of the world. Or, to make essentially the same point in a slightly different way: if one fills all the posts with one's own nominees, one is not likely to meet with much opposition. And the fact that neither Warham nor Nix was a nominee of Wolsey's and, indeed, each had been made bishop at about the time that Wolsey secured his first benefice back in 1500, may in a negative way help to make this point. It also helps to introduce a note of caution into any consideration of Wolsey's ecclesiastical patronage. The usual impression given, perhaps especially by A. F. Pollard in his sustained attack on Wolsey's 'despotism' over the English Church,[1] is that during the 1520s Wolsey monopolized ecclesiastical patronage. Such an impression needs to be seriously modified. To take episcopal appointments first: from early 1514 to his appointment as legate *a latere* in May 1518, a period during which Wolsey had considerable influence in royal government but was not master of the English Church, there were only three appointments to English sees, apart from his own to Lincoln and York in 1514 – those of William Atwater to Lincoln in 1514, of West to Ely in 1515 and of Booth to Hereford in 1516. From May 1518 until his downfall in October 1529, eleven appointments or translations were made, three of which involved himself: Bath and Wells in 1518, Durham in 1523 and Winchester in 1529, all held *in commendam* with York. Three others – those of Giulio de' Medici to Worcester in 1521, of Geronimo de Ghinucci to that same see in 1523, and of Campeggio to Salisbury in 1524 – involved the appointment of foreigners, a practice much favoured by Henry VII and continued by Henry VIII and Wolsey as a way of rewarding foreign churchmen who had proved, or might prove, useful to the English Crown, especially in any negotiations with the Curia. These changes left the core of the episcopal bench very much as it had been before Wolsey's 'despotism': Warham at Canterbury, Sherburne at Chichester, Blythe at Coventry and Lichfield, Nix at Norwich, and Fisher at Rochester remained throughout the 1520s, and Fox at Winchester until 1528.

Of the seven new appointments to English sees from 1514 to 1529 there is direct evidence of Wolsey's involvement in two cases only, that of Cuthbert Tunstall to London in 1522 and of John Clerk to succeed him at Bath and Wells in 1523; and as regards the former the evidence is somewhat misleading. It comes in a letter from Warham in January 1522 in which he thanks Wolsey for advising the king to promote Tunstall who, 'in [his] poor opinion' was 'a man of so good learning, virtue, and sadness' and therefore 'right meet and convenient to entertain ambassadors and other noble strangers at that notable and honourable city' in the absence of the king and Wolsey.[2] The reason why Warham wrote was that until 1515 Tunstall had been

---

[1] A.F. Pollard, pp.165-216.
[2] LP,iii,1972.

his protégé, serving as one of his leading archiepiscopal officials. After 1515, admittedly, Tunstall became heavily involved in royal service as diplomat and administrator, and inevitably came into close contact with Wolsey.[1] Presumably he would not have been so fully employed if he had not won Wolsey's respect, but then Tunstall won the respect of everyone he met, for not only was he a most successful ecclesiastical lawyer and diplomatist but he was also part of the great humanist network centring on Erasmus. Tunstall was destined for a highly successful career in the Church, whether Wolsey had come along or not, and even if he was subsequently, but most reluctantly, to temporize over religious changes with which he was not in sympathy, he was in no obvious sense a yes-man to Wolsey, or anyone else.[2]

Much the same can be said of the other new appointments. John Veysey, in September 1519 appointed bishop of Exeter, was like Wolsey a Magdalen man, although he had resigned his fellowship in 1496, a year before Wolsey took his up. His early patron had been John Arundel, bishop of Coventry and Lichfield from 1496 to 1502, and of Exeter from 1502 until his death in 1504. Veysey acted as his vicar-general in both sees, continuing in that post under the new bishop of Exeter, Henry Oldham, until in 1509 he became dean of Exeter. It is just possible that Wolsey had a hand in what was clearly the vital appointment in Veysey's career, that to the deanery of the Chapel Royal in 1514; but his subsequent appointments, culminating in his bishopric, were probably at the king's initiative. Veysey had been a major spokesman for Henry both in the debates over the Standish affair in 1515 and over the legal position of sanctuaries in 1519. Given his earlier connections with Exeter, he was an obvious choice for that see. Veysey was older than Wolsey, as were the pre-1518 appointments, West and Booth, neither of whom had any close connections with Wolsey; so also was John Kite, appointed to Carlisle in 1521. Tunstall was almost Wolsey's exact contemporary. All these men were therefore well-established on the ladder of clerical promotion before Wolsey could have had any decisive say in church appointments. And there is a further point to bear in mind. Wolsey's rise was so rapid that there was no time for him to have gathered a group of clerical administrators or household officials who could have been immediately considered for episcopal office. It is thus not surprising that he only ever had a limited influence over episcopal appointments. His protégés, people like Stephen Gardiner and Rowland Lee, were to become bishops only after he himself had fallen.

Still, there are two episcopal appointments in which Wolsey may have had a considerable say. One is John Clerk's who became bishop of Bath and Wells in 1523. Like Tunstall, Clerk attended Bologna university, where in 1510 he became a doctor of canon law. He had then been snapped up by Cardinal Bainbridge as part of the talented team he surrounded himself with during his five-year embassy at Rome, a team which also included Richard Pace, the future royal secretary, and William Burbank who was to become one of Wolsey's leading legatine officials.[3] On

---

[1] His first embassy was to Brussels in 1515, an embassy made famous because it was during it that More wrote some of *Utopia*.

[2] For Tunstall's opposition to Henry's religious changes but eventual submission see Scarisbrick, *Henry VIII*, pp.276-7, 330-1.

[3] Chambers, 'English representation', pp.379 ff.

Bainbridge's death in 1514 Wolsey took over this team, and this undoubtedly accelerated Clerk's promotion, as it did Pace's and Burbank's. Clerk's experience of Rome no doubt explains why in 1521 he was sent on an important embassy there in 1521, one of the purposes of which was to present to the pope Henry VIII's defence of the Catholic Church against Martin Luther, the *Assertio Septem Sacramentorum*. He returned to England in the autumn of 1522, and it was early in 1523 that he became bishop. By the end of that year he was back in Rome on another important mission, and it was from there that, on 2 December, he wrote to Wolsey to inform him that he was about to be consecrated as bishop, adding: 'I pray God send me grace to behave myself henceforth accordingly in the high and holy order whereunto most unworthily I have been called only by your grace.'[1] Even allowing for the element of flattery, the remark may well have been somewhere near the truth.

There is no direct evidence for the appointment of John Longland to Lincoln in 1521, but there are good reasons for thinking that it owed something to Wolsey.[2] They had been exact contemporaries at Magdalen, and their surviving correspondence, most of it admittedly for the period following Longland's appointment as bishop, suggests a genuine friendship within the limits set by their different positions in the Tudor hierarchy. And that Wolsey respected Longland is indicated by the fact that he chose him to deliver the sermon to the monks of Westminster at his joint-legatine visitation of the abbey in January 1519, which signalled his intention to embark on reform. It should be said, though, that by that date Longland was already a distinguished doctor of theology, and probably did not need Wolsey's influence to bring him to the king's attention; from 1518 he was a regular preacher at court and thus well known to the king, well before he became bishop. Be that as it may of all his episcopal colleagues, Longland was probably the closest to Wolsey. But that does not mean that he was Wolsey's 'creature', or even that he owed his appointment entirely to him.

What emerges, therefore, is that a significant number of bishops owed nothing to Wolsey as regards their appointment; one, John Longland, was personally close to him and no doubt owed something to him, but only one, John Clerk, owed a great deal. Moreover, given his academic qualifications and diplomatic skills, even if Clerk had not had the good fortune to be taken up by Wolsey in 1514, he would almost certainly have risen to a high position in the Church. In other words, there was nothing odd about Clerk's appointment, and the same can be said about all the others. The chief characteristic of those appointed to English bishoprics between 1514 and 1529 was simply the suitability of their qualifications, which differed very little from bishops of earlier periods, except insofar as not one of them was of noble birth, and not one of them was incompetent. In fact, if one takes Wolsey's episcopal colleagues as a whole, it is fair to say that they were an exceptionally able and conscientious group.[3] With Fisher as its star, any group that also included Warham, Tunstall and Fox must be awarded high marks. Longland was a theologian by training and an outstanding preacher. Sherborne of Chichester a first-rate diocesan administrator.[4] Even those who at first glance do not appear to be promising

[1] *LP*,iii,3594.
[2] Bowker, *Henrician Reformation* is the major source for all aspects of Longland's life.
[3] O'Day and Heal, p.20 for a similarly optimistic view.

episcopal material improve on closer inspection. In some ways Veysey of Exeter looks like a typical court appointment, but his earlier diocesan experience should not be forgotten, nor that he had been an active preacher in his earlier days.[1] Although West of Ely had been at one time heavily involved in diplomacy, this did not prevent him from earning the praise of Fisher, not only for his learning but for being a good bishop.[2] Only Booth of Hereford has nothing particular to recommend him – apart from his residency – and perhaps Kite of Carlisle, though he had been very active in royal government before his appointment. It is not a bad line-up. Only Fisher, it is true, gave his life for the Catholic Church, but in their different ways Clerk, Nix, Sherborne, Tunstall, Warham, West and Standish all attempted to resist the 'break with Rome'.[3] And it certainly cannot be argued that the reason why there was so little opposition to Wolsey's legatine powers was because the bishops were either too sycophantic or too afraid to put up more resistance.

There is a coda to this survey of episcopal appointments and one that will serve to emphasize something that may have been read between the lines, namely, the king's involvement. The most detailed information on the subject to have survived relates not to an English see, but to a Welsh one. When early in 1518 the see of St Asaph became vacant, Richard Pace, the royal secretary, then with the king at Abingdon, wrote to Wolsey to recommend as new bishop the abbot of Valle Crucis.[4] Meanwhile, Wolsey had made his own choice: William Bolton, prior of St Bartholomew's, London, whose main claim to fame was that he was an excellent supervisor of major building works, one of which was Henry VII's chapel at · Westminster.[5] It was this that enabled Henry to have some fun at Wolsey's expense, for as it happened, he had already made his own decision about who was to become bishop of St Asaph – none other than Friar Standish, the great champion in 1515 of the royal position vis-à-vis the Church. In considering Wolsey's choice, Henry admitted that masters of works had previously risen to high position in the Church – William of Wykeham was one he could have mentioned – but on the whole, he thought, not for their skill in building but for such good qualities as profound learning; and when it came to learning, Henry had no doubt that Standish was more profound than Bolton.[6] Pace was very upset at Henry's choice of a man who, he reported, was very popular in the royal household because of his efforts to subvert the English Church[7] – an interesting piece of evidence for anticlericalism in high places. Whether Wolsey was quite so upset does not emerge, but since, as was mentioned earlier, the two men were to get on perfectly well together during the 1520s, it does not look as if he was. But what is beyond argument is that as regards St Asaph Wolsey did not get the bishop of his choice. Neither was this his only failure. In October 1528, Richard Fox died and Wolsey asked Henry if he might not himself

[4] S.J. Lander, 'Diocese of Chichester'; 'Church courts'.

---

[1] S. Thompson, 'English and Welsh bishops', p.168 for his preaching; more generally Pill.
[2] In the dedication to West of his Defensio regie assertionis, quoted by Heal in her 'Bishops of Ely', p.9.
[3] Scarisbrick, Henry VIII, pp.273 ff; 'Conservative episcopate', pp.72 ff.
[4] LP, ii, 4070.
[5] Henry Ellis, 3 ser, i, pp.184-5 (LP, ii, 4083).
[6] Ibid.
[7] LP, ii, 4074, 4083.

succeed to Winchester on the grounds that Winchester's geographical position would enable him to play a personal role in his diocese while continuing in Henry's service.[1] The fact that Winchester was the wealthiest see may also have come into his calculation, though Durham, which he proposed to surrender, was not significantly less wealthy.[2] But Wolsey had in mind a scheme by which he would have effectively retained control of Durham, for he suggested that it should be given to Thomas Winter. Wolsey did get Winchester, but Winter did not get Durham.

Henry VIII's interest in the appointment of bishops should come as no surprise, for it is a commonplace of medieval history that the Crown's wishes played a decisive factor in such appointments. How far this relates to the comparative lack of opposition to Wolsey's legatine powers will be discussed shortly. For the moment, what needs to be stressed is the more obvious point that it must seriously modify the generally accepted view of Wolsey exercising a 'despotism' over the English Church, especially since it can be shown that Henry's interest extended to a wide range of church appointments, apart from bishops'. If there had been a 'despotism', it would have been exercised jointly by king and cardinal. However, a search through the bishops' registers (which is where most church appointments were recorded) leaves the overwhelming impression that during the 1520s they were being made in more or less the same way as they always had been – that is by the bishops themselves, the Crown, and by the very great number of lay and monastic holders of benefices. Wolsey's legatine powers, which included the right, by virtue of the papal *plenitudo potestatis* invested in his office, to override the rights of existing patrons and to appoint, or, as it was technically called, to prevent whom he liked,[3] hardly figure at all. This runs counter to the usual impression given by historians, following perhaps a reference to 'divers benefices' in the articles brought against Wolsey at his fall, that he did prevent on a large scale.[4]

But before we tackle the question of Wolsey's preventions, we need to look at the church patronage that Wolsey exercised in perfectly traditional ways. The extent of a bishop's patronage – that is, his right to appoint, or to collate, to prebends, collegiate churches and livings within his diocese – varied from one to another, but was never a very high percentage of the total patronage, most of which was exercised by monastic institutions or laymen. Recently it has been suggested that only about 6 per cent of all livings were in the bishops' gift.[5] But Wolsey was unique amongst English bishops by virtue of the fact that he held more than one see at a time: from 1518 to 1523 he combined Bath and Wells with his archbishopric of York, from 1523 to 1529 he held Durham, and from 1529 and thereafter Winchester. Moreover, for much of this time he effectively controlled patronage in the name of the foreign bishops who had been appointed to the sees of Worcester

---

[1] *LP*,iv,4824.

[2] Durham's revenue in the Valor Ecclesiaticus was £3,023, Winchester's £3,888.

[3] For preventions or, as earlier they were more frequently called, provisions see Southern, pp.156-69 for a good introduction.

[4] *LP*,iv,6075, art.7,though probably Pollard's views have been even more influential; see A.F. Pollard, pp.204 ff.

[5] S. Thompson, 'English and Welsh bishops', p.26 though there were wide variations; for instance 5 per cent for York, 26 per cent for Durham.

and Salisbury. As abbot of St Albans from 1521 he controlled the abbey's extensive patronage.[1] Finally, in his capacity as lord chancellor, he had the right to appoint to all Crown livings valued at under twenty marks a year, a limit which Wolsey raised to £20.[2] The chancellor also claimed the right to prevent to livings in Calais, though in 1527 Henry queried it – another demonstration of his personal interest in church patronage.[3] It has proved very difficult to calculate what all this added up to, but from the end of 1524 when Campeggio, and thus effectively Wolsey, became bishop of Salisbury, Wolsey may have had about 380 church dignities and livings in his gift.[4]

The extent of Wolsey's non-legatine patronage was undoubtedly great; and, for instance, more than double the amount at Warham's disposal when he was lord chancellor.[5] Nevertheless, with the number of livings alone running at over eight thousand, Wolsey's holding in no sense constituted a monopoly, and moreover, for him as for anyone else just how much patronage it gave him depended on the mortality rate amongst the holders of those dignities and livings. For instance, although there were forty-one Salisbury prebends, only one can be shown to have become vacant during the four and a half years that Wolsey had a say in appointments to them.[6] And he was probably fortunate that during his sixteen years as archbishop of York he was able to make thirty-four appointments to prebends there, though even that figure is one less than the total number.[7]

In discussing Wolsey's non-legatine church patronage, a balance has to be struck between emphasizing its considerable and in all probability unique extent, while at the same time avoiding exaggeration. When looking at what he did with it, the same care has to be exercised. In most respects he did the same as every other bishop: he shared it amongst members of his family and household and his leading diocesan officials, while much of what was left over he gave to anyone whose request he had some reason for complying with. Wolsey was always being approached by people seeking preferment, either for themselves or others,[8] but until more detailed work has been done on Wolsey's church patronage, it is impossible to say what proportion of it was used to satisfy such requests; probably a considerable amount. It is also impossible to say how far political considerations influenced his use of patronage, but here the guess would be not as much as might be expected. The appointment of William Boleyn, a cousin of Anne, in December 1529 as a prebend of York and in January 1530 archdeacon of Winchester, no doubt had everything to do with the importance of the Boleyn family and with Wolsey's own fall from

---

[1] I have failed to discover the total number of livings in the abbey's gift, but there were 26 in the counties of Hertfordshire and Lincolnshire; see Bowker, *Secular Clergy*, pp.67-8

[2] Croke, ii, p.819, quoting from BL Lansdowne 163, fo.141, where the number of livings at his disposal is put at 40. See also O'Day.

[3] *LP*, iv, 3304.

[4] My suggested breakdown is York 120 appointments, Durham 60, Salisbury, 80, Worcester 30, St Albans 50, lord chancellor 40, but I must stress that these are very rough and ready figures.

[5] M.J. Kelly, 'Canterbury jurisdiction', p.10 for his estimate of 135 appointments in his gift, to which should be added the putative 40 as lord chancellor.

[6] *Fasti*, iii. The certainty is Peter Vannes to the prebend of Grantham australis in 1528; there are 10 possible appointments.

[7] *Fasti*, vi.

[8] See *inter alia LP*, ii, 3834; iii, 2136; iv, 1385-6, 2576, 4135, 4647, 5069, 5410.

favour. However, most of Wolsey's appointments to York prebends had no obvious political overtones. The key man in the York administration was Brian Higden. Not only was he Wolsey's vicar-general, but from June 1516 dean of York, when he was also rewarded with a prebend. Also active either in the diocese or, more generally, in northern affairs, were Hugh Ashton, Thomas Donyngton, William Franklyn, Cuthbert Marshall, Edward Kellet and William Tate – all made prebendaries of York by Wolsey. Two of them, Franklyn and Tate, along with Brian Higden, were appointed to the Council of the North in 1525.

Another category of people whom Wolsey appointed prebendaries were academics who had close connections with him. These, in order of appointment, were Thomas Linacre, the famous humanist and medical man; John London, warden of New College, Oxford from 1526; Robert Shorton, master of Pembroke Hall, Cambridge, from 1516, but also at some time dean of Wolsey's chapel and almoner to Catherine of Aragon; Richard Duke, a fellow of Exeter College, Oxford, and also at some time dean of Wolsey's chapel; John Higden, brother of the dean of York, president of Magdalen from 1516 to 1525, and then first and last dean of Cardinal College; Robert Nooke of Eton and King's College, where he was a fellow from 1504 to 1526; and Laurence Stubbs, the controversial president of Magdalen, reinstated by Wolsey's legatine authority in 1527 and used by him in the setting-up of Cardinal College.

Then there were those who were closely connected with either legatine or royal administration. Robert Toneys was registrar of the joint-prerogative court. Edward Fox, after Eton and King's, became Wolsey's secretary, did much to organize the propaganda campaign in favour of the divorce, and in 1535 became bishop of Hereford. Richard Sampson, a future bishop of Chichester and of Coventry and Lichfield, spent a long time in Wolsey's household, only to become, like so many of Wolsey's servants, increasingly involved in royal service. Neither Cuthbert Tunstall nor Edward Lee was ever directly in Wolsey's service, but both worked very closely with him, especially in diplomatic affairs. In a category of his own was Reginald Pole, who in the 1520s was very much a favourite scholar of the king, to whom he was related. In 1525 he had written from Italy, where he was studying, that he hoped he would not be forgotten, or alone thought ungrateful amongst the many who had received Wolsey's favours, and on his return to England he was rewarded with a York prebend.[1]

Last but not least there is the ubiquitous Thomas Winter, who was given the prebend of Fridaythorpe in 1522 but was quickly switched to the more valuable one of Strensall. Since, in addition, he was made archdeacon of York in 1523 and of Richmond in 1526, by the late 1520s he was receiving about £350 a year from the dean and chapter revenues. He also received innumerable dignities and livings in other dioceses, including the deanery of Wells, the archdeaconries of Suffolk and Norfolk, the chancellorship of Salisbury, and prebends at Bath and Wells, Beverley, Lincoln, Salisbury and Southwell.[2] His annual income, as stated in the articles brought against Wolsey in 1529, was £2,700.[3] There is thus no question but

[1] LP,iv,1529.
[2] A.F. Pollard, pp.308-12 for a useful summary.
[3] LP,iv,6075, art.27.

that Winter was extremely well provided for, but it is necessary to point out that he was neither the first nor the last to benefit greatly from having a bishop for a close relative. William Warham, a so-called nephew but perhaps like Winter an illegitimate son, was given by his uncle the archdeaconry of Canterbury, worth £163 a year, the provostship of a college worth £56, and various other benefices and lay farms.[1] Nicholas Hawkins, nephew of Bishop West of Ely, became archdeacon of Ely in 1527.[2] In 1528 Longland made his nephew, Richard Pate, a prebendary of Lincoln offering Wolsey £200 for Cardinal College to ensure that he retained it.[3] At Coventry and Lichfield various members of the Blythe family held important ecclesiastical posts: the chancellorship of Lichfield Cathedral, two archdeaconries and two prebends were divided up amongst four of the bishop's relatives. Even the saintly Fisher saw no objection to helping his brother, though admittedly he was a layman.[4]

All in all, then, it would appear that nepotism was widespread, if not universal, amongst Wolsey's episcopal colleagues – which may suggest that it was not considered a great evil. True, in the 1530s a petition was presented to parliament criticizing the practice, but then in the 1530s the Church was fair game for lay prejudice.[5] Moreover, the notion of helping one's relatives so saturated the secular world that it would have been very odd if it had not permeated into the ecclesiastical – as it had done long before Wolsey appeared on the scene. Even such a critic of the early sixteenth-century Church as John Colet thought it perfectly reasonable that a quarter of a bishop's revenue should be spent on his family, and in this he was only following St Augustine.[6] With nepotism so out of fashion, it is easy to overlook that the practice was not merely a means of gratifying one's relatives' desires. Given the very narrow limits to their patronage, bishops had a real problem in exercising effective control in their dioceses, and the appointment of suitable relatives to important positions offered one solution, for they at least could usually be relied upon to further the bishops' own interests. Winter, of course, was not of an age to contribute anything directly to Wolsey's ecclesiastical administration, but the many positions that were obtained for him, especially those which were not in Wolsey's direct gift, did in a roundabout way further the cardinal's control over the English Church. Another way that Wolsey might have sought to control it was by making use of his legatine power to prevent. As has been suggested already, historians have tended to exaggerate the extent to which Wolsey made use of this, and in doing so have heaped much criticism on him. It is thus a matter of some importance to try to establish what the facts are – but first some background.

The practice of prevention had been common in England throughout the Middle Ages, reaching a peak in the fourteenth century when, it has been estimated, an average of about forty-four parochial benefices were filled each year in this manner,

[1] M.J. Kelly, 'Canterbury jurisdiction', pp. 27-30.

[2] For West asking Wolsey to promote his nephew to the living of East Dereham see LP, iii, 1030.

[3] LP, iv, 4527. Pate did retain the prebend but there is no evidence of whether Wolsey accepted the bribe. For Pate see Bowker, Henrician Reformation, pp. 79-80.

[4] His brother Robert Fisher was his steward.

[5] Lehmberg, p. 84.

[6] Lupton, pp. 301-2.

as well as many of the more important church dignities such as cathedral prebends.[1] But as the practice grew, so did opposition, resulting in the fourteenth century in a number of statutes of provisors and praemunire designed to exclude papal interference of all kinds.[2] The wider aim was not achieved, but by the middle of the fifteenth century preventions had ceased. Thus, in making use of them, Wolsey was reviving a practice which had not been seen in England for about seventy years, and, given its previous history, was unlikely to be popular – but with some important qualifications. Although theoretically it was the pope who prevented, in practice he only did so when asked to by all manner of people and institutions, but especially by the English Crown, which had found it a useful way of, in effect, extending its own patronage. It is not therefore surprising that the Crown's opposition to prevention had been to say the least ambivalent. Moreover, although in its most aggressive and theoretical moods, the papacy claimed the right to appoint to all dignities and benefices, as a general rule it was careful not to interfere with the rights of lay patrons. It was the ecclesiastical patronage that was plundered, but as it was churchmen who were in receipt of the plunder, by being prevented to benefices, it is not surprising that there had been a certain ambivalence about the English Church's response as well.

Given this background, certain suggestions about Wolsey's approach to a revival of the practice can be made. The most important is that it is highly unlikely that Wolsey would have interfered in the rights of lay patrons, and if this is so, then the scale of his preventions was limited from the start, more than half of all available benefices being in lay hands. It is also likely that his approach would have been in general rather cautious, because any sudden large-scale interference, even in ecclesiastical patronage, would have led to considerable opposition. And that he was cautious is shown by the way episcopal rights to patronage were specifically safeguarded in the compositions made between Wolsey and the bishops.[3] There was also another limitation imposed upon him, at least for a time, by the specific terms of his legatine commissions. It was not until July 1521 that he was granted any right to prevent,[4] and nearly three years later, in February 1524, he was still complaining that he found 'somewhat more strangeness to be showed to me than my merits require, that there hath been difficulty made to amplify my faculties *pro non familiaribus* [those not in his household or legatine administration], and such other things contained in my instructions'.[5] In August John Clerk was writing from Rome that the pope had at last agreed to most of Wolsey's requests, but unfortunately what precisely had been agreed does not emerge.[6] Still, it looks as if after 1524 Wolsey was authorized to prevent whom he liked, for prevent such people he did – and even if one takes the worst view of him, to have done so illegally would have raised so many complications as to make such a step very counter-productive for all those involved.

[1] Pantin, *English Church*, pp.47-102 for the most useful treatment but see also Deeley.

[2] The statutes of provisors are dated 1351 and 1390, the statutes of praemunire 1353, 1365 and 1393, the last being the 'Great Statute of Praemunire'.

[3] LRO Bishops' Possessions, Manorial, unnumbered box.

[4] M.J. Kelly, 'Canterbury jurisdiction', p.171.

[5] St.P,vi, p.257 (LP,iv,126).

[6] LP,iv,568, 610.

At any rate, it is important to realize that there were restraints, both technical and tactical, on Wolsey's freedom of action in this area, because they go a long way to explaining why so very few examples of prevention by Wolsey have been discovered. The two most important are those that were used in drawing up the praemunire charge against him in October 1529.[1] One was his prevention of John Allen – as a leading legatine official covered by the provisions of the 1521 commission – to the living of Galby in Leicestershire in the gift of the hospital of Burton Lazars; and the other was the prevention of James Gorton, who does not appear to have had any close connection with Wolsey, to the living of Stoke-next-Guildford in Surrey in the gift of the priory of St Pancras, Lewes.

There are, in fact, worries about both these charges, especially as regards the first. The bishop of Lincoln's register records that on 10 January 1527 John Allen was presented to Galby by Thomas Allen, a valet of Henry VIII, who had been given the presentation by the masters and fellows of Burton Lazars. Later in the same year, John Allen was given permission by the masters and fellows to give the living to a certain Thomas Hykman.[2] There was nothing unusual about either of these transactions; and certainly no mention of Wolsey or of his legatine authority. What these formal entries do not tell us is why the hospital chose to do what it did – and it could be that pressure was brought by Wolsey for it to reward his hardworking official. But even if that were so, that does not make what happened into a prevention. This raises a number of questions, including the possibility of Allen's collusion with the Crown in 1529 in framing Wolsey – and with the fall of his master Allen was in no position to resist such an invitation. Before, however, considering the other questions raised, the second charge needs to be looked at. There is no reference in either Fox's or Wolsey's register – the living was in the diocese of Winchester – to Gorton's acquisition of Stoke. This in itself may indicate that he was prevented. On the other hand, there appears to be no good reason why Wolsey would have wanted to favour Gorton in this way, while the priory of St Pancras had some reason to dislike Wolsey. In 1526 the priory had agreed to part with some of their manors to help endow Cardinal College.[3] The next year there was an attempt to remove the prior – a move not normally attempted without good reason – but in this case it does not seem to have been successful, and thus in 1529 the priory would have been run by a man who had no reason to like Wolsey.[4] In addition, St Pancras was a Cluniac monastery, exempt from episcopal jurisdiction. It was, therefore, particularly affected by Wolsey's legatine powers to visit exempt monasteries. The evidence concerning St Pancras is all too thin, but given the serious doubts about the first charge, there has to be some doubt about the second.

---

[1] LP,iv,6035.

[2] I owe this information to Bowker's kindness, taken from LAO Register 27 (Longland), fos.148v-9; the register actually refers to 'Alyn'. Another oddity is that the charge stated that Allen was prevented on 2 Dec. 15 Hen. VIII, that is in 1523 (PRO KB 29/161/ m.37), but all the evidence suggests that Woderuffe was rector of Galby until his death in either late 1526 or early 1527 and that only then did Allen succeed him.

[3] LP,iv,2340.

[4] LP,iv,3277. For those obsessed with the notion of faction, Norfolk's involvement in this episode will be of interest, but he seems to have been in favour of the removal, so presumably, on this occasion at least, not antagonistic to Wolsey.

And why, if so many preventions had taken place, were only two used by the Crown in making its accusations against Wolsey? Of course, it was anxious to move quickly, and these two cases may have been the ones most readily to hand – though even more readily if they were essentially fabrications. It is also true that legally one case would have been sufficient, but then why produce two, and if two why not more? After all, the case against Wolsey was a political one, and to produce more examples would have been a successful propaganda exercise – if, that is, there were more to produce. There was certainly one which the Crown knew all about, for on 7 July 1528 Dr Bell informed Wolsey that Henry wished him to confer the vicarage of Thaxted, in the gift of the college of Stoke-by-Clare, whose patron was Catherine of Aragon, on a royal chaplain, Nicholas Wilson, by 'his legatine prerogative and prevention'[1] – but one can quite see why this prevention might not have been thought compelling evidence of Wolsey's guilt!

The prevention to Thaxted was one of eight recorded in the register of Cuthbert Tunstall, bishop of London.[2] Of these, seven were inserted at a later date, following an entry recording the presentation on 10 December 1526 of Oliver Vessy to the living of South Ockendon, on Wolsey's legatine authority but with the consent of the patrons who were laymen – a fact which would seem to go against the earlier assertion that Wolsey was unlikely to have interfered with the rights of lay patrons. That it happened here, allegedly with the consent of the lay patrons, is a further complication. If Wolsey had obtained consent, what need was there for legatine interference? One possible explanation is that there had been a dispute over who the lay patrons were, which had been brought before the legatine court, and that this curious form of appointment was a way of implementing its judgment. And that this happened on more than one occasion will be suggested when a series of court cases brought just after Wolsey's fall is discussed. The scribe also recorded that the seven additional preventions were made without the consent of the bishop of London, and added, though not without an element of contradiction, that it was because of their acceptance of the exercise of Wolsey's legatine powers that the bishops and clergy had been found guilty of praemunire and consequently forced to pay a subsidy of £100,000.

Eight preventions for the diocese of London over a period of seven or eight years is not a lot, and on close inspection the number begins to dwindle. Other evidence in Tunstall's register indicates that in the 1520s appointments to four of these livings – Purleigh, Alphamstone, Edmonton and Lammarsh – took place in an entirely regular way.[3] As regards one, the living of Moreton, there is no evidence of any appointment between 1484 and 1532, and as it was in the gift of the Crown, any prevention could only have taken place with Henry's knowledge. This leaves one living so far unmentioned, that of Barnston. Like Moreton, it was in the gift of the Crown. In 1526, a William Borne was appointed without any aid from Wolsey.[4] But nine years later a James Hampton resigned, and as there is no record of when he succeeded Borne it is possible that he was prevented, though it would again have

[1] GRO MS 9531/10/fo.31v.
[2] 'The pardon of the clergy' agreed to on 24 Jan. 1531.
[3] GRO MS 9531/10/fos.22, 23, 28, 29.
[4] Ibid, fo.26.

had to be with the consent of the Crown.

Thus the eight London preventions appear to dwindle to at the most four, and in three of those the most significant feature is that the Crown was closely involved. Other preventions are hard to come by. In March 1524, Warham complained that one of Wolsey's chaplains had entered into All Hallows, Lombard Street without the consent of the patrons, the prior and convent of Christ Church, Canterbury, which could indicate a prevention, though Warham made no mention of any legatine authority for the chaplain's action.[1] In July 1528, Wolsey informed Henry that following the death of the dean of Lincoln, the gift of the vicarage of Wirksworth in the diocese of Coventry and Lichfield was Wolsey's 'by prevention'. What he meant by this is uncertain but perhaps, unlike All Hallows, Wirksworth should be counted as an example of a legatine appointment.[2] In May 1529, there were preventions to two livings in the gift of the bishop of Bangor, though in fact made in person by one of Wolsey's commissaries in Wales, Edward Johns.[3] There is also something a little suspicious about John Laylond's resignation of the rectory of Laverstoke in the diocese of Winchester on 10 November 1529 – this, of course, very shortly after Wolsey's fall. In resigning, Laylond stated that he had been collated to the rectory by Wolsey, suggesting thereby that it was in Wolsey's gift, presumably as bishop of Winchester.[4] But in fact it was in the gift of Hyde Abbey, so that Laylond could only have received the rectory from Wolsey by prevention, and, if so, may have decided to get out before he found himself facing a charge of praemunire.

Finally, there are six possible preventions that are known about as a result of legal proceedings brought before King's Bench in 1530, at least four of which seem to have involved a dispute between patrons settled by Wolsey's legatine court and then, after his fall, reopened.[5] But even if this suggestion is wrong and they were all in the strict sense preventions, that only six cases came to light after Wolsey's fall hardly supports the view that Wolsey was making preventions on a large scale. Neither, of course, does the total number that have been discovered. Accepting every possible prevention, the total is twenty; a stricter definition reduces it to under double figures,[6] and this over a period of eight years. Even if these figures were trebled, it would still be difficult to argue that preventions played a significant part in Wolsey's 'despotism'. Indeed, it is more reasonable to ask whether it played any.

But in emphasizing the very small number of preventions one might give a false impression. There is, for instance, the undoubted fact that Wolsey was able to secure for his illegitimate son, Thomas Winter, a very large number of ecclesiastical dignities and livings, many of which were not his to give. Remember Bishop Nix having to battle to prevent Winter obtaining the archdeaconry of Norfolk, an office that was wholly in the bishop's gift. Other bishops also suffered. In 1518 Nicholas

---

[1] *LP*, iv, 193.

[2] *LP*, iv, 4521.

[3] *LP*, iv, 5533; see also Glanmor Williams, pp. 310 ff. The episode provided the centre-piece of Pollard's attack on Wolsey's use of preventions; see A. F. Pollard, pp. 206-8.

[4] *Registrum Thome Wolsey*, p. 59.

[5] Baker, ii, p. 69, where full documentation is provided.

[6] This would be to exclude 4 out of the 8 London preventions, 4 out of the King's Bench cases, Galby, Laverstoke, and Wirksworth.

West was asked to appoint somebody of Wolsey's choosing to one of the benefices in his gift, even though, as bishop of Ely, he had 'the fewest benefices of any value that any bishop hath in this realm'; and this was not the only occasion that he was asked to do so.[1] In 1528 Wolsey was hoping to make Thomas Winter dean of Lincoln, but Bishop Longland, anxious for a resident dean, had someone else in mind.[2] As with Nix, Longland got his way, but in both cases the impression is that Wolsey, in allowing the bishops' choices to stand, was granting them a favour, and was thereby exercising some control over episcopal patronage, if only indirectly. He may even have been making use of his legatine powers to prevent in order to force bishops to consult with him over important appointments, the threat being that if they did not do so he would make the appointments himself. However, two difficulties stand in the way of such a suggestion. In his composition with the bishops, Wolsey specifically excluded legatine interference by prevention,[3] while there is no extant evidence that he did use such a threat. What, therefore, seems more likely is that the kind of pressure that Wolsey did exert on bishops, and indeed on anyone else, was of a much more general kind, deriving not from any specific office or legatine commission but from his position as the leading servant of the Crown – which brings us back, as so often, to Henry VIII.

It has already been stressed that like his predecessors, Henry took a personal interest in episcopal appointments, but his interest extended wider than that. The need to appoint a new dean of Lincoln in 1528 resulted from the death of John Constable in the July of that year, a death which freed not only the deanery, but a number of other church dignities and livings. And at about the same time, there were other comings and goings which offer some insight into the realities of church patronage.

Let us start with the appointment of Edward Staples, a royal chaplain, to the mastership of the hospital of St Bartholomew's, West Smithfield. The election of a new master had been compromitted to, or given into the hands of, the bishop of London, Cuthbert Tunstall.[4] However, it emerges that Staples was not Tunstall's choice, for when on 10 July 1528 he reported to Wolsey that Staples had been appointed, he referred to it having been done in accordance with Wolsey's letter and, more importantly, with the king's pleasure.[5] In the previous month, Thomas Heneage, who had just transferred from Wolsey's to the king's household, reported to Wolsey that Henry had discussed with him the question of the mastership and was anxious that either Dr Nicholas Wilson 'or some other good man' should secure the post.[6] The 'good man', as it turned out, was Staples, but on becoming master he relinquished some of his ecclesiastical positions, including a prebend attached to Tamworth College, and livings at Covington and Thaxted. What happened at Thaxted has already been explained: at Henry's request, Dr Wilson was prevented to it. Henry's suggestion for the Tamworth prebend and Covington was another

---

[1] See Heal, 'Bishops of Ely', pp.6-7.

[2] *LP*,iv,4527.

[3] Always assuming that the compositions followed the pattern of the only surviving copy, that for Lincoln.

[4] GRO MS. 9531/10/fos 87-101.

[5] *LP*.iv,4489. The episode is a good example of the formal record concealing the truth.

[6] *LP*,iv,4335.

of his chaplains, Dr Robert Dingle.[1] When Winter failed to become dean of Lincoln, he was compensated with the mastership of St Leonard's, York. He then resigned his prebend in Ripon, whereupon Wolsey immediately offered the right to fill the vacancy to the king, who accepted with alacrity.[2] Meanwhile, Wolsey gave the vicarage of Wirksworth, formerly held by the dean of Lincoln and which, it will be remembered, Wolsey claimed to be his to give 'by prevention', to Nicholas Wilson, because he remembered 'how gladly your highness' would have him promoted.[3] But more was yet to come for Wilson. In August, Henry was asking Wolsey to appoint someone of his choice to the living of Hurworth in the diocese of Durham, which was in Wolsey's gift, not because he was bishop but because he was the guardian of the patron, Sir George Tailboys. Henry considered that the £25 a year the living was worth not sufficiently valuable for Wilson, so he suggested Richard Croke, the duke of Richmond's tutor.[4] What could be found suitable for Wilson? The answer was the archdeaconry of Oxford, relinquished by Heneage when he had become dean of Lincoln.[5]

There happens to be rather more information about the comings and goings of church patronage in July and August 1528 than for other periods during Wolsey's ascendancy, but there is no reason to suppose that what happened then was not typical. It is true that the deanery of Lincoln did not fall vacant every month of the year, but similar vacancies occurred at fairly frequent intervals, and there were always plenty of royal chaplains in need of promotion. In attempting to draw some conclusions from this survey of Wolsey's church patronage, royal chaplains do provide a valuable clue. It has been shown that what may be called Wolsey's ordinary patronage was indeed ordinary except in one respect, its scale. Other bishops promoted their relatives, their diocesan administrators and members of their households. They also appointed candidates of the Crown and of anyone else who could influence their decisions.[6] Wolsey just had more dignities and livings to give, and, moreover, did have this advantage over his episcopal colleagues, that he did not have to suffer from his own interference!

The main conclusion of this survey of Wolsey's patronage is the important part played by the king. There was nothing new in this royal interest in appointments: most of Henry's predecessors had shared it, but none more so apparently than Henry VII who, when in 1495 he moved Oliver King from Exeter to Bath and Wells, had secured a promise that all the important episcopal appointments in that see – and there were over fifty prebends – should be made by himself.[7] It may be that this was an ad hoc arrangement facilitated by the fact that King, as royal secretary, was close to his royal master, and if similar promises were extracted from other bishops no evidence of them has so far come to light. On the other hand, if there were, it

---

[1] LP,iv,4476.

[2] LP,iv,4521.

[3] LP,iv,4521.

[4] LP,iv,4562, 4605.

[5] LP,iv, 4546; Fasti,i,p.14.

[6] For Fisher complying with a royal request in 1523 see S. Thompson, 'Bishop in his diocese', p.73.

[7] J.A. Robinson, pp.5-8 for Henry VII's letter to Sir Reginald Bray dated 1501/2 in which the king gave an account of the promise. Sadly both Henry VII's and Edward IV's involvement with the Church has been inadequately treated by recent biographers.

would come as no surprise. It was Henry VII who began on any regular basis the practice, continued by his son, of appointing foreigners to English bishoprics. This was a means not only of securing the aid of people with some influence at the Roman Curia, but also of placing the bishopric under royal control, whether that control was exercised by a Richard Fox under Henry VII or a Wolsey under Henry VIII. It is also the case that Henry VII had pushed his leading minister's role in church affairs in the same way as his son was to do. John Morton was made archbishop of Canterbury in 1486; in the following year he secured a bull, *Quanta in Dei Ecclesia*, giving him powers to reform the exempt monasteries; and in 1493 he was made a cardinal. Of course, it was the papacy who formally bestowed both the bull and the cardinal's hat but, as with Wolsey's successes with the papacy, what was needed was royal support, and this Morton received.[1] When to all this is added the critical attitude taken by both kings towards the Church's defence of its 'liberties',[2] the broad continuity of policy adopted by father and son towards the English Church becomes apparent. And the direction was towards greater royal control – of which church patronage was one part. One of Wolsey's principal tasks was to ensure that the royal wishes in church matters were carried out, and as such he, amongst other things, performed the role of church patronage secretary.

It has seemed right to emphasize the Crown's involvement in the Church, partly because it has been too much overlooked, and partly because it provides one answer to the question why there was so little opposition to Wolsey's legatine powers. What has misled in the past has been the concentration on Wolsey to the exclusion of his chief source of power, Henry VIII. In fact, it was his close association with the king, rather than his legatine powers, that enabled him so easily to dominate the English Church, something that emerges clearly from a brief look at the fate of previous legates *a latere*, the most famous of whom was Henry Beaufort. Despite being a grandson of Edward III and probably the wealthiest man in England, both in 1417 and 1428 his appointment as legate was strongly resisted, on the first occasion by Henry V and Archbishop Chichele and on the second by Protector Gloucester and the royal Council.[3] When a hundred years later Leo X proposed sending Cardinal Bainbridge, archbishop of York but resident at Rome, to England as papal legate there had again been opposition, with this time Wolsey and Fox pointing out to the pope that it was not the practice of English kings to allow legates *a latere* to enter their territory.[4] The point about these episodes is that the initiative in sending the legate had not come from the king or royal government. But in 1518 it was different. Henry had wanted Wolsey to become papal legate, so that he could carry out not the pope's wishes, but his own.

What did Henry hope to obtain from his own papal legate? Certainly, not just a greater control over church patronage, because, as has been shown, though Wolsey's legatine powers probably did strengthen the king's hands in this matter, it was not by very much, if only because earlier kings had anyway exercised a considerable control. Still, there does seem to be a difference between Henry VII

---

[1] Harper-Bill, *JEH*, 29, a most important and not sufficiently well-known article.
[2] See pp.43 ff. above.
[3] McFarlane.
[4] *LP*, i, 2611.

having to extract a promise from one of his bishops to place all his episcopal patronage in his hands, and Henry VIII's assumption in 1528 that the archdeaconry of Oxford, theoretically in the gift of the bishop of Lincoln, was in the royal gift; and maybe Wolsey's legatine powers explain the difference. At any rate, when on 7 July 1528 Dr Bell wrote to Wolsey that 'his said highness commanded me to signify to your grace his pleasure and desire to your said grace by virtue of your legatine prerogative and prevention to confer to his chaplain, Mr Wilson, the vicarage of Thaxted',[1] there is just a hint that Henry believed that Wolsey was authorized to appoint anybody to anywhere.

However, the chief advantages of Wolsey's legatine powers to Henry were of a more general kind. In an earlier chapter it was argued that the early sixteenth century witnessed in England a jurisdictional conflict between Church and state, in which the first two Tudor monarchs had played an active part. Their intentions had not been to destroy the 'liberties' of the Church, nor, indeed, had they been looking for any 'break with Rome'. Instead they had been anxious to prune back 'liberties', but to recover ground which, during the fifteenth century, they felt the Crown had lost, and to ensure that where there was a clash of interests the Crown's interests would prevail. When in 1515 the Church had attempted to interpret its right to 'benefit of clergy' in the widest possible sense, perhaps in an effort to reverse the royal policy, a major battle had taken place. There had been no outright winner; neither side was ready for, or even wanted, a fight to the death, but it was the Church that had lost the argument. However, the fact that his archbishop of Canterbury had talked of Becket and of martyrdom can only have encouraged Henry to look for ways to secure a more compliant Church, and the way that he found was Wolsey and his legatine powers. The great advantage to the king of this arrangement was that since Wolsey's supremacy over the English Church derived in theory from the Church itself – that is, from the pope – it was difficult for the Church to challenge it. Indeed, they could only have done so by appealing to the king which, given his support for Wolsey's legatine powers, was not a course of action open to them. Thus, as long as Henry felt that he could trust Wolsey, the legatine powers were an ideal solution to the problem of securing a subservient Church; and it is notable that during the 1520s there was no more conflict between Church and state. That the stated purpose of legatine commissions was to facilitate the reform and correction of the Church raises the question of whether Henry had any real interest in such matters.[2] Given his sustained involvement in many aspects of the Church's life, which led him, amongst other things, to write a work of theology, the famous *Assertio Septem Sacramentorum*, the possibility that he did should not be completely discounted, even if positive evidence is hard to come by. In March 1525 it had been his intention to accompany Wolsey on his visitation of the London Greyfriars, but, as we have seen, in the end this did not take place – and this non-event is about all there is. However, when writing to Wolsey in January 1519, Richard Fox argued that there would be less difficulty in carrying through church reform because 'our most Christian king who had, I think, exhorted,

---

[1] St. P.i, p.311 (*LP*,iv,4476).
[2] *LP*,iii,600, a letter of Henry's to Leo X of 20 Jan. 1520 in which he acknowledged that reform was their purpose.

encouraged, and advised you to undertake the task, will lend his authority and help your godly desires'.[1] Of course, in associating the king with Wolsey and reform, an element of flattery was intended, but Fox does seem to have been making a genuine point as well. Moreover, the fact that virtually no evidence of Henry's interest in reform has survived is partly explained by his having no 'constitutional' part to play in its implementation; Henry and Wolsey could well have talked about it, but there would have been no resulting records. Perhaps this argument should not be pushed too far, but it does seem permissible to remark that if there was going to be church reform, Henry would have preferred it to be carried out under the aegis of his favourite minister rather than of his somewhat tiresome archbishop of Canterbury – all of which brings one back to the central question of Wolsey's intentions towards the Church.

By stressing Henry's involvement in church matters, and his responsibility for securing Wolsey's legatine powers, it is possible to reject much of the more extreme criticism of Wolsey's churchmanship. Far from being the ego-trip that it is frequently portrayed as, in which the attraction of the clothes and the crosses were the dominant feature, it should be seen as yet another aspect of his work as leading royal servant. One feature of that work was clerical taxation. Kings had always seen the Church as a possible source of revenue, and the first two Tudors were no exception. The whole question of clerical taxation is a complicated one best left to the experts; and even they find it hard to come up with very precise figures.[2] What does emerge is that Wolsey made some innovations – though, as in so many other areas, he had been partially anticipated by Archbishop Morton. It was Morton who, for the so-called *magnum subsidium* of 1489, had started to overhaul the method of assessment and collection which had remained essentially unaltered since the *taxatio ecclesiastica* of 1291.[3] In 1522 Wolsey continued Morton's work when he instructed the commissioners for the 'general proscription' – an enquiry into England's military potential – to discover 'the values of all spiritual dignities and benefices . . . in tithes, portions, annuities, and oblations'.[4] Their findings provided the basis for the clerical subsidy voted by convocation in the following year.

There were other features of this subsidy which, if not entirely new, were at least unusual. It was a graduated tax which included at the lower end a large number of people who, under previous clerical tenths, would have been exempt from payment; and neither were curates any longer exempt. Dispensing these exemptions contributed to the most novel feature of the 1523 subsidy, its size. The clergy were being asked to provide, according to Wolsey, £120,000, in five annual portions of £24,000; his estimate for the clerical loan of the previous year had been £60,000.[5] On top of all this, there was the Amicable Grant of 1525, for which the clergy were supposed to contribute a sum equivalent to one-third of their income. Comparisons with previous payments by the clergy are hard to make, given in particular the uncertainty about how much of the required amount was actually collected – and

[1] Richard Fox, p.116 (*LP*,iii,1122).
[2] The most useful treatment is M.J. Kelly, 'Canterbury jurisdiction', pp. 292-315, but see also Salter; Scarisbrick, *JEH*, 12.
[3] Harper-Bill, *JEH*, 29, pp.2-4.
[4] Goring, *EHR*, lxxxvi, p.693.
[5] *LP*,iv,2483 (3), but in the end only £56,252 0s. 8d. may have been paid; see *LP*,iv, app.37.

there were indeed difficulties in collecting the 1523 subsidy.[1] What is certain is that the resident papal legate was asking the clergy to contribute annually in taxation to the king about half as much again as they had been accustomed to pay.[2] As in the case of patronage, it is difficult to assess just how far Wolsey's new powers contributed to this achievement, and, as was indicated earlier, it is not even certain that in 1523 Wolsey had been able to make use of a legatine convocation to persuade the clergy to pay. However, insofar as the legatine powers did increase the king's minister's authority over the Church, they may have made it marginally easier for large financial demands to be made.

If Wolsey as legate was to act effectively on the king's behalf, it was obviously necessary for him to assert his legatine authority. The ways in which he did this have already been described, but given the emphasis in this account on the royal involvement, a further point emerges. In the traditional picture of Wolsey's churchmanship, his insistence on his legatine rights had a largely financial motivation. And those rights did indeed bring financial gain. As was mentioned earlier, one result of his composition with the bishops was that he secured a third of their annual revenues from spiritualities. A third of the £3,450 arrived at in the 1535 Valor Ecclesiasticus produces a figure of £1,150, and from this must be deducted the spiritualities of the sees that Wolsey himself held – for most of the relevant period York and Durham – and also those of Canterbury, which appear to have been left untouched by Wolsey's composition with the archbishop. This gives us an annual income from this source of about £800. From the joint-prerogative court he was receiving just over £300 a year, and there would also have been revenue from the proving of wills reserved for his sole legatine jurisdiction. There are no figures for this, nor indeed for the revenues derived from his legatine court of audience, but he was receiving about £200 a year from the granting of dispensations and other licences. Legatine visitations of monastic and collegiate institutions in the dioceses of Coventry and Lichfield, Lincoln, Salisbury and Worcester in 1524-5 resulted in about £440, and similar visitations in and around London about £200.[3] Another source of revenue derived from his right to conduct *sede vacante* visitations, but only in the case of Winchester in 1528, on the death of Fox and before his own accession, does he seem to have asserted the right, and even then he may have arrived at some financial compromise with Warham who, as archbishop of Canterbury, had a better established right to conduct such a visitation.[4]

It will be obvious from the many uncertainties surrounding these figures that only a most impressionistic indication of the amount Wolsey derived from his legatine powers can be given. In February 1524 he himself estimated that 'all the profits that may rise of my legation, . . . will not be worth one thousand ducats (£300) by the year, whatsoever report may be made to his Holiness to the contrary by such as might suppose and think great revenues might grow'.[5] One thing, at

---

[1] Many of the bishops' registers bear witness to this but see especially Fisher's (KAO DR c/R7/fo. 113).

[2] Using Kelly's figures, the amount paid between 1490 and 1520 was £205,000, or £6,800 a year. In the 1520s it was £8,000 a year this little less than for 1445-53 when it was £8,250; see Griffiths, *Henry VI*, p.384.

[3] *LP*,iv,964.

[4] M.J. Kelly, 'Canterbury jurisdiction', p.194; *Registrum Thome Wolsey*, p.xxvi.

least, that this survey of his legatine revenues shows is that Wolsey was here being very economical with the truth, because something approaching £1,500 would be nearer the mark.[1] Does such a figure confirm the view that 'great revenues' would ensue? The answer has to be yes, since few people in Tudor England had an income of more than this amount – but with one important qualification. Such a figure was a great deal of money for almost everyone but Wolsey himself. After 1526 he was receiving about £7,500 a year from his French pension alone, while Thomas Winter's income, which was effectively his own, was alleged to be £2,700. Then there were the revenues from his sees of York and Durham, amounting to nearly £5,000, about £2,000 from St Albans, and the lord chancellorship brought him at least £2,000 – and these are just the more obvious sources of revenue. In 1519 the Venetian ambassador had estimated Wolsey's income at about £9,500, while in 1531 a successor reported that it had been about £35,000 – but this figure left out of the reckoning his French pension.[2] In such a context, a legatine income of about £1,500, at the most 8 per cent of his total income, cannot explain Wolsey's motivation for wanting to become legate. Moreover, by concentrating on the financial aspects, one can too easily ignore the fact that his legatine authority could most easily and effectively be expressed in terms of jurisdiction, and it was from jurisdiction that revenue derived.[3] Wolsey could only effectively assert his legatine powers by insisting on his jurisdictional rights, because it was only they which gave reality to his theoretical claim. If he was successful, money would inevitably accrue. It may be going too far to see the money as merely a symbol, but to argue thus is nearer the truth than to see it as an end in itself – especially when a new claim to authority is being asserted, which is precisely what Wolsey was doing.

It is not, therefore, the love of money or of glory that provides the key to Wolsey's churchmanship, but rather the desire to further his master's interests: this at least has been the argument so far. Now the task is to try to discover what such a desire entailed and, if possible, to arrive at some assessment of his personal attitude towards religion. It is, for instance, most unlikely that Wolsey ever had a religious vocation. As mentioned earlier,[4] for a person of his social standing, with any aptitude for learning, university followed by the Church provided the obvious and well-tried route not only to financial success but to a more interesting life. There are similar if more varied routes today, but then as now, a passionate devotion to the steps along the way – to learning while at university or to the mechanics of the law while one is being articled – is not required, and indeed is probably unusual. Similarly for Wolsey, university and Church were likely to have been the means to an end – which is not to say that he would have had any emotional or intellectual difficulties in accepting the means. And the point has been made before that what is interesting about Wolsey is his decision not to read for the canon or civil law, courses which the brightest and most ambitious students of his day would have more

---

[5] St.P,vi, p.257 (LP,iv,115).

[1] In Wolsey's defence it should be stressed that the amount would vary considerably, depending especially on whether any large-scale visitations had taken place.

[2] Ven.Cal.,iv, p.600. These figures are mainly taken from A.F.Pollard, pp.320-5.

[3] See Southern, pp.111 ff., 164 for perceptive comments on this most important general point.

[4] See pp.25-6 above.

naturally chosen.[1] Perhaps he was a slow developer, or perhaps, as will be suggested shortly, he did have a genuine interest in academic study? The great sadness for his biographer is the dearth of evidence. What, however, need not be accepted is the view that sees all career churchmen as time-servers, men with no sincerity in their religious beliefs. For whatever their youthful attitudes, it would have been hard for people in their position not to develop an attachment and loyalty to the institution that had done so much for them. Of course, its size and diversity may not have helped in this respect. On the other hand, the Church did have a great tradition which, combined with the ceremonial and sacramental dimension, must have made its influence very hard to resist – and this would have been as true for Wolsey as anyone else. Another attempt will be made later to discover more about Wolsey's personal attitude to religion. The point being made here is simply this: even if Wolsey saw his major role as that of royal servant, it does not exclude the possibility that he had, if no vocation, at least a genuine interest in the affairs of the Church. And whether he did or not, he could never escape from the fact that he was a churchman, and this in itself may be of some importance.

What that importance is was suggested in the chapter on the Hunne and Standish affairs, where it was argued that Wolsey, while essentially working in the king's interest, was also anxious to minimize the conflict between Church and state; and that this involved keeping open the channels of communication with the clerical party and looking at all times for compromise. Since such a posture made political sense, it does not necessarily tell us very much about his religious beliefs, but it may serve to reiterate the point that neither Church nor state was anxious for a fight to the death. So the ambiguities in his position, which Wolsey had expressed to Henry on bended knee in 1515 – that though he owed everything to his king, he had also, along with all the bishops, taken an oath of loyalty to the pope – need not and, once the dust of 1515 had settled, did not, create for him a major problem. Wolsey as royal servant was not expected to lead an all-out attack on the Church and in fact the most likely effect of Wolsey's increasing domination of the Church would be in the opposite direction. With his own man in charge, Henry could relax.

From the bishops' point of view, too, there were some advantages in Wolsey's legatine ascendancy. Of course, they were shrewd enough to appreciate that Wolsey was first and foremost the king's man as, indeed, in many respects they were. What they wanted was protection from the Crown lawyers, from fellow clergy such as Veysey and Franciscans such as Standish, who took the Crown's side in any jurisdictional conflict; and this they hoped someone with Wolsey's influence with the king could achieve. Here Fox's letter to Wolsey in January 1519 is again helpful, for after he had stressed the importance of the king's support in carrying out reform, he went on:

> As far as I can see this reformation of the clergy and religions will so abate the calumnies of the laity, so advance the honour of the clergy, and so reconcile our sovereign lord the king and his nobility to them and be the most acceptable of all sacrifices to God, that I intend to devote to its furtherance the few remaining years of my life.[2]

[1] Storey, BP, 16, pp.15-7, qualified in R.G. Davies, pp.55-64.
[2] Richard Fox, p.116 (LP, iii, 1122).

One thing that emerges from this passage – as from the position he took up in the Standish affair[1] – is that, despite having been a career churchman and royal servant *par excellence*, he had still retained, or perhaps had developed, a strong attachment to the Church. But what matters here is that he clearly perceived that what Wolsey was about to do had some relevance to the current conflict between Church and state and, by implication at any rate, that he saw Wolsey as being on the Church's side. It is not known whether other bishops took a similar view, but it is conceivable that they did. And if so, this would provide a further explanation of why they did not oppose Wolsey's legatine authority with the vigour that might have been expected. Perhaps even Nix took the point in the end; he of all the bishops had suffered most from royal interference, with his officials being systematically accused of praemunire by Henry VII's attorney-generals. In attempting to combat this interference he had looked to Warham for support, but it does not look as if his support was very effective. This did not prevent Nix from backing Warham in early 1519, when they had both tried to resist Wolsey's legatine authority. However, what may have in the end helped both men to accept it was the realization that it might offer some protection to what they saw as a beleaguered Church.

But whatever the reasons for supporting legatine reform, there was one thing that Richard Fox at least was in no doubt about, and that was that serious reform was intended. Indeed, in a moving passage that surely exceeds the requirements of decorum, Fox described his reaction to Wolsey's summoning of a legatine council on the subject:

> This day I have truly longed for, even as Simeon in the Gospel desired to see the Messiah, the expected of men. And in reading your grace's letter I see before me a more entire and whole reformation of the ecclesiastical hierarchy of the English people than I could have expected, or ever hoped to see completed, or even so much attempted in this age.[2]

Fox's words may have been a little excessive, but they do convey a genuine excitement about Wolsey's intentions, which, it has to be said, most historians have not shared. The bare bones of what Wolsey achieved have already been outlined: the new legatine constitutions for the secular clergy and new statutes for the Benedictine and Augustinian orders, along with some kind of legatine supervision over the remaining ones. The time has now come to try to assess the quality of these reforms. New legislation and new machinery are all very well, but did anything change for the better as a result of their introduction?

It will come as no surprise if it is admitted from the start that there are great difficulties in answering this question. These have not only to do with limitations of the evidence, but perhaps even more so with the criteria to use for judging success. To take one point about evidence: the question was raised earlier whether the legatine constitutions were widely published. The answer given was that probably they were, although only about half a dozen references to them have survived. Must one therefore conclude that they made no impact? In the end that is a judgment that everyone must make for themselves, but what must be borne in mind is that

[1] See p.52 above.
[2] Richard Fox, pp.114-15 (*LP*,iii,1122).

immediately after his fall, Wolsey's legatine constitutions could only have been an embarrassment to the Church, and for this reason one would not expect to find any reference made to them in the discussions about reform in the early 1530s.[1] After the 'break with Rome' they would have become an irrelevance. It would also be surprising to find references to them, once they had been locally published, in the diocesan archives. What a bishop and his officials required records for were particular judicial and administrative actions, and the connection between these and any set of constitutions would, in most cases, be too remote to deserve a mention. Since the lack of documentary references cannot, therefore, be taken as a measure of their success or failure the problem – and it is probably insoluble – is to find another yardstick. The verdict of the considerable amount of recent work on the activities of the early Tudor bishops and their administrations has been favourable, and certainly not one that lends support to the common notion of a Church suffering from a terminal illness.[2] There were regular visitations of both parishes and monastic institutions, effective church courts, some efforts to supervise the suitability of candidates for ordination, and considerable worries about heresy – though mostly of a Lollard rather than a Lutheran variety. And a feature of the 1520s that has been particularly commented upon is the considerable degree of involvement in the health of their diocese shown by a majority of the bishops. Fisher at Rochester, Fox at Winchester, Longland at Lincoln, Nix at Norwich, Sherborne at Chichester, Veysey at Exeter, Warham at Canterbury and West at Ely, all in their differing ways were much concerned with what went on in their dioceses, and even someone like Blythe of Coventry and Lichfield, not an obvious choice as a distinguished bishop, is known to have preached three visitation sermons and in 1511-12 was actively involved in one of the largest heresy trials to have taken place in England.[3] How far the publication of Wolsey's legatine constitutions helped them in the successful administration of their dioceses, it is impossible to say. Most of them had been involved in drawing them up, and if the evidence of Fisher's contribution to the legatine council of 1519 can be accepted, they had approached their task with a proper seriousness. At the very least the new constitutions were a statement of intent, and in this respect may have helped to create a climate in which reform and correction could more easily be carried out.

All this is very speculative. For positive evidence of Wolsey's reforming intentions one has to turn to the monastic institutions. These, it will be remembered, had been the particular concern of the legatine commission of August 1518, the first that Wolsey had secured after throwing off any pretence of intending to further the pope's plans for a crusade. And insofar as many of these institutions were exempt from episcopal control, they offered scope for a resident legate to make a real contribution. In addition, both the election and deprivation of the heads of monasteries and visitations were administrative and judicial actions whose

---

[1] It is slightly surprising that both in his thesis and published article Kelly completely ignored the legatine constitutions when discussing those of 1532, an indication, perhaps, of just how strong the view is that the English Church was violently hostile to all that Wolsey had done.

[2] The best starting point for this recent work is O'Day and Heal, pp.13-29, but see also S. Thompson, 'English and Welsh bishops'.

[3] *Visitations, c.1515-1525*, p.xiv; Fines, JEH, 14, pp.160-74.

proceedings were recorded; and some of the resulting documents have survived. Admittedly, Wolsey's involvement in the choice of monastic heads had very little to do with his legatine powers. Many monastic institutions had long been entitled to 'compromit' – that is, to entrust the choice of a new head to whomsoever they pleased. Moreover, of the three ways of choosing a new head, that of 'compromise' seems to have been every bit as common as the other two: 'acclamation', or by way of the Holy Spirit, in which a new head was unanimously chosen by the chapter, and 'scrutiny', in which what would now be considered a proper election took place. Pollard's passionate concern for democratic procedures led him to denounce the despotism of Wolsey's intervention in monastic elections, but his onslaught was unfair and misleading.[1] The medieval and early modern world did not share Pollard's concerns, and monastic institutions were no exception. What they were ideally looking for was unanimity in the choice of a new head. Not only was election by 'scrutiny' an admission that this did not exist, but it was probably the best way of ensuring that none would exist. Furthermore, the virtues of leaving the election to members of a usually very small, inward-looking and perhaps complacent body of men do not seem quite so self-evident as Pollard considered them to be.

The real problem of interpretation should have nothing to do with the virtues of democracy as against despotism, but with whether or not Wolsey deliberately set out to use a recognized procedure by which to appoint monastic heads in order to ensure that men of high calibre were chosen. I have discovered twenty occasions, after he became legate, on which Wolsey was closely involved in a monastic election, and on all but two of these the election appears to have been actually compromitted to him.[2] The number is quite large, but until much more work is done on monastic elections in the decades immediately preceding Wolsey's ascendancy, it would be dangerous to attach too much importance to numbers alone. As bishop, at various times, of four sees, and in virtual control of two more, a large number of elections would have been compromitted to Wolsey, whatever his intentions. What we really need to know is all the circumstances surrounding the elections, because only then would it be possible to make a qualitative judgment about the people Wolsey was appointing and arrive at some conclusion about his intentions. As it is, one has to make do with rather fragmentary evidence, just enough to be worth some attention, but not such as to allow any definite conclusion to be reached.

Glastonbury Abbey was one of the oldest and wealthiest monasteries in the country. It was also one of the select number of Benedictine houses which were exempt from episcopal control. On 20 January 1525 its distinguished abbot, Richard Bere, died. Three weeks later the chapter chose William Benet, an auditor of Wolsey's legatine court of audience, as director of the election for a new abbot, and then proceeded to compromit the choice to Wolsey, though with the proviso that

[1] A.F. Pollard, pp.200-4.
[2] The 20 occasions in alphabetical order: Athelney (1526); Barlinch (1524); Bristol, St.Augustine's (1525); Bruerne (1529); Butley (1529); Chester (1524, 1527); Fountains (1526); Glastonbury (1525); Haltenprice (1528); Milton (1525); Newcastle (1523); Pershore (1526); Peterborough (1528); Rievaulx (1529); Selby (1526); Taunton (1523); Wherwell (1529); Wigmore (1518); Wilton (1528). Newcastle, Wherwell and Wilton were Benedictine nunneries.

the person chosen should be a member of their house.[1] Although such internal appointments were frequently desired by monastic institutions, they were not necessarily in their best interests, especially if the institution was a small one with few to choose from, or if the religious life of the community was in a bad way. Neither of these things was true of Glastonbury in 1525, and Wolsey, at least, thought that in choosing Richard Whiting from amongst them he had appointed 'an upright and religious monk, a provident and discreet man, and a priest commendable for his life, virtues, and learning'; and moreover, someone who would protect the laws and liberties of the monastery.[2] And however difficult it may be to interpret the causes of Whiting's eventual 'martyrdom' in 1539, there is nothing at all to suggest that Wolsey's choice was not a good one.[3] How far Glastonbury had freely delivered up their choice to Wolsey is impossible to determine. The choice of Benet as director of the election might suggest some pressure from above, especially since he played the same role at the priory of Taunton in 1523 and of Barlinch in 1524, both houses, like Glastonbury, in the diocese of Bath and Wells.[4] So perhaps, although not all elections in the diocese were compromitted to Wolsey, Benet had some watching brief from Wolsey over monastic elections in the diocese.

The elections that took place at St Augustine's, Bristol, in 1515 and 1525, are interesting if only because they help to modify Pollard's picture of decorous democracy being blown away by Wolsey's despotic tendencies. In the course of the first election, Richard Fox informed Wolsey, not as yet either cardinal or legate, of 'the inordinate, heady, and unreligious dealings of the canons of St Augustine's besides Bristol'. Because of 'the evil example that may come thereof', he asked Wolsey to intervene, offering various suggestions about how this could best be done.[5] It is not known whether Wolsey acted on his advice, only that a Robert Eliot became the new abbot. When in 1525 Eliot died, the ensuing election resulted in just the same kind of 'unreligious dealings' as the previous one. According to Thomas Hannibal, the absentee bishop of Worcester's vicar-general,[6] dissension amongst the canons had reached such a pitch and 'the laity were no less audacious', that he had scarcely dared to enter the chapter 'for fear of the assemblage of retainers and others'. However, in the end he persuaded the canons to compromit the election to Wolsey, together with deans of the Chapel Royal and of Canterbury, and subsequently a William Burton was chosen.[7] It is clear from Hannibal's letter to Wolsey that Wolsey had been anxious to intervene in St Augustine's election, and the reason why is also clear: he wished to ensure that amongst all the factions jockeying for power within the monastery, activities in which important laymen were closely involved, the well-being of the abbey was not completely lost to view. There was much more to monastic elections than a few saintly men sitting down to

[1] The formal records of the election are set out in *Registers of Thomas Wolsey, John Clerke, etc.*, pp.84-8; for a detailed account see Gasquet, *Last Abbot of Glastonbury*, pp.17-23.

[2] Domerham,i,pp.c-ci (*LP*,iv, app.22).

[3] Knowles, *Religious Orders*, iii, pp.483-91; Paul, *BIHR*, xxxiii, pp.115-18.

[4] *Registers of Thomas Wolsey, John Clerke, etc.*, pp.76-9.

[5] Richard Fox, pp.79-80 (*LP*,ii,730); see also *LP*,ii,904, 906, 990.

[6] Jerome de Ghinucci from 1523-1535. St Augustine's was in the diocese of Worcester and subject to its bishop's jurisdiction.

[7] *LP*,iv,1544 for Hannibal's letter, dated 3 Aug. 1525, but see also *LP*,iv,1816, 1828.

choose from amongst themselves the most saintly, something that needs to be borne in mind when considering Wolsey's interference.

That said, it has to be admitted that amongst the elections that Wolsey is known to have had a hand in, St Augustine's is exceptional insofar as it is possible to demonstrate that there was a need for his interference. What can be shown in at least some of the other elections is that he was anxious to ensure a good appointment. This is true of Fountains in 1526, after the death of the eminent Marmaduke Huby, who had been not only abbot but for many years an abbot-commissary of the Cistercian order.[1] Probably the election of a new abbot was not formally compromitted to Wolsey, and if it had been it would have been unusual, for it was not the practice of the Cistercians, or indeed of any order except the Augustinians and Benedictines to do so. However, the involvement in the election of Brian Higden, the resident dean of York and one of Wolsey's most active ecclesiastical administrators – an involvement which was to be repeated at Rievaulx in 1529 at an election that was said to have been submitted to Wolsey[2] – does raise the suspicion that past forms were concealing new ways. This suspicion becomes a certainty when in September 1526 we find Higden and his fellow supervisors of the election, the abbots of Rievaulx and Roche, replying to a request from Wolsey for a full report on the abbot-elect before he confirmed his appointment.[3] Here is proof that Wolsey's confirmation was not a mere formality, and that he was concerned to appoint a good abbot. What remains uncertain is why his confirmation was required. As a Cistercian abbey, Fountains was exempt from episcopal jurisdiction so that the fact that it was in the diocese of York is no explanation, though it no doubt does explain Wolsey's interest. What gave him his legal standing in the matter must have been his legatine powers.

There is other evidence that Wolsey was concerned to see good appointments made. In 1526 the dean of York advised him to appoint as abbot of Selby someone from within the monastery: as there were four or more able candidates, he felt that the election of a stranger would only add an unnecessary complication.[4] Wolsey's reaction is not known, but what is of interest is the tone of the letter. It shows someone with a genuine concern for the interests of the abbey, that he assumed was shared by the recipient of his advice, Wolsey – and it does look as if Wolsey went ahead and made an internal appointment.[5] What also emerges from the dean's letter is that he himself had been to Selby and that it was at his suggestion that the election had been compromitted to Wolsey – evidence, perhaps, of a policy of getting monasteries to do this, at least in the diocese of York.

Further evidence for Wolsey's concern to make good appointments survives for elections to the famous Cistercian abbey of Rievaulx,[6] the Augustinian house of Haltenprice and St Bartholmew's nunnery, Newcastle,[7] but since, like Fountains

---

[1] Knowles, *Religious Orders*, iii, pp.35-7.
[2] *LP*,iv,5445.
[3] *LP*,iv, app.85.
[4] *LP*,iv, app.73.
[5] *LP*,iv,2083, 2277, 2412. The new abbot was called Robert Selby.
[6] *Inter alia Fountains*, pp.252 ff. My belief is that Elton's interpretation of this election and subsequent events there (Elton, *JEH*, 7) is seriously misleading but space has not allowed me to develop my criticisms.

and Selby, they were in dioceses of which Wolsey was bishop – Durham and York – they cannot provide compelling evidence for a national policy of interfering in monastic elections. Moreover, even as regards those elections in the diocese of Bath and Wells with which Wolsey was involved, it could be argued that there was a personal connection. He had, after all, been bishop there from 1518 to early 1523, and it has been shown already that his successor, John Clerk, was close to him. During the period in which the monastic elections there were compromitted to Wolsey, from September 1523 to March 1525, Clerk was abroad on a mission to Rome, so Wolsey's involvement is not altogether surprising. And, as was mentioned earlier, there were special circumstances surrounding the elections at St Augustine's, Bristol, for not only were they unusually contentious, but the abbey was in the diocese of Worcester, and its bishops were, during this period, absentee Italians.

As regards the election in January 1528 of a new prior of Butley, an Augustinian house in the diocese of Norwich, there appear to be no special reasons for Wolsey's involvement. According to Bishop Nix, the canons were just about to choose Sir Thomas Sudborne as their new prior, 'per viam Spiritus Sancti', when Wolsey's commissaries intervened, threatening to sequester all the goods of the house if they proceeded.[1] Not surprisingly, the priory decided to compromit the election to Wolsey, only for him to choose Sir Thomas Sudborne.[2] In passing, it is worth mentioning, as a reminder that Wolsey was by no means the first person to intervene in monastic elections, that in 1509 Bishop Nix had secured the election to Butley of a prior who had not been the canons' first choice.[3] What may have been new, though, is the scale and scope of Wolsey's interventions. In the case of Butley, it does look as if he was merely concerned to make a point. There was nothing seriously wrong with the religious life of Butley. The canons appear to have made a good choice. The only reason for Wolsey's action was that he wanted to have a say in monastic elections.

The trouble with the Butley election is that it is the only one in which the evidence convincingly points to such a conclusion; and one example does not seem quite enough to conclude that Wolsey sought to control all elections, especially when so many were not compromitted to him. For instance, of the five that took place in the diocese of Winchester from the beginning of 1523 to the death of Richard Fox in October 1528, none were.[4] The same is true throughout the 1520s of Rochester. The Butley case may merely be further evidence of the unhappy relationship between Wolsey and Nix, which made Wolsey take every opportunity to interfere in the affairs of the diocese of Norwich. On the other hand, the date of the Butley election may be of some significance. By January 1528 Wolsey could have felt sufficiently in control of the English Church to risk intervention of this kind. In a strong position in his own diocese or in those dioceses where there were absentee bishops, it was easy enough for him to get elections compromitted to him there; less

---

[7] LP,iv,3878 for Haltenprice; LP,iii,3171, 3189, 3193 for St Bartholomew's.

[1] LP,iv, app.230.
[2] Butley Priory, pp.55-7.
[3] Ibid, p.8.
[4] Registrum Thomas Wolsey, pp.xix ff.

easy where there was an active and influential bishop such as Fox at Winchester or Fisher at Rochester. Prudence and tact, both of which qualities Wolsey could use when necessary, may explain why he did not interfere in their dioceses. This need not mean that he would not have liked to have intervened more generally, and was not by the late 1520s planning to do so more often.

The suggestion here is that it is this view which comes nearest to the truth, and the main reason for thinking this is the real concern that Wolsey appears to have shown in monastic elections. Never mind that there were particular reasons for his interest that were not all directly related to the good health of the houses involved. The important point is that his concern would have encouraged him to seek greater control, and here the outstanding example is the election in 1528 of a new abbess of Wilton.[1] Wilton, in the diocese of Salisbury, with an absentee bishop (since late in 1524) in Campeggio, was effectively run on Wolsey's behalf by Thomas Benet, the vicar-general, and it is this which probably explains Wolsey's initial involvement with the election of the new abbess. Thus, unlike Butley, the Wilton election does not bear directly on the question of the intended scope of Wolsey's interference in such matters. What is remarkable about Wilton is the evidence it provides of his determination to appoint the best candidate, because here the opposition to his choice was supported by none other than Henry himself. Wolsey and, at least according to Thomas Benet, the majority of the nuns favoured Dame Isabel Jordan, already prioress of the house, and, again according to Benet, reported to be 'ancient, wise, and discreet'.[2] A minority of the nuns supported Dame Eleanor Carey, sister to William Carey, a gentleman of the privy chamber and in close attendance on the king. Even more important than his position was the fact that he was married to Mary Boleyn, a former mistress of the king and sister to the woman who, if she could not be called the king's current mistress, was the person with whom he was passionately in love. Thus Eleanor had, from outside the abbey, the most influential support possible in Anne Boleyn, and very quickly the king himself. She may even have had Wolsey's support until he got to know more about the qualifications and qualities of the two candidates,[3] and therein lay Dame Eleanor's Achilles' heel. Under cross-examination by Wolsey himself, she confessed that she had had two children by two different priests, and had recently been kept by a servant of the late Lord Broke. On the other hand, accusations of incontinence against Dame Isabel turned out to be at least unproven and, as even Henry admitted to Anne, she was anyway 'so old that of many years she could not be as she was named'.[4]

To do Henry justice, once he had learnt of Dame Eleanor's misdemeanour, he withdrew his support. However, so as to lessen the blow to his loved one and her friends and relatives, he decided that Dame Isabel should not be made abbess but 'rather some other good and well disposed woman'.[5] This decision Wolsey proceeded to ignore, pretending that he knew nothing about it.[6] The result was a royal rebuke 'written with the hand of him that is and shall be your loving

[1] Knowles, *BIHR*, xxxi for the best account of this.
[2] *LP*,iv,4197.
[3] *LP*,iv,4408.
[4] *LP*,iv,4477 an undated letter of Henry's to Anne Boleyn.
[5] *LP*,iv,4477.

sovereign'. If, as these words indicate, the tone of Henry's letter was not too unfriendly, there was not the slightest doubt of his displeasure, not only at Wolsey's refusal to comply with his wishes but at his pretence that he had known nothing of them: 'My lord, it is a double offence both to do ill, and colour it too, but with men that have wit, it cannot be accepted so, wherefore good my lord use no more that way with me for there is no man living that more hateth it.' And to underline his displeasure, Henry took the opportunity, though 'upon no other ground, but for the wealth of your soul and mine', to draw Wolsey's attention to the many criticisms he was hearing about money being wrongfully exacted from monastic institutions to pay for the setting up and financing of Cardinal College.[1] However, in the same letter Henry conceded that Dame Isabel would become the next abbess, although the confirmation of her election did not take place until four months later, on 13 November 1528.[2] A discussion of those aspects of this important letter that bear on Henry's relationship with 'his best beloved servant and friend', must be deferred until a later chapter. For the moment, what is important is the light it sheds on Wolsey's attitude to the religious orders and to reform.

In thwarting the wishes of the king and of Anne Boleyn and her friends, Wolsey obviously took a risk. One might argue that the risk was easily calculated, in that he was still sufficiently confident of his influence with Henry to believe that he could happily survive his master's temporary displeasure. One might even argue that it was deliberately calculated to thwart the growing Boleyn circle,[3] though if so, it was an unusually stupid miscalculation on his part, given that his major task at this time was to secure an annulment of Henry's first marriage so as to enable him to marry Anne. In fact, neither line of argument is as convincing as the position that Wolsey himself appears to have taken up in letters to Henry and his acting secretaries.[4] Put simply, Wolsey's view was not only that Dame Isabel was a better candidate than Dame Eleanor, but that she happened to be the right person for the necessary task of 'reforming' the nunnery of Wilton. Things had obviously become a little lax during the forty-odd years of the previous abbess's rule. Moreover, in a nunnery noted for its wealth and for the high birth of its inmates, too much laxity, especially as regards the movement of the nuns in and out of the house, was always likely to be a danger. At any rate, it was stricter enclosure that Wolsey wanted from the new abbess and, moreover, he instructed Thomas Benet to go to Wilton to see that it was enforced. This proved easier said than done, for despite Benet's actual residence there for some time and despite putting three or four of the leading resisters 'in ward' and closing up 'curtains, doors and ways', the opposition to reform continued, so that Benet was forced to pin all his hopes on a visit of the attorney-general, Richard Lister, who had promised to help Wolsey in this matter.[5] The evidence is,

---

[6] St.P,i, p.314 (LP,iv,4488), a letter to Wolsey in which Henry's displeasure at his decison to go ahead with the election of Dame Isabel is reported to him.

---

[1] LP,iv,4488.
[2] LP,iv,4950.
[3] So presented in D.R.Starkey, Henry VIII, pp.97-8, but not by that other great believer in faction, Ives, for whose views see Anne Boleyn, pp.121-2.
[4] These have to be surmised from the replies to them; see LP,iv,4488, 4507.
[5] LP,iv,4950 (St.P,i, p.314, n.1 for a full transcript).

therefore, quite convincing that Wolsey stuck by Dame Isabel because he considered that her appointment was in the best interests of Wilton – and it should be said that he came to this conclusion after having personally examined all the inmates.[1] Moreover, he may have gone some way to convincing Henry of the wisdom of his decision. Henry did not, of course, admit this openly, but he did admit that he had been informed that 'her age, personage, and manner' showed her to be a person of some weight, which he prayed 'God it be so indeed seeing that she is preferred to that room'.[2] It was all very grudging, but there is just a hint that he realized that in supporting an obviously unsuitable candidate he had made a bit of a fool of himself; and that even if he had the best possible excuse for his error – his devotion to Anne – nevertheless it was now time for Wolsey to get on with the job of looking after the well-being of the nunnery of Wilton.

All in all, 'the matter of Wilton' is the best example of Wolsey's genuine concern for the health of the religious orders, even if some problems of interpretation remain. It is, for instance, a little surprising, given his intention of enforcing enclosure at Wilton, that only eighteen months previously Wolsey had been chiding Bishop Fox for being too strict with the nuns in his diocese over just this issue.[3] Presumably, the degree of inconsistency in Wolsey's attitude on these two occasions depends to a great extent on how strict was strict: and the impression is that in 1528 Wilton was in a particularly bad way and thus in need of treatment which in other circumstances might have been too severe. Nevertheless, a worry remains. It may also have been the case – though it is not a view accepted here – that Wolsey's zeal for reform may have been encouraged by the Boleyn opposition to his choice. And it is certainly not the case that Wolsey usually resisted royal intervention in church appointments, but then there was rarely any obvious clash between the king's wishes and the good of the Church. In the case of Wilton there was, and it is striking that on this occasion he chose the Church.

Arguably, Wolsey's involvement in the deposition or resignation of the heads of religious houses offers a better way of assessing his genuine concern for their well-being than his involvement in appointments, where it has been difficult to arrive at any convincing assessment of the quality of the people chosen. At least with an outgoing head, there is almost always some specific evidence of unsatisfactory conduct, even if the validity of the evidence is hard to confirm.

But before looking at particular cases, the general point needs to be made that it was extremely difficult to remove anyone from the headship of a religious house. It could only be done by a judicial process in which the case against the incumbent would have to be proved, and this was a hard and costly process.[4] Wolsey's legatine commission in this respect made very little difference. It is true that his and Campeggio's joint commission to visit and reform the religious orders gave them the power to depose delinquent abbots and priors, but only if their houses' income was under 200 ducats[5] – that is, roughly £45 a year. This meant that as regards about 70

[1] *LP*,iv,4477, this Henry's report to Anne.
[2] Fiddes, *Collections*, p.174 (*LP*,iv,4507).
[3] Richard Fox, pp.150-1 (*LP*,iv,3815).
[4] Knowles, *Religious Orders*, ii, p.252, but I confess to having had great difficulty in finding any very satisfactory secondary reading on this subject, and I just hope that my treatment is not misleading.

per cent of all monastic houses Wolsey had no special powers, and that any deposition could only take place by the due process of canon law. The fact, therefore, that, rather than dismissing him outright, Wolsey was usually to be found attempting to negotiate the resignation of an unsatisfactory abbot or prior, should not be taken by itself for evidence of a lack of serious intent. Even though these negotiations usually resulted in the equivalent of the present-day golden handshake, in the form of a pension and somewhere to live, this was the most effective and, in most cases, the only way of removing such a person.

There is evidence of Wolsey having been closely involved in negotiations to secure the removal of eight heads of religious houses,[1] and there is the suspicion that he was involved in at least two other attempts.[2] Of the six, there is most evidence about the resignations of John Birchenshawe, abbot of St Werburg's, Chester, in 1524, and Edmund Kirton, abbot of Peterborough, in 1528. Both appear to have been powerful personalities; both were builders – their additions to their abbeys, in both cases subsequently cathedrals, can still be enjoyed; both were involved in jurisdictional disputes with the governing bodies of the towns in which their abbeys were situated; and both presided over their abbeys' affairs for a considerable time, Birchenshawe having been elected in 1493 and Kirton three years later.[3] The removal of Birchenshawe is of particular interest, because of all the cases in which Wolsey participated this one came nearest to being a formal deposition – and, indeed, it may even have been one. Certainly in 1534, in a letter to Thomas Cromwell, Birchenshawe referred to a time 'when I was put from my abbey by the late lord Cardinal'.[4]

Birchenshawe's problem seems to have been that he could not resist a quarrel. Between 1507 and 1509 he was in conflict with the mayor and corporation of Chester over rival claims to jurisdiction in the city. He was a defendant in a Star Chamber case for the alleged eviction of a family from their smallholding, in the course of which he had all their household goods thrown 'into a great pond of water'.[5] But his real battle was with the bishop of Coventry and Lichfield, Geoffrey Blythe, over two related matters: Birchenshawe's right to a mitre and pontifical staff, and the right of his monastery to exemption from all episcopal jurisdiction. It is easy enough to see why the second matter, in particular, could have led to disagreement, for the prospect of being denied the supervision of a leading institution within his diocese must have been irksome to any bishop. It cannot, therefore, be assumed that the conflict was all of Birchenshawe's making; and in fact both the matters under dispute had been decided in the abbey's favour by the end of the fourteenth century, and it was the bishop who was challenging the status quo when he took the abbot to the Roman Curia.[6] However, Birchenshawe's refusal to

---

[5] KCA DR c/R7/fo.100v.

[1] Chester, Hyde, King's Langley, Peterborough, Spalding, Tywardreth, Vale Royal and Wenlock.
[2] Lewes and Oseney.
[3] For Birchenshawe see Burne. For Edmund Kirton see *Peterborough Monastery*. Birchenshawe's most important addition to his abbey was the west front and south west porch, Kirton's the 'New Building' at the east end.
[4] *LP*, vii, 854.
[5] *Lancashire and Cheshire Cases in Star Chamber*, p. 74.
[6] *VCH, Cheshire*, iii, p. 143.

produce the relevant documents, his subsequent excommunication by the pope, and the absolution he arranged for himself by a local priest 'in contempt and derision of the apostolic see', all point to his abrasive personality being at the root of the problem. Wolsey was first drawn into the dispute, at the pope's request, in December 1516 in order to deal with the abbot's uncanonical behaviour, but it appears that he initially had no more success in bringing about peace than the Curia had had.[1] But when the abbot, in an effort to strengthen his position, sued for a papal confirmation of the abbey's exemption from episcopal jurisdiction, Wolsey seized his opportunity, threatened him with praemunire for appealing to a foreign jurisdiction, and in this way forced his resignation.[2] There is an obvious irony in Wolsey's use of praemunire; but it also shows his confidence that his own theoretical reliance on papal authority would not be challenged. The important point is that Birchenshawe's offence had given Wolsey a specific lever with which to bring pressure on him – something which most other cases lacked. Whether an abbot had or had not sued for a papal bull was easily proved; whether he had, or had not, slept with someone was not.

What it is impossible to say is whether Birchenshawe's rule had been detrimental to the well-being of the abbey, because there is no evidence one way or the other. Neither is there evidence of any moral lapse on his part. It may be, therefore, that his forced resignation hardly served the interests of reform. Moreover, it has been suggested that Wolsey had a personal grievance against him for his part in a land transaction harmful to the interests of his concubine's husband, George Legh of Adlington,[3] and favourable to another member of the local gentry, Sir John Stanley. At any rate, article 38 of the charges drawn up against Wolsey at his fall accused him of wrongfully imprisoning Sir John until he had returned a lease to the abbot of Chester for him to reconvey it to Legh.[4] Whatever the truth of this allegation, as regards the central matter of Birchenshawe's dispute with Bishop Blythe, all one can say is that on general grounds Blythe – and Wolsey – were in the right. Monastic exemptions were liable to lead to just this kind of disagreement which could harm the religious life of a diocese, especially when the monastery concerned was as influential as the abbey of St Werburg. Furthermore, its earlier history – for instance, in 1437 it had had to be placed in royal custody 'by reason of it having been wasted by misrule' – does not inspire confidence that Abbot Birchenshawe's resistance to the bishop's claim to jurisdiction was in the best interests of either abbey or diocese.[5]

The removal of Abbot Kirton from Peterborough presented Wolsey with rather different problems. Technically, Birchenshawe had committed an offence, which, fairly or not, could be used to lever him out. Kirton had not, and was therefore in a much better position to resist the manoeuvres to oust him. On the other hand, that he deserved to be removed can be shown much more clearly than in Birchenshawe's case, because of the survival of a long list of complaints made at the time of Bishop

[1] LP,ii,2692.

[2] LP,iv,546 [19], 1278.

[3] The concubine being Mistress Lark; see A.F. Pollard, p.306, though in fact very little is known about her.

[4] LP,iv,6075. For a discussion of the allegation see p.137 above.

[5] VCH, Cheshire,iii, pp.140-2.

Atwater's visitation of the abbey in June 1518.[1] Of course, complaints are by their nature partial, and the autocratic Kirton's hot temper, plus his insistence on the strict observance of the daily offices, no doubt encouraged a jaundiced view of him amongst his fellow monks. Moreover, it should be stressed that no complaint was ever made about his private life. What was wrong with Kirton was that he had systematically broken all the customs of the house, had gained complete control of its finances, had occupied every important office, and had then used the concomitant power and money to further his own ends. These were not necessarily bad in themselves. A lot of the money had, for instance, been spent on the so-called 'new building' at the east end of the abbey and on other improvements to its fabric, but a lot had also been spent on improving his private accommodation.[2] And this seems to have been the problem. The ends envisaged were entirely his own, and not those of his fellow monks. As a result he had succeeded in destroying any sense of community. The complaints against him were made in 1518, long before either Wolsey or Bishop Longland was involved in efforts to secure his resignation, so that, whatever their reasons for reviving the opposition to him, the case against the abbot was not their invention. Their efforts, beginning at least by August 1526,[3] were to continue until March 1528, when Kirton finally resigned, though not before he had secured for himself a reasonable pension.[4] He may also have paid a substantial contribution to Cardinal College. It is, of course, this that throws doubt on the genuineness of Wolsey's desire to further the interests of Peterborough Abbey, and the historian's problem is to try and decide how far his undoubted wish to obtain money for his college dominated the negotiations with Kirton.

The evidence, as so often, permits no certainty and, indeed, it is not even known whether in the end a contribution was made, despite the considerable and entirely frustrating haggling that went on. Perhaps the wisest course is to concentrate on the one undoubted fact – that in the end Kirton did resign, so if he was hoping to prevent that happening by offering the bribe, the tactic failed, even if it did win him delay. What may have happened is this: Wolsey and Longland decided that it was time Kirton went. Kirton responded by offering a large sum of money for Cardinal College, initially as much as 2,000 marks (£1,333 6s 8d).[5] However, he then discovered that though Wolsey jumped at the offer, he was not very willing to pay the *quid pro quo* – Kirton's continuation as abbot. This put Kirton on the spot, for to withdraw his offer immediately would expose his real intention in making it in a rather humiliating way. The result was an elaborate farrago, during which Kirton repeatedly lowered the amount, mainly by conveniently forgetting how much he had previously offered. But he could hardly end up by offering nothing, because there were such matters as the size of his pension to be considered. At one point he offered 400 marks, which, after a short pause for consideration, he raised to 500.[6] Longland obviously considered the reduction of the original offer by as much as £1,000 to be unacceptable. Kirton, in his view, was only trying to waste

---

[1] *Visitations in the Diocese of Lincoln,*, xxxvii, pp. 76-83.
[2] *Peterborough Monastery*, p. ix, n.2.
[3] LP, iv, 2391, Longland to Wolsey, 11 Aug. 1526.
[4] LP, iv, 4047, 4279.
[5] LP, iv, 2378.
[6] LP, iv, 2378, 2391.

time and he argued that if he continued to 'swerve and warble', he should be made to resign almost immediately – that is, by Michaelmas 1526.[1]

Does Longland's advice imply that if Kirton had kept to his original promise, all attempts to remove him would have been dropped – a course of action which would reflect no credit on Wolsey? The suggestion is no: it was merely the timing of his resignation and the various other conditions he was insisting on, such as that his successor should be someone from within the abbey, that were at stake. If it were otherwise, it is odd that Kirton should have been in the end offering so little, unless he had come to the conclusion that he was in such a strong position to resist removal that he need not bother with a bribe. And one thing that does emerge from all these negotiations is that it was much easier for Longland to propose Kirton's resignation than to achieve it. Ten months later, in June 1527, the bishop was still trying to remove him.[2] By then he had come up with a new strategy, the appointment of two coadjutors who would take over the administration of the abbey on the grounds that Kirton, because of his age, was no longer able to carry this out. Such a procedure was not uncommon and had been used, for instance, in 1519 for St Albans in Abbot Ramrige's case.[3] It would have been easier to implement than a formal dismissal, because there was no requirement to prove that any crime had been committed, and because easier, it would have posed a greater threat for Kirton. However, if it did have the effect of making him reconsider his position, he nevertheless took his time for it was only eight months after Longland had devised the strategy – that is, in March 1528 – that he eventually resigned.[4]

One of the complaints that Longland made about Kirton during these lengthy negotiations was that he was doing everything possible to persuade the prior of Spalding, Thomas White, not to resign; 'thus secretly he works, not like a wise and kind man, to study to abridge your grace of your honourable pleasure and purpose'.[5] What Wolsey's precise 'pleasure and purpose' was is uncertain. No mention of any direct financial advantage accruing to Wolsey from the prior's resignation has survived. On the other hand, Spalding was a wealthy house with an income of about £880, so there may have been some financial motive involved. There was also a persistent rumour that Wolsey intended to appoint the prior of Tynemouth in White's place.[6] But there were also criticisms of Prior White. Longland, it is true, in a letter to Wolsey called him 'good and gentle', but added that he was led by others,[7] an observation which mirrors almost precisely those made at the time of Bishop Atwater's visitation in 1519. Then the bishop had ordered the prior to take the advice not of two laymen, whom White clearly relied on far too much, but of the majority of the brothers.[8] Without knowing a great deal more about the state of the

---

[1] *LP*,iv, 2378.

[2] *LP*,iv,3175.

[3] VCH, *Hertford*, iv, p. 409 – and with Pace's deaneries when he went mad.

[4] *LP*,iv,4047.

[5] PRO SP 1/39/fo.58 (*LP*,iv,2391).

[6] *LP*,iv, 3478, 4708. John Stonywell was prior of Tynemouth until 1526, when he became abbot of Pershore and Thomas Gardiner was prior by 1528. Which of these was the man who may have been intended for Spalding is not certain.

[7] *LP*,iv,4796.

[8] *Visitations in the Diocese of Lincoln*,, xxxvii, p.98.

priory, it is impossible to say whether this criticism should have provided sufficient grounds for attempting to force his resignation. It certainly did not provide a sufficient case in law, as Longland himself admitted.[1] Thus, when the good prior, for all his gentleness, refused to give way to pressure, there was nothing that either Wolsey or Longland could do, and he remained at the head of his house until well into the 1530s.[2]

What Wolsey's efforts to secure the resignations of the heads of the monastic houses of Chester, Peterborough and Spalding make abundantly clear is how difficult they were to remove. This means that even if the worst possible view is taken of Wolsey's intentions, there were severe limits to what he could do – and this despite his legatine authority. But, in fact, none of these three cases suggests that Wolsey's intentions were wholly bad. There were, it is true, financial considerations involved – and what is thought of these depends very much on what view is taken of Cardinal College, because it was this that was to be the main beneficiary of money accruing from monastic appointments and resignations. But even if these considerations arouse suspicion, it cannot be denied that there were genuine grounds for considering the removal of all three men from high office; and the same can be said about most of the other people in whose removal, or attempted removal, Wolsey played some part. The usual defect was old age and the consequent inability to cope with the demands of an exacting office. In 1526, Wolsey wrote to Richard Romsey, abbot of the large Benedictine abbey of Hyde in Winchester, suggesting that though in the past he had managed his house discreetly and well, he could no longer do so given his age and imbecility. Not surprisingly, the abbot hotly denied this. However, since he had been abbot since 1509, he must have been of a considerable age, and even he had to admit that he was 'somewhat diseased'. This, he said, would prevent him from travelling to see Wolsey but did not, in his opinion, prevent him from exercising his office. He had therefore no intention of resigning, but trusted that Wolsey would rather conserve and aid him than 'experiment any sharper means' to remove him[3] – and in March 1529 Romsey was to die in office. Wolsey also attempted to remove the prior of St Andrew's, Tywardreth, because 'by reason of your great age and impotency you neither may nor can take such pain and diligence . . . as you have done in time past'. He should therefore relieve himself 'of the great burden of office, live restfully and at ease in this your great age, and, as we verily think, do a great deed of good merit to the pleasure of Almighty God and weal of your said house.'[4] The letter shows some tact, quite unlike the marquess of Exeter's peremptory request, made after Wolsey's fall, for the prior to make way for the marquess's own candidate. But Prior Collins, whether or not, as was later alleged, he had taken to drink, was quite sober enough to resist both these approaches, and he is last encountered writing off to his friends amongst the

[1] PRO SP 1/50/fo.90 (LP,iv,4708): 'The prior will on no condition resign, yet all lawful ways has been attempted'.

[2] VCH, Lincoln, ii, p.124.

[3] LP,iv,2394 Romsey's letter to Wolsey 12 Aug. [1526]. It is the only source for this episode, although episcopal injunctions of 1522 suggest that all was not well with the house; see Liber Monasterii de Hyda, p.lxiii. For Fox's possible worries about Hyde see p.272 above.

[4] Monasticon diocesis Exonienses, pp.45-6.

diocesan administrators of Exeter to rally support.[1]

However much one may sympathize with Prior Collins or with the abbot of Hyde, an ageing head who had held office for many years – and both Romsey and Collins had held it for about thirty[2] – was probably no good thing for the 'weal' of the community, and arguably what was required were greater powers to remove such a person. A tactful letter, hints about the possible loss of a pension, or even the start of more direct moves to depose might do the trick, but if the head was determined to resist, his likelihood of success was great. For Hyde and Tywardreth, this may not have been too disastrous. Things may have been a little lax at Hyde, but there is no evidence that anything was seriously wrong with either. At the Augustinian abbey of Wigmore in Herefordshire, the situation was more serious. Its abbot, John Smart, had in fact been appointed by Wolsey in June 1518, and for once Wolsey's choice did not turn out well.[3] At any rate, by 1537 the then bishop of Hereford, Edward Fox, was forced to issue a set of injunctions critical of the behaviour both of Smart and the canons under him.[4] Worse was to follow, for in the following year one of the canons accused Smart of every crime under the sun, of which rape, murder and robbery were the most heinous.[5] One of the lesser charges was that he had paid Wolsey £100 in order to obtain his appointment as abbot. It should be said that the canon's evidence was very partial and, in the view of the new bishop, Rowland Lee, incapable of proof, so there is no compelling reason to accept it now. But if money did pass hands at the election, this did not in any way prevent Wolsey from working to secure his removal,[6] and according to Wolsey's agent in the matter (none other than the same Rowland Philipps who had allegedly led the opposition to Wolsey in the 1523 legatine convocation), Smart's removal was necessary if the house was not to be destroyed.[7]

Smart apparently felt confident enough to tell Phillips that he trusted to the extinction of Wolsey's legatine powers to escape removal, and so it proved.[8] But the remark itself was surely some acknowledgement, if unintentional, of Wolsey's genuine concern for the good of the monastic houses, a concern that emerges most clearly from the last case to be discussed. In 1528, the prior of King's Langley, Hertfordshire, was Robert Miles. He was also provincial of the Dominican order and thus a man of some importance. Unfortunately he had a weakness, which was women, or rather, one particular woman, Agnes Pastloo. It was a relationship which he had attempted to disguise by marrying her off to one of his servants, but without success, and one of the people who got to know about it was none other than the queen who, since the house was a royal foundation, had every right to show her concern. The 'honest people' of Dunstable were also concerned, though

---

[1] Ibid, pp.45-7; for the allegation of drunkenness see Baskerville, pp.55-6.
[2] Romsey had been abbot of Hyde since 1509, Collins prior of Tywardreth since 1507.
[3] For this episode see Knowles, 'Last abbot of Wigmore'; also Froude, pp.363-7.
[4] LP,xii [1],742 [1].
[5] LP,xii [1],742 [2,3].
[6] LP,iv,5121.
[7] LP,iv,5898.
[8] LP,iv,5898 'I have been with the abbot of Wigmore and showed him your gracious mind towards him, . . . but now, as he trusts to a great change, and specially the extinction of your authority, he refuses the offer.' Phillipps to Wolsey, 31 Aug. 1529.

why this should have been so is not at all clear. Although in an adjoining county, Dunstable was not especially close geographically,[1] and neither this nor the fact that Dunstable had a Dominican priory of its own appears quite to explain the town's interest. Be that as it may, they had gone to the trouble of drawing up a list of 'detections' against Miles.[2] Longland, who as diocesan bishop had been drawn into the matter, admonished the prior both in a private interview and by letter, but to no effect. Despite the warnings, the prior and Agnes had obviously remained rather more than 'just good friends'.

Longland's problem was that, as a Dominican house, King's Langley was exempt from his jurisdiction. Private remonstrations were thus the only course of action available to him, other than appealing to Wolsey as legate, which he did. In fact his letter to Wolsey is the only evidence for this episode which has survived.[3] It is not known what action, if any, Wolsey took. It is not even known when Miles ceased to be prior, though by 1530 he was no longer there which may suggest that some action against him was taken.[4] How, then, is it possible to consider this episode to be important evidence of Wolsey's genuine interest in the welfare of the religious orders? The answer lies in the tone of Longland's letter. The bishop obviously felt strongly that something must be done, 'for it is a pity such a man should be head of Christ's Church'. Moreover, it was not just Miles's sexual lapses that worried him, for he reported that there 'is little religion kept at his house, and it is in utter decay'.[5] When Longland wrote this letter on 1 June 1528 he had known Wolsey for about thirty years, and for the previous seven had worked closely with him in all manner of ways. It would therefore seem most unlikely that he would have bothered to express himself in this way unless he was reasonably certain that Wolsey would share his concern for the well-being of King's Langley and of the Dominican order over whose affairs the incontinent prior presided.

On 10 January 1519 Wolsey, in company with his fellow legate Cardinal Campeggio, conducted a visitation of the great Benedictine monastery of St Peter's, Westminster that was intended to herald the start of a new era of legatine reform of the religious orders. The episode provided Polydore Vergil with the occasion for one of his most vicious assaults on Wolsey:

> He dealt with the business extravagantly and confused and disturbed them in order to frighten the other monks, to show his power, to represent himself as even more terrible. The whole performance tended to one result: that the monks who had been called to judgment should prefer voluntarily to pay cash rather than change their way of life. His view was not mistaken. The monks easily comprehended why the physician who was so forgetful of his own health was so careful of that of others.[6]

Following Vergil, most other historians have suspected that Wolsey saw his legatine

---

[1] Dunstable is in Beds, King's Langley in Herts.
[2] Mentioned in Longland's letter to Wolsey; for which see PRO SP 1/48/fo.86 (*LP*,iv,4315).
[3] *LP*,iv,4315.
[4] Of course, he may just have died. He is known to have been in the Oxford convent in 1497, so he was well into middle-age by the late 1520s; for the biographical details see Emden, *Oxford, 1540*.
[5] PRO SP 1/48/fo.86 (*LP*,iv,4315).
[6] Vergil,p.259.

powers only as a means of raising revenue,[1] and no aspect of these powers has done more to arouse these suspicions than that which enabled him to visit monastic houses, and as a consequence to charge a procuration fee. One reason for this may be that post-medieval historians are not very familiar with procurations, even though they continued to be paid in England after the Reformation. Reading Pollard, one might even think that Wolsey had invented them which, of course, is in no sense true.[2] Although in theory they were supposed to cover the expenses of any ecclesiastical official in the conduct of his business, usually when carrying out a visitation, but also when acting as papal nuncio or legate, they had in the course of time become a standard charge for every kind of church visitation, not just those of monastic institutions.[3] So large sums of money were involved: Morton, for instance, as archbishop of Canterbury, obtained from ten *sede vacante* visitations the sum of £1,416 15s 3d, of which £402 12s 4d came from visitations of monastic houses. Given this background, it was both inevitable and acceptable that Wolsey should, in his legatine capacity, charge a procuration fee. The only possible objection can be to the amount.

Wolsey calculated his procuration fee at one twenty-fifth of an institution's annual income, which was considerably more than anyone else charged. To make one direct comparison, in March 1525 Wolsey's commissary, John Allen, visited Tewkesbury Abbey, whose income was put at £761 7s 2d, and he charged a procuration fee of £30 9s 1d.[4] For the *sede vacante* visitation of Archbishop Warham in 1522, Tewkesbury had paid only £3 6s 8d[5] – which seems, incidentally, at least in the diocese of Worcester, to have been the fixed rate for all larger monasteries, irrespective of their precise income. It should be said that the institutions – which included colleges and hospitals as well as monasteries – were allowed to pay their legatine procurations in manageable instalments. Prior William More of Worcester paid his personal contribution to the £40 owed for Allen's visitation in April 1525 in five instalments of £3;[6] Winchester College, whose annual income was put at £628 13s 6d, was charged £8 for Allen's visitation in March 1527, but was still paying it off after Wolsey's fall.[7] But though payment by instalments would have eased the burden, procuration fees were heavy, so it is not surprising that they were made the subject of one of the articles brought against Wolsey in 1529.[8] Moreover, there were additional sums of money involved. Prior More's journal records that for his visitation Allen was given £5, William Clayton 26s 8d and their servants 20s, plus additional expenses of 6s 8d;[9] and Winchester College gave Allen 30s.[10] But such

---

[1] *Inter alia* Elton, *Reform and Reformation*, p.90: 'money and the assertion of personal power constituted the cardinal's overriding concern', this in connection with his legatine rule.

[2] A.F. Pollard, pp.198-200.

[3] Harper-Bill, *JEH*, 29, p.14. *Sede vacante* visitations were those carried out by archbishops where an episcopal vacancy occurred in their province.

[4] PRO SP 1/32/fo.268 (*LP*,iv,964).

[5] William More, p.4.

[6] Ibid, pp.221, 238, 254, 263, 278.

[7] *Registrum Thome Wolsey*, pp.189-91. It is rather typical of Henry that the college was still having to pay, even though it was Wolsey's exercise of his legatine authority which provided the excuse for his disgrace.

[8] *LP*,iv,6075, art.25.

[9] William More, 207-8.

gifts of this kind were nothing new. In 1494 the bishop of Winchester's visitation had cost Winchester College £6 13s 4d over and above the procuration fee of 13s 4d, of which 3s 4d had been distributed amongst the bishop's officials.[1]

None of this is meant to be an apology for legatine extortion. But before pronouncing judgment, one needs to consider the historical context. Undoubtedly Wolsey made money out of the legatine visitations, but how much is impossible to say. The legatine visitations made in the London area during the spring and early summer of 1525 brought in £189 8s 5d; and those of about the same time in the dioceses of Salisbury, Worcester, Coventry and Lichfield, and Lincoln £439 12s 2d.[2] Apart from one or two isolated examples, such as Winchester College, these are all the visitations that are known to have taken place, and my guess would be that if many others had occurred, some record of them would have survived. If so, during a period of ten years, Wolsey received about £630. It does not seem to have been an exorbitant charge on the religious orders of England. And when it comes down to it, the only thing that was unusual about Wolsey's visitations was their legatine nature. Even then we must remember that only about thirty years earlier Archbishop Morton, although not a legate *a latere* and not yet even a cardinal, had been granted a bull in 1487 authorizing him to visit exempt monasteries if the regular authority, such as the order to which the house belonged, failed to act within six months.[3]

But how was the undeniably high rate of one twenty-fifth of any given institution's income arrived at? There is no reference to any procuration fees in Wolsey's various legatine commissions. On the other hand, it is most unlikely that he just plucked the figure out of thin air. This is not because he was especially saintly, but because it was just not how such matters were decided. The workings of the Church were dominated by precedent and legal requirements. Whatever advantage his position as resident legate *a latere* may have offered him, Wolsey almost always played by the book, whether he was obtaining wider or more specific legatine powers from the papacy, or working out his elaborate compositions with the bishops. The problem is, and no doubt was, that none of the precedents in this matter quite fitted or, if they did, they derived from a very long time ago: procurations for visiting papal nuncios and legates had ceased in the early fifteenth century but to find a legatine visitation of a monastic institution one has to go back to the second half of the thirteenth century.[4] By 1300 the going rate for important papal nuncios and legates, which seems in practice to have meant those who were cardinals, was 4d in the mark, or one fortieth, except for institutions with incomes of £200 or more, who were charged a flat rate of £8. Thus, for an income of precisely £200, the rate was one twenty-fifth. Could this be the source of Wolsey's figure? Perhaps – and, at any rate, it is as near to finding one that I have been able to get.[5]

[10] *Registrum Thome Wolsey*, p.190.

---

[1] Kirby, p.296.
[2] LP,iv,964.
[3] Harper-Bill, *JEH*, pp.6-8. The bull, *Quanta in Dei Ecclesia*, was granted in 1487 and reissued in 1490.
[4] By my reckoning Cardinal Ottobuono's visitations during his legation of 1265-8 were the last but this may well prove to be wrong. In 1459, Francesco Coppini, bishop of Terni, was appointed legate *a latere* to England with powers 'to visit the whole of the said realm and reform abuses', but he does not seem to have actually done this (Constance Heal, pp.149-50).

But that there was some source I have little doubt, for to have produced an arbitrary figure would have been out of keeping with the way that Wolsey normally worked, and would anyway have probably been challenged.

But to put the financial aspects of Wolsey's legatine visitations into some kind of context still leaves us with the even more difficult task of assessing their contribution to reform. It was, after all, in order to reform the religious orders that Wolsey had first asked for legatine powers, so it is of some importance to decide whether he made effective use of them. Vergil, in his castigation of Wolsey's 1519 visitation of Westminster Abbey, was for the most part unfair, but insofar as he recognized that it was its propaganda effect rather than any particular good it might do for Westminster Abbey, he had grasped the essential point. There is no reason to suppose that the abbey was in any special need of a visitation; what evidence there is suggests that all was reasonably well.[1] But it was conveniently placed and, moreover, it happened to be one of the most prestigious monastic houses in England. It was also, despite being a Benedictine house, exempt from episcopal jurisdiction. In all these respects it could hardly have been better suited for Wolsey's purpose, which was to serve warning on the monastic orders that he had every intention to 'castigate and punish' each and every house that was in need of such treatment, whether exempt or not.[2] Unfortunately, it is not possible to calculate whether the visitation had the intended effect, for no comments have survived. What has is the sermon with which John Longland opened the proceedings, a sermon that he thought sufficiently important to have published, and which gave so much pleasure to Archbishop Warham.[3]

Longland's text from Genesis 18:18, where God informs Abraham that he intends to visit Sodom and Gomorrah to 'see whether they have done altogether according to the outcry against them which has come down to me', was appropriate to the wider ends in view, if a little unfair to Westminster Abbey. After expounding on the monastic vows of poverty, charity and obedience, Longland exhorted the monks of Westminster to live by their vows them in order that there could be no outcry against them. He also made a more general call for church reform:

> Today the Church, whose former devotion has cooled, is injured. And is she not injured by herself? Certainly by herself. Our true predecessors, both monks and secular clergy, led a holy and hard life, we a much easier and softer one, we who have stained her pristine beauty and devotion with worldly desires.[4]

[5] It is to be hoped that someone with a greater knowledge of continental practice will be able to solve this problem. Meanwhile, I would like to thank Professor C.R. Cheney for his kind assistance. The major source in English on this subject is Lunt, *Financial Relations to 1327*, pp.532-70; *Financial Relations, 1327- 1534*, pp.621-92.

---

[1] The impression is gained from the respect with which John Islip, abbot of Westminster from 1500 to 1532, was held and the active role that he played in government, and for the lack of any surviving adverse comment; but see Knowles, *Religious Orders*, iii, pp.96-9 for a slightly jaundiced account of Islip's life. For the visitation, see WAM, Register 2, fos. 129-130v. No visitation articles or injunctions have survived. I am grateful to N.H. MacMichael for making the Abbey archives available.

[2] Rymer, xiii, p.739-40 from the 1521 amplification but quoting from the earlier commission.

[3] Longland; and for Warham's pleasure see LAO Register 26, fo. 206, quoted extensively in Bowker, *Henrician Reformation*, pp.11-12.

[4] Taken from Bowker, *Henrician Reformation*, p.11.

It was up to the monastic orders and the church authorities to bring the Church back to her 'pristine beauty'. He did not actually say, as Bishop Fox had written only a few days earlier,[1] that this would best be achieved under Wolsey's leadership as legate, but, given the occasion, the implication was surely there.

Given this rousing start, what followed may seem a little disappointing. As we have already seen, the number of legatine visitations was not all that great. Moreover, as with Westminster, in most cases there is no reason to suppose that there was anything especially wrong with the places visited. The visitations were, therefore, in part at least, an assertion of Wolsey's legatine authority, in the same way as his compositions with the bishops were – which is not to say that they were merely a formality.

The only details we have are a set of injunctions dated 17 April 1525 in connection with a visitation of Worcester Priory, later revised because they were 'frequently occasion of strife and controversy from ambiguous and obscure language', and not, apparently, ratified by Wolsey until November 1526.[2] Contrary to the generalization that has just been made, all was not entirely well at Worcester. Prior William More had been in dispute with his sub-prior, Neckham, and his cellarer, Fordham, and in the revised injunctions Wolsey's usual legatine visitor, John Allen, sided with the prior, confirming their dismissal from office, as well as that of two 'scholastics'.[3] That he did so could be taken as evidence that the prior's 'gifts' had taken effect.[4] Moreover, it has to be said that the character of the prior which emerges from his journal is not that of a zealous reformer. Neither is it, however, that of a villain.[5] William More liked his country pursuits and entertainments, and was at ease with the local gentry, but he also cared a great deal for the well-being of his priory. When in the 1530s – a time when the opportunities for settling scores were easily come by – the two dismissed monks, along with another who had been imprisoned by More for stealing, caused him considerable trouble, both the local gentry and most of the monks of Worcester supported their prior. Indeed, twenty-eight of them wrote to Cromwell saying that they had no wish to have Fordham back as cellarer, because not only was he 'a troublesome person', but he had also contracted 'the pox'.[6] As so often, there is not enough available detail for the rights and wrongs of what was going on at Worcester to be fully established, but the burden of the surviving evidence points to the conclusion that Allen had been right to back the prior in 1525. Moreover, even if Wolsey's legatine injunctions in their final form were more lenient than they had been initially, they do show that considerable attention had been paid to the specific problems of the priory.

If Allen's visitation of Worcester Priory was typical of legatine visitations as a whole – and there is no reason to suppose that it was not – then it would be possible to argue that, though perhaps not strictly necessary, they did make some contribution to reform – perhaps even a rather specific one. It has already been

---

[1] Richard Fox, pp.114-17 (*LP*,iii,1122).
[2] Wilson, pp.359-64; Knowles, *Religious Orders*, iii, p.83, n.3.
[3] Wilson, p.360.
[4] See p.331 above.
[5] William More; Knowles, *Religious Orders*, iii, pp.108-26.
[6] *LP*,ix,653; Knowles, *Religious Orders*, pp.342-5.

stressed that, despite the troubles at Worcester, there is no reason to suppose that houses visited were specially in need of reform. What may be significant is their geographical location. If the London houses are excluded, there remain forty-nine that Allen visited. Of these, four were in the diocese of Lincoln, seven in the diocese of Coventry and Lichfield, nine in the diocese of Salisbury, and twenty-nine in the diocese of Worcester. It emerges from this that it was the dioceses which had foreign and absentee bishops that saw the greatest number of visitations, which is to say Salisbury and Worcester, and this suggests another reason for them – to compensate for their lack of close episcopal supervision. In other words, it was a sensible, if rather limited, use of Wolsey's authority, and certainly neither as selfish nor as arbitrary as has sometimes been alleged.

There remain one or two legatine visitations which were the result of particular circumstances. Longland's request to Wolsey for help with the Cistercian, and therefore exempt, house of Thame, and the consequent visitation in 1526 of the abbot of Waverley acting as Wolsey's legatine commissary, has already been mentioned.[1] In the same year, there was a legatine visitation of the college of Stoke-by-Clare in Bishop Nix's diocese of Norwich. Like everything in which Wolsey and Nix were brought into contact with, this episode provides a complicated and messy story, the rights and wrongs of which are impossible to unravel. It seems unlikely, though, that it brought Wolsey, as has been alleged, into conflict with Catherine of Aragon, patroness of the College; for his chief agent in the matter was Robert Shorton, not only her almoner but, as future events were to prove, her very devoted servant. Equally unlikely is the allegation that Wolsey intended to suppress the college, since he had no papal authority to suppress an institution of this wealth and size.[2] True, he did not keep strictly to the conditions laid down in the only relevant papal bull that has survived,[3] but even so Stoke-by-Clare would have represented a striking departure from the normal run of houses he suppressed.[4] What appears to have been involved was a genuine effort by both Wolsey and Catherine to do something about the state of the college, whose statutes even Nix admitted in a letter to Wolsey, were in need of reform. Admittedly their efforts came to nothing; at least no new statutes resulted, although Shorton's appointment as dean, which unfortunately cannot be precisely dated, may have been due to their efforts.

The last legatine visitation to be looked at here is that of the Cluniac priory of Wenlock, Herefordshire, in September 1523; and for once quite a lot of documentation has survived.[5] The difficulties in 1523 can be traced back to the election of Roland Gosenell as prior in 1521 – the first election since a bull of 1494 had given the priory the right to choose its own head.[6] A party in the priory, with

---

[1] See p.273 above

[2] *Visitations of the Diocese of Norwich*, pp.227-8; VCH, *Suffolk*, ii, p.147, which is the most detailed account of Wolsey's suppressions to date.

[3] Rymer, xiv, pp.23-5, 11 Sept. 1524.

[4] It was worth over £300 a year, and of the 30 houses suppressed none was worth that, only two were over £200, one of which being St Frideswide, Oxford, for which special papal provision was made. For a complete list see Knowles, *Religious Orders*, iii, p.470.

[5] Graham, pp.125-45, where the injunctions and 'counsels' are printed; also Knowles, *Religious Orders*, iii, pp.82-3. For the prior's answers to the complaint brought against him see LP,iv,954.

[6] At the same time, the house was placed directly under papal jurisdiction and subject only to the visitation of the papal collector in London.

some outside support, had strongly opposed the choice of Gosenell. As a result he had appealed to Wolsey, who had supported his election, subject to the bishop of Hereford's confirmation that it had been properly conducted. But opposition to Gosenell continued, and in 1523 he had again appealed to Wolsey – and hence the legatine visitation. The resulting injunctions, drawn up by Allen, who as usual had carried out the visitation, were designed to steer a middle path between Gosenell and his opponents. Like other heads who found themselves in conflict with their subordinates, Gosenell was ambitious; he had, for instance, secured for himself the use of the bishop's mitre, thus putting himself in the top league of abbots and priors. And in furthering his ambition he may well have ignored the best interests of his house. At any rate, his contention that by placing on his mitre one of the priory's holy relics, an ivory cross of St Milburg, along with other of the priory's jewels, he would augment 'the honour of God and the house', was surely rather partial.

At the same time, Allen's injunctions leave no doubt that there was a good deal of slackness in the observance of regulations – perhaps the result of the very long rule of the previous prior – and there could therefore be something in Gosenell's argument that the monks only objected to his rule because he was trying to tighten up. To assist this process Allen laid down that the necessary silences should be observed, that doors should be kept closed to prevent free access, that young boys should not be in and out of the monks' dormitories and that there should be adequate provision made for the teaching of the young monks. The playing of cards, chess, or marbles for money was forbidden and better singing in the chapel was called for. The monks were also advised to consult 'the new legatine constitutions'; presumably he had in mind those issued for the Benedictine order in 1520,[1] since they would have been most relevant to a Cluniac priory. And this suggests that they were readily available and that they were not, as is usually implied, mere window-dressing. But Allen also took the prior to task, exhorting him to be moderate in his criticisms of his fellow monks, in the manner of a father to his sons. He was also urged not to spend too much on hospitality, so as not to 'incur the stigma of luxurious living'. It is not known precisely what transpired concerning the charges brought against Gosenell by his monks. Gosenell maintained that they had already been rejected by the bishop of Hereford, but this did not inhibit Allen from referring them to Wolsey for a decision, while in the meantime Gosenell was suspended from office. The decision must have gone in Gosenell's favour, because he was formally restored to office in the following June. Whether this was because Wolsey genuinely believed that he was a good prior or just that the case against him could not be proved, is another matter. Certainly, within three years – that is, before Wolsey's fall – Gosenell was no longer prior, and since he was to spend a considerable amount of time and effort in trying to get his office back, one must assume that he had not gone willingly. Indeed, when his successor and the sub-prior wrote to Cromwell in 1534 to ask him to put an end to these efforts, they pointed out that Gosenell had been 'deposed' both for bringing the house into debt and for his 'execrable living'.[2] On the other hand, as he was in receipt of a pension, this

---

[1] Worcester priory obtained a copy in 1520 (William More, p.108), and presumably they were issued to all Benedictine houses.

[2] LP, vii, 1066.

may suggest that they were writing rather loosely. But the important point here is that whatever the precise nature of his departure, it seems reasonable to surmise that but for the pressure brought upon him by virtue of Wolsey's legatine authority, Gosenell would have continued his unpopular rule at Wenlock for much longer than he did.

Wolsey is known to have intervened in twenty monastic elections, to have taken part in at least eight attempts to remove a monastic head – though on only four occasions were these efforts successful[1] – and to have authorized 72 legatine visitations. By and large, his involvement would seem to have been beneficial. It is true that financial gain did accrue to him, but then most interventions by church authorities involved the payment of money. It is also true that some of his interventions had rather more to do with the assertion of his legatine authority than with the health of the institution concerned – but then he would have argued that such an assertion was a prerequisite for any real reform. It can hardly be stressed too often that the surviving evidence permits only the most cautious of conclusions, because so often the detail necessary to unravel the ins and outs of a particular episode is lacking. But whatever the qualifications, the overall impression is of Henry's cardinal legate making a genuine attempt to further the best interests of the religious orders.

But is it possible to go beyond this rather low-key, almost negative conclusion? To state that, by and large, Wolsey's rule was beneficial hardly earns for him the title of reformer, or justifies the enormous powers acquired in order to bring about reform. Is it really the case, for instance, that out of the roughly 820 heads of religious houses in England, only eight deserved to be removed? Even bearing in mind all the legal difficulties in the way of removing anyone, it seems an almost derisory figure – or perhaps not? In answering such questions, so much depends on one's assumptions. If the view is taken that the religious houses were indeed dens of iniquity, then of course the figure is worryingly low. If, on the other hand, one considers that, given the close scrutiny that the religious houses were submitted to, of a kind no institution could undergo without faults emerging, they come out of it reasonably well, then eight deliquent heads may seem about right. To suggest a modern parallel, there can be very few headmasters today about whom criticisms could not be made, and yet how many should be sacked and, more relevantly, how many are? Outstanding heads of anything are rare, and the temptation to expect the impossible is one that historians should resist. It is this, hopefully more realistic, view of the religious orders that is taken here. From this it follows that Wolsey's efforts to remove nine heads in what was effectively under six years[2] – for the legatine machinery was not really set up until the beginning of 1523 – reflect not a dereliction of duty but the very small number of obvious candidates for removal.

[1] Birchenshawe at Chester; Kirton at Peterborough; Butler at Vale Royal (*VCH, Cheshire*, iii, p.162); and probably Gosenell at Wenlock.

[2] Admittedly Wolsey had visitorial powers from 1518, but 1524 is probably a fairer starting date. Only by then had the new constitutions for the religious orders been drawn up and published, his legatine powers been granted him for life and, following the compositions with the bishops, his legatine machinery established and it was not until 1525 that an important number of legatine visitations took place.

What this small number also helps to confirm is an aspect of Wolsey's use of his legatine authority which has underlain much of the interpretation so far. It never seems to have been Wolsey's intention to intervene on a day-to-day basis in the running of the Church. As we have seen, the legatine powers had given him overall control of all aspects of the English Church, and the series of new constitutions and statutes that he had issued were his declaration of intent. This achieved, his role was to intervene only when it would be helpful to do so, which is to say usually only when he was requested to. For example, in 1519 it was at the request of the dean, John Colet, that he became involved in deciding what should be the proper function and rewards of the canons of St Paul's.[1] In 1523 he intervened in the affairs of Wenlock Priory only at the request of Prior Gosenell. In 1526 he intervened in the affairs of the Cistercian abbey of Thame only at the request of Bishop Longland, and it was that same bishop who in 1528 asked him to investigate the Dominican house of King's Langley. On the other hand, Wolsey did nothing at all in 1527 when there was serious trouble at the Benedictine abbey of Malmesbury. Instead, the order's machinery for coping with such emergencies was activated in the normal way by the then president of its chapter, John Islip, abbot of Westminster. The abbot of Gloucester was called upon to conduct a visitation of Malmesbury, with the result that at least six of the 'rebels' ended up excommunicated.[2] Malmesbury was an exempt monastery and, given that it is the existence of such monasteries that has been used to justify Wolsey's acquisition of legatine powers, it is reasonable to ask why in this case they were not used. The simple answer seems to be that nobody asked him to, and since the matter was adequately dealt with, there was no other reason for intervening.

It is important to grasp just how cautious and circumscribed was Wolsey's approach to the exercise of his legatine powers. Certainly he was sufficiently determined to take on Warham when, in the winter of 1518-19, the archbishop had attempted to challenge them, but he was far too skilful a politician to overplay his hand. If, as has been suggested here, he saw it as his task to provide leadership and a sense of overall direction, and in other ways to act as a long-stop or final court of appeal, then it becomes all the more urgent to tackle the question of his claim to be called a reformer. It is also high time to consider what was meant by reform in the early sixteenth century.[3] The word is always a loaded one, and in attempting any final assessment of Wolsey's achievement it is important to bear this in mind.

Well before anyone in England had heard of Martin Luther, reform of the English Church was a matter for serious concern. It may be that John Morton's concern was characterized by an aggressive assertion of his own rights as archbishop of Canterbury, but, if only as a byproduct of this, it also led him to to try to tackle the problem of the exempt monasteries.[4] Warham shared Morton's concern for the rights of Canterbury, but then a concern for one's rights seems to be strongly implanted in all of us, and was very much part of the tradition of the English episcopacy. Not surprisingly, therefore, Warham's assertion of his rights was

[1] *Registrum Sancti Pauli*, pp.xiv ff. 416 ff.
[2] Pantin (ed.), *English Black Monks*, pp.124-36; *VCH, Wilts.*, iii, p.225.
[3] I have found the following especially useful: Duggan, Gleason; Oakley; O'Malley.
[4] Harper-Bill, *JEH*, 29.

strongly resisted by a group of his suffragans, led by Bishop Fox, a conflict that has been briefly touched upon at various stages in this book.[1] Here the point to make is that it cannot have helped the process of reform, though it did not prevent all discussion of it. In 1510 convocation had set up a committee for reform, and out of this committee emerged three new canons. One gave powers to the bishops to suspend stipendiary chaplains who persistently failed to celebrate the services that they had been appointed to perform. Another attempted to tackle the problem of the sale of church offices, or, as it was called, simony. The third condemned the wearing of improper dress. One member of that committee was John Colet, and it was at the opening of the 1510 convocation that he made his celebrated indictment of the state of the English Church.[2] Not nearly so well known is the very similar indictment made by John Taylor in the convocation of 1514 – and for the historian at any rate it is more interesting. Colet's attack can be passed off as *sui generis* – the kind of thing one might expect from a great Christian 'humanist', but from no one else. Not so John Taylor's, for he seems to fall very clearly into that category of careerist churchman that usually come in for criticism. But this did not prevent Taylor making a passionate plea for the Church to reform itself,[3] which suggests that the demand for reform was fairly widespread, at least amongst the better educated clergy.

The call for 'reform' was not confined to England, and nowhere did it surface more strongly than at the Fifth Lateran Council of 1512-17, where in session after session leading churchmen lamented the existing state of affairs, sometimes in apocalyptic terms.[4] The picture of a sleepy and complacent Church caught unawares by the criticisms of a German friar will not do. Indeed, if anything, the self-condemnation of the Church in the years just prior to the Diet of Worms and Luther's decision to reject the authority of the Catholic Church was over-strained, over-scrupulous and almost certainly exaggerated.[5] It came in many varieties, not all of it of the Erasmian kind that in the past has, perhaps, tended to monopolize historians' imaginations – but then Erasmus's magic is very hard to resist. In more recent years the pendulum may have swung too far in the other direction,[6] and the intention here is not to cast doubt on the importance of the Christian humanism so much associated with Erasmus, but to suggest that it should not be used as the only yardstick for judging a person's concern for the well-being of the Church. In an earlier chapter it was argued that Bishop Fitzjames has always suffered in comparison with his recalcitrant dean, John Colet, because of his lack of interest in biblical scholarship, although he seems to have taken his episcopal duties extremely seriously.[7] Robert Sherburne, bishop of Chichester from 1508 to 1536, venerated the saints, especially Thomas Becket and Richard of Chichester, believed devoutly in intercession for the souls of the dead and in the merits of 'good works'. He was

---

[1] M.J. Kelly, 'Canterbury jurisdiction', pp.42-94.

[2] Ibid, pp.95-147.

[3] Brock, pp.27, 309-15; see also p.46 above.

[4] Jedin, i, pp.117-38.

[5] The theme of Ozment, *Reformation in the Cities*.

[6] Thus Scarisbrick in *Reformation*, p.47: 'Erasmus . . . has received more attention from historians than he did from his contemporaries.'

[7] See pp.36-7.

also opposed to a vernacular bible. None of these things should be allowed to obscure the fact that he was a very active diocesan bishop who worked extremely hard to improve the standards and efficiency of his clergy.[1]

What separated a Fitzjames or Sherburne from a Colet was not a lack of concern for reform, but a belief that it should not involve any changes in doctrine or in the intellectual and scholarly substructure, or any challenge to the existing authority of the Church. Rather, they seem to have had in mind what Richard Fox, in his ecstatic response to Wolsey's summoning of a legatine council in 1519, called 'the primitive integrity of the clergy, and especially in the monastic state', which he had found to be everywhere 'perverted either by dispensation or corruptions, or else had become obsolete from age or depraved owing to the iniquities of the times'.[2] In fact cries for a return to this 'primitive integrity' came from every quarter, and what was needed to achieve it was not any pulling up by the roots or drastic cutting down, but careful pruning; not the making of new laws but the strict enforcement of the old; not theological innovation but a moral reawakening.

What makes it difficult for the historian is that both radicals and conservatives tended to use the language of renovation and renewal to mean different things; and these differences could and, in the case of Colet and Fitzjames, did lead to conflict. And in reality the divisions were not clear-cut. Erasmus felt constantly threatened by conservatives, while receiving support from such as Warham and Leo x, who can hardly be called radical. And though both Colet and Erasmus were critical of many aspects of the Church's 'paraphernalia', and stressed, in a way that worried many conservatives, a spiritual renewal rather than more formalized routes to salvation, neither of them challenged directly the basic tenets or authority of the Church. Indeed, as was pointed out in a previous chapter,[3] there was no greater defender of the clerical orders than Colet, whose passionate concern for reform arose precisely from his belief that the clergy were mediators between God and man. And whatever difficulties he may have had with Fitzjames, it is clear that the Church hierarchy was by no means opposed to everything he stood for. He was, after all, asked by Warham to preach to the 1510 convocation and to sit on its committee for reform. He was also asked by Wolsey to preach at his installation as cardinal in 1515. The picture of reform on the eve of the Reformation is, thus, a confusing one, and no doubt it is partly this confusion that has helped to hide the considerable and widespread interest in it. What matters here, however, is not the differences but the similarities, and above all the simple fact that a movement for reform was alive, if not in every respect well, in England at the time when Wolsey acquired his legatine power. The question now arises of where precisely Wolsey fits into this picture.

The tragedy for anyone with an interest in Wolsey is that the lack of evidence makes it very difficult – some might say impossible – even to attempt an answer. Something of his personal beliefs is recorded by Cavendish, of which more later, but there is nothing on which to base a convincing history of his intellectual or religious life – not even, for instance, any direct evidence of any one book that he may have read. It might be tempting to conclude that there is no evidence because there

[1] S.J. Lander, 'Diocese of Chichester', pp.14 ff. for his conservatism.
[2] Richard Fox, p.115 (LP,iii,1122); the translation from Taunton, p.63.
[3] See p.45.

never was a history. But before we do that, there is some indirect evidence that needs to be looked at. It is not only that Wolsey went to university; many people without any intellectual, let alone religious, inclinations have done that. More important is the fact that he read theology, became a fellow of Magdalen, a college arguably then at the intellectual heart of Oxford, and in 1498 was chosen to be master of the college's famous school. This provided what today would be called a secondary education, preparing its pupils for entry into the college in the same way as Winchester did for New College, Oxford, and Eton did for King's College, Cambridge. If Wolsey himself had been a pupil there, he would have been taught by John Anwykyll, the distinguished master of the school from 1481 to 1488. His successor, John Stanbridge, gave his name to the first Latin grammar written in English. Both men were at the top of their profession, presiding over a school with a first-class reputation. Too much cannot be made of Wolsey's headmastership, for it only lasted a year, and it looks as if the appointment was always intended to be a stop-gap measure.[1] Still, that he was appointed at all is likely to be evidence of some genuine interest in education, as, indeed, is the last post that he held at Magdalen, that of dean of divinity, an academic post, similar to a modern director of studies.[2]

Given this busy academic start to his career – and even in the 1520s, when he was overwhelmed with work, he took a considerable interest in the affairs of Oxford and Cambridge – it is difficult to believe that Wolsey had no interest in or knowledge of intellectual and religious matters. Then there are his foundations of Cardinal College and Ipswich. Admittedly, these were intended to perform a public function, and it is perfectly possible to believe that education is good for the common weal without being much interested in it oneself. Moreover, a concern for fame and reputation is always likely to lead the wealthy would-be patron to the merely fashionable, and in the early sixteenth century the founding of Oxford and Cambridge colleges was just that.[3] And there was the additional attraction that founding a college did not only ensure earthly fame, but the founder's chances of heavenly salvation were greatly increased by the provision of prayers to be said for his or her soul; indeed, a large proportion of the endowments of such colleges was set aside for this purpose. There were, therefore, plenty of reasons for founding a college that which for the present purpose will not do. What will is the almost obsessional nature of Wolsey's involvement in his colleges, which seems to have gone beyond the merely fashionable. Even so, to state that he had some interest in intellectual and religious matters is not, perhaps, to say very much and, however difficult, some attempt at a sharper definition must now be made.

Erasmus's reiterated praise of Henry VIII's court for its patronage of 'humane studies' is well-known, and though in his search for wealthy patrons he may have occasionally allowed himself to relax his standards a little, there are reasons for believing that he meant it.[4] There is, first of all, the known intellectual quality of the people whom he cited in support of his praise, pre-eminently Colet, Fisher and

---

[1] Stanier, pp. 1-63.
[2] *Statutes of the Colleges of Oxford*, ii, pp. 24-5, 34-5.
[3] At Cambridge there was Jesus College founded by Bishop Alcock in 1496, and Christ's in 1506 and St. John's College founded in 1516 by Lady Margaret Beaufort and John Fisher; at Oxford Brasenose College founded by Bishop Smith and Sir Richard Sutton in 1509, and Corpus Christi founded in 1517 by Bishop Fox.

More, but also the likes of Linacre, Longland, Mountjoy, Pace, Tunstall, and Warham. It is an impressive collection by any standards, and moreover, the language in which he expressed his praise seems to go beyond the requirements even of Erasmian rhetoric. Anyway, one of the Englishmen whom Erasmus singled out for praise was Cardinal Wolsey, and for the following reasons:

> The study of the humanities, hitherto somewhat fallen, is rebuilt; the liberal arts, still struggling with the champions of ancient ignorance, are supported by your [Wolsey's] encouragement, protected by your power, gilded in your reflected glory, and nourished by your magnificence, as you offer princely salaries to attract outstanding scholars to come and teach. In the getting-together of libraries richly furnished with good authors of every kind, you rival Ptolemy Philadelphus himself, who owes his fame to this even more than to his crown. The three ancient tongues, without which all learning is handicapped, are revived among us by you, for I regard the generous benefactions now offered to the famous university of Oxford a blessing to the whole of Britain . . . I see, I see a kind of golden age arising, if once that spirit of yours enters a certain number of princes.[1]

Erasmus wrote this in May 1519, at a time when he was prone to visions of a golden age; but the fact that it was Wolsey who, not only as a patron of learning but as the author of a universal peace, made the visions possible is often forgotten. Of course, the praise is excessive, but the essential point that Erasmus was making is correct. The 'generous benefaction' was the recent setting up of public lectureships at Oxford. Their precise details are difficult to arrive at but in 1518 it was announced that Wolsey intended to provide the money for six such lectureships,[2] and in the autumn of that year John Clements was lecturing in the humanities,[3] that is in Greek and Latin literature, and in 1519 Thomas Brinknell, a leading Oxford academic, was lecturing in theology.[4] If other lecturers were appointed at this time no trace of them has survived. What we do know is that Wolsey was well aware that if the new studies were to catch on, more was required than just the setting up of lectureships; the current degree courses were so heavily weighted towards logic and moral philosophy that students would have neither the time nor much incentive to attend them. So in 1519 Wolsey asked the heads of colleges to consider making attendance at the lectures compulsory. This they refused to do, but in the following year he had better luck with the regent masters – in charge of the degree courses – who agreed to rearrange their timetables to accommodate the new studies.[5]

These negotiations with the university authorities are perhaps better evidence of Wolsey's genuine interest in university education than the more obvious successes;

---

[4] Best expressed in a letter to the Italian humanist Paulo Bombace in July 1518; see CWE, 6, pp.61-2; see also ibid, 3, pp.86-7, 94-5; 5, pp.392-3, 411; 6, pp.62-3, 356-8, 364-5, 377-80, 387, 405.

[1] Ibid, 6, pp.366-7 Erasmus to Wolsey 18 May [1519].

[2] Fowler, pp.87-9; McConica, Collegiate University, pp.336-9 which sadly appeared too late for me to make best use of it. The problem is that they get muddled up with Fox's lectureships at Corpus Christi, where the lectures probably took place, and Wolsey's subsequent public lectureships attached to Cardinal College.

[3] CWE, 6, p.215 (LP,ii, app.56).

[4] Mitchell, p.90.

[5] Ibid, pp.95-6; 376-7; J.M. Fletcher, p.54.

but there were some of these as well. In 1523, for instance, he obtained the services, probably as lecturer in the humanities, of the Spaniard, John Vives, who according to Erasmus was so skilled in the classics that 'when he writes he reproduces in our own time the example of the ancients'.[1] Nor was he just a Ciceronian or stylist, for in the year before his appointment he had brought out an edition of St Augustine's *City of God*. And in the coming years he was to write a number of 'humanist' or Erasmian works, the most famous of which was his *Instruction of a Christian Woman*, dedicated to Catherine of Aragon, whose cause in the divorce he was to support – and was to lead to his leaving England for good in 1528 in some disgrace.[2] Nevertheless, Vives's appointment to Oxford in 1523 demonstrates Wolsey's concern to find the best people. In practice it proved difficult to attract good people from abroad, so that at one point Wolsey was advised 'to be contented with our learning in England, although it be somewhat more rude'.[3] And in fact his English appointments were not all that bad. John Clements, Wolsey's first lecturer in the humanities, had been a pupil of the famous schoolmaster, William Lily, at Colet's recently founded St Paul's school, and subsequently a tutor in More's household. The humanist pedigree of Clements's successor, Thomas Lupset, was if anything even more impeccable: having been brought up in Colet's household, on going up to Cambridge in 1513 he had helped the great Erasmus himself with two of his most famous undertakings, an edition of St Jerome's works and his *New Testament*.[4]

Turning from people to books, the evidence is again of considerable efforts to obtain the best, which included having copies made of works in libraries at Rome and Venice. Unfortunately there is little information about what exactly Wolsey was after, though it seems as if Greek texts were a priority.[5] These copies were meant for Cardinal College, and it was the setting up of this college, the building of which was under way by at least early 1525, that Wolsey saw as his greatest contribution to the religious and intellectual life of the country; and it was to be in many ways a decidedly humanist contribution. His professor of the humanities, one of six new public professorships attached to the college, was to deliver two lectures a day, one on the works of Cicero, Quintilian, Trapezuntius or some other rhetorician, the other on the works of Isocrates, Lucian, Philostratus, Homer, Aristophanes, Euripides, Sophocles, Pindar, Hesiod, or some other Greek poet or orator,[6] while in the college itself Plautus and Terence were to be taught.[7]

This was a massive injection of classical literature into the formal teaching of the university, which was heavily weighted towards philosophy and logic – that is, towards scholasticism. But Wolsey's humanistic intentions need to be qualified in a number of ways. The degree courses would have remained heavily weighted towards

[1] *CWE*, 6, pp.251-2. For his appointment, the details of which remain obscure, see Fowler, pp.87-9; Mitchell, pp.154-6.
[2] Vives is not well treated in English, but see Emden, *Oxford 1540*, pp.594-6; R.P. Adams, pp.220 ff; Mitchell, p.7 passim, for his Oxford career.
[3] The advice came from John Clerk in Nov. 1525; see *LP*,iv,1777. For Wolsey's efforts to secure European scholars see *LP*,iv,2149, 2158, 2222, 5224.
[4] For Clement and Lupset at Oxford see McConica, *Collegiate University*, pp.67-8, 337-8.
[5] For these efforts see *LP*,iv,2149, 2158, 2181, 2240, 2272, 2296; Ven.Cal.,iii,1187. (p. 515).
[6] *Statutes of Oxford*, ii, p.127.
[7] Ibid, pp.71-2.

scholasticism and, indeed, even the majority of Wolsey's new academic courses were devoted to the old ways.[1] And in the significant area of theology, Wolsey showed a continuing faith – or it might be more accurate to call it a revival of faith – in the scholastic methods. For the new professor of theology was to spend only half of his time in biblical studies, for a humanist the key to that subject; the other half he was to spend interpreting the 'subtle questions' of Duns Scotus, the *bête noire* of all self-respecting humanists.[2] And since his works already provided the backbone of much of the intellectual life of the university, it is all the more surprising to find Wolsey promoting them in this way. The explanation is that he believed that scholastic skills had a particular part to play in the fight against heresy, and he began to fear that, given the increasing emphasis on classical literature, these skills would be devalued and eventually lost.

Inevitably the rapid spread of Lutheranism on the continent introduced a note of caution into the initially rapturous reception of humanism in English intellectual circles, but especially amongst its slightly older members. As the 1520s advanced, both Longland and Tunstall, for instance, showed increasing unease about the effects of some of Erasmus's writings, and were not afraid to tell him so.[3] The climate was changing. The mockery and satire had been all very well when the only enemy had been the immoral and the hidebound within, but now the obvious danger was that Erasmus's weapons would get into the hands of the much more dangerous enemy without. When even More began to have doubts, not just about his 'darling's [Erasmus's] books' but his own,[4] it is not surprising that Wolsey followed suit. And that he did is suggested not only by his provision of more Duns Scotus but by the lengthy defence of a new edition of the *Colloquies* that in April 1526 Erasmus felt it expedient to send him.[5] But if doubts crept in, it remains true that Wolsey envisaged a central role in the university's curriculum for the study of classical literature, so that, as Longland explained to the queen in January 1525, men would come from all parts of Christendom to benefit from the new college's learning. At the same time Longland spoke of the special provisions which Wolsey had made for the study of the Bible there.[6] Classical literature and the Bible – were not these two at the heart of the programme for Christian renewal that humanists had been calling for during the two decades before the founding of Cardinal College? Wolsey was not the first Englishman to give active support to this programme at the universities: both Fisher at Cambridge and Fox at Oxford, to name only the most obvious, had preceded him. However, the scale of his new foundation signalled Wolsey's intention to give the programme a major boost. And nothing may be more indicative of this than the differences in salary of his new professors. Four were to receive £20 a year, but the professors of theology and of the humanities were to receive £40.[7]

[1] Sophistory, logic or dialectics, and philosophy.
[2] *Statutes of Oxford*, ii, p.127.
[3] Erasmus, *Colloquies*, pp.xxix-xxx, 314, 623-37; Sturge, pp.121-7.
[4] CWM, 8, p.179; see also More's passionate plea to Erasmus in Dec. 1526 for Erasmus to continue his fight against Luther following rumours that he had lost his nerve.
[5] LP,iv,2121.
[6] LP,iv,995.
[7] *Statutes of Oxford*, ii, p.132.

The suggestion being put forward here is that, despite the severe limitations of the evidence, it is possible to assign Wolsey a position within that broad movement for church 'reform' whose existence was argued for earlier. It was, to use the current jargon, a little left of centre, nearer to Colet than to Fitzjames – at least as regards educational and intellectual matters. As for his personal preferences, there is no evidence that he was in love with classical literature, nor do his letters display any great knowledge of the Bible – but then diplomatic correspondence hardly lends itself to biblical quotation. Erasmus did send him a copy of the 1519 edition of his *New Testament*, bearing a Latin epigram written by More in which much was made of Wolsey's 'preoccupation' with 'the Law of Christ' which More equated with Erasmus's work.[1] Still, this is not proof that Wolsey ever read the proffered gift, and in fact no acknowledgement of its receipt has survived. Moreover, as an undergraduate and fellow of Magdalen in the last two decades of the fifteenth century, neither classical literature nor the Bible would have figured prominently, though perhaps more at his college than elsewhere in the university.[2] What Wolsey would have been trained in were scholastic skills, and a letter that Thomas Winter wrote in December 1528 suggests that he retained his interest in scholasticism. Winter, then resident in Paris, was giving his father an account of his studies. What pleased him most, he wrote, were scholastic questions, because of their 'intellectual subtilty';[3] other authors merely skimmed the surface, but the schoolmen really got to the bottom of things.[4] Such remarks were hardly calculated to win the heart of a committed humanist, but there was method in them, and method that may have had very little to do with Winter's own likes and dislikes. What had happened was that the Venetian ambassador in Paris, none other than that earlier Wolsey-watcher, Sebastian Giustinian, had remarked to Winter that any real learning was dependent on the schoolmen, adding that this was something of which 'your patron was not ignorant'[5] – 'patron' being an ambassadorial euphemism for natural father. Winter did what was expected of him and passed on the compliment, at the same time stressing his own interest in the subject. One could take the view that, like Giustinian's remark, Winter's letter was no more than an exercise in insincerity but, even as such, it would have made no sense if there had been no substance to the Venetian ambassador's view of Wolsey's intellectual interests. It looks, therefore, as if Wolsey never completely deserted his training as a schoolman, and that, although he came to accept the relevance of humanism to the Church's current needs, unlike those around him, such as More and Tunstall, he was never personally reanimated by it.

Such a view is supported by the scraps of evidence that do throw some light on Wolsey's inner religious life. In 1517 he went on a pilgrimage to the shrine of our Lady of Walsingham. So did Erasmus, but, unlike him, Wolsey was not prompted to

[1] CWE, 6, p.372; Thomas More, *Latin Epigrams*, pp.124-5. In it More calls the New Testament 'the law of Christ, which has ever been your [Wolsey's] preoccupation. That law provides you with the skill by means of which you are enabled to render decisions in the face of the Mocker, for, to the amazement of people, you resolve intricate differences in such a way that even the loser cannot complain.'
[2] J.M. Fletcher, pp.47 ff., 179 ff.
[3] 'ingeniosa subtilitate'.
[4] PRO SP 1/52/fos.157-8 (*LP*,iv,5019).
[5] *LP*,iv,5019.

write a satire about what he found there. Instead, he seems to have made the pilgrimage for the time-honoured reason that he had vowed to do so if he recovered from a serious attack of the 'sweating sickness'.[1] And if humanists were not supposed to take pilgrimages very seriously, neither were they supposed to believe very much in relics. Yet Wolsey, so Cavendish tells us, wore a piece of the 'true cross' on a chain around his neck, and a hair-shirt[2] – though whether this was only in the exceptional circumstances following his political disgrace is not certain; probably it was, but then exceptional circumstances offer a good testing ground for a person's beliefs. At any rate, penitential aids are more easily associated with the monastery than the humanist's stamping ground of court and university, although the fact that More also wore one is a useful reminder that humanists, like every other category of person, came in all shapes and sizes! It is Cavendish again who tells us that Wolsey 'heard commonly every day two masses in his privy closet. And there then said his daily service with his chaplain and, as I heard his chaplain say (being a man of credence and of excellent learning), that the cardinal, what business or weighty matters so ever he had in the day, he never went to his bed with any part of his divine service unsaid, yea not so much as one collect, wherein I doubt not but he deceived the opinion of divers persons.'[3] His view that behind the public persona in all its pomp and glitter lay hidden a truly devout Christian carries some conviction, in part because of the way it emerges in his account: he provides a source – Wolsey's chaplain – while the fact that he does not feel the need to elaborate on the subject gives his judgement additional credibility. And what none of Cavendish's comments provides is evidence of any interest on Wolsey's part in 'humane studies'. Admittedly, as one whose job it was to further the smooth running of Wolsey's household, he was not in the best position to comment upon his master's intellectual concerns, but his silence on the subject at least corroborates the view being offered here that Wolsey's humanism was a matter of policy rather than private conviction. At the same time, his extensive patronage of humanism makes it impossible not to think that he genuinely believed in the policy.[4]

But is one not entitled to expect rather more 'policy' from him? Erasmus had a vision of a time when the Bible, having been translated into the vulgar tongue, would be sung by the farmer walking behind his plough and hummed by the weaver in time with the movement of his shuttle, and when travellers would tell stories from it to lighten their journeys.[5] More cautiously Thomas More could write in 1531 that he

> never yet heard any reason laid why it were not convenient to have the Bible translated into the English tongue, but all those reasons seemed they never so gay and glorious at the first sight, yet when they were well examined they might in effect as well be laid

---

[1] LP,ii,3655; ii, app.38.

[2] Cavendish, p.103 for the relic; ibid pp.130, 162, 182 for the hair-shirt.

[3] Ibid, pp.22-3; cf. ibid, pp.58-9 for Wolsey working from 4 am. until 4 pm. without a break, while all the time his chaplain was waiting to say mass, which he did immediately after the letters to the king had been despatched.

[4] Cf. M.J. Kelly, 'Canterbury jurisdiction' pp.33 ff. for the view that despite his patronage of humanists, including Erasmus, even Warham's intellectual and theological interests were essentialy conservative. See also Headley.

[5] From his Paraclesis; see inter alia Olin, pp.96-8.

against the holy writers that wrote the scripture in the Hebrew tongue.[1]

If only Wolsey had agreed with him and, instead of leaving it to heretics such as William Tyndale to meet the demand, had authorized a vernacular Bible, then the Reformation in England might never have occurred – or so it can be argued. And it is precisely his failure to come up with this kind of major innovation, so the argument continues, that makes it difficult to justify his legatine rule of the English Church. At the very least it was a glorious opportunity missed – and most historians have been more severe than that!

In rejecting such a view, the first point to make is that it is based largely on an assumption that the battle for the hearts and minds of the English people was lost by the Catholic Church on account of its own failings. If, on the other hand, there would have been no Reformation in England but for the betrayal of the Catholic cause by the English Crown, then the argument that an English Bible was a necessary 'reform' does not look so strong. The second point to make is that it was not just Wolsey who failed to see the need for an English Bible. There is no evidence before the 1530s for anyone of orthodox beliefs advocating an English Bible – and this should have given pause for thought. For instance, it is a striking fact that nowhere in Colet's writings or sermons is there any call for an English Bible and yet it is Colet who is supposed to have brought the new biblical scholarship to England. The same is true of Fisher's writings and sermons, and yet not only did he believe that scripture was the spiritual food of the soul but he had so encouraged Erasmus's biblical studies that the great Dutch humanist had considered dedicating to him his famous 1516 edition of the New Testament.[2] Moreover, even More's advocacy of an English Bible in 1531 was so circumspect as to be almost off-putting. It is not only that he insisted that any such Bible must be authorized, but that even then it should only be allowed to people whom a bishop considered 'honest, sad and virtuous'.[3] Of course, in 1531 with the Church under threat both from the king and Lutheranism, one can understand his circumspection. But the fact is that in the 1520s he, along with Fisher, had been silent on the subject, and it is difficult not to escape the conclusion that but for the advent of William Tyndale's translation of the New Testament in early 1526 he would have remained so. It is therefore not just a case of having to explain why Wolsey showed no interest in an English Bible, which could easily be ascribed to his moral failings and lack of interest in anything genuinely religious. Instead, the question that has to be tackled is why it was on nobody's agenda, not even those whose good intentions are usually considered beyond reproach.

The most usual explanation is that since such Bibles were already associated with the Lollard heresy, even the best English Catholics were prejudiced against them[4] – and undoubtedly the association was commonly made. One of the reasons why the church authorities had taken Richard Hunne to be a Lollard was that he possessed 'the Apocalypse in English, epistles and gospels in English, Wyclif's damnable works, and other books containing infinite errors', while at his

---

[1] CWM, 6, p.337.
[2] CWE, 3, p.293; Surtz, *John Fisher*, pp.114 ff.
[3] CWM,6, pp.331-44.
[4] *Inter alia* Dickens, *English Reformation*, p.9; Lander, *Government and Community*, pp.132-3.

posthumous trial article 13 stated that 'he defendeth the translation of the Bible and the holy Scripture into the English tongue, which is prohibited by the laws of our mother, holy Church'.[1] How far they were actually prohibited is another matter. It has been estimated that by 1500 at least 29 editions of vernacular Bibles had appeared on the continent, with little or no opposition from the church authorities[2] – not that this prevented the Reformation! The English Church did take a different line. Such Bibles in themselves were never banned, but as a direct result of Wyclif and Lollardy, anyone wishing to read an English Bible had to obtain the approval of a bishop, and the possession of an unauthorized English bible, as in the case of Hunne, was taken as evidence of heterodoxy.[3] Does it have to be concluded that fear of Wyclif's Bible drove the English bishops into a blinkered resistance to something that their flocks were everywhere hungering after?

The simple fact is that it is virtually impossible to find any demand for an English Bible before the 'break with Rome', except amongst the Lollards. Admittedly the church authorities' alarm at the appearance of Tyndale's *New Testament* in 1526 is evidence that they anticipated some demand for it. And people did buy it. Indeed, there was in the 1520s an illicit trade in heretical works, amongst which was Tyndale's *New Testament*, but the notion that these sold like hot cakes should be treated with a good deal of scepticism. For instance, following the arrest of Thomas Garrard in 1528 for his efforts to subvert the undergraduates of Oxford with such literature, about six Tyndale's *New Testaments* were discovered, which, in view of the thoroughness of the searches that were carried out, does not seem all that many.[4] And what of the evidence of Robert Necton's confession of the same year, which reveals that over a period of eighteen months he managed to sell thirty-five copies of that same work, mostly to people with known Lollard connections?[5] My own feeling is that it was a highly selective trade, the booksellers using almost exclusively their connections with Lollard groups and the few at the universities who were interested in the new heresy from abroad.

The answers one gives to the questions that these controversial matters raise depend very much upon one's assumptions, in particular about the state of the English Church on the eve of the Reformation and the inclination, or otherwise, of the English nation to embrace Protestantism. It is hardly surprising that most English historians, brought up in a Protestant and Whig tradition, have argued, to use the current jargon, for a 'fast' Reformation, one fuelled by a genuine popular desire for the new faith. Yet even the most passionate believers in such a view have had great difficulty in finding many avid readers of an English Bible, even though by the late 1530s the provision of such a Bible in every parish church had become a government requirement.[6] And the lack of demand cannot be unconnected with the fact that, as More rightly pointed out, only a very few people could read.[7] One

---

[1] Foxe, iv, pp.184, 186.

[2] Duggan, pp.12-4; see also Dickens, *English Reformation*, p.9.

[3] The statutes against heresy are conveniently printed in CWM, 9, pp.249-60; prohibitions against translations of the Bible into English, and against their possession, unless licensed by a bishop in A.W.Pollard, pp.79-81. See also Thomson, *Later Lollards*, pp.220 ff.

[4] Foxe, v, app 6 for the list of books found and number; also CWM, 8, p.1173. On the general subject of English translations A.W.Pollard is still essential.

[5] The confession printed in A.W. Pollard, pp.155-9.

suspects, anyway, that Bible-reading has only ever appealed to the committed, who tend to be few. And if there was so little demand, it can hardly be held against Wolsey, along with such champions of reform as Colet, Fisher and More, that he made no effort to meet it.

Part of the difficulty in assessing the demand for an English Bible on the eve of the Reformation derives from the great differences between Catholics and Protestants about the importance to be attached to the Bible itself. As the authentic word of God, for Luther and his followers the Bible provided the only touchstone for all matters of doctrine and practice. For a Catholic such as More this position was untenable. The Church was a living organism sustained by Christ's promise to the disciples that he would remain with them until the end of time. As such, it could speak with even more authority than the Bible, for it was able to produce, so to speak, the most up-to-date edition. It naturally followed that the possession of a Bible, particularly in one's own language, was of more importance to a Protestant than to a Catholic. Indeed, for the former it became something of a membership card, not necessarily read but evidence of belonging, and it is this that has caused the confusion. After all, it is doubtful that every Chinese who acquired Mao Tse-tung's Little Red Book was necessarily a fervent supporter of Mao, and thus the distribution of Little Red Books might not be very reliable evidence of the demand. Similarly, the fact that Thomas Cromwell ordered that an English Bible be kept in every parish church is not reliable evidence that lots of people wanted to read it. But since in England the Protestants were to win, it has been assumed that they had a better case, and one that most people believed in. The suggestion here has been that most people in the 1520s held no such belief.

The distortions of the Protestant tradition have led to bad history, and have created en passant the very critical view of Wolsey as a churchman that it has been the purpose of this chapter to revise. What the Catholics of the early sixteenth century thought of as necessary 'reforms' have been downgraded, if not ignored completely, thereby creating a false perspective. For instance, by giving the impression that Catholics were opposed to the Bible, historians have ignored the enormous amount of money and effort being expended by leading churchmen on better provision for biblical studies. Both Fisher at Christ's and St John's, Cambridge, and Fox at Corpus Christi, Oxford, made detailed provision for it, the latter going out of his way to point out that in interpreting the Bible his reader in theology should not make use of medieval authorities, who were 'posterior and inferior in learning, but the holy and ancient Greek and Latin doctors'.[1] For Cardinal College Wolsey did not specify what authorities should be consulted. Probably he felt that it was no longer necessary to do so, and certainly the emphasis in his statutes on the usefulness of Latin and Greek for a proper understanding of the Bible suggests that he expected a humanist approach. True, he insisted that the professor of theology spend half of his time in scholastic pursuits, but that left the

<hr>

[6] On the English Bible and the Reformation by such a believer see Dickens, *English Reformation*, pp.70 ff., 129 ff., 189 ff.

[7] CWM, 9, p.13.

<hr>

[1] Fowler, pp.51-2, quoting from the statutes. For Fisher at Cambridge see Rackham, pp.91, 109; Mayor, pp.313, 315, 335, 376.

other half for Old and New Testament studies.[1] Moreover, as Fisher and Fox had done at their colleges, Wolsey insisted that a portion of the Bible should be read out each day at dinner, and then expounded upon by a suitably qualified person.[2]

Something else that the Protestant tradition has tended to obscure is the fact that most medieval men and women liked sermons; one thinks not only of the great audiences that a Bernardino of Sienna or a Savonarola could command, but also of the great number of medieval sermons delivered in England by much less charismatic preachers.[3] And after all, it was as early as 1216 that the Dominican order had been established, with preaching as its principal task. Thus, whatever special significance he may have attached to it as the principal means, alongside the Bible, by which the 'Word of God' was revealed to man, the sermon was not the invention of Martin Luther, and what is to be noted is the concern being shown in England in the first decades of the sixteenth century to provide a preaching ministry. As Fisher reminded the university of Cambridge in 1528, it had been his intention and that of the university's great patroness, Lady Margaret Beaufort, that its graduates should 'spread Christ's Gospel throughout the confines of the whole of Britain',[4] and to ensure this he laid down that a quarter of the fellows of St John's should preach to the people in English at least eight times a year.[5] Wolsey's provision for preaching by the fellows of Cardinal College was, if anything, more extensive. Four public sermons were to be delivered in the college chapel each year, to which the citizens of Oxford were to be summoned by the 'ringing of the largest bell for a notable space of time'. Furthermore, for the ten years after obtaining their doctorates the college's five doctors of theology should preach publicly seven times a year. Anyone studying theology who left the college before becoming a doctor and sought to become one at a later date, as Wolsey himself did, was to deliver one public sermon a year.[6] It looks therefore as if in any one year Wolsey was intending to fund about forty public sermons,[7] surely by any standards an impressive contribution to the spreading of Christ's gospel?

Fisher, Fox and Wolsey all felt that a better knowledge of the Bible and the preaching of Christ's gospel were vital to any programme of church reform, and went to great lengths to ensure that both were encouraged. More generally, all three saw the education of the clergy, rather than doctrinal or administrative changes, as being at the heart of the matter which is why their colleges must be assigned a major role in any assessment of the state of the English Church on the eve of the 'break with Rome'. The purpose of this education was to bring about a moral reformation. This could only be achieved by beginning at the top, for as Colet put it in 1510, 'if the priests and bishops, that should be as lights, run in the dark way of the world, how dark then shall the secular people be? Wherefore St Paul said chiefly unto priests and bishops: be you not conformable to this world, but be ye reformed.'[8]

---

[1] *Statutes of Oxford*, ii, p.127.

[2] Ibid, p.69.

[3] Owst.

[4] Quoted in Surtz, *Works and Days*, p.56.

[5] Mayor, pp.313-5.

[6] *Statutes of Oxford*, ii, pp.78-81.

[7] The rumour that he personally preached 40 sermons a year is sadly unfounded. Indeed, he seems not to have preached any.

Colet saw no use for new laws: 'The way whereby the Church may be reformed into better fashion is not for to make new laws, for there be laws many enough and out of number; as Solomon saith: nothing is new under the sun.'[1] Instead, what he wanted was an inward spiritual regeneration and it was his sources for this, such as neo-platonism, St Paul's epistles and a humanist approach to the Bible, which displeased conservative churchmen, just as their concern for the veneration of saints and the efficacy of good works displeased Colet. However, both conservatives and humanists could agree that what was essential to any programme of moral regeneration was a tightening up of the existing church machinery and enforcement of existing laws.

> [The evils] that are now in the Church were before in time past, and there is no fault but that the fathers have provided very good remedies for it. There are no trespasses but there be laws against them in the body of the canon law. Therefore it is no need that new laws and constitutions be made, but that those that are made already be kept.[2]

Thus spoke Colet but so also spoke almost everybody with any interest in the well-being of the Church.

But if in the 1520s the call was for 'moral regeneration' rather than for innovation, was Wolsey really a suitable person to make it? Colet, yes. Fisher, yes. Even a layman like More, yes. But surely not Wolsey? After all, no one could have been more 'conformable to this world', the very evil that Colet believed was destroying the Church, an evil for Colet even more dangerous, because more insidious, than heresy itself. In some obvious ways, it has to be admitted, Wolsey was not suitable. Even if one can discount some of the more extreme criticisms of his allegedly excessive love of pomp and ceremony made by such as Skelton and Vergil at the time, and many people since, there is no escaping the fact that, as the leading royal servant for fifteen years, Wolsey was heavily involved in secular affairs including the conduct of war and diplomacy. To achieve such a position he must have been ambitious, and, undoubtedly, his position made him extremely wealthy. There is also the matter of his 'concubine', Mistress Lark, and their two children – a daughter, Dorothy, placed in the wealthy nunnery at Shaftesbury, and the son Thomas Winter, on whom he lavished, according to his critics, far too much wealth and church patronage. On the whole Wolsey seems to have managed his sex life very discreetly. True, Skelton makes some rude remarks on the subject, though compared with what he wrote about other aspects of the cardinal's life he is surprisingly restrained[3] – perhaps because it was not a convincing line to take? There is also article 6 of the charges drawn up after his fall from power, which accused him of endangering the king's person, for while knowing he had 'the foul and contagious disease of the great pox broken out upon him in divers places of his

---

[8] Lupton, p.294.

---

[1] Ibid, p.299.

[2] Ibid, p.300.

[3] 'He foynes and he frygges;/Spareth neither mayde ne wyfe.' From 'Why come ye nat to Court' (Skelton, p.284); and for guidance in interpreting all Skelton's criticism of Wolsey's moral failings see Walker, pp.124-53.

351

body, [Wolsey] came daily to your grace rowning in your ear and blowing upon your most noble grace with his perilous and infective breath'.[1] Wolsey was to dismiss these charges out of hand, and it will be argued later that he was right to do so. Interestingly, very little was dredged up at that time about Mistress Lark – just the case of Sir John Stanley, allegedly bullied into surrendering a tenancy to the man whom Wolsey had married her off to. Neither was there anything about other mistresses, which, if there had been, would have been just the kind of thing to help blacken Wolsey's name. Moreover, nothing of Mistrss Lark, or even a hint of any other sexual peccadilloes, is to be found in the reports of foreign ambassadors; and one suspects that even diplomatic caution would not have excluded such subject matter if there had been anything serious to report.[2] Still, however discreetly Wolsey behaved, the fact remains that Mistress Lark should not have been or, at least, not if one is directing a programme of 'moral regeneration'. Unlike Fisher, Wolsey was not a saint; but then a saint was probably not what the English Church needed at its head.

In arriving at any assessment of Wolsey's achievement, some allowance must be made for the political realities of the time. The Church constituted a number of extremely powerful and wealthy interest groups, none of which would welcome interference in its affairs from any quarter. It is difficult to say what made life more difficult for a reformer: the ability of any one of these groups to resist intervention, or the existence of the groups themselves and the consequent rivalries between them. As regards the former, it is worth recalling the almost successful efforts of the Observant Franciscans who had powerful enough friends at Rome to obtain the support of the pope himself to prevent a legatine visitation of the Greenwich house. The problem of conflicting interest groups, although implicit in much of the discussion, may not so far have been sufficiently highlighted, but, arguably, it was Warham's inability to dominate these groups that undermined his efforts at reform. Despite a theoretical primacy, an archbishop of Canterbury's authority over the English Church was very limited. For all practical purposes York's northern province was outside his control. Over the religious orders, he had no more jurisdiction than any other bishop, which is to say that he could intervene only in the affairs of the non-exempt monasteries in his own diocese and, for a brief period, in any diocese in which there was an episcopal vacancy. He could, indeed, summon southern convocation, though in practice he only did this when a parliament was called, but his efforts to push through reform there were not very successful, in part at least because he became embroiled in a major row over competing jurisdictions with a group of his suffragans led by the extremely influential Richard Fox. Moreover, what this conflict showed up was that Warham did not have the support of the king, and, indeed, in 1515 he found himself in direct conflict with Henry over the Standish affair.

What Wolsey brought to the task of reform were just those things that Warham lacked: immense political skill and Henry's full support. It was easy enough for the likes of Colet and Fisher, with their limited responsibilities and scholarly interests,

---

[1] LP,iv,6075.
[2] LP,iv,6075, art.38 with its reference to 'one Lark's daughter which woman the said lord cardinal kept, and had with her two children'.

to deplore the the way in which the Church had become so enmeshed in the affairs of Caesar as to leave precious little time or room for the affairs of God. But while a yearning for the 'purity' of the early days of the apostles was understandable, whether the reality of being a small persecuted sect would have fulfilled these yearnings is another matter. And in the early sixteenth century the reality was that religious and secular life were so intertwined, and the need of both Church and Crown for each other so established, that, while there was room to argue about the nature of the relationship, divorce or disestablishment was not a possibility. Thus, it was precisely what in 1519 Bishop Fox called his 'great skill in business, whether divine or human' that enabled Wolsey during the 1520s to provide the right conditions for the Church to flourish. There were no more attacks from the Crown lawyers. There were no damaging disputes between different interest groups within the Church. The standards expected from its various members were publicly restated and it was made clear that where necessary the legatine authority was available to ensure that these were enforced. Far from being 'despotic', a possible criticism of Wolsey is that he was not willing enough to ignore the legal restraints that, for instance, made the removal of unsatisfactory heads of religious houses so difficult. It may also be that he did not attempt enough, though the force of such a criticism derives from, in this account, the mistaken notion that everything was terribly wrong with the English Church. In fact, during his last eighteen months in power Wolsey did embark upon some major reforms, prompted, so it will be argued, by a growing fear of the Lutheran threat. It was a threat that Wolsey took extremely seriously, but then the argument here has been that Henry's cardinal legate always had the best interests of the English Church at heart.

CHAPTER NINE

THE GREAT ENTERPRISE

O**N 29 MAY 1522 FRANCIS I RECEIVED HENRY VIII'S FORMAL DECLARATION OF** war and for the next three years these two kings, who only two years before had celebrated their 'perpetual friendship' on the Field of Cloth of Gold, were to do battle with one another. Superficially it might look as if the Hundred Years War had been revived with an English king, once again in partnership with his Burgundian allies, asserting his ancient claim to the throne of France. For Henry the play-acting was over: he could now discard the always rather uncomfortable character of *Rex Pacificus* which his cardinal had tried to coach him in, and resume his more natural role as 'the flower and glory of all knighthood'. In doing so he would not only be following in the footsteps of his great ancestor and namesake, Henry v, but also reviving the ancient claims of the kings of England to the throne of France.[1]

Such a view of Henry's mood in the spring and summer of 1522 has something to be said for it. It was hardly possible for there to be a war with France without playing the old tunes; and perhaps it was impossible for a king of England not to be somewhat stirred by them. In the September of that year Sir Thomas More reported to Wolsey a conversation with Henry during the course of which the king had declared 'that he trusted in God to be there [in France]', and to be 'governor himself', and that the French should 'make way for him as King Richard did for his father'.[2] It might seem quite a bellicose remark, but perhaps in the circumstance of an existing war with France not exceptionally so. It had been prompted by a report from Surrey, then in command of an expeditionary force in France, that the French Council were thinking of 'retiring' Francis and appointing a governor; and to contemplate acceptance of the throne as the gift of a committee is not evidence of excessive machismo; even his 'unheroic' father had had to win the English crown on Bosworth Field. More's hope, that if Henry's becoming governor of France should 'be good for his grace and for this realm that then it may prove so, and else in the stead thereof I pray God send his grace one honourable and profitable peace',[3] may be evidence of the kind of restraints that a Christian humanist laboured under as a royal councillor. But, as his literary battles with the French poet, Germain de Brie, indicate, More could be as anti-French as any other Englishman, and both his and Henry's comments on this occasion reflect the degree of ambiguity that always lay behind the Great Enterprise.

That there was ambiguity should come as no surprise. Enough has already been explained about Wolsey's approach to foreign policy to suggest that there was nothing very chivalric about it – not, at least, if that meant a lot of charging about on white horses. Henry may have been rather more fond of equestrian pursuits, but

---

[1] Gunn, 'French Wars', pp. 36-7; Scarisbrick, *Henry* viii, pp. 21-4, 128; L.B. Smith, *Henry* viii, pp. 145 ff.
[2] Thomas More, *Correspondence*, p. 263 (*LP*, iii, 2555).
[3] Ibid.

as his approach to the campaign of 1523 will show, he was in military matters extremely cautious. Moreover, the argument to date has been that in matters of substance there was no conflict between master and servant, which in the present context would suggest that Wolsey was not about to spend his time restraining a monarch concerned only to win honour on the battlefields of France. Of course, Henry's honour was always a major concern, but, as we have already seen, this was a fairly flexible notion, able to incorporate a number of contradictory activities, such as seeking peace or waging war. Furthermore, it will greatly help to understand the ambiguities of English foreign policy in the three years that elapsed between the signing of the Treaties of Windsor and Bishop's Waltham with the emperor in July 1522 and the signing of the Treaty of the More with the French in August 1525 if the reasons for the Imperial alliance are firmly borne in mind. Powerless to prevent conflict between Habsburg and Valois, Henry and Wolsey had been forced either to opt out of European affairs or to make a choice between the contending royal houses. As the first course of action was virtually unthinkable, because so detrimental to Henry's honour, a choice had to be made. In the end it was the Imperial alliance that appeared to have more to offer, on the assumption that Charles was likely to be more compliant than Francis. As events were to prove, the assumption was wrong, for despite the care that Wolsey had taken to draw up an agreement that would be binding upon him, the emperor was to find it remarkably easy to escape. But the central purpose of the Imperial alliance had never been the conquest of France; indeed, not until the emperor's resounding victory over the French at Pavia in early 1525 was the conquest of France discussed – and then, it will be argued, not very seriously. Instead, the intention was to use any military success that might result from the war to establish a European order dominated by Henry and his leading councillor. It was, in other words, very much the same policy as before, except that this time circumstances had dictated that England's partner should be not, as in 1514 and 1518, a king of France but rather a Holy Roman Emperor and king of Aragon and Castile, Charles v. All the same, it remains the case that from Wolsey's return from Calais in November 1521 until at least the spring of 1524, English foreign policy did have a consistency of purpose unlike what had gone before, and indeed what was to follow; the reason for this was the Great Enterprise. War with France was what all England's efforts were directed towards and to that end in March 1522 commissioners had been sent to every county in order to establish the extent of her ability to conduct it.

The so-called 'general proscription' of 1522 is perhaps the most important piece of evidence for the seriousness of the government's commitment to the Great Enterprise.[1] In fact the first reports from the commissioners were considered incomplete and inaccurate, and in July new instructions had to be sent out, which incidently make it clearer that financial rather than more directly military matters were the government's chief concern. Nevertheless, as a result of the exercise, for the first time for centuries the Crown had a reasonably accurate notion of the number of able-bodied men available to fight, and the potential size of any retinue that any given leading figure could raise; and it needs to be remembered that such

[1] Goring, EHR, lxxxvi for all aspects of the general proscription.

retinues, rather than any professional force, still comprised a major part of any royal army. The survey had also discovered to what extent people's obligations under the statute of Winchester of 1285 to provide armour and weapons were being fulfilled, and in the following year an effort was made to remedy the many deficiencies that had come to light. All in all, it was an impressive achievement, and in its close targeting on the practical problems of waging war perhaps unparalleled. By the spring of 1523 the information obtained concerning people's wealth had made it possible to raise two loans from the laity amounting to over £200,000, and one from the Church of over £55,000. Moreover, a parliament had been summoned to meet in April 1523 so that yet more money might be raised, for if one thing was certain it was that the Great Enterprise would cost a lot of money, for there has never been a more expensive activity than war.

No medieval or early modern king could finance war from his own resources.[1] Henry VII, and indeed his Yorkist predecessors, had undoubtedly strengthened the royal finances, especially as regards the management of the royal estates, which, along with the customs revenue, by Henry VIII's accession had come to provide about 80 per cent of the Crown's annual income. Precisely how great this income was has been disputed, but it was somewhere in the region of £110,000. By 1522 there had probably been a decline; certainly, revenue from both customs and land had decreased, and there is no reason to suppose that the shortfall had been made up from other sources.[2] All the same, there is no evidence that in peacetime the Crown was experiencing any major financial difficulty, though both in 1519 and in 1525-6 some concern was shown to restrict royal expenditure, especially in the household departments. What is certain, however, is that £110,000 was not enough in wartime. Even the supposedly financially prudent Henry VII managed to spend some £108,000, though admittedly over four years, ostensibly in defence of Breton independence. His son's early interventions in France were even more expensive. Between the spring of 1511 and the autumn of 1514 Henry VIII spent a staggering £892,000 on wages, provisions and ordinance, though even this does not compare with the £560,000 that he spent on warfare in the space of of twelve months in the 1540s.[3] Nor was it only English kings who spent colossal sums in this way. Within two years of his succession Francis I found himself in debt to the tune of something approaching four million *livres* (about £400,000), the result very largely of his first, and it should be stressed very successful, invasion of Italy.[4] Almost the same amount was to be provided by the kingdom of Naples alone to finance Imperial forces in Northern Italy in the late 1520s, and even this was not enough to prevent large-scale mutiny amongst the Imperial forces for lack of pay, leading amongst other things to the sack of Rome.[5]

It was undoubtedly to Henry's disadvantage that both Francis and Charles were in receipt of much larger sums. It has been estimated that in 1523 Francis's revenue was in the region of 7,800,000 *livres* (£780,000) a year.[6] Because of the autonomy of

[1] See Hale for an excellent introduction.
[2] Wolfe, *Crown Lands*, pp.66 ff; EHR, lxxix.
[3] Bernard, *War, Taxation and Rebellion*, p.53 for all these figures.
[4] Knecht, p.117.
[5] Koenigsbergher, p.50.
[6] Knecht, p.128.

the various parts of his empire, Charles's revenue is much harder to calculate, but merely as king of Aragon and Castile, he received somewhere in the region of 1,000,000 ducats, or £225,000 a year.[1] Moreover, in differing ways, both rulers were in a better position than Henry to draw upon a greater proportion of their subjects' wealth by way of taxation. There was, for instance, nothing in England to compare with such important indirect taxes as the *gabelle* in France or the *alcabala* in Spain; and the beauty of such taxes was that they did not require the subject's consent. Another difference was that both Francis and Charles borrowed money on a much greater scale than Henry – especially Charles, who was fortunate to be able to make use of the increasingly large amounts of revenue from South American bullion to serve as security for large loans from the great finance houses of Europe such as the Fuggers of Augsburg. He also borrowed from his own subjects on an increasingly large scale by the sale of annuities. Francis also borrowed from his subjects, but more usually from very particularly wealthy men such as his own finance minister, Semblançay. He also very much extended the practice of creating offices for the express purpose of selling.

Something all three monarchs agreed upon was that the Church was a suitable case for financial exploitation, Charles obtaining from just one Spanish clerical source, the *cruzada*, 150,000 ducats, or over £30,000 a year.[2] Curiously, however, in the secular field the English Crown was not nearly so innovative or various in its approaches to the obtaining of money. Admittedly, in the 1540s Henry, like Charles, was to borrow large sums from the Fuggers,[3] but in Wolsey's time there was very little borrowing either from foreign bankers or, except in special circumstances such as applied in 1522 and 1525, from private individuals. Indeed, the strong impression is that private individuals were much more likely to be in debt to the Crown rather than the other way round. Some money does seem to have passed hands on the appointment to offices, and the practice was to grow as the century progressed, while under James I the sale of titles was to be introduced in a systematic way. But the sale of neither title nor office made any real contribution to Henry VIII's revenues. What did was taxation, of which more shortly. First, though, some comment is needed upon the great disparity between the financial resources of the English monarchy and those of its European counterparts, a comment that may come quite naturally at a moment when England was about to embark upon a Great Enterprise.

If one first asks why the disparity, the obvious answers have to do with size and resources. It is easy to forget just how big a political unit France was in the sixteenth century. Although in area just a little behind her nearest rival, Spain,[4] in other respects she was way ahead. Population figures are largely a matter of guesswork, but it looks as if France contained about fifteen million, Castile and Aragon together about seven and half million. As for revenue, Francis I could expect perhaps three times the amount that Charles V received from his Spanish kingdoms.[5] Compared with both these, England and Wales together could muster only two and half

[1] Elliott, p.198.
[2] Elliott, p.193.
[3] Dietz, *English Government Finance*, p.173.
[4] The approximate figures are 180,000 sq. miles for France and 194,000 for Castile and Aragon.
[5] Knecht, p.119; Elliott, p.198.

million people, with royal revenues amounting to about one-fifth the French.[1] But lack of size and numbers was no reason for not attempting to sell offices or adopting other such financial stratagems, and it has to be said that the impression is that in the first two decades of his reign Henry does not seem to have been under any great financial strain, and hence there was little incentive to seek for new sources of revenue.

Why this was so is not as clear as it used to be when the belief was that Henry VII had left his son great financial surpluses, and it may still be the case that quite large sums of money, some of it in the form of jewels and plate, had been channelled into such private repositories as the rather shadowy king's coffers.[2] But whatever the reality, for at least the first decade of his reign, Henry was considered by foreigners to be a wealthy king, the Venetian ambassador, Giustinian, calling him not only 'the best dressed sovereign in the world' but also 'very rich indeed'.[3] Moreover, in 1513 not only had he been able to finance one of the largest expeditionary forces ever to have set sail from England, but he had also had to finance an army to meet the Scots. And for Henry even peace could be quite expensive, the famous meeting with Francis at the Field of Cloth of Gold costing about £15,000, or roughly one-seventh of the Crown's annual revenue.[4] But the money for all this expenditure was apparently found with comparative ease; and the conclusion would seem to be, therefore, that there was no great pressure to seek new sources of revenue because it was thought that there was money enough to conduct even the kind of ambitious foreign policy that both Henry and Wolsey believed in. And it is the connection between finance and foreign policy that has to be looked at now.

It was apparently Wolsey's practice to answer criticism of his forward foreign policy by recounting one of Aesop's fables. A few wise men were attempting to escape the consequences of a 'great rain the which should make them all fools' by retreating into a cave, hoping that when the rain had passed they would re-emerge to hold sway over those foolish enough to stay out in the rain. The stratagem did not work for 'the fools would none of that, but would have the rule themselves' for all the wise men's craft.[5] In other words, Wolsey was arguing that whatever the wisdom of isolationist and pacifist policies, there are just too many 'foolish' or, alternatively, ruthless, people who will take advantage of passivity. The sensible policy can only be for a government to get its hands dirty or, to continue the metaphor of the fable, get wet, and hope to beat the 'fools' at their own game. It is the classic defence of *realpolitik* which may offer a different perspective on the rationale of Wolsey's foreign policy from that provided by 'honour' and the chivalric trappings of a Field

---

[1] For perceptive comments on the relationship between resources and foreign policy see Mattingly, *Renaissance Diplomacy*, pp.115-25.

[2] Wolfe, *Crown Lands*, p.86 for scepticism about Henry VII's 'mighty treasure', while for the view that he took his scepticism too far see Starkey, 'King's privy chamber', pp.393 ff., usefully summarized in Elton, *Reform and Reformation*, p.30.

[3] Rawdon Brown, ii, p.313 (*LP*,iii,402).

[4] Elton, *Reform and Reformation*, p.84.

[5] Thomas More, *Correspondence*, pp.512-13 in a letter allegedly from Margaret Roper to her step-sister Lady Alington, in which she recounts More's reaction to use of this same fable to persuade him not to continue his opposition to Henry's 'break with Rome'. It should not, therefore, be taken as a final statement of More's view of Wolsey's foreign policy.

of Cloth of Gold. It may, nevertheless, not convince everyone, for the difficulty is that it is not very obvious that during the 1520s the 'fools' were anxious to invade or in other ways to threaten the interests of Henry's kingdom. Moreover, as one contemporary who may not have been altogether happy with Wolsey's foreign policy, or indeed with the moral implications of the fable whereby to rule the 'fools' one had to become a 'fool' oneself, wryly commented, it was a fable that in Wolsey's time had helped 'the king and the realm to spend many a fair penny'.[1]

The implication behind More's comment that the pennies had been badly spent by Wolsey, together with something of his 'puritanism' – if one may use such a term in relation to a Catholic saint – has remained lurking behind much of the criticism of Wolsey's foreign policy. It has been thought too grandiose, too extravagant, too much a reflection of his own self-glorification.[2] From a certain viewpoint such criticism must be true, but it is the point of view that is controlling the judgement. For some people, all expenditure on foreign policy is so much vanity and wickedness. For others, any amount spent in the pursuit of a country's self-interest is money well spent. And what of money spent on more nebulous, and perhaps nowadays unfashionable, concepts, such as honour and glory? By their very nature such things are not very amenable to accounting criteria. For both Henry and Wolsey the king's honour and the best interests of the common weal were hardly divisible, and both needed to be promoted with all the resources at the kingdom's disposal. It is perfectly legitimate to be critical of the foreign policy that resulted from this, as long as one tries to understand the attitudes that lay behind it and to appreciate how all-pervasive they were. It has already been mentioned that the English spent about £15,000 on the Field of Cloth of Gold. What should also be mentioned is that the French spent about £20,000.[3] As much in peace as in war conspicuous display was expected of a sixteenth-century monarch, and it would have been a very brave and probably foolish king who did not try and fulfil such expectations. And it needs to be stressed that the argument of this book has been that Wolsey was just as much concerned for his master's honour as his master was. It was not the case that he was having to spend all his time restraining a more chauvinistic and chivalric Henry.[4] Indeed, as will be shown in this chapter, Henry could on occasions be considerably more cautious than Wolsey. Thus, if there is criticism to be made of the extravagance, not to say fecklessness, of English foreign policy during the 1520s, Wolsey must take his fair share, and insofar as he was more concerned with the administrative and financial consequences of the policy, perhaps the lion's share.

What has already been made clear is that England's resources were nowhere near equal to those of her two main rivals. What is equally true, however, is that her commitments were nowhere near as great, if only because she was not involved in the battle for Italy. In preparation for his first and, as it turned out, most successful Italian campaign, culminating in his famous victory at Marignano, Francis I had spent in the region of 1.8 million *livres* (£180,000), and the diplomacy which

[1] Ibid, p.518.
[2] *Inter alia* C.S.L. Davies, *Peace, Print and Protestantism*, p.160; Elton, *Studies*, 1, pp.122-3.
[3] Knecht, p.121.
[4] This an underlying theme of Scarisbrick's treatment; see *Henry VIII*, pp.125-47.

followed cost him almost as much. In the aftermath of the Treaties of Noyon and Fribourg in 1516 he had had to find well over £200,000 for the Swiss, at least £45,000 for the Emperor Maximilian, and £20,000 for the dispossessed duke of Milan; and despite English opposition to much of what he was doing, he continued to pay Henry a pension of £10,000 a year.[1] As for Charles, he was having to provide armies to put down rebellions in Spain, to defend all his Mediterranean possessions from naval attack by the Turks and Barbary pirates, to fight campaigns in Italy, to maintain his own position in Germany as Holy Roman Emperor and to help his brother, the Archduke Ferdinand, defend Habsburg lands in Austria and Hungary from Turkish attack.

The fact that Francis's and Charles's resources were more stretched than Henry's helped to lessen the disparity between them. Moreover, the secret of the successful financing of war was not so much how much credit one might eventually obtain but how quickly and efficiently one could get large sums of money to a particular spot at a particular time; and arguably the English were rather better, at any rate than Charles, at doing this. It was, after all, an Imperial army that in 1527 sacked Rome for lack of pay, not an English one. And when for the only time during the Great Enterprise English and Imperial armies co-operated on any scale, for the 'march on Paris' in October and November 1523, it was the Imperial army, not the English, that failed to receive its wages.[2] Not so many months later the emperor was recording in a private memo that 'however much I save and scrape, it is often difficult for me to find the necessary means'.[3] None of this is meant to suggest that if either Francis or the emperor, or the two of them together, chose to concentrate their resources against England, she would not have been outgunned, and it will be argued later that as regards the vital matter of Henry's divorce, Charles was to prove to have a few too many guns for Wolsey's good. But in assessing the viability of Wolsey's foreign policy it is important to bear in mind that England's main rivals had as many financial difficulties as she did, and that in most circumstances they were not prepared to concentrate their resources against her. Both these factors enabled Henry and Wolsey to play a much greater role in European affairs than their comparatively slender resources might, at first glance, appear to have allowed.

What Henry and Wolsey could not have done, however, was to play such a role without a fairly massive contribution from the English taxpayer. Moreover, recently it has been argued very persuasively that in 1525 vital decisions were forced upon them by a lack of money, as taxpayers finally revolted against having to finance their too ambitious plans.[4] In what follows such an argument will be resisted, but however convincing the refutation may be, the revolt did take place and has to be taken as evidence of some unusual strain on the body politic, a strain undoubtedly imposed by war. Thus, if England could indeed finance her foreign policy with comparative ease, as was earlier claimed, emphasis needs to be placed upon the

[1] Knecht, pp.121-2.
[2] Gunn, *EHR*, ci, pp.622-3.
[3] Brandi, p.218.
[4] The central argument of Bernard, *War, Taxation and Rebellion*. Much of what follows is a commentary on this work. The fact that I am one of its dedicatees is, I hope, an indication of my respect for the argument, despite my disagreement with it.

qualification. And the general proscription of 1522 has to be evidence of some concern about England's ability to pay for enterprises abroad. So also do the efforts made, at about this time, to modernize a system of parliamentary taxation that had seen little alteration in some hundred and fifty years.

The usual practice in the late Middle Ages was for a parliamentary grant to be made in the form of 'tenths' and 'fifteenths' – representing the rate at which the tax had been levied, that is, at one-tenth of the wealth of those individuals residing within a borough and at one-fifteenth for the remainder.[1] But ever since 1334 all attempts to reassess an individual's wealth each time the tax was levied had been abandoned. Instead, each local community was allocated a fixed sum, based upon what had been customarily raised from the area, and was then left to its own devices as to how to raise the amount. It was a system that had advantages for both Crown and taxpayer. From the Crown's point of view, it was simple to administer and the revenue was certain. For the taxpayer, its initial advantage lay in the fact that his personal wealth was not submitted to frequent scrutiny by central government. But as the years went by, the system acquired the additional advantage that the fixed sums, anyway significantly reduced in 1433 and 1446 and subject to a great number of exemptions, increasingly underestimated real wealth.[2] Of course, it was possible for the Crown to compensate for this shortfall by asking for more and more fifteenths and tenths, but to do so was politically difficult. For one thing, the Crown had to provide a convincing reason for any request for money – virtually the only acceptable one being the need to provide for the defence of the kingdom – and this was not always possible. For another, in such a sensitive matter as taxation, people were very quick to react to novelty of any kind. One case had been the famous poll tax of 1381, and the result had been the Peasants' Revolt. Another had been Henry VII's 'subsidies' of 1489 and 1497. Both had resulted in rebellions – the first in Yorkshire and the second, while starting in Cornwall, had only been ended on the battlefield of Blackheath. One way and another, then, the existing system of parliamentary taxation was not to the Crown's advantage: the yield from any one grant was less and less, but any attempt at change met with great resistance.

It is evidence of the self-confidence of Henry VIII's government that it was prepared to make a new attempt, despite the disastrous results that had attended Henry VII's efforts. The way chosen was to return to something not unlike an individual assessment of wealth, but without insisting upon a precise figure. Instead, certain bands of taxation were laid down, so that all that had to be established was what band any particular person was in. Thus both over-complexity and too much interference in an individual's financial affairs were avoided. Moreover, the source of any person's wealth was divided into three categories – land, moveable goods and wages – and an individual was liable only for that category which yielded the largest amount. Again this must have eased the task of assessment, while the fact that not all an individual's wealth was liable to tax may have helped to reconcile tax-payers to the new set-up. It was also a graduated tax, those in the higher bands paying at a higher rate. Whether the fact that the yield was not fixed had any advantages for the Crown is unclear. Probably not, for any kind of budgeting is made more difficult

[1] Most of what follows derives from Schofield, 'Direct lay taxation'.
[2] Hoskins, *Age of Plunder*, pp.214-15; Schofield, *EcHR*, 2 ser, xviii.

by uncertainty; and attempts at a similar form of taxation in Henry VII's reign had raised very much less than had been expected. Be that as it may, the Tudor 'subsidy', when first introduced, was a more flexible tax than the old one, and one that corresponded much more accurately to the real wealth of the country, so that even at a lower rate, more money would accrue to the Crown. Thus the subsidy of 1515 at 6d. in the pound, or a fortieth, had brought in about £44,900, as compared with the £29,800 that a fifteenth and tenth traditionally yielded. The fact that the Commons accepted the new tax has to be considered a major victory for the Crown. But what part did Wolsey play in its introduction?

No precise answer to this question can be given. Clearly, Henry VII's subsidies prefigure the more successful innovations of 1512 and 1515, and as regards the former especially, it would be surprising if Wolsey had played a major role, if only because his influence was not yet fully established. Moreover, the only remotely financial office he ever held was that of king's almoner, whose function was peripheral to the main business of administering the Crown's finances. True, the lack of specialization amongst early Tudor officials may disguise the amount of financial expertise that Wolsey had acquired, and his deep involvement in the organization of the war effort in 1512 and 1513 meant that he could hardly have avoided acquiring some. Still, there were many leading officials, such as Sir Thomas Lovell and Sir John Heron, whose involvement in the Crown's finances, going back well into the previous reign, was much more extensive than Wolsey's, and it is on such people that the search for the authors of the new tax should concentrate – though any search will quickly come up against a lack of evidence. So far all that has been discovered is an original draft of the subsidy Act drawn up for the 1513 parliament by a future baron of the Exchequer, John Hales.[1] The suspicion must be that it is to his skill in drafting rather than to his financial expertise that this discovery bears witness, but in any event there is no evidence to associate him closely with Wolsey.

There seems, therefore, to be no compelling reason to think of Wolsey as the originator of the Tudor subsidy; but insofar as what was important was not so much the idea – which even in Henry VII's reign was not original – but the political will to persist with it, then his connection looms rather larger. It is probably significant, for instance, that in 1523, when Wolsey's central role in government is unquestionable, the request for a subsidy was not, as it had been earlier, coupled with one for a fifteenth and tenth. The earlier coupling suggests a lack of confidence – which was to be justified – that a subsidy alone would bring in the required amount. In 1523 no such safety net was thought necessary, in part because the general proscription had provided the government with a much more accurate assessment of the country's wealth and hence of what a subsidy would bring in. Moreover, the 1523 subsidy Act appears to have been so well drawn up that it became the blueprint for successive Acts. It also included some important new features. For the first time local collectors were to receive payment, which may have made their difficult task more palatable. The assessment of the nobility was transferred from the hands of local commissioners to those of a high-powered committee, presided over by Wolsey himself as lord chancellor. The purpose of this measure was not to do down the nobility; indeed, it has been suggested that it may

[1] Schofield, 'Direct lay taxation', p.203.

even have appealed to their *amour propre* by freeing them from having to submit their financial affairs to the scrutiny of local gentry. On the other hand, it would be much more difficult to deceive such a committee, and the measure bears all the hallmark of Wolsey's concern, as shown in the search for 'indifferent justice', to ensure that the nobility lived up to the obligations that their high rank imposed.

Before we consider how much the country was asked to contribute towards the Great Enterprise, some attempt must be made to sum up Wolsey's attitude to the Crown's finances. As was mentioned earlier, the impression is often conveyed of a rather profligate Wolsey, who while failing to build upon Henry VII's careful housekeeping, lacked the bureaucratic flair and 'modern' methods of his successor, Thomas Cromwell. In fact, character judgement need play no part in explaining the different financial approaches of these three men. Given the collapse of royal revenue in the early years of his reign, Henry VII's close involvement in financial administration is readily understandable. Cromwell, for his part, had to cope with the problem of processing the enormous influx of money that resulted from Henry VIII's assault on the Church. Thus both men were faced with problems that needed immediate attention, and there is no reason to suppose that in similar circumstances Wolsey would not have risen to the challenge. As it was, his circumstances were different, and the way that he responded reflects this much more than any alleged character defect.

Henry VII's greatest contribution to the successful management of the royal finances was not his willingness to devote his own time to auditing the accounts, though no doubt this helped, but his decision early in his reign to return to the highly successful Yorkist system of chamber finance, thereby bypassing the ministrations of an increasingly moribund Exchequer.[1] Despite the very significant increases in royal revenue that resulted, in which admittedly luck played a part, an attempt has been made to portray chamber finance as somehow old-fashioned, allegedly because it was short on that apparently modern characteristic, bureaucratic procedure.[2] Quite why this should be considered modern is not entirely clear, for to label as modern the labyrinthine workings of Byzantium – a fair description of the medieval Exchequer – does not altogether convince. Still, as long as its normative connotations are ignored, the distinction may serve. Compared with what it replaced, the chamber system was not very bureaucratic. This was its strength and its weakness. It undoubtedly gave to the financial administration of the Crown a greater flexibility both in the collection and, perhaps even more importantly, in the disbursement of royal revenues; its leasing policies could more easily be adjusted to current economic practice, and a much more financially orientated supervision and auditing of the accounts could be introduced. What was not so good for the common weal was the uncertainty and, perhaps, arbitrariness that the abandonment of the Exchequer practices introduced. Securing the Crown's revenues was a difficult business. It was not just that people might fail to pay what was owing, or even that they might challenge what the Crown alleged they owed, but inevitably there were some royal officials who were bent on cheating the Crown

[1] Wolfe, *Crown Lands*, pp.66-75.
[2] Central to Elton's 'Tudor Revolution'; see his *Tudor Revolution*, pp.160 ff.

and whom it would wish to bring to book. All these matters were traditionally dealt with in the court of Exchequer, which, most importantly, was a 'court of record' whose decisions had full legal standing and whose procedures for ensuring attendance and such matters were formally established.

It was because the chamber and the court of general surveyors, which in practice had taken on many of the functions of the Exchequer court, lacked full legal standing that they came under threat at the beginning of Henry VIII's reign, as part of a general reaction to the first Tudor's allegedly arbitrary methods. For a short time the Exchequer recovered much of its control over the collection and processing of the royal revenues, but with predictable results: the old problems returned and revenues declined. What then occurred was a gradual restoration of the chamber system of finance, so that by 1523 it was more or less performing as it had under Henry VII. In particular, the general surveyors could act once again as a court of law, summoning people to appear before them on their own initiative and able to enforce their decisions by, amongst other measures, the hated recognizance, by which the defendant concerned promised to perform what he was ordered to on pain of a fine, though now with an upper limit of £100. Moreover, this return to the chamber system had been brought about by successive Acts of parliament, which gave it just the kind of legal standing that previously had been lacking.[1]

One might be forgiven for thinking that the compromise that had emerged by 1523 offered the best of all possible worlds: the greater flexibility and efficiency of the chamber system had been restored, but the resulting potential for arbitrary government had been greatly reduced. And insofar as the government might deserve some credit for such a development, one might also be forgiven for supposing that Wolsey would enjoy a share of it. In fact most historians have not been very complimentary, the usual judgment being that while the chamber was no longer the ruthless debt-collecting agency that it had been under Henry VII, it had not been replaced by the modern financial departments that Cromwell was supposedly to introduce. Leaving aside some of the rather dubious normative judgements previously touched upon, the main cause for doubts about the compromise is that revenues do appear to have declined while at the same time expenditure was rising – never a very happy state of affairs. However, the case would be more compelling if it was based upon more evidence. As it is, except for the very specific loan account book for 1522-3, very little information about the Crown revenues at this time has survived. For instance, for the period 1509-36 there are none of the chamber receipt books that have survived for Henry VII's reign. Instead, one has to make do with the occasional financial survey, and, of these, none falls within the period 1516-29. It is thus impossible to be too dogmatic about the success or failure of Wolsey's supervision of royal finances. The drop in overall revenue indicated by the surviving surveys does point, though, to a decline in income from Crown lands, amounting to as much as £15,000 a year.[2]

One reason may be that disruption to the system of chamber finance already described, and which the government had by 1523 restored. But there was a more important reason, and one that it was more difficult to do anything about – royal

[1] For much of the above see Wolfe, *Crown Lands*, pp. 76 ff.
[2] Ibid.

generosity. In the survey designed to show the loss of annual revenue following Henry VIII's accession, it was stated that Crown lands worth £7,500 a year had been given away, £3,000 a year was having to be found to pay for additional annuities and fees, and £1,000 a year in payments due from Crown lands was being remitted. In other words, some £11,000 a year had been lost to the Crown by Henry VIII's exercise of royal patronage. What is not clear is whether such generosity was necessarily a bad thing. However one characterizes Henry VII's methods, there seems little doubt that, at least towards the end of his reign, he had been pressing a little too hard on his subjects for the house of Tudor's ultimate good. With his son there had come a relaxation. Kings were, after all, expected to give, and Henry VIII performed this function with an affability and skill which did his standing amongst the political nation no harm at all. In the process people such as Sir William Compton, a leading figure in his household, may have made a fortune, but they also gave very loyal service.

However, while suggesting that it is wrong to judge the administration of early Tudor finance from a Gladstonian or Thatcherite standpoint, I am not trying to make excuses for laxity or incompetence, for the evidence, admittedly rather scanty, would not support such a charge. A modified return to Henry VII's system of chamber finance was the best policy decision that could have been made, and that there was a genuine concern to make the system work is shown by the number of Acts that were introduced to bring about that return – including two in 1515 and one in 1523 that Wolsey must have been involved with – and by the surviving surveys, designed, it would seem, to show that the change in direction was desirable.[1] Moreover, there was some realization that in strict accounting terms Henry's generosity was a growing liability. In 1515 an Act of resumption was passed whereby a certain number of royal grants – though not of land – were revoked, and this may have saved the Crown somewhere between £5,000 and £10,000 a year.[2] And both in 1519 and again in the so-called Eltham ordinances of January 1526, Wolsey tried to do something about the mounting expenditure in the royal household.

Wolsey's attempts at household reform have frequently attracted attention, but sometimes for the wrong reasons. English historians' obsession with trying to chart and weigh the significance of the constant changes in the composition of the king's Council has inevitably led them to that provision in the Eltham ordinances for a group of twenty of the most prominent councillors to be in constant attendance upon the king. More recently, interest has centred upon the possible factional concerns that may have lain behind the attempts at reform. Both these matters are discussed elsewhere.[3] What will be suggested here is that there is no very good reason why what Wolsey was attempting to do should not be taken at its face value as a genuine effort to put the royal household in 'honourable, substantial and profitable order without any further delay'.[4] After all, the matter had been a major

[1] Ibid, pp.79-80 for the suggestion that the Acts of 1515 bore 'the stamp of Chancellor Wolsey's clear legal and administrative mind'; see also Elton, *Tudor Revolution*, pp.45 ff. The statutes were 6 Hen. VIII cap.24; 7 Hen. VIII cap.7; 14 & 15 Hen. VIII cap.18.

[2] Gunn, 'Act of resumption', p.106.

[3] See pp.204 ff., 561 ff.

concern of Edward IV's government in the 1470s,[1] was to occupy the attention of Cromwell in the 1530s,[2] and then for the next hundred years was to be always somewhere near the top of the agenda for every leading minister of the Crown.[3] The chief reason for this is that the running of the royal household was increasingly expensive. In Edward IV's reign the annual running costs were about £13,000.[4] By the beginning of Henry VIII's reign they had risen to about £19,000, creeping ever upwards through the 1520s and 30s so that by 1545-6 they stood at £45,000;[5] and by the middle of James I's reign the total was about £77,500.[6] Some of the reasons for this increase had very little to do with the household itself, or the competence of those who ran it. Sixteenth-century inflation is an obvious one; also much depended upon the size of the royal family: wives, ex-wives and children, in practice all with their separate households but all with a claim on what might be called the household account, were an additional, unavoidable and unpredictable burden.

But the real problems of administering the royal household with any degree of efficiency were inherent in its function as the National Theatre of the country's political life. As such, it had to provide lavish and virtually open hospitality, magnificent ceremonial and varied and colourful entertainment, to mention but the most obvious. And all this went on not in one location but on tour! In every way it was an administrator's nightmare. Exact numbers are difficult to estimate, but if the retinues of the royal servants are included – for these were men of rank themselves and so were attended by their own servants, as indeed were courtiers and distinguished visitors to court – then one should probably be thinking in terms of about two thousand individuals.[7] Not all of these were officially supposed to have their accommodation and food provided but, given the belief that the king had always to be available to his subjects, it was virtually impossible to prevent exploitation by 'rascals and vagabonds now spread, remaining and being in all the court'.[8] And whatever the success of such efforts, the numbers were always going to be large, and the tendency would be for them to increase as the court became more and more the focus of the political nation's ambitions.[9]

What Wolsey was trying to do in 1519 and 1525-6 was to bring Edward IV's household ordinances up to date.[10] Abuses that had crept in, especially in what might be called the expense account area to do with the entitlement of members of the royal household to free board and lodging, were to be eliminated. New lists of legitimate claimants and of precisely what they were entitled to were drawn up.[11]

---

[4] BL Titus B i, fo.188 (*LP*,iii,576).

[1] J.R. Lander, *Crown and Nobility*, p.188; Myers.

[2] Elton, *Tudor Revolution*, pp.380-414.

[3] *Inter alia* Prestwich, pp.206 ff. for household reform in James I's reign.

[4] Ross, p.372.

[5] Dietz, *English Government Finance*, p.89; Elton, *Tudor Revolution*, pp.399-400.

[6] Dietz, *English Public Finance*, pp.412-20; Prestwich, p.207.

[7] L.B. Smith, *Henry VIII*, pp.77 ff; also Newton.

[8] *Royal Household*, pp.137-61 is the most convenient, but not the best text for the Eltham ordinances. For a discussion of the various versions see Elton, *Tudor Revolution*, p.375, n.4.

[9] *Inter alia* Stone.

[10] Newton is still probably the best account, but see also Elton, *Tudor Revolution*, pp.370 ff; D.R. Starkey, 'King's privy chamber', pp.133 ff.

Something that was certainly on the increase was the 'delight' that 'sundry noblemen, gentlemen and others' took in dining 'in corners and secret places, not repairing to the king's chamber nor hall, . . . by reason whereof . . . such viand as is allowed to be spent in the king's house appeareth not to be employed and dispensed to the king's honour'.[1] In other words, dining in the royal hall was becoming unfashionable, thereby removing the original reason for the lavish provision of food and drink. What had not been removed was the possibility for pecuniary gain by such practices as selling off the unwanted food. Provision was also made for a much closer supervision of the household officials, and there was a new determination that they should actually carry out the duties assigned to them, rather than delegating them to deputies.[2] The excessive use of deputies may have been new, or at any rate a growing practice and, if so, just the kind of abuse to prompt Wolsey to embark upon household reform.

Wolsey's determined effort to slim down the establishment included that reduction in the numbers in the privy chamber from twenty-two to fifteen that has given rise to the suspicion that the whole exercise was principally a political one.[3] But the seven who lost their jobs in that department in 1526 were but a tiny fraction of the hundreds from elsewhere who suffered the same fate and who, incidentally, as would be the case today, had to be compensated in some way.[4] In pointing this out the intention is not to deny the Eltham ordinances any political significance, but to put the emphasis in the right place. What is being suggested is that while the household did present a real administrative problem that would have to be tackled, the precise timing of any attempt was likely to have a political dimension to do not with any factional struggle but rather with the strains that war imposed upon the political fabric. As the preamble of the Ordinances put it:

> the king's highness soon after his first assumption of his crown and dignity royal was enforced and brought unto the wars, wherein his grace . . . hath much travailed and been occupied in such wise as many of the officers and ministers of his household being employed and appointed to the making of provisions and other things concerning the wars, the accustomed good order of his said household hath been greatly hindered and in manner subverted.[5]

This was undoubtedly true. Members of the household were very much caught up in the mechanics of war, and at the very least this would have distracted them from their household duties. But the more general point, for obvious reasons, was not made: namely, that when a king is asking his subjects to make a great financial contribution to war, then it becomes politically expedient for him to put his own house in order. Indeed, the very notion that the king should 'live of his own' and not trouble his subjects for money save in exceptional circumstances arose very

---

[11] The so-called bouge, bouche or, as Skelton entitled one of his poems, 'Bowge of Court'.

[1] *Royal Household*, cap.52, p.153, quoted in Newton, p.251.

[2] *Royal Household*, cap.40, p.149.

[3] D.R. Starkey, 'King's privy chamber', pp.133 ff.

[4] Newton, pp.242-3 where he suggests the removal of a hundred gentlemen ushers, fifty-four grooms and an unspecified but greater number of guardsmen.

[5] *Royal Household*, p.137.

largely out of the final phase of the Hundred Years War and the financial incompetence of Henry VI's government. This led Edward IV to embark upon financial and administrative reforms, amongst which figured prominently reform of the household, which may have been particularly stimulated by the 1475 invasion of France.[1] Turning to the early seventeenth century, one again sees a connection between household reform and the Crown's financial difficulties, and its consequent desire to obtain more money in both direct and indirect taxation.[2] It seems reasonable to suppose that there was some such connection in the 1520s. The Crown had made unusually large demands on the taxpayers' pockets. The difficulties encountered over the Amicable Grant in the spring of 1525 sounded a warning that they should not be pushed any harder. In these circumstances household reform made a lot of sense, both as a way of conciliating the taxpayers by making a show of prudent management of money, and more directly as a way of saving money so that further recourse to them would not be necessary.

How successful the Eltham ordinances were is difficult to assess. Politically they may have been, though there is precious little evidence one way or another. At any rate, there seems to have been no widespread demand for the repayment of the 1522-3 loans, as Wolsey was relieved to note in the summer of 1527 as he journeyed through Kent, one of the most troubled areas in 1525, *en route* to Amiens.[3] Although only a dozen or so years later Cromwell felt the need to look at the matter again, which might suggest that the impact of the ordinances had not been very great, it must be borne in mind that the household running costs continued to grow throughout the 1530s, perhaps precisely because the cardinal's hand had been removed.[4] The truth is that it was the kind of problem to which there would never be any final solution. All that a leading minister could do was to worry away at it in the hope of keeping the costs within reasonable limits. This is what Cromwell tried to do. So also did Wolsey, and that he did so provides further evidence that the view of Wolsey as a man totally unconcerned with the mundane world of administration and finance is one that does not stand up to close examination.

It ought perhaps to be stressed here that there is not the slightest doubt that Wolsey was personally involved in drawing up the Eltham ordinances, as he had been in 1519 when he headed the committee set up to look into the underlying problem.[5] In August 1525 he wrote to Sir Henry Guildford for the relevant papers, while one of the drafts of the ordinances has amendments in his own hand, as have other working papers.[6] What has also been shown is that he was directly responsible for that major administrative and financial exercise of 1522, the general proscription. And although his personal involvement in the two other aspects of

---

[1] In this I am following Wolfe, *Crown Lands*, pp.1-28, but for criticism of this view see Harriss's review in *EHR*, lxxxvii, p.172 and ibid, xciii, p.723, n.1.

[2] Prestwich, pp.206 ff.

[3] *LP*,iv,3231, 3243.

[4] For 1530-1 the figure was £24,908, for 1539-40 £32,933, with some variation in between. What the figure was during the 1520s is not known, but in 1526 Wolsey seems to have hoped that the statutory allocation of £19,394 (1 Hen. VIII c.16) would be sufficient; for all of which see Elton, *Tudor Revolution*, pp.39, 399 ff.

[5] For 1519 see BL Titus B i,fo.188 (*LP*,iii,576).

[6] *LP*,iv,1572, 1939 [4].

financial policy and administration I have already discussed, the return to the highly successful chamber system of finance and the introduction of the Tudor subsidy, is less certain, the timing of both these moves would seem to connect them with his increasing influence in royal government. Moreover, when in March 1515 Wolsey is to be found personally checking through the accounts of the recently deceased general surveyor of Crown lands, Sir Robert Southwell,[1] or when in 1525 in connection with the Amicable Grant he queried with the duke of Norfolk the varying amounts being promised by the wealthiest men in the county of Norfolk and the city of Norwich,[2] the impression is very much of a man in control of the detail of financial administration.

What now needs to be stressed is that for Henry to cut the kind of figure that he wished to cut upon the European scene, much more than prudent financial administration was required. Earlier it was made clear that there was no way in which Henry's ordinary revenues could bear the enormous cost of war. What was required was a quite different source of revenue, the pockets of the king's subjects, whether lay or clerical. The main skill of any leading minister would have to be to persuade Henry's subjects to part with their money in quite large amounts. This was the task that Wolsey was faced with in 1522 and 1523, as he had been in a lesser capacity in connection with the earlier French wars. It was for this reason that he had instituted the general proscription, and it was for this reason that in April 1523 a meeting of parliament was summoned and with it the convocations of the two provinces of the English Church.

Like so many other aspects of his career, Wolsey's attitude towards and management of parliament has not been looked upon very kindly by historians. It is hardly surprising that Pollard's Wolsey, with his obsession with the papacy and his unbridled egotism, had no time for anything that smacked of government by consent.[3] For Pollard's successor as the doyen of Tudor studies, Sir Geoffrey Elton, the problem has always been complicated by his wish to award to Thomas Cromwell the prize for having first realized England's sacred mission to act as the standard-bearer of parliamentary democracy. It has suited him to draw the contrast between Wolsey,'the uncomplicated activist, a magnificent if often extravagant manipulator of what was available',[4] and a Cromwell who was sufficiently creative to realize the full potential of this hitherto sadly under-used institution – for Elton yet another illustration of the divide between the old and the new world that the careers of these two leading ministers are supposed to epitomize. The argument here will be that both these views, and any others that take their lead from them, both over- and under-estimate the importance of parliament in the early sixteenth century, while at the same time being unfair to Wolsey.[5]

---

[1] LP,ii,3313; see also Gunn, 'Act of Resumption' for other examples of Wolsey's involvement in the detail of financial administration.

[2] LP,iv, app.36.

[3] 'No minister with such opportunities left so little trace upon the statute-book, and his single parliament of 1523 was one of the most barren in English history.' (A.F. Pollard, p.337).

[4] Elton, Studies, i, p.128.

[5] For other critical assessments see C.S.L. Davies, Peace, Print and Protestantism, p.169; Graves, pp.43, 61-2; Lehmberg, p.1. Guy's 'Wolsey and the parliament of 1523' appeared too late to be fully considered but it is by and large critical.

The first point to make is that by any criteria the parliament of 1523 was an extremely successful one, at least from the Crown's point of view. From it the king received what both Thomas Cromwell and an anonymous correspondent of the duke of Norfolk considered to be an unprecedentedly large amount of money.[1] To some extent, they exaggerated. In the previous decade some £287,000 had been raised in taxation, its collection spread over a period of five years. The 1523 subsidy was to raise about £152,000 over four years. Thus, the annual rate of taxation was slightly less than it had been earlier. However, the taxation of the 1510s had not been voted all at one time, and what made the situation in 1523 unprecedented was that the subsidy was granted immediately after the enormous loans of 1522-3, amounting to no less than £204,000. If one counts this as tax – and it was never in fact to be repaid – the annual rate of taxation shot up to £89,000 compared with the already high 1510s figure of £57,000.[2] All in all, there is no doubt that Henry's subjects – with what degree of enthusiasm will be discussed shortly – had been extremely generous. For the Crown, money was the chief motive in calling a parliament; and this was no peculiarity of Henry's – or indeed of Wolsey's. But parliament also passed statutes whose pre-eminent legal standing, it should be stressed, had been established well before the reign of Henry VIII. This being so, it was in the interests of both king and subjects from time to time to have their wishes and actions sanctioned by parliamentary consent, and in 1523 both parties took advantage of the opportunity to do so. Fifteen public Acts were passed, this very much in line with previous numbers, along with an unusually large number of private ones.[3]

The claim has been made that none of the public Acts was of much importance,[4] and there is some truth in this: bits and pieces to do with the cloth trade and apprenticeship, a consolidating Act to do with the organization of chamber finance and an Act to prevent the tracing of hares in the snow, apparently brought in because so many hares were being caught by this method that there were not enough left for the king and noblemen to hunt![5] However, the mix is not that different from those passed by other parliaments, and it would be wrong to read anything very sinister into it. Important social legislation depends upon there being important social problems. Undoubtedly the one problem that contemporaries identified had to do with enclosure, but the statutory aspects of this had been dealt with by two Acts in the previous parliament,[6] the provisions of the second having been made permanent, unlike so many statutes which had effect only until the following parliament. Thus the absence of legislation in 1523 on this important matter is neither evidence for Wolsey's lack of concern, which in the following chapter will be shown to have been considerable, nor, more relevantly, a lack of respect for parliament. What he did secure was a quite important modification in the existing law by which offenders were pardoned for past transgressions of the enclosure Act, so long as they had made these good by a specific date. This,

[1] *LP*, iii, 3024, 3249.
[2] Bernard, *War, Taxation and Rebellion*, pp. 119 ff. is excellent on all this.
[3] Even Elton in *Reform and Reformation*, p. 89 concedes this point.
[4] Ibid.
[5] 14 & 15 Hen. VIII c. 10; for all these acts see *SR*, iii, pp. 206 ff.
[6] 6 Hen. VIII c. 5, 7 Hen. VIII c. 1.

however, was achieved not by a new statute but by provisos in the General Pardon which, as was customary, brought the parliament to an end. That Wolsey made use of it in this way is not, of course, evidence of any great love of parliament, but at least he did not dislike it so much that he was unable to take advantage of the possibilities it presented.[1]

The view that Wolsey and parliament did not agree with each other rests on three foundations, not one of which on close inspection proves sound. The first is provided by a brief passage in a letter Wolsey wrote to Henry in December 1515, which can be paraphrased as follows: 'I send as requested the Act of apparel and accompanying papers; please examine them and send back your amendments as quickly as possible so that we can get on and dissolve parliament.'[2] Apart from the fact that it must be dangerous to read anything much into such a passing reference to parliament, the circumstances in which the letter was written lend little weight to the usual interpretation given to it.[3] This was that the parliament's main business, the provision of further sums of money consequent upon the failure of the grants of the first session to raise what was required, had been achieved.[4] Henry's sister Margaret, the dowager queen of Scotland, was expected any minute and her visit required the court's full attention, as did the approaching feast of Christmas. Indeed, the proximity of Christmas is probably sufficient to explain any urgency Wolsey felt as regards the dissolution of parliament. No Tudor parliamentary session continued through the Christmas period for the obvious reason that, then as now, it was a time when people wished to be with their families, not kicking their heels in London. Thus, it is very likely that in December 1523 everyone concerned would have been as anxious as Wolsey for a prompt dissolution.

But what, more generally, was the attitude of Wolsey's contemporaries to parliament? It is an almost impossible question to answer, for virtually no direct comments on the institution have come down to us. One that has was made by none other than Thomas Cromwell and in connection with the 1523 parliament. Writing to a friend in August 1523, he referred to the fact that

> by long time I amongst others have endured a parliament which continued by the space of xvii whole weeks where we communed of war, peace, strife, contention, debate, murmur, grudge, riches, poverty, penury, truth, falsehood, justice, equity, deceit, oppression, magnanimity, activity, force, attemprance, treason, murder, felony, conciliation, and also how a commonwealth might be edified and also continued within our realm. Howbeit in conclusion we have done as our predecessors have been wont to do; that is to say as well as we might and left where we began.[5]

We have been warned, quite rightly, not to take this passage too seriously, [6] but given the dearth of evidence one cannot help but try to make something of it – and

---

[1] But for a different view of the provisos see Scarisbrick, 'Cardinal Wolsey', pp.63-4.

[2] BL Caligula D vi, fo.115 (LP,ii,1223).

[3] A.F. Pollard, pp.51-2, 343-4, but see also C.S.L. Davies, Peace, Print and Protestantism, p.169; Elton, Reform and Reformation, p.58; Roskell, p.320, none of whom make specific reference to the letter but can only have it in mind, or Pollard's use of it.

[4] Two subsidy Acts and one fifteenth and tenth had been granted.

[5] Merriman, i, p.313 (LP,iii,3249).

[6] Elton, Studies, i, p.224.

that something hardly suggests that Cromwell thought parliament all that important. It is the sort of thing that today might be said about the United Nations: issues, both large and small, are there discussed, but in the end nothing much results because real power does not lie in that assembly. Much the same was true of early Tudor parliaments. Although the early Tudor parliament did have some important functions and, as Cromwell's comments make clear, could provide a useful talking shop, it had nothing to do with the making of policy or its execution, something that the statistics concerning the frequency and duration of its meetings help to confirm.

From 1485 to 1523 there were eleven parliaments, meeting, therefore, on average only once every three and a half years. Moreover, when parliament did meet, it did not meet for long. No session lasted more than nine weeks, and two for less than five; the average was about seven. During the mid-Tudor period parliament sat more often, with twenty-one sessions in the thirty years between 1529 and 1559; but the reason for this is not that Tudor monarchs or their advisers had grown to love parliament, or indeed that the institution had become sufficiently powerful to warrant or insist upon more frequent meetings. Rather it was the particular circumstances of this unsettled period. The dramatic religious changes requiring statutory confirmation, the need to cajole the political nation into accepting them, the fact that there were two short reigns and that a new reign customarily began with a parliament, and that for ten of these years England was at war – all these things rendered it inevitable that parliament would meet more often. With the long and comparatively more settled reign of Elizabeth, the figures return more or less to the early Tudor norm, with parliament meeting on average every three and a half years, though admittedly the sessions tended to be a little longer.[1]

What these statistics make abundantly clear is that while parliament did have a recognized role, the government could get on for quite long periods without it, and usually did. Only in rather exceptional circumstances did the Crown need 'extraordinary' revenue, and only then did it need to consult or inform. As for new laws, the demand was not all that great: witness the fact that so many early Tudor statutes were merely restatements of old ones. And from the subjects' point of view there were not many advantages – and some disadvantages – in holding a parliament. After all, it invariably meant that they were going to have to pay out quite large sums of money, not only in taxation but also, for those who resided in a parliamentary borough, in expenses for their MP's travel to and from London and for food and lodging while there.[2] In return, an MP might be able to get through a private bill promoting his constituency's interests, so the expense might not all be loss. As for the MP himself, there was usually plenty for him to do in London by way of legal and other business. Moreover, as will be shown, MPs took a considerable interest in the amount of money the Crown was asking for at any given time and were quite prepared to argue strongly about it. But to spend long periods there on matters which for the most part could have been of little concern, was in no one's interest, so that once the question of taxation had been settled their inclination would be to return home as soon as possible. Neither would they wish to attend too

---

[1] Graves, pp. 7, 41, 159-60 as a useful check for my arithmetic.
[2] Ibid, pp. 73-6; Lehmberg, pp. 31-5.

often. Thus, when in 1504 Henry VII announced that 'for the ease of his subjects' he would not call another parliament for a long time, unless for 'great, necessary and urgent causes', his words almost certainly did not displease his subjects.[1]

The statistics on the frequency of parliamentary sessions also undermine the second foundation for the view that Wolsey was hostile towards parliament. If sessions were only ever occasional and brief, and if no one was especially keen on them, the comparative lack of such meetings in this period cannot have the significance as regards Wolsey's attitude that is usually implied. Admittedly, an average of only one parliament in every seven years between 1515 and 1529 is well below the early Tudor norm of one every three and a half years, but there are quite straightforward explanations for the difference. From 1511 to 1518 England was either formally at war or paying other people to fight on her behalf. The result was a series of parliamentary sessions in which money was voted, the last being a subsidy agreed to in 1515 but not levied until two years later.[2] In 1518 the Treaty of London inaugurated a brief period of European peace, but by 1521 war had broken out again and by the end of the year England was committed to the Great Enterprise against France. Again, the consequence was the calling of parliament, in 1523, which sanctioned the raising of a large sum of money spread over four years – the last portion was levied in 1527. In fact, by 1525 the Great Enterprise had failed and England had made peace with France, so there was no need to apply for further sums. Admittedly in January 1528 England had formally declared war on the emperor, but this, it will be shown, was largely a diplomatic manoeuvre with no fighting intended.[3] But if a large-scale war had been seriously contemplated, no doubt a parliament would have been called – which brings us to the nub of the matter.

Nine times out of ten parliaments were called when the Crown needed money to finance a war, and Wolsey's period in high office was no exception. The explanation for the apparent lack of parliaments is partly that between 1518 and 1522 England was at peace, and partly that the parliaments of 1515 and 1523 were so generous that, with the addition of the loans of 1522-3, further grants were not required, or at least were not considered politically viable.[4] There was therefore nothing odd about the fact that between 1515 and 1529 only one parliament was called. Wolsey – and one should almost certainly include Henry VIII in this – called a parliament at precisely the moment when one would have expected him to do, and there was no obvious occasion when he failed to call one.[5]

There remains the evidence of the various literary accounts of the handling of the 1523 parliament – those written by Hall, Vergil and, perhaps above all, by

---

[1] Quoted in Graves, p.42. See also Speaker Audley's request to Henry in March 1532 to dissolve parliament considering 'what pain, charge and cost his humble subjects of the Nether house had sustained since the beginning of this parliament'.

[2] There were two parliaments, 1512-4 and 1515, and five sessions, Feb.-March, Nov.-Dec. 1512, Jan.-March 1514, Feb.-April and Nov.-Dec. 1515.

[3] See p.542 below.

[4] The resistance to the Amicable Grant in 1525 would have discouraged any attempt to ask for money.

[5] In April 1521 thought was given to calling a parliament in order to finance Surrey's military activities in Ireland and resistance to a possible Scottish invasion. The idea was rejected because in this 'hard and dear year' people were not in a position to pay and anyway such money that might be granted could not have been raised in time or so at least Surrey was informed; see St.P,iii, p.67 (LP,iii,1252).

William Roper in his celebrated life of his father-in-law, Thomas More. Irrespective of its intrinsic merits, this evidence is bound to loom large, because institutional or archival records for 1523 are virtually non-existent, which is to say that no Lords Journal for this parliament has survived. [1] One should, perhaps, not make too much of this, for in many ways we are lucky to have such extensive literary evidence, but the lack of any formal archive by which to monitor it is a pity, especially given that bias against Wolsey that both Vergil and Hall so notably exhibit. As for Roper, his intention was to present his father-in-law in as good a light as possible, and one of the ways he chose to do this was by highlighting More as the virtuous Speaker standing up for the liberties of the House of Commons against the wicked and tyrannical Wolsey. Amongst other things, he portrays a Wolsey so angry with More's behaviour during the parliament that he plotted to send him off to Spain as ambassador – a fate which, according to Roper, More considered would lead to his certain death. [2] In fact some of the best Tudor councillors were sent to Spain, including Tunstall, Richard Sampson and Richard Wingfield, and though, while on his embassy in 1525, Wingfield did fall ill and die, it is not possible to argue that such a posting was thought to be a journey to certain death. Roper must be wrong about this, and thus may well be wrong on other matters. And as regards Wolsey's view of More's performance as Speaker, it is known that he went out of his way to praise More to Henry for 'the faithful diligence . . . in all your causes treated in this your late parliament', and as a consequence requested that More be paid an additional sum of £100 as a reward being 'the rather moved to put your highness in remembrance thereof because he is not the most ready to speak and solicit his own cause'. [3]

Thus, though the literary evidence must be treated with caution, what does emerge without any shadow of doubt from it and from other bits of evidence, in particular that account of the parliament written to Surrey, is that there was considerable opposition to the very large sum of money requested. [4] It is also the case that Wolsey asked for more than he was to obtain, and that in order to obtain what was eventually granted he had to indulge in a good deal of politicking. This probably involved two addresses to the Commons, which occasioned much unfavourable comment by both Roper and Hall; and arguably Wolsey did offend against the traditions of the House, at least insofar as he tried to engage the members in direct argument rather than merely stating his case. At any rate, his efforts were foiled by a combination of the MPs' 'obstinate silence' and More's tact. [5] In addition, Hall recounts that when a delegation of the House asked Wolsey 'to move the king's highness to be content with an easier sum, he currishly answered that he would rather have his tongue plucked out of his head with a pair of pincers

[1] A Commons' Journal did not begin until 1547. For a good introduction to the sources see Graves, p.44.
[2] Roper, p.19.
[3] St.P,i,124 (LP,iii,3267). For More's thank you, see St.P,i,125 (LP,iii,3270).
[4] See also Imperial ambassador's report of 1 June: 'Parliament has been postponed from the eve of pentecost to the 10th of this month because there are divers opinions and several difficulties have arisen. . . What is worse it seems likely the opposition will be greater this time than before. Wolsey is incredibly unpopular here and matters will not go so easily as he and Henry seem to believe.' (Sp.Cal., F.S., p.235).
[5] Roper, pp.16-19; Hall, p.655.

than move the king to take any less sum'.[1] He also allegedly lied to the Commons about the Lords' attitude to the subsidy, claiming that they had accepted the original amount requested, an allegation which seems a little improbable given that the Commons' superiority in matters of taxation was already well established. So whether true or not[2] – and Surrey's correspondent made no mention of it – the statement was bound to be counter-productive. What does seem to have occurred was a split between the shire MPs and those representing the boroughs, the former having, however reluctantly, agreed to the payment of an additional sum from those with landed incomes of £50 and over, but on condition that those with a non-landed income of the same value should contribute a similar amount. Insofar as the county MPs were successful, this was clearly to the Crown's advantage. What is not so clear is whether the division was engineered by it, and in particular by Wolsey. Hall says that the suggestion for an extra contribution from the wealthy landed gentry came from Sir John Hussey in order 'to please the Cardinal'.[3] This is not quite the same as saying that Wolsey initiated the move and, given that the division might well have jeopardized the whole subsidy, it seems unlikely. On the other hand, most of the sources state that considerable pressure was brought to bear upon what might be called the royal affinity in the House, which is to say the councillors, courtiers and household officials, first to secure their agreement to the subsidy and then to use their influence to get it through. Indeed, Surrey's correspondent suggested that the subsidy was only passed in a thin House in which the royal affinity predominated, a manoeuvre which could probably only have been achieved with More's connivance.[4]

If the details and especially the tone of the evidence that have come down to us are sometimes questionable – did the Commons, for instance, really discuss whether Wolsey should be allowed to address them 'with all his pomp', or is this just a 'Utopian' embellishment on Roper's part – it is undoubtedly true that Wolsey had to battle to achieve the subsidy. What is in dispute is how skilfully he went about winning the battle, because win it he did. The great success of the 1523 parliament from the Crown's point of view, resulting as it did in the granting of a very large sum of money, makes it hard to sustain any serious criticisms of Wolsey's management of it – though not entirely impossible. If, for instance, parliaments had always been in the habit of happily granting the Crown large sums of money, then the difficulty in 1523 could be held against him. What is now required is a little more context in which to place the events of the 1523 parliament, in the course of which it will be necessary to modify some of the generalizations about this institution already made.

What emerges from even the briefest survey of parliament's earlier history is that money had always been a bone of contention – not altogether surprising, since it derived its existence from the Crown's need to extract money more frequently and from a much wider constituency than it had been able to do before parliament came into existence. Parliament was primarily a negotiating chamber where, in return for a sum of money, the Crown's subjects could secure certain concessions. As such it

---

[1] Hall, p.656.
[2] But both Hall and Vergil do; see Hall, p.657; Vergil, p.307.
[3] Hall, p.657.
[4] Henry Ellis, I ser, i, pp.220-1 (*LP*,iii,3024).

was a place where conflict frequently arose. Looking back to an earlier period, for instance to Edward III's or Henry IV's reign, there was more or less one parliament every year, in contrast to the one every three and a half years referred to earlier as the early Tudor norm, though the sessions were equally brief. Moreover, there is evidence of conflict between Crown and parliament that is more usually associated with the seventeenth century, including impeachment proceedings against the Crown's ministers and favourites, and an insistence that the Crown account to parliament on the way that taxes had been spent. It is always a mistake to see the conflict between Crown and parliament in purely constitutional terms, and a worse one to think in terms of an ever-increasing crescendo of conflict in which parliament slowly but inexorably gained the upper hand. Both in the fourteenth and the seventeenth centuries, the background to conflict was provided by heavy financial demands from the Crown, the detail by any number of things, such as the, at least perceived, incompetence of the Crown and its ministers and an unpopular foreign policy. The conflict was not confined to parliament – it was in the Council and court that the real power lay and where the main drama was played out – but parliament provided a natural, if occasional, theatre for any competing directors to present their case – and well before 1523.[1]

What all this means is that in the earlier discussion to some extent the importance of parliament was underplayed, or at any rate the extent to which it had a life of its own and was not just an adjunct of royal power. But there was a reason, or at any rate an excuse, for doing so. The success of Edward IV and Henry VII in both political and financial terms undoubtedly lessened the occasion for conflict, and this in turn meant that not only was there no need to summon parliament so often, but when it did meet less conflict arose. What it does not mean is that there was no conflict, or that the potential for parliament to play a political role had suddenly ceased. And insofar as conflict existed, it was undoubtedly about money. The parliament of 1472-5 had proved extremely reluctant to provide Edward IV with the necessary funds for war with France, and when it did, it hedged the grants around with all sorts of conditions.[2] The 1489 parliament was no less suspicious of Henry VII, and when in 1504 he asked for the customary feudal aids for the knighting of his eldest son and the marriage of his daughter, initially they turned the request down.[3] Thus, if in comparison with what had gone before, the parliaments of these two kings were rather more malleable, they were never completely so, and undoubtedly needed some management.[4] And to make some direct comparisons with what Wolsey did in 1523: on at least two occasions his predecessor as lord chancellor, William Warham, spoke directly to the House of Commons in an effort to persuade them to give money, on both occasions being accompanied by a large entourage.[5] Furthermore, in 1512 he had used precisely the same tactic as Wolsey

---

[1] *Inter alia English Historical Documents*, pp.360-8 for a good introduction. Anything by Harriss is illuminating, but see especially *Journal of Medieval History*, ii.

[2] Ross, pp.214-8.

[3] Chrimes, pp.200-1.

[4] Almost certainly the meagreness of the records make them appear more quiescent than they were. For instance, it is known that on a number of occasions the City of London mounted vigorous campaigns in the Commons of which the official records give no indication; see Elton, *Studies*, i, pp.84-6; Kennedy, pp.35 ff., 130 ff.

had in 1523, that of asking for a much larger sum than in the end he was willing to settle for.[1]

The conclusion has to be that the opposition to the request for a large subsidy in 1523 was neither unusual nor unexpected. And within the severe limitations set by the meagre evidence, the conclusion must also be that Wolsey's response to the problem of raising money was neither unusual nor unexpected. Since it was his job to get the money that the king wanted, his attitude would inevitably be different from that of the majority of MPs and taxpayers. But to turn up in the Commons to plead the king's case, to bargain, even occasionally to lie, was not only what his predecessors had done but what his successors were to do, never more than in the parliaments of the 1530s. Then, however, in part perhaps because the leading minister, Thomas Cromwell, was not lord chancellor or cleric, and thus was in one sense but another MP, the task of making the dramatic appearances devolved upon Henry.[2] The kind of silliness that has singled out Wolsey's management of the Commons for special condemnation must be put aside. Sadly, it is not possible to replace it with a more sophisticated criticism, because the evidence will not allow it. If at one stage in the proceedings he did lie to the Commons about the Lords' attitude to the subsidy, one may feel that this was foolish, because so easily detectable. But given that the episode is mentioned by his critics, Hall and Vergil, it would also be foolish to make too much of it. Anyway, an attempt to isolate the Commons by suggesting that their elders and betters were all in favour was probably a gambit worth trying, even if it backfired. And what none of the contemporary comment, including that emanating from Wolsey and the king, suggests is that the government saw the outcome of the 1523 parliament as in any way a defeat; indeed, rather the contrary impression is given. Both Cromwell and Surrey's unknown correspondent commented upon the unprecedented sum that had been granted, and it seems unlikely that Wolsey would have been anxious for Thomas More to be rewarded for his work as Speaker if he had felt that his management of the House had been a disaster. Thus, when in bringing the parliament to a close, Wolsey thanked it for granting a 'right large subsidy' and for 'taking long pain, travail, study, costs and charges' in devising statutes for the common weal, there is no reason to suppose that he was having to grit his teeth, or indulging in irony.[3]

By mid-August 1523, a whole two years after the plan had first been discussed at Bruges, Wolsey was at last in a position to embark upon the Great Enterprise, if that was indeed what he and Henry intended to do. The length of time it had taken to obtain the necessary resources and England's refusal to commit to any major military intervention against France for another year are but two of the most obvious

---

[5] *Lords*, pp.12-3, 21; Graves, p.61.

---

[1] *Trevelyan Papers*, p.8 for Warham's initial request of £600,000. He eventually obtained £126,745; see also Bernard, *War, Taxation and Rebellion*, pp.120-1.

[2] Lehmberg, pp.137-8, 254-5.

[3] PRO SP 1/2/7/fos.187-8 (*LP*,iii,2957), a draft in Tuke's hand. Wolsey's failure to deliver the opening speech to parliament, a task usually performed by the chancellor, led Elton to comment that he had 'apparently extended his dislike of parliaments to the point of suppressing his normal delight in the sound of his own voice'; see *Parliament of England*, p.27. But, as Henry informed the Venetian ambassador, the explanation was that Wolsey was ill (*Ven.Cal.*,iii, p.313).

pointers that suggest that, whatever the propaganda, king and minister approached the Great Enterprise with considerable caution. More ambiguous is the rather cautious tone of the propaganda: much emphasis was placed upon the impossible behaviour of the French king that had prevented the continuation of peace, but very little was said about the conquest of France, or Henry's rights to its throne. Of course, as time passed, so the circumstances that had led to the Anglo-Imperial alliance altered. When it had been first discussed, the French were still in control of the duchy of Milan, Francis and Charles were campaigning against each other on the north-east borders of France, major revolts in both Castile and Valencia were still grumbling on and the strategically important town of Fuentarrabia, situated on the Atlantic coast close to the borders of France, Spain and the disputed territory of Navarre, had just been captured by the French. Insofar as all this meant that the emperor was in need of English help, it resulted in the balance of the new partnership being, if not quite in England's favour, at least much more so than it quickly became. On 27 April 1522 the French defeat at the battle of La Biococca confirmed her loss of the duchy of Milan the previous November. And when on 16 July Charles landed on Spanish soil again, his rebellious subjects were almost everywhere defeated. More generally, Charles's residence in Spain during the next seven years inevitably meant that the Imperial centre of gravity went south with him, and this on the whole was bad news for Wolsey. There was first of all the emperor's anxiety to recapture Fuentarrabia, but more importantly there was his need to achieve a satisfactory settlement in Italy. This meant finding a ruler for the duchy of Milan who, at the very least, would not be opposed to his interests, and persuading the pope to crown him emperor. What it did not mean, and never seems to have meant, as far as Charles and his leading adviser, the grand chancellor Mercurino Gattinara, were concerned, was any serious invasion of France. In other words, they had no real intention of keeping to the promises they had solemnly made at Windsor and Bishops Waltham in the early summer of 1522, just prior to their return to Spain.[1]

What of Henry and Wolsey? Had they any intention of keeping their word? The answer already given is that the enormous efforts made by them during 1522 and 1523 to prepare for war indicate that some notable exploit against France was contemplated; but, that said, the qualifications press in on all sides. To begin with, war with France brought with it the renewal of Albany's interference in Scotland. England's northern border had to be put on a war footing and her most experienced military commander, the earl of Surrey, was to spend much of 1523 and 1524 at the head of a large army fending off the constantly threatened Scottish invasion. Moreover, some people, including apparently Thomas Cromwell, considered that it was against Scotland that the full weight of English resources should be concentrated, while Surrey's unknown correspondent suggested that £10,000 or £12,000 of the 1523 subsidy should be set aside 'on the building up again of the piles and castles on our English borders'.[2] But if Scottish affairs were an unavoidable

---

[1] *LP*,iii,2322, 23333; *Sp.Cal.*,ii, pp.438-40; 449-51. When Charles addressed the Castilian cortes in July 1523 he appears to have failed to mention the Great Enterprise! For this and, more generally for Charles's policy at this time see Brandi, pp.194 ff.

[2] Henry Ellis, 1 ser, i, p.223 (*LP*,iii,3023).

distraction, what is more difficult to interpret is the fact that from the outset both Henry and Wolsey entertained the strongest suspicions, constantly fuelled by the reports of the English ambassadors at the Imperial court, of Charles's intentions. Time and again these warned of the emperor's lack of money, of his failure to make any warlike preparations, of his preoccupation with Italian affairs, and of his intention to make use of English support merely to further his own interests.[1]

There was thus nothing starry-eyed about England's attitude towards the Great Enterprise. Moreover, as has already been suggested, despite its grandiose title, it did not really represent any dramatic change in Wolsey's underlying approach to foreign policy. The conquest of France was never very high on the agenda, and indeed when dining with the Imperial ambassadors on Christmas day 1522, Wolsey ventured the opinion that there was little likelihood that the allies would ever conquer France, for the French king would be able to fortify his cities while at the same time refusing to give battle.[2] He was almost certainly being deliberately pessimistic in order to test the Imperial commitment, but that such a remark could even be made is an indication that England's approach to the Great Enterprise was far from straightforward. What does seem to have been looked for was some notable exploit by which France would be forced to make terms even more favourable to England than those she had made in 1518, this in turn leading to a new European settlement that Wolsey could claim had been brought about under England's aegis. Thus, in September 1522 the English ambassadors to the emperor were informed that while the present French offers of peace might seem favourable, they would be much more favourable once the war against them had been successfully prosecuted.[3]

But though the title Great Enterprise may in one sense mislead, it may nonetheless help to capture the mood of the mid-1520s which was anything but pessimistic or defensive; hence the large amounts of money sought from the English taxpayers, hence the immediate despatch in the summer of 1522 of an expeditionary force under the earl of Surrey, and hence, in part at any rate, the willingness to commit a force of some eleven thousand men under the duke of Suffolk to what became, briefly, a march on Paris. Whatever view of Henry's and Wolsey's mood is taken affects the interpretation of the policy that they adopted. If, for instance, one believes, according to the most persuasive and only detailed account of these events in recent years, [4] that their main concern was with damage-limitation, which in effect meant trying to ensure that England ended up on the winning side, then what happened was something of a disaster. It was the Imperialists who, in February 1525, were to win the decisive battle of Pavia and who in the process captured the French king, but by August it was the French who were to be England's closest ally – not only because Charles had conspicuously failed to do anything that Henry and Wolsey asked him to do, but also because the English taxpayers had refused to shell out any more money, thereby forcing king and minister to bring the Great Enterprise to an end. In the account that follows, the fruits of Pavia will be

---

[1] For Henry's and Wolsey's suspicions see LP,iii,1810, 2551, 2567, 3302, 3326, 3346; for the English ambassadors' suspicions see LP,iii,3246-7, 3559.

[2] Sp.Cal., F.S., p.180.

[3] LP,iii,2567. Cf. Charles's comment in March 1523 that a good peace could only be obtained by a good war; see Sp.Cal., F.S., p.197.

[4] Bernard, War, Taxation and Rebellion, pp.3-52.

considered to have been much more satisfactory. Indeed, as a consequence of the new French alliance, England was arguably in an even better position to dominate European affairs than in either 1514 or 1518, until, that is, Henry's matrimonial concerns completely undermined it.

There is obviously some contradiction between an optimistic Wolsey and a Wolsey highly suspicious of Imperialist intentions, but the contradiction lies in the situation and not in the interpretation. One way of describing English policy is to say that until the collapse of Suffolk's expedition in December 1523, optimism was dominant. The main evidence for this is the speed and energy with which Wolsey attempted to take advantage of what in a letter to Henry of 10 August 1523 he called the 'so many concurrances'.[1] These included the detachment of Venice from the French side, partly thanks to the efforts of England's ambassador to the Republic, Richard Pace,[2] the decision by the new pope Adrian VI finally to commit himself to the Anglo-Imperial side,[3] but above all the severing of the allegiance to the French Crown of the constable of France, Charles duke of Bourbon.

The precise reasons for this dramatic event are obscure, but it had something to do with the death of the duke's wife in April 1521, the complicated problems of her inheritance that ensued, and the decision of both Francis I and his mother, Louise of Savoy, to lay claims to that inheritance. Bourbon's unhappiness about this was known to the Imperialists as early as August 1522, and by the following May serious negotiations were under way, which in the following month Henry and Wolsey were to join in, when first William Knight and then John Russell were sent on embassies to Bourbon.[4] Thus, by the late summer of 1523 a leading French nobleman at the head of three duchies, seven counties, two vicomtés and seven lordships, not to say several fortresses, was poised to rebel, and with the real prospect that a number of his fellow noblemen would join him. The opportunity to inflict severe damage upon Francis was just too good to miss, even though the Great Enterprise was not scheduled until the following year; and, indeed, Wolsey had been seeking to put it off until 1525.[5]

Still, however good the prospects, the speed with which England acted is worth stressing. On 1 June 1523 the Imperial ambassador, de Praet, could write that English preparations were so tardy that he strongly advised his master not to bother with their help for this year.[6] But by the end of August the duke of Suffolk and his expeditionary force were in France – and despite the fact that not only had no formal agreement yet been signed between England and Bourbon,[7] but a large English army under Surrey was already engaged in counter-measures against the Scots.[8] That Henry and Wolsey were prepared to be committed on two fronts is a

---

[1] St.P,i, p.117 (LP,iii,3231).

[2] LP,iii,3207 for the treaty between Venice, Charles, Henry and Archduke Ferdinand.

[3] 3 Aug. 1523 a complicated story involving the 'treasonable' activities of the pro-French cardinal, Soderini; see Knecht, p.147; Pastor, ix, pp.185 ff.

[4] Russell left England in early August and the agreement with Bourbon was signed on 6 Sept. For Bourbon's treason see Knecht, pp.146-9.

[5] Sp.Cal., F.S., p.253. For the effect of Bourbon's treason see Bernard, War, Taxation and Rebellion, pp.11-12; Gunn, EHR, ci, pp.608-11.

[6] Sp.Cal., F.S., p.240.

[7] Not until 6 Sept. The agreement with Charles and Margaret was reached on 2 July; see LP,iii,3149; Sp.Cal., F.S., pp.208, 216.

measure of that optimism already referred to. But what can also be concluded is that their priority was some notable exploit in France. An English invasion of France in the summer of 1523 could easily have been avoided. In the event not only was there an invasion, but also a march on Paris.[1]

The march on Paris in the autumn and early winter of 1523 was the occasion for probably the best-known disagreement between king and cardinal. The original plan, accepted reluctantly by the Imperialists on 2 July, had been to besiege Boulogne.[2] Situated on the English Channel and close to Calais, it was accessible to the English from land and sea. Moreover, it would make rather more sense of England's toe-hold in France, the area around Calais called the English Pale, if Boulogne could be added to it. Thus, whenever there was an English invasion of France at this time, an attack on Boulogne usually featured in it, and indeed in 1544 Henry was to capture the town.[3] However, sometime between 12 and 20 September Wolsey changed his mind. Instead, he accepted the wisdom of what was really an Imperial plan, though one that had apparently been contemplated the previous year, to march deep into French territory, along a line close to the borders of Flanders, crossing the Somme a little to the east of Amiens. That accomplished, the English army would contrive to link up both with Bourbon's forces in the Champagne and with a contingent of German cavalry, or *landsknechts*, whose cost Henry and Charles had agreed to share.[4]

There were obvious worries about this new strategy. Pushed by the regent Margaret and the commander of her forces that were to co-operate with the English, Floris Egmont count of Buren, there was a very real possibility, recognized by Wolsey as well as by Henry, that its main purpose was to defend the Burgundian border from French attack at England's expense.[5] And to this general worry Henry added a number of what might be called technical or military ones. It was too late in the year to mount such a campaign, what with the 'wet weather and rotten ways'. Capturing the small towns in their path would be much harder than the Imperialists were suggesting, especially given the difficulty of manoeuvring heavy artillery in bad weather. The logistical problems, which even for a stationary army around Boulogne were difficult enough, especially given the all too justified doubts about Margaret's ability and willingness to provide the vital supplies she had promised, would be ten times worse for an army marching deep into French territory. If, as Bourbon was insisting, the allied forces were to pose as an army of liberation and that as a consequence no 'profit of spoil' was allowed, the soldiers would have 'evil will to march far forward, and their captains shall have much ado to keep them from crying Home ! Home !' Most importantly, there was a very real danger that with the English lines of communication overextended, with the effectiveness of Bourbon's support difficult to calculate, and the likelihood that his treason would force Francis

---

[8] Eaves, pp.126 ff.

[1] Cf. Scarisbrick, *Henry VIII*, pp.125 ff. who argues for a divergence of view between Henry and Wolsey from the start.
[2] *LP*,iii,3149.
[3] Gunn, 'French wars', p.33.
[4] Gunn, *EHR*, ci, pp.607-9.
[5] *St.P*,i, p.132 (*LP*,iii,3320).

to give up his invasion of Northern Italy, to concentrate on defeating the rebellious duke and his allies, Suffolk's army could find itself deep in enemy country, isolated and alone, an easy prey to a French attack.[1]

Reading Henry's sane and all too prescient analysis, one is immediately struck by how little it seems to relate to the gung-ho figure sometimes portrayed, who if, in some accounts at least, he had not been restrained by such as Wolsey, would have been constantly charging into battle. In this case it was Wolsey who was being more gung-ho than Henry, and to explain this curious reversal of roles on the grounds that Wolsey felt that if his master insisted on having a war, then the sooner the better, does not entirely convince.[2] It seems more likely that this apparent disagreement is rather evidence of an essential unity of purpose between king and minister. Henry had thought it necessary to acquaint Wolsey with 'these considerations . . . to the entent that the same by your high prudence advised and considered, such final determination may be taken by his grace and yours'. That this was to accept the new plan is not evidence that, despite his better judgment Henry had given way to a dominant minister; it is more likely that in the light of the assessment of the commanders in the field, Suffolk and Buren, and, perhaps even more, of Russell's report of his meeting with Bourbon he decided that it was, on balance, worth the greater risks involved.[3] The point is that if there had been real tension between king and minister, the tone of Henry's letter would have been very different,[4] and indeed the issue might well have blown them apart, especially when many of Henry's points turned out to be all too true. However, there is no hint that Henry ever held the ultimate failure of the expedition against Wolsey, and no doubt for the good reason that he had in the end, like Wolsey, accepted the very compelling reasons for embarking upon it.

Just how great a failure the expedition was is a matter of judgment, and probably the tendency has been to exaggerate it.[5] It is true that by the second week in November, with the onset of weather more wintery than any in living memory, mutiny in the English army was rife: 'it was no worse being hanged in England than dying of cold in France', was apparently the feeling. If anything, things were worse with the Imperial contingent under Buren, who for at least six weeks had received no money. By 13 November the pressure to order an immediate withdrawal could no longer be resisted, though Suffolk's intention was still to overwinter in France. Indeed, only a few days before, he had received instructions to that effect, together with the news that substantial reinforcements and money were on the way. But it was not to be. The continuing bad weather and the almost immediate disbandment of Buren's forces forced Suffolk on the 22nd to instruct his troops to make their own way back to Calais as best they could, and most of them seem not to have bothered to stop there. If not exactly a rout, it was not far off, and for a brief moment, at least, Suffolk appears to have wondered what sort of reception he would receive on his return. Interestingly, it was not at all bad, and no feeling of disgrace prevented him

---

[1] St.P, i, pp.135-40 (LP,iii,3346).

[2] Scarisbrick, pp.128-9 for this explanation.

[3] LP,iii,3346; Sp.Cal., F.S., p.275.

[4] I call it Henry's, but his letters at this time were written by More, acting as royal secretary in the absence of Pace.

[5] For instance called a débâcle by Scarisbrick, Henry viii, p.130.

before leaving Calais from exercising his privilege as a commander in the field of rewarding some of his men with knighthoods. Moreover, in the following year, and again in 1528, he was appointed to command new expeditionary forces to France, though in the event they were never sent. Thus his military reputation, in Henry's eyes at least, does not appear to have suffered – and in a sense why should it have? In the space of six weeks, eight towns had fallen to him, and he had found himself only seventy miles from Paris and in a position seriously to contemplate its capture. On the very day that the withdrawal was ordered, the defences of that city had been put on full alert, every bell silent so that when one did ring the citizens would know that the attack had begun. For a moment it had looked as if Suffolk had secured 'unrestricted entry into the bowels of France', and even that the English Crown's ancient right to the throne of France might be enforced.[1] It was not quite like 1419-20 when Henry v had entered Paris as heir to the king of France, but the similarity made it all seem for a time quite exciting. And even when, early in the following year, both Henry and Wolsey knew the worst, they nevertheless felt able to make the point that this near-success with such a small force showed the golden opportunities that awaited, if only their allies would come up to the mark.[2]

Thus, in Henry and Wolsey's eyes the failure of Suffolk's expedition was a qualified one, and the qualifications are of great importance. They felt, and with some justification, that England had been badly let down by every one of her allies. Margaret had failed to provide money for her own troops and the promised carts and horses for Suffolk's. Buren had failed to prevent his troops from looting and pillaging, thus creating great difficulties for the English command, which at Bourbon's request had pledged itself not to permit such activity. Neither had the sudden disbanding of his troops, when all that had been agreed was withdrawal, helped very much. Meanwhile, the absence of any contribution at all from Bourbon had been even more disastrous. Not only had the rest of France singularly failed to come to his support, even in those areas where his family influence could have been expected to be decisive, but his promised invasion of the Champagne from over the border in the Franche-Comté came to nothing, while the *landsknechts* supposedly hired to help him never got very far.[3] And what had Charles been doing all the while? Well, according to Henry and Wolsey, not a damned thing, or at least nothing that helped them. Indeed, it looked very much as if he had been using English money and men merely to further his own ends. In March 1524 he recovered Fuentarrabia, and in the following month the French were yet again driven out of Northern Italy, but none of this could be said to have been to England's advantage. Moreover, as Henry and Wolsey were unlikely to forget, one consequence of the alliance with the emperor had been the giving up of the very considerable French 'pension'. Back in Bruges in August 1521, Charles had promised to compensate the English for this loss by the payment of what was called the 'indemnity', to the tune of 133,305 gold crowns (nearly £30,000) a year.[4] The only trouble was that not a penny of it had come England's way – and indeed never

---

[1] For all of this see Gunn, *EHR*, ci, pp.611 ff.
[2] *LP*,iv,8; *Sp.Cal., F.S.*, p.318.
[3] Gunn, *EHR*, ci, pp.611 ff; Knecht, pp.152-6.
[4] *Sp.Cal.*,ii,355. It was confirmed at Windsor in June 1522 (*Sp.Cal.*,ii,441).

was to come. Thus, by early 1524 Henry and Wolsey had a whole series of complaints to put to England's allies, and they were not backward in putting them, either then or during the months that followed. Indeed, for the next year and a half they were to dominate the relationship between king and emperor, and they go a long way to explain why by the summer of 1525 that relationship had broken down.[1]

It would be wrong, of course, to take these complaints entirely at their face value; to some extent they were merely part of the bargaining process, and indeed it could be argued that far from showing that Henry's and Wolsey's belief in the Great Enterprise was disintegrating, they suggest a continuing commitment. There is, after all, nothing like putting people in the wrong to make them anxious to do what you want. The argument here, however, will be that the complaints were to a great extent only a smoke screen to disguise Wolsey's increasing lack of faith in the Great Enterprise as a whole and his desire to extricate his master, if only a favourable opportunity arose – but one must emphasize the last point. Wolsey did not suddenly decide in January 1524 that in August 1525 he would make an alliance with the French; that was not his way, nor in the real world can it be anybody's. What happened is that at about that time he came to the decision that the strategy that had emerged in Bruges in the summer of 1521 of using an Imperial alliance to forge a new European settlement was unlikely to be successful, and he began actively to look for a new way forward.

That Wolsey's approach had changed significantly can be shown by his reaction to the opportunities for another invasion of France in the late summer and autumn of 1524. On the face of it, the prospects looked good. The French defeat and expulsion from Northern Italy in April had been followed up by an invasion of French territory by an army led by Bourbon. True, it did not move north towards Lyons as Wolsey had hoped, but by the middle of August it was besieging Marseilles, reached on the 26th. On the way there, rather as with Suffolk's army the previous year, one French town after another had surrendered to it.[2] Admittedly, after his success in March in capturing Fuenterrabia, Charles had not done much to help Bourbon, but at least until late May he had put on some pretence of being keener on concerted action than he had shown himself to be earlier.[3] As regards Scotland, however, things had dramatically improved with the departure of Albany to France in June, which led almost immediately to negotiations for peace and thus removed the threat, very much a reality the previous year, of a war on two fronts.[4]

The fact is that by the summer of 1524 the situation was more favourable for an English invasion of France than it had been the previous year, and indeed there was some pretence at making such an invasion. On 25 May an agreement was made with Bourbon to that effect;[5] on 2 September Wolsey reported to Norfolk, then still in the North, that on the strength of the good news of Bourbon's successes in the south of France, a decision to invade had been taken; and on the 10th circular letters had been sent out to the relevant people instructing them to prepare for war.[6] But even

[1] LP,iv,8,61, 186, 684, 1628-9; Sp.Cal., F.S., pp.298-304.
[2] St.P,iv, p.333 (LP,iv,605).
[3] LP,iv,349, 356-7, 365.
[4] Eaves, pp.160 ff; Rae, pp.157 ff. In fact peace was not formally concluded until Jan. 1526 but a series of truces beginning on 4 Sept. 1524 produced much the same effect.
[5] LP,iv,365.

in the letter to Norfolk, Wolsey had made an important qualification: England would invade, but only in the event of 'the matters prosperously succeeding'.[1] As almost every letter that Wolsey wrote in 1524 on this subject made abundantly clear,[2] the qualification was all-important, and nowhere does this emerge more clearly than in the letters he wrote to Pace.[3]

Like so many of his fellow English diplomats, Pace was pro-Imperialist. Furthermore, his was a very emotional, not to say unstable, nature. So it is not surprising that no sooner had he arrived at Bourbon's camp than a hero-worship of the French king's rebellious subject set in.[4] Bourbon had, he reported, 'so faithful and so steadfast mind without vacillation to help the king to his crown of France that if he be assuredly entertained, the king shall assuredly obtain his crown in France', and even if he would not, Bourbon's valiant army would get it for him.[5] Wolsey had to put up with a good deal of such hyperbole, even being threatened at one point that if he refused to accept Pace's advice, he would be held responsible by him for any failure to obtain the crown of France for their master – all of which Wolsey took in surprisingly good part.[6]

What he would not do was accept the advice, neither, indeed, as he pointed out to Pace, would the king or other members of the Council. Victories in Provence were all very well, but it was well known to be a very weakly defended area, and moreover the only two strongholds there, Arles and Marseilles, remained in French hands. There was little doubt that Francis's decision not to engage with Bourbon was deliberate; he was merely allowing him to waste the allies' money there so that in the end Bourbon would have to retreat without the French king having to lift a finger. Writing on 31 August, Wolsey showed himself to be not at all impressed with Bourbon's achievement so far, nor was he especially amused to hear that in Provence the French were giving their allegiance to Bourbon and not to Henry, thereby undermining Henry's claim to the French throne, which had been a matter of negotiation between Bourbon and the English from the start.[7] On the other hand, Wolsey did make it clear that if Bourbon crossed the Rhone, marched on Lyons and then on into 'the bowels of France', achieving there 'a notable victory with a general revolution', Henry would be willing to invade. But even then further conditions would have to be met. Under the provisions of the May agreement, once England invaded, Charles had to take on the full burden of paying for Bourbon's army, and it was vital, so Wolsey informed Pace, for Bourbon to confirm that this condition would be fulfilled by the emperor. He also thought it vital that the promised Imperial reinforcements for Bourbon should materialize before England committed herself. And if all this was not enough to dampen even Pace's enthusiasm, Wolsey raised the suspicion that even if Bourbon successfully moved

---

[6] LP,iv,615; Hall, p.684.

[1] LP,iv,615; Hall, p.684.
[2] LP,iv,420-1, 440-2, 503, 510, 589.
[3] For his posting to Bourbon see LP,iv,361-2, 374, 420-1, 456.
[4] He arrived on 13 June.
[5] St.P,vi, p.313 (LP,iv,420).
[6] St.P,vi, p.314 (LP,iv,442).
[7] On this point see LP,iii,3123, 3154, 3217.

north, the duke's intention would be to secure not some 'notable revolution' but rather his own lands in the Auvergne and Bourbonnais – which would hardly be to England's advantage.[1]

What all this adds up to is that Wolsey had no intention of being taken for a ride by the Imperialists, as to some extent he had been the previous year. On the other hand – and this is important for the argument that follows – he could not afford to miss out on any notable Imperial success, for the obvious reason that in any settlement that followed he would have a very weak hand to play. But it looks as if in 1524 he had little faith in any such success, and he was indeed proved right; on 29 September Bourbon was forced to raise his siege and one month later Francis i was back again in Milan![2]

But Wolsey's reluctance in 1524 to take any military action to further the Great Enterprise is not the only curious feature of his conduct of policy at this time. Perhaps even more so, and especially to the Imperialists, was the appearance in London in April of a Genoese friar, one Jean-Joachim de Passano. Moreover, as it turned out, during the next eighteen months he was very rarely to be out of London.[3] Ostensibly he had come on a business trip to a fellow Genoese settled in London, Antonio Bonvisi, but in fact he was Louise of Savoy's *maître d'hôtel*, sent by her to England to begin negotiations for peace. Quite how serious these were lies at the heart of the interpretative problem that a study of Wolsey's foreign policy during these years presents. For some it is crucial evidence of Wolsey bending yet again to the dictates of the papacy, for was not the new pope, Clement vii, at this very time working hard for a peace that might prevent Northern Italy from being a permanent battlefield between the French and Imperialists? Thus loyally taking his cue from his spirtual head, Wolsey too sought peace.[4] And there was a more personal reason for this decision. Clement's election to the papacy in November was a second rebuff in two years to Wolsey's ambitions to obtain the papal tiara for himself. It was also sure proof of the emperor's unwillingness to honour the promise he had made at Bruges in 1521 to support Wolsey's candidature in any future papal elections. Thus, so it has been alleged, his determination to get his own back on the emperor by coming to terms with France.[5] For yet others it demonstrates Wolsey's lack of genuine commitment to the Great Enterprise from the start, deriving in part from an attachment to peace that supposedly was always threatening to separate him from his more bellicose master.[6] More recently the negotiations have been seen as merely an insurance policy, to be activated only when it looked as if the French might be winning. Moreover, according to this view, in the weeks just before Pavia they were anyway in the process of breaking down. Thus, the dramatic Imperial victory there, far from disrupting Wolsey's well-laid plans for a diplomatic revolution, was genuinely welcomed by him, the negotiations with the French being only

---

[1] St.P,vi, pp.333 ff. (LP,iv, 605). For their full correspondence see LP,iv,420-1, 440-2, 503, 512, 589.

[2] St.P,vi, p.333, n.1; ibid, p.364, n.2; Knecht, pp.163 ff.

[3] Jacqueton, pp.53-4 for a biographical sketch. The work is of great importance because it makes full and highly intelligent use of material not otherwise readily available. My one complaint concerns the many highly critical comments on Wolsey!

[4] A.F. Pollard, pp.137-8; Wilkie, pp.114 ff.

[5] A.F. Pollard, pp.137-8.

[6] Scarisbrick, Henry viii, pp.131 ff.

reluctantly resumed when neither the emperor nor Henry's subjects proved as co-operative as Wolsey had hoped.[1]

The fact that all these interpretations will be rejected here is not to say that there is not a good deal to be said in favour of all of them. It is the case that in the spring of 1524 Clement was actively working for peace and that by the end of the year he had entered into secret agreements with the French king, so that a Wolsey dedicated to peace might have been inclined to follow his lead. Moreover, as already stressed, at no time during 1524 did Wolsey show any enthusiasm for war against France. And as regards the 'insurance policy', it may well be true that in the weeks leading up to Pavia the Anglo-French negotiations were not on the verge of success. But there are serious objections to be made to all three interpretations – not least, of course, that if one is right, the others must be wrong.

The chief objections to the first two have in effect already been presented. The notion of Wolsey as a lackey of the papacy is unconvincing, in part because even the obvious link with it, his legatine authority, was obtained very much to further Henry's policies, and in part because on close examination the necessary links between papal and English diplomatic initiatives are missing. Moreover, it was suggested earlier that, when Wolsey first put his name forward at a papal election in December 1521, he was prompted to do so out of concern for Henry's prestige rather than any personal ambition; and this seems to have been equally true when in the late autumn of 1523 he stood again. True, in the October he had graciously responded to intimations that both Charles and Margaret of Austria were eager for him to become pope by agreeing that if they were willing to write on his behalf, he would put himself forward – and put himself forward he did. However in doing so he again stressed that it was Henry who desired him to obtain the dignity. Furthermore, the word from Rome was that it was Giulio de' Medici who would be the successful candidate. If this indeed was the case, the English envoys at Rome were not to put Wolsey's name forward but instead were to make use of letters in support of de' Medici, who was not only officially the cardinal-protector of England but was considered to be genuinely sympathetic towards her interests. Wolsey's response, when informed of de' Medici's success, makes it difficult to believe that he had suffered any great disappointment at his own lack of success.[2]

As regards Wolsey's commitment to peace, the essence of the rebuttal has been that no one who wished to dominate the European scene in the way that Wolsey did, could have afforded the luxury of truly pacifist sentiments.[3] Neither have any serious divisions between him and his master in the conduct of foreign policy been discerned so far, nor is there much evidence for thinking there were any in 1524 or 1525. It is true that on 25 March 1524 Wolsey wrote to the English envoys in Rome that he would not refrain 'to study, devise and set forth, as much as may stand with my duty to my Sovereign Lord and master, all such things [that] in my conceit may be thought upon or imagined for to conduce everything to the best purpose', and by emphasizing the scruple about his duty to the king it is possible to see what follows

---

[1] Bernard, *War, Taxation and Rebellion*, pp.24 ff.

[2] *LP*, iii, 3372, 3377, 3389, 3587, 3592, 3609, 3659; *Sp.Cal., F.S.*, p.276; also Chambers, 'English representation', pp.512 ff; Scarisbrick, *Henry VIII*, pp.109-10.

[3] See pp.98 ff., 144 ff. above.

in the letter as an attempt to distance himself from Henry's views, especially in view of the ensuing references to the papal peace initiatives.[1] For a number of reasons, however, such a reading must be rejected. To begin with, Wolsey gave his own 'conceit' because he had been asked to by the pope, so it cannot in itself provide evidence that he was embarking on an independent, not to say clandestine, policy. The main emphasis throughout the letter, even in that part which allegedly contained his real thoughts, was not on any new peace initiative but on the continuing need to maintain military pressure on the French. The problem, however, as Wolsey made clear to the envoys, was that it was becoming increasingly unlikely that such pressure could be maintained. The Imperialists had already let him down badly and the new pope was not nearly as opposed to the French as had been expected. It was all this, not any love of peace, that was forcing Wolsey to look for a new policy – something that emerges more clearly from the way he left it to the envoys to decide whether circumstances in Northern Italy made this the right moment to launch it.[2]

Wolsey's willingness to give the envoys such a free rein hardly suggests that he was asking them to do something that he knew their king disapproved of, for surely the longer the delay in implementing it, the more likely that Henry would get wind of it? But in this instance there is no need to speculate. Henry did know about the pope's desire for peace because back in February the pope had written to him about it; and, what is more, at the same time as Wolsey had presented his own 'conceits', Henry had made his favourable response.[3] And at this stage it may be helpful to reiterate the general point that for Wolsey to have conducted a clandestine policy he would have needed to set up a private courier service, of which there is no evidence. As it was, almost all the diplomatic correspondence was either seen by the king or made known to him in digest form. He was extremely well briefed for his audiences with foreign ambassadors. When important decisions had to be made he usually contrived a meeting with Wolsey, and letters were daily passing between them.[4] None of this means that Wolsey's advice did not carry great weight. After all, advice was what he was paid to give and all the evidence is that for fifteen years or more Henry for the most part took it. But this in itself provides another reason for disbelieving that Wolsey was having to conduct a clandestine policy; the more Henry is thought to have trusted his judgement, the less need would there have been for any secrets.

It is almost certainly true that on occasions Wolsey may have been quicker to grasp the appropriate means by which to achieve his master's ends. It is difficult to believe, given the recent fate of Suffolk's expedition, that anyone in England in the first few months of 1524 could have been very enthusiastic for war or the Imperial alliance, and in March Henry's favourable response to the papal feelers for peace underlines this. Admittedly, there is some evidence for a rather bellicose Henry, but there were good reasons why he should want to appear so. First there was the need to keep up diplomatic appearances. England was, after all, still formally

---

[1] St.P,vi, p.282 (LP,iv,185). For Scarisbrick's interpretation see Scarisbrick, Henry VIII, p.132.
[2] St.P,vi, p.282 for Wolsey giving them freedom to decide when the right moment was; for the whole letter see St.P,vi, 278-86 (LP,iv,185).
[3] LP,iv,6, 184.
[4] See pp.205 ff. above; also Bernard, War, Taxation and Rebellion, pp.40-5.

committed to the Great Enterprise, and nothing was to be served by letting her ally think otherwise, especially not if she was thinking of deserting! Thus, Wolsey's statements about how bellicose the king and Council were and Henry's suitably warlike noises when he met the Imperial ambassador should not be taken as the truth.[1] In addition, as has already been pointed out, Wolsey was very ready, in order to clinch a deal quickly and on the most favourable terms, to put pressure on any foreign power he was negotiating with by stressing that he was the only person in England on their side. Most commonly it was a ploy he used with the French, but when sometime in May or early June he instructed Clerk to inform Clement that he, Wolsey, had had to labour hard to persuade king and Council to listen to the papal pleas for peace, 'they now being fixed upon matters of war', it looks very much as if he was using it with the pope too, if only because Henry would almost certainly have known the contents of Wolsey's letter.[2]

The difficulty in early 1524 was not in realizing that the Great Enterprise was going badly but in finding some attractive alternative. Merely to have given it up would have been an unthinkable admission of failure and would have anyway left England totally isolated. On the other hand, the alternative of a French alliance and the consequent imposition of a European settlement in which 'all the glory and the incense' would fall to Henry and Wolsey seemed a long way off.[3] What seems to have happened is that Wolsey took advantage of, and indeed subtly encouraged, the new pope's desire for peace in order to get into direct negotiations with the French without having himself to make the first approach. The vital evidence for this is provided by a letter from the English envoys in Rome of 21 March in which they reported that, as instructed, they had suggested to Clement that he should persuade the French to send someone to England with a view to furthering the peace process that he had already embarked upon, and for the success of which, it was to be stressed, Clement was to get all the honour – though in reality this was something that Wolsey would have had no intention of allowing.[4] For the moment, however, the important thing was for the process to start, and it seems that Clement took the bait. When his envoy, the archbishop of Capua, arrived at the French court on 27 March he brought with him the very suggestion that Wolsey had put to Clement. Louise had responded favourably, and the result was that appearance in London already mentioned of a Genoese friar ostensibly on a business trip but really to begin negotiations with Wolsey for a peace with France.[5] It is difficult not to admire the skill with which Wolsey had achieved this vital first step, and in particular the way in which he had minimized the risks. After all, he could not have known what the French response would be, and there was the very real possibility that any hint that England was willing to make a separate peace with them might have been exploited, by, for instance, their informing the emperor. But by making it a papal suggestion, Wolsey had more or less pre-empted such a manoeuvre because he could, and indeed would, always maintain that Joachim's arrival had had nothing to do with him.[6] As it was, all sorts of stratagems had to be used to allay the inevitable

---

[1] LP,iii,3659; iv,26; Sp.Cal., F.S., p.318; made use of in Scarisbrick, Henry VIII, p.131.

[2] LP,iv,446, Clerk to Wolsey, 25 June.

[3] That this was what they sought was Giberti's view in 1525; see LP,iv, 1467.

[4] LP,iv,170.

[5] Jacqueton, pp. 42 ff. for a fuller account.

suspicions of, in particular, the Imperial ambassador in England, Louis de Praet, suspicions that inevitably increased the longer Joachim stayed.

The cheekiest of the stratagems used by Wolsey to try and throw his allies off the scent was the pretence that Joachim was a French spy,[1] but none of them should encourage the notion that Wolsey was working behind Henry's back. For one thing, there is direct documentary evidence that the king was well aware of Joachim's presence in England and very interested in the negotiations that were taking place.[2] What, of course, he could not do, in any public way at any rate, was take part in them. Whatever the actual state of play, the French in 1524 were still ostensibly the enemy whose territory Henry had committed himself to invade. It was just about all right for there to be suspicions that his leading minister was involved in clandestine meetings with Genoese friars who might or might not be in the service of the French queen-mother – and, after all, not all the Imperialists' negotiations were above suspicion – but it would not do at all for such suspicions to be attached to the person of the king. Indeed, it would have been very unseemly if, involved in the Great Enterprise against France, Henry had not appeared more bellicose than his minister. Still, none of this helps to answer the question how seriously these negotiations were taken.

At the very least, one has to assume some seriousness. After all, they had been difficult to set up and, given that any hint of them would undermine the alliance and place England in a very exposed position,[3] it would have been foolish to embark on them just on the off chance that something good might come of it. Moreover, the mere fact that Joachim's visit was so prolonged and that he was eventually joined by the chancellor of Alençon, Jean Brinon, must indicate that Wolsey was looking for something substantial.[4] The question remains, what? If it was neither a papal blessing nor the sixteenth-century equivalent of the Nobel peace prize, could it have been that most recently favoured answer, some kind of insurance policy against the possibility of French success, which in the early months of 1524 and again the following winter, as Francis followed Bourbon's retreating army back into Northern Italy, might have seemed a real possibility? For such an answer to carry conviction it would have to be shown that, as during early 1525 the prospects of French success in Northern Italy dwindled, so Wolsey took his negotiations with the French less and less seriously. And it would certainly make a nonsense of the view that an audience planned for the French envoys with Henry VIII on 9 March was intended to be the occasion for reaching some kind of Anglo-French agreement.[5]

In fact, it will never be known for certain what was intended, for on that very day confirmation of the overwhelming nature of the Imperial victory at Pavia arrived in London, and the audience was cancelled even as the envoys were on their

---

[6] *Inter alia Sp.Cal.*,iii (i), p.78.

[1] *LP*,iv,394, 684, 1083.

[2] *LP*,iv,882, 1018.

[3] *LP*,iv,671, 684, 841, 1083, 1132, 1190; *Sp.Cal.*, F.S., pp.335 ff. for Imperial concern; *LP*,iv,1002, 1017 for papal concern; *LP*,iv,1072 for Venetian concern.

[4] His first visit appears to have been brief, but he was back again in June and then stayed for over a year.

[5] Scarisbrick, *Henry VIII*, p.139; but also Hall, p.693.

way.[1] All the same, the view put forward here is that the negotiations with the French were serious enough, and had become increasingly so. One reason for thinking this is the kind of terms that were being discussed. Back in the summer of 1524 the English demands, by Wolsey's own account at any rate, had been ludicrously high – nothing less, indeed, than 'the whole realm of France'.[2] Since, this piece of information was only for Imperial consumption, it may well have been disinformation, but be that as it may, by the time Joachim had been joined by the chancellor of Alençon in late January 1525 the demands were of a much more realistic kind: the counties of Boulogne and Guisnes and the town of Ardres, which is to say an area of land adjoining Calais and the English Pale, together with an annual pension of 100,000 crowns. It is true that the French appear to have been determined not to surrender any territory and thought that the financial demands were on the high side, but on the other hand the possible gains for them were great: if they could break the Anglo-Imperial alliance, Milan might be theirs once again, and perhaps even Naples – in which case a bit of land around Calais might not seem too high a price. As for the money, it was only a little more than they were paying before war broke out, and as it turned out, was to be precisely the amount agreed to a few months later at the Treaty of the More. From the English point of view, it appears to be not nearly so good a deal, for by giving up the Great Enterprise they were in theory giving up the opportunity of conquering France. On the other hand, they would at least be sure of getting some money, which they had singularly failed to do from the emperor. They also stood to recover that dominant position in European affairs which, as it became increasingly obvious how little influence they had over their present allies, was rapidly slipping away – but more of this later. For the present the point to be made is not that the terms on the table were especially liked by either party, but that they were not so unacceptable as to suggest that neither side took them seriously. There are other reasons, too, for believing that the contrary was true.[3]

One of the things that anyone who thinks otherwise has to account for is the enormous damage that the presence of Joachim in England for so lengthy a period did to Anglo-Imperial relations. From the moment in June 1524 when Wolsey, in order to assuage Imperial worries, reported that he had sent the French emissary packing after only half an hour, to well after Pavia when, at least by some accounts, the English were very keen to revive the Great Enterprise, the negotiations with Joachim were a stumbling block which all Wolsey's diplomatic inventions did little to remove.[4] Thus, when the English ambassador at the Imperial court first presented the English congratulations for Pavia, he had to report that Charles's response had not been altogether gracious. One reason for this was Joachim's long stay in England which, according to the emperor, could only mean that Henry had chosen to desert him – and by implication deserved no share in the spoils of victory.[5] No doubt it suited Charles at this moment to play down his ally's contribution, but in truth it had not been very great, nor was this by any means the first time that he had

[1] Jacqueton, pp.90-1.
[2] LP,iv,394; see also LP,iv,684.
[3] LP,iv,1093, 1160; Jacqueton, pp.66-96.
[4] See Sp.Cal.,iii (i), pp.23-4, 40, 52, 76, 160.
[5] LP,iv,1190.

expressed his disappointment.[1] Why, if Wolsey was still *au fond* committed to the Great Enterprise, did he let the negotiations with Joachim drag on so that they became a real bone of contention with England's partner? Even a merely wary Wolsey might have been a little more careful not to provide the emperor with such an obvious excuse for not co-operating. It was very curious behaviour, as was his failure to ensure that Charles's special envoy, Beaurain, was not granted, while he was in London, an audience with the king – something that Henry had expressed himself perfectly amenable to.[2] As it was, the failure to do so provided Charles with another reason for his lack of graciousness in March.

Yet another arose from Wolsey's treatment of the Imperial ambassador in England, Louis de Praet. Whether Wolsey deliberately set out to engineer a diplomatic incident with the emperor by the seizure on 11 February, against all diplomatic conventions, of de Praet's correspondence, or whether it came into his hands accidentally, will probably always remain an open question. But it has to be said that Wolsey's relationship with the Imperial ambassador was already bad, and he was certainly quite capable of such a move.[3] However, the relevant point is how he chose to react; and this was to make as much out of the incident as possible. De Praet was banished from court and put under virtual house arrest. Even Pavia made no difference to Wolsey's view that if the Imperialists wanted a resident ambassador, they must send a new one.[4] One result of this was that Wolsey's negotiations became bogged down in acrimonious exchanges about de Praet at the very time when Henry was supposedly hell bent on an invasion of France in company with his 'dear brother', the emperor. Admittedly, de Praet had not been reporting back very complimentary things about Wolsey – and, given the negotiations going on with Joachim, why on earth should he have been? Even so, if Wolsey still believed in the Imperial alliance, his behaviour in the months leading up to and immediately after Pavia was more than inept. It was downright foolish.

Does the notion of an insurance policy against French success save Wolsey from such a charge, or, to put it another way, did Wolsey think the potentially harmful consequences of that success sufficient to justify jeopardizing England's relationship with her allies ? Obviously nobody likes to end up on the losing side, but it would have been curiously naïve of Wolsey, and indeed of Henry, to assume that something like the Great Enterprise could proceed without any setbacks, and, given the will to succeed, one might have expected any reversals to be countered with more, rather than less, co-operation with England's allies. Moreover, it is certainly not true that when, back in March 1524, the Anglo-French negotiations began, the French success was such that sheer survival demanded that England consider reapproachment. In fact, the French army, which had crossed into Northern Italy in the previous autumn, had barely survived a harsh winter holed up at Abbiategrasso, in early March was threatened not only by an Imperial army but also by plague, and by the end of April was in full retreat.[5] Even allowing for some time

[1] *LP*,iv,671.
[2] *St.P*,i, p.152 (*LP*,iv,882).
[3] Bernard, *War, Taxation and Rebellion*, pp.28-9 for the view that it was accidental. For Wolsey's detailed account see *St.P*,vi, pp.386 ff. (*LP*,iv,1083).
[4] *Sp.Cal*,iii (i), pp.75 ff.
[5] Knecht, pp.160-1.

lag for the news to reach England, English diplomatic correspondence throughout the first half of 1524 was much more concerned about what her allies had not done than what the French were doing.[1] Moreover, it would have been perfectly possible to have sent Joachim packing, once news of the French defeat was certain but this was not at all what happened.

But might it not be that the return in October 1524 of a French army to Northern Italy, this time led by Francis in person, was sufficiently alarming for Wolsey to want to pursue his negotiations with the French with even greater urgency?[2] Given the almost total lack of detail concerning any of the negotiations up until this point, it is very difficult to answer such a question. It is clear, however, that Wolsey, worried by the effect of French success on England's at least theoretical allies in Northern Italy, the papacy and Venice, made moves to counter their possible defection[3] – arguably curious behaviour for one on the verge of being frightened into defecting himself. But although he was receiving some fairly gloomy assessments of the allied position there, at no point did he show great alarm.[4] Perhaps his most worrying moment occurred in mid-January 1525 when he was informed by the French of their newly formed alliance with the papacy, Venice, Sienna and Lucca, but significantly his advice to Henry was that it should be treated with some scepticism. At the same time he permitted himself the revealing prayer that 'good resistance may be made against the French king while we shall be treating with [the ambassador] that cometh now out of France [that] our bargain shall be like to be the better wherein to have some good success'.[5] In other words, what bothered Wolsey about French success was not that it was directly harmful to English interests. The spectre of a rampant France in alliance with Scotland and even with Richard de la Pole, the Yorkist claimant to the English throne, was never raised by him, presumably because he never saw it as a possibility.[6] Moreover, from a defensive point of view, the more the French were drawn into Italy the better, while Albany's participation in the campaign there prevented his active intervention in Scottish affairs. More interestingly, Wolsey never even expressed regret that French success might signal the end of the Great Enterprise. What did worry him about it was that it weakened his bargaining position, and to that extent prevented him making an acceptable deal with the French.

It is always dangerous to believe that one document offers the answer to a historical problem, and perhaps especially so as regards foreign policy in which the circumstances are always changing, and with them the answer. At the very least, however, Wolsey's letter of 12 February 1525 provides some insight into the way he operated. In the course of the letter he gave Henry the latest news from Italy, including the French failure to detach Venice from the Anglo-Imperial camp and the Imperial commanders' decision to do immediate battle with a French army that for over two months had been tied down outside Pavia and still, Wolsey was happy

---

[1] LP,iv,8, 26, 30, 61, 170, 186, 356.

[2] Bernard, *War, Taxation and Rebellion*, pp.24-5; Jacqueton, pp.63 ff.

[3] LP,iv,882, 1002, 1015, 1017.

[4] His letter to Sampson of 19 Nov. was perhaps the most pessimistic (LP,iv,841), but as against this see LP,iv,882.

[5] Thomas More, *Correspondence*, pp.314-16 (LP,iv,1018).

[6] Cf. Bernard, *War, Taxation and Rebellion*, pp.7-8.

to report, showed no sign of taking it. Indeed, what with one thing and another, Wolsey felt able to venture the opinion that 'thanked be to Almighty God, the affairs there be in very good train' – and this which ever side won the impending battle! It is a very curious statement for an ally of Bourbon and the emperor to have made, but then the burden of the argument here has been that by now this was precisely what Wolsey was not. Admittedly, his expectation was of an Imperial victory, and this was marginally the preferred outcome. But, even so, it was not so much the victory itself that was to be welcomed, but 'the good effect which shall come of this matter may well, and is to be, ascribed unto your highness, who in the time of extreme desperation of the emperor's affairs in Italy, have been the only reviver of the same'. Henry was to get the credit, and the implication was that he would then be in a position to dominate the outcome of such a victory.[1] What Wolsey did not feel it necessary to spell out was the kind of settlement he would have envisaged imposing upon the French. Obviously one favourable to England, but whether much more favourable than the one he was negotiating at the time may be doubted; for, as has been indicated, what in the letter seems to be his chief concern is to secure for Henry, not any particular gains, but some kind of hold over his ostensible ally, the emperor.

To interpret the letter in this way may be to strain too hard for something that was not meant. Moreover, it must be pointed out that this same letter has been seen as vital evidence that the negotiations with France were only ever an insurance against French success because, as Wolsey wrote, if by any chance they were to be successful in battle 'your affairs be by your high wisdom in more assured and substantial train by such communications as be set forth with France apart than others in outward places would suppose'.[2] Thus, if Francis I had won the battle of Pavia, the French envoys in England, instead of being denied an audience with Henry on 9 March would have been welcomed with open arms, and the Treaty of the More would have been signed seven months earlier.[3] The difficulty in accepting this interpretation is that it appears to ignore the important qualification that Wolsey made about a French victory – that it could only be achieved at such great cost to them that even in victory they would be forced to look for support from England, and thus submit to English direction. At any rate, this seems to have been what he had in mind when declaring that any battle would be 'well and highly to the benefit of your grace's purpose'.[4] Nowhere in the letter or, I would suggest, anywhere else, is there any hint of genuine fears that a French victory would pose a serious threat to vital English interests.

It is really for this reason that the notion of an 'insurance policy' seems to mislead. Honour and reputation are what Henry and Wolsey dealt in, not insurance; if the latter is what they had chiefly been concerned with, then they would never have embarked upon the Great Enterprise in the first place. French success in 1525 would have been unwelcome, not because of the harm that it was doing to the Great Enterprise but because the more successful the French were, the

[1] St. P,i, p.157 (LP,iv,1078).
[2] St. P,i, p.158 (LP,iv,1078).
[3] Bernard, War, Taxation and Rebellion, p.30.
[4] St. P,i, p.157 (LP,iv,1078).

less they would be prepared to pay for England's switch to their side; and in bringing an end to the Great Enterprise it would be necessary for Wolsey to show not only that the emperor had continually let England down, but that there were substantial advantages to be gained from an alliance with the former enemy. As his letter of 12 February indicates, Wolsey believed that events in Northern Italy were playing into his hands: whatever happened there, all the leading participants were likely to want English support, and this put him in a strong position to reassert the English king's role as the arbiter of European affairs. It was for this reason that the negotiations with the French continued; during the first week of March one or other of the French envoys appears to have been continually with Wolsey. Neither did Wolsey feel much need to conciliate his allies. In interviews on the 7th and 8th, Margaret's newly arrived envoys, sent to persuade England to take military action against France, found Wolsey 'intractable' – something of an understatement since they had found his conditions for any English invasion of France totally unacceptable.[1] As every new report was indicating Imperial success, this was curious behaviour on Wolsey's part if, that is, he saw the French negotiations only as an insurance policy. But then the argument here has been that, if that was really all it ever was, almost everything he had done during the last ten or so months was very curious – especially since as early as 4 March he appears to have used unconfirmed reports of Pavia to raise his terms with the French envoys.[2]

If, on the other hand, the main thrust of his policy is interpreted as seeking to create a situation that would enable him to extract England from an enterprise which was clearly not working, while retaining a dominant position in European affairs, then his behaviour, especially towards his ostensible allies, makes much more sense. Not only can one afford to be a little rude towards an ally whose help is no longer wanted, but also it is useful to have a long list of complaints with which to justify one's desertion; and this Wolsey had little trouble in compiling, helped by the unexpected – or perhaps not so unexpected – access to the rude remarks that the Imperial ambassador had been writing home about him.[3] Since the spring of 1524 Wolsey's policy had been to do the minimum to further the allied cause consistent with the need to maintain sufficient pressure on the French to come to terms with him – precisely the policy he had used to persuade the French to sign the Treaty of London in 1518.[4] The difficulty, as always, was to get the timing right, for to have moved too soon and thereby miss out on any advantage that might accrue from Imperial success would have been a pity, to say the least. It may well be that only an hour or so had stood between Wolsey and a decision to jump too soon. Given that England was still formally at war with France, it is difficult to see why Henry would have been willing to grant the French envoys an audience unless there had been some major breakthrough in the negotiations, perhaps even the renouncing of any territorial claim by England. On the other hand, it would have been surprising if Wolsey had been willing to show all his hand before receiving definite news from Italy – this an argument for thinking that whatever the purpose of the audience it

---

[1] *Sp.Cal.*,iii (i), pp.75-82.

[2] *LP*,iv,1160.

[3] *LP*,iv,1628-9 for a list drawn up in Sept. to be used against Imperial objections to England's seperate peace.

[4] See pp.78 ff. above.

was not to make any final agreement.[1] But whichever scenario is correct, the important thing was that the French were in play, ready to be hooked when the right moment came. What temporarily threw all Wolsey's plans awry was the extent of the Imperial victory at Pavia and in particular the capture of the French king; once he had full knowledge of it some fairly fancy footwork would be needed, if only to buy himself a little time to weigh up the new possibilities.

It is hoped that in this account the notion that Pavia might cause Wolsey considerable worry will not come as too much of a surprise. True, it was suggested earlier that his preferred solution was some kind of allied victory, but because this would put considerable pressure on the French to do his bidding. Immediately after Pavia, it must have seemed as if there would be no French for him to negotiate anything with. The cards would have appeared to be now all with Charles, who was in a position to make what terms he liked with the French and finally to impose his will on Northern Italy. In doing this he might have chosen to show some gratitude to England for past services, though, despite what Wolsey was going to maintain, the English contribution to the final victory had been paltry in the extreme and, in this account, deliberately so. Moreover, in the new situation such grievances as Joachim's lengthy residence in England and the seizure of de Praet's letters would not have enhanced England's standing with the emperor.[2]

But for Henry and Wolsey Charles's generosity was beside the point. They were not in the business of making do with crumbs from the Imperial table; on the contrary, it was they who wished to dole out the crumbs and from this point of view Pavia threatened to be a disaster. But if so, why was it that the news of the Imperial victory was greeted with such rapture? Bonfires were ordered to be lit, Wolsey led the English nation in a service of thanksgiving in St Paul's, and Henry was allegedly so excited that he compared the messenger who brought him the news to the Angel Gabriel.[3] And if all these gestures had only to do with appearances, rather more substantial was the decision to send new ambassadors to Spain with grandiose proposals for Henry to lead an army into France to help remove that kingdom from the map of Europe![4] And what is more, to give some substance to these proposals, the nation was called upon to donate to their king a free gift of money so that he might lead an English army over the Channel to recover his rightful throne of France. Do not all these things suggest at the very least the revival of a genuine commitment to the Great Enterprise – in which case, of course, the interpretation so far presented of Wolsey's conduct of foreign policy must be seriously flawed? Many people have thought so. Henry's reaction to Pavia – for some would have a doubt about Wolsey's[5] – was perfectly genuine: any suspicions previously harboured about the emperor's behaviour were apparently blown away by the euphoria surrounding the great Imperial victory, and Henry really did think that the time had

---

[1] Jacqueton, pp.90-1 and Scarisbrick, Henry VIII, p.139 for the view that an agreement was about to be made; Bernard, War, Taxation and Rebellion, p.30 for the view that it was not.

[2] Bernard, War, Taxation and Rebellion, p.31 for the view that the smallness of England's contribution was a serious flaw in Wolsey's policy; also Jacqueton, pp.107-8. For Imperial attitudes see LP,iv,1190, 1213, 1237-8; Sp.Cal.,iii (i), pp.75 ff.

[3] Bernard, War, Taxation and Rebellion, p.32 for the Angel Gabriel; also Sp.Cal.,iii (i), pp.82 ff.

[4] LP,iv,1212.

[5] Scarisbrick, Henry VIII, p.141.

come to recover his French throne. And if one then asks why the euphoria was so short-lived, two straightforward explanations are forthcoming. The first is that the emperor notably failed to share in the euphoria, so that in any conquest of France, England would have had to go it alone. This in itself might have put an end to England's grandiose plans but, as it happened – and this is the second reason – Henry's subjects made it very clear that they had no intention of giving the Amicable Grant, thereby ruling out any serious military activity.[1]

Whatever view is correct, some chronology is called for, taking as a starting point the cancellation of Henry's meeting with the French envoys on 9 March, the day that confirmation of Pavia reached England. Things then began to happen fairly quickly, except for the departure of the French envoys, which did not take place until the 21st.[2] Still, this curious delay did not prevent Wolsey informing Margaret's envoys on the 10th that Henry himself was to lead an invasion of France. On the 21st commissioners were appointed to secure the Amicable Grant, and on the 26th Tunstall and Richard Wingfield received their commission to go to Spain.[3] In fact they did not leave Southampton until 18 April, having been held up by bad weather,[4] by which time the decision that Henry would immediately lead an army over to France had been rescinded – the first hint, perhaps, that all was not quite as it seemed.[5] Nevertheless, some kind of imminent English invasion was still, apparently, to take place. On 11 April Wolsey wrote to Norfolk, chosen to lead it, giving him details of his command, and on the 14th Norfolk wrote a modest thank-you for the honour, while promising to do his best. He was also able to report good progress in the county of Norfolk with the initial negotiations for the Amicable Grant.[6] Meanwhile on the 12th Fitzwilliam and Robert Wingfield had been sent to Margaret with instructions to present the same aggressive line that Tunstall and Richard Wingfield were taking to the emperor and as Wolsey was employing with her envoys in England.[7] But, over a week before Norfolk's letter of the 14th, Warham had already reported resistance to the Amicable Grant in Kent,[8] and by the 26th this had spread sufficiently for the government to modify their original demands – though, as will be shown, in a curiously uneven way. Not until 14 May were attempts to obtain money called off, by which time a minor uprising in the area of Suffolk around Lavenham, Sudbury and Hadleigh had had to be put down. Almost immediately after came the first clear indications that the Great Enterprise had been abandoned.

In the ten days following the cancellation of the grant Wolsey wrote a number of letters to English representatives abroad containing secret instructions. Unfortunately these have not survived but their gist can perhaps best be illustrated by the fact that immediately after receiving his, Clerk had an interview with the pope during the course of which his Holiness was informed that it had always been

---

[1] This is the central theme of Bernard, War, Taxation and Rebellion.
[2] Sp.Cal, iii (i), p.8. 95, with its reference to 'last Tuesday', the 24 March 1525 being a Friday.
[3] Sp.Cal., iii (i), pp.82 ff; LP,iv,1199, 1200, 1212.
[4] LP,iv,1249, 1255.
[5] LP,iv,1249, 1255.
[6] LP,iv,1261, 1265.
[7] LP,iv,1301; Sp.Cal.,iii (i), pp.86 ff.
[8] LP,iv,1243.

Henry's wish that the Imperial victory at Pavia should be 'moderately used' and that anyway his principal reason for taking part in the war had only ever been to save Northern Italy from French domination.[1] The degree of double-talk is almost breathtaking but the message was surely clear enough. And if one needs more certainty, Wolsey's letter to Henry of 27 May provides it. Its chief purpose was to explain why Margaret's envoys, who had just taken leave of the king in readiness for their return home, had suddenly decided to stay on. Wolsey ventured to add that he did not doubt

> but of your profound and great wisdom your grace will and can facilely conject what this manner of proceeding doth imply; and partly your grace shall take some conjecture thereof by such letters as Master Sampson now writeth which were delivered unto me by the said ambassadors. Your grace shall receive the same herewith, and right soon shall understand thereby that such war as the said emperor intendeth to provoke your highness unto shall little or nothing be to your commodity, profit or benefit. And whereas your highness hath lately been advertised that the said emperor would be moderate in his requests and demands of the French king to the intent that your bargain might be the better, I can perceive little or no appearance that he is minded so to do.[2]

The notion that at this time Charles was intent on provoking Henry into any kind of war is ripe indeed, but clearly by this date England's grandiose plans of only two months earlier were no more. Indeed it is more likely that negotiations with the French had been renewed. At any rate, sometime during the first week in June Joachim left Lyons *en route* for London, where he arrived on the 23rd. Just over a month later the chancellor of Alençon was also back and by the end of August a treaty between the two former enemies was signed, perhaps appropriately at the More, one of Wolsey's country houses.

Presented thus, the chronology very much supports the interpretation that is to be rejected here. Everything appears to hinge on the failure of the Amicable Grant and the government's recognition of this on, or near to, 14 May. Before this date English diplomacy shows every appearance of working towards an invasion of France. Only after it was cancelled was there a rapid change-about. And if this were not enough to clinch the argument, there is the undoubted fact that Wolsey himself was to inform the English ambassadors with the emperor that 'the king's coffers are not furnished for a continuance of war, and his subjects cannot help him'.[3] Why then reject it? The immediate answer is that if the earlier interpretation of English foreign policy prior to Pavia was correct, then anything that has as its groundwork a euphoric reaction to the Imperial victory makes no sense. Henry's and Wolsey's suspicions of the way in which the Imperialists had sought to use England for their own purposes were just too great to be blown away, even by a victory on such a scale. However, what the scale did mean was that, for the moment, plans for any immediate desertion of the emperor had to be abandoned. There was little point in joining a sinking ship, and moreover, if France really was sinking, then there could

---

[1] *LP*,iv,1443 Clerk's report of his interview dated 22 June. Wolsey's letter to him, brought by Casale, must have been written on or about 19 May; at any rate letters delivered by Casale to Russell and Pace were dated 18 and 19 May respectively; see *LP*,iv, 1410, 1419.

[2] *St.P*,i,160 (*LP*,iv,137); for its dating see Bernard, *War, Taxation and Rebellion*, p.51,n.210.

[3] BL Vespasian C iii, fo.76v (*LP*,iv,1488).

certainly be no question of leaving the salvage to the emperor. This last point needs to be stressed. The argument that follows is not that the revival of the Great Enterprise in March 1525, and the consequent request for an Amicable Grant, was a complete fiction. The circumstances were such that an invasion of France might have had to have been mounted. Charles might have been so fired up by Pavia that he might, after all, wish to invade France. Some provision had to be made for Bourbon, one of the victors of Pavia, who at the very least would be expecting to recover his lands in France and who might feel entitled to more. Moreover, there was even the possibility that as a result of the crushing defeat and the capture of its king, the French state might disintegrate, leaving a power vacuum that would have been too dangerous for Charles to ignore. In other words, even though Charles had never been keen on a conquest of France, the logic of the new situation might have compelled him to embark on one. And if France was to be dismembered, there was no way in which Henry's honour would have allowed him not to play a leading part and for this to happen money would be needed immediately. However, there was never any real euphoria; long before the Amicable Grant was called off, it was clear that there was going to be no immediate invasion, and by the time it was, Wolsey, if not actively in negotiations with the French, would have been fairly confident that an approach by Louise was about to be made. It will also be argued that it is not as certain as is sometimes suggested that the resistance to the Amicable Grant was such that it had to be cancelled.

There are a number of reasons for believing that, whatever diplomatic noises they were making in the aftermath of Pavia, Henry and Wolsey had no real desire to invade France. In the first place, the degree of military preparation seems not to have been commensurate with the enormous amount of talk about it, which lends some weight to Francis's observation the following year that he 'knew right well that it was but ceremoniously done'.[1] It is also strange that it was not until 16 May – that is, not until after the Amicable Grant had been called off – that there was any effort to contact Bourbon; and yet, as all the paper plans make clear, his contribution to any invasion of France was supposedly crucial. Moreover, even before Tunstall and Wingfield ever set sail for Spain, the plans that they were originally to have presented to Charles had already been scaled down, and an invitation to meet Henry in Paris had been withdrawn, or at least delayed, because Henry was no longer going to be leading the initial invasion force. When, as early as 7 April, Wolsey informed them of this decision, he gave as the chief reason that it was clear that the emperor would not agree to a personal invasion, or to any great feat of war, at least until after he had seen how his negotiations with the French were progressing.

Wolsey's concern about these negotiations may help to direct attention away from the fantasy world of chivalric exploits on the fields of France to his real worries. More importantly, his assessment that the emperor was not, for the moment, interested in war is evidence that, almost before anybody had been asked to contribute to the Amicable Grant, the likelihood of any English invasion of France had enormously diminished, for there is no evidence anywhere of any desire by the English to go it alone. Wolsey gave as his source for this assessment a letter of

[1] Henry Ellis, 2 ser, i, p.335 (*LP*,iv,2033).

Clerk's from Rome, but it was something that his own negotiations with Margaret's envoys throughout April and May would only have confirmed.

The role that Wolsey chose to play in these was that of a man consumed with a desire to satisfy his master's dream of an invasion of France and consequently filled with righteous indignation at the series of obstacles being put forward by the pusillanimous representatives of the emperor and his aunt. But that it was a performance is suggested not only by the views he had expressed on 7 April, but by the way he made certain throughout that his demands were pitched in such a manner as to render their acceptance highly unlikely. For instance, on 8 March, before news of Pavia had been confirmed, when they were still anxious to obtain some military aid from the English, the Imperial envoys had made it plain that they were opposed to an invasion of Normandy, and by the 30th Margaret had categorically rejected the idea, as she was to again a week or two later.[1] In fact, it was not until the end of April that Wolsey gave way[2] – a curiously late concession if the English effort was designed to get an invasion of France off the ground as quickly as possible. On the other hand, if it was Wolsey's intention to steer clear of any invasion while continuing to appear to want one, it was eminently sensible. At an earlier interview he had contrived to turn the tables on the envoys by playing a game of 'let's pretend for the sake of argument that we will give up a Normandy invasion'. He was rewarded with five reasons why an invasion of Picardy was also unacceptable![3] Thus, when later on he formally conceded the point, he already knew that this would not further the invasion plans – and hence the willingness to concede.

Anybody interested in witnessing Wolsey at work should study the envoys' account of their negotiations with him. They present a picture of Wolsey very much on top of his form, forcing the ever more embarrassed envoys in one meeting after another to justify the rejection of a whole number of requests from their erstwhile and, they still hoped, future ally. Finally, in some desperation, on 2 May Margaret and her councillors signed an agreement on Anglo-Burgundian military co-operation, but in practice all it amounted to was the promise of 100 hoys, plus, as its *pièce de résistance*, the promise of a hundred transport ships – this in lieu of the thousand that had been asked for! It was an offer that would have finally convinced Wolsey, if nothing else had, that there was nothing to be hoped for from the Imperialists by way of real military aid – but then in my view he had long ago lost all faith in that.[4]

When Wolsey received news of this non-agreement, there was no display of histrionics, as there had been earlier. Instead, he merely ventured the comment that he 'should have wished for a better answer, but since Madame is not willing to give it we shall have patience and wait'.[5] He may also have permitted himself a quiet smile. Margaret and her envoys had not come out well from these negotiations. On every possible issue they had been put into a position which made them appear to have let their ally down, thereby providing Wolsey with the perfect

[1] *Sp.Cal.*,iii (i),p.132.
[2] *Sp.Cal.*,iii (i), p.135.
[3] *Sp.Cal.*,iii (i), pp.111-2.
[4] *LP*,iv,1301, 1307.
[5] *Sp.Cal.*,iii (i), p.153.

justification for double-crossing them. So by 7 May, when making this comment, he could afford to be a little gracious. He could also call to a halt the Amicable Grant without any real loss of face and without giving any obvious signal to anyone about his real intentions. England, as he told Margaret's envoys on the 7th, was still keen on invading France but, alas, her allies had not seen fit to support her.[1] This being so, there was no point in continuing the attempt to raise further sums of money, and a week later the Amicable Grant was brought to an end.

It will be seen that in this account the question of whether or not Wolsey had been forced to come to this decision because of widespread opposition to the grant is almost irrelevant. Instead, the question becomes why it was not called off sooner – why, even, it had been called for in the first place. It could hardly have come as a complete surprise that an unexpected request for yet more money would result in some resistance, particularly since the second instalment of the 1523 subsidy was still being collected.[2] Would Wolsey have dared to risk such resistance, perhaps even widespread rebellion, if he had not been genuinely determined on reviving the Great Enterprise? In answering this question it must again be pointed out that when the grant was called for in March there was no certainty that there would not be military action. That said, it surely cannot have escaped Wolsey's notice that here was a golden opportunity to raise money in order more generally to finance a foreign policy which, given his own and his master's ambitions, was never likely to be inexpensive. Both theory and practice dictated that when the king was risking his life in a rightful cause, it was his subjects' duty to support him financially, even if the request lacked parliamentary authorization. In 1475 and 1481-2 Edward IV, and in 1491 Henry VII had secured such support in the form of 'benevolences', but if any of Henry VIII's subjects had cared to dwell on these precedents, they might have been a little perturbed. True, both kings did get across to France but in 1475 it had taken Edward just over a month, and in 1495 Henry considerably less, to come to some satisfactory financial settlement with the supposed enemy. And in 1482 Edward had not, as promised, led an invasion of Scotland – not, it should be said, the first time he had reneged on a commitment to his subjects to fight. No wonder questions have been raised about exactly what these kings' intentions were in asking for money, and neither should Henry's and Wolsey's escape scrutiny.[3]

To be over-cynical is not my intention: armies needed to be fed and paid reasonably promptly, and if war was even to be contemplated, financial provision had to be made in advance. But what is being suggested is that the calling of the Amicable Grant cannot, in itself, be proof of a strong commitment to the Great Enterprise. The decision to postpone the king's personal involvement in the invasion had been taken a fortnight before instructions alleging his continued commitment to such an invasion were sent to the commissioners for the grant.[4] And, whatever Wolsey's real intentions, there were diplomatic advantages to be

---

[1] *Sp.Cal.*, iii (i), p.153.

[2] Due on 9 Feb. but not paid until considerably later though interestingly, given the widespread pleas of poverty, almost in full; see Bernard, *War, Taxation and Rebellion*, pp.125-9.

[3] Harriss, *HJ*, 6; J.R. Lander, *Crown and Nobility*, pp.220-41; Ross, pp.205-38, 278-95.

[4] The decision to postpone was taken sometime before 7 April and the instructions went out on 21st; see *LP*, iv, 1249; *LP App*, 34.

gained from the Amicable Grant. After all, England was proposing to carve up the kingdom of France, something that the Hundred Years War and any amount of money had failed to bring about. It would, therefore, have been odd indeed to have made such a proposal without making any special financial provision.[1] As it was, in all his negotiations with the Imperialists Wolsey was able to stress the efforts taken by the English to prosecute the Great Enterprise, efforts notably absent on her allies' part.[2] But when, by 7 May at the latest, the allies had made it so clear that there would be no support for military action, then any diplomatic advantage to be gained from continuing with the Amicable Grant ceased. This made it easy for the Crown to back down as the resistance stiffened. Whether it was forced to back down is another matter.

Much will probably always remain problematical about the Amicable Grant. It is not even known precisely how much Henry's subjects were asked to pay: the clergy certainly one-third of their income, or of the value of their moveable goods, if this came to more than £10, and a quarter if it was less; the laity less certainly a sixth, though Hall at one point describes a complicated sliding scale.[3] Our knowledge of how people reacted to the request is confined very largely to those living in London, Kent and East Anglia, with only one or two snippets from elsewhere. In London and in Kent there was considerable opposition, and from the latter no promise of any money; it is also worth mentioning that it was only ever a promise that was sought or ever obtained.[4] On the other hand, in Norfolk and Suffolk people were generally willing to contribute, even before any concessions about amounts to be contributed were made.[5] Even where, as in Ely, there was much 'dolour and lamentation', in the end most people had been won over.[6]

It is hard at this distance in time and on such little evidence to judge how seriously to take the considerable dismay, in some areas at least, caused by the grant. It must also be true that at the time considerable political judgement would have been required in assessing the risks involved in pushing on with it. We have no real insights into Wolsey's view, no letters between him and Henry or indeed any one else, which shed much light on real feelings or intentions. What is known is that probably after a consultation with leading commissioners such as the dukes of Norfolk and Suffolk sometime before 25 April,[7] a decision was taken to make concessions, but these were curiously uneven. While some, such as Londoners, were to be allowed to contribute what they thought they could afford, thereby making the grant into a 'benevolence', others such as the inhabitants of Norfolk had the request reduced from one-sixth to one-twelfth. Yet others, such as the inhabitants of Kent had no reductions made until 5 May, some ten days after the concessions granted to others.[8] The inconsistency of the government's reaction is

---

[1] Charles was anyway to be offered about £40,000. He was also advised to ask his own subjects for a benevolence; see St. P, vi, pp.421-3, 427-8 (LP, iv, 1212).

[2] LP, iv, 1301 (1); Sp. Cal, iii (i) 92, 109-12, pp.125, 131-6, 146.

[3] Hall, p.694; Bernard, War, Taxation and Rebellion, p.56.

[4] Bernard, War, Taxation and Rebellion, pp.76 ff.

[5] On 1 April Norfolk reported some initial opposition in Norwich, but by 14th Lynn and Yarmouth had agreed, while three days earlier most of Suffolk was 'conformable'; see LP, iv, 1235, 1260, 1265.

[6] LP, iv, 1272.

[7] The St George's day celebrations on and around 23 April would have provided the opportunity.

bizarre enough to deserve a little more attention shortly. But whatever the reasons, it could not have helped the commissioners one little bit as news of the uneven treatment travelled and was used as ammunition against the new request. Nevertheless, a considerable amount was promised; and even in Kent, the search for money was not abandoned. Warham may not have thought much of Wolsey's advice to try asking for it at small meetings rather than at the large ones so far attempted, but his response of 12 May to this suggestion was not so desperate as to have forced Wolsey to call off the Amicable Grant altogether.[1] What may have done is a rising centring on the Suffolk towns of Lavenham, Sudbury and Hadleigh, close to the Essex border.

In the present context the most interesting thing about this rising is that it probably had little to do directly with the Amicable Grant. Of 525 people indicted for riot and unlawful assembly as a consequence of the rising, 390 were not, according to the 1524 assessment, worth more than one pound, and so were probably not being asked to pay anything in 1525.[2] What seems to have happened is that workers, but especially those in the cloth industry – and it was a considerable cloth-making area – feared for their livelihoods as a consequence of their employers trying to recoup the amount by cutting down on their labour force. Whether their fears were justified or not hardly matters. In Hall's version the clothiers had started to lay people off, and the Norwich authorities' warning to Norfolk that this would happen may confirm this.[3] On the other hand, the warning could have been merely a bargaining counter, played in order to encourage the Crown to call off the grant; and there was hardly time for lay-offs to have have taken place. Moreover, the fact that no money had changed hands by the time the decision to end the grant was taken might suggest that there was a lot of rumour but no actual unemployment – but then rumour is often a potent cause for rioting. Anyway, the suggestion that is being made here is that it would be wrong to call the rising in Suffolk in 1525 a taxpayers' revolt, because by and large it was not they who were directly involved. But does that matter? A rising is a rising and must be viewed by authority as extremely dangerous – and dangerous enough in this instance for the government to have decided to call off the offending demand for more money. Less than thirty years previously the men of Cornwall had marched on London in response to a demand for money, so that it is perfectly conceivable that in May 1525 it was felt that there was no option but to give way. But there is no direct evidence that either Wolsey or Henry felt this. Moreover, the fact that it was not, by and large, the taxpayers who were rebelling must make a difference to how one views the matter – and in two respects.

The first is that it was not from the cloth workers of Suffolk, or anywhere else,

---

[8] Bernard, *War, Taxation and Rebellion*, pp.56-60.

[1] *LP*,iv,1332.

[2] Bernard, *War, Taxation and Rebellion*, pp.138-40. According to Hall the poorest category asked to pay consisted of those worth between £20 and £1. In Kent no one worth less than £20 appears to have been approached (*LP*,iv,1306). In Norfolk they were, but a clear distinction was made between those worth over and under £20, which seems a high dividing line if those under £1 were to be included (*LP*,iv,1241, 1265).

[3] Hall,pp.699-700; *LP*,iv,1236.

that the government was hoping to obtain the bulk of the money, but from much wealthier people. In 1475 it was precisely these wealthier people that Edward IV had approached to obtain his benevolence, and in the process had raised, at the lowest estimate, £21,656, while probably from the same class Henry VII had raised in excess of £48,000 in 1491.[1] In 1525 these people may have grumbled – and in London and Kent may have grumbled a lot – but, as we have seen, there is enough evidence to suggest that in the end they would have paid up if pressed to do so. The second, and perhaps more relevant, point is that risings become revolts, and thus even more serious, when some section of the political nation is involved. Insofar as they were taxpayers, the Cornishmen of 1497 fall into that category. They even found a nobleman, Lord Audley, to lead them and, even if they were not part of a White Rose conspiracy, Perkin Warbeck was at the time alive and reasonably well, hoping to persuade James IV to invade England.[2] But there seems to have been nothing remotely political about the happenings of May 1525 in Suffolk, and insofar as the insurgents there were below the tax level they cannot even be said to have been part of the political nation, however widely defined. Neither is there any evidence that they were being made use of by leading clothiers or gentry to frighten the government into giving way. And that the rising in Suffolk was not as serious as all that is confirmed by the speed with which it was put down. It began at Lavenham on 4 May; by the 8th Norfolk and Suffolk appear to have felt that they had the matter well in hand, and by the 11th it was all over, apparently without a blow being struck.[3]

What the two dukes were certainly concerned about was what might happen elsewhere. On 8 May they suggested a watch might be kept on those potentially dissident noblemen, the Lords Bergavenny and Stafford – and here was the only hint in the whole episode that the political nation might not entirely rally to the Crown.[4] More seriously, on the very day that they were reporting the first humble submissions from the rebels of Lavenham, they received alarming reports that not only other parts of Suffolk, but also Essex and Cambridgeshire, including both the town and university of Cambridge, were on the verge of rebellion, and that as many as twenty thousand might be involved.[5] On the following day there was no mention of twenty thousand, but 'continually more and more knowledge' was coming in of a 'confederacy with evil disposed persons', extending to many other counties in addition to those already mentioned.[6] Despite reporting also that the submission of the original rioters was proceeding according to plan, the two dukes were obviously increasingly worried, and would have been even more so if they had been able to read Longland's letter to Wolsey of the same date, which reported that rumours had just reached his diocese of a rising in Norfolk and Suffolk, adding that 'such rumours in these parts, where so late was lightness of the commonalty used, doth not well'.[7]

Was it these rumours that finally convinced the government that it must give up

[1] Ross, p.217; Chrimes, Henry VII, pp.203-5.
[2] Chrimes, Henry VII, pp.88-92.
[3] LP,iv, 1319, 1323, 1325; Bernard, War, Taxation and Rebellion, pp.136-49.
[4] LP,iv,1319.
[5] BL Cleopatra F vi, fo.261 (LP,iv,1323) a document which for once was inadequately calendared.
[6] PRO SP 1/34/fo.196 (LP,iv,1329).
[7] LP,iv,1330.

its attempt to raise money? If the suggestion here is that it was not, this is not because the fears that such rumours would have caused are underestimated. But if governments are really determined on something they are usually prepared to take risks, and Henry VIII's government was no exception. After all, the much greater opposition, in which elements of the political nation were certainly involved, did not prevent the king from divorcing Catherine and 'breaking' with Rome. If, as has been argued here, the Amicable Grant had long ceased to have any real justification, the question that needs to be asked is why it was persisted with for so long. One answer could be that Henry and Wolsey were just greedy. Once the exercise had begun, why not continue and see what could be obtained? Of course, some awkward explanations would be called for when a peace treaty with France was announced, but perhaps they felt strong enough to ride out any resulting political storm, or did until they realized the extent of the opposition. It is never easy to turn down large sums of money and, as has been noted, the kind of foreign policy that Henry's and Wolsey's ambitions demanded was not cheap. Still, as an explanation it does not altogether convince, if only because the possible gains do not seem to have been commensurate with the risks involved. In that same year, 1525, they were anyway to obtain somewhere in the region of £80,000 by way of lay and clerical taxation, so that it would have been excessively greedy, and thus politically very unwise, to go ahead in the knowledge that no military activity was to take place.

Here it is appropriate to recall the curiously inconsistent way that the government handled the concessions it embarked on from 25 April onwards; for there is not the slightest doubt that they did considerable damage to the prospects of success, so much so that in their letter to Wolsey of 12 May the dukes called for a meeting of the Council to iron out the discrepancies.[1] For some this ineptness strengthens the case for a Wolsey at odds with his master and so determined to prevent any revival of the Great Enterprise that he was willing to sabotage the Amicable Grant by more or less engineering a taxpayers' revolt; or it shows, at the very least, that because his heart was not in it, he made mistakes.[2] But any view based on the notion of a major divergence between master and servant is suspect, and in this instance the evidence points in the opposite direction. Indeed, it is worth stressing that there can be no question but that Henry was fully informed about the Amicable Grant and about the uprising in Suffolk.[3]

Another possible explanation for Wolsey's inept performance is to see it as the desperate effort of someone so keen to obtain money that he was reluctantly forced into making concessions as he encountered first one, then another point of resistance. In such a scenario it might be expected that far from keeping Warham in the dark for so long, Wolsey would have informed him before anyone else of any concession, because it was in Kent that the strongest resistance by taxpayers was encountered. Or was it that the ineptness – and whatever the explanation, ineptness it certainly was – resulted from Wolsey's knowledge all along that the

[1] *LP*,iv,1329.
[2] Scarisbrick, *Henry VIII*, pp.138-9; Bernard, *War, Taxation and Rebellion*, pp.66-7 for a rejection of such a view.
[3] Bernard, *War, Taxation and Rebellion*, pp 60-6 for a full treatment of this important point.

pressure could and indeed would be released? In this scenario his chief concern was not the day-to-day management of the grant but choosing the moment when giving it up would cause least damage to his diplomatic negotiations.

It has already been pointed out that at least a week before 14 May and the calling off of the Amicable Grant, one of the reasons for continuing with it had disappeared. The Imperialists had made it so clear that they had no intention of engaging in any military activity that Wolsey could call a halt to any English military preparations while still maintaining that an invasion of France was what his master wanted. He now needed to establish that the prospects for negotiations with the French were encouraging, and it is tempting to think that this was what the delay in calling off the grant was about. Of course, it would have had to emerge sooner or later that some such negotiations had begun – but all the more reason for advancing them as far as possible while still pretending to be France's greatest enemy, for there was no doubt that the negotiations were contrary to both the spirit and the letter of Henry's treaty obligations to the emperor. It is not possible to ascertain precisely when these negotiations began, and it probably never will be. What has survived is an undated letter that Joachim wrote to Thomas Lark, his host for much of his earlier visit to England and, as brother of Wolsey's former mistress, close to Wolsey. Its purpose was to persuade Wolsey that with the emperor now in such a strong position, this was the moment 'rather to strengthen than relax the arrangements with France that by so doing he may turn an afflicted neighbour into a most obliged friend'. In the rest of the letter Joachim was anxious to get across the message that France had rallied to Louise and remained powerful.[1] No doubt his intention was primarily to try to strengthen a weak hand in any resulting negotiations, but in doing so he provided Wolsey with just the information he was looking for, because a France on the verge of collapse was not a viable ally. And clearly the letter did please Wolsey. By 8 June Joachim had left Lyons and Louise, and he was in London by the 23rd. It is very frustrating that these two June dates are the only certainties. Letters between Lyons and London took about a fortnight and this pushes back the possible date for a reply from Wolsey to about 24 May, though even that presents one with the problem that in a letter to Henry on the 27th there is no mention of French negotiations.[2] On the other hand, there might well have been an earlier exchange of letters, for Joachim's surviving letter was so informal as to make it very unlikely it was the first. Moreover, given that their two countries were still formally at war, the reference in that letter to 'arrangements' is tantalizingly suggestive of some secret understanding that Pavia had not destroyed. Still, none of this proves that there were any new negotiations between England and France before the Amicable Grant was called off on about 14 May. All that is certain is that by the 18th there was a definite change of direction in English foreign policy, signalled by those secret instructions from Wolsey to English diplomats already referred to. They suggest that by then Wolsey had some knowledge of Joachim's original letter, or at the very least was very confident that an approach

---

[1] LP,iv,1233. This much mutilated letter is printed in Jacqueton, pp.316-20. He dates it to the first fortnight of May (ibid, p.112). In LP it is placed at the beginning of April.

[2] LP,iv,1371, dated by Bernard 27 May (*War, Taxation and Rebellion*, p.51, n.210); *Ven.Cal.*,iii, p.446 for Joachim's departure from Lyons; Braudel, i, p.362 for the speed of letters.

from France would shortly be made. What has also been shown is that as early as 7 April he was sufficiently suspicious of the emperor's intentions to scale down his proposals for an invasion of France. Lastly, there is evidence that by 21 April he was making plans that his supposed ally would not have approved of.

It comes in a reply of John Clerk's from Rome to a letter of the 21st in which Wolsey had disclosed to him 'the whole platte [plan] of the king's highness and your grace's determinate and resolute mind'.[1] It is frustrating, of course, that Wolsey's letter has not survived; even more so that because Clerk felt that the time was not ripe 'to wade any further with his Holiness in the disclosing of any secret matter concerning the King's mind contained in your grace's letter, the Emperor not concurring with his Highness or being otherwise too much studious of his own advantage', we are never told what the 'platte' was. What does emerge, though, is that Wolsey was hoping to use the pope as 'mediator for the bringing to pass of your grace's desires', which, if past precedent was anything to go by, was another way of saying that he was looking for some alliance with the French.[2]

No more than any of the other evidence cited is Clerk's letter of 14 May proof that long before the failure of the Amicable Grant the Great Enterprise had been dead and buried, but that is the conclusion to which it points. And what is inescapable is that the deep suspicion of Imperial intentions which had so characterized English policy in the weeks before any knowledge of Pavia continued unabated afterwards. This makes it hard to take very seriously the grandiose plans of conquest that for a brief time Wolsey was conjuring up, like rabbits out of a hat. And that these plans never meant much is suggested by the speed and comparative smoothness with which the negotiations with the French proceeded after Joachim's arrival, culminating in the Treaty of the More of 30 August. The key to this was England's willingness to give up all territorial claims to France, and to accept instead the resumption of the annual French pension of 100,000 gold crowns (about £20,000) – and £4,000 more than she had gained from the Treaty of London.[3] Such an increase must have gratified Henry's purse, if not his honour; and, indeed, on the face of it it does seem small recompense for all the time and effort expended on the Great Enterprise, not to mention all the taxpayers' money. As against this, it was Louise's opinion that her envoys had conceded too much.[4] And what the terms of the Treaty of the More tend to confirm is something that has been central to my interpretation of Wolsey's conduct of foreign policy: that it was always position rather than possessions that Wolsey was seeking. The position that he had engineered in the summer of 1525 offered his master the possibility of continuing to play a leading role in European affairs, as a brief look at his relations with the emperor and with Margaret during the time leading up to the signing of the treaty with France will show.

There is always a danger of presenting the conduct of foreign policy as if it consisted of a simple choice between allies: for England in the early sixteenth century, between the emperor and the French; or nowadays between America and

[1] BL Vitellius B vii, fo.116 (LP,iv,1336).
[2] BL Vitellius B vii, fo,126 (LP,iv,1336).
[3] LP,iv,1600-6, 1609; Jacqueton, pp.113 ff.
[4] LP,iv,1609, 1617.

Russia. Sometimes, of course, it does boil down to this, and at any rate most of us find it easier to make sense of a policy in which there are obvious friends and enemies. For those responsible for the conduct of foreign policy the scenario can look rather more complicated, leading nowadays to what is sometimes rather dismissively referred to as the 'Foreign Office view'. If the phrase implies an over-cautious approach, it may not be readily applied to Wolsey. On the other hand, for him Europe was not, as it was for such as Pace and Tunstall, peopled with goodies and baddies, for if it had been, he would not have been able to conduct the kind of secret diplomacy that he was involved in during 1524 and the first half of 1525. Furthermore, there is the curious phenomenon that, as the new French alliance began to look more certain, so his attitude towards the emperor appeared to mellow. This can best be shown by his reaction to Charles's, on the face of it, rather provocative proposal to reject the hand of the Princess Mary in favour of Isabella of Portugal. As it happened, this suited England quite well. Charles had always been rather old for Mary, who in 1525 was still only nine to his twenty-five. More importantly, it freed her for a possible French match, another bargaining counter in the negotiations with France. Nevertheless, it would have been well within English rights to kick up an enormous fuss at the emperor's reneging on a solemn promise concerning a matter that touched Henry's honour so closely – and that Wolsey could kick up a fuss is shown all too clearly by his earlier treatment of de Praet, while apparently in December 1524 he had informed another Imperial envoy that his master was a liar, Margaret a ribald, the Archduke Ferdinand (aged twenty-one) a child, and Bourbon a traitor.[1] However, when in June Henry and Wolsey first got wind of Charles's intention, they took it all remarkably calmly.[2] And that they were increasingly concerned to maintain a good relationship with the emperor, despite their secret negotiations with France, emerges from a series of marginal comments to one of Tunstall's and Sampson's reports from the Imperial court.

When they wrote them on 11 August, the two English envoys were becoming increasingly worried at the pro-French direction that English foreign policy was taking, and did not hesitate to express their worries – so much for Wolsey's dictatorial behaviour! Their particular concern was that if England made a separate treaty with France before Charles had ended his negotiations, 'you in so doing shall lose the emperor for ever'.[3] It was a fair enough assessment – and it could well have been that what Wolsey was after was some kind of conflict with the emperor to pay him back for all the frustration and disappointment of the last few years. But according to Wolsey they had simply got it wrong: there was no reason, he explained to Henry, why Charles's friendship should be lost, 'seeing your grace is minded to continue your old amities with him'. For one thing, 'nothing is done by the treaty with France to the emperor's prejudice'. For another, 'your amity is as beneficial to the emperor as his to your grace'.[4] In other words, Wolsey had every intention that the 'old amities' should continue, but only on his terms, not the emperor's.

[1] LP,iv,1379.
[2] LP,iv, 1390, 1484, 1557, 1559.
[3] St.P,vi, pp.468-71 (LP,iv,1557). The comments are in Tuke's handwriting, but are clearly Wolsey's views for Henry's benefit.
[4] St.P,vi, pp,469-70.

It may be felt that, in teasing out an explanation for Wolsey's policy during the period that the Great Enterprise was supposedly England's aim, there has been too much supposition and guesswork and not enough attention to the evidence. This may be so, though it is one of the *sine qua nons* of this work that all the evidence needs a great deal of interpretation, not least because there are so many gaps in it. What, however, the surviving reports of Tunstall and Sampson permit is the construction of a viable alternative policy to the one, it has been argued, Wolsey adopted.[1] Instead of trying to tell Charles what to do with his great victory, would it not have been much better for England to have adopted a more modest posture? Pavia could, and should, have been good news for her. If she had only been willing to please her victorious ally just a little, she would have been in a good position to gain from the resulting peace settlement – probably, in fact, rather more than she was going to from the Treaty of the More, though Tunstall and Sampson never said this. There is no evidence that Charles wanted to do England down. Indeed, it was, as Wolsey had pointed out, very much in his interests to continue his friendship with her, but only as long as he was not asked to do too much. Thus, for Tunstall and Sampson at least, the straightforward and honourable course was to fulfil England's treaty obligations to the emperor in the reasonable expectation that he would reciprocate. Moreover, it was their belief that the policy that they now perceived Wolsey to have embarked upon was so dangerous, threatening an alliance between the emperor and Francis against England, that it had made them 'more bold to write thus plainly in discharging of our duty to your highness' – to which Wolsey had appended the comment: 'Being in this fear and perplexity they know not the bottom of your affairs, nor the force of your puissance, thinking that all dependeth upon the emperor's string'.[2]

Put like that, it is difficult not to feel a little sorry for the simple-minded English envoys! And at the same time it may serve as a warning to those of us who have tried to get to the bottom of what Wolsey was after – and it is worth pointing out *en passant* that Wolsey's comment makes it clear that Henry certainly had. Whether the interpretation that has been presented here is correct only the dead will know for certain, but at least it does allow for the complexity of Wolsey's approach. His secret diplomacy with the French had been specifically designed to free England from dependence upon the emperor, and for two reasons. Unlike Tunstall and Sampson, and probably others at the English court, Wolsey had come to believe nothing that the emperor said; and it has to be said that Charles's record of broken promises was justification enough for this view. At the same time – and much more importantly – any policy that resulted in vital decisions affecting Henry's honour and interests being made by someone other than Henry and himself was unacceptable. Wolsey had always been aware that in any alliance with the emperor Henry might be forced into a subsidary role, and it was to prevent this happening that the Great Enterprise had been invented. Henry had had to appear bullish and provide money and armies because only by drawing Charles into a conquest of France could he force him to treat him as an equal, while at the same time putting

---

[1] Most informative is probably the one just discussed (*LP*,iv,1557), but see also *LP*,iv,1380, 1421-2, 1555, 1655.

[2] St.P,vi,470 (*LP*,iv,1557).

the maximum pressure on Francis so as to persuade him once again to come to Henry's heel.

This, in general terms, was the policy Henry and Wolsey adopted in the years 1522-5, and, as was the case between 1515 and 1518, it was by no means an unmitigated success. Charles and the unexpected ally, Bourbon, proved to be extremely difficult, if not impossible, to manage. Francis, as usual, was very reluctant to be brought to heel. And by 1525 the situation had become, as far as England was concerned, something of a stalemate, with neither the French nor the Imperialists prepared to do what she wanted them to do. Pavia broke this up. Potentially it had been a moment of great danger, if dependence upon the emperor was what was feared. Wolsey's immediate response, as in 1522-3, had been to be more bullish than ever, in a desperate effort to prevent Charles from making all the decisions. Meanwhile, he waited to see what had happened to France. If she had not collapsed completely there was a strong possibility that she would be willing to accept England's predominance as never before. And this was how it turned out. Wolsey with his accustomed flair had been able to execute a diplomatic volte-face which could well have put England in a stronger position than ever before. What with an alliance with a suitably chastened France, the strong possibility of an anti-Imperial alliance, orchestrated by himself, emerging in Northern Italy, and an emperor who, though victorious, was increasingly desperate for money and, as always, dreadfully overcommitted, the scene looked set for Wolsey to execute another diplomatic triumph similar to that of 1518 – in other words, a settlement of the affairs of Europe directed from London. It was never to be. One reason was that Charles, whatever the weaknesses of his position, still had a great number of cards to play, including the person of the French king. Another would result from the fact that, all too soon, Henry would make the momentous decision to seek a divorce. For Wolsey this was a devastating stroke of ill-luck, for nothing could have been better calculated to undermine all his efforts to make his master the dominant sovereign of Europe.

Chapter Ten

Wolsey and the Common Weal

It would be to make no judgement on his moral worth to state that Wolsey took a great interest in the well-being of the king's subjects: what he and his contemporaries called 'the common weal'. Whatever his private shortcomings, as a leading royal councillor he could hardly have avoided doing so. Unhappy subjects are dangerous, or at the very least uncooperative, and even the most cynical of regimes is inclined to avoid trouble if it can. The lord chancellor's special responsibility for the poor, discussed earlier, devolved to him from the king, whom both theory and tradition enjoined to 'seek the profit of the people as much as his own'.[1] Tradition and theory can, of course, be ignored, but unless necessity compels otherwise most people are conventional enough to go along with them, even to believe in them! As a starting point, therefore, it seems reasonable to assume that Henry viii and his councillors, including Wolsey, were no exceptions.[2] It was also the case that both late medieval and early modern governments very much favoured state regulation over the workings of the free market. Whether, as a consequence, it makes sense to talk of them having an economic policy – what for the early modern period has been called mercantilism – is much disputed; most recent historians have tended to be sceptical, in part because so much government intervention in social and economic matters was apparently so half-hearted and ineffective.[3] In what follows this larger issue cannot be ignored, but a warning is called for. By its very nature, it is a wide and open-ended debate, for the subject matter ranges from the minutiae of village life to the complexities of the European money markets, taking in on the way the size and quality of pieces of cloth, the question of whether people should be allowed to play cards, what they should be allowed to wear, what Thames watermen should be allowed to charge, and so on. The terrain is vast, the existing maps unclear, and the danger of getting lost very great. Furthermore the problem of trying to define Wolsey's contribution in this area is even more acute than elsewhere. No writings or memoranda by him on social or economic matters have survived, and it is even quite hard to connect him directly with any social or economic legislation. But in two matters, enclosure and the combination of bad harvests and the dislocation of trade during 1527-9, the government's involvement was so great that, given his position and personality, it is not possible to doubt his personal involvement. Indeed, he seems to have instituted major government initiatives, and, furthermore, to have gone to considerable efforts to try to ensure their success.

It was in May 1517 that commissioners were appointed to inquire into the extent of

---

[1] Thomas Smith, p.53.
[2] But see Hoskins, *Age of Plunder*, in which Henry is presented as the 'Stalin of Tudor of England'.
[3] There is a large literature but Ramsey still provides an excellent starting point. See also Coleman; Elton, *Studies*, i, pp.285-93.

depopulation and enclosure in all but the four most northern counties.[1] They, in turn, were to summon juries of local men whose task was to report on

> which and how many towns and hamlets, and how many houses and buildings, have
> been destroyed since the feast of St Michael the archangel in the 4th year [1488] of the
> reign of the illustrious Lord Henry VII, late king of England, our dearly beloved father,
> and how many and how large the lands which were then in tillage and have now been
> put down and converted to pasture, and also how many and how large parks have been
> emparked since the feast for the preservation of game, and what lands have been
> enclosed in any park at any time.[2]

For those who have seen Wolsey as power-hungry, self-obsessed and essentially frivolous, this apparent concern for the poor and dispossessed has been inconvenient, so it has been necessary for them to undermine his efforts. Pollard thought that they were ineffective and possibly illegal.[3] More recently they have have been cited as evidence of a 'crass absence of political sensitivity and an unflinching refusal to look reality in the face'.[4] However, Wolsey has also had one recent champion in J.J. Scarisbrick, who in a very important essay, whose title this chapter deliberately echoes, sought to show that Wolsey deserved the plaudits and the tears bestowed on him by the poor commons on his final journey, for he had truly laboured on their behalf. It is this view that will be accepted here; indeed, much of what follows is but a commentary on Scarisbrick's pioneering work.[5]

The charge of political insensitivity derives from the provision under the still operative statutes of 1489 and 1515, that held the landowners responsible for any infringements,[6] so that it was on the whole important people who found themselves facing prosecution. This included not just the gentry, but heads of important religious houses such as Peterborough and Reading; Wolsey's own episcopal colleagues, including his former patron, Richard Fox; and at least nine noblemen, amongst whom were the dukes of Norfolk and Suffolk.[7] But it is a point that can be overstressed. Since very few of these people were personally involved in enclosure and the charges against them were thus technical, the offence having been committed by tenants who were probably not even known to them, there was little personal blame attached to the prosecutions, nor was any slight intended. Indeed, those who were closely involved in government, which is to say the most powerful of them, were presumably as anxious as Wolsey that the government's efforts to tackle the problem should succeed – and this is not entirely speculation.

The views on enclosure of only two royal councillors have survived. One, John

---

[1] LP,ii,3297.

[2] Leadam, *Domesday*, i, pp.9-10.

[3] A.J. Pollard, pp.85-7.

[4] Elton, *Reform and Reformation*, p.69.

[5] Scarisbrick, 'Cardinal Wolsey'. Not only does this essay provide the starting point for what follows, but I owe an enormous debt to its author not only for much fruitful discussion and a visit to Wormleighton, but also for making available his detailed notes.

[6] 4 Hen VIIc.19; 6 Hen.VIIIc.5; 7 Hen.VIIIc.1.

[7] Scarisbrick, 'Cardinal Wolsey', p.63 for his 'nine peers, three bishops, thirty-two knights and fifty-one heads of religious houses'. My own list of peers numbers eleven together with two aristocratic ladies: dukes of Norfolk and Suffolk, marquess of Dorset, earls of Derby, Devon and lords Cobham, Ferrers, Fitzwarren, Mountjoy and Zouche; also the countesses of Devon and Oxford.

Longland bishop of Lincoln, was positively in favour of what the government was doing, while the other, Sir Thomas More, was the author of a famous attack on enclosers. Both may have been prosecuted for enclosure! This does not, however, make them hypocrites. Longland himself may have escaped prosecution, but, if so, his predecessor William Atwater did not, which is to make the point that either would have been prosecuted not as active enclosers, but as, by virtue of their office, the chance owners of the land concerned.[1] There is no doubt at all, though, that in Hilary term 1527 More did appear in court as a defendant in an enclosure case, but, as he had acquired the property in question only two years earlier, on the death of Sir Thomas Lovell, it is difficult to attach any blame to him.[2] This is not to suggest that having to answer in court, even for an offence one had not committed, was not without embarrassment. It could also be tedious and costly, and may well have dampened enthusiasm for what the Crown and its leading minister were doing. But these prosecutions do not amount to a serious attack on the political nation, such as might justify the accusation of gross political insensitivity. This is especially so since, as will shortly emerge, the number of eminent people for whom enclosure was an important financial concern was probably very small.[3]

But why did Wolsey go for the owners if they were not in any real sense responsible? Probably he thought that a landlord was in a much better position than the Crown to ensure that the wrongs were remedied. Moreover, because most landlords were financially so little affected, they were less likely to try to deceive the courts and the more distinguished they were, the more they had to lose if they were found out doing so. What does emerge, even from a cursory look at the evidence, is a serious intention on the government's part – and one sustained long after the initial inquiry – to achieve results. There is, first of all, the sheer scale of the administrative exercise begun in May 1517, seeking out information about thousands of acres of land and about the fates of countless properties and individuals. What is also striking is the altruistic nature of the exercise. With other national inquiries, including Wolsey's own general proscription of 1522, the intention had usually been to establish royal rights and thus incur financial and political advantages. In this case the Crown would in theory make some slight financial gain – under the provision of the enclosure Acts it received half the income from land during the period that it had been wrongfully enclosed. However, this only applied where it could be shown that the land was held directly from the Crown; and furthermore the whole thrust of the government's action was to provide every incentive for the enclosure to be brought to an end, thereby eliminating any possible financial claim by the Crown.

The whole question of intention will have to be looked at again, but for the moment the assumption will be that, when embarking upon the enclosure inquiry of 1517, Wolsey wanted to do something for the common weal, and to that end some 260 people are known to have been brought to court. This in itself is remarkable, when one remembers how rarely anybody appeared in court.[4] It is even more

---

[1] For the bishop of Lincoln being cited see PRO E 159/298, ro.xviii, the date Michaelmas 1519, two years before Longland became bishop. The subsequent history of the case is unknown, but if others are anything to go by, it could well have dragged on into Longland's time.

[2] LP,iv,1525; also Scarisbrick, 'Cardinal Wolsey'.

[3] Here I am taking issue not only with Elton but also Scarisbrick, 'Cardinal Wolsey', pp.65-6.

remarkable that some 188 of the cases (and the actual figure was almost certainly greater) are known to have been brought to a conclusion. In addition, seventy-four people are known to have pleaded guilty and, as a consequence, entered into large recognizances to remedy the fault.[1] On the face of it, all this unusually successful legal activity is yet more evidence of serious intent.

In 1518 and 1519 further commissions of inquiry were set up, while in 1523 the General Pardon, which traditionally brought a parliament to an end, contained an important provision designed to further the thrust of government policy on enclosure.[2] In 1526 there was a new initiative. On 14 July a proclamation was issued in which it was admitted that despite the 'industry and diligence' of the government 'to reform, remove and repress the aforesaid great enormities and inconveniences . . . very little reformation thereof as yet is had'.[3] This may have been a deliberately pessimistic assessment designed to encourage more effort, but Wolsey was not content with mere words. New commissioners were sent out, and on 30 September one of them, John Longland, was reporting back to Wolsey that he had had no time to write earlier because he had been

> so occupied in the view of these enclosures according unto the king's commission . . . And tomorrow do ride to Northampton and all the week to be occupied in that part of the shire. And the week after that in Leicestershire and Rutland. My Lord Brudenell and Sir William Fitzwilliam hath taken great labour therein with as good a mind as any men might. And we most humbly beseech the king's highness and your good grace to give us a further time for much part of it is so intricate and large it cannot be well done in little time. Our books will be far greater than hath been and much things will come to light that yet hath not been known.[4]

Then in November two Chancery decrees were issued ordering all those named by the commissioners to appear in court and make recognizances whereby they promised to remedy their errors on pain of considerable financial penalties.[5] And the pressure continued. In May 1528 there was a further decree ordering all the king's subjects

> being relaters and furtherers of the commonwealth . . . that they by writing and bills secretly disclose unto the lord legate, his chancellor of England, the name of all such persons . . . who hath and keepeth in his hands and possession . . . any more farm than one; and moreover by the same bill to disclose to the same lord chancellor the names of such person as do enclose any grounds or pastures to the hurt of the commonwealth of this the king's realm.

Two masters of chancery were deputed to receive the information and a promise was made that the names of the informers would be kept secret.[6] In the following

---

[4] See p.110 above.

[1] Scarisbrick, 'Cardinal Wolsey', pp.51-4.
[2] Kerridge, EHR, lxx, pp.214-15; SR, iii, p.244.
[3] TRP, no.110.
[4] PRO SP 1/50/fo.151 (LP, iv, 4796).
[5] TRP, nos.113-14.
[6] Ibid, no.119.

February it was further ordered that anyone obtaining profit from land enclosed

> contrary to the statutes and law of the realm . . . that they and every of them, at this side the 15th of Easter next coming [11 April], without any further delay or contradiction, clearly break and cast down all and singular the said hedges, ditches and enclosures so made and enclosed as is aforesaid upon pain to them and every of them not following the king's commandment to run into his high indignation and displeasure.[1]

If anybody dared to ignore such a warning, the sheriffs were instructed to tear down the enclosures themselves.[2] And in the previous month Wolsey had ordered the sheriff of Northamptonshire to intervene in a long-running dispute between the inhabitants of Thingden (now Finedon) and the lord of the manor, to the point of destroying the hedges and ditches which the lord had apparently wrongfully erected. In none of this is there any evidence of a lack of determination on Wolsey's part. Indeed, it has been argued, especially as regards the last episode, that he was verging on the over-zealous.[3]

So determination and effort there certainly were, but to what ends? The various statutes, proclamations, decrees and government instructions provide a number of answers, but in trying to make sense of them, it may be helpful to begin with a source less directly bound up with the propaganda requirements of government policy, Thomas More's well-known analysis of the problem in Utopia. More's literary skill and sharp intelligence must always command attention, but what is particularly relevant here is the timing. Published in December 1516, it appeared only six months before the setting up of the enclosure inquiry, just when More was entering royal service and coming into close contact with Wolsey. This does not mean that Wolsey would have read More's book, but he could hardly have been ignorant of its contents, and to that extent, it may bring us as close to the workings of Wolsey's mind on this and related economic and social concerns as it is possible to get.[4] The effectiveness of More's analysis derives in part from one striking passage in which, by reversing the expected order of things and making sheep devour human beings, he created an image that has been difficult to forget.[5] It may also, however, have focused attention in the wrong place, that is, on the sheep.[6] But for More, at any rate, there was no doubt that sheep were at the heart of the problem, and in the following way: sheep meant wool, wool meant cloth, and cloth, as England's major export, meant profits, not just for the merchants but for the producers of the wool. The profitability of sheep farming encouraged farmers to convert from arable to pasture. This in turn encouraged enclosure because farmers would not want other people's sheep grazing their pasture. It also encouraged an

---

[1] Ibid, no.123.

[2] Ibid.

[3] Select Cases in Star Chamber, pp.36 ff. For Wolsey's over-zealousness see p.439.

[4] CWM, 4, pp.65 ff; Hexter, pp.146-55 for interesting comments on the relationship between the two men, and its relevance to More's decision to accept a career in royal service.

[5] 'Your sheep . . . which are usually so tame and so cheaply fed, begin now according to report to be so greedy and wild that they devour human beings and devastate and depopulate fields, houses and towns.' (CWM, 4, pp.65-7).

[6] Blanchard; Thirsk, Rural Economy, pp.73-5; Thirsk (ed.), Agrarian History, pp.238-9.

accompanying evil, legislated against in the enclosure Acts – that of engrossing the consolidation of two separate farming units into one, the consequent rationalization bringing with it the eviction of tenants and farm labourers and the destruction of property. In this way large sheep runs could be created, a form of farming that was profitable not only because the demand for wool was so great, but because it was far less labour-intensive than arable farming. If a farmer could not physically enclose or engross, he could, if powerful enough, eliminate or at any rate seek to limit, the right of others to graze their stock on the common fields.[1]

This, very simply, was More's analysis, and much the same view was taken by other writers and social commentators in the sixteenth century and later.[2] The most serious consequence for More was the enforced idleness that came from people being driven off the land. It led them into bad ways such as drinking and gaming, and these in turn led to crime. Indeed, it was his preoccupation with crime and what he saw as the Crown's failure to tackle its underlying causes that had led him to a discussion of enclosure. But other, more mundane, ills were mentioned. He blamed the obsession with sheep for the high price of food and raw materials, including wool. The overstocking of sheep resulted in disease and death and the breeding of cattle was neglected. More generally, prices had been kept artificially high by greedy farmers and middlemen combining to ensure that output always lagged behind demand. The result was large profits for the few but misery for the many.[3]

Clearly there was much more than economics involved in More's analysis of the ills of early Tudor society, and if one turns to official pronouncements on enclosure this is, if anything, even more marked.[4] For instance, many were concerned that the depopulation of the villages and the disappearance of the small tenant farmer or yeoman would seriously impair the Crown's ability to raise an army. How far such men did provide the backbone of Henry VIII's armies is a moot point, but certainly the perception was that they did. They were also thought to be vital to the stability and moral health of the kingdom, for as the instructions to the 1517 commissioners put it, 'husbandry and householding' were together 'the stepmother of the virtues'.[5] Moreover, depopulation resulted in dwindling or non-existent congregations, inadequate church services, deteriorating church buildings and disrespect for the dead: for to quote More, the only thing the churches were being used for was 'to pen the sheep in'.[6]

Arguably, if there was no congregation but plenty of sheep, to use churches in this way made a lot of sense, which is but a flippant way of emphasizing the curious and not very happy pairing of economic realism with moral concern that was so

---

[1] CWM, 4, pp.65-9.

[2] *Tudor Economic Documents*, iii, pp.20 ff. for extracts from A. Fitzherbert's *The Book of Husbandry*, Thomas Lever's St Pauls Cross sermon and C. Armstrong's 'A treatise concerning the Staple and Commodities of this Realme' and 'Howe to Reforme the Realme in settyng them to work and to restore Tillage'; Lamond; Thomas Starkey, pp.95-7, 155-6.

[3] CWM, 4, pp.67-9.

[4] A good way into these is through the preamble to the 1517 instructions, for which see *English Historical Documents*, pp.929-30.

[5] Ibid, p.930.

[6] CWM, 4, p.67. See also SR, ii, p.542; iii, pp.127, 176; TRP, nos.75, 110.

characteristic of contemporary attitudes. But it probably only strikes historians as curious from a vantage point of supposed superiority, the assumption being that sixteenth-century man did not understand economics, hence his quaint tendency to get into an intellectual muddle. In fact, the muddle is alive and well in present-day Britain, what with the idle British worker and his cups of tea, the wicked property speculator, and most recently the yuppie, a character that More would have no difficulties in understanding – or inventing. But governments are always being faced with the need to reconcile the irreconcilable. A show of moral concern can be a useful tool here, and certainly to favour exclusively the economic interests of a particular group, even if powerful, can be politically unwise – which again may be too cynical. For what emerges from all the pronouncements on enclosure, whether by private individuals or by government, is a vision of an ideal commonwealth in which arable farming organized around the village community and the open field system played a central and time-honoured part. It provided the necessary food, especially corn for that staple commodity, bread. It provided settled employment. It provided the tenant farmer and labourer, as much as the landowner, with a stake in the land. Such people did not riot, nor were they likely to embark upon a life of crime. It is not, therefore, surprising that the Crown should have shown concern for them, and that insofar as it believed enclosure to threaten their existence, it worked to prevent this from happening.

Yet these same pronouncements also indicate that Tudor government was perfectly aware that there were many areas of England where the vision had little basis in reality; indeed, it was really only in parts of Norfolk and the Midland counties that it had.[1] Neither can it have escaped its notice that pasture farming in general and sheep in particular played a vital part in the economy and that the export of wool and increasingly cloth was a major source of revenue. Moreover, if only on the evidence of the returns of the enclosure commissioners, the government would have been forced to accept that enclosure increased the value of the land, for the good reason that it resulted in more efficient farming practices. And that Wolsey understood this can be deduced from the proclamation of 1526 which stated that anyone who could prove that their enclosures were 'not prejudicial, hurtful nor to the annoyance of the king's subjects, nor contrary to the laws and commonwealth of his realm' need not destroy them[2] – and at least four people accepted the challenge.[3] The fact that they lost does not invalidate the point being made that Wolsey and his colleagues were aware of the possibility that the common weal could be served by enclosure. It is not that they were visionaries determined to recapture some golden age in which the profit motive did not exist. Instead, in full awareness of the arguments for and against, they had concluded that any large-scale changes in agricultural practices would have harmful consequences for the many, whatever the benefits to the few. It is not so surprising that they took this view. Governments have usually been wary of economic innovation, knowing that it is likely to result in social unrest. Moreover, in this particular case there appeared to be no compensating financial or military advantage. It would not be appropriate,

---

[1] Thirsk (ed.), *Agrarian History*, pp. 1-112 for a detailed survey of the different farming regions.
[2] TRP, no.155.
[3] The four were Sir Edward Belknap, Thomas Haselrig, Thomas Purfrey and John Spencer.

therefore, to conclude that idealism was the chief component in the resistance of Wolsey and his colleagues to enclosure, if it were not for the emotional language that they employed and the intensity with which they tackled the problem.

It could be, of course, that what they were exhibiting was not idealism but anxiety. Because enclosure touched upon so many nerve ends to do with law and order and the safety of the realm, its emotional charge was bound to be high – indeed, so high that as respectable a member of society as the high sheriff of Northamptonshire, Sir John Spencer, could be classified as one of More's 'insatiable gluttons' and be ordered to remove all enclosures from his land.[1] But here another difficulty looms, and one so serious that it threatens to undermine everything that has been said so far. Quite simply, recent work in this area points increasingly to the conclusion that in the twenty or so years before the setting up of the enclosure commissions very little enclosure had taken place, even in the Midlands, an area previously alleged to have been peculiarly sensitive to market forces and thus to enclosure. Furthermore, this same work suggests that those supposedly most threatened, far from suffering had probably 'never had it so good'. Reduced rents, readily available land, rising wages, larger holdings, more stock, this, rather than the nightmare vision of More's carnivorous sheep, now appears to be the true picture of rural life in fifteenth- and early sixteenth-century England.[2] Nor, insofar as arable had been converted to pasture, had it been the consequent enclosure that had caused depopulation and 'deserted villages'. Instead, it was the dramatic decline in population of the fourteenth century that was largely responsible for enclosure: with a reduced demand for corn and a shrinking labour market, farmers were more or less forced to look for an alternative to arable farming, or leave their land lying idle.[3] This being so, it is hardly surprising that what was previously thought of as a late sixteenth-century phenomenon, the so-called 'peasant enclosure' whereby often quite humble people enclosed the open fields, has been discovered as early as the late fourteenth century.[4] This points up a general consequence of all these findings, which is that the moral dimension begins to recede. Gone are the wicked entrepreneurs seeking to maximize the profits offered by large-scale sheep-farming, and in their place are a bunch of sleepy yokels sucking on straws and being pushed reluctantly to change their ways. Someone whose reputation has benefited from this seachange is the high sheriff of Northamptonshire. Undoubtedly John Spencer owned a lot of sheep, but it now looks as if he was not personally responsible for the widespread enclosure and decay of properties that the enclosure commissioners found on his estates and which was a prerequisite for the scale and success of his farming activities. Rather, what seems to have happened is that he and his uncle had deliberately acquired land already enclosed.[5]

But, if there were no villains, why the statutes and proclamations, why the commissioners and the court cases, and why the moral outrage? In facing up to the findings of recent research one is forced almost to conclude that Wolsey and his

---

[1] CWM, 4, p.67: Thorpe.
[2] Blanchard; C. Dyer, *Lords and Peasants*, pp.218 ff; *EcHR*, 2 ser., 35. Dyer's work underlies much of what follows; and I must also thank him for taking the trouble to comment on it.
[3] C Dyer, *Lords and Peasants*, p.244 ff.
[4] C. Dyer, Dugdale Society, 27, pp.25 ff.
[5] Thorpe, pp.55-6; also C. Dyer, Dugdale Society, 27, p.18.

colleagues suffered from some kind of collective madness such as obviously does afflict groups of people from time to time, leading them to invent here a 'popish plot' or there a 'world-wide Jewish conspiracy'. On the other hand, they have not so far struck one as people likely to be afflicted in this way, and to believe that they were would require that the hundreds of entries in enclosure commissioners' findings were a complete fabrication, and that the seventy-four people known to have pleaded guilty to offences contrary to the Acts of enclosure had thereby perjured themselves. One way and another, there is so much contradiction between what contemporaries thought was happening and what present-day historians would have us believe, that it is far from easy to see how best to reconcile the two views.

One relevant consideration may be that while statistics are known to lie, they may also anaesthetize. Two or three people and one or two acres may not show up as much of a percentage, but they nevertheless remain people who can weep and acres which once grew corn and then sustained sheep.[1] Moreover, the fact that according to current estimation, between 1455 and 1607 only an additional 1.98 per cent of the twenty-four counties investigated by the enclosure commissioners was enclosed still means that well over 600,000 acres were affected.[2] And what has always been recognized is that some areas were much more affected than others. In Leicestershire, Northamptonshire, Rutland and Warwickshire, the four counties that witnessed the greatest amount of enclosure, the percentage of land affected was as high as 8.95 (compared with the average of 1.98) and even within these counties it was only certain areas that bore the brunt. In Warwickshire, for instance, it has been estimated that between 1488 and 1517 one in five of the villages in the hundred of Kineton, lying in the so-called Felden area south-east of the River Avon, was seriously affected by enclosure, while other areas of the county escaped very lightly.[3] And, though depopulation leading sometimes to a deserted village did usually take place over a long period and without any significant help from enclosure, it does seem that in some instances enclosure finished the process off, and occasionally played a larger role.[4] For example, it has been calculated that in Leicestershire between 1485 and 1550 twenty-one villages were wholly enclosed. Of these only six witnessed a significant decline in population prior to enclosure, which is but another way of saying that fifteen were destroyed by it.[5] So there do appear to be some villains after all.

In the 1480s the inhabitants of the village of Quinton in Warwickshire suffered from the activities of one John Salbrygge who, at least according to the vicar, was driving them off arable land that they had customarily occupied, and had ploughed up some of the common pasture for his own use. In this case, the villain may have got his come-uppance for in response to the vicar's complaint the lord of the manor,

---

[1] In the enclosure findings the people affected are usually said to have departed in tears,or rather, since they were written in Latin, 'lacrimando', 'lamentando', or adverbially 'lacrimose' or 'dolorose'; see Leadam, Domesday.

[2] Wordie, pp.491-4, where he modifies Gay's much used findings; see Gay, TRHS, new ser, xiv; Quarterly Journal of Economics, xvii.

[3] C. Dyer, Dugdale Society, 27, pp.10-12.

[4] Ibid, pp.18 ff; C. Dyer, Dugdale Society, 27, pp.18 ff; Lords and Peasants, pp.244 ff; EcHR, 2 ser., 35, p.30.

[5] Parker, 'Enclosure', pp.30 ff.

the governing body of Magdalen College, Oxford, replaced Salbrygge with a group of lessees.[1] Another Warwickshire villain was Sir Edward Belknap. Like John Spencer, he had attempted to defend himself in court on the grounds that enclosure was of benefit to the common weal. It was at one time thought that he had not been personally responsible for the land enclosed, but with the recent reopening of the file it now appears that he lied to to the commissioners and courts and that conversion and enclosure were carried out in 1496, when he first obtained full possession of his estate.[2] . What is interesting about Belknap's case is the recent metamorphosis: from the innocent legatee of ineluctable forces to thrusting entrepreneur. He has become, in the process, just the kind of person whom the government said they were out to get, and so despite the general direction of modern research the moral dimension begins to creep back! And at this point it seems right to quote a little more from that letter of 26 September 1526 to Wolsey from Bishop Longland. The good bishop was extremely busy as a commissioner for some of the Midland counties – not that he minded, for as he explained,

> I assure your good grace there was never thing done in England for a more common weal than to redress these enormous decays of towns and making of these enclosures, for if your grace did at the eye see as I have now seen, your heart would mourn to see the towns, villages, hamlets and manor places in ruin and decay, the people gone, the ploughs laid down, the living of many honest husbandmen in one man's hands, the breed of mannery [manors] by this means suppressed, few people there stirring, the commons in many places taken away from the poor people, whereby they are compelled to forsake their houses and so wearied out and wot not where to live, and so maketh their lamentation.[3]

The apocalyptic vision returns, and from one who, though a conscientious bishop and royal servant, is not obviously to be associated with visions of any kind.

If, therefore, Longland's letter forces one to the conclusion that there was a real problem, nevertheless the emotional intensity still worries. Yes, there were some villains and some villages were depopulated by enclosure, but not, one would have thought, on a large enough scale to justify the degree of overdrive that Wolsey and his colleagues went into. And there are other difficulties. Despite the emotional reaction, very little seems to have been done for those supposedly made to depart in tears. Houses were to be rebuilt, enclosures were to be removed, land was to be restored to its former use as arable, but there was never any attempt to return the dispossessed to their former properties.[4] It may be that such an exercise would have been administratively too complicated, or even legally impossible and, indeed, the accusation was never that anyone had been evicted illegally. Alternatively, it may be that there were very few people to be put back. At the very least, it seems to have been quite easy for people to find alternative accommodation for the evidence is that mobility and rapid changes in the composition of villages were a feature of late medieval rural life.[5] It is also worth making the point that not all those affected by

---

[1] Magdalen College Muniments, Quinton, 56, 60.
[2] Alcock, *Records of Social and Economic History*, new ser., iv, p.35, this a revision of his earlier views in *Warwickshire History*, 3.
[3] PRO SP 1/57/fo.151v (*LP*,iv,4796).
[4] Blanchard, p.438 comments on this, but mostly it has been ignored.

enclosure were poor. During the course of a law suit in 1496 it was deposed that when the village of Keythorpe had been 'taken down' and enclosed a certain Thomas Skeffington had physically transported his house and set it up on land he held elsewhere. Also, he had refused to sell to the encloser a piece of land he owned in Keythorpe and continued to pasture some of his cattle there. So had his grandson, and it was this that had led the owner of Keythorpe to go to law. Nowadays one associates the transporting of buildings more with wealthy Americans than with the poor and dispossessed, but then Skeffington cannot have been all that poor if he owned land elsewhere on which to put the house, and certainly the family suffered no mortal blow from the activities of the encloser of Keythorpe. The grandson was knighted for his services to the Crown and was, in fact, that Sir William Skeffington sent to Ireland as the king's deputy in 1529.[1] Of course, one cannot draw too many conclusions from one example; but the real point is that there should be many more examples of what happened to the dispossessed and almost none have come to light. Even Longland's moving description has much more to do with property than with people.

A better known difficulty is that there is no precise correlation between the peak period of enclosure and that of government intervention, and recent research has done nothing to improve it.[2] Indeed, the more one emphasizes the long-term causes of the phenomenon, especially the drastic decline in population in the second half of the fourteenth century, the more difficult it is to explain the precise timing of the government intervention and in a study of Wolsey it is the question of timing that is of most concern. Put simply, the question that needs answering is why, if much more enclosure went on before 1489 than after, was any serious attempt to do anything about it delayed until 1517? We need to look for some crisis or new factor that could explain the sudden urgency in tackling the problem. An obvious area to look at first is the corn supply, for any shortfall there, leading to high bread prices would have immediate and serious repercussions. It would also focus attention on enclosure, since at this period it was nearly always accompanied by conversion to pasture, and if there is one thing in all this uncertainty that shines out it is that during the fifteenth and early sixteenth centuries the Midlands witnessed a significant increase in the amount of land put to pasture, for the raising of stock of all kind but especially sheep. Nobody would have minded this as long as corn stocks proved adequate, but if there was, for instance, a bad harvest – which had a nasty tendency to occur in sequences of three – or if the demand for corn increased, most obviously as a result of a rising population, then the apparent overreaction of Wolsey and colleagues becomes much more understandable. It is possible to argue that both these things occurred, and indeed the notion that rising population is the key to an understanding of contemporary attitudes towards enclosure is still something of an orthodoxy.[3] And the strength of this orthodoxy is precisely that it does help to explain the discrepancy between reality and perception that is at the

[5] C. Dyer, EcHR, 2 ser., 35, p.31; B.M.S. Campbell.

[1] Skillington, pp.95-8; Hoskins, Leicestershire History, p.85.
[2] Inter alia C. Dyer, EcHR, 2 ser., 35; Ramsey, pp.26 ff.
[3] The view is particularly associated with Thirsk and popularized in her Tudor Enclosures, but see also Thirsk (ed.), Agrarian History, pp.200-55.

heart of the interpretative problem. The fact that very little enclosure took place at the relevant time no longer matters. What had activated the Crown's concern was a new factor: an increase in population which meant that what had been acceptable when there were no people to fill the decaying properties or to work on the arable fields no longer was. Instead, demand for everything now rose, but especially for food, housing and jobs. And, since even the poorest families on the land usually owned some livestock, any increase in population led to an increase in the number of animals.[1] More animals led to increased pressure on the common pastures and the serious likelihood of overgrazing. To cope with this the practice of stinting – that is, regulating the number of animals each person could graze on the common pasture – was more frequently employed; but inevitably there was a great temptation for the more powerful either to manipulate such regulation to their advantage or just to ignore it, even perhaps by unilaterally enclosing parts of the common land.[2]

It goes without saying that there is a good deal of evidence in support of this orthodoxy; in particular trouble was caused by attempts to limit access to a town's common fields, often by erecting hedges and ditches. For instance, ever since the 1460s there had been a running battle between the citizens of Coventry and certain local farmers concerning such access, culminating in the Lammas Day Conspiracy of 1525, and the government's subsequent insistence that the citizens' lawful access should be restored to them.[3] Some years earlier none other than Sir Reginald Bray, a leading councillor of Henry VII, had apparently advised the tenants of Enfield, near London, forcibly to remove enclosures, which, given the deeply entrenched antipathy towards any riotous behaviour, is evidence of his great sympathy for their plight and a clue perhaps to Wolsey's feelings.[4] Be that as it may, it is by directing attention away from the physical act of enclosure and towards the more general consequences of population growth and the resulting pressure on resources, that this view of enclosure appears to make much more sense of the intensity of the Crown's response. Its great weakness, as its proponents would readily admit,[5] is that its statistical foundations are shaky. Lack of data makes population figures for the mediaeval and early modern periods largely guesswork. What is clear is that during the sixteenth century the population in England rose from somewhere in the region of two million to about four million.[6] The real difficulty comes in deciding on the timing and it is perhaps better appreciated now that the rate of increase fluctuated quite markedly, both geographically and chronologically. Though it is hardly possible to talk of consensus on the question of when the rise began, there seems to be an increasing tendency to locate it in the 1520s rather than, say, the 1470s.[7] If the former date is correct, a rise in population may help to explain why the Crown continued to be concerned about enclosure during the middle decades of the

---

[1] Thirsk (ed.), *Agrarian History*, pp.412-17.

[2] Ibid, pp.200-12.

[3] M. Dormer Harris, pp.169-211; Phythian-Adams, pp.254; see also p.449 below.

[4] Pam, p.4.

[5] Ramsey, p.22; Thirsk (ed), *Agrarian History*, p.204.

[6] Hoskins, *Age of Plunder*, pp.219-20; Palliser, *Age of Elizabeth*, pp.29-38.

[7] In writing thus I may be too much under the influence of C. Dyer, *Lords and Peasants*, pp.218 ff., but see also Blanchard, pp.436-45; B.M.S. Campbell, pp.145-54. Campbell produces a figure of 1,843,568 for the population of early Tudor England, significantly lower than other estimates.

century. But it does not explain why Wolsey and his colleagues showed so much interest in it in 1517. What may do, though, are the bad harvests of 1511-13.

Admittedly, these harvests were not as bad as those of 1527-9 or even those of 1519-21, and in Hoskins's classification they are only considered 'deficient', when they might have been 'bad' or 'dearth'.[1] Nevertheless, prices did rise, and that of wheat quite dramatically: whereas in 1509 the index number for wheat stood at 69, in 1512 it had shot up to 144.[2] And it is worth repeating that while it is possible to average out the figures so that they do not appear all that alarming, particular and often quite wild fluctuations must have posed considerable difficulties for the bulk of the population, operating as they did within financially very narrow margins. The estimate is that about 90 per cent of the poor's income went on food and drink, making them extremely vulnerable to any rapid price increases.[3] Nor would it have helped that, despite the political fluctuations, as regards economic indicators the second half of the fifteenth century was remarkably stable. In the 1510s prices did rise and were to continue to do so in 1520s using the price index, the figures are 100 for 1491-1500, 106 for 1501-10 and 116 for 1511-20.[4] The reasons for government anxiety become apparent. The trigger, though, was not a rise in population, but the bad harvests of 1511-13, compounded by the even worse ones of 1519-21 and 1527-9.

This switch from population growth to bad harvests as the underlying explanation for the timing of the government intervention, and even of its emotional nature, makes more sense. After all, the rise in population would only have had a gradual effect on scarcity and prices, and yet there was More in 1515 writing as if something cataclysmic had just taken place. If there was a good deal about high prices and scarcity in his account, just as there was in the statutes of 1515, in the instructions to the enclosure commissioners, and in all subsequent government pronouncements, the reason is that this was precisely what the bad harvests suddenly produced. This explanation also saves Wolsey and his colleagues from the charge of failing to realize that the population was rising, while at the same time making much more sense of contemporary comments that the country was under-populated.[5] In addition, it would explain why so little help was offered to the dispossessed: they did not exist, or at least not in any significant numbers. What it does not solve, though, any more than the notion of rising population did, is why the poor encloser was singled out for blame. Wicked he may have been, but he was hardly responsible for the weather! Even if both phenomena affected the corn supply, and therefore its price, it is a little surprising that the two factors were apparently so confused. After all, it must have been obvious that harvests had a much more dramatic effect on prices than enclosure, and that in anything other than a bad year there was plenty of corn, and the harvests of 1514, 1516, 1517 and 1522-6 produced above-average yields. Moreover, though the removal of recent enclosures would have marginally increased the amount of corn available, even in a bad year, it would not have prevented the fluctuations in prices that were at the root of the problem.[6]

[1] Hoskins, *Age of Plunder*, p.87.
[2] Ibid, p.247.
[3] Ibid, p.116; see also Thirsk (ed.), *Agrarian History*, pp.275-7.
[4] Hoskins, *Age of Plunder*, pp.218-19.
[5] Palliser, *Age of Elizabeth*, p.35.

What may have helped to bring about this confusion is that the years 1503-18 had seen a return to the situation in which the price of wool rose more sharply than that of grain. The differential was not as great as it had been between 1462 and 1486, but it may have been enough to encourage some farmers to make further enclosures, and would at least lend support to the notion that greedy farmers would be looking to sheep to secure their profits.[1] It may help us to understand the confusion to take a brief look at when and how attitudes towards enclosure hardened.

Apparently, two petitions against enclosure were presented to parliament as early as 1414,[2] but it seems to have been the Warwickshire antiquarian, John Rous, who in 1459 first put forward the notion that enclosers were the number one public enemies, when he presented the first of a number petitions to parliament. Interestingly, these appear to have fallen upon stony ground, but he did not give up. In his *Historia Regum Angliae*, written at the beginning of Henry VII's reign, he devoted a lengthy passage to denouncing 'the lovers or inducers of avarice, . . . murderers of the poor, destroyers of human sustenance', whom he accused of being responsible for the destruction, or at least the severe depopulation, of sixty-two villages within a twelve-mile radius of his home town, Warwick.[3] This time he seems to have made more of an impact, or perhaps it was just that informed opinion was coming round to his point of view. In 1483, the lord chancellor, Bishop Russell, had intended to include in a general denunciation to parliament everyone who 'severally studieth to his own singular avail, and the accomplishing of his own particular affection', all those responsible for 'closures and emparking' and for the 'driving away of tenants and letting down of tenantries'.[4] In the event the speech was never delivered, but it was shortly afterwards, in 1488 and 1489, that the first statutes against enclosure were passed.[5] It was only after a gap of twenty-five years that the issue was taken up again, with a proclamation in 1514 and two statutes in 1515. But for the next thirty years it was to remain at the top of the agenda of all those interested in the common weal.[6]

The interesting thing about Rous's reaction to enclosure is that it was strongly rooted in some kind of reality, or at least more so than, say, More's. The area he wrote about is one that modern research confirms was seriously affected by enclosure. Admittedly, in some of the deserted villages he mentioned the rot had set in many years previously, but in others it may well have been as sudden and dramatic as his portrayal.[7] Paradoxically, however, this greater reality may not have helped his cause. Truth is rarely palatable if it involves criticism of people whose interests one is inclined to identify with, and what, after all, Rous was trying to do was convince a House of Commons full of country gentry that some of their number

---

[6] Hoskins, *Age of Plunder*, p.87 for the harvest figures.

[1] Palliser, *Age of Elizabeth*, p,171 for a table of relative movements of grain and wool prices. But for the argument that there was no financial advantage to be obtained from conversion see Blanchard.

[2] Thirsk (ed.), *Agrarian History*, p.214.

[3] Translated in *English Historical Documents*, pp.1014-16.

[4] Nichols, *Grants from the Crown*, pp.li-lii; also in *English Historical Documents*, p.1016.

[5] 4 Hen. VII c.16; 4 Hen. VII c.19.

[6] Thirsk (ed.), *Agraian History*, pp.217-38; Palliser, *Age of Elizabeth*, pp.178-85.

[7] C. Dyer, *EcHR*, 2 ser., 35, p.25.

were behaving badly. At the same time, since enclosure was such a localized phenomenon, it would have been difficult for even an impartial body of men to get too incensed about it, especially since the majority of those working on the land were prospering. Possibly, however, what Rous, and perhaps others unknown to us, did achieve was to provide a blueprint which, just because it did touch upon all those sensitive nerve ends discussed earlier, did not go away. Moreover, one characteristic of decaying properties is that they remain visible for a long time. The sight of the ruined houses helped to keep the blueprint in people's minds.

The bad harvests would have provided the occasion to return to it. Thus, Bishop Russell's reference to the evils of enclosure, the first evidence that the Crown was taking the problem seriously, was made in the year following the exceptionally bad harvest and high prices of 1482.[1] That harvest turned a localized problem caused by particular changes in farming practice in the Midlands into an issue of national proportions, or so, at least, it seemed to an increasing number of people. Rous's rhetoric, with its talk of scarcity and high prices and a countryside overrun with animals, made a good deal of sense. More importantly, it suggested a course of action. One could not legislate against bad harvests, but one could against enclosure. Thus, when bad harvests returned in 1511-13, so did more enclosure legislation. Still, legislation is one thing, but a nation-wide inquiry followed by sustained government action through the law courts is another – and perhaps it is at this point that Wolsey himself may begin to put in more of an appearance!

The notion that in explaining events it is not so much the circumstances as people's changing perception of them that needs to be taken into account is better understood now than it used to be. In the context of enclosures it has obvious attractions since it provides another explanation for the overreaction of Tudor government to a very limited problem. The new sensitivities of humanists such as More or 'commonwealth men' such as Hugh Latimer would not tolerate a level of social distress that had been accepted in the late fifteenth century – or so the argument runs – and such men were now in a position to influence government action.[2] There is, admittedly, something worrying about a view that posits an ever-increasing sensitivity amongst the English ruling classes. Medieval man was quite capable of recognizing a social evil and, as the works of Langland and Chaucer show, he was even capable of writing about them! And to quote a historian of medieval responses to poverty, 'a modern textbook on sociology will pose few fundamental problems that did not arise in one form or another in the theological *Summa* of Aquinas or in the canonistic *Commentaria* of Hostiensis'.[3] At the same time there are always objections to be made against any kind of label, and historians have spilt an enormous amount of ink in trying to decide whether the subspecies 'humanist' ever existed. What is undeniable, however, is that from his intellectual and literary luggage More was able to fashion an attack on enclosure. Someone who shared some of the luggage is that other royal councillor of the 1520s whose views on enclosure have survived, John Longland. What about Wolsey? Or, to put it another

---

[1] The index price of wheat shot up from 132 in 1481, a figure which was anyway high, to 177, the highest it had been for over thirty years, and a figure not passed until 1543; see Thirsk (ed.), *Agrarian History*, pp. 815-19.

[2] C. Dyer, *EcHR*, 2 ser., 35, p. 24.

[3] Tierney, p. 22

way, has humanism got anything to do with his approach to enclosure?

The question has to be asked. The commissions of inquiry of 1517-19 and 1526 and the resulting legal action constitute an unusually ambitious exercise in social and economic policy. It seems therefore to require some novel ideological underpinning, and humanism is the obvious possibility.[1] As already stated, there is no surviving evidence for Wolsey's views on social and economic matters other than that which can be derived from government action during the period in which he held high office. The best that we have been able to do so far is to suggest that he would probably have been aware of More's views on enclosure, but especially since it is possible that More's concern itself had been prompted by government action – and the 1514 proclamation did predate his writing of *Utopia* – is does not dramatically advance our understanding! Moreover, whatever More's standing as an intellectual at this time, he was very much a new man in government circles, and thus perhaps with only limited influence. So, though it was suggested earlier that, for want of anything better, More's views provided a way in to Wolsey's, what they do not do is provide a complete explanation for Wolsey's decision to set up the 1517 inquiry. The general change in public opinion, for which More's writing is part of the evidence, probably played a decisive part. And there was also Wolsey's own experience in government. In 1516 the City of London authorities were pressing the government to do something about the shortage of corn, despite the fact that the 1514 harvest had been adequate and that of 1515 only just below average.[2] Back in 1513 the task of providing large amounts of food and drink, not to mention men, for the military campaigns of that year would also have brought the problems of supply and scarcity to Wolsey's attention, especially as in 1513 the harvest was bad and consequently prices were high. And it is worth recalling that one of the supposed evils of enclosure was that the resulting depopulation weakened the country's ability to defend itself.[3] Scarcity of corn, high prices, recruitment of men were, then, all matters which Wolsey was familiar with before he set up the 1517 inquiry. They may all have helped to focus his mind on the problem of enclosure, and at the very least have persuaded him of the need to discover its extent. Any disturbances arising from enclosure that came before Star Chamber would also have contributed, and in 1516 there was such a disturbance. The inhabitants of Draycott and Stoke Gifford were accused of riotously pulling down the lawful enclosures of their landlord, Sir John Rodney, and even of threatening his person. In defending themselves against this charge, they managed to accuse Sir John of almost every evil that the archetypal wicked encloser could possibly be guilty of: arbitrary financial exactions, wrongful dispossessing of tenants, tampering with the legal evidence as regards tenure, misuse of his tenants' horses and preventing them from defending their crops against the ravages of grazing deer. However, very much at the top of the list was the enclosure of Stoke Moor and a further 200 acres elsewhere. It has to be said that Rodney's counter defence is not unconvincing and, as so often with Star Chamber cases, it is difficult to reach any firm conclusions about the rights and

---

[1] For a still useful introduction to the vast literature on the relationship between humanism and politics see Elton, *Reform and Renewal*, pp.1-8.

[2] Gras, pp.223-6; Thirsk (ed.), *Agrarian History*, pp.214-15.

[3] Both the 1515 Acts mention it.

wrongs of the matter, nor is it possible to ascertain how much detailed knowledge of the episode – if any – Wolsey possessed. What is known is that in July 1516 a commission headed by Lord Fitzwarren and the abbot of Glastonbury was instructed to investigate; and it may be surmised that in a year just after the passing of two statutes against enclosure it would have taken very few such episodes to galvanize Wolsey into action.[1]

The reason for saying this has nothing to do with any commitment Wolsey may have had to a particular set of beliefs, but with his personality, in particular with his enormous confidence in his own ability to get things done. In 1516, the year before the first enclosure inquiry, as the new lord chancellor he had declared his intention of imposing 'indifferent justice' upon the whole realm, and just one year later he determined to impose a legatine authority on the English Church the better to reform it. Then in 1522 he set in motion the general proscription in order to obtain an up-to-date assessment of England's ability to wage war, and in 1527 he introduced the first nation-wide attempt to regulate corn supplies in an effort to cope with the severe shortages that yet another bad harvest threatened. The corn commissions will be looked at in more detail shortly, but the immediate point about all these major initiatives is their scale. Enormous amounts of information were collected from every corner of England, many sections of the community were roped in as commissioners or jurors, and a great many administrative actions resulted. It does not seem unreasonable to suppose that the driving force behind much of this activity was Wolsey himself.

A further point is worth making. This explanation fits a pattern that can be discerned in the build up to many other major government initiatives. It took at least fifty years to come about. It required the coming together of a whole number of often unconnected phenomena which certain assumptions mingled together in a potent mix. The way in which those decayed buildings, largely the result of the decimation of the population by plague in the second half of the fourteenth century, came to be taken as crucial evidence of the evil consequences of enclosure is a good example. A recent parallel is provided by the changing attitudes towards trade unions whereby since the Second World War trade unions have declined from their once accepted status as the fifth estate to almost, under the energetic direction of Mrs Thatcher, a proscribed organization. And like the enclosers of the sixteenth century, the trade unionists' crime has been, allegedly, to sacrifice the nation's interests in the selfish pursuit of their own. There may be some reality in this view, just as there was behind the sixteenth-century obsession. Yet, when all the other possible reasons for England's recent decline are considered, it may come to seem as curious that, in an effort to arrest it, so much political energy was directed in this one particular direction as it now seems curious that so much energy was directed against enclosers.

It remains to attempt some assessment of the effectiveness of Wolsey's activity. In doing so we come up against the fundamental objection that if it was wrongly conceived in the first place it could never have been effective. It is a fair enough

[1] For this episode see PRO STAC 2/13/183-4 printed in *Tudor Economic Documents*, i, pp.29 ff. The dating of the episode can be ascertained from the documents, but not when the case appeared in Star Chamber, which for the present argument is unfortunate.

point, and will in part be accepted here, but first the exercise needs to be judged on its own terms, which is to ask the question: insofar as there was enclosure, was it fully brought to light by the commissioners, and were the enclosers themselves successfully brought to book and made to reverse what they had done? It has been estimated that for the twenty-four counties inquired into and for which records have survived, the commissioners reported that 101,293 acres of land had been adversely affected, 647 houses had either been destroyed or allowed to decay, and 6,931 people had been displaced. Even if this does not constitute a very high percentage of the acreage and population of those counties, it is an impressive administrative effort.[1] What was also impressive, as we noted earlier, was the willingness of the courts, contrary to their usual practice, to reach a decision, not to mention their success in getting people to appear or be represented. There is other evidence of immense pains being taken. Properties were inspected more than once, sometimes by new juries, sometimes by the original jury returning to a site to check their original findings. At the same time considerable care was taken to check that defendants who had sworn that they had remedied all the wrongs they were accused of had in truth done so.

Sir Richard Knightley was to find himself accused of all manner of misdemeanours in Northamptonshire involving the destruction of at least seventeen properties and the conversion to pasture of four hundred acres. The charges against him were the work of the commissions of both 1517 and 1518. While admitting the bulk of the charges, he defended himself against others, and apparently with some success. Still, this left him having to rebuild a good number of houses and to restore a great many acres to arable on pain of a recognizance of £100. This, according to the findings of one of the most active enclosure commissioners in the Midlands, Roger Wigston, he did, though it did not prevent him from being reported for further misdemeanours in 1526.[2] It is a highly complicated story, but the impression is certainly of a great deal of effort both to discover what precisely had taken place and then to put it to rights.

The same can be said about the case of Thomas Haselrig of Noseley in Leicestershire, even though in the end there is an ambiguity about what happened that raises some worrying questions. Haselrig was one of that select band of four who had attempted to defend their enclosing on the grounds that it had been of benefit to the common weal. He subsequently decided to accept the charges, while pleading that in the meantime he had remedied everything – this in the court of Exchequer where the defendants in enclosure cases first appeared, after the findings of the commissioners had been processed in Chancery. What happened next is unclear, but by November 1526 he was in real trouble. Back before the barons of the Exchequer, he was forced to confess that, despite his earlier plea, he had not repaired or rebuilt the affected houses or restored the land to arable, and consequently he was committed to the Fleet.[3] At first glance, this looks like a success for the lord chancellor and the legal and administrative machinery that he

---

[1] Gay, *Quarterly Journal of Economics*, xvii, p.581.

[2] PRO E 159/298, Mich., 11 Hen. VIII, m.xiv; C 43/28/6, no.24; C 47/7/2/3, no.7; Scarisbrick, 'Cardinal Wolsey', p.48.

[3] Scarisbrick, 'Cardinal Wolsey', p.61; Parker, 'Enclosure', pp.51 ff.

presided over: someone had tried to lie their way out of trouble, but had been found out. The worry derives from the fact that Haselrig seems to have been the only one found out. Of course, this could merely mean that the machinery was so effective that people did not dare to try to beat it, and certainly the Crown went to considerable lengths to confirm the truth. The question of whether or not buildings or land had been returned to their former condition, as Haselrig had claimed, was frequently the point at issue, and not just in those hundred cases in which the defendant pleaded that all had been put to rights.[1] This was especially so after the General Pardon of 1523 allowed people to escape any prosecution if they could show that the land and buildings in question had indeed been restored.[2] It also became, in effect, the issue in all those seventy or so cases in which the defendant had pleaded guilty and entered into a recognizance to put everything to rights, for all that was then required was some confirmation from a local source that this had happened.[3] Sometimes the word of one person sufficed, usually one of the enclosure commissioners; more often the confirmation came from a panel of 'trustworthy men'.

Frequently, however, the Crown refused to accept the defendant's plea, in which case he or she had to make good the claim before a formal jury, either in King's Bench or at a local assize court. Formal juries would also frequently end up deciding those cases in which a defendant denied the validity of the charges brought against him. Sometimes this involved just a flat denial that the houses had ever been in disrepair or the land taken out of arable; sometimes it was claimed that the enclosure had occurred outside the period covered by the statutes and that therefore no offence had been committed. In other cases the defendant denied that he was the owner of the land, again with the consequence that no case could be brought against him.[4] There were also one or two idiosyncratic pleas, such as that made by one Eusibius Isham that he had indeed destroyed a house, but only because it was already in such a terrible state of repair, and anyway it was far too isolated and the land was not up to much, either![5] However, the fact remains that whenever or however the Crown sought to show that a defendant was in the wrong, it never succeeded except, apparently, in the case of Haselrig. Even then it seems that the confession was brought about not so much by the Crown's efforts, and certainly not because a jury found against him, but because for some unknown reason, perhaps to do with an impending Star Chamber case, he chose to admit that he had lied.[6]

What conclusion can be drawn? Unless one posits a very elaborate conspiratorial theory in which all the juries were handpicked by the government, which, despite all appearances to the contrary, was happy to let all enclosers get off, it is difficult to blame the government machinery for the reluctance of juries to ferret out the truth. Instead, what seems to be at work is merely the perennial difficulty of having to achieve results with the means available. And in this instance it could

[1] For this estimate see Scarisbrick, 'Cardinal Wolsey', p.56. It was, incidently, the plea that Thomas More made.
[2] Ibid, pp.63-4.
[3] Ibid, p.52.
[4] Ibid, pp.53-4.
[5] PRO C 43/28/6/4. What the court made of his defence does not emerge.
[6] PRO E 368/297, m.xxiv; see also Scarisbrick, 'Cardinal Wolsey', p.61; Parker, pp.55-7.

well be that the jurymen and commissioners, having similar social backgrounds and economic interests to those whose actions they were investigating, were not the best people to achieve results. At the same time, even with the best will in the world, there were genuine difficulties in arriving at the truth.[1] Juries were being asked to comment accurately on changing farming practices over a perod of thirty years – and these were not by any means fixed in some immemorial routine. One of the practices that must have considerably complicated the work of both commissioners and juries was the not infrequent one of convertible husbandry, whereby land was sometimes put down to pasture and sometimes ploughed for arable crops. Interestingly, and surely to the Crown's credit, there is at least one case in which the fact of convertible husbandry was recognized and allowed to continue, though the defendant was asked to restore the houses.[2]

Establishing the true facts was a difficult exercise and there is no doubt that on a number of occasions the government failed and may even have been seriously duped. Sir Edward Belknap's deliberate lying about the origins of enclosure on his estates has already been mentioned.[3] He may also have seriously misled the courts about the extent of the land enclosed;[4] and, if so, he would not have been alone. The descendants of William Ashby appear to have convinced both commissioners and courts that he had only enclosed 120 acres of his lordship of Lowesby when in fact he had probably enclosed the whole, amounting to well over eight hundred acres.[5] Then there is Haselrig who, though willing to admit that he had lied in some of his claims, was apparently more successful in bamboozling the courts into taking into account only half the amount of land he had enclosed![6] It is also the case that some estates in which large-scale enclosure took place were completely overlooked.[7] What of the final total? Are the 260 or so people who were made to appear in court and the seventy-odd of these who pleaded guilty and entered into recognizsances to restore buildings and land to their former condition an impressive enough number to justify a successful verdict for Wolsey's endeavour?[8]

It has been suggested, and by someone who took a favourable view of what Wolsey was trying to do, that in the end the evidence permits him to be credited with the restoration of only ninety-seven houses, two barns and 3,260 acres.[9] It is not a lot, but, then, as was argued earlier, there was probably never a lot to be restored anyway, so that these numbers may reflect the misguided purpose of the exercise more than any lack of efficiency. What has to be a comment on the latter, though, is the fate of those few large-scale enclosures such as occurred at Burton Dassett and Wormleighton in Warwickshire and Cotesbach and Lowesby in

---

[1] It cannot have helped that there was considerable uncertainty whether 1 Hen. VII(1485-6) or 4 Hen. VII(1489-90) should be taken as the *terminus a quo* for illegal enclosure.

[2] Scarisbrick, 'Cardinal Wolsey', p.60; also PRO STAC 2/6/176; STAC 2/22/352 for other cases in which convertible husbandry was used as a defence. For convertible husbandry itself see Kerridge, *Agricultural Revolution*. pp.188 ff; Dyer, Dugdale Society, 27, pp.28 ff.

[3] See p.420 above.

[4] Alcock, *Warwickshire History*, p.182.

[5] Parker, 'Enclosure', pp.35-8, 188.

[6] Ibid, pp.51 ff.

[7] Ibid, p.187.

[8] Scarisbrick, 'Cardinal Wolsey', p.52 for these figures.

[9] Ibid, p.62.

Leicestershire, of which the government had at least some knowledge. It was precisely these, quite often the work of successful livestock farmers and affecting whole communities, that the government's policy was designed to put an end to. For a short time it may have succeeded, for if it did not, then none of the evidence can be trusted, not even those seventy or so recognizances by which defendants promised to put things to rights or else be liable to fines of up to £200. That said, however, it has proved nigh on impossible to find any instance where enclosure, once it had occurred on any scale, was reversed for any length of time. Certainly there was no reversal at Wormleighton, where the Spencers' sheep continued to graze large areas of enclosed land for centuries to come, even if Althorp in Northamptonshire was to become their main residence. At Haselrig's Noseley the story is no better, for by 1584 at the latest the whole lordship was enclosed.[1] It looks more and more as if the conclusion must be that, even taken on its own terms, Wolsey's policy was unsuccessful. If one then adds the suggestion that the policy may anyway have been misconceived, one is left with quite a lot of explaining to do if the cardinal is to be portrayed as a successful maintainer of the common weal.

At this point the evidence becomes less important than the criteria used to judge it. Anyone with high expectations of the state's ability to intervene successfully in economic and social affairs will be disappointed in Wolsey's efforts to do something about enclosure. Anyone, who, like the present writer, is a sceptic in such matters may, while ruing the attempt, be nevertheless quite impressed at the way in which Wolsey approached his task. The statistics can, on the face of it, be used to show that Wolsey's policy was extremely successful. Precise figures for the rate of enclosure may not be worth very much, but the trend is not in doubt. During the middle decades of the century very little new enclosure took place: it has been suggested that of all the enclosure in Leicestershire between 1485 and 1607 (and it was one of the counties most affected) only 9 per cent occurred between 1530 and 1580.[2] At first glance, therefore, it would appear that a policy started by Wolsey may almost have killed enclosure stone-dead. Alas, this is most unlikely. In the fifty-six years from 1462 to 1518 only sixteen saw grain prices rising more quickly than wool. In the fifty-five years from 1518 to 1573 there were only twelve in which wool prices rose faster than grain. Insofar as in this period enclosure was normally accompanied by conversion of arable to pasture much of the explanation for the dramatic decline in enclosure in the mid-century must be that the financial incentive to turn to pasture farming had disappeared. Moreover, when the rate of enclosure picked up – and this, until the bad harvests of 1594-7, with very little government disapproval – it seems to have been fuelled by the rapidly increasing demand and rising prices for all agricultural products but especially grain, with the result that enclosure no longer involved conversion to pasture on anything like the same scale.[3]

The picture is getting worse. Not only does Wolsey appear to have tried to slay a dragon that hardly existed, but any wisp of smoke it may have left behind was blown

[1] In arguing that no permanent reversal occurred I rely heavily on Parker, 'Enclosure', the most detailed and convincing study of sixteenth-century enclosure yet to appear.

[2] Parker, *Trans. of the Leicestershire Archaeological Society*, xxiv, p.42, n.2; 'Enclosure', pp.26 ff; also Ramsey, pp.26-7; Wordie, pp.41-76.

[3] Palliser, *Age of Elizabeth*, pp.171, 178-85; Thirsk (ed.), *Agrarian History*, pp.227 ff.

away, not by Wolsey's intervention but by a few Midland farmers responding to market forces! Perhaps, but it would be wrong, and grossly unfair to Wolsey, to leave it there. For one thing, whatever the final verdict, the general impression that an enormous amount of effort was taken by him to get results is only strengthened by some of the supposed shortfalls. For instance, that the commissioners came up with different findings for the same properties is surely more to their credit than otherwise? Their willingness to look again suggests that they were trying to get at the truth, and the later inquiries usually did discover more. Moreover, if some enclosure was overlooked, it does not look as if much was. In Leicestershire, the one county for which a detailed study exists, only six large-scale enclosures appear to have been missed, four of which probably took place too early to have come within the commissioners' terms of reference. To have missed only two, in a county which saw more enclosure than most, seems to be rather to the government's credit.[1]

And by and large, the detail is convincing. In the autumn of 1519 a Robert Lee appeared in Chancery, in order to show that everything in Fleet Marston in Buckinghamshire had been put to rights: a hundred acres had been sown with beans, he had built a new barn, and the only hedges that remained were those that had been there forty years or more.[2] Another Lee was involved, though only as a tenant, in a case to do with a house called Clarks Place in Thorpacre, Leicestershire, which had been allowed to fall into disrepair, with twenty-four of its acres having been converted to pasture. Two points about this case are worthy of comment. Firstly, the owner, the abbot of Garendon, was sufficiently frightened by the activities of the first commission of inquiry immediately to order his tenant to rebuild the house and restore the land to arable. The second point is that the government did not believe the abbot and forced him to prove his case at the assize court.[3] In the case of William Willington of Barcheston (now Barston) in Warwickshire, Chancery was informed that some of the jury sitting at Kenilworth in September 1518 had made an on-site inspection to confirm the truth of the inquisition.[4] The abbot of Thame had his recognizance cancelled when he persuaded Wolsey that a rebuilding programme in the village of Odington, Oxfordshire, had provided better housing for the villagers than the house that he was accused of destroying.[5] On 20 October 1520 in Wolsey's presence, Robert Wighthill swore that he had rebuilt a house and barn on his property in Wighthill, Oxfordshire, but that the land had never been taken out of arable as the findings of the inquiry had stated. There was John Godwin who, having first tried to escape any legal consequences of enclosure by claiming that the forty acres in question in Woburn, Buckinghamshire, were owned by the bishop of Lincoln, then maintained that 'since time out of mind' the land had never been out of arable. As for the house involved, it was only left empty because, since every winter it was flooded for up to four or five days and to a depth of a yard, nobody wanted to live in it – which seems reasonable enough![6]

[1] Parker, 'Enclosure', p.187.
[2] PRO C 43/28/3/3; Scarisbrick, 'Cardinal Wolsey', p.54.
[3] PRO E 368/296, Mich. 14 Hen.VIII, m.ix; Scarisbrick, 'Cardinal Wolsey', p.56, n.24.
[4] PRO E 368/298, Hil. 16 Hen.VIII.
[5] PRO C 54/388/32.
[6] PRO C 43/28/3/9.

Finally in this survey, there is the case of Catherine, countess of Devon's property in Waddesdon, Buckinghamshire. On 10 October 1517 the enclosure commissioners found that two of her houses had been destroyed and some seventy acres had been converted to pasture. This she subsequently denied, and the assize jury agreed with her. Admittedly, one of the houses had been accidentally destroyed by fire, but it had been rebuilt, as had the other. They also found that, just as the countess had maintained, all the land was down to arable and no distress had been caused.[1] A victory for the truth? It is diffcult to say, but, as in the other cases, the detail probably suggests that it was. What is a little worrying is that the houses were only rebuilt in the month prior to inquiry taking place, creating the impression of a rushed job, the only purpose of which was to escape prosecution – but then it was the results rather than how they were achieved that seem to have been the government's chief concern. It is this that probably explains the government's decision to include a clause in the General Pardon of 1523, whereby enclosers could escape any financial penalty if they could show that they had put matters to rights by a certain date. This has been seen as a *quid pro quo* by which Wolsey secured the support of the landowners in the House of Commons for a large subsidy in return for an easing of the government's attack on enclosure, and certainly the Crown would stand to lose what little money accrued to it from enclosure prosecutions.[2] But, if producing results was what mattered, it made a lot of sense. Instead of the courts getting bogged down in the details of ownership and farming practices of the previous thirty years, only the current situation was at issue. The object of the exercise was thereby achieved with the minimum amount of time and money being expended.

Some support for the view that results were Wolsey's chief concern is provided by his correspondence with the bishop of Winchester, Richard Fox, in the late autumn of 1518. Apparently the bishop's lawyers had just appeared before Wolsey in Chancery to swear that the findings of the enclosure commissioners concerning one of the bishop's estates were 'all and every of them untrue', and they had promised to produce evidence to support their contention. However, Wolsey had then declared that by reason of his 'old accustomed favour' towards Fox he was willing to accept his written assurances, and it was these that the bishop's letter was seeking to provide. Fox admitted that he had 'not been personally present upon the grounds and lands surmized to be enclosed', but he felt able to give Wolsey the assurances he had asked for because he believed that his officials' word could always be relied on.[3] One question that immediately arises is whether the assurances of a soon to be blind and deaf old bishop were worth very much. Estate officials were notorious for deceiving their masters, and Fox looks like a potentially easy target, even if he had once been one of Henry VII's outstanding ministers. Of more interest is Wolsey's willingness to make the approach. Is it, perhaps, evidence, if not exactly of an old boy network, at least of two prominent members of the establishment getting together to ensure that, whatever the outcome, their convenience and interests would take priority? Or is it, even worse, an indication that the whole exercise was a

---

[1] PRO E 159/302, Mich. 15 Hen. VIII, m. xix.
[2] Scarisbrick, 'Cardinal Wolsey', pp. 63-4. For the money accruing see p. 413 above.
[3] Richard Fox, pp. 112-14 (*LP*, ii, 4540) for all the quotations.

put up job in which the Crown staged an elaborate charade of appearing to further the common weal by hauling 'the great and the good' before the courts, while working behind the scenes to ensure no real harm would come to them? In other words, was it all either a fix or a conspiracy ? A third possibility is that Wolsey wrote to Fox because he believed it to be the most effective way of getting at the truth.

It is surely the last possibility that is the most likely. In part, of course, this is so because of the view of these two men, especially of Wolsey, that this book has sought to establish: namely, that they were both genuinely concerned to promote the common weal. There is, admittedly, a circularity about such an argument which will not help to convince the sceptic. Neither, perhaps, will that defence against all conspiracy theories: that they are just too complicated to carry great conviction. Still, the tone of Fox's letter gives no hint of a conspiracy, and to what end would such an exercise be directed, anyway? Although enclosure did normally increase the value of land,[1] any increase would be unlikely to filter through to the landlord, who did not benefit from the increased production for some considerable time; and with an annual revenue of well over £3,000, a bishop of Winchester had no great need to lie about a possible increase in rent from a property worth only £5 a year. At this point it is worth recalling that for the comparatively few important people who were at all affected by the government's efforts, the consequences were marginal in the extreme, rarely amounting to much more than it cost to hire a lawyer. The only people who might have suffered financial hardship were those, such as the Spencers of Wormleighton, heavily committed to livestock farming; and it is interesting that it was they who, rather than disputing the facts, tried in the first instance to rest their defence on the merits of enclosure. Still, the relevant point here is that these people were neither numerous nor powerful enough for it to have been necessary or expedient for Wolsey to indulge in any kind of charade or conspiracy. The conclusion here is that Wolsey was trying to do what the official pronouncements declared, and for roughly the reasons given. The problem was that the intentions were, in part, misguided. It is difficult to see, for instance, how making John Spencer give up sheep-farming would have solved any of the problems that the government maintained it would.

But there is another kind of reality that politicians have to grapple with. To call it public opinion has obvious dangers; there were no Gallup polls in the 1520s and no newspapers. On the other hand, people did have opinions, and there were forums, including parliaments, which had passed anti-enclosure legislation, in which those opinions were expressed. To repeat here that what Wolsey had done in 1517 was to put himself at the head of a growing body of opinion that saw enclosure as an evil, is not to imply that he only took the issue up because it was popular, though successful politicians have a happy knack of taking such issues and making them their own, hence the frequent accusations of opportunism. In Wolsey's case the evidence hardly permits much speculation into his motives, but an entirely cynical explanation seems unlikely, if only for the reason that it is very difficult to see how he could have sustained his efforts without a degree of genuine commitment. There is no reason to suppose that Wolsey did not believe a good deal at least of the propaganda that he was orchestrating. It is true that a public concern

---

[1] Dyer, Dugdale Society, 27, pp.19ff; Lamond, pp.49,122; Thirsk (ed.), *Agrarian History*, pp.207-8.

for enclosure would do the Crown no harm at all, especially since enclosure appeared to threaten the livelihood of the yeomen of England. That such a body of men are not just a romantic fiction is suggested by the words of the sober mid-Tudor royal servant, Sir Thomas Smith, who in his *De Republica Anglorum* wrote that

> those whom we call yeomen next unto the nobility, the knights and squires, have the greatest charge and doings in the commonwealth, or rather are more travailed to serve in it than all the rest. . . these tend their own business, come not to meddle in public matters and judgments, but when they are called, and glad when they are delivered of it, are obedient to the gentlemen and rulers, and in war can abide travail and labour as men used to it, wish it soon at an end that they might come home and live of their own. . . These were they which in the old world got that honour to England.[1]

Such men were worth taking a good deal of trouble about, and it is this that may provide the chief explanation, as well as the chief justification, for Wolsey's determination to grapple with enclosure.

In comparison with the government's response to enclosure, its other interventions into economic and social matters have a distinct air of *déjà vu*. Statutes were passed and proclamations issued laying down maximum wages, compelling all those out of work to take up whatever jobs were offered; confirming the usual rates for Thames watermen; insisting that Venetian merchants brought in a certain proportion of bowstaffs with any other merchandise imported; providing victuals for London; regulating the kind of games people could play; prohibiting the use of crossbows and handguns; issuing new coins and so on.[2] Not surprisingly, many Acts and proclamations had to do with England's most important exports, wool and cloth, and with the maintenance of standards and the defence of English merchants from foreign competition.[3] One such Act was concerned to ensure that the clothmakers of Great Yarmouth and Lynn observed the regulations, because the making of worsteds 'hath much increased and been multiplied in the city of Norwich and divers towns and places in the county of Norfolk'.[4] Another Act allowed the cordwainers of London to resume the selling of shoes on a Sunday.[5] Both Acts are a reminder that much legislation was promoted, as it is now, by sectional interests, whether a particular craft or town. Many other Acts dealt with purely private concerns. But economic regulation did not depend wholly on statutes and proclamations; letters patent from the king granting licences and so forth were commonly used, though not as commonly as at the end of the century when the practice of granting monopolies in this way became a political issue. Still, contrary to existing regulations, towns, as well as favoured courtiers, were receiving export licences on quite a large scale. In 1517 Sir William Compton was granted a licence to export eight hundred 'weys' of beans and peas,[6] and in 1526 Sir Thomas More was licensed to export one thousand cloths.[7] In 1523 the city of York, with Wolsey's

---

[1] Thomas Smith, pp. 74-5.
[2] 6 Hen. VIII c.5; 6 Hen. VIII c.11; 14 & 15 Hen. VIII c.7; *TRP*, nos. 86, 108, 112, 118.
[3] 6 Hen. VIII c.8; 6 Hen. VIII c.12; 14 & 15 Hen. VIII c.3; 15 Hen. VIII c.11.
[4] 14 & 15 Hen. VIII c.3.
[5] 14 & 15 Hen. VIII c.9.
[6] Bernard, *EHR*, xcvi, p. 770, n.4.

active support, received a licence to export wool and fells from various parts of Yorkshire, thereby escaping the staplers' monopoly.[1] But such licences were no innovation, and indeed there was nothing new about the mix of statute, proclamation and letters patent, or about the matters that they dealt with.

An area of people's lives that the government legislated for had to do with the clothes that people of different status could wear and the food they could eat.[2] In these more egalitarian times when informality in dress and the free interchange of fashion between social groups is now quite accepted, this concern may come as some surprise and, as will emerge, I have some difficulty in understanding it![3] One striking feature was the obsession with detail. Not only were the types of material prescribed but also the precise fashion, so that, for instance, in 1515 it was stated that only knights and their superiors could wear 'guarded or pinched shirts'. In 1517 the exact number of dishes of food permitted at any meal to each category of person from a cardinal downwards was set out. The result was that, in theory at any rate, the Tudor nanny controlled every aspect of what a person wore or ate, and not only in public. But in fact ever since the late thirteenth century sumptuary legislation had been passed throughout Western Europe. The first English Act was in 1337 and from then on they were passed with some regularity. Perhaps the most comprehensive came in 1463, but this did not prevent two more appearing in 1483 and 1510, before those of 1515, which were by no means the last. Moreover, between 1516 and 1593 there were no fewer than nineteen proclamations. And to what end? The Acts of 1510 and 1515 claimed 'great and costly array and apparel . . . hath been the occasion of great impoverishing of divers of the king's subjects, and provoked many of them to rob and do extortion and other unlawful deeds to maintain thereby their costly array'[4] – which brings us back, as did enclosure, to that obsession of Tudor government with law and order. Another way in which this expenditure on luxuries impoverished not so much the individual but the country as a whole, was in its adverse effect on the balance of payments: so many luxury goods, those 'Apes and japes and marmusettes tailed,/ Nifles and trifles that little availed' of *The Libelle of Englyshe Polycye*,[5] came from abroad and English exports were not sufficient to pay for them, or so it was alleged. But it is another contemporary obsession that is usually seen as the motor behinds these Acts and proclamations. There were many names for it, 'degree', 'order', 'place', 'rank'. Considered an essential ingredient both of heaven and earth, of the natural world and civil society, it came in many shapes and guises, but what was certain was that without it there was only hell and chaos.[6]

My suspicion is that we have become so familiar with the popular wisdom on this subject that we may have some difficulty in imaginatively comprehending it,

[7] LP,iv,2248.

[1] Palliser, *Tudor York*, p.47.
[2] 6 Hen. viiic.1; 7 Hen. viii c.7; *TRP*, nos.80-1.
[3] N.B. Harte is my chief source of information.
[4] Quoted in N.B. Harte p.139.
[5] *Libelle of Englyshe Polyce*, p.18.
[6] Essentially a paraphrase of Sir John Fortescue quoted in Tillyard, p.39, but examples can be found in every kind of writing and government pronouncement of the sixteenth and seventeenth centuries.

but it is easy, though, to see how dress comes into this, for nothing more easily distinguishes different 'orders' of men, whether religious, chivalric, or whatever. Wolsey's alleged defence of the outward signs of office, his 'pillars and pollaxes', that they were necessary 'to maintain the commonwealth',[1] is of some relevance here, but more so are the words of someone who worked under him, Sir Thomas Elyot:

> Apparel may be well a part of majesty. For as there hath been ever a discrepance in vesture of youth and age, men and women, and as our Lord God ordained the apparel of priests distinct from seculars, as it appeareth in Holy Scripture, also the Gentiles had of ancient times sundry apparel to sundry estates, as to the senate and dignitaries called magistrates. And what enormity should it now be thought, and a thing to laugh at, to see a judge or sergeant at law in a short coat, garded and pounced after the galyard fashion, or an apprentice of the law or pleader come to the bar with a Milan bonnet or French hat on his head, set full of plumes, powdered with spangles. So is the apparel comely to every estate and degree and that which exceedeth or lacketh, procureth reproach, in noblemen specially. For apparel simple or scanty reproveth him of avarice. If it be always exceeding precious, and oftentimes changed, as well into charge as strange and new fashions, it causeth him to be noted dissolute of manners.[2]

But laughter or reproach is one thing, elaborate legislation is another, and in trying to understand the reasons for it we are again faced with the problem which dominated the discussion of enclosure: the wild overreaction on the part of government to a problem which at this distance in time hardly seems to have existed.

Two main explanations for sixteenth-century sumptuary legislation are usually offered. Both involve defensive responses to alarming new developments. First, there was more social mobility. Second, there was more fashion. And the two things were supposedly connected: a greater and more widely spread prosperity led to greater social mobility and more money for the socially mobile to spend on fashion.[3] The result was confusion. Clothes no longer distinguished a lord from a peasant, and this encouraged the latter to think that he was a lord, which would never do. The worry is that social mobility and fashion had been facts of life for a long time, and so, as we have just seen, had the measures taken against them. Since previous Acts had clearly not been effective, was it not time for governments to recognize their impotence in this matter? Moreover, having lived with them for so long, surely governments would have ceased to feel threatened? The point of these questions is to raise doubts about whether social mobility or changing fashion do provide a convincing explanation for Wolsey's interest in the subject, for interested he certainly was. Not only do the Acts and proclamations of 1515 and 1517 suggest this, but in December 1515 he had sent Henry 'as well of Act of apparel as well also articles of the same containing in effect the whole substance of the same Act that it may like your grace to change, restore and correct such parts as shall be thought to your great wisdom not meet to pass'.[4] The fact that both king and minister showed such interest in the detail of the Act is some kind of testimony to the curious

[1] CW8, pp.1378-9.
[2] Elyot, p.102.
[3] N.B. Harte, pp.139-40. Du Boulay, pp.61-79 is a useful introduction to class in late medieval England.
[4] BL Caligula D vi, fo.115 (LP,iv,1223).

obsession of the age with sumptuary legislation – without, unfortunately, explaining it!

If the reader detects a note of desperation creeping in, he or she would be right, and the problem is not helped by there being virtually no evidence for any prosecutions occurring as a result of these Acts, despite the Act of 1463 having introduced a scale of fines. However, the one piece of evidence to the contrary, though admittedly only literary, does concern Wolsey who, according to Hall, took it upon himself to confiscate 'an old jacket of crimson velvet and divers brooches'. Hall commented that 'this extreme doing caused him to be greatly hated' and led to 'many cruel officers for malice' following his example, of whom he instanced the mayor of Rochester who had a young man placed in the stocks 'for wearing a riven shirt'.[1] We may detect here Hall's usual jaundiced view of the cardinal's doings, but perhaps, as a London lawyer, he was just the kind of upwardly mobile person that the legislation aimed to keep in his place! On the other hand, when writing of the so-called 'purge' of 1519, he was happy to point out that one reason for the 'purged' courtiers' unpopularity was that they were 'all French in eating, drinking and apparel, yea, and in the French vices and brags',[2] proving that clothes did have some moral connations for him. Someone else who commented unfavourably on French fashion was Thomas More, who in one of his epigrams portrayed a man who was only happy strutting about in French clothes, even down to his underpants, and beating his servants![3] More could be almost as francophobic as Hall, but behind the satire was a more serious concern for the vanity of all conspicuous display. Thus in *Utopia* cloth of gold and ropes of pearls were only worn by prisoners, as the Anemolian ambassadors found to their cost.[4] In trying to understand the attractions of sumptuary legislation it is, as with enclosure, the mix of ingredients that is important. After all, xenophobia and protectionism go well together, as do morality and law and order. Add to these a belief that 'from man down to the meanest worm' there is no 'creature which is not in some respect superior to one creature and inferior to another',[5] and we may begin to make a little sense of sumptuary legislation. It would be easier to understand, though, if it had been accompanied by a little more action on the government's part and if it had not coexisted with quite so much social mobility, such a delight in ostentation and new fashions and such a willingness in practice to let in from abroad all manner of luxury goods.

The lack of prosecutions was not, however, confined to sumptuary legislation, for very few prosecutions are known to have resulted from any Tudor social and economic legislation. To trot out the usual explanation that the government lacked the necessary enforcement machinery is not altogether convincing, partly because there was in the JPs, town officers and local constables considerable machinery, and even the often denigrated system of informers is not unknown today, and is used precisely when government is most concerned to produce results. At any rate, lack of machinery cannot be the whole answer, because if it was, it would have been as apparent to sixteenth-century man as it seems to be to twentieth-century historians;

---

[1] Hall, p. 583.

[2] Ibid, p. 597.

[3] Thomas More, *Latin Epigrams*, no. 70. I owe this reference to Walker.

[4] CWM, 4, pp. 153-4.

[5] Quoted in Tillyard, p. 39.

all of which leaves us with the puzzle of why so much legislation that nobody, apparently, paid much heed to.[1]

It has been suggested that Wolsey did exhibit some impatience with this lack of effectiveness, enough at any rate 'to stretch the proclaiming power to its outermost limits and possibly even beyond, if necessary, without seeking parliamentary authority' in order to remedy it.[2] This he, allegedly, did most blatantly in his efforts to prevent people from playing unlawful games and using handguns and crossbows. The efforts to prevent the games seem almost as mysterious as those to dictate what clothes people should wear. On the face of it there is little to object to in the occasional game of bowls or quoits, which along with cards and dice (perhaps more obviously worrying)[3] were on the proscribed list. Admittedly, almost any game can involve an element of gambling and drinking, possibly resulting in violence and the occasional rumpus or riot. But even so, what is difficult to understand is how the authorities ever thought that such games could be effectively banned, though perhaps this is no more mysterious than the endlessly unsuccessful efforts of present-day schoolteachers to prevent their pupils from smoking and drinking. Anyway, clearly Wolsey felt that the existing legislation relating to games and illegal weapons was not working well, and in a series of proclamations issued ever more dire threats against those who were breaking it; so that, according to Hall, 'the people murmured against the cardinal, saying he grudged at every man's pleasure saving his own'.[4] By December 1528 so impatient had Wolsey become that he authorized people 'to take and burn the said tables, dice, cards, bowls, closhes, tennis balls and all other things pertaining to the said unlawful games', while anyone who saw a handgun or crossbow being used was ordered to seize it and break it up. Furthermore, right of entry was granted to anyone who suspected that such weapons were being kept in another's house. There is just a little evidence that Wolsey really did mean business, for at any rate in London and New Romney, Kent, searches were carried out, and some people were prosecuted.[5]

Earlier we saw a similar escalation in the government's response to enclosure, culminating with the proclamation of February 1529 empowering sheriffs and enclosure commissioners to destroy the enclosures of anyone failing to comply with the law. What is not true, however, is that Thomas More, on succeeding Wolsey as lord chancellor, pronounced such action to be illegal. Admittedly, the landlord involved in the Thingden case did make such claim, but More's judgment was that it was only the subsequent actions of the inhabitants, not those of the sheriff, that were against the law.[6] Thus, in arriving at his judgment, More was making no adverse comment on Wolsey's constitutional propriety, for the good reason that none was called for. And recent attempts to draw a distinction between his

[1] Ramsey, pp.146 ff. and P. Williams, *Tudor Regime*, 139 ff. for useful discussions of this extremely difficult subject.

[2] Heinze, pp.108-9.

[3] I am reminded of the resistance to the introduction of bridge at Winchester College in the 1960s – and in the original statutes all these games were banned.

[4] Hall, p.712.

[5] TRP, no.121; Heinze, pp.89-94.

[6] Heinze, p.98 for the accusation. My interpretation rests on my reading of the documents printed in *Select Cases in Star Chamber*, pp.123-42.

unconstitutional and Thomas Cromwell's constitutional behaviour should surely be resisted.[1] The use of parliament in the 1530s had everything to do with matters of high policy, nothing to do with more general concerns for the common weal – and if one truly wants to see unconstitutional behaviour, then it is to the 1530s that one should turn. Or to put it another way, nobody in the sixteenth century would have called a parliament to pass legislation about unlawful games, enclosure or the like, so that the fact that Wolsey did not either should not be a matter for comment. What should be, though, is the evidence that these proclamations provide of his persistence in trying to grapple with the problems of the common weal. It may also be true that, as Hall suggests, his efforts may not always have been popular, but then neither would have been the frequent calling of parliament!

Wolsey's efforts to combat the plague and other epidemics may not have been popular either, despite his obvious good intentions. What is interesting is that these did involve a new departure.[2] What may have prompted Wolsey here was the sweating sickness. All epidemics are alarming, but while the bubonic plague, and even typhus and smallpox, all of which were present in England at this time, had more devastating effects on the mortality rates, the Sweat did have a number of features that made it especially feared. The first attack probably occurred in 1485, and the second in 1508-9, but when it broke out in 1517 and then again in 1525-6 and 1528 it was still a new phenomenon. That it was apparently confined to England, hence its title, 'English Sweat', cannot have helped morale, especially for those who saw illness as a judgment from God. It was no respecter of persons, so that its victims included noblemen and courtiers such as Lords Clinton and Grey in 1517 and Sir William Compton in 1528. There remains a mystery about precisely what kind of disease it was. Probably it was not bubonic, but viral, and so in some ways more infectious than the plague, though not, as it happened, so lethal. Its main symptom, profuse sweating, led within twenty-four hours either to death or to a fairly rapid recovery so that, as Hall put it, one could be 'merry at dinner and dead at supper'.[3] Henry considered himself something of an expert on its treatment and, when in June 1528 first Anne Boleyn and then Wolsey were struck down, he bombarded them both with advice. His prescription was 'small suppers' and little wine, 'once in the week to use the the pills of Rasis; and if it come in any wise to sweat moderately the full time, without suffering it to run in; which by your grace's physicians, with a possetale, having certain herbs clarified in it, shall facilly, if need be, be provoked and continued'. Of course, it would have been better if they had avoided catching it in the first place, and Henry was quite clear that the key to that was 'to keep . . . out of all air where any of that infection is'.[4] When anybody anywhere near him went down with it, Henry was the first to take his own advice by removing himself as quickly as possible. Brian Tuke, on the other hand, seems to

---

[1] It is Elton who has argued for the constitutional Cromwell in all his writings on him, but he has been followed by Heinze; see Heinze, pp.108-9.

[2] Slack, *Impact of the Plague*, pp.199 ff; 'Mortality Crises', pp.9 ff; also useful is Palliser, *Age of Elizabeth*, pp.46-54.

[3] Hall, p.592; dinner was usually taken between 10 am and 12 noon and supper about 6 pm. For other good descriptions see Rawdon Brown, ii, pp.113, 126-7 (*LP*,ii,3558, 3638).

[4] Byrne, p.73 (*LP*,iv,4408).

have thought that the illness was largely psychosomatic, noting that it only needed a rumour of its presence in London for everyone to believe they had it. This did not stop him from thinking that it was better to avoid contact with the infection if possible and to prevent people congregating in large numbers when the disease was known to be present.[1]

Isolation was also at the heart of Wolsey's preventative measures, as it had been on the continent; indeed, it is quite possible that it was continental measures that provided him with his model for the royal proclamation of January 1518, for in many respects it was similar to plague orders issued in Paris and other French towns not long before. In fact the continent was way ahead of England in its management of epidemics, Italian towns having made elaborate provisions to cope with them in response to the Black Death of the mid-fourteenth century.[2] Why nothing similar had been introduced in England is a mystery, but one thing that may have prompted Wolsey to make the first public provision for combating major epidemics was his close contact with England's leading medical man, Thomas Linacre, an academic of great distinction and for a time Wolsey's own doctor. Not only did Linacre dedicate one of his translations of Galen, De pulsuum usu, to Wolsey, but he also obtained his help in founding a college of physicians in 1518.[3]

The proclamation of January 1518 ordered that all infected houses in London should be marked by bundles of straw attached to ten-foot poles overhanging the streets, these to be left out for forty days. For thirty-eight days after an attack any member of an infected household was to carry a white stick when they went out, while infected clothes were not to be worn for three months.[4] These were stringent measures, imposing some inconvenience and financial burden. When in April Thomas More discovered the Sweat in Oxford he decided to enforce Wolsey's decree there, and received the Council's approval for doing so. However, after much debate, it advised against the banning of the Austin Friars' fair shortly to be held there. Since it would be attended by merchants from London, to hold it would, admittedly, result in the spread of more infection, but the Council feared 'grudges and murmurs' of Londoners, who 'would think that men went about utterly to destroy them'.[5] However, it was Wolsey who was allowed the last word, which was only right because, unlike the king and those of the Council in attendance on him, he had remained in London and therefore more in touch with the mood of the City. Undoubtedly, some Londoners were hostile to the measures taken to combat the Sweat and the City authorities had been forced to seek out those who had uttered seditious words against the proclamation and, interestingly, against the king for having so conspicuously fled the City.[6] Whether Wolsey's remaining behind was entirely to his credit is not entirely clear, for London was the obvious centre of operations for his chief preoccupation at this time, the complicated negotiations with the French that led to the Treaty of London. But this did not prevent him from taking a close interest in the problems of the City and not just those caused by the

[1] LP,iv,4510.
[2] Slack, Impact of the Plague, pp.44 ff.
[3] Webster.
[4] Ibid, p.208; Slack, Impact of the Plague, p.201.
[5] LP,ii,4124-5.
[6] Slack, Impact of the Plague, pp.41 ff. for current debates on the morality of fleeing from the plague.

Sweat. Food appears to have been scarce, prices were high, and above all the riots of the previous year were a reminder that London's problems could never be ignored.[1]

It could be that more people have heard of Evil May Day than have heard of Wolsey. At any rate, it is one of those events in English history, like, perhaps, the Field of Cloth of Gold, that have somehow caught the imagination without it being very clear why. It may have something to do with ingrained fears of the 'many-headed monster', for riots and revolts do seem to be remembered, even when, like those associated with the earl of Essex or Lord George Gordon, they did not in the end amount to much. At any rate on the eve of May Day 1517 substantial numbers of Londoners, mainly apprentices and journeymen, went on the rampage, their anger directed against the many foreign residents in the City who were involved not only in trade but also, and more importantly, in manufacture. The estimate is that there were some three thousand aliens in London at this time. Some were wealthy merchants and/or bankers such as More's Italian friend Antonio Bonvisi, or the German merchants of the Hanseatic League with their important trading privileges, and in the Steelyard, not far from London Bridge, there was a very visible symbol of those privileges. In 1493, when a trade war with the Netherlands was breaking out, the Steelyard had been attacked by an angry mob. In 1517, though, it was not the wealthier foreign merchants who were the principal problem, even though certain commercial interests within the City were pushing, as they always did, for some curbing of their powers, but the less wealthy artisans and skilled craftsmen, especially those in tanning and brewing. The great bulk of these came from the Low Countries, in the past mostly Dutch speaking but more recent arrivals tended to speak French. The result was just that mix required to bring about racial antagonism, in which often quite realistic fears about losing out economically to the new arrivals, who in early sixteenth-century London were often highly skilled and thus very competitive, combine with much more irrational fears of the unknown. Anti-semitism is one manifestation of this. Nowadays, it is more usually associated with colour, but language can be just as divisive. Moreover, then, as now, immigrants tended to congregate in the same areas, thereby maintaining a much higher profile than if they had been scattered randomly through the City. And by living together the process of assimilation was slowed down.[2]

Evil May Day has all the appearance of a race riot. It did not come out of a cloudless sky. There had been similar riots throughout the Middle Ages, not only in London but in places such as Southampton where there were also large foreign communities. Foreigners had often been a target of rioters and rebels – for instance, in the Peasants' Revolt in 1381 and Jack Cade's rebellion in 1450. As for the Crown, it took up then, as many governments take up now, a very ambiguous position. It was perfectly aware that foreigners were unpopular and that foreign competition might be harmful. Yet it also knew that the English economy and standard of living could not be maintained without a large input of money, goods and skills from abroad. Moreover, foreigners were an invaluable source of cash, either as bankers or

---

[1] Kennedy, pp. 203 ff for London and the plague. I have found Kennedy's thesis on London an enormous help; and it ought to be much better known.

[2] This account owes much to Holmes; but see also Giuseppi; Pettegree, pp. 1 ff. For Giustinian's excellent account and other contemporary material see Rawdon Brown, ii, pp. 69 ff.

because they could be sold privileges, such as rights of denizenship, enabling them to live and work in England, or be made to pay special duties on the goods they traded in. The result was that foreigners were allowed into the country in quite large numbers both to trade and to seek employment, but their activities were closely regulated. In Wolsey's time, even in the aftermath of Evil May Day, the Crown seems to have performed the same kind of balancing act as it had previously. Through much of the 1520s the City was pushing hard to restrain foreign merchants at least enough to ensure that money accrued to the City from their activities. In 1523 an Act was passed compelling foreign tradesmen to employ at least one English apprentice and not more than two foreign journeymen, though this may have been a relaxation of previous Acts prohibiting the employment of foreigners.[1] When in 1526 Londoners were forbidden to trade with certain foreign merchants who, in the opinion of the City authorities, had been evading trading regulations, these merchants complained to the king. Wolsey was brought in to mediate, and with some success in that both sides dropped their complaints. On the other hand, when in the same year French merchants complained of the City's treatment, he seems to have supported the French. This cannot have helped his popularity at a time when he was anyway thought of as far too pro-French and it does seem that xenophobia was running high throughout the decade. But Wolsey's action on this occasion probably had very little to do with any great desire to please the French. Instead, his principal concern was almost certainly to resist attempts by the City to interfere in the regulation of foreign trade, which the Crown considered to be its own preserve.[2]

But what there was not in 1517 was any major dispute between the City, or any particular interest group within it, and foreign merchants that might directly explain the explosion of racial antagonism; nor does there appear to be any other obvious reason, such as a sudden dislocation of trade or a catastrophic harvest. It is true that England's efforts to bring the French to heel without actually declaring war against them were failing, and, as was suggested earlier, this may have led to some unease at court.[3] But it is not immediately clear why this unease should have transferred itself to City circles, for England's trading position was not affected. On the other hand, some accounts of the rioting do suggest that the mob's anger was especially directed against the French, which could have reflected the anti-French stance that the government was taking abroad. Still, foreign policy hardly provides a full explanation for Evil May Day, and more to the point may have been a series of minor incidents going back at least to the previous spring, when anti-alien placards had been posted on the doors of some London churches.[4] There was almost certainly some deliberate stirring by particular people or interest groups, though only scraps of information have survived. In February or early March the Mercers' Company had sought the help of the earl of Surrey 'to subdue all strangers that be breakers of the privileges of the said City'.[5] At the instigation of a certain John Lincoln, the preacher at the Easter Monday sermon at St Mary's Spital in London, had played upon anti-alien feeling, declaring that it was the duty of all Englishmen

[1] 14 & 15 Hen. viii c.2.
[2] Kennedy, pp.168-81.
[3] See pp.88 ff. above.
[4] LP,ii,1832, quoted in Kennedy, pp.196-7.
[5] Mercers' Company, pp.443-4.

'to hurt and grieve aliens for the common weal'.[1] Then on the day that the riot began certain citizens including a skinner, William Daniel, had been bound on pain of death not to hurt any Frenchmen or strangers, while their servants were not to be allowed 'to go forth May day now next coming'.[2]

As so often, there is the problem of deciding to what extent the rioting was spontaneous or had been deliberately incited. After it was over Henry did tell a delegation from the City that 'you never moved to let them nor stirred once to fight with them . . . but you did wink at the matter'.[3] Whether he really believed this is not clear; he could just have been seeking a bargaining position, or at least trying to ensure that next time they did a little better. Whatever particular groups or individuals were doing, the City authorities had been anxious to prevent trouble. Indeed, as so frequently happens, it may have been some of the preventive measures that in the end provoked the riot. In particular, there seems to have been a very late decision to proclaim a curfew, to begin at 9.00 p.m. On the eve of a major public holiday, when the City was traditionally en fête, any curfew was bound to cause some resentment, but the lateness of the decision led only to uncertainty and confusion, and thus to even greater resentment. Minor incidents quickly escalated, and in a very short time hundreds of people were on the rampage. In fact, though a lot of property was destroyed, nobody was killed, and the trouble was over before dawn. This may have been partly because much of the rioting had more to do with high spirits than with anything very vicious or planned. On the other hand, it may reflect the success of the steps taken, which to some degree were organized by Wolsey, to deal with the expected trouble. Important places, including apparently Wolsey's residence at York Place, were protected, and troops under the command of the duke of Norfolk, in company with his son, the earl of Surrey, and the earl of Shrewsbury, were standing by, though it is probable that calm had been restored by the time they entered the City.

Almost immediately severe punishment was meted out against a dozen or so of the most prominent rioters; then on 22 May the famous scene was acted out at Westminster Hall in which Wolsey pleaded with Henry to grant a royal pardon to four hundred penitents dressed, as was traditional on such occasions, in only their shirts and with halters round their necks. At the first time of asking Henry declined,

> whereupon the said right reverend cardinal, turning towards the delinquents, announced the royal reply. The criminals, on hearing that the king chose them to be hanged, fell upon their knees, shouting 'Mercy!', when the cardinal again besought his majesty most earnestly to grant them grace, some of the chief lords also doing the like, so at length the king consented to pardon them, which was announced to these delinquents by the said right reverend cardinal with tears in his eyes; and he made them a long discourse, urging them to lead good lives and comply with the royal will which was that strangers should be well treated in this country . . . It was a very fine spectacle and well arranged, and the crowd of people present was innumerable.[4]

And the emphasis has to be on 'arranged'. As with the other great set-pieces of

---

[1] Holmes, pp.643-4.
[2] Kennedy, p.198.
[3] Kennedy, p.200.
[4] Rawdon Brown, ii, 74-5, an account written by the Venetian ambassador's secretary, Nicolo Sagudino.

Wolsey's time, when for instance he had knelt before Henry at Baynard's Castle apparently to defend the clerical cause in the Standish affair, what was taking place was state theatre, in which the speeches had been prepared beforehand. Rather than the spotlight being on the kneeling Wolsey, it ought to be on Henry, sitting in state surrounded by his court, because the whole point of the exercise was to emphasize the aweful power of majesty; hence the purpose of the initial refusal to grant a pardon was to increase the dramatic effect of the eventual consent.[1] Be that as it may, the image of Wolsey as mediator between City and king is an appropriate one with which to convey his relationship with the City during his fifteen years in high office. And an image is required because here the detail will largely be ignored, partly because the work has been done by others with a much better knowledge of London's affairs, but also because much of the detail has little to do with social or economic matters. Wolsey's main preoccupation was patronage and Henry's attempts to provide offices and favours in the gift of the City or large livery companies on his own nominees. Wolsey's task was largely to put into effect the royal wishes. Naturally, royal interference was resented in the City and indeed resisted. Wolsey could try to bully, but tact was as effective, and in the cut and thrust of negotiations Wolsey was, as always, the supreme master. He did have things to give that the City wanted, most obviously their charter of liberties. This Henry at the start of his reign had been slow to renew, no doubt because the City was anxious to win back some of the ground it had lost to Henry VII, and the new king saw no good reason to concede. However, when in the summer of 1513 he suddenly gave way, the City chamberlain was instructed to deliver £20 to 'Mr Wolsey, the king's almoner, for his labour and good will and for the confirmation of the liberties of the City'.[2]

That the City was pleased with Wolsey on this occasion, and at least pretended to be on a number of subsequent ones, may come as a surprise. Some conflict there undoubtedly was, though: significantly, however, it arose over essentially national issues such as the request for a forced loan in 1522 and for the Amicable Grant in 1525. On both these occasions the principal bargaining with the City was conducted by Wolsey in person, and on both occasions he took an extremely tough line. He had much more success in 1522 than in 1525; indeed, it is not certain that he was having any at all when the attempt to raise the Amicable Grant was called off. Certainly, he had quickly made a significant concession to Londoners, allowing them to pay what they felt able to instead of the fixed rate originally asked, but this had not prevented all opposition. When reminded that by a statute of Richard III all benevolences had been declared illegal, he marvelled that anyone dared to mention a man who 'was a usurper and a murderer of his own nephews', a good debating point but one that, at least according to Hall, still failed to secure any definite promise of money.[3] Even if the earlier argument is correct, that the eventual calling off of the Amicable Grant was not the defeat it appears to have been, these negotiations cannot have helped Wolsey's relationship with the City. Whether it

---

[1] That Wolsey did make efforts to arrange matters is suggested by the number of meetings between himself and the City authorities; see Kennedy, pp. 200-1.
[2] Kennedy, p. 33; but more generally ibid, pp. 29 ff.
[3] Hall, pp. 698-9.

was permanently impaired is another matter,[1] and there is perhaps something a little bit too whiggish about a view of a gradually worsening relationship. For instance, the reason why Wolsey negotiated in person with the City authorities and took such a strong line had nothing to do with a growing animus against them. Instead, the most simple explanation is that, being mainly resident in the City, he was the obvious person to conduct the negotiations. It was vitally important for the success of the overall policy that the City should pay up, as is indicated by the fact that as soon as concessions were made, they were used elsewhere to resist the grant. Thus, though one may well have doubts about the way Wolsey handled the City, to accept too easily what is essentially Hall's version of an arrogant bully boy trying to browbeat the good burghers of London is a mistake. Yes, Wolsey could take an aggressive stance, but he could also be charming and helpful, as the City was well aware. Or to put it another way, it was policy rather than personality that was involved. If the king's policy was unpopular, then Wolsey would have problems, as in 1522 and in 1525. From late 1526 a combination of events – bad weather, bad harvests, plague and sweating sickness, an unpopular divorce leading to an anti-Imperial stance with inevitable repercussions on England's vital trade with the Netherlands – did make life very difficult for Wolsey, but they would have done so for any minister. And, where national issues did not obtrude too much, Wolsey and the City authorities remained capable of doing business together right up until his fall. It can, of course, be countered that Wolsey must take his share of responsibility for the unpopular policies – some would want him to take sole responsibility. But he surely cannot be blamed for the weather and in this account he will not be blamed for Henry's wish for a divorce. Moreover, in the autumn of 1529 no one in the City sought to provide the king with amunition against the fallen minister, and Henry was then on the look out for anything to blacken Wolsey's name. Moreover when one looks back at the City's relationship with the Crown in previous reigns, in particular at the history of conflict in Henry vii's reign, when in the five years before his death in 1509 three former lord mayors were imprisoned and heavily fined, the election of a sheriff was quashed, various royal nominees to important offices were foisted on them – the truth seems to be that, despite a difficult brief, Wolsey managed the City of London not at all badly.[2]

What of Wolsey's management of other cities and towns? In fact, it is an absence of management on his part that offers the most interesting line of inquiry, in particular his failure to remedy or even to recognize what some historians have seen as a crisis in England's urban life. The failure is undoubted. There was, for instance, no legislation in the 1523 parliament that touched upon the subject, and neither did any proclamations during Wolsey's time. Admittedly, he did seek to ameliorate 'the great decay, poverty and calamity of your poor city of York',[3] but as archbishop of York, Wolsey would have been expected to act as the city's 'good lord' and, indeed, did so. It is also true that he saw enclosure and in particular depopulation as having a deleterious effect on urban life, believing that a town's prosperity depended on the demand for its goods and services generated by the agricultural activity of the

---

[1] This suggested in Kennedy, pp.212 ff.
[2] Kennedy, pp.30-1. For Henry vii and the City see Cooper, pp.106-8, 110, 126.
[3] PRO SP 1/4/6/fo.160 (LP,iv,3843).

surrounding countryside. Of course, then as now, towns varied considerably as to function and style. York, for instance, was an important administrative centre for both Church and state; Bristol was a thriving port; boom-time Lavenham or pushy Newcastle were heavily dependent on a particular product respectively cloth and coal. Most English towns were small. Outside London, only Bristol, Exeter, Norwich, Salisbury and York could claim 8,000 people, and of the six hundred or so towns that deserve to be so classified, five hundred had populations of no more than 600 to 1,500.[1] They all functioned to some extent as market towns in a country in which agriculture and its related products, especially wool, dominated the economy. Thus, it made sense for Wolsey to believe that in doing something about enclosure, he was doing something to ease the plight of the towns which, in the 1526 proclamation concerning enclosure, were described as 'brought to desolation, ruin and decay'. Yet, if there was an urban crisis, as some historians have claimed, Wolsey's response was totally inadequate, so whether there was one is of some importance.

The language of the 1526 proclamation raises the same question about early sixteenth-century language, and the government's use of it, that arose when considering the problems of law and order. Perhaps it should have been raised earlier, for even Longland's description of what he supposedly witnessed with his own eyes – the evil effects of enclosure in the Midlands – may well have shown the symptoms of that disease of hyperbole to which sixteenth-century man seems particularly prone. The difficulty is in finding an answer, for if things had really been as Tudor statutes and proclamations suggest, life would have been intolerable. Meanwhile, the existence of the disease furnishes one reason for being sceptical of any urban crisis, which is not to say that there were no urban problems.

The inability or unwillingness of a town's crafts and industries to adapt to changing techniques and fashions was one. This certainly occurred in the cloth industry, which for various reasons tended to migrate to the countryside, or to different urban areas, to the detriment of older centres such as Winchester and, to a lesser extent, York. Some of the reasons, for example the increasing need for water power, were outside anybody's control. Moreover, unlike the countryside, where there was much under-employment, towns found it difficult to provide enough of the right kind of part-time labour that certain of the most important textile processes, such as spinning and weaving, required. Something that town authorities might have done more towards was to free industry, and more generally civic life, from unnecessary and harmful regulation; this does seem to have been tried, but with little success, and it increasingly looks as if it could only ever have brought about marginal improvements. Also, towns were burdened with heavy expenses. There was an enormous amount of civic entertaining and ceremonial to be paid for. If it was an incorporated town, it would have to pay an annual fee-farm to the Crown, or to whomever the Crown had granted it. Thus, much of York's theoretical £160 fee farm was paid not to the Crown but to the Manners family and St Stephen's Chapel, Westminster.[2] Another expense was sending MPs to parliament. Above all, there was taxation. For the 1522 loans Coventry raised £1,195 and for the 1523

[1] Palliser, *Age of Elizabeth*, pp. 217-18.
[2] Palliser, *Tudor York*, p. 48.

subsidy £974.[1] Admittedly, these large sums were mainly found by the wealthy, and some of Coventry's merchants were amongst the wealthiest in England, but nonetheless a considerable burden was imposed on the town. Then there were the many endemic problems of urban life: it is difficult to provide enough food and employment; disease spreads more easily; poverty is a common feature, in part for the paradoxical, but perhaps significant, reason that towns are also seen as centres of hope and prosperity for the rural poor, who thus migrate to them in great numbers.

Such were some of the slings and arrows that afflicted early sixteenth-century towns; but neither they nor the accompanying complaints were new – and anyway if one is going to complain, there is little point in not laying it on thick. So, when in January 1528 the dean of York suggested to Wolsey that the city would disappear unless it secured some financial relief, he was obviously writing nonsense.[2] What is true is that by the 1520s York, having once been second only to London, had declined to about sixth in the urban pecking order.[3] One of the reasons was that its cloth industry was losing out to towns in the West Riding such as Halifax, Leeds and Wakefield. It did not like this, so it squealed. Moreover, it saw no reason not to take advantage of the fact that the present incumbent of the archiepiscopal seat happened to be one of the most important men in England. York was also suffering from a significant decline in population, from about 12,000 in 1400 to about 8,000 in the 1520s,[4] and the same is true for every other major town. One inevitable consequence was that they were left with a lot of empty houses, something that almost every complaint or petition from a town made great play of. Thus, in 1452 the Winchester authorities cited as evidence of its poverty that 997 houses stood empty, while in 1518 a sheriff of Bristol lamented that 800 houses were unoccupied.[5] But while these memorials to the Black Death and subsequent epidemics may have been an eyesore, and may also have begun in the 1530s to create legal problems, as a rising urban population sought to reclaim the ruined properties,[6] they are no more evidence of genuine poverty than those empty houses in the rural areas were. Moreover, it is suspicious that these complaints about empty houses came not only from towns, such as Winchester, which had been in decline for about two hundred years, but also from towns such as Bristol, which appear to have been flourishing.[7]

In assessing the urban crisis, historians have perhaps too often ignored the simple point that a declining population and consequent decline in the gross national product does not have to mean a decline in *per capita* wealth. As a result they have taken too gloomy a view of late medieval economic activity. But if the volume of economic activity undoubtedly had declined from the high levels of the thirteenth century, there are plenty of signs that England's economic health was in good order, fuelled from the 1460s onwards by a buoyant foreign trade spearheaded

---

[1] Pythian-Adams, p.63; Hoskins, *Age of Plunder*, p.13.

[2] *LP*,iv,3843.

[3] Palliser, *Tudor York*, pp.201-2.

[4] Ibid.

[5] Bridbury, pp.13-14; Elton, *Reform and Renewal*, pp.107-8; Lander, *Government and Community*, p.19.

[6] Bridbury, p.23 whose scepticism about urban decline I find convincing.

[7] Admittedly her cloth and wool exports were not as buoyant as in the 1490s boom, but the flourishing trade in wine may have compensated for there was no significant fall in customs revenue; see Hoskins, *Age of Plunder*, p.181.

by a booming textile industry. In such a context it is difficult to believe in crisis. What may be true is that the decline in population had a disproportionately adverse effect on civic finances. Incomes from rents would have been directly affected, while the decline in the volume of trade would have meant less revenue from tolls. At the same time, many of a town's financial commitments, for instance the payment of a fee-farm and parliamentary taxes, remained the same. Moreover, the decline in population had been accompanied by a tendency for people to move into suburbs, outside the jurisdiction and financial control of the town authorities. None of this has to mean that urban prosperity was declining, but it might well explain the numerous petitions to the Crown from the towns for tax relief, many of which were favourably received. It may also be true that some towns were facing particularly severe problems. Lincoln had suffered badly from the silting up of the River Witham. Hull's export trade to the Baltic was destroyed by the Hanseatic League's increasing stranglehold on all trade to that area; Boston's export trade, too, seems to have considerably diminished, though in both cases the volume of coastal traffic may have increased.[1] The long-term decline of Winchester as a result of the collapse of its cloth industry has already been mentioned. But it is Coventry that has been advanced as the main instance of urban crisis: a town, allegedly, not only suffering a chronic illness, but by 1525 in its death-throes. The cause was apparently a combination of difficulties in its own textile industry, a short-term but severe slump in cloth exports, high food prices and heavy taxation.[2] Perhaps, but there must be serious doubts about a crisis whose chief symptom was a 'conspiracy' of no more than fifty people, and for which no one was executed. In fact, far from being Coventry's death-throe, the conspiracy was no more than an enclosure riot, which at Coventry had, during the previous fifty years, traditionally taken place on Lammas day (1 August), as some of its citizens sought to ensure that the town-fields were made available for common pasturage, which by custom they should have been.[3]

The number of citizens who sought exemption from civic office on the grounds that they could not afford the expense or face up to the responsibility of handling a town's shaky finances might seem to support the notion of an urban crisis. But there were a number reasons for declining office, including the reluctance of successful entrepreneurs to waste their time in local politics. It looks also as if some people were asked to stand for office against their own wishes, in order that they might be persuaded to buy an exemption – which at the very least complicates any interpretation of the figures of those seeking exemption, as does the fact that there was never any serious difficulty in filling civic offices.[4] Moreover, that Wolsey showed no sign of believing in an urban crisis may in itself be a reason for not believing in one, for there has so far been nothing to suggest that he was one to duck a problem – rather the opposite.

[1] Hoskins, *Age of Plunder*, p.180.
[2] Pythian-Adams, pp.51 ff. One of my many worries about his interpretation is that the national slump is difficult to find, and even his figures for high food prices are not all that convincing: 2s. 3d. a bushel in 1520 but under 1s in 1522 and 1523 and only 1s. 5d. in 1524.
[3] The account in Pythian-Adams, pp.253 ff. needs to be checked against M. Dormer Harris, pp.155 ff.
[4] Dobson, pp.13-14; Kermode.

The Tudor poor laws have been seen as important milestones on the way to the welfare state, and they have commanded a good deal of mostly sympathetic attention.[1] Wolsey's lack of involvement with any of them may, as a consequence, be held against him, especially as only a few years later Thomas Cromwell was able to grasp their importance – but then he was a very 'modern' man! The present writer's scepticism of anything 'whiggish' will already be apparent, and the fact that these laws were largely the work of Elizabethan councillors, such as William Cecil, not otherwise noted for their modernity, does not encourage him to revise his views. Instead, the suggestion would be that the poor laws were in part a pragmatic response to a probably growing problem, and, as with enclosure and indeed with most social legislation, there was also a less rational side to them, in which the obsession with 'order' and 'degree' and an ingrained fear of those without fixed abode or employment, were the most obvious features. Again as with enclosure, the long incubation period and the way in which successive Acts built upon each other need to be stressed. Much of the theory, including that distinction between the 'undeserving' and 'deserving' poor, was around long before the 1530s, and not just in canon law. It appears in the statute of 1349 which forbade the giving of alms to able-bodied beggars, and in that of 1388, which not only provided for their punishment but also sought to control the movement of the 'impotent poor'.[2] Claims that the poor law Act of 1536, even in its draft form, was revolutionary seem a little excessive. Even the notion of some form of graduated income tax to finance schemes for setting the able-bodied poor to work may have had its origins in fifteenth-century canonists' views that contributions to poor relief should be compulsory, and anyway this notion did not survive the passage of the bill through parliament.[3] Still, in its draft form at least, it was an imaginative attempt to tackle a perennial problem, and certainly nothing like it was considered in Wolsey's time.

However, the absence of a poor law Act should not be taken to indicate that Wolsey and his fellow councillors showed no concern for the poor. Their efforts to do something about enclosure are alone evidence to the contrary, as are the strenuous attempts to grapple with food shortages and high prices in 1527-9. Moreover, existing poor laws, admittedly having more to do with the control of 'vagabonds' and 'sturdy' beggars than the relief of the impotent poor, were very much in force, as the proclamations of 1517 and 1527 make clear.[4] More interestingly, in early 1518, when, it will be remembered, there was much worry about the Sweat, the Council was actively involved with the City authorities in measures to combat poverty in the capital. A new official was appointed with the specific duty to seek out the able-bodied 'vagabonds and beggars', while the 'impotent' beggars were to be licensed. Those suffering from the 'great pox', or who were in any way 'loathsome or abhorrent to be looked at', were to be sent to hospital. Throughout the 1520s there were frequent 'searches' of the City to round up 'idle, vagrant and suspicious persons'.[5] These may have had more to do with a

[1] For useful recent introductions and bibliographies see Beier and Pound. Slack's important *Poverty and Policy* appeared too late to be fully assimilated.
[2] Tierney, pp.128-9.
[3] Elton, *EcHR*, 2 ser, vi; *Reform and Renewal*, pp.122 ff. Tierney, pp.125 ff. for fifteenth-century canonists.
[4] *TRP*, nos.80, 118.

concern for law and order than with a desire to relieve poverty, but then much the same can be said about all government intervention in social matters. What needs to be borne in mind is that there already existed elaborate, if what would now be called private or voluntary, provision for the poor. Parishes, monastic institutions, hospitals and guilds not only provided money, food, housing, medical attention and clothing, but also the means to administer these. They in turn were constantly provided with the wherewithal by the generosity of individuals, especially in their wills.[1] It has been fashionable to play down the efforts of the medieval world to relieve its poor and sick. An estimate derived from the Valor Ecclesiasticus of 1535 gives only 3 per cent of monastic income as being set aside for charitable purposes; a more realistic figure might be 6.25 per cent. But even the smaller 3 per cent would still put the annual figure at about £4,000. And, when all is said and done it is not at all clear that more recent government efforts to eradicate poverty have been any more successful.[2]

The point here, though, is not to mount an apology for the medieval world but to make a suggestion about the Tudor poor law. Much of medieval giving was tied up with the notion of 'good works' and the role these played in the process of salvation. The Reformation in England, however it is defined, attacked this notion and thereby undermined both people's willingness to give to good causes and, perhaps more importantly in this context, the existing machinery for poor relief.[3] It is, therefore, not altogether surprising that the secular state was increasingly drawn in. What may also be true is that this machinery was probably anyway proving inadequate for dealing with the ever-growing problems of poverty in the large cities. The first secular poor laws were drawn up in the large European cities such as Venice, but even in England it was in the towns rather than in the rural areas that secular measures for poor relief first appeared.[4] And as the sixteenth century advanced, so the population increased and prices rose. It may be that there has been a tendency to exaggerate the harmful consequences of these trends, but it does seem likely that the poor became poorer and that there were more of them and thus the Tudor poor laws.[5] But in Wolsey's time not only were the medieval provisions for poor relief very much in place but the demographic and inflationary spirals were not yet under way, so that at the very least the need for more direct intervention by the state was not so obvious.

So far the emphasis in this chapter has been on the social rather than the economic. To some extent this reflects the government's greater concern with social issues, because, however much it may have regulated trade and industry, its direct participation was limited. Regulation of the coinage was more obviously an

[5] Kennedy, pp.204-5; also Leonard, pp.25 ff.

[1] Beier, pp.2-4, 19-23; Scarisbrick, *Reformation* , pp.51-4; Youings, *Seventeenth Century*, pp.254 ff.
[2] Knowles, pp.264-7. My feeling is that there is a lot more to be discovered about medieval provision for the poor.
[3] Palliser, *Age of Elizabeth*, pp.116-29; Pound, pp.68-75 on what is a controversial matter, much of the debate centring on Jordan's findings, for which see Jordan.
[4] Palliser, *Age of Elizabeth*, pp.126-9; Pound, pp.56-67 but can one really believe that Gloucester was the first English town to take action?
[5] But see Palliser, *Age of Elizabeth*, pp.118-29 for a quietly revisionist view.

economic matter, though, as we shall see, the Crown did have other reasons for intervention. There were two aspects to this regulation, one to do with the denominations available, the gold and silver content and such like, and the other to do with the exchange rates. During the 1520s both were a preoccupation of government, and in 1526 so much action was taken that that year has been called 'a remarkable one for English coinage'.[1] The subject is highly technical, but the main point is that, compared with other European currencies, the English coinage was too pure for its own good: that is, its gold and silver content was virtually unalloyed. As European bullion prices rose, the English coinage was increasingly undervalued and, as a result, was allegedly being bought up and exported. At the same time the financing of military activity abroad, such as Suffolk's expedition in late 1523, accelerated the flight of English money abroad. By April 1525 the Venetian ducat, which in 1522 had been given a nominal value of 4s. 6d., was fetching anything between 4s. 9d. and 5s. 2d., and in August the following year the government was forced to act.

What it did was technically an 'enhancement' – that is, it raised the exchange rate without altering the gold or silver content of the coinage. As a result the ducat was valued at 4s. 8d., while the crown of the sun, in 1522 valued at 4s. 4d., rose to 4s. 6d. At the same time the value of the sovereign and noble was raised, and new coins were introduced, including the George noble, worth 6s. 8d., and the crown and half-crown. When first issued in August, the crown had been worth 4s. 6d., to be the exact equivalent of the crown of the sun, but it quickly became apparent that, despite the August increases, the English coinage was still undervalued. So in November many values were raised, one consequence being that the new crown became 5s., and the half-crown, therefore, 2s. 6d., at which value it was to remain until the early 1970s, when decimalization broke this little known link with Wolsey.[2]

The coins mentioned so far were all gold. Silver ones, the most common of which was the groat, worth 4d., were also causing concern, and in 1522 there was some experimentation with a new silver coinage of less weight. Initially unsuccessful, in 1526 it was made even lighter, and this seems to have done the trick: during the next four years production significantly increased, while the unsatisfactory pre-1526 silver coinage soon dropped out of circulation.[3] Modern experts have on the whole been favourably impressed by Wolsey's scheme. 'Wolsey's coinage' was to have a long history, and led to an increase in the volume of coin minted, gold as well as silver. Given the talk of scarcity in 1525, this must have been a good thing. The new exchange rates were to remain unaltered until 1538. In the light of the subsequent history of currency manipulation in Henry's reign, it needs to be stressed that the motives behind the changes of 1526 were entirely proper. Their purpose was to create a coinage whose bullion content and resulting rate of exchange made it no longer so financially attractive to export. And though the stimulation of coin production did lead to increased revenue for the

---

[1] Challis, pp.70-1, a book which should be consulted for all that follows. See also Feaveryear, pp.46 ff; Gould.

[2] Challis, pp.68 ff. Did any of Thomas Cromwell's reforms have a longer history?

[3] Ibid, pp.70-1, 168.

royal mint, the intention was never, as it was to be later, to make a quick buck by coining debased money.

There remains the difficult question of the extent of Wolsey's direct involvement in the reforms. That detailed instructions were drawn up in his name does not necessarily mean that he was personally responsible for them. Despite the tendency for most royal councillors to be jacks-of-all-trades, there were some who were financial experts. Sir John Heron, treasurer of the chamber from 1492 to 1521, is an obvious example, as is Sir John Daunce, who in the autumn of 1526 chaired an important committee on monetary reform.[1] But if the expertise came from others, it seems fair to assume, given his personality and leading position, that the implementation of the currency reforms owed a good deal to his support.[2]

It was mentioned earlier that economic considerations were not the only reason for the Crown's interest in the coinage. The need to have ready cash to pay for military and naval requirements was probably of greater concern to it than, for instance, any overwhelming desire to boost English exports. Indeed, an undervalued currency would have been good for exports, for it would have meant that English goods were comparatively cheap. Thus to praise Wolsey for his reform of the coinage is still not to credit him with any great interest in economic activity. Moreover, what has already emerged from the study of his foreign policy is that furthering economic prosperity was not his chief priority. But it would be wrong to conclude that economic considerations played no part. Indeed, in June 1525 that doughty champion of the Imperialist cause, Sir Robert Wingfield, not liking the pro-French direction that England's foreign policy was taking, suspected that it arose out of a desire to please the merchants who 'have more mind to their case and singular profit than the weal of Christendom'.[3] His suspicions were ill-founded, but what is significant here is that he could have held them at all.

Like most people, English merchants in the early sixteenth century were quite happy to make their own decisions, until, that is, they found themselves in dispute with a foreign merchant, or needed protection for their ships. Thus in September 1522 it was recorded in the minute book of the Mercers' Company that Wolsey was to be consulted over the capture by the French of a ship called *The Windsor* and some compensation obtained; and in the following month the Company was seeking protection for their Zeeland fleet.[4] Requests such as these must have frequently ended up on Wolsey's table. Like any royal councillor, Wolsey would have seen it as his duty to further the interests of English merchants. This was partly because they brought in a significant proportion of the annual £30-40,000 in customs revenue. It was partly because the export trade, especially cloth, which made up three-quarters of it, provided much needed employment. And it was partly because the export trade stimulated the ship-building industry, which in turn provided ships for the royal navy. But over and above all these tangible reasons for royal concern, the king's honour demanded that the interests of English merchants, as his subjects, were vigorously pursued. And if money, defence and honour are put

---

[1] *LP*,iv,2595.

[2] *LP*,iv,2541 Knight to Wolsey, 1 Oct. 1526 re. the issuing of the November proclamation. For this and the August proclamation see *TRP*, nos.111-12.

[3] BL Galba B viii, fo.192 (*LP*,iv,1400).

[4] *Mercers' Company*, pp.544, 548.

together, one has what might be called a policy, one that might even pass as mercantilism. All it really means is that there were certain general considerations that governed the Crown's attitude towards trade. It was slightly defensive. It was suspicious of foreign competition. It paid more attention to national security than to economic growth.

Almost certainly Wolsey shared these attitudes and saw no reason for any radical departures. It is true that during the 1520s customs revenue fell, from an annual average of £42,643 during the previous decade to £35,305, and for the years 1530-8 it was to fall even further, to just over £32,000.[1] It is also true that, with the disruption to trade caused by the outbreak of war with France and subsequent naval activity in the English Channel, 1522 was a particularly bad year, revenue dropping to just below the £30,000 mark for the first time since 1492. There was also going to be a temporary crisis in the first half of 1528, as a result of the albeit reluctant declaration of war against the emperor. Since wool had been the chief export when custom duties were first introduced, the duties on wool were traditionally greater than on anything else, so that as the export of wool declined, the customs revenues increasingly underestimated the volume of English trading. Thus, if instead of customs revenue, one takes as an indicator the number of cloths leaving London, a more buoyant picture emerges. In 1515 some 59,000 cloths were being exported, rising to 67,000 in 1519. There was then a drop to 50,000 in 1521, but after that there were successive rises, until in 1527 the number had reached 81,000. The 1528 declaration of war resulted in a dramatic drop, but the next year the number was still over 70,000, as, apart from 1528, it had been since 1524. One can, of course, play around with the figures endlessly, but even if the cloth trade was not quite so booming as it had been in the last years of Henry VII's reign (and this is by no means certain) by and large it continued to flourish, and with it the rest of England's foreign trade, this despite the efforts of a leading minister who allegedly had no interest in such things![2]

In most circumstances Wolsey did his best to further the interests of English merchants, but there were occasions when these conflicted with other concerns. Then the other concerns were quite often given priority, though any such generalization oversimplifies an often very complicated picture. To begin with the merchant community itself was very heterogeneous, with, for instance, those in the outports such as Bristol and Exeter having quite different interests from those in London, and increasingly it was the last, especially members of the Merchant Adventurers' Company with its virtual monopoly of the cloth trade, that dominated government thinking. And if we turn to a particular episode, the picture becomes no less complicated. The well known disagreement between Henry and Wolsey in 1521 over whether the English merchants should sail to Bordeaux for the autumn shipment of wine is an example of a conflict of interest, and one in which the king may be said to have taken the merchants' part against his chief minister. At any rate, at a time of increasing international tension he was very reluctant to let them run the risk of sequestration by the French. Wolsey, however, took the view that to

[1] Hoskins, *Age of Plunder*, pp.181-2.
[2] For the figures see Carus-Wilson and Coleman; Hoskins, *Age of Plunder*, pp.177-91; for the cloth trade Bowden.

prevent them sailing would alert the French to his deception during the lengthy Calais and Bruges negotiations. His priority was for everything to appear as normal, and to this end he was prepared to jeopardize the merchants' ships, though he never considered the risk of sequestration to be very great.[1]

On this occasion it was an anti-French alliance with the emperor that was being negotiated behind Francis I's back. A pro-French alliance would be more damaging to England's foreign trade because of its strong bias towards the Low Countries, particularly Antwerp, and insofar as Wolsey was pursuing such a policy from 1525 onwards it could be seen as a much more significant example of his lack of interest in mere trade. But on closer inspection it is not nearly so obvious that this is so. It so happens that when, in January 1528, war was formally declared between Henry and the emperor, England was also facing serious economic and and social problems at home, largely the consequence of the disastrous harvest in 1527 followed by two more with low yields. This combination of difficulties provides an excellent opportunity for studying Wolsey, the promoter of the common weal, in action, and of arriving at some final assessment of his performance.

It will be shown later that in 1528 Wolsey had no real wish for a war with the emperor, and that the formal declaration of war made in Spain on 22 January was not of his choosing.[2] Nevertheless, he must have been aware that if Charles refused to make any concessions to Anglo-French pressure, war was a possibility. During the summer of 1527 he took steps to encourage English merchants to make use of Calais as their main mart, rather than Antwerp, and while at Amiens he sought to obtain important concessions for English merchants trading with France, which suggests that he was trying to minimize the harmful economic consequences of a war with Charles some time before it took place.[3] Not surprisingly, most English merchants resisted, pointing out that 'as a town of war' Calais was unsuitable as a centre of trade, nor could the harbour cope with the 'great hulks and carracks that come to a mart'.[4] Interestingly, Wolsey appears to have listened to them. At any rate, when the war came, instead of putting even more pressure on the merchants to use Calais, he moved quickly to keep the trading routes to the Low Countries open. As early as 25 February 1528 Margaret was aware of Wolsey's wishes in this respect, and expressed herself willing to comply.[5] An exchange of envoys took place in March and negotiations continued until 15 June when a truce between England, France and the Low Countries was signed, the main purpose of which was to allow trade to continue as normal.

That it took so long for a truce to be signed was not Wolsey's fault. The French proved awkward; but, then, not having a vital cloth trade with the Low Countries and being desperately anxious to maintain pressure on the emperor in order to recover the French princes held by him as surety for their observance of the Treaty of Madrid, there was little in it for them.[6] Undoubtedly the fact that in all three countries merchants had been taken into custody and their goods seized

---

[1] LP,iii,1533, 1544, 1558, 1577, 1594, 1611, 1630; see also Scarisbrick, Henry VIII, pp.89-92.
[2] See p.542 below.
[3] LP,iv,3449, 3451 (2); TRP, no.115; Hall, p.729.
[4] Hall, p.729.
[5] LP,iv,3959, 3966; Sp.Cal.,iii (ii), p.603.
[6] LP,iv, app.153, 158-60, 162-9, 175.

complicated matters.[1] There was also some suspicion on the English side that Margaret was dragging her feet: Imperialist and French forces were fighting in Italy so there was every reason for her not to make life easier for the French, or indeed the English.[2] Still, there were disadvantages for her own subjects in any prolonged disruption to trade, and the English suspicions may have been exaggerated. What is certainly not the case is that Wolsey was dragging his feet.[3] He must have approached Margaret almost immediately news of the defiance in Spain reached England: when precisely that was is not known, but there could have been no knowledge of it before the middle of February, and by the 24th Margaret was writing of Wolsey's expressed concern that trade should continue as normal.[4] A little later he was to show himself sufficiently determined to secure the truce to stand up to Henry's criticisms. It was not that the king was opposed to a truce on principle – he too had been quick to recognize the importance of obtaining one[5] – but he thought the final terms were far too generous to the Imperialists, especially disliking the lack of any provision for the restitution of English goods seized in Spain. Wolsey, on the other hand, believed that he had obtained the best deal possible and that delay was not in England's interests. Rather grudgingly, Henry came round, but as a result of his opposition the proclamation of the truce was delayed until 27 June.[6]

In the spring of 1528 the interests of English merchants trading abroad were not Wolsey's chief priority; securing his master's divorce occupied that position, and would do so until his dismissal from office in October 1529. This meant that there was no question of giving up the French alliance, seen by him, and indeed by Henry, as vital for the securing of the divorce. But the alliance seems to have been disliked by almost everybody else in England, especially by merchants with interests in the Low Countries. Wolsey did his best to minimize its harmful economic consequences. Even in normal circumstances he would have wanted to to do this, but in early 1528 the situation was decidedly abnormal, and not just because of the requirements of the divorce, which put added pressure on him to intervene. From September 1526 to June 1527 it rained virtually without ceasing.[7] The result was a disastrous harvest; in the whole of the century only the harvests of 1556 and 1596 were worse.[8] The index figure for wheat rose from 110 in 1526 to 227 in 1527: in money terms, from £6.53s. per quarter to £13.37s. The situation appears to have been much worse in eastern England than in the west, and wheat suffered more than other grain. Other arable crops such as peas and beans were not so badly affected, the index figure rising from 148 to 195. Livestock prices hardly seem to have been affected at all.[9]

These qualifications need to be borne in mind when trying to assess the

---

[1] LP,iv,3958, 4009, 4018, 4069, 4147, 4071, 4286; Hall, pp.744-5.

[2] St.P,i, p.294 (LP,iv,4404).

[3] As suggested in Herbert, p.196, probably following Hall, pp.747-9.

[4] LP,iv,3959; Sp.Cal.,iii (ii), p.603.

[5] LP,iv,4080.

[6] LP,iv,4376, 4389, 4404, 4409, 4426.

[7] Ven.Cal.,iv,188; Hall, pp.721, 736; Stow, p.885.

[8] Hoskins, Age of Plunder, p.87.

[9] Harrison, AHR, xix, pp.148, 152; Hoskins, AHR, xii, pp.33-4; Thirsk (ed.), Agrarian History, pp.817, 835.

seriousness of the crisis. It seems unlikely that famine stalked the land. Bread and ale provided the staple diet and both involved grain; but bread did not have to be made from wheat, it could even be made, in part at any rate, from beans and peas, while ale was normally made from barley, which, if there were some local shortages, was overall in plentiful supply.[1] Still, in the winter and spring of 1527-8 the situation must have seemed desperate, as it became apparent that there was not enough wheat to go round. The Venetian ambassador was reporting rising prices and great scarcity in London, and was even having to defend his own servants from attack when they bought his bread.[2] Hall also recorded alarming shortages,[3] and in Norwich, 'there was so great scarceness of corn that about Christmas the commons of the city were ready to rise upon the rich men'.[4] Wolsey was not long in taking action. As early as 26 September the JPs in Kent were ordered to take themselves 'into sundry places and parts of the said county and not only to view, search and try what grains and corns be in the houses, barns, garners or ricks' but also to force all those with surplus grain to sell it on the open market. Anyone who refused was to be imprisoned.[5] Whether similar orders went out to other counties is uncertain, but by 12 November a national response to the crisis had been planned. Similar tasks were now to be performed in every county of England by specially appointed commissioners, and any statute that might have some bearing on the matter was to be vigorously enforced.[6]

The fact that Wolsey was prepared to contemplate having every single barn in England searched is rather impressive. Even more so is the fact that probably every barn in England was searched, and all within a surprisingly short time. The names of any who refused to release their surplus were to be presented to king and Council in Star Chamber before 21 January, and the surviving returns of the commissioners indicate that by that date not only was this achieved but that a census of all the available grain in the country had been drawn up. How accurate the census was is another matter: the surviving returns appear to be complete, even if some of the maths is occasionally awry. A calculation was made of the amount of grain needed to provide sufficient bread and ale until the next harvest as well as enough seed in times of scarcity there was always considerable pressure not to make such provision. Then, the actual amount of grain discovered was recorded, and from these two sets of figures the amount of surplus or shortfall was calculated. Armed with this information, the government could then take appropriate action.[7]

The usual policy at times of scarcity was to prevent the entrepreneur from acting in a way that would aggravate the situation. This he could do in a number of ways, but essentially by selling at the highest price, which would not necessarily be to the local community. In November 1528 the inhabitants of Yaxley and Holme in

---

[1] Hoskins, *Age of Plunder*, p. 86 calls 1527-8 the famine years, but see Dymond, pp. 31-4 for important qualifications. See *Ven. Cal.*, iv, 208 for the fact that bean flour was used.

[2] *Ven. Cal.*, iv, 188, 205, 210, 212, 235.

[3] Hall, p. 736.

[4] Hoskins, *AHR*, xii, p. 34, quoting from the mayor's register.

[5] Heinze, p. 99.

[6] *TRP*, no. 118.

[7] *LP*, iv, 3544 (Notts), 3587 (Northants), 3665 (Essex, Northants, Wilts), 3712 (Northants), 3819 (Notts), 3822 (N. Ridings). Dymond is invaluable but see also Heinze, pp. 100-2.

Huntingdonshire were greatly angered that local peas and beans were being bought up by merchants in Lynn and then sold to Scotland, with the result, so they claimed, that in their local markets the price rose and 'some died for very hunger'.[1] In acting in this entrepreneurial way, the Lynn merchants may have been guilty of the crime of 'forestalling', that is, of deliberately preventing produce coming to the local market and thereby affecting its price. They would have been more obviously guilty if their intention had been to play the local market by sitting on the produce only to sell when the price had risen sufficiently for them to make a fat profit. If, instead of buying it up beforehand, they had waited for the produce to get to the local market and had then bought it only to resell at a later date, they would have been guilty of the related crime of 'regrating'. What they were accused of was 'engrossing', that is, of buying up produce while it was still growing in the fields.[2] Of course, if the Crown had systematically enforced the legislation against these activities, it would have put a stop to a sophisticated agricultural economy whereby produce was being transported long distances, often to supply rather specialized markets, and, for instance, the fifty thousand or so inhabitants of London would have starved. One has, therefore, to assume that this legislation, along, perhaps, with some of the Acts which caused puzzlement earlier on, such as the banning of certain games, were quite consciously thought of as providing reserve powers for use in special circumstances. In late 1527 such circumstances had arisen.

It follows from all this that there was nothing very new about what Wolsey was trying to do in the winter and early spring of 1527-8. The statutes against forestalling and related matters date from at least the thirteenth century, while as early as 1204 it had been laid down that grain could not be exported without licence. In 1437 a slightly different approach was tried: no licence was required as long as certain conditions were met, most importantly that grain did not exceed the specified rates. It was these conditions that were in force in the 1520s, and with the price of grain well above the specified rates 6s. 8d. per quarter for wheat, that meant, quite sensibly, that none could leave the country. But the main point that is being stressed here is that the idea of regulation was very well accepted long before 1527.[3] What was striking about Wolsey's efforts were their scale and thoroughness. Never before had there been a nation-wide investigation into grain stocks, and without that knowledge it would have been impossible to judge how serious the problem was and where the government should direct its efforts. As it was, the commissioners for Staffordshire were able to report a genuine shortage, with no grain being hoarded or otherwise forestalled, and they therefore asked for the restraint on the movement of grain from county to county to be lifted in their case, so that they could obtain necessary supplies. On the other hand, some of the Northamptonshire commissioners reported that all was well,[4] while in Norfolk there was found to be a sufficient surplus for some of it to be released for other counties.[5]

---

[1] *Select Cases Star Chamber*, pp.178 ff.

[2] For these definitions see Heinze, p.100, n.36; but cf Gras, pp.130-1 and the terms do seem to have been rather interchangeable.

[3] Gras, pp.130 ff.

[4] *Select Cases in Star Chamber*, pp.165-8. But for parts of Nottinghamshire reporting a surplus see Heinze, p.102, n.40.

Given the reported distress of the inhabitants of Norwich at the scarcity of corn, the fact that the county of Norfolk was in surplus comes as a surprise. It may also serve as a warning against taking too alarmist a view. Shortages were indeed discovered. In ten villages along the Essex side of the river Stour, not all that far from Norfolk, the calculation in the returns was that there was a shortage of some 572 quarters of grain for bread making and some 451 quarters for ale; and this, according to a recent calculation, meant that on average these villages could raise only 53 per cent of their requirements.[1] But there is really no evidence to suggest that the shortages had any devastating consequences, which may merely mean that, as was suggested earlier, people did find sufficient alternatives to grain. It may also be that the measures that Wolsey took were successful. By being able to move any surpluses to areas especially in need, the worst consequences of the bad harvest may have been averted; though the corollary to this would also have to be that in a normal year English arable farmers were producing very large surpluses. What complicates any assessment is the conjunction of the bad harvest with that temporary severance of trade with the Low Countries already discussed and the resulting threat of widespread unemployment in the cloth industry. Undoubtedly, this made things much more difficult for Wolsey. The interesting point is that, as regards the quite considerable unrest reported in the early part of 1528, it seems to have been the the trade embargo rather than the bad harvest that played the major part – another reason for not believing that there was anything remotely approaching a famine.

The surviving evidence is so patchy that no detailed study of the unrest of 1528 is possible. As in 1525, unemployment was at the heart of it and most of the trouble seems to have been in East Anglia and Kent. In other respects too it was a re-run of those previous disturbances with very much the same principals – namely, the dukes of Norfolk and Suffolk in East Anglia and Warham, Boleyn and the Guildford brothers in Kent – doing and writing in very much the same vein. So yet again Warham found himself having to deal with angry crowds converging on Knole, complaining of their poverty, and, most worryingly, again asking awkward questions about when the loan of 1522 would be repaid[2] – and this when only the previous year, Wolsey, on his way through Kent en route for Amiens, had been relieved to find that the matter had been forgotten.[3] In East Anglia the two dukes were once again having to keep a very high profile in an effort to keep a restless populace under control. A rising was planned at Bury St Edmunds in late February, but it was nipped in the bud. Earlier there had been unrest in Stowmarket and Norwich, and in April at Colchester.[4] In Kent the worst trouble came in May, and then was chiefly confined to that area in the Weald around Cranbrook that was

[5] LP,iv,3883.

---

[1] Dymond, p.32.
[2] LP,iv,4188; for Norfolk's worries about such questions see LP,iv,4192.
[3] LP,iv,3231, 3234.
[4] LP,iv, 3664, 4012-13, 4129, 4145. See also Bernard, War, Taxation and Rebellion, p.143-4; MacCullough, pp.298-9 though his redating of the Stowmarket trouble to 1526 must be wrong because of the specific references in the relevant documents to the 1527 commission and to Francis Pointz's return from Spain.

always a thorn in the establishment's flesh. The plan there was to capture various leading local gentry, including Sir Edward Guildford, but ultimately Wolsey as well. The rebels had even worked out how to dispose of the cardinal once he was taken: to kill him with their own hands would have brought down the wrath of the pope, so he was to be put to sea in a boat 'in the which shall be bored four great holes', temporarily filled with large pins. Once out into the Channel, these were to be knocked out and Wolsey was to have met a watery death, but one that could have been passed off as an accident.[1]

In fact, the trouble at Cranbrook seems never to have amounted to much; the Guildfords' considered view was that no more than twenty were involved, and these only 'light persons'.[2] And as with the rising in Bury, the authorities had got wind of it before anything happened, and had no difficulty in dealing with it. The same appears to be true of other parts of the country. In March Lord Sandys was informed by the king that 'certain light persons have assembled themselves in an unlawful number about Westbury', and unrest was also reported in Devizes, Taunton and Bridgewater.[3] But the impression is never of a situation out of control, partly because, as soon as the extent of the disastrous harvest was realized, trouble of some kind was prepared for. The proclamation of November 1527 which announced the setting up of the corn commissions had also, it will be remembered, called for the strict enforcement of a whole range of statutes, most of which, however indirectly, had to do with the maintenance of law and order. Consequently, the commissioners were ordered to carry out 'privy searches' of their areas to round up all 'vagabonds and idle beggars', and to follow this up with a twice weekly sweep of all the ale-houses.[4] The assumption, not borne out by what happened, was that in times of difficulty it was just such people who would cause most trouble. Still, the fact that the law enforcement machinery had been put on red alert and, perhaps most importantly, that leading noblemen and gentry such as the two dukes and Thomas Boleyn, who might otherwise have expected to spend more time at court, had been sent back to their localities in order to supervise the government response to the difficulties, must offer one explanation for the situation never having got out of hand. Another is provided by the fact that however serious the shortages, it was not starving thousands or 'idle beggars' who caused the unrest, but a few hundred temporarily unemployed clothworkers.

In 1527 the role of the clothworkers is even clearer than in the 1525 disturbances. For one thing, in all the areas where trouble was reported a considerable amount of clothmaking took place, and most of the reports made the connection between the unrest and unemployment. Moreover, in 1528 there was no question, as there had been in 1525, of the employers inventing a problem merely to avoid having to accede to an unpopular request for money. If cloth could not be sold to the Low Countries, then the industry would be in real difficulty. As has already been shown, Wolsey was quick to realize this, and by negotiating immediately for a truce with Margaret of Savoy he showed a determination to do

---

[1] *LP*,iv,4310.
[2] *LP*,iv,4301.
[3] *LP*,iv,4043, 4058, 4085.
[4] *LP*,iv,3625, 3664, 3712, 3822; *Select Cases in Star Chamber*, p.168.

something about it. Meanwhile, both he and the men on the spot did their best to persuade clothiers that the situation was only temporary and that there was no need to dismiss their workers. Thus Norfolk, after a meeting with forty of the most substantial clothiers in his area at which he had informed them, quite wrongly, that there was no truth in the rumour that English merchants in Spain and the Low Countries had been detained, strongly advised Wolsey to pressure the London merchants into continuing to buy East Anglian cloth.[1] It is doubtful whether Wolsey would have needed this advice, but certainly he did intervene, writing to the City authorities to secure their help.[2] He is also known to have instructed Lord Sandys not to allow clothiers to lay off people in Hampshire and Wiltshire.[3]

Hall reports a rather unsatisfactory meeting that Wolsey had with the London merchants,[4] and as late as 4 May Norfolk was still writing to him of the Norfolk clothiers' inability to sell their cloth.[5] That Wolsey's negotiations were not very successful is not altogether surprising, for until London merchants could be assured of a market for their cloth there was no good reason why they should venture their capital. The key to the problem was the truce with the Low Countries, and until this was signed and the uncertainty about markets abroad was removed, which, it will be remembered, was not achieved until the end of June 1528,[6] the situation was bound to remain tense. How far English merchants and clothiers were deliberately stirring up trouble in order to force Wolsey to reverse the pro-French policy that they saw as so destructive to their trading interests is another matter. In February the French ambassador reported that this was precisely what was happening, but then, in order to explain away the widespread francophobia, he was prone to think in conspiratorial terms.[7] In April a Colchester clothmaker, under cross-examination, stated that a London merchant had told him that there would be no buying of cloth 'except we could cause the commons to arise and complain to the king's grace and show him how the people be not half set awork', and he had heard something similar from another source.[8] But it is very easy to imagine such talk going the rounds without there being very much substance to it, and the surviving evidence is anyway a little thin. More to the point, there is no need for a conspiracy theory in order to explain the unrest. England's main outlet for cloth had been stopped, merchants were reluctant to buy, employers were laying people off, or were about to, and in such circumstances clothworkers had good reasons to be restless.

In emphasizing unemployment, or the threat of it, rather than scarcity or indeed famine, as the chief cause of the unrest in 1528, one is to some extent playing down the seriousness of the situation that Wolsey had to grapple with, and to that extent removing some of the credit due to him for coping with it so successfully. But something that undoubtedly contributed to the heightened tension, especially

---

[1] LP,iv,4044.

[2] Kennedy, p.220; also Mercers Company, Acts of Court, ii, fo.10, the reference to which I owe to I. Archer.

[3] LP,iv,4058.

[4] Hall, pp.745-6.

[5] LP,iv,4239.

[6] It was signed on the 15th but not proclaimed until the 27th.

[7] LP,iv,3930.

[8] LP,iv,4129, 4145; and quoted in Bernard, *War, Taxation and Rebellion*, 144.

perhaps in London, was the deepening political crisis brought about by Henry's desire for a divorce, which was never popular. And all these difficulties were connected, if in rather complicated ways, as the government's efforts to secure imports of grain from both France and the Low Countries demonstrate. As it happened, though French grain was promised, it never materialized, while that from the Low Countries did.[1] This only fuelled the general dissatisfaction with a French alliance, and this in turn made the conduct of foreign policy more difficult, because the alliance was vital for any success in the divorce negotiations.

A difficult economic situation, the divorce and an unpopular foreign policy were what Wolsey was faced with from the autumn of 1527 onwards, and the impression one gets is of someone coping remarkably well, and with him the whole apparatus of government. Nobody could have worked harder at this time than the dukes of Norfolk and Suffolk, whether organizing the corn commissioners, talking to clothworkers, interrogating potential rebels or just giving advice. And it was not only leading royal councillors and noblemen who were involved, but every JP, every mayor and alderman, and every local constable. What is most impressive is the sense of a government that knew what it was about: detailed information on a national scale was sought and obtained, instructions were issued, difficulties were foreseen and steps taken to anticipate them. But the question remains of just how effective all this activity was. Some scepticism is probably justified, especially if the suggestion here is correct that supplies were probably never so short that market forces could not have coped. Still, as has also been pointed out, there is more to government than cold logic and in times of difficulty any government's action may have some beneficial effect, if only on morale. And the scepticism may be unfounded. In judging Wolsey's achievement, it is the totality of what he was doing that needs to be remembered, including that these years saw renewed efforts to grapple with enclosure, a problem that was thought to bear very directly upon the question of scarcity of corn. And the fact is that Wolsey showed himself just as concerned to grapple with the problem of unemployment as with that of scarcity, so he cannot be accused of making a wrong diagnosis; and anyway the one problem must have compounded the other. The trouble in Cranbrook in late May does seem to have been primarily the result of unemployment but, in the depositions of those arrested, shortage of corn was also mentioned.[2] Very soon after helping to put down the trouble there Sir Edward Guildford was writing to Wolsey about local complaints of scarcity and high prices, urging that even greater efforts should be made to tackle the wicked 'regraters' who were responsible.[3] So he, at least, had sufficient belief in the beneficial effects of government intervention to want more of it.

What of Wolsey's overall contribution to the common weal? The very diversity of the subjects that come under such a label, few of which are easily quantifiable in terms of success or failure, makes such an assessment difficult. What does emerge, though, despite the many gaps in the evidence, is Wolsey's enormous concern to achieve something: the enclosure and corn commissions alone are proof of this. Add to these his reforms of the royal household and of taxation, his massive

[1] *LP*,iv,4018, 4107, 4147, app.156; Hall, p.736.
[2] *LP*,iv,4310.
[3] *LP*,iv,4414.

intervention in all areas of the English Church and his concern for 'indifferent' justice, and the final result in terms just of energy expended is remarkable, but especially so in one who, if he is not being portrayed as the gifted and self-indulgent amateur, usually emerges as more anxious to adorn a Field of Cloth of Gold than to master the complexities of the exchange rates, or to counter the effects of bad harvests. But if there is a seriousness about Wolsey's concern for the common weal that cannot be gainsaid, this does not go very far to explaining his motivation. Because of the lack of direct evidence for his personal views they will probably always remain uncertain. Certainly, the things he was attempting show no striking new departures, neither do they suggest that he was driven by any deep ideological commitment such as might have been provided by Christian humanism. All the same, the possible effect on him of that admittedly rather nebulous concept, the climate of opinion, should not be underestimated, for after all, when in 1519 Erasmus had announced the dawn of a golden age, he had the court of Henry VIII much in his mind. And at the very least, Wolsey's efforts suggest an enormous confidence in the efficacy of government intervention and more specifically in the usefulness of detailed information. Nevertheless, as always with Wolsey, it is his temperament that most catches the eye, and in particular that boundless energy and determination which he brought to bear on any problem. In December 1527, the duke of Norfolk, having ventured to give Wolsey some advice on the current problems, was so moved by the cardinal's thanks that he promised that 'from time to time I shall be so bold, as long as I shall know your grace content with the same, not only with my tongue and pen to give your grace my best poor advice to do that thing that may best and most sound to your honour, but also with my words and reports advance the same to the best of my little wit and power'. And why should he do this? Because he knew Wolsey 'to be so firmly determined to do all things that may sound to the king's high honour and the universal wealth of this realm'.[1] Not a bad verdict from one who was supposedly his arch-enemy.

---

[1] PRO SP 1/4/5/fo.193 (*LP*,iv,3663).

CHAPTER ELEVEN
REFORM AND REFORMATION

During 1528 and the first half of 1529 Clement VII appears to have been willing to give Wolsey more or less anything that he asked for – except, that is, what he wanted above all else, his consent to Henry's divorce from Catherine. Over twenty papal grants of one sort or another were made during this period. Many had to do with Wolsey's two colleges at Oxford and at Ipswich; others concerned his translation as bishop from Durham to Winchester. All these might be considered personal concerns of Wolsey, though it was argued earlier that his colleges were very much part of his plans for reform.[1] Definitely of public concern was a bull dated 12 May 1529 which made it easier to degrade those in holy orders who had committed serious crimes, so that they could be tried in the secular courts.[2] The background and purpose of this measure has already been discussed,[3] but it provides important evidence for that combination of persistence and political tact – in this case a determination to meet the criticisms of the Crown lawyers concerning the abuse of 'benefit of clergy' without offending too much the susceptibilities of the clergy themselves – already singled out as typical of Wolsey's approach to reform of the Church. However, at the centre of this reform were four bulls intended to tackle two major areas much in need of attention – the size and composition of English dioceses and the multiplicity and general health of monastic institutions. And it was concern for the latter that had been one of the stated reasons for Wolsey's original acquisition of legatine powers.

These two matters were closely connected, as a brief summary of the bulls concerning the creation of new dioceses makes clear. The first, dated 12 November 1528, empowered Wolsey to inquire into the expediency of suppressing certain monasteries in order that their buildings and revenues might be used to create new cathedrals and dioceses.[4] The second, obtained the following May, gave him the executive powers to proceed. It is particularly unfortunate that many of the details of the bulls have not survived,[5] as I believe they would have provided vital evidence of Wolsey's serious commitment to the welfare of the English Church. All, however, is not lost, and the first thing to do is to see how much of his plans can be recovered.[6]

---

[1] See pp. 343 ff. above.

[2] Rymer, xiv, p. 239; Wilkins, iii, p. 713. Both place it in 1528, but suggest uncertainty about the date. I prefer 1529 because of what I take to be a reference to it in a letter from Gardiner to Henry of 4 May 1529; see *LP*, iv, 5318.

[3] See p. 53 above.

[4] Rymer, xiv, pp. 273-4.

[5] Ibid, pp. 291-4 for the bull, which is, however, chiefly concerned with providing legal limits for Wolsey's actions.

[6] Almost the only serious treatment of them is in Gasquet, *Henry VIII and the English Monasteries*, pp. 29 ff.

What is known is that they received a mixed reception at Rome. Clement did show some interest; at any rate, he asked a number of questions, including the most relevant, which was whether there was any need for new dioceses.[1] But at least some of his cardinals and curial officials took a more partial view, fearing that in one way or another the proposals would be detrimental to both their honour and their pocket. There was more justification for their worries about Wolsey's insistence on the deletion of a clause stating that it was necessary to obtain the agreement of all those with a rightful interest in any of the institutions concerned.[2] Moreover, curial suspicion of Wolsey's intentions was not surprising. At the very least, he was out to secure the best possible financial bargain – which meant from the Curia's point of view the worst – and to be given the freest possible hand.

By and large Wolsey seems to have got what he was after. As regards the offending clause, he explained that he wanted it deleted, not so that he could ride rough-shod over other people's interests, but in order to prevent factious and malicious opposition to his well intentioned plans.[3] This the Curia accepted and the clause, though not removed, was so qualified as to become meaningless.[4] No limits were imposed on the number of monastic institutions that could be affected by the scheme, and none to the number of dioceses to be created. Indeed, there was no reference to numbers at all, even though the cardinals had expressed worries on this point.[5] The organization of the new dioceses was placed entirely in Wolsey's hands. The major decision facing him was whether their presiding cathedrals should be left as essentially monastic institutions, as so many English cathedrals, such as Benedictine Winchester and Augustinian Carlisle, already were. Alternatively, he could go for the compromise of allowing both secular and religious canons, as was already the case at Bath and Wells and at Coventry, or make them entirely secular on the model of Lincoln and London. The obvious advantage of retaining some monastic or 'religious' features is that any changes would meet with less opposition, but clearly Wolsey was prepared to be ruthless. He was permitted to appoint the heads of the existing monastic institutions as the new bishops, but he did not have to; indeed, in the first instance he was specifically empowered to appoint as bishop anyone Henry chose, only subsequent appointments having to be made in the normal way, by papal provision.

What was involved here was almost certainly not the *de facto* rights of English kings to choose their own bishops, for this had not been challenged for over a century, but finance. If bishops were not 'provided', no annates, or more correctly 'common services', would be due to the pope and Curia. On the face of it, then, it looks as if Wolsey had secured an important financial concession, which no doubt would have also helped him to sell the idea politically at home. In fact, the opposition of the cardinals was successful, to the extent that at one stage in the negotiations for the bulls Wolsey had felt compelled to promise that nothing that he intended would result in financial loss to the papacy.[6] In the final bull, it was laid

[1] Rymer,xiv, p.273; *LP*,iv,4900.

[2] *LP*,iv,5226, 5638-9.

[3] *LP*,iv,5639.

[4] Rymer, xiv, p.293. To the original clause was added: 'unless it seems to you after mature and diligent consideration necessary to do otherwise'.

[5] *LP*,iv,5638 for their worries.

down that the apostolic camera was to be informed of the annual revenues of the new dioceses as soon as possible so that the necessary calculations could be made, and the figure proved to be owing was to be paid within six months of the new bishop being appointed, or everything to do with the creation of the new diocese would be declared of 'no force or moment'. [1]None of these technicalities, nor the arguments they resulted in, are of great moment in themselves.[2] But they help to make the point that the reforms Wolsey was contemplating constituted a minefield which was liable to erupt at any moment. A lot of people, and not just greedy curial officials and cardinals – and there were, it should be said, altruistic reasons for not wanting papal revenues to fall – were likely to have strong objections to the changes that Wolsey was proposing. Existing English bishops would lose part of their revenues – not, it is true, from land, because the dioceses were to be funded out of former monastic land, but from the loss of large areas over which they had had jurisdiction and had therefore drawn fees of various kinds. And there was more than money involved. One of the strongest traditions of the English episcopacy had to do with the intense loyalty of its members to the dioceses over which they presided. Anselm's *cri de coeur* at the end of the eleventh century, that he 'would not dare to appear before the judgment seat of God with the rights of [his] see diminished' expresses an attitude that was very much alive in early sixteenth-century England.[3] Whether this was 'well' depends on one's point of view, but it was certainly central to the serious quarrels discussed earlier between both Morton and Warham as archbishops of Canterbury and their suffragans.

So for one reason or another, some opposition could be expected from the existing bishops. The position of the monastic institutions to be affected was more complicated. If they were to close down altogether, then serious objections, perhaps even physical resistance, might be forthcoming. When in the summer of 1525 the Premonstratensian monastery of Bayham in Sussex was suppressed in order that its revenues might form part of the endowments of Cardinal College, some of the monks staged a forcible reoccupation of their former home. Admittedly it only lasted for a week, but if it could happen at a comparatively small house such as Bayham, what might not result if more powerful houses were to come under the axe? Moreover, a feature of 'the riot of Bayham' was the close involvement of local laymen, in particular the head of a leading local family, that controversial figure, Lord Bergavenny.[4] This may serve as a reminder of the close connection between religious houses and local inhabitants at every level. Apart from any spiritual pull that they may have exercised, the religious houses provided employment and were a source of loans and gifts of charity. Many leading families had a long tradition of involvement with a particular house: perhaps an ancestor had founded it, or at any rate there was a family tradition to be buried there. Families like the Nevilles at Bayham would have expected to act as protectors to the house they were associated with, so that anyone with designs on a monastic house was not just taking on a

[6] *LP*,iv,5235.

[1] Rymer,iv, p.294.
[2] It may be that I have not understood all of them, despite generous help from Dr P. Chaplais.
[3] Southern, p.186.
[4] Goring, *Sussex Archaeological Collections*, CXVI.

small, isolated group of unworldly individuals, but a whole nexus of vested interests which might include some of the most powerful in the land. And it is worth recalling that the most serious rebellion that the Tudors ever faced, the Pilgrimage of Grace of 1536-7, had a lot to do with the suppression of monasteries.

What Wolsey was proposing to do was fraught with difficulty, both politically and legally. A modern parallel would be the public inquiries set up in response to government schemes for building major roads or airports, at which every conceivable kind of objection is raised, almost all of them partial. And in the end, whatever the modifications or concessions made as a result, for the scheme to be implemented some of the objections have to be ignored or overridden. Faced with this kind of situation, Wolsey would have had no illusions about the difficulties. Hence his concern to exclude the clause in the bull which insisted on the agreement of all those with a rightful interest – a clause which in effect would have prevented any changes taking place. Although it is not known what constitutions he intended for the new cathedrals, by allowing for the possibility that they might retain a monastic character he was in a position not only to threaten but also to bribe. It was one thing for a monastery to be suppressed, but quite another for it to be turned into a cathedral presided over by the former abbot as bishop with the monks as canons.

It may be felt that this interpretation of Wolsey's negotiations with the Curia and of the resulting bulls has been much too favourable to him. One could just as easily cite these same things as evidence of the megalomaniacal Wolsey determined to trample upon other people's rights. Powerful figures attract such conflicting opinions that probably no amount of evidence can resolve them because value judgements are so much involved. For some people any degree of arbitrariness is unacceptable, but in doing so they preclude almost any achievement. Most are prepared to put up with some, and reserve most concern for the ends in view, which in this case brings us back to the question that Clement himself raised, whether or not there was any need for the major reorganization of diocesan boundaries that Wolsey was proposing.

The answer can only be guess-work. None of the surviving evidence throws any light on the matter. Indeed, there appears to be no pre-history to Wolsey's plans: no previous discussions in convocation or any other clerical assembly, and no reference by anyone to the need for such an increase. This is both frustrating and surprising. Many English bishoprics were large, those of York and Lincoln especially so.[1] The larger the diocese, the more difficult it was for the bishop to make a personal impact and to be, as Colet wanted, 'living unto us'.[2] One who seems to have shared Colet's views was John Fisher. In a dedicatory letter to his fellow bishop, Richard Fox, he wrote that he did not envy his colleagues their wealthier sees – and Fox was the occupant of the wealthiest. Fisher was quite happy with his poor see of Rochester because it permitted him to exercise a close personal supervision; and since he stayed at Rochester for so long he probably meant what he wrote.[3] What he never seems to have done was to draw any general conclusions from this and advocate the

---

[1] Hughes, p.33 for the size of English dioceses.
[2] Lupton, p.299 from Colet's convocation sermon.
[3] Richard Fox, pp.153-4; Surtz, *Works and Days*, pp.54 ff; S. Thompson, 'Bishop in his diocese', pp.69-70.

kind of diocesan reform that Wolsey envisaged. That Longland, bishop of Lincoln, did not do so is less of a surprise, for any reform would have resulted in just that diminution in the wealth and privileges of his diocese that bishops saw it as their duty to resist. Nevertheless, it was almost certainly the very size of his huge diocese of Lincoln, with its 1,736 parishes and 111 religious houses, extending from the Thames to the Humber, that forced him to limit his personal role in diocesan life. At any rate, he seems to have confined his personal interventions to the religious houses in his diocese and to the cathedral itself. Yet Longland took his episcopal office seriously, and he must have had some inkling that he could have been a much better bishop if his diocese had been smaller, as indeed in the 1540s it was to become.[1]

Before condemning the episcopal bench of the 1520s for their self-interest and lack of imagination, it is necessary to point out that what may be involved is not their failings but rather the inadequacy of the surviving evidence. Just as almost nothing of what went on at Wolsey's legatine meetings has been preserved, so it is with any episcopal correspondence that might touch upon diocesan life. Thus silence on this particular issue cannot be made too much of: the sampling is just too small. Moreover, for Wolsey to have got his scheme for diocesan reform to the stage of conducting lengthy negotiations with pope and Curia, some discussion must surely have gone on with leading churchmen at home, even if the initiative came from him. Moreover there is a prima facie case for stating that almost any scheme for diocesan reform was a good one. If a bishop was to be the active shepherd of his flock, as Colet and Fisher wished him to be, he would have to involve himself in regular visitations of his parishes and monastic houses. With a diocese the size of Lincoln or York, this was virtually impossible.[2] With a diocese like Rochester, or even one a little larger, such as Chichester where Robert Sherburne was a very active resident bishop, it was a much more practical proposition.[3]

It is only possible to make an informed guess at how radical a change in the size of the dioceses Wolsey had in mind. When plans for the creation of new ones were revived in the late 1530s, two men who had been very close to Wolsey, namely Stephen Gardiner and Richard Sampson, took a leading part in drawing them up. Given that in April 1529 Gardiner had discussed Wolsey's plans with the pope, it seems inconceivable that ten years later when he and Sampson were asked to provide new plans they did not draw heavily on the old ones. Gardiner's list of 1539 indicates that as many as sixteen new dioceses were considered; another, in Henry's own hand, named thirteen. What seems to have been envisaged was that diocesan boundaries should coincide as far as possible with those of the counties. Thus, in Henry's list the county, or in some cases two, are given first. Then come the religious house or houses that were to be used to form the new diocese; the abbey church – and if more than one was involved a choice would have to be made – would become the new cathedral, its lands would provide the necessary endowments. For example, Westminster Abbey and its lands would be used to

---

[1] Bowker, *Henrician Reformation*.

[2] But Longland's predecessor, Atwater, made a good attempt, helped by the fact that, unlike Longland, he was free of court commitments; see Bowker, *Secular Clergy*, pp.85-154.

[3] For Fisher at Rochester see S. Thompson, 'Bishop in diocese'; for Sherburne see S.J. Lander, 'Diocese of Chichester'.

create a diocese of Middlesex, while to create a diocese of Bedfordshire and Buckinghamshire, two monasteries, Dunstable and Newnham, and one nunnery, Elstow, were to be used. In the event Henry's ardour for diocesan reform quickly peaked, and only six new dioceses were formed, one of which, Westminster, was quickly abandoned. However, there is no doubting the radical nature of the plans as put forward in 1539, and there is only slightly less doubt that these were the same plans that Wolsey had drawn up ten years earlier.[1]

It could be that, like Henry's, Wolsey's ardour might have cooled when faced with the task of implementing such a major undertaking, but if so, there would at least have been some justification. As far as Henry was concerned, the monasteries were to go anyway, so that the very real argument that such a major undertaking would cause too much disruption, and therefore opposition, could hardly have been used. With Wolsey, though, the very selectivity of the exercise would make resistance easier, as each monastery put up a case for its own salvation and another house's destruction. The prospect of such resistance would have encouraged Wolsey to be cautious. On the other hand, he was not faced with the temptation that faced Henry, and to which he succumbed, of using the revenues of religious houses not for the creation of new dioceses but for much more secular purposes. And it is perhaps worth making the point that none of Wolsey's reforms ever envisaged the wholesale transference of ecclesiastical funds to secular, or indeed private, purposes – and this can be extended to Catholic reform in general. Still, the main point remains that the evidence of the schemes put forward in 1539 strongly suggests that what Wolsey had in mind was a dramatic increase in the number of dioceses and a consequent decrease in their size, thereby providing the English bishops with a much better opportunity of making a personal impact on their dioceses.

The second major reform that Wolsey was planning to undertake in the last eighteen months before he lost office was some change in the size and number of monastic houses. As with the plans for the dioceses, information about what precisely he had in mind is very meagre, essentially just the relevant bulls and one or two references in letters between himself and the English envoys at Rome. The original bull of 12 November 1528 enabled Wolsey to unite any monastic institution with less than twelve inmates with one that had more.[2] Nine months later, and after considerable badgering, Wolsey persuaded the pope to grant him a second bull, empowering him to unite houses with less than twelve people with similar houses, in order to create a house of more than twelve.[3] Obviously, Wolsey intended to take some action, but the bulls themselves do not greatly help to answer the more interesting question of what precisely he had in mind. He could have been merely seeking reserve powers enabling him to take action when the need arose, perhaps just to tidy up the odds and ends after the new dioceses had been created. Alternatively, he may have intended a major reorganization. Marginally, it is the latter that seems the more likely, for the efforts taken to obtain the necessary powers, and especially the insistence on the second bull giving that greater

---

[1] Transcripts and some facsimiles of the 1539 plans are to be found in Cole; see also *LP*,xiv (2), 428, 430. There are considerable variations; hence the difficulty in arriving at a final total.

[2] Rymer, xiv, pp.272-3.

[3] Ibid, p.345; for the badgering see *LP*,iv, 5607, 5639.

flexibility, would otherwise look disproportionate.

The reason why the number twelve was fixed upon was almost certainly because it had traditionally been taken as the ideal, being the number of Christ's disciples. The Cistercian order, in particular, insisted that no house should consist of less than twelve together with the head, extending the analogy to include Christ, and by and large they kept to it. Sometimes the ideal was more honoured in the breach than in the observance, especially by the Augustinian order, amongst whose houses were many very small ones, often with as few as two or three canons. About 55 per cent of its houses would have been liable to reorganization under the provision of Wolsey's bulls,[1] and it may be that it was precisely in order to do something about the small Augustinian houses that the bull was obtained. Be that as it may, there does, as in the case of the diocesan bulls, seem to be a prima facie case for believing that Wolsey's intentions were honourable. There was to be no financial gain for himself, and conversely no loss to the orders affected, not even by diversion of their revenues to other quasi-religious ends. Moreover, and most compelling, the bulls did seem to address themselves to a genuine problem.

Not all small religious houses were composed of unsatisfactory inmates, while many large ones had their fair share. When in July 1514 Bishop Nix visited the Augustinian priory of Walsingham, he found its affairs in grave disorder largely because of the prior, who not only had a mistress but was also very much under the influence of two disreputable servants.[2] Clearly, neither its size – in 1514 there were twenty-nine canons and two novices – nor its prestige as the home of one of the most famous shrines in England had done anything to improve the religious life of the community. On the other hand, in the same year Hempton, with only a prior and three canons and with an annual revenue of £32 as compared with Walsingham's minimum of £400, was found to be in reasonably good order, the only complaint being that on days when the canons were not occupied in manual work they received nothing to eat until after High Mass, which could be thought to have been rather to its credit.[3] Size, therefore, was not everything, but there was something in the point made in the preamble to Wolsey's two bulls, that if numbers and income fell below a certain level then even the very minimal observance of the daily round of services and intercession was more difficult to perform. If more was expected, then the problems multiplied. The smaller the community the more difficult it was for any kind of scholarly or intellectual life to flourish, because not only were the chances of there being someone with the requisite ability, to act as teacher for instance, much less than in a large establishment, but it was more difficult to provide what we nowadays refer to as 'resources', primarily in the early sixteenth century manuscripts and, increasingly, the comparatively new educational resource, the printed book. Moreover, it needs to be stressed that members of the regular orders were not supposed to be hermits leading solitary lives of prayer and ascetic practices. Rather, their task was to play an active role in a corporate life governed by a rule, and the very notion of a corporate life suggests more than two or three people.

---

[1] My own rough calculation based on Knowles and Hadcock.
[2] *Visitations of Norwich*, pp.113-22.
[3] Ibid, pp.112-13.

An anonymous late sixteenth-century writer lovingly recreated the daily life of the Benedictine monks of Durham Cathedral Priory on the eve of the Reformation. Not only were they surrounded by a kaleidoscope of colour from the gold and marble and precious jewels, by images and shrines, by pyxes and candles, by solemn services and holy anthems, but they were 'always most virtuously occupied, never idle, but either writing of good and godly works or studying the Holy Scriptures to the setting forth of the honour and glory of God, and for the edifying of the people'.[1] Undoubtedly the picture is all the more idealized for the writer by the destruction and disappearance by his time of the corporate life it describes, but the ideal is worth bearing in mind when we try to understand likely attitudes to the great number of small religious houses that coexisted with the larger ones like Durham. Admittedly, not all religious orders placed the same emphasis on liturgical display as the Benedictines, but it was the Carthusians, interestingly, with their quite different emphasis on private devotion and study who more than any other order adhered to the ideal of twelve.[2] The ideal number for a successful corporate life, whether of ritual or private devotion, is, of course, debatable. But it is difficult not to believe that Durham represented considerably more 'prayer power' – and at the heart of all forms of the religious life was, after all, prayer – than, say, the little priory of Weybourne in Norfolk with, in 1514, just two canons.[3] And even if a large house like Walsingham could go spectacularly wrong, it also stood a much better chance of living up to the ideal of its rule, and acting as a beacon of spiritual light.

There was, therefore, a lot to be said for a comprehensive reorganization of the monastic institutions. Moreover, this is not just a twentieth-century view. The need for a complete overhaul was discussed in almost all the important reform proposals of the fifteenth and sixteenth centuries. Pierre d'Ailly had raised the matter in his *Tractatus de Reformatione ecclesiae* presented to the Council of Constance in 1416.[4] It is also to be found in the *Libellus ad Leonum x* presented by Tommaso Giustiniani and Vincenzo Quirini to the Fifth Lateran Council in 1513,[5] and then again in probably the most famous of all proposals for Catholic reform, the *Consilium de emendanda ecclesia* of 1537.[6] All these proposals touched upon much more than just the problem to which Wolsey's bulls addressed themselves, that of the size of religious houses; and now may be the right moment to widen the discussion in an effort to answer the question of what Wolsey's attitude to the monastic orders as a whole might have been, and this in turn will lead on to a serious attempt to assess Wolsey as a religious reformer.

A central concern of all these proposals for monastic reform had to do with the relationship between the religious orders and the secular clergy, and in particular with the way this was affected by the exemption from episcopal jurisdiction possessed by so many religious orders. Most Catholic reformers considered such exemption to be harmful, so that in using his legatine powers to override it, Wolsey

---

[1] *Durham*, but much of it in Knowles, *Religious Orders*, iii, pp.129-37.
[2] Knowles, *Religious Orders*, ii, p.259.
[3] VCH, Norfolk, ii, 405, *Visitation of Norwich*, p.123-4.
[4] Oakley, pp.307-8.
[5] Jedin, i, pp.129-30.
[6] Ibid, i, pp.424-6.

was going with the current of reform, if in an idiosyncratic way: the bishops were still barred from intervening directly, but they were now in a position to call upon Wolsey to do so and, as was shown earlier, at least one bishop, Longland, is known to have done so, and more than once. Another concern was with the multiplicity of the religious orders themselves, and there was a general consensus that a good deal of weeding out might profitably be done. There is no direct evidence that Wolsey had any plans in this direction, but if he was seriously thinking of redrawing the monastic map of England, it would have simplified his task of regrouping the smaller houses if the orders to which they belonged could be ignored; and in this way one reform would have suggested another.

What also worried reformers is that not nearly enough effort was being taken to ensure that those who entered the religious orders were suited for what should be a demanding life. Inevitably the quality of that life declined and, especially worrying, the orders' rule had to be accommodated to the low standard of entry. The severest critics had come from within the orders, and one result had been the emergence of the 'observant' orders dedicated to the recovery of the spirit and form of the original rule. These had attracted the patronage of wealthy laymen, including many of the rulers of Europe. It is possible to be cynical about this; just as with cars, the wealthy like to be seen with the latest model, and no doubt a desire for kudos was involved. Alternatively, and perhaps only a little less cynically, it may be that they were in search of an insurance policy against damnation, and if they could buy the best, why not! More relevant here is the possibility that the rulers at least saw the Observants and such associated orders as the famous 'Congregation of Windesheim' as the driving force for more wide-ranging reform. Certainly periods of religious revival were often associated with the religious orders. In the tenth and eleventh centuries it had been Cluny and the Benedictines who had led the way, and in the thirteenth it had been the Friars. Could the same thing happen in the sixteenth century? There were people, both then and since, who have thought no; the religious orders had served their turn and had become obsolete. But the enormous success of the Jesuits in second half of the sixteenth century is proof positive that it could.

But what of Wolsey? Did he see the religious orders as an instrument of reform? Well, not if his treatment of the Observant Franciscans is anything to go by, and, with the possible exception of the Carthusians, it was this order, much favoured by both Edward IV and Henry VII, that would have been the most obvious choice to perform such a role. A reformer worth his salt should surely have made use of them, but on the contrary we have seen how Wolsey had become embroiled in conflict with them over his right to conduct a legatine visitation of their Greenwich house, and in the end went to considerable lengths to put them in their place.[1] Moreover, his readiness to use monastic endowments for his educational foundations, and his proposal to use them to create new dioceses suggests that, far from assigning the religious orders a special role, he was disenchanted with them. One could cite this as yet another example of his lack of genuine Christian concern were it not for the fact that fellow countrymen, whose credentials were beyond reproach, seem to have shared his disenchantment.

When the great historian of the religious orders in England, David Knowles,

[1] See p.275 ff. above.

came to answer the question of whether or not those of the Tudor age had deserved their fate, he came as near as makes no difference to saying that they did. It is not that he concluded that all was bad, but rather that there was just not enough that was good to resist the onslaught when, in the 1530s, it came. As a member of a religious order himself, he must have found this a painful conclusion, but it may also be that his very membership led him to be over-critical because his expectations were too high. It is also true that in the 1950s when he was writing the last volume of *The Religious Orders* a much gloomier view of all aspects of the late medieval Church was taken than is the case today. By and large, it is no longer felt that that Church was failing to meet spiritual and pastoral needs, or, to put it another way, that it was out of date – and behind Knowles's disappointment lurks the notion that the religious orders had become just that. If the work was to be done again from today's different perspective, a more optimistic view might emerge. That said, however, Knowles's conclusions still remain persuasive.

Even for Knowles there were bright spots. These included the Franciscan Observants and the Carthusians, and also the Bridgettines, represented in England, however, by only one house, albeit the most distinguished abbey of Syon, home not only of Richard Whitford, one of the few published defenders of the religious against the attacks of Luther and Tyndale, but also of the martyr Richard Reynolds.[1] And if martyrdom is a test of the vitality of religious belief, it is a test which points precisely to these three orders.[2] Of those monks who took part in the Pilgrimage of Grace, the most open resistance to the religious changes of the 1530s, the Cistercians were the most prominent. Admittedly they were much more strongly represented in the North than elsewhere, and statistically one would expect to find quite a high percentage of them in any sample of Northern monks. Nevertheless, there are some grounds for thinking that the Cistercians were in reasonably good health and in Marmaduke Huby, abbot of Fountains from 1494 to 1526, they could claim one of the most distinguished monastic figures of the early sixteenth century.[3] What may also tell in their favour is that in the early 1530s Cromwell was prepared to go to some lengths to bring down a successor of Huby at Fountains, William Thirsk, and the abbot of nearby Rievaulx, Edward Kirkby, both of whom took some part in the Pilgrimage.[4] Finally, it is worth mentioning that even the possibly complacent and compliant Benedictines included at least three 'martyrs' and, if this seems too few, they were at least some of the most eminent representatives of their order. One was Richard Whiting who presided over Glastonbury, the second wealthiest abbey in England, and under his rule a model of what a Benedictine abbey should have been.[5]

But when all is said and done, nowhere in England was there the kind of spiritual intensity and rigorous discipline to be found at this time on the continent, in particular in those houses that came into contact with the Augustinian canons of

---

[1] Knowles, *Religious Orders*, iii, pp.212-21. Curiously Knowles made no mention of Whitford's *The Pype or Tonne of the Lyfe of Perfection*.

[2] Knowles, *Religious Orders*, pp.182-91, 206-11.

[3] Ibid, pp.28-38.

[4] This my own interpretation of these episodes, which unfortunately space has not allowed me to develop; but for a different view see Elton, *JEH*, 7.

[5] Paul, *BIHR*, xxxiii, pp.115-19.

Windesheim in the Low Countries. It was a group of these canons led by Jan Mombaer, author of a famous spiritual treatise, the *Rosetum*, that in 1496 had been summoned to France by Jean Standonck, principal of the College of Montaigu, to spearhead that movement for reform behind which, as legate *a latere* from 1501 to 1510, Cardinal d'Amboise was to put his own authority and that of the French Crown. The similarities between d'Amboise and Wolsey are many, not least that behind the acquisition of both men's legatine authority lay the desire of their respective monarchs to dominate the Church. However, in his reliance on the Windesheimers and other monastic reform movements in France d'Amboise clearly differs, as he does in another important respect. Whatever the virtues of d'Amboise's support for monastic reform, it was met by so much opposition both from the religious orders and the parlement of Paris that for his last six years he was virtually a lame-duck legate. In contrast, Wolsey, as we saw earlier, experienced little opposition from anyone, least of all from the religious orders, amongst whom only the Franciscan Observants showed any real unease. Should this be taken as evidence of a lukewarm Wolsey who, unlike his French counterpart, was unwilling to grapple with the real problems of reform, or is it merely that he was a more skilful operator than d'Amboise? In fact, neither a moralistic nor an expediential judgment is appropriate, for the answer probably lies in the very different circumstances. While the French religious orders may have been more vigorous and more powerful and so better able to resist any interference, they also showed many more signs of grave disorder. Consequently, there was not only a greater need to intervene but also a much greater likelihood that any intervention would result in conflict, especially in view of the powerful opposition of the French parlement, an institution for which there was no equivalent in England.[1]

While d'Amboise was battling with the problems of reform in France, another and more famous cardinal was doing the same in Spain. Like his French counterpart but unlike Wolsey, Cardinal Ximenes saw the religious orders as the key to reform. At a comparatively late stage in his life he had become a Franciscan Observant and was always noted for his extreme asceticism. There can be little doubt that Ximenes's religion was very different from either d'Amboise's or Wolsey's, despite the latter's hairshirt, but differences in the Spanish background too are also very important. In Ximenes's time the religious life of the Spanish peninsula was dominated by the continuing presence of a large Muslim population, given both a real and symbolic focus by the Moorish kingdom of Granada until its reconquest by Ferdinand and Isabella in 1492. The enormous crusading energy unleashed by the *reconquista* continued to fuel the engine of Spanish imperialism throughout the sixteenth century. It also, and more relevantly, explains much about the religious sensibilities of Spain. Ximenes himself was both a product and an architect of this crusading spirit. A zealot himself, he could count upon considerable grass-roots support for the kind of fervent reform associated with the Observant movements. What is also true is that, given the imperatives of reconquest, there was a close identification between the Spanish Crown and Church, which made opposition to reform more difficult than, for instance, in France.[2]

---

[1] The *locus classicus* for all this is Renaudet; and for opposition to d'Amboise see ibid, pp.326 ff. For a useful introduction to the Windesheim canons see Oakley, pp.102 ff.

To state that the particular conditions in the Spanish peninsula and in France have to be taken into account may seem to be stating the obvious, but it is curious how often the obvious is overlooked. People like their religious reformers to look the part, and in this respect Ximenes scores heavily over both his French and English counterparts. But in France and England there was no Moorish kingdom and hence no crusade, and in neither of these countries is it conceivable that a Franciscan Observant zealot could ever have become the monarch's chief adviser. What is also true is that in comparison with France and Spain even the best of English monasticism appears a little low key, which may provide one reason why Wolsey did not make significant use of it to further reform.

Another reason may have a lot to do with chronology. Even by the time of d'Amboise's death in 1510, serious doubts were being entertained in some quarters of France, not just about the likelihood of the success of monastic reform but its value. One reason for this was the growing influence of Erasmus and the humanist movement associated with him; and with the increasing number of humanist publications in the decade after d'Amboise's death the doubts could only have grown. Indicative of this is the fact that in the preface to the 1518 edition of his *Enchiridion*, dedicated to the Benedictine abbot of Hügshofen, Paul Volz, Erasmus felt obliged to defend himself against the accusation that his book was intended to turn men's minds against the monastic life – not that the defence could have carried much conviction, since only a few paragraphs later he launched into one of his most sustained attacks on the religious orders.[1] It was in that year, 1518, that Wolsey first acquired his legatine powers and began seriously to turn his attention to the problems of the English Church. If he read Erasmus's preface, he would not have been encouraged to place monastic reform of the kind that d'Amboise and Ximenes had envisaged at the top of his agenda. But if, as seems more likely, he did not read it, there were plenty of people in England who almost certainly did, people who were not only friends of Erasmus but who were also known to, and in some cases worked closely with, Wolsey. Given that so little that offers any insight into Wolsey's mind has survived, these people's thoughts on such matters may be the nearest that we can get to his.

Someone who was close to Wolsey and at least corresponded with Erasmus, was John Longland, and of all the English humanists it is he who has the best claim to be called a friend of the religious orders. It will be remembered that in 1519 he delivered to the monks of Westminster Wolsey's and Campeggio's visitation sermon, a passionate exhortation for them to live up to the high ideals of their rule. On becoming bishop of Lincoln in 1521 he spent a good deal of time trying to improve the quality of life of the religious in his diocese, amongst other things probably providing the nuns of his diocese with a compendium of the rule of St Benedict drawn up by the famous abbot of Wincombe, Richard Kidderminster. That said, however, it remains difficult to become very excited by Longland's efforts. The impression is very much of a conscientious bishop in an over-large diocese deciding to concentrate on an area in which he felt he could make the best

[2] Elliott, pp. 33 ff. and Oakley, pp. 247-51.

[1] ECW, 6, pp. 86-90.

use of his time. Of monastic reform as a means by which to inspire a religious revival in his diocese, let alone his country, there is no hint.[1]

Much closer to Erasmus was Thomas More, though in his earlier days at least he was much more attracted to the religious life than his friend was. At any rate, far from having to battle to free himself of it as Erasmus had, for a time More may have even have contemplated entering the Carthusian order. Yet when some years later a Carthusian presumed to attack Erasmus's *New Testament*, he received the full force of More's scorn, not only for his lack of learning but also for his very calling as a monk, 'as if to reside for ever in the same spot and, like a clam or sponge, to cling eternally to the same rock were the ultimate of sanctity'.[2] And when, in the late 1520s and early 1530s, More felt compelled to take up his pen in defence of the Catholic Church, he had very little to say in defence of the religious life, even though wherever in Europe the Protestant reformers had gained control that life had been destroyed. Admittedly, when he came to be imprisoned in the Tower he informed his daughter, Meg, that if his captors had thought to displease him by locking him up, they had made a great mistake because, but for the love of his family, he 'would not have failed long ere this to have closed myself in as strait a room and straiter, too'.[3] To see this, however, as compelling evidence of a deep yearning for the monastic life is probably to ignore More's love of irony and his concern to comfort Meg.[4] Indeed, his *A Dialogue of Comfort* written while in the Tower is essentially a defence of the active life.

But what of More's fellow martyr and saint, John Fisher? Like Longland, he seems to have taken a genuine interest in the religious houses in his diocese, especially in his cathedral priory, but neither in his great polemical writings nor in his two famous sermons against Luther did he choose to make any significant defence of the monastic ideal. Moreover, like Wolsey he was quite prepared to have religious houses suppressed, although on nothing like the same scale, in order to help finance new university colleges.[5] Perhaps even more to the point, the purpose of these colleges was not to fit men for the life of the cloister, but, as Fisher himself reminded the university of Cambridge in 1528, to enable them to go out into the world and preach the Gospel of Christ.[6]

More modest in his intellectual and spirtual attainments than More and Fisher, though to that extent a more representative figure, was Richard Fox. However, his thirty years at the centre of politics had not prevented him from taking an interest in religious matters. As bishop of Winchester he had been no enemy to the religious orders, except insofar as he endeavoured to impose a stricter observance of their rules which, as we saw earlier, earned him a mild rebuke from Wolsey, who wondered whether more allowances should not be made for human fraility.[7] As we have also seen, Fox was the founder of Corpus Christi, Oxford, whose outstanding

---

[1] My assessment is based on Bowker, *Henrician Reformation*, pp.13-28.

[2] Thomas More, *Selected Letters*, p.137, but the whole letter needs to be read. For the identification of the monk see Knowles, *Religious Orders*, p.469.

[3] Roper, p.76.

[4] For such a view see Marius, p.465, in my opinion an almost perverse interpretation of More's life.

[5] Knowles, *Religious Orders*, p.157. For Wolsey's involvement in Fisher's suppressions see *LP*, iii,1690.

[6] Surtz, *Works and Days*, pp.180-93.

[7] See p.323 above.

feature was its promotion of humanist learning. Apparently his original intention had been to establish a college for the monks of his cathedral priory, similar to other monastic colleges such as Durham and Gloucester, until he had the following conversation with Hugh Oldham, bishop of Exeter:

> 'What! My lord, shall we build houses and provide livelihoods for a company of buzzing monks, whose end and fall we ourselves may live to see? No, no. It is more meet to provide for the increase of learning and for such as who, by their learning, shall do good in the Church and commonwealth'.[1]

Oldham's prescience about the fate of the monasteries is suspicious, and the story may well be an invention of the editor of the 1577 edition of Holinshed's *Chronicles*, in which it first appeared. On the other hand, there is evidence that Fox did originally make plans for a monastic college, while Oldham was a close enough friend of his to contribute a large sum towards it, so the story cannot be dismissed out of hand. And whether true or false, it is undeniable that in the early sixteenth century the foundation of Oxbridge colleges was more fashionable than the foundation of new monasteries.

What has emerged so far is that not only was there nothing much about the English religious orders to suggest that they could be used as a jumping-off point for widespread reform, but that this was appreciated by those in a position to influence policy making. Wolsey could hardly have been unaffected by this disenchantment amongst at least some sections of informed opinion. What one really wants to know is how far this disenchantment fuelled his specific proposals for major reform in 1528-9, which brings us back to the question raised in chapter 8 of whether it makes any sense to call Wolsey a humanist reformer. The very cautious answer then was that while there was no evidence for any strong commitment to humanism at a personal level, at the level of policy there was enough to suggest that he was anxious to make use of humanist ideas to further reform.[2] Could it be that his schemes for 1528-9 provide more evidence of this?

One way of tackling the question is to try to calculate the consequences to monastic life of all the proposals that Wolsey was considering in 1528-9. Such an exercise involves a good many variables but to begin with we will assume the worst. By this reckoning, the creation of the new dioceses would have resulted in a loss of monastic revenue of about £19,500 a year.[3] To provide endowments for Cardinal College and Ipswich, Wolsey had by the time of his fall suppressed twenty-nine houses whose total annual revenue amounted to about £2,220, a sum equivalent to the revenues of one of the larger abbeys, such as St Albans. In addition, in November 1528 Wolsey obtained a bull enabling him to suppress monasteries to the total value of 8,000 ducats (about £1,750) to provide further endowments for the royal colleges of Eton and Cambridge. All this adds up to a potential loss for the religious orders in the region of £23,500, or 17 per cent of their total annual revenue

---

[1] Quoted in Mumford, p.108.
[2] See pp.340-6 above.
[3] In arriving at this figure I have assumed that all the new cathedrals would have been staffed by secular canons and that all 25 houses mentioned in the 1539 proposals would have been used.

of £136,361, as assessed in the Valor Ecclesiasticus of 1535. About a hundred monastic institutions would have ceased to exist, though in some cases their buildings would have continued to be put to religious purposes. A much larger but unknowable number would have been affected by Wolsey's plans to reorganize all houses containing less than twelve people. At the very least, therefore, such changes would have been noticed, particularly since some of the most famous religious houses in England would have ceased to function.

Is this unambiguous evidence, at last, for the kind of radical and humanist reform that the English Church was supposedly in need of? Perhaps not, but, even if we make a much more modest calculation of the possible effects of his 1528-9 proposals, it is indisputable that Wolsey did not see religious houses as inviolable, but rather as institutions whose usefulness needed to be periodically reassessed and whose wealth could be diverted if the need arose. In thinking thus he differed little from Thomas Starkey, the young humanist product of his own former college, Magdalen, who having spent time in one of the magic circles of European intellectual life, the household in Padua of Henry's cousin and future cardinal, Reginald Pole, had returned to England in the early 1530s to offer his services to the cause of reform. Starkey never advocated the complete destruction of the monasteries, but instead assigned to them a modest role as places where, on reaching the age of thirty, the select few could spend their remaining years in study and prayer. He envisaged the great bulk of monastic wealth being reallocated by the Crown to current educational and social needs – a reallocation which, he argued, the original founders and subsequent benefactors would be sympathetic to, as long as it was to the benefit of the common weal.[1] Admittedly Starkey envisaged using some of the money for such essentially secular purposes as poor relief. Wolsey did not, but, given that he was willing to make that most difficult first step of reinterpreting past benefactors' wishes, in the very different circumstances of the 1530s he might well have come to agree with Starkey that such purposes were godly enough to justify widespread suppression.

All this is speculation. What is not is that there are some similarities between what both Wolsey and Starkey were proposing to do with the monasteries. This does not make Wolsey into a fully-fledged humanist reformer; there are just too many qualifications for that, including the almost total lack of evidence for the kind of personal involvement with classical literature, the early Fathers, or the new biblical scholarship that are the humanist's hallmark. Moreover, the radical nature of Wolsey's 1528-9 proposals has so far been deliberately exaggerated in order to raise questions that have been too frequently ignored. The 17 per cent reduction in monastic revenues that they could have resulted in was very much an optimum figure: it need not have been anywhere near as much. Even if he had been aiming so high, the assets of the religious orders would have remained considerable. All that Wolsey's proposals would have resulted in, even at their most ambitious, was a slimmer and sounder version of the existing set-up – and this does seem a little different from the 'certain monasteries and abbeys' that Starkey wished to retain merely as a 'great comfort to many feeble and weary souls which have been oppressed with worldly vanity'.[2] That there were differences is not nearly so

---

[1] Thomas Starkey, p.140; Herrtage, pp.liii ff.

surprising as the fact that there were similarities. Wolsey was, after all, a considerably older man, whose formative years were free of the Erasmian influences that coloured Starkey's views. More importantly, however much he may later have been attracted by such influences, Wolsey remained first and foremost a man of affairs who had to take reponsibility for the effects of any changes he might make, unlike Starkey, who at most only ever became a propagandist and backroom adviser. Responsibility encourages caution. The suggestion here would be that when he became legate in 1518 Wolsey had no blueprint for reform, whether of the religious orders or other areas of the Church. Rather, he was anxious to ensure that everything was functioning as well as possible; and, as we have seen, in a number of ways he worked to that end: new constitutions were drawn up, care was taken over appointments to religious houses, some unsatisfactory heads were removed and, above all, no religious house could hide behind its right to exemption from episcopal jurisdiction. It was a measured and by and large conservative approach, deliberately designed to minimize opposition. On the other hand, Wolsey was sufficiently influenced by humanist ideas to see the provision of education, in which the new studies were assigned a prominent part, rather than any dramatic revival of the religious orders, as the way forward. Or to put it more simply, it was on the fellows of Cardinal College rather than on the friars of Greenwich that Wolsey pinned his hopes. But in the late 1520s the pace quickened, as he contemplated redrawing the diocesan map of England, funding the changes from monastic wealth. The question is, why?

It would be wrong to ignore the possibility that no more is required to explain the 1528-9 proposals than that Wolsey's interventions in church affairs had built up a momentum of their own. Not only might Wolsey have needed time to assess what reforms were needed, but he also had to ensure that the legatine machinery was securely in place, and it should be remembered that, though Wolsey first acquired his legatine powers in 1518, it was not until 1524 that they were granted to him for life and that his compositions with the bishops were finally secured. Admittedly, there was then a three-year pause before the momentum picked up again, but it is not all that long a time, especially since the Church was by no means Wolsey's only concern. Nevertheless, there is a further, and probably more compelling, explanation: the threat of Lutheranism, which, though present since 1521, was not a dominant concern until the arrival in England of William Tyndale's New Testament in early 1526. In the fight against this new heresy the bishops would be expected to play a leading part, just as they had for many years in the fight against Lollardy.[1] More often than not the early sixteenth-century bishop took personal control of any heresy trial within his diocese. He was also responsible for the detection and suppression of heretical literature. The larger the diocese, the more difficult it was for a bishop effectively to perform this role of defender of the Faith, something which was explicitly acknowledged by southern convocation in 1532 when it explained the necessity for bishops to appoint preachers to act as their pastoral representatives: 'in these dangerous times', it was vital that people heard the true

---

[2] Thomas Starkey, p.140.

[1] S. Thompson, 'English and Welsh bishops', pp.121-44.

word of God and the size of his diocese made it impossible for a bishop alone to bring it to them.[1] Moreover, the greater the threat of heresy, the more anxious was the Church to forestall criticism, and perhaps royal intervention, by carrying out reform itself. Arguably, the many small monasteries were an easy target for such criticism and thus the pressure on Wolsey to do something about them.[2] The reform proposals of 1528-9 are thus best understood in the context of a number of measures designed to counter the threat of Lutheranism. But for such an argument to carry conviction it is necessary to believe that Wolsey took the Lutheran threat seriously, and this most historians have been reluctant to do.

There are many reasons for this. Some have been reluctant to believe that Wolsey could take seriously anything that was not directly related to his own self-interest and personal aggrandizement. On the other hand, some have taken the view that, unlike so many of contemporaries, Wolsey was far too sane and sensible to want to burn people, and, indeed, under his benign rule nobody was or so (wrongly) they have alleged.[3] Since Wolsey's supposed toleration of heresy is one of the few aspects of his character that called forth praise, it may seem perverse for a sympathetic biographer to cast doubt on it, but doubt there has to be, especially since the benign view is most frequently advanced to make a stick with which to beat Sir Thomas More, who, unlike Wolsey, was supposedly a fanatic.[4] The fanatical More is a curious construct, designed to make it easier for the Protestant or secular mind to come to terms with the opposition by someone with as high a reputation as More to something they see as self-evidently better than what it sought to replace. It is a travesty of the truth, and should not be allowed to obscure the fact that Wolsey took the threat of Lutheranism extremely seriously.

It was on 12 May 1521 that Wolsey publicly opened the campaign against Luther when he presided over a burning of Lutheran books in St Paul's courtyard. But although it appears to have been carried out with due solemnity, even this episode has been taken as evidence for his lack of enthusiasm for defending Catholicism: it was too late, and anyway his main reason for holding it had everything to do with his foreign policy and very little with his hatred of heresy.[5] Neither proposition will be accepted here.

The first point to make is that it was not until Luther's works were officially pronounced heretical that there was any reason, let alone obligation, for Wolsey to act at all; indeed until this was done it would have been hard for him to make any

---

[1] M.J. Kelly, *TRHS*, 5 ser, xv, p.100.

[2] Ibid, pp.208 ff. for the relationship between heresy and reform in southern convocation in the early 1530s. It is also possible that convocation would have been prepared to hand over the smaller monasteries to the Crown but for an intervention by Fisher; see Ortory, pp.342-4; Surtz, *Works and Days*, p.87.

[3] Guy, *More*, pp.104-5, A.F. Pollard, p.208, and for the contrast between the tolerant Wolsey and fanatical More see Marius, pp.336-8; Ridley, *The Statesman and the Fanatic*, pp.163-5. A little depends on how you assign responsibility. No heretics were burnt in a Wolsey diocese because none were found but heretics were burnt during his chancellorship, including at least four in 1521-2 in the Lincoln diocese; see Dickens, p.27; S. Thompson, 'English and Welsh bishops', p.125. The confusion has been caused by the fact that none of those burnt in the 1520s were Lutheran.

[4] Marius, pp.386-406; Ridley, *The Statesman and the Fanatic*, pp.238-62.

[5] Meyer.

kind of assessment of the dangers inherent in Luther's writings. Academics with new ideas – Jacques Lefèvre in France and Johann Reuchlin in Germany – would be contemporary examples, as perhaps also Colet, had always faced the threat of being labelled heretics by their conservative colleagues, but this in no way implied that the Church's foundations were being threatened. No one in England could have immediately appreciated that Luther, who until at least 1517 was an unknown academic at one of the newer and less distinguished German universities, was a different proposition. Precisely when Wolsey first heard of Luther is not known. By early 1519 his works were on sale in England, and a letter from Erasmus to Wolsey written in the May of that year seems to assume that Wolsey was well acquainted with him. Erasmus's intention was to distance himself a little from the new theologian, but this did not prevent him from offering some praise. Moreover, he presented Luther as but one of a number of controversial German academics, such as Reuchlin and Ulrich von Hutten, and as of posing no more of a threat than they did.[1] By the following year this could no longer be anybody's attitude. In May 1520, Silvestro Gigli reported to Wolsey from Rome that after long debate Luther had been declared a heretic; and on 15 June the famous bull, *Exsurge Domine*, was published.[2] Forty-one of Luther's ninety-five theses were condemned, and the faithful were called upon to destroy his works. It is the fact that it took Wolsey almost a year from this date to organize the English Church's response that underlies the suggestion that it lacked conviction.

Some authorities did act more quickly. Bonfires of Luther's works were lit at Louvain on 8 October 1520 and at Cologne on 12 November. On the other hand, it was on 15 April, only a month before Wolsey formally declared his hand, that in France the Sorbonne condemned them, and it was at about the same time that action was taken in Venice and Naples.[3] Thus, if Wolsey was dilatory, he was in good company, but perhaps company that, like he himself, was concerned only to make diplomatic signals? It seems unlikely, and becomes even more so when it is realized that such responses as the lighting of bonfires required a good deal of preliminary work. This made them unsuitable instruments for conducting diplomacy, for by the time the bonfires had been lit, the situation was likely to have changed. Unfortunately it is difficult to establish precisely when Wolsey began the preparations for 12 May 1521. It rather looks as if Tunstall's letter to him of 21 January provides the *terminus a quo*. Writing from the battleground of Worms, where on 18 April Luther had defied his emperor and pope by refusing to retract one jot of his teachings, Tunstall begged Wolsey to summon 'the printers and booksellers and give them straight charge that they bring none of his [Luther's] books into England nor that they translate none of them into English, lest thereby might ensue great trouble to the realm and Church of England, as is now here'.[4] It does not look as if any steps had yet been taken in England, though as Tunstall had been out of the country since the previous September it could be that he was out of date.[5] However, by the end of February rumours were circulating that Henry himself

[1] ECW, 6, pp.368-72.
[2] LP,iii,847.
[3] Meyer, p.179, n.4; Hempsall, p.296.
[4] Sturge, pp.360-1. It was never calendared.
[5] LP,iii,969.

was contemplating a work against the heresiarch,[1] and seven months later his defence of the seven sacraments, the *Assertio Septem Sacramentorum adversus Martin Lutherum* was presented to the pope. On 16 March Leo x thanked Wolsey for forbidding the importation of Lutheran works, which puts the ban in late February at the latest, but also specifically suggested a burning of Luther's works.[2] Wolsey's reaction was to wonder whether he possessed sufficient powers to do this, and though he was informed that his doubts were groundless, it looks as if further powers were sent.[3] And whether groundless or not, there is no real reason to believe that his doubts were not genuine. Legal niceties were always a major concern, and the more important the matter, the more important it was to get them right.[4] Moreover, even before the pope had written, preparations for some considerable response to the new heresy were under way. On 3 April Warham thanked Wolsey for sending various Lutheran and Lollard works, and promised to consult with him about them on his return to London on the 11th.[5] On the 16th Henry was reported to be anxious to meet with theologians, already summoned to a conference to consider the orthodoxy of Luther's works, so as to be able to discuss his own reply to Luther.[6] On the 21st Oxford appointed four of their leading theologians to attend the conference, and Cambridge, at presumably about the same time, did likewise.[7] The date it took place and precisely who attended it has proved difficult to establish, but for the moment the most relevant point is that the conference was being planned at least a month before the bonfire took place which makes it difficult to attach the diplomatic significance to the episode that some have wanted.

What Wolsey is supposed to have intended in lighting a bonfire was to signal to the emperor and pope that in the armed conflict that had just broken out in Europe he was on their side. Given the large number of bonfires that were being lit at this time, it might be thought that amidst so much smoke any particular signal would be hard to pick up. Moreover, in giving such a signal it is important to know what the recipient wants. Charles v's condemnation of Luther was not given until 19 April. It was not a foregone conclusion, so for Wolsey to have started upon elaborate arrangements for a message that the emperor might have found unwelcome would surely have been a curious way of conducting foreign policy. Of course, there was no doubting that a bonfire would please the pope, but pleasing the pope was never a major priority of Wolsey's foreign policy. Moreover, in April 1521 it could not have been clear that in pleasing the pope he would have been pleasing the emperor, because it was not until 28 May that the two came to their unexpected agreement.[8] But above all even by 12 May England was still trying to act the honest broker between the emperor and Francis I, and it was not until a month later that she made

---

[1] CWM, 5, p.718

[2] *LP*, iii, 1197.

[3] *LP*, iii, 1210, 1233-4.

[4] Meyer, p.181 for a different view.

[5] *LP*, iii, 1218.

[6] *LP*, iii, 1233.

[7] Oxford University, Reg. H, fo.60. For Cambridge see Mullinger, p.571. There has been considerable confusion about the university burnings. Following Chester, *Library Chronicle*, pp.69-71 my own belief is that none occurred, but if there was one in Cambridge it was certainly in 1521.

[8] Pastor, viii, pp.17-36.

any significant move in the direction of the emperor.[1] Thus, if by any any chance Charles saw the burning as a friendly signal, he would have been reading far too much into it!

The notion that the ceremonies of 12 May 1521 were some kind of diplomatic signal has virtually nothing to commend it, and need not have been considered at all were it not indicative of just how pervasive has been the notion that Wolsey was soft on heresy. In fact diplomatic considerations played no part in the moves to condemn Luther. The reason why some states acted more quickly than others is that the papal condemnation of Luther in June 1520 had been hasty and ill-prepared, and that Luther had been given sixty days to admit his errors. As it happened, he did no such thing, but instead sat down to write three of his most influential works. The *Address to the Christian Nobility of the German Nation* appeared in August. The *Babylonian Captivity of the Church*, the work that Henry set out to refute, followed a month later and finally in November appeared *The Liberty of a Christian Man*. It took this marvellous riposte for the extent to which he had moved into direct conflict with the Catholic Church and the seriousness of the threat that he posed to be widely appreciated. For those who did not read such works for themselves, it might have taken Luther's public burning of the papal condemnation on 10 December and the coming into effect, on 3 January, of the sentence of excommunication against him to make the position absolutely clear and by the following month Henry was planning his counter-attack.

In the light of this, it is difficult to argue that the English response to Luther was dilatory or unimpressive. One estimate puts the number of spectators at the ceremony as high as thirty thousand, but if this seems incredible – it would have meant that about half the population of London had turned up – the attendance was certainly good.[2] Wolsey, processing under a canopy 'as if', according to the Venetian ambassador, 'the pope in person had arrived', was much in evidence, but then as cardinal and papal legate so he should have been. However, the centrepiece was a two hour sermon by John Fisher in which, lamenting 'this most pernicious tempest of heresy that Martin Luther hath now stirred', he sternly warned his audience of the terrible fate that would befall all those who would 'give faith to Martin Luther, or any such heretic, rather than to Christ Jesu and unto the spirit of truth'.[3] Fisher's sermon was quickly published, and instructions were sent out to the bishops to promulgate in their dioceses the forty-two errors of Luther identified by the English theologians, while a fifteen-day amnesty was to be proclaimed to allow everyone time to hand in heretical literature without suffering any penalty.[4] The English Church had been put on a red alert for the forthcoming battle with the Lutherans, although it is far from clear that in 1521 there were any Lutherans in England with whom to fight!

The one notable absentee on 12 May was the king – an enforced absence because of illness. And in a sense he was very much present, for throughout the proceedings Wolsey clutched in his hands the as yet unfinished manuscript of the

[1] See p.147 ff. above
[2] *Ven. Cal.*, iii, p.124 for Spinelli's estimate, but more generally ibid, pp.121-5; *LP*, iii, 1275.
[3] Fisher, *English Works*, pp.313, 347-8 for the quotations; see also Surtz, *Works and Days*, pp.302 ff.
[4] Wilkins, iii, pp.690-2.; GRO MS 9531/10/fo.139; KCA DR c/R7/fo.107v.

Assertio Septem Sacramentorum, a work which Fisher in his sermon declared would deliver them all 'from the slanderous mouth and cruelty that Martin Luther hath set upon them'.[1] There has been a tendency to be dismissive of Henry's theological enterprise, though this has not prevented doubts being raised, both at the time and since, about its authorship, on the grounds that the work was too good to have been written by him.[2] Any such doubts should be rejected. Letters written by his secretary, Richard Pace, provide clear evidence of Henry's deep involvement in the project,[3] while the interest in and grasp of theological matters that he showed throughout his life make it plain that he was quite capable of writing such a work.[4] The doubts arise because of the assistance he received – from More and Fisher, from the Oxford and Cambridge theologians summoned to give their judgement on Luther, and perhaps even from Wolsey[5] – but then any major polemical work by a reigning monarch could never have been a purely private matter. Far too much was at stake. Indeed, it needs to be stressed that the writing of the *Assertio* gave the fight against Luther a priority in government circles that could not be ignored by any of his councillors, whatever their private views. There was the kind of editorial work that many books require; and Thomas More insisted, when he described himself as 'only a sorter out and placer of the principal matters', that this was the only part he had ever played in the *Assertio*.[6] There was what would now be called research assistance, presumably from the university theologians – but many much more professional writers than Henry have made use of such help. Then there were the publishing aspects of the book, to do with production and distribution. These included the preparation of the beautifully illuminated manuscript copy for Leo x presented to him by the English ambassador in Rome, John Clerk, on 2 October 1521 at a consistory specially summoned for the purpose. Apparently the ceremony was not quite as spectacular as Clerk would have wished, though his disgruntlement might have been the result of having to deliver the book, and an oration, while on his knees! Still, Leo was full of praise for Henry, declaring that in writing the book he had 'rendered himself no less admirable to the whole world by the eloquence of his style than by his great wisdom'.[7] He also conferred upon Henry the much coveted title of Defender of the Faith, thereby enabling him to keep company on equal terms with the Most Christian king of France and the Catholic king of Spain.[8]

One thing that Leo very much approved of was the decision to give the book as wide a circulation as possible. The princes of Europe were to receive special copies, and in addition at least three editions were produced in 1522 and two more the following year.[9] Two German editions were prepared by leading Catholic polemicists, Thomas Murner and Jerome Emser.[10] All this testifies to the work's

---

[1] Fisher, *English Works*, p.327.

[2] For a good example of damning with faint praise see Elton, *Reform and Reformation*, pp.75-6, while a standard work on the English Reformation gives it a sentence; see Dickens, *English Reformation*, p.95.

[3] *LP*,iii,1220, 1233.

[4] Scarisbrick, *Henry VIII*, pp.110-16; 245 ff., 403 ff. is good on this.

[5] *LP*,iii,1233; *CWM*, 5, pp.720-1.

[6] Roper, p.67.

[7] Quoted in Doernberg, p.19; see also Tjernagel, pp.9-10 and E. Gordon Duff, important for the book's bibliographical history. For the presentation and and the pope's reply see *LP*,iii,1574, 1654, 1656.

[8] Scarisbrick, *Henry VIII*, pp.115-17.

[9] *LP*,iii,1574.

popularity, but this should come as no surprise, for the entry of a reigning monarch into the polemical lists was bound to cause a stir. It was also bound to generate a great deal of anxiety among the monarch's councillors, especially since it was almost inevitable that Luther would reply, as sure enough he did. In his *Antwort deutsch* of August 1522 – a Latin version, *Contra Henricum*, appeared the following month – he made no concessions to royal authorship, of which anyway he chose to be sceptical. According to him, Henry's work only proved the old adage that there were no greater fools than kings and princes – and Henry was also an ass, a pig, a drunkard, a dreamer, a mad and most ignorant monster, and much else besides![1]

Such a reply would have to be answered, though in what manner would require a good deal of thought. For the king of England to get involved in a protracted slanging match with a heretical ex-monk and university lecturer would have been altogether too undignified. Moreover, it so happened that the ex-monk in question was one of the most brilliant polemicists that Europe had ever seen, and it would not have done at all for the king to be worsted in a theological and literary battle. The solution was to call in Sir Thomas More, as the most distinguished writer, and John Fisher, as the most distinguished theologian in England, to write the replies. Henry could then confine himself to composing a dignified letter to the two princes of Saxony, the Elector Frederick and Duke George, calling upon them to eradicate the poison of Lutheranism in their territories before it got out of hand. He also took the opportunity to inform them, and the rest of Europe, that he had no intention of personally answering what he referred to as the ravings of a madman, not least because there was nothing in Luther's reply that had not been sufficiently dealt with in the royal book.[2]

The complex story of More's and Fisher's replies to Luther need not delay us long.[3] More was to write two versions of his *Responsio ad Lutherum*, the first appearing early in 1523 under the pseudonym Ferdinand Baravellus, the second, written in the autumn but probably not appearing until early in 1524, under the better known pseudonym, William Ross. Fisher's *Defensio regie assertionis contra Babylonicam captivitatem* did not appear until June 1525, long after his *Assertionis Lutheranae confutatio*, a refutation of Luther's *Assertio omnium articulorum* of early 1521, his defence against the papal condemnation of his works. As such, Fisher's work had nothing directly to do with the government's response to Luther's attack on Henry, but the preface contained much praise of Henry's *Assertio*, and its publication in January 1523 could hardly have been better timed. It also happened to be probably the most important defence of the Catholic faith to appear anywhere at this time. It was not, however, the only one to be written in England, for the good reason that the government was very anxious to encourage such works. Not all the details of these have survived. Catholic apologetics were not likely to last long in Protestant England but they included work by Edward Powell, a leading Oxford theologian and one of those chosen by the university in April 1521 to consider Luther's teachings, and Alphonso de Villa Sancta, one of Catherine of Aragon's

[10] *CWM*, 5, p.719.

[1] Tjernagel, pp.17-22.
[2] *LP*,iv,40, where misdated to 1524.
[3] Very fully treated in *CWM*, 5, pp.715 ff.

confessors.[1]

Just as Henry's *Assertio* has been too often ignored or belittled, so also has the English contribution to Catholic apologetics. That same English Protestant tradition that has been so unkind to Wolsey and ambivalent to Thomas More – and its treatment of More is of great relevance here – is largely responsible for this. The impression has been created that More was somehow the only person in England who was in the least bit worried by Luther, and, in most recent interpretations, only because he was mad or sexually disturbed. One result of this is that scant justice has been done to the bishop of Rochester, whose three most important works in defence of the Catholic Church (to the two already mentioned should be added *De veritate corporis et sanguinis in Eucharistia . . . adversus Johannem Oecolampedium* of 1527) together with his two show sermons against Luther of 1521 and 1526, published in English as well as Latin, were a massive contribution to that cause. They were well known on the continent and, like Henry's *Assertio*, some or parts of them were translated into German, some indication that they were considered as vital weapons in the battle against the new heresy.[2] They were also the works that the early English Protestants, especially William Tyndale in his *The Parable of the Wicked Mammon* and *The Obedience of a Christian Man*, felt they must refute. With the exception of his defence of Henry's *Assertio*, virtually all More's polemical works appeared after Wolsey's downfall, and, thus, another effect of the over-concentration on More has been to create the impression that under Wolsey's leadership no defence of Catholicism was launched. The result has been to ignore not only Fisher's outstanding contribution and the work of those university theologians specifically commissioned to write against Luther, but above all the king's. In fact, it is difficult to see what greater efforts could have been made, and though, as we have seen already, Henry's direct participation meant that inevitably the whole machinery of government was brought to bear, Wolsey's role as leading royal councillor and cardinal legate had to be of central importance.

Wolsey himself wrote no books, but according to Henry it was he who had 'moved and led' him to write the *Assertio*. He therefore deserved to be the 'partner of all honour and glory he hath obtained by that act', a suggestion which Wolsey did not reject![3] It is difficult to get behind this exercise in mutual flattery; my guess would be that Wolsey's role in initiating the project was small and incidental. But his involvement in the publishing and marketing of the book was considerable. He had first to find someone to produce the beautiful manuscript copy for the pope, and then to provide Henry with a choice of verses to be placed at the front of it.[4] He sent copious instructions to John Clerk at Rome concerning its presentation,[5] as well as on the distribution of other copies 'to the regions, universities and other countries as they were to you addressed and ordered'.[6] How far he was directly responsible for the planning of the English response to Luther's reply to Henry cannot be discovered,

---

[1] Mitchell, pp.109-14 *CWM*, 5, p.792.
[2] Surtz, *Works and Days* is essential for Fisher's writings.
[3] *LP*,iii,1659 (2), 1772.
[4] *LP*,iii,1450; E. Gordon Duff, pp.3-4.
[5] *LP*,iii,1510, 1574.
[6] Henry Ellis, 3 ser, i, pp.283-4 (*LP*,iii,1760).

but since it involved a good deal of diplomatic activity, such as corresponding with the Saxon princes, he could hardly have escaped being drawn in, and my guess would be that he was in charge of the whole operation. What is certain is that the English diplomats kept him fully informed about the polemical warfare that was raging on the continent and sent him copies of the latest works.[1] When in 1526 Henry came to consider his reply to a letter from Luther, which though full of contrition for any offence he might have caused the king in the past, was very rude about his leading councillor, calling him 'that pernicious plague and desolation of your majesty's kingdom', he received the benefit of Wolsey's advice: no reply should be sent without a copy of the original letter being attached, 'for that Luther, who is full of subtlety and craft, hereafter might perchance deny that any such letter hath been sent by him . . . as that the said answer, not having the said copy adjoined should be, for want thereof, to the readers and hearers thereof somewhat obscure'.[2] The advice is a good example of the trouble Wolsey took to get things right. It also serves to underline the point already made that Henry's personal involvement in the polemical battle made it a matter of major public concern, for the king's honour was just as much at stake here as, say, at the Field of Cloth of Gold. Wolsey's role, therefore, had to be of the greatest importance, as Henry's reply to Luther made clear when he went out of his way to stress that one of the reasons why Wolsey was so much in royal favour was that 'according to my commandment, [Wolsey] studiously purgeth my realm from that pestilent contagion of your factious heresies'.[3]

Of course, it could be argued that it was only because of the royal involvement that Wolsey showed any interest in the fight against heresy, and certainly he does not appear to have concerned himself nearly so much with arguably more vital but less conspicuous tasks such as, for instance, grappling with England's indigenous heretics, the Lollards. However, this is not as significant an indication of a lack of genuine concern for heresy as might at first appear. The ground-rules for combating Lollardy had been established by Archbishop Arundel about a hundred years earlier, and if Wolsey's episcopal colleagues could be trusted (and there is every reason for thinking that they could) there was no need for him to intervene, or to make use of his legatine powers. Luther and his followers were quite another matter. Here there were very few ground-rules: hence Wolsey's rapid and very public intervention in the spring of 1521. Admittedly, after the opening shots on the home front there was something of a lull, but this was not because Wolsey had become bored with the problem, but because for the next two or three years there was no problem. No Lutherans could be found, for the good reason that very few, if any, existed.

Two events changed all this. The Peasants' Revolt in Germany in 1524-5 provided proof positive that heresy and insurrection went hand in hand, and thus fears about Lutheranism dramatically increased.[4] And in the same year that the revolt was put down William Tyndale completed his translation into English of the

---

[1] LP,iii,2714, 3025; iv,2652, 2677, 2933.

[2] St.P,i, p.175 (LP,iv,2445); see also LP,iv,2371, 2420.

[3] LP,iv,2446, quoted in Doernberg, p.56; see also CWM, 8, pp.1135-6.

[4] For More's writing on this theme see Thomas More, *Correspondence*, p.323 in his *Letter to Bugenhagen*, and CWM, 8, pp.56 ff., 483 ff. in his *Confutation of Tyndale's Answer*. See also Cavendish, p.179-81 for Wolsey's views.

New Testament, though the disruption of its printing in Cologne and Tyndale's flight to Worms delayed its appearance in England until 1526.[1] But as soon as Wolsey received news of its imminent arrival, he went into action. With Henry's approval he decided to institute a 'secret search' for all Lutheran literature, but especially Tyndale's New Testament, to be followed by a burning of books like that of May 1521. And as in 1521, he ordered an amnesty for all those who would surrender heretical literature within a set period, insisting, in addition, that all printers and likely merchants should take out recognizances binding them not to import such literature.[2] In other words, he had decided upon a major government initiative, and one that led directly on 26 and 27 January 1526 to the famous raid on the Steelyard, the London home of the Hanse merchants, and to that ceremony at St Paul's Cathedral on 11 February, presided over by Wolsey, at which Robert Barnes, and probably five Hanse merchants abjured and did public penance, and where heretical works were burnt and Fisher delivered the second of his great sermons against Luther.[3] The battle had been reopened in earnest, and this time there were people and books to battle with, but even now not very many. Indeed, it has been suggested that there was great difficulty in finding enough books to burn and almost certainly no copies of the one that had stirred Wolsey into action, Tyndale's New Testament.[4] However, by the autumn these were arriving in such numbers that in October Tunstall, as bishop of London, was able to light a bonfire of his own, taking the opportunity to warn the London book trade against importing any copies.[5] At the same time heretical works by other English authors who, like Tyndale, were having to live and publish on the continent, were being smuggled in, despite all the English authorities' efforts to prevent them. And not only were there English Lutherans to be found abroad, but some were now discovered living in England.

Because it has become an interpretative crux, before we proceed, it must be stressed again that the Steelyard raid was not, as it is so often portrayed,[6] a private initiative of the heresy-hunter Thomas More, but a government initiative organized by Wolsey, with Henry's knowledge and consent. True, More did take part in it, but on both days he was accompanied by a number of other royal councillors and church officials.[7] The suspects were then interrogated by a commission of leading churchmen, set up by virtue of Wolsey's legatine authority, and on which, on at least one occasion he himself sat[8] – this providing the pattern for most subsequent heresy proceedings. In using his legatine powers in this way, Wolsey was usurping episcopal jurisdiction, and there is evidence that Cuthbert Tunstall, in whose diocese of London most of the heretics were to be found, was unhappy with this. At

[1] CWM, 8, pp.1068, 1159-10 for a good starting point to a complicated story.

[2] Henry Ellis, 1 ser, i, pp.179-84 (LP,iv,995), a most important letter, redated to 1526 in Chester, HLQ, 14, pp.214-5.

[3] Hall, p.708 says that only two Hanse merchants abjured, but see Chester, HLQ, 14, pp.211-21 for five. For the raid see Kronenburg; for Fisher's sermon see Surtz, Works and Days, pp.330-2.

[4] Chester, HLQ, 14 p.221. CWM 8, p.1160, for the suggestion that they first reached England in March.

[5] CWM, 8, pp.1161-2.

[6] See Elton, Studies, i, 148; Marius, p.316.

[7] Kronenberg, p.26.

[8] LP,iv,1962 (1-5); for his personal presence see LP,iv,1962 (5); Barnes, HLQ, 14, p.217.

any rate on 21 November 1527, the opening day of probably the most famous of these early heresy trials, that of 'Little Bilney' and Thomas Arthur, after Wolsey had made a formal declaration of his legatine jurisdiction over heresy Tunstall objected that, as bishop of the diocese in which the heretical activity was alleged to have taken place, he already possessed sufficient authority to try the defendants. Wolsey's immediate reaction is not known, but, when the trial resumed on 1 December, it was not at Westminster where it had begun, but at the London home of the bishop of Norwich, where the presiding judges were Tunstall, Fisher and West of Ely. The record does not state whether they were acting as Wolsey's commissaries, suggesting that they were not. When, however, the two defendants came to abjure, they did so to Tunstall as Wolsey's commissary but also as their 'ordinary and diocesan', while Tunstall's fellow judges are referred to as legatine commissaries.[1]

It seems, therefore, that if initially Wolsey had been insensitive to episcopal *amour-propre*, he had quickly recovered his touch. By admitting Tunstall as bishop to a share in the jurisdiction, he had successfully asserted his own legatine authority, without apparently seriously offending the bishop. Shortly after the trial a distressing interest in Lutheranism was discovered amongst some Oxford under-graduates, especially at Cardinal College. Along with Longland, in whose diocese of Lincoln Oxford lay, it was Tunstall who shouldered the main burden of the investigations, because of the involvement of a London curate in the distribution of heretical literature at Oxford, one Thomas Garrard.[2] That Wolsey's pride and joy had been found to be infected with heresy, made this a particularly sensitive matter and one which brought him and Tunstall into close contact. If Turnstall had borne Wolsey a serious grudge about what had happened over Bilney and Arthur, one might expect some evidence of it in the surviving correspondence, but on the contrary both men appear to be wholly concerned with how best to deal with the matter in hand.[3] Moreover, Garrard's eventual trial was conducted under the same arrangements as had finally prevailed at Bilney's and Arthur's, as were Geoffrey Lome's and John Tewkesbury's: Tunstall took part both as Garrard's bishop and as Wolsey's commissary, while the other judges were there solely as his commissaries.[4]

Something else which suggests that Tunstall's remonstrations at the Bilney and Arthur trial were only a hiccup is the co-operation between Wolsey and the bishops which became such a feature of the fight against Lutheranism during 1520s. It is impossible to arrive at exact figures for the turn out of bishops at the two famous book-burnings of 1521 and 1526, but one description of the earlier one states that 'the most part' were there, while one of 1526 has it that thirty-six bishops and abbots attended.[5] Certainly, at least nine bishops, Warham, Tunstall, Fisher, Clerk, Longland, Veysey, Standish, West and Kite took part in heresy trials as Wolsey's commissaries. Moreover, though Fisher's great sermons against Luther are rightly well known, those which Tunstall and Longland delivered are not. Tunstall's, as we

[1] GRO MS 9531/10/fos.130v-6, printed in Foxe, iv, app; Walker, *JEH*, 40 appeared too late to be assimilated here, but it needs to be consulted.

[2] Sometimes Garret or Garrett.

[3] *LP*, iv, 4004, 4017, 4073, 4125, 4150, 4418, printed in Foxe, v, app. vi.

[4] GRO MS 9531/10/fos.136v-8 for Garrard's and Lome's trials; Foxe, iv, pp. 689-90, curiously not to be found now in Tunstall's register.

[5] *LP*, iii, 1275; Chester, *HLQ*, 14, p. 211.

have seen, was delivered in October 1526 at a specifically London book-burning ceremony. Longland's was given at a meeting of bishops on 27 November 1527, which coincided with the opening of the Bilney and Arthur trial.[1] And there may have been a meeting earlier in the year specifically to work out a response to the threat posed by the imminent arrival of Tyndale's *New Testament*. Unfortunately, the only reference to this appears in a satirical poem, the principal purpose of which was to pour scorn on the bishops' reaction to that work, so it is hardly a reliable source.[2] On the other hand Tunstall's chaplain, Robert Ridley, mentioned in February 1527 that Tyndale's Bible had been 'accursed and damned by the consent of the prelates and learned men and commanded to be burnt'.[3] This could well be a reference to such a meeting, and at least points to joint episcopal action. Further evidence is provided by the instructions sent out to the bishops of the southern province to take action against heretical works,[4] and not just by the instructions themselves, for one imagines that any list of such works would have had to be drawn up by a committee of bishops and other experts, as had happened in 1521 just before the first book-burning. Moreover, as early as October 1524, if not before, the task of vetting all imported books for their heretical views had been assigned not only to Wolsey but also to Warham, Tunstall and Fisher.[5]

One of Lord Darcy's accusations against Wolsey in 1529 was that 'he and other bishops have counselled together, often secretly'.[6] He did not say whether they did so in order to promote the fight against heresy, but there is no doubt that the defence of the Church against the onslaught of Luther and his English followers frequently resulted in precisely that. Such co-operation will come here as no surprise, for the notion of a legatine 'despotism' has already been rejected. What should also be rejected is the notion of a beleaguered Thomas More battling almost alone to stem the heretical tide, for, as we have seen, it was the full apparatus of Church and state that was quickly mobilized to that end. Moreover, it is unlikely that More's horror of heresy was significantly stronger than anyone else's, for it was a horror that was widely shared – at least until the divorce and 'break with Rome' greatly muddied the waters. What was special about More, as Tunstall implied when licensing him to read Lutheran works in order to write against them, was that he could 'play the Demosthenes in our native tongue just as well as in Latin' and was therefore well qualified to put forth 'some writings in English which will reveal to the simple and uneducated the crafty malice of the heretics'.[7] In other words, it was not More's fervour but his literary skills that Tunstall wished to mobilize though whether Tunstall was the prime mover is another matter. When More had first been asked to take up his pen in the Catholic cause, in 1523, the initiative had almost certainly been Henry's. It may have been his in 1528 also, or perhaps, More himself asked to do so. But it is most likely that the request came from Wolsey, perhaps after

[1] Longland, fo.35 ff., not referred to in Bowker, *Henrician Reformation*, but see ibid, pp.57-64 for his concern about heresy.
[2] Barlowe, p.120.
[3] *LP*,iv,3960, transcribed in Arber, p.54.
[4] *LP*,iv,2607; S. Thompson, 'English and Welsh bishops', p.127.
[5] Reed, pp.165-6.
[6] *LP*,iv, p.2549.
[7] Thomas More, *Correspondence*, pp.387-8; (*LP*,iv,4028).

consultation with his fellow bishops, including Tunstall. What is most unlikely is the scenario of the two old chums, More and Tunstall, getting together to do something off their own bat, because they felt no one else was making an effort. Apart from anything else, it would have been incredibly foolish to have embarked upon a private crusade; and there is no reason why they should even have contemplated doing so, for both would have been well aware of how much was already being done to combat Lutheranism, not least by the king and his cardinal legate.

There was, however, one area of the fight against heresy in which Wolsey played a special role. The threat from Lutheranism came primarily from abroad, with the corollary that much of the government's effort in combating it had to be directed there, and increasingly so as English Lutherans, such as Tyndale, went into exile. It was vitally important to neutralize their activities, either by securing their arrest and extradition, or if this proved too difficult, by at least disrupting their publishing activities. But the point about all such efforts, whether made through normal diplomatic channels or clandestinely, was that because any intervention in a foreign country's affairs is a sensitive matter, it required authorization and direction from above; and it was this that Wolsey provided. We will ignore the details, which are anyway difficult to unravel, in part because much of the activity was clandestine. We know that particular use was made of the English ambassador in the Low Countries, Sir John Hackett, who had the difficult job of persuading Margaret of Austria's government to arrest obscure Englishmen on flimsy evidence.[1] The most successful coup was achieved in the autumn of 1525 by Hermann Rinck, a leading citizen of Cologne, whose contacts with the English court reached back into Henry VII's reign. Acting on a tip-off from the famous Catholic polemicist, John Cochlaeus, he successfully persuaded the Cologne authorities to disrupt the publication of Tyndale's New Testament, so that the editor and his collaborator, William Roye, were forced to start more or less from scratch at Worms.[2] Three years later, he brought off another coup, this time at Frankfurt, already a great centre of the book trade, where he bought up a whole run of Roye's A Brief Dialogue between a Christian Father and his Stubborn Son, a mix of anticlericalism and sacramentarian views, and James Barlowe's The Burial of the Mass, a racy attack in verse on Wolsey and the English Church. In doing so, however, he may have accidentally forestalled an even more dramatic coup by one Friar West who, acting as Wolsey's 'heresy-hunter' abroad, appears to have been cooking up a scheme to secure the capture of the authors themselves.[3] In any event, these three, Hackett, Rinck and West, were extremely active in carrying out Wolsey's instructions to suppress English Lutheranism at its source.

Wolsey has earned few marks for all this effort. In particular, it has been suggested that he gave insufficient support to Sir John Hackett in his attempt to secure the extradition of Richard Harman, an agent for heretical literature active in the Low Countries, his wife, and a former priest, Richard Akreston, all of whom

---

[1] For biographical information and full transcripts of his letters see Hackett.

[2] CWM, 8, p.1068; Arber, pp.18 ff. For Rinck see LP,iv,4810 his letter to Wolsey of 4 Oct. 1528.

[3] The evidence in letters of West to Hackett and Rinck to Wolsey in Hackett, pp.173-5; Arber, pp.32-6 (LP,iv,4693, 4810).

had been arrested by the Antwerp authorities in July 1528.[1] If the suggestion is true, it would go some way to undermine the view of Wolsey as a committed champion of Catholicism that is being put forward here, so the episode calls for a little attention. Undoubtedly, the English ambassador would have liked more support than he got. In almost every letter he complained of lack of instructions and a failure to send him the documents which the Antwerp authorities were insisting upon before they would even consider handing over the prisoners. Whether they ever had any intention of doing so is another matter. Requests for extradition are rarely treated with great enthusiasm, and in this case there was the complication that by having had himself made a burgess of Antwerp, Harman was in a strong legal position to resist the English government's efforts.[2] Neither was the evidence for his alleged heretical activities all that strong. So if Wolsey was not as eager to help as Hackett would have liked, it was probably because he realized that there was not a great deal that could be done. Neither is it likely that Wolsey attached as much importance to Harman's fate as Hackett did, if only because in the summer and autumn of 1528 there were a number of pressing matters claiming his attention such as his master's divorce! Wolsey also had to bear in mind the importance of maintaining good relations with Margaret of Austria at a time when, partly because of the divorce, he was anxious to secure her support. Such wider considerations did not bear so heavily upon the hard-pressed English ambassador in whose eyes the fate of Harman must have loomed very large, especially when for a short time the hunted turned hunter and he found himself under arrest at Harman's instigation![3]

However, in attempting to explain Wolsey's and Hackett's different perspectives, the intention is not to excuse Wolsey's lack of concern, because no excuses are required. Wolsey did write letters to Hackett about Harman, including two very shortly after he first heard of his arrest.[4] He also wrote more than one letter to Margaret of Austria, adopting, interestingly, precisely the strategy that Hackett had suggested, of stressing Harman's treasonable activities rather than his involvement in heresy.[5] And when Friar West was sent over to intensify the campaign against English heretics abroad, he brought further instructions as regards Harman.[6] All in all, the impression that the surviving evidence creates, despite Hackett's many laments, is that Wolsey acted as effectively as the situation allowed, and not only in Harman's case. True, the Antwerp authorities never agreed to his extradition, while Friar West failed in his schemes to secure the arrest of other English Lutherans. True, also, that books continued to be published abroad and to cross back into England. On the other hand, Harman's activities were greatly checked; he spent just over six months in prison, and all his books and documents were confiscated.[7] There had been Hermann Rinck's successes in delaying the publication of key heretical works, and in the winter of 1526-7 even Hackett

---

[1] Ridley, *The Statesman and the Fanatic*, 168.

[2] Hackett, p.169 (*LP*,iv,4650), but for Harman episode as a whole see ibid, pp.155 ff.

[3] *LP*,iv,5461.

[4] The letters are not extant, but are referred to by Hackett in Hackett, p.167 (*LP*,iv,4650).

[5] *LP*,iv, 4714, 5078, 5402.

[6] Hackett, p.180 (*LP*,iv,4714).

[7] He was arrested in July 1528 and was out of prison the following April; see Hackett, pp.156, 251 (*LP*,iv,4511, 5462). For the search see ibid, pp. 173 ff. (*LP*,iv,4693-4).

managed to persuade the Antwerp authorities to move swiftly against the printers of a pirated edition of Tyndale's *New Testament*, with the result that many copies were burnt.[1] And for this success Wolsey deserves some of the credit, for it was he who had prompted Hackett to act.[2]

Insofar as all the evidence so far presented points to Wolsey's very serious commitment to the fight against heresy both at home and abroad, it becomes all the more necessary to try and understand how it is that a contrary impression has been given by so many writers. Much has to do with general perceptions about Wolsey, for neither the picture of a fun-loving, overweight cardinal nor even that of a Machiavellian power-broker suggest that a defence of the Catholic Church would mean very much to him. And, as has already been pointed out, the obsession with Thomas More has not helped: indeed, a whole book has been written in order to bring out the contrast between the fanatical saint and the tolerant statesman. But there are other factors that may shed light, if sometimes indirectly, on Wolsey's attitude.

That the government feared heretical literature will come as no surprise. Books do have a worrying potential for filling people's heads with the wrong ideas, which once there prove difficult to remove. But why the fear in the 1520s of an English Bible – or more specifically Tyndale's *New Testament* – especially if the earlier argument, that there was very little demand for one, is correct? The notion that there was some kind of conspiracy by the wicked church authorities to deprive the people of the truth need not be accepted. Their real problem was that the majority of their flock were unequipped to grapple with a cerebral religion, even if they desired one. Of course, the essence of the Bible is that it is a story and one need not be theologically trained, let alone literate, to follow it. But every story contains interpretative cruxes, especially if it has been translated from one language to another; and therein lay the danger in an unauthorized version. People quite innocent of theological niceties would be confronted with a Bible in which there was no mention of 'priests', no mention of 'the Church', no mention of 'charity', indeed, no mention of many other words that had come to be closely associated with the Catholic Faith. How could they understand that, far from reading the word of God, or of the Catholic Church, they were reading only the word of Tyndale and Luther?[3] The same problem arose with any heretical work written in English. It was dangerous because it was popular – which is not to say that there was any great demand for it, but that it was written for a non-academic audience in no position to evaluate the ideas that were being put forward.

This distinction between a popular and an academic audience was an old one. The latter, as much in the past as nowadays, is used to controversy; indeed it thrives on it. During the Middle Ages such controversy had often led to accusations of heresy, but usually without any very dire consequences. It was only when an academic or his supporters looked for an audience outside the confines of the university precinct that a harsher line was taken, and even then it was often the

---

[1] Hackett, pp.63-72 (*LP*,iv,2797).

[2] Hackett, pp.41-2 (*LP*,iv,2649).

[3] In writing thus I am to a great extent paraphrasing More; see especially Thomas More, *Correspondence*, p.441; *CWM*, 6, pp.284 ff., 508 ff; *CWM*, 8, pp.143 ff. For similar worries of Tunstall's chaplain, Robert Ridley, in a letter to Henry Gold see *LP*,iv,3960.

political circumstances of the time rather than the precise nature of the views expressed that were the decisive factor as regards the severity of the response. The career of that earlier Oxford academic, John Wyclif, exemplifies the point, as indeed does that of the Erfurt graduate, Martin Luther. So also do the careers of many English Lutherans of the 1520s and 1530s. As up-and-coming academics, it would have seemed perfectly in order for them to be treated with a certain leniency – at least on the first occasion that they had got into trouble. They were merely naughty schoolboys who would outgrow their youthful indiscretions and go on to make important contributions to the common weal.

Robert Barnes's own account of his examination before Wolsey and his legatine commissioners has very much this flavour about it, though it is written from the schoolboy's point of view. It was during it that Wolsey allegedly made his well known defence of his 'pillars and Pollaxes and other ceremonies' on the grounds that such outward symbols were necessary in order 'to maintain the commonwealth' – to which Barnes made the excellent rejoinder that as the commonwealth had got on perfectly well before Wolsey had displayed them, it could no doubt do so again.[1] At this point Wolsey could well have become angry. Instead, he congratulated Barnes on a good answer. Moreover, at the end of the interview he offered him the opportunity of making an informal submission to him as legate, thereby avoiding the stress, and more serious consequences, of a formal trial.[2]

Our information on this point comes from the great chronicler of the English Protestant martyrs, John Foxe, and it is perhaps not surprising that he has Barnes rejecting the easy way out. Apparently Thomas Bilney, around whom so many English Reformation cruxes seem to cluster, did not.[3] More's comment on what he saw as a kindness by Wolsey which in the light of Bilney's subsequent activities had been misplaced was that it arose from the cardinal's 'tender favour' to the university of Cambridge;[4] and it is one that very much supports the present argument. Wolsey may have offered the same opportunity to another leading light of the English Reformation, Hugh Latimer, like Barnes and Bilney a Cambridge academic, and it was probably accepted.[5] There has also survived an account of an interview that Latimer had with Wolsey in the spring of 1528 which shows many similarities to his interview with Barnes. The cardinal is alleged to have been much taken with Latimer. Not only did he admire Latimer's skill in outshining his own chaplains in scholastic theology, but he even approved of his exposition of a bishop's duties. Since it was just such an exposition that had got Latimer into trouble with his bishop, Nicholas West, Wolsey's conclusion that 'if the bishop of Ely cannot abide such doctrine as you have here repeated, you shall have my licence, and shall preach into his beard, let him say what he will' was, if it was ever made, a remarkable victory indeed for the future Protestant bishop.[6]

That both this account and the one concerning Barnes present Wolsey in an

[1] CWM, 8, p.1379.

[2] Foxe,v, p.417.

[3] Admitted under interrogation at his trial in 1527; see GRO MS 9531/10/fos.130v.; Foxe, iv, app.vi.

[4] CWM, 6, p.268.

[5] The evidence is difficult to interpret but see Chester, *Hugh Latimer*, pp.22 ff.

[6] This from the only source for the interview, Ralph Morice's near contemporary account; see BL Harleian 422, fos.84-7, printed in Foxe, vii, app.iv.

unexpectedly sympathetic light is interesting even if, despite having been written not long after the events they describe, they need to be treated with caution. For instance, that Wolsey is portrayed in a favourable light does not prevent both Barnes and Latimer winning the arguments. Surely, if they could convince even the great cardinal, then they must have been right? This seems to be the message, and to get it across the facts may well have been massaged, which would not have been too difficult given that when the accounts were written Wolsey, being dead, could not challenge their veracity. He had also ceased to be the enemy. When Barlowe wrote *The Burial of the Mass* and Tyndale *The Practice of Prelates* Wolsey was very much alive, and both these works contained savage attacks on him.[1] So the suggestion here would be that the benign Wolsey of these two accounts is to some extent the invention of the propaganda requirements of the early Protestants, but this does not entirely dispose of him. When in 1527 Bilney was in trouble – again like Latimer, he had on the first occasion escaped a formal charge of heresy – he asked to be 'brought before the tribunal seat of my Lord Cardinal, before whom I had rather stand than before any of his deputies'.[2] And there are other bits of evidence to suggest that people in trouble for heresy did believe that they stood more chance with Wolsey than before a formal tribunal. May it not therefore be the case that this notion of a Wolsey who, for whatever reason, never took heresy very seriously is the truth?

The answer is no, and here we must hark back to that disinction made earlier between the academic world, where differences of opinion were generally tolerated, and the world outside, where they were not. Whatever happened between Wolsey and people such as Barnes, Bilney and Latimer, it would never have been his intention to persecute them. But then neither in the first instance would it have been anybody's intention, not even Thomas More's. It was, after all, a requirement, and one that in England appears to have been generally met,[3] that everything possible should be done to win back erring sheep to the true faith, and it was only those who wilfully and maliciously resisted who were to be treated with severity. In the case of 'simple folk', the working assumption was that it was ignorance that had led them astray. In the case of academics it was assumed to have been intellectual curiosity and youthful high spirits; hence the significance of Wolsey's alleged remark to Latimer on first seeing him: 'You are of good years, nor no babe, but one that should wisely and soberly use yourself in all your doings.'[4] In other words, 'You should have known better!'

The people whom Wolsey was out to get were the pedlars of heretical literature, the colporteurs. In the Oxford round-up of early 1528 it was only Thomas Garrard, responsible for bringing such literature to Oxford, who was formally charged and made to abjure, while scholars such as John Frith were not. Similarly at Cambridge, although the evidence for what occurred there is even less certain than for Oxford,[5] it was not someone like Latimer, but Sygar Nicholson, the bookseller, who was

---

[1] Tyndale's work appeared in 1530, and thus after Wolsey's fall. But since he expected Wolsey's triumphant return, I hope the point being made holds.
[2] In a letter to Tunstall; see Foxe, iv, p.638.
[3] Thomson, *Later Lollards*, pp.227-36.
[4] Foxe, vii, app.iv.
[5] But see Chester, *Hugh Latimer*, p.36.

proceeded against.[1] Then there was Geoffrey Lome, another distributor of books, and Richard Bayfield, a monk of Bury, who acted as a link in the passage of books between London and Cambridge.[2] Of the twenty-four articles alleged in May 1528 against Henry Monmouth, Tyndale's first patron, thirteen had to do with the production and distribution of heretical literature.[3] In April 1529 it was the turn of John Tewksbury to stand trial for his part in the sale of heretical works, but especially Tyndale's *Parable of the Wicked Mammon*.[4] True, Garrard's rector, Dr Forman, who may have been at the centre of this book trade, did escape a formal trial; and no doubt it helped him that he had been president of Queens' College, Cambridge, though the more important reason was probably that in the end not enough evidence could be found against him. But the fact that he was very closely investigated by Tunstall and may even have been personally interrogated by Wolsey tends to strengthen the present argument that it was the colporteurs who were seen as the arch-enemies.[5]

That this was so is not surprising, though it has been very much underplayed. A modern parallel can be found in the concentration on drug-traffickers rather than the drug-users. The latter are seen as victims, while it is the former who are villains, partly because they make a lot of money from their activities, as to a lesser extent did the traffickers in heretical literature. And without the drugs, or books, there would be no problem, though this is not quite so true of books, since people could be contaminated by word of mouth. Nevertheless, books and, given the Lutheran emphasis upon its privileged position, especially the Bible, did play a part in the success of the Reformation. In calling upon his archdeacons to search out and destroy heretical works, Tunstall declared them to be the source of a 'pestiferous and most pernicious poison',[6] and it was as a poison that More saw them. Not only did he seek in his writings to provide an antidote, but on becoming lord chancellor he did his utmost to prevent the poison being spread by the likes of George Constantine, who incidently was on Friar West's list of wanted heretics, and Richard Bayfield – but then Wolsey had done the same. In fact, their attitudes were entirely similar. Heresy was an evil to be eradicated, but there were degrees of evil: the foolish young scholar temporarily seduced by intellectual curiosity or emotional instability, such as More's own son-in-law, William Roper, appears to have been, was a very different proposition from someone who persisted in his foolishness despite all the efforts of the Church to persuade him otherwise, not to mention those who sought by their writings or preaching, or by the distribution of other people's writings, to infect the nation with their disease.

Wolsey treated Bilney leniently on the occasion of his first offence partly no doubt because it has never proved easy to decide whether his views were heretical or not, but chiefly because it was proper for him to behave thus towards a much respected and much loved Cambridge scholar.[7] When Bilney not only persisted in

---

[1] No record of his trial has survived but see Foxe,iv, p.586; v, p.27; CWM, 9, pp.119-20.

[2] GRO MS 9531/10/fos136v-7.

[3] LP,iv,4260.

[4] Foxe,iv, pp.688-91; see also J.F. Davis, 'Heresy and Reformation', pp.269-71.

[5] Foxe, v, app.vi (LP,4073, 4175).

[6] From his instructions to his archdeacons in Oct. 1526, quoted in Foxe, iv, p.667, but see GRO MS 9531/10/fo.45,where the date is 24th rather than 28th, but everybody produces a slightly different date!

his errors, but compounded them by proceeding to stump the pulpits of East Anglia and London denouncing the worship of saints and images, Wolsey reacted with much greater severity. Bilney was brought to a formal trial, abjured, albeit reluctantly, and was for a time placed in custody. When, after his release, he not only could not keep silent but proceeded to distribute Tyndale's *New Testament*, at least to a Norwich anchoress, then there was little that could be done to save him. In August 1531 he was tried before the bishop of Norwich's chancellor, found guilty, and, since he had already abjured, was sentenced to death by burning. What needs to be understood is that whether or not he made a full confession of his errors before he was burnt – a question that has been endlessly debated both at the time and since[1] – had no bearing on his ultimate fate, for the legal position was quite clear: anyone convicted of holding heretical views who acknowledged his errors and showed himself truly penitent was to be set free and readmitted to full membership of the Church. But there was no second chance. If he or she relapsed into heresy, once having abjured, then the penalty was death by burning, whether or not on this second occasion contrition was shown, and this was the case with Bilney. During More's chancellorship five Lutherans were burnt.[2] During Wolsey's none were, but, since some Lollards suffered that fate, it cannot be that he was in principle against burning. In fact there is a very simple explanation for Wolsey's apparent leniency: of the ten or so against whom proceedings were initiated, all were facing trial for the first time and all either abjured or fled before sentence was given.

This failure to understand the legal position has been another reason why Wolsey's attitude towards heresy, and indeed More's, have been misunderstood. And if the comparison between the two men is extended, yet another one emerges. Put at its simplest, by the time of More's chancellorship it had become so much more obvious that the erring scholar had a strong propensity to turn into the persistent heretic. When, following the round-up of Oxford Lutherans in 1528, Wolsey had considered the case of John Frith, he was faced with someone who, apart from being by all accounts a most attractive personality, may well have done nothing more heinous than to read Tyndale's *New Testament* and dip into other heretical works. By December 1532, when More sat down to write A *Letter* against him, Frith had himself become the author of heretical works, but even so More's tone was far less abrasive than the one he adopted towards other English heretics.[3] By 1532 the battle was much further advanced, people were more committed to their views, and in England the stakes could not have been higher. However, none of this indicates any fundamental difference between More and Wolsey. It was the circumstances that had changed, and from the Catholic point of view much for the worse, if only because the king's position had become so ambiguous. And even in 1530 Henry may not have been all that receptive to Wolsey's death-bed message to

---

[7] See Dickens, *English Reformation*, pp. 79-81 for a sympathetic pen portrait, but for a more streetwise Bilney see Walker, *JEH*, 40.

[1] J.F. Davis, *HJ*, 24 is the best starting point.
[2] In chronological order of their sentence there were Thomas Hitton, Thomas Bilney, Richard Bayfield, John Tewkesbury and James Bainham.
[3] Though the reader may think it abrasive enough; see Thomas More, *Correspondence*, pp. 441-2; also Marius, pp. 429-30.

him, if he ever received it, or indeed if it was ever uttered, for we only have Cavendish's word for it. Still, as reported by his first biographer, the message was clear: Henry should 'have a vigilant eye to depress this new perverse sect of Lutheranism, that it do not increase within his dominions through his negligence'.[1] The argument of this chapter has been that he had very much followed his own advice. What remains to be decided is how effective his defence of Catholicism had been. In arriving at an answer there are, as always, enormous difficulties, to do partly with evidence or lack of it, partly with the criteria used – of special importance for a subject which remains an emotive one. Still, how you answer the question must depend to a great extent on how many heretics, whether Lutheran or Lollard, you think there were in the 1520s. The number of known Lutherans is very small indeed, even if one takes a generous view of what constitutes an attachment to Lutheranism at this early stage, when distinctions were still blurred. There were the frequenters of the White Horse Inn at Cambridge, and the Oxford Lutherans discovered in 1528, most of them from Cardinal College and many of them recent imports from Cambridge. In close contact with these was a London group, and it was from here, perhaps under Dr Robert Forman's leadership, that the heretical book trade was organized. It is difficult to push the total to above fifty individuals. Connected with these, though in ways that are both uncertain and disputed, were the Lollards. My own view is that very few of them converted or graduated to Protestantism; and even those who are confident that they did, have found it difficult to name names.[2] What is known is that some Lollards were interested in Tyndale's *New Testament* and that Robert Necton, for instance, was providing books for both Lollards and Lutherans.[3] And there were certainly more Lollards than Lutherans, though just how many is another much disputed question.

In his visitations of 1527 and 1528 Tunstall and his officials detected about 140, and it was in his London diocese that by the late 1520s most Lollard activity seems to have been concentrated, especially in the Colchester area. Fifteen years earlier about fifty had been discovered in Kent and another seventy or so in Coventry. In 1521-2 some three hundred and fifty were detected in the area around Great Missenden in Buckinghamshire, and the occasional Lollard turns up elsewhere.[4] It is interesting that in these clamp-downs the same names keep cropping up. This suggests to me an isolated and ageing group, though others have seen it merely as indication of the inadequacies of the detection process and the skill with which Lollards minimized the damage caused by it. The same may have been true of the early Lutherans – and when arrested most of them did name names but, as with the

---

[1] Cavendish, p.179.

[2] For a recent account of early Tudor Lollards, see Hope; but also see M. Aston, *Lollards and Reformers*, pp.119 ff; Davis, *Heresy and Reformation*, passim; Dickens, *English Reformation*, pp.33-7. I must confess to finding it very difficult to take early sixteenth-century Lollards as seriously as no doubt they should be, but even Hope wrote that 'there remains something insubstantial about Lollardy on the eve of the Reformation' (Hope, p.24).

[3] For Lollards and the New Testament in general see M. Aston, *History*, lxii; for the Lollard deputation from Steeple Bumstead to Robert Barnes while in custody to buy Tyndale's *New Testament* see CWM, 8, pp.1384 ff; for Robert Necton's sale of Protestant literature to Lollards see *LP*,iv,4030, printed in A.W. Pollard, pp.155-9. See also J.F. Davis, *Heresy and Reformation*, pp.59-60.

[4] For a useful survey of all heresy trials at this time see see S. Thompson, 'English and Welsh bishops', pp.121 ff; see also Dickens, *English Reformation*, pp.26-33.

Lollards, usually the same ones. Thus the final figure would vary according to how easily one thinks the church authorities were conned. And, however arrived at, it is difficult to get the figure into thousands. The Lollards were composed of comparatively small communities of mostly humble folk. The Lutherans were chiefly to be found in academic circles, with some spill-over into London's mercantile community, and totalling probably under the hundred. Any organization was chiefly confined to the distribution of heretical literature, and there was nothing approaching a coherent command structure presiding over a dedicated body of people bent on reformation.

In suggesting that there were few heretics I am very much following in the footsteps of recent historians.[1] There has been a reaction away from a Protestant view of the English Reformation, which has been an enormously healthy corrective. Still, revisionism can go too far and numbers are not everything. In an earlier chapter it was argued that, while the extent of anti-clericalism in the early sixteenth century has been greatly exaggerated, there was nevertheless a lot of it around, and amongst such important people as courtiers and Crown lawyers. This was not because the clergy were especially wicked but because the Church as an institution was wealthy, powerful and pervasive, and was bound to have its critics at all levels of society. However, what turned something endemic into an epidemic had little to do with the state of the Church, which, under Wolsey's leadership at least, may never have been so healthy, but with other factors, such as the popularity of a particular monarch or the degree of social unrest. It was these that created the right conditions for the bacilli of anticlericalism to multiply, but what was also needed was a catalyst. In 1515 there had been a major battle in the long-running war between Church and state over disputed areas of jurisdiction, during the course of which Henry VIII had made it very clear that he expected to preside over a Church that was subservient to his will. To ensure this, he had put at its head a man whom he trusted above all others, and for a dozen or so years there was no more conflict. Then came the divorce and the Church's refusal to grant Henry what he believed was rightly his. Of course, it was not initially the English Church that had refused to do his bidding, but far too many important members of it had shown themselves either lukewarm or downright contrary. So it was borne in on him that 'the clergy of our realm be but half our subjects, yea, and scarce our subjects'.[2] For Henry this was intolerable, and thus the king who in the 1520s had quite justifiably earned for himself the title of Defender of the Faith became the Church's greatest enemy. The jurisdictional battle was renewed, the man who had done so much to secure the peace, the king's own cardinal legate, was jettisoned, and anticlericalism was given its head, this time with the potential to ally with the new heresy from Germany.

In fact, despite the endemic anticlericalism, the nation seems to have been in no hurry to follow its prince's lead. Instead, it took a good deal of bullying and bribery to bring about the so-called Henrician Reformation, and not before substantial resistance had been offered. For some, such as the thousands of 'pilgrims'

[1] See especially Haigh, *PP*, 93; *HJ*, 25; and Scarisbrick, *Reformation*. For a spirited counter-attack to this recent work see Dickens, *Archiv fr Reformationsgeschicte*, lxxviii, where he mentions that for the period 1525-8 3,000 names included in J. Fines's Biographical Register of Early English Protestants; see ibid, p.191.

[2] Hall, p.788.

in 1536, this meant out-and-out rebellion, for others martyrdom, and for yet others merely the writing of letters or the hiding of their parish church's furnishings and plate.[1] What would Wolsey have done? The usual answer has been that he was not of the stuff of martyrs, and his death-bed admission that he had all his life served his king more diligently than his God tends to confirm this. However, if, as has been argued here, he had devoted so much of his time and energy to the reform and defence of the English Church, then at least a moment's hesitation is in order. Moreover, it does not follow that because he worked so hard to secure the divorce that he should be thought of as some kind of proto-protestant. There was nothing heretical about making the request, just as long as in the end the pope's decision was accepted – and that decision did not come until after Wolsey's death. Wolsey had frequently warned Clement of the consequences of refusing to give Henry what he wanted, schism and the English conversion to Lutheranism, but there is not the slightest indication that he welcomed such a prospect, either for the country or for himself. On his death-bed his major concern had been to warn Henry of the horrors of heresy, while his personal beliefs seem to have been of a very traditional kind.

Nevertheless, after due pause, the conclusion must be that probably Wolsey would have followed his monarch into schism but he would have hated doing so. This is not because he would have missed dressing up in red, or any of the perks that went with being a cardinal. After all Henry was going to be quite happy to put a layman, Thomas Cromwell, in charge of the Church; and if Wolsey had retained the king's confidence, he might have had to acquire a new title, but his position would have remained effectively the same. In trying to understand not only Wolsey's reaction to 'the break with Rome', but that of all those who were close to the court, including such as Thomas More, we must bear in mind the strength of the bonds that attached them, both emotionally and intellectually, to the figure of the king. It is not just that it was Henry, or his predecessors, who had granted them office, lands, honours, and so on. In all aspects of their life they were programmed to serve him; and one of the most powerful forces behind this programming was the Church, which was constantly expounding the virtues of loyalty and obedience. So it is not all that surprising that, when Church and king found themselves in a fight to the death, the majority of the political nation, however reluctantly, sided with the king. The suggestion, therefore, that Wolsey would have done so too in no way contradicts the argument that he was devoted to the best interests of the English Church and had fought hard to ward off the threat from Martin Luther. There was always an element of ambiguity in his dual role as both the king's and the Church's leading servant – an ambiguity that has applied to countless other churchmen both before and since. Wolsey himself was lucky to have died just before he would have had to choose where his allegiance lay, but his own downfall was intimately involved with the battle between king and pope that was to force that decision upon the English nation – a battle that was to destroy all the work that he had done for the English Church during the 1520s. Thus, if not a martyr, Wolsey has a claim to be considered the first important victim of the Henrician Reformation.

---

[1] Scarisbrick, 'Reformation', pp.61 ff. for a brilliant corrective to the more usual whitewash.

Chapter Twelve

The King's Great Matter

B Y THE SPRING OF 1527 HENRY VIII WAS MUCH TROUBLED BY A 'SCRUPLE' concerning his marriage to Catherine of Aragon. He had become aware that not only was the marriage technically invalid, but what was far worse, that it was contrary to divine law. This being so, the very salvation of his soul was in jeopardy unless the Church acted swiftly to free him from a marriage that should never have been. Wolsey's task as the king's leading servant and, by virtue of his legatine powers, head of the Church in England was to see that it did so but, as everyone knows, he failed, and in failing destroyed himself. But more than personal loss was at stake. The pope's refusal to grant a divorce led almost directly to the 'break with Rome' and to the creation of a Protestant England.[1] It is, thus, one of the most significant failures in English history, which brings with it the, in some ways unfortunate, consequence for a biographer of Wolsey that the story has been much told, and in the greatest detail. Usually the storytellers have been emotionally involved, taking sides with the personalities and with their religious beliefs, and as a result the evidence has not been impartially treated. Perhaps more importantly, in a climate in which the religious divisions are no longer so dominant as they once were, the evidence itself is very difficult to interpret.

To begin with there is its bulk. For six years the divorce was Henry's government's priority and a matter of some interest in all the courts of Europe, not least at Rome. Every kind of official, lawyer and academic was dragged into it, and this generated an enormous quantity of paper, much of it highly technical and requiring specialist interpretation.[2] It is a daunting prospect and there can be no attempt here to give a full account of Henry's 'great matter'. Instead, what follows is a highly selective commentary from which it is hoped that Wolsey's private attitude to his master's predicament will emerge, though in a matter in which the king's personal wishes and royal policy were so powerfully intertwined it was very difficult for any of his servants, as pre-eminently Thomas More found, to have views of their own, or if they did, they might wish to keep them to themselves. And perhaps this must be the first point to make: that considering Wolsey's position as the king's chief servant, he could hardly have afforded the luxury of a personal view, even if it had occurred to him to have one. But before we become too lost in interpretation, a brief chronological framework is called for.

Wolsey's first documented involvement with the divorce was the holding of a legatine court, which met secretly at Westminster on 17 May 1527, to pronounce on

---

[1] Technically what Henry was seeking would be called a decree of nullity, but it would be too perverse not to use the word divorce.

[2] My account is very dependent on H. A Kelly, *Matrimonial Trials*; Parmiter; and Scarisbrick, *Henry VIII*, pp. 147 ff., where very full documentation is to be found. For letters and instructions of 7,000 words and more see *inter alia LP*, iv, 4897, 4978, 5050, 5270, 5428, 5523.

the validity of Henry's marriage.[1] When, on the 31st, the trial was adjourned without sentence being passed,[2] there followed an uneasy period during which Henry and Wolsey appear to have adopted differing tactics. At any rate, Wolsey spent much of the summer in France trying to grapple with the additional complication of the pope's captivity, begun when on 5 June an Imperial army sacked Rome and ended only with Clement's escape to Orvieto on 8 December. Meanwhile Henry, acting in the first instance without Wolsey's knowledge, had instructed his secretary William Knight somehow to gain access to the pope and persuade him to grant a dispensation enabling the king to remarry, despite the fact that, at least in the eyes of the Church, he was legally married to somebody else.[3]

But Henry's request to be free to marry someone to whom he was related in the first degree of affinity could only confirm the rumour that his 'scruple' had little to do with God and more to do with Anne Boleyn, who as a consequence of Henry's affair with her sister, Mary, was related to the king in just that degree. It was a curious, not to say foolish, first step, as Wolsey was quick to realize as soon as he got wind of it. This was not until early September, while he was still in France and when Knight had already started for Rome and, despite his best efforts, he was unable to persuade Henry to rescind Knight's instructions, only to modify them.[4] A perfectly useless dispensation was in fact obtained,[5] but only at the expense of destroying Henry's moral credibility, for by drawing attention to Anne it made it difficult for the pope to take seriously any more acceptable reasons that might be advanced later for dispensing with the first marriage.

The one good thing that emerged from Knight's mission was that it brought Henry and Wolsey together again. The king accepted that, however impatient he might be, the divorce of a queen, with all its many implications, including those concerning the succession, could not be rushed. Every kind of legal propriety needed to be observed,[6] or rather to appear to be observed, for what also soon became apparent was that the pope, in whose jurisdiction matrimonial matters ultimately lay, was not as convinced of the rightness of Henry's case as he himself was. Moreover, Clement was faced with very difficult political choices, for while he was anxious not to offend Henry unnecessarily, circumstances made it even more important for him not to offend Catherine's nephew, the emperor Charles v. What was required on the English side were patient and persistent negotiations with the pope to overcome the many legal and political obstacles which stood in the way of a decision in Henry's favour. These began in earnest with the dispatch of Edward Fox and Stephen Gardiner to Italy in February 1528, and to begin with they were very successful. It is true that what Wolsey wanted above all else, a decretal

---

[1] LP,iv,3140.

[2] LP,iv,3140.

[3] LP,iv,3420.

[4] LP,iv, 3400, 3422, 3423. For Henry modifying his instructions see his uncalendared letter to Knight in Gairdner, *EHR*, xi, pp.685-6.

[5] Ehses, *Römische Dokumente*, pp.14-16. It was dated 23 Dec. 1527. LP,iv,3749-51 for Knight's negotiations. For Wolsey's view that it and the commission that Knight had also secured for Wolsey to act in the matter were 'as good as none at all' see LP,iv,3913.

[6] The chief evidence for this is the five or more years that passed before Henry broke with the papacy, but for a specific recognition of the point see Pocock,i, p.153 (LP,iv,4251); also LP,iv,5156.

commission, of which more later, eluded him, and that he had to put up with a 'secret' one, which was not the same thing at all, though a gain of sorts. He was also granted a general commission under the terms of which he and Cardinal Campeggio were empowered to conduct a second legatine trial. In addition, Wolsey obtained what was called a 'pollicitation', in which the pope promised to do nothing to hinder the execution of the commission. Taken together, these concessions did offer Wolsey and Henry a chance of success. On 25 July Campeggio left Italy for London, and early in August Anne Boleyn wrote to Wolsey that 'the great pains and troubles that you have taken for me, both night and day, is never likely to be recompensed on my part, but only in loving you, next unto the King's grace, above all creatures living'.[1] That no irony was intended is suggested by the fact that she persuaded the king to write a postscript which he signed as Wolsey's 'loving sovereign and friend'. Shortly afterwards Henry wrote to Anne: 'touching our other affairs', by which he meant the divorce, 'I assure you there can be no more done, or more diligence used, nor all manner of dangers better foreseen and provided for'.[2] Wolsey may not have been quite as optimistic as his master, but the patient negotiations begun in the early part of the year had borne some fruit, and he must have hoped that he would soon be deserving of even more of Anne's love if that is what he wanted? But as it turned out the summer of 1528 was to be the nearest that Wolsey got to success in this matter.

Campeggio's journey to London was agonizingly slow; for Campeggio on account of the severe gout from which he suffered, and continued to do so for most of his stay in England; for Henry, Anne, and Wolsey just because it was so slow. When on 8 October he did eventually arrive, instead of proceeding immediately with the trial, as Henry and Wolsey expected, he did what Clement had instructed, which was to waste yet more time, first by trying to reconcile Henry to Catherine, and then, when a four-hour interview with Henry had convinced him that not even an angel from heaven could succeed in that task, by trying to persuade Catherine to take a vow of chastity, a step which, according to some interpretations, would have released Henry from his marriage vows. It is doubtful whether Henry or Wolsey ever believed that such a move on Catherine's part could provide a satisfactory solution, but she soon resolved their doubts by refusing to comply, despite Wolsey going down on bended knee in one of the many attempts to persuade her. Not long afterwards she brilliantly counter-attacked by producing from out of the blue, or rather from Spain, a copy of a dispensation for her marriage to Henry of which the English had been hitherto unaware. The so-called 'Spanish brief' had been sent in 1504 as a special favour to Catherine's mother, Isabella of Castile, who was dying and wished to have some of the uncertainties surrounding her daughter's second marriage resolved.[3] It differed slightly from the one provided for the English court, and some of these differences added extra legal complications; but the real complication was its very existence. Since the commission drawn up for Wolsey and Campeggio to try the case made no mention of it, any sentence passed by them

---

[1] LP,iv,4360, where it is placed in early June. But Henry's worry that Campeggio had not arrived in France suggests that he knew that the cardinal had set off from Italy, which he did on 25 July. None of the Henry/Anne love letters are dated but see Byrne, pp.53-85, 430-1.

[2] LP,iv,4648.

[3] Parmiter, p.73, n.1.

could have no bearing on its validity, and thus it could be claimed that the marriage remained good even if it was found that the 'English brief' was defective. By suddenly producing this document in early November, Catherine achieved not only a *coup de théâtre* but a real setback to Henry's and Wolsey's plans. Either they would have to prove that the 'Spanish brief' was a forgery, and its opportune appearance at least raised a presumption that it might be, or failing that, they would have to get their commission altered so that the brief came within its terms of reference. Wolsey tried both approaches, but all negotiations with the Curia were slow, for it took about a month for letters from London to get there and back. In this case the problem was greatly complicated by Clement's illness, which began in January 1529 and continued until the summer. Early on, when Clement seemed about to die, Wolsey made his third and last attempt to become pope, in the belief that if he succeeded he would be in a position to solve Henry's problem. In the event Clement recovered, but his recurring ill health meant that he could not always be visited by the English envoys. This was a nuisance, but it also meant that he could not be visited by Imperial ambassadors either, which, as the diplomatic situation turned increasingly against the English, had its advantages.

The reasons for England's changing fortunes will be analysed more fully later. All that needs to be mentioned now is that by early 1529 there were many reasons why Clement should want to commit himself more fully to the Imperial side. And there were good reasons, in law as well as in what might be best called natural justice, for taking the case out of Wolsey's and Campeggio's hands and advoking it to Rome. This the Imperialists had been begging Clement to do ever since the matter first arose in 1527, but by early 1529 it was really only a question of time before he would give in to them. Realizing this, in early May Wolsey decided to go ahead with the trial, even though there were many loose ends and the prospects for success were not all that good. He was still uncertain whether Clement had agreed to alter his and Campeggio's commission so as to allow for the existence of the 'Spanish brief'. In fact, Clement had, and by the time the trial began, or very shortly afterwards, Wolsey would have known this. But other problems remained unresolved. In particular there were Fisher's many powerful interventions on Catherine's behalf, especially his famous address to the legatine court on 28 June. Moreover, as he had always feared, the issue of whether or not Catherine's first marriage, to Henry's brother, Arthur, had been consummated increasingly dominated the court's proceedings, and it was not a winning issue for Henry. On 23 July the legatine court was adjourned and it was on 9 October that Wolsey was dismissed from office.

This, then, in brief, is the story of the divorce from its beginnings in early 1527 to the failure of the second legatine court and Wolsey's downfall in the summer and autumn of 1529. Not surprisingly, there have been many different views of Wolsey's role. Some have argued that he was so unsound on the divorce as to have been secretly sabotaging his own and the king's efforts to obtain it and hence his dismissal.[1] Others have gone to the opposite extreme, seeing Wolsey as the man

---

[1] This the view of the Imperial ambassador, Mendoza (*Sp. Cal.*, iii (ii), pp. 432-3, 790, 847, 877) and the Venetian ambassador, Falier (*Ven. Cal.*, iv, p. 212). Cavendish has Wolsey going down on bended knee to persuade Henry not to seek a divorce.; see Cavendish, pp. 74-5. For Henry's statement in court that

who first advanced the idea that Henry's marriage to Catherine was invalid, and hence as the true author of the divorce.[1] Some, even, have wished to have the best, or worst, of both views and have portrayed him as one who, having started something, found it proceeding in a direction that he did not like and decided that he would have to suppress it. This last and most complex of scenarios goes something like this:[2] Wolsey was determined to gain his revenge on Charles v for failing to carry out his promise to support his candidature for the papacy, a promise he had first made at Bruges in August 1521 and had broken both on the death of Leo x in the December of that year and again on the death of Adrian vi in the autumn of 1523.[3] The divorce of the emperor's aunt would serve Wolsey's purpose not only because Charles and his family would be greatly dishonoured by it, but because it would leave the way open for Henry to marry into the French royal family. Such a marriage, probably to Renée, a daughter of Louis xii, would serve as a cornerstone for a permanent alliance between England and France, thereby delivering a severe blow to Habsburg power and pretensions. A secondary, or alternative, purpose, was simply to get rid of Catherine because, it has been alleged,[4] Wolsey never got on with her, and this antagonism had hampered his domination of the king. The first part of Wolsey's master plan succeeded all too well. Henry was quickly convinced that his marriage to Catherine had been invalid from the start, and that, therefore, he had been living in sin for almost twenty years. However, instead of being amenable to a French marriage he had promptly fallen head over heels in love with Anne Boleyn, the one queen, so this scenario goes, whom above all others Wolsey might have hoped to be spared. Why this was so will be discussed more fully in the following chapter, but Cavendish had grasped the essence of it when he wrote that 'the great lords of the Council, bearing a secret grudge against the cardinal because that they could not rule in the commonweal as they would,' realized that Anne 'should be for them a sufficient and an apt instrument to bring their malicious purpose to pass', that purpose being none other than Wolsey's overthrow.[5] Wolsey, it has been argued, saw this danger. He was also aware that in affairs of the heart Henry was very mutable. So he did everything in his power to drag out the matrimonial proceedings in the hope that Henry would cool towards Anne and either return to Catherine or marry someone who, if not a French princess, would at least be more sympathetic towards himself than Anne was.

In fact, no view of the divorce which sees Wolsey either as its author or as one who worked to prevent it, whether from the very beginning or only after he grasped Henry's intentions towards Anne, works very well. One reason is that there was

---

Wolsey 'had been rather against me in attempting and setting forth thereof', see Scarisbrick, *Henry VIII*, p.153.

[1] The chief source for such a view is to be found in More's biographers, Nicholas Harpsfield and William Roper; see Harpsfield, *Life and Death*, pp.40-4; *Pretended Divorce*, p.175; Roper, pp.29-31.

[2] Very much a composite account, so difficult to footnote, but recent historians have tended to favour some version of it, perhaps in part because it makes it easier to reconcile the conflicting evidence; see Elton, *Reform and Reformation*, pp.104-11; Ives, *Anne Boleyn*, pp.131 ff.; Mattingly, *Catherine of Aragon*, pp.178-9, 188-9; A.F. Pollard, pp.221-3.

[3] For Charles himself making use of this explanation see *LP*, iv, 3844.

[4] Harpsfield, *Life and Death*, pp.42-3; Mattingly, pp.178-9.

[5] Cavendish, p.35.

almost certainly no aristocratic faction using Anne in the way that Cavendish and many others believed, and so there was no need for Wolsey to be frightened of her; but more of this when Wolsey's downfall is discussed. Other reasons can be dealt with immediately. It was shown earlier that Wolsey was never anxious to become pope, that he never took very seriously Charles's offer in 1521 to further his candidature and that it was certainly not the reason for the Anglo-Imperial alliance of that year.[1] This being so, Charles's failure to honour his promises can hardly bear the weight of interpretation that in so many accounts it has to. The timing of Wolsey's diplomatic initiatives lends no support to the view that sees him consumed with a desire for revenge on the emperor. The Anglo-Imperial alliance continued with some vigour until after Pavia in 1525, and there was no formal break until January 1528. For a man allegedly consumed with dark thoughts of revenge, surely Wolsey waited rather too long to put them into action? Moreover, one of the themes of this book has been that Wolsey did not conduct foreign policy in order to further his private interests; and after Pavia, for instance, there were strong reasons for believing that a French alliance was the best means of achieving Henry's wishes. If all this is so, and if Wolsey was not consumed with a hatred of Charles, or at least did not allow it to dominate his conduct of affairs, then the main reason for believing him to be the author of the divorce disappears.

What of his alleged dislike of Catherine, irrespective of her relationship with Charles? The theory that Wolsey and Catherine were always enemies hardly stands up to close examination, if only because very little evidence concerning their relationship has survived. Such as there is, has mainly to do with their shared interest in education, and in particular Oxford university. If Wolsey did indeed visit that university in 1518 it was in her company,[2] while perhaps the most distinguished of all the academics whom Wolsey appointed to his newly founded professorial chairs at Oxford, the Spanish humanist, Juan Luis Vives, was also closely connected with Catherine. And a letter of 1525 in which Longland describes Catherine's reaction to the founding of Cardinal College suggests that queen and cardinal had a warm regard for each other.[3] It is true that Tyndale in his *The Practice of Prelates* alleged that Wolsey kept spies in her household, but since that book consists largely of a diatribe against Wolsey, and since, also, he could have had very little, and certainly no first-hand, knowledge of the workings of the royal households, he can hardly be a reliable source.[4] It is also true that very occasionally Imperial ambassadors hint that all was not well between Catherine and Wolsey,[5] but then, of course, they would. When Wolsey was acting against the interests of Spain they naturally hoped that Catherine would try and influence Henry in the opposite direction; and what one hopes for, one may come to believe. Perhaps, Catherine did sometimes put in a good word for her uncle, and it may even be that in 1520 she tried, as has been alleged,[6] to prevent the Field of Cloth of Gold taking place. What

---

[1] See pp.156 ff., 387.
[2] Maxwell-Lyte, *University of Oxford*, p.422; Mitchell, pp.74-7, 78-81 for evidence that such a visit took place, but it is difficult to fit it into Wolsey's known itinerary.
[3] *LP*,iv,995.
[4] Tyndale, *Exposition and Notes*, p.309.
[5] *LP*,iii, 728; *Sp.Cal.*, iii (ii), p.110.
[6] Mattingly, *Catherine of Aragon*, pp.152-60.

is more certain is that she can hardly have welcomed the direction that English foreign policy took after Pavia, when the French rather than the Imperialists became increasingly England's main ally. But the point is that whatever Imperial ambassadors or Catherine may have hoped, she never had any influence over the conduct of foreign policy, and even the ambassadors really knew this. On his arrival in March 1527 the new Imperial ambassador, Mendoza, commented on the fact that he was being deliberately prevented from having a private conversation with Catherine, but it cannot be said that this worried him greatly because, he added, although she might wish to preserve the 'old alliance', she lacked the means.[1] Later in the year he gave as a reason for Wolsey's secret opposition to the divorce that, unlike Catherine, a new queen would not be incapable of doing him an injury.[2] And surely there can be no better confirmation of Catherine's lack of influence than Charles's almost total failure to communicate with her during the 1520s,[3] so that by November 1526 she had come to the conclusion that he must be angry with her.[4] He was not angry. He just did not consider her important enough to write letters to.

But if Catherine had no influence over the conduct of foreign policy and so was in this respect no worry to Wolsey, it could nevertheless be argued that in 1527 the mere fact that she was married to Henry stood in his way, because it prevented him from marrying the king off to a French princess. There is a great deal that is worrying about this view, not least the unconvincing evidence. All the same, Francesco Guicciardini in his *History of Italy* believed that this was indeed Wolsey's intention, and the view of this very experienced contemporary diplomat deserves some respect.[5] However, in 1527 Guicciardini was in Italy, trying his best to stave off Bourbon's Imperialist army, and was thus far removed from Amiens and Compiègne where Wolsey was negotiating with the French. At the very best, therefore, he would only have been reporting high gossip. Other evidence is derived from the reports of someone with first-hand knowledge of Wolsey, the French ambassador du Bellay. In August 1528 he surmised, and it was only a surmise, that Wolsey had hoped to marry Henry to Madame Renée, but that Henry's love for Anne had prevented him.[6] Two months later he reported a conversation in which Wolsey had apparently admitted to him that he was responsible for starting the search for the divorce[7], and this could, of course, be taken as conclusive proof that he was indeed its author. It should be stressed that this was the only time that Wolsey ever made such an admission, while on a number of other occasions both he and Henry denied it.[8] It may also, on reflection, seem a rather curious, not to say dangerous, thing to have told a foreign ambassador unless, that is, he had good reason for admitting authorship, which Wolsey did. The admission came in the course of an interview concerning the payment of an English contribution to the French military effort, and he had been 'very cold' on the subject because, as he explained to du Bellay at

---

[1] *Sp.Cal.*, iii (ii), pp.110-11.
[2] *Sp.Cal.*, iii (ii). p.433.
[3] *Sp.Cal.*, iii (i), p.108.
[4] *Sp.Cal.*, iii (i), p.1018.
[5] Guicciardini, p.401.
[6] *LP*, iv, 4649.
[7] Le Grand, iii, p.186 (*LP*, iv, 4865).
[8] Scarisbrick, *Henry VIII*, p.153.

some length, the French had grossly mishandled the military situation in Italy. Was this, demanded Wolsey, the way to reward someone who had done everything possible to bring about a perpetual union between England and France, a union which he had promised Louise of Savoy at Compiègne she would herself see if only she lived to be a year older?[1] It was at this point that he mentioned the divorce, for it was in order to bring about this union that Wolsey alleged his desire to free Henry from his marriage to the Imperialist Catherine. In this context Wolsey's remark appears to be merely a variant on his usual tactics towards the French, which were to make out that he was the only pro-French person in England and so they had better do what he advised if they wished to maintain good relations with her. 'Look what I have done and am doing for you, even as far as getting the king to change his wife, but in return you will have to help me, and, in particular, you will have to stop going on about the money you think we owe you': that was Wolsey's message to du Bellay, and if a diplomatic lie concerning his authorship of the divorce increased its impact, so be it.

It should be remembered that the French were well aware of the English desire for a divorce, so that the lie gave nothing away. It should also be remembered that the negotiations at Amiens and Compiègne were indeed about a perpetual union, and one that did involve a marriage: not, however, between Henry and Renée but between the Princess Mary and the duke of Orleans. What is more likely than that, given the rumours of Henry's desire for a divorce that were already circulating in the courts of Europe, people not directly involved would assume that a marriage for Henry was intended? The chief reason for believing that this was the case, however, is that in all the extensive English correspondence to do with Wolsey's embassy to France in 1527 there is nowhere the faintest hint of such a marriage. True, if Wolsey had been scheming behind Henry's back one would hardly expect any mention of it, but is it really conceivable that Wolsey would have dared to do such a thing? Given the view advanced in this book that it was Henry who was the dominant partner, the answer must be no, but it is difficult to conceive of any view of the relationship that would lead to a different answer. To go about arranging a marriage without the king's knowledge would have been too risky a manoeuvre to contemplate unless, that is, the king was putty in one's hands. Even so, it would have made much more sense for him to explain to Henry what he was planning before leaving for Amiens, rather than casually announcing to Henry on his return that, by the way, he was to marry a French princess. And if Henry had been putty in Wolsey's hands how does one explain Anne Boleyn?

One of the most remarkable aspects of the divorce is the behaviour of the two leading ladies, Anne and Catherine. It was Anne's refusal to take the easy option and become, as her sister had, yet another mistress that had precipitated the crisis. Almost as remarkable was Catherine's decision to resist Henry's efforts to obtain a divorce. The pressure on her to comply with the king's wishes must have been enormous, at no point more than in November 1527 when her very life seemed threatened by an accusation of what might best be called 'constructive treason'. It had been brought to the king's notice that 'divers personages do intend to conspire and imagine the death of the king's grace's most royal person and that of the lord

[1] Le Grand, iii, p.186 (*LP*,iv,4865).

legate. And this is surely thought to be enterprised for your grace's [Catherine's] sake, or for your grace's occasion by such as be favourers of the emperor'. If any such conspiracy should be attempted, Catherine was told, she would be held directly responsible even though she 'be nothing guilty therein'.[1] She would make no answer to such an abominable accusation, Catherine apparently replied, for the thought that she might commit treason against her lord and husband was beneath contempt;[2] and here she exhibited a dignity and courage characteristic of her behaviour throughout the difficult last years of her life. But on this occasion there were mitigating circumstances for her treatment. The totally unexpected appearance of the 'Spanish brief' just before the accusation was made, seemingly by her contrivance, had succeeded in destroying much of the work of the previous six months to achieve a divorce, and this must have been intensely provoking. There is also some evidence that at about this time king and minister were genuinely worried by information coming out of Spain and France that treasonable activity was being contemplated on Catherine's behalf, so the accusation was not a total fabrication.[3] Moreover, it needs to be borne in mind that however much we may admire Catherine's courage and deplore Henry's discarding of a woman who had loved and served him so loyally for so long, the fact remains that in deciding to resist the king's wishes she became an enemy of the English Crown, and an extremely dangerous one. This was not only because of her Imperial connections, but because she could not help but become a focus of any discontent within the kingdom. Any moves, either by herself or by others acting on her behalf, would have to be most sternly countered by the king's leading councillor.

In fact, given the threat that Catherine's opposition posed, what is only marginally less surprising than her bravery in offering it is the restraint shown by Henry and Wolsey in resisting it. She may have been threatened with constructive treason and subjected to lengthy harangues on the reasons why she should comply with Henry's wishes, but she was allowed to take legal advice from foreigners and to appoint to her legal council men of the highest calibre who, whatever her occasional suspicions about them,[4] seem to have prosecuted her case for the most part with sincerity and vigour. John Fisher is the outstanding example, but his episcopal colleagues, John Clerk and Henry Standish, were not far behind.[5] That this was allowed to happen is not entirely to Henry's and Wolsey's credit, just as the pressure placed on her to comply is not entirely to their discredit. Given the need to secure for Henry as legally and politically sound a marriage as possible, appearances had to be very important, and thus it was difficult not to allow her at least some of

---

[1] Pocock, i, p. 212 (*LP*,iv,4981) instructions to Warham, Tunstall and other councillors deputed to conduct the interview with Catherine; see also Gairdner, *EHR*, xii, p.238 for some corrections to Pocock.

[2] *Sp.Cal.*,iii (ii), pp.884-5 for Mendoza's account of the interview.

[3] In information sent from both the English ambassador to France and from Sylvster Dario returning from a mission to the emperor; *LP*,iv,4961; see also *LP*,iv,4909, 5016; *Sp.Cal.*,iii (ii), pp.878, 887.

[4] The point is worth making that, in public at any rate, Catherine was bound to suspect their genuineness, because one of the central planks of her defence was that she could never receive a fair trial in England.

[5] Also Warham, Tunstall, Veysey, George de Athequa bishop of Llandaff, Robert Shorton; and this is not a complete list; see Pocock, ii, pp.432, 612 for their signatures; also Paul, *Catherine of Aragon*, pp.92 ff.

her legal rights. Catherine's treatment had little to do with morality and everything to do with expediency; and it must be judged accordingly. But in order to understand Wolsey's position we must remove the spotlight for a moment from the wronged but defiant queen and focus it on a figure whose overriding responsibility was to the king. It has been suggested here that Wolsey would have been unlikely to see any political advantage for himself or for the Crown in trying to remove Catherine. This alone means that he is a most unlikely candidate for the role of author of the divorce, and it will be suggested shortly that in his heart of hearts he would have been much more likely to be opposed to it because of the great difficulties it would so obviously present. But his personal views were neither here nor there. It was his duty to carry out the king's wishes to the best of his ability. In the way of those wishes stood Catherine, who had so singularly failed to see where her duty as a loyal subject lay. This being so, she became the enemy who must be treated in whatever way the Crown found expedient.

Why Catherine chose to resist remains something of a mystery. It is not enough to say that she was fighting for her daughter's interests, for, as Wolsey more than once pointed out,[1] compliance with Henry's wishes would have done much more to further them. It is also the case that nothing stood in the way of good relations between Henry and Charles more than Catherine's unwillingness to yield gracefully to her husband's wishes. Thus, what might be called the sensible reasons for taking the stand she did are not all that credible. What seems to have sustained her was a strong sense of the rightness of her position: that her marriage being holy and good, no power on earth could dissolve it. Whether this belief was coupled, as has been suggested,[2] with an intense bitterness at being rejected by a man of whom she had deserved nothing but good, and whether this bitterness translated itself into a determination to thwart his every wish, a not uncommon reaction to the break up of a marriage, must remain speculation, though there are reasons for rejecting it.

One reason is that her comments about Henry's behaviour towards her reveal distress and sadness, not anger. Her anger was reserved for Wolsey, whom she blamed for what had happened. It was he, she told Campeggio, who had 'blown this coal' between herself and Henry,[3] and it is her views that provide the most convincing evidence that Wolsey was the author of her troubles, even if in the end they must be rejected. It is easy enough to see why she thought as she did. Whatever Wolsey's responsibility for instigating the divorce, much of its management was bound to fall to him. It was he who presided over the two legatine courts which tried the matter. It was he whose task it usually was to persuade her to comply with Henry's wishes; he who was chiefly responsible for the divorce negotiations with the Curia and other European courts; and, in particular, it was he who was most clearly asssociated with the new francophile policy that coincided with, and was in part dictated by, the search for a divorce. It must have seemed to Catherine at this time that everywhere she turned the figure of the cardinal blocked her way. And not only

---

[1] Ehses, p.60 in the second of two interviews he and Campeggio had with Catherine in Oct. 1528.

[2] Mattingly, *Catherine of Aragon*, p.198, though this rather contradicts his earlier assessment that she could never bring herself to blame Henry for anything; but then Catherine probably had contradictory feelings; see ibid, p.179.

[3] *Sp.Cal.*, iii (ii), p.841; see also Hall, p.755; for Wolsey being aware of Catherine's view of his part in the matter see *St.P*,i, p.200 (*LP*,iv,3231).

was her conclusion that he was responsible for both the conception of the divorce and its management a very natural one, but it was probably psychologically necessary too. What Catherine had to explain to herself, and in the least hurtful way possible, was Henry's rejection of her. The wiles of a younger and more attractive rival were not by themselves enough. For one thing, there had been other rivals in the past, but none had previously threatened her marriage.[1] For another, such an explanation would attach rather more blame to Henry as willing accomplice of these wiles than she was prepared to allow. What was required was an Iago-like figure, powerful and sinister enough fatally to corrupt her husband, and this Wolsey provided. Moreover, by blaming him, she gave herself the hope that if only his evil influence could be removed, Henry would return to his senses and come back to her. Wolsey thus became the scapegoat who hid from her the unbearable truth that Henry himself was the author of all her misfortunes.

That Henry was the author, if something of a simplification, must surely be the truth. None of the arguments and evidence that point to Wolsey in the end convince. Moreover, other suggested candidates turn out to be men of straw. One such is John Longland, bishop of Lincoln and one of the king's confessors; but what he could possibly have been up to in taking the initiative in such a sensitive matter defies the imagination. Then there is Gabriel de Grammont, bishop of Tarbes, of whom more shortly, but he is no more likely an author than Longland: in such a matter no foreign ambassador's view could have carried sufficient weight. Unless one sees Henry as at the mercy of every passing whim and fancy that blew in his direction, it is only he himself who could have been the author of his own divorce: he was the king and it was his marriage.

Why did he want a divorce? Both at the time and since a number of reasons have been put forward, some more creditable to him, and more credible, than others. It is, of course, likely that there was more than one reason, but what was surely central was his passion for Anne Boleyn. In making this perhaps not very controversial statement there are, nevertheless, problems of evidence. It is not even possible to ascertain when their relationship began: nearly twenty love letters have survived, but none of them is dated.[2] As for what it was about Anne that attracted him, that too remains something of a mystery. She was no obvious beauty, apart from her dark almond-eyes, about which most people commented.[3] She had spent some time at the French court, so perhaps it was her sophisticated French ways that enticed him; at any rate, she was probably a great deal more fun than Catherine, who in 1527 was in her early forties, and even ten years previously had been considered 'rather ugly than otherwise'.[4] Moreover, not only did Catherine lack beauty, but she also lacked sons; and as her last pregnancy had occurred as long ago as 1518, by 1527 it was certain that she would never bear one.[5] This cannot have helped the marriage, but

[1] They include Anne's sister, Mary Boleyn, and Elizabeth Blount.

[2] For a possible chronology placing the begining of the courtship in the spring of 1526 see Ives, *Anne Boleyn*, pp.108-9; see also Scarisbrick, *Henry VIII*, pp.147-9.

[3] Ives, *Anne Boleyn*, pp.49-53. It needs to be consulted on all matters relating to Anne though on particular episodes I find myself often in disagreement and it is especially good on her early life. But Friedmann still remains very useful.

[4] *Ven.Cal.*,ii,p.248, quoted in Mattingly, *Catherine of Aragon*, p.132.

whether it destroyed it is another matter. In Mary, Catherine had produced a legitimate female heir. There also existed an illegitimate male heir in Henry Fitzroy, the son of an early mistress, Elizabeth Blount. In 1525 Fitzroy, aged six, had been created duke of Richmond, and appointed nominal head of the Council of the North. There was, thus, no question of him remaining a skeleton in the cupboard, but whether Henry ever seriously contemplated naming him his heir it is impossible to tell.[1] As for a legitimate male heir, of course Henry talked about the need for one, but not quite as often as historians have done; and, when he did so, it appears to have been for tactical reasons rather than out of concern that the lack was proof that God was against his marriage, or that it endangered the future well-being of his kingdom. For instance, as we shall shortly discover, one of Henry's problems, when he tried to make use of the Levitical prohibition against a marriage to one's brother's widow, was the very existence of Mary. Proof of this prohibition was supposedly that such a marriage would be childless. Fortunately, there was a way round this, not invented by Henry, which was to argue that only the lack of a male child was relevant, even though that was not strictly what the text said.[2] This being so, Henry had to stress such a lack, whether it really bothered him or not. When it suited him he was perfectly happy not to stress it.

When, in November 1528 he addressed a meeting of notables in a major propaganda exercise to prove to his audience that his 'great matter' was entirely motivated by a concern for the common weal, he concentrated only on the effect on Mary's legitimacy, put in doubt by his invalid marriage, and on her right to succeed, at no stage suggesting that her gender was any impediment.[3] He did not convince his audience, and he should not convince us. The trouble with all seemingly altruistic reasons for the divorce is that they appear to be entirely geared to the demands of the moment. And the course of his relationship with Anne does nothing to strengthen the view that concern for a male heir was uppermost in Henry's mind. If it had been, a more compliant lady might have served his purpose better and, while it is true that Anne's miscarriage in January 1536 may well have had something to do with her downfall in the following April, the marriage was under stress well before then, and, unlike Catherine, she was still capable of bearing him other children. But though Henry's concern for a male heir does not carry great conviction, it is possible that in 1527 Catherine's inability to bear him more children and Anne's potential to do so, may have played some part in Henry's thinking.

Again care needs to be taken about the role assigned to the bishop of Tarbes both at the time and since. During the course of the Anglo-French negotiations in

---

[5] Parmiter, pp.8-9 for a useful chronology of her miscarriages and childbearing.

[1] It was quite usual practice for kings and noblemen to acknowledge illegitimate sons: two contemporary examples would be Charles Somerset, created earl of Worcester, an illegitimate son of Henry Beaufort, 2nd duke of Somerset, and Arthur Plantagenet, created Viscount Lisle, an illegitimate son of Edward IV. It is therefore dangerous to read too much significance into Henry Fitzroy's elevation – it is not in itself evidence for concern for the lack of a male heir.

[2] Murphy, p.28 on the scholarly support for this interpretation of Leviticus.

[3] Hall, pp.754-5; see also LP,iv,3913, 4977-8, 5050, 5377 for important statements of the king's position in which the lack of a male heir could have been used but was not, concern about the succession being expressed, as in Henry's speech, in connection with Mary's legitimacy.

the early spring of 1527 he does seem to have raised the question of Mary's legitimacy, this in response to English questioning about Francis I's precise marital status following his pre-contract to Eleanor of Austria.[1] Given that one of the options being discussed was a marriage between the French king and Mary, such diplomatic manoeuvring was to be expected, but, it is possible that the bishop's question triggered in Henry a chain of thought that made it easier for him to question his marriage. If the French could challenge its validity there must be something wrong with it. But that the bishop's intervention played only an accidental part is suggested by the way it was made use of in the months ahead. Wolsey mentioned it in that first tricky interview with Fisher on the subject of the divorce in July 1527, presumably because it offered a neutral explanation of how a scruple about the marriage had entered Henry's head at that particular time[2] and certainly it was better than talking to Fisher about Anne! It was also used, this time by Henry, at that meeting of notables already referred to.[3] On the other hand, when explaining the origins of Henry's 'scruple' to the pope or emperor it was more usual to stress that it had first arisen out of the king's own biblical studies, an edifying picture indeed![4] As with the arguments about the lack of a male heir, so with the bishop of Tarbes's role, it was the circumstances that dictated whether or not they were used, and this in turn suggests that scepticism is called for. The one argument for the divorce that Henry never made in public was that he had fallen in love with Anne, for to have done so would have been tactically foolish. Yet in February 1529 Campeggio was to say that Henry's love was 'something amazing, and in fact he sees nothing and thinks nothing but Anne. He cannot stay away from her for an hour; it is really quite pitiable, and on it depends his life, and indeed the destruction or survival of this kingdom.'[5] Surely Campeggio had got to the heart of the matter, for without the intensity of that love, or perhaps it should be called infatuation, it is difficult to see how Henry could have sustained the campaign for the five and half years that were needed, or that he would have jeopardized so much in order to do so.

Henry was the author of his own divorce. So where does that leave Wolsey? Perhaps as an opponent of it, if not from the start, though Cavendish said he was,[6] at least from the moment he realized that Henry was in deadly earnest about Anne? There are reasons for believing this. The most important is that the divorce confronted him with enormous problems, for which there may never have been any satisfactory solutions. This alone suggests that it was a foolish thing to wish for – unless, like Henry, one was in love. As regards the succession to the throne, it raised more questions than it solved. As regards foreign policy, it meant that England became a hostage to the other European powers, for once it became apparent that there was something that Henry wanted almost regardless of the cost, they were in the strongest of positions to raise their terms. The possibility that the divorce would

---

[1] LP,iv, pp.1398, 1400.

[2] St.P,i, p.199 (LP,iv,3231).

[3] LP,iv,4942; this is the French ambassador's account of Henry's speech.

[4] Inter alia LP,iv,3913; Wolsey's instructions for the important Fox, Gardiner mission to Rome in Feb. 1528; also LP,iv,5156, instructions to English envoys with the emperor in Jan. 1529, though in Aug. 1527 the Tarbes version had been used with him; see LP,iv,3327.

[5] Ehses, Romische Quartalschrift, xiv, p.267, translated by R.Roberts.

[6] Cavendish, p.74-5.

lead to schism unless Clement complied was a threat that Wolsey was to use frequently, but it was also a real possibility and one that would have worried Wolsey a good deal. Religious divisions would enormously complicate the conduct of foreign policy, leaving Henry dangerously exposed to attack from his two main rivals, Francis and Charles. In addition, they would undermine the internal peace of the kingdom, and at the same time make a mockery of the Christian faith. Wolsey was never a papalist, and, despite what was said earlier about his churchmanship, might just have accepted an English Church free of Rome's authority; but he was no friend of heresy and his acceptance would have been extremely reluctant. With his firm grasp of all the implications, Wolsey must have had many misgivings about a policy dictated to him by his master's foolishness. And there is the possibility that he may have feared for his own position if Anne ever became queen and, as a result, her faction ruled. Against all this, however, there is one compelling argument: that failure to obtain what the king so passionately wanted was the quickest route to his own destruction. It is this argument which should be borne in mind while we consider the episode that has lent most support to the opposite point of view.

The importance of William Knight's mission to the Pope in the autumn and winter of 1527 is that not only was he chosen as emissary to the pope against Wolsey's advice, but the king did not inform Wolsey of the true purpose of his mission, which was to obtain for Henry a dispensation to remarry irrespective of his existing marital status.[1] In the event, Wolsey got to know about the purpose, was intensely critical of it, but failed to prevent the mission going ahead. It is evidence of a lack of confidence between king and leading councillor more serious than any that had occurred before, for previous differences had been stated, not hidden, and had never concerned such a central matter. Henry's doubts probably set in in June 1527, when Wolsey had pointed out the difficulties for Henry's case if consummation of Catherine's first marriage could not be proved,[2] and were certainly over by the following May, when Wolsey's tactics were beginning to bear fruit. But that these doubts existed does not prove that Wolsey was an opponent of the divorce. Most people have felt, mistakenly, that because Henry had been anxious to keep the information from him, Wolsey was slow to appreciate that what he really wanted was a marriage to Anne.[3] In support of this view has been that contention that while Wolsey was in France during the summer of 1527 he had been working on his own plan to marry Henry off to a French princess. Since it has been argued here that he never had such a plan, it cannot be used as evidence that he was in the dark about Anne. And is it probable that he would have been? Since at least April of that year he had been heavily involved in Henry's great matter, presiding over the first legatine trial and discussing it at length with Warham, Fisher and Richard Sampson, not to mention the king himself. He must have thought a great deal about why, after all these years, Henry should suddenly be so anxious to discard Catherine. Whatever respect he may have had for Henry's biblical interests and the ensuing 'scruple', he would surely also have taken the trouble to check up on who

[1] See p.502, n.5.
[2] *LP*,iv,3217.
[3] *Inter alia* Elton, *Reform and Renewal*, p.105; Parmiter, pp.18-24; Scarisbrick, *Henry VIII*, pp.161-2.

his current favourite was, and so could hardly have failed to find out about Anne.

All this is, of course, to assume that Henry would not have told Wolsey about Anne, and, given Wolsey's major role in obtaining the king what he wanted, it is surely a curious assumption to make. And there is one piece of evidence which suggests quite strongly that Henry had indeed informed him, and at an early stage. While Wolsey was in France, he received a letter from Sampson, already deeply involved in the divorce, which informed him that:

> The great matter is in very good train; good countenance, much better than was in mine opinion; less suspicion or little; the merry visage is returned not less than was wont. The other party, as your grace knoweth, lacketh no wit, and so showeth highly in this matter. If that I perceive otherwise or more, I shall not fail to advertise your grace with diligence. The 23rd day the king's highness departed from Hunsdon to Beaulieu. And though his grace was ready to depart by a good space, and yet he tarried for the queen. And so they rode forth together. [1]

There are a number of ways of interpreting this passage, but the suggestion here is that the 'merry visage' refers to Catherine, the 'other party' to Anne. What is being described is a deliberate deception of Catherine to which Wolsey was privy, and for which, indeed, he was probably responsible. Catherine had not in the first instance been told of Henry's 'scruple', or even about the first legatine trial, the intention being to present her with a *fait accompli* that she could not have reversed. However, it was soon realized that the case was too complicated to be rushed through in this way. On 31 May the trial had been called off, and on 22 June, Catherine was informed by the king himself of his 'scruple':[2] no doubt this became necessary because rumours were already circulating and had, for instance, been picked up by the Imperial ambassador as early as 18 May.[3] Of course, the calling off of the trial was not intended to end the matter. It was simply that difficulties had been encountered, and time was needed to resolve them. Meanwhile, Henry had a deeply unhappy and potentially dangerous wife on his hands, and the question was how best to manage her. Not surprisingly, it was decided to play the whole thing down and to induce in her a false sense of security: the 'scruple' needed to be cleared up (the bishop of Tarbes's raising of the subject would have been useful here) but Catherine need not worry because it would all quickly be sorted out and Henry would end up more securely married to his dear wife than ever. With Catherine's fears allayed, negotiations could proceed at Rome without any interference from her. This, at any rate, was the plan.

Wolsey knew about Anne from the start. So it was not any sudden discovery that so upset him when he divined the true purpose of Knight's mission, nor, of course, could it have been Henry's intention, in sending him to Rome, to keep knowledge of Anne from Wolsey. So why did Henry send Knight, and, in particular, why did he send him while trying to keep from Wolsey any knowledge of the instructions he had given him? Something that has so far perhaps been underplayed is the extreme foolishness of those instructions. There was first the point that Wolsey had felt able to put directly to the king, which was that Knight

---

[1] Pocock, i, p.11 (*LP*,iv,3302).
[2] *Sp.Cal.*, iii (ii), p.276.
[3] *Sp.Cal.*, iii (ii), pp.193-4.

was poorly qualified to conduct such negotiations with the pope.[1] There was also the obstacle that Wolsey had spent so much of the summer trying to get round: namely, that Clement was a prisoner of the Imperial army in Rome, so that even access to him was extremely difficult. But the real foolishness was the one already mentioned: by seeking to secure a dispensation to remarry before securing an annulment of his first marriage, Henry had effectively blown any cover of respectability that his case might have had. The rumours circulating in Rome, one of which was that Anne was already expecting Henry's child,[2] must be true, for why else would Henry want such a dispensation? What was at stake was not a 'scruple' but lust, and lust was not something that the Vicar of Christ should encourage, especially when the legal arguments for doing so were not very strong.

That Henry's credibility with the pope had been destroyed at the outset was quite clear to Wolsey. In a letter dated 5 December 1527 to Gregory Casale, the permanent English representative at the Curia, he tried his best to rebuild it. Casale was told:

> how the king, partly by his assiduous study and learning, and partly by conference with theologians, has found his conscience somewhat burdened with his present marriage, and out of regard to the quiet of his soul, and next to the security of his succession and the great mischiefs likely to arise, he considers it would be offensive to God and man if he were to persist in it, and with great remorse of conscience has now for a long time felt that he is living under the offence of the Almighty, whom in all his efforts and actions he always sets before him.[3]

Casale was to make all this known to the pope, and in every way to try and further the king's 'great matter' with him. What Wolsey did not tell him was that the notion of a conscience-stricken Henry had already been exploded by Knight, but at least it could be made clear to Clement, lest by chance he had got a different impression, that Anne was not a harlot. Rather, 'the approved, excellent, virtuous qualities of the said gentlewoman, the purity of her life, her constant virginity, her maidenly and womanly pudicity, her soberness, chasteness, meekness, humility, wisdom, and laudable qualities and manners, apparent aptness to the procreation of children, with her other infinite good qualities' justified Wolsey believed – or said he did – the request that Henry was making.[4] One may squirm at the hypocrisy, but at the same time admire the way in which Wolsey set about trying to restore the right tone to the proceedings after it had been so foolishly sullied by Henry's half-cocked effort to obtain a speedy resolution to what could only ever have been half of his problem.

Wolsey was upset by Knight's secret mission not because he suddenly perceived the threat to his position that Anne posed, but because it seriously impaired the chances of the king's eventual success. But in stating that Wolsey was determined the intention is not to deny those doubts about the wisdom of the king's wishes that have already been raised. Two pieces of evidence support the notion of an unhappy Wolsey. Cavendish states that when Wolsey first heard of Henry's intentions he

---

[1] St.P,i, pp.270-1 (LP,iv, 3400).

[2] Pocock, i, p.144 (LP,iv,4251).

[3] LP,iv,3641; for the Latin original see Burnet,iv, pp.19-33.

[4] LP,iv,3641.

went down on bended knee in an effort to persuade him to change his mind.[1] Wolsey in such a posture is not always evidence of sincerely held belief. Moreover, given that Cavendish likened the destructive power of 'this pernicious and inordinate carnal love' of Henry for Anne to the plague,[2] he could hardly have portrayed his hero supporting it. But if there is room for scepticism, it seems likely that, if Wolsey did have doubts, he would have expressed them before the matter became public and before unalterable positions had been taken up and to that extent Cavendish's account rings true. More convincing is Campeggio's assessment, made not years afterwards as Cavendish's was, but as events were still unfolding. On 9 January he wrote:

> As far as I can make out the cardinal is actually not in favour of the affair, but your lordship can be sure that he would not dare to admit this openly, nor can he help to prevent it; on the contrary he has to hide his feelings and pretend to be eagerly pursuing what the king desires. I talk freely with the cardinal, since I know his opinion is as I have described it. In the end he shrugs his shoulders, and says there is nothing he can say except that the only course open is somehow to satisfy the king whatever the consequences, since in time some remedy will be found.[3]

Campeggio may have been clutching at straws; it would, after all, have been comforting for him to believe that secretly his fellow legate was on his side, despite his occasional bullying. For his part, Wolsey was quite astute enough to present a sympathetic face or hint that he believed something that he did not, if he thought that he could thereby get what he wanted. Nevertheless, there is something about Campeggio's assessment that is convincing. Wolsey was not the author of the king's 'great matter', and probably he always had reservations about its wisdom and may just possibly have had worries about how it would affect his own position. But if at the outset he had dared, as Cavendish maintained, to persuade the king to change his mind, he had thereafter kept his doubts to himself and done everything possible to bring about what Henry wanted. Campeggio understood that Wolsey had no choice. If his position depended upon his personal relationship with Henry, it needed to be reinforced by frequent proof that he was still the best man to put into effect the royal wishes. The more Henry wanted something, the more necessary it was for Wolsey to provide it, for if he did not, there were plenty of others who would. But it was not just a matter of self-interest; one does not serve a person or institution, and Henry was both, for over fifteen years without developing strong attachments, and no doubt the magic of kingship would also have cast its spell. Carrying out the king's wishes was what in every sense Wolsey was programmed to do, and if one studies the letters and instructions that were drawn up by him in the pursuit of the divorce, very rarely less than five thousand words, and occasionally twice that length, and if one considers the ingenuity with which he grappled with the legal problems involved and the complexity of the diplomatic initiatives that he undertook, there can be no reason to doubt that, whatever his reservations, he did everything in his power to free Henry from his unwelcome marriage. All that remains to be considered is how skilfully he went about it, and we shall approach

---

[1] Cavendish, pp. 74-5.
[2] Cavendish, p. 79.
[3] Ehses, *Römische Dokumente*, p. 69, translated by R. Roberts.

this on two fronts. The first to be considered will be the legal issues, which, though ultimately less important than the second – his negotiations with the pope and other European rulers – are every bit as complicated.

The most important point to make, and one which touches on both aspects, is that getting rid of a queen, especially the mother of the (albeit female) heir to the throne, was a serious undertaking with all kinds of political consequences. To take one minor point: under the terms of the Treaty of Amiens, Mary was to marry the duke of Orleans, Francis's younger son; but what would become of this marriage if Mary, instead of being heir to the throne, became merely an illegitimate daughter? The more serious point concerned the English succession itself and the rival claims to the throne that a second marriage could create. To try and prevent such rivalry it was vitally important to achieve the divorce in the most legally binding way possible. There was also the question of decorum. One could not just dump a queen: not only because she might be, as Catherine was, popular and therefore a potential focus of opposition, but because as queen she shared in the divinity of kingship – a dangerous thing to tamper with. Moreover, there were standards of behaviour which Henry, not only as king but as a chivalrous knight and Renaissance gentleman, would be expected and would want, if at all possible, to conform to. Rigging an ecclesiastical trial and rushing into marriage with the sister of a former mistress could hardly be said to be doing that. Technically, it is true, a court sitting under Wolsey as cardinal legate would have had a legal status of sorts, and would have given Henry's actions a veneer of respectability. However, it would not have created a good impression that one of the parties had no knowledge of the trial, and the more arbitrary and precipitate the efforts to get rid of Catherine were, the thinner that veneer became.

Almost certainly Wolsey was the first fully to appreciate that a successful outcome to the king's 'great matter' demanded the direct involvement of the pope. Henry in the early stages was less certain, which is why in the summer of 1527 he and Wolsey appear to have been working in different directions; but it was only the route, not the end in view that was different. Wolsey favoured the slow but sure approach; Henry was all for speed. But even Knight's disastrous mission is evidence that the king had realized that to get rid of his queen he needed the pope's help and however disagreeable and inconvenient the matter was to him, the pope could not wash his hands of it. Both men needed each other: Henry to prove to the world that he was indisputably in the right, Clement to show that the Church's authority in this vital area of the canon law was being upheld. This being so, short cuts, however tempting, were to be avoided as far as possible. Not everyone took this view all the time, and on at least two occasions Clement himself appears to have suggested that Henry should present Europe with a *fait accompli* and divorce Catherine by virtue of Wolsey's legatine authority. And considering the cost of the divorce to everyone concerned, especially to the Catholic Church and to Wolsey, would it not have made sense to do just that: divorce Catherine, marry Anne, produce a male heir, and challenge the rest of Europe to do something about it? We know nothing of the English reaction to Clement's supposed invitation to go it alone, in December 1528.[1] But this in itself seems significant: if it had been taken seriously, surely some evidence would have survived? Certainly, when in the previous December the pope had first made the suggestion, the English envoys in Rome advised against accepting it, because in their view it had only been made by him and his advisers so that they 'would not be noted of counsel in the beginning of the matter or be privy to any speciality thereof in the commencement'.[1] And if it is correct, as Campeggio seems to have suggested, that in September 1528 Stephen Gardiner had brought back with him from Rome a draft document enabling Henry to take unilateral action, Henry's and Wolsey's reaction was unenthusiastic[2] – odd, if such a move could have been the answer to their problem. They did not take Clement's suggestions seriously because they were never meant to be taken seriously. Instead, they were the pope's desperate efforts to put off for as long as possible having to choose between Henry and the emperor, a choice that he did not want to make but knew that he could not avoid if both stuck to their guns. There was no way in which the pope could avoid getting involved in the divorce of a queen, just as there was no satisfactory solution from the king's point of view that did not have the pope's seal of approval. That Wolsey made this the cornerstone of his approach is not evidence of procrastination; despite being a slow convert to the view, even Henry continued to see it in this way for long after Wolsey's fall.

The one problem to this approach was that it did not guarantee what Henry was insisting upon – namely, success – for the good reason that the law never does permit of certainty. Moreover, Henry's case was not especially good. There were two main grounds for maintaining that his marriage to Catherine was invalid. The first was to argue that the impediment to it had been imposed directly by God and · therefore it could not under any circumstances be dispensed with by the Church. Thus the dispensations granted by Julius II before it took place had no authority, Henry and Catherine had never been married in the eyes of God, and therefore both were free to marry to marry whom they liked. The evidence for God's prohibition was derived from Leviticus, the source for all the Church's regulations of the marital state, and in particular from two verses: 'Thou shalt not uncover the nakedness of thy brother's wife: it is thy brother's nakedness', was a view confirmed by the later statement that 'if a man shall take his brother's wife, it is an impurity: he hath uncovered his brother's nakedness; they shall be childless'. Apart from the objection that Henry's marriage had not been childless, a more serious difficulty was the text in Deuteronomy which stated that 'when brethren dwell together, the wife of the deceased shall not marry to another; but his brother shall take her, and raise up seed for his brother'. The way round this was to argue that it was a specifically Jewish custom with only local application, which since the coming of Christ had no validity for the rest of the Christian world. Both texts had their protagonists, who over the years had defended their point of view with great skill and learning, and there was no telling which view a particular court would take.

On what came to be the main issue, the status of the Levitical prohibitions and whether or not the pope could dispense with them in special circumstances, there

---

[1] *LP*, iv, 5038 made in an interview with England's envoy, John Casale, in which Clement showed the greatest agitation.

[1] *LP*, iv, 3802 for the suggestion; Pocock, i, p.114 (*LP*, iv, 4120) for the English envoys' advice.

[2] Ehses, *Römische Quartalschrift*, xiv, pp.259-60 for this, based on his interpretation of Campeggio's letter to Salviati of 18 Feb. 1529; see ibid, p.266.

had over the years been a significant change, and it was not one helpful to Henry.[1] Although for some time after the Fourth Lateran Council in 1215 these prohibitions had usually been taken in the way that Henry favoured, that is, being of divine origin, they could not be dispensed with, the writings of John Andreae, a professor of canon law at Bologna who had died in 1348, had encouraged a tendency to give increasing scope to the pope's dispensing powers in this area, as in many others. In 1411 John XIII had issued a dispensation to the duke of Clarence, a younger son of Henry IV, enabling him to marry within the second degree of affinity, which had previously been considered indispensable. Martin V followed his precedent in giving permission for Count John I of Foix to marry his deceased wife's sister, but Martin's successor Eugenius IV refused to allow the future Louis XI of France to marry one of his deceased wife's sisters; and the reason given was precisely that the Levitical prohibitions because ordained by God could not be dispensed with, even by the pope. And when in 1485 Richard III had been anxious to marry Elizabeth, the daughter of his brother, Edward IV, he had been strongly advised against it on similar grounds. Then, in the space of eight years three requests for dispensations within the Levitical degrees were granted, the last by Julius II to enable Henry to marry Catherine.

The position in the late 1520s was this. Henry could appeal to a canonical tradition which for much of the Middle Ages had been the dominant one, but the most recent precedents went against him. Moreover, even that older tradition had tended to admit an exception, the one laid down in the verse from Deuteronomy already quoted, which specifically commanded a younger brother to marry the wife of a deceased elder brother when that first marriage had been childless. As has been mentioned, Deuteronomy could be attacked, but nevertheless it did not help Henry that the most usual exception to the canon law prohibition against marriage to a widowed sister-in-law was the one that so closely fitted his own situation. It was, therefore, not the case, however attractive the notion was to Henry, that God was on his side, that a reliance on Leviticus provided the degree of certainty that he wished for. Moreover, there were two serious additional problems, the one factual, the other tactical. To take the former first: in canon law affinity was said to result from the consummation of a marriage, not from any contractual arrangement. Therefore, for God to be on Henry's side Catherine must not only have married his brother Arthur, which was indisputable, but she must also have had sexual intercourse with him, which was not. Indeed, Catherine was always to deny it, and the fact that she did so on oath, even on occasions when it was not in her interests to do so, strongly suggests that she was telling the truth. Her difficulty was to prove it, but it would be equally difficult for Henry to disprove and if he failed, his case collapsed.

That was one additional difficulty. The tactical one was this: since the point of going to the pope was to get his approval, it was counterproductive to argue that in this matter the pope had no authority. Moreover, by and large popes were reluctant to admit that they lacked authority in any sphere, and so if Clement's support was what was wanted, again it would not do to push the Levitical argument too strongly. This brings us to the second grounds for maintaining that Henry's marriage to

[1] For these developments see especially H.A. Kelly, *Matrimonial Trials*, pp.5-14; *Traditio*, xxiii.

Catherine was invalid, which was to argue that the original dispensation granted by Julius II was seriously defective. The great advantage of this approach was, first, that it would obviate the need to get too immersed in the uncertain seas of the canon law. More importantly, it avoided a direct challenge to papal authority and was therefore much more likely to be successful. Its great weakness, though, was that, in admitting the pope's competence to dispense, it made it difficult to reject the solution that Clement would have been all too happy to provide, which was to admit the original defects but to offer to remedy them. In an important statement of his position set out in a letter to Henry of 7 October 1529, Clement made precisely such an offer: he was willing to grant new dispensations to clear up any uncertainty.[1] He also put the point most forcibly that in cases where different views could be advanced about the validity of a marriage, the onus of proof lay very much with those who challenged its validity. And in stating the legal position Clement was also exposing Henry's hypocrisy. A marriage which had been assumed to be good for nearly twenty years should, according to Clement, continue to be thought good unless very compelling reasons were found to the contrary. Everything possible should be done to rectify any technical difficulties that had come to light and to assuage any resulting crisis of conscience. But, of course, Henry had no real concern about his conscience, and the last thing he wanted was to have the validity of his marriage confirmed.

These two strategies, the reliance on Leviticus and a concentration on the defects in the original dispensation, need not be, nor were they, considered mutually exclusive. It is vitally important to bear in mind that Henry and Wolsey were engaged in negotiations which only in the end needed to be translated into a legal decision. In negotiations, any bargaining counter is worth playing. By all means threaten the pope with all manner of dire outcomes; maintain that he had no competence, or then again, if his views are favourable, declare that he has. It was all a question of tactics, and for this reason it is a mistake to try to attribute a particular approach to a particular person. It has been usual to identify Henry with the strategy that relied upon Leviticus, and it has recently been shown that in the submission that he made to the second legatine trial the divine nature of the Levitical prohibition was very much to the fore. The conclusion drawn is that this was because Henry really believed in Leviticus, while others, such as Wolsey, did not.[2] In fact, there were obvious advantages in ascribing the Levitical argument to the king. His dubious enterprise needed to be cloaked in the greatest amount of principle possible to have any chance of carrying conviction and, anyway, it was fitting for kings to concern themselves with such lofty matters; the technicalities could be left to the clerks. It was also tactically convenient to keep the Levitical argument, essentially a threat with which to force Clement into an agreement about the technicalities, away from the day-to-day negotiations, only to be brought out on the big occasions or when the going got rough; and for such a purpose the king was an ideal repository. None of this can be proved because we have no clear insight

---

[1] Theiner, p.566 (*LP*,iv,5994); see also H.A. Kelly, *Matrimonial Trials*, pp.139-40.

[2] This the central argument of V. Murphy's work, now essential reading for the textual history of the divorce, but see especially Murphy, pp.70 ff. I am most grateful to her for an early look at her thesis, now more readily available in her introduction to Surtz and Murphy.

into Henry's mind, but if we believe that it was his passion for Anne which fuelled the divorce and if we consider the multiplicity of arguments put forward during the search for it, then the argument advanced here seems the best way of explaining the available evidence. That being so, it may seem perverse to try to ascribe a particular version of the second strategy, that which concentrated on the technical defects, to Wolsey, but the evidence points in that direction.

Virtually nothing is known about the first legatine trial in May 1527, but the fact that it was so soon abandoned suggests that Wolsey quickly realized that what Henry had asked for would prove very difficult to achieve and could only be done with the pope's personal intervention. The particular worry that must have pointed Wolsey towards this conclusion was the difficulty of proving that Catherine's marriage to Arthur had been consummated. How this affected Henry's case has already been mentioned. The point being stressed here is that it was Wolsey who first spotted the problem and, incidentally, got few thanks from Henry for doing so.[1] Indeed, it appears to have been Wolsey's raising the matter that encouraged him in the summer of 1527 to ignore his minister's advice and look for a quick solution. As it was, the issue was to dominate the second legatine trial in a disastrous way for Henry, as will shortly be shown. Neither can it have been the only difficulty that Wolsey foresaw. Soon after raising it with Henry, he conducted the famous interview with Fisher in which the bishop made it abundantly clear that he saw no grounds for believing that Henry's marriage was invalid or at least none that could not be easily remedied by the pope.[2] This news must have been very depressing for Wolsey, however brave a face he might put on it, because since Fisher was by far and away England's leading theologian, his view that there were no grounds for a divorce suggested strongly that there were none, or none sufficient to produce the cast-iron case that his master so desperately required. Probably it was this realization that convinced Wolsey that a decretal commission from the pope offered the best solution to the king's 'great matter'.

A decretal commission enabled the pope to pronounce sentence upon a particular case, conditional only upon certain facts being established by those to whom the commission was granted.[3] As Wolsey had every intention of drawing up the commission himself, one may begin to see the point of the exercise: Wolsey could choose the battlefield.[4] Another great advantage was that it would be difficult for Catherine to appeal against the judgment of the commissioners – a course of action that she was almost bound to take, as indeed she did, against any unfavourable sentence passed in England – because that judgment was already the pope's. Not surprisingly, given that the whole exercise depended upon the pope's close co-operation, Leviticus did not get a look in. Instead, the focus was to be entirely on the original dispensation, and in particular on three points of fact. The first was whether it was true, as the dispensation implied, that the marriage between Henry and Catherine had been necessary to preserve the peace between England

---

[1] St.P,i, pp.194-5 (LP,iv,3217) Wolsey to Henry, 1 July 1527.

[2] St.P,i, pp.198-201 (LP,iv,3231).

[3] Parmiter, p.44 for a brief history and definition of a decretal commission.

[4] For convincing arguments that the decretal commission granted in June 1528 had in effect been drawn up by Wolsey see Thurston, pp.639-40; for Wolsey's drafts see H.A. Kelly, Matrimonial Trials p.57, n.4.

and Spain. The second was whether the young Henry had desired the marriage for the reason stated in the dispensation, which was that he wanted to preserve that peace. The third was whether any of the three monarchs named in the dispensation, Henry VII, Ferdinand and Isabella, had died before the dispensation came into effect, which was taken to be when the marriage had been solemnized in June 1509.

To take the last point first, it is obvious that the answer was easy: by 1509 both Henry and Isabella were dead and therefore in no position to have any views on the subject of peace. This being so, the stated motive of those asking for the dispensation collapsed. But if the factual answer was easy, one might reasonably wonder what it had to do with the genuineness of Henry's marriage; Julius II can hardly be blamed for the long delay between his granting the dispensation and the deaths of two of those who had requested it. He had acted in good faith, believing that the preservation of peace between royal families, in which dynastic marriages played an important role, was an honourable policy. Surely there was nothing in all this that a reasonable man could take exception to? But an unreasonable man might argue, and hence the significance of the first matter to be inquired into, that in the case in question it made no sense to maintain that the marriage served such a purpose because peace already existed between the two kingdoms. Everyone agreed that the stated motive was a very important part of a dispensation.[1] Whatever one's view of the dispensability or otherwise of the Levitical prohibition, nobody doubted that an impediment deriving from a relationship in the first degree of affinity – that is, a relationship with a brother or sister of the intended spouse – was a grave one, and that even a pope could only dispense with it for some compelling reason. If there was already peace, and no obvious reason why that peace should not continue whether or not the marriage took place, then it could hardly be argued that the marriage provided such a reason; or so the unreasonable man might argue. The second question to be investigated by the commissioners is susceptible to the same kind of analysis. At first sight it may not seem exceptionable to state, as the original dispensation did, that Henry had wanted the marriage in order to conserve peace. But the unreasonable man – and lawyers are trained to be such – might point out that at the time that the dispensation had been granted and the marriage treaty drawn up, Henry was only eleven, so not of an age to have views on such a topic. Therefore the statement in the dispensation must be false, and the dispensation itself invalid.

The purpose of the above discussion is to show with what skill Wolsey had attempted to choose the battleground on which the case was to be fought and won.[2] The questions were so posed that not only was it easy to arrive at the factually correct answers, but the answers themselves would be precisely those that would most effectively undermine the validity of the dispensation. And to underline how little Wolsey intended leaving to chance, it was to be laid down in the decretal commission that it required the facts in only one of the three matters to be investigated to prove inconsistent with what was stated in the dispensation, for the

---

[1] See especially Thurston, pp.643-4.

[2] A fact acknowledged in Clement's pollicitation, which stated that he had issued the decretal commission in order to 'clearly certify to the said King Henry our desire to administer speedy justice . . . and render it more secure against a labyrinth of judicial proceedings'. Since the decretal commission itself was destroyed, the pollicitation is an essential source for what it contained.

marriage to be declared invalid.[1] To have reduced the legal complexities raised by the king's 'great matter' to these three simple questions of fact, only one of which needed to be answered in a way favourable to Henry, was a remarkable conjuring trick. No wonder Wolsey fought so hard to persuade Clement to grant such a document.

As we have seen, he got remarkably close. Clement did draw up such a document, but at the same time instructed Campeggio not to hand it over to Henry or Wolsey. Meanwhile, the case was to be tried by the two cardinals by virtue of a general commission, which was not the same thing at all. This was not only because it would be easier for Catherine to appeal against their judgment, but, much more serious, because the legal battleground under such a commission would not be controlled by Wolsey. Absolutely any argument for or against the validity of the marriage could be raised, and in such a free-for-all the many weaknesses in Henry's case could be exposed, in particular the question that had first worried Wolsey back in June 1527: whether it could be proved that Catherine's first marriage had been consummated. If it could not, it will be remembered, Henry's case would suffer a severe setback: no consummation, no impediment of affinity, and therefore no reason why Henry should not have married Catherine. In fact, there did remain one, the impediment of public honesty, which was created by the existence of any kind of former marriage contract, such as there had certainly been for Catherine and Arthur. And if this impediment had existed, should it not have been dispensed with before Catherine had married Henry? It was Wolsey who late that same June had first noted this failure in the original dispensation, and saw how this could in certain circumstances be used to Henry's advantage.[2] However, the failure did not, as has been alleged, provide Wolsey with a winning line that only Henry's obsession with Leviticus had prevented him from playing.[3]

According to the then generally accepted view, the omission of any reference to the impediment of public honesty in the dispensation would only have had serious consequences if the marriage had not been proceeded with and, thus, consummated. Otherwise it could be assumed that the dispensation for the impediment of affinity also covered that of public honesty. As there could be no consummated marriage without a prior marriage contract, a dispensation for the latter was considered redundant. And that a dispensation for public honesty had been considered redundant was to be presumed from the fact of its omission, especially from the English bull, the only one that the English accepted as authentic, for in that a doubt concerning consummation was admitted. The issue of public honesty was not so obscure as to have been easily overlooked, and indeed was specifically mentioned by the English and Spanish commissioners for the marriage treaty of 1503.[4] If the view in Julius II's time was that there was no legal requirement

---

[1] Thurston, p.642.

[2] St.P,i, pp.194-5 (LP,iv,3217).

[3] Central to Scarisbrick's discussion of Wolsey's handling of the divorce, but see especially Henry VIII, pp.194-7. In rejecting it, I am very dependent on the arguments in H.A. Kelly, Matrimonial Trials, pp.30-1, 109, 114-18; 129-31, 137-8, 146-7, 152-6. One of the most telling points he makes is that much more use was made of the impediment of public honesty than Scarisbrick allowed, though only in situations in which other lines were proving unsuccessful.

[4] Rymer,xiii, p.81; see also H.A. Kelly, Matrimonial Trials, p.115.

for it to be mentioned, there was no very compelling reason why Clement should think differently. It was, therefore, most unlikely to have been a winning line. Moreover, there were tactical reasons for not playing it, for to focus on it would have been more or less to concede that consummation had not taken place, and thus to abandon the Levitical argument. It was also open to the same response as any other argument that rested on the defects of the original dispensation: that there was nothing God-given about it and so any omissions or defects could easily be put right by the pope. It was precisely to guard against this weakness that it was so important not to jettison Leviticus.

Wolsey only ever saw the omission of any reference to the impediment of public honesty in the original dispensation as of any use if the case for the consummation of Catherine's original marriage was to give way in the face of her persistent denial. What is clear, however, is that he always feared that this might happen, and hence the insistence on a decretal commission. It is, therefore, most unlikely that he viewed the outcome of the second legatine trial with as much optimism as most historians have implied.[1] It had only been the fear that, if he delayed any longer, the Imperialists would succeed in persuading the pope to advoke the case to Rome that had forced him to set it in motion. One reason for his preference for delay was the continuing uncertainty about the Spanish brief, but right up until the last moment he was still instructing the English envoys in Rome to secure yet wider powers for himself and Campeggio in an effort to make it as difficult as possible for Catherine.[2] There is not the slightest doubt that, when on 31 May 1529 the trial at length got under way, Wolsey was a worried man, and the next six or seven weeks were to give ample proof that his fears were well founded. The trial went so badly for Henry that Campeggio's adjournment on 23 July probably came as something of a relief.[3] The more usual interpretation sees it as an unexpected and devastating blow to Henry's cause, contrived by Campeggio who was desperately worried that he would have to pass judgment in Henry's favour even though his instructions from Rome were to do no such thing. There are sound reasons for such a view: Campeggio's instructions were on no account to proceed to a judgment and there is no doubt that by 21 June he was worried that he would be unable to comply with them, so great was the pressure to proceed.[4] Three weeks later he reported that things were speeding up 'now faster than a trot', and that it would be impossible for him to withhold his opinion, adding, however, that in doing so he would have before his eyes only God and the honour of the Holy See.[5] Was this merely an excuse for going against Clement's wishes, or was it a hint that he would not, after all, have to come down in Henry's favour? There are grounds for thinking that the

---

[1] See *inter alia* Ives, *Anne Boleyn*, p.140, but even Scarisbrick's comment in *Henry VIII*, p.227, that 'at Blackfriars, the king's case had been going badly, for reasons that are not clear', implies that the expectation was that it would go well.

[2] *LP*,iv,5523, 5575 for Wolsey's instructions of 7 and 20 May.

[3] In suggesting this I have again relied heavily on H.A. Kelly's work; see *Matrimonial Trials*, pp.75 ff. which needs to be consulted, especially for a detailed discussion of the sources; but see also V. Murphy's introduction to Surtz and Murphy.

[4] A PS to Campeggio's letter of 21 June in Ehses, *Römische Dokumente*, pp.107-10, translated in Gairdner, *EHR*, xii, pp.249-52 the PS is not in *LP*. The treatment of all Campeggio's letters in *LP* needs to be checked with Ehses, *Römische Dokumente*.

[5] Ehses, *Römische Dokumente*, p.120 (*LP*,iv,5775), though not a calendar of the complete letter.

latter was the case, the chief one being that John Fisher's powerful intervention on 28 June turned the climate against Henry. Moved, he maintained, by Henry's personal appeal on the 21st for anyone to speak their mind who could help relieve the burden of his conscience, Fisher proceeded to tell the court that two years of study had convinced him that Henry's marriage was good; indeed, so convinced was he that, like John the Baptist, whose death had been brought about by his criticisms of Herod's matrimonial plans, he was willing to lay down his life in the defence of his conviction.[1] According to a friend of Campeggio's secretary, Fisher was held in such esteem that after this intervention it would be quite impossible for the court to pronounce against the validity of the marriage.[2] This may have been an exaggeration, but the immediate adjournment of the court for a week suggests that Fisher made an impact, and that in consequence Wolsey was anxious for time to take stock.[3]

According to Cavendish's admittedly garbled account,[4] Fisher made his speech, or perhaps it was another of his interventions, at a moment when the question of consummation was under scrutiny – this, of course, the topic that Wolsey had most feared, but it had not needed Fisher's intervention to bring it to the forefront, for Catherine had seen to that. Back in November 1528 she had issued a public statement denying it,[5] and in doing this she was only repeating what she had most forcibly declared to both Wolsey and Campeggio in private.[6] Then, on 21 June 1529, she did something even more dramatic. In her one and only appearance in court she knelt before her king and husband and affirmed that 'when you had me at the first, I take God to be my judge, I was a true maid without touch of man'.[7] This public declaration was a great embarrassment. Of course, it was true, as Wolsey and others pointed out,[8] that because she and Arthur had lived together for five months and had undoubtedly gone to bed, though according to Catherine on only seven occasions,[9] did create a presumption that intercourse had taken place. There were also a number of people willing to swear that on their wedding night intercourse had occurred.[10] But this had been almost thirty years earlier and all most people were in a position to remember was court gossip. There were really only two people who could provide authoritative testimony: one was Catherine, who had made her views all too plain, both in public and on oath, and the other was Henry, and therein lay further difficulties. In his younger days, apparently, Henry had been inclined to boast that he had found his wife a virgin.[11] Now, this was the kind of thing that any

[1] Ehses, *Römische Dokumente*, pp.116-17 (*LP*,iv,5732), though a letter by Campeggio's secretary, not, as stated in *LP*, by Campeggio). For du Bellay's account see *LP*,iv,5741.

[2] Ehses, *Römische Dokumente*, pp.117-18.

[3] H.A. Kelly, *Matrimonial Trials*, p.97.

[4] Cavendish, p.85.

[5] *LP*,iv, app.21.

[6] Ehses, *Römische Dokumente*, pp.58-9.

[7] Cavendish, p.81; see also Ehses, *Römische Dokumente*, pp.108-9.

[8] *LP*,iv,4685 for Wolsey's assertion.

[9] Ehses, *Römische Dokumente*, p.59 said by Catherine to Campeggio when taking confession.

[10] *LP*,iv,5774, 5778, 5783, 5791; see also Kelly, *Matrimonial Trials*, pp.112 ff.

[11] Scarisbrick, *Henry VIII*, p.188, n.3. In addition to the references cited there see *Sp.Cal.*, *F.S.*,p.450. And in October 1529 Chapuys reported Henry allowing Catherine's claim, admittedly only in order to convince her that the marriage would still be invalid because the original dispensation had made no

husband might want to boast about, even in the special circumstances of a marriage to one's brother's widow, and anyway the boast might well have been untrue. Still, it was very awkward that he had made it and, worse, that it probably was true! At any rate, Henry never dared to answer Catherine's direct challenge to declare on oath in what condition he had found her on their wedding night.[1] Moreover, following the trial those who supported the king were forced to argue, against the generally accepted view, that the issue of consummation did not in any way invalidate the Levitical prohibitions.[2] It also does not help one to believe in Henry's view that vital evidence he presented to the court was suppressed from the official record before his case was retried by Thomas Cranmer at Dunstable in 1533.[3]

If considerable time has been spent on this rather than on any other aspect of the second legatine trial, it is because it does seem to have been a losing line for Henry, and one which, if lost, would fundamentally undermine his case that any dispensation granted for his marriage had been invalid from the start. It would then be very difficult, as we saw earlier, for him to resist the argument that any faults in the original dispensation could be easily remedied, and after twenty years of marriage even that was probably not required. Once the question of consummation had become central, Wolsey would be in difficulty; and there are indeed signs that, despite the pressure to conclude lest the case be advoked to Rome, proceedings were becoming bogged down. At one point it had been Wolsey's and Campeggio's intention to have all the relevant material on which to base their judgment presented to them on 14 July. But the documents were not presented until the 19th, and there are some indications that, even then, all was not as it should be, for though sentence was to have been given on the 21st, there was yet another postponement, which led only to Campeggio's 'unexpected' adjournment on the 23rd.[4] It is difficult to believe that these delays can be ascribed entirely to Campeggio's machinations, for if all had been going well there would have been enormous pressure from the king's side to come to judgment as soon as possible. But what appears to have happened is that Henry's lawyers were having trouble in presenting a winning line – and if that was so, then the adjournment may not have been quite the disaster that is usually assumed.

There has always been something surprising about the passivity with which Wolsey accepted the allegedly unilateral declaration of an adjournment by his

---

reference to public honesty, an argument that interestingly Chapuys dismissed as being as thin as 'la glace d'une nuit'; see Sp.Cal., iv (i), p.275.

[1] Catherine's challenge was made in her mandate to the pope of 10 May 1529 and passed on to Henry in Clement's letter of 7 Oct. 1529; see LP,iv,5994. See also H.A. Kelly, Matrimonial Trials, pp.135-47.

[2] H.A. Kelly, pp.224-9.

[3] H.A. Kelly, Matrimonial Trials, pp.95-6. It looks as if, in answer to the question whether he had found her a virgin, he had admitted uncertainty, may even have said she was a virgin, an admission too damaging to have been left on the record. For the evidence of Campeggio's secretary for Henry's answer see LP,iv,6694; also Sp.Cal.,iv (i), p.656.

[4] H.A. Kelly, Matrimonial Trials, pp.120. Scarisbrick in Henry VIII, p.227, n.2 assigned the adjournment to the 31st. This would help to solve some of the puzzles surrounding Wolsey's letter of 27th (LP,iv,5797), which implies that the trial was still in progress, but the record of the trial does not support his suggestion, and a scribal error does not seem very likely; see H.A. Kelly, Matrimonial Trials, pp.127-8.

fellow judge, especially when it is usually further alleged that it was this declaration that destroyed him. And the idea that the adjournment was either unexpected or disastrous is not supported by the letter which Wolsey wrote to the English envoys at Rome on 27 July. Admittedly there are problems about it, one being the date, for written apparently after the adjournment, it anticipates it! Moreover, it is a signed letter which must raise a doubt about whether it was ever sent, since outgoing letters have usually only survived in draft form. Neither is there any reference to it having been received by the envoys, nor do any of its instructions appear to have been carried out.[1] On the other hand, the fact that all but the first two sentences were written in an apparently unique cipher suggests that, whether sent or not, Wolsey considered its contents of some importance.[2] He began by thanking the envoys for their efforts in trying to prevent the advocation until:

> such time as you supposed, celerity being used, sentence might have been given . . . Howbeit, to show unto you in great and secret counsel, and to be in any wise reserved to yourselves without disclosing thereof to the pope or any other person, such discrepant contrareity of opinions hath here ensued in the said cause, that no manner of hope in the same opinions can be in any brief time groundly trutinate, weighed, and every part to the point pondered, but that it must require more long demur and tract of time for the profound digesting of the same. So, as no certain time being known how long it shall be before the said opinion shall now be well resolved, remembering furthermore that now within one week the days judicial shall expire wherein it is by law used and appointed to proceed in such causes, and so the course of the process must needs of force cease for two months or thereabouts, it is here taken for a thing not feasible so long to protract and put over the signature of the said advocation.[3]

Wolsey then instructed the envoys to act on the assumption that the advocation would go ahead, whether or not it had been signed by the time they received this letter. The adjournment, which Wolsey does not even associate with Campeggio, let alone blame him for, was thus merely an addendum to Wolsey's main point: that it had proved impossible to come to any speedy conclusion to the trial. There seems to have been no good reason for Wolsey to make this point unless it was the truth; he seems merely to have wanted to put the envoys in the picture, while naturally being anxious that the difficulties should not too quickly become common knowledge at Rome. And, of course, the picture that Wolsey presented here fits well with the delays and difficulties that have been shown to have existed.

If Wolsey was speaking the truth and there really was 'no manner of hope' that the trial would be quickly concluded, and by that must be understood concluded in Henry's favour, then it is most unlikely that Campeggio's adjournment would have been unexpected, or indeed unwelcome. This view receives some confirmation from a letter which the French ambassador wrote on 22 July, just a day before the adjournment was announced. His assessment was that, while on the 19th, when all the documents had been finally presented to the legates, the king's supporters had been hopeful of success, already by the 22nd the situation had changed and they

---

[1] For instance, Wolsey asked for the instant recall of Peter Vannes, but this does not seem to have happened until October.

[2] St.P,vii, p.193, n.1.

[3] St.P, vii, pp.193-4 (LP,iv,5797).

were now worried that Campeggio would not do as they wished.[1] The ambassador's explanation for this turn of events was that Campeggio was so anxious to profit from Imperial favour now that Charles v was the virtual master of Italy, that he would do nothing to disappoint him. There could be something in this, although his loyalty to the pope was probably more significant. Both explanations, however, obscure an aspect that is of great relevance. To secure an adjournment Campeggio would have needed to secure the agreement of his fellow judge. Furthermore, his fellow judge was probably aware of the dates of curial holidays and, as his letter of 27 July proves, did know that these dates were not binding in the case of special commissions such as he and Campeggio were acting under.[2] To assume otherwise is to assume that Wolsey had been grossly negligent in his preparation, and this is so unlike him as to be inconceivable, and Englishmen had been dealing with the Roman courts from time out of mind. No, the only credible scenario is that Campeggio adjourned the court with Wolsey's agreement and Henry's prior knowledge. The question then arises of how that agreement was obtained.

The answer has more or less been given already. On the evidence presented it would have been quite easy for Campeggio to show that sentence could not be given in Henry's favour, or at the very least that there were so many difficulties that a speedy decision was not possible. But time was not on Wolsey's side, for by the end of July the advocation, which Clement had agreed to on the 13th,[3] was expected any minute.[4] In these circumstances it was vital for Wolsey not to allow knowledge of the true state of the legal position to become public, let alone to allow a sentence in favour of the marriage, legally the most correct outcome of the trial, to be passed. Far better to create the impression that all would have been well if only Campeggio had not intervened. And why would Campeggio have been prepared to shoulder the blame? Because it averted the more difficult alternative of having to pass a sentence that would have infuriated his hosts, and at the same time it enabled him to carry out the only specific instruction that he had from Rome, which was to prevent any sentence being passed. The adjournment was a compromise that gave just enough to all sides for it to be acceptable.

But what, then, becomes of the duke of Suffolk's one moment of fame? It may be remembered that when Campeggio had announced the adjournment, so great apparently was his fury that the duke had shouted out what, according to most accounts, all Henry's loyal subjects were thinking at this time: that 'it was never merry in England whilst we had cardinals amongst us'.[5] There is no reason to doubt that Suffolk made the remark, but if it should be thought a little too theatrical and apposite to ring completely true, there is an explanation. According to Cavendish, Suffolk's declaration was made at the king's command and, although there are

---

[1] *LP*,iv,5789.

[2] For the fact that the dates were not binding see H.A. Kelly, *Matrimonial Trials*, p.78.

[3] But formally agreed to on the 16th; see Ehses, *Römische Dokumente*, pp.122-5; H.A. Kelly, *Matrimonial Trials*, p.136.

[4] Wolsey's instructions to the English envoys at Rome of 27 July were for them to act on the assumption that the advocation had been granted; see *St.P*, vii, p.194, but then the decision back in May to go ahead with the legatine trial had been taken on the basis that an advocation was likely.

[5] This in Cavendish, p.90; but see also Hall, p.758, who has Suffolk making 'a great clap on the table with his hand'.

problems about Cavendish as a source, in this instance he probably got it right: there is nothing else in Suffolk's career to suggest that he was capable of taking a political initiative, and the alternative interpretation, that he merely lost his temper, is undermined by the argument put forward here that the adjournment could not have come as a surprise to Henry and his leading councillors, of whom Suffolk was one.[1] Thus, Suffolk's outburst was probably entirely premeditated: an official protest made for propaganda effect, and one entirely compatible with the kind of compromise that it has been suggested was arrived at, with the king's full knowledge, between Campeggio and Wolsey. Moreover, though the failure of the legatine court was a setback – and following the optimism of the previous September, one severe enough to convince Henry that the time had come to disgrace his cardinal legate – Wolsey did not see it as the end of the road. He was to spend the next two months conducting a skilful damage limitation exercise, the aim of which was to persuade the pope to take the matter into his own hands and give a personal judgment in Henry's favour.[2] It was the continuation of the existing policy in another guise, and, as before, it meant that somehow the pope would have to be fixed, but in a way that could not be proved, for appearances were almost more important than reality. The best solution had been the decretal commission, and with its failure the prospects for any kind of success greatly diminished. But because, as Wolsey put it, the king's cause suffered no negative,[3] the search for a solution had to go on. And if there was a solution, it had probably far less to do with the complexities of the canon law than with the equally complex issues of foreign policy.

The task that Henry set Wolsey in the spring of 1527 was the hardest he had ever asked his cardinal legate to perform. Insofar as the pope held the key, it meant that it was Italian politics that Wolsey would have to try and dominate, and one does not have to be too influenced by Burckhardt to appreciate that the Italian peninsula was something of a quicksand in which even the best laid plans could quickly disappear without trace. Moreover, for England, as has been pointed out before, for what were essentially logistic reasons, it was probably the most difficult area of Europe on which to exert pressure. But the alternative was to rely on allies, and after fifteen years of involvement in foreign affairs Wolsey did not need to read Machiavelli to appreciate that allies were unreliable and at best a crude instrument with which to achieve one's ends. Admittedly, he did not have to look for lasting success in Italy. All that was needed was to apply a half-nelson for just long enough to persuade Clement that it was worth his while to agree to Henry's request. It would be entirely a question of timing, and, given that in the late 1520s Clement was much in need of help, it might just be possible to pull it off.

One thing in Wolsey's favour was that, as a result of the Imperial victory over the French at Pavia in February 1525, the rulers of Italy were extremely suspicious of Charles's intentions. King of Naples and effective ruler of both Genoa and Milan,

---

[1] Hall's version is a little more complicated but in it Henry knew of the postponement before it occurred and ordered Norfolk, Suffolk and 'other nobles of the Council' to intervene; see Hall, p.758. For Chapuy's report see *Sp.Cal.*10 (i), p.263.

[2] See pp.591-2 below.

[3] For his actual words see Burnet,iv, p.84 (*LP*,iv,5428).

and for the moment without the French to act as a restraining influence, Charles did seem to be in a strong position to establish some kind of sovereignty over the whole peninsula, although the assumption that he wanted to was probably a mistake. Threatened from within by the spread of Lutheranism and from without by the army of Suleiman the Magnificent, his hold over the Holy Roman Empire, never strong, was increasingly precarious. All he wanted in Italy was a settlement which safeguarded his position sufficiently to allow him to turn his attention to overcoming these threats. But if Charles saw his policy towards Italy as essentially defensive, her rulers, given the opportunities that Pavia had created, may be excused for not sharing his view. For them the immediate task was to resist further Imperial advancement, and to that end they were very much in the market for allies, even one who could give as little help as England. This underlying point needs to be borne in mind as the complex story of Wolsey's negotiations with the papacy is unravelled. It was this that gave him his chance to exert some influence on Italian affairs and thus to obtain the divorce; for, of course, one of the most important of the Italian states was presided over by Clement VII, the only person able to grant it.

When, however, the news of Pavia had first reached Wolsey, the divorce had not yet been thought of. Instead he had to contend with the more general problem of deciding how this Imperial victory, and the unusual circumstances that resulted from the capture of the French king, affected England's chances of continuing in the dominant role in European affairs that both he and his master considered rightfully hers. At first sight Pavia might have appeared to confirm the wisdom of the Imperial alliance and the Great Enterprise against France decided upon at Bruges way back in 1521. In fact, as we saw earlier, Wolsey had begun to have serious doubts about the alliance sometime before Pavia, and these were soon confirmed when it became clear that Charles had no intention of seizing the opportunity to launch an all-out attack on France. The result was the volte-face described in a previous chapter and the signing, on 30 August, of the Treaty of the More.[1]

The most obvious purpose of this was to secure Francis's release from captivity in Spain on reasonable terms. In return for English help, his mother, Louise of Savoy, was prepared, albeit reluctantly, to pay quite a high price: in money terms about £20,000, and she was also at last to come to some satisfactory financial settlement of what was owing to Henry's sister, Mary, as dowager queen of France, and to settle yet another long-standing grievance by forbidding Albany to return to Scotland. In making this treaty, Wolsey had no intention of allowing England to become involved in a full-scale war with the emperor, but to achieve a position somewhat similar to the one he had secured in 1518 by the Treaty of London: a European peace presided over by Henry and himself, and underpinned and dominated by the Anglo-French alliance of which England was to be the senior partner.[2] The difficulty, even before the king's 'great matter' complicated everything, was that this time neither Francis nor Charles was especially anxious for peace. Once Francis had been released in March 1526, he was determined to re-establish himself as a leading figure

---

[1] See pp.386 ff. above for a very full discussion of this volte-face.
[2] The treaty is well summarized in Knecht, p.185; for the financial terms see *LP*,iv,1602-4; for Louise's reluctance see *LP*,iv,1609.

in Europe, while at the same time attempting to recover the two sons whom he had had to surrender to Charles as a guarantee of his good behaviour. Both these ambitions meant intervening in Italian affairs. Charles's position, although arguably more defensive, did have a curious tendency to end in war-like behaviour. Moreover, though he may not have been anxious for further gains in Italy, he was faced with some difficult decisions there which were always likely to provoke opposition. First, there was what to do about Milan whose puppet duke, Francesco Sforza, and his adviser, Girolamo Morone, had proved to be less compliant to his wishes than he had hoped. He was also most anxious to be crowned emperor by the pope, which would necessitate a personal visit to Italy, and this could only arouse the gravest suspicions about his long-term intentions. The Venetians and Clement – if his chief advisers at the time, Gian Giberti bishop of Verona and Francesco Guicciardini, could persuade him to make any decision – were likely to resist even Charles's modest plans for Italy. All in all, the prospects for peace in 1525 and 1526 were not good, but especially not for one arranged by Wolsey, since one undoubted consequence of Pavia was that Charles was in no mood to be dictated to. Somehow or other, Wolsey would have to prove to the emperor that England was a force to be reckoned with, and this was not going to be easy.

Francis's release was accomplished in March 1526, but it has to be admitted that the part played by Wolsey was not all that great, for it was Charles's priorities in Italy and Germany and thus his desire to conciliate France that applied the pressure. Still, insofar as Wolsey had promised to obtain the French king's freedom, it was an auspicious start, but no more than that. France was weak in 1526, and though up to a point this suited Wolsey it would not do if she was so weak that even the combined strength of England and France could pose no threat to the emperor. Further allies would have to be sought, and the obvious place to look was among the Italian states anxious to resist further Imperial encroachments. The result was that in May 1526 the League of Cognac was formed, consisting of France, the papacy, Venice, Florence and the duke of Milan, who was being besieged at the time by Imperial forces in the castle of Milan, and was in effect a duke without a duchy.[1] For the Italians it was his restoration that was the major purpose of the league, for this was the most practical way of limiting Imperial power. For Wolsey, however, Milan was but a small brick in a much larger edifice. Although he was much involved in bringing the league into existence, it did not suit his purpose to be too obviously connected with it. Henry was to be given the deliberately shadowy title of 'protector', but for the moment that was all. The actual fighting was to be left to the members of the League, especially to the Venetians, for to begin with Francis was almost as reluctant to fight as Wolsey was, and anyway, what with the setbacks of the last year and a half, including the payment of a large ransom to Charles, he was hardly in a position to do so. However, some fighting was essential to Wolsey's plans. What Wolsey hoped was that Charles would become so embroiled in fighting the league that he would be only too willing to take up Wolsey's offer to act as honest broker. Once he could get Charles to the conference table, then he was confident that he could engineer a settlement of Europe's problems acceptable to all, but most of all to England: a subordinate France paying England a large annual

---

[1] Knecht, pp.209-10 for the terms.

sum for the privilege of being number two; a contained Charles, content to surrender more dangerous ambitions so as to concentrate on what was, after all, the task of a Holy Roman Emperor, the defence of Christendom from the Infidel; and a grateful Italy freed from the threat of the rapacious Imperialists. The plan has all the hallmarks of its author: a mix of bluff and real pressure, of stick and carrot, a combination that had served him well in the past. It was ambitious, but with a little luck and his usual good judgement it might not be impossible to bring it off.

One characteristic feature of the plan was that it required only the minimum use of England's own military and financial resources. This had the disadvantage that the more the fighting was left to his allies, the more difficult it would be for Wolsey to prevent them from dictating the terms of any peace settlement that might emerge. The advantage was that, when the right moment occurred, England's non-involvement in the fighting would lend credibility to Wolsey's claim to the role of honest broker and it was this that was central to his strategy of dominating any general European settlement. Moreover, there was the important further consideration that money to finance any major contribution to a war against the emperor was lacking. Whatever Henry and Wolsey's real intentions as regards the Amicable Grant, the undoubted resistance to it was a warning that the country was in no mood to accept further heavy financial demands; a mood which could not have been improved now that the enemy was no longer to be the French but the more popular Imperialists. It is possible to make too much of this shortage of money: it was, after all, a weakness shared by every European power, yet it very rarely prevented them from engaging in war. But it was a further complication for Wolsey in what was already a very complicated scenario.

Just how complicated it was, and how difficult it was going to be for Wolsey to achieve success, was already apparent before Henry's 'great matter' doubled his difficulties. The trouble was that during 1526 the new league had not had much success in Italy; indeed, one member, Clement, had had to endure the indignity of being besieged in his castle of St Angelo in Rome by a small force organized, with Imperial help, by his arch-rival Cardinal Pompeo Colonna. And in early 1527 a large force of German and Spanish troops, commanded by the duke of Bourbon, had moved into Northern Italy and was posing a real threat to the continued existence of the league. It was obvious that, if it was to survive, much more would have to be done by England and France, and the result was a series of diplomatic initiatives culminating in Wolsey's famous mission to Amiens and Compiègne in the summer of 1527. By the Treaty of Amiens, signed on 18 August, England agreed to make a monthly financial contribution to support a French army led by Odet de Foix, sieur de Lautrec, which had, in fact, already left for Italy.[1] As Wolsey explained to Henry, it was now necessary for there to be 'a real and actual prosecution of the war',[2] but it is important to realize that for Wolsey this was something of a setback. The evidence lies in the otherwise curious fact that while negotiating an offensive alliance against the emperor, Wolsey spent much of his time at Amiens trying to persuade Francis to modify the terms that were to be put to Charles, so that there was some prospect of them being acceptable.[3]

---

[1] Lautrec left Paris on 2 July (LP,iv,3215, 3225) and was rumoured to be at Asti on 2 Aug. (LP,iv,3329).
[2] St.P,i, p.255 (LP,iv,3350).

The point was that over a period of a year Wolsey had failed even to get close to any sort of settlement between these two monarchs. In order to secure his release, the French king had been forced to sign the treaty of Madrid.[1] This had included his agreement to the restoration of Burgundy to its nominal duke, Charles V, and to the reinstatement of the rebel duke of Bourbon. Neither of these was in the long run acceptable to him, and, short of being compelled by armed force, he had no intention of keeping his word on either account. More negotiable was his renunciation of any claims to the duchy of Milan, though this was only because, not being in control of the duchy, he had little choice. Furthermore, the fact that Charles had taken the precaution of insisting on hostages, the dauphin, François, and Henri duke of Orléans, forced him at least to pretend to negotiate. Meanwhile, he was hoping to use his alliance with England and the League of Cognac to bring pressure on Charles to return the princes without having to pay too high a price. By securing a yet larger English commitment at Amiens, he was in a stronger position vis-à-vis Charles, and therefore less likely to make concessions – none of which was good news for a Wolsey trying to occupy the pivotal position. But Wolsey needed Amiens to bring pressure on Charles, who even less than Francis was showing no inclination to make concessions.

Wolsey's problem was that, as a consequence of Pavia, it was very difficult to get a firm hold on Charles. True, the emperor's difficulties in Germany and with the Turk, further complicated by his brother Ferdinand's newly acquired claims to the kingdoms of Bohemia and Hungary, which needed his support if they were to be made a reality, did impose certain restraints on his freedom of action. For instance, while he was anxious that Francis should comply with as many of the terms of the Treaty of Madrid as possible, he was even more anxious that he should not cause him too much trouble in Italy, which he needed to have firmly under his control before he could safely move on to Germany. As we have seen, in Italy his two priorities were, first, to ensure that Milan should be securely held in the Imperial interest and his determination to be crowned emperor by the pope. The problem here was that Clement had been a founder member of the League of Cognac, and although in September 1526 Charles had been able to compel him to sign a four-month truce, the pope was in no mood to do his bidding.

The dramatic events of May 1527 drove the wedge between the two men even deeper, though their consequences were more complex than might at first appear.[2] The rape and pillage of the Holy City by Bourbon's unpaid and mutinous army, and the consequent imprisonment of the Holy Father in St Angelo for the second year running, may appear to have reduced Clement to the role of Charles's puppet. However, when all is lost it is sometimes easier to be brave, and this even the timid Clement determined to be. Thus, in the summer of 1527 Charles was faced with the hostility of a battered but unbowed pope, and the imminent arrival of a French army in Northern Italy, which after Pavia he had probably hoped never to see again. What would he do? One option was immediately to buy Francis off by offering to

---

[3] LP, iv, 3337, 3343, 3362-4, 3381, 3400; amongst other things Wolsey had to fend off Henry's worry that he was allowing Francis to make too many concessions to Charles.

[1] Knecht, p.189.
[2] Hook, pp.155 ff. for an excellent treatment of the sack of Rome.

return his sons on the most generous terms, however much he might lose face by it. Another was to respond more favourably to Wolsey's overtures. This too would have meant the return of the French princes, but on more advantageous terms for himself than could probably be obtained by direct negotiations with the French, while much talk of European peace, his cousin Henry's good offices, and such like, would let him off the hook as far as loss of face was concerned. The third option was to hope that the French army could be defeated and Clement and his other opponents in Italy forced to come to terms, thereby eliminating the need to make concessions to either Francis or Wolsey. It was this last option that in the autumn of 1527 Charles felt strong enough to pursue, but he would have quickly to reconsider his position if Lautrec's army proved successful.

What has been described is a very fluid situation in which neither Francis nor Charles was willing to give away too much too soon, in the hope that their bargaining positions would improve. On the other hand, they might at any moment have been persuaded to come to the conference table by the ever persuasive Wolsey, especially if things began to go wrong for them. For Wolsey it was the usual juggling act, but by the summer of 1527 his priority was no longer the glorious settlement of Europe's problems under the aegis of his king, but the much more specific, and, if truth be told, rather sordid, matter of getting that king a divorce. Before we examine how this change of priority affected Wolsey's plans, it needs to be stressed how seriously it weakened his position in Europe, as he himself was quick to appreciate. Writing from Amiens on 11 August, he explained to Henry that he had 'forborn to make any overture of your secret matter, fearing that by disclosing thereof the same might cause the said French king to be more slack and stand further aloof'. Only when he had put Henry's affairs 'in assured perfection and train', that is, only after the terms of the Treaty of Amiens had been settled, would it be wise to bring the subject up.[1] Undoubtedly, Henry's matrimonial problems were a godsend to Francis. As a result of his recent humiliations, he and his mother had had to come to the English cap in hand. Overnight the relationship had been, if not reversed, at least put on a more equal footing. Henry was now very much in need of Francis's help, and Francis was, of course, going to make quite sure that he paid for it.

For Charles too, Henry's matrimonial problems brought advantages. What he really thought of Henry's proposed rejection of his aunt is not at all clear. He and Catherine met only three times, briefly at Canterbury and Gravelines in 1520, and for a little longer in June 1522 when Charles had paid a visit to England in order to finalize plans for the Great Enterprise. On these occasions they appear to have got on perfectly well, but there was a fifteen-year difference in their ages, and, apart from the fact that Catherine was the sister of his mother, Joanna the Mad, whom Charles had hardly known, having been brought up in the household of another aunt, Margaret of Savoy, they had little in common. Charles was a son of Burgundy who became a king of Spain. Catherine, a daughter of Spain, became a queen of England who, when she first met her nephew, had not been anywhere near Spain for fifteen years. And whatever their feelings, Charles had been a most dilatory

---

[1] St.P,i, p.254 (LP,iv,3340).

correspondent. Of course, Henry's behaviour towards his aunt did touch upon the family honour, and the Habsburgs took their honour extremely seriously. However, when in January 1529 Campeggio had put this precise point to Wolsey, the answer he got was that 'the Emperor will not in fact be concerned about the affair, and once it is done there will be a thousand ways of being reconciled to him'.[1] It looks as if Wolsey was right, for Charles would not object in principle to Henry becoming a signatory to the Treaty of Cambrai in August 1529, nor in February 1535, when Catherine, though divorced, was still alive, would he be against putting out feelers to Henry for an alliance, for the good reason that he felt very much in need of support and was therefore not too fussy where it came from.[2] Whatever Charles's feelings towards his aunt, Henry's matrimonial difficulties suited him well, just because they seriously weakened England's position, and put a bridle on any schemes of Wolsey's to do him down. Or, to put it another way, they provided him, as every other ruler in Europe, with a bargaining counter, to be used however and in whatever way, and whenever he wished – and in 1527 and 1528 he saw no overwhelming reason to let Henry off the hook by meekly accepting the English king's wish for a divorce.

The divorce not only weakened Wolsey's position, but it seriously affected the direction of his strategy. Hitherto, the League of Cognac had been essentially a means to force Charles to the conference table. In the new situation the wishes of the league's members, and above all Clement's, had to become his chief concern. This meant involving himself even more in the affairs of Italy, which was not good news. It also meant having to adopt a more aggressive stance towards Charles, the declared enemy of the league, than ideally he would have wished. Firm pressure rather than all-out war was what he had wanted, but the overriding necessity to comply with papal wishes would make it much more difficult to achieve the one without the other. Of course, all this only applied if Charles opposed the divorce, but Wolsey did not have to wait long to find out. At the end of July, despite all the government's efforts to prevent it, a private messenger from Catherine had put Charles in full possession of the facts, at least as far as they were known to Catherine, including her determination to resist Henry's wishes.[3] He immediately informed Henry of his support for his aunt, and at the same time dispatched the general of the Franciscan order, Francisco Quiñofies, to Rome in order to register his strong protest at what had already occurred and to insist that if there was to be a trial it should not take place in England, where Catherine could hardly expect an impartial hearing.[4]

Since Clement was still a prisoner of an Imperial army Charles was in a reasonable position to insist on his request being acted upon, though not in quite such a good position as might at first appear. The destruction of the Holy City and the humiliating treatment of the Holy Father and his cardinals was a matter of some embarrassment to the Holy Roman Emperor, even if he could truthfully claim this had happened without his knowledge or consent.[5] In order to avoid even greater

[1] Ehses, *Römische Dokumente*, 69.
[2] Brandi, pp.352-3.
[3] For this episode involving Francisco Felipez see Mattingly, *Catherine of Aragon*, pp.185-6.
[4] *LP*, iv, 3312.
[5] *LP*, iv, 3322 for Charles's apologia to Henry for the sack of Rome.

odium, he was forced to move with circumspection, or, to put it another way, Clement, although physically helpless, was in a strong moral position to resist unwarranted demands from Charles. And there remained for Charles the further embarrassment that, while his troops remained in what threatened to become a chronic state of mutiny, he was not fully in control of events in Rome, and, therefore, not best placed to negotiate with a pope who was his army's prisoner rather than his own.

For Wolsey, on the other hand, the pope's captivity offered an outside chance of obtaining the divorce without Clement becoming directly involved. Given that Henry's case was by no means certain in law, and given Clement's inevitable fears about offending the emperor, such a possibility had its attractions, and he tried two ways of bringing it about. One was to summon a council of cardinals to Avignon, whose ostensible task would be to administer the Church during this emergency, but en passant they might be persuaded to pass sentence in Henry's favour.[1] The other way was to have himself appointed the pope's vicar-general with full authority to act on his behalf; once in that office he could then himself pass sentence. Having completed the main negotiations with Francis and Louise, Wolsey spent his remaining time in France attempting to accomplish one or other of these ends.[2] As he himself realized all too well, his chances were never good.[3] What is also clear is that both schemes were only ever a reluctant response to an extraordinary situation, for throughout this time he was working even harder for Clement's release.[4] One might think this a little surprising, and certainly not in line with the usual picture of an egotistical Wolsey always anxious to push himself forward; but, in fact, neither scheme, even if it could be achieved, offered a satisfactory solution to his problem. Any divorce pronounced either by himself alone as vicar-general or by a council of cardinals could only have ever been considered partial and provisional, and certainty was what he was after. Of course, if Clement was going to remain in captivity for long, then alternatives would have to be sought, but it was not to be. On 7 December, with some connivance from his gaolers, Clement escaped to Orvieto, and both schemes became redundant, for it was now possible to negotiate with Clement directly.

Admittedly the flight to Orvieto only marginally increased Clement's room for manoeuvre, for his position remained extremely fraught.[5] Before escaping he had been forced to accept humiliating terms from the Imperial commanders. These included the surrender not only of some papal towns but also of a number of cardinals, who were to serve as security for the large sums of money that he had promised and that the Imperial commanders needed to pay their troops with, but which, because of the havoc wrought by those troops and by the endemic feuding of the Orsini and Colonna families, was not available. Clement was left with no

[1] LP,iv,3247, 3311.

[2] St.P,i, p.271 (LP,iv,3400); see also LP,iv,3401, 3423. For the view that these plans are evidence for Wolsey's increasing megalomania see Scarisbrick, Henry VIII, pp.157-8.

[3] St.P, pp.230-1, 270-1 (LP,iv,3311, 3400).

[4] In his letter to Henry of 29 July Wolsey made it clear that the pope's release was his chief priority, while as early as 2 June he had pointed out that the pope's death or captivity would hinder the king's affairs; see St.P,i, pp.189, 230-1 (LP,iv,3147, 3311). See also LP,iv,3179.

[5] For this and much of what follows see Hook, pp.219 ff.

money, no Rome and no Papal States. And with the havoc came famine and disease. But, despite everything, he remained the Vicar of Christ, and this was a negotiable commodity. During the months ahead he was to exploit it for all it was worth, with everyone, but especially with the emperor. Meanwhile, although he was reasonably secure in Orvieto, it was fear of the Imperial army, whether paid or unpaid, that preoccupied him. This state of mind was by no means entirely to Wolsey's disadvantage, but, as always, everything would depend on getting the timing and balance right. If Clement was too frightened, he would only do what Charles told him to do; but if he had no fears at all, he might well not do what Wolsey wanted. What Wolsey needed was a Clement who remained both grateful and beholden, at least long enough for him to decide in Henry's favour over the divorce. The instrument by which Wolsey was to bring this about was the existing League of Cognac, but more especially Lautrec's army, which at Amiens in August he had agreed to help finance.

What Lautrec's army could do was provide Clement with the prospect of real protection against the Imperial army, and it was a prospect which became increasingly real with Lautrec's new success. By early November he had reached Parma on the southern fringe of the Po valley, and Genoa and most of the duchy of Milan, though not the city itself, were already in the league's hands. These successes were enough to persuade Alfonso d'Este duke of Ferrara to change sides and on 14 November he formally joined the League. Would Clement follow suit? Having recovered his freedom, he could again receive foreign envoys, and those of the league immediately began to pressure him into rejoining. Even without his inherent caution there were good reasons why Clement should hesitate, but as during the spring of 1528 Lautrec proceeded to mop up the cities of the kingdom of Naples, so that by 26 April virtually only Naples itself was left to the Imperialists, the reasons for rejoining grew more compelling. One early bonus was that during 16 and 17 February the Imperial army, after nearly eight months of occupation, left Rome, enabling Clement to contemplate a return. And as the league's successes continued, and the likelihood of his rejoining increased, so did the likelihood of his granting what Wolsey wanted as regards the 'divorce'.

There has been some debate about how far Clement's attitude towards Henry's 'great matter' was governed by political and temporal considerations rather than legal and ethical ones. The great historian of the papacy, Ludwig Pastor, took pains to emphasize that it was the latter;[1] but even if it is admitted, as it is here, that Henry's case was poor and that, therefore, there was no overwhelming legal or moral reason why Clement should have supported him, the facts do not appear to endorse Pastor's view. It was only during the spring and summer of 1528 that Clement was prepared to make significant concessions to Henry: the dispensations enabling him to marry within the prohibited degrees, and thus to marry Anne, the general commission of 13 April enabling the divorce to be decided in England; the regranting of this commission on 9 June, and in that same month the 'secret' decretal commission; and finally in July the 'pollicitation', by which he promised not to interfere with any decision reached in England. The granting of the decretal commission, of which the content but not its potential application satisfied Wolsey,

[1] Pastor, x, pp. 256 ff.

is particularly relevant. As we saw earlier, by this document Clement was in effect giving judgment in Henry's favour, provided only that three highly selective and easily ascertainable facts could be established. In doing this he made it impossible for Catherine to mount a defence, which, given that certainly as regards natural justice and probably in law she was in the right, was a monstrous act of injustice, and one that can only be explained by his wish to take advantage of the league's successes. For Clement it was a comparatively cheap way of signalling to an important constituent of the league that he was on its side, but without having as yet to commit himself. The fact that the decretal commission was only granted in a secret and limited form only confirms that political considerations were uppermost in his mind when taking this step.

By mid-1528 it was by no means certain that the league's successes would continue. Lautrec and his army had been encamped around Naples for some time without the city falling, and, as the summer advanced, so did the heat, and with the heat plague and typhoid. Meanwhile, for the defenders of Naples the only serious problem appears to have been the lack of wine for the thirsty German troops who made up a large part of the Imperial army. It was also becoming clearer that, owing to insensitive handling on their part, the French were in imminent danger of losing the services of the Genoese naval *condottiere*, Andrea Doria, whose support had given them vital naval supremacy off the west coast of Italy. Moreover, as early as April a second Imperial army, led by the duke of Brunswick, had entered Northern Italy and linked up with those Imperial forces that had remained in possession of the city of Milan. Admittedly, this new threat had been countered by a second French army led by the count of St-Pol, but the situation in the north was by no means promising for the league. One way and another, Clement would have been extremely foolish to commit himself wholeheartedly to it at this point. He would also have been foolish not to make some concessions to Henry. The decretal commission was a large concession but, given the manner in which it had been granted, one that could easily be withdrawn. And how right Clement was to move cautiously. On 4 July Doria left the French service, on 16 August Lautrec died of the plague, and by the end of the month what was left of the French army in the kingdom of Naples surrendered. In the north it took a little longer for things to turn decisively against the league, but by the end of October the French had lost control of Genoa and nearby Savona. Only a toe-hold in Northern Italy remained to them. Venice, for her part, was just able to cling on grimly to what was her own, or, in some cases, to what only she considered to be her own. The League of Cognac was, in effect, no more.

When Campeggio had set off for England towards the end of July 1528, the death of Lautrec and the other disasters to befall the league were still in the future, but some at least could have been predicted. At any rate, Clement's native caution served him in good stead. Ostensibly Campeggio would be doing the king of England's bidding, or, more correctly, he was to act as Wolsey's fellow judge in the 'great matter'. In fact, as we noted earlier, his instructions were first of all to persuade Henry to change his mind, and, failing that, to persuade Catherine to take religious vows. Only if both moves were unsuccessful was he to exercise his commission and, with Wolsey, to proceed to a trial. Underlying these instructions was the need to play for time for, as he was informed in September, 'every day stronger reasons are discovered which compel the Pope to remind you that you are to act cautiously'.[1] By December, with the virtual disappearance of the league, the situation had become much clearer, and it did not encourage Clement to look favourably upon Henry's cause. No wonder that he was driven to distraction, perhaps even to illness,[2] by Wolsey's pestering to be allowed to make more use of the decretal commission.[3] Now Clement deeply regretted that he had granted it even in limited form.[4] He need not have worried. Campeggio had allowed Henry and Wolsey one glimpse of the document, had read it out to them once, but that was all.[5] In January 1529 the pope's chamberlain, Campano, arrived in England with orders for Campeggio to destroy the document, which he duly did. He also brought instructions for Campeggio on no account to proceed to a judgment, or so Clement maintained. In June Campeggio was to deny that he had ever received them, but by then he was under such pressure from Henry and Wolsey to decide in the king's favour that he was doubtful of being able to avoid doing so, whatever Clement desired.[6] What is not in doubt is that by the end of 1528, perhaps even as early as August,[7] Clement had decided to make terms with the emperor – and part of the price he would have to pay would almost certainly be a settlement in Catherine's favour, however much it would offend his erstwhile Defender of the Faith.

It is important to stress that Clement came to this decision not so much out of fear of the emperor, but because he had come to the conclusion that it was the emperor who had the most to offer him. The sack of Rome and the resulting collapse of papal authority had inevitably led to chaos in the Papal States, and there were plenty of people around to take advantage of this. Amongst them were the Venetians who had moved in when in June and July 1527 the cities of Ravenna and Cervia were disrupted by factional fighting stirred up by Imperial intrigue, and had in effect claimed both cities for their own.[8] As for many years they had belonged to the Venetians and had only been lost to the papacy in 1509, it could be argued that they were merely reclaiming their own, but this did not prevent their action from being a bitter blow to Clement. Perhaps as bitter to him had been the decision in November 1527 of his great rival, the duke of Ferrara, to join the league, but at a price – and the price that he had demanded was the surrender of all papal rights to Modena, Reggio and Rubiera.[9] However, the bitterest blow of all concerned Florence which ever since Giovanni de' Medici had become Pope Leo x in 1513, had been virtually part of the Papal States. There on 17 May 1527, as an almost direct result of the sack of Rome, the Medici family had been requested to leave, and the last Florentine republic was established.[10]

[1] *LP*, iv, 4737).
[2] He fell ill on 9 Jan. 1529; for a useful chronology of the illness see Hughes, i, p.182, n.1.
[3] *St.P*, vii, pp.104-6, 132-4 (*LP*, iv, 4897, 4978); *LP*, iv, 5038, 5073, 5151-2
[4] *LP*, iv, 5038.
[5] Ehses, pp.54-5, 108; Gairdner, *EHR* xii, p.250; Parmiter, pp.66-7.
[6] Ehses, p.108; Gairdner, xii, pp.250-1.
[7] Hook, p.239.
[8] Hook, pp.198-9.
[9] *LP*, iv, 4737).
[10] Hook, pp.201 ff; Stephens, pp.203 ff.

For Clement, who for so long had been virtual ruler of a Florence that had been in effect his family's patrimony for a hundred years, all this had been almost harder to bear than the horrendous happenings in Rome. Thus, the recovery of Florence was at the top of his shopping list. And by the autumn of 1528 it had become apparent to him that the best way of obtaining most of what he wanted was to seek Imperial aid, which strange to say, he was in quite a good position to obtain. Since Charles was so heavily committed in a number of areas, there would be great advantages for him in arranging the affairs of Italy as quickly as possible, even if this meant making concessions to its leading states, including the papacy. Moreover, Charles's aims of being crowned emperor could only be achieved with any dignity if he and Clement were on good terms. And there were other useful things that Clement as head of the Church could do for him. Most importantly, he could grant him a *cruzada*, which would enable him to raise a considerable amount of much needed money. So, one way and another Clement had quite a few good cards to play, and Charles might well be willing to pay quite a lot for them. He would be sorry if any deal with Charles meant that he would have to deny Henry what he wanted, and thereby, perhaps, precipitate England's withdrawal from the Catholic Church, but it would hardly be his fault, given that what Henry wanted was both unreasonable and unnecessary.[1] That, at least, was how things must have looked to Clement when he made his decision to side with Charles, and by the Treaty of Barcelona of 29 June 1529 he gained most of what he wanted.[2] Charles, it is true, was to renege on his promise to force the duke of Ferrara to return Modena and Reggio, but an Imperial army did restore Medici rule in Florence and got Venice to return Ravenna and Cervia. As a result, Clement emerged from one of the most disastrous episodes in papal history with the Papal States virtually intact, if greatly impoverished, and the interests of his own family well served. It was a remarkable performance, but one that helped Wolsey not at all.

Of course, the danger that Clement and Charles would come to some agreement was not unperceived by Wolsey. In particular, he appreciated the damage that was being done to his chances of success by his failure to obtain the restoration to Clement of Ravenna and Cervia. Indeed, 'this blessed matter', as du Bellay called it on one occasion,[3] was one of Wolsey's chief preoccupations throughout his negotiations for the divorce: special embassies to Venice such as Gardiner's in July 1528,[4] pressure on France to lean on Venice,[5] stormy interviews with the Venetian ambassador,[6] and promises to the pope,[7] all were tried, but to no avail. Venice would not budge, and this was to cost Wolsey dear. On the other hand, it is hard to see what more he could have done. The league needed Venice's military and financial help; her contribution in both men and money was probably greater than

---

[1] *LP*,iv,5038.

[2] Pastor,x, pp.56-7.

[3] *LP*,iv,5133.

[4] *LP*,iv,4482, 4553.

[5] *LP*,iv,5016, 5421; *LP*,iv,app.145, 158, 177, 180, 196,203.

[6] *LP*,iv,5133; *LP*,iv, pp.2178, 2200. See also *LP*,iv,3989 for Henry's letter to the doge in Feb. 1528; also *LP*,iv,5538â

[7] *LP*,iv,3957. The return of the two cities was central to Wolsey's peace plans of December 1528; see *LP*,iv,5028.

France's, and certainly greater than England's.[1] So she had a perfect right to seek some reward, and she did have some claim to Ravenna and Cervia, while Clement's very ambiguous policy towards the league offered her little incentive to return them. For Henry and Wolsey, however, the consequences of her refusal were very damaging. Clement was determined to get them back. If his supposed friends and allies could not bring this about, then he was willing to turn to his supposed enemy, Charles v.[2]

Wolsey's response to the increasing likelihood of agreement between Clement and Charles was to return to those plans for a European peace settlement which had been central to his strategy before the divorce had arisen. When that divorce made Clement the focus of his attention, the priority had to be to free him from Imperial control. However, ideally Wolsey had always wanted at the very least to secure Charles's acquiescence to Henry's divorce, and it needs to be stressed that at no time during these years, despite his heavy involvement in the French invasion of Italy, did his negotiations with the emperor cease. True, in January 1528 the English ambassadors in Spain had been manouvred by their French colleagues into making a formal declaration of war against the emperor.[3] But they received no thanks from Wolsey, such is the lot of ambassadors, and he was very quick to try to minimize the consequences of their actions.[4] By April he had drawn up new peace proposals, and in May he sent to Spain Sylvester Darius, an Italian who had made a career for himself in England, to obtain Charles's agreement.[5] He also began to negotiate with Margaret of Savoy in order to minimize any possible disruption to England's vital trade with the Low Countries, and a truce was signed on 15 June.[6] No such success attended Darius, for Charles, already involved in serious negotiations with Clement, was in no mood to be dictated to by Wolsey.[7] And it was the possibility that these negotiations might prove successful that in December forced Wolsey to unfurl yet another plan for European peace. As a first step, the pope was to declare a general truce. There was then to be a meeting of representatives of the leading European states, probably at either Nice or Avignon, where it would be possible for both Charles and Francis to keep in close touch with the proceedings. Wolsey's hope was that there would be enough in any such meeting to tempt everyone to attend. Charles might obtain his Imperial coronation at the hands of the pope, though not necessarily in Italy; he might also be assured of receiving the ransom money from France in return for releasing the French princes. It would be his sons' return that would be the chief attraction of such a conference for Francis. Milan might be restored to Francesco Sforza, probably the solution that offended the fewest people. Other Italian states might be guaranteed their territorial independence in return for handing back territory that did not belong to them,

---

[1] On all this see Mallet and Hale, pp.225-9.

[2] For an assessment that Clement would turn to the devil if that would help get them back, see LP,iv,4900; for Clement's secretary's view in April 1529 that Henry could expect no remedy while Venice retained papal territory see LP,iv,5447.

[3] LP,iv,3826-7.

[4] LP,iv,4564.

[5] LP,iv, app.162, 164.

[6] LP,iv,3959, 3966, 4376; see also pp.455-6 above.

[7] Sp.Cal., iii (ii), pp.802-3, 808-14; LP,iv,4909-10.

which would mean that Clement would recover his beloved Ravenna and Cervia. In fact, it would be a settlement with Clement very much in mind. To him, rather than to Wolsey, would go all the honour of calling and presiding over the meeting: evidence of how far the divorce had weakened Wolsey's position. The prospect of the emperor setting foot in Italy was something that Clement, like most Italian rulers, greatly feared, and this was now ruled out. Wolsey also proposed that Clement should receive the protection of a 'presidiary', of two thousand men, to be paid for by England and France. Finally, it was to be made clear to Charles that if he refused to agree to the meeting, or in any other way behaved unreasonably, then England and France would mount a major invasion of Spain.[1]

In this way Wolsey hoped, even at the last moment, to tempt Clement away from the Imperial embrace. At the same time he was intensifying the arguments that had been his stock-in-trade ever since the search for the divorce began. The well-being of Henry's kingdom as well as his personal salvation depended upon it being granted, he told Clement. If it was not, Henry would be forced to act independently of the pope, with disastrous consequences for the Catholic Church at a time when the Lutheran heresy was gaining ground. Moreover, it would do the Church no good in England if his papal legate was shown to be powerless to bring about his temporal master's wishes, especially if his failure led to his dismissal from the king's service. And, anyway, Clement was under a particular obligation to Henry for his famous book denouncing Luther's heresies, the *Assertio Septem Sacramentorum*.[2] And if all these arguments, and variations on them, were the constant refrain, in late 1528 Wolsey was adding all the new ones he could think of in order to work upon Clement's natural suspicions of the emperor. In particular, the English envoys were instructed to make as much as possible of a prophecy apparently circulating in Rome, that Clement would be succeeded by a pope named Angelo. This, they were to say, could only be a reference to the general of the Franciscan order, the Spaniard Francisco Quiñones, otherwise called de los Angeles.[3] It will be remembered that he had been used by Charles back in the autumn of 1527 to notify Clement of his opposition to the divorce, and he was to figure in most of the subsequent negotiations between the two men, a fact that lent some weight to Wolsey's interpretation of the prophecy that had Charles deposing Clement and putting the Spaniard in his place. Not very surprisingly it does not appear to have impressed Clement very much. But by this stage almost any argument was worth trying. The league's position in Italy had collapsed and the incentives for Clement to throw in his lot with the emperor were multiplying daily. Meanwhile, it had become apparent that Campeggio's arrival in England at the beginning of October was not going to lead to any speedy legal solution to the divorce question; Clement's instructions to him had seen to that. Then, early the following month, Catherine had produced her bombshell, the Spanish brief, and, since Clement was the only person who could diffuse this, it put him in a strong position. But then a satisfactory solution to Henry's 'great matter' could only ever

[1] LP,iv,5050 for Wolsey's detailed presentation of them, but see also LP,iv,4897, 5028, 5053, 5133, 5179; LP,iv,5138-9, 5148 for papal reactions.
[2] *Inter alia* LP,iv, 3641, 3913, 3921, 4251, 4897, 5417.
[3] LP,iv,4977, 5014; Hook, p.239.

have been found with Clement's active support; and by the late autumn of 1528 that was looking increasingly unlikely.

It is difficult not to admire the energy, courage and skill with which Wolsey faced up to this worsening situation; and before concluding it is worth dwelling on that skill for just a little longer. The central plank of the new initiatives presented to the pope during the winter of 1528-9 was undoubtedly the plan for a settlement of all outstanding European problems. Its attractions for Clement have just been outlined, but what should not be forgotten is that if he had adopted the role allotted him, which included acceding to Henry's rather than Charles's wishes as regards the divorce, he would have had to offend the man whose armies were most in a position to do him harm. Wolsey's task was to persuade him that what he had to offer was worth risking that man's wrath. He needed both to emphasize the threat to papal and Medici power of any increase in Imperial influence in Italy and promise immediate military aid. Admittedly, two thousand men would be of little help if fighting on any scale were to break out again, but, of course, the intention was that the peace settlement would prevent this. Meanwhile, even a small force could provide Clement with useful protection from the marauding bands of unpaid and undisciplined Imperial troops which now constituted the main threat to his safety. It would also be symbolic of a genuine commitment to him by England and France, which, if Charles proved intransigent and the peace negotiations broke down, was in theory to be translated into a massive military strike against the emperor. In fact, neither England nor France was in much of a position to make such a strike, but the fact that no one knew better than Clement of Henry's single-mindedness in his search for a divorce made it difficult for him entirely to discount the possibility that Wolsey would feel obliged somehow or other to provide the much larger force that an invasion of Spain necessitated. There was also the possible damage to the Catholic Church and to his own spiritual authority, if his siding with the emperor resulted in Henry doing what Wolsey threatened: namely, to take the English Church into schism. This was a price that Clement proved to be willing to pay, but it was a very high price, and it must have given him pause for thought which was exactly what Wolsey wanted. The loss of England – and might not England's ally, France, who after all was no stranger to schism, follow her example? – would not only have religious consequences, but would make the papacy worryingly dependent upon the emperor. Rather than let this happen, would it not be worth taking up Wolsey's initiatives, at the same time making it clear to the emperor that he was not going to be his lackey, by granting Henry what he could make out to Charles was only the English king's legal due, judgment in his favour? During the winter of 1528-9 Wolsey was harping on the difficulties of the choices facing Clement, while at the same time offering him an attractive alternative. It was pressure diplomacy of a high order. In the end it did not succeed. Did it ever stand a realistic chance?

The answer is probably yes, though it was always a slim one. One thing that suggests this is that, whatever the strength of Clement's commitment to the emperor, it in no way prevented him from behaving very generously towards Henry and Wolsey. Between 2 November 1528 and 4 June 1529 he issued, at their request, at least five important bulls.[1] Now it can be argued, with some justification, that it

---

[1] See p. 464 ff. above.

was precisely because he was unwilling to grant Henry the one thing he really wanted that he was prepared to be so compliant about other matters. Nevertheless, these bulls are evidence that at this time Clement had in no sense broken with England, was still anxious to please, and was hoping to keep his options open for as long as possible. He showed a good deal of interest in Wolsey's plans for a general European settlement – in fact, far too much for the peace of mind of the various Imperial representatives in Rome.[1] Moreover, Charles came to Wolsey's aid by being dilatory in responding to Clement's proposals to him, and when at length, in December, he did, his answers were not very satisfactory.[2] Three months later the Imperialist party in Rome was still worried that the various efforts (for Venetian and French envoys were at work as well) to prevent Clement from joining with Charles might be successful.[3] Indeed, it was probably not until April 1529 that Clement finally decided to take the plunge. Although the Medici had been driven out of Florence in May 1527, the new ruling faction, led by Niccolo Capponi, had opened up negotiations with Clement, so that by the winter of 1528-9 there was some possibility of compromise. On 17 April any such chance ended when a new group, deeply antagonistic to Medici interests, seized power.[4] The only way back for the Medici was now by force, and this could only be provided effectively by the Imperialists. On 9 May Clement sent a special envoy to Charles with instructions to reach an agreement with him. The result was that Treaty of Barcelona already referred to, and the end of Wolsey's hopes. But the point is that it did take Clement some time to come to a final decision. Obviously his long illness was one explanation, but so also was Wolsey's diplomatic activity. If only Venice could have been persuaded to hand back Ravenna and Cervia, or if the coup in Florence had not occurred, then Clement's decision might have been different.

What of Charles? Was it ever likely that he would accept Wolsey's European settlement, and in doing so abandon his aunt? As we have seen, in January 1529 Wolsey told Campeggio that he did not believe that Charles would allow his concern for Catherine to stand in the way of achieving other more vital ends. On 20 February he repeated his view in a letter to the English envoys at Rome,[5] and on 6 April he explained to them why he thought that Charles would in the end be willing to fall in with his proposals: events had gone so well for him in Italy that a peace that would confirm his main achievement, the expulsion of the French from the peninsula, would be sufficiently attractive to outweigh some of the less appealing aspects of the proposals.[6] With the advantage of hindsight it is easy to say that Wolsey's assessment was over-optimistic. But given that Henry demanded a solution, there was no point in him being anything else. The various treaties that Charles made in 1529 show that he was in the mood to make concessions, both to the French and to the Italian states, in order to clear the decks for a settlement of his

---

[1] *LP*,iv,5138 for Clement's favourable response; for Imperial worries see *Sp.Cal*, iii (ii), pp.922-3, 929-30.

[2] Hook, pp.244-6; Pastor, x, pp.32-67.

[3] *LP*,iv,5387; *Sp.Cal.*, iii (ii), pp.911, 915, 921-2, 929-30.

[4] Hook, pp.246-8; Pastor, x, p.53; for Casale's assessment to Wolsey of 21 April see *LP*,iv,5478; also *Sp.Cal.*,iii (ii), 924 for the importance of events in Florence.

[5] *LP*,iv,5314.

[6] *LP*,iv,5428.

affairs in Germany. Still, whether or not Wolsey really believed in his own assessment, it showed a serious underestimate of the cards that Charles would be able to play in the spring of 1529.

When, early in May, Wolsey asked the English envoys to inform the pope that the trial was about to begin, he also instructed them to inform him of an Anglo-French decision to mount a major campaign against Charles.[1] This could have been just what was needed to stiffen Clement's resolve to side with Henry, but not, perhaps, if during the previous month rumours had reached Rome that the French were on the point of making a separate peace with Charles.[2] It was just such a possibility that had been the Achilles heel in all Wolsey's plans since 1526. Charles would always wish to sell the return of the dauphin and his brother for the highest price possible, while Francis would wish to pay the lowest, and it was the difficulty of arriving at a figure acceptable to both which, as was argued earlier, had given Wolsey an outside chance to dominate events. The snag was that if the moment ever came when Charles felt he had to break the Anglo-French alliance and so neutralize France, then he had only to lower his price and Francis was more or less bound to accept, for his honour demanded that his sons be returned to him sooner rather than later.

During the winter and early spring of 1528-9 as Charles's difficulties in Germany mounted, so the need to get the French off his back brought that moment ever closer. At the same time the failure of Lautrec's expedition and the virtual collapse of the league's resistance made any reasonable offer by Charles especially attractive to Francis, for after two years of fighting and negotiation there appeared little likelihood that the alliance with England would bring about the return of his children. The negotiations culminating in August 1529 in the 'ladies' peace' of Cambrai, so-called because they were supervised by the two ladies of Savoy, Louise and Margaret, need not concern us. What does need to be stressed, because so often a contrary impression is given,[3] is that the Treaty of Cambrai did not take Wolsey by surprise. Rumours of talks were reaching him as early as November 1528.[4] The fact that both he and Henry often spoke as if no separate agreement between Charles and Francis would be signed is not in itself evidence that they did not take the negotiations seriously: to have said anything else in public would have been a terrible admission of defeat which could have served no purpose, except, perhaps, to frighten Clement off.[5] As it was, Wolsey did his best to buy off the French by offering them military support, something that he had studiously refrained from doing up until this point, and more money, his efforts culminating in Suffolk's and Fitzwilliam's mission to France in late May.[6] There is some indication that Wolsey's

---

[1] LP,iv,5523.

[2] Pastor, x, p.52.

[3] Inter alia Elton, Reform and Reformation, pp.110-11; Scarisbrick, Henry VIII, pp.232-3.

[4] LP,iv,4945, 4985; for Tuke's suspicions on 9 Dec. see LP,iv,5018; also LP,iv,5137, 5163, 5231 for early English awareness of Franco-Imperial negotiations.

[5] See especially Wolsey's boast to du Bellay in early December that England would not be left in the lurch by the emperor and Francis in LP,iv,5016; also LP,iv,5572, 5636, 5701. As against this one needs to look at Tuke's prescient analysis of why Francis and Charles needed peace, sent to Wolsey on 4 March.

[6] They left England on 17 May; see LP,iv,2462. See also LP,iv,5523, 5535, 5582, 5601; I assume the military proposals would be along the lines outlined to du Bellay in December, to be put into effect if

inducements had some effect, and, at any rate, Francis was not sure until the very last moment that Charles's terms were acceptable.[1] In the end, however, the prospect of the speedy return of his sons was more compelling than anything Wolsey had to offer, and in that respect the English could never have prevented Cambrai. Moreover, it was only the necessity of obtaining the divorce that made it the severe setback that it was. In other respects Cambrai resembled the Treaty of Noyon of 1516. This, too, had appeared to signal a major setback, as Wolsey's ostensible allies made their peace with the then enemy, France, but in fact it turned out to be the prelude to his greatest diplomatic triumph, the Treaty of London. Similarly, in 1529 Wolsey might well have been able to recover lost ground, given more time, because, as he pointed out himself, it was most unlikely that Francis and Charles would remain allied for long, and the return of the princes was a card which could only be played once.[2] But time was not on Wolsey's side, and Cambrai was undoubtedly a serious blow to his hopes of obtaining a divorce.

Cambrai is but one of the ways in which Charles was able to escape the noose which Wolsey had so strenuously striven to catch him in, but in the end not only did he have more to offer than Wolsey did, but, perhaps even more important, he was better placed to deliver it. For Francis there was the return of his sons, for Clement the return of papal territory and the restoration of Medici control over Florence. Charles, for his part, was able to secure better terms for himself by picking off his potential opponents one by one than by submitting to the outcome of a summit conference which would have had its ground plans drawn up in advance by Wolsey. Another gain was that he was not compelled to desert his aunt's cause.

In surveying the story of Wolsey's efforts to find a solution to Henry's matrimonial difficulties, it is tempting to think that he could never have been successful. Henry did not have a good case in law. For him to win, Wolsey needed to secure the pope's connivance to an act of injustice that would have been at the expense of a close relation of the most powerful man in Europe. Moreover, this act needed to be so dressed up that it could convincingly be presented as being entirely just. In other words, the deck was stacked against Wolsey from the start. However, what has been argued here is that there were times when the cards might have fallen the right way, especially in the spring and early summer of 1528 when Lautrec's military successes were putting pressure on Clement to acquiesce to Henry's and Wolsey's wishes. Lautrec's death and the collapse of the French invasion of Italy were terrible setbacks, and ones which, like so many others, was essentially outside Wolsey's control. The French handling of affairs in Italy was unsure, leading to the defection of Andrea Doria and the consequent loss of Genoa and Savona; and, on Wolsey's own admission, the loss of the latter broke his heart.[3] The refusal of Venice to hand back Ravenna and Cervia has been given more prominence in this account than

Charles proved intransigent, see LP,iv,5028. It was typical of Wolsey to become more bullish the heavier the going became.

---

[1] Bellay, Correspondence, pp.25-30 (LP,iv,5601); also LP,iv,5704; Knecht, p.219. It is clear that as late as 26 May Wolsey held some hope of averting Cambrai, but only some; see St. P,i, p.334 (LP,iv,5595).
[2] LP,iv,5801 Wolsey's own assessment of 30 July.
[3] LP,iv,5016

usual, for if Venice had not refused, then Clement might have rejoined the League of Cognac, and this in turn might well have secured his support for the divorce. It was not to be, but short of going to war with Venice, who just happened to be a leading member of the League, it is difficult to see what more Wolsey could have done to persuade Venice to comply with Clement's wishes. But while the fickleness of *Fortuna* and the realities of Imperial power help to explain Wolsey's failure, what of his own contribution? It is possible to argue that a completely different strategy, in which the emphasis had been on speed and in which there had been little concern for appearances, might possibly have succeeded and without what was in the end necessary for success, a 'break with Rome'. Here this argument has been rejected. Given the hostility to the divorce in England, and the overriding need to safeguard the succession, appearances were of the utmost importance. This being so, the only feasible strategy was to apply the kind of pressure diplomacy and attention to legal detail that Wolsey so determinedly displayed. The task that Henry presented him with was one that in his heart of hearts he may not have approved of, but nonetheless he loyally devoted all his considerable intelligence and negotiating skills to it. When he failed, he was made to pay a very high price.

Chapter Thirteen
Wolsey's Downfall

IN MAY 1519 SEBASTIAN GIUSTINIAN, THE VENETIAN AMBASSADOR, REPORTED from England: 'Within the last few days his majesty has made a very great change in the court here, dismissing four of his chief lords-in-waiting.'[1] According to some accounts, both at the time and since, the man behind this 'purge' was Cardinal Wolsey. Some six and a half years later in the Eltham Ordinances of January 1526, he allegedly attempted another. In the meantime he had worked hard to ensure that Richard Pace, appointed royal secretary in 1516, was kept from the king's presence by being despatched to Italy in December 1521, on a mission from which he did not return until November 1525, by which time he was insane. Thomas Howard, who became 3rd duke of Norfolk in 1524, was made of sterner stuff. Wolsey tried the same tactics with him: from 1520 to 1525 Norfolk was kept well away from the king by almost full-time employment in Ireland or on the Scottish border. But after 1524 potential trouble spots to which to banish him ran out, and Norfolk returned to court to begin his plotting against the cardinal. By 1527 Henry had fallen desperately in love with the duke's niece, Anne Boleyn, and this provided him with his opportunity. Combining with the Boleyn family and other members of the nobility, in some accounts with almost all of them but certainly with Charles Brandon duke of Suffolk, he managed by October 1529 to persuade a weak-minded and dithering Henry to dismiss his lord chancellor from office. And, when Henry showed signs of restoring him, Norfolk and his allies were able to convince him of Wolsey's treason, so that only his death from natural causes on 29 November 1530 saved him from the executioner's axe. There have been many variations of this scenario, but always at their core is a simple model: an unpopular royal favourite constantly having to fight to retain his hold on a king all too easily manipulated by those around him. In the end Wolsey lost the fight, the nobility took their revenge and yet another meddlesome priest had been taught a lesson.

It will be immediately apparent that this scenario has already been considerably undermined. Wolsey, it has been argued, was not a royal favourite, or certainly not to the exclusion of other royal councillors. He had not set out to antagonize the nobility, or in any way to harm its interests, except when they directly conflicted with those of Crown and common weal, which was not all that often. Moreover, he was far too skilful a political animal needlessly to offend anybody, nor is there any evidence that he did so on anything like the scale that the scenario requires. Above all, Henry was quite capable of making up his own mind about whom he consulted and when, and whom he rewarded and by how much. Thus, if there was faction fighting at court, his role would have been that of puppeteer rather than puppet. All this makes it highly unlikely that any conspiracy theory could explain Wolsey's downfall – and that it did not will be the main thrust of what follows. However,

---

[1] Rawdon Brown, ii, p.270 (*LP*,iii,235).

before the question of the downfall is confronted, the earlier episodes involving Richard Pace and members of the privy chamber must be dealt with.

The picture of the scholarly Pace being hounded into an abyss of paranoia and despair by one so much more politically adept than himself is not a pleasant one, and, if it were true, would have seriously to modify the view of Wolsey that has so far emerged. What is true is that in the autumn of 1521 Wolsey was cross with Pace. He was at Calais, heavily involved in complicated negotiations with the French and Imperialists while Pace had remained with the king in England, where his principal task as secretary was to act as a channel of communication between king and cardinal. This was not easy, especially as there were disagreements between the two. These, it was argued earlier,[1] had been to do merely with tactical matters, but they were nevertheless genuine; and given the complexities of the negotiations and the logistical problems involved in any communications, it is not surprising that misunderstandings occurred and that Pace received some of the blame. He was very much the pig in the middle, and things only got worse when Thomas More, who had been with Wolsey in Calais, informed him on his return that there were two more personal matters that Wolsey was annoyed about. In both these Pace was accused of interfering with Wolsey's patronage. As regards the appointment of a new prior of Marton, a small Augustinian house in Wolsey's diocese of York, Pace's defence was that it was Henry who had recommended a particular canon for the office;[2] and, given Henry's interests in all such matters, that defence rings true. With the other appointment, to a minor office in Chancery, Pace maintained that there had been a genuine misunderstanding. He had been led to believe by the candidate that it was in the gift of the master of the rolls, whose candidate had therefore secured the office.[3] Again, the secretary's defence seems convincing: just the kind of muddle that can cause trouble, however benign the intentions of those involved.

What lay behind the friction was the separation of king and cardinal, plus the enormous pressure imposed upon Wolsey, who was having to pretend to conduct an even-handed policy between the French and the Imperialists when he was doing nothing of the sort. Henry appears not to have been very sensitive to the circumstances, and hence the disagreements and poor Pace's troubles. When appointments which Wolsey believed to be in his own gift had been made without his consent, and with Pace's knowledge, it was the last straw, but not one that was likely to break his back. One thing that suggests this is that Pace did get to hear of Wolsey's displeasure, and the matter came out into the open. How we interpret this depends to some extent on whether Wolsey had told More to give Pace a ticking off, or whether, as Pace's friend, More had passed on Wolsey's grumbles on his own initiative.[4] The latter seems unlikely, but in either case surely Wolsey was being a little careless, even silly, in signalling his displeasure to someone who might be emerging as his arch-rival for the king's favours? Alternatively, he saw him not as an

---

[1] See p.153 above.

[2] *LP*,iii,1717.

[3] *LP*,iii,1717.

[4] It is Pace who mentioned that it was More who had informed him of Wolsey's displeasure, which rather suggests that More was deputed to; see *LP*,iii,1717.

arch-rival but as someone who was making a bit of a mess of things and needed to be told as much. Given that Wolsey was usually neither silly nor careless, it is the latter view that best fits the known facts.

Wolsey arrived back from Calais at the end of November 1521, and by the end of December Pace was on his way to Rome and insanity. The price he paid for incurring Wolsey's displeasure was heavy indeed – or so it has been alleged.[1] A closer look suggests another interpretation. The first point to be made is that royal secretaries frequently went on diplomatic missions; indeed, until Thomas Cromwell's appointment in 1533 these were very much part of the job description.[2] There was thus nothing odd in sending Pace abroad, and in fact he was an excellent, if rather obvious choice, for the mission that he was sent on. Before being recruited to Wolsey's household in 1514 he had spent over fifteen years in Italy, during the last five of which, as Cardinal Bainbridge's secretary, he had been heavily involved in curial politics.[3] He had many friends in Italy, and his reputation as a published scholar would have boosted his standing in a milieu in which humanist studies were fashionable. It was for these reasons that he had been sent to Northern Italy with the important task of organizing opposition to the French, first in 1515 and then again in December 1521. On the second occasion there was a further reason, and one that explains the precise timing of his mission: namely, the death on 2 December of Leo x and the decision to nominate Wolsey in the ensuing election. In fact, Wolsey's candidature was not very serious,[4] and it was important foreign policy considerations that really explain the choice of Pace. Wolsey, it may be remembered, had come back from Calais with an alliance with the emperor and plans, at least in embryo, for that major offensive against the French, the Great Enterprise. In these plans the situation in Italy was of vital importance, and it would be especially helpful if the alliance between France and Venice could be broken. It was this that soon became Pace's main task, and by the end of July 1523 he had accomplished it. A fortnight later Pope Adrian vi died, and Pace was asked to stay in Italy to help promote Wolsey's second candidature for the papacy, and to ensure that, if Wolsey failed, Giulio de' Medici, considered favourably disposed towards the Anglo-Imperial alliance, did not. Once this had been achieved, it had been Wolsey's intention to let Pace return home. Indeed, he did get as far as the Low Countries, but was then diverted back to Northern Italy to act as England's representative with the rebel duke of Bourbon, whose co-operation was seen as essential to allied success.[5]

Pace, it should be stressed, made it quite clear that this new task was one he welcomed.[6] Like so many of his colleagues in the upper echelons of royal service, he was a committed Imperialist and entirely approved of the notion of bringing Francis I to his knees. Arriving at Bourbon's camp, he was soon writing glowing reports of the duke's personal qualities, and making optimistic assessments of his chances of success. Pace's judgement in this matter was of vital concern to Wolsey because

[1] Scarisbrick, Thought, 52, p.253.
[2] Elton, Tudor Revolution, pp.32, 56-9; Higham.
[3] Chambers, English Representation, pp.390-3.
[4] See p.156 above.
[5] Wegg, pp.225 ff for the above and for much of what follows.
[6] St.P,vi, p.288 (LP,iv,374).

upon it would depend whether or not Henry himself invaded France. Wolsey made all this very clear to Pace, itself evidence of Wolsey's continuing confidence in him.[1] It is also true that he was well aware that Pace's enthusiasm for the Imperialist cause coloured his judgement. Commenting in a letter of 31 August on Pace's desire that Henry should invade, Wolsey allowed himself a little irony: 'For the helping whereof, you desire me to lay my cardinal's hat, crosses, maces, and myself in pledge.'[2] He also warned Pace: 'In this matter necessary it is that you look substantially to yourself that by fair words, promises,or demonstrations you be not seduced, nor, giving over-much credence to them, provoked to allect the king's highness or his army over the sea.'[3] Pace, for his part, accused Wolsey of taking a remark of his too seriously, though, as it had been to the effect that if Henry failed to gain the French crown, the responsibility would be Wolsey's, his seriousness is understandable.[4]

In September 1508 Erasmus had described Pace thus:

> a young man so well versed in knowledge of Greek and Latin letters that his intellect would enable him unaided to bring fame to the whole of England; and who is of such high character, and so modest withal, that he wholly deserves the favour of yourself, and those who resemble you.[5]

The praise could hardly have been more generous, and undoubtedly Pace did win favour amongst a lot of people, including both Henry and Wolsey at home, and the Venetian signory abroad, as well as the devotion of people such as Thomas Lupset and Reginald Pole. But as a colleague, his over-anxiousness and hyperactivity, which by March 1525 had begun seriously to undermine his sanity, caused problems. In August 1524 the Imperial ambassador at Rome commented that Pace wrote '"in a thousand colours"'. In one letter he says that the Imperial army is prosperous beyond all expectation . . . and in another he pretends that all is ruined, and the army is lost. Such letters do much harm.'[6] In November Pace had told a Venetian friend that when he returned to England he would be urging Henry to invade France in person, and had then added 'whole sackfuls of bravadoes'.[7] In December the Imperial diplomat, Nicholas Schomberg, archbishop of Capua, told the Venetian Gasparo Contarini that 'he did not approve of Pace because he was too vehement'.[8] These comments, it should be stressed, were from people to whose cause Pace was wholly committed. What some may find surprising, particularly given Wolsey's own detached attitude towards the Imperialists, is the patience that he showed throughout the summer and autumn of 1524 in dealing with Pace's outpourings. If there was criticism, there was also much praise, and always Wolsey emphasized how great was his and Henry's trust in him. There was also some acute probing behind Pace's over-involvement with Bourbon in order to arrive at a

[1] *LP*,iv,605.
[2] *St.P*,vi, p.334 (*LP*,iv,605).
[3] *St.P*,vi, p.341 (*LP*,iv,605).
[4] *St.P*,vi, p.314 (*LP*,iv,442).
[5] *CWE*,2, pp.141-2.
[6] *Sp.Cal.*,ii, p.660.
[7] *Ven.Cal.*,iii,897.
[8] *Ven.Cal.*,iii,899.

realistic assessment of the duke's chances of success.[1]

By the end of September Bourbon's army was in retreat from Marseilles. By October Francis had entered Milan. The Great Enterprise was in ruins, and with it Pace's dreams. He was ordered back to Venice with the important task of trying to prevent the republic from reverting to its former ally. At the same time, though, he was increasingly having to deny rumours that his own master was involved in serious negotiations with the French. Not surprisingly he found this painful, especially as he suspected, rightly, that the rumours were true.[2] If the French defeat at Pavia on 25 February 1525 caused him some happiness, it was short-lived, because by 5 March he was seriously ill.[3] In a letter to Wolsey of the 12th of that month he described his illness as a fever,[4] but it soon transpired that the problem was mental. One symptom was insomnia, and he may also have been suffering delusions.[5] Shortly after Pace's return to England in November paranoia had set in. He was melancholy, and thought that the king had taken all his possessions and that he had been left penniless.[6] Some of his paranoia may have focused upon Wolsey. In October 1524 Pace had apparently blamed the failure of Bourbon's mission on Wolsey and suspected that, lured by generous bribes and his own 'base nature', he had come to some secret understanding with the French.[7] In the following April the signory advised their newly appointed ambassador to England not to praise Pace too highly in Wolsey's presence, for they understood that he was not in great favour with the cardinal[8] which suggests that Pace's criticisms of Wolsey were common knowledge in Venice.

Pace's criticisms are not surprising, but they should not be misinterpreted. They centred not upon any deep grievance about his blighted career, for given the office of royal secretary and his many church preferments, including the deaneries of St Paul's, Salisbury and Exeter, blighted it could hardly be said to have been. Rather, they stemmed from his completely different attitude towards the conduct of foreign policy. As has been frequently mentioned, the view that England's interests were best served by a close alliance with the emperor was a commonplace amongst the English ruling classes, but for Pace it had been reinforced by his early Italian experiences, especially his service with Cardinal Bainbridge whose four and a half years at the papal court had been devoted to doing the French down at every conceivable opportunity.[9] There was also a moral dimension, an attachment to some kind of Imperialist *pax christiana* in which the emperor served as protector, perhaps even as reformer, of the Church, if the papacy would not take up this task.[10]

---

[1] See pp. 385-6 above.

[2] Ven. Cal., iii, 888.

[3] Ven. Cal., iii, 947.

[4] LP, iv, 1178.

[5] See Erasmus's reference to Pace's 'love-affairs' in LP, iv, 1547; see also LP, iv, 2252 for Pace's own references to love. For his insomnia see LP, iv, 1546, 1678.

[6] Ven. Cal., iii, 1175, 1187.

[7] Ven. Cal., iii, 888.

[8] Ven. Cal., iii, 975.

[9] Chambers, *Cardinal Bainbridge*, pp. 22 ff. For Pace's francophobia see his comment to Wolsey in Feb. 1523: 'We shall soon leave the French king without a friend; the Gallic eagle will not have a single feather to fly with.' (LP, iii, 2847).

[10] Headley, *Emperor and his Chancellor*, pp. 86 ff. is interesting on this.

For Wolsey, on the other hand, foreign policy was not a matter of sentiment or of morality, except insofar as pursuing the best interests of one's monarch was in itself a good. Wolsey's only commitment was to the pursuit of those interests, and if this meant, as in 1525, sacrificing the Imperial alliance, so be it. But with that sacrifice went all Pace's efforts of the last three years. Given his temperament, the feeling of having been let down by Wolsey, perhaps even deceived by him, might easily lead to madness and paranoia, which would only have reinforced and exaggerated his feelings of betrayal. It is possible to argue that in this sense Wolsey was responsible for Pace's insanity, though given the complexity of the human personality and the continuing uncertainties about the origins of mental illness, it might be a little unfair to do so. What it is not possible to do is to argue that Wolsey deliberately set out to destroy Pace because he had perceived him to be a dangerous rival. There is nothing sinister in the use that Wolsey, and Henry also, made of Pace's services from 1521 to 1525. Indeed, that they drove him so hard during these years is evidence of their continuing trust and confidence.

There is a coda to this story. On his return to England in November 1525 Pace's condition worsened. On the 24th the Venetian ambassador reported that he was no longer allowed visitors, and a month later he wrote of those delusions already referred to. Sometime in 1526 he was replaced as king's secretary by William Knight, and Wolsey took steps, for which he was commended by the king, to ensure that Pace's three deaneries were properly administered by appointing coadjutors:[1] a normal procedure when holders of church offices were unable for reasons of ill-health or old age to carry out their duties. Shortly afterwards Pace went to reside at the famous Brigettine monastery of Syon.[2] In October 1527, having switched allegiance in the king's 'great matter' from Henry's side to Catherine's, he tried to arrange a clandestine meeting with the Imperial ambassador, Mendoza, which the latter claimed he had avoided precisely because he believed Pace to be mad. Be that as it may, the government got to hear of Pace's plan, and he was arrested. And probably the madness had returned, for Pace was surprisingly free with his criticisms not only of Wolsey but of Henry.[3] At any rate, after a short spell in the Tower, he was placed in the custody of the abbot of Beaulieu, who was a relation, perhaps even a brother. This did not prevent the abbot coming to the conclusion that Pace was incurable, 'for in his rage and distemperance, renting and tearing his clothes, no man can rule him'.[4] By November 1528 poor Pace was very mad indeed, and, moreover, the abbot's prognosis seems on the whole to have been correct. During Pace's eight remaining years there were temporary respites, but he was never able to resume a normal life.[5]

In all the circumstances, Wolsey's treatment of Pace was both considerate and patient. His wild accusations against Wolsey have been taken too much at their face value. They must have been highly embarrassing to Wolsey personally, as well as detrimental to the search for the divorce. Yet he made great allowances, going to some lengths to obtain the best treatment for him. And interestingly, Pace could

[1] *LP*,iv,2420, 2434.
[2] *Ven.Cal.*,iv,144
[3] *LP*,3233, 3235-6; *Sp.Cal*,iii (ii), 224, 442; see also Wegg, pp.273 ff.
[4] Henry Ellis, 3 ser.,ii, p.151 (*LP*,iv,4927).
[5] Wegg, pp.285-8.

also praise Wolsey, writing, probably in 1527 at the time of his arrest, that 'whatsoever is spoken here of my lord cardinal's evil mind against me it is untrue, for he hath nothing done against me but that is to my high contentation, and rather advancement than hindrance'.[1] Where mental illness is concerned, there can be no compelling reason for believing one statement rather than another; but if the record of Wolsey's behaviour towards Pace throughout the 1520s is considered in detail, what may surprise is not any harm that Wolsey may have done, but that he put up with so much.

The reason for focusing so long on Pace is that it tells us so much about Wolsey's treatment of his colleagues. What has emerged is not some power-crazed paranoid – indeed it was Pace who was paranoid – but one who, though expecting a lot, treated them with respect and decency. Moreover, and this was commented upon earlier in connection with his conduct of foreign policy,[2] he was quite prepared to listen to different viewpoints. Wolsey did not control royal patronage, did not surround himself with yes-men, nor was he hated by everybody: that has been the argument so far. What is true, however, is that as royal secretary Pace resided, when in England, in the royal household and was therefore in the kind of intimate contact with the king that Wolsey, with his many duties at Westminster, could not be. As such he was well placed to undermine Wolsey's position. In an even stronger position, because in even closer contact, were members of a newly created department of the household, the privy chamber. It is upon these people that our attention must now focus.

As the name suggests, the function of members of this department was to wait upon the king in the privy chamber, a private apartment to which he could withdraw in order to escape the hurly-burly of the great chamber and the only slightly less public presence chamber. At one level, their duties were what one would nowadays expect of a servant: seeing to it that when the king got up in the morning the fires were lit and the room 'pure, clean, wholesome, and meet without any displeasant air'.[3] By 1526 such duties were being performed by the grooms of the privy chamber. The ushers controlled the entrances, allowing only those with royal permission to enter, though the great chamber was open to almost anyone. The gentlemen of the privy chamber were particularly responsible for dressing the king, and two of them attended him throughout the night. During the day they were to 'have a vigilant and reverent respect and eye to his grace so that by his look and countenance they may know what lacketh, or is his pleasure to be had or done'.[4] But though their duties were mundane enough, the object of their attentions was not, which meant that they had to be men of discretion and of a certain social standing, accomplished in the ways of the court. Being so close to the king they would overhear all sorts of conversations, some very personal, others to do with important matters of state. They were used as royal messengers, and not only within the environs of the court, for as the 1526 Eltham ordinances put it, they were to be 'well languaged, expert in outward parts, and meet and able to be sent on familiar messages, or otherwise, to

---

[1] LP,iv,3234.
[2] See pp.72-3, 205, 551-2 above.
[3] *Royal Household*, p.155.
[4] Ibid, p.156.

outward princes, when the case shall require'.[1] And they were not only the king's servants and messengers but also the companions of his leisure, whether snowball fights, playing cards and dice, hunting, jousting or performing masques and disguisings. Of course, they were not the only people who took part in these entertainments. At the start of his reign the royal companions had not been organized into a privy chamber, but they performed essentially the same role of servant *cum* courtier that the sons of the nobility and leading gentry had performed ever since courts first existed. All that was new was the formality.

As it happened, the original group of royal companions was quickly dispersed: two of its most prominent members, Sir Thomas Knyvet and Sir Edward Howard, were killed in naval engagements, and perhaps more significantly for what follows, others, such as Charles Brandon, created duke of Suffolk in 1514, received promotions and rewards which made it more difficult for them to perform their earlier role. Consequently, new companions had to be sought. In September 1518 took place a grand French embassy which included amongst its entourage six leading 'gentilzhommes de la Chambre'. To complement these, six Englishmen were given similar titles: Sir Edward Neville, Arthur Pole, Nichlas Carew, Francis Bryan, Henry Norris, and William Carey, just those younger companions who had been emerging during the previous two or three years, and of whom all but Neville had fought in Henry's 'band' at the great joust on 7 July 1517.[2] To these six should be added Sir William Compton who from 1510 occupied the office of groom of the stool and, as such, was head of the privy chamber, with special responsibilities not only, as the name suggests, for Henry's lavatorial requirements but for his day-to-day expenditure, which by the 1520s was running at about £10,000 a year, and for the safe-keeping of his jewels and plate. Like Richard Pace, all these men have been seen as rivals to Wolsey, and we must now look and see if this was so.[3]

On 18 May 1519 the Venetian ambassador, Giustinian, wrote:

> Within the last few days his majesty has made a very great change in the court here, dismissing four of his chief lords-in-waiting who enjoyed extreme authority in this kingdom, and were the very soul of the king; he has likewise changed some other officials, replacing them by men of greater age and repute, a measure which is deemed of as vital importance as any that has taken place for many years.[4]

In an effort to discover the reason for this 'great change' Giustinian had consulted the Venetian organist, Dionysius Memo, whose playing since his arrival in England in September 1516 had so impressed both Henry and Wolsey that he had been given a permanent post at court. Memo came up with various explanations, one of which was that those who had been removed were considered to be too French, through having taken part in an embassy to France during which they had spent some time with Francis I 'throwing eggs, stones, and other foolish trifles' at the unsuspecting Parisians. Another view, and one which had the seal of approval from none other than the duke of Norfolk, was that these young men by their obsession with gambling had been leading Henry astray, and that he, 'resolving to lead a new life,

---

[1] Ibid, p.155.
[2] For all this see D.R. Starkey, 'King's Privy Chamber', pp.89-111.
[3] Central to all Starkey's writing on the privy chamber, but see especially *History Today*, 32.
[4] Rawdon Brown, ii,270 (*LP*,iii,235).

. . . of his own accord removed these companions of his excesses'.[1] Giustinian also consulted the French ambassador and those French hostages who under the terms of the Treaty of London were resident at the court as security for the French payments for the return of Tournai. While admitting that the changes might have had something to do with English suspicions of the French, they came up with quite a different explanation: it was Wolsey who had got rid of them, believing that they had become 'so intimate with the king that in the course of time they might have ousted him from government'.[2] Meanwhile, across the Channel the French court was abuzz with gossip about the changes, and Francis was able with some accuracy to inform the English ambassador at his court, Thomas Boleyn, of the names of those dismissed: Carew, Bryan, Neville, the two Guildfords, Sir John Peachey, Francis Pointz and one other whose name he did not know.[3] Of these, Carew, Bryan and Neville had been named as gentlemen of the privy chamber in 1518, while Edward and Henry Guildford and Peachey had a long record of service in the royal household. Here they were, being unceremoniously bundled out of the court, and, at least according to the French ambassador, all because Wolsey had become jealous. On the face of it, it does look as if something quite important had taken place, but as so often closer scrutiny raises doubts.

In order to explain the precise dating of this purge, our attention has recently been directed to Wolsey's failure in the autumn of 1517 to secure for one of his household servants the hand in marriage of the recently widowed Margaret Vernon. Instead, the prize was won by a member of the privy chamber, William Coffin who, with the help of his colleague, Nicholas Carew, had obtained royal letters in his favour. The gossip at court, and the source was none other than Compton, was that Wolsey was not best pleased.[4] In May 1519 he took his revenge – or so it can be argued. One difficulty with this interpretation is that if it was revenge that Wolsey was after, he was peculiarly unsuccessful, for one of the curious things about the 'expulsions' is that those expelled did rather well. Carew, the rising star of the royal jousts, was made captain of Rysbank, a castle at the entrance to Calais harbour. Sir Edward Guildford was made marshal of Calais. Sir John Peachey, whom Carew had replaced at Rysbank, was appointed deputy-lieutenant of Calais, replacing Sir Richard Wingfield, one of Wolsey's so-called 'creatures' who replaced the expelled in the privy chamber.[5] And in exchanging one Calais office for another in getting Rysbank, Carew was given an increase in his annual salary of some £100, while Peachey's new office was one of some distinction, more usually held by a nobleman.[6] For the others expelled there are no details of promotions, though Sir Henry Guildford retained his important office of master of the horse, which hardly suggests that he was in any serious disgrace. What is true of all those expelled is that the event did not seriously interrupt their already successful careers; in fact, they can hardly be said to have been away from court. Only four months later, Carew and Bryan were taking part in a great masque at the newly acquired palace of Beaulieu in

---

[1] Rawdon Brown, ii, p.271 (LP,iii,235).
[2] Ibid.
[3] LP,ii,246.
[4] D.R. Starkey, Henry VIII, pp.73-4; LP,ii,3807 for Wolsey's displeasure.
[5] LP,iii,247, 261, 259, 265.
[6] Morgan, p.94.

Essex, while the chance survival of the houshold accounts shows that for October and November they were both in receipt of breakfasts and liveries as members of the royal household, as were Sir Henry Guildford, and someone spelt either as Poynes or Poyntes,[1] and my suggestion is that they never lost these privileges. Sir Edward Neville does appear to have left the household at this time, but did not lose royal favour until his alleged treason and consequent execution in 1538, but that event surely cannot be blamed on Wolsey!

And can Wolsey's failure to obtain the hand of a widow in marriage for one of his household servants really be a convincing explanation for the events of May 1519? It was shown earlier that the main recipients of royal favour were precisely members of the royal household, such as William Coffin, a fact of life which Wolsey may not have liked, but certainly had to lump. In the Vernon case Wolsey had probably acted for his servant in a fairly routine way, without initially being aware of Coffin's interest. Moreover, Wolsey was by no means the only person being asked to put in a good word with the king, and so had to take his chances with the rest. On this occasion, his servant lost, but not even the king won all the time; and Wolsey himself does not appear to have done too badly, for he secured 'the wardship of young Mr Vernon and Mr Clifton'.[2] If the failure to secure the young man's mother for his servant had led to the severe bout of paranoia concerning members of the privy chamber that has been alleged, one cannot help feeling that Wolsey would have had to have been certified long before his master dispensed with his services, for quite other reasons, in 1529.

One way and another the 'purge' of 1519 appears to have been something of a storm in a tea-cup, and not one that Giustinian, for all his excitement about the 'very great change', ever mentioned again. Probably on reflection he realized that it had not been so significant, but may be his initial excitement had been fuelled by the French ambassador and his compatriots at court, for what seems to have happened is this: although a French alliance was never popular in England, since the previous summer it had become the cornerstone of English foreign policy. Relations between the two countries were thus in a particularly sensitive state in which possible slights and misunderstandings were likely. People were saying that the changes at court reflected anti-French feeling. To counter this, the French ambassador was putting it about that it was Wolsey who was behind the changes, and it needs to be stressed that it was only ever the French, as reported by Giustinian, who associated Wolsey with this 'purge'; and the fact that two such hostile commentators as Hall and Vergil did not, helps to confirm the account given here.

What convinced Giustinian that the 'French view' was right was the provenance of those brought in to replace the expelled. They were Sir Richard Wingfield, Sir Richard Jerningham, Sir Richard Weston and Sir William Kingston. Interestingly, they were given the new and rather grand title of 'knights for the body in the king's privy chamber'. What has more usually caught the attention has been Giustinian's comment that they were 'creatures of Cardinal Wolsey'.[3] Edward Hall

---

[1] *LP*,iii,pp.1551; Hall, p.599.
[2] *LP*,ii,3807.
[3] Rawdon Brown, ii, p.271 (*LP*,iii,235).

took a different view, describing them merely as 'sad and ancient knights',[1] and in doing so he seems to have been more accurate. All four had been in royal service for a considerable time. About ten years older than Wolsey, Weston had entered the royal household by 1505 at the latest as groom of the chamber. Wingfield had been an esquire of the body as early as 1500, when Wolsey was still at Oxford, and was made marshal of Calais in 1511. Kingston had been a yeoman of the chamber as early as 1497 and a gentleman usher in 1504. Less is known about the early career of Jerningham, but by 1511 he was sufficiently important to be sent on a mission to Venice. All these men had begun their careers in the royal service before Wolsey could have acted as their patron. Their rise was not as spectacular as his, or, indeed, as Brandon's or Compton's. Instead, they were typical royal servants of the second rank: competent, hard-working and loyal, they had climbed slowly but steadily up the ladder of promotion, and their appointments in 1519 were but the next rung. They may have got on well with Wolsey; there is no obvious evidence either way. As loyal servants of the Crown they would undoubtedly have tried their best to co-operate with him and to carry out his instructions, but this hardly makes them his 'creatures'.

Why, then, were they appointed to these new posts in the privy chamber? What all four men did possess was a certain age and experience, and so perhaps it was a certain gravitas that was their attraction. The privy chamber was, in a formal sense at any rate, a very new department, and what seems to have been felt was that in order to get it established it needed greater status. This was best provided by putting at its head more senior men, at the same time giving them a grander title. It may also be true, and was certainly said at the time, that the likes of Carew and Bryan had been behaving in too frolicsome a fashion and needed a touch of the reins, perhaps even a little experience of the less glamorous side of royal service.[2] In this context a letter that the earl of Surrey wrote to Wolsey in October 1523 is of some interest. At Newcastle in command of a royal army raised to defend the North from invasion by the duke of Albany, he was finding it such a worrying business that, as he had written earlier, he was quite decayed in body as well as worn out in purse.[3] Such feelings no doubt encouraged him to speak his mind. Please, he wrote, could 'some noblemen of the king's house and the south parts' be sent to help him.

> God knoweth, if the poorest gentleman in the king's house were here, and I at London and were advertised of this news, I would not fail to kneel upon my knees before the king's grace to have licence to come hither in post to be at the day of battle. And if young noblemen and gentlemen be not desirous and willing to be at such journeys and take the pain and give the adventure, and the king's highness well contented with those that will so do, and not regarding others that will be but dancers, dicers and carders, his grace shall not be well served when he would be; for men without experience shall do small service, and experience of war will not be had without it be sought for and the adventure given.[4]

---

[1] Hall, p.598.
[2] Walker's reappraisal of this episode appeared too late to be seriously considered here, but he argues for a genuine desire for a reformation of the court's lifestyle, pushed not by Wolsey but other royal councillors such as Norfolk; see Walker, HJ, 32, pp.12-16.
[3] LP,iii,3384.
[4] Henry Ellis, 1 ser, i, pp.225-6 (LP,iii,3405).

Given that Surrey had spent so much of his life fighting for the king, the emotional force of this passage is very understandable. It also made a good deal of sense. But in the present context it is what it has to tell of the likes of Bryan and Carew and others in the privy chamber that is of most interest. The impression is not of politically powerful figures, but rather of young men being trained, though in Surrey's view not very well, to be effective royal servants. One aspect of this training should have been active campaigning, but in May 1519 there was none to be had, and so the young men had perhaps got a little out of control. Now in 1523, the time for dancing and dicing was over. On 23 October Surrey was reporting the arrival of the marquess of Dorset and 'all the gentlemen of the king's house,' and among them none other than Sir Francis Bryan and Sir Nicholas Carew.[1]

Someone who was not sent up North that October was Sir William Compton, but this was no doubt only because he had been there earlier in the year. It was Vergil who first suggested that Compton had been deliberately sent to the war because Wolsey disliked the fact that 'Henry found him most agreeable', and because Compton 'disliked Wolsey's ruthless nature'.[2] Recently this suggestion has been revived and elaborated upon, in order to promote a conspiracy-theory view of the conduct of foreign policy, this an off-shoot of the factional view of Henrician politics that has become almost an orthodoxy. According to this, the decision to go to war against France in 1522 – which also meant war with Scotland, and hence the presence of the royal army on the northern border in 1523 – was taken primarily in the interests of Wolsey's factional fighting against members of the privy chamber.[3] Despite the 'purge' of 1519, they had become too big for their boots. The only way Wolsey could devise to get rid of them was to have a war, because then there could be no excuse for them to hang around the court. The real reasons for the war have already been discussed, and included among them was no desire to separate Henry from his courtiers. It is also most unlikely that war would have achieved what Wolsey is supposed to have wanted. Rather, it would probably have provided just the occasion for such men to shine, and thereby to gain yet more influence over a king who was always attracted by the martial arts.

There is, in fact, no direct evidence why Compton went to war in the spring of 1523, but Surrey's letters written that autumn again provide important clues: people such as Compton should 'be at such journeys' because it was expected of them. The nobility were for fighting, and if Compton was not strictly a nobleman, he was the next best thing, a gentleman close to the king with an ever-expanding landed estate. That Compton, who, incidentally, had gone with Henry on the French campaign of 1513 and had been knighted after the capture of Tournai, had joined Surrey on the Scottish border thus hardly needs an explanation. Indeed, what surprised – and annoyed – Surrey was that more people like Compton had not accompanied him: and it needs to be stressed that it was Surrey who was clamouring for members of the household to be sent up to him, not Wolsey who was anxious to see them go. In fact, their staying at court probably had nothing to do, as Surrey thought, with their love of courtly pleasures, nor with any machinations of

---

[1] *LP*,iii,3458; also *LP*,iii,3421, 3424.
[2] Vergil, p.309.
[3] D.R. Starkey, *History Today*, 32, p.19; see also his 'King's privy chamber', pp. 161 ff.

Wolsey's, but with the more mundane fact that Henry was expecting at any moment to launch an army across the Channel for which they would be needed, especially if he himself was to go. And this highlights a serious weakness in the factional view of Henrician politics. It completely ignores the practicalities – that armies have to be raised and that men have to be sent on embassies not because somebody wants to be rid of them but because they are the best, or perhaps even the only, people available. In the real world the exigencies of the moment usually dictate what happens, and in so doing make life very difficult for the conspirator – even one as wicked and as wily as Wolsey! And even if the above interpretation of Compton's journey north were wrong, and it was all a plot by Wolsey, it would have been one that Henry approved of, for why else would he write to Surrey to thank him for having 'lovingly entertained' Compton while he had been in the North? Furthermore, Surrey replied that he had done no more than his duty, for he was 'bound to make much of all such that I know your grace should favour', especially since 'at my coming from your highness, your grace showed me your pleasure was I should so do, and to make the more of him for your sake'.[1] In this exchange there is not even a whiff of any machinations by Wolsey.

If it is true, as has been argued here, that neither in 1519 nor in 1523 did Wolsey set out to remove men of standing from the king's presence, it becomes less likely that he attempted to do so in 1525-6, though not, of course, impossible. It has been suggested that he did precisely this,[2] and it could well be that, as these people became better established, Wolsey would have resorted to more Machiavellian tactics in order to retain his own influence with the king. Moreover, by mid-1525 things were not going particularly well. The Amicable Grant had failed, the Great Enterprise had had to be called off, and the result was a return to the always unpopular alliance with the erstwhile enemy, France. All this could have weakened Wolsey's position with the king and made him more sensitive to competition. There is no evidence that at this date it did, but what has given rise to speculation that Wolsey did attempt to exclude his rivals from court are his efforts to reform the royal household, culminating with the Eltham ordinances of January 1526. One consequence of these was that not only was the privy chamber thinned down from about twenty-two to fifteen, but that some of its leading lights, including Compton, Bryan and Carew, were excluded. Thus, it can be argued that what Wolsey had failed to do in 1519 and 1523 he at last achieved in January 1526.[3]

In fact, the argument is no more convincing than those put forward for the earlier episodes. For one thing, in 1526 as in 1519, none of the people removed was in any way disgraced. Indeed, most of them received, or had recently received, rather lucrative offices. The marquess of Dorset, who had always been a close friend of the king without exercising any very obvious influence, did not immediately receive a compensatory office, but later in the year he became lord master of Princess Mary's Council in the Marches of Wales, an appointment which hardly suggests that he had earlier been 'purged'. Moreover, he continued to receive marks

---

[1] *LP*,iv,149, quoted in Bernard, *EHR*, xcvi, p.775, but since Surrey was not in Newcastle in March 1524 the *LP* dating must be wrong.
[2] D.R. Starkey, 'King's privy chamber', pp.161 ff; *Henry VIII*, pp.86-9.
[3] For non-factional aspects of the Eltham ordinances see pp.365-9 above.

of royal favour, including, in 1528, a share in the constableship of Warwick Castle with his former privy chamber colleague, Sir Francis Bryan. He was also frequently at court and was placed fifth in the list of the twenty leading royal councillors as set out in the very instrument of his purging, the Eltham ordinances; the only people above him being Wolsey, Norfolk, Tunstall and Suffolk. His position could hardly have been more pre-eminent.

Sir Richard Weston has been mentioned already as one of 'the creatures of Cardinal Wolsey' brought into the privy chamber in 1519, along with another person purged in 1526, Sir William Kingston. That Wolsey would then wish to remove them in 1526 might, therefore, seem a little odd. Of course, six years is a long time in politics, and perhaps Wolsey had grown to distrust them. But there is probably nothing odd about it at all, for just as their original appointment to the privy chamber probably had nothing to do with Wolsey's factional interests, so neither had their removal. In the autumn of 1525 Weston had been appointed treasurer of Calais. This was quite an important post, with a salary of £100 and apparently requiring residence in Calais.[1] At any rate, Weston went, and this provides the most obvious explanation for why he ceased to be a member of the privy chamber. Kingston, though, did not leave court, for he retained his office of captain of the guard, which meant, as the Eltham ordinances made clear, that he had important duties to perform in the royal household. Moreover, in 1524 he had been made constable of the Tower of London, another office with real responsibilities, one of which would be to escort the arrested Wolsey down from the North in 1530. In 1525 he had been given the duchy of Lancaster stewardships, previously retained by the chancellor of the duchy but not given to More when he was appointed to that office.[2] It looks as if Kingston had been given quite enough, both to do and by way of reward, and he was probably quite happy to be relieved of his privy chamber duties. And if Wolsey was planning to cut down expenditure on the household, discontinuing Kingston's membership of the privy chamber would have made sense.

Of the three who might be considered to have possessed rather more political importance, Carew, Bryan and Compton, least is known about Carew. He seem to have received no office or grant of royal favour to compensate him for loss of privy chamber membership, but as master of the horse from 1522 he remained a significant figure at court, and when in 1527 Francis I was made a knight of the garter it was Carew who conveyed it to him. And he was to remain significant enough at Court to have his head cut off in 1539! Bryan also seems to have received nothing. Perhaps it was felt that with an annual income of some £400 he was in no need of further remuneration. But he is an interesting figure if, as befits his sobriquet of 'the Vicar of Hell', a rather shadowy one.[3] Related to Anne Boleyn, his return to the privy chamber in the summer of 1528 may be connected with her increasing influence. It was he who was sent to Paris in the summer of 1528 to escort Campeggio across the Channel and to Rome on an important mission in connection with the divorce in November, with instructions to submit regular

---

[1] Morgan, pp.94, 295.
[2] See pp.194 ff. above.
[3] For both Bryan and Carew see D.R. Starkey, *Henry viii*, pp.69-70; for his income see *LP*,iv,2972.

reports for the king's eyes only;[1] and some of these reports were critical of the way the divorce had been handled. Here, at last, is something with a whiff of faction about it, but it is only a whiff, and it could be a false trail. One would need something a bit more definite before it was possible to argue convincingly that Wolsey saw Bryan, along with the others removed from the privy chamber in 1526, as a serious rival, and thus interpret the Eltham ordinances in a factional sense. Moreover, if, as was suggested earlier,[2] Henry made his own appointments, then presumably he would have controlled dismissals as well, especially as regards so intimate a matter as a personal servant and companion. So, even if he had wanted to, it is most unlikely that Wolsey was ever in a position to conduct a purge of the royal household.

What is also clear is that, whatever his intentions, Wolsey never succeeded in keeping Bryan, or anyone else, away from the king for any length of time, and it is worth making the point that even after 1526 Compton and Carew continued to be provided with lodgings in the royal household, as indeed did Dorset, Kingston and Weston, presumably, therefore, still well placed to influence the king, if that was what they were bent on. Wolsey was far too intelligent not to have quickly realized the impossibility of doing away with people whom the king liked. Both his instinct and his practice were to conciliate, and there is no reason to suppose that members of the privy chamber were the exception. Neither is there any evidence that he and Bryan did not get on well. He accompanied the cardinal on both his great embassies abroad, to Bruges and Calais in 1521 and to Amiens and Compiègne in 1527, which suggests that Wolsey trusted him and appreciated his diplomatic skills. If, on the other hand, it is argued that on these occasions the choice of Bryan was not Wolsey's, then this hardly suggests that Wolsey would have been able to remove him from the privy chamber against the king's wishes. A letter that Bryan wrote to Wolsey in connection with his escorting Campeggio to England in 1528 is very much a friendly exchange between people who knew and respected each other[3] – a view which is not necessarily contradicted by what can be taken to be veiled criticisms of Wolsey in his reports from Rome in the spring of 1529.[4] Spurred on by both Henry and Wolsey to obtain from the pope something that they realized would not be forthcoming, he and his colleagues were in a difficult position. They had therefore little option but to criticize their instructions or to admit their own incompetence. In the strained atmosphere of those months criticisms were bound to surface, but they should not be taken as evidence of an endemic rivalry between Wolsey and the likes of Bryan.

The overwhelming impression is that the dismissals of 1526 made a good deal of sense, both for those removed and for the more cost-effective running of the royal household, which, after all, was the stated purpose of the exercise. A conspiracy theorist would wish to ignore the stated purpose, but that would seem a little cavalier. Reform of the royal household was to be a leitmotiv of sixteenth- and seventeenth-century politics. The institution itself was an administrator's

---

[1] St.P,vii, p.166 (LP,iv,5481).
[2] See.pp.190-201.
[3] LP,iv,4656.
[4] See p.589 below.

nightmare, in some ways consciously designed to be wasteful and corrupt, because it was one of the purposes of kingship to be bountiful. But given that Tudor and Stuart kings were always short of money, if not desperately in need of it, it was inevitable that attempts would periodically be made by those in charge of government to limit the drain on money that the royal household always was. In 1525 money was a problem for Henry, so there is nothing at all sinister in the fact that Wolsey turned his attention to household reform.

A brief look at Sir William Compton's position in 1526 will help us to a proper understanding of the role of the privy chamber in this period and of its relationship with Wolsey. Having presided over the first ten years of its existence, as groom of the stool, Compton was the privy chamber member *par excellence*.[1] In the late summer of 1525, he had wished to become chancellor of the duchy of Lancaster, one of the major offices of state, and if he had obtained it, he would certainly have had to give up his privy chamber post. As it was, he obtained a post not quite so important but nevertheless perfectly respectable and well paid, that of undertreasurer of the Exchequer.[2] Whatever his disappointment, it has to be assumed that Compton was by 1525 anxious to escape from the burdensome duties of groom of the stool, and saw this office as promotion. And the notion of promotion is the key to understanding. The royal household and, if you were fortunate, the privy chamber was where you started your career, not where you hoped to end it. For this reason entry into the privy chamber was largely for the young, and the exceptions, such as Wolsey's four 'creatures', do not disprove the rule. These older men, it was argued earlier, gave to the newly formed institution that status and distinction that, probably following the French model, Henry perceived a body so intimately associated with the king to require. In fact the appointment of four hard-working senior royal servants was not a great success. Kingston and Weston remained until 1526 when both went on to more important things, but Wingfield and Jerningham had dropped out much earlier, being far too busily employed in foreign embassies to perform satisfactorily duties that involved close and permanent attendance upon the king.

Service in the royal household provided an excellent training in all kinds of skills, lots of good perks and, above all, a golden opportunity to form a personal relationship with the king, which would obviously further one's career; a modern equivalent would be the post of personal private secretary to a cabinet minister. But personal private secretaries do not exercise great power, and neither did members of the the privy chamber, as is suggested by the fact that they were rarely mentioned by foreign ambassadors, one of whose main jobs was, after all, to detect who was and was not important. Compton, it is true, occasionally rated a mention. In 1511 the French ambassador even reported that he enjoyed more 'credit' with the king than anyone else, and should therefore be granted a pension, advice that was later to be acted upon.[3] All the same, Giustinian in his four years at the English court never once mentioned Compton, and when he came to report the 'purge' of 1519 he failed to provide the names of those who had been removed, almost certainly because he

---

[1] Bernard, *EHR*, xcvi for Compton's career.
[2] For the detail see pp.194 ff. above.
[3] *LP*, i, 734, 3502; iii, 1321.

did not know them. The people whom he felt to be important, apart from Wolsey, were Norfolk, Suffolk, Fox, and occasionally Pace and More. Now, it would ill behove one as sceptical of the value of ambassadorial reports as the present writer to set too much store by this, but it does seem unlikely that Giustinian would have completely failed over a four-year period to detect a whole group of people, if indeed they did possess great influence. Later ambassadors did not spot them either. And, when, from 1527 onwards, they began to speculate about an anti-Wolsey faction, it was one composed not of privy chamber members, but of two dukes and one viscount. Even if, as will shortly be argued, they were wrong about this, they were surely right to think that any threat to Wolsey's position would come from such people, because only they had the authority to force the king's hand?

By and large it was the 3rd Duke of Norfolk who was singled out by the ambassadors as Wolsey's chief opponent, and so it is a little surprising to find that during the 1520s he was given an enormous amount of responsibility. Sent to Ireland in 1520, he was recalled in 1522 because of the imminent outbreak of war with France, and by the July of that year he was in charge of an expedition to Brittany. War with France meant war with Scotland, and in February 1523 Surrey, as he was then, was made lord lieutenant of the king's army against Scotland, his brief to defend the Northern border from invasion by the duke of Albany. By the end of 1524 the threat of invasion was no more, and Surrey, who had by then succeeded his father as 3rd duke of Norfolk, was allowed to return south. But he was not given much rest. In 1525 he was heavily involved in efforts to secure the Amicable Grant in East Anglia and in putting down the accompanying unrest. If, as a result of Pavia, there had been an English invasion of France, it was he who would have led it, but in fact the year brought peace with France, and though there was occasional talk of English armies, Norfolk's military skills were not required again in Wolsey's time. Since 1522 he had been lord treasurer of England, and by the end of the decade he was on virtually every commission of the peace, a distinction he shared with Wolsey alone. It must be assumed from this that Henry and Wolsey, who as lord chancellor was responsible for the appointment of JPs, considered that the duke's name alone added such distinction and authority to a commission that it was worth putting him on it, whether he had any connections with the county or not. As has already been shown, in areas such as East Anglia where he did have strong connections much more than his name was required. In 1525 and from late 1527 through much of 1528 his presence there was considered vital for carrying out government policy and for maintaining law and order.

Norfolk's contribution at these critical times offers the best illustration of the importance to royal government of a loyal nobility. It also provides important evidence of his good relationship with Wolsey. Not only did he make no effort to exploit what might have been considered a heaven-sent opportunity to bring Wolsey down, but the tone of his correspondence with the cardinal at this time reveals two conscientious servants of the king, with different roles to play, but both co-operating to do their very best for their master in difficult circumstances. And what there is certainly no sign of, even in 1527 and 1528, is that Norfolk was at the head of a faction that was striving night and day to bring the cardinal down. Admittedly, tone is a notoriously difficult matter to reach a judgement about and it would be very odd if Norfolk had chosen in his correspondence to let Wolsey know that he was plotting against him! Moreover, one of the charges against Wolsey is that he deliberately kept Norfolk in exile in order to deny him political influence, and for a conspiracy theorist the fact that Norfolk was ordered, even if by the king, to remain in East Anglia in 1528 could be seen as part of Wolsey's machinations. Similar charges levelled against him in connection with Richard Pace and Sir William Compton were refuted, and so will this one be. But it has this much to be said for it: Norfolk, being a nobleman who was prepared to work hard at being a royal servant, was potentially a much more serious threat to Wolsey's position than anyone so far mentioned.

It was the decision to send Norfolk to Ireland in 1520 which, for Polydore Vergil at least, provided the decisive evidence that Wolsey was determined to keep him as far away as possible from the king;[1] and in support of this view is the idea, as much a commonplace of Tudor and Stuart politics as it is of today's, that if one wants to ruin a man's reputation one sends him to sink in the quagmire of Irish politics. What this view ignores is that Ireland has presented successive English governments with real problems which, however reluctantly, have had to be faced up to. This was so in 1520, and in the particular circumstances of that year Norfolk was so obviously the candidate for the post of lord lieutenant of Ireland that no other explanation for the appointment is required. It can also be shown that at that time Henry was taking a direct interest in Irish affairs, and that, given his keen interest in all military matters, he was almost certainly responsible for Norfolk's appointment.[2] And what is true of Norfolk's appointment to Ireland is even more the case, because of his experience of Scottish warfare, of his appointment to command the army against Scotland in 1523 and 1524. The fact is that of the two obvious candidates for any important military command at this time – whether they liked it or not – Norfolk was one. The other was the duke of Suffolk, according to some a fellow conspirator against Wolsey.

Even if Norfolk's appointments to these important commands cannot be evidence of a plot on Wolsey's part to do him down, this does not, of course, prove that no such plot existed. Moreover, it is not only Polydore Vergil and the foreign ambassadors who saw the two men as enemies. In October 1526 the young Henry Percy wrote a letter to his brother-in-law, the earl of Cumberland, in which he reported a conversation between his father the 5th earl of Northumberland and Wolsey, to the effect that Wolsey should put no trust in Cumberland because he was 'all with my lord of Norfolk'.[3] On the face of it, here is convincing evidence that, in leading Northern circles at least, Norfolk and Wolsey were thought to be rivals, and one can see why this might be so. It was during his defence of the Northern border in 1523-4 that Norfolk had been so critical of the stay-at-home courtiers, and no doubt he sometimes made rude remarks about Wolsey too, and what anxious military commander has not criticized civilian leaders who have failed to provide him with the necessary men and money and have obstinately refused to appreciate all the difficulties of waging war? Some of Norfolk's remarks would have gone the rounds and might easily have been misinterpreted – and in this particular instance

[1] Vergil, p.265.
[2] See Quinn, pp. 234-5.
[3] *Clifford Letters*, p.106.

were probably being deliberately misinterpreted. Northumberland was never really trusted by Henry or Wolsey, and when this conversation with Wolsey took place, he was on bad terms with both his son and his son-in-law. And its purpose was not to provide Wolsey with an objective assessment of factional groupings in the North, but to create trouble for his son-in-law. This makes him an unreliable source for the true relationship between Norfolk and Wolsey – something that his son, who had been brought up in Wolsey's household and was thus well placed to make a judgement, seems to have realized. At any rate, the burden of his letter to Cumberland was to warn him not of the awful consequences of a too close attachment to Norfolk but only of Northumberland's efforts to do him down.

But what is one to make of the confession of one William Stapleton who in the late 1520s was called in by a servant of Norfolk to free his master from a spirit allegedly conjured up by Wolsey's enchantment? And what of the Scotsman who, while in France in 1527, got to hear of rude remarks against the duke that Wolsey had apparently made to the French at Amiens, and then reported them to Norfolk? As regards Stapleton, it is necessary to bear in mind he was a professional 'conjuror' who had previously been up before Sir Thomas More for trying to find treasure by magical means, and it looks rather as if Norfolk had been deliberately leading him on in order to discover more about his activities.[1] As regards the Scotsman, there was no doubt some truth in the anecdote, but only insofar as he was reporting that favourite gambit of Wolsey with foreigners in which he portrayed himself as the only Englishman who favoured their cause.[2] A feature of both episodes is that Norfolk did not attempt to conceal them from Wolsey. This may have been mere prudence: he would no doubt have borne in mind the salutary example of his father-in-law, the duke of Buckingham, whose secret consultations with the Carthusian prophesier of Henton Priory had led to his destruction in 1521. Still, if he was seriously planning Wolsey's destruction, why get involved with the likes of Stapleton, only then to rat on him? And if he had to tell somone, why not go straight to the king, who after all was the man he had to persuade that Wolsey was up to no good if he was going to bring the cardinal down? In fact, on both occasions Norfolk behaved very correctly, and in a way that does not suggest that he believed Wolsey to be his evil genius. Twenty years later, however, he was to maintain, if not quite that, at least that Wolsey had spent all his political life plotting against him.

On the face of it this statement would appear decisively to refute the claim being made here that Wolsey and Norfolk got on perfectly well. Here is Norfolk himself saying quite the opposite, and why should we not believe him? One reason might be that twenty years is a considerable time. Wolsey was long dead and much discredited, so that it did not really matter what Norfolk said about him. Moreover, the accusation was made in a letter to the Council written from the Tower where he had just been placed, along with his eldest son, on a charge of treason.[3] Its purpose was to show that he who had done so much for his sovereign had been misunderstood and wronged by almost everyone at court, especially those who had

---

[1] LP,iv,5096.

[2] LP,iv, app.125-6, 128.

[3] Burnet,vi, p.276 (LP,xxi,554).

in the end proved unfaithful to their master: his two nieces, Anne Boleyn and Catherine Howard; Buckingham; and the two great ministers of the Crown, Cromwell and Wolsey. The price of his loyalty had been their opposition to him, so how was it that this man who had suffered so much on behalf of his king could now be considered a traitor? This at any rate was Norfolk's argument, and, of course, the truth about the opposition to him was not his greatest concern. Moreover, what he had to say about Wolsey's plotting against him does not fit in very well with the usual interpretations of his part in the downfall of Wolsey. For one thing, he had learnt of it from Wolsey himself, and only after he had been removed from office, so it cannot have provided the motivation for his alleged machinations against Wolsey. For another, what according to Norfolk Wolsey had confessed to was that he had been put up to his plotting by an aristocratic faction, which had included none other than the duke of Suffolk, who is usually supposed to have been working with Norfolk against Wolsey! It is all very confusing, and in the end cannot be very convincing evidence of what was really going on between the two men during the 1520s.

It is begins to look as if there were two Norfolks. On the one hand there was the Norfolk 'small and spare in person, and his hair black',[1] a Machiavellian figure who not only destroyed Henry's Wolsey and Cromwell but who may have attempted to murder his second wife while she was pregnant! Such a Norfolk deserves the judgement of a great Tudor historian that he was 'one of the most unpleasant characters in an age which abounded in them'.[2] What is interesting about this version is that it is based largely on the evidence of foreign ambassadors and the like, who, as we have seen, often had some axe to grind. The other Norfolk, emerging largely from his own correspondence, was the conscientious duke co-operating fully with Wolsey to ensure the good government of the realm. And in other respects his correspondence is relevant to our present concerns. In October 1523 he wrote to the cardinal a rather sad letter from Newcastle, asking to be discharged from his responsibilities in the North: by the end of the month the campaigning season would be over so that for the time being Albany would be no threat; the affairs of the North were generally in good order, but he himself was not, because after four years of almost continual fighting, in Ireland, France and the Far North, he was desperately in need of some respite.[3] The letter that he wrote a month later to Henry was even more emotional, for he made the dramatic announcement that another winter in the North would kill him.[4] He followed this up with another letter to Wolsey, in which he explained that 'the little flesh that I had is clean gone, and yet I am not sick, but in a manner I eat very little, and these five week days I never slept one whole hour without waking, my mind is so troubled for fear that anything should frame amiss'.[5] On the face of it this all adds up to dramatic evidence not only that Wolsey was deliberately keeping poor Norfolk away from court, but that he was trying to kill him off!

Undoubtedly Norfolk was in a bad way, and, as we have suggested, may have

[1] Ven. Cal., iv, 694.
[2] Elton, Studies, i, p.189.
[3] LP, iii, 3384.
[4] LP, iii, 3508.
[5] St. P, iv, p.55 (LP, iii, 3515).

permitted himself the occasional rude remark about a cardinal sitting comfortably in front of his own fire. But momentary anger need not indicate long-term enmity, and as their replies to Norfolk's passionate requests for a discharge indicate, both Henry and Wolsey believed that he was performing a vital service, for as the former wrote: 'Considering that for your wisdom, prowess and experience no man is more meet to match him [Albany]', Norfolk must 'possess himself with patience' until such time as the situation on the Border had become clearer.[1] But if his continuing presence in the far North was deemed essential for the success of royal policy there, this did not mean that his actions were beyond criticism. Indeed, Wolsey was often critical: Norfolk had been warned; he should have foreseen that; unnecessary expense could have been avoided if only; and, above all, if only he had carried out his instructions.[2] But no more than Norfolk's momentary anger, should these criticisms to 'his loving friend' be taken as Wolsey's final judgement on Norfolk, for just as often he praised the duke, some of the praise in marginal notes intended for Henry's eyes only[3] – not the best way of doing down his arch-rival! What elicited the particular response were the particular circumstances, and it is precisely these that a conspiratorial view of Henrician politics ignores. Every scrap of evidence is dragged in to support the view that leading figures were always at one another's throats and, in this instance, the fact that it was the overriding necessity of defeating Albany that explains Wolsey's critical comments is ignored. Moreover, the leitmotiv of Wolsey's criticisms was that Norfolk was failing to carry out instructions which he himself had helped to draw up.[4] And when Henry and Wolsey at last agreed to let him return south, it was not out of any great concern for his health, but because they wished to consult with him in person about the king's affairs. Wolsey never saw Norfolk as merely an executant of royal policy, but as one involved in its making at the highest level. As lord treasurer from 1522, he was one of the principal ministers of the Crown, and despite his frequent absences on active service, he emerges as one of the most regular attenders of Council meetings. No wonder that in 1525 the Imperial ambassador wrote to Margaret of Austria: 'You know how powerful the cardinal and Norfolk are in this kingdom and how much confidence their master places in them.'[5] Does it not become ever more difficult to sustain the belief that the two men were bitter enemies?

What it is also difficult to sustain is a belief in the Machiavellian Norfolk, for if there is one thing which his many letters from the North make abundantly clear, it is that he found responsibility a great worry, which makes him an unlikely candidate for the role of leader of a faction. Of course, one has to be extremely careful. Writing in the 1530s, his wife provided the text for the Machiavellian Norfolk when she alleged that he could 'speak fair, as well to his enemy as to his friend, and that I perceive by them that be dead and them that be alive'.[6] But given the unhappy state of the marriage at this time the text does not have to be believed; and it may be

[1] St.P,iv, p.48 (LP,iii,3394) Henry to Norfolk, 5 Oct. 1523.
[2] BL Caligula B ii,fos.31-2 (LP,iii,3477), marginal notes for Henry's benefit to a letter written by Surrey to Wolsey in Oct. 1523.
[3] St.P,iv, pp.53-6 (LP,iii,3515).
[4] St.P,iv, p.100 (LP,iv,571).
[5] Sp.Cal, F.S., p.432.
[6] LP,xii (2),1049.

relevant that in their quarrels not only their children, but her own brother, who refused even to have her in his house, took the duke's side.[1] And it is very difficult to believe that when on 23 October 1523 Norfolk 'scribbled' a note to Wolsey 'at 11 at night' desperately seeking further instructions,[2] he was only pretending to be worried in order to disguise his ambitious plans to usurp Wolsey's place. Norfolk was always worrying about something, usually about whether he was carrying out his instructions properly, so that on occasions he drove Wolsey to distraction. Yet this is the man who is supposed to have successfully plotted to bring down first Wolsey and then Cromwell, so that he could be, under Henry, the first man in the land. It really will not do. Norfolk was loyal, conscientious, hardworking, reasonably intelligent, though, as du Bellay commented on more than one occasion,[3] not nearly as intelligent as Wolsey. If this makes him seem too good to be true, there are criticisms that can be made. Thomas Magnus, a close observer of Norfolk's rule of the North during 1523 and 1524, believed that, while the duke always took great pains to serve the king, he was 'some deal suspicious, . . . and soon will be moved to be hasty',[4] and the observation seems a shrewd one. Norfolk was a little suspicious, towards the end of his life even a little paranoid, as his letter from the Tower in 1546 indicates, though perhaps one should be allowed a little paranoia when in the Tower! Still, his efforts always to do the right thing may well have been only part of a strategy to deflect all possible criticism from himself. He may also have felt that his great services to Henry had not always been appreciated, even that Wolsey had not always appreciated him. Norfolk was no saint, but there is nothing in his character to suggest that he had either the ability or the desire to be a ruthless manipulator of the political scene. Why then did people as shrewd as the Imperial and French ambassadors think that he was just that? Part of the explanation is that as one of the two or three most important men in the kingdom, Norfolk was bound to be thought of as Wolsey's rival. It has also to do with the particular circumstances of the years 1527 to 1529. More will have to be said about both these things, but before this is done it is necessary to consider whether, any more than his fellow duke, Suffolk emerges as someone who had it in him to bring Wolsey down.

There are three aspects to Suffolk's career and character that are relevant. The most obvious is that he seems to have always got on well with Wolsey; indeed, in their younger days they were probably close friends.[5] The hiccup to Suffolk's career in early 1515 brought about by his initially unauthorized marriage to the king's sister Mary may have placed some strain on the friendship, but the strain was inherent in the situation; Henry to begin with was furious, as well he might be, and Wolsey had no choice but to represent that fury to Suffolk. However, it appears that Wolsey did his best to restore Suffolk to royal favour, and, that achieved, continued to give help and advice, especially on his very complicated financial affairs. One

[1] For the marriage see B. Harris, *Journal of Social History*, 15; see also *Letters of Royal and Illustrious Ladies*, ii, p.367; iii, p.96.

[2] *LP*,iii,3458.

[3] *LP*,iv, 5210, 5679 – though other opponents of Wolsey, under Norfolk's leadership, were included in this judgement.

[4] *LP*,iii,3625.

[5] Gunn, *Charles Brandon*, pp.27, 32-3.

consequence of his becoming duke in 1514 and being set up as a great East Anglian magnate, was that Suffolk was less frequently at court, so that he did not see as much of Wolsey as previously. However, one of his close advisers in East Anglia, Humphrey Wingfield, was also close to Wolsey, which must have helped to continue the good relations between duke and cardinal.[1] Certainly, as late as 1527 and at least during the first half of 1528, the two were corresponding in a friendly way, with Suffolk asking Wolsey the usual mixture of favours, and Wolsey doing his best to provide them.[2] In fact, the increasing importance to England at this time of the French alliance involved Wolsey and Suffolk, known for his francophile sentiments, working closely together on plans for possible military action against the emperor.[3] Their co-operation was also called for over the difficulties in East Anglia, for, like Norfolk, Suffolk was doing everything possible to ensure that the government measures to alleviate distress and to maintain law and order were put into effect there.[4] And, as with Norfolk, there is no hint in all this of any attempt by Suffolk to take advantage of the government's difficulties to embarrass a Wolsey who on the face of it remained his friend.

The second point to make is that Suffolk emerges as an even less likely candidate for the leadership, or even membership of a faction, than Norfolk. Indeed, the chief impression is of a man who, despite almost as dramatic a rise as Wolsey's – from 'stable boy into a nobleman', as Erasmus, with a good deal of exaggeration, had put it[5] – was as near as anybody in his position could have been to being apolitical. His elevation to a dukedom had been entirely due to his friendship with the young Henry, with whom he shared an interest in military matters. He showed himself to be a competent enough soldier, who was, as has already been noted, along with Norfolk, the natural choice to command a royal army in the 1520s, and indeed during most of the reign. But what really seems to have brought him and Henry together was their mutual passion for the joust, at which they both excelled. And sport is perhaps the key to Suffolk's character: today he would have been very much the 'good chap', almost a 'hooray Henry', excelling at most games, enjoying his field sports, not especially bright but loyal and courageous. Suffolk, wrote the Venetain ambassador in 1531 was

> sixty-one years of age, very robust, and although not of very noble lineage, yet as he has for his wife his Majesty's sister, widow of the King Louis of France, much honour and respect are paid him; and he has the second seat in his Majesty's Council, which he rarely enters, save for discussion of matters of certain importance, passing his time more pleasantly in other amusements.[6]

Not for Suffolk the loss of weight and sleep that his fellow duke had to endure in the service of his king, nor indeed frequent attendance at the no doubt often tedious Council meetings. Instead, what Suffolk seems to have wanted was the honour and respect due to a personal friend of the king whose family's record of service to the

[1] Ibid, pp.50, 59.
[2] LP,iv,2807, 3884, 3997, 4324; LP,iv, app.11.
[3] LP,iv,3105; LP,iv, app.173.
[4] Inter alia LP,iv,3760, 3883.
[5] CWE,2, p.278.
[6] Ven.Cal., iv, p.294.

Tudors was outstanding, but not too much responsibility or hard work. This is not a man who hungered after Wolsey's job, or who would have taken any initiative to bring him down.

The third point to make is that while there is plenty of evidence that Suffolk and Wolsey were friends, there is little to show that Suffolk and Norfolk were.[1] Indeed, there is quite a lot to suggest that they were not. Even Suffolk's elevation in 1514 probably did not help. The 3rd duke's father's great victory at Flodden virtually demanded that he be restored to the dukedom of Norfolk which he had lost on his attainder in 1485 for having fought at Bosworth for Richard III. But to ease the slight embarrassment that such a step involved, it may have helped to raise to a similar rank someone whose Tudor credentials were impeccable, Suffolk's father having achieved the ultimate distinction of death on the field of Bosworth at the hands of Richard himself! And if the Howards' reaction to being paired with Suffolk in this way must in the end remain speculation, in the following year Suffolk definitely saw them as rivals.[2] Moreover, it so happened that a large part of the de la Pole lands, which had been granted to Suffolk on his elevation, had previously been granted to the 3rd duke of Norfolk. Some extremely complicated negotiations ensued, in which Wolsey was much involved and which resulted in Suffolk having to buy back some of his own land, while renting the rest for the considerable sum of £413 6s. 8d., to be paid annually, either until Norfolk died or forty years had elapsed, when the land would revert to him.[3] Given their importance, considerable efforts must have been taken to make this settlement as acceptable as possible to both men, but it cannot have been pleasing to Suffolk, especially given the parlous state of his finances, to be paying out such large sums for land that was nominally his. This did not prevent him from co-operating with Norfolk in the affairs of East Anglia, but the assumption, at least implicit in so many accounts of Wolsey's downfall, that the two men were natural allies should be resisted. Their characters and careers were very different, and indeed one of the few things they had in common was that neither was the kind of man to have taken upon himself the destruction of Wolsey. Such a conclusion flies in the face not only of most historians' interpretations of Wolsey's downfall, but also, and more worryingly, of a good deal of contemporary evidence, especially that of two very acute observers of the English political scene, the Imperial ambassador, Mendoza, and Jean du Bellay, bishop of Bayonne, since November 1527 the French ambassador in London. Why is it then, that so many people have got it so wrong? An examination of three particular moments in the story of Wolsey's downfall may help to provide an answer.

The traditional story really begins with Mendoza's reports of May 1527. It was at this time that he first got wind of Henry's desire for a divorce, but even before then he was describing a London seething with discontent, a discontent directed particularly against Wolsey. His main explanation for this was a severe attack of francophobia brought on by the recent visit to England of an important French embassy. Much hard bargaining throughout April had at length resulted in new treaties, providing, amongst other things, for the marriage of Princess Mary either

[1] Gunn, *Charles Brandon*, pp.15, 33, 36, 98.
[2] *LP*,i,3376.
[3] Gunn, *Charles Brandon*, pp.41-2.

to Francis himself, or to his second son, the duke of Orléans, a prospect which seems to have been especially unpopular. The treaties also increased the likelihood of an out-and-out war with the emperor, one consequence of which would be severe, if not complete, disruption of the vital trade with the Low Countries. But what concerns us for the moment is the report that Wolsey was about to be relieved of some of his duties; and one rumour had Tunstall, whom Mendoza anyway saw, along with Norfolk, as a secret opponent of Wolsey, succeeding to the office of lord chancellor. Wolsey was on the way out, and in support of this assessment Mendoza pointed to the fact that lately he had absented himself from court, pleading, what was for Mendoza at least, a purely diplomatic illness.[1]

How much truth was there in all this? Well, to begin with, Mendoza's suspicions about the illness seem to have been groundless; at any rate, a reliable French source states that during the second half of April Wolsey was ill for about a week with a 'tertian fever'.[2] But if Wolsey had really been ill, he had also been exceptionally busy. There was, first, the negotiations with the French: these had lasted for over a month, had involved a great deal of hard bargaining, with himself very much in the thick of things, and there is nothing to indicate, whatever the citizens of London, or even Norfolk and Tunstall, may have thought, that Henry was at all unhappy with the outcome. Indeed, the French alliance was such an essential part of the strategy to achieve the divorce that Henry was bound to approve of it. Indeed, it is the emergence of the divorce as the dominant issue in English politics that makes it highly unlikely that Henry was contemplating getting rid of Wolsey in the spring of 1527. Put at its simplest, his own cardinal legate was his best weapon in the struggle to obtain the Church's authorization for the divorce. Wolsey was already in April busy preparing the case which in May was to be presented to a court called by virtue of his legatine powers, over which he would preside. Arguably there had never been a time when the king needed Wolsey more, and so it can be said with reasonable certainty that on the matter of Wolsey's position, Mendoza had got it wrong. What he almost certainly did not get wrong was Wolsey's, and indeed Henry's, un-popularity – but more of that in a moment.

Most later historians, while picking up on the general notion that Wolsey's position first began to be threatened in the spring of 1527, have not followed Mendoza in thinking that Wolsey's absence from Court at this time had any special significance. Instead they have focused their attention on his absence during the summer of that year on his famous mission to Amiens and Compiègne, seeing this as the moment when the aristocratic faction first began to put its act together.[3] The main reason for doing this is the company that Henry was keeping while he was on progress and Wolsey was away; and it was indeed very distinguished, including the marquess of Exeter, the earls of Oxford, Essex and Rutland, and viscount Fitzwalter;[4] plus the triumvirate of Norfolk, Suffolk and Boleyn, with whom, it was reported to Wolsey, Henry usually took supper.[5] Obviously there could have been something very significant in all this, but the point that will be stressed here is that

[1] *Sp.Cal.*, iii (ii), pp.190-3.
[2] *LP*,iv, p.1410.
[3] *Inter alia* Scarisbrick, *Henry VIII*, pp.158-162.
[4] *LP*,iv, 3318.
[5] *LP*,iv,3318.

there does not have to be.

To begin with, Wolsey was not in the habit of accompanying Henry on progress, so there would have been nothing unusual in his not being with him, even if he had not been in France. Noblemen, on the other hand, usually did, especially those whose estates lay in the parts of the country that Henry had chosen to visit. In the previous summer his progress had taken him through Surrey, Sussex and Hampshire, and so he had been accompanied by the earl of Arundel, Viscount Lisle, and the Lords Dacre of the South, de la Warr and Sandys, men whose chief residences lay in these counties. Their attendance upon the king had been duly reported to Wolsey,[1] but nobody so far has suggested that they comprised an aristocratic faction! In 1527 Henry chose to centre his progress on his own palace of Beaulieu, or New Hall, near Chelmsford in Essex. It is not, therefore, all that remarkable that he was surrounded on this occasion by his East Anglian noblemen, who happened to include pre-eminently the dukes of Norfolk and Suffolk, and Boleyn, who had sold Beaulieu to the king.[2] And, given that these three were with the king, it is hardly surprising that they supped with him – much more remarkable if they had not. It is only with hindsight or if one already believes in the existence of the aristocratic faction that their presence at Beaulieu appears significant.

In the previous chapter it was suggested that at this time an elaborate charade was being acted out, to which Wolsey was privy, the purpose of which was to allay the queen's fears about Henry's intentions towards her and also to try and disperse any rumours about a possible divorce. In this sense there may have been some political significance in the progress of 1527, but it had nothing to do with any cabal to bring Wolsey down. Admittedly, there was criticism being voiced at Beaulieu at his suppression of monasteries to endow his new college at Oxford, and this criticism focused on two men closely associated with him, his leading legatine official, John Allen, and a member of his household, Thomas Cromwell.[3] But to turn this very natural reaction into evidence for an aristocratic plot to destroy the cardinal is to stretch the evidence quite unjustifiably. The search for the divorce was increasingly to introduce an unsettling element into English politics, but whatever else the triumvirate of Norfolk, Suffolk and Boleyn were doing at Beaulieu, they were not, or at least not according to the royal secretary, William Knight, taken into Henry's confidence on the one matter that most concerned him.[4] It may be true, though, that on this particular progress Henry had desired a specially good turn-out in order to demonstrate what was clearly not the case – that it was business as usual: with the queen at his side, and his noblemen arrayed around them, all was supposed to be well with the world.

A year later the French ambassador was describing a series of lengthy interviews with Wolsey in which the cardinal had appeared to be more than usually expansive and personal.[5] He stressed his deep commitment to the French alliance, which in his usual fashion he claimed had cost him a great deal of popularity, a view which, it should be said, du Bellay fully endorsed. Wolsey also talked much about his own

[1] *LP*,iv,2368, 2377, 2407.
[2] *King's Works*, p.172, n.1.
[3] *LP*,iv,3360.
[4] *LP*,iv,3360.
[5] Bellay, *Ambassades*, pp.359–65 (*LP*,iv,4649).

future: if only he could bring about a perpetual amity between England and France, if only he could reform the laws and customs of England, and if only he could resolve all possible doubts about the royal succession, then he could retire, a happy man, in order to devote himself to the service of God. In his patron Fox and in Archbishop Warham, there were, indeed, recent precedents for such honourable retirements, but Wolsey in 1528 was a good ten years younger than both these men had been when they had resigned. Moreover, there were rather too many 'ifs' in Wolsey's conversation for his words to carry great conviction, nor did du Bellay entirely believe them. Wolsey might be thinking of retirement, though not because he was hungering for a life of devotion to God, but because he was frightened of what would happen if Anne became queen even though, according to him, Wolsey was not fully apprised of Henry's intentions as regards the divorce. Moreover, du Bellay reported 'on good authority', though he could not give it 'as certain', that recently 'the king used terrible language [to Wolsey] because he seemed desirous to cool [the king], and show him that the pope would not consent to [the divorce]'. Of course, it is impossible to prove that such an episode did not take place, and Wolsey must frequently have had to counsel patience, something that Henry cannot have been eager to listen to. But as we saw earlier, there is substantial evidence to suggest that in the summer of 1528 king and minister had never been closer, and that at least until October and Campeggio's arrival in England, expectations of success were high, at least on Henry's part, and that until the second legatine court had taken place, there was no way in which he was going to dismiss Wolsey. So, like Mendoza a year earlier, du Bellay got it wrong, deceived by a more than usually brilliant performance put on by Wolsey to delay, even to avoid, the payment then due, of an English contribution to the French war effort.

But if neither Norfolk nor Suffolk was a likely candidate for the role of factional leader, why, we must ask again, have so many intelligent people thought that they were? Part of the explanation is that whatever their character and ability, these two men were great figures on the political scene, and thus bound to be the focus of speculation and rumour. Moreover, it was always likely that they would be seen as Wolsey's rivals, especially by foreign ambassadors. Since it was with the cardinal that the ambassadors did most business, it was natural for them to identify the current policy with him, and to some extent they were right: Wolsey was very much in charge of the conduct of foreign policy, and thus in a very good position to influence its direction. But it has been one of the themes of this book that the direction was of the king's choosing, and that both he and Wolsey consulted with other councillors, including Norfolk and Suffolk. The temptation for the resident foreign ambassadors was to ignore this and to concentrate too much upon the figure of the cardinal, and in this way to get a slightly distorted picture of what was going on at court. Thus, for Mendoza, Wolsey was the emperor's sole enemy against whom he hoped and believed Charles's many friends in England were plotting. For du Bellay, he was the one friend of France surrounded by her many enemies. Both saw him much as it suited them to, as an isolated figure opposed by everyone else in England, but most significantly by the likes of Norfolk and Suffolk. Thus both ambassadors ended up with a similar picture of the politics of the late 1520s, but one that was sufficiently out of focus to have seriously misled subsequent historians as to the reasons why Wolsey fell from power. However, this would not have happened if their picture had been totally unrecognizable, and it is just as important to discover in what ways they got it right as how they got it wrong.

It would not have displeased Mendoza to report in May 1527 a London near to rebellion, especially angered at the prospect of a French marriage for Mary. Handbills opposing it were being circulated at night, and pasquinades critical of both Henry and Wolsey were appearing all over the city.[1] And although Mendoza was probably exaggerating, the government was taking the situation extremely seriously. Edward Hall records 'a great watch' being ordered throughout the city on the last day of April,[2] while on 30 June Henry wrote to all the great livery companies warning them against 'divers persons of light disposition which study to raise and bring up seditious, untrue, and slanderous rumours', ordering them to do everything possible to suppress their activities.[3] At the same time a massive propaganda exercise, including an exchange of the highest chivalric honours the English and French kings could grant, the orders of the garter and St Michael, in order to win people over to the new alliance was undertaken. For his part, Wolsey appears to have made two lengthy speeches in Star Chamber, one shortly after his return from France, presumably in October 1527,[4] and the other in February 1528 following the formal declaration of war against the emperor.[5] On both occasions the audience was large, including, at least on the first, not only representatives of the city of London but JPs from all over the country. But on neither occasion, at least according to Hall and he is about the only source for these two speeches, was the audience very impressed:

> Some knocked the other on the elbow and said softly he lieth, others said that evil will said never well, others said that the French crowns made him speak evil of the emperor, but they that knew all that you have heard before said that it was a shame for him to lie in such an audience.[6]

Hall's chronic francophobia calls for caution in interpreting his account, but it receives support from too many sources for it to be ignored or explained away.[7] Nor did the unpopularity of the French alliance stem only from the traditional francophobia, which, after all, had not prevented the nation from earlier becoming increasingly reluctant to pay for a war against France, which had cost some £470,000. And having shown every sign of refusing to pay the Amicable Grant of 1525, now, in 1527, they were faced not only with the prospect of further taxation for war against England's traditional friends, but also with a disruption of the vital trade with the Low Countries. What with the disastrous harvest of that year, bringing with it the likelihood of severe grain shortages and high prices, and, on top of all this, rumours that Henry was determined to get rid of his popular, 'Imperialist'

[1] *Sp.Cal.*, iii (ii), pp.190-1.
[2] Hall, p.721.
[3] *Mercers' Company*, pp.749-50.
[4] Hall, p.723.
[5] Ibid, pp.742-4.
[6] Ibid, p.744.
[7] The reports of both Imperial and French ambassadors are an obvious source; see *inter alia* Bellay, *Ambassades*, p.365 (*LP*,iv,4649); *Correspondence*, 324 (*LP*,iv,5679); *Sp.Cal.*, iii (ii), pp.178-85.

queen, no wonder the government felt under some pressure!

Before we discuss the consequences of this pressure upon Wolsey, it will be useful to dispose of the question of whether or not it was being in any way manipulated by his potential rivals, particularly Norfolk and Suffolk. Much of the argument already presented would suggest that the answer must be no. But that the two dukes turned down the opportunity afforded by the troubles in East Anglia to further a plot to topple Wolsey does not in itself settle the matter. To have come out in support of, or to have attempted to manipulate, the 'many-headed monster' that the poorer classes became when restless would have been to play with the kind of fire that Tudor noblemen on the whole avoided. On the other hand, to try to persuade the king that his chief adviser was advocating a foreign policy wholly detrimental to the king's own interests would have been merely to perform the good office of a royal councillor. It is just conceivable that a dislike of the pro-French direction of foreign policy, which it would have been easy to blame on Wolsey, could have united enough important people in moves to change that direction by advocating the removal of the man so closely identified with it.

The notion that this was what the triumvirate tried to do depends largely on the belief that Norfolk was at this time pro-Imperialist. But the evidence is slight and, such as it is, difficult to interpret. Given his assumption that everyone except Wolsey was on his side, the fact that Mendoza saw Norfolk as being sympathetic to the emperor is not very conclusive. Similarly du Bellay, who saw everybody as anti-French, included Norfolk in this category. So also did members of an important French mission to England in the spring of 1527. Moreover, a French account of that embassy appears at first sight to offer proof not only that Norfolk was pro-Imperialist, but that he was prepared to fight for a pro-Imperialist policy in direct opposition to Wolsey's wishes, even as far as launching an attack, in the king's presence, on both Wolsey and the policy he was pursuing.[1] The only trouble with this as evidence is that it was supplied to the French by none other than Wolsey himself, and one does not go around advertising such opposition unless one has a specific purpose in mind which, of course, Wolsey did. He was up to his usual ploy with the French, and here one can see it working in a rather precise way. For the French envoys rushed a courier back to Francis to warn him that, because of the extent of the opposition to the alliance, further bargaining and delay could result in no treaty at all. Francis took the hint, the French duly settled, and Wolsey had won a small diplomatic victory of the kind he was rather good at winning.[2] The price of victory, however, was almost certainly a little exaggeration, if not a downright lie, for it is highly improbable that there would have been serious opposition amongst royal councillors to a French alliance, whatever their natural inclinations, and whatever the evidence to the contrary.

The attachment to France was fully discussed earlier, and all that needs to be stressed here is that to obtain the divorce it was essential, for it was only with French support that enough pressure could be exerted on the pope to grant it.[3] This being so, to oppose the alliance would have been in effect to oppose the king in the matter

---

[1] LP, iv, pp.1410-11.
[2] LP, iv, pp.1410-13.
[3] LP, iv, 5862 for du Belley's assessment to this effect.

nearest to his heart, not a very sensible move for anyone aiming to bring down the king's leading minister. Admittedly, it could be argued that, since in those negotiations with the French in April 1527 the effect of the divorce on the conduct of English foreign policy would not have been obvious, the alliance might at least have been questioned, but even that is not very likely. The argument of this book has been that, if many of the tactical decisions were Wolsey's, Henry controlled the general direction of foreign policy, so that talk of opposition to Wolsey's policy has to be misleading. This does not exclude the possibility that different points of view were being put to Henry by different councillors, indeed, it was their duty to do so,[1] but if Henry decided the policy, then the only person to be toppled, if that policy was not to one's liking was the king himself and the loyal and over-conscientious Norfolk was not likely to contemplate that! The French alliance had been the cornerstone of English policy for almost two years, and there is no evidence to suggest that in early 1527 Henry was having serious doubts about it.

What should also be remembered is that the tactics being used by Wolsey at this time were not crudely anti-Imperial; and at no point during this period, despite the reluctant declaration of war in January 1528, was Wolsey not engaged in some kind of negotiations with the emperor. Moreover, he had moved quickly to obviate the problems that a dislocation of trade with the Low Countries would bring, by making a separate truce with the regent, Margaret of Austria.[2] Norfolk may not always have followed the intricacies of Wolsey's foreign policy, but he would have been well aware of its broad outlines and of how far the popular caricature of Wolsey as one who had sold himself to the French was from the truth. None of this means that the duke may not have had some worries – when did he ever not! In 1531 it was the departing Venetian ambassador's assessment that Norfolk bore ill-will to all foreigners;[3] and there was always something of the Little Englander about him, a characteristic which combined happily with the Howard caution. So it would be understandable if he had expressed some concern about where a military commitment to France might lead to, and none knew better that the discontent in East Anglia was not unconnected with the current direction of English foreign policy – but to express such concern is a long way from plotting and caballing.

Dislike of the French alliance does not explain the plotting itself, but insofar as it greatly contributed to the growing unpopularity of Henry's government from mid-1527 onwards, it does help to explain the widespread belief in such plotting, both at the time and since. Also contributing were the bad harvests, the disruption in foreign trade, and increasingly the divorce. Quite why the country came to Catherine's defence in the remarkable way that almost every scrap of evidence suggests it did, is not entirely clear. She can hardly be called charismatic, but then perhaps merely by being a queen she acquired charisma. Moreover, she had been a devoted and loyal queen and wife for almost twenty years, and the injustice of her situation may have earned her the esteem of ordinary people, as well as many at court. True that it was perfectly possible under canon law to secure an annulment, and there may have been people, including, it would seem, Archbishop Warham,[4]

---

[1] See Tunstall's comments to this effect in Dec. 1525 in *LP*,iv,1800.

[2] See p.455 above.

[3] *Ven.Cal.*,iv, p.295.

who genuinely believed that Henry had a case in law. But the common perception seems to have been, and surely quite rightly, that his case was mere casuistry, designed to enable him to marry the woman he loved or, more plainly, to bed his whore with a slightly better conscience. Not enough is usually made of the unpopularity of the divorce, or, indeed, of the general unpopularity of Henry's government in the late 1520s, but it is a vital part of the present story, for it was bound to focus on the man who, as the king's leading minister and cardinal legate, appeared to be responsible for much of what was going wrong. Criticisms of the king were also made,[1] but it was much safer to lay the blame on one of his councillors; and anyway the whole panoply of kingship made it difficult to confront the man behind it. When the Amicable Grant had made royal government a target in the spring of 1525, Warham in an effort to console Wolsey had pointed out that 'it hath been and ever shall be that whatsoever be in most favour and most of counsel with a great prince shall be maligned and ill spoken of, do he never so well'.[2] If the remark fitted Wolsey's situation in 1525, how much better did it fit it two years later.

And what the many problems facing Henry's government in the late 1520s may have encouraged is that strain of anticlericalism which, it was suggested earlier, was endemic at court.[3] In August 1527 the king's secretary, William Knight, wrote to Wolsey, then in France, to warn him that since 'the king and noblemen speak things incredible of the acts of Mr Allen and Cromwell', it would be sensible for Wolsey to use someone other than Allen as his messenger to the king.[4] The 'Mr Allen' was John Allen, Wolsey's chief legatine commissary, who had carried out the visitations of monastic houses. Cromwell was at this time a leading member of Wolsey's household, his principal task being the setting up of Wolsey's colleges at Oxford and Ipswich. The suppression of the thirty-odd largely small monastic houses in order to provide endowments for these colleges had been unpopular, unleashing a combination of local sentiment and genuine religious feeling, as well as self-interest on the part of laymen with rights and interests in those houses.[5] The following summer, in letters to Wolsey, Henry referred to the 'great murmuring' throughout England against Wolsey's legatine officials, especially in connection with their work for his colleges, adding that he thought the murmuring justified. He had been informed that people were being forced to give money and land for the colleges in order to secure Wolsey's favour, and, he alleged, many of these so-called gifts were illegal. Moreover, if, as reported, exempt monasteries were being allowed to buy back from Wolsey the right to be visited by members of their own order, this was to make a mockery of the whole purpose of Wolsey's legatine powers. 'If your legacy is a cloak *apud homines*', warned Henry, 'it is not *apud Deum*', and he told Wolsey in no uncertain terms to mend his ways, and those of his officials,

---

[4] At least he was alleged to have had doubts about the validity of the original dispensation; see Scarisbrick, *Henry VIII*, p.13.

[1] *Inter alia* Mendoza mentions hostility to the king in May 1527; see *Sp.Cal.*, iii (ii), p.190; also Hall, p.754. For hostility to government as a whole, see *Sp.Cal.*, iii (2), p.444, 845-6, 862.

[2] *LP*,iv, app.39.

[3] See p.298.

[4] *St.P*,i, p.261 (*LP*,iv,3360).

[5] See Knowles, *Religious Orders*,iii, pp.161-3, 470; Goring, *Sussex Archaeological Collections*, cxvi.

immediately.[1]

Wolsey never accepted that these criticisms were valid,[2] and neither does the present writer. Even Henry may have been merely venting his anger on Wolsey for preventing his beloved Anne from getting her way in the Wilton affair; at any rate the criticism came as part of a royal blast concerning Wolsey's behaviour during that episode.[3] But however unfair, and indeed hypocritical, Henry's charges were, what is indisputable is that the criticism was being voiced in high places, and that Henry was showing himself not averse to using it against his cardinal. In this respect it is different from, and, from Wolsey's point of view more worrying, than the probably much more widespread criticism being levelled against the alliance with France, where he was very much putting into effect the king's policy, and could therefore feel confident of his protection. As regards the criticisms being made of his legatine powers, the king was showing himself to be not very protective, and this might encourage other people to work against him. It might even encourage Norfolk and Suffolk, especially as they were both affected by Wolsey's suppressions, Norfolk because an earlier duke had founded Felixstowe Abbey, Suffolk by virtue of an earlier duke of Suffolk's alleged refoundation of Snape Priory.

Both these houses were suppressed to provide endowments for Wolsey's college at Ipswich, and both the suppressions led to complicated negotiations in which Cromwell, on Wolsey's behalf, played a leading role. Whether the dukes got the worst of it is not clear, but it seems unlikely. The interests of the new college would not have been best served by alienating the leading men in the locality, and Norfolk, at any rate, seems to have done quite well out of it since he obtained possession of the lands of Felixstowe at an annual rent of £20, when it was worth double.[4] It is true that in April 1529 the dean of the college, William Capon, reported that on a recent visit Norfolk had at first been 'very rough' because he had heard that Felixstowe's lead and stone had been used on the college's buildings. However, when it was pointed out that this was not the case, he had ended up by being 'very kind'.[5] A year earlier he had also been kind, for in March 1528 he had written to Wolsey to say that he had seen the plans for the new college and had thought of ways in which Wolsey might save on building costs.[6] Admittedly, this seems to have been before he knew that Felixstowe was to be suppressed, but it is clear that he had no objections in principle to the new foundation, indeed rather the opposite. As for Suffolk, although in January 1529 he and his wife agreed to renounce all their rights in Snape without, it would seem, getting anything in return, not even the honour bestowed upon Norfolk of being made a co-founder of Ipswich College, there is no evidence that he felt hard done by.[7] And in becoming a co-founder, Norfolk had joined a select band including not only Wolsey but also the king and the archbishop of Canterbury. That he was granted this distinction is evidence of Wolsey's customary tact and good sense in such matters. For the success

---

[1] LP,iv,4507, 4509.
[2] LP,iv,4513.
[3] See pp.321 ff. above for the Wilton affair.
[4] LP,iv,5985; Knowles, *Religious Orders*, iii, p.470.
[5] LP,iv,5458.
[6] LP,iv,4044.
[7] Gunn, *Charles Brandon*, pp.102-3.

of his college, the support of such an important local figure as Norfolk, and indeed of Suffolk, would be an enormous advantage. So he had every incentive to ensure that neither of the two dukes felt any grievance, and such evidence as there is suggests that he was successful.

But if it seems unlikely that Norfolk and Suffolk were amongst those making rude remarks about Wolsey in August 1527, it remains true that criticisms were being made in the king's presence and that he had chosen to take notice of them by telling Wolsey off in no uncertain terms. And that they had to do with ecclesiastical matters is of some significance. It is almost certainly wrong to exaggerate the strength of anticlericalism, for much of the time it probably amounted to no more than the occasional anticlerical joke amongst the young bucks at court. But it would not take all that much for such jokes to turn into something more serious, and some anticlericalism was anyway a bit more serious than that. As we saw earlier, relations between Church and state were not especially happy in the early Tudor period, and in 1515 it had taken a good deal of effort on Wolsey's part to prevent a serious rift. It had been precisely so as to obtain a firmer control over the English Church that Henry had been happy for Wolsey to seek extensive legatine powers, thereby allowing the man he most trusted to have more control over the English Church than probably anyone had ever enjoyed. It has been one of the central arguments of this study that Wolsey's legatine rule brought the Church considerable gains, amongst them protection from the unwelcome interference of the Crown lawyers. But there was a price to be paid, not only by the Church but by Wolsey personally, for what Henry would expect in return was that in matters close to his heart the Church would do what he wanted. Of course, English kings had always expected this, but insofar as Henry's close relationship with Wolsey had increased his expectations, the resulting disappointment, not to say anger, if the Church refused, would be that much greater. In 1527 the moment came for Henry to collect. He wanted a divorce and only the Church could give it to him. He realized that there would be difficulties, and he was prepared to give it a little time to overcome them. In the end, however, he would go to any lengths to secure the payment, even if this meant schism, and with it the destruction of his cardinal legate.

The argument put forward here is that though Wolsey's dismissal did not come out of a cloudless sky, the effect of the many difficulties crowding in on every side should not be exaggerated. Wolsey had shown himself to be a past master at getting himself and his king out of tight corners: witness the volte-face that he had achieved in 1525 by exchanging the dead-end of the Imperial alliance for a profitable one with France. In the spring of 1528 he was quick to minimize the economic effects of the declaration of war with the emperor by securing a truce with Margaret and the Low Countries. He had also seen to it that the government had intervened on what may have been a hitherto unprecedented scale to minimize the effects of the bad harvests of 1527 and 1528. These bad harvests are a reminder that luck plays a large part in politics, and Wolsey was unlucky not to have survived into the early 1530s when the harvests improved. Moreover, it was suggested in the previous chapter that if the cards had fallen a little bit more kindly, he might even have obtained the divorce, and in that case the unpopularity of the years 1527 to 1529 would have seemed neither here nor there. After all, perhaps Wolsey's greatest triumph, the Treaty of

London of 1518, had been preceded by two years of failure. In the end, Dame Fortune did not serve Wolsey well, but an awareness of this should not lead us to believe that Wolsey was from early 1527 on a downward slide from which it was impossible to get off. Things were going badly. Speculation was rife. This led some people to believe that the dukes of Norfolk and Suffolk had allied with the Boleyns to bring him down. In reality they had done no such thing. Instead, Wolsey's fate depended entirely on the continuance of Henry's confidence, and in particular in his confidence that Wolsey would be successful in his efforts to obtain for him a divorce. Indeed, once Henry had decided to get rid of Catherine and marry Anne, everything in English politics was subordinated to that end.

Interestingly, even the timing of rumours concerning an aristocratic faction supports the notion of the primacy of the divorce in this matter of Wolsey's downfall. Mendoza's first references to an anti-Wolsey faction led by Norfolk in May 1527 came in the same letter in which he first mentioned the divorce, describing it as 'the finishing stroke' of all Wolsey's 'iniquities'.[1] He next mentioned the faction in October, by which time, in his account, the Boleyns had been enlisted.[2] Then something rather curious happened. The faction disappeared, or at least for over a year none of the ambassadors mentioned its existence. Admittedly in July 1528 the French ambassador du Bellay reported the cardinal as, by his own account, having to use a 'terrible alchemy' to defeat the machinations of unspecified people,[3] but it was not until the following January that Norfolk and the Boleyns occupied the centre stage again,[4] and not until the following month that they were joined in the ambassadors' reports, and for the first time, by Suffolk.[5]

Not everything that Mendoza and du Bellay wrote has survived, so it would be wrong to make too much of this apparent hiatus, but it does look as if the existence of an aristocratic faction coincided in the ambassadors' minds with the ups and downs of the divorce. At first, it must have seemed that such an unexpected and unusual event needed rather more than a king's infatuation to explain it. High politics must assuredly come into it somewhere; and if so, and the divorce presaged important changes, then the obvious person to be affected would be Wolsey. When he did not go, and, at any rate during much of 1528, it looked increasingly as if Henry might get his divorce, then there was no need to invent any faction. However, in the autumn of that year the situation changed yet again. Campeggio's arrival did not precipitate a sentence in Henry's favour, and by January 1529 it must have been fairly obvious to even a casual observer of the political scene that Wolsey's efforts to secure a divorce were in disarray. It would also have been obvious that this spelt trouble for him – and hence the aristocratic faction made a reappearance. In fact, though, it was no more a reality in January 1529 than it had

---

[1] *Sp.Cal.*, iii (ii), p.193.

[2] *Sp.Cal.*, iii (ii), pp.432-3.

[3] Bellay, *Ambassades*, p.360 (*LP*,iv,4649 where placed wrongly in August). Du Bellay himself commented that if Wolsey were to stumble, there were plenty on the watch to pick him up which is surely not quite the same as saying that there was a faction plotting his overthrow. It is also true that in Sept.1528 Mendoza suggested that Wolsey was increasingly fearful of Anne's growing influence; see *Sp.Cal.*, iii (ii), p.790.

[4] *LP*,iv,5210.

[5] *LP*,iv,5255. *Sp.Cal.*, iii (ii), pp.885-6.

been in May 1527. What did spell danger for Wolsey was Henry's growing impatience. As early as autumn 1527 he had been impatient enough to attempt his own short cut. His failure had enabled Wolsey to get things moving in what he hoped would be a better direction. But having suggested that there was a better way, Wolsey only compounded the more general difficulty just referred to, that as Henry's 'tame' churchman he would be expected to be able to obtain from the Church whatever his master wanted.[1] Now he had really put his head on the line, for if the better way proved unsuccessful, then Henry would have every justification for getting rid of him – and in January 1529 Mendoza heard that Henry was beginning to blame Wolsey for his failure to fulfil his promises.[2]

Whether January 1529 was the moment when Henry seriously began to contemplate the possibility of removing Wolsey will be considered shortly. Meanwhile it is the obvious that needs to be emphasized. It was Henry who was in love, it was Henry who wanted a divorce, and however weak a character he is assumed to be, he really did not require a faction to tell him that, or even that Wolsey's divorce plans were not succeeding. It is this simple fact that should have always alerted historians to the fallacy of believing in an aristocratic faction. In terms of Wolsey's downfall, it is an almost entirely superfluous notion. Perhaps it could be allotted a minor role if Henry were thought so weak and incompetent that he could not have organized the mechanics of Wolsey's removal, but in view of the large number of people, not to mention heads, that he did remove during the course of his reign, such a belief would be curious. And in fact the Henry I have portrayed in this study was much more able to make decisions than at least two supposed leaders of the faction, Norfolk and Suffolk.

But what about the Boleyns, father and daughter? Their part in this story, especially Anne's, has to be rather privileged; and that a scheming Anne plotted Wolsey's downfall is a commonplace, best exemplified by Cavendish's account of Wolsey's last meeting with Henry.[3] For almost two months after the adjournment of the legatine court on 23 July 1529 Wolsey had been firmly but politely refused a meeting with the king. Then Henry relented, and Wolsey was allowed to accompany Campeggio on his farewell visit to Grafton, where the king then was. Not unnaturally it had been assumed by those at court that Wolsey's enforced absence from the royal presence was a prelude to his dismissal, so that his arrival at Grafton came as a surprise. Apparently the betting was that Henry would not actually speak to Wolsey, and the fact that no accommodation was provided for him must have shortened the odds. Everything pointed to a very frosty reception, but in fact Henry greeted him as warmly as ever. And even more worryingly for those who wished the cardinal ill – and in Cavendish's account this seems to have included everybody – he proceeded after dinner to have a lengthy private meeting with him. Suddenly it looked as if the old wizard was once again casting his spell, but the next day it was the young and beautiful witch whose spell proved the more binding. She suggested a picnic. Henry could not resist. He cancelled the planned further meeting with Wolsey, and was never to see his cardinal again. As told by

[1] Bellay, *Correspondence*, p.19 (*LP*,iv,5582) for du Bellay's assessment to this effect of 22 May 1529.

[2] *Sp.Cal.*, iii (ii), p.877 (*LP*,iv,5177).

[3] Cavendish, pp.92-6.

Cavendish, it is a very good story, but, at least as regards Anne's part in it, a story is just what it is. For one thing, as will be shown shortly, it is almost certain that for once the court gossip was right and Henry had made his decision to dismiss Wolsey sometime before this last meeting, which from Henry's viewpoint made it a charade from start to finish. This being the case, there was no need for Anne to have laid on a picnic. And probably the picnic never happened. At any rate, a contemporary account of the Grafton meeting by a member of Wolsey's household has it that while Henry in Cavendish's account was supposedly enjoying it, he was in fact closeted with Wolsey and his Council. In the afternoon, indeed, he went hunting, but only after he had taken his leave of Wolsey in what appears to have been a perfectly normal way.[1]

It should be remembered that for Cavendish Anne was an undoubted she-devil, so that even if he did not invent her role at Grafton he would have been happy to make use of any rumour or apocryphal story of her guileful ways there. He is also the source for Anne's 'privy indignation' against Wolsey for having broken up her early affair, perhaps even a precontract of marriage, with Henry Percy, and the decision to get her own back if ever the opportunity arose.[2] Some kind of affair with Henry Percy does seem to have occurred,[3] but it has to be admitted that Cavendish's version gains much of its effect from an awareness of subsequent events, so much so that the suspicion must be that at least some fiction was again involved. Still, Cavendish is not the only source for Anne's dislike of the cardinal. In October 1527 Mendoza reported that it derived from Wolsey at some time having been instrumental in depriving her father of promotion to high office.[4] Earlier it was shown that though in 1519 Boleyn may have had some cause for feeling momentarily aggrieved for his failure to obtain a promised household appointment, it is most unlikely that this would have provoked his daughter's desire for revenge, for the good reason that Wolsey's role in the episode vis-à-vis Boleyn was entirely benign, and likely in the end to have been seen as such by him.[5] Of course, resentments are not necessarily very rational so that this attempt to try and play down the episode may be misplaced. And what cannot be denied is that in the summer of 1528 Wolsey did prevent the election of the Boleyn candidate for the office of abbess of Wilton. Moreover, earlier in the same year she had given her support to Sir Thomas Cheyney, a member of the privy chamber, whose overreaction to Wolsey's grant of of a wardship to Sir John Russell had not endeared him to the cardinal or, for that matter, to the king.[6]

If one adds all the evidence for Anne disliking Wolsey to the belief, held by du Bellay and Mendoza, that he feared that Anne as queen would mean the end of his

---

[1] BL Vitellius B xii, fos,168-9 (LP,iv,5953), Thomas Alvard to Thomas Cromwell, 23 Sept.1529.

[2] Cavendish, pp.29-34.

[3] Suggested by Henry's wish in 1527 for a dispensation allowing him to marry a woman who had already contracted to marry someone else provided there had been no consummation, and by the need in 1532 to obtain a statement from Henry Percy that no formal precontract had been entered into.

[4] Sp.Cal., iii (ii), p.432.

[5] See pp.192-3 above.

[6] LP,iv,4081, 4584, 5210; see also Ives, Anne Boleyn, pp.126-7. I should perhaps mention that my account of Wolsey's downfall was written before Ives's biography appeared, and differs from it in a number of respects.

influence with Henry,[1] there does seem to be some reason for thinking that she did play an important, perhaps even decisive part in Wolsey's downfall, but in the end not enough. There is first the same difficulty that was encountered with the two dukes' opposition to Wolsey, which was that, like them, she was bound to be seen as Wolsey's enemy whatever her real attitude. It is a difficulty to which there is no solution, except perhaps by giving more credence not to what people were saying about their relationship, but to the relationship itself.

On 3 March 1528 Thomas Heneage, recently transferred from Wolsey's household to the king's, wrote that Anne had complained that Wolsey had sent her no 'token' by his recent messenger.[2] Wolsey took the hint, and by 16 March Heneage was conveying to Wolsey Anne's thanks 'for his kind and favourable writing unto her', while at the same time reporting her sorrow that Sir Thomas Cheyney should have earned Wolsey's displeasure.[3] In this little exchange there is almost a hint of flirtation in Anne's behaviour; and at the very least a relationship of some sort is implied, even one that might be expected between royal 'mistress' and elder statesman. And clearly Wolsey was in the habit of writing to her, because in July she herself replied to a letter of his, thanking him not only for a present but also for his help, 'of which I have hitherto had so great plenty that all the days of my life I am most bound of all creatures, next the king's grace, to love and serve your grace'.[4] Perhaps this merely illustrates the hypocrisy of court life, but it is quite an interesting letter for her to have written while the Wilton affair, in which Wolsey did undoubtedly oppose her wishes, was still in progress – and need she have written quite as warmly as she did?

There were other expressions of her fond regard, and why not?[5] As we have seen, in the summer of 1528 Wolsey's plans for the divorce did appear to be coming to fruition; a decretal commission of sorts had been obtained and Campeggio was on his way to England to start what Anne hoped would be successful legal proceedings. No wonder she wrote loving letters to Wolsey. But that is not to say, of course, that she was a close friend, for what would a young lady enjoying a love affair with her king, from which, if she played her cards right, she had so much to gain, have in common with the elder statesman, conscious as he was of all the dangerous implications of the course she and Henry had embarked upon? Moreover, if she was as sympathetic to Lutheranism as some have maintained,[6] then the mere fact that Wolsey was a cardinal was an added complication. In fact, it seems more likely that it was political advantage rather than genuine conversion that might have inclined her to encourage reform, and the Lutheran Anne is probably more of an invention of a subsequent Protestant tradition, in which her role as Elizabeth I's mother was important. What is not in doubt, though, is that Anne was a very determined lady; there would have been no 'great matter' if she had not been, and there is no reason to suppose that her determination would have stopped at trying to remove Wolsey if

---

[1] Inter alia LP,iv,4649; Sp.Cal., iii (ii), p.790.

[2] LP,iv,4005.

[3] LP,iv,4081.

[4] LP,iv,4480.

[5] LP,iv,4360; see p.503 above.

[6] Dowling, JEH, 35; Ives, Anne Boleyn, pp.302-31, though both place the emphasis on a biblical humanism rather than on a commitment to Lutheran doctrine.

she had felt he stood in her way. But since until very late in this story he must have seemed the one man in England capable of realizing her wishes, far from organizing an anti-Wolsey faction she had every incentive to try to get on with him; hence the 'loving' letters. Equally there was every incentive for Wolsey to get on with her. Theirs was surely a perfectly good working relationship, with the one proviso that Wolsey had to obtain the divorce? There is no more need to invent a conspiracy led by Anne than one by Norfolk, or anyone else.

And if there was no plot to destroy Wolsey, then Anne's father could hardly have been part of one! Moreover, even if logic did not insist upon this conclusion, the evidence would. Earlier it was shown that the notion that Wolsey had done his utmost to thwart Sir Thomas Boleyn's career cannot be sustained, whatever occasional misunderstandings may have occurred.[1] And Boleyn's was a highly successful career, which in 1525 had resulted in his elevation to the peerage as Viscount Rochford. True that this was probably a consolation for Henry's and Wolsey's failure, so far, to persuade the Butler family to surrender to Sir Thomas the earldom of Ormond, then in their hands, but to which Boleyn had a claim. But that Henry bothered to further the Boleyn claim, ironically by trying to arrange a marriage between James Butler and none other than Anne, and was willing to to ennoble Sir Thomas indicates his high standing with the king, a high standing that preceded any interest in his daughters. One way or another, it is hardly possible that in 1527, when Henry decided that he was going to marry the younger Boleyn daughter, Sir Thomas can have had much reason for wanting to get rid of Wolsey. Moreover, he would no doubt have shared Anne's and Henry's belief that Wolsey was the most likely person to bring about their marriage.

What the foreign ambassadors make clear is that in the period just before and after Wolsey's dismissal, Boleyn, even more than either Norfolk or Suffolk, was constantly in attendance upon the king, and here they are reporting the evidence of their own eyes rather than gossip and rumour. Whether this means that his influence at this time was significantly greater than those two is another matter. Du Bellay thought it was: on 4 October he reported that it was Boleyn 'who leads the dance expressly against the dukes and Wolsey',[2] and on the 12th he launched into a tirade against him, calling him 'vainglorious', only anxious to show that 'none of the others have influence except insofar as his daughter is prepared to allow it'.[3] The report of the new Imperial ambassador, Chapuys, of his first meeting with Henry and the English court at Grafton in September also gives the impression that Boleyn's influence was dominant, even if by the end of October he was clear that the dukes, especially Norfolk, were the real powers at court.[4] But Boleyn's constant attendance upon the king at this time should hardly come as a surprise. As the father of the woman Henry loved and intended to marry, it was inevitable that he should be more intimately involved than either Norfolk or Suffolk in the search for a divorce, which, while it was on one level a most important matter of state, on another was a private concern in which he was a principal party. This does not

[1] See pp.192-3 above.
[2] Bellay, *Correspondence*, p.94 (*LP*,iv,5983).
[3] Bellay, *Correspondence*, pp.104-5 (*LP*,iv,6003).
[4] *Sp.Cal.*, iv (i), pp. 220-39, 292, 303.

necessarily mean that Henry took him in to his confidence about his intentions towards his leading minister, but what must be true is that once the decision was made he was bound to make more use than ever not only of Boleyn, but of Norfolk and Suffolk. There may have been some element of calculation on Henry's part here. Wolsey's dismissal, especially in the circumstances of the divorce, was a potentially dangerous moment for him, so he would have been anxious for the great men of the kingdom to show their support by keeping a high profile. More simply, they happened to be the men available to Henry, great not only in status but in experience of the conduct of affairs. And there was also an element of optical illusion. With Wolsey no longer there to mask them, they appeared more prominent; but they had always been there.

It is easy to see why the belief in an aristocratic faction was, and is, so pervasive, but it is hoped that by this stage it will be just as easy to see why it is wrong. At any rate, the argument here has been that Wolsey fell because at a certain moment Henry came to the conclusion that he was not going to get him what he most wanted in the world, a pronouncement by the Church that his marriage to Catherine had never had any validity, thereby leaving him free to marry Anne. The only question remaining is exactly when he made that decision: not an easy task for by its very nature it was not something which he would have wanted to make very public, and certainly not to commit to paper.

It was in January and February 1529 that Mendoza reported having been told that Henry was beginning to blame Wolsey for his failure to fulfil his promises concerning the divorce. Could this be the moment that Wolsey's fate was decided? It is possible, but there is quite a bit of evidence to suggest that Henry's confidence in Wolsey had not yet been completely eroded. It was only at the very end of the previous November that an important embassy, carrying with it new divorce proposals, had set off for Rome, and when in mid-January it eventually arrived, it found Clement supposedly on his deathbed. This had resulted in Stephen Gardiner being rushed out to promote Wolsey's candidature for the prospective vacancy, for if he could have become pope, Henry's problems would have been over. Meanwhile Campeggio was still in England, his ostensible task to preside with Wolsey over a trial to consider the validity of Henry's marriage. And however poor the king's prospects in the trial, it would have been foolish to move against Wolsey without seeing the outcome. When in March the English envoys at Rome sent back extremely gloomy reports about the chances of obtaining anything from the now no longer dying pope,[1] Henry joined with Wolsey in berating them for being far too pessimistic,[2] which he would have been unlikely to do if he had not still believed in Wolsey's ability to bring about a divorce. By the end of May he was no longer confident, despite the legatine court having at last got under way.

That Henry had lost confidence in Wolsey is proved by a letter that the duke of Suffolk wrote to him from Orléans on 4 June. He and Fitzwilliam had been sent there in a rather desperate attempt to prevent a long-threatened and increasingly likely accord between Francis and the emperor. Their mission had been planned

---

[1] *LP*,iv,5213, 5302, 5348.
[2] *LP*,iv,5427 for Henry's letter; *LP*,iv,5428 for Wolsey's.

with Wolsey's knowledge and approval, but what he did not know was that Suffolk had been given a 'secret charge', which was to pump Francis for any views and information about the reliability of Campeggio in the matter of the divorce.[1] Having discovered that Francis had always mistrusted him, Suffolk then asked if he 'knew any other that in like case doth dissemble'. When Francis failed to take the hint, Suffolk was forced to be more direct: 'Sir,' he asked, 'what say you by the cardinal of England in this matter ?' Francis's initial reply was, not unnaturally, cautious: when he had met Wolsey at Amiens in the summer of 1527 he told Suffolk, 'I assure you, as far as I could perceive in him, he would the divorce should go forth and take effect, for he loved not the queen'.[2] Not too damaging an answer as far as Wolsey was concerned, but then Francis became rather more mischievous.

Why he did is not entirely clear. It was not at all what his ambassador in London, du Bellay, would have wanted: his advice almost to the very end was that the French should stick by Wolsey as the one man in England who could ensure the continuance of an Anglo-French alliance.[3] Probably Francis's assessment was that, with or without Wolsey, Henry was going to require French support, and that the removal of such a skilled negotiator as Wolsey could only strengthen the French position. He may also have felt that if Wolsey was anyway on the way out, he could only gain credit with Henry by advancing the process. At any rate his next remarks could have done Wolsey no good at all:

> Mine advice shall be to my good brother that he shall have good regard and not put so much trust in no man, whereby he may be deceived as nigh as he can. And the best remedy for the defence thereof is to look substantially upon his matters himself, as I hear say he doth, which I am not a little glad of.

So far not very good, but Francis then proceeded to touch upon a very sensitive nerve: he understood that Wolsey

> had a marvellous intelligence with the Pope, and in Rome, and also with Cardinal Campeggio. Whereof, seeing that he hath such intelligence with them, which have not minded to advance your matter, he thinketh it shall the more need for your grace to have the better regard to your said affair.[4]

As was shown in the previous chapter, Francis's remarks were very unfair: in fact, Wolsey was battling against enormous odds to persuade Clement to do something that was bound to offend an emperor who happened to be in a much better position to affect the fortunes of the papacy for good or ill than Henry and Wolsey were. No wonder there were delays; but, as they continued, the implication behind Francis's remarks that the reason for them could only be that Wolsey was deceiving Henry, or at least not doing his best to bring about the divorce, must have crossed the English king's mind. And, after all, what was the point of Henry having his own cardinal legate if he could not obtain from the pope what he wanted?

Suspicion and resentment were lodged in Henry's mind by the end of May, for

---

[1] St.P,vii,p.182 (LP,iv,5635).
[2] St.P,vii,p.183 (LP,iv,5635).
[3] LP,iv,5862, 5582, 6011.
[4] St.P,vii, p.183 (LP,iv,5635).

otherwise why the 'secret charge' to Suffolk? It was hardly usual to ask another monarch whether one's leading servant was deceiving one. Moreover, further reports from Rome, addressed to the king rather than to Wolsey, would have helped to fuel these feelings, may even have triggered it off, for they probably reached England just before Suffolk set off for France.[1] In the first, written on 21 April, Sir Francis Bryan (incidently, a distant relation of Anne's)[2] who had recently returned to the privy chamber and had by his own account been sent to Rome with a special brief to keep Henry personally informed of what was going on, made it quite clear that in his opinion Clement 'will do nothing for your grace', adding ominously for Wolsey that 'whosoever hath made your grace believe that he would do for you in this cause hath not, as I think, done your grace the best service'.[3] Bryan devoted his letter of 5 May to an attack on Campeggio who, he understood, was reporting back to the pope that he had merely indulged in diplomatic pleasantries with Henry, but had never promised anything specific as regards the divorce, nor had he any intention of doing so. Then Bryan repeated his earlier warning that 'all that is told you there [England] that the pope will do for your grace in this cause, I assure you they tell you the gloss and not the text'.[4]

It is worth stressing that Bryan was not taking a 'privy chamber' or factional view of the matter, but, as he put it in this same letter, was merely reporting what seemed to be the truth as seen from Rome.[5] That this was so is confirmed by someone who was neither a relative of Anne's nor a member of the privy chamber, and indeed was probably still technically in Wolsey's household: Stephen Gardiner.[6] Writing on 4 May, he first warned Henry that it looked very much as if Clement would revoke his commission to Wolsey and Campeggio to try the divorce and then remarked how sorry he was to see that Henry's case had not been handled according to his merits by the pope, 'or some other'.[7] It is not clear whether by this Gardiner meant Wolsey. Much of his letter was an attack on Campeggio, so probably he was intended, just as it is possible that Bryan in his comments to Henry had only Campeggio in mind. But in a sense it hardly matters. Campeggio's presence in England had become an essential part of Wolsey's plans to achieve Henry's ends. How certain he himself was of the Italian's soundness is difficult to judge; any confidence he had in him must have taken a severe knock during those first few weeks after his arrival in England, when he had blatantly failed to do what Wolsey and Henry had expected him to. But by now they simply had to make the best of him; and for all Campeggio's reluctance he very nearly was pressurized into doing what Henry and Wolsey wanted. But in this matter a near miss was no good, and as the months went by and nothing happened, Henry must have grown increasingly

---

[1] Suffolk set off on 17 May. On 21 May Wolsey reported receiving letters from Rome of 4 May (LP,iv,5576). Admittedly seventeen days was fast; the norm from Venice was twenty-four, the fastest nine; see Braudel, i, p.362.

[2] Usually referred to as a cousin, but only a half-cousin: one of Bryan's grandmothers was also Anne's, but their mothers were only half-sisters; see Ives, *Anne Boleyn* for genealogical table.

[3] St.P, vii, pp.166-7 (LP,iv,5481).

[4] St.P, vii, p.170 (LP,iv,5519).

[5] St.P, vii, p.167 (LP,iv,5519).

[6] As Wolsey's secretary, though ever since the previous February he had been working almost full time on the divorce, and was to become royal secretary in July.

[7] LP,iv,5518.

impatient with the Church in general and the two cardinal legates in particular, impatient enough to instruct the duke of Suffolk to make discreet inquiries of Francis about them.

Again, it must be stressed that this does not show that the duke was plotting Wolsey's downfall, however much it might appear to be so. Because of his francophile sentiments he had been much involved with Wolsey in drawing up plans for a possible Anglo-French campaign against the emperor,[1] and since the main purpose of his mission was to persuade Francis not to come to terms with the emperor by promising to make a much greater English contribution to the present war, the duke was an obvious choice as envoy. If he was being sent on such a mission, then he was also an obvious choice, as a personal friend of both monarchs, to perform the 'secret charge'. And that the initiative came from Henry is confirmed by an episode that occurred on Suffolk's return. Apparently du Bellay had fed Wolsey a rather garbled version of Suffolk's interview, in which the duke had done his best to put him out of favour with Francis.[2] Wolsey was naturally annoyed and complained to Henry, who then solemnly asked Suffolk in Wolsey's presence whether there was any truth in the allegation. Suffolk duly denied that there was. Strictly speaking his denial was correct, for to have asked those questions does not have to be interpreted as trying to create bad blood between Wolsey and Francis. But by indicating to Francis that Wolsey was no longer trusted by his king, he was doing something at least as harmful. Still, it is Henry's part in the episode that is most interesting, for there can be no doubt at all that he was acting, and acting very well. Even if one believed, unlikely as it is, that he was putty in Suffolk's hand, he knew perfectly well that Suffolk had asked questions that could only have damaged Wolsey's credit with Francis. Yet here he was playing the innocent, asking Suffolk questions to which he already knew all the answers. And if Henry was capable of stage-managing this little charade, it really does not look as if he needed many lessons in the art of political infighting, from Suffolk, or indeed from anyone else.

The suggestion being put forward here is that at some time during April and May 1529 Henry began to take seriously the possibility that it might be in his best interests to disgrace his cardinal legate. He would, of course, want to wait for the outcome of the legatine trial which had at length got under way on 31 May, and if all went well the time bomb would be defused. However, as was shown in the previous chapter, there was little optimism about its outcome. And once the embarrassing question of the consummation of Catherine's first marriage, upon which so many of the legal issues turned, came more and more to dominate the proceedings, and after Fisher's powerful intervention on Catherine's behalf, Henry would have had to face the fact that the initiative begun very early in the previous year was increasingly likely to fail. The news from Rome was increasingly that Clement would recall the case to the Curia, which almost certainly meant that he would decide in Catherine's favour. At the same time all the diplomatic signals were unfavourable. Since Charles had managed to bring both Clement and Francis to heel, any chance of Henry getting his way seemed for the time being out of the question. The Henry of this book was no fool: he would have been perfectly aware

---

[1] LP,iv, app.173; also Gunn, *Charles Brandon*, pp.101-2.
[2] Bellay, *Correspondence*, pp.64-9 (LP,iv,5862) for this episode.

how badly things were going. Once the court had adjourned on 23 July, it had to be made clear to the pope that he was not going to take no for an answer. One way of doing this would be publicly to humiliate the pope's English legate, Cardinal Wolsey, and he began in a small way by sending Suffolk down to inform the court that 'I see that the old saw is true that never a cardinal or legate did good in England'. But then for two months he stayed his hand. Campeggio was allowed to depart in peace, and publicly Wolsey's position remained unchanged. Since in this account Henry had been contemplating the possibility of dispensing with Wolsey's services since at least May, this curious hiatus needs some explanation.

In fact, the ending of the legatine court did more or less immediately affect Wolsey's position. For almost two months Henry skilfully kept him at arm's length, politely turning down all his efforts to arrange a meeting. And, when in the middle of September Henry relented, it was only to allow Wolsey to accompany Campeggio on that leave taking at Grafton already described. Meanwhile, Gardiner, appointed royal secretary on 28 July, was conducting much of the day-to-day business of the Crown previously carried out by Wolsey. Amongst other things this involved him in writing a good many letters to Wolsey, and this correspondence with his former master – he had been Wolsey's secretary – offers some indication of the change in their respective relationships with the king. Gardiner's letters were often brief, sometimes off-hand, and by the end of August openly critical. Thus on 31st he wrote: 'Your grace's qualifications, to say truly to your grace, doth no more serve the king's purpose than as the treaty is now couched',[1] and four days later he warned Wolsey not to blame others for his mistakes.[2] But the real problem for Wolsey was precisely his banishment from the king's presence; nor, indeed, was Gardiner, at Henry's express command, allowed to visit him.[3] Even foreign ambassadors had now to obtain permission before doing so.[4] Wolsey did not require the rumours which were reaching him of his imminent disgrace to realize that his position was extremely precarious.[5] His letters if not abject, were by now entirely lacking in their usual confidence. Late in July he referred to his perfectly sensible comments to Brian Tuke on the Treaty of Cambrai as his 'poor fantasies' which he hoped would be taken 'in agreeable part'.[6] Three weeks later he wrote to Gardiner that he would not approach Catherine until he 'be advertised how the king's highness and you of his Council do like the same'.[7] And when he used one of his chaplains as a messenger, he advised him to consult with Gardiner before seeing Henry[8] – a clear indication of Wolsey's recognition that his former secretary was in greater favour with the king than he was.

During August and September Wolsey was fighting for survival. He had never been under any illusion about how badly Henry wanted a divorce, or the effect on

[1] St.P,i, p.343 (LP,iv,5894) but for Tuke's defence to Wolsey of the brevity of Gardiner's letters see LP,iv,5885.
[2] LP,iv,5918.
[3] LP,iv,5844.
[4] LP,iv,5865; Sp.Cal.,iv (i), p.189.
[5] Or at least reaching Wolsey's household; see Thomas Alvard's reference to them in LP,iv,5953.
[6] LP,iv,5801.
[7] LP,iv,5867.
[8] LP,iv,5882.

his own position if he failed to obtain it. What he was not aware of was that his battle for survival was already lost. How could he be, when his advice and help were still in such demand? In fact, it is the very nature of the advice that he was now being asked for which lends support to the view that Henry had already made his decision to get rid of him sometime earlier. True, what Wolsey was being consulted about concerned the major issue of the day: namely, how did the Treaties of Barcelona and Cambrai affect Henry's chances of obtaining the divorce? Should he still rely chiefly upon the French alliance, or did the new peace with the emperor open the way to some deal over the future of his aunt? Wolsey appears to have recommended the former, but only as long as the price was not too high.[1] However, that Wolsey was not being retained in office in order to obtain such advice is suggested by the way in which it was received. On 30 August Gardiner wrote to thank him for his 'excessive pains and labour . . . Nevertheless, for speedy speaking with the King, and to speak at leisure, I reckon great difficulty, and, as for this night, I am out of hope by reason the king's highness is out on hunting . . . but I shall do therein the best I can'.[2] Gardiner's response to advice on the major issue of the day from England's greatest expert on foreign affairs appears a little cavalier, not to say downright dismissive; and it is evident that Henry no longer wanted Wolsey's opinions on such matters. What he still needed Wolsey for was something much more tangible. The advocation of his case to Rome had been both a bitter blow to his reputation and a great impediment to his chances of victory. Having got him into this mess, Wolsey must now get him out of it, or at least minimize the damage. This meant, in the first place, ensuring both that Henry was not served with any formal summons and that the standard financial penalties for non-observance of such summonses, should he be served with any, were not demanded. That achieved, it might then be possible to persuade the pope to take the case into his own hands and give a personal judgment in Henry's favour. In this way the more formal proceedings in the papal courts, the outcome of which it would be impossible to control, could be bypassed, but at the same time any accusation of bias inevitably to be attached to any sentence given in England could be avoided. This at least was how Wolsey saw the way forward,[3] but it was not advice that Henry really wanted now. His more pressing concern in August and September was to overcome the legal and technical consequences of the advocation, and it would not have helped him one bit to have moved precipitously against either of the two papal legates then present in England. Indeed, in persuading both the pope and Catherine to dispense with the formal summons, their help was essential.

As was mentioned in the previous chapter, Henry's immediate ends were achieved. During the second week of September Wolsey was able to report that Catherine's legal advisers were willing to waive the formal summons on Henry,[4] and shortly afterwards a papal brief arrived by which all financial penalties were removed, and the hearing of the case in Rome was suspended until Christmas.[5]

---

[1] Incidently the policy that, after the failure Thomas Boleyn's mission to the emperor in early 1530, was to be pursued, but for Wolsey's advice see *LP*,iv, 5801, 5875, 5881, 5890, 5891, 5893.

[2] *St.P*,i, pp.341-2 (*LP*,iv,5890).

[3] *LP*,iv,5797, 5864-5, 5878 (2), 5966; 5995 (Ehses, *Römische Dokumente*, pp.132-5).

[4] *LP*,iv,5928, 5936.

[5] Ehses, *Römische Dokumente*, p.134 (*LP*,iv,5995).

Henry's honour had been saved and valuable time gained. Meanwhile, Campeggio had agreed to sign a document by which he promised to keep his mouth shut concerning any privileged information he may have gained as judge in the case, and to work wholeheartedly to advance the king's interests.[1] This done, the way was left open for Henry to bid not only him but also Wolsey a gracious farewell, which he neatly accomplished at Grafton on 20 September. On 9 October a first indictment of praemunire was brought against Wolsey in King's Bench, and on the 20th a second,[2] while on the 17th he had surrendered the great seal, thus ceasing to be lord chancellor.[3] On the 22nd he admitted his fault, and on the 30th he formally submitted himself to the mercy of the king.[4] His downfall was complete.

There seem to be two possible explanations, not mutually exclusive, for the interval of almost three weeks which elapsed between Wolsey's last meeting with the king and the first formal charges being brought against him. The simpler one is that since the new law term did not open until 9 October, that day was the first opportunity after the leave-taking for charges to be brought. The second is that it would be preferable if Campeggio were out of the country before the moves against his fellow legate became public, and the calculation probably was that three weeks would allow sufficient time. As it was, bad weather delayed Campeggio in Canterbury until 26 October, so that, rather to Henry's embarrassment, news of Wolsey's disgrace reached the Italian cardinal before he set sail.[5] Poor Campeggio also suffered the indignity of having his luggage searched, perhaps in a last despairing effort to lay hands on that elusive decretal commission which he had taken the precaution of destroying sometime before, or perhaps merely to get hold of any other documents that might further the king's case.[6] When Campeggio justifiably protested to Henry, he got a flea in his ear.[7] Henry had obtained all that he could immediately hope for from his papal legates: the real battle was with the pope himself. In this, Campeggio's goodwill might have been of some help, but his concern to hang on to the see of Salisbury would probably ensure that anyway. For the moment a little rough handling might help him to convey to the pope just how annoyed Henry was; something that Wolsey's disgrace would help to make crystal-clear.

That Wolsey's downfall was intended as a signal to the pope is suggested by the means Henry chose to achieve it. He could, after all, merely have removed him from office without bringing any charges. Both Fox and Warham before him had retired to their dioceses, and if Wolsey's retirement would not have been quite as voluntary as theirs, it is difficult to see how he could have resisted the suggestion. On the other hand, Henry could have mounted a full-scale attack on Wolsey's 'personal rule', and he certainly went to the lengths of preparing, or rather inventing, evidence for just such an attack. Articles against Wolsey were prepared, and in his opening address to the Reformation Parliament, his successor as lord

---

[1] *LP*,iv, 5820.
[2] For both see *LP*,iv,6035.
[3] *LP*,iv,6025.
[4] *LP*,iv,6017, 6035, A.F. Pollard, pp.242-5 for full documentation.
[5] *LP*,iv,6050.
[6] *LP*,iv,6003, 6016.
[7] *LP*,iv,6016.

chancellor, Sir Thomas More, made his celebrated reference to 'the great wether, which is of late fallen', and who had 'so craftily, so scabbedly, yea and so untruly juggled with the king'.[1] In the end the articles were never formally presented, but instead were used as a weapon in the elaborate negotiations with Wolsey after his dismissal from office, and probably this was all they were ever intended for.[2] As it is, Henry's decision to prosecute Wolsey for praemunire, the basis of the charge being his prevention, by virtue of his legatine authority, of clerics to two totally unimportant benefices, seems at first sight extraordinary. The punishment seems so disproportionate to the crime. And it was also hypocritical of Henry to make the charge, because it was he who had asked Wolsey to make use of his legatine powers in this way. Added to which, the basis for the charge was almost certainly a fabrication; for, though Wolsey had occasionally made preventions, such evidence as there is suggests that in the two instances cited he had not.[3] All this points to there being something very deliberate about Henry's choice of praemunire to bring Wolsey down. As well as leading royal servant, Wolsey had been in a very public sense the pope's chief representative in England, and it was the pope whom Henry was now anxious to get at. Furthermore, if a charge of praemunire had become merely a technicality in the English law courts, it was also part of an English tradition of opposition to papal pretension, and in the fourteenth century, when the praemunire statutes originated, opposition in particular to the papal power to prevent. So Henry's use of this charge against Wolsey was not only deliberate; it was also very appropriate.

In the first place, it would remind Clement of the independent traditions of the English Church which not even a papal legate as powerful as Wolsey could withstand, and which Clement, by refusing to do his duty by Henry in the matter of the divorce, was ignoring at his peril. Secondly, it would remind the English Church, which earlier in the reign had appeared to require some reminder, that, if it owed a double allegiance, to pope and king, the first claim on its loyalty should be to the latter. And if any member of the Church showed any inclination to ignore this, it was always possible to use the Church's acceptance of Wolsey's legatine powers to bring a charge of praemunire against that member, as indeed was going to happen.[4] Meanwhile, Henry had summoned a parliament in which he could manipulate any latent anticlericalism in order to put yet further pressure on the Church to stick closely by him as his quarrel with the pope escalated. All this means that Wolsey's downfall marked the opening of, if not exactly a new strategy, because Wolsey's had contained a good deal of the stick as well as carrot, certainly one in which the stick came more and more to dominate. It was a strategy which was to lead to the 'break with Rome', and the declaration in 1533 by an English Church, 'sufficient and meet of itself',[5] that his marriage to Catherine had always been invalid.[6] In 1529 Henry did not intend this outcome, but only because he hoped that the sacrifice of his papal legate would help to make more extreme measures unnecessary.

---

[1] Hall, p.724.
[2] See p.617 below.
[3] See pp.303-4 above for both points.
[4] See p.623 below.
[5] From the famous preamble to the Act in restraint of appeals of 1533.
[6] Archbishop Cranmer's judgment at Dunstable, 23 May 1533.

In the months prior to Wolsey's downfall Henry emerges very much as the Machiavellian prince, in full control of himself and of those close to him, and so skilled in the arts of manipulation and deception that his decision to dispense with his services appears to have taken Wolsey by surprise. It was an extraordinary achievement, especially since from at least January 1529 Wolsey had been well aware that his position was under threat. How did Henry manage it?

For some people the explanation may be found in Wolsey's supposed arrogance: in the end he just ignored all the signs because he believed himself to be indispensable. There could be something in this, though it would be a little unfair to concentrate on the arrogance. Henry and Wolsey had survived through good times and bad for over fifteen years, and the notion that the reward for his devoted service, particularly in this matter of the divorce, would be humiliation and disgrace, must have been very hard for Wolsey to contemplate. Thus, if reason pointed in one direction, his heart probably pointed in another, especially as Henry skilfully fed the heart with just enough to keep the hope alive that before long he would be restored to his master's full confidence. The masterstroke does seem to have been Grafton, for just when Wolsey's services could be entirely dispensed with, Henry appeared to welcome him back into the fold. When Wolsey left Grafton, his keeper of the wardrobe was able to reassure Cromwell that, despite the many rumours to the contrary, all was well;[1] and probably Wolsey did believe that the worst was over. At any rate, right up until the last moment the king was still consulting him, while on 6 October, only two days before his indictment for praemunire, he took a leading role in an interview with the new Imperial ambassador, Chapuys, despite both Norfolk and Suffolk being present.[2] When on 9 October the blow came, it must have taken Wolsey by surprise, but it should not surprise us. It was the same with all Henry's leading ministers and courtiers when the time for their destruction came, because in every case it was Henry who made the decision, and he kept it very close to his chest. So there could be no leaks, only endless speculation and rumour which, though alarming, did allow the victim to hope that all would be well, right up until the moment that Henry struck.

Some may find this interpretation of Wolsey's downfall too simple. By concentrating on one issue, the divorce, and on one agent of Wolsey's destruction, Henry himself, it may be felt that too much has been ignored. After all, the courts of sixteenth-century kings were notoriously treacherous places, where everyone was looking for any opportunity to do his or her rival down, or so at least the courtier poets of the time would have us believe.

> Say to the Court it glows,
> and shines like rotten wood,
> . . . Tell potentates, they live
> Acting by others' action,
> Not loved unless they give,
> Not strong but by a faction:
> . . . Tell men of high condition,
> That manage the estate,

[1] LP, iv, 5953.
[2] Sp.Cal., iv (i), pp. 276-7.

> *Their purpose is ambition,*
> *Their practice only hate:*
> *And if they once reply,*
> *Then give them all the lie.*[1]

So instructed Sir Walter Raleigh; while earlier Sir Thomas Wyatt, who as a member of the king's household throughout the 1520s would have had ample opportunity to observe Wolsey at first hand, explained thus his reasons for leaving the court: 'I cannot speak and look like a saint,/ Use wiles for wit and make a deceit a pleasure/ And call craft counsel, for profit still to paint[2] – and much else besides. Literature is not life, but there is enough evidence around to suggest that the poets had a point: ministers and courtiers were executed or disgraced in some numbers, and even queens lost their heads. And surely a man like Wolsey, a royal favourite for over a decade, a man who had risen from 'butcher's cur' to become lord chancellor and cardinal legate and in the process amassed a fortune, such a man must have excited envy, and made dangerous enemies? And would not those enemies come from the English nobility, whose natural role as leading royal councillors he had so blatantly, by some accounts, usurped? Faction and intrigue must have existed if only because they are the very stuff of high politics, and any analysis of Wolsey's downfall that ignores them must be seriously flawed.

Perhaps; but whatever generalizations are made about the workings of high politics, the historian has to pay attention to the particular circumstances and to the surviving evidence. It has been argued in this chapter that the evidence for Wolsey being destroyed by an aristocratic faction is slight, and that what there is of it is unconvincing. The truth is that not enough can be known about what the leading members of that supposed faction thought about Wolsey to conclude that they wanted to plot his overthrow. To state that they did is, therefore, at best a guess, at worst an invention. Of course, much of history has to be guesswork, and, however great the wealth of evidence, must in the end involve the historian in a judgement. Here the judgement has been that Wolsey got on perfectly well with individual nobles such as Norfolk and Suffolk, but also with the nobility as a group. This was not because Wolsey was a particularly 'nice guy', but because he was a good politician, who could see no advantage in antagonizing people upon whom the good government of the kingdom depended, and who, if he got on the wrong side of them, could have made things very difficult for him. In this matter of Wolsey's downfall, the danger has always been to accept too readily the views of foreign ambassadors with their inevitably very partial vision, and it is hoped that here this danger has been avoided. A new danger has derived from recent interpretations of Henry's character and the workings of his court. Despite the efforts of his most outstanding modern biographer, the prevalent view is that Henry was a king who was easily manipulated; indeed, so weak was he that he needed to be manipulated for anything to happen. This view has been attacked here. It was Henry who had made Wolsey, and it was Henry who destroyed him, just as he was to make and destroy Thomas Cromwell. He made all the important decisions and appointments. In every sense he ruled.

---

[1] From *The Lie*; but Raleigh's authorship is not certain.
[2] From the *Epistolatory Satires*.

If this is so, then the interpretation of Wolsey's downfall offered here is not as naïve as it might at first appear. Serious fighting usually only breaks out when there is weakness at the centre, which in the case of a monarchy means when the king is a minor or has some obvious character defect – the reigns of Henry III, Edward II, Richard II, and Henry VI are all instances of this. Henry VIII, though at seventeen technically a minor when he ascended the throne, never behaved as one. From the start he caught people's imagination as the very model of what a king should be. Moreover, he succeeded to the throne of a kingdom which, though driven rather too hard by his father who had been faced with the unenviable task of establishing a new dynasty, was essentially in good order.

It could be said of Henry and Wolsey that, as these things go, they had a fairly easy ride. It is true that there were Yorkist rivals about, but despite the occasional alarm, the 'White Rose', Richard de la Pole, never posed a serious threat, and anyway he had the good manners to die at the Battle of Pavia in 1525. Scotland was a nuisance, but the scale of the English victory at Flodden and the resulting minority of James V ensured that it was never much more than that for all the efforts of the duke of Albany. And if Scotland was a nuisance, Ireland was only a minor irritation. The European powers presented greater problems, but they were mainly of Henry's own choosing, a consequence of his determination to play a major role in Europe. They offered no major threat to his throne. There was indigenous heresy in the shape of Lollardy, but on a scale small enough for Wolsey not to have to bother with it personally. Lutheranism, though potentially much more serious, in the 1520s was certainly containable. There were bad harvests, plague and the Sweat, and short periods of economic distress, not helped by the heavy taxation required to support Henry's European ambitions. A case can be made for the situation getting worse as the 1520s progressed, but even so most problems were temporary and manageable, and the strains on the political nation were never very great.

In the 1530s things would be very different. Henry's marriages and the ensuing dynastic confusion, together with the 'break with Rome' and the religious conflict that followed, did impose enormous strain. Some say that it was during this decade that a 'Tudor Revolution' occurred, and whatever doubts have been cast, probably correctly, on this notion, it does at least draw attention to the extraordinary nature of the decade. The times were out of joint. Henry was faced with a major rebellion, which for a time presented him with a much larger force than he could raise himself. In addition, the threat of foreign intervention became for the first time in his reign a reality. Everything was more difficult, and as a result even a strong king would have to become more Machiavellian, might even have to play off rival factions in order to get his way. It is possible to argue that Wolsey was the first victim of this new political climate: indeed, insofar as this climate was created by Henry's desire to marry Anne, the argument contains an obvious truth. But while any interpretation of Wolsey's downfall must always be speculative, the one that seems to fit best all the known facts and probabilities is that it was the ruthless act of a strong king determined to get his way.

One thing that this interpretation would seem to challenge is a central theme of this study: that Henry's and Wolsey's relationship had been a genuine marriage of minds and personalities. As late as June 1528 Henry wanted Wolsey to know that with the Sweat threatening he was anxious for him to stay as close as possible, so that 'every hour one of you might hear of the other, and that his physicians might be as well for his grace as for him if any chance should fortune'.[1] And in the following May du Bellay's view was that Wolsey loved his master more than himself.[2] But if there was so much love and concern, why did the marriage break down? A final assessment of their relationship must await the last chapter, but as regards Wolsey's downfall this much may be said. Henry's 'great matter' was not any old issue which, after fifteen years of wear and tear and plenty of opportunity for either party to become bored or irritated by the other, just happened to be the final straw. It was 'great' just because it combined a number of powerful ingredients. These included Henry's latent anticlericalism, and the belief that what was right for him was right for his country. But above all it included love, and one way of explaining Wolsey's downfall is that in the end Henry loved Anne more than he loved Wolsey.

[1] St.P,i, pp.303-4 (LP,iv,4438).
[2] Bellay, Correspondence, p.20 (LP,iv,5610).

Chapter Fourteen

The Final Year

THE GREAT FRUSTRATION FOR ANYONE TRYING TO FATHOM WHAT WOLSEY was up to during the last year of his life is that it is a story without an end. Or rather there is an end: Wolsey's death on 29 November 1530, but it is precisely his death that prevents one from knowing why, almost four weeks earlier, Henry had had him arrested on a charge of treason. Was he really intending to put a cardinal and archbishop to death? True, there were precedents of a kind. Over three hundred and fifty years earlier an archbishop of Canterbury had been murdered in his own cathedral, and though the then king, Henry II, may not have been directly responsible, he had felt sufficiently implicated to do penance. In 1405 Henry IV had had an archbishop of York, Richard Scrope, executed for treason, a more precise parallel, obviously, but with one important difference: whatever the justification for his actions, Scrope's treason was undoubted. There can be no such certainty about Wolsey. And whatever the precedents, the death of a prince of the Church at the hands of laymen, however princely, was so unusual and threatened such dangerous political consequences that it immediately raises the question of whether Henry VIII could ever have seriously considered taking such a step. Sadly, Wolsey's death before Henry was forced to declare his hand means that no definitive answer can ever be given, for the vital piece in the jigsaw is missing. This is all the more frustrating because in many ways no period of Wolsey's life is better documented. There are innumerable letters, both to and from him. There is also Cavendish.

Cavendish's account of Wolsey's last months can claim to be one of the great passages of English prose. It is not that it is fine writing; indeed, some may find almost all early Tudor English a little clumsy. But in some rather magical way Cavendish has got the mix right: plenty of lively detail is combined with moral reflections to generate a powerful emotional charge. It helped that for him it was the story not only of the fall of a great man who happened to have been his master, but also of a nation brought low by the lust of a king for his mistress. At this level there is little point in trying to compete with Cavendish, and no such attempt will be made here. This does not mean that his account of these months needs to be accepted, and in what follows in some important respects it will not be. But, given the many criticisms made earlier about him as a historical source, it is only fair to state that for the last months of Wolsey's life he has to be considered much more reliable than for any other period. This is not surprising. Wolsey was no longer the statesman grappling with the affairs of the nation, the intricacies of which his servant would not have been privy to, even if he had wished to be. The spotlight now focused on the man and his household, and with both of these Cavendish was intimately concerned. He was probably with Wolsey throughout this period. He was certainly one of the few to accompany him on his fateful journey south following his arrest at Cawood, near York, on 4 November, and he was present at his death. Cavendish is, therefore, an important eyewitness of much that took place, and in the rather special circumstances of his close attendance upon a man both physically and mentally under great stress, he is likely to have been more than usually privy to that man's thoughts. Not that eyewitnesses are always reliable; and, certainly, by the time that he came to write his biography Cavendish had a very committed view of his former master's part in England's destiny. But his usefulness as a source for what actually took place cannot be denied, and to unravel what did take place will be the main purpose of this chapter.

There are three main possibilities, though each of them spawns a number of mutants. Firstly, and most excitingly, Wolsey may have been involved in some kind of conspiracy, perhaps to overthrow Henry himself and replace him with Princess Mary, but at any rate to bring about his own restoration to full power. At the other extreme it is possible that there was no real conspiracy, merely one invented by Henry and/or the 'Boleyn faction', with the duke of Norfolk to the fore. There could have been a number of reasons for such a set-up. If Henry was its principal author, then his campaign against the Church in order to force it to embrace his view of his marital status would provide the motivation; if the faction was behind it, then the motivation could have been a determination to prevent a comeback by Wolsey. In the middle lies what might be called the 'sensible view'. There was no conspiracy, but Wolsey was giving Henry and his advisers genuine grounds for believing that a recently dismissed lord chancellor, apparently winning for himself ever more golden opinions in that always slightly worrying part of the kingdom north of the Trent, constituted a threat that in the rather special circumstances of 1530 was too great to ignore. Such a view has an obvious attraction for one as suspicious of conspiracy theories as the present writer. But people are not always sensible, and there is plenty of evidence that would point to either extreme.

If quantity of evidence alone was the criterion, probably the first view would prevail. It also has going for it, or against, it the fact that it was the official line as, for instance, expounded in correspondence between Henry and his ambassador at the French court, Sir Francis Bryan.[1] According to the king, Wolsey's plot was as follows. First, the French were to encourage England to engage in a war with both emperor and pope. War against the former would result in the collapse of English foreign trade, against the latter in Henry's excommunication and an interdict whereby almost any kind of hostile action against the English Crown would receive the Church's blessing. The French would thereby be discharged of the need to repay their debts to England, and they would also be provided with a justification for invading the pale of Calais, while the Scots would be enabled to march into Northern England. Both these things, according to Henry, Wolsey had countenanced; but that was only the beginning of it. To counter these invasions the English people would be asked to provide both men and money in great amounts. Henry would then be faced with large-scale unrest, not to say insurrection, on the part of his own subjects. In desperation he would turn against the advisers who had got him into such a mess, and would recall the fallen minister. And as if all this were not enough, something even more miraculous would happen. At an instant Henry's enemies would cease causing him trouble, and peace and prosperity would reign

[1] Elizabethan copies of three letters from Henry to Bryan recently discovered in the British Library by L.R. Gardiner; see Gardiner. The reference numbers are BL Add MS 48066. fos. 184,186-7.188.

again. However, just in case the plot did not quite work out, Wolsey would at the same time have been establishing a fall-back position whereby foreign powers, but especially the papacy and France, would put subtler pressure upon Henry to secure his restoration. What precisely was meant by this is not clear, but at least Wolsey's full enjoyment of his rights as bishop of Winchester and abbot of St Albans, which he had been forced to surrender when he had accepted that he was guilty of praemunire.

This, then, was what Henry alleged Wolsey was plotting, and the main evidence was apparently provided by members of Wolsey's own household, especially his Venetian doctor, Agostino Agostini.[1] How much of the evidence can be believed will be considered shortly, but there is no doubt that Agostini was extremely active on Wolsey's behalf at this time, and was in personal contact with the French ambassador, Joachim, and the Imperial ambassador, Chapuys. Moreover, if Agostini's evidence is to be believed, then the case for a conspiratorial Wolsey must prevail. It is certainly supported by Joachim's and Chapuys's dispatches as well as those of the Venetian and Milanese ambassadors. What is interesting, though, is that reports of Wolsey's plotting were circulating, and in government circles, a long time before he was arrested. Thus, in July Norfolk informed Chapuys that all Wolsey's machinations were known to the government, having apparently been revealed by the three men in whom Wolsey had most confidence, though Chapuys mentioned no names.[2] And even if one were inclined to take Norfolk's statement with a pinch of salt, it is harder to dismiss Chapuys's account in the previous month of Wolsey's advice, as conveyed to him by Agostini, that now was the moment to take the strongest possible action on Catherine's behalf.[3] On the face of it, Chapuys's evidence alone would provide incontrovertible proof of a plot, but it is not alone. When in November Henry informed Sir Francis Bryan of Wolsey's arrest he sent also, as proof of the cardinal's mendacity, a copy of an extract from a letter that Agostini would have written on his master's behalf to the French ambassador in England if he had not had the great sense to perceive that it was 'maliciously contrived', and had therefore, without telling Wolsey, not sent it.[4] Agostini's confession, which included his total recall of the letter, was and remains at the heart of the case against Wolsey. If its validity could be undermined, then the rest of the evidence might not be quite as incontrovertible as at first it appears.

Agostini was arrested at the same time and place as Wolsey, but unlike his master he was hurried back to London for questioning, where he quickly turned king's evidence – if indeed he had not always been a mole, acting on the Crown's behalf while posing as a loyal servant of the cardinal. The reason for supposing that Agostini was not quite what he seemed to be is the treatment that he received once he got to London. On 13 November Chapuys reported that the doctor had been sent to the Tower on a charge of treason,[5] but on the 27th the picture he presented was

[1] For Agostini see A.F. Pollard, p.295, n.3.
[2] Sp.Cal, iv (i), p.630. One of them must have been Agostini. Another seems to have been a chaplain arrested while crossing the Channel; see Mil.Cal, 832. Could the third have been Cromwell?
[3] Sp.Cal, iv (i), pp.600-1, 619.
[4] Gardiner, p.103.
[5] Sp.Cal, iv (i), p.805.

very different: 'The said physician, ever since the second day of his coming here, has been, and still is, treated as a prince in the house of the duke of Norfolk, which clearly shows that he has been singing to the right tune.'[1] Writing just a few days later the Milanese ambassador gave a similar account; only he reported that Agostini 'immediately, from the very first, . . . found great favour'.[2] It was 'undeniable', he added, that a few days before his arrest letters of Agostini's, probably to the French ambassador, had been intercepted, and that these had contained some lines in cipher.

The Crown's treatment of one supposedly guilty of treasonable activity, if only on another's behalf, is a little curious. True, its kindness may have produced a lot of useful information, but if Agostini had indeed been involved in even half the activities he said he had, is it probable that he would have been treated quite so well? After all, merely the threat of a conviction for high treason was enough to make most people quite talkative. But even more curious is the recognizance that Agostini signed on 22 December, in which he promised on pain of a £100 fine never to disclose to anyone the 'matter as is mentioned in a book written with his own hand concerning the late cardinal of York'.[3] Why hide anything about what Wolsey had been up to? After all, he was already a disgraced minister, and really the more that was broadcast about his wicked activities the more convincing would have been the Crown's justification for having him arrested. And when he died, all the Crown could manage was a short press release, largely for foreign consumption, giving a brief explanation and justification for Wolsey's arrest. To have missed such a golden opportunity for berating not only Wolsey but all those people he had allegedly been in treasonable negotiations with, could suggest some difficulty in making out a convincing case for treason.

And what none of this does is help to confirm that the aspects of the plot that the Crown did choose to release had very much to do with the truth. It is also worrying that the one bit of hard evidence it produced was a letter supposedly written on Wolsey's behalf but never sent. Whatever the reason – and one might think that a conspiracy on the alleged scale and complexity of this one might have generated a little more evidence and of a kind less easily undermined – the fact that the letter was stored only in Agostini's mind must make it easier for it to have been invented. And what of Norfolk's three-month delay in acting on the information from sources close to Wolsey that he was up to no good? A possible explanation might be that the Crown deliberately stayed its hand to allow Wolsey to dig an ever deeper pit for himself, but if so, this must make Agostini into a mole, working for the Crown while posing as the close confidant of the Cardinal. Now, of course, what moles say is not necessarily untrue, but there must be a temptation for them to report what they think their real masters want to hear; and it could well be that this particular mole was instructed to put the worst possible construction on what Wolsey was up to.

Agostini's evidence is flawed; there can be no doubt about that. The only question is to what extent. In support of its essential veracity, that is that there was

[1] *Sp.Cal,* iv (i), p.819.
[2] *Mil.Cal,* 833.
[3] *LP,* iv, 6763 (PRO SP1/58/fo.215).

some kind of conspiracy afoot, is the fact that before accompanying Wolsey north in early April Agostini did visit both Chapuys and Joachim and did ask for favours of their respective sovereigns on his master's behalf.[1] Then in the second week of June he wrote Chapuys that letter already referred to, in which he apparently conveyed Wolsey's advice that now was the moment to intensify the campaign on Catherine's behalf, to the extent even of calling upon the 'secular arm, since so little nerve is shown on the other side', which is to say Henry's.[2] It has to be assumed that Agostini did write the letter, since Chapuys reported receiving it and summarized its content. He did, however, admit that the advice had been written *'assez obscurément'*, which no doubt was as annoying to him as it is to the historian.[3] It was not, however, the only advice that Chapuys received from Wolsey. On 20 August he informed Charles that he was receiving daily communications from Wolsey.[4] It is also clear that the French were being similarly bombarded, and just before Wolsey left for York, Joachim spent a few days with him at Richmond.[5] Not quite so certainly – because, as will be shown shortly, there is no hard evidence for it – he was in communication with the pope. If all the evidence for Wolsey's contacts with foreign powers is pooled, some kind of pattern does emerge, but one that is not quite so damning as regards conspiratorial activity as might at first appear.

To take first Agostini's letter and its reference to 'the secular arm'. It may be remembered that one of the last tasks that Wolsey performed for Henry was to minimize the effects of the advocation of the divorce to Rome: the substantive gain had been to secure a delay to the opening of legal proceedings at Rome, and delay was to remain a principal aim of English policy through 1530-1. A sub-plot to this was to prevent the summons to Rome being formally served upon Henry in the first place, but also to nullify any consequences of that summons, should it be served, the worry being that failure to comply would result in Henry's excommunication, 'incurring into contempt, *vel cum invocatione bracchi secularis aut penis pecuniaris'.*[6] Wolsey's reference to 'the secular arm' had thus to do with this last point. It was the practice of the secular courts to lend aid to the Church in cases concerning excommunication,[7] and this is what Wolsey was apparently suggesting should happen on this occasion. At any rate, according to Chapuys, he was pushing for the legal proceedings to go ahead with the greatest speed and stringency, declaring himself in favour of a papal prohibition against Anne's, or indeed any woman's, cohabitation with Henry while the divorce proceedings were in train.[8] All this was music to the Imperial ambassador's ears, for it was precisely such a measure, though not always with Catherine's full approval, that he was after.[9] And no doubt it was precisely because it was such sweet music that Wolsey was playing it. This is not

[1] Bradford, p.306-7; *Sp.Cal,*iv (i),pp.448, 486, 514.

[2] *SP.Cal,*iv (i), pp.600-1 (*'plus grandes censures et a la invocacion du bras seculier, cart maintenant yl ny a nul nerf.'*).

[3] *SP.Cal,*iv (i), p.600.

[4] *SP.Cal,*iv (i), p.692.

[5] *SP.Cal,*iv (i), 486.

[6] St.P,vii, p.194 (*LP*,iv,5797).

[7] Logan, p.13 ff.

[8] *Sp.Cal,*iv (i), pp.599-601. It was not until Jan. 1532 that Clement formally rebuked Henry for cohabiting with Anne, and not until that November that he threatened excommunication.

[9] Ibid, pp.601, 673, 736.

mere surmise. On 23 April Chapuys recorded the first of Agostini's visits to him on Wolsey's behalf. The ambassador's reaction was cool: before he could really advise his master to put in a good word for Wolsey with the king he wanted proof of his genuine desire to help Charles.[1] Then, lo and behold, Wolsey started to give lots of advice about how Catherine should go about thwarting Henry's plans. That the one followed the other so immediately is instructive; but before we follow this up, we need to examine more closely Wolsey's advice to Chapuys, for the light it sheds on the whole notion of a conspiracy.

The important point to make is that it was not treasonable. As we have seen, the Crown went to considerable lengths to give at least the appearance of legality and fairness to the divorce proceedings. Catherine had been allowed the best possible legal advice, and she was still receiving it long after the second legatine trial had come to an end, and by a council which included such eminent people as the bishop of Bath and Wells, John Clerk.[2] In August 1530 a chaplain of Catherine's, almost certainly Thomas Abel, was hauled before the royal Council for having publicly stated that all those who favoured Henry in the divorce were wicked; but he was then released, even though on being interviewed he had called most of the royal councillors present 'traitors'.[3] On a number of later occasions Abel was to be banished to the Tower and was eventually to die there; but then, as the events that make up the 'break with Rome' unfolded, to defend Catherine or the Catholic Church was made a treasonable offence by act of parliament. Before then, to what must have been Henry's absolute fury, Fisher was able to write treatise after treatise on her behalf. Considerable pressure was brought to bear upon him to shut up, but in fact it was for his connection with the Nun of Kent, attainted and then executed in February 1534, that he was first accused of treasonable activity. And his execution the following year, like More's, resulted from a refusal to take the oath attached to the Act of Succession of 1534, such refusal having been made a treasonable offence, under a further Act of that year.

In 1530 to give advice about the conduct of Catherine's case was not treasonable. It may nonetheless be considered strange coming from someone who had played such a leading part in trying to destroy her marriage, and who on 16 June 1530 had signed a letter to the pope virtually demanding that the marriage be declared null and void.[4] If much of the evidence of conspiracy on Wolsey's part is suspect, it must be stressed that some of his actions at this time were far from straightforward. Still, if to be for Catherine was not to be a traitor, neither was it treasonable for Wolsey to ask foreign powers to put in a good word for him with Henry, as, through Chapuys, he had asked Charles to do. Even more so did he appeal to Francis. Wolsey's tendency to side with the French had not endeared him to the majority of his fellow countrymen, and it is easy to see why he might have thought that the French owed him something. On the French side, du Bellay, at least, always saw Wolsey as important for the promotion of a mutually satisfactory relationship between the two countries. It also looks as if he came to respect, and

---

[1] Ibid, pp.514-5.
[2] Inter alia LP,v,62; Sp.Cal,iv (i), p.690; Sp.Cal, iv (ii), p.40.
[3] Sp.Cal,iv (i), p.672.
[4] Herbert, pp.331 ff. (LP,iv,6513); for further details see A.F. Pollard, p.287.

perhaps even to like, Wolsey, and was even in a sense taken in by him.[1] This was never true of Francis himself: his rather ambiguous role in Wolsey's initial fall was to continue after it. He had always thought, Francis remarked, when Bryan broke the news of Wolsey's arrest to him, that 'so pompous and ambitious a heart, sprung out of so vile a stock, would once show forth the baseness of his nature'. By his 'outrageous behaviour' Wolsey 'had well merited either a life worse than death, or else of all deaths the most cruel'.[2] This might well seem unnecessarily harsh; but if Wolsey had appeared to Englishmen to be over-fond of the French, to the French, as he squeezed them for all they were worth, it would have looked very different. And there was no reason at all for Francis to shed tears over the English king's fallen minister when his main concern was to secure favourable terms from that king. Indeed, it rather looks as if his ambassador, Joachim, had informed Henry of Wolsey's communications with him,[3] thereby winning favour with Henry and strengthening the French position in the current negotiations, without giving anything away. Moreover, it may be that well before Wolsey's arrest Joachim was getting annoyed with the cardinal; at any rate this was the view of the papal nuncio to England, Antonio Borgho, who had apparently been instructed by Clement to be guided by Joachim concerning his own relations with Wolsey.[4] Of course, Joachim may have been deliberately misleading the nuncio; he may, as Chapuys usually suspected, have been working closely with Wolsey, had then realized that Wolsey's plotting was about to be uncovered, thought he had better get in on the act and so had told Henry something of Wolsey's negotiations with him. All this is perfectly possible, and it has to be stressed that what was actually going on between Wolsey and the French, or indeed anyone else, will always remain obscure. Such a view, however, does not seem best to fit all the facts.

What may help to clarify the picture is a brief account of the state of Anglo-French relations at this time. The governing factors were Henry's desire for French support for his divorce, and Francis's determination to reassert French power and influence after the crippling setback of Pavia, and of his own and his sons' captivity. For both kings there were great advantages in good relations. The question, as always, was at what price, complicated in this instance by the Treaty of Cambrai, whereby Francis had decided that a temporary peace with the emperor was worth the immediate return of his sons. The English had had little option but to follow in Francis's wake, and the peace did offer Henry a glimmer of hope that in order to cement it Charles might waive his objections to the English king's abandonment of his aunt.[5] All this introduced a good deal of fluidity into European relations. Everyone was jockeying for pole position, but within the framework imposed by Henry's and Francis's major concerns. Francis got his sons back – and a Habsburg wife – in July 1530, but Henry was still no nearer getting a divorce. This placed Francis in a stronger position, though Henry's desperation to be free of Catherine

---

[1] *Inter alia* his letters to Montmorency of 12 and 17 Oct 1529; see *Correspondence*, pp. 104-11 (*LP*,iv,6003, 6011).

[2] *St. P*, vii, p.213 (*LP*,iv,6733).

[3] *St. P*, vii, p.213 (*LP*,iv, 6733).

[4] *Sp. Cal*,iv (i),p.805.

[5] Boleyn's embassy to the emperor early in 1530 was an attempt to take advantage of this opportunity; see Parmiter, pp.133-5.

had given the French king the upper hand for some time. With his immediate needs satisfied, here was the opportunity to claw back some of the money that, as a result of the Treaty of the More and the subsequent alterations to it, he owed the English king: of course Francis would help his dear brother obtain satisfaction from Rome and bring pressure on the University of Paris to come out in favour of Henry, but in return it was only fair that Henry should be lenient about the payment of the French pension. The day-to-day negotiations between the two monarchs were, thus, largely concerned with money, with the French enjoying yet another advantage in that it is always easier to withold payment than to obtain it.[1] And there was always the opportunity to haggle over the marriage contract between Princess Mary and Francis's second son, the duke of Orléans. It is not clear that either side was desperate for the marriage to take place, but it was something further to bargain about; and yet again, because Mary might at any moment be declared illegitimate, the French were at an advantage.

In deciding what effect these negotiations had on Wolsey's position, it is important to realize that despite the relations being generally good between the two kingdoms, there were moments when they were bad. One such seems to have occurred in the autumn of 1530, obviously an interesting period in view of Wolsey's arrest. Given that there was no reason why the French should lose much sleep over his fate – unless that is, there was some very concrete advantage to be derived either from his return to favour or from his final destruction – for Joachim, informing on Wolsey was but another ploy in his rather sticky negotiations with Henry. What may also have been the case is that Henry was making use of Wolsey in order to resist French pressure.

When Joachim had visited Wolsey in March the main topic of conversation was apparently the cardinal's French pension, which was in arrears. As, however, under the terms of Henry's agreement with Wolsey made the previous month, this pension would now go to the Crown, it has been quite plausibly suggested that during this visit Wolsey was negotiating on Henry's behalf, not his own. The suggestion is supported by the fact that the visit was allowed to take place at all; a meeting between an accredited French ambassador and a fallen minister could hardly have taken place without the king's knowledge.[2] And if Henry had been willing to make use of Wolsey in March in order to get as much money out of the French as possible, might he not also have been trying to do so in October and November when negotiations with the French were at a critical stage and when he had few cards to play? This time, however, the tactics were to be a little different. Instead of Wolsey's close relationship with the French being a plus, it was to be presented as something treasonable, the aim being to thereby embarrass the French and make them more compliant. It is all very speculative, but at least it may serve to alert us not to take Henry's account of Wolsey's treasonable contacts with the French entirely at its face value.

The main difficulty, however, in accepting Henry's version is that it made no sense at all for the French to become involved in a war with the English, which was,

[1] This was Chapuys's assessment (Sp.Cal,iv (i), 712); and almost all du Bellay's reports confirm it.
[2] LP,iv,6271, 6273, 6307; Sp.Cal,iv (i),p.486; Rymer, xiv,p.372 for the agreement; also Friedmann,i, pp.110-2.

according to him, what Wolsey was proposing. If Anglo-French relations were not all sweetness and light at this time, the two countries had many more shared interests than opposing ones. Moreover, the French had good relations with the Boleyns, the father having been a resident ambassador in France, and Anne herself having been in part educated at the French court. So if they had lost a friendly, though always formidable, royal servant, they had gained a royal mistress, an exchange that cannot have been too much to their disadvantage. Furthermore, since they were in such a strong position vis-à-vis the English, there was no incentive for them to destroy this by going to war. And although the possibility that Wolsey suggested a conspiracy cannot be ruled out, one has to continue to work on the assumption that Wolsey's intelligence had not completely deserted him, unless, that is, his fall had unhinged him in some way. If it had not, he would have appreciated, just as much as we do, if not more, that the French were not about to embark on some hare-brained scheme to put him back in power. What he might reasonably have expected was that they put in a good word for him, and in suggesting this he might well have promised that if he were restored to favour, he would be even more francophile than he was alleged to have been hitherto. Such promises could have been misinterpreted, deliberately or otherwise, by both the French and Henry, and hence the talk of conspiracy. But that the French were involved in anything like a conspiracy, or that Wolsey suggested one, is the least likely of the many possible hypotheses.

It will be remembered that in the official version of Wolsey's conspiracy the French had a very positive role to play; and, indeed a letter intended for Joachim, though in fact only stored in Agostini's head, had been the main, if not the only, exhibit in the case against Wolsey. If a conspiracy with the French was unlikely, then the case for a conspiracy of any kind is seriously undermined. Arguably, however, the person most likely to have been interested in conspiring with Wolsey was the emperor, in order to make life as difficult as possible for the man who was behaving so dishonourably towards his aunt. But it has already been suggested that his attachment to his aunt was largely a calculated one, which he did not allow to stand in the way of other more pressing interests. In 1530 Charles did have such interests, in Germany and elsewhere, and though quite prepared to cause a little trouble for England in order to prevent her causing mischief, in particular with France, it is difficult to see how a full-scale conspiracy could have been of much help to him. Moreover, not only does nothing Chapuys reported give any indication that the emperor was interested in such a conspiracy, but if the mention of bringing in 'the secular arm' is interpreted as it has been here, there is not even any suggestion that Wolsey ever proposed one. Admittedly, Wolsey's and Agostini's arrests must have alarmed Chapuys momentarily because he had been in frequent communication with both. However, when on 27 November he wrote to Charles that even should Agostini 'repeat every word that has passed between him and me, he could say nothing for which I should be liable to be impugned or calumniated',[1] there is no reason to suppose that he was not telling the truth; neither did Henry ever try to contradict Chapuys on this point. The significance of his clean bill of health is worth underlining. It is only from Chapuys's detailed reports that we have

---

[1] Bradford, pp.326-7. (SP.Cal,iv (i), p.820).

any inside information of Wolsey's dealings with foreign powers at this time. The French evidence is far less complete; there is Joachim's account of his stay with Wolsey, but it lends no support to any conspiratorial theory.[1] If, therefore, a search of Chapuys's reports draws a blank, then again the case for a conspiracy by Wolsey is considerably undermined.

But it was the pope, not the French, who was given the leading role in the official account of the plotting, for according to Henry's first letter to Bryan on the subject, 'the particularities [of the plot] most specially concern sinister practices made and set forth to the court of Rome'.[2] There were obvious tactical advantages for Henry in stressing the papal connection, for Clement was hardly a favourite with him. However, these advantages would operate whether there had been any 'sinister practices' or not, so that Clement's star billing does not help much to unravel the truth. Moreover, as with both Francis and Charles, it is difficult to see what advantages such plotting would have had for Clement. It was argued in a previous chapter that during the winter of 1528-9 he had come to the conclusion that there was more to be gained from co-operating with Charles than not. Such co-operation of necessity entailed some resistance to Henry's anyway rather importunate demands for a divorce; that said, Clement had no wish to become merely the emperor's puppet, and, as the whole history of the divorce shows, he bent over backwards to be as amenable to Henry as possible. What Clement would have loved most of all was for the problem to go away, and conspiring with Wolsey, who had done precious little for him, was not going to bring that about. So there was no strong reason for him to be receptive to feelers from Wolsey concerning any serious conspiracy. And there is virtually no evidence of it. The Venetian ambassador in Rome stated on 6 December that some people there were reporting the discovery of letters from Wolsey to the pope in which, according to some accounts, he had asked to be reappointed legate, while according to others he had been making proposals about the divorce.[3] Rumours of this kind do not really add up to much, while the assertion sometimes made that Henry had asked his envoys at Rome to search for any incriminating evidence against Wolsey does not stand up to close scrutiny.[4] It depends upon a passage from a letter of one of the English envoys, William Benet, to Henry on 27 October 1530 in which he declared that 'as concerning those things that your Highness in your last letter commanded to Dr Carne and to me to search for, we shall not by God's grace omit no labours nor diligence for the searching thereof. And such things as we shall find with all diligence we shall advertise your Highness thereof.'[5] Henry's command has not survived, but nowhere in this nor in Benet's subsequent letter is there any reference to Wolsey. On the other hand, the English envoys were constantly being asked to chase up various matters to do with the divorce, and it seems likely that it was some such matter that this particular command had to do with.[6]

[1] Sp.Cal.,iv (i), pp.486-7; and following Wolsey's arrest Joachim was cleared of any suspicion of plotting by Henry and the Council; see LP,iv,6720.

[2] Gardiner, p.102.

[3] Ven.Cal.,iv, 638.

[4] A.F. Pollard, p.291; Scarisbrick, Henry VIII, p.239.

[5] BL, Add, 25114, fos.47-8 (LP,iv,6705).

[6] For full details see Scarisbrick, Bibl.d'Humanisme et Renaissance, xxiv, pp.212-5.

Positive evidence for any plotting by Wolsey with the pope is, then, negligible; foreign ambassadors in London might say otherwise, but as they were merely reporting gossip or information fed to them by the Crown, what they had to say is hardly more convincing than the Rome rumours. Moreover, that there was no plotting nor even much communication of any kind between Wolsey and the pope is strongly suggested by some negative evidence. When in the late summer of 1530 the papal nuncio, Antonio de Pulleo baron de Burgho, was sent to London, ostensibly to discuss proposals for a defence of Christendom against the infidel Turk but inevitably with divorce matters on his agenda, he was instructed to be guided in his conduct towards Wolsey by Joachim.[1] Since he found that the French ambassador and Wolsey were not on good terms, this was not very helpful, but more to the point, it hardly suggests that Clement had any plans for secret negotiations with Wolsey. Neither does the fact that Wolsey was apparently desperately anxious to discover from Chapuys whether the nuncio had brought any instructions about him.[2] And in a long letter that the nuncio wrote on 16 September he made no mention of Wolsey whatsoever.[3] In some ways all this is curious. It might be thought that Clement would have shown more concern about the fate of a papal legate, an attack on whom – which was, it has been argued, what Henry intended it to be – was an attack on himself, and more generally on the liberties of the Church. In fact, Wolsey's fate seems to have been a very low priority for the pope, his difficult relations with Henry being of much more importance. No doubt he was approached in some way by Wolsey, but quite how is not known. Almost certainly, any approach would have had to do with Wolsey's restoration not so much to royal favour but to a full enjoyment of his rights as bishop of Winchester and abbot of St Albans. Perhaps, also, his help was sought in connection with Wolsey's strenuous efforts to save his colleges, though it is more likely that Wolsey would have realized that in the circumstances papal help would have been counterproductive. Again, in the complete absence of any real evidence all this has to be speculation. Nevertheless, the strong probability is that, as with both Francis and Charles, there was nothing between cardinal and pope that deserves to be called a conspiracy.

It is beginning to look as if the first possibility mentioned at the start of this chapter does not stand up to close scrutiny, and what may deliver the *coup de grâce* is an aspect of Wolsey's arrest not so far mentioned. It will be remembered that it took place at Cawood on 4 November and that Wolsey died three and a half weeks later, by which time he and the accompanying entourage had got as far as Leicester, about half way between Cawood and London. The journey up had taken Walter Walsh, the groom of the privy chamber sent to arrest him, four days,[4] so that Wolsey's progress south was by any standards slow. Admittedly, he was increasingly ill, but even the concern shown for his health tells against the view of Wolsey as a dangerous threat to Henry's security. Cavendish reports, though one cannot be too certain about his accuracy, that on this last journey Wolsey was accompanied by people 'weeping and lamenting . . . crying "God save your grace, God save your

---

[1] Sp.Cal,iv (i),p.805.
[2] Ibid.
[3] Ibid, pp.718-20.
[4] He left Greenwich on 1 Nov.

grace, my good Lord Cardinal."[1] This is really not the kind of reception that the king would have liked to see given to a traitor, and the slow, almost stately, progress of the cavalcade bringing Wolsey to the Tower, which included eighteen days at Sheffield Park, a home of the earl of Shrewsbury, seems almost calculated to make it easy for anyone involved in a conspiracy to co-ordinate their plans. In fact, nobody stirred, probably for the very good reason that there was nobody to stir. In fact, there is not one piece of evidence that connects anyone in England, outside Wolsey's household, with a plot of any kind.

There was no conspiracy. Moreover, the Crown's handling of Wolsey's arrest hardly suggests that it really believed in one, which may in turn cast the first doubt on what was referred to at the beginning of this chapter as the 'sensible view': that there was in truth no conspiracy, but that the Crown had reasonable grounds for believing that Wolsey was up to no good. Given this scenario, its actions do make some kind of sense. The slow journey south is explained by the fact that Henry and his councillors were quite happy to take their time in deciding whether or not there was a conspiracy, and to pronounce on Wolsey's future accordingly. It has to be said that this was not how Henry presented the matter to Bryan, but then there was no particular reason why, when instructing one of his ambassadors, Henry should have concerned himself with the truth, which is unfortunately not always helpful in the successful conduct of affairs. More interestingly, and this is where the first doubts creep in, the slowness of journey south makes even more sense if Henry's intention was to continue to use Wolsey as a weapon in his attack on the Church, even if this meant inventing a conspiracy, this, of course, being precisely what the second possibility suggested earlier entailed. Still, the 'sensible view' is nevertheless attractive, partly just because it avoids a conspiratorial view of life. Much has to be muddle and misunderstanding. Henry had created a most difficult situation for himself in which anxiety, if not paranoia, could well have come to dominate his judgement, fuelled, as it is known to have been, by reports of Wolsey's increasing popularity in the North and his never ending complaints about shortage of money and the fate of his colleges.[2] At the same time, no one would have understood better than the king that his former lord chancellor knew his way around the courts of Europe better than any man living. Wolsey was potentially dangerous, and it was surely only sensible to bring him down from the North, though if this were the case why let him go there in the first place?

At this stage it may be helpful to try to approach the matter from Wolsey's point of view. How had he come through the enormous strain of the events of October 1529 when, accused of praemunire, he had been dismissed as lord chancellor, and then banished, first to the bishop of Winchester's palace at Esher, and then in the following March to Richmond? Not surprisingly, his mood appears to have oscillated. In a letter that he wrote to Henry shortly after the original charges of praemunire were made against him he referred to himself as 'your poor, heavy, and wretched Priest'.[3] According to Chapuys, he managed to remain in control of himself until the day after the great seal was removed from him, that is to say 18

[1] Cavendish, p.163.
[2] LP,iv,6335, 6344, 6436, 6447, 6496, 6545, 6571.
[3] St.P,i,p.347 (LP,iv,5999).

October, at which point 'all his bravadoes turned suddenly into bitter complaints, tears, and sighs which are unceasing night and day'.[1] Chapuys also reported that Henry had sent Wolsey a ring 'by way of consolation'.[2] According to Cavendish, on receiving it from the groom of the stool, Sir Henry Norris, Wolsey, 'incontinent, kneeled down in the dirt upon both his knees, holding up his hands for joy', where he was joined by Norris. . .

> And talking with Master Norris upon his knees in the mire, he would have pulled off his cap of velvet, but he could not undo the knot under his chin. Wherefore with violence he rent the laces and pulled it from his head and so kneeled bareheaded. And that done, he covered again his head and arose, and would have mounted his mule, but he could not mount again with such agility as he lighted before, where his footmen had as much ado to set him in his saddle as they could have.[3]

Here are obvious signs of emotional stress, and if one is tempted to think that Cavendish had embroidered the scene a little, it has to be said that the same signs are very much present in Wolsey's own letters of the next two or three months, especially those that he wrote to the man he was most relying upon to conduct his negotiations, Thomas Cromwell. He was for Wolsey his 'only aider in this mine intolerable anxiety and heaviness',[4] and any delay in communications with him sent Wolsey into utter despair, in December writing that 'the furthering and putting over of your coming hither hath so increased my sorrow, and put me in such anxiety of mind that this night my breath and wind by sighing was so short that I was by the space of three hours as one that should have died'.[5] How far these symptoms resulted only from stress is hard to say, for by late January he was very ill. Agostini, a doctor himself, wrote a hurried note to Cromwell for Dr Butts, the king's own doctor, and one other, to be sent immediately, and ordered a good supply of leeches.[6] Cromwell seems to have passed the request on to Henry, and, at least according to Cavendish, the royal response was both prompt and friendly. Not only was Butts sent, but four other doctors as well. In addition, and perhaps a far better medicine than any doctor could have provided, Henry sent another ring 'for a token of our good will and favour', and with it the message that he was in no way offended by Wolsey, who should therefore 'be of good cheer, and pluck up his heart and take no despair'. And as if this was not enough, Henry also persuaded Anne to send a token, and with it 'very gentle and comfortable words'.[7] All this royal concern on behalf of one who only a few months before had been dismissed from office and charged with praemunire seems rather curious, all the more so since a few months later he would be arrested for treason. Still, the concern seems to have been effective, for when Joachim visited him late in March he found a Wolsey who was not only physically well but 'so completely resigned and so armed with patience' that there was no need for the French ambassador to console him[8] – but by then Henry had at last made up

---

[1] *Sp.Cal.*, iv (i), p.303.
[2] Ibid.
[3] Cavendish, p.102-3.
[4] St.P,i, p.352 (*LP*,iv,6098), but see also St.P,i, pp.351-2, 354, 359(*LP*,iv,6114, 6203-4).
[5] St.P,i,351 (*LP*,iv,6114).
[6] *LP*,iv,6151.
[7] Cavendish, pp.120-2.

his mind about what to do with Wolsey.

When in October 1529 Wolsey confessed to being guilty of praemunire, legally he lost everything but his life. He had no income, no property and no position. His continued existence depended entirely upon what Henry chose to give back to him, and Henry had shown himself to be in no hurry to come to a decision. A general pardon was not granted until 10 February 1530,[1] and though Wolsey was at the same time informed about the major decisions concerning his future, in the following weeks negotiations continued, and indeed in a sense they never ceased until the day he was arrested. These decisions can be briefly summarized as follows.[2] Wolsey was to be allowed to enjoy all his rights and revenues as archbishop of York, with the exception of a few wealthy collations which were to be placed at the king's disposal. But York Place, the London residence of the archbishops of York and very much Wolsey's centre of his operations, was to be forfeited to the Crown, shortly to emerge as Whitehall.[3] As regards St Albans and Winchester the situation was more complicated. He was to retain the titles of abbot and bishop, but his rights and duties were to be exercised by others. At the same time his income from the two, which in the case of Winchester had amounted to nearly £4,000 a year, was to go to the Crown, in return for which he was to be allowed a pension of 1,000 marks, to be drawn out of Winchester's revenues.[4] He also forfeited to the Crown his French and Spanish pensions. However, he did receive an estimated £6,374 3s. 7d., of which £3,000 was in ready money, and the rest in goods and chattels, urgently required since being stripped of everything that he had previously owned, right down to the sheets and pillow cases.[5] Despite this, ready money appears to have remained an acute problem for Wolsey, so that during the next few months he asked for and obtained further sums.[6]

The result of this agreement was that Wolsey was going to enjoy something approaching the £4,000 a year which he had at an early stage in the negotiations accepted as the least he could survive on.[7] It might be thought that such a sum was a rather high 'pension' for an apparently disgraced minister, but there are signs, not least the requests for further sums, that Wolsey was not altogether happy with it. And what was certainly making him very unhappy were Henry's designs on his colleges at Oxford and Ipswich. It quite quickly became apparent that there was no chance of Wolsey saving the latter, though a final decision was not made until September 1530.[8] The fate of Cardinal College, which at Wolsey's downfall had been much more of a going concern and was in every way the more important

[8] *Sp.Cal.*, iv (i), p.486.

---

[1] Rymer, xiv, p.366 (*LP*, iv, 6313).

[2] Rymer, xiv, pp.371-4 (*LP*, iv, 6220).

[3] *King's Works*, pp.300-8.

[4] Rymer, xiv, p.373 (*LP, iv, 6220*); see also *Registrum Thome Wolsey*, pp.184-7.

[5] Rymer, xiv, pp.374-5 (*LP*, iv, 6214 (ii)) for a schedule of what was given.

[6] *Inter alia* £500 for 'the defraying of my servants' (*LP*, iv, 6226); and perhaps a further gift of £1,000 (Cavendish, p.132).

[7] *St. P*, i, p.354 (*LP*, iv, 6204), a figure apparently first suggested by Gardiner.

[8] *LP*, iv, 6663, William Capon's to Wolsey of 4 Oct. outlining steps taken to dissolve the college on the king's command; but as early as 20 July he was reporting that the decision had been taken (*LP*, iv, 6523).

institution, hung much more finely in the balance, and during the summer of 1530 Wolsey devoted much of his energies to trying to save it. Cromwell was his chief agent in this, but almost anybody who was anybody was approached, including Norfolk and Gardiner, but also More who was reported in October to be 'very good in this matter', though rather pessimistic.[1] The details of the negotiations can be passed over, but in the end More's pessimism was justified. Wolsey was undoubtedly heart-broken by his failure to preserve an institution on which he had expended so much energy, time and money. Amongst other things, the failure threatened his good relations with Cromwell, whom he began to suspect of not having done enough to save it.[2] What effect the outcome had on his relationship with Henry no document discloses, but it surely could have left Wolsey by October 1530 extremely bitter: perhaps even bitter enough, when his other disappointments concerning Henry's arrangements for his future are borne in mind, to have contemplated treason?

In asking this question the intention is not to revive the just discarded theory of the conspiratorial Wolsey, but to draw attention to that aspect of his attitude during his last year that has been generally overlooked. It could, after all, be argued that Wolsey had absolutely no reason for being bitter or disappointed. Indeed, should he not have been immensely grateful that as a disgraced minister he was allowed to remain archbishop of York, enjoying what was by the standards of the day an almost princely income? The loss of the colleges was obviously a great blow, but Henry's decision to refound Cardinal College meant that something might be saved from the wreckage. And anyway, just to be alive and comparatively free to do what he liked was surely, in all the circumstances, something to be going on with? In fact, Wolsey never seems to have viewed the matter in this light. It is true that at the time of his fall he did write that fairly cringing letter to Henry already referred to[3] and that he admitted his guilt as to the praemunire charges, though there was much that was tactical about this.[4] He was quite prepared to write begging letters and to solicit help from all and sundry, and he exhibited to his close associates a degree of self-pity. All that said, however, his general stance was not of a man conscious of having escaped a terrible fate or even of one experiencing guilt and thus deserving of what had befallen him – and this surely is a little strange?

So far very little has been said about the charges brought against Wolsey, either officially by members of both houses of parliament, or unofficially by Lord Darcy and John Palsgrave; and in fact not a lot will be said, for in a sense much of this book has been a reply to them. The point to bear in mind about both Darcy and Palsgrave is that, rightly or wrongly, but probably wrongly, they felt that they had been badly treated by Wolsey. Darcy was aggrieved with his former 'bedfellow' at court for, in

---

[1] LP,iv,6679 for More's invlovement; but see also LP,iv,pp.6377, 6510, 6574-5, 6579, 6666.

[2] Bodleian Library, MS Jesus Coll, 74, fo.194v (otherwise known as the Masters MSS); Lord Herbert's often detailed summaries of letters between Wolsey and Cromwell for his Life and Reign of King Henry the Eighth, useful where, as in this case, the original has not survived.

[3] St. P,i,pp.347-8 (LP,iv,5999). It begins: 'Though that I, your poor, heavy and wretched priest, do daily pursue, cry and call upon your royal majesty for grace, mercy, remission and pardon, . . .'

[4] As Wolsey explained to Cavendish, by confessing to something that Henry knew that he was not guilty of, 'the king (I doubt not) had a great remorse of conscience, wherein he would rather pity me than malign me'. (Cavendish, pp.136-7).

his view, so woefully under-using him in the government of the North and of starving him of the fruits of royal patronage;[1] indeed, one of the charges that he levelled against Wolsey in 1529 was that he had deprived him of royal offices.[2] In 1524 his eldest son was summoned before the Council for unknown offences.[3] In 1525 he was not appointed to the new Council of the North, while in 1526 he was worried that Wolsey was displeased with him, though in fact another of his sons assured him that this was not the case.[4] The main reason why Darcy was not made more use of was almost certainly because his power base was not sufficiently strong to make him an effective leader in the North, nor did he possess the requisite legal experience to make him an automatic choice as a member of the Council there.[5] He may also have been a rather curmudgeonly old stick with a natural disposition to be 'agin the government'; at any rate Wolsey's passing was to bring him no closer to the centre of power, and in 1537 he was to be executed for his part in the Pilgrimage of Grace. Be that as it may, during the 1520s Darcy was a man who felt that he had been cold-shouldered by a former friend and colleague. It is not therefore surprising that in 1529 he came forward with a list of greivances amounting almost to a formal indictment against Wolsey.

Unlike Darcy, Palsgrave did not volunteer his voluminous charges, but their existence was either known about or strongly suspected, and for the following reason. When Henry's illegitimate son was created duke of Richmond and set up as nominal head of the Council of the North, Palsgrave had been appointed his tutor. However, he was soon complaining that he was not being allowed to educate the child as he wished, because of interference from members of the duke's own council, who were much more interested in the knightly arts than in book learning.[6] He had looked to Wolsey for support, but far from being forthcoming he found himself very quickly out of the job, which pleased him not at all. The obvious target for his displeasure was Wolsey, and in what was almost certainly intended to be an essentially private and therapeutic exercise, he let off steam by working upon a very literary attack upon the king's leading minister, in which ironic praise was the main weapon. Thus, quite unlike Darcy's, it was not drawn up in anything approaching a legal form. On the other hand, steam there does seem to have been, not all of which he had managed to retain in his study. The result was that on 11 April 1528 he was formally bound 'to demean and behave himself discreetly, soberly and wisely in his words towards the king's highness and his most honourable Council, and not to use or to speak any seditious words against them'.[7] It was thus well known that Palsgrave was a man with a grievance, so that when the time came to look for material to use in drawing up charges against Wolsey his study was an obvious place to search.[8]

---

[1] LP,iv,2576 Darcy to Wolsey, 15 Jan. 1514, a passionate plea for Wolsey not to forget 'such as were your lovers and friends'.

[2] LP,iv, 5749, p.2554 'Item, voiding me upon his promise to recompense me of the offices of treasurer, chamberlain and customer of Berwick . . .'

[3] LP,iv,541.

[4] LP Add,538.

[5] See pp.228-9.

[6] Palsgrave, pp.ix-liv for still probably the best account of his life, though G. Bernard has suggested to me that his charges may predate his dismissal from Richmond's household and most of the specific things he mentioned are earlier than 1522.

[7] PRO, C54/396, m.31 I owe this reference to S.J. Gunn.

Why the Crown was anxious to lodge further charges, given that Wolsey had quickly admitted to the offence of praemunire, will be discussed shortly. What is most relevant here is Wolsey's attitude to them, and it emerges very clearly in a letter that he wrote to Cromwell: 'As touching the articles laid unto me, whereof a great part be untrue, and those which be true are of such sort that by the doing of them no malice nor untruth can be justly arrected unto me, neither to the prince's person, nor to this realm.'[1] This was an extraordinarily bold defence to have made, all the more so because it was intended not only for Cromwell's ears, but for the king's as well.[2]

In trying to make sense of Wolsey's conduct during his last year this lack of contrition must somehow be fitted into the increasingly complicated picture. For most of the time he appears to have been unwilling even to put on a show of contrition which, given his situation, might be thought at the very least to have been tactless; but then tact was not a feature of his conduct during the last months of his life, as his friends were only too well aware. Early in June Thomas Heneage, on being asked yet again to approach the king on his former master's behalf, advised that if only Wolsey would content himself 'with that you have', there was no doubt that Henry would be 'good and gracious' to him.[3] Three or four weeks later Peter Vannes, who like Heneage had been close to Wolsey for many years before entering royal service, was advising him to keep a low profile.[4] So also, and on more than one occasion, did Thomas Cromwell. His long letter of 18 August was devoted to this theme, and included a philosophical passage which he would have done well to have paid more attention to himself. Having urged great restraint as to Wolsey's building programme in the diocese of York, and specifically at Southwell where he was then residing, he supposed Wolsey was 'right happy that you be now at liberty to serve God and to learn to experiment how you shall banish and exile the vain desires of this unstable world', which people with Wolsey's gifts were especially afflicted by. In the end, though, these brought only 'sorrow, anxiety and adversity', so he assumed that Wolsey would not wish to return to the political fray, though he 'were to win a hundred times as much as ever you were possessed of'.[5]

Given that Cromwell was just as much a political animal as Wolsey, it is difficult to take this passage too seriously; though such people do seem to have moments when release from the burdens of office is the only thing they crave, however much they regret it if it comes.[6] Here, however, the main purpose of the homily was

---

[8] That there was a search is indicated by the endorsements to the charges; see *LP*,iv,5750,pp.2561, 2562.

---

[1] *LP*,iv, 6204.

[2] At least as summarized by Lord Herbert: 'As touching the articles laid unto me, whereof a great part be untrue, and those which be true are of such sort that by the doing of them no malice nor untruth can justly be arrected unto me . . . This may be urged to the king.' (Bodlean Library, MS Jesus Coll, 74, fo.193v). The letter itself is more ambiguous, partly because defective, but certainly Cromwell was urged to be 'plain' with Fitzwilliam and Gardiner, both involved in drawing up the details of his pardon.(*St.P*,i, p.354).

[3] As reported to Wolsey by a messenger, Robert Smythe; see *LP*,iv,6447.

[4] *LP*,iv,6496.

[5] *St.P*,i,p.367 (*LP*,iv,6571).

[6] Both Bismarck and Gladstone had such moments, but not apparently Mrs Thatcher!

probably to convert Wolsey to a view that Cromwell was all too well aware he did not hold. Some aspects of Wolsey's allegedly ostentatious conduct, such as his much criticized building programme, were undoubtedly exaggerated by enemies at court, but it was nonetheless a very substantial cavalcade that moved north with him to Southwell. At Peterborough on Maundy Thursday he washed the feet of fifty-nine poor men. When he got to Southwell

> he kept a noble house and plenty both of meat and drink for all comers, both for rich and poor, and much alms given at his gate . . . He made many agreements and concords between gentleman and gentleman, and between some gentlemen and their wives that had been long asunder and in great trouble, and divers other agreements between other persons; making great assemblies for the same purpose and feasting of them, not sparing for any costs where he might make peace and amity, which purchased him much love and friendship in the country.[1]

And if he was extremely prominent on what might be called the secular front, he was equally so as regards his episcopal duties. On one occasion, Cavendish reports, he personally confirmed about two hundred children, while Richard Morison shortly after Wolsey's death gave this account of his activities:

> There were few holydays but he would ride five or six miles from his house, now to this parish church, now to that, and there cause one or other of his doctors to make a sermon unto the people. He sat amongst them and said mass before at the parish. He saw why churches were made. He began to restore them to their right and proper use . . . He brought his dinner with him, and had divers of the parish to it. He inquired whether there was any debate or grudge between any of them; if there were, after dinner he sent for the parties to the church and made them at one.[2]

Wolsey the great pastoral bishop is not a Wolsey that most people know of, though an attempt was made in an earlier chapter to show that the picture is not so improbable. Here, however, the emphasis is on his great visibility during his last months. He may have been a recently disgraced minister; may have confessed to being guilty of praemunire, with all the dire consequences that this was supposed to bring; but in his conduct in his diocese of York there was not the slightest hint of any of these things. Instead he was every inch the great cardinal bishop, merely taking a little time off from the more hectic affairs of state to minister to his flock.

Wolsey's high profile in the North is, on the face of it, the most obvious reason for believing in the 'sensible view', for surely it must have forced the Crown to be suspicious of what he was up to, even to wonder whether he was not deliberately courting popularity in this always sensitive region only so as to be able to bring pressure upon Henry to restore him to power. Perhaps it did, but there are serious difficulties in accepting that this was the chief reason for Wolsey's arrest. To begin with, would any government, however anxious, have felt seriously threatened by a previously absentee bishop with no particular ties with the Northern gentry, whose support he would surely have needed to bring any pressure to bear. And if there had been any question mark about the loyalty of the Northern gentry, why deliberately

---

[1] Cavendish, p.138-9.
[2] Morison, p.E 11v.

banish the fallen minister to that region? This question keeps obtruding, and for the very good reason that it is so difficult to answer. After all, no archbishop of York could have kept a low profile, if only because the office made its holder a leading, if not the leading, representative of the Crown in the area. As such, it was his duty to keep open house and to try to settle disputes in precisely the way that Wolsey actually did. All this Henry would have been well aware of. Moreover, the figure that Wolsey cut there was largly dictated by the amount of cash that the Crown had been willing to provide; and that he was given £150 to furnish his household with ninety horses and their trappings and £300 for his own clothing hardly suggests that he was expected to be invisible!

Why send Wolsey north, thus becomes a key question. Perhaps it was simply because Henry had no option but to do so, and in offering such an answer we come up against the strangest aspect of the whole story. As the time for Henry's decision on his future approached – and it appears that Wolsey had been promised that it would be made shortly after parliament was prorogued in December 1529[1] – he was naturally anxious that as many important people as possible should put in a good word for him with the king.[2] Pre-eminent among these were the dukes of Norfolk and Suffolk, and it was they whom Cromwell was especially urged to approach, but not just because of their leading positions at court. They were also, Wolsey explained to Cromwell, men who 'knoweth honour, and what is convenient to be done with the king's honour in this behalf, and can call to remembrance what hath been promised unto me upon the trust and confidence whereof I have done and made my submission, putting me wholly in the king's most gracious hands, who by the rigour of his laws could not have had so much as his Grace now hath'.[3] As it turned out their honour could not prevent Wolsey losing, at least for all practical purposes, both Winchester and St Albans, and when this became evident he made very clear his hurt and surprise because, as he explained in another letter to Cromwell, he had 'never thought, and so I was assured at the making of my submission, to depart from any of my promotions'.[4] Neither, apparently, had he expected to lose all his ecclesiastical apparel, and again for the good reason that at the time of his submission Norfolk and Suffolk had promised that he would not.[5] Just how much of a shock it was that their word, indirectly the king's, had not been entirely kept is not clear; certainly, his great anxiety about the final settlement does not suggest that he had really hoped to hang on to everything. What he was quite prepared to do was to use the original promises as bargaining counters in the negotiations, by, for instance, insisting that he secured the pension out of Winchester's revenues.[6] But the very fact that the story of Wolsey's last months can be seen as a whole series of negotiations has to be considered as very odd, for what other disgraced minister of Henry's was allowed such a say in what was to become of him?

That he was allowed it explains a lot about what has so far been puzzling about

---

[1] St. P,i,352 (LP,iv,6098).
[2] Inter alia LP,iv, 6098, 6112, 6114, 6181, 6182.
[3] St. P,i,p.352 (LP,iv,6098).
[4] St. P,i,p.355 (LP,iv,6181).
[5] St. P,i,p.356 (LP,iv,6181).
[6] St. P,i,p.355 (LP,iv,6181).

Wolsey's state of mind at this time. The high profile, the lack of contrition, the surprising degree of confidence that all would be well, make sense just because he had been promised that all would indeed be well. He would, of course, have had in certain respects to toe the line: this would have meant accepting the loss of secular office, at least for the time being, and making no attempt to resist his indictment for praemunire; for, given Henry's own deep involvement in the legatine powers and the shakiness of the charges, any resistance could have proved embarrassing for the king, and certainly would not have given the clear message to the Church that Henry intended.[1] It would, of course, be wrong to exaggerate the strength of Wolsey's position. Henry could have crushed him just whenever he wished, by, for instance, bringing an act of attainder against him. As it was, he contented himself with a mere petition from both houses of parliament containing a list of the many heinous offences the fallen minister was guilty of.[2] This could very easily have been converted into a formal attainder, but Henry's hope was that this would not be necessary. Wolsey should have got the message and behaved accordingly, which is to say that he should have accepted gratefully any terms that Henry chose to offer him. The purpose of the forty-four charges brought against him was to exert pressure on him while negotiations about his future were still going on. They were part of a bargaining process, and never intended to be taken too seriously, something which helps to explain some of the more far-fetched articles, that, for instance, Wolsey had infected Henry with the pox by 'rouning' in his ear and blowing upon him 'with his perilous and infective breath'.[3] Unfortunately for Henry, Wolsey realized this only too well, called the king's bluff by dismissing the charges out of hand, and continued to bargain for the best terms possible. But the only reason why he felt in a strong enough position to do this was because of the earlier promises made to him that he would be treated well, and more importantly because of what lay behind these earlier promises: Henry's realization that his former minister might still be of use to him.

In the last chapter it was argued that Wolsey's dismissal from office was neither the work of a faction nor the king's impulsive reaction to the failure of the second legatine court. Instead, it was seen as a calculated act of policy on Henry's part to further the divorce negotiations. The argument here is that after he had been dismissed Wolsey continued to figure in those calculations, with the result that he was in quite a strong position for as long Henry continued to see a use for him. If this argument is correct then important consequences follow, for by focusing attention on Henry rather than on Wolsey the second possibility mentioned at the start of this chapter looms ever larger: that Wolsey's arrest and the accusation of conspiracy was a set-up quite unrelated to what he was actually doing. Or to put it another way, if Henry had been prepared to dismiss him from office on a trumped-up charge of praemunire in October 1529, there seems no good reason why he should not have had him arrested on a trumped-up charge of treason in November 1530 if, that is, a good enough reason for doing so can be discovered. In looking for that reason the

---

[1] Cavendish, p.136 for the statement that even some of Henry's legal advisers thought the grounds for Wolsey's indictment for praemunire shaky.

[2] Herbert, pp.294-302 (*LP*, iv, 6075); see Pollard, p.261 for a discussion of the status of the charges.

[3] Art. 6.

timing must be important. There would have been little point in sending Wolsey off to York if it was known that he was shortly to be arrested. This means that it is most unlikely that any decision to arrest him had been made before April 1530. Moreover, on 16 June Wolsey had dutifully signed a letter to be sent to the pope by English notables requesting him promptly to do what they saw as the only right and proper thing: to grant Henry a divorce.[1] In fact, Wolsey's signature heads the list, and it would not have made much sense to ask him to sign if by that date the decision to arrest him had already been taken. So we are looking for a change of plan that occurred after 16 June, and probably much nearer the time when Walter Walsh was sent north to arrest him on 1 November. Furthermore, one would expect the change to have had something to do with the divorce; there would have been little point in arresting Wolsey in connection with anything less than this all-engrossing issue. Thus, what had been happening in the divorce negotiations since Wolsey's dismissal from office becomes a matter of some importance.

From Henry's point of view things had not gone well. One year after the advocation in July 1529 the position remained exactly the same: the case was still to be heard in Rome, and nothing that Henry had thrown at the pope, not even the dismissal and disgrace of his papal legate, had persuaded Clement to change tack. Someone else who had not budged was Catherine's nephew, Charles V, and this despite both the Treaty of Cambrai, which had meant that, in a formal sense at least, he and Henry were allies again, and an embassy, headed not altogether tactfully by Anne's father, sent specially to persuade him that it was in Catherine's best interests to give way gracefully. Lastly and as regards Wolsey's arrest, most relevantly there was little indication that Henry's own subjects had changed their minds and become in any way reconciled to the loss of their queen. True, parliament had been called, and a certain amount of anticlerical feeling had been stirred up which could be made use of in any future bargaining with the English Church. However, at least according to Chapuys, this feeling was in no way associated with any sympathy for the divorce.[2] Of course, Chapuys is no impartial source here but, as we saw earlier, almost all the evidence points to the great majority of the English nation being behind Catherine.[3] This was obviously bad news for Henry, but especially given Clement's continuing obstinacy.

Until recently at any rate, it has been rather assumed that the key to obtaining the divorce was the realization, probably by either Cromwell or Cranmer, that the pope's consent was not required.[4] Everything so far in this study has pointed to the inadequacies of this assumption, and it will continue to do so. Earlier it was

---

[1] Pollard, p.287.

[2] Sp.Cal,iv (i), p.387.

[3] See pp.578-9. See also outgoing Venetian ambassador's report to the senate, 10 Nov. 1531: Catherine was 'so loved and respected, that the people already commence murmuring; and were the faction to produce a leader, it is certain that the English nation, . . , would take up arms for the queen.' (Ven.Cal, iv, p.300.)

[4] Cromwell's significance has been especially pushed by Elton; see Reform and Reformation, pp.130 ff. for a summary of his views, but see inter alia Parmiter, pp.144 ff. A strong counter was provided by Scarisbrick in his Henry VIII, pp.241 ff, but I suspect that the orthodoxy would still be that Henry was incapable of engineering a 'break with Rome' on his own. Significantly, however, Dr Guy, an Elton pupil, who, in his Sir Thomas More, p.130, accepted his master's view, now rejects it; see inter alia his EHR, xvii, passim.

emphasized that papal consent was sought not out of some kind of conventional piety or concern for justice, but for reasons of state: that is, in order to bolster up an unpopular, and, as regards the succession, politically unwise decision, which without the papal blessing might not have been made to stick. And just how politically necessary the pope's consent was considered to be is suggested not only by the enormous lengths that Henry went to in order to obtain it, but by the fact that whenever Clement himself had hinted that the best thing would be for Henry to go it alone, his advice was never acted upon.[1] On the other hand, if the pope would not grant a divorce, then an alternative way of freeing himself would, however reluctantly, have to be found. What this did not mean was that Henry could just fling Catherine aside, for the political problem of making acceptable the essentially unacceptable remained – indeed, was made much worse by the lack of papal authorization. A substitute had to be found for the pope. There was obviously parliament, but an essentially secular body was not best suited to pass judgment on a matter that had traditionally been the preserve of the ecclesiastical courts. Better, perhaps, to confine its role to authorizing some other body to give judgment; but even as regards this supporting role there remained the little matter of whether or not it would be amenable to Henry's wishes. And this, as has been indicated, was not at all certain.

The obvious substitute for the pope, with or without parliamentary backing, was the English Church, but the fact that it was obvious did not make it easy to put into effect. For one thing, there remained that obstacle that Wolsey, despite all his ingenuity and effort, had found insurmountable: namely, that Henry's case was weak in law, especially if, as appeared to be the case, he could not prove that Catherine's marriage to his brother had been consummated. It is true that some churchmen (amongst the more senior perhaps Warham,[2] and amongst a younger generation Gardiner and Edward Fox, used extensively by first Wolsey and then Henry in the divorce negotiations)[3] appear to have genuinely believed in Henry's case. And by the summer of 1530 Oxford and Cambridge, as well as a number of European universities, had pronounced in Henry's favour, and this obviously strengthened his position.[4] Against this, in order to obtain these verdicts a considerable amount of pressure had had to be exerted, nowhere more than at the English universities.[5] Given that at any trial Henry would have to deal with men of the calibre of Fisher and Clerk who would not be nearly so easily dictated to, this did not bode well. Moreover, it was one thing to give an opinion, or even to write to the pope on Henry's behalf, as some of his leading subjects had done, though even getting people to sign this letter had proved very difficult.[6] But to give a judgment against the express command of the pope would be quite another matter. In order to persuade people to do this Henry would have to find some totally convincing theoretical justification, and then, no doubt he would also have to do a lot of arm twisting as well.

[1] See p.518.
[2] H.A. Kelly, p.123.
[3] Surts and Murphy, pp.xxii.
[4] Parmiter, p.124; Cambridge on 9 Mar., Oxford 8 April.
[5] Ibid; Sp.Cal.,iv (i), pp.475-6.
[6] St.P,iv (i), pp.598-9.

The theoretical justification was already to hand, and Henry needed no prompting to make full use of it. After all, it was back in 1515 that he had informed his assembled bishops that 'by the ordinance and sufferance of God we are king of England, and the kings of England in time past have never had any superior but God only', which, amongst other things, meant that no one other than God could force him to stand trial at Rome. Moreover, both in 1515 and again in 1519 the Crown's legal advisers had argued that papal decrees had no standing in England unless they had the consent of the Crown and were compatible with 'the customs of England'.[1] But to stress the lack of novelty, is not to play down the particular circumstances of 1530. Whatever may be said about the seriousness of those earlier conflicts between Church and state, Henry had not then been challenging the express command of a pope on a specific issue, and moreover one that could not have been more important to him, both emotionally and politically. This was precisely the situation in 1530, and so the theoretical arguments in defence of the royal position would have to be all the more presented and, of course, tailored to Henry's particular need, which were to prevent his matrimonial cause being tried at Rome.

The continuing refusal of both Charles and Clement to accede to his wishes compelled Henry in the summer of 1530 to enter upon not exactly a new policy, but rather a new phase, in which these theoretical arguments would have to play an increasingly important part.[2] The threat that if Henry did not get his way he would have to proceed without the pope's consent had been there from the very beginning, and, as we have seen, Wolsey had been just as happy to use it as anyone else.[3] At the same time it must be stressed that what is not being said here is that it was in the summer of 1530 that Henry decided to 'break with Rome'. The threat continued to be, as it had been before, part of a bargaining process in which Henry's main purpose was still to persuade Clement to do his bidding. But given Clement's continuing refusal to oblige, Henry was now faced with the prospect either of giving up or of turning the threat into a reality. Not to proceed was for him unthinkable, and the result was that he took a number of decisions which, it will be argued here, led directly to Wolsey's arrest.

According to Chapuys, the new phase began at the meeting of notables held on 15 and 16 June to draw up that letter to the pope in which they called upon Clement to accede to their master's wish. The letter itself made no mention of what was going to be the continual cry during the months ahead, that Henry's case could only be tried in England. What signalled the new phase was the kite which was flown when it was asked at the meeting whether, now that Henry had secured the favourable verdict of 'many competent judges', Henry might not remarry immediately 'without waiting any further approval of his conduct'.[4] In fact, the kite had to be hauled down immediately because so few spoke out in its favour, but the lesson that Henry learned from this was not that he should give up but that he would have to try a good deal harder.

In describing Henry's efforts over the next few months it will be helpful to

---

[1] See pp.49-50.
[2] Scarisbrick, *Henry VIII*, pp.261 ff. still seems to me to be the best account.
[3] See p.53-5.
[4] *Sp.Cal*,iv (i), p.599.

separate them into two strands. First, there were the continuing negotiations with the pope, but with the emphasis now on the 'customs of England', which the English envoys were instructed to inform Clement forbade any Englishman to appear in a foreign court against his will, but especially a king of England who had never acknowledged any superior but God! Given that at the same time they were instructed to threaten Clement with that anathema to all popes, a General Council, it is not altogether surprising that their initial reaction was to balk, explaining to Henry that they did not feel that either proposition would cut much ice with Clement just at that moment. [1] In this, of course they were quite right, but their explanation impressed Henry not at all. He much regretted, he informed them on 7 October, that they had refrained from alleging the 'customs of England', which he then proceeded to restate and justify at length, explaining that there was just as much evidence for them as for papal authority, and that, therefore, by some rather curious logic, to question one was to question the other. All of this he now ordered them to put to the pope as vigorously as possible. [2]

Meanwhile, early in September the papal nuncio, Antonio Borgho, had arrived in England just in time for the publication of a royal proclamation forbidding Henry's subjects from trying to obtain anything from Rome 'containing matter prejudicial to the high authority, jurisdiction, and prerogative royal of this his said realm'. [3] It may be that, as some ambassadors suggested, this prohibition was not directly related to the campaign for the divorce, but to the appeal to Rome by three English bishops against the anticlerical legislation of the first session of the Reformation parliament. And given that it did not prohibit the pope from summoning people to Rome, the issue that was most germane to the divorce, this is probably correct. [4] However, the bishops in question were Fisher, Clerk and West, all three Catherine's staunch defenders, which only serves to underline that at this time anticlericalism and the search for a divorce were inseparable, as Borgho was quickly to find out. When, quite understandably, he protested against the proclamation, Suffolk and Boleyn informed him that they 'cared neither for pope or popes in this kingdom, not even if St Peter should come to life again', and that Henry 'was absolute both as emperor and pope in his own kingdom'. Just in case the nuncio had failed to take the point, Suffolk apparently ended the interview by graciously admitting that despite all this, Henry was quite willing to be the pope's most devoted and obedient servant if only he would grant the divorce. [5]

The poor papal nuncio was going to endure a good deal of this kind of treatment in the following months, as Henry and his councillors tried every possible means to persuade him that any trial of Henry's matrimonial cause could only take place in England. [6] Meanwhile, every effort was made to widen the king's support. A second appeal to the universities of Europe was made, this time to secure their agreement to the proposition that it had always been the practice of the early Church to allow all

[1] LP,iv, app.262.
[2] LP,iv,6667 he continued, however,to keep his options open, instructing that if Clement would not accept their arguments they were to continue to press for delay.
[3] TRP, p.197.
[4] Bernard, JEH, 37, p.265 for best account, though he is sceptical of the ambassadors' reasons.
[5] Sp.Cal.,iv (i), pp.734-5.
[6] Ibid, pp.760-1, 797, 832-3.

causes to be tried in their country of origin, and that therefore the present practice of citing people to Rome was a gross usurpation of power.[1] At the same time the hard-pressed English envoys, already faced with the prospect of informing Clement of Henry's unacceptable views, were instructed to comb the Vatican Library for anything that touched upon this new obsession with the king's 'authority imperial', which, what with the sheer quantity of the material and the inevitable suspicions of the librarians, was, as they pointed out, a somewhat Herculean task and insofar as they did it, it produced quite the wrong answers.[2] Still, the point is that by the autumn of 1530 Henry was generating an enormous head of steam in his effort to prove, not only to the pope but to his own subjects, that his request to pronounce on the divorce in England was perfectly legitimate. But, of course, all this would avail him nothing if when it came to the point he could find nobody in England willing to grant it to him. If only to convince Clement that he really meant business, Henry had to ensure, and in a very public fashion, that the English Church, the most obvious alternative to the papacy as a sanctioning body, would do his bidding. His efforts to achieve this constitute the second strand of the new phase in the divorce campaign, and the one that was to affect Wolsey most.

On 11 July 1530 the attorney-general personally filed informations against fourteen leading churchmen accusing them of praemunire. The reason given was that by virtue of the financial compositions they had made with Wolsey – with which, it may be remembered, they had bought back from him their jurisdictional rights[3] – they had all connived in his illegal legatine authority.[4] Informations were subsequently filed against two others, one of whom was a notary public and lawyer, Anthony Husye, who practised in the court of arches. Why Husye was singled out is not entirely clear, but it looks as if his role was that of notional layman acting as a warning to all Henry's subjects that it was not only those in clerical orders who were liable to prosecution for praemunire.[5] Indeed, the point that was being made in the summer of 1530 was that anyone who had had anything to do with the Church during the period of Wolsey's papal legateship might suddenly find himself facing the possibility of imprisonment and the loss of all his goods and, given that Wolsey had admitted his guilt, with little prospect of mounting a successful defence.

Praemunire had always been in theory a potent weapon in the hands of the Crown, but like all such weapons its destructive power could be counterproductive, so it was not frequently used. In normal circumstances it benefited the Crown not at all to be at war with its subjects over the jurisdictional powers of an institution which by and large conferred upon it many more gains than losses. Henry's use of this weapon against fifteen members of that institution, amongst whom were eight bishops and three abbots, indicates both the intractability of the problem and his determination to overcome it. It has been pointed out that not all the fifteen

---

[1] Scarisbrick, *Henry VIII*, p. 267.

[2] Scarisbrick, *Bibl. d'Humanisme et Renaissance*, xxiv, pp. 211-5.

[3] See pp. 280-1.

[4] For this important episode see Bernard, *JEH*, 37; Guy, *EHR*, xcvii, and Scarisbrick, *Cambridge Historical Journal*, xii, and his 'Conservaive episcopate', pp. 114 ff. In the controversy between Bernard and Guy, I very much side with Bernard.

[5] Guy, *EHR*, xcvii, pp. 486-7; the discovery of these two was Guy's.

accused can be shown to have been passionate defenders of Catherine,[1] and indeed four had signed the recent letter to Clement imploring him to respond to Henry's rightful request.[2] But to conclude from this that the divorce was not the main reason for the praemunire charges is surely to miss the very large wood for a small group of trees? For one thing it ignores the fact that people sign things under pressure which they do not truly assent to, and there is evidence, at least in Sherburne's case, that this is what happened.[3] More importantly, such a conclusion suggests a misunderstanding of what Henry was after. It was not a case of getting his own back on particular people, but of frightening a powerful body of opinion into agreeing to what he wanted. What better way of doing this than to point a finger at three of the most senior abbots in the land, one of whom, John Islip of Westminster, was a very busy royal councillor? And there was no harm in throwing in the aged and not very influential Sherburne as a warning to all his episcopal colleagues to keep in line during the difficult months ahead, when the rival claims of king and pope to their alliegance were bound to cause them increasing worries.[4] What Henry was looking for was maximum impact, and his sacrificial lambs were well chosen. And with Fisher, Standish, West and Clerk included, who were all close to Catherine, there could not have been the slightest doubt in anybody's mind what his purpose was.

Then there was the question of influencing lay opinion. A leitmotiv of Henrician propaganda during the early 1530s was the highlighting of the enemy within: that is to say, the clergy whom Henry, as he himself, on one celebrated occasion in May 1532, was to point out to a parliamentary delegation, had thought to be 'our subjects wholly, but now we have well perceived that they be but half our subjects, yea, scarce our subjects'.[5] It was an effective tactic, because by appealing to a gut xenophobia – had not the accused sought the intervention of a foreign jurisdiction? – it distracted people from thinking too hard about what Henry was really up to: namely, ditching his wife and in the process destroying a whole set of beliefs and practices which most of his subjects were happy with. And from the propaganda point of view it did not really matter who was accused, though it would help if they were reasonably distinguished.

When on 11 July the first move against the accused was made, Henry was already aware that the vital component of his new tactics, the 'customs of England' and his 'authority imperial', had not gone down well with his leading subjects. At the meeting of 12 June about the letter to the pope, they had made their opposition clear.[6] What must have been all the more worrying for Henry is that dislike of the new tactics was coming not from partisans of Catherine such as Fisher and Clerk, who had not been invited to the meeting, but from the solid ranks of the Tudor establishment. If Henry was to succeed in any battle with the papacy, it was vital for him to win them over, and it was this that encouraged him to make an assault on the Church – or that at least is the suggestion being made here. Very little is known

[1] Ibid, p.484.
[2] Fuller, Islip, Melford and Sherburne.
[3] Bernard, JEH, 37, p.285.
[4] Chapuys was in no doubt about the connection between the praemunire charges and the divorce; see Sp.Cal.,iv (i), p.673.
[5] Hall, p.788.
[6] Sp.Cal.,iv (i), pp.598-9.

about Henry's meeting with his leading councillors at Hampton Court in August: only that it lasted five days, that Warham was amongst those summoned, and that at least for some of the time the French envoy, Joachim, was present.[1] Chapuys, our source for the meeting, believed that its chief purpose was to decide the next move in the divorce campaign, and even if negotiations with the French were also on the agenda, as the presence of Joachim suggests and as some of those present later alleged, this was hardly unrelated to the divorce. Moreover, on 17 August, the day after the meeting, a courier was dispatched to Rome possibly carrying with him instructions for the English envoys outlining the new tactics.[2] And whatever may have taken place there, the following weeks were to see a quickening of activity and, it has to be confessed an increase in the mystery, a reflection, in part, of Henry's success in preventing Council 'leaks',[3] as throughout August and September negotiations with the papal nuncio, Burgho continued. Needless to say, this gentleman was quite good at spinning things out, apparently going along with some of the suggestions put to him but without committing his master to anything, which must have been very frustrating.[4] Meanwhile, on 31 August a ban had been imposed preventing anyone leaving the Kent ports except for authorized business in Calais. There was much speculation about the reasons for this. Some even thought that it was a preventive measure against any attempt by Wolsey to flee the country, an idea which Chapuys rather pooh-poohed, believing that the current tricky stage of negotiations with the French was a sufficient explanation.[5]

However that may be, the ban was an unusual step to have taken, and indicative of the increasing strain that failure to secure a divorce was imposing upon Henry and his councillors. So much activity had resulted in so little progress, as letters that Henry received from his envoys in Rome on 30 September would have made all too clear to him.[6] Indeed, given that the wretched envoys had not even dared to carry out his most recent instructions, Henry might well feel that there had been no progress at all. Certainly, he felt in no position to meet parliament, which was due to reassemble on 1 October, but which he had prorogued until the 22nd.[7] Before it met he called yet another meeting to consider the divorce. Chapuys refers only to clergy and lawyers being present,[8] which suggests a more specialized gathering than at some of the previous meetings. And the question before them was in a sense a technical one: 'whether in virtue of the privileges possessed by this kingdom, parliament could and would enact that notwithstanding the pope's prohibition, this cause of the divorce be decided by the archbishop of Canterbury'.[9] Henry's problem was that, whatever view was taken of English privileges, it was most unlikely that they permitted an English bishop to decide upon a matter which the pope had

---

[1] Ibid, p.690.

[2] Ibid, p.690-1; this Chapuys's surmise, but since the envoys do not appear to have replied until 17 Sept. he may have been wrong (LP,iv,6667; LP App, 262.

[3] Sp.Cal.,iv (i), p.727.

[4] LP,iv,6618; Sp.Cal.,iv (i), pp.712, 719, 721-6, 734-6, 760-2.

[5] Ibid, p.709; also the view of the Milanese and Ventian ambassador (Mil.Cal.,827; Ven.Cal., iv, 629).

[6] LP App,262.

[7] LP,iv,6469; Sp.Cal.,iv (i), p.712, 719.

[8] Ibid, p.758.

[9] Ibid.

specifically forbidden anyone other than himself to consider. And that was precisely the view that the meeting took. No wonder that

> the king was very angry, and adopted the expedient of proroguing parliament till the month of February in the hope, as may be supposed, that in the meanwhile he may hit upon some means of bringing over to his opinion the said lawyers as well as some members of his parliament, with whose power he is continually threatening the pope, and see whether by compulsion or persuasion he can ultimately gain his end.[1]

And on the day that Henry learned the unwelcome verdict of his clergy and lawyers he was telling the papal nuncio that he was being very strongly urged to summon

> parliament for the punishment of the clergy who were indeed so hated throughout his kingdom, both by the nobles and the people, that but for his protection they would be utterly destroyed, and yet in spite of this urgent request he had determined to prorogue parliament till the month of February next, to see whether the pope would in the meantime adopt a different course of action towards him.[2]

This assessment of Henry's tactics is Chapuys's, as is the report of the meeting itself, for which he is the only source. The view here is that it is in essence correct, which, given the scepticism with which so many ambassadorial reports in this book have been greeted, calls for further comment. Chapuys's assessment convinces for two reasons. It ties in with the known facts concerning both the English negotiations at Rome and events at home, and particularly with the fact that parliament was indeed prorogued, though until January and not February as Chapuys first thought. It also makes a lot of sense. Henry was trying to threaten the pope with talk of parliament and the independent jurisdictional powers of the English Church, when neither body were quite as willing to do his bidding as he was pretending. To ensure that they were, the cardinal archbishop of York might be of some use to him.

When the October meeting took place, the sixteen praemunire charges were public knowledge, and it would have been understood how easy it would be for Henry to use the same weapon against anyone. It is thus all the more surprising, and rather to its credit, that the meeting chose not to come up with the answer that Henry was looking for. One explanation for why the threat did not work must surely be that many members of the Tudor establishment were rather more principled than has usually been allowed. It has been no part of the Protestant tradition to publicize opposition to the coming of the true religion, and although such events as More's and Fisher's executions have had to be incorporated into the story, that really large numbers of people were very unhappy with what was going on has been suppressed. But another explanation may be that Wolsey's pardon and subsequent generous treatment did not give the threat of praemunire quite the force that it would otherwise have had. It may even not have helped the legal case, because what the sixteen were accused of was participating with Wolsey in something that he had been forgiven for. All this is speculative,[3] but whatever the legal niceties, what was important for Henry was to create a climate of opinion which would make it more difficult for the sixteen, and for the Church as a whole, to resist his wishes; and it

---

[1] Ibid.

[2] Ibid, p.759. It is impossible to give a precise date for the meeting, but Chapuys's report is dated 15 Oct.

would not have helped to have the man most guilty of the crime of praemunire swanning around the diocese of York, while his so-called accomplices stood trial. Very much more to Henry's purpose would have been the spectacle of that man standing trial for treason, for there could hardly have been a more effective way of demonstrating that the Church was a thoroughly untrustworthy institution whose members were deserving of little sympathy from Henry's subjects.

The argument that Wolsey was arrested on an essentially trumped-up charge of conspiracy (the second possibility referred to earlier) makes an enormous amount of sense in the context of Henry's continuing campaign, and not only as regards motivation. It has already been pointed out that if the surviving evidence is taken at its face value, one has to explain why a government which was well aware of Wolsey's 'conspiratorial' activities by mid-July waited until the beginning of November to arrest him. If, on the other hand, there was no conspiracy, then there is far less difficulty in explaining the timing of the arrest. By the end of October it would have been clear to Henry that he would have to bring additional pressure to bear if he was going to persuade both Church and parliament to his point of view. Moreover, on 31 October nine of the sixteen accused of praemunire had failed to appear in King's Bench, amongst them three of Henry's most distinguished opponents, Clerk, Fisher and West. This act of defiance required some immediate counter-measure by the government:[1] accordingly the following day Walter Walsh was sent north to expedite Wolsey's arrest – this, at any rate, is the suggestion. Before looking at the many possible objections to it, two more points in its favour must be briefly touched upon.

When the nine failed to appear in court on 31 October they were summoned to appear on 20 January, by which time, according to Henry's latest decision on the matter, both parliament and southern convocation would have been in session for a week. What this meant was that when these bodies first met, the sword of Damocles would still be hanging over many of their members, inducing, it was to be hoped, the right frame of mind on all those issues relating to the divorce about which, to date, they had shown themselves to be so unco-operative. What it also meant was that once Wolsey was arrested there was no need for any urgency in proceeding against him. Indeed, the longer the delay the greater the tension that would build up amongst those under threat. Henry may also have been anxious to keep a number of options open, one of which may even have been Wolsey's restoration to the Council in return for doing Henry's bidding in the matter of the divorce. It would have been quite a desperate expedient, and there is no evidence to indicate that Henry was planning to make use of Wolsey in this way, unless, that is, there is some hint of it in a report by both Chapuys and the Milanese ambassador that shortly before Wolsey's arrest was ordered Henry exclaimed 'I miss the cardinal of York every day.'[2] Be that as it may, what Henry was looking for was a tame but

[3] See pp.623-4 were the opposite was suggested. One problem here is my lack of legal expertise; but it must also have been rather unchartered waters for the Crown lawyers, making contrary legal opinions possible.

[1] It is worth making the point that even if their non-appearance was not an act of defiance, the mere fact that Henry was anxious for a delay in both the prosecutions and the resummoning of parliament, suggests the weakness of his position and therefore a greater incentive to make use of Wolsey.

nonetheless important churchman to give credibility to a divorce secured without papal consent, a job description that the cardinal archbishop of York might be said to fit! And as we have seen, not only was Wolsey's journey southwards in all the circumstances surprisingly leisurely, but also he was treated remarkably well, being assured by his custodians more than once that the king meant him no harm. Now, of course, it is well recognized that a contented prisoner is one who will give his custodians no trouble, and clearly these assurances do not prove that in return for granting him a divorce Henry intended to let Wolsey off the charge of treason. All that can be said is that given Henry's manipulation of people such as Cranmer and Gardiner in the 1540s,[1] it is not inconceivable that in the autumn of 1530 Henry contemplated making use of Wolsey in this way.

Finally, the scenario that is being proposed does help to make more sense of the extraordinary nature of the conspiracy that Wolsey was allegedly at the head of – the very extraordinariness, it was argued earlier, that helps to make such a conspiracy so unlikely. But as a government invention it makes considerable sense. The reason for the emperor's and pope's alleged complicity in it hardly needs any comment: in the matter of the divorce they were the enemy, and anything that embarrassed them or told against them was grist to the mill. But why implicate the French, on whose support Henry was very much relying? More specifically, why was it that the only bit of concrete evidence that the Crown ever produced for Wolsey's conspiratorial activity was that letter which he had supposedly asked Agostini to write to the French ambassador detailing the plot, and why, whatever its validity, show it to the French king ? It was an odd way of maintaining good relations between the two countries, though not so odd when it is borne in mind that, as was mentioned earlier, they were at this time engaged in difficult negotiations over their complicated financial arrangements. There was a whole series of diplomatic missions, with much huffing and puffing on both sides, and it may well be that the embargo of 31 July on people leaving the country had something to do with these missions.[2] During much of October Joachim was to be found holidaying at Dover, not a very usual way for a foreign envoy to pass the time.[3] Meanwhile, all the foreign ambassadors were reporting that the negotiations between England and France were going badly.[4] Thus Chapuys, writing on 31 October, referred to the French having made 'so many and such exorbitant conditions' that Henry had become exceedingly angry, but now they were 'trying to make matters straight again, and have the conditions demanded by the French modified'.[5] In this context it did make some sense politely to draw the attention of the French to the embarrassing fact of Wolsey's treasonable negotiations with them. It also made sense for the French to

---

[2] Mil.Cal. 833; Sp.Cal.,iv (i), p.819 [His report of 27 Nov.]. See LP,xvi,590 for rather similar remarks about Cromwell after his fall.

[1] See especially L. Baldwin Smith, 28 ff, though one needs to bear in mind that the politics of the 1540s is much disputed.

[2] So thought Chapuys and the Milanese ambassador (Sp.Cal.,iv (i), pp.711, 720-1; Mil.Cal., 827; the suggestion being that in order to strengthen his hand with the French envoys Henry was anxious temporarily to cut the links between them and Francis.

[3] Sp.Cal.,iv (i), pp.737, 788.

[4] Ibid, 711-2; Mil.Cal., 827; Ven.Cal.,iv,618.

[5] Sp.Cal.,iv (i), pp.790-1.

distance themselves from Wolsey as much as they could; hence Francis's remarks about his 'pompous and ambitious' heart and humble origins.[1]

The view being put forward here, that Wolsey's arrest was but another ploy in Henry's desperate quest for a divorce, rests upon no direct evidence, and neither has it found favour with historians, who have all more or less accepted that, as the Crown maintained, Wolsey had been involved in a conspiracy. Furthermore, if this alone is not considered to deal the view a fatal blow, there are some weaknesses in the argument that must be tackled now. First, the question of timing. Much importance has been attached in this account to the connection between Wolsey's arrest and the praemunire charges against the sixteen. Indeed, it has even been suggested that it was the failure of nine of them to appear in court that led directly to it. A difficulty in accepting this view arises from Cromwell's letter to Wolsey of 21 October – incidentally the last communication that has survived between the two men – in which he wrote that 'the parliament is prorogued until the sixth day of January. The prelates shall not appear in the praemunire. There is another way devised in place thereof as your grace shall further know.'[2] Cromwell's 'other way' has usually been taken to refer to a decision to bring pressure upon the Church through parliament rather than through the law courts, a decision which was to result in the famous Act for the Pardon of the Clergy of March 1531.[3] If this is so, it can then be argued that the Crown would have had very little interest in whether those accused of praemunire showed up or not, and indeed it is possible that those who defaulted dared to do so only because they were aware of the government's change of plan.[4] In such a scenario Wolsey's arrest would not have had much significance: it was Henry's manipulation of parliament that was going to provide the pressure, not Wolsey's final humiliation. And even if it is countered, as it will be, that the one does not preclude the other and that in any scenario parliament was going to play an important part, what would be extremely difficult to argue is that the final decision to arrest Wolsey was a consequence of the nine's decision not to appear.

There are no easy rejoinders to these criticisms, but given that the large gaps in the evidence make any interpretation very provisional, they are not such that the view put forward here has to be rejected. In the first place, what Cromwell meant by this piece of information, or what authority should be attached to it, is not as clear as it has sometimes been taken to be. Whatever his precise position in royal government at this time, he was not involved in the making of major policy decisions, nor is there any reason to suppose that he had access to any privileged information.[5] One reason for being so confident about both these things is that the closer Cromwell became to Henry the less likely it is that he would have either

---

[1] St. P, vii, p.213.

[2] PRO Cotton app, xlviii, fo.110 (LP, iv, 6699).

[3] Guy, *Sir Thomas More*, pp.136-8, but revised in *EHR*, xcvii, pp.487-8; see also Scarisbrick, *Henry VIII*, 274 ff. and Elton, *Reform and Reformation*, pp.130-140, where he makes little of Cromwell's letter, but is anxious to connect the new direction in Henry's campaign for a divorce in the autumn of 1530 with Cromwell and his fellow radicals.

[4] Guy, *EHR*, xcvii, p.487.

[5] When Cromwell assumed a leading position is a crux that may never be resolved, but see *inter alia*, Elton, *Tudor Revolution*, pp.71-91. However, it really cannot have been until at least late 1531.

dared or wished to pass on confidential information to his former master, particularly if he had any reason to believe that the former master was about to be arrested for high treason. Secondly, it is most unlikely that any very dramatic decision had been made as regards the praemunire prosecutions. The notion that the government had decided to drop them in favour of a charge against the whole of the English clergy cannot be sustained, for the simple reason that this did not happen.[1] Instead, at least the nine who had defaulted would be appearing in court on 20 January, shortly after parliament had reassembled. As suggested earlier, there could hardly have been a better way of encouraging MPs to think carefully before opposing the royal wishes; but the point is that the government had always seen a connection between the prosecutions and parliamentary pressure on the Church, since what it was looking for was some kind of parliamentary authorization for the Church to grant a divorce. The original cases had been timed to coincide with the sitting of parliament, and Cromwell's cryptic remark probably only referred to the fact that the recent prorogation had made a nonsense of that timing, which now needed to be adjusted. But an alternative explanation does present itself. What Henry had done in October by proroguing parliament was to buy himself a little time – time in which, perhaps, to tighten the screws by moving against Wolsey, or even to make use of him to pronounce his first marriage null and void? If this is so, then it may be that Cromwell was trying to convey some kind of coded message to his former master, something he might have attempted just because he was not in the inner ring of royal advisers. A possible scenario might be that he knew of the prorogation, for that after all was public knowledge. He would have deduced that this might affect the praemunire prosecutions. He may have heard rumours that some of the accused bishops had decided not to turn up; he could hardly have known for certain that they would not because that decision was the bishops', not, as in some accounts is assumed, the Crown's. He may also have picked up rumours of a decision affecting Wolsey. Putting all these things together, he might then have written as he did, not daring to be more explicit about what he had gleaned concerning Wolsey's fate. It is a scenario that may appear bizarre, but it seems to make at least as much sense as any other, particularly of Cromwell's remark that Wolsey would 'further know' about the praemunire prosecutions. This is unlikely to have been a reference to some new parliamentary tactics which the Crown had decided upon *vis-à-vis* the Church. Even if it is assumed that the government had just made some important decision about the prosecutions, and that, contrary to the view advanced earlier, Cromwell was privy to the decision, there is no earthly reason why Wolsey would have received any information about something that was inevitably of a confidential nature until, that is, it was put into effect some three months hence. That 'as your grace shall further know' suggests something more immediate than this, and, moreover, something that might affect Wolsey more closely.

Another criticism of the view of events being advanced is that it ignores some important evidence concerning Wolsey's arrest that in most accounts has been given some prominence. When in mid-July 1530 Norfolk had informed Chapuys of

---

[1] The notion was originally Scarisbrick's in *Cambridge Historical Journal*, xii, 27-9, but in my view successfuly challenged by Guy in *EHR*, xcvii, 488-90.

Wolsey's plotting, he had made a point of saying that, come what may, the cardinal 'would never again either see or speak with the king', adding that the information about the conspiracy had only been revealed to him by those closest to Wolsey, because they knew that it could harm no one but himself, the duke.[1] Three months later, and only about a fortnight before Wolsey's arrest, a former member of Wolsey's household, Thomas Arundel, reported to Wolsey a conversation with Norfolk, who had told him that he did not believe that Wolsey no longer aspired to any position of authority, 'for he said that he had both your grace's hand to the contrary, and knew three messages, sent by three divers persons, of your grace to the king, whereby it might well appear that you desired as much authority as ever you did'.[2] And that this was not entirely an invention of Norfolk's paranoia is indicated by the fact that at one point Henry himself had informed Cromwell that he understood that Wolsey had been trying to stir up trouble between himself and the duke.[3]

That Wolsey's arrest was the result of Norfolk's and his supporters' fear that he might make a come-back was an explanation put forward, though not with any great conviction, by both Chapuys and the Milanese ambassador.[4] For Cavendish there was no uncertainty:

> My lord's accustomed enemies in the court about the king had now my lord in more doubt than they had before his fall, considering the continual favour that the king bare him; [they] thought at length the king might call him home again and, if he so did, they supposed that he would rather imagine against them than remit or forget their cruelty which they most unjustly imagined against him. Wherefore they compassed in their heads that they would either by some means dispatch him by some sinister accusation of treason, or to bring him into the king's high indignation by some other ways.[5]

And if this was Cavendish's mature assessment, it was no doubt based, in part at least, on his recollection of Wolsey's own words to Walter Walsh immediately after his arrest:

> I doubt not for my part but I shall prove and clear myself to be a true man against the expectation of all my cruel enemies. I have an understanding whereupon all this matter groweth . . . Put therefore the king's commission and your authority in execution, in God's name, and spare not, and I will obey the king's will and pleasure. For I fear more the cruelty of my unmerciful enemies than I do my truth and allegiance.[6]

In Cavendish's account, Wolsey probably meant by his 'enemies' the Boleyns, especially a certain 'serpentine enemy . . . (I mean the night crow)',[7] alias Anne, rather than Norfolk; and Chapuys too at one point placed the emphasis upon 'the lady', whom he reported as threatening to leave Henry if he ever allowed Wolsey to

[1] *Sp.Cal*,iv (1), p.630.
[2] *LP*,iv,6688.
[3] Bodleian Library, MS Jesus Coll 74, fo.194; see also Pollard, *Wolsey*, p.288.
[4] Bradford, pp.323-7 (*Sp Cal*,iv (i), pp.819-21); *Mil.Cal.*, 832, a view he ascribes to those more friendly to Wolsey, 'who attribute everything to the envy and fear of his rivals'.
[5] Cavendish, p.150.
[6] Ibid, p.156.
[7] Ibid, p.137.

return.[1] . As most accounts assume that the Boleyns and Norfolk were still at this stage as one, this multiplication of Wolsey's enemies hardly matters; essentially it is the old aristocratic faction back to its dirty tricks again. What, of course, does complicate matters is the argument of the previous chapter that this faction had not existed: its alleged members were in no sense committed enemies of Wolsey's, and even if they had been, they lacked the necessary skill and determination to bring him down. Above all, and despite the king's all too obvious infatuation for Anne, they were never the king's masters.

How to get over this problem? On the one hand, there is the particular evidence of a paranoid Norfolk and a 'serpentine' Anne's determination to prevent any come-back by Wolsey. On the other, there are the conclusions already reached concerning those who were supposedly Wolsey's enemies, which suggest that they would have been neither able nor especially anxious to prevent his return. One oddity about the particular evidence has already been pointed out: that Norfolk by his own account was in full command of all the facts about Wolsey's alleged conspiracy by mid-July, but that no action was taken about it until early November. Another is that he was willing to tell a foreign ambassador about it, especially one who was known to have been in contact with Wolsey and whose master was supposedly involved in the plotting. And why did he talk in the rather aggressive way that he did about Wolsey's continuing political ambitions to someone like Arundel, who was almost certainly going to report what he was saying back to Wolsey? It was all very indiscreet, not to say downright foolish, for it makes no sense to tip off one's political opponent just before destroying him. If, on the other hand, he is not much of a threat, and one is not about to destroy him, it might make more sense and in two ways. First, it could be a way of obtaining information. Secondly, it could be a way of conveying messages. What Wolsey was up to had to be of concern to Norfolk, not because Wolsey was a lifelong enemy whom he was determined to do down at all costs, but because as a leading royal servant it was Norfolk's job to keep his eye on all potential troublemakers, which as a recently disgraced minister of the Crown Wolsey had to be. His contacts with foreign governments were known about, as was his popularity in the North. Probably all this was quite harmless, but it was worth monitoring from time to time. By mentioning a conspiracy, or by making some provocative remark about Wolsey's continuing ambitions, Norfolk would have hoped to elicit a reaction from his listener which might be informative. It would also be a gentle way of warning everybody concerned that the government was not stupid, and that therefore they should resist any temptation to do anything silly.

There are further reasons for doubting whether this evidence adds up to much. Norfolk's mention of Wolsey's plotting occurred very much *en passant* in the course of a long interview with Chapuys. What happened was that the role that the French, and in particular the bishop of Tarbes, might play in furthering the divorce had come up, and this had given Norfolk the opportunity to launch an attack on the bishop's remarks on his and his fellow councillors' competence to the effect that they were not a patch on the former lord chancellor. Moreover, Chapuys had been stirring things up by suggesting that at any moment Wolsey would return courtesy of

[1] *Sp.Cal.*, iv (i), p.819.

the French, a suggestion given some credibility by the cardinal's close relationship with the French while in power. Wolsey's presence in the wings undoubtedly made life more difficult for Norfolk because it could be made use of by foreign powers and not only for Norfolk. It did not do Henry's reputation much good either for rumours to be circulating that he was so in the pocket of the French king that he was likely to recall a disgraced minister at their request. Little wonder that Norfolk was anxious to scotch all such rumours: not only was Wolsey not going to return to power, but all his secret negotiations with the French were already known to the government, who could put an end to them whenever it liked. This is what Norfolk told Chapuys,[1] but in doing so it is highly unlikely that he was disclosing information of any great significance concerning a serious threat to Henry's throne, masterminded by Wolsey. Rather, he was simply making use of the continuing contact between Wolsey and Joachim, which it should be remembered the government had authorized, to try to put an end to harmful diplomatic gossip. And that this is how Chapuys perceived it is suggested by the fact that he made no further comment to the emperor about Wolsey's plotting, which if he had ever taken it seriously, he surely would have done. And as a coda it is worth pointing out that however suspicious Norfolk had shown himself to be to Arundel about Wolsey's continuing political ambitions, it had not prevented him from promising that 'in all reasonable causes' he would be as good a friend to Wolsey as Arundel could desire.[2]

As was suggested in the previous chapter, most interpretations of Norfolk's role in Wolsey's destruction derive from preconceptions about his relationship with Wolsey which should probably be dispensed with. Moreover, whatever Norfolk's personal views about Wolsey, it is highly unlikely that they would have figured uppermost in his day-to-day conduct of Henry's business, or that he would have gone out of his way to tell Chapuys, or indeed Arundel, about them; the conduct of the king's affairs was a rather more serious business than that. First and foremost, Wolsey was for Norfolk but one factor in the conduct of the king's affairs, and it is in this light that one should evaluate the evidence of what he said about Wolsey in the months before his arrest. And if this is done, the evidence will be seen to lend little weight to the theory that the arrest was a pre-emptive strike to prevent the cardinal's return to power.

It will have been noticed that in arriving at this conclusion the question of whether or not there was a conspiracy led by Wolsey could not be kept out. This is not surprising, since everything in this chapter turns on the answer. If there was a conspiracy, then the interpretation of Wolsey's last months is relatively straightforward. Interesting problems would be raised about the motivation of all those involved. There would remain some worries about its extent, and whether it was precisely as the Crown alleged. But that Henry was forced to move against his former lord chancellor, who had repaid his generous treatment by plotting with various foreign powers against him, would provide the bare bones of a simple story. But although it is a story that clearly Henry wanted everyone to believe, and for which the greatest amount of evidence has survived, here it has been rejected. So, also, has the 'sensible view', which has it that there was no conspiracy by anybody,

---

[1] Ibid, p.630.
[2] PRO SP1/58/fo.135v (LP,iv,6688).

just a good deal of mutual suspicion and misunderstanding. It may be felt that not enough attention has been paid to this view, but once Wolsey is freed from suspicion it is hard to take a benign view of Henry. After all, if there was no conspiracy, then the case that he made against Wolsey to Bryan was a pack of lies,[1] in support of which he had been prepared to bribe and bully a former confidant of Wolsey's into providing false evidence. There was nothing naïve or muddled in all this, nor indeed should one expect it. By insisting against all the odds on marrying Anne, and in the process changing his kingdom's religious practice and beliefs, Henry took enormous risks. That he succeeded in getting his way suggests that he was a ruthless and skilful political operator, not at all a man to have overlooked the dangers inherent in allowing Wolsey to take up his duties as archbishop of York, or, once he had allowed this, to have been easily panicked into having him arrested. To accept the 'sensible view' one would have to revise completely the picture of Henry that has so far been drawn, and the evidence in its favour by no means calls for such a revision.

We are left with the second possibility, that it was Henry who conspired against Wolsey, as the only credible interpretation, despite the fact that the evidence is almost entirely circumstantial. The reasons for believing in it are, nevertheless, strong. Given the continuing unhappiness about, not to say opposition to, his desire for a divorce both at Rome and amongst his leading subjects, both lay and clerical, it would have been remarkable if Henry had not tried to make some use of a cardinal archbishop with whom he could do more or less as he wanted. That the story as put out by Henry could belong only to the world of Walter Mitty merely increases the suspicion that he did precisely that. But for those who like their evidence cut and dried it will not convince. And Wolsey's death before Henry's intentions could be revealed makes any interpretation more than usually provisional. Still, it would be very surprising if any direct evidence for what Henry was up to had survived, since it would have served him not at all for it to have got out that a conspiracy had been a set-up. One possible danger was Agostini, who in this scenario would have been all too well aware of the lengths to which the government had gone to invent a case against Wolsey. The way round it was that curious recognizance by which Agostini promised on pain of a fine of £100 not to reveal to anyone what was contained in a book 'written with his own hand concerning the late cardinal of York'.[2] It was also probably fear of what might emerge about the set-up that explains why surprisingly – whatever one's interpretation of the events – the government did so little to exploit the propaganda value of Wolsey's 'treason', which by no means needed to disappear with his death. Interestingly, insofar as it was exploited at all, it was very briefly used with the French who, just because they were more anxious than the others to keep in with Henry, were the least likely to challenge the official story. What is also true is that a dead Wolsey provided Henry with neither the room for manoeuvre nor the impact

---

[1] BL Add. MS 48066, fos.184, 186-7; St.P,vii, pp.211-5 (LP,iv,6733).

[2] PRO SP1/58/fo.215 (LP,iv,6763); also A.F. Pollard, p.295, n.3. His suggestion that the bond was extracted because the government was anxious to prevent anything coming out that would in some way jeopardize England's relations with foreign powers could have some truth in it, but any embarrassment would have been much greater if they had learnt that the conspiracy they were supposed to be involved in was Henry's invention!

that he had hoped for. A posthumous trial would have been an anti-climax, while a dead man could hardly grant him a divorce. One way and another, it probably seemed better to let the matter drop.

As this book draws to a close, it is proper that the focus of attention should return to the man whose political career has been its subject. Wolsey had reached Southwell, in the south of his very extensive diocese of York, on 28 April, and there he remained for the next three months. He was extremely busy, performing both the role of pastoral bishop and that of leading representative of the Crown, keeping open house for the important families of the area and helping to settle their disputes.[1] The high point was to have been his enthronement as archbishop in the great abbey church of St Mary's, York, on Monday 7 November, when he had hoped also to open northern convocation. As it was, his arrest on the 4th intervened, prompting some people to argue that it was precisely to prevent his enthronement that it occurred when it did. Far from being unpopular in the North, he had won golden opinions from almost everybody; and almost everybody of importance would have been present at York for his enthronement. This surely was the moment for him to declare his hand, and in the name of Catherine, or the pope, or the emperor, or Francis, or perhaps in the name of all of them – it is all so unlikely that it hardly matters who it was – to declare war upon his former master.[2] In this version of events Wolsey's performance as the good bishop is entirely hypocritical, calculated only to secure for himself a power base from which to attack the king. But there is no inconsistency between Wolsey the active resident bishop and Wolsey the cardinal legate and lord chancellor. There has been no attempt in this study to portray him as a deeply religious man, but he certainly believed that active intervention in the affairs of the day, whether national or local, was to the benefit of the common weal. It was very much in his nature to get involved. He also had great confidence in his own ability to put things right, and justifiably so. Negotiator *par excellence*, it mattered little to him whether the dispute was between humble villagers or pope and emperor. So it is not at all surprising that, having been denied the larger theatre, he threw all his energies into the life of his diocese.

And if one has to admit that his conduct in the North would have been the same even if more Machiavellian motives had lain behind it, the same can hardly be said of the many other matters which occupied him at this time. He was still embroiled in trying to rescue as much from his initial downfall as possible: organizing a defence of his colleges, which involved trying to secure the support of all those supposedly his enemies such as Norfolk and the Boleyns;[3] fighting off attempts to exploit his conviction for praemunire in order to secure the title to archiepiscopal land;[4] and coping with demands from hither and yon for the payment of past bills and debts, the inevitable consequence of his loss of political clout and credit-worthiness.[5] Moreover, he found that the lack of a resident archbishop, whatever its effect on

[1] Cavendish specifically mentions that between the Tempests and the Hastings; see Cavendish, p.145.
[2] Pollard, *Wolsey*, p.297. For the belief that he would be unpopular but was not see *inter alia Sp.Cal.*, iv (i), p.515; *LP*,iv,6571; *Mil.Cal.*, 817.
[3] *Inter alia, LP*,iv,6330, 6377, 6510, 6523, 6578-9, 6663, 6666.
[4] *LP*,iv,6475, 6554, 6555, 6571.
[5] *LP*,iv,6302, 6335, 6344, 6545.

the spiritual life of the diocese, had certainly done nothing for the archiepiscopal properties. Many repairs were needed, which Wolsey maintained were of an extremely modest and essential kind, while to his enemies they smacked of his usual extravagance and love of magnificence.[1] Then in August he was faced with the demands of a former comptroller of his household, Thomas Strangeways. For some reason, perhaps because in a quarrel between him and Thomas Cromwell Wolsey had sided with the latter, this man appears to have formed a grudge against the cardinal. At any rate, Wolsey's political disgrace gave him an opportunity to appeal to the Council concerning the sum of £700 which he claimed Wolsey owed him in connection with a wardship. It was all extremely aggravating, not least because any claim for money at this time was an acute embarrassment.[2]

In none of these matters did Wolsey show many signs of giving in to the pressures imposed by his new circumstances. True, he had to write letters to former colleagues seeking their help, and to that extent he had to be conciliatory. During the 1520s he had usually signed himself in letters to Norfolk as his 'loving friend',[3] but by August 1530 he had become 'your daily chaplain and bedesman'.[4] What he did not do – despite much prompting – was to give in on what he considered to be matters of substance. As we have seen, many people, including Norfolk, had advised him to stop badgering the king and to be content with what he had got.[5] But the very last thing Wolsey was during the last months of his life was content, nor was he at all averse to letting people know it, including foreign ambassadors. Earlier it was suggested that what Wolsey was hoping to gain from these contacts was the support of their masters for his efforts to recover everything he had lost at his downfall, in return for which he would do his utmost to further their causes. With Chapuys, at least, he frequently raised the issue of the divorce, apparently offering advice very favourable to Catherine. If that advice is taken at its face value, it will incline one to the view that he was up to no good though, as was pointed out earlier, to be in favour of Catherine at this time was technically no crime. What was also suggested was that it would be wrong to take this particular evidence at face value. All Wolsey was doing was making noises that he knew would please Chapuys who would then favour his cause, but in the full knowledge that his advice was neither here nor there and that he was not giving anything away. This was more or less what the Milanese ambassador reported Wolsey had been up to,[6] and it makes a good deal of sense, especially when the very public nature of Wolsey's contacts with these foreign ambassadors is borne in mind. There is little to suggest that Wolsey's or his chaplain's letters to Chapuys were clandestine ones, nor that Chapuys took Wolsey's suggestions very seriously. One way and another, for supposedly one of the best political operators in Europe, Wolsey seems to have gone about organizing his conspiracy in a curious way. Short of writing to Henry to tell him of it, he could hardly have behaved with greater stupidity, on the one hand drawing attention to himself by his constant complaints and high profile, and on the other making no

---

[1] LP,iv,6329, 6341, 6344, 6447, 6545, 6571.
[2] LP,iv,6571, 6582, 6583-8.
[3] Inter alia St.P,iv,145, 152 (LP,iv, 662, 687).
[4] St.P,i,p.368 (LP,iv,6582).
[5] See p.615.
[6] Mil.Cal., 838.

secret of his many contacts with foreign powers. It really makes no sense at all – unless the truth is that he felt no need to behave in a Machiavellian way because he did not believe that what he was up to was in any way treasonable.

This was certainly Wolsey's own view, for on his arrest on 4 November he immediately declared his innocence to the two men to whom the task of making the arrest had been delegated, the earl of Northumberland and Walter Walsh.[1] And it was a declaration that he was to repeat to each of his new custodians in turn. The earl of Shrewsbury, whose treatment of him could hardly have been more courteous and sensitive, received many protestations of his innocence, and to this effect: if someone who owed everything to Henry's favour and who now, when his enemies had gained the upper hand, was more in need of his support than ever before, should have set about conspiring against him, then, indeed, 'all men might justly think and report that I lacketh not only grace, but also both wit and discretion'.[2] All he now wanted to do was to prove his innocence by confronting his so far unnamed accusers in the king's presence, 'when I doubt not but you shall see me acquit myself of all their malicious accusations and utterly confound them'.[3]

It was while he was staying with Shrewsbury that the first symptoms of the illness that was to kill him appeared, difficult to diagnose at this distance in time, but he himself seems to have thought that he was suffering from some form of dysentery,[4] and certainly diarrhoea and sickness were the most obvious symptoms. He had no illusions about his chances of surviving, and was to predict the exact hour of his death the day before it occurred,[5] if that is not a literary embellishment of Cavendish's. In a final interview with Sir William Kingston, keeper of the Tower, who had recently arrived to escort him on the last part of his journey south, he was very conscious of his impending death, and that it was going to be God rather than the king to whom he would have to answer, and that God could in no way be deceived.[6] His remarks were, therefore, much more than a defence against a specific charge; and in fact his last words were a warning of the dangers of 'this new perverse sect of the Lutherans' who, like past heretical sects, would destroy not only the clergy but the whole natural order of things, unless Henry moved swiftly against them. As for what had befallen him, he saw it as God's judgment; for, in those much quoted words, he felt sure that if he had served him 'as diligently as I have done the king, he would not have given me over in my grey hairs. Howbeit this is the just reward that I must receive for my worldly diligence and pains that I have had to do him service, only to satisfy his vain pleasures, not regarding my godly duty'.[7] He then ventured to issue Kingston a warning, which has perhaps been too often ignored by historians. Henry, he told his custodian, was

> *a prince of royal courage, and hath a princely heart; and rather than he will either miss or want any part of his will or appetite, he will put the loss of one half of his realm in danger. For I assure you I have often kneeled before him in his privy chamber on my*

[1] Cavendish, p.156.
[2] Ibid. p.165.
[3] Ibid, p.166
[4] Ibid, pp.167, 178.
[5] Ibid, p.181-2.
[6] Ibid, pp.178-81.
[7] Ibid, p.178-9.

knees the space of an hour or two to persuade him from his will and appetite; but I could never bring to pass to dissuade him therefrom. Therefore, Master Kingston, if it chance hereafter you to be one of his privy council (as for your wisdom and other qualities ye be meet so to be) I warn you to be well advised and assured what matter ye put into his head; for ye shall never pull it out again.[1]

The picture is of a Henry that readers of this book will recognize. It is hoped that what also emerges is a Wolsey who will be recognized, not least the man who, even at this unpropitious time, in his complimenting of Kingston did not fail to show his accustomed charm. It may be objected that what is being presented here is fiction. The source for this last scene, as indeed for Wolsey's arrest and subsequent journey south, is almost entirely Cavendish, and it can be argued that he could hardly have remembered the conversations he purported to have had with Wolsey when, nearly thirty years later, he sat down to write. At worst, the whole account could have been a white lie. The truth that Cavendish was concerned with was not the kind that the professional historian of today spends much time worrying about; and, particularly where Wolsey's downfall and the destruction of the Catholic Church in England merge, it may well be that he thought the message was more important than any literal report. Be that as it may, I find his account of Wolsey's last weeks on the whole convincing; and without wanting to be paradoxical, it is fair to say that even those aspects of his account that have not been accepted help to reinforce this conviction. In the circumstances that Wolsey found himself in, it would be surprising if he had not come to believe that there were enemies at work determined to destroy him. That someone to whom one has devoted one's life no longer needs one is the kind of unbearable fact that many people have chosen to ignore, even when the evidence is there for all to see. Moreover, when that person is a sixteenth century king it becomes even harder, for built into the panoply of sixteenth century kingship was the notion that he could do no wrong. And, of course, if Wolsey did believe that it was his enemies who destroyed him, then Cavendish was right to record the fact. That he accepted it is no more surprising than that Wolsey believed it – none of which, however, is proof that either man was right.

As an account of what took place, and of what Wolsey was thinking Cavendish's rings true, and, for what it is worth, receives some support from the very few other surviving accounts of Wolsey's last days, especially as regards the issue that has been of most concern: whether or not he had conspired against the king. On 4 December Chapuys noted that Wolsey had 'prepared for his death like a good Christian. At the time of receiving the holy sacrament he protested that he had never undertaken anything to his sovereign's prejudice'.[2] Two days earlier the Milanese ambassador had sent home a somewhat fuller account. Like Cavendish, he refers to Kingston's sympathetic treatment of the cardinal, and his account of the medical symptoms is very similar. As for the deathbed scene itself, the Milanese ambassador's was, in fact, the more dramatic:

According to report, his mind never wandered at the last, and on seeing Captain Kingston, he made his attendants raise him in his bed, where he knelt, and whenever he

---

[1] Ibid, p.179.
[2] Bradford, p.336 (*Sp.Cal.*,iv (i), p.833).

heard the king's name mentioned, he bowed his head, putting his face downwards. He then asked Captain Kingston where his guards were, and being answered that lodging was provided for them in several chambers on the ground floor of the palace, he requested that they might all be sent for into his presence. As many having entered as the place would hold, and having raised himself as much as he could, he said that on the day before he had taken the sacrament and expected to find himself soon before the supreme judgment seat, and that in such extremity he ought not to fail in speaking the truth, or leave any other opinion of him than such as was veracious. He added, I pray God that that sacrament may be the damnation of my soul if ever I thought to do disservice to my king.[1]

According to Cavendish, Wolsey had spent all his remaining energies in his final interview with Kingston, so that by the time the guards were summoned to witness the end he was already almost unconscious. Moreover, in that interview he had been less concerned with the issue of his guilt as regards the particular charge of treason. Instead, he took a longer view, asking to be

commended unto his royal majesty, beseeching him in my behalf to call to his most gracious remembrance all matters proceeding between him and me from the beginning of the world unto this day, and the progress of the same. And most chiefly in the weighty matter yet depending (meaning the matter newly begun between him and good Queen Catherine) then shall his conscience declare whether I have offended him or no.[2]

The answer that Wolsey wanted and expected is the answer that this book has ended up providing. Unfortunately, what has also emerged is that it was a terrible error of judgement for him to have believed that his king would take his past record into consideration when deciding on his future. But then, as one of the most perceptive observers of the English political scene, the French ambassador du Bellay, had realized, the key to an understanding of Thomas Wolsey is that he loved his master more than himself.[3]

---

[1] Mil. Cal., 833.
[2] Cavendish, p.179.
[3] Bellay, Correspondence, p.20 (LP,iv,5610).

Bibliography

Adams, R.P. *The Better Part of Valour* (Seattle, 1962).

Adams, S. 'Eliza enthroned? The court and its politics' in *The Reign of Elizabeth I*, ed. C. Haigh (1984).

Alcock, N.W. 'Enclosure and depopulation in Burton Dassett: a 16th century view', *Warwickshire History*, 3 (1977).

'Warwickshire grazier and London skinner, 1532-1555', *Records of Social and Economic History*, new ser., iv (1981).

Allen, P.S. 'Dean Colet and Archbishop Warham', *EHR*, xvii (1902).

Anderson, Andrew H. 'Henry, Lord Stafford (1501-63) and the lordship of Caus', *Welsh History Review*, 6 (1972-3).

Angelo, S. *Spectacle, Pageantry and Early Tudor Policy* (1969).

Arber, E. (ed.) *The First Printed English New Testament* (1871).

Associated Architectural Societies Reports and Papers, xxviii (1905-6).

Aston, M. *Lollards and Reformers: image of literacy in late medieval England* (1984).

—'Lollards and literacy', *History*, lx (1977).

Aston, T.H. 'Oxford's medieval alumni', *PP* 74 (1977).

Aston, T.H., Duncan, G.D. and Evans, T.A.R. 'The medieval alumni of the university of Cambridge', *PP*, 86 (1980).

Baker, J.H. (ed) *The Reports of Sir John Spelman*, Selden Society, (2 vols, 1977-8).

Bangor, the Diocese of, being a digest of the Registers of the Bishops, A.D. 1512-1646, ed. A.I.Pryce (1923).

Baldwin, J.F. *The King's Council in England during the Middle Ages* (1913).

Barlowe, Jerome *The Burial of the Mass* (Arber reprint, 1871).

Barraclough, G. *Papal Provisions* (1935).

Baskerville, G. *The English Monks and the Suppression of the Monasteries* (1937).

Bean, J.M.W. *The Estates of the Percy Family, 1416-1537* (1958).

Behrens, B. 'The office of the English resident ambassador: its evolution as illustrated by the career of Sir Thomas Spinelly, 1509-22', *TRHS*, 4th. ser, xvi (1933).

Beir, A.L. *The Problem of the Poor in Tudor and Early Stuart England* (1983).

Bellamy, J.G. *The Law of Treason in England in the Later Middle Ages* (1970).

—*Crime and Public Order in England in the Later Middle Ages* (1973).

—*Criminal Law and Society in Late Medieval and Tudor England* (1984).

Bellay, Jean du *Ambassades en Angleterre de* , ed. V.-L. Bourilly and P. de Vaissire (Archives de l'histoire religieuse de la France, 1905).

—*Correspondence du Cardinal Jean du*, ed R. Scheurer (Société de l'Histoire de France, 1969).

Beresford, M. and Hurst, J.G. (eds) *Deserted Medieval Villages* (1971).

Bernard, G.W. *The Power of the Early Tudor Nobility* (1985).

—*War, Taxation and Rebellion in Tudor England* (1986).

—'The fortunes of the Greys, earls of Kent in the early sixteenth century', *HJ*, 25 (1982).

—'The rise of Sir William Compton, early Tudor courtier', *EHR* , xcvi (1981).

—'Pardon of the clergy reconsidered', *JEH*, 37 (1986).

—'Politics and government in Tudor England', *HJ* 31 (1988).

—'The fourth and fifth earls of Shrewsbury: a study in the power of the English nobility' (D.Phil, Oxford, 1978).

Bindoff, S.T. (ed.)*The History of Parliament: The House of Commons, 1509-1558* (3 vols, 1982).

Black, Ladbrooke (ed) *The Love Letters of Henry the Eighth* (1933).

Blanchard, I. 'Population change, enclosure and the early Tudor economy', *EcHR* , 2nd ser, 23 (1970).

Blatcher, M. *The Court of King's Bench, 1450-1550* (1978).

Blomefield, F., *History of Norfolk* (2nd ed. 11 vols, Norwich 1805-10).

Boersma, F.L. *An Introduction to Fitzherbert's Abridgement* (1981).

Bowden, P.J. *The Wool Trade in Tudor and Stuart England* (1962).

Bowker, Margaret *The Secular Clergy in the Diocese of Lincoln 1495-1558* (1968).

—*The Henrician Reformation: The Diocese of Lincoln under John Longland, 1521-1547* (1981).

—'Some archdeacons' court books and the Commons supplication against the ordinaries' in *The Study of Medieval Records*, ed. D.A. Bullough and R.L. Storey (1971).

Bradford, W. (ed.) *Correspondence of the Emperor Charles v* (1850).

Bradshaw, B. *The Irish Constitutional Revolution of the Sixteenth Century* (1975).

Brand, J. *History of Newcastle* (1789).

Brandi, Karl *The Emperor Charles v*, trans. C.V. Wedgwood (1965).

Braudel, F. *The Mediterranean and the Mediterranean World in the Age of Phillip II* (2 vols, 1972).

Bridbury, A.R. 'English provincial towns in the later Middle Ages', *EcHR*, 2nd ser, xxxiv (1981).

Brigden, S.E. 'Tithe controversy in Reformation England', *JEH*, 32 (1981).

—'The early Reformation in London, 1522-1547: the conflict in the parishes' (D. Phil., Cambridge, 1979).

Brock, R.E. 'The career of John Taylor, master of the rolls, as an illustration of early Tudor administrative history (MA. London, 1950).

Brown, A.L. 'The kings' councillors in fifteenth century England', *TRHS*, 5 ser, xix (1969).

Brown, K.D. 'The Franciscan Observants in England 1482-1559 (D.Phil, Oxford, 1986).

Brown, J.M. 'Henry VIII's book, "Assertio septem sacramentorum", and the royal title of "Defender of the Faith"', *TRHS*, 1st ser, viiii (1880).

Brown, Rawdon (ed) *Four years at the court of Henry VIII* (2 vols, 1854).

Burne, R.V.H. 'The dissolution of St Werburgh's abbey', *Journal of the Chester and North Wales Architectural, Archaeological and Historical Society*, n.s., xxxvii (1948).

Burnet, Gilbert *History of the Reformation of the Church of England*, ed. N. Pocock (7 vols, 1865).

Bush, M.L. 'The Tudors and the royal race', *History*, lv (1970).

—'The problem of the Far North: a study of the crisis of 1537 and its consequences', *NH*, 6 (1971), pp. 40-63.

Butley Priory, Suffolk, 1510-1535, The Register and Chronicle of, ed. A.G. Dickens (1951).

Byrne, Muriel St C. (ed) *The Letters of King Henry VIII* (1936).

Calais, The Chronicle of, ed J.G. Nichols, CS, xxxv (1846).

Calendar of State Papers, Spanish, ed. G.A. Bergenroth, and P. de Gayangos (1862-86).

Calendar of State Papers, Spanish, Further Supplement to, ed. G. Mattingly (1947).

Calendar of State Papers, Venetian , ed. R.Brown, C. Bentinck, H. Brown (9 vols, 1864-1898).

Cameron, T.W. 'The early life of Thomas Wolsey', *EHR* , iii (1888).

Campbell, B.M.S. 'The population of early Tudor England: a re-evaluation of the 1522 muster returns and 1524 and 1525 lay subsidies', *Journal of Historical Geography*, 7 (1981).

Campbell, L. 'The authorship of the *Recueil d'Arras*', *Journal of the Warburg and Courtauld Institutes*, xl (1977).

Carew Manuscripts, Calendar of, 1515-74, ed J.S. Brewer and W. Bullen (1867).

Carus-Wilson, E.M. and Coleman, 0. *England's Export Trade, 1275-1547* (1963).

Catto, J. 'The king's servants' in *Henry V: the Practice of Kingship*, ed G.L. Harriss (1985).

—'Religious change under Henry V' in *Henry v: the Practice of Kingship*, ed G.L. Harriss (1985).

Cavendish, George *The Life and Death of Cardinal Wolsey*, ed. R.S. Sylvester, EETS (1959).

Challis, C.E. *The Tudor Coinage* (1978).

Chambers, D.S. *Cardinal Bainbridge in the Court of Rome, 1509 to 1514* (1965).

—'Cardinal Wolsey and the papal tiara', *BIHR*, xxviii (1965).

—'English representation at the court of Rome in the early Tudor period' (D. Phil., Oxford, 1962).

Chapters of the Augustinian Canons , ed. H.E. Salter, OHS, lxxiv (1920).

Chapters of the Black Monks, ed. W.A. Pantin, CS, 3 ser, liv (1937).

Cheney, C.R. 'William Lynwoode's *Provinciale*', *The Jurist*, 21 (1961).

Chester, A.G. *Hugh Latimer: Apostle to the English* (Philadelphia, 1954).
—'A note on the burning of Lutheran books in England', *Library Chronicle*, 18 (University of Pennsylvania, 1952).
—'Robert Barnes and the burning of books', *HLQ* 14 (1951).
Chrimes, S.B. *An Introduction to the Administrative History of Medieval England* (1959).
—*Henry VII* (1972).
Churchill, I, *Canterbury Administration* (1933).
Clark, P. *English Provincial Society from the Reformation to the Revolution* (1977).
Clark, P. and Slack, P. (eds.) *Crisis and Order in English Towns 1500-1700* (1972).
Clifford Letters of the Sixteenth Century, ed A.G. Dickens, Surtees Society, clxxii (1962).
Cole, H. (ed) *King Henry the Eighth's Scheme of Bishopricks* (1838).
Coleman, D.C. 'Merchantilism revisited', *HJ*, 23 (1980).
Colvin, H.M. *The White Canons* (1951).
Condon, M.M. 'Ruling elites in the reign of Henry VII' in *Patronage, Pedigree and Power in Later Medieval England*, ed C. Ross (1979).
Cooper, J.P. 'Henry VII's last years reconsidered', *HJ* 2 (1959).
Councils and Synods with other documents relating to the English Church, II, 1205-1265, ed. F.M. Powicke, C.R. Cheney (1964).
Corpus Iuris Canonici, II: Decretales Gregorii IX, ed. A. Friedberg (Leipzig, 1881).
Cosgrave A. (ed.), *A New History of Ireland: Medieval Ireland, 1169-1534* (1987).
Coward, B. *The Stanleys, Lords Stanley and Earls of Derby, 1385-1672: the Origins, Wealth and Power of a Landowning Family* , Chetham Society, 3 ser, xxx (1983).
Creighton, Mandell *Cardinal Wolsey* (1891).
Croft, R. 'Books, reform and the Reformation', *Archiv für Reformationsgeschichte*, 71 (1980).
Croke, Sir A. *The Genealogical History of the Croke Family* (1823).
Cruickshank, C.G. *Army Royal: Henry VIII's Invasion of France 1513* (1969).

Davies, C.S.L. *Peace, Print and Protestantism 1450-1558* (1977).
—'The Pilgrimage of Grace reconsidered', *PP*, 41 (1968).
—'Bishop John Morton, the Holy See and the accession of Henry VII', *EHR*, cii (1987).
Davies, R.G. 'The episcopate' in *Profession, Vocation and Culture in later Medieval England*, ed. C.H. Clough (1982).
Davies, R.R. *Lordship and Society in the March of Wales 1280-1400* (1978).
Davis, E.J. 'The enquiry of the death of Richard Hunne', *The Library*, 3 ser, xviii (1914).
—'The authorities for the case of Richard Hunne', *EHR*, xxx (1915).
Davis, J.F. *Heresy and Reformation in the South-East of England* (1983).
—'The trials of Thomas Bylney and the English Reformation', *HJ*, 24 (1981).
—'Heresy and Reformation in the South-East of England, 1520-1559' (D. Phil., Oxford, 1968).
Deeley, A. 'Papal provision and royal rights of patronage in the early fourteenth century', *EHR*, xliii (1928).
Derrett, J.D.M. 'The affair of Richard Hunne and Friar Standish' in *CWM*, 9 (1979).
Dickens, A.G. '*The English Reformation* (1964).
—'The shape of anti-clericalism and the English Reformation' in *Politics and Society in Reformation Europe*, ed E.I. Kourie and T. T Scott (1987).
Dietz, F.C. *English Government Finance 1485-1558* (Urbana, 1920).
—*English Public Finance, 1558-1641* (New York, 1932).
Dobson, R.B. 'Urban decline in late medieval England', *TRHS*, 5 ser, xxvii. (1977).
Doernburg, E. *Henry VIII and Luther* (Stanford, 1961).
Domerham, Adam de *Historia de rebus Glastioniensibus*, ed. T. Hearne (2 vols, 1727).
Dowling, M. 'Anne Boleyn and reform', *JEH*, 35 (1984).
Du Boulay, F.R.H. *An Age of Ambition* (1970).
Duff, E. Gordon 'The Assertio Septem Sacramentorum' in *The Library*, new.ser., ix (1908).
Dudley, Edmund, *The Tree of Commonwealth*, ed. D.M. Brodie (1948).
Duggan, L.G. 'The unresponsiveness of the late medieval church: a reconsideration', *Sixteenth Century Journal*, ix (1978).
Dumont, J. *Corps universel diplomatique du droit des gens, etc.* (Amsterdam, 1726).

Durham, Rites of, ed. J.T. Fowler, Surtees Society, cvii (1903).

Dyer, A.D. 'Growth and decay in English towns 1500-1700', *Urban History Yearbook* (1979).

Dyer, C. *Lords and Peasants in a Changing Society; the Estates of the Bishopric of Worcester. 680-1540* (1980).

—'Warwickshire farming 1349-c.1520: preparations for agricultural revolution', *Dugdale Society, Occasional Papers* 27 (1981).

—'Deserted medieval villages in the West Midlands', *EcHR,* 2nd ser, 35 (1982).

Dymond, D. 'The famine of 1527', *Local Population Studies,* xxvi (1981).

Eaves, R.G. *Henry VIII's Scottish Diplomacy, 1513-24* (New York, 1971).

Ehses, S. *Römische Dokumente zur Geschichte der Ehescheidung Heinrichs VIII von England, 1527-1534* (Paderborn, 1893).

—'Zur ehescheidung Heinrichs VIII von England' , *Römische Quartelschrift,* xiv (1900).

Elliott, J.H. *Imperial Spain, 1496-1716* (1963).

Ellis, Henry (ed) *Original Letters Illustrative of English History* (11 vols in 3 ser, 1824-46).

Ellis, S.G. *Tudor Ireland* (1985).

—*Reform and Revival: English Government in Ireland 1470-1534* (1986).

—'Tudor policy and the Kildare ascendancy in the lordship of Ireland, 1496-1534), *IHS,* xx (1976-7).

Elton, G.R. *The Tudor Revolution in Government* (1960).

—*Henry VIII: an Essay in Revision* (Historical Association Pamphlet, 1962).

—*Reform and Renewal* (1973).

—*Reform and Reformation* (1977).

—'An early Tudor poor law', *EcHR,* 2nd ser, 6 (1953).

—'The quondam of Rievaulx', *JEH,* 7 (1956).

—'State-planning in early Tudor England', *EcHR,* 2nd ser, 13 (1961).

—*Studies in Tudor and Stuart Politics and Government* (3 vols, 1974, 1983).

    [Vol.One includes: 'Henry VII: rapacity and remorse', *HJ,* (1958); 'Henry VII: a restatement', *HJ,* (1961); 'The king of hearts', *HJ,* 12 (1969); 'Cardinal Wolsey', intro. to A.F. Pollard's *Wolsey* (Fontana, 1965).

    Vol.Two includes: '"The Body of the Whole Realm": parliament and representation in medieval and Tudor England', *Jamestown Essays on Representation,* ed. A.E. Dick Howard (Virginia, 1969); 'The political creed of Thomas Cromwell', *TRHS,* 5 ser, vi (1956); 'The political creed of Thomas Cromwell, *TRHS,* 5th ser, vi (1956); 'Reform by statute: Thomas Starkey's *Dialogue* and Thomas Cromwell's policy', *Proceedings of the British Academy,* (1968).

    Vol.Three includes 'Tudor government the points of contact, the Council', *TRHS,* 5 ser, xxv (1974).

Elton, G.R. (ed) *The Tudor Constitution* (rev.ed., 1982).

Elyot, Sir Thomas, *The Book Named the Governor,* ed. S.E. Lehmberg (1962).

Emden, A.B. *A Biographical Register of the University of Oxford to 1500* (1957-9).

—*A Biographical Register of the University of Cambridge to 1500* (1963).

—*A Biographical Register of the University of Oxford, 1501-40* (1974).

English Historical Documents, IV, 1327-1485, ed. A.R. Myers (1969).

Erasmus, Desiderius, *The Collected Works of* (Toronto, 1974—):.

    Vol 2 *The Correspondence of, 1501 to 1514,* ed. and trans. W.K. Ferguson, R.A.B. Mynors and D.F.S. Thompson (1975).

    Vol 3 *The Correspondence of, 1514 to 1516,* ed. and trans. J.K. McConica, R.A.B. Mynors and D.F.S. Thompson (1976).

    Vol 5 *The Correspondence of,* 1517-18, ed. and trans. P.G. Bietenholz, R.A.B. Mynors and D.F.S. Thompson.

    Vol 6 *The Correspondence of* , 1518-19, ed. and trans. ed. and trans. P.G. Bietenholz, R.A.B. Mynors and D.F.S. Thompson (1982).

The Praise of Folly (Univ. of Michigan, 1958).

The Colloquies of, ed. C.R. Thompson (Chicago, 1965).

Fasti Ecclesiae Anglicanae, 1300-1541:

    Vol. i, *Lincoln* , comp. H.P.F. King (1962).

Vol. iii, *Salisbury*, comp. J.M. Horn (1962).

Vol. iv, *Monastic Cathedrals*, comp. B. Jones (1963).

Vol. vi, *Northern Province* , comp. B. Jones (1963).

Vol. x, *Coventry and Lichfield*, comp. B. Jones (1964).

Feavearyear, Sir A. *The Pound Sterling; a History of English Money* (2nd edn, 1963).

Febvre, L. 'The origins of the French Reformation: a badly-put question?' in *A New Kind of History and Other Essays*, ed. P. Burke (New York, 1973).

Fenlon, Dermot *Heresy and Obedience in Tridentine Italy* (1972).

Ferguson, A.B. *The Indian Summer of English Chivalry* (North Carolina, 1960).

Fiddes, Richard, *The Life of Cardinal Wolsey* (1724).

Fines, J. 'The post-mortem condemnation for heresy of Richard Hunne', *EHR*, lxxviii (1963).

—'Heresy trials in the diocese of Covemtry and Lichfield', *JEH*, (1963).

Firth, C.B. 'Benefit of clergy in the time of Edward IV', *EHR*, xxxii (1917).

Fish, Simon 'The supplication for the beggars' in Thomas More, *The Supplication of Souls* (Primary publication, 1970).

Fisher, John, *Assertionis Lutheranae Confutatio* (Antwerp, 1523).

—*Defensio Regie Assertionis contra Babylonicam Captivitatem* (Cologne, 1525).

—*Sacri sacerdoti defensio contra Lutherum* (1525).

—*English Works*, ed. J.E.B. Mayer, EETS, extra ser, xxvi (1876).

Fitzgerald, B. *The Geraldines: an Experiment in Irish Government, 1169-1601* (1951).

Fletcher, A., *Tudor Rebellions* (3rd edn, 1983).

Fletcher, J.M. 'The teaching and study of arts at Oxford, c.1400-1520' (D. Phil., Oxford, 1961).

Fletcher, J.R., *The Story of the English Bridgettines of Syon Abbey* (1933).

Fonblanque, E.B. de *Annals of the House of Percy* (2 vols, 1887).

Fountains, Memorials of St Mary's Abbey of, ed. J. Walbran, Surtees Society, xlii, (1863).

Fowler, T. *The History of Corpus Christi College*, OHS, xxv (1893).

Fox, A. and Guy, J. *Reassessing the Henrician Age* (1986).

Fox, Richard *The Letters of*, ed. P.S. and H.M. Allen (1929).

Foxe, John *The Acts and Monuments of*, ed. J. Pratt (8 vols, 4 ed, 1877).

Friedmann, P. *Anne Boleyn, a Chapter of English History, 1527-1536* (2 vols, 1884).

Froissart, The Chronicles of Jean, in Lord Berners's translation, ed G. and W.Anderson (1963).

Froude, J.A. *Short Studies in Great Subjects* (1907).

Gabel, L.C. 'Benefit of Clergy in the later Middle Ages', *Smith College Studies in History*, 14 (Northampton, Mass., 1928-9).

Gairdner, J. 'New lights on the divorce of Henry VIII', *EHR*, xi (1896); xii (1897).

Galbraith, V.H. 'Alfred Frederick Pollard', *Proceedings of the British Academy*, xxxv (1954).

Gardiner, L.R. 'Further news of Cardinal Wolsey's End', November—December 1530', *BIHR*, lvii (1984).

Garrett-Goodyear, H. 'The Tudor revival of the quo warranto and local contribution to state building',in *On the Laws and Customs of England*, ed M.S. Arnold, S.A. Selby and S.D. White (Univ. of North Carolina, 1981).

Gasquet, F.A. *The Eve of the Reformation* (1900).

—*The Last Abbot of Glastonbury and other Essays* (1908).

—*Henry VIII and the English Monasteries* (8th edn.,1925).

Gay, E.F. 'The inquisitions of depopulation in 1517', *TRHS*, new.ser., xiv, (1900).

—'Inclosures in the sixteenth century', *Quarterly Journal of Economics*, xvii (1903).

—'The rise of the English county family: Peter and John Temple to 1603', *HLQ*, i (1938).

Giuseppi, M.S. 'Alien merchants in England in the fifteenth century', *TRHS*, ns, ix (1895).

Glamorgan County History, vol. 111, the Middle Ages, ed T.B. Pugh (1971).

Gleason, E.G. 'On the nature of sixteenth-century Italian evangelism: scholarship, 1953-1978', *Sixteenth Century Journal*, ix (1978).

Goodman, A. *The Wars of the Roses, Military Activity and English Society, 1452-97* (1981).

Goring, J.J. 'The general proscription of 1522', *EHR*, lxxxvi (1971), .

—'The riot at Bayham abbey, June 1525', *Sussex Archaeological Collections*, cxvi (1978).

Gould, J.D. *The Great Debasement* (1970).

Graham, R. 'Roland Gosenell, prior of Wenlock, 1521-6' in R. Graham *English Ecclesiastical Studies* (1929).

Gras, N.S.B. *The Evolution of the English Corn Market* (1915).

Graves, M.A.R. *The Tudor Parliaments: Crowns, Lords and Commons, 1485-1603* (1985).

Griffith, R.A. *The Principality of Wales in the Later Middle Ages*, Board of Celtic studies, History and Law series 26 (1972).

—*The Reign of Henry vi* (1981).

Guicciardini, Francesco *The History of Italy*, ed. and trans. S. Alexander (New York, 1972).

Gunn, S.J. *Charles Brandon, Duke of Suffolk c.1484-1545* (1988).

—'The regime of Charles duke of Suffolk in North Wales and the reform of Welsh government', *Welsh Historical Review* , 12 (1985).

—'The duke of Suffolk's march on Paris in 1523', *EHR*, ci (1986), pp.000.

—'The French wars of Henry VIII' in *The Origins of War in Early Modern Europe*, ed. J. Black (1987).

—'The Act of Resumption of 1515' in *Early Tudor England*, ed D. Williams (1989).

Guy, J.A. *The Cardinal's Court* (1977).

—*The Public Career of Sir Thomas More* (1980).

—'Wolsey's Star Chamber: a study in archival reconstruction', *Journal of the Society of Archivists*, v (1975).

—'Wolsey, the council and the council courts', *EHR*, ccclx (1976).

—'Henry VIII and the praemunire manoeuvres of 1530-1531', *EHR* , xvii (1982).

—'The privy council: revolution or evolution?' in *Revolution Reassessed: Revisions in the History of Tudor Government and Administration*, ed. C. Coleman and D. Starkey (1986).

—'The development of equitable jurisdiction' in *Law, Litigants and the Legal Profession*, ed E.W. Ives and A.H. Manchester (1983).

—'The King's Council and political participation' in *Reassessing the Henrician Age*, ed A. Fox and J.A. Guy (1988).

—'Wolsey and the parliament of 1523' in *Law and Government under the Tudors*, ed C. Cross, D. Loades and J.J. Scarisbrick (1988).

—'The court of Star Chamber during Wolsey's ascendancy' (D.Phil, Cambridge, 1973).

Guy, J.A. (ed) *Christopher St German on Chancery and Statute*, SS, supl. ser. vi (1985).

Gwyn, P.J. 'Wolsey's foreign policy: the conferences of Calais and Bruges reconsidered', *HJ*, 23.

Hackett, Sir John, *The Letters of*, ed. E.F. Rogers (Morgantown, 1971).

Haigh, C., *Reformation and Resistance in Tudor Lancashire* (1975).

—'The recent histiography of the English Reformation', *HJ*, 25 (1982).

—'Anticlericalism and the English Reformation', *History*, lxviii (1983).

Hale, J.R. *War and Society in Renaissance Europe 1450-1620* (1985).

Hall, Edward *The Union of the Two Noble and Illustre Famelies of York and Lancaster* , ed. H. Ellis (1809).

Harcourt, L.W. Vernon *His Grace the Steward and the Trial Peers* (1907).

Hare, C. *Maximilian the Dreamer* (1913).

Hargrave, F.(ed) *A Collection of Tracts relative to the Law of England*, (1787).

Harper-Bill, C. 'Archbishop John Morton and Canterbury, 1486-1500', *JEH*, 29 (1978).

—'Dean Colet's convocation sermon and the pre-Reformation Church', *History*, lxxiii (1988).

Harpsfield, Nicholas *A Treatise on the Pretended Divorce between Henry VIII and Catherine of Aragon*, ed. N. Pocock, CS, 2nd ser, xxi (1878).

—*The Life and Death of Sir Thomas More, Knight*, ed. E.V. Hitchcock and P.E. Hallett, EETS, orig. ser, clxxxxvi (1932).

Harris, B. *Edward Stafford, Third Duke of Buckingham, 1478-1521* (Stanford, 1986).

—'The trial of the third duke of Buckingham: a revisionist view', *AJLH*, xx (1976).

—'Marriage sixteenth century style: Elizabeth Stafford and the third duke of Norfolk', *Journal of Social History*, 15 (1981-2).

Harris, M. Dormer, *The Story of Coventry* (1911).

Harrison, C.J. 'The petition of Edmund Dudley', *EHR*, lxxxvii (1972).

Harriss, G.L. 'Aids,loans and benevolences', *HJ*, 6 (1963).

—'War and the emergence of the English parliament, 1297-1360', *Journal of Medieval History*, 2 (1976).

—'Thomas Cromwell's new principal of taxation', *EHR*, xciii (1978).

Harte, N.B. 'State control of dress and social change in pre-industrial England' in *Trade, Government and Economy in Pre-industrial England; Essays presented to F.J. Fisher*, ed. D.C. Coleman and A.H. John (1976).

Harte, W.J.(ed) *Gleanings from the Common Place Book of John Hooker relating to the City of Exeter (1485-1590)* (1926).

Harvey, B. *Westminster Abbey and the Estates in the Middle Ages* (1977).

Harvey, J.H. 'The building works and architects of cardinal Wolsey', *Journal of the British Archaeological Association*, 3 ser, viii (1943).

Hastings, M. *The Court of Common Pleas in Fifteenth Century England* (New York, 1947).

Hay, D. 'The life of Polydore Vergil of Urbino', *JWCI*, xii (1949).

Headley,J.M. *The Emperor and his Chancellor; a Study of the Imperial Chancery under Gattinara* (1983).

—'Gattinara, Erasmus and the Imperial configurations of humanism', *Archiv für Reformationisgeschicte*, (1980).

Heal, Constance 'Pope Pius II and the Wars of the Roses', *Archivum Historiae Pontificiae*, 8 (1970).

Heal, F. *Of Prelates and Princes* (1980).

—'The bishops of Ely and their diocese during the Reformation period' (D. Phil., Cambridge, 1972).

Heath, P. *The English Parish Clergy on the Eve of the Reformation* (1969).

—'The treason of Geoffrey Blythe, bishop of Coventry and Lichfield, 1503-1531', *BIHR*, xlii (1969).

Heinze, R.W. *The Proclamations of the Tudor Kings* (1976).

Hembry, P. 'Episcopal palaces 1535 to 1660' in *Wealth and Power in Tudor England*, ed. E.W. Ives, R.J. Knecht, J.J. Scarisbrick (1978).

Hempsall, D. 'Martin Luther and the Sorbonne, 1519-21', *BIHR*, xlvii (1973).

Herbert, Lord Edward of Cherbury, *The life and raigne of King Henry the eighth* (1672).

Herrtage, S.J. (ed) *England in the Reign of Henry VIII*, EETS, extra ser, xxxii (1878).

Hexter, J.H. *More's Utopia; the Beginning of an Idea*, (Nw York, 1965).

Higham, F.M.G. 'A note on the pre-udor secretary' in *Essays in Medival . History presented to T.F Tout*, ed A.G. Little and F.M. Powicke (1925).

Historical Mauscripts Commission, Tenth Report (1885).

Historical Mauscripts Commission, Welsh (1898).

Hocquet, A. 'Tournai et l'occupation Anglaise (1513-19), *Annales de la Société Historique et Archéologique de Tournai*, (1900).

Hodgson, J. *A History of Northumberland* (1820).

Holinshed, Raphael *Chronicles of England, Scotland and Ireland*, ed H. Ellis (6 vols, 1806-8).

Holmes, M. 'Evil May-Day, 1517', *History Today*, 15 (1965).

Hook, Judith *The Sack of Rome* (1972).

Hope, A. 'Lollardy: the stone the builders rejected' in *Protestantism and the national Church in Sixteenth Century England*. ed P. Lake and M. T Dowling (1987).

Hoskins, W.G. *Essays in Leicestershire History* (1950).

—*The Age of Plunder: King Henry's England 1500-1547* (1976).

—'Harvest fluctuations in English economic history, 1480-1619', *AHR*, xii (1964).

Houlbrooke, R. *Church Courts and the People during the English Reformation, 1520-70* (1979).

—'The decline of ecclesiastical jurisdiction under the Tudors' in *Continuity and Change*, ed. R. O'Day and F. Heal (1976).

Hoyle, R.W. 'The first earl of Cumberland: A reputation reassessed', *NH*, 22 (1986).

Hughes, P. *The Reformation in England, I*, (1950).

Hurstfield, J. 'Was there a Tudor despotism after all?' in *Freedom, Corruption and Government in Elizabethan England* (1973).

Ives, E.W. *Anne Boleyn* (1986).

—*Faction in Tudor England* (Historical Association Pamphlet, 2 edn, 1986).

—'The common lawyers in Prereformation England', *TRHS*, 5 ser, xviii (1968).

—'Patronage at the court of Henry VIII: the case of Sir Ralph Egerton of Ridley', *Bulletin of the John Rylands Library*, 52 (1969-70).

—'Court and county palatinate in the reign of Henry VIII: the career of William Brereton of Malpas', *Trans. of the Historical Society of Lancashire and Cheshire*, cxxiii (1972).

—'"Agaynst taking away of Women": the inception and operation of the Abduction Act of 1487', in *Wealth and Power in Tudor England*, ed. T E.W. Ives, R.J. Knecht and J.J. Scarisbrick (1978).

—'Crimes, sanctuary and royal authority under Henry VIII: the exemplary sufferings of the Savage family' in *On the Laws and Customs of England; Essays in Honor of Samuel E. Thorne*, ed. M.S. Arnold, T.A. Green, S.A. Scully and S.D. White (Univ. of North Carolina, 1981).

Ives, E.W. (ed) *Letters and Accounts of William Brereton of Malpas*, Record Society of Lancashire and Cheshire, cxvi (1976).

Jacqueton, G. *La Politique Extéreiure de Louise de Savoie* (Paris, 1892).

James, M.E. *Family Lineage and Civil Society* (1974).

—'Change and continuity in the Tudor North', *BP*, 27 (1965).

—'A Tudor magnate and the Tudor state', *BP*, 30 (1966).

—'The first earl of Cumberland (1483-1542) and the decline of Northern feudalism', *NH*, 1 (1966).

—'Obedience and dissent in Henrician England: the Lincolnshire Rebellion 1536', *PP*, 48 (1970).

Jedin, H. *History of the Council of Trent* (2 vols, 1957-61).

Jones, D. 'Sir Rhys ap Thomas, a study in family history and Tudor politics', *Archaelogia Cambrensis*, 5 ser, ix (1892-3).

Jones, Theophilus *A History of the County of Brecknock* (1805).

Jones, Thomas 'A Welsh chronicler in Tudor England', *Welsh History Review*, 1 (1960).

Jones, W.J. *The Elizabethan Court of Chancery* (1967).

Jorden, W.K. *Philanthropy in England, 1480-1660* (1959).

Kaufman, P.I. 'John Colet and Erasmus' Enchiridion' in *Church History*, 46 (1977).

Keilway, Robert, *Reports . . .*, ed. John Croke (1688).

Kelly, H.A. *The Matrimonial Trials of Henry VIII* (Stanford, 1976).

—'Canonical implications of Richard III's plans to marry his niece', *Traditio*, xxiii (1967).

Kelly, M.J. 'The submission of the clergy', *TRHS*, 5 ser, xv (1965).

—'Canterbury jurisdiction and influence during the episcopate of William Warham, 1503-1532' (D. Phil., Cambridge, 1965).

Kennedy, J. 'The city of London and the crown c.1509-c.1529' (M.A., Manchester, 1978).

Kermode, J.I. 'Urban Decline? The flight from ofice in late medieval York', *EcHR*, 2 ser, xxxv (1982).

Kerridge, E. *The Agricultural Revolution* (1967).

—'The returns of the inquisitions of depopulation', *EHR*, lxx (1955).

Kingsford, C.L. (ed.) *The First English Life of of King Henry the Fifth* (1911).

—*King's Works, 1485-1660, History of the*, IV (pt. ii), gen. ed. H.M. Colvin. (1982).

Kirby, T.F. *Annals of Winchester College* (1892).

Kitching, C. 'The prerogative court of Canterbury from Warham to Whitgift' in *Continuity and Change*, ed. R. O'Day and F. Heal (1976).

Kitson Clark, G.S.R. *An Expanding Society: Britain 1830-1900* (1967).

Knecht, R. *Francis I* (1984).

Knowles, D. *The Religious Orders in England* (3 vols, 1947-59).

—'The last abbot of Wigmore' in *Medieval Studies presented to Rose Graham*, ed. V. Ruffer and A.J. Taylor (1950).

—'The case of St Albans in 1490', *JEH*, 3 (1952).

—'"The Matter of Wilton" in 1528', *BIHR*, xxxi (1958).

Knowles, D. and Hadcock, R.N. *Medieval Religious Houses, England and Wales* (1971).

Koenigsburgher, H.G. *The Habsburgs and Europe 1516-1660* (Ithaca, 1971).

Kronenberg, M.E. 'A printed letter of the London Hanse merchants (3 March 1526)', *Oxford Bibliographical Society Publications*, n.s., i (1948).

Lamond, E. (ed) *A Discourse of the Common Weal of this Realm of England* (1954).

Lancashire and Cheshire Cases in the Court of Star Chamber, ed. R. Stewart-Brown, Record Society of Lancashire and Cheshire, lxxi (1916).

Lander, J.R. *Crown and Nobility 1450-1509* (1976).

—*Government and Community: England 1450-1509* (1980).

Lander, S.J. 'Church courts and the Reformation in the diocese of Chichester' in *Continuity and Change*, ed. R. O'Day and F. Heal (1976).

—'The diocese of Chichester, 1508-1558: episcopal reform under Robert Sherburne and its aftermath' (D. Phil., Cambridge, 1974).

Leadam, I.S. *The Domesday of Enclosures* (2 vols, 1897).

—'The inquisitions of 1517: inclosures and evictions', *TRHS*, n.s., vi, vii, viii (1893-4).

Le Glay, E.A.J. *Négotiations diplomatiques entre la France et l'Autriche* (Paris, 1845).

Le Grand, Joachim, *Histoire du Divorce de Henry VIII* (3 vols, Paris, 1688).

Lehmberg, S.E. *The Reformation Parliament, 1529-1536* (1970).

Leonard, E.M. *The Early History of English Poor Relief* (1900).

Letters and Papers, Foreign and Domestic, of the reign of Henry VIII, 1509-47, ed. J.S. Brewer, J. Gairdner, R.H. Brodie (21 vols, 1862-1910).

Letters and Papers, Foreign and Domestic, of the reign of Henry VIII, 1509-47, Addenda, ed. R.H. Brodie (1929-32).

Letters and Papers Illustrative of the reigns of Richard III and Henry VII, ed. J. Gairdner, Rolls Series (2 vols, 1861-3).

Letters of Royal and Illustrious Ladies of Great Britain, ed M.A.E. Wood (3 vols, 1846).

Levine, M. 'The fall of Edward duke of Buckingham' in *Tudor Men and Institutions*, ed. A.J. Flavin (Louisiana, 1972).

Libelle of Englyshe Polycye, The, ed Sir G.F. Warner (1926).

Liber Monasterii de Hyda, ed. E. Edwards, Rolls Series, (1866).

Lloyd, John M. 'The rise and fall of the house of Dinefwr' (M.A., Cardiff, 1963).

Lodge, E. *Illustrations of British History* (3 vols, 1791).

Logan, F.D. 'Excommunication and the secular arm in medieval England', *Pontifical Institute of Medieval Studies*, 15 (1968).

Longland, John, *Tres Conciones* (?1527).

Lords, Journals of the House of, (10 vols, 1846).

Lunt, W.E. *Financial Relations of the Papacy with England to 1327* (Cambridge, Mass, 1939).

—*Financial Relations of the Papacy with England, 1327-1534* (Cambridge, Mass, 1962).

Lupton, J.H. *A Life of John Colet* (1887).

Lydgate, John *Lydgate's Fall of Princes*, ed. H. Bergen, *EETS*, extra ser, cxxi (1924 for 1918).

Lydon, J.F. *The Lordship of Ireland in the Middle Ages* (1972).

Lynwood, W. *Provinciale* (1679).

Lytle, G.F. 'Patronage patterns and Oxford colleges, c.1300-1530' in *The University in Society*, ed. L. Stone (2 vols, Princeton, 1975).

—'Universities as religious authorities in the later middle ages and Reformation' in *Reform and Authority in the Medieval and Reformation Church*, ed. G.F. Lytle (Catholic Univ. press, 1981).

McConica, J. *English Humanists and Reformation Politics under Henry VIII and Edward VI* (1965).

—'Scholars and Commoners' in *The University and Society*, ed L. Stone (1975).

McConica, J. (ed.) *The Collegiate University; the History of the University of Oxford* (1986).

MacCullough, D.N.J. *Suffolk and the Tudors* (1986).

Mcfarlane, K.B. 'Henry V, Bishop Beaufort and the red hat, 1417-21', *EHR*, lx (1945).

McKisack, M. *The Fourteenth Century, 1307-1399* (1959).

—*Medieval History in the Tudor Age* (1971).

Macray, W.D. *A Register of the Members of St Mary Magdalen College, Oxford from the Foundation of the College* (7 vols, 1894-1911).

Madden, F. (ed) *Privy Purse Expenses of the Princess Mary* (1831).

Mallet, M.E. and J.R. Hale *The Military Organisation of the Renaissance State, Venice c. 1400 to 1617* (1984).

Marius, Richard, *Thomas More* (1985).

Martene, E and U. Durand, *Veterum Scriptorum et Monumentorum amplissima collectio* (9 vols, Paris, 1724-33).

Martin, J. 'Enclosures and inquisitions of 1607: an examination of Dr. Kerridge's article, "The returns of the inquisitions of depopulation"', *Agricultural History Review*, xxx (1982).

Mattingly, G. *Catherine of Aragon* (1963).

Renaissance Diplomacy (1965).

—'An early non-aggression pact', *Journal of Modern History*, x (1938).

Mayer, T.F. 'Faction and ideology: Thomas Starkey's *Dialogue*', *HJ*, (1985).

Maxwell-Lyte, H.C. *A History of the University from the earliest times to the year 1530* (1886).

—*Historical Notes on the Use of the Great Seal of England* (1926).

Mayor, J.E.B. (ed) *Early Statutes of the College of St John the Evangelist in the University of Cambridge* (1859).

Mercers' Company, 1453-1527, Acts of Court of the, ed. L. Lyell and F.D. Watney (1936).

Merriman, R.B. *The Life and Letters of Thomas Cromwell* (2 vols, 1902).

Metzger, F. 'The last phase of the medieval chancery' in *Law-making and Law-makers in British History*, ed A. Harding (1980).

—'Das Englische kanzleigericht unter Kardinal Wolsey, 1515-29' (D.Phil, Erlangen, 1976).

Meyer, Carl S. 'Henry VIII burns Luther's books', *JEH*, 9 (1958).

Miller, H. *Henry VIII and the English Nobility* (1986).

—'The early Tudor peerage, 1485-1547 (M.A., London, 1950).

Milsom, S.F.C. 'Richard Hunne's "praemunire"', *EHR*, lxxvi (1961).

Mitchell, W.T. (ed) *Epistolae Academicae, 1508-1596*, OHS, new.ser., 26 (1980).

Monasticon diocesis Exoniensis, ed. G. Oliver (1846).

Monumenta Franciscana, ed. R. Howlett, Rolls Series, 4b (1882).

More, Thomas *The Workes . . . in the Englysh Tonge* (1557).

—*Complete Works of St*, (Toronto, 1963—):.

   Vol 4 *Utopia*, ed. E. Surtz, J.H. Hexter (1965).

   Vol 5 *Responsio ad Lutherum*, ed. J.M. Headley (1969).

   Vol 6 *A Dialogue Concerning Heresies*, ed. T.M.C. Lawler, G. Marc'hadour and R.C. Marius (1981).

   Vol 8 *The Confutation of Tyndale's Answer*, ed. L.A. Schuster, R.C. Marius, J.P. Lusardi and R.J. Schoek (1973).

   Vol 9 *The Apology*, ed. J.B. Trapp (1979).

   Vol 12 *A Dialogue of Comfort against Tribulation*, ed. L.L. Martz and F. Manley (1976).

—*The English works of*, ed. W.E. Campbell and A.W. Reed (1931)

—*Correspondence of*, ed. E.F. Rogers (Princeton, 1947).

—*The Latin Epigrams of*, ed. and trans. L. Bradner and C.A. Lynch (Chicago, 1953).

—*Selected Letters of*, ed. E.F. Rogers (New Haven, 1961).

—*The Supplication of Souls* (Primary Publications,1970).

More, William *Journal of*, Worcestershire Historical Society (1914).

Morgan, P.T.J. 'The government of Calais, 1485-1558' (D. Phil, Oxford, 1966).

Morison, Richard, *A Remedy for Sedition* (London, 1536).

Mullinger, J.B. *The University of Cambridge from the earliest times to the Royal Injunction of 1535* (1873).

Mumford, A.A. *Hugh Oldham* (1936).

Murphy, V. 'The debate over Henry VIII's divorce; an analysis of the contemporary treatises' (D.Phil, Cambridge, 1984).

Myers, A.R. *The Household of Edward IV: The Black Book and Ordinances of 1478* (1959).

Neale, J.E. 'Albert Frederick Pollard', *EHR*, lxiv (1949).

Newton, A.P. 'Tudor reforms in the royal household', *Tudor Studies presented to A.F. Pollard*, ed R.W. Seton-Watson (1924).

Nichols, J.G. (ed) *Grants from the Crown during the reign of Edward v*, CS, 60 (1854).

—*Inventories of the wardrobes, plates, chapel stuff, etc of Henry Fitzroy duke of Richmond*, CS, 61 (1855).

Northern Convocation, Records of, ed. G.W. Kitchen, Surtees Society, cxiii (1906).

Norwich, The Records of the City of, ed. W. Hudson and J.C. Tingey (2 vols, 1906).

Oakley, F. *The Western Church in the Later Middle Ages* (Cornell, 1979).
O'Day, R. 'The ecclesiastical patronage of the lord keeper, 1558-1642', *TRHS*, 5 ser, xxii (1973).
O'Day, R. and Heal, F.(eds.) *Continuity and Change: Personnel and Administration of the Church in England, 1500-1642* (1976).
O'Faolain, Sean *The Great O'Neill* (1942).
Ogle, A. *The Tragedy of the Lollards' Tower* (1949).
Olin, J.C. *Christian Humanism and the Reformation: Desiderius Erasmus* (Harper Torchbooks, 1965).
O'Malley, J.W. *Giles of Viterbo on Church and reform; a Study in Renaissance Thought* (Leiden, (1968).
Ormond Deeds, Calendar of, ed E. Curtis (1937).
Ortory, F. van 'Vie du bienheureux martyr Jean Fisher', *Analecta Bollandiana*, x (1891).
Otway-Ruthven, A.J. *History of Medieval Ireland* (1968).
Owen, G.D. *Elizabethan Wales: the social scene* (1962).
Owst, G.W. *Literature and Pulpit in Medieval Society* (2nd edn, 1961).
Oxley, J.E. *The Reformation in Essex* (1965).
Ozment, S. *The Reformation in the Cities* (1975).
—*The Age of Reform 1250-1550* (1980).

Palliser, D.M. *Tudor York* (1979).
—*The Age of Elizabeth: England under the Later Tudors 1547-1603* (1983).
—'A crisis in English towns? The case for York, 1460-1640', *NH*, xiv (1978).
Palsgrave, John *The Comedy of Acolastus*, ed P.L. Carver, EETS orig. ser, ccii (1937 for 1935).
Pam, D.O. 'The fight for common rights in Enfield and Edmonton 1400-1600', *Edmonton Hundred Historical Society Occasional Papers*, n.s., 27 (1974).
Pantin, W.A. *The English Church in the Fourteenth Century* (1955).
—'The general and provincial chapters of the English black monks, 1215-1540', *TRHS* , 4th ser, x (1927).
Pantin, W.A. (ed.) *Documents illustrating the activities of the General and Provincial Chapters of the English Black Monks, 1215-1540,* CS, 3 ser, liv (1937).
Parker, L.A. 'The agrarian revolution at Cotesbach, 1501-1612', *Trans. of the Leicestershire Archaelogical Society* , xxiv (1948).
—'Enclosure in Leicestershire, 1485-1607' (D. Phil., London, 1948).
Parmiter, G. de C. *The King's Great Matter* (1967).
Pastor, L. von *The History of the Popes*, trans. F.I. Antrobus, R.F. Kerr (23 vols, 1891-1933).
Paul, J.E. *Catherine of Aragon and her Friends* (1966).
—'The last abbots of Reading and Colchester', *BIHR* , xxxiii (1960).
Perry, G. 'The visitation of the monastery of Thame, 1526', *EHR*, iii (1888).
Peterborough Monastery, The Last Days of, ed. W.T. Mellows, Northants Record Society, 12 (1947).
Pettegree, A. *Foreign Protestant Communities in Sixteenth-Century London* (1986).
Pill, D.H. 'The administration of the diocese of Exeter under Bishop Veysey', *Trans. of the Devonshire Association*, xcviii (1966).
Pocock, Nicholas (ed.) *Records of the Reformation, the Divorce 1527-1533* (2 vols, 1870).
Pollard, A.F. *Wolsey* (1929).
Pollard, A.W. *Records of the English Bible* (1911).
Porter, H.C. *Reformation and Reaction in Tudor Cambridge* (1958).
Pound, John *Poverty and Vagrancy in Tudor England* (2nd edn., 1986).
Prestwich, M. *Cranfield: Politics and Profits under the Early Stuarts* (1966).
Pronay, N. 'The Chancellor, the Chancery and the Council at the end of the fifteenth century' in *British Government and Administration*, ed. H.Herder and H. R. Loyn (1974).
Public Records, Third Report of the Deputy Keeper of the, (1842).
Pugh, T.B.(ed.) *The Marcher Lordships of South Wales, 1415-1536,* Board of Celtic Studies, History and Law Series, xx (1963).

—'"The Indenture for the Marches" between Henry VII and Edward Stafford (1477-1521), duke of Buckingham', *EHR*, lxxi (1956).

Pythian-Adams, C. *Desolation of a City: Coventry and the Urban Crisis of the Late Middle Ages* (1979).

Quinn, D.B. 'Henry VIII and Ireland, 1509-1534', *IHS*, xii (1960-1).

Rackham, H. (ed) *Early Statutes of Christ's College, Cambridge* (1927).

Rae, T.I. *The Administration of the Scottish Frontier, 1513-1603* (Edinburgh, 1966).

Ramsey, P. *Tudor Economic Problems* (1963).

Rawcliffe, C. *The Staffords, Earls of Stafford and Dukes of Buckingham, 1394-1521* (1978).

Redstone, V.B. 'Wulcy of Suffolk', *Suffolk Institute of Archaelogy and Natural History*, xvi (1918).

Reed, A.W. *Early Tudor Drama* (1926).

Rees, W. 'The union of England and Wales', *Trans. of the Honourable Society of Cymmrodorion* (1937).

Register of Henry Chichele, ed E.F. Jacobs, CYS, xlii (1943).

Register of the University of Oxford, ed C.W. Boase, OHS, i (1885).

Registers of Richard Fox while Bishop of Bath and Wells, 1492-4 ed. E.C. Batten (1889).

Registers of Thomas Wolsey, John Clerke, etc., ed. H.C. Maxwell-Lyte, Somerset Record Society, lv (1940).

Registrum Caroli Bothe, Episcopi Herefordensis, A.D. MDXVI-MDXXXV, ed. A.J. Bannister, CYS, 28 (1921).

Registrum Ricardi Mayew, ed. A.T. Bannister, CYS 27 (1919).

Registrum Statutorum et Consuetudinem Ecclesiae cathedralis Sancti Pauli Londiniensis, ed. W.S. Simpson (1873).

Registrum Thome Bourgchier, ed. F.R.H. Du Boulay, CYS, liv (1957).

Registrum Thome Wolsey, ed. H. Chitty, CYS, 32 (1926).

Reid, R.R. *The King's Council in the North* (1921).

Renaud, F. 'Contributions towards a history of the ancient parish of Prestbury in Cheshire', Chetham Society, 1st ser, xcvii (1876).

Renaudet, A. *Préréforme et Humanisme à Paris pendant les premières guerres d'Italie (1494-1527)* (2nd edn., Paris, 1953).

Richardson, W.C. *Tudor Chamber Administration, 1484-1547* (Baton Rouge, 1952).

Ridolfi, R. *The Life of Francesco Guicciardini*, trans. C. Grayson (1967).

Ridley, Jasper, *Thomas Cranmer* (1966).

—*The Statesman and the Fanatic* (1982).

Roberts, P.R. 'The union with England and the identity of "Anglican" Wales', *TRHS*, 5 ser, 22 (1972).

Robinson, J. Armitage 'Correspondence of Bishop Oliver King and Sir Reginald Bray', *Proc. of the Somerset Archaelogical and Natural History Society*, 60, pt. 2 (1915).

Robinson, W.R.B. 'Marcher lords of Wales 1525-1531', *Bulletin of the Board of Celtic Studies*, 26 (1974-6).

Roper, William, *The Lyfe of Sir Thomas More, knight*, ed. E.V. Hitchcock, EETS, orig, ser, cxcvii (1935).

Roskell, J.S. *The Commons and their Speakers in English Parliaments, 1376-1523* (1965).

Ross, Charles *Edward IV* (1974).

Rosser, A.Gervase *Medieval Westminster 1200-1540* (1989).

Roth, F. *The English Austin Friars, 1249-1538* (New York, 1966).

Royal Household, A Collection of Ordinances and Regulations for the Government of, Society of Antiquaries (1790).

Roye, William *A Briefe Dialogue between a Christian Father and his Stubborn Son* (Stasburg 1527).

Russell, J.G. *The Field of Cloth of Gold* (1969).

—'The search for universal peace: the conferences at Calais and Bruges in 1521', *BIHR*, xliv (1971).

Rymer, Thomas (ed), *Foedera, Conventiones, Litterae, etc* . (edn. 1704-35).

St German, Christopher, *Doctor and Student*, ed T.F.T. Plunkett and J.L. Baldwin, SS, xci (1974).

—'A treatise concerning the division between the spirituality and temporality' in CWM, 9 (1979).

Salter, H.E. (ed.) A Subsidy Collected in the Diocese of Lincoln in 1526, OHS, lxiii (1909).

Sanctuarium Dunelmense et Sanctuarium Beverlacense, Surtees Society, v (1837).

Savine, A. The English Monasteries on the Eve of the Dissolution (1909).

Sayer, J.E. Papal Judges Delegate in the Province of Canterbury, 1198-1254 (1971).

Scarisbrick, J.J. Henry VIII (1968).

—The Reformation and the English People (1984).

—The pardon of the clergy, 1531', Cambridge Historical Journal , xii (1956).

—'Henry VIII and the Vatican Library', Bibliothèque d'Humanisme et Renaissance, xxiv (Geneva, 1962).

—'Thomas More: the king's good servant', Thought, 52 (1977).

—'Cardinal Wolsey and the Common Weal', in Wealth and Power in Tudor England, ed. E.W. Ives, R.J. Knecht, J.J. Scarisbrick (1978).

—'Clerical taxation in England, 1485-1547', JEH, 29 (1978).

—The conservative episcopate in England, 1529-1535' (D.Phil, Cambridge, 1955).

Schoek, R.J. 'Common law and canon law in their relation to Thomas More' in St Thomas More: Action and Contemplation, ed. R.S. Sylvester (1972).

—'The Fifth Lateran Council' in Reform and Authority in the Medieval and Reformation Church, ed. G.F. Lytle (Catholic Univ. of America Press, 1981).

Schofield, R.S. 'The geographical distribution of wealth in England 1334-1649", EcHR, 2nd ser, 18 (1965).

—'Direct Lay Taxation under the Early Tudors' (D.Phil., Cambridge, 1962).

Schoeder, H.J. Disciplinary Decrees of the General Councils (1937).

Scofield, C.L. The Life and Reign of Edward iv (2 vols, 1923).

Select Cases before the King's Council, 1243-1482, ed I.S. Leadam and J.F. Baldwin, SS, xxxv (1918).

Select Cases before the King's Council in Star Chamber, 1509-1544, ed I.S. Leadam, SS, xxv (1911).

Select Cases in the Council of Henry VII, ed. C.G. Bayne and W.H. Dunham, SS, lxxv (1958).

Sharpe, J.A. 'The history of crime in late medieval and early modern England: a review of the field', Social History, 7 (1982).

Simpson, A.W.B. 'Keilwey's reports, temps Henry VII and Henry VIII', Law Quarterly Review, 73 (1957).

Skeel, C.A.J. The Council in the Marches of Wales (1904).

Skelton, John, The Complete English Poems, ed. J. Scattergood (1978).

Skillington, S.H. 'The Skeffingtons of Skeffington', Trans. of Leicestershire Archaelogical Society, xvi (1929-31).

Slack, Paul The Impact of the Plague in Tudor and Stuart England (1985).

—Poverty and Policy in Tudor England (1988).

—'Mortality crises and epidemic disease' in Health, Medicine and Mortality in the Sixteenth Century, ed C. Webster (1979).

Smart, S.J. 'John Foxe and "The Story of Richard Hunne, Martyr"', JEH, 37 (1986).

Smith, J.B. 'Crown and community in the principality of North Wales in the reign of Henry Tudor', Welsh History Review, 3 (1966-7).

Smith, L.B. Henry VIII: the Mask of Royalty (1971).

—'English treason trials and confessions in the sixteenth century', Journal of the History of Ideas, xv (1954).

Smith, R.B. Land and Politics in the England of Henry VIII (1970).

Smith, Thomas, De Republica Anglorum, ed. M. Dewar (1982).

Somerville,R. History of the Duchy of Lancaster (1953).

—'Henry VII's "Council Learned in the Law"', EHR, liv (1939).

Southern, R.W. Western Society and the Church in the Middle Ages (1970).

Stainer, R.S. Magdalen College School, OHS, n.s., iii (1940).

Starkey, D.R. The Reign of Henry VIII (1985).

—'From feud to faction', History Today, 32 (Nov., 1982).

—'Privy secrets: Henry VIII and the lords of the Council', History Today, 37 (Aug., 1987)).

—'The king's privy chamber, 1485-1547' (D.Phil., Cambridge, 1973).

Starkey, Thomas *A Dialogue between Reginald Pole and Thomas Lupset*, ed. K.M. Burton (1948).

State Papers of the Reign of Henry the Eighth (1830-52).

Statutes of the Colleges of Oxford (3 vols, 1853).

Statutes of the Realm, ed A.D. Luders *et al* (11 vols, 1810-28).

Stephens, J.N. *The Fall of the Florentine Republic, 1512-1530* (1983).

Stone, L. *The Crisis of the Aristocracy, 1558-1641* (1965).

Storey, R.L. *The End of the House of Lancaster* (1966).

—*The Reign of Henry VII* (1968).

—'The wardens of the marches of England towards Scotland, 1377-1498', *EHR*, lxxii (1957).

—'Diocesan administration in Fifteenth-century England', *BP*, 16 (2nd edn., 1972).

—'Gentleman-bureaucrats' in *Profession, Vocation and Culture in Later Medieval England*, ed. C.H. Clough (1982).

Stow, John, *Annales* (1582).

Stoyel, A.D. 'The lost buildings of Otford Palace', *AC*, c (1984).

Strong, Roy, *The National Portrait Gallery: Tudor and Stuart Portraits* (1969).

Sturge, C. *Cuthbert Tunstal* (1938).

Surtz, E. *The Works and Days of John Fisher* (Cambridge, Mass, 1967).

—'St Thomas More and his utopian embassy of 1515', *Catholic Historical Review*, xxxix (1953-4).

Surtz, E. and V. Murphy (eds.), *The Divorce Tracts of Henry VIII* (Angers, 1988).

Taunton, E.L. *Thomas Wolsey, Legate and Reformer* (1902).

Theiner, A. *Vetera Monumenta Hibernorum et Scotorum Historia Illustrantia* .

(Rome, 1864).

Thirsk, J. *Tudor Enclosures*, Historical Association (1959).

—*The Rural Economy of England* (1984).

Thirsk, J. (ed) *The Agrarian History of England and Wales, IV, 1500-1640* (1967).

Thompson, A. Hamilton, *The English Clergy and their Organisation in the Later Middle Ages* (1957).

Thompson, E.M. *The Carthusian Order in England* (1930).

Thompson, S. 'The bishop in his diocese' in *Humanism, Reform and Reformation: the career of Bishop John Fisher*, ed B. Bradshaw and E. Duffy (1989)â.

—'The pastoral work of the English and Welsh bishops 1500-1558' (D.Phil., Oxford, 1984).

Thomson, J.A.F. *The Later Lollards* (1965).

—*Popes and Princes, 1417-1517* (1980).

— 'Tithe disputes in later medieval London', *EHR*, lxxviii (1963).

Thornley, I.D. 'The destruction of sanctuary' in *Tudor Studies presented to A.F. Pollard*, ed. R.W. Seton-Watson (1924).

Thorpe, H. 'The lord and the landscape', Birmingham Archaelogical Society, 80 (1965).

Thurston, H. 'The canon law of divorce', *EHR* xix (1904).

Tierney, B. *Medieval Poor Law* (Berkeley, California, 1959).

Tillyard, E.M.W. *The Elizabethan World Picture* (Peregrine, 1963).

Tjernagel, N.S. *Henry viii and the Lutherans* (St Louis, 1965).

Trapp, J.B. and H.S. Herbrggen (eds) *'The King's Good Servant' Sir Thomas More 1477/8-1535* (National Portrait Gallery, 1977).

Trevelyan Papers , ed. W.G. Trevelyan and C.E. Trevelyan, *CS*, cv (1872).

Tucker, M.J. *The Life of Thomas Howard, Earl of Surrey and Second Duke of Norfolk* (The Hague, 1964).

Tudor Economic Documents, ed. R.H. Tawney and E. Power (3 vols,1924).

Tudor Royal Proclamations, ed. P.L. Hughes and J.F. Larlin (3 vols, New Haven, 1964-9).

Two Early Tudor Lives, ed. R.S. Sylvester and D.P. Harding (New Haven, 1962) [Modernized versions of Cavendish's *Life* of Wolsey and Roper's *Life* of More.].

Tyndale, William *Parable of the Wicked Mamon* (Marburg, 1528).

—*The Obedience of a Christian Man* (Antwerp, 1528).

—*Exposition and Notes on sundry portions of the Holy Scriptures, together with the practice of prelates*, ed. H. Walker, Parker T Society, xliii (1849).

Ullmann, W. 'The realm of England is an empire', *JEH*, 30 (1979).

Underhill, N. *The Lord Chancellor* (1978).

Vergil, Polydore *The Anglica Historia of*, ed D. Hay, CS, lxxiv (1950).
Virgoe, R. 'The recovery of the Howards in East Anglia, 1485-1529' in *Wealth and Power in Tudor England*, ed E.W. Ives, R.J. Knecht and J.J. Scarisbrick (1978).
Visitations, c.1515-1525, Bishop Geoffrey Blythe's, ed P. Heath, Historical Collections, Staffordshire, 4th ser, 7 (1973).
Visitations in the Diocese of Lincoln 1517-1531, ed. A.H. Thompson, Lincoln Record Society, xxxiii, xxxv, xxxvii (1940, 1944, 1947).
Visitations of the Diocese of Norwich, 1492-1532, ed. A. Jessop, CS, n.s.,xliii (1888).

Wales and Monmouthshire, Report of the Royal Commission on Land in (1896).
Walker, Greg *John Skelton and the Politics of the 1520s* (1988).
—'The "expulsion of the minions" of 1519 reconsidered', *HJ*, 32 (1989).
—'Saint or schemer? The 1527 heresy trial of Thomas Bilney reconsidered', *JEH*, 40 (1989).
Ware, James, *The Antiquities and History of Ireland* (1708).
Warham, William, 'Letters of,' AC , i, ii (1858-9).
Webster, C. 'Thomas Linacre and the foundation of the college of physicians' in *Linacre Studies*, ed. F. Maddison, M. Pelling and C. Webster (1977).
Wegg, J. *Richard Pace: a Tudor Diplomatist* (1932).
Wernham, R.B. *Before the Armada* (1966).
Whitford, Richard *The Pype or Tonne of the Lyfe of Perfection* (?1532).
Whiting, R. "'For the health of my soul": prayers for the dead in the Tudor south-west', *SH*, 5 (1983).
Wilkie, W. *The Cardinal Protectors of England* (1974).
Wilkins, David *Concilia Magnae Britanniae et Hibernia* (4 vols, 1737).
Williams, G. *The Welsh Church from Conquest to Reformation* (1976).
Williams, P. *The Council in the Marches of Wales under Elizabeth I* (1958).
—*The Tudor Regime* (1979).
Williams, W.L. 'A Welsh insurrection', *Y Cymmrodor*, xvi (1902).
Williamson, D.M. 'Some aspects of the legation of Cardinal Otto in England, 1237-41', *EHR* , lxiv (1949).
Wilson, H.A. *Magdalen College* (1899).
Wilson, J.M. 'The visitations and injunctions of Cardinal Wolsey and archbishop Cranmer to the priory of Worcester', *Associated Architectural and Archaeological Reports*, xxxvi (2) (1922).
Wolfe, B.P. *The Crown Lands, 1461-1536* (1970).
—'Henry vii's land revenues and chamber finance', *EHR*, lxxix (1964).
Woodcock, B.L. *Medieval Ecclesiastical Courts in the Diocese of Canterbury* (1952).
Wordie, J.R. 'The chronology of English enclosure, 1500-1914', *EcHR*, 2nd ser, 37 (1983).
Wright, T. *Three Chapters of Letters relating to the Suppression of Monasteries*, CS, 26 (1843).
Wriothesley, C.A. *A Chronicle of England*, ed W.D. Hamilton, CS, new ser, xi (1875).
Wunderli, R. 'Pre-Reformation London summoners and the murder of Richard Hunne', *JEH*, 33 (1982).

Youings, Joyce, *The Dissolution of the Monasteries* (1971).
—*Sixteenth Century England* (1984).

Zeeveld, W.G. *Foundations of Tudor Policy* (Cambridge, Mass., 1948).

INDEX